List of Statutory Instruments

together with the List of Statutory Rules
of Northern Ireland
for

1994

LONDON: HMSO

Contents

Preface iii
List of abbreviations v
Out of print publications vi
Customer service vi
List of statutory instruments by subject headings 1
Numerical list of statutory instruments with subject headings 200
List of statutory instruments having subsidiary numbers 236
Alphabetical index of statutory instruments 240
List of statutory rules of Northern Ireland by subject headings 317
Numerical list of statutory rules of Northern Ireland with subject headings 342
List of statutory rules of Northern Ireland having commencement order nos. . . . 348
Alphabetical index of statutory rules of Northern Ireland 349
HMSO catalogues and information vii
Enquiries viii
Orders ix
SI-CD ROM information x
HMSO Books terms & conditions of sale xi

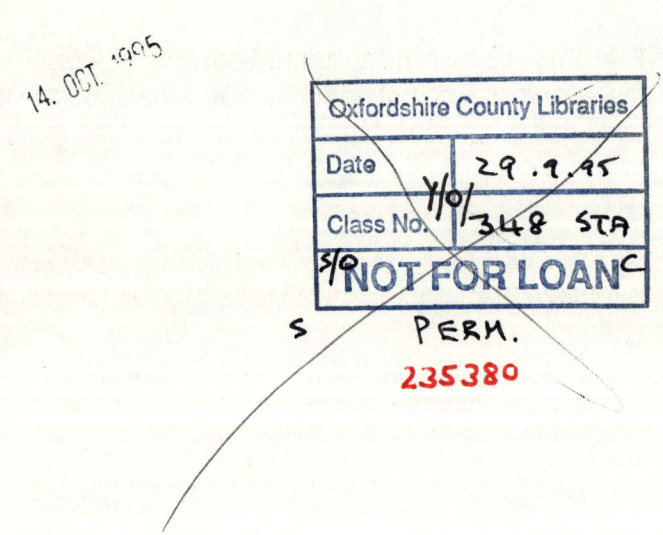

© Crown copyright 1995
Applications for reproduction should be made to HMSO
First published 1995

ISBN 0 11 500415 7
ISSN 0267-2979

Preface

This annual *List of Statutory Instruments* contains particulars of all statutory instruments registered in 1994 (including those not issued until 1995). It includes both those which were issued (i.e. printed and published) by HMSO and those which were not printed by HMSO. The details of the statutory rules of Northern Ireland included in this *List* can be found on pages 317-342.

This *List* contains:

(a) a list of the general and local statutory instruments (printed and non-printed), arranged under subject headings. Each entry includes, where available or appropriate: the enabling power, as set out in italics; the date when the instrument was issued, made and laid and comes into force; a short note of any effect; territorial extent and classification; pagination; ISBN and price;

(b) a numerical list of the same instruments, with their subject headings;

(c) a list of instruments which have subsidiary numbers (C for commencement orders; L for instruments relating to court fees or procedure in England and Wales; NI for orders in Council relating only to Northern Ireland; S for instruments that extend only to Scotland);

(d) an alphabetical subject index;

(e) a list of Northern Ireland statutory rules and associated indexes.(see pages 313-357)

Details of later statutory instruments (printed and non-printed) may be found in the monthly *List of Statutory Instruments*. The *Daily List* of publications from HMSO contains particulars only of those issued by HMSO. Details of previous years' annual lists which are still available appear on the inside back cover.

The full text of the general statutory instruments appears in the annual edition of *Statutory Instruments*. This is issued in three consecutive parts, each of which has an index and table of effects. Part III also contains a classified list of the local statutory instruments (both printed and non-printed).

Copies of local instruments issued recently by HMSO may be obtained from the addresses on the back cover. Copies of local instruments unobtainable from HMSO, may be obtained at prevailing prices from

- Statutory Publications Office, America House, 6-8 Spring Gardens, London SW1A 2BP (from 1922 onwards – except for the years 1942, 1950, 1951 and up to SI no. 940 of 1952)
- Head of Search Department, Public Record Office, Chancery Lane, London WC2A 1LR (as before, up to 1960)
- British Library, Official Publications and Social Sciences Service, Great Russell Street, London WC1B 3DG (as before, up to 1980)

To find out what general statutory instruments are in force on a given subject, or under a particular act, refer to the *Index to Government Orders*. This is published every two years, with a supplement in the intervening year. To ascertain whether a particular general statutory instrument is still in force, refer to the *Table of Government Orders* published annually with a noter-up during its currency. Alternatively, contact HMSO's enquiries section (see p. viii).

iv *Preface*

Net prices are quoted, exclusive of VAT, and include despatch by first class post or carrier in the UK and the cheapest method of despatch to overseas destinations. Customers requiring despatch by by other methods will be charged in full at the appropriate rate. The publications referred to in this catalogue shall be supplied to the customer only on HMSO's terms and conditions (see p. xi-xii) and not on any additional terms which may be included with the customer's order.

Prices are subject to change without notice.

List of abbreviations

accord.	accordance
art(s).	article(s)
c.	chapter
C.	Commencement
C.I.	Channel Islands
E.	England
EEC	European Economic Community
G.	Guernsey
G.B.	Great Britain
GLC	Greater London Council
IOM	Isle of Man
J.	Jersey
L.	Legal: fees or procedure in courts in E. & W.
N.I.	Northern Ireland*
para(s).	paragraph(s)
reg(s).	regulation(s)
s(s).	section(s)
S.	Scotland
sch(s).	schedule(s)
S.I.	Statutory instrument(s)
S.R.	Statutory rule(s) of Northern Ireland
S.R. & O.	Statutory rules and orders
U.K.	United Kingdom
W.	Wales

* Northern Ireland: to distinguish between acts of Parliament (Westminster) and acts of the Northern Ireland Parliament (Stormont) the former are shown Year Chapter no. (N.I), and the latter Year (N.I.) Chapter no.

Out-of-print publications

Photocopies of out-of-print Parliamentary, statutory and regulatory publications can be obtained by HMSO from the British Library Document Supply Centre. Customers requiring this service should order through
   HMSO Books (Photocopies section)
   PO Box 276
   London SW8 5DT
   (Tel. 0171 873 8455)

The section will advise the current rate for this service.

Copyright

Most HMSO publications are Crown or Parliamentary copyright. A letter of guidance on the circumstances where it is necessary to request permission to reproduce Crown or Parliamentary copyright material has been widely promulgated, and additional copies are available from the following address (to which requests for permission to reproduce material should also be sent):
   HMSO
   Copyright Unit
   St Crispins
   Duke Street
   Norwich NR3 1PD
   (Tel. Norwich 01603 695506)

RAISING THE STANDARD

Customer Service

We aim to provide a courteous and efficient service at all times. We have set targets for our service to our customers and monitor the performance achieved.

MAIL, TELEPHONE AND FAX ORDERS
We aim to despatch publications to customers within five days of receiving an order. Goods are despatched by first class post or carrier in the United Kingdom, and usually by accelerated surface post to overseas destinations. Special despatch services are available at extra cost.

STANDING ORDERS
We aim to despatch all standing order publications within two days of publication date.

SUBSCRIPTIONS
We aim to despatch all subscription publications on or before the day of publication.

PROBLEMS?
If you have not received your goods, and would like to ask about your order, or if you have already received your order and found it unsatisfactory in any way, please contact the HMSO address to which your order was sent. The addresses and telephone numbers are given on the back cover of this catalogue.

QUALITY
HMSO's quality policy is to earn a reputation for excellence in satisfying customers' expectations through continual improvement and innovation.

We welcome comments on our service, and any suggestions for improvement.

LIST OF STATUTORY INSTRUMENTS BY SUBJECT HEADING

ACQUISITION OF LAND

The Compulsory Purchase of Land Regulations 1994 No. 2145. Enabling power: *Acquisition of Land Act 1981, ss. 7 (2), 10 (2), 11 (1), 12 (1), 15, 22, sch. 1, paras. 2 (1), 3 (1), 6, sch. 3, para. 9.* Issued: 02.09.94. Made: 11.08.94. Coming into force: 01.10.94. Effect: S.I. 1990/613 revoked. Territorial extent & classification: E/W. General. – 24p. – 0 11 045145 7 £4.15

The Land Compensation (Additional Development) (Forms) (Scotland) Regulations 1994 No.1187 (S. 63). Enabling power: *Land Compensation (Scotland) Act 1963, ss. 32 (2), 33 (2), 34 (3), 36.* Issued: 09.05.94. Made: 11.04.94. Laid: 04.05.94. Coming into force: 25.05.94. Effect: None. Territorial extent & classification: S. General. – 8p. – 0 11 044187 7 £1.95

ACQUISITION OF LAND: COMPENSATION

The Acquisition of Land (Rate of Interest After Entry) Regulations 1994 No. 468. Enabling power: *Land Compensation Act 1961, s. 32 (1).* Issued: 08.03.94. Made: 28.02.94. Laid: 01.03.94. Coming into force: 23.03.94. Effect: S.I. 1992/3183 revoked. Territorial extent & classification: GB. General. – 2p. – 0 11 043468 4 £0.65

The Acquisition of Land (Rate of Interest After Entry) (Scotland) Regulations 1994 No.469. Enabling power: *Land Compensation (Scotland) Act 1963, s. 40 (1).* Issued: 08.03.94. Made: 28.02.94. Laid: 01.03.94. Coming into force: 23.03.94. Effect: S.I. 1992/3225 revoked. Territorial extent & classification: S. General. – 2p. – 0 11 043469 2 £0.65

AGRICULTURE

The Aberdeen and District Milk Marketing Board (Residual Functions) Regulations 1994 No.2589 (S. 125). Enabling power: *Agriculture Act 1993, s. 14 (2) (3) (6).* Issued: 19.10.94. Made: 05.10.94. Laid: 10.10.94. Coming into force: 01.11.94. Effect: S.I. 1984/464 amended. Territorial extent & classification: S. General. – 24p. – 0 11 045589 4 £4.15

The Agricultural Marketing Act 1958 Part I (Certification of Cessation of Effect in Relation to Milk) Order 1994 No. 2922. Enabling power: *Agriculture Act 1993, s. 21 (3).* Issued: 25.11.94. Made: 16.11.94. Coming into force: 16.11.94. Effect: 1958 c. 47 amended. Territorial extent & classification: E/W/S. General. – 2p. – 0 11 043098 0 £0.65

The Agriculture Act 1986 (Amendment) Regulations 1994 No. 249. Enabling power: *European Communities Act 1972, s. 2 (2).* Issued: 28.03.94. Made: 07.03.94. Laid: 08.03.94. Coming into force: 01.03.94. Effect: 1986 c. 49 amended. Territorial extent & classification: E/W/S. General. – 2p. – 0 11 043249 5 £0.65

The Apple Orchard Grubbing Up (Amendment) Regulations 1994 No. 2731. Enabling power: *European Communities Act 1972, s. 2 (2).* Issued: 10.11.94. Made: 19.10.94. Laid: 24.10.94. Coming into force: 25.10.94. Effect: S.I. 1991/3 amended. Territorial extent & classification: E/W/S. General. – Implements REG 1200/90 [L 119/90] as last amended by REG 1890/94 [L 197/94], & REG 2604/90 [L 245/90] as amended by REG 2264/94 [L 246/94]. – 6p. – 0 11 045731 5 £1.55

The Arable Area Payments (Amendment) Regulations 1994 No. 2287. Enabling power: *European Communities Act 1972, s. 2 (2).* Issued: 05.10.94. Made: 31.08.94. Laid: 05.09.94. Coming into force: 26.09.94. Effect: S.I. 1994/947 amended. Territorial extent & classification: E/W/S. General. – 2p. – 0 11 045287 9 £0.65

The Arable Area Payments Regulations 1994 No. 947. Enabling power: *European Communities Act 1972, s. 2 (2).* Issued: 13.04.94. Made: 24.03.94. Laid: 28.03.94. Coming into force: 18.04.94. Effect: None. With correction slip dated June 1994 Territorial extent & classification: E/W/S. General. – 24p. – 0 11 043947 3 £4.15

The Beef Carcase (Classification) (Amendment) Regulations 1994 No. 2853. Enabling power: *European Communities Act 1972, s. 2 (2).* Issued: 14.11.94. Made: 31.10.94. Laid: 08.11.94. Coming into force: 29.11.94. Effect: S.I. 1991/2242 amended. Territorial extent & classification: E/W/S. General. – Implements REG 2191/93 (L 196/93) which amends art. 1 (1) of REG 344/91 (L 41/91). – 4p. – 0 11 043039 5 £1.10

The Beef Special Premium (Amendment) Regulations 1994 No. 3131. Enabling power: *European Communities Act 1972, s. 2 (2).* Issued: 22.12.94. Made: 08.12.94. Laid: 09.12.94. Coming into force: 01.01.95. Effect: S.I. 1993/1734 amended. Territorial extent & classification: E/W/S. General. – Give effect to EC Council REG 805/68 art 4g4a as amended re: REG 3611/93 art. 1 (3). – 4p. – 0 11 043732 2 £1.10

The Common Agricultural Policy (Wine) Regulations 1994 No. 674. Enabling power: *European Communities Act 1972, s. 2 (2).* Issued: 13.04.94. Made: 08.03.94. Laid: 11.03.94. Coming into force: 01.04.94. Effect: S.I. 1993/517, 3071 revoked. Territorial extent & classification: GB. General. – 31p. – 0 11 043674 1 £5.60

The Countryside Access Regulations 1994 No. 2349. Enabling power: *European Communities Act 1972, s. 2 (2).* Issued: 05.10.94. Made: 05.09.94. Laid: 08.09.94. Coming into force: 29.09.94. Effect: None. Territorial extent & classification: E/W. General. – 8p. – 0 11 045349 2 £1.95

The Environmentally Sensitive Areas (Avon Valley) Designation (Amendment) Order 1994 No.927. Enabling power: *Agriculture Act 1986, s. 18 (1) (4).* Issued: 29.04.94. Made: 24.03.94. Laid: 29.03.94. Coming into force: 30.04.94. Effect: S.I. 1993/84 amended. Territorial extent & classification: E. General. – 4p. – 0 11 043927 9 £1.10

Price/availability are liable to change without notice

AGRICULTURE

The Environmentally Sensitive Areas (Blackdown Hills) Designation Order 1994 No. 707. Enabling power: *Agriculture Act 1986, s. 18 (1) (4)*. Issued: 13.04.94. Made: 03.03.94. Laid: 16.03.94. Coming into force: 06.04.94. Effect: None. Territorial extent & classification: E. General. – 8p. – 0 11 043707 1 £1.95

The Environmentally Sensitive Areas (Breckland) Designation (Amendment) Order 1994 No.923. Enabling power: *Agriculture Act 1986, s. 18 (1) (4)*. Issued: 29.04.94. Made: 24.03.94. Laid: 29.03.94. Coming into force: 30.04.94. Effect: S.I. 1993/455 amended. Territorial extent & classification: E. General. – 4p. – 0 11 043923 6 £1.10

The Environmentally Sensitive Areas (Cambrian Mountains - Extension) Designation (Amendment) Order 1994 No. 240. Enabling power: *Agriculture Act 1986, s. 18 (1) (4)*. Issued: 01.03.94. Made: 01.02.94. Laid: 08.02.94. Coming into force: 01.03.94. Effect: None. Territorial extent & classification: W. General. – 8p. – 0 11 043240 1 £1.95

The Environmentally Sensitive Areas (Clun) Designation (Amendment) Order 1994 No.921. Enabling power: *Agriculture Act 1986, s. 18 (1) (4)*. Issued: 29.04.94. Made: 24.03.94. Laid: 29.03.94. Coming into force: 30.04.94. Effect: S.I. 1993/456 amended. Territorial extent & classification: E. General. – 4p. – 0 11 043921 X £1.10

The Environmentally Sensitive Areas (Clwydian Range) Designation Order 1994 No. 238. Enabling power: *Agriculture Act 1986, s. 18 (1) (4)*. Issued: 01.03.94. Made: 01.02.94. Laid: 08.02.94. Coming into force: 01.03.94. Effect: None. Territorial extent & classification: W. General. – 8p. – 0 11 043238 X £1.95

The Environmentally Sensitive Areas (Cotswold Hills) Designation Order 1994 No. 708. Enabling power: *Agriculture Act 1986, s. 18 (1) (4)*. Issued: 13.04.94. Made: 03.03.94. Laid: 16.03.94. Coming into force: 06.04.94. Effect: None. Territorial extent & classification: E. General. – 10p. – 0 11 043708 X £2.40 Replaced by ISBN 0110523806

The Environmentally Sensitive Areas (Dartmoor) Designation Order 1994 No. 710. Enabling power: *Agriculture Act 1986, s. 18 (1) (4)*. Issued: 13.04.94. Made: 03.03.94. Laid: 16.03.94. Coming into force: 06.04.94. Effect: None. Territorial extent & classification: E. General. – 10p. – 0 11 043710 1 £2.40

The Environmentally Sensitive Areas Designation (Radnor) (Welsh Language Provisions) Order 1994 No. 1989. Enabling power: *Agriculture Act, s. 18 (1) (4) (11)*. Issued: 02.08.94. Made: 21.07.94. Laid: 02.08.94. Coming into force: 01.09.94. Effect: None. Includes text in Welsh. Territorial extent & classification: W. Local. – 8p. – 0 11 044989 4 £1.95

The Environmentally Sensitive Areas Designation (Ynys Môn) (Welsh Language Provisions) Order 1994 No. 1990. Enabling power: *Agriculture Act, s. 18 (1) (4) (11)*. Issued: 02.08.94. Made: 21.07.94. Laid: 02.08.94. Coming into force: 01.09.94. Effect: None. Includes text in Welsh Territorial extent & classification: W. Local. – 8p. – 0 11 044990 8 £1.95

The Environmentally Sensitive Areas (Essex Coast) Designation Order 1994 No. 711. Enabling power: *Agriculture Act 1986, s. 18 (1) (4)*. Issued: 13.04.94. Made: 03.03.94. Laid: 16.03.94. Coming into force: 06.04.94. Effect: None. Territorial extent & classification: E. General. – 8p. – 0 11 043711 X £1.95

The Environmentally Sensitive Areas (Exmoor) Designation (Amendment) Order 1994 No.928. Enabling power: *Agriculture Act 1986, s. 18 (1) (4)*. Issued: 29.04.94. Made: 24.03.94. Laid: 29.03.94. Coming into force: 30.04.94. Effect: S.I. 1993/83 amended. Territorial extent & classification: E. General. – 4p. – 0 11 043928 7 £1.10

The Environmentally Sensitive Areas (Lake District) Designation (Amendment) Order 1994 No.925. Enabling power: *Agriculture Act 1986, s. 18 (1) (4)*. Issued: 29.04.94. Made: 24.03.94. Laid: 29.03.94. Coming into force: 30.04.94. Effect: S.I. 1993/85 amended. Territorial extent & classification: E. General. – 4p. – 0 11 043925 2 £1.10

The Environmentally Sensitive Areas (Lleyn Peninsula) Designation (Amendment) Order 1994 No.241. Enabling power: *Agriculture Act 1986, s. 18 (1) (4)*. Issued: 01.03.94. Made: 01.02.94. Laid: 08.02.94. Coming into force: 01.03.94. Effect: None. Territorial extent & classification: W. General. – 10p. – 0 11 043241 X £2.40

The Environmentally Sensitive Areas (North Kent Marshes) (Amendment) (No. 2) Order 1994 No.918. Enabling power: *Agriculture Act 1986, s. 18 (1) (4)*. Issued: 29.04.94. Made: 24.03.94. Laid: 29.03.94. Coming into force: 30.04.94. Effect: S.I. 1993/82 amended. Territorial extent & classification: E. General. – 4p. – 0 11 043918 X £1.10

The Environmentally Sensitive Areas (North Peak) Designation (Amendment) Order 1994 No.922. Enabling power: *Agriculture Act 1986, s. 18 (1) (4)*. Issued: 29.04.94. Made: 24.03.94. Laid: 29.03.94. Coming into force: 30.04.94. Effect: S.I. 1993/457 amended. Territorial extent & classification: E. General. – 4p. – 0 11 043922 8 £1.10

The Environmentally Sensitive Areas (Pennine Dales) Designation (Amendment) (No. 2) Order 1994 No. 930. Enabling power: *Agriculture Act 1986, s. 18 (1) (4)*. Issued: 29.04.94. Made: 24.03.94. Laid: 29.03.94. Coming into force: 30.04.94. Effect: S.I. 1992/55 amended & S.I. 1994/253 revoked. Territorial extent & classification: E. General. – 4p. – 0 11 043930 9 £1.10

The Environmentally Sensitive Areas (Preseli) Designation Order 1994 No. 239. Enabling power: *Agriculture Act 1986, s. 18 (1) (4)*. Issued: 01.03.94. Made: 01.02.94. Laid: 08.02.94. Coming into force: 01.03.94. Effect: None. Territorial extent & classification: W. General. – 10p. – 0 11 043239 8 £2.40

The Environmentally Sensitive Areas (Scotland) Orders Amendment Order 1994 No. 3067 (S. 161). Enabling power: *Agriculture Act 1986, s. 18 (1) (4) (11)*. Issued: 12.12.94. Made: 29.11.94. Laid: 09.12.94. Coming into force: 30.12.94. Effect: S.I. 1992/1919, 1920; 1993/996, 997, 2345, 2767, 2768, 3136, 3149, 3150 amended. Territorial extent & classification: S. General. – 4p. – 0 11 043325 4 £1.10

The Environmentally Sensitive Areas (Shropshire Hills) Designation Order 1994 No.709. Enabling power: *Agriculture Act 1986, s. 18 (1) (4)*. Issued: 13.04.94. Made: 03.03.94. Laid: 16.03.94. Coming into force: 06.04.94. Effect: None. Territorial extent & classification: E. General. – 12p. – 0 11 043709 8 £2.80

Price/availability are liable to change without notice

The Environmentally Sensitive Areas (Somerset Levels and Moors) Designation (Amendment) (No. 2) Order 1994 No. 932. Enabling power: *Agriculture Act 1986, s. 18 (1) (4).* Issued: 29.04.94. Made: 24.03.94. Laid: 29.03.94. Coming into force: 30.04.94. Effect: S.I. 1992/530 amended & S.I. 1994/251 revoked. Territorial extent & classification: E. General. – 6p. – 0 11 043932 5 £1.55

The Environmentally Sensitive Areas (South Downs) Designation (Amendment) (No. 2) Order 1994 No. 931. Enabling power: *Agriculture Act 1986, s. 18 (1) (4).* Issued: 29.04.94. Made: 24.03.94. Laid: 29.03.94. Coming into force: 30.04.94. Effect: S.I. 1992/52 amended & S.I. 1994/252 revoked. Territorial extent & classification: E. General. – 6p. – 0 11 043931 7 £1.55

The Environmentally Sensitive Areas (South Wessex Downs) Designation (Amendment) Order 1994 No. 924. Enabling power: *Agriculture Act 1986, s. 18 (1) (4).* Issued: 29.04.94. Made: 24.03.94. Laid: 29.03.94. Coming into force: 30.04.94. Effect: S.I. 1993/86 amended. Territorial extent & classification: E. General. – 4p. – 0 11 043924 4 £1.10

The Environmentally Sensitive Areas (South West Peak) Designation (Amendment) Order 1994 No.926. Enabling power: *Agriculture Act 1986, s. 18 (1) (4).* Issued: 29.04.94. Made: 24.03.94. Laid: 29.03.94. Coming into force: 30.04.94. Effect: S.I. 1993/87 amended. Territorial extent & classification: E. General. – 4p. – 0 11 043926 0 £1.10

The Environmentally Sensitive Areas (Suffolk River Valleys) Designation (Amendment) Order 1994 No. 920. Enabling power: *Agriculture Act 1986, s. 18 (1) (4).* Issued: 29.04.94. Made: 24.03.94. Laid: 29.03.94. Coming into force: 30.04.94. Effect: S.I. 1993/458 amended. Territorial extent & classification: E. General. – 4p. – 0 11 043920 1 £1.10

The Environmentally Sensitive Areas (Test Valley) Designation (Amendment) Order 1994 No.919. Enabling power: *Agriculture Act 1986, s. 18 (1) (4).* Issued: 29.04.94. Made: 24.03.94. Laid: 29.03.94. Coming into force: 30.04.94. Effect: S.I. 1993/459 amended. Territorial extent & classification: E. General. – 4p. – 0 11 043919 8 £1.10

The Environmentally Sensitive Areas (The Broads) Designation (Amendment) (No. 2) Order 1994 No. 929. Enabling power: *Agriculture Act 1986, s. 18 (1) (4).* Issued: 29.04.94. Made: 24.03.94. Laid: 29.03.94. Coming into force: 30.04.94. Effect: S.I. 1992/54 amended & S.I. 1994/254 revoked. Territorial extent & classification: E. General. – 6p. – 0 11 043929 5 £1.55

The Environmentally Sensitive Areas (Upper Thames Tributaries) Designation Order 1994 No.712. Enabling power: *Agriculture Act 1986, s. 18 (1) (4).* Issued: 13.04.94. Made: 03.03.94. Laid: 16.03.94. Coming into force: 06.04.94. Effect: None. Territorial extent & classification: E. General. 12p. 0 11 043712 8 £2.80

The Environmentally Sensitive Areas (West Penwith) Designation (Amendment) (No. 2) Order 1994 No. 933. Enabling power: *Agriculture Act 1986, s. 18 (1) (4).* Issued: 29.04.94. Made: 24.03.94. Laid: 29.03.94. Coming into force: 30.04.94. Effect: S.I. 1986/2251 amended & S.I. 1994/250 revoked. Territorial extent & classification: E. General. – 4p. – 0 11 043933 3 £1.10

The Farm and Conservation Grant (Variation) Scheme 1994 No. 1302. Enabling power: *Agriculture Act 1970, ss. 28, 29.* Issued: 12.07.94. Made: 13.05.94. Laid: 16.05.94. Coming into force: 30.06.94. Effect: S.I. 1989/128 amended. Supersedes SI of same no. & ISBN published on 06.06.94. Territorial extent & classification: E/W. General. – 4p. – 0 11 044302 0 £1.10

The Feeding Stuffs (Amendment) (No.2) Regulations 1994 No. 2510. Enabling power: *Agriculture Act 1970, ss. 66 (1), 68(1) (1A), 69(1), 70(1), 74A, 84.* Issued: 13.10.94. Made: 05.09.94. Laid: 09.09.94. Coming into force: 01.10.94, for regs. 1-3, 4 (1) (b) (2) (3) and the schedules. 01.01.95, for the remainder. Effect: S.I. 1991/2840 amended. Territorial extent & classification: E/W/S. General. – 12p. – 0 11 045510 X £2.80

The Feeding Stuffs (Amendment) Regulations 1994 No. 499. Enabling power: *Agriculture Act 1970, ss. 74A, 84 & European Communities Act 1972, s. 2 (2).* Issued: 10.03.94. Made: 01.03.94. Laid: 10.03.94. Coming into force: 31.03.94. Effect: S.I. 1994/2840 amended. Territorial extent & classification: E/W/S. General. – 4p. – 0 11 043499 4 £1.10

The Feedingstuffs (Sampling and Analysis) (Amendment) Regulations 1994 No. 1610. Enabling power: *Agriculture Act 1970, ss. 66 (1), 79 (2), 84.* Issued: 06.07.94. Made: 06.06.94. Laid: 20.06.94. Coming into force: 11.07.94. Effect: S.I. 1982/1144 amended. Territorial extent & classification: E/W/S. General. – 20p. – 0 11 044610 0 £3.70

The Fertilisers (Sampling and Analysis) (Amendment) Regulations 1994 No. 129. Enabling power: *Agriculture Act 1970, ss. 66 (1), 79 (2), 84.* Issued: 23.02.94. Made: 26.01.94. Laid: 27.01.94. Coming into force: 17.02.94. Effect: S.I. 1991/973 amended. Territorial extent & classification: E/W/S. General. – 24p. – 0 11 043129 4 £4.15

The Habitat (Broadleaved Woodland) (Wales) Regulations 1994 No. 3099. Enabling power: *European Communities Act 1972, s. 2 (2).* Issued: 05.01.95. Made: 12.12.94. Laid: 14.12.94. Coming into force: 09.01.95. Effect: None. Territorial extent & classification: W. Local. – Implements in part REG 2078/92 [OJ L215 1992]. – 8p. – 0 11 043812 4 £1.95

The Habitat (Coastal Belt) (Wales) Regulations 1994 No. 3101. Enabling power: *European Communities Act 1972, s. 2 (2).* Issued: 05.01.95. Made: 12.12.94. Laid: 14.12.94. Coming into force: 09.01.95. Effect: None. Territorial extent & classification: W. Local. – Implement in part REG 2078/92 [OJ L215 1992]. – 8p. – 0 11 043811 6 £1.95

The Habitat (Former Set-Aside Land) Regulations 1994 No. 1292. Enabling power: *European Communities Act 1972, s. 2 (2).* Issued: 10.06.94. Made: 12.05.94. Laid: 16.05.94. Coming into force: 06.06.94. Effect: None. Territorial extent & classification: E. General. – 8p. – 0 11 044292 X £1.95

Price/availability are liable to change without notice

AGRICULTURE

The Habitat (Salt-Marsh) Regulations 1994 No. 1293. Enabling power: *European Communities Act 1972, s. 2 (2)*. Issued: 10.06.94. Made: 12.05.94. Laid: 16.05.94. Coming into force: 06.06.94. Effect: None. Territorial extent & classification: E. General. – 6p. – 0 11 044293 8 £1.55

The Habitat (Species-Rich Grassland) (Wales) Regulations 1994 No. 3102. Enabling power: *European Communities Act 1972, s. 2 (2)*. Issued: 05.01.95. Made: 12.12.94. Laid: 14.12.94. Coming into force: 09.01.95. Effect: None. Territorial extent & classification: W. Local. – Implement in part REG 2078/92 [OJ L215 1992]. – 8p. – 0 11 043816 7 £1.95

The Habitats (Scotland) Regulations 1994 No. 2710 (S. 138). Enabling power: *European Communities Act 1972, s. 2 (2)*. Issued: 01.11.94. Made: 17.10.94. Laid: 01.11.94. Coming into force: 22.11.94. Effect: None. Territorial extent & classification: S. General. – Implements in part REG 2078/92 [L 215/92]. – 16p. – 0 11 045710 2 £3.20

The Habitat (Water Fringe) Regulations 1994 No. 1291. Enabling power: *European Communities Act 1972, s. 2 (2)*. Issued: 10.06.94. Made: 12.05.94. Laid: 16.05.94. Coming into force: 06.06.94. Effect: None. Territorial extent & classification: E. General. – 12p. – 0 11 044291 1 £2.80

The Habitat (Water Fringe) (Wales) Regulations 1994 No. 3100. Enabling power: *European Communities Act 1972, s. 2 (2)*. Issued: 05.01.95. Made: 12.12.94. Laid: 14.12.94. Coming into force: 09.01.95. Effect: None. Territorial extent & classification: W. Local. – Implements in part REG 2078/92 [OJ L215 1992]. – 8p. – 0 11 043819 1 £1.95

The Hill Livestock (Compensatory Allowances) (Amendment) Regulations 1994 No. 94. Enabling power: *European Communities Commission Act 1972, s. 2 (2)*. Issued: 01.02.94. Made: 20.01.94. Laid: 21.01.94. Coming into force: 22.01.94. Effect: S.I. 1993/2631 amended. This SI has been made in consequence of a defect in SI 1993/2631 and is being sent free of charge to all known recipients of that SI. Territorial extent & classification: E/W/S. General. – 2p. – 0 11 043094 8 £0.65

The Hill Livestock (Compensatory Allowances) Regulations 1994 No. 2740. Enabling power: *Euorpean Communities Act 1972, s. 2 (2)*. Issued: 11.11.94. Made: 20.10.94. Laid: 25.10.94. Coming into force: 15.11.94. Effect: S.I. 1993/2631, 2924; 1994/94 revoked. Territorial extent & classification: E/W/S. General. – Complies with Dir 75/268 as amended by Dir 80/666 & Dir 82/786, & with arts. 17 to 19 of Reg.(EEC) no. 2328/91 as amended by Regs. no. 870/93, 1992/93 & 3669/93. Also makes provision for administration & enforcement of provisions for payment of compensatory allowances in Commission Reg. no. 3887/92. – 12p. – 0 11 045740 4 £2.80

The Integrated Administration and Control System (Amendment) Regulations 1994 No.1134. Enabling power: *European Communities Act 1972, s. 2 (2)*. Issued: 13.05.94. Made: 21.04.94. Laid: 22.04.94. Coming into force: 15.05.94. Effect: S.I. 1993/1317 amended. Territorial extent & classification: GB. General. – 4p. – 0 11 044134 6 £1.10

The Marketing Development Scheme 1994 No. 1403. Enabling power: *Agriculture Act 1993, s. 50 (1) (2) (3)*. Issued: 24.06.94. Made: 24.05.94. Laid: 25.05.94. Coming into force: 15.06.94. Effect: None. Territorial extent & classification: E/W/S. General. – 6p. – 0 11 044403 5 £1.55

The Marketing Development Scheme (Specification of Activities) Order 1994 No. 1404. Enabling power: *Agriculture Act 1993, s. 50 (2) (c)*. Issued: 24.06.94. Made: 24.05.94. Laid: 25.05.94. Coming into force: 15.06.94. Effect: None. Territorial extent & classification: E/W/S. General. – 2p. – 0 11 044404 3 £0.65

The Milk Marketing Board (Residuary Functions) Regulations 1994 No. 2759. Enabling power: *Agriculture Act 1993, ss. 14 (2) (3) (6), 62 (1) (2)*. Issued: 29.11.94. Made: 27.10.94. Laid: 28.10.94. Coming into force: 01.11.94. Effect: S.R. & O. 1933/789 amended. Territorial extent & classification: E/W. General. – 32p. – 0 11 045759 5 £5.60

The Milk Marketing Board Scheme of Reorganisation (Further Extension of Period for Application) Order 19194 No. 951. Enabling power: *Agriculture Act 1993, s. 2 (7)*. Issued: 13.04.94. Made: 28.03.94. Coming into force: 31.03.94. Effect: None. Territorial extent & classification: E/W. General. – 2p. – 0 11 043951 1 £0.65

The Milk Marketing Board Scheme of Reorganisation (Third Party Rights) Regulations 1994 No. 2460. Enabling power: *Agriculture Act 1993, s. 62 (1) (2), sch. 2, paras. 42 (3) (a), 43 (3), 44 (2) (a)*. Issued: 25.10.94. Made: 16.09.94. Laid: 19.09.94. Coming into force: 20.09.94. Effect: None. Territorial extent & classification: E/W. General. – 4p. – 0 11 045460 X £1.10

The Milk Marketing Scheme (Certification of Revocation) Order 1994 No. 2921. Enabling power: *Agriculture Act 1993, s. 1 (5)*. Issued: 25.11.94. Made: 16.11.94. Coming into force: 16.11.94. Effect: S.R. & O. 1933/789 amended. Territorial extent & classification: E/W. General. – 2p. – 0 11 043099 9 £0.65

The Milk Marketing Schemes (Certification of Revocation) (Scotland) Order 1994 No. 2900 (S. 146). Enabling power: *Agriculture Act 1993, s. 1 (5)*. Issued: 23.11.94. Made: 09.11.94. Coming into force: 01.11.94. Effect: None. Territorial extent & classification: S. General. – 2p. – 0 11 043089 1 £0.65

The Milk Marketing Schemes (Substitution of Date of Revocation) (Scotland) Order 1994 No. 685 (S. 33). Enabling power: *Agriculture Act 1993, s. 1 (3)*. Issued: 18.03.94. Made: 08.03.94. Coming into force: 11.03.94. Effect: 1993 c. 37 amended. Territorial extent & classification: S. General. – 2p. – 0 11 043685 7 £0.65

The Milk Marketing Scheme (Substitution of Date of Revocation) Order 1994 No. 282. Enabling power: *Agriculture Act 1993, s. 1 (3)*. Issued: 09.03.94. Made: 08.02.94. Coming into force: 09.02.94. Effect: None. N.B. Postpones the revocation of the Milk Marketing Scheme 1993 from 01.10.94 to 01.01.95. Territorial extent & classification: E/W. General. – 2p. – 0 11 043282 7 £0.65

The Nitrate Sensitive Areas Regulations 1994 No. 1729. Enabling power: *European Communities Act 1972, s. 2 (2)*. Issued: 08.08.94. Made: 01.07.94. Laid: 01.07.94. Coming into force: 26.07.94. Effect: None. Territorial extent & classification: E. General. – 16p. – 0 11 044729 8 £3.20

Price/availability are liable to change without notice

The North of Scotland Milk Marketing Board (Residual Functions) Regulations 1994 No.2590 (S. 126). Enabling power: *Agriculture Act 1993, s. 14 (2) (3) (6).* Issued: 19.10.94. Made: 05.10.94. Laid: 10.10.94. Coming into force: 01.11.94. Effect: S.R. & O. 1934/703 amended. Territorial extent & classification: S. General. – 24p. – 0 11 045590 8 *£4.15*

The Organic Aid (Scotland) Regulations 1994 No. 1701 (S. 75). Enabling power: *European Communities Act 1972, s. 2 (2).* Issued: 08.07.94. Made: 27.06.94. Laid: 01.07.94. Coming into force: 22.07.94. Effect: None. Territorial extent & classification: S. General. – 8p. – 0 11 044701 8 *£1.95*

The Organic Farming (Aid) Regulations 1994 No. 1721. Enabling power: *European Communities Act 1972, s. 2 (2).* Issued: 08.08.94. Made: 29.06.94. Laid: 01.07.94. Coming into force: 22.07.94. Effect: None. The Incorrect no. 1994/1712 appears on the document - 1994/1721 is the correct number. With correction slip to this effect, issued 22.09.94 Territorial extent & classification: E/W. General. – 12p. – 0 11 044712 3 *£2.40*

The Pig Carcase (Grading) Regulations 1994 No. 2155. Enabling power: *European Communities Act 1972, s. 2 (2).* Issued: 20.09.94. Made: 09.08.94. Laid: 22.08.94. Coming into force: 12.09.94. Effect: 1967 c. 22 amended & S.I. 1988/1180; 1989/644 revoked. Territorial extent & classification: E/W/S. General. – 12p. – 0 11 045155 4 *£1.55*

The Potato Marketing Scheme (Amendment) Order 1994 No. 2404. Enabling power: *Agricultural Marketing Act 1958, s. 2, sch. 1.* Issued: 11.11.94. Made: 07.09.94. Coming into force: 08.09.94. Effect: S.I. 1955/690 amended. Territorial extent & classification: E/W/S. General. – 6p. – 0 11 045404 9 *£1.55*

The Preserved Tuna and Bonito (Marketing Standards) Regulations 1994 No. 2127. Enabling power: *Food Safety Act 1990, ss. 17 (2), 26, 48 (1).* Issued: 26.09.94. Made: 05.08.94. Laid: 12.08.94. Coming into force: 02.09.94. Effect: S.I. 1984/1305; 1519 amended. Territorial extent & classification: E/W/S. General. – 4p. – 0 11 045127 9 *£1.10*

The Scottish Milk Marketing Board (Residual Functions) Regulations 1994 No. 2591 (S. 127). Enabling power: *Agriculture Act 1993, s. 14 (2) (3) (6).* Issued: 19.10.94. Made: 05.10.94. Laid: 10.10.94. Coming into force: 01.11.94. Effect: S.I. 1989/1806 amended. Territorial extent & classification: S. General. – 24p. – 0 11 045591 6 *£4.15*

The Set-Aside Access (Scotland) Regulations 1994 No. 3085 (S. 165). Enabling power: *European Communities Act 1972, s. 2 (2).* Issued: 16.12.94. Made: 05.12.94. Laid: 07.12.94. Coming into force: 28.12.94. Effect: None. Territorial extent & classification: S. General. – Implements in part REG no. 2078/92 [OJ L215/92]. – 8p. – 0 11 043378 5 *£1.95*

The Sheep Annual Premium (Amendment) Regulations 1994 No. 2741. Enabling power: *European Communities Act 1972, s. 2 (2).* Issued: 12.12.94. Made: 20.10.94. Laid: 25.10.94. Coming into force: 15.11.94. Effect: S.I. 1992/2677 amended. Territorial extent & classification: E/W/S. General. – Gives effect to article 5 (d) of REG 3013/89 (OJ L 289/89) & REG 233/94 (OJ L 30/94). – 4p. – 0 11 045741 2 *£1.10*

The Sheep Annual Premium and Suckler Cow Premium Quotas (Amendment) Regulations 1994 No. 2894. Enabling power: *European Communities Act 1972, s. 2 (2).* Issued: 01.02.95. Made: 14.11.94. Laid: 14.11.94. Coming into force: 15.11.94. Effect: S.I. 1993/1626 amended. Territorial extent & classification: GB. General. – The regulations make further provision for the implementation of the Community instruments - REG 805/68; 3013/89 [OJ L289/89]; 3567/92 as amended by REG 2527/94 [OJ L269/94], 2869/93 [OJ L262/93], 1720/94 [OJ L181/94]; 3886/92 as amended by REG 2526/94 [OJ L269/94], 489/94 [OJ L62/94], 1719/94 [OJ L181/94] & implements REG 826/94 [OJ L95/94] (following 233/94 [OJ L30/94]) and REG 2078/92. – 4p. – 0 11 043936 8 *£1.10*

The Suckler Cow Premium (Amendment) Regulations 1994 No. 1528. Enabling power: *European Communities Act 1972, s. 2 (2).* Issued: 24.06.94. Made: 10.06.94. Laid: 10.06.94. Coming into force: 01.07.94. Effect: S.I. 1993/1441 amended. Territorial extent & classification: E/W/S. General. – 4p. – 0 11 044528 7 *£1.10*

AGRICULTURE: CEREALS MARKETING

The Home-grown Cereals Authority (Rate of Levy) Order 1994 No. 1424. Enabling power: *Cereals Marketing Act 1965, ss. 13 (3), 23 (1), 24 (1).* Issued: 10.06.94. Made: 20.05.94. Laid: 10.06.94. Coming into force: 01.07.94. Effect: None. Territorial extent & classification: GB. General. – 4p. – 0 11 044424 8 *£1.10*

AGRICULTURE: COMMON AGRICULTURAL POLICY

The Organic Products (Amendment) Regulations 1994 No. 2286. Enabling power: *European Communities Act 1972, s. 2 (2).* Issued: 05.10.94. Made: 19.08.94. Laid: 05.09.94. Coming into force: 26.09.94. Effect: S.I. 1992/2111 amended. Territorial extent & classification: GB. General. – 4p. – 0 11 045286 0 *£1.10*

AGRICULTURE: HORTICULTURE

The Farm and Conservation Grant (Amendment) Regulations 1994 No. 3003. Enabling power: *European Communities Act 1972, s. 2 (2).* Issued: 05.12.94. Made: 25.11.94. Laid: 29.11.94. Coming into force: 30.11.94. Effect: S.I. 1991/1630 amended. Territorial extent & classification: E/W/S. General. – Implements provisions in Title IV of REG 2328/91 (OJ L 218/91). – 2p. – 0 11 043244 4 *£0.65*

The Farm and Conservation Grant (Variation) (No. 2) Scheme 1994 No. 3002. Enabling power: *Agriculture Act 1970, ss. 28, 29.* Issued: 05.12.94. Made: 25.11.94. Laid: 29.11.94. Coming into force: 30.11.94. Effect: S.I. 1989/128 amended. Territorial extent & classification: E/W/S. General. – Complies with art. 12 of REG 2328/91 (OJ L 218/91). – 2p. – 0 11 043243 6 *£0.65*

Price/availability are liable to change without notice

AGRICULTURE: PESTICIDES

The Pesticides (Maximum Residue Levels in Crops, Food and Feeding Stuffs) Regulations 1994 No. 1985. Enabling power: *European Communities Act 1972, s. 2 (2) & Food and Environment Protection Act 1985, ss. 16 (2) (k) (1) (15), 24 (1) (3)*. Issued: 05.08.94. Made: 25.07.94. Laid: 24.05.94. Coming into force: 26.07.94. Effect: S.I. 1988/1378 revoked. Territorial extent & classification: E/W/S. General. – Implements DIR 90/642 (L 350/90) as amended by DIR 93/57 & 58 (L 211/93). – 43p. – 0 11 044985 1 £6.75

ANCIENT MONUMENTS

The Ancient Monuments (Class Consents) Order 1994 No. 1381. Enabling power: *Ancient Monuments and Archaeological Areas Act 1979, ss. 2, 3, 60*. Issued: 01.06.94. Made: 19.05.94. Laid: 24.05.94. Coming into force: 14.06.94. Effect: S.I. 1981/1302; 1984/222 revoked. With correction slip dated June 1994. Territorial extent & classification: E/W. General. –6p.– 0 11 044381 0 £1.55

ANIMALS

The Spongiform Encephalopathy (Miscellaneous Amendments) Order 1994 No. 2627. Enabling power: *Animal Health Act 1981, ss. 1, 8 (1), 11, 15 (4), 83 (2) (5), 88 (2) (4)*. Issued: 02.11.94. Made: 10.10.94. Coming into force: 02.11.94. Effect: S.I. 1985/1765; 1991/1155, 2246 amended. Territorial extent & classification: E/W/S. General. – Implements DEC 94/381 [L 172/94] and art. 3 (1) (b) of DEC 94/474 [L 194/94]. – 4p. – 0 11 045627 0 £1.10

ANIMALS: ANIMAL HEALTH

The Bovine Spongiform Encephalopathy Compensation Order 1994 No. 673. Enabling power: *Animal Health Act 1981, ss. 32 (3), 34 (7)*. Issued: 28.03.94. Made: 08.03.94. Laid: 11.03.94. Coming into force: 01.04.94. Effect: S.I. 1990/222 revoked. Territorial extent & classification: E/W/S. General. –4p. – 0 11 043673 3 £1.10

The Brucellosis (England and Wales) (Amendment) Order 1994 No. 2762. Enabling power: *Animal Health Act 1981, ss. 1, 15 (4)*. Issued: 19.12.94. Made: 26.10.94. Coming into force: 17.11.94. Effect: S.I. 1981/1455 amended. Territorial extent & classification: E/W. General. – Implements those provisions of DIR 64/432 [OJ L121/64] as amended, & DIR 77/391 [OJ L145/77] as amended. – 4p. – 0 11 043412 9 £1.10

The Brucellosis (Scotland) Amendment Order 1994 No. 2770 (S. 140). Enabling power: *Animal Health Act 1981, ss. 1, 15 (4)*. Issued: 07.11.94. Made: 26.10.94. Coming into force: 17.11.94. Effect: S.I. 1979/1596 amended. Territorial extent & classification: S. General. – Implement provisions of DIR 64/432 (L 121/64) & 77/391 (L 145/77) which require monitoring/testing for maintenance of officially brucellosis free status achieved in Scotland. –4p. – 0 11 045770 6 £1.10

The Diseases of Animals (Approved Disinfectants) (Amendment) Order 1994 No. 2965. Enabling power: *Animal Health Act 1981, ss. 1, 7 (1) (a) (b) (c) (2), 23 (f) (g)*. Issued: 13.12.94. Made: 21.11.94. Coming into force: 22.11.94. Effect: S.I. 1978/32 amended & S.I. 1993/1194, 3086 revoked. Territorial extent & classification: E/W/S. General. –6p. – 0 11 043368 8 £1.55

The Diseases of Poultry Order 1994 No. 3141. Enabling power: *Animal Health Act 1981, ss. 1, 7, 8 (1), 15 (5), 17 (1), 23, 25, 35 (1), 83 (2), 87 (5) (a), 88 (4)*. Issued: 12.01.95. Made: 08.12.94. Coming into force: 01.01.95. Effect: S.I. 1983/344; 1991/1168 amended & S.I. 1952/437; 1956/11; 1958/1344, 1442, 1611; 1963/1956; 1983/941; 1986/1755; 1994/944 revoked. Territorial extent & classification: E/W/S. General. – Implements DIR 92/40 & DIR 92/66. – 12p. – 0 11 043888 4 £2.80

The Importation of Animal Products and Poultry Products (Amendment) Order 1994 No. 2920. Enabling power: *Animal Health Act 1981, ss. 1, 10, 87 (5) (a)*. Issued: 20.12.94. Made: 16.11.94. Laid: 17.11.94. Coming into force: 14.12.94. Effect: S.I. 1980/12, 14 amended & S.I. 1980/1934; 1981/1238 revoked. Territorial extent & classification: E/W/S. General. –4p. – 0 11 043474 9 £1.10

The Marek's Disease (Restriction on Vaccination) (Revocation) Order 1994 No. 472. Enabling power: *Animal Health Act 1981, ss. 1, 72, 88 (4) (a)*. Issued: 14.03.94. Made: 28.02.94. Coming into force: 25.03.94. Effect: S.I. 1987/905 revoked. Territorial extent & classification: E/W/S. General. – 2p. – 0 11 043472 2 £0.65

The Rabies (Importation of Dogs, Cats and Other Mammals) (Amendment) Order 1994 No.1716. Enabling power: *Animal Health Act 1981, ss. 1, 10 (1) (2) (3) (5), 95 (l)*. Issued: 25.07.94. Made: 30.06.94. Laid: 30.06.94. Coming into force: 01.07.94. Effect: S.I. 1974/2211 amended. Territorial extent & classification: E/W/S. General. – 4p. – 0 11 044716 6 £1.10

The Racing Pigeons (Vaccination) Order 1994 No. 944. Enabling power: *Animal Health Act 1981, ss. 1, 8 (1), 88 (4) (a)*. Issued: 04.05.94. Made: 25.03.94. Coming into force: 01.04.94. Effect: None. Territorial extent & classification: E/W/S. General. – 2p. – 0 11 043944 9 £0.65

The Welfare of Animals During Transport Order 1994 No. 3249. Enabling power: *Animal Health Act 1981, ss. 1, 7, 8 (1), 37, 38 (1), 39, 83 (2), 87 (2) (3) (5) (a)*. Issued: 20.01.95. Made: 13.12.94. Coming into force: 23.01.95. Effect: S.I. 1975/1024; 1981/1051 amended & S.I. 1992/3304 revoked. Territorial extent & classification: E/W/S. General. – Implements DIR 91/628 on the protection of animals during transport [OJ L340 1991]. – 12p. – 0 11 043914 7 £2.80

ANIMALS: PREVENTION OF CRUELTY

The Welfare of Livestock Regulations 1994 No. 2126. Enabling power: *European Communities Act 1972, s. 2 (2) & Agriculture (Miscellaneous Provisions) Act 1968, s. 2*. Issued: 17.08.94. Made: 27.07.94. Laid: 14.06.94. Coming into force: 10.08.94. Effect: 1954 c. 46 amended & S.I. 1978/1800; 1987/2020, 2021; 1990/1445; 1991/1477 revoked. Supersedes Draft ISBN 0110459385 published 27.06.94. Territorial extent & classification: E/W/S. General. – 16p. – 0 11 045126 0 *£3.20*

ARMORIAL BEARINGS, ENSIGNS AND FLAGS

The Lyon Court and Office Fees (Variation) Order 1994 No. 201 (S. 7). Enabling power: *Public Expenditure and Receipts Act 1968, s. 5*. Issued: 10.02.94. Made: 27.01.94. Laid: 10.02.94. Coming into force: 01.04.94. Effect: 1867 c. 17 amended & S.I. 1993/298 revoked. Territorial extent & classification: S. General. – 4p. – 0 11 043201 0 *£1.10*

ARMS AND AMMUNITION

The Firearms (Amendment) Rules 1994 No. 3022. Enabling power: *Firearms Act 1968, ss. 27 (2) (3), 53 (a), 57 (4)*. Issued: 06.12.94. Made: 28.11.94. Coming into force: 01.01.95. Effect: S.I. 1989/854 amended. Territorial extent & classification: E/W. General. – 2p. – 0 11 043261 4 *£0.65*

The Firearms (Period of Certificate) Order 1994 No. 2614. Enabling power: *Firearms Act 1968, s. 26 (3A)*. Issued: 13.10.94. Made: 06.10.94. Laid: 13.10.94. Coming into force: 01.01.95. Effect: None. Territorial extent & classification: E/W. General. – 2p. – 0 11 045614 9 *£0.65*

The Firearms (Scotland) Amendment Rules 1994 No. 3198 (S. 178). Enabling power: *Firearms Act 1968 ss. 27 (2) (3), 53 (a), 57 (4)*. Issued: 22.12.94. Made: 12.12.94. Coming into force: 01.01.95. Effect: S.I. 1989/889 amended. Territorial extent & classification: S. General. – 2p. – 0 11 043549 4 *£0.65*

The Firearms (Variation of Fees) Order 1994 No. 2615. Enabling power: *Firearms Act 1968, s. 43 & Firearms (Amendment) Act 1988, s. 15 (4)*. Issued: 13.10.94. Made: 06.10.94. Laid: 13.10.94. Coming into force: 01.01.95. Effect: 1968 c. 27; 1988 c. 45 amended & S. I. 1990/290 revoked. Territorial extent & classification: E/W. General. – 4p. – 0 11 045615 7 *£1.10*

The Firearms (Variation of Fees) (Scotland) Order 1994 No. 2652 (S. 134). Enabling power: *Firearms Act 1968, s. 43 & Firearms (Amendment) Act 1988, s. 15 (4)*. Issued: 20.10.94. Made: 06.10.94. Laid: 13.10.94. Coming into force: 01.01.95. Effect: 1968 c. 27; 1988 c. 45 amended & S.I. 1990/325 revoked. With correction slip dated November 1994. Territorial extent & classification: S. General. – 4p. – 0 11 045652 1 *£1.10*

ATOMIC ENERGY AND RADIOACTIVE SUBSTANCES

The Nuclear Installations (Increase of Operators' Limits of Liability) Order 1994 No. 909. Enabling power: *Nuclear Installations Act 1965, s. 16 (1A)*. Issued: 07.04.94. Made: 24.03.94. Laid: 16.02.94. Coming into force: 01.04.94. Effect: 1965 c. 57 amended. Supersedes Draft ISBN 0110458842 issued 25.02.94. Territorial extent & classification: GB. General. – 2p. – 0 11 043909 0 *£0.65*

BANKS AND BANKING

The Accountants (Banking Act 1987) Regulations 1994 No. 524. Enabling power: *Banking Act 1987, s. 47 (5)*. Issued: 14.03.94. Made: 03.03.94. Coming into force: 01.05.94. Effect: None. Supersedes Draft ISBN 0110458559 published on 17.01.94. Territorial extent & classification: GB. General. – 2p. – 0 11 043524 9 *£0.65*

BETTING, GAMING AND LOTTERIES

The Gaming Act (Hours and Charges) (Amendment) Regulations 1994 No. 958. Enabling power: *Gaming Act 1968, ss. 14 (2), 51*. Issued: 06.04.94. Made: 25.03.94. Laid: 06.04.94. Coming into force: 01.05.94. Effect: S.I. 1984/248 amended & S.I. 1993/968 revoked. Territorial extent & classification: E/W. General. – 2p. – 0 11 043958 9 *£0.65*

The Gaming Act (Variation of Monetary Limits) (No. 2) Order 1994 No. 957. Enabling power: *Gaming Act 1968, ss. 21 (8), 51 (4)*. Issued: 06.04.94. Made: 25.03.94. Laid: 06.04.94. Coming into force: 01.05.94. Effect: 1968 c. 65 amended & S.I. 1992/429 revoked. Territorial extent & classification: E/W. General. – 2p. – 0 11 043957 0 *£0.65*

The Gaming Act (Variation of Monetary Limits) Order 1994 No. 956. Enabling power: *Gaming Act 1968, ss. 20 (8), 51 (4)*. Issued: 06.04.94. Made: 25.03.94. Laid: 06.04.94. Coming into force: 01.05.94. Effect: 1968 c. 65; S.I. 1993/967 amended. Territorial extent & classification: E/W. General. – 2p. – 0 11 043956 2 *£0.65*

The Gaming Act (Variation of Monetary Limits) (Scotland) Order 1994 No. 1043 (S. 53). Enabling power: *Gaming Act 1968, ss. 20 (8), 21 (8), 51*. Issued: 15.04.94. Made: 07.04.94. Laid: 08.04.94. Coming into force: 01.05.94. Effect: 1968 c. 65; S.I. 1992/751; 1993/1037 amended. Territorial extent & classification: S. General. – 2p. – 0 11 044043 9 *£0.65*

The Gaming Clubs (Bankers' Games) Regulations 1994 No. 2899. Enabling power: *Gaming Act 1968, ss. 13 (2), 15 (2), 51*. Issued: 22.11.94. Made: 13.11.94. Laid: 22.11.94. Coming into force: 01.01.95. Effect: S.I. 1970/803, 804 revoked. Territorial extent & classification: E/W/S. General. – 12p. – 0 11 043080 8 *£2.80*

The Gaming Clubs (Hours and Charges) (Scotland) Amendment Regulations 1994 No. 1042 (S. 52). Enabling power: *Gaming Act 1968, ss. 14 (2) (3), 51*. Issued: 15.04.94. Made: 07.04.94. Laid: 08.04.94. Coming into force: 01.05.94. Effect: S.I. 1984/470 amended & S.I. 1993/1040 revoked. Territorial extent & classification: S. General. – 2p. – 0 11 044042 0 £0.65

The National Lottery etc. Act 1993 (Commencement No. 2 and Transitional Provisions) Order 1994 No. 1055 (C. 16). Enabling power: *National Lottery etc. Act 1993, s. 60 (5)*. Bringing into operation various provisions of this act on 03.05.94, 03.10.94. Issued: 20.04.94. Made: 10.04.94. Effect: None. Territorial extent & classification: E/W/S. General. – 4p. – 0 11 044055 2 £1.10

The National Lottery etc. Act 1993 (Commencement No. 3) Order 1994 No. 2659 (C. 58). Enabling power: *National Lottery etc. Act 1993, s. 65*. Bringing into operation various provisions of the 1993 act on 14.11.94. Issued: 19.10.94. Made: 10.10.94. Effect: None. Territorial extent & classification: E/W/S. General. – 2p. – 0 11 045659 9 £0.65

BRITISH NATIONALITY

The British Citizenship (Designated Service) (Amendment) Order 1994 No. 556. Enabling power: *British Nationality Act 1981, s. 2 (3)*. Issued: 11.03.94. Made: 05.03.94. Laid: 11.03.94. Coming into force: 01.04.94. Effect: S.I. 1982/1004 amended. Territorial extent & classification: GB. General. – 2p. – 0 11 043556 7 £0.65

The British Nationality (South Africa) Order 1994 No. 1634. Enabling power: *British Nationality Act 1981, s. 37 (2)*. Issued: 04.07.94. Made: 22.06.94. Laid: 04.07.94. Coming into force: 26.07.94. Effect: 1981 c.61 amended. Territorial extent & classification: GB. General. – 2p. – 0 11 044634 8 £0.65

BROADCASTING

The Broadcasting (Foreign Satellite Programmes) (Specified Countries) Order 1994 No.453. Enabling power: *Broadcasting Act 1990, s. 79 (5)*. Issued: 07.03.94. Made: 24.02.94. Coming into force: 14.03.94. Effect: S.I. 1991/2124; 1993/3047 revoked. Territorial extent & classification: GB. General. – 2p. – 0 11 043453 6 £0.65

The Broadcasting (Prescribed Countries) Order 1994 No. 454. Enabling power: *Broadcasting Act 1990, s. 43 (4)*. Issued: 07.03.94. Made: 24.02.94. Coming into force: 14.03.94. Effect: S.I. 1991/1820; 1993/3046 revoked. Territorial extent & classification: GB. General. – 2p. – 0 11 043454 4 £0.65

The Broadcasting (Restrictive Trade Practices Act 1976) (Exemption for Networking Arrangements) Order 1994 No. 2540. Enabling power: *Broadcasting Act 1990, s. 194 (1)*. Issued: 07.10.94. Made: 28.09.94. Laid: 03.10.94. Coming into force: 24.10.94. Effect: None. Territorial extent & classification: GB. General. – 4p. – 0 11 045540 1 £1.10

The Broadcasting (Unlicensed Television Services) Exemption Order 1994 No. 3172. Enabling power: *Broadcasting Act 1990, ss. 13 (2), 200*. Issued: 22.12.94. Made: 07.12.94. Laid: 15.12.94. Coming into force: 05.01.95. Effect: None. Territorial extent & classification: GB. General. – 2p. – 0 11 043442 0 £0.65

The Wireless Telegraphy (Guernsey) Order 1994 No. 1064. Enabling power: *Wireless Telegraphy Act 1949, s. 20 (3), & Marine, etc., Broadcasting (Offences) Act 1967, s. 10, & Telecommunications Act 1984, s. 108, & Broadcasting Act 1990, s. 204 (6)*. Issued: 25.04.94. Made: 13.04.94. Coming into force: 01.06.94. Effect: S.I. 1991/1709 amended. Territorial extent & classification: Guernsey. General. – 6p. – 0 11 044064 1 £1.55

BUILDING AND BUILDINGS

The Building (Prescribed Fees) Regulations 1994 No. 2020. Enabling power: *Building Act 1984, ss. 1, 16 (10), 34, 35, 50 (3), sch. 1, paras. 1 (b), 5, 10 (c)*. Issued: 09.08.94. Made: 01.08.94. Laid: 03.08.94. Coming into force: 01.10.94. Effect: S.I. 1985/1576; 1986/2287; 1988/871; 1989/1118; 1990/2600; 1992/741, 2079 revoked. Territorial extent & classification: E/W. General. – 16p. – 0 11 045020 5 £3.20

The Building Regulations (Amendment) Regulations 1994 No. 1850. Enabling power: *Building Act 1984, ss. 1 (1), 3 (1), 126, sch. 1, paras. 1, 2, 4, 7, 8, 10*. Issued: 22.07.94. Made: 12.07.94. Laid: 15.07.94. Coming into force: 01.10.94, for the purposes of reg. 2 (3)/ 01.01.95, for purposes of reg. 2 (2) (a) (4) (5) (b) (c). 01.09.94, for all other purposes. Effect: S.I. 1991/2768 amended. Territorial extent & classification: E/W. General. – 4p. – 0 11 044850 2 £1.10

The Building Standards (Scotland) Amendment Regulations 1994 No. 1266 (S. 65). Enabling power: *Building (Scotland) Act 1959, ss. 3, 24 (1) (b), 29 (1), sch. 4*. Issued: 19.05.94. Made: 09.05.94. Laid: 19.05.94. Coming into force: 30.06.94. Effect: S.I. 1990/2179 amended. With correction slip dated June 1994 Territorial extent & classification: S. General. – 4p. – 0 11 044266 0 £1.10

The Construction Products (Amendment) Regulations 1994 No. 3051. Enabling power: *European Communities Act 1972, s. 2 (2)*. Issued: 08.12.94. Made: 30.11.94. Laid: 08.12.94. Coming into force: 01.01.95. Effect: S.I. 1991/1620 amended. Territorial extent & classification: GB. General. – Gives effect to DIR 93/68 (OJ L 220/93). – 4p., ill. – 0 11 043291 6 £1.10

BUILDING SOCIETIES

The Building Societies (Accounts and Related Provisions) (Amendment) Regulations 1994 No.2459. Enabling power: *Building Societies Act 1986, ss. 73 (6) (7) (8), 74 (3) (4) (6), 75 (1) (b)*. Issued: 07.10.94. Made: 23.09.94. Laid: 03.10.94. Coming into force: 01.01.95. Effect: S.I. 1992/359 amended. Territorial extent & classification: GB. General. – 6p. – 0 11 045459 6 £1.55

Price/availability are liable to change without notice

The Building Societies (Aggregation) (Amendment) Rules 1994 No. 2458. Enabling power: *Building Societies Act 1986, s. 20 (9) (10).* Issued: 07.10.94. Made: 28.09.94. Laid: 03.10.94. Coming into force: 01.11.94. Effect: S.I. 1993/2833 amended. Territorial extent & classification: GB. General. – 2p. – 0 11 045458 8 *£0.65*

The Building Societies (Auditors) Order 1994 No. 525. Enabling power: *Building Societies Act 1986, s. 82 (9).* Issued: 14.03.94. Made: 03.03.94. Coming into force: 01.05.94. Effect: None. Supersedes Draft ISBN 0110458540 published on 17.01.94. Territorial extent & classification: GB. General. – 2p. – 0 11 043525 7 *£0.65*

The Building Societies (Designated Capital Resources) (Amendment) Order 1994 No. 750. Enabling power: *Building Societies Act 1986, s. 45 (5).* Issued: 29.03.94. Made: 11.03.94. Laid: 18.03.94. Coming into force: 15.04.94. Effect: S.I. 1992/1611 amended. Territorial extent & classification: GB. General. – 2p. – 0 11 043750 0 *£0.65*

The Building Societies (Designation of Qualifying Bodies) (Amendment) Order 1994 No. 2457. Enabling power: *Building Societies Act 1986, s. 18 (2) (3).* Issued: 07.10.94. Made: 28.09.94. Laid: 03.10.94. Coming into force: 01.11.94. Effect: S.I. 1993/985; 2706 amended. Territorial extent & classification: GB. General. – 4p. – 0 11 045457 X *£1.10*

The Building Societies (EFTA States) Order 1994 No. 655. Enabling power: *Building Societies Act 1986, s. 14.* Issued: 18.03.94. Made: 08.03.94. Coming into force: 09.03.94. Effect: None. Territorial extent & classification: GB. General. – 4p. – 0 11 043655 5 *£1.10*

The Building Societies (General Charge and Fees) Regulations 1994 No. 656. Enabling power: *Building Societies Act 1986, ss. 2 (2), 116 (2).* Issued: 08.04.94. Made: 08.03.94. Laid: 09.03.94. Coming into force: 01.04.94. Effect: S.I. 1993/546 revoked. Territorial extent & classification: GB. General. – 8p. – 0 11 043656 3 *£1.95*

The Building Societies (Undated Subordinated Debt) Order 1994 No. 749. Enabling power: *Building Societies Act 1986, s. 45 (5).* Issued: 30.03.94. Made: 11.03.94. Laid: 18.03.94. Coming into force: 15.04.94. Effect: S.I. 1991/702 amended. Territorial extent & classification: GB. General. – 8p. – 0 11 043749 7 *£1.95*

CARIBBEAN AND NORTH ATLANTIC TERRITORIES

The Virgin Islands (Constitution) (Amendment) Order 1994 No. 1638. Enabling power: *West Indies Act 1962, s. 5, 7.* Issued: 04.07.94. Made: 22.06.94. Laid: 04.07.94. Coming into force: On a day to be appointed under s. 1 (4). Effect: None. Territorial extent & classification: GB. General. – 2p. – 0 11 044638 0 *£0.65*

CHANNEL TUNNEL

The Channel Tunnel (Amendment of the Fisheries Act 1981) Order 1994 No. 1390. Enabling power: *Channel Tunnel Act 1987, ss. 11 (1) (d) (2) (b) (3) (b), 13 (1) (2).* Issued: 10.06.94. Made: 23.05.94. Laid: 10.06.94. Coming into force: 01.07.94. Effect: 1981 c. 29 amended. Territorial extent & classification: E/W/S. General. – 2p. – 0 11 044390 X *£0.65*

The Channel Tunnel (Application of Road Traffic Enactments) (No. 2) Order 1994 No. 1667. Enabling power: *Channel Tunnel Act 1987, s. 23.* Issued: 30.06.94. Made: 22.06.94. Laid: 30.06.94. Coming into force: 22.07.94. Effect: S.I. 1994/970 amended. This SI has been made in consequence of a defect in SI 1994/970 and is being sent free of charge to all known recipients of that SI. Territorial extent & classification: E. Local. – 6p. – 0 11 044667 4 *£1.10*

The Channel Tunnel (Application of Road Traffic Enactments) Order 1994 No. 970. Enabling power: *Channel Tunnel Act 1987, s. 23.* Issued: 06.04.94. Made: 29.03.94. Coming into force: 05.04.94. Effect: None. Territorial extent & classification: E. Local. – 2p. – 0 11 043970 8 *£0.65* Replaced by ISBN 0110459393

The Channel Tunnel (Miscellaneous Provisions) Order 1994 No. 1405. Enabling power: *Channel Tunnel Act 1987, s. 11.* Issued: 02.06.94. Made: 24.05.94. Laid: 02.06.94. Coming into force: In accord. with art. 1. Effect: S.I. 1974/2211; 1984/2041; 1989/1813; Prvention of Terrorism (Temporary Provision) (Places of Detention) Direction 1989; 1990/2167; 1993/1813; 1994/311; Immigration (Places of Detention) Direction 1994 amended. Territorial extent & classification: E/W. General. – 20p. – 0 11 044405 1 *£3.70*

The Channel Tunnel (Security) Order 1994 No. 570. Enabling power: *Channel Tunnel Act 1987, s. 11.* Issued: 14.03.94. Made: 04.03.94. Laid: 07.02.94. Coming into force: 05.03.94. Effect: 1978 c. 26; 1984 c 60; 1991 c. 24; S.I. 1989/1341 (NI. 12) amended. Supersedes Draft ISBN 0110458745 published on 11.02.94. Territorial extent & classification: GB. General. – 36p. – 0 11 043570 2 *£6.10*

The Channel Tunnel (Shop and Liquor Licensing Hours Requirements) (Disapplication) Order 1994 No. 2478. Enabling power: *Channel Tunnel Act 1987, s. 11.* Issued: 03.10.94. Made: 21.09.94. Laid: 23.09.94. Coming into force: 14.10.94. Effect: None. Territorial extent & classification: E. Local. – 2p. – 0 11 045478 2 *£0.65*

The Channel Tunnel (Sunday Trading Act 1994) (Disapplication) Order 1994 No. 3286. Enabling power: *Channel Tunnel Act 1987, s. 11.* Issued: 04.01.95. Made: 19.12.94. Laid: 29.12.94. Coming into force: 19.01.95. Effect: None. Territorial extent & classification: E. Local. – 2p. – 0 11 043820 5 *£0.65*

CHARITIES

The Charitable Institutions (Fund-Raising) Regulations 1994 No. 3024. Enabling power: *Charities Act 1992, ss. 64, 77 (3).* Issued: 06.12.94. Made: 28.11.94. Laid: 06.12.94. Coming into force: 01.03.95. Effect: None. Territorial extent & classification: E/W. General. – 6p. – 0 11 043258 4 *£1.55*

Price/availability are liable to change without notice

The Charities Act 1992 (Commencement No. 2) Order 1994 No. 3023 (C. 69). Enabling power: *Charities Act 1992, ss. 77 (3), 79 (2). Bringing into operation various provisions of the 1992 act on 28.11.94.* Issued: 06.12.94. Made: 28.11.94. Effect: None. Territorial extent & classification: E/W. General. – 2p. – 0 11 043257 6 £0.65

The Charities (The National Trust for Places of Historic Interest or Natural Beauty) Order 1994 No. 2181. Enabling power: *Charities Act 1993, s. 17 (2).* Issued: 25.08.94. Made: 16.08.94. Coming into force: 30.08.94. Effect: None. Supersedes Draft ISBN 0110459342 published on 14.06.94. Territorial extent & classification: E/W. General. – 4p. – 0 11 045181 3 £1.10

The Charities (The Royal Philanthropic Society) Order 1994 No. 1235. Enabling power: *Charities Act 1993, s. 17 (2).* Issued: 13.05.94. Made: 06.05.94. Coming into force: 20.05.94. Effect: 1806 c.cxliv; 1823 c.18; 1848 c.cix revoked. This SI supersedes Draft SI ISBN 0110458869 previously published on 08.03.94. Territorial extent & classification: E/W. General. –8p. – 0 11 044235 0 £1.95

The Exempt Charities Order 1994 No. 1905. Enabling power: *Charities Act 1993, sch. 2, para. (c).* Issued: 29.07.94. Made: 19.07.94. Coming into force: 01.08.94. Effect: None. Territorial extent & classification: E/W. General. – 2p. – 0 11 044905 3 £0.65

The Exempt Charities Order (No. 2) 1994 No. 2956. Enabling power: *Charities Act 1993, sch. 2, para. (c).* Issued: 02.12.94. Made: 24.11.94. Coming into force: 01.01.95. Effect: None. Territorial extent & classification: E/W. General. – 2p. – 0 11 043208 8 £0.65

CHILDREN AND YOUNG PERSONS

The Child Abduction and Custody Act 1985 (Isle of Man) Order 1994 No. 2799. Enabling power: *Child Abduction and Custody Act 1985, s. 28 (2).* Issued: 14.11.94. Made: 02.11.94. Laid: 14.11.94. Coming into force: 06.12.94. Effect: None. Territorial extent & classification: GB. General. – 2p. – 0 11 045799 4 £0.65

The Child Abduction and Custody (Parties to Conventions) (Amendment) (No. 2) Order 1994 No.1063. Enabling power: *Child Abduction and Custody Act 1985, s. 2.* Issued: 21.04.94. Made: 13.04.94. Coming into force: 01.05.94. Effect: S.I. 1994/262 amended. Territorial extent & classification: GB. General. – 2p. – 0 11 044063 3 £0.65

The Child Abduction and Custody (Parties to Conventions) (Amendment) (No. 3) Order 1994 No.1322. Enabling power: *Child Abduction and Custody Act 1985, s. 2.* Issued: 25.05.94. Made: 18.05.94. Coming into force: 18.05.94. Effect: S.I. 1993/3144 amended & S.I. 1994/262, 1063 revoked. Territorial extent & classification: GB. General. – 2p. – 0 11 044322 5 £0.65

The Child Abduction and Custody (Parties to Conventions) (Amendment) (No. 4) Order 1994 No.1889. Enabling power: *Child Abduction and Custody Act 1985, s. 2.* Issued: 29.07.94. Made: 19.07.94. Coming into force: 01.08.94. Effect: S.I. 1993/3144 amended & S.I. 1994/1322 revoked. Territorial extent & classification: GB. General. – 2p. – 0 11 044889 8 £0.65

The Child Abduction and Custody (Parties to Conventions) (Amendment) (No. 5) Order 1994 No.2792. Enabling power: *Child Abduction and Custody Act 1985, s. 13.* Issued: 11.11.94. Made: 02.11.94. Coming into force: 02.11.94. Effect: S.I. 1986/1159 amended & S.I. 1993/1243 revoked. Territorial extent & classification: GB. General. – 2p. – 0 11 045792 7 £0.65

The Child Abduction and Custody (Parties to Conventions) (Amendment) (No. 6) Order 1994 No.3201. Enabling power: *Child Abduction and Custody Act 1985, s. 2.* Issued: 21.12.94. Made: 14.12.94. Coming into force: 01.02.95. Effect: S.I. 1993/3144 amended & S.I. 1994/1889 revoked. Territorial extent & classification: GB. General. – 4p. – 0 11 043587 7 £1.10

The Child Abduction and Custody (Parties to Conventions) (Amendment) Order 1994 No.262. Enabling power: *Child Abduction and Custody Act 1985, s. 2.* Issued: 18.02.94. Made: 08.02.94. Coming into force: 01.03.94. Effect: S.I. 1993/3144 amended. Territorial extent & classification: GB. General. – 2p. – 0 11 043262 2 £0.65

The Children's Homes Amendment Regulations 1994 No. 1511. Enabling power: *Children Act 1989, sch. 4, para. 4 (1) (2) (b), sch. 5, para. 7 (1) (2) (b), sch. 6, para. 10 (1) (2) (b) (c).* Issued: 13.06.94. Made: 06.06.94. Laid: 13.06.94. Coming into force: 04.07.94. Effect: S.I. 1991/1506; 1993/3069 amended. This SI has been made to correct an error in SI 1993/3069 & is being issued free of charge to all known recipients of that SI. Territorial extent & classification: E/W. General. – 2p. – 0 11 044511 2 £0.65

The Family Law Act 1986 (Dependent Territories) (Amendment) Order 1994 No. 2800. Enabling power: *Family Law Court Act 1986, s. 43.* Issued: 14.11.94. Made: 02.11.94. Laid: 14.11.94. Coming into force: 06.12.94. Effect: S.I.1991/1723 amended. Territorial extent & classification: GB. General. – 2p. – 0 11 045800 1 £0.65

The Parental Responsibility Agreement (Amendment) Regulations 1994 No.3157. Enabling power: *Children Act 1989, ss. 4 (2), 104.* Issued: 21.12.94. Made: 08.12.94. Laid: 12.12.94. Coming into force: 03.01.95. Effect: S.I. 1991/1478 amended. With correction slip dated January 1995. Territorial extent & classification: E/W. General. – 4p. – 0 11 043477 3 £1.10

CINEMAS AND FILMS

The European Convention on Cinematographic Co-production (Amendment) (No. 2) Order 1994 No.3218. Enabling power: *Films Act 1985, sch. 1, para. 4 (5).* Issued: 21.12.94. Made: 14.12.94. Coming into force: 04.01.95. Effect: S.I. 1994/1065 amended. Territorial extent & classification: E/W/S. General. – 2p. – 0 11 043552 4 £0.65

Price/availability are liable to change without notice

The European Convention on Cinematographic Co-production (Amendment) Order 1994 No.1904. Enabling power: *Films Act 1985, sch. 1, para. 4 (5).* Issued: 26.07.94. Made: 19.07.94. Coming into force: 10.08.94. Effect: S.I. 1994/1065 amended. Territorial extent & classification: E/W/S. General. – 2p. – 0 11 044904 5 *£0.65*

The European Convention on Cinematographic Co-production Order 1994 No. 1065. Enabling power: *Films Act 1985, sch. 1, para. 4 (5).* Issued: 21.04.94. Made: 13.04.94. Coming into force: 14.04.94. Effect: None. Territorial extent & classification: GB. General. – 2p. – 0 11 044065 X *£0.65*

The Films Co-Production Agreements (Amendment) Order 1994 No. 3222. Enabling power: *Films Act 1985, sch. 1, para. 4 (5).* Issued: 21.12.94. Made: 14.12.94. Coming into force: 15.12.94. Effect: S.I. 1985/960 amended. Territorial extent & classification: E/W/S. General. – 2p. – 0 11 043583 4 *£0.65*

CIVIL AVIATION

The Access for Community Air Carriers to Intra-Community Air Routes (Second Amendment and Other Provisions) Regulations 1994 No. 1731. Enabling power: *European Communities Act 1972, s. 2 (2).* Issued: 11.07.94. Made: 30.06.94. Laid: 01.07.94. Coming into force: 01.07.94. Effect: S.I. 1992/2993; 1989/2004 & 1980 c. 19 amended. Territorial extent & classification: GB. General. – 4p. – 0 11 044731 X *£1.10*

The Aeroplane Noise (Limitation on Operation of Aeroplanes) (Amendment) Regulations 1994 No.1734. Enabling power: *European Communities Act 1972, s. 2 (2).* Issued: 11.07.94. Made: 30.06.94. Laid: 01.07.94. Coming into force: 01.07.94. Effect: S.I. 1993/1409 amended. Territorial extent & classification: GB. General. – 2p. – 0 11 044734 4 *£0.65*

The Air Fares (Third Amendment) Regulations 1994 No. 1735. Enabling power: *European Communities Act 1972, s. 2 (2).* Issued: 11.07.94. Made: 30.06.94. Laid: 01.07.94. Coming into force: 01.07.94. Effect: S.I. 1992/2994 amended. Territorial extent & classification: GB. General. – 2p. – 0 11 044735 2 *£0.65*

The Air Navigation (Dangerous Goods) Regulations 1994 No. 3187. Enabling power: *S.I. 1989/2004, arts. 47 (1), 106 (5).* Issued: 22.12.94. Made: 06.12.94. Coming into force: 01.01.95. Effect: S.I. 1985/1939; 1986/2129; 1988/2133; 1990/2531; 1993/179 revoked. Territorial extent & classification: GB. General. – 10p. – 0 11 043733 0 *£2.40*

The Air Navigation (Restriction of Flying) (Ballahulish) Regulations 1994 No. 3235. Enabling power: *Air Navigation Order 1989, art. 74.* Made: 07.12.94. Coming into force: 07.12.94. Effect: None. – *Unpublished*

The Air Navigation (Restriction of Flying) (Ballahulish) (Revocation) Regulations 1994 No. 3236. Enabling power: *Air Navigation Order 1989, art. 74.* Made: 09.12.94. Coming into force: 09.12.94. Effect: S.I. 1994/3235 revoked. – *Unpublished*

The Air Navigation (Restriction of Flying) (Bournemouth) Regulations 1994 No. 2159. Enabling power: *Air Navigation Order 1989, art. 74.* Made: 08.08.94. Coming into force: 08.10.94. Effect: None. – *Unpublished*

The Air Navigation (Restriction of Flying) (Brentwood) Regulations 1994 No. 904. Enabling power: *Air Navigation Order 1989, art. 74.* Made: 18.03.94. Coming into force: 18.03.94. Effect: None. – *Unpublished*

The Air Navigation (Restriction of Flying) (Brentwood) (Revocation) Regulations 1994 No.905. Enabling power: *Air Navigation Order 1989, art. 74.* Made: 18.03.94. Coming into force: 18.03.94. Effect: None. – *Unpublished*

The Air Navigation (Restriction of Flying) (Chequers) Regulations 1994 No. 2493. Enabling power: *Air Navigation Order 1989, art. 74.* Made: 20.09.94. Coming into force: 24.09.94. Effect: None. – *Unpublished*

The Air Navigation (Restriction of Flying) (Coventry) Regulations 1994 No. 3322. Enabling power: *Air Navigation Order 1989, art. 74.* Made: 21.12.94. Coming into force: 21.12.94. Effect: None. – *Unpublished*

The Air Navigation (Restriction of Flying) (Coventry) (Revocation) Regulations 1994 No.3323. Enabling power: *Air Navigation Order 1989, art. 74.* Made: 22.12.94. Coming into force: 22.12.94. Effect: S.I. 1994/3322 revoked. – *Unpublished*

The Air Navigation (Restriction of Flying) (Cowden) Regulations 1994 No. 2712. Enabling power: *Air Navigation Order 1989, art. 74.* Made: 15.10.94. Coming into force: 15.10.94. Effect: None. – *Unpublished*

The Air Navigation (Restriction of Flying) (Cowden) (Revocation) Regulations 1994 No.2713. Enabling power: *Air Navigation Order 1989, art. 74.* Made: 17.10.94. Coming into force: 17.10.94. Effect: S.I. 1994/1712 revoked. – *Unpublished*

The Air Navigation (Restriction of Flying) (Cranfield) Regulations 1994 No. 784. Enabling power: *Air Navigation Order 1989, art. 74.* Made: 14.03.94. Coming into force: 01.07.94. Effect: None. – *Unpublished*

The Air Navigation (Restriction of Flying) (Edinburgh) Regulations 1994 No. 1392. Enabling power: *Air Navigation Order 1989, art. 74.* Made: 19.05.94. Coming into force: 20.05.94. Effect: None. – *Unpublished*

The Air Navigation (Restriction of Flying) (Epsom Racecourse) Regulations 1994 No.1154. Enabling power: *Air Navigation Order 1989, art. 74.* Made: 19.04.94. Coming into force: 01.06.94. Effect: None. – *Unpublished*

The Air Navigation (Restriction of Flying) (Exhibition of Flying) (No. 1) Regulations 1994 No. 327. Enabling power: *Air Navigation Order 1989, art. 74.* Made: 08.02.94. Coming into force: 15.03.94. Effect: None. – *Unpublished*

The Air Navigation (Restriction of Flying) (Exhibition of Flying) (No.2) Regulations 1994 No.1157. Enabling power: *Air Navigation Order 1989, art. 74.* Made: 19.04.94. Coming into force: 21.05.94. Effect: None. – *Unpublished*

Price/availability are liable to change without notice

12 CIVIL AVIATION

The Air Navigation (Restriction of Flying) (Exhibition of Flying) (No. 3) Regulations 1994 No. 1991. Enabling power: *Air Navigation Order 1989, art. 74.* Made: 11.07.94. Coming into force: 17.09.94. Effect: None. – *Unpublished*

The Air Navigation (Restriction of Flying) (Exhibition of Flying) (No. 3) (Amendment) Regulations 1994 No. 1992. Enabling power: *Air Navigation Order 1989, art. 74.* Made: 22.07.94. Coming into force: 22.07.94. Effect: S.I. 1994/1991 amended. – *Unpublished*

The Air Navigation (Restriction of Flying) (Exhibition of Flying) (No.3) (Second Amendment) Regulations 1994 No. 2160. Enabling power: *Air Navigation Order 1989, art. 74.* Made: 08.08.94. Coming into force: 08.08.94. Effect: S.I. 1994/1991 amended. – *Unpublished*

The Air Navigation (Restriction of Flying) (Exhibition of Flying) (No. 3) (Third Amendment) Regulations 1994 No. 2260. Enabling power: *Air Navigation Order 1989, art. 74.* Made: 26.08.94. Coming into force: 26.08.94. Effect: S.I. 1994/1991 amended. – *Unpublished*

The Air Navigation (Restriction of Flying) (Fairford) Regulations 1994 No. 1612. Enabling power: *Air Navigation Order 1989, art. 74.* Made: 14.06.94. Coming into force: 27.07.94. Effect: None. – *Unpublished*

The Air Navigation (Restriction of Flying) (Farnborough) Regulations 1994 No. 1969. Enabling power: *Air Navigation Order 1989, art. 74.* Made: 11.07.94. Coming into force: 30.08.94. Effect: None. – *Unpublished*

The Air Navigation (Restriction of Flying) (Finningley) Regulations 1994 No. 1968. Enabling power: *Air Navigation Order 1989, art. 74.* Made: 11.07.94. Coming into force: 16.09.94. Effect: None. – *Unpublished*

The Air Navigation (Restriction of Flying) (Gawcott) Regulations 1994 No. 3072. Enabling power: *Air Navigation Order 1989, art. 74.* Made: 26.11.94. Coming into force: 26.11.94. Effect: None. – *Unpublished*

The Air Navigation (Restriction of Flying) (Gawcott) (Revocation) Regulations 1994 No. 3073. Enabling power: *Air Navigation Order 1989, art. 74.* Made: 27.11.94. Coming into force: 27.11.94. Effect: S.I. 1994/3072 revoked. – *Unpublished*

The Air Navigation (Restriction of Flying) (Glen Ogle) (No. 2) Regulations 1994 No. 2491. Enabling power: *Air Navigation Order 1989, art. 74.* Made: 04.09.94. Coming into force: 04.09.94. Effect: None. – *Unpublished*

The Air Navigation (Restriction of Flying) (Glen Ogle) (No. 2) (Revocation) Regulations 1994 No. 2492. Enabling power: *Air Navigation Order 1989, art. 74.* Made: 04.09.94. Coming into force: 04.09.94. Effect: SI 1994/2491 revoked. – *Unpublished*

The Air Navigation (Restriction of Flying) (Glen Ogle) Regulations 1994 No. 2489. Enabling power: *Air Navigation Order 1989, art. 74.* Made: 01.09.94. Coming into force: 01.09.94. Effect: None. – *Unpublished*

The Air Navigation (Restriction of Flying) (Glen Ogle) (Revocation) Regulations 1994 No. 2490. Enabling power: *Air Navigation Order 1989, art. 74.* Made: 02.09.94. Coming into force: 02.09.94. Effect: SI 1994/2489 revoked. – *Unpublished*

The Air Navigation (Restriction of Flying) (Great Longstone) Regulations 1994 No. 2161. Enabling power: *Air Navigation Order 1989, art. 74.* Made: 08.08.94. Coming into force: 22.08.94. Effect: None. – *Unpublished*

The Air Navigation (Restriction of Flying) (Guidon Ceremony) Regulations 1994 No. 785. Enabling power: *Air Navigation Order 1989, art. 74.* Made: 14.03.94. Coming into force: 10.05.94. Effect: None. – *Unpublished*

The Air Navigation (Restriction of Flying) (Hackney) Regulations 1994 No. 352. Enabling power: *Air Navigation Order 1989, art. 74.* Made: 16.02.94. Coming into force: 20.03.94. Effect: None. – *Unpublished*

The Air Navigation (Restriction of Flying) (Higher Chisworth) Regulations 1994 No. 3237. Enabling power: *Air Navigation Order 1989, art. 74.* Made: 08.12.94. Coming into force: 08.12.94. Effect: None. – *Unpublished*

The Air Navigation (Restriction of Flying) (Higher Chisworth) (Revocation) Regulations 1994 No. 3238. Enabling power: *Air Navigation Order 1989, art. 74.* Made: 09.12.94. Coming into force: 09.12.94. Effect: S.I. 1994/3237 revoked. – *Unpublished*

The Air Navigation (Restriction of Flying) (Inverness) Regulations 1994 No. 1155. Enabling power: *Air Navigation Order 1989, art. 74.* Made: 19.04.94. Coming into force: 11.05.94. Effect: None. – *Unpublished*

The Air Navigation (Restriction of Flying) (Kensington) Regulations 1994 No. 2065. Enabling power: *Air Navigation Order 1989, art. 74.* Made: 26.07.94. Coming into force: 26.07.94. Effect: None. – *Unpublished*

The Air Navigation (Restriction of Flying) (Kensington) (Revocation) Regulations 1994 No. 2066. Enabling power: *Air Navigation Order 1989, art. 74.* Made: 27.07.94. Coming into force: 27.07.94. Effect: S.I. 1994/2065 revoked. – *Unpublished*

The Air Navigation (Restriction of Flying) (Kintyre) Regulations 1994 No. 1521. Enabling power: *Air Navigation Order 1989, art. 74.* Made: 02.06.94. Coming into force: 02.06.94. Effect: None. – *Unpublished*

The Air Navigation (Restriction of Flying) (Kintyre) (Revocation) Regulations 1994 No. 1522. Enabling power: *Air Navigation Order 1989, art. 74.* Made: 06.06.94. Coming into force: 06.06.94. Effect: S.I. 1994/1521 revoked. – *Unpublished*

The Air Navigation (Restriction of Flying) (Leicester) Regulations 1994 No. 1764. Enabling power: *Air Navigation Order 1989, art. 74.* Made: 26.06.94. Coming into force: 26.06.94. Effect: None. – *Unpublished*

The Air Navigation (Restriction of Flying) (Leicester) (Revocation) Regulations 1994 No. 1765. Enabling power: *Air Navigation Order 1989, art. 74.* Made: 26.06.94. Coming into force: 26.06.94. Effect: S.I. 1994/1764 revoked. – *Unpublished*

Price/availability are liable to change without notice

The Air Navigation (Restriction of Flying) (Middle Wallop) Regulations 1994 No. 783. Enabling power: *Air Navigation Order 1989, art. 74.* Made: 14.03.94. Coming into force: 13.05.94. Effect: None. – *Unpublished*

The Air Navigation (Restriction of Flying) (Official Opening of the Channel Tunnel) Regulations 1994 No. 1194. Enabling power: *Air Navigation Order 1989, art. 74.* Made: 27.04.94. Coming into force: 06.05.94. Effect: None. – *Unpublished*

The Air Navigation (Restriction of Flying) (Piper Bravo) Regulations 1994 No. 1229. Enabling power: *Air Navigation Order 1989, art. 74.* Made: 02.05.94. Coming into force: 02.05.94. Effect: None. – *Unpublished*

The Air Navigation (Restriction of Flying) (Piper Bravo) (Revocation) Regulations 1994 No.1264. Enabling power: *Air Navigation Order 1989, art. 74.* Made: 02.05.94. Coming into force: 02.05.94. Effect: S.I. 1994/1229 revoked. – *Unpublished*

The Air Navigation (Restriction of Flying) (Portsmouth and D day 50th Anniversary Commemoration Flypast) Regulations 1994 No. 1197. Enabling power: *Air Navigation Order 1989, art. 74.* Made: 19.04.94. Coming into force: 03.06.94. Effect: None. – *Unpublished*

The Air Navigation (Restriction of Flying) (Portsmouth and D Day 50th Anniversary Commemoration Flypast) (No. 2) Regulations 1994 No. 1393. Enabling power: *Air Navigation Order 1989, art. 74.* Made: 18.05.94. Coming into force: 03.06.94. Effect: S.I. 1994/1197 revoked. – *Unpublished*

The Air Navigation (Restriction of Flying) (Rememberance Day Ceremony) Regulations 1994 No. 2630. Enabling power: *Air Navigation Order 1989, art. 74.* Made: 05.10.94. Coming into force: 13.11.94. Effect: None. – *Unpublished*

The Air Navigation (Restriction of Flying) (Ripon) Regulations 1994 No. 1171. Enabling power: *Air Navigation Order 1989, art. 74.* Made: 21.04.94. Coming into force: 21.04.94. Effect: None. – *Unpublished*

The Air Navigation (Restriction of Flying) (Ripon) (Revocation) Regulations 1994 No.1172. Enabling power: *Air Navigation Order 1989, art. 74.* Made: 21.04.94. Coming into force: 21.04.94. Effect: S.I. 1994/1171 revoked. – *Unpublished*

The Air Navigation (Restriction of Flying) (Runnymede) Regulations 1994 No. 1395. Enabling power: *Air Navigation Order 1989, art. 74.* Made: 17.05.94. Coming into force: 31.05.94. Effect: None. – *Unpublished*

The Air Navigation (Restriction of Flying) (Silverstone Aerodrome) Regulations 1994 No.1394. Enabling power: *Air Navigation Order 1989, art. 74.* Made: 12.05.94. Coming into force: 10.07.94. Effect: None. – *Unpublished*

The Air Navigation (Restriction of Flying) (State Opening of Parliament) Regulations 1994 No.2629. Enabling power: *Air Navigation Order 1989, art. 74.* Made: 05.10.94. Coming into force: 16.11.94. Effect: None. – *Unpublished*

The Air Navigation (Restriction of Flying) (State Visit of the King and Queen of Norway) Regulations 1994 No. 1391. Enabling power: *Air Navigation Order 1989, art. 74.* Made: 17.05.94. Coming into force: 05.07.94. Effect: None. – *Unpublished*

The Air Navigation (Restriction of Flying) (State Visit of the President of Zimbabwe) Regulations 1994 No.1153. Enabling power: *Air Navigation Order 1989, art. 74.* Made: 19.04.94. Coming into force: 17.05.94. Effect: None. – *Unpublished*

The Air Navigation (Restriction of Flying) (Stevenage) Regulations 1994 No. 1766. Enabling power: *Air Navigation Order 1989, art. 74.* Made: 13.06.94. Coming into force: 13.06.94. Effect: None. – *Unpublished*

The Air Navigation (Restriction of Flying) (Stevenage) (Revocation) Regulations 1994 No.1767. Enabling power: *Air Navigation Order 1989, art. 74.* Made: 13.06.94. Coming into force: 13.06.94. Effect: S.I. 1994/1766 revoked. – *Unpublished*

The Air Navigation (Restriction of Flying) (St Mawgan) Regulations 1994 No. 1970. Enabling power: *Air Navigation Order 1989, art. 74.* Made: 20.07.94. Coming into force: 02.08.94. Effect: None. – *Unpublished*

The Air Navigation (Restriction of Flying) (The Queen's Birthday Parade) Regulations 1994 No.1156. Enabling power: *Air Navigation Order 1989, art. 74.* Made: 19.04.94. Coming into force: 28.05.94. Effect: None. – *Unpublished*

The Air Navigation (Restriction of Flying) (Tour de France (United Kingdom Stages)) Regulations 1994 No. 1396. Enabling power: *Air Navigation Order 1989, art. 74.* Made: 17.05.94. Coming into force: 06.07.94. Effect: None. – *Unpublished*

The Air Navigation (Restriction of Flying) (Visit of the President of the United States of America) Regulations 1994 No. 1514. Enabling power: *Air Navigation Order 1989, art. 74.* Made: 03.06.94. Coming into force: 04.06.94. Effect: None. – *Unpublished*

The Air Navigation (Restriction of Flying) (Wigan) Regulations 1994 No. 3332. Enabling power: *Air Navigation Order 1989, art. 74.* Made: 30.12.94. Coming into force: 30.12.94. Effect: None. – *Unpublished*

The Airports Slot Allocation (Second Amendment) Regulations 1994 No. 1736. Enabling power: *European Communities Act 1972, s. 2 (2).* Issued: 11.07.94. Made: 30.06.94. Laid: 01.07.94. Coming into force: 01.07.94. Effect: S.I. 1993/1067 amended. Territorial extent & classification: GB. General. – 2p. – 0 11 044736 0 *£0.65*

The Civil Aviation (Canadian Navigation Services) (Fifth Amendment) Regulations 1994 No.1601. Enabling power: *Civil Aviation Act 1982, s. 73 (1) (a) (4) (6) (a).* Issued: 24.06.94. Made: 16.06.94. Laid: 17.06.94. Coming into force: 01.07.94. Effect: S.I. 1986/1202 amended. Territorial extent & classification: GB. General. – 2p. – 0 11 044601 1 *£0.65*

Price/availability are liable to change without notice

The Civil Aviation (Canadian Navigation Services) Regulations 1994 No. 2325. Enabling power: *Civil Aviation Act 1982, ss. 73 (1) (a) (3) (4) (6) (a) (9), 74 (4) (a) (5).* Issued: 15.09.94. Made: 06.09.94. Laid: 09.09.94. Coming into force: 01.10.94. Effect: S.I. 1986/1202; 1988/772; 1989/2220; 1991/198; 1993/2320; 1994/1601 revoked. Territorial extent & classification: GB. General. – 6p. – 0 11 045325 5 £1.55

The Civil Aviation (Joint Financing) Regulations 1994 No. 3055. Enabling power: *Civil Aviation Act 1982, ss. 73 (1) (3) (4) (6) (a) (9), 74 (4) (a) (5), 102 (2) (b).* Issued: 09.12.94. Made: 29.11.94. Laid: 09.12.94. Coming into force: 01.01.95. Effect: S.I. 1988/2151; 1989/2221; 1990/2514; 1991/2792; 1992/3039; 1993/2975 revoked. Territorial extent & classification: GB. General. – 6p. – 0 11 043312 2 £1.55

The Civil Aviation (Navigation Services Charges) (Fourth Amendment) Regulations 1994 No.503. Enabling power: *Civil Aviation Act 1982, ss. 73 (1) (a) (3) (4), 6 (a).* Issued: 08.03.94. Made: 01.03.94. Laid: 08.03.94. Coming into force: 01.04.94. Effect: S.I. 1991/470 amended. Territorial extent & classification: GB. General. – 4p. – 0 11 043503 6 £1.10

The Civil Aviation (Personnel Licences) Order 1992 (Amendment) Regulations 1994 No.1733. Enabling power: *European Communities Act 1972, s. 2 (2).* Issued: 11.07.94. Made: 30.06.94. Laid: 01.07.94. Coming into force: 01.07.94. Effect: S.I. 1992/2673 amended. Territorial extent & classification: NI. General. – 2p. – 0 11 044733 6 £0.65

The Civil Aviation (Route Charges for Navigation Services) Regulations 1994 No. 3071. Enabling power: *Civil Aviation Act 1982, ss. 73 (1) (a) (1A) (3) (4) (6), 74 (4), 102 (2) (b).* Issued: 09.12.94. Made: 01.12.94. Laid: 09.12.94. Coming into force: 01.01.95. Effect: S.I. 1993/1965, 3098; 1994/1468 revoked. Territorial extent & classification: GB. General. –12p. – 0 11 043304 1 £2.80

The Civil Aviation (Route Charges for Navigation Services) (Third Amendment) Regulations 1994 No. 1468. Enabling power: *Civil Aviation Act 1982, ss. 73 (1) (a) (1A) (a), 6 (b) (i).* Issued: 09.06.94. Made: 02.06.94. Laid: 09.06.94. Coming into force: 01.07.94. Effect: S.I. 1993/1965 amended. Territorial extent & classification: GB. General. – 8p. – 0 11 044468 X £1.95

The Licensing of Air Carriers (Third Amendment and Other Provisions) Regulations 1994 No.1732. Enabling power: *European Communities Act 1972, s. 2 (2).* Issued: 11.07.94. Made: 30.06.94. Laid: 01.07.94. Coming into force: 01.07.94. Effect: 1982 c. 16; S.I. 1992/2992; 1991/1672; 1989/2004 amended. Territorial extent & classification: GB. General. – 4p. – 0 11 044732 8 £1.10

The Rules of the Air (Third Amendment) Regulations 1994 No. 1444. Enabling power: *S.I. 1989/2004, art. 69 (1).* Issued: 08.06.94. Made: 26.05.94. Coming into force: 01.07.94. Effect: S.I. 1991/2437 amended. Territorial extent & classification: GB. General. – 4p. – 0 11 044444 2 £1.10

CLEAN AIR

The Ozone Monitoring and Information Regulations 1994 No. 440. Enabling power: *European Communities Act 1972, s. 2 (2).* Issued: 07.03.94. Made: 24.02.94. Laid: 28.02.94. Coming into force: 21.03.94. Effect: None. Territorial extent & classification: GB. General. – 2p. – 0 11 043440 4 £0.65

CLERK OF THE CROWN IN CHANCERY

The Crown Office Fees Order 1994 No. 600. Enabling power: *Great Seal (Offices) Act 1874, s. 9.* Issued: 11.03.94. Made: 07.03.94. Coming into force: 08.03.94. Effect: S.I. 1990/2319 revoked. Territorial extent & classification: E/W. General. – 2p. – 0 11 043600 8 £0.65

COAL INDUSTRY

The Aire and Calder Navigation Act 1992 (Amendment) Order 1994 No. 3065. Enabling power: *Coal Industry Act 1994, s. 67 (2) (3) (4).* Issued: 05.01.95. Made: 01.12.94. Laid: 01.12.94. Coming into force: 24.12.94. Effect: 1992 c. iv amended. Territorial extent & classification: E. Local. – 4p. – 0 11 043817 5 £1.10

The British Coal Staff Superannuation Scheme (Modification) Regulations 1994 No. 2576. Enabling power: *Coal Industry Act 1994, s. 22 (1), para. 2 (1) (2) (3) (4) (5) (6) (7) (8) (11), sch. 5, para. 5 (1) (2).* Issued: 26.10.94. Made: 04.10.94. Laid: 07.10.94. Coming into force: 31.10.94. Effect: None. Territorial extent & classification: E/W/S. General. – 112p. – 0 11 045576 2 £10.35

The Coal Industry Act 1994 (Commencement No. 1) Order 1994 No. 2189 (C. 45). Enabling power: *Coal Industry Act 1994, s. 68 (4) (5). Bringing into operation various provisions of this Act on 19.09.94.* Issued: 01.09.94. Made: 21.08.94. Effect: None. Territorial extent & classification: GB. General. – 4p. – 0 11 045189 9 £1.10

The Coal Industry Act 1994 (Commencement No. 2 and Transitional Provision) Order 1994 No.2552 (C. 53). Enabling power: *Coal Industry Act 1994, s. 68 (4) (5). Bringing into operation various provisions of the 1994 act on 31.10.94.* Issued: 13.10.94. Made: 29.09.94. Laid: 05.10.94. Effect: None. Territorial extent & classification: GB/IOM. General. – 6p. – 0 11 045552 5 £1.55

The Coal Industry Act 1994 (Commencement No. 3) Order 1994 No. 3063 (C. 71). Enabling power: *Coal Industry Act 1994, s. 68 (4) (5). Bringing various provisions of the 1994 act into operation on the 24.12.94.* Issued: 05.01.95. Made: 01.12.94. Effect: None. Territorial extent & classification: E/W/S. General. – 4p. – 0 11 043837 X £1.10

Price/availability are liable to change without notice

The Coal Industry Act 1994 (Consequential Modifications of Local Acts) Order 1994 No.3081. Enabling power: *Coal Industry Act 1994, s. 67 (2) (3) (4).* Issued: 16.01.95. Made: 03.12.94. Laid: 05.12.94. Coming into force: 27.12.94. Effect: 1953 c.xx; 1959 c.xliv; 1969 c.xlix, c.xxxiv; 1971 c.xiii, c.xvi; 1972 c.xxviii, c.xxxix, c.xliv, c.xlvi; ; 1973 c.xxix, c.xxxi, c.xxxii; 1976 c.xxv; 1981 c.ix, c.xxiii, c.xxxv; 1983 c.xviii; 1985 c.xv; 1987 c.vii, c.viii amended. Territorial extent & classification: E/W/S. Local. – 12p. – 0 11 043901 5 £2.80

The Coal Industry Act 1994 (Consequential Modifications of Subordinate Legislation) Order 1994 No. 2567. Enabling power: *Coal Industry Act 1994, s. 67 (2).* Issued: 17.10.94. Made: 03.10.94. Laid: 06.10.94. Coming into force: 31.10.94. Effect: S.I. 1966/1471; 1969/1843; 1970/1152; 1977/815; 1981/15, 1468; 1983/506; 1984/457; 1985/698; 1986/625, 1078, 2194; 1987/433, 1343, 1345, 1532; 1988/646, 900; 1989/1796, 2203, 2204, 2205; 2206; 1990/426; 1992/656, 1703, 2902; 1993/323; 1994/1381 amended. Territorial extent & classification: E/W/S. General. – 8p. – 0 11 045567 3 £1.95

The Coal Industry (Protected Persons) Pensions Regulations 1994 No. 3070. Enabling power: *Coal Industry Act 1994, s. 22, sch. 5, paras. 4, 5.* Issued: 03.01.95. Made: 01.12.94. Laid: 02.12.94. Coming into force: 24.12.94. Effect: None. Territorial extent & classification: E/W/S. General. – 16p. – 0 11 043740 3 £3.20

The Coal Industry (Restructuring Date) Order 1994 No. 2553. Enabling power: *Coal Industry Act 1994, s. 7 (1).* Issued: 13.10.94. Made: 29.09.94. Coming into force: 31.10.94. Effect: None. Territorial extent & classification: GB/IOM. General. – 2p. – 0 11 045553 3 £0.65

The Coal Industry (Restructuring Grants) Order 1994 No. 1422. Enabling power: *Coal Industry Act 1987, s. 3 (2) (a) (3) (4) (a) (6).* Issued: 06.06.94. Made: 25.05.94. Laid: 21.04.94. Coming into force: 28.05.94. Effect: None. Supersedes Draft ISBN 0110458990 previously published on 29.04.94. Territorial extent & classification: E/W/S. General. – 4p. – 0 11 044422 1 £1.10

The Coal Industry (Retained Copyhold Interests) Regulations 1994 No. 2562. Enabling power: *Coal Industry Act 194, sch. 7, para. 3 (1) (a) (7).* Issued: 17.10.94. Made: 03.10.94. Laid: 06.10.94. Coming into force: 31.10.94. Effect: None. Territorial extent & classification: E/W. General. – 4p. – 0 11 045562 2 £1.10

The Coal Mining Subsidence (Arbitration Schemes) Regulations 1994 No. 2566. Enabling power: *Coal Industry Act 1994, s. 47 (2) (7) (8) (10) & Coal Mining Subsidence Act 1991, s. 50.* Issued: 19.10.94. Made: 03.10.94. Laid: 06.10.94. Coming into force: 31.10.94. Effect: None. Territorial extent & classification: E/W/S. General. – 10p. – 0 11 045566 5 £2.40

The Coal Mining Subsidence (Blight and Compensation for Inconvenience During Works) Regulations 1994 No. 2564. Enabling power: *Coal Industry Act 1994, sch. 10, para. 13 (3) & Coal Mining Subsidence Act 1991, s. 25, 29, 50.* Issued: 20.10.94. Made: 03.10.94. Laid: 06.10.94. Coming into force: 31.10.94. Effect: None. Territorial extent & classification: E/W/S. General. – 4p. – 0 11 045564 9 £1.10

The Coal Mining Subsidence (Land Drainage) Regulations 1994 No. 3064. Enabling power: *Coal Mining Subsidence Act 1991, ss. 36 (7), 50.* Issued: 22.12.94. Made: 30.11.94. Laid: 01.12.94. Coming into force: 24.12.94. Effect: S.I. 1958/1486 revoked. Territorial extent & classification: E/W. General. – 4p. – 0 11 043532 X £1.10

The Coal Mining Subsidence (Provision of Information) Regulations 1994 No. 2565. Enabling power: *Coal Industry Act 1994, s. 45 (1) (3), sch. 10, para. 3 & Coal Mining Subsidence Act 1991, s. 46 (5), 50.* Issued: 20.10.94. Made: 03.10.94. Laid: 06.10.94. Coming into force: 31.10.94. Effect: None. Territorial extent & classification: E/W/S. General. – 4p. – 0 11 045565 7 £1.10

The Coal Mining Subsidence (Subsidence Adviser) Regulations 1994 No. 2563. Enabling power: *Coal Industry Act 1994, s. 46 (1) (2) (3) (5) (6) (7) & Coal Mining Subsidence Act 1991, s. 50.* Issued: 19.10.94. Made: 03.10.94. Laid: 06.10.94. Coming into force: 31.10.94. Effect: None. Territorial extent & classification: E/W/S. General. – 6p. – 0 11 045563 0 £1.55

The Doncaster Area Drainage Act 1929 (Amendment) Order 1994 No. 3062. Enabling power: *Coal Industry Act 1994, s. 67 (2) (3).* Issued: 05.01.95. Made: 01.12.94. Laid: 01.12.94. Coming into force: 24.12.94. Effect: 1929 c. xvii amended. Territorial extent & classification: E. Local. – 4p. – 0 11 043813 2 £1.10

The Industry-Wide Coal Staff Superannuation Scheme Regulations 1994 No. 2973. Enabling power: *Coal Industry Act 1994, sch. 5, paras. 3 (1) (6), 5 (1) (2).* Issued: 05.12.94. Made: 22.11.94. Laid: 24.11.94. Coming into force: 15.12.94. Effect: None. Territorial extent & classification: E/W/S. General. – 112p. – 0 11 043192 8 £10.35

The Industry-Wide Mineworkers' Pension Scheme Regulations 1994 No. 2974. Enabling power: *Coal Industry Act 1994, sch. 5, paras. 3 (1) (6), 5 (1) (2).* Issued: 05.12.94. Made: 22.11.94. Laid: 24.11.94. Coming into force: 15.12.94. Effect: None. Territorial extent & classification: E/W/S. General. – 84p. – 0 11 043186 3 £8.70

The Mineworkers' Pension Scheme (Modification) Regulations 1994 No. 2577. Enabling power: *Coal Industry Act 1994, s. 22 (1), para. 2 (1) (2) (3) (4) (5) (6) (7) (8) (11), sch. 5, para. 5 (1) (2).* Issued: 26.10.94. Made: 04.10.94. Laid: 07.10.94. Coming into force: 31.10.94. Effect: None. Territorial extent & classification: E/W/S. General. – 84p. – 0 11 045577 0 £8.70

The Opencast Coal (Compulsory Rights, Drainage and Rights of Way) (Forms) Regulations 1994 No. 3097. Enabling power: *Opencast Coal Act 1958, ss. 4 (1A) (b), 15A (1) (1A) (4) (5) (c) (10), 16 (2A) (c), 49 (1) & Acquisition of Land Act 1981, ss. 10 (2), 11 (1), 1, 15, 22, 29.* Issued: 09.12.94. Made: 02.12.94. Laid: 09.12.94. Coming into force: 31.12.94. Effect: S.I. 1987/1915 revoked. Territorial extent & classification: E/W/S. General. – 20p. – 0 11 043348 3 £3.70

Price/availability are liable to change without notice

COMMUNITY CHARGES, ENGLAND AND WALES
The Community Charges (Administration and Enforcement) (Amendment) Regulations 1994 No.504. Enabling power: *Local Government Finance Act 1988, s. 146 (6), sch. 4, paras. 1, 2, 26.* Issued: 09.03.94. Made: 24.02.94. Laid: 09.03.94. Coming into force: 01.04.94. Effect: S.I. 1989/438 amended. Territorial extent & classification: E/W. General. – 2p. – 0 11 043504 4 £0.65

COMPANIES
The Companies Act 1985 (Audit Exemption) (Amendment) Regulations 1994 No. 2879. Enabling power: *Companies Act 1985, s. 257.* Issued: 06.12.94. Made: 05.11.94. Laid: 11.11.94. Coming into force: 12.11.94. Effect: S.I. 1994/1935 amended. Territorial extent & classification: E/W/S. General. – 2p. – 0 11 043269 X £0.65

The Companies Act 1985 Audit Exemption Regulations 1994 No. 1935. Enabling power: *Companies Act 1985, s. 245 (3) to (5), 257.* Issued: 01.08.94. Made: 19.07.94. Laid: 21.07.94. Coming into force: 11.08.94. Effect: 1985 c. 6; 1993 c. 10: S.I. 1990/2570 amended. Territorial extent & classification: E/W/S. General. – 8p. – 0 11 044935 5 £1.95

The Companies Act 1985 (Bank Accounts) Regulations 1994 No. 233. Enabling power: *Companies Act 1985, s. 257.* Issued: 21.02.94. Made: 02.02.94. Laid: 07.02.94. Coming into force: 11.02.94. for regs. 1, 2, 4 & 7; 28.02.94. for the remainder. Effect: 1985 c. 6; 1989 c. 40 amended. Territorial extent & classification: E/W/S. General. – 4p. – 0 11 043233 9 £1.10

The Companies (Fees) (Amendment) Regulations 1994 No. 2217. Enabling power: *Companies Act 1985, s. 708.* Issued: 14.09.94. Made: 23.08.94. Laid: 30.08.94. Coming into force: 20.09.94. Effect: S.I. 1991/1206 amended. Territorial extent & classification: E/W/S. General. – 2p. – 0 11 045217 8 £0.65

The Companies (Welsh Language Forms and Documents) (Amendment) Regulations 1994 No.727. Enabling power: *Companies Act 1985, ss. 710B (3), 744.* Issued: 11.08.94. Made: 09.03.94. Coming into force: 01.04.94. Effect: S.I. 1994/117 amended. For the Welsh language version of SI 1994/727, see ISBN 0110701815 issued 13.04.94. Supersedes SI of same no. & ISBN published on 25.03.94. With correction slip dated August 1994. Territorial extent & classification: E/W/S. General. – 2p. – 0 11 043727 6 £0.65

The Companies (Welsh Language Forms and Documents) Regulations 1994 No. 117. Enabling power: *Companies Act 1985, ss. 287 (3), 288 (2), 363(2), 710B (3), 744 & Welsh Language Act 1993, s. 26 (3).* Issued: 01.02.94. Made: 25.01.94. Coming into force: 01.02.94. Effect: None. Territorial extent & classification: E/W. General. – 20p. – 0 11 043117 0 £3.70 Replaced by 0110430174

The Foreign Companies (Execution of Documents) Regulations 1994 No. 950. Enabling power: *Companies Act 1989, s. 130 (6).* Issued: 18.04.94. Made: 24.03.94. Laid: 30.03.94. Coming into force: 16.05.94. Effect: None. Territorial extent & classification: E/W/S. General. – 4p. – 0 11 043950 3 £1.10

The Welsh Language Act 1993 (Commencement) Order 1994 No. 115 (C.5). Enabling power: *Welsh Language Act 1993, s. 36 (2). Bringing into operation various provisions of this act on 25.01.94, 01.02.94.* Issued: 01.02.94. Made: 24.01.94. Effect: 1985 c.6 amended. Territorial extent & classification: E/W/S. General. – 2p. – 0 11 043115 4 £0.65

COMPETITION
The Anti-Competitive Practices (Exclusions) (Amendment) Order 1994 No. 1557. Enabling power: *Competition Act 1980, s. 2 (3) (4).* Issued: 01.08.94. Made: 14.06.94. Laid: 14.06.94. Coming into force: 14.08.94. Effect: S.I. 1980/979 amended. Supersedes SI of same no. & ISBN published 22.06.94. Territorial extent & classification: GB. General. – 4p. – 0 11 044557 0 £1.10

CONSUMER CREDIT
The Consumer Credit (Exempt Agreements) (Amendment) Order 1994 No. 2420. Enabling power: *Consumer Credit Act 1994, ss. 16 (1) (4), 182 (2) (4).* Issued: 26.09.94. Made: 13.09.94. Laid: 19.09.94. Coming into force: 10.10.94. Effect: S.I. 1989/869 amended. Territorial extent & classification: GB. General. – 2p. – 0 11 045420 0 £0.65

CONSUMER PROTECTION
The Cosmetic Products (Safety) (Amendment) Regulations 1994 No. 1529. Enabling power: *European Communities Act 1972, s. 2.* Issued: 08.07.94. Made: 08.06.94. Laid: 09.06.94. Coming into force: 30.06.94 except for regs. 2 (b), 2 (d), 2 (f) (ii), 2 (g) (ii) which come into force on 01.07.94 in the case of supply by manufacturers or importers, on 30.06.95 in the case of supply by retailers and all other cases. Effect: S.I. 1989/2233 amended. Territorial extent & classification: GB. General. – 4p. – 0 11 044529 5 £1.10

The Dangerous Substances and Preparations (Safety) (Consolidation) Regulations 1994 No.2844. Enabling power: *Consumer Protection Act 1987, s. 11.* Issued: 24.11.94. Made: 04.11.94. Laid: 10.11.94. Coming into force: 01.01.95. Effect: S.I. 1980/136, 958; 1985/127, 128; 1987/2116 revoked. Territorial extent & classification: GB. General. – Implement DIR 89/677 (L 398/89) amending DIR 76/769 (L 262/76). – 4p. – 0 11 043093 X £1.10

The Electrical Equipment (Safety) Regulations 1994 No. 3260. Enabling power: *European Communities Act 1972, s. 2 (2) & Consumer Protection Act 1987, s. 11.* Issued: 25.01.95. Made: 15.12.95. Laid: 16.12.94. Coming into force: 09.01.95. Effect: S.I. 1992/2932 amended & S.I. 1989/728 revoked (save in respect of electrical equipment placed on the market before 01.01.97.) Territorial extent & classification: GB. General. – Implements DIR 73/23 (L 77/73) as amended by 93/68. – 10p. – 0 11 043917 1 £2.40

The General Product Safety Regulations 1994 No. 2328. Enabling power: *European Communities Act 1972, s. 2 (2).* Issued: 21.09.94. Made: 05.09.94. Laid: 08.09.94. Coming into force: 03.10.94. Effect: 1987 c. 43 amended & S.I. 1987/1911 revoked. Territorial extent & classification: GB. General. – 8p. – 0 11 045328 X £1.95

The Medical Devices Regulations 1994 No. 3017. Enabling power: *Consumer Protection Act 1987, ss. 11, 27 (2) & European Communities Act 1972, s. 11 (5).* Issued: 06.12.94. Made: 28.11.94. Laid: 30.11.94. Coming into force: 21.12.94, for the purposes of reg. 17.; 01.01.95 for all other purposes. Effect: S.I. 1988/1586; 1992/2932, 2966; 1993/2360 amended. Territorial extent & classification: GB. General. – Implements DIR 93/42 (OJ L 169/93). – 20p. – 0 11 043255 X £3.70

The Motor Vehicles Tyres (Safety) Regulations 1994 No. 3117. Enabling power: *Consumer Protection Act 1987, s. 11 (5) & European Communities Act 1972, s. 2 (2).* Issued: 15.12.94. Made: 07.12.94. Laid: 08.12.94. Coming into force: 01.06.97 for reg. 5, 01.06.95 for regs. 7 & 10 & 01.01.95 for remainder. Effect: S.I. 1984/1233; 1992/3087; 1993/2877 revoked. Territorial extent & classification: GB. General. – In accordance with UN ECE Reg 30, 54, 75 & DIR 92/23/EEC. – 12p. – 0 11 043399 8 £2.80

The Personal Protective Equipment (EC Directive) (Amendment) Regulations 1994 No.2326. Enabling power: *European Communities Act 1972, s. 2 (2).* Issued: 15.09.94. Made: 05.09.94. Laid: 08.09.94. Coming into force: 01.10.94. for reg. 2; 01.01.95. for all other purposes. Effect: S.I. 1992/2932, 2966, 3139; S.R. 1993/20 amended & S.I. 1993/3074 revoked. Territorial extent & classification: GB. General. – 4p., ill. – 0 11 045326 3 £1.10

The Plugs and Sockets etc. (Safety) Regulations 1994 No. 1768. Enabling power: *Consumer Protection Act 1987, s. 11.* Issued: 21.07.94. Made: 05.07.94. Laid: 06.07.94. Coming into force: 03.08.94.; 01.02.95.; 01.02.96; in accord. with reg. 1 (2) (3) (4). Effect: S.I. 1969/310; 1970/811; 1977/931; 1987/603: S.R. 1970/31, 180; 1977/301 revoked. Territorial extent & classification: GB. General. – 12p. – 0 11 044768 9 £2.80

The Price Indications (Resale of Tickets) Regulations 1994 No. 3248. Enabling power: *Consumer Protection Act 1987, s. 26.* Issued: 05.01.95. Made: 14.12.94. Laid: 15.12.94. Coming into force: 20.02.95. Effect: None. Territorial extent & classification: E/W/S. General. – 4p. – 0 11 043836 1 £1.10

The Unfair Terms in Consumer Contracts Regulations 1994 No. 3159. Enabling power: *European Communities Act 1972, s. 2 (2).* Issued: 05.01.95. Made: 08.12.94. Laid: 14.12.94. Coming into force: 01.07.95. Effect: None. Territorial extent & classification: GB. General. – Implement DIR 93/13 [OJ L95 1993]. – 6p. – 0 11 043784 5 £1.55

CONTRACTS

The Contracts (Applicable Law) Act 1990 (Amendment) Order 1994 No. 1900. Enabling power: *Contracts (Applicable Law) Act 1990, s. 4 (1).* Issued: 29.07.94. Made: 19.07.94. Coming into force: In accord. with art. 1. Effect: 1990 c. 36 amended. Territorial extent & classification: GB. General. – 4p. – 0 11 044900 2 £1.10

COPYRIGHT

The Copyright (Application to Other Countries) (Amendment) Order 1994 No. 263. Enabling power: *Copyright, Designs and Patents Act 1988, s. 159.* Issued: 18.02.94. Made: 08.02.94. Laid: 18.02.94. Coming into force: 11.03.94. Effect: S.I. 1993/942 amended. Territorial extent & classification: GB. General. – 4p. – 0 11 043263 0 £1.10

The Copyright (Certification of Licensing Scheme for Educational Recording of Broadcasts and Cable Programmes) (Educational Recording Agency Limited) (Amendment) Order 1994 No. 247. Enabling power: *Copyright, Designs and Patents Act 1988, s. 143.* Issued: 28.02.94. Made: 02.02.94. Coming into force: 01.04.94. Effect: S.I. 1990/879 amended. Territorial extent & classification: GB. General. – 4p. – 0 11 043247 9 £1.10

COUNCIL TAX, ENGLAND AND WALES

The Council Tax (Additional Provisions for Discount Disregards) (Amendment) Regulations 1994 No. 540. Enabling power: *Local Government Finance Act 1992, s. 116 (1), sch. 1, para. 9.* Issued: 10.03.94. Made: 02.03.94. Laid: 10.03.94. Coming into force: 01.04.94. Effect: S.I. 1992/552 amended. Territorial extent & classification: E/W. General. – 2p. – 0 11 043540 0 £0.65

The Council Tax (Administration and Enforcement) (Amendment) Regulations 1994 No.505. Enabling power: *Local Government Finance Act 1992, s. 113 (1) (2), sch. 2, paras. 2, 3, sch. 4, paras. 1 to 3, 6, 12, 17.* Issued: 09.03.94. Made: 24.02.94. Laid: 09.03.94. Coming into force: 01.04.94. Effect: S.I. 1992/613 amended. Territorial extent & classification: E/W. General. – 4p. – 0 11 043505 2 £1.10

The Council Tax (Alteration of Lists and Appeals) (Amendment) Regulations 1994 No.1746. Enabling power: *Local Government Finance Act 1992, ss. 24, 113 (1).* Issued: 15.07.94. Made: 02.07.94. Laid: 04.07.94. Coming into force: 11.07.94. Effect: S.I. 1993/290 amended. Territorial extent & classification: E/W. General. – 4p. – 0 11 044746 8 £1.10

The Council Tax (Discount Disregards) (Amendment) Regulations 1994 No. 543. Enabling power: *Local Government Finance Act 1992, s. 113, sch. 1, paras. 2, 4.* Issued: 10.03.94. Made: 02.03.94. Laid: 10.03.94. Coming into force: 01.04.94. Effect: S.I. 1992/548 amended. Territorial extent & classification: E/W. General. – 2p. – 0 11 043543 5 £0.65

The Council Tax (Exempt Dwellings) (Amendment) Order 1994 No. 539. Enabling power: *Local Government Finance Act 1992, s. 4.* Issued: 10.03.94. Made: 02.03.94. Laid: 10.03.94. Coming into force: 01.04.94. Effect: S.I. 1992/558 amended. Territorial extent & classification: GB. General. – 4p. – 0 11 043539 7 £1.10

Price/availability are liable to change without notice

The Council Tax Limitation (Sheffield City Council) (Maximum Amount) Order 1994 No. 1419. Enabling power: *Local Government Finance Act 1992, s. 54 (2).* Issued: 06.06.94. Made: 25.05.94. Coming into force: 26.05.94. Effect: None. Supersedes Draft ISBN 0110459164 previously published on 25.05.94. Territorial extent & classification: E. General. –2p. – 0 11 044419 1 £0.65

The Council Tax (Situation and Valuation of Dwellings) (Amendment) Regulations 1994 No. 1747. Enabling power: *Local Government Finance Act 1992, ss. 1 (3), 21 (2), 113 (1).* Issued: 15.07.94. Made: 02.07.94. Laid: 04.07.94. Coming into force: 11.07.94. Effect: S.I. 1992/550 amended. Territorial extent & classification: E/W. General. – 4p. – 0 11 044747 6 £1.10

The Council Tax (Transitional Reduction Scheme) (England) Regulations 1994 No. 135. Enabling power: *Local Government Finance Act 1992, ss. 13, 113 (1) (2).* Issued: 03.02.94. Made: 26.01.94. Laid: 27.01.94. Coming into force: 17.02.94. Effect: None. Territorial extent & classification: E/W. General. – 4p. – 0 11 043135 9 £1.10

COUNCIL TAX, SCOTLAND

The Council Tax (Discounts) (Scotland) Amendment Order 1994 No. 626 (S. 26). Enabling power: *Local Government Finance Act 1992, s. 113 (1), sch. 1, paras. 2, 4.* Issued: 17.03.94. Made: 04.03.94. Laid: 11.03.94. Coming into force: 01.04.94. Effect: S.I. 1992/1408 amended & S.I. 1993/343 revoked. Territorial extent & classification: S. General. – 2p. – 0 11 043626 1 £0.65

The Council Tax (Discounts) (Scotland) Amendment Regulations 1994 No. 629 (S. 28). Enabling power: *Local Government Finance Act 1992, ss. 113 (1), 116 (1), sch. 1, para. 9.* Issued: 17.03.94. Made: 04.03.94. Laid: 11.03.94. Coming into force: 01.04.94. Effect: S.I. 1992/1409 amended. Territorial extent & classification: S. General. – 2p. – 0 11 043629 6 £0.65

The Council Tax (Exempt Dwellings) (Scotland) Amendment Order 1994 No. 628 (S. 27). Enabling power: *Local Government Finance Act 1992, ss. 72 (6) (7), sch. 11, para. 7 (2) (3).* Issued: 17.03.94. Made: 04.03.94. Laid: 11.03.94. Coming into force: 01.04.94. Effect: S.I. 1992/1333 amended. Territorial extent & classification: S. General. – 2p. – 0 11 043628 8 £0.65

The Council Tax (Reduction of Liability) (Scotland) Regulations 1994 No. 3170 (S. 177). Enabling power: *Local Government Finance Act 1992, ss. 80, 84 (3), 113 (1), 116 (1), sch. 2, paras. 1 (1), 2 (4) (e).* Issued: 21.12.94. Made: 12.12.94. Laid: 21.12.94. Coming into force: 12.01.95. Effect: S.I. 1992/1330, 1332 amended. Territorial extent & classification: S. General. – 4p. – 0 11 043438 2 £1.10

COUNTRYSIDE

The Conservation (Natural Habitats, &c.) Regulations 1994 No. 2716. Enabling power: *European Communities Act 1972, s. 2 (2).* Issued: 31.10.94. Laid: 13.07.94. Coming into force: 30.10.94. Effect: None. Supersedes Draft ISBN 0110459458 published on 18/07/94. Territorial extent & classification: E/W/S. General. – Implements DIR 92/43 [L 206/92]. – 60p. – 0 11 045716 1 £8.70

COUNTY COURTS

The Civil Courts (Amendment No. 2) Order 1994 No. 1536. Enabling power: *Supreme Court Act 1981, s. 99 (1) & County Courts Act 1984, ss. 2 (1), 26 & Insolvency Act 1986, ss. 117 (4), 374.* Issued: 24.06.94. Made: 09.06.94. Laid: 13.06.94. Coming into force: 04.07.94. Effect: S.I. 1983/713 amended. Territorial extent & classification: E/W. General. – 4p. – 0 11 044536 8 £1.10

The Civil Courts (Amendment No. 3) Order 1994 No. 2626. Enabling power: *Supreme Court Act 1981, s. 99 (1) & County courts Act 1984, ss. 2 (1), 26 & Insolvency Act 1986, ss. 117 (4), 374.* Issued: 26.10.94. Made: 11.10.94. Laid: 11.10.94. Coming into force: 02.11.94. Effect: S.I. 1983/713 amended. Territorial extent & classification: E/W. General. – 2p. – 0 11 045626 2 £0.65

The Civil Courts (Amendment No. 4) Order 1994 No. 2893. Enabling power: *Supreme Court Act 1981, s. 99 (1) & County Court Act 1984, ss. 2 (1), 26 & Insolvency Act 1986, ss. 117, 374.* Issued: 25.11.94. Made: 14.11.94. Laid: 14.11.94. Coming into force: 05.12.94, except for art. 5 (a). 09.01.95, for art. 5 (a). Effect: S.I. 1983/713 amended. Territorial extent & classification: E/W. General. – 2p. – 0 11 043095 6 £0.65

The Civil Courts (Amendment) Order 1994 No. 706. Enabling power: *County Courts Act 1984, s. 2 (1).* Issued: 17.03.94. Made: 10.03.94. Laid: 14.03.94. Coming into force: 05.04.94. Effect: S.I. 1983/713 amended. Territorial extent & classification: E/W. General. – 2p. – 0 11 043706 3 £0.65

The County Court (Amendment No. 2) Rules 1994 No. 1288 (L.7). Enabling power: *County Courts Act 1984, s. 75.* Issued: 26.05.94. Made: 11.05.94. Coming into force: 06.06.94. Effect: S.I. 1981/1687 amended. Territorial extent & classification: E/W. General. – 8p. – 0 11 044288 1 £1.95

The County Court (Amendment No. 3) Rules 1994 No. 2403 (L. 15). Enabling power: *County Courts Act 1984, s. 75.* Issued: 30.09.94. Made: 08.09.94. Coming into force: 03.10.94. Effect: S.I. 1981/1687 amended. Territorial extent & classification: E/W. General. – 6p. – 0 11 045403 0 £1.55

The County Court Fees (Amendment) Order 1994 No. 1936 (L. 9). Enabling power: *County Courts Act 1984, s. 128.* Issued: 28.07.94. Made: 19.07.94. Laid: 20.07.94. Coming into force: 15.08.94. Effect: S.I. 1982/1706 amended. Territorial extent & classification: E/W. General. – 4p. – 0 11 044936 3 £1.10

The County Court (Forms) (Amendment) Rules 1994 No. 1289 (L.8). Enabling power: *County Courts Act 1984, s. 75.* Issued: 26.05.94. Made: 11.05.94. Coming into force: 06.06.94. Effect: S.I. 1982/586 amended. Territorial extent & classification: E/W. General. – 8p. – 0 11 044289 X £1.95

The Family Proceedings (Amendment) (No. 2) Rules 1994 No. 2165 (L. 13). Enabling power: *Matrimonial and Family Proceedings Act 1984, s. 40 (1).* Issued: 24.08.94. Made: 11.08.94. Laid: 24.08.94. Coming into force: 01.11.94. Effect: S.I. 1991/1247 amended. Territorial extent & classification: E/W. General. – 20p. – 0 11 045165 1 £3.70

The Family Proceedings (Amendment) (No. 3) Rules 1994 No. 2890 (L. 17). Enabling power: *Matrimonial and Family Proceedings Act 1984, s. 40 (1).* Issued: 21.11.94. Made: 25.10.94. Laid: 14.11.94. Coming into force: 06.12.94. Effect: S.I. 1991/1247 amended. Territorial extent & classification: E/W. General. – 4p. – 0 11 043077 8 £1.10

The Family Proceedings (Amendment) (No. 4) Rules 1994 No. 3155 (L. 21). Enabling power: *Matrimonial and Family Proceedings Act 1984, s. 40.* Issued: 22.12.94. Made: 08.12.94. Laid: 12.12.94. Coming into force: 03.01.95. Effect: S.I. 1991/1247 amended. Territorial extent & classification: E/W. General. – 92p. – 0 11 043515 X £9.40

The Family Proceedings (Amendment) Rules 1994 No. 808 (L. 4). Enabling power: *Matrimonial and Family Proceedings Act 1984, s. 40 (1).* Issued: 25.03.94. Made: 21.03.94. Laid: 21.03.94. Coming into force: 11.04.94. Effect: S.I. 1991/1247, 21113 amended. Territorial extent & classification: E/W. General. – 8p. – 0 11 043808 6 £1.95

COUNTY COURTS: PROCEDURE

The County Court (Amendment) Rules 1994 No. 306 (L. 1). Enabling power: *County Courts Act 1984, s. 75.* Issued: 16.02.94. Made: 10.02.94. Coming into force: 07.03.94. Effect: S.I. 1981/1687 amended. Territorial extent & classification: E/W. General. – 2p. – 0 11 043306 8 £0.65

The County Court (Forms) (Amendment No. 2) Rules 1994 No. 2110 (L. 11). Enabling power: *County Courts Act 1984, s. 75.* Issued: 01.09.94. Made: 06.08.94. Coming into force: 01.09.94. for rule 2 & 01.10.94. for the remainder. Effect: S.I. 1982/586 amended. Territorial extent & classification: E/W. General. – 24p. – 0 11 045110 4 £4.15

COURT OF SESSION, SCOTLAND

Act of Sederunt (Fees of Messengers-at-Arms) 1994 No. 391 (S. 12). Enabling power: *Execution of Diligence (Scotland) Act 1926, s. 6 & Court of Session Act 1988, s. 5.* Issued: 02.03.94. Made: 18.02.94. Coming into force: 23.03.94. Effect: S.I. 1990/379; 1991/291; 1992/87, 529; 1993/118 revoked. Territorial extent & classification: S. General. – 6p. – 0 11 043391 2 £1.55

Act of Sederunt (Fees of Messengers-at-Arms) (No. 2) 1994 No. 3268 (S. 188). Enabling power: *Execution of Diligence (Scotland) Act 1926, s. 6 & Court of Session Act 1988, s. 5.* Issued: 10.01.95. Made: 16.12.94. Coming into force: 09.01.95. Effect: S.I. 1994/391 amended. Territorial extent & classification: S. General. – 4p. – 0 11 043814 0 £1.10

Act of Sederunt (Registration Appeal Court) 1994 No. 2483 (S. 115). Enabling power: *Representation of the People Act 1983, s. 57.* Issued: 30.09.94. Made: 22.09.94. Coming into force: 01.10.94. Effect: S.I. 1990/1972 revoked. Territorial extent & classification: S. General. – 2p. – 0 11 045483 9 £0.65

Act of Sederunt (Rules of the Court of Session 1994 Amendment No. 1) (Commercial Actions) 1994 No. 2310 (S. 112). Enabling power: *Court of Session Act 1988, s. 5.* Issued: 13.09.94. Made: 25.08.94. Coming into force: 20.09.94. Effect: S.I. 1994/1443 amended. Territorial extent & classification: S. General. – 6p. – 0 11 045310 7 £1.55

Act of Sederunt (Rules of the Court of Session 1994 Amendment No. 2) (Human Fertilisation and Embryology) (Parental Orders) 1994 No. 2806 (S. 143). Enabling power: *Court of Session Act 1988, s. 5; Adoption (Scotland) Act 1978, s. 59.* Issued: 09.11.94. Made: 21.10.94. Coming into force: On the date of the coming into force of the Parental Order (Human Fertilisation and Embryology) (Scotland) Regulations 1994. Effect: S.I. 1994/1443 amended. Territorial extent & classification: S. General. – 12p. – 0 11 045806 0 £2.80

Act of Sederunt (Rules of the Court of Session 1994 Amendment No. 3) (Miscellaneous) 1994 No. 2901 (S. 147). Enabling power: *Children Act 1975, s. 48 (1) & Presumption of Death (Scotland) Act 1977, s. 15 & Adoption Act 1978, s. 59 (1) & Civil Jurisdiction and Judgements Act 1982, s. 48 & Copyright, Designs and Patents Act 1988, ss. 114 (3), 204 (3), 231 (3) & Trade Marks Act 1994, s. 19 (3).* Issued: 23.11.94. Made: 10.11.94. Coming into force: 05.12.94. Effect: S.I. 1994/1443 amended. Territorial extent & classification: S. General. – 8p. – 0 11 043091 3 £1.95

Act of Sederunt (Rules of the Court of Session Amendment No. 1) (Fees of Solicitors) 1994 No.1139 (S. 59). Enabling power: *Court of Session Act 1988, s. 5.* Issued: 03.05.94. Made: 21.04.94. Coming into force: 24.05.94. Effect: S.I. 1965/321 amended. Territorial extent & classification: S. General. – 4p. – 0 11 044139 7 £1.10

Act of Sederunt (Rules of the Court of Session Amendment No. 2) (Shorthand Writers' Fees) 1994 No. 1140 (S. 60). Enabling power: *Court of Session Act 1988, s. 5.* Issued: 03.05.94. Made: 21.04.94. Coming into force: 24.05.94. Effect: S.I. 1965/321 amended. Territorial extent & classification: S. General. – 2p. – 0 11 044140 0 £0.65

Act of Sederunt (Solicitor's Right of Audience) 1994 No. 221 (S. 8). Enabling power: *Court of Session Act 1988, ss. 5, 48.* Issued: 09.02.94. Made: 06.01.94. Coming into force: 07.01.94. Effect: None. Territorial extent & classification: S. General. – 2p. – 0 11 043221 5 £0.65

Price/availability are liable to change without notice

The Court of Session etc. Fees Amendment Order 1994 No. 3265 (S. 185). Enabling power: *Courts of Law Fees (Scotland) Act 1895, s. 2.* Issued: 12.01.95. Made: 08.12.94. Laid: 20.12.94. Coming into force: 01.02.95. Effect: S.I. 1984/256 amended & S.I. 1993/427 revoked. Territorial extent & classification: S. General. – 8p. – 0 11 043868 X £1.95

CRIMINAL LAW, ENGLAND AND WALES

The Bail (Amendment) Act 1993 (Commencement) Order 1994 No. 1437 (C. 24). Enabling power: *Bail (Amendment) Act 1993, s. 2 (2). Bringing into force various provisions of this Act on 27.06.94.* Issued: 06.06.94. Made: 25.05.94. Effect: None. Territorial extent & classification: E/W. General. – 2p. – 0 11 044437 X £0.65

The Bail (Amendment) Act 1993 (Prescription of Prosecuting Authorities) Order 1994 No.1438. Enabling power: *Bail (Amendment) Act 1993, s. 1 (2) (b) (11).* Issued: 06.06.94. Made: 25.05.94. Laid: 06.06.94. Coming into force: 27.06.94. Effect: None. Territorial extent & classification: E/W. General. – 2p. – 0 11 044438 8 £0.65

The Criminal Justice Act 1988 (Crown Servants) Regulations 1994 No. 1759. Enabling power: *Criminal Justice Act 1988, s. 93 G (1).* Issued: 11.07.94. Made: 01.07.94. Laid: 08.07.94. Coming into force: 01.08.94. Effect: None. Territorial extent & classification: E/W/S. General. – 2p. – 0 11 044759 X £0.65

The Criminal Justice Act 1988 (Designated Countries and Territories) (Amendment) Order 1994 No. 1639. Enabling power: *Criminal Justice Act 1988, s. 96.* Issued: 04.07.94. Made: 22.06.94. Laid: 04.07.94. Coming into force: 01.08.94. Effect: S.I. 1991/2873 amended. Territorial extent & classification: E/W. General. – 2p. – 0 11 044639 9 £0.65

The Criminal Justice Act 1988 (Reviews of Sentencing) Order 1994 No. 119. Enabling power: *Criminal Justice Act 1988, s. 35 (4).* Issued: 02.02.94. Made: 24.01.94. Laid: 02.02.94. Coming into force: 01.03.94. Effect: None. Territorial extent & classification: E/W. General. – 2p. – 0 11 043119 7 £0.65

The Criminal Justice Act 1991 (Commencement No. 4) Order 1994 No. 3191 (C. 77). Enabling power: *Criminal Justice Act 1991, s. 102 (2). Bringing into operation various provisions of the 1991 act on 09.01.95.* Issued: 20.12.94. Made: 11.12.94. Effect: None. Territorial extent & classification: E/W. General. – 2p. – 0 11 043517 6 £0.65

The Criminal Justice Act 1993 (Commencement No. 4) Order 1994 No. 71 (C. 1). Enabling power: *Criminal Justice Act 1993, s. 78 (3) (4). Bringing into force various provisions of this act on 15/02/94.* Issued: 25.01.94. Made: 14.01.94. Coming into force: 15.02.94. Effect: None. Territorial extent & classification: GB. General. – 6p. – 0 11 043071 9 £1.55

The Criminal Justice Act 1993 (Commencement No. 5) Order 1994 No. 242 (C. 7). Enabling power: *Criminal Justice Act 1993, s. 78 (3) (4). Bringing into operation various provisions of this act on 01.03.94.* Issued: 10.02.94. Made: 04.02.94. Effect: None. Territorial extent & classification: GB. General. – 4p. – 0 11 043242 8 £1.10

The Criminal Justice Act 1993 (Commencement No. 6) Order 1994 No. 700 (C. 12). Enabling power: *Criminal Justice Act 1993, s. 78 (3) (4). Bringing into operation various provisions of the 1993 act on 01.04.94.* Issued: 18.03.94. Made: 10.03.94. Effect: None. Territorial extent & classification: GB. General. – 6p. – 0 11 043700 4 £1.55

The Criminal Justice Act 1993 (Commencement No. 7) Order 1994 No. 1951 (C. 36). Enabling power: *Criminal Justice Act 1993, s. 78 (3) (4). Bringing into operation various provisions of this Act on 22.08.94.* Issued: 28.07.94. Made: 20.07.94. Effect: None. Territorial extent & classification: UK/CI/IOM. General. – 6p. – 0 11 044951 7 £1.55

The Criminal Justice and Public Order Act 1994 (Commencement No. 1) Order 1994 No.2935 (C. 66). Enabling power: *Criminal Justice and Public Order Act 1994, s. 172 (2). Bringing into operation various provisions of the 1994 act on 19.12.94.* Issued: 28.11.94. Made: 19.11.94. Effect: None. Territorial extent & classification: GB. General. – 2p. – 0 11 043113 8 £0.65

The Criminal Justice and Public Order Act 1994 (Commencement No. 2) Order 1994 No.3192 (C. 78). Enabling power: *Criminal Justice and Public Order Act 1994, s. 172 (2). Bringing various provisions of the 1994 act into operation on 09.01.95.* Issued: 21.12.94. Made: 11.12.94. Effect: None. Territorial extent & classification: E/W/S. General. – 4p. – 0 11 043511 7 £1.10

The Criminal Justice (International Co-operation) Act 1990 (Crown Servants) Regulations 1994 No. 1756. Enabling power: *Criminal Justice (International Co-operation) Act 1990, s. 23A (1).* Issued: 11.07.94. Made: 01.07.94. Laid: 08.07.94. Coming into force: 01.08.94. Effect: None. Territorial extent & classification: GB. General. – 2p. – 0 11 044756 5 £0.65

The Criminal Justice (International Co-operation) Act 1990 (Enforcement of Overseas Forfeiture Orders) (Amendment) Order 1994 No.1640. Enabling power: *Criminal Justice (International Co-operation) Act 1990, s. 9.* Issued: 04.07.94. Made: 22.06.94. Laid: 04.07.94. Coming into force: 01.08.94. Effect: S.I. 1991/1463, 1464 amended. Territorial extent & classification: E/W/NI. General. – 4p. – 0 11 044640 2 £1.10

The Drug Trafficking Offences Act 1986 (Crown Servants and Regulators etc.) Regulations 1994 No. 1757. Enabling power: *Drug Trafficking Offences Act 1986, s. 36B (1) to (5).* Issued: 11.07.94. Made: 01.07.94. Laid: 08.07.94. Coming into force: 01.08.94. Effect: None. Territorial extent & classification: E/W. General. – 2p. – 0 11 044757 3 £0.65

The Drug Trafficking Offences Act 1986 (Designated Countries and Territories) (Amendment) Order 1994 No. 1641. Enabling power: *Drug Trafficking Offences Act 1986, s. 26.* Issued: 04.07.94. Made: 22.06.94. Laid: 04.07.94. Coming into force: 01.08.94. Effect: S.I. 1990/1199 amended. Territorial extent & classification: E/W. General. – 2p. – 0 11 044641 0 £0.65

Price/availability are liable to change without notice

The Northern Ireland (Emergency Provisions) Act 1991 (Crown Servants and Regulators etc.) Regulations 1994 No. 1760. Enabling power: *Northern Ireland (Emergency Provisions) Act 1991, s. 55A (1) to (5).* Issued: 11.07.94. Made: 01.07.94. Laid: 08.07.94. Coming into force: 01.08.94. Effect: None. Territorial extent & classification: GB. General. – 2p. – 0 11 044760 3 *£0.65*

The Prevention of Terrorism (Temporary Provisions) Act 1989 (Crown Servants and Regulators etc.) Regulations 1994 No. 1758. Enabling power: *Prevention of Terrorism (Temporary Provisions) Act 1989, s. 19A (1) to (5).* Issued: 11.07.94. Made: 01.07.94. Laid: 08.07.94. Coming into force: 01.08.94. Effect: None. Territorial extent & classification: GB. General. – 4p. – 0 11 044758 1 *£1.10*

CRIMINAL LAW, NORTHERN IRELAND

The Criminal Justice Act 1993 (Commencement No. 4) Order 1994 No. 71 (C.1). Enabling power: *Criminal Justice Act 1993, s. 78 (3) (4). Bringing into force various provisions of this act on 15/02/94.* Issued: 25.01.94. Made: 14.01.94. Coming into force: 15.02.94. Effect: None. Territorial extent & classification: GB. General. – 6p. – 0 11 043071 9 *£1.55*

The Criminal Justice Act 1993 (Commencement No. 5) Order 1994 No. 242 (C. 7). Enabling power: *Criminal Justice Act 1993, s. 78 (3) (4). Bringing into operation various provisions of this act on 01.03.94.* Issued: 10.02.94. Made: 04.02.94. Effect: None. Territorial extent & classification: GB. General. – 4p. – 0 11 043242 8 *£1.10*

The Criminal Justice Act 1993 (Commencement No. 6) Order 1994 No. 700 (C. 12). Enabling power: *Criminal Justice Act 1993, s. 78 (3) (4). Bringing into operation various provisions of the 1993 act on 01.04.94.* Issued: 18.03.94. Made: 10.03.94. Effect: None. Territorial extent & classification: GB. General. – 6p. – 0 11 043700 4 *£1.55*

The Criminal Justice Act 1993 (Commencement No. 7) Order 1994 No. 1951 (C. 36). Enabling power: *Criminal Justice Act 1993, s. 78 (3) (4). Bringing into operation various provisions of this Act on 22.08.94.* Issued: 28.07.94. Made: 20.07.94. Effect: None. Territorial extent & classification: UK/CI/IOM. General. – 6p. – 0 11 044951 7 *£1.55*

The Criminal Justice and Public Order Act 1994 (Commencement No. 1) Order 1994 No.2935 (C. 66). Enabling power: *Criminal Justice and Public Order Act 1994, s. 172 (2). Bringing into operation various provisions of the 1994 act on 19.12.94.* Issued: 28.11.94. Made: 19.11.94. Effect: None. Territorial extent & classification: GB. General. – 2p. – 0 11 043113 8 *£0.65*

The Criminal Justice (International Co-operation) Act 1990 (Crown Servants) Regulations 1994 No. 1756. Enabling power: *Criminal Justice (International Co-operation) Act 1990, s. 23A (1).* Issued: 11.07.94. Made: 01.07.94. Laid: 08.07.94. Coming into force: 01.08.94. Effect: None. Territorial extent & classification: GB. General. – 2p. – 0 11 044756 5 *£0.65*

The Criminal Justice (International Co-operation) Act 1990 (Enforcement of Overseas Forfeiture Orders) (Amendment) Order 1994 No. 1640. Enabling power: *Criminal Justice (International Co-operation) Act 1990, s. 9.* Issued: 04.07.94. Made: 22.06.94. Laid: 04.07.94. Coming into force: 01.08.94. Effect: S.I. 1991/1463, 1464 amended. Territorial extent & classification: E/W/NI. General. – 4p. – 0 11 044640 2 *£1.10*

The Northern Ireland (Emergency Provisions) Act 1991 (Crown Servants and Regulators etc.) Regulations 1994 No. 1760. Enabling power: *Northern Ireland (Emergency Provisions) Act 1991, s. 55A (1) to (5).* Issued: 11.07.94. Made: 01.07.94. Laid: 08.07.94. Coming into force: 01.08.94. Effect: None. Territorial extent & classification: GB. General. – 2p. – 0 11 044760 3 *£0.65*

The Prevention of Terrorism (Temporary Provisions) Act 1989 (Crown Servants and Regulators etc.) Regulations 1994 No. 1758. Enabling power: *Prevention of Terrorism (Temporary Provisions) Act 1989, s. 19A (1) to (5).* Issued: 11.07.94. Made: 01.07.94. Laid: 08.07.94. Coming into force: 01.08.94. Effect: None. Territorial extent & classification: GB. General. – 4p. – 0 11 044758 1 *£1.10*

CRIMINAL LAW, SCOTLAND

The Confiscation of the Proceeds of Drug Trafficking (Designated Countries and Territories) (Scotland) Amendment Order 1994 No. 1644 (S. 72). Enabling power: *Criminal Justice (Scotland) Act 1987, s. 30.* Issued: 08.07.94. Made: 22.06.94. Laid: 04.07.94. Coming into force: 01.08.94. Effect: S.I. 1991/1467 amended. Territorial extent & classification: S. General. – 2p. – 0 11 044644 5 *£0.65*

The Criminal Justice Act 1988 (Crown Servants) Regulations 1994 No. 1759. Enabling power: *Criminal Justice Act 1988, s. 93 G (1).* Issued: 11.07.94. Made: 01.07.94. Laid: 08.07.94. Coming into force: 01.08.94. Effect: None. Territorial extent & classification: E/W/S. General. – 2p. – 0 11 044759 X *£0.65*

The Criminal Justice Act 1993 (Commencement No. 4) Order 1994 No. 71 (C.1). Enabling power: *Criminal Justice Act 1993, s. 78 (3) (4). Bringing into force various provisions of this act on 15/02/94.* Issued: 25.01.94. Made: 14.01.94. Coming into force: 15.02.94. Effect: None. Territorial extent & classification: GB. General. – 6p. – 0 11 043071 9 *£1.55*

The Criminal Justice Act 1993 (Commencement No. 5) Order 1994 No. 242 (C. 7). Enabling power: *Criminal Justice Act 1993, s. 78 (3) (4). Bringing into operation various provisions of this act on 01.03.94.* Issued: 10.02.94. Made: 04.02.94. Effect: None. Territorial extent & classification: GB. General. – 4p. – 0 11 043242 8 *£1.10*

The Criminal Justice Act 1993 (Commencement No. 6) Order 1994 No. 700 (C. 12). Enabling power: *Criminal Justice Act 1993, s. 78 (3) (4). Bringing into operation various provisions of the 1993 act on 01.04.94.* Issued: 18.03.94. Made: 10.03.94. Effect: None. Territorial extent & classification: GB. General. – 6p. – 0 11 043700 4 *£1.55*

The Criminal Justice Act 1993 (Commencement no. 7) Order 1994 No. 1951 (C. 36). Enabling power: *Criminal Justice Act 1993, s. 78 (3) (4)*. Bringing into operation various provisions of this Act on 22.08.94. Issued: 28.07.94. Made: 20.07.94. Effect: None. Territorial extent & classification: UK/CI/IOM. General. –6p. – 0 11 044951 7 £1.55

The Criminal Justice and Public Order Act 1994 (Commencement No. 1) Order 1994 No.2935 (C. 66). Enabling power: *Criminal Justice and Public Order Act 1994, s. 172 (2)*. Bringing into operation various provisions of the 1994 act on 19.12.94. Issued: 28.11.94. Made: 19.11.94. Effect: None. Territorial extent & classification: GB. General. – 2p. – 0 11 043113 8 £0.65

The Criminal Justice and Public Order Act 1994 (Commencement No. 2) Order 1994 No.3192 (C. 78). Enabling power: *Criminal Justice and Public Order Act 1994, s. 172 (2)*. Bringing various provisions of the 1994 act into operation on 09.01.95. Issued: 21.12.94. Made: 11.12.94. Effect: None. Territorial extent & classification: E/W/S. General. – 4p. – 0 11 043511 7 £1.10

The Criminal Justice (International Co-operation) Act 1990 (Crown Servants) Regulations 1994 No. 1756. Enabling power: *Criminal Justice (International Co-operation) Act 1990, s. 23A (1)*. Issued: 11.07.94. Made: 01.07.94. Laid: 08.07.94. Coming into force: 01.08.94. Effect: None. Territorial extent & classification: GB. General. – 2p. – 0 11 044756 5 £0.65

The Criminal Justice (International Co-operation) Act 1990 (Enforcement of Overseas Forfeiture Orders) (Scotland) Amendment Order 1994 No. 1645 (S. 73). Enabling power: *Criminal Justice (International Co-operation) Act 1990, s. 9*. Issued: 08.07.94. Made: 22.06.94. Laid: 04.07.94. Coming into force: 01.08.94. Effect: S.I. 1991/1468 amended. Territorial extent & classification: S. General. – 2p. – 0 11 044645 3 £0.65

The Criminal Justice (Scotland) Act 1987 (Crown Servants and Regulators Etc.) Regulations 1994 No. 1808 (S. 80). Enabling power: *Criminal Justice (Scotland) Act 1987, s. 46A (1) to (5)*. Issued: 15.07.94. Made: 06.07.94. Laid: 11.07.94. Coming into force: 01.08.94. Effect: None. Territorial extent & classification: S. General. – 4p. – 0 11 044808 1 £1.10

The Northern Ireland (Emergency Provisions) Act 1991 (Crown Servants and Regulators etc.) Regulations 1994 No. 1760. Enabling power: *Northern Ireland (Emergency Provisions) Act 1991, s. 55A (1) to (5)*. Issued: 11.07.94. Made: 01.07.94. Laid: 08.07.94. Coming into force: 01.08.94. Effect: None. Territorial extent & classification: GB. General. – 2p. – 0 11 044760 3 £0.65

The Prevention of Terrorism (Temporary Provisions) Act 1989 (Crown Servants and Regulators etc.) Regulations 1994 No. 1758. Enabling power: *Prevention of Terrorism (Temporary Provisions) Act 1989, s. 19A (1) to (5)*. Issued: 11.07.94. Made: 01.07.94. Laid: 08.07.94. Coming into force: 01.08.94. Effect: None. Territorial extent & classification: GB. General. – 4p. – 0 11 044758 1 £1.10

CROFTERS, COTTARS AND SMALL LANDHOLDERS

The Crofters etc. Livestock Purchase Loans (Scotland) Revocation Scheme 1994 No. 1014 (S. 46). Enabling power: *Crofters (Scotland) Act 1993, ss. 42 (1) (2) (3), 46 (4)*. Issued: 13.04.94. Made: 29.03.94. Laid: 08.04.94. Coming into force: 15.04.94. Effect: S.I. 1966/1298 revoked. Territorial extent & classification: S. General. – 2p. – 0 11 044014 5 £0.65

The Crofting Counties Agricultural Grants (Scotland) Amendment Scheme 1994 No. 1013 (S. 45). Enabling power: *Crofters (Scotland) Act 1993, ss. 42 (1) (2) (3), 46 (4)*. Issued: 13.04.94. Made: 29.03.94. Laid: 08.04.94. Coming into force: 15.04.94. Effect: S.I. 1988/559 amended. Territorial extent & classification: S. General. – 4p. – 0 11 044013 7 £1.10

CULTURAL OBJECTS

The Return of Cultural Objects Regulations 1994 No. 501. Enabling power: *European Communities Act 1972, s. 2 (2)*. Issued: 09.03.94. Made: 01.03.94. Coming into force: 02.03.94. Effect: None. Supersedes Draft ISBN 0110358821 previously published on 06.01.94. Territorial extent & classification: GB. General. – 8p. – 0 11 043501 X £1.95

CUSTOMS AND EXCISE

The Aircraft Operators (Accounts and Records) Regulations 1994 No. 1737. Enabling power: *Customs and Excise Management Act 1979, ss. 118A, 172 & Finance Act 1994, sch. 6, para. 1 (1)*. Issued: 07.07.94. Made: 01.07.94. Laid: 01.07.94. Coming into force: 01.11.94. Effect: None. Reprinted to include corrections previously printed as a correction slip, dated August 1994. Territorial extent & classification: GB. General. – 4p. – 0 11 044737 9 £1.10

The Air Passenger Duty (Connected Flights) Order 1994 No. 1821. Enabling power: *Finance Act 1994, ss. 30, 42*. Issued: 19.07.94. Made: 08.07.94. Laid: 11.07.94. Coming into force: 01.11.94. Effect: None. With correction slip dated August 1994 Territorial extent & classification: GB. General. – 4p. – 0 11 044821 9 £1.10

The Air Passenger Duty (Prescribed Rates of Interest) Order 1994 No. 1820. Enabling power: *Finance Act 1994, sch. 6, para. 11*. Issued: 19.07.94. Made: 08.07.94. Laid: 11.07.94. Coming into force: 01.11.94. Effect: None. Territorial extent & classification: GB. General. – 2p. – 0 11 044820 0 £0.65

The Air Passenger Duty Regulations 1994 No. 1738. Enabling power: *Finance Act 1994, ss. 31 (3) (6), 32 (2) (3), 33 (4) (7) (8), 34 (5), 35 (1) (2), 38 (1) (2), 42, 43 (1)*. Issued: 07.07.94. Made: 01.07.94. Laid: 01.07.94. Coming into force: 01.08.94. Effect: None. Territorial extent & classification: GB. General. – 8p. – 0 11 044738 7 £1.95

Price/availability are liable to change without notice

The Alcoholic Liquor Duties (Beer-based Beverages) Order 1994 No. 2904. Enabling power: *Alcoholic Liquor Duties Act 1979, s. 1 (10).* Issued: 07.12.94. Made: 29.11.94. Coming into force: 30.11.94. Effect: S.I. 1988/1684 revoked. With correction slip, dated June 1995. Territorial extent & classification: GB. General. – 2p. – 0 11 043285 1 *£0.65*

The Bingo Duty (Exemptions) Order 1994 No. 2967. Enabling power: *Betting and Gaming Duties Act 1981, sch. 3, para. 7.* Issued: 29.11.94. Made: 23.11.94. Laid: 23.11.94. Coming into force: 01.01.95. Effect: S.I. 1993/752 amended. Territorial extent & classification: GB. General. – 2p. – 0 11 043149 9 *£0.65*

The Customs Duties (ECSC) (Quota and other Reliefs) (No. 2) Order 1994 No. 1739. Enabling power: *Customs and Excise duties (General Reliefs) Act 1979, ss. 1, 4.* Issued: 19.08.94. Made: 01.07.94. Laid: 04.07.94. Coming into force: 02.07.94. Effect: S.I. 1994/1692 revoked which was never published. Territorial extent & classification: GB/IOM/CI. General. – 10p. – 0 11 044739 5 *£2.40*

The Export of Goods (Control) (Amendment No. 7) Order 1994 No. 534. Enabling power: *Import, Export and Customs Powers (Defence) Act 1939, s. 1.* Issued: 29.03.94. Made: 01.03.94. Coming into force: 02.03.94. Effect: S.I. 1992/3092 amended. With correction slip. Territorial extent & classification: GB/IOM. General. – 6p. – 0 11 043534 6 *£1.55*

The Export of Goods (Control) (Croatian and Bosnian Territories) (Revocation) Order 1994 No. 2972. Enabling power: *Import, Export and Customs Powers Act 1939, s. 1.* Issued: 30.11.94. Made: 18.10.94. Coming into force: 19.10.94. Effect: S.I. 1993/1189 revoked. Territorial extent & classification: GB/IoM. General. – 2p. – 0 11 043153 7 *£0.65*

The Export of Goods (Control) Order 1994 No. 1191. Enabling power: *Import, Export and Customs Powers (Defence) Act 1939, s. 1.* Issued: 25.05.94. Made: 24.04.94. Coming into force: 04.05.94. for the issue of general licences, 25.05.94. for all other purposes. Effect: S.I. 1992/3092 amended & S.I. 1993/1020, 1692, 1825, 2515, 3264, 3305; 1994/534 revoked. Territorial extent & classification: GB/IOM. General. – 168p. – 0 11 044191 5 *£14.30*

The Export of Goods (Control) Order 1994 (Amendment No. 2) Order 1994 No. 2518. Enabling power: *Import, Export and Customs Powers (Defence) Act 1939, s. 1.* Issued: 10.10.94. Made: 23.09.94. Coming into force: 24.09.94. Effect: S.I. 1994/1191 amended. Territorial extent & classification: GB/IOM. General. – 2p. – 0 11 045518 5 *£0.65*

The Export of Goods (Control) Order 1994 (Amendment No. 3) 1994 No. 2711. Enabling power: *Import, Export and Customs Powers (Defence) Act 1939, s. 1.* Issued: 09.11.94. Made: 19.10.94. Coming into force: 10.11.94. Effect: S.I. 1994/1191 amended. With correction slips dated November 1994 and February 1995. Territorial extent & classification: GB/IOM. General. – 4p. – 0 11 045711 0 *£1.10*

The Export of Goods (Control) Order 1994 (Amendment) Order 1994 No. 1632. Enabling power: *Import, Export and Customs Powers (Defence) Act 1939, s. 1.* Issued: 07.07.94. Made: 17.06.94. Coming into force: 18.06.94. Effect: S.I. 1994/1191 amended. Territorial extent & classification: GB/IOM. General. – 2p. – 0 11 044632 1 *£0.65*

The Finance Act 1993, s. 4 (Appointed Day) Order 1994 No. 2968 (C. 67). Enabling power: *Finance Act 1993, s. 4 (8).* Bringing various provisions of the 1993 act into operation on 01.01.95. Issued: 29.11.94. Made: 23.11.94. Effect: None. Territorial extent & classification: GB. General. – 2p. – 0 11 043150 2 *£0.65*

The Finance Act 1994, Part I, (Appointed Day etc.) Order 1994 No. 2679 (C. 59). Enabling power: *Finance Act 1994, s. 19.* Bringing various provisions of the 1994 act into operation on 01.11.94, 01.01.95. Issued: 24.10.94. Made: 17.10.94. Effect: None. Territorial extent & classification: GB. General. – 4p. – 0 11 045679 3 *£1.10*

The Finance Act 1994, section 7, (Appointed Day) (No. 2) Order 1994 No. 2143 (C. 43). Enabling power: *Finance Act 1994, s. 19.* Bringing into operation various provisions of the 1994 act on 31.08.94. Issued: 25.08.94. Made: 15.08.94. Effect: None. Territorial extent & classification: GB. General. – 2p. – 0 11 045143 0 *£0.65*

The Finance Act 1994, section 7, (Appointed Day) Order 1994 No. 1690 (C.31). Enabling power: *Finance Act 1994, s. 19.* Bringing into operation various provisions of the 1994 act on 01.07.94. Issued: 04.07.94. Made: 27.06.94. Effect: None. Territorial extent & classification: GB. General. – 2p. – 0 11 044690 9 *£0.65*

The Free Zone (Birmingham Airport) (Substitution of Responsible Authority) Order 1994 No. 2509. Enabling power: *Customs and Excise Management Act 1979, s. 100A (4) (b).* Issued: 04.10.94. Made: 23.09.94. Coming into force: 24.09.94. Effect: None. Territorial extent & classification: GB. General. – 2p. – 0 11 045509 6 *£0.65*

The Free Zone (Humberside) Designation Order 1994 No. 144. Enabling power: *Customs and Excise Management Act 1979, s. 100A.* Issued: 03.02.94. Made: 26.01.94. Coming into force: 01.02.94. Effect: None. Territorial extent & classification: E. Local. – 2p. – 0 11 043144 8 *£0.65*

The Free Zone (Port of Sheerness) Designation Order 1994 No. 2898. Enabling power: *Customs and Excise Management Act 1979, s. 100A.* Issued: 22.11.94. Made: 15.11.94. Coming into force: 16.11.94. Effect: None. Territorial extent & classification: E. Local. – 2p. – 0 11 043008 5 9 *£0.65*

The Free Zone (Port of Tilbury) Designation (Variation) Order 1994 No. 2216. Enabling power: *Customs and Excise Management Act 1979, s. 100A (4) (a) (ii).* Issued: 31.08.94. Made: 24.08.94. Coming into force: 25.08.94. Effect: S.I. 1992/1282 amended. Territorial extent & classification: E. Local. – 2p. – 0 11 045216 X *£0.65*

The Free Zone (Prestwick Airport) Designation (Variation) Order 1994 No. 143. Enabling power: *Customs and Excise Management Act 1979, s. 100A (4) (a) (ii).* Issued: 03.02.94. Made: 26.01.94. Coming into force: 01.02.94. Effect: None. Territorial extent & classification: S. Local. – 2p. – 0 11 043143 X *£0.65*

The Free Zone (Southampton) Designation (Variation) Order 1994 No. 1410. Enabling power: *Customs & Excise Management Act 1979, s. 100A.* Issued: 02.06.94. Made: 24.05.94. Coming into force: 01.06.94. Effect: S.I. 1991/1740 amended. Territorial extent & classification: E. General. – 2p. – 0 11 044410 8 *£0.65*

Price/availability are liable to change without notice

The Hydrocarbon Oil (Amendment) (No. 2) Regulations 1994 No. 694. Enabling power: *Hydrocarbon Oil Duties Act 1979, s. 24, sch. 4.* Issued: 08.04.94. Made: 10.03.94. Laid: 11.03.94. Coming into force: 16.03.94, for regs. 1 & 2. 18.03.94, for the remainder. Effect: S.I. 1973/1311 amended & S.I. 1994/361 revoked. Territorial extent & classification: GB. General. – 2p. – 0 11 043694 6 *£0.65*

The Travellers' Allowances Order 1994 No. 955. Enabling power: *Customs and Excise (General Reliefs) Act 1979, s. 13 (1) (3).* Issued: 06.05.94. Made: 28.03.94. Laid: 29.03.94. Coming into force: 01.04.94. Effect: S.I. 1968/1558; 1972/1770; 1978/1883; 1979/1551; 1982/1591; 1984/718; 1985/1375; 1986/2105; 1989/2252; 1991/1286; 1992/3192 revoked. This SI supersedes SI of same number & ISBN previously published on 05.04.94. With correction slip. Territorial extent & classification: GB. General. – 4p. – 0 11 043955 4 *£1.10*

DANGEROUS DRUGS

The Criminal Justice (International Co-operation) (Anguilla) Order 1994 No. 1635. Enabling power: *Criminal Justice (International) Co-operation Act 1990, s. 32 (4).* Issued: 29.06.94. Made: 22.06.94. Coming into force: 14.07.94. Effect: Anguilla Ordinance no. 1988/14, 17 amended. With correction slip dated July 1994. Territorial extent & classification: GB. General. – 16p. – 0 11 044635 6 *£3.20*

The Misuse of Drugs (Licence Fees) (Amendment) Regulations 1994 No. 535. Enabling power: *Misuse of Drugs Act 1971, ss. 30, 31, 37 (1).* Issued: 11.03.94. Made: 03.03.94. Laid: 11.03.94. Coming into force: 01.04.94. Effect: S.I. 1986/416 amended. Territorial extent & classification: E/W/S. General. – 2p. – 0 11 043535 4 *£0.65*

DEFENCE

The Army, Air Force and Naval Discipline Acts (Continuation) Order 1994 No. 1903. Enabling power: *Armed Forces Act 1991, s. 1 (2).* Issued: 29.07.94. Made: 19.07.94. Coming into force: 19.07.94. Effect: None. Territorial extent & classification: GB. General. – 2p. – 0 11 044903 7 *£0.65*

The International Headquarters and Defence Organisations (Designation and Privileges) (Amendment) Order 1994 No. 1642. Enabling power: *International Headquarters and Defence Organisations Act 1964, s. 1.* Issued: 29.06.94. Made: 22.06.94. Coming into force: 01.07.94. Effect: S.I. 1965/1535 amended. Territorial extent & classification: GB. General. – 2p. – 0 11 044642 9 *£0.65*

The Visiting Forces and International Headquarters (Application of Law) (Amendment) Order 1994 No. 1643. Enabling power: *Visiting Forces Act 1952, s. 8 (6).* Issued: 29.06.94. Made: 22.06.94. Coming into force: 01.07.94. Effect: S.I. 1965/1536 amended. Territorial extent & classification: GB. General. – 2p. – 0 11 044643 7 *£0.65*

DEREGULATION

The Deregulation and Contracting Out Act 1994 (Commencement No. 1) Order 1994 No.3037 (C. 70). Enabling power: *Deregulation and Contracting Out Act 1994, s. 82 (4). Bringing into operation various provisions of the 1994 act on 01.12.94.* Issued: 08.12.94. Made: 28.11.94. Effect: None. Territorial extent & classification: E/W/S. General. – 2p. – 0 11 043315 7 *£0.65*

The Deregulation and Contracting Out Act 1994 (Commencement No. 2) Order 1994 No.3188 (C. 76). Enabling power: *Deregulation and Contracting Out Act 1994, s. 82 (4). Bringing various provisions of the 1994 act into operation on 03.01.95 and 01.04.95.* Issued: 22.12.94. Made: 09.12.94. Effect: None. Territorial extent & classification: GB. General. – 4p. – 0 11 043736 5 *£1.10*

DESIGNS

The Designs (Convention Countries) Order 1994 No.3219. Enabling power: *Registered Designs Act 1949, s. 13 (1), 37 (5).* Issued: 23.12.94. Made: 14.12.94. Coming into force: 13.01.95. Effect: S.R. & O. 1901/1799; 1938/767, 768; 1946/170; S.I. 1948/104, 872, 1006; 1949/2338; 1950/522, 1653; 1952/2107; 1953/394, 971, 1899; 1956/1003; 1957/600; 1958/263, 1053, 1054; 1960/201, 437, 1651, 1958; 1962/1083; 1963/366, 1326, 1487, 1757, 1919, 2082; 1964/265, 692, 998, 1196; 1965/977, 1123, 1711, 1304, 2013; 1966/80, 81, 396; 1967/158, 481, 1492, 1681, 1682; 1969/865; 1972/972; 1973/773; 1974/2146; 1975/2195; 1976/1785; 1977/1633, 1634, 2161; 1978/187; 1982/162; 1983/1709; 1984/367, 1694; 1985/173, 456, 457; 1988/1856; 1992/2672; 1993/1257 revoked. Territorial extent & classification: GB/IOM. General. – 6p. – 0 11 043741 1 *£1.55*

DIPLOMATIC SERVICE

The Consular Fees (Amendment) Order 1994 No. 3202. Enabling power: *Consular Fees Act 1980, s. 1 (1).* Issued: 21.12.94. Made: 14.12.94. Coming into force: 04.01.95. Effect: S.I. 1994/2793 amended. Territorial extent & classification: GB. General. – 4p. – 0 11 043649 0 *£1.10*

The Consular Fees Order 1994 No. 2793. Enabling power: *Consular Fees Act 1980, s. 1 (1).* Issued: 11.11.94. Made: 02.11.94. Coming into force: 24.11.94. Effect: S.I. 1989/152, 844; 1991/2291, 2629; 1992/2669; 1993/1781 revoked. Territorial extent & classification: GB. General. – 10p. – 0 11 045793 5 *£2.40*

ECCLESIASTICAL LAW, ENGLAND

The Church Representation Rules (Amendment) Resolution 1994 No. 3118. Enabling power: *Synodical Government Measure 1969 No. 2. s. 7 (1).* Issued: 16.12.94. Made: 29.11.94. Laid: 08.12.94. Coming into force: 01.01.95. Effect: Synodical Government Measure 1969 No. 2 amended. Territorial extent & classification: E. General. – 16p. – 0 11 043408 0 *£3.20*

Price/availability are liable to change without notice

The Ecclesiastical Judges and Legal Officers (Fees) Order 1994 No. 2009. Enabling power: *Ecclesiastical Fees Measure 1986, s. 4.* Issued: 05.08.94. Made: 08.07.94. Laid: 29.07.94. Coming into force: 01.01.95. Effect: S.I. 1993/1842 revoked. Territorial extent & classification: E. General. –6p. – 0 11 045009 4 *£1.55*

The Grants to the Redundant Churches Fund Order 1994 No. 962. Enabling power: *Redundant Churches and Other Religious Buildings Act 1969, s. 1 (1) (2).* Issued: 31.03.94. Made: 28.03.94. Coming into force: 01.04.94. Effect: None. This SI supersedes Draft SI ISBN 011045877X previously published on 17.02.94. Territorial extent & classification: GB. General. –2p. – 0 11 043962 7 *£0.65*

Incumbents (Vacation of Benefices) Rules 1994 No. 703. Enabling power: *Incumbents (Vacations of Benefices) Measure 1977, s. 18.* Issued: 21.03.94. Made: 24.01.94. Laid: 11.03.94. Coming into force: In accord with rule 1. Effect: None. Territorial extent & classification: E. General. –10p. – 0 11 043703 9 *£2.40*

The Parochial Fees Order 1994 No. 2011. Enabling power: *Ecclesiastical Fees Measure 1986, s. 1.* Issued: 05.08.94. Made: 12.07.94. Laid: 29.07.94. Coming into force: 01.01.95. Effect: S.I. 1993/1844 revoked. Territorial extent & classification: E. General. –6p. – 0 11 045011 6 *£1.55*

ECCLESIASTICAL LAW, ENGLAND: FEES

The Legal Officers (Annual Fees) Order 1994 No. 2010. Enabling power: *Ecclesiastical Fees Measure 1986, s. 5.* Issued: 05.08.94. Made: 08.07.94. Laid: 29.07.94. Coming into force: 01.01.95. Effect: S.I. 1993/1843 revoked. Territorial extent & classification: E. General. –8p. – 0 11 045010 8 *£1.95*

EDUCATION, ENGLAND AND WALES

The Cleveland College of Further Education and Sir William Turners' Sixth Form College, Redcar (Dissolution) Order 1994 No. 1755. Enabling power: *Further and Higher Education Act 1992, s. 27.* Issued: 22.07.94. Made: 05.07.94. Laid: 05.07.94. Coming into force: 01.08.94. Effect: None. Territorial extent & classification: E. Local. –2p. – 0 11 044755 7 *£0.65*

The Cleveland Tertiary College (Government) Regulations 1994 No. 1435. Enabling power: *Further and Higher Education Act 1992, ss. 20 (2), 21 (1) (2), 61 (1), 89 (4), sch. 4.* Issued: 08.07.94. Made: 26.05.94. Laid: 27.05.94. Coming into force: 29.06.94. Effect: None. Territorial extent & classification: E. Local. –16p. – 0 11 044435 3 *£3.20*

The Cleveland Tertiary College (Incorporation) Order 1994 No. 1434. Enabling power: *Further and Higher Education Act 1992, s. 16 (1), 17.* Issued: 08.07.94. Made: 26.05.94. Laid: 27.05.94. Coming into force: 29.06.94. Effect: None. Territorial extent & classification: E. Local. –2p. – 0 11 044434 5 *£0.65*

The Coleg Menai (Government) Regulations 1994 No. 1450. Enabling power: *Further and Higher Education Act 1992, ss. 20 (2), 21 (1), 61 (1), 89 (4), sch. 4.* Issued: 15.06.94. Made: 28.05.94. Laid: 07.06.94. Coming into force: 30.06.94. Effect: None. Territorial extent & classification: W. General. –16p. – 0 11 044450 7 *£3.20*

The Diocese of Bangor (Educational Endowments) Order 1994 No. 937. Enabling power: *Education Act 1973, s. 2 (1).* Made: 22.03.94. Coming into force: 28.03.94. Effect: None. –*Unpublished*

The Diocese of Bangor (Educational Endowments) (Variation) Order 1994 No. 1385. Enabling power: *Education Act 1973, s. 2 (1).* Made: 18.05.94. Coming into force: 25.05.94. Effect: S.I. 1994/937 amended. –*Unpublished*

The Diocese of Canterbury (Educational Endowments) Order 1994 No. 934. Enabling power: *Education Act 1973, s. 2.* Made: 24.03.95. Coming into force: 15.04.95. Effect: None.. –*Unpublished*

The Diocese of Carlisle (Educational Endowments) Order 1994 No. 349. Enabling power: *Education Act 1973, s. 2.* Made: 18.02.94. Coming into force: 10.03.94. Effect: None. –*Unpublished*

The Diocese of Chelmsford (Educational Endowments) Order 1994 No. 2845. Enabling power: *Education Act 1973, s. 2.* Made: 14.11.94. Coming into force: 25.11.94. Effect: None. –*Unpublished*

The Diocese of Ely (Educational Endowments) (Amendment) Order 1994 No. 2449. Enabling power: *Education Act 1973, s. 2 & Education Act 1944, s. 111.* Made: 14.09.94. Coming into force: 05.10.94. Effect: S.I. 1990/88 amended. –*Unpublished*

The Diocese of Guildford (Educational Endowments) (No 2) Order 1994 No. 1135. Enabling power: *Education Act 1973, s. 2.* Made: 21.04.94. Coming into force: 12.05.94. Effect: None. –*Unpublished*

The Diocese of Guildford (Educational Endowments) (No. 3) Order 1994 No. 1290. Enabling power: *Education Act 1973, s. 2 & Reverter of Sites Act 1987, s. 5.* Made: 12.05.94. Coming into force: 02.06.94. Effect: None.. – *Unpublished*

The Diocese of Guildford (Educational Endowments) (No. 4) Order 1994 No. 2855. Enabling power: *Education Act 1973, s. 2.* Made: 04.11.94. Coming into force: 25.11.94. Effect: None.. –*Unpublished*

The Diocese of Guildford (Educational Endowments) (No. 3) Order 1994 No. 1290. Enabling power: *Education Act 1973, s. 2 & Reverter of Sites Act 1987, s. 5.* Made: 12.05.94. Coming into force: 02.06.94. Effect: None. –*Unpublished*

The Diocese of Guildford (Educational Endowments) (No. 4) Order 1994 No. 2855. Enabling power: *Education Act 1973, s. 2.* Made: 04.11.94. Coming into force: 25.11.94. Effect: None. –*Unpublished*

The Diocese of Norwich (Educational Endowments) Order 1994 No. 2037. Enabling power: *Education Act 1973, s. 2 & Reverter of Sites Act 1987, s. 5.* Made: 01.08.94. Coming into force: 22.08.94. Effect: None. –*Unpublished*

The Diocese of Oxford (Educational Endowments) (No 2) Order 1994 No. 1136. Enabling power: *Education Act 1973, s. 2.* Made: 21.04.94. Coming into force: 12.05.94. Effect: None. –*Unpublished*

EDUCATION, ENGLAND AND WALES

The Diocese of Oxford (Educational Endowments) Order 1994 No. 532. Enabling power: *Education Act 1973, s. 2.* Made: 03.03.94. Coming into force: 24.03.94. Effect: None. – *Unpublished*

The Diocese of St Asaph (Prevention of Reverter) Order 1994 No. 1615. Enabling power: *Education Act 1973, s. 2 (1).* Made: 13.06.94. Coming into force: 24.06.94. Effect: None. – *Unpublished*

The Diocese of Truro (Educational Endowments) (No. 2) Order 1994 No. 2892. Enabling power: *Education Act 1973, s. 2.* Made: 11.11.94. Coming into force: 02.12.94. Effect: None. – *Unpublished*

The Diocese of Truro (Educational Endowments) Order 1994 No. 2450. Enabling power: *Education Act 1973, s. 2.* Made: 14.09.94. Coming into force: 05.10.94. Effect: None. – *Unpublished*

The Diocese of Wakefield (Educational Endowments) Order 1994 No. 1196. Enabling power: *Education Act 1973, s. 2 & Reverter of Sites Act 1987, s. 5.* Made: 29.03.94. Coming into force: 20.05.94. Effect: None. – *Unpublished*

The Diocese of Wakefield (Educational Endowments) (No. 2) Order 1994 No. 1544. Enabling power: *Education Act 1973, s. 2.* Made: 10.06.94. Coming into force: 01.07.94. Effect: None. – *Unpublished*

The Education Act 1993 (Commencement No. 2 and Transitional Provisions) (Amendment) Order 1994 No. 436 (C. 13). Enabling power: *Education Act 1993, ss. 301 (6), 308 (3).* Bringing into operation various provisions of the 1993 act on 18.02.94. Issued: 14.03.94. Made: 18.02.94. Effect: S.I. 1993/106 amended. Territorial extent & classification: E/W. General. – 2p. – 0 11 043436 6 £0.65

Education Act 1993 (Commencement No. 3 and Transitional Provisions) Order 1994 No.507 (C. 10). Enabling power: *Education Act 1993, ss. 301 (6), 308 (3), sch. 20, para. 2.* Bringing into operation various provisions of this act on 03.03.94, 01.04.94. Issued: 24.03.94. Made: 01.03.94. Effect: None. Territorial extent & classification: E/W. General. – 12p. – 0 11 043507 9 £2.80

Education Act 1993 (Commencement No. 4) Order 1994 No. 1558 (C. 28). Enabling power: *Education Act 1993, s. 308 (3).* Bringing into operation various provisions of the 1993 act on 15.06.94 for s. 279 & 01.04.95 for provisions specified in the 1st column of the schedule to this order. Issued: 12.07.94. Made: 14.06.94. Effect: None. Territorial extent & classification: E/W. General. – 8p. – 0 11 044558 9 £1.95

The Education Act 1993 (Commencement No. 5 and Transitional Provisions) Order 1994 No.2038 (C. 39). Enabling power: *Education Act 1993, s. 301 (6), 308 (3).* Bringing into operation various provisions of this Act on 01.08.94, 01.09.94, 01.12.94. Issued: 23.09.94. Made: 28.07.94. Effect: None. This SI was amended by SI 1994/2248 (C. 47) before publication and therefore published SIMULTANEOUSLY. Territorial extent & classification: E/W. General. – 16p. – 0 11 045248 8 £2.80

The Education Act 1993 (Commencement No. 5 and Transitional Provisions) (Amendment) Order 1994 No. 2248 (C. 47). Enabling power: *Education Act 1993, s. 301 (1), 308 (3).* Bringing into operation various provisions of this Act on 01.08.94, 01.09.94, 01.12.94. Issued: 03.10.94. Made: 25.08.94. Effect: SI 1994/2038 (C. 39) amended. This SI has been made in consequence of a defect in SI 1994/2038 which INCLUDED copies of this SI 1994/2248 [ISBN 0110452488]. Territorial extent & classification: E/W. General. – 2p. – 0 11 045038 8 £0.65

The Education Act 1994 (Commencement) Order 1994 No. 2204 (C. 46). Enabling power: *Education Act 1994, s. 26.* Bringing various provisions of this Act into operation on 21.09.94, 01.04.95. Issued: 09.09.94. Made: 23.08.94. Effect: None. Territorial extent & classification: E/W. General. – 2p. – 0 11 045204 6 £0.65

The Education (Amount to Follow Permanently Excluded Pupil) Regulations 1994 No. 1697. Enabling power: *Education Act 1993, s. 262 (2) (4).* Issued: 07.07.94. Made: 28.06.94. Laid: 07.07.94. Coming into force: 01.09.94. Effect: None. Territorial extent & classification: E/W. General. – 2p. – 0 11 044697 6 £0.65

The Education (Annual Consideration of Ballot on Grant-Maintained Status) (Wales) Order 1994 No. 1861. Enabling power: *Education Act 1993, ss. 24 (1), 301 (6).* Issued: 26.07.94. Made: 13.07.94. Laid: 15.07.94. Coming into force: 01.09.94. Effect: None. Territorial extent & classification: W. General. – 2p. – 0 11 044861 8 £0.65

The Education (Assisted Places) (Amendment) Regulations 1994 No. 2034. Enabling power: *Education Act 1980, ss. 17 (6) (7), 35 (4).* Issued: 26.08.94. Made: 30.07.94. Coming into force: 26.08.94. Effect: S.I. 1989/1235 amended. Territorial extent & classification: E/W. General. – 2p. – 0 11 045034 5 £0.65

The Education (Assisted Places) (Incidental Expenses) (Amendment) Regulations 1994 No.2035. Enabling power: *Education Act 1980, ss. 18, 35 (4).* Issued: 26.08.94. Made: 28.07.94. Laid: 03.08.94. Coming into force: 26.08.94. Effect: S.I. 1989/1237 amended. Territorial extent & classification: E/W. General. – 2p. – 0 11 045035 3 £0.65

The Education (Bursaries for Teacher Training) Regulations 1994 No. 2016. Enabling power: *Education (No. 2) Act 1986, ss. 50, 63.* Issued: 09.09.94. Made: 28.07.94. Laid: 01.08.94. Coming into force: 22.08.94. Effect: S.I. 1988/1397; 1989/451; 1990/1599; 1991/1804, 2589; 1993/1775 revoked. Territorial extent & classification: E/W. General. – 6p. – 0 11 045016 7 £1.55·

The Education (Chief Inspector of Schools in England) Order 1994 No. 1633. Enabling power: *Education (Schools) Act 1992, s. 1 (1) (4).* Issued: 04.07.94. Made: 22.06.94. Laid: 04.07.94. Coming into force: 31.08.94. Effect: S.I. 1992/1295 revoked. Territorial extent & classification: E. General. – 2p. – 0 11 044633 X £0.65

The Education (Chief Inspector of Schools in Wales) Order 1994 No. 2957. Enabling power: *Education (Schools) Act 1992, s. 5 (1) (4).* Issued: 06.12.94. Made: 24.11.94. Laid: 06.12.94. Coming into force: 31.12.94. Effect: S.I. 1992/1739 revoked. Territorial extent & classification: W. General. – 2p. – 0 11 043211 8 £0.65

The Education (Distribution by Schools of Information about Further Education Institutions) (Wales) Regulations 1994 No. 1321. Enabling power: *Education Act 1993, ss. 265, 301 (6), 305 (1) & Further and Higher Education Act 1992, ss. 50, 89 (4).* Issued: 24.05.94. Made: 17.05.94. Laid: 18.05.94. Coming into force: 07.06.94. Effect: S.I. 1993/2169 amended. Territorial extent & classification: W. General. – 4p. – 0 11 044321 7 £1.10

Price/availability are liable to change without notice

The Education (Exclusions from Schools) (Prescribed Periods) Regulations 1994 No.2093. Enabling power: *Education Act 1993, s. 301 (6), sch. 19, para. 99.* Issued: 22.08.94. Made: 04.08.94. Laid: 08.08.94. Coming into force: 01.09.94. Effect: None. Territorial extent & classification: E/W. General. – 4p. – 0 11 045093 0 *£1.10*

The Education (Fees and Awards) Regulations 1994 No. 3042. Enabling power: *Education (Fees and Awards) Act 1983, ss. 1, 2.* Issued: 13.12.94. Made: 30.11.94. Laid: 01.12.94. Coming into force: 01.01.95. Effect: S.I. 1993/559; 3183 amended & S.I. 1983/973; 1984/1201; 1985/1219; 1987/1364; 1988/1391; 1991/830, 1839 revoked. Territorial extent & classification: E/W. General. – 12p. – 0 11 043353 X *£2.80*

The Education (Financial Delegations to Schools) (Mandatory Exceptions) Regulations 1994 No.277. Enabling power: *Education Reform Act 1988, s. 38 (4) (c) (d).* Issued: 25.02.94. Made: 08.02.94. Laid: 14.02.94. Coming into force: 07.03.94. Effect: None. Territorial extent & classification: E/W. General. – 4p. – 0 11 043277 0 *£1.10*

The Education (Further Education Corporations) Order 1994 No. 1449. Enabling power: *Further and Higher Education Act 1992, ss. 16 (1) (a) (4) (5), 17 (2).* Issued: 15.06.94. Made: 28.05.94. Laid: 07.06.94. Coming into force: 30.06.94. Effect: None. Territorial extent & classification: W. General. – 2p. – 0 11 044449 3 *£0.65*

The Education (Government of Groups of Grant-maintained Schools) Regulations 1994 No.2281. Enabling power: *Education Act 1993, ss. 127 (5) (c), 187 (c).* Issued: 02.11.94. Made: 01.09.94. Laid: 05.09.94. Coming into force: 01.10.94. Effect: 1993 c. 35 amended. Territorial extent & classification: E/W. General. – 4p. – 0 11 045281 X *£1.10*

The Education (Governors of New Grant-maintained Schools) Regulations 1994 No. 654. Enabling power: *Education Act 1993, ss. 60 (6), 61 (4), 78, 301 (6), sch. 5, para. 10 (4).* Issued: 16.05.94. Made: 08.03.94. Laid: 10.03.94. Coming into force: 01.04.94. Effect: None. Territorial extent & classification: E/W. General. – 4p. – 0 11 043654 7 *£1.10*

The Education (Grant) (Amendment) Regulations 1994 No.2102. Enabling power: *Education Act 1944, s. 100 (1) (b).* Issued: 26.08.94. Made: 05.08.94. Laid: 09.08.94. Coming into force: 01.09.94. Effect: S.I. 1990/1989 amended. Territorial extent & classification: E/W. General. – 2p. – 0 11 045102 3 *£0.65*

The Education (Grant) (Henrietta Barnett School) Regulations 1994 No. 156. Enabling power: *Education Act 1944, s. 100 (b) (3).* Issued: 07.02.94. Made: 31.01.94. Laid: 07.02.94. Coming into force: 28.02.94. Effect: None. Territorial extent & classification: E. Local. –2p. – 0 11 043156 1 *£0.65*

The Education (Grant-maintained Schools) (Finance) Regulations 1994 No. 938. Enabling power: *Education Act 1993, ss. 81 (2), 82, 83 (1) (2), 84 (2) (6), 94, 301 (6).* Issued: 16.05.94. Made: 27.03.94. Laid: 28.03.94. Coming into force: 01.04.94. Effect: S.I. 1993/568 amended. Territorial extent & classification: E/W. General. – 40p. – 0 11 043938 4 *£6.10*

The Education (Grant-maintained Schools) (Finance) (Wales) Regulations 1994 No. 610. Enabling power: *Education Act 1993, ss. 81 (2), 82 (2), 8 (2), 88, 89, 90, 94, 301 (6).* Issued: 20.04.94. Made: 14.03.94. Laid: 14.03.94. Coming into force: 01.04.94. Effect: S.I. 1990/549 revoked. Territorial extent & classification: W. General. – 20p. – 0 11 043610 5 *£3.70*

The Education (Grant-maintained Schools) (Initial Governing Instruments) (Amendment) Regulations 1994 No. 2094. Enabling power: *Education Act 1993, s.56 (1) (3), 301 (6).* Issued: 17.08.94. Made: 04.08.94. Laid: 11.08.94. Coming into force: 01.09.94. Effect: None. Territorial extent & classification: E/W. General. – 8p. – 0 11 045094 9 *£1.95*

The Education (Grant-maintained Special Schools) (Amendment) Regulations 1994 No.1231. Enabling power: *Education Act 1993, ss. 183 (6) (9), 186, 301 (6).* Issued: 17.06.94. Made: 03.05.94. Laid: 05.05.94. Coming into force: 01.06.94. Effect: S.I. 1994/653 amended. This SI has been made in consequence of a defect in SI 1994/653 and is being sent free of charge to all known recipients of that SI. Territorial extent & classification: E/W. General. – 6p. – 0 11 044231 8 *£1.55*

The Education (Grant-maintained Special Schools) (Finance) Regulations 1994 No. 2111. Enabling power: *Education Act 1993, ss. 81 (2), 82 (2), 83 (1), 84 (2) (6), 94, 301 (6).* Issued: 09.09.94. Made: 09.08.94. Laid: 10.08.94. Coming into force: 01.09.94. Effect: None. Territorial extent & classification: E/W. General. – 16p. – 0 11 045111 2 *£3.20*

The Education (Grant-maintained Special Schools) (Initial Governing Instruments) Regulations 1994 No. 2104. Enabling power: *Education Act 1993, s. 301 (6), sch. 11, para. 2 (1) (3).* Issued: 30.08.94. Made: 06.08.94. Laid: 09.08.94. Coming into force: 01.09.94. Effect: None. Territorial extent & classification: E/W. General. – 34p. – 0 11 045104 X *£6.10*

The Education (Grant-maintained Special Schools) (No. 2) Regulations 1994 No. 2247. Enabling power: *Education Act 1993, sch. 11, para. 14.* Issued: 09.09.94. Made: 26.08.94. Laid: 31.08.94. Coming into force: 21.09.94. Effect: None. Territorial extent & classification: E/W. General. – 2p. – 0 11 045247 X *£0.65*

The Education (Grant-Maintained Special Schools) Regulations 1994 No. 653. Enabling power: *Education Act 1993, ss. 183 (3) (6) (9), 186, 301 (6), sch. 11, paras. 12, 14.* Issued: 31.03.94. Made: 10.03.94. Laid: 11.03.94. Coming into force: 01.04.94. Effect: 1944 c.31; 1948 c.40; 1972 c.70; 1973 c.23; 1975 c.75; 1976 c.74; 1977 c.49; 1978 c.44; 1980 c.20; 1982 c.30; 1986 c.61; 1988 c.40; 1989 c.41; 1990 c.43; 1991 c.49; 1992 c.13; 1993 c.10, c.35; S.I. 1989/398, 954, 1181, 1261; 1991/751, 752, 1511, 1658, 1681, 2562, 2563; 1992/156, 597, 598, 757, 758, 1857, 2274; 1993/398, 835, 1502, 2077, 2190, 2191, 3072, 3182 amended. Territorial extent & classification: E/W. General. – 20p. – 0 11 043653 9 *£3.70* Replaced by ISBN 0110459350

Price/availability are liable to change without notice

EDUCATION, ENGLAND AND WALES

The Education (Grants for Education Support and Training) (Amendment) Regulations 1994 No.2446. Enabling power: *Education (Grants and Award) Act 1984, ss. 1, 3 (4)*. Issued: 17.10.94. Made: 14.09.94. Laid: 16.09.94. Coming into force: 06.10.94. Effect: S.I. 1994/612 amended. Territorial extent & classification: E/W. General. – 2p. – 0 11 045446 4 *£0.65*

The Education (Grants for Education Support and Training) Regulations 1994 No. 612. Enabling power: *Education (Grants and Awards) Act 1984, ss. 1, 3 (4)*. Issued: 31.03.94. Made: 06.03.94. Laid: 10.03.94. Coming into force: 01.04.94. Effect: S.I. 1992/3275 revoked. Territorial extent & classification: E/W. General. – 8p. – 0 11 043612 1 *£1.95*

The Education (Grants) (Music and Ballet Schools) (Amendment) Regulations 1994 No.2036. Enabling power: *Education Act 1944, ss. 100 (1) (b) (3)*. Issued: 26.08.94. Made: 26.07.94. Laid: 03.08.94. Coming into force: 26.08.94. Effect: S.I. 1989/1236 amended. Territorial extent & classification: E/W. General. – 4p. – 0 11 045036 1 *£1.10*

The Education (Groups including Grant-maintained Special Schools) Regulations 1994 No.779. Enabling power: *Education Act 1994, s. 187*. Issued: 05.05.94. Made: 15.03.94. Laid: 17.03.94. Coming into force: 08.04.94. Effect: None. Territorial extent & classification: E/W. General. – 2p. – 0 11 043779 9 *£0.65*

The Education (Groups of Grant-maintained Schools) (Finance) Regulations 1994 No.1195. Enabling power: *Education Act 1993, s. 126 (2)*. Issued: 13.05.94. Made: 27.04.94. Laid: 03.05.94. Coming into force: 01.06.94. Effect: None. Territorial extent & classification: E/W. General. – 2p. – 0 11 044195 8 *£0.65*

The Education (Groups of Grant-maintained Schools) (Initial Governing Instruments) Regulations 1994 No. 2896. Enabling power: *Education Act 1993, ss. 118 (1), 119, 124*. Issued: 23.11.94. Made: 11.11.94. Laid: 16.11.94. Coming into force: 07.12.94. Effect: None. Territorial extent & classification: E/W. General. – 20p. – 0 11 043078 6 *£3.20*

The Education (Groups of Grant-maintained Schools) Regulations 1994 No. 1041. Enabling power: *Education Act 1993, ss. 117 (5), 127, 187 (2), 301 (6)*. Issued: 16.05.94. Made: 08.04.94. Laid: 08.04.94. Coming into force: 01.05.94. Effect: None. Territorial extent & classification: E/W. General. – 28p. – 0 11 044041 2 *£4.70*

The Education (Gwynedd Technical College and Coleg Pencraig) (Dissolution) Order 1994 No.1478. Enabling power: *Further and Higher Education Act 1992, s. 27*. Issued: 15.06.94. Made: 28.05.94. Laid: 07.06.94. Coming into force: 01.08.94. Effect: None. Territorial extent & classification: W. General. – 2p. – 0 11 044478 7 *£0.65*

The Education (Individual Pupils' Achievements) (Information) (Wales) Regulations 1994 No.959. Enabling power: *Education Reform Act 1988, ss. 22, 232 (5) (6)*. Issued: 19.04.94. Made: 29.03.94. Laid: 31.03.94. Coming into force: 22.04.94. Effect: None. Territorial extent & classification: W. General. – 10p. – 0 11 043959 7 *£2.40*

The Education (Information as to Provision of Education) (England) Regulations 1994 No.1256. Enabling power: *Education Act 1993, s. 21, 301 (6)*. Issued: 21.07.94. Made: 09.05.94. Laid: 10.05.94. Coming into force: 31.05.94. Effect: None. Territorial extent & classification: E. General. – 12p. – 0 11 044256 3 *£2.80*

The Education (Initial Government of Grant-maintained Special Schools) Regulations 1994 No.2003. Enabling power: *Education Act 1993, ss. 183 (6) (9), 301 (6), sch. 11, paras. 13, 14*. Issued: 26.08.94. Made: 26.07.94. Laid: 28.07.94. Coming into force: 19.08.94. Effect: 1993 c.35; S.I. 1994/653 amended. Territorial extent & classification: E/W. General. – 8p. – 0 11 045003 5 *£1.95*

The Education (Inner London Education Authority) (Property Transfer) (Amendment (No. 2) Order 1994 No. 2163. Enabling power: *Education Act 1988, s. 231 (2) (3) (d)*. Issued: 24.08.94. Made: 17.08.94. Laid: 24.08.94. Coming into force: 19.09.94. Effect: S.I. 1990/124 amended. Territorial extent & classification: E. General. – 2p. – 0 11 045163 5 *£0.65*

The Education (Inner London Education Authority) (Property Transfer) Order 1994 No.1255. Enabling power: *Education Reform Act 1988, s. 231 (2) (3) (d)*. Issued: 02.06.94. Made: 09.05.94. Laid: 10.05.94. Coming into force: 01.06.94. Effect: None. Territorial extent & classification: E/W. General. – 2p. – 0 11 044255 5 *£0.65*

The Education (Inter-authority Recoupment) Regulations 1994 No. 3251. Enabling power: *Education (No. 2) Act 1986, ss. 51, 63 (3)*. Issued: 23.12.94. Made: 15.12.94. Coming into force: 01.04.95. Effect: None. Territorial extent & classification: E/W. General. – 4p. – 0 11 045980 6 *£1.10*

The Education (Lay Members of Appeal Committees) Regulations 1994 No. 1303. Enabling power: *Education Act 1993, s. 267 (2)*. Issued: 25.05.94. Made: 12.05.94. Laid: 16.05.94. Coming into force: 06.06.94. Effect: None. Territorial extent & classification: E/W. General. – 2p. – 0 11 044303 9 *£0.65*

The Education, (London Residuary Body) (Property Transfer) (Amendment) (No. 2) Order 1994 No.3105. Enabling power: *Education Reform Act 1988, ss. 187 (5) (6), 231 (2), 232 (5)*. Issued: 15.12.94. Made: 06.12.94. Laid: 07.12.94. Coming into force: 01.01.95. Effect: S.I. 1992/587 amended. Territorial extent & classification: E. General. – 2p. – 0 11 043386 6 *£0.65*

The Education (London Residuary Body) (Property Transfer) (Amendment) Order 1994 No.3078. Enabling power: *Education Reform Act 1988, s. 187 (5) (6), 231 (2), 232 (5)*. Issued: 13.12.94. Made: 05.12.94. Laid: 06.12.94. Coming into force: 30.12.94. Effect: S.I. 1991/2778 amended. Territorial extent & classification: E/W. General. – 2p. – 0 11 043357 2 *£0.65*

The Education (London Residuary Body) (Transfer of Property etc.) Order 1994 No. 580. Enabling power: *Education Reform Act 1988, ss. 187 (5) (a), 231 (2), 232 (5) & Local Government Act 1985, s. 77*. Issued: 11.03.94. Made: 08.03.94. Laid: 08.03.94. Coming into force: 29.03.94. Effect: S.I. 1991/439; 1992/2257 amended. Territorial extent & classification: E/W. General. – 4p. – 0 11 043580 X *£1.10*

Price/availability are liable to change without notice

The Education (Maintained Special Schools becoming Grant-maintained Special Schools) (Ballot Information) Regulations 1994 No. 1232. Enabling power: *Education Act 1993, s. 28 (3) (a), 301 (6)*. Issued: 16.06.94. Made: 03.05.94. Laid: 05.05.94. Coming into force: 01.06.94. Effect: None. Territorial extent & classification: E/W. General. – 2p. – 0 11 044232 6 £0.65

The Education (Mandatory Awards) (Amendment) (No. 2) Regulations 1994 No. 3043. Enabling power: *Education Act 1962, ss. 1, 4 (2)*. Issued: 13.12.94. Made: 30.11.94. Laid: 01.12.94. Coming into force: 01.01.95. Effect: S.I. 1993/2914 amended. Territorial extent & classification: E/W. General. – 4p. – 0 11 043354 8 £1.10

The Education (Mandatory Awards) (Amendment) Regulations 1994 No. 1606. Enabling power: *Education Act 1962, ss. 1, 4 (2)*. Issued: 05.07.94. Made: 16.06.94. Laid: 17.06.94. Coming into force: 08.07.94. Effect: S.I. 1993/1850, 2914 amended. Territorial extent & classification: E/W. General. – 2p. – 0 11 044606 2 £0.65

The Education (Mandatory Awards) Regulations 1994 No. 3044. Enabling power: *Education Act 1962, ss. 1, 4 (2), sch. 1, paras. 3, 4, & Education Act 1973, s. 3 (1) (3)*. Issued: 15.12.94. Made: 30.11.94. Laid: 01.12.94. Coming into force: 01.09.95. Effect: S.I. 1993/2914, 3183; 1994/1606, 3043 revoked. Territorial extent & classification: E/W. General. – 33p. – 0 11 043355 6 £6.10

The Education (Middle Schools) (Amendment) Regulations 1994 No. 581. Enabling power: *Education Act 1964, s. 1 (2)*. Issued: 31.03.94. Made: 05.03.94. Laid: 10.03.94. Coming into force: 01.04.94. Effect: S.I. 1980/918 amended. Territorial extent & classification: E/W. General. – 2p. – 0 11 043581 8 £0.65

The Education (National Curriculum) (Assessment Arrangements for English, Welsh, Mathematics and Science) (Key Stage 1) (Wales) (Amendment) Order 1994 No. 646. Enabling power: *Education Reform Act 1988, ss. 4 (2) (c) (5) (6) (7) (8), 232 (5) (6)*. Issued: 05.04.94. Made: 10.03.94. Coming into force: 01.04.94. Effect: S.I. 1993/2190 amended. Territorial extent & classification: W. General. – 2p. – 0 11 043646 6 £0.65

The Education (National Curriculum) (Assessment Arrangements for English, Welsh, Mathematics and Science) (Key Stage 1) (Wales) (Amendment) Order 1994 No. 2226. Enabling power: *Education Reform Act 1988, ss. 4 (2) (c) (5) (8), 232 (5) (6)*. Issued: 07.09.94. Made: 24.08.94. Coming into force: 31.08.94. Effect: S.I. 1993/2190 amended. Territorial extent & classification: W. General. – 4p. – 0 11 045226 7 £1.10

The Education (National Curriculum) (Assessment Arrangements for English, Welsh, Mathematics and Science) (Key Stage 2) (Wales) Order 1994 No. 2227. Enabling power: *Education Reform Act 1988, ss. 4 (2) (c) (5) (6) (8), 232 (5) (6)*. Issued: 07.09.94. Made: 24.08.94. Coming into force: 31.08.94. Effect: None. Territorial extent & classification: W. General. – 4p. – 0 11 045227 5 £1.10

The Education (National Curriculum) (Assessment Arrangements for English, Welsh, Mathematics and Science) (Key Stage 3) (Wales) (Amendment) Order 1994 No. 647. Enabling power: *Education Refrom Act 1988, ss. 4 (2) (c) (5) (6) (7) (8), 232 (5) (6)*. Issued: 05.04.94. Made: 10.03.94. Coming into force: 01.04.94. Effect: S.I. 1993/2191 revoked. Territorial extent & classification: W. General. – 2p. – 0 11 043647 4 £0.65

The Education (National Curriculum) (Assessment Arrangements for English, Welsh, Mathematics and Science) (Key Stage 3) (Wales) Order 1994 No. 2228. Enabling power: *Education Reform Act 1988, ss. 4 (2) (c) (5) (6) (8), 232 (5) (6)*. Issued: 07.09.94. Made: 24.08.94. Coming into force: 31.08.94. Effect: S.I. 1993/2191; S.I. 1994/647 revoked. Territorial extent & classification: W. General. – 4p. – 0 11 045228 3 £1.10

The Education (National Curriculum) (Assessment Arrangements for the Core Subjects) (Key Stage 1) (Amendment) Order 1994 No. 2099. Enabling power: *Education Reform Act 1988, s. 4 (2) (c) (5), (6) (8), 232 (5) (6)*. Issued: 05.09.94. Made: 04.08.94. Coming into force: 08.08.94. Effect: S.I. 1993/1983 amended. Territorial extent & classification: E. General. –4p. – 0 11 045099 X £1.10

The Education (National Curriculum) (Assessment Arrangements for the Core Subjects) (Key Stage 2) (England) Order 1994 No. 2100. Enabling power: *Education Reform Act 1988, s. 4 (2) (c) (5), (6) (8), 232 (5) (6)*. Issued: 05.09.94. Made: 04.08.94. Coming into force: 08.08.94. Effect: None. Territorial extent & classification: E. General. – 4p. – 0 11 045100 7 £1.10

The Education (National Curriculum) (Assessment Arrangements for the Core Subjects) (Key Stage 3) (England) Order 1994 No. 2101. Enabling power: *Education Reform Act 1988, s. 4 (2) (c) (5), (6) (8), 232 (5) (6)*. Issued: 05.09.94. Made: 04.08.94. Coming into force: 08.08.94. Effect: S.I. 1993/1984 revoked. Territorial extent & classification: E. General. –4p. – 0 11 045101 5 £1.10

The Education (National Curriculum) (Attainment Targets and Programmes of Study in Geography) (England) (Amendment) Order 1994 No. 1817. Enabling power: *Education Reform Act 1988, s. 4 (2) (a) (b) (4)*. Issued: 21.07.94. Made: 06.07.94. Laid: 11.07.94. Coming into force: 01.08.94. Effect: S.I. 1991/2562 amended. Territorial extent & classification: E. General. – 2p. – 0 11 044817 0 £0.65

The Education (National Curriculum) (Attainment Targets and Programmes of Study in Geography) (Wales) (Amendment) Order 1994 No. 1744. Enabling power: *Education Reform Act 1988, ss. 4 (2) (a) (b), 232 (5) (6)*. Issued: 19.07.94. Made: 07.07.94. Laid: 11.07.94. Coming into force: 01.08.94. Effect: S.I. 1991/751 amended. Territorial extent & classification: W. General. – 2p. – 0 11 044744 1 £0.65

The Education (National Curriculum) (Attainment Targets and Programmes of Study in History) (England) (Amendment) Order 1994 No. 1816. Enabling power: *Education Reform Act 1988, s. 4 (2) (a) (b) (4)*. Issued: 22.07.94. Made: 07.07.94. Laid: 11.07.94. Coming into force: 01.08.94. Effect: S.I. 1991/681 amended. Territorial extent & classification: E. General. – 2p. – 0 11 044816 2 £0.65

EDUCATION, ENGLAND AND WALES

The Education (National Curriculum) (Attainment Targets and Programmes of Study in History) (Wales) (Amendment) Order 1994 No. 1743. Enabling power: *Education Reform Act 1988, ss. 4 (2) (a) (b), 232 (5) (6).* Issued: 19.07.94. Made: 07.07.94. Laid: 11.07.94. Coming into force: 01.08.94. Effect: S.I. 1991/752 amended. Territorial extent & classification: W. General. – 2p. – 0 11 044743 3 *£0.65*

The Education (National Curriculum) (Attainment Targets and Programmes of Study in Modern Foreign Languages and Technology at Key Stage 4) (England) (Amendment) Order 1994 No. 1815. Enabling power: *Education Reform Act 1994, s. 4 (2) (a) (b) (4), 232 (5) (6).* Issued: 22.07.94. Made: 07.07.94. Laid: 11.07.94. Coming into force: 01.08.94. Effect: S.I. 1991/2563 amended. With correction slip. Territorial extent & classification: E. General. – 2p. – 0 11 044815 4 *£0.65*

The Education (National Curriculum) (Attainment Targets and Programmes of Study in Science) (Amendment) Order 1994 No. 1520. Enabling power: *Education Reform Act 1988, ss. 4 (2) (a) (b) (4).* Issued: 17.06.94. Made: 28.05.94. Coming into force: 01.08.94. Effect: S.I. 1991/2897 amended. Territorial extent & classification: E/W. General. – 2p. – 0 11 044520 1 *£0.65*

The Education (National Curriculum) (Exceptions in Welsh at Key Stage 4) Regulations 1994 No.1270. Enabling power: *Education Reform Act 1988, s. 17.* Issued: 24.05.94. Made: 30.04.94. Laid: 19.05.94. Coming into force: 01.08.94. Effect: None. Territorial extent & classification: W. General. – 2p. – 0 11 044270 9 *£0.65*

The Education (National Curriculum Exceptions) Regulations 1994 No. 2112. Enabling power: *Education Reform Act 1988, ss. 17, 232 (5) (6).* Issued: 26.08.94. Made: 09.08.94. Laid: 10.08.94. Coming into force: 01.09.94. Effect: S.I. 1992/155, 156, 157 revoked. Territorial extent & classification: E/W. General. – 4p. – 0 11 045112 0 *£1.10*

The Education (National Curriculum) (Exceptions) (Wales) Regulations 1994 No. 2206. Enabling power: *Education Reform Act 1988, ss. 17, 232 (5) (6).* Issued: 20.09.94. Made: 22.08.94. Laid: 26.08.94. Coming into force: 01.09.94. Effect: None. Territorial extent & classification: E/W. General. – 4p. – 0 11 045206 2 *£1.10*

The Education (National Curriculum) (Foundation Subjects at Key Stage 4) Order 1994 No.1814. Enabling power: *Education Reform Act 1988, s. 3 (4) (a).* Issued: 22.07.94. Made: 07.07.94. Coming into force: 01.08.94. Effect: 1988 c. 40 amended. Territorial extent & classification: E/W. General. – 2p. – 0 11 044814 6 *£0.65*

The Education (National Curriculum) (Modern Foreign Languages) (Amendment) Order 1994 No.1818. Enabling power: *Education Reform Act 1988, s. 3 (2) (b), 232 (5) (6).* Issued: 21.07.94. Made: 07.07.94. Laid: 11.07.94. Coming into force: 01.08.94. Effect: S.I. 1991/2567 amended. Territorial extent & classification: E. General. – 2p. – 0 11 044818 9 *£0.65*

The Education (No. 2) Act 1986 (Amendment) (No. 3) Order 1994 No. 2732. Enabling power: *Education (No. 2) Act 1986, s. 30 (5).* Issued: 03.11.94. Made: 24.10.94. Laid: 25.10.94. Coming into force: 16.11.94. Effect: SI 1994/692 amended. This SI has been made in consequence of a defect in SI 1994/692 and is being sent free of charge to all known recipients of that SI. Territorial extent & classification: E/W. General. – 2p. – 0 11 045732 3 *£0.65*

The Education (No. 2) Act 1986 (Amendment) Order 1994 No. 692. Enabling power: *Education (No. 2) Act 1986, s. 30 (5).* Issued: 25.03.94. Made: 10.03.94. Laid: 11.03.94. Coming into force: 01.04.94. Effect: 1986 c. 61 amended. Territorial extent & classification: E/W. General. – 2p. – 0 11 043692 X *£0.65* Replaced by ISBN 0110430190

The Education (No. 2) Act 1986 (Amendment) (No. 2) Order 1994 No. 2092. Enabling power: *Education (No. 2) Act 1986, s. 63 (3), sch. 3, para. 5.* Issued: 22.08.94. Made: 04.08.94. Laid: 08.08.94. Coming into force: 01.09.94. Effect: 1986 c. 61 amended. Territorial extent & classification: E/W. General. – 4p. – 0 11 045092 2 *£1.10*

The Education (Northern School of Contemporary Dance, Leeds Further Education Corporation) (Transfer to the Higher Education Sector) Order 1994 No. 2018. Enabling power: *Education Reform Act 1988, s. 122A.* Issued: 17.08.94. Made: 28.07.94. Laid: 01.08.94. Coming into force: 01.10.94. Effect: None. Territorial extent & classification: E. Local. – 2p. – 0 11 045018 3 *£0.65*

The Education (Norwich School of Art and Design Further Education Corporation) (Transfer to the Higher Education Sector) Order 1994 No. 2017. Enabling power: *Education Reform Act 1988, s. 122A.* Issued: 17.08.94. Made: 28.07.94. Laid: 01.08.94. Coming into force: 01.10.94. Effect: None. Territorial extent & classification: E. Local. – 2p. – 0 11 045017 5 *£0.65*

The Education (Particulars of Independent Schools) (Amendment) Regulations 1994 No.537. Enabling power: *Education Act 1944, s. 70 (4) (4A).* Issued: 26.04.94. Made: 27.02.94. Laid: 07.03.94. Coming into force: 01.04.94. Effect: S.I. 1982/1730 amended. Territorial extent & classification: E/W. General. – 2p. – 0 11 043537 0 *£0.65*

The Education (Payment for Special Educational Needs Supplies) (Amendment) Regulations 1994 No. 2156. Enabling power: *Education Act 1993, ss. 162 (2), 301 (6).* Issued: 09.09.94. Made: 16.08.94. Laid: 17.08.94. Coming into force: 07.09.94. Effect: S.I. 1994/650 amended. Territorial extent & classification: E/W. General. – 2p. – 0 11 045156 2 *£0.65*

The Education (Payment for Special Educational Needs Supplies) Regulations 1994 No.650. Enabling power: *Education Act 1993, ss. 162 (2), 301 (6).* Issued: 05.04.94. Made: 09.03.94. Laid: 10.03.94. Coming into force: 01.04.94. Effect: None. Territorial extent & classification: E/W. General. – 4p. – 0 11 043650 4 *£1.10*

The Education (Publication of Notices) (Special Schools) Regulations 1994 No. 2167. Enabling power: *Education Act 1993, ss. 72 (4), 73 (5) (6), 301 (6).* Issued: 09.09.94. Made: 17.08.94. Laid: 18.08.94. Coming into force: 08.09.94. Effect: None. Territorial extent & classification: E/W. General. – 2p. – 0 11 045167 8 *£0.65*

Price/availability are liable to change without notice

The Education (Pupil Referral Units) (Application of Enactments) Regulations 1994 No.2103. Enabling power: *Education Act 1980, ss. 8 (5B) (7), 35 (4) & Education Act 1993, ss. 298 (8), 301 (6), sch. 18, para. 3.* Issued: 18.08.94. Made: 05.08.94. Laid: 09.08.94. Coming into force: 01.09.94. Effect: None. Territorial extent & classification: E/W. General. – 8p. – 0 11 045103 1 *£1.95*

The Education (Registered Inspectors of Schools Appeal Tribunal) (Procedure) Regulations 1994 No. 717. Enabling power: *Education (Schools) Act 1992, s. 12 (5), sch. 3, para. 2.* Issued: 05.04.94. Made: 10.03.94. Laid: 14.03.94. Coming into force: 15.04.94. Effect: None. Territorial extent & classification: E/W. General. – 12p. – 0 11 043717 9 *£2.80*

The Education (School Curriculum and Assessment Authority) (Transfer of Functions) Order 1994 No. 645. Enabling power: *Education Act 1993, s. 252.* Issued: 05.04.94. Made: 10.03.94. Laid: 11.03.94. Coming into force: 01.04.94. Effect: None. Territorial extent & classification: W. General. – 2p. – 0 11 043645 8 *£0.65*

The Education (School Financial Statements) (Prescribed Particulars etc.) Regulations 1994 No.323. Enabling power: *Education Act 1988, ss. 42 (4) (6) to (8), 232 (5).* Issued: 11.03.94. Made: 15.02.94. Laid: 16.02.94. Coming into force: 01.03.94. Effect: None. Territorial extent & classification: E/W. General. – 20p. – 0 11 043323 8 *£3.70*

The Education (School Information) (England) (Amendment) Regulations 1994 No. 2387. Enabling power: *Education Act 1944, s. 55 (5) & Education Act 1980, ss. 8 (5) (5A) (5B) (6) (7), 35 (4) & Education (Schools) Act 1992, ss. 16, 19 (3) & Education Act 1993, ss. 153 (1), 301 (6).* Issued: 03.11.94. Made: 11.09.94. Laid: 12.09.94. Coming into force: 01.10.94. Effect: S.I. 1994/1421 amended. This is SI has been made in consequence of a defect in SI 1994/1421 and is being sent free of charge to all known recipients of that SI. Territorial extent & classification: E. General. – 4p. – 0 11 045387 5 *£1.10*

The Education (School Information) (England) Regulations 1994 No. 1421. Enabling power: *Education Act 1944, s. 55 & Education Act 1980, ss. 8 (5) (5A) (5B) (6) (7), 35 (4) & Education Reform Act 1988, ss. 22, 232 (5) (6) & Education (Schools) Act 1992, ss. 16, 19 (3) & Education Act 1993, ss. 153 (1), 301 (6).* Issued: 27.06.94. Made: 25.05.94. Laid: 26.05.94. Coming into force: 21.06.94. Effect: S.I. 1993/1502, 2824 revoked. Territorial extent & classification: E. General. – 16p. – 0 11 044421 3 *£3.20* Replaced by ISBN 0110430182 @TS D = **The Education (School Information) (Wales) Regulations 1994 No. 2330.** Enabling power: *Education Act 1944, ss. 55 (5), 111A & Education Act 1980, ss. 8 (5) (5A) (5B) (6) (7), 35 (4) (5) & Education Reform Act 1988, ss. 22, 232 (5) (6) & Education (Schools) Act 1992, s. 16, 19 (3) & Education Act 1993, ss. 153 (1), 301 (6), sch. 18, s. 298 (8).* Issued: 30.09.94. Made: 07.09.94. Laid: 09.09.94. Coming into force: 10.10.94. Effect: S.I. 1991/1658, 1813; 1993/998 revoked. Territorial extent & classification: W. General. – 16p. – 0 11 045330 1 *£3.20*

The Education (School Performance Information) (England) Regulations 1994 No. 1420. Enabling power: *Education Reform Act 1988, ss. 22, 232 (5).* Issued: 08.06.94. Made: 25.05.94. Laid: 26.05.94. Coming into force: 21.06.94. Effect: S.I. 1993/2077 revoked. Territorial extent & classification: E/W. General. – 12p. – 0 11 044420 5 *£2.80*

The Education (School Performance Information) (Wales) (Amendment) Regulations 1994 No.1912. Enabling power: *Education (Schools) Act 1992, ss. 16, 19 (3).* Issued: 22.07.94. Made: 10.07.94. Laid: 22.07.94. Coming into force: 15.08.94. Effect: S.I. 1994/1186 amended. This SI has been made in consequence of a defect in SI 1994/1186 and is being sent free of charge to all known recipients of that SI. Territorial extent & classification: W. General. – 2p. – 0 11 044912 6 *£0.65*

The Education (School Performance Information) (Wales) (No. 2) Regulations 1994 No.2254. Enabling power: *Education Reform Act 1988, ss. 22, 232 (5) (6) & Education (Schools) Act 1992, ss. 16, 19 (3).* Issued: 30.09.94. Made: 26.08.94. Laid: 05.09.94. Coming into force: 30.09.94. Effect: S.I. 1993/2194; 1994/1186, 1912 revoked. Territorial extent & classification: W. General. – 10p. – 0 11 045254 2 *£2.40*

The Education (School Performance Information) (Wales) Regulations 1994 No. 1186. Enabling power: *Education (Schools) Act 1992, ss. 16, 19 (3).* Issued: 09.05.94. Made: 21.04.94. Laid: 29.04.94. Coming into force: 20.05.94. Effect: None. Territorial extent & classification: W. General. – 4p. – 0 11 044186 9 *£1.10* Replaced by ISBN 0110430166

The Education (Schools Conducted by Education Associations) (Initial Articles of Government) (Amendment) Regulations 1994 No. 1085. Enabling power: *Education Act 1993, ss. 223 (3) (4), 301 (6).* Issued: 02.06.94. Made: 13.04.94. Laid: 18.04.94. Coming into force: 09.05.94. Effect: S.I. 1993/3101 amended. Territorial extent & classification: E/W. General. –4p. – 0 11 044083 8 *£1.10*

The Education (Schools Conducted by Education Associations) (Amendment) Regulations 1994 No.1083. Enabling power: *Education Act 1993, ss. 228 (1) (6), 301 (6).* Issued: 02.06.94. Made: 13.04.94. Laid: 18.04.94. Coming into force: 09.05.94. Effect: S.I. 1993/2194; 3103 amended. Territorial extent & classification: E/W. General. – 6p. – 0 11 044085 4 *£1.55* Replaced by ISBN 0110523067

The Education (Schools Conducted by Education Associations) (Initial Articles of Government) Regulations 1994 No.2849. Enabling power: *Education Act 1993, ss. 223 (3) (4), 301 (6).* Issued: 21.11.94. Made: 05.11.94. Laid: 10.11.94. Coming into force: 01.12.94. Effect: S.I. 1993/3101 revoked. Territorial extent & classification: E/W. General. – 20p. – 0 11 045849 4 *£3.70*

The Education (School Teachers' Pay and Conditions) (No. 2) Order 1994 No. 1673. Enabling power: *School Teachers' Pay and Conditions Act 1991, ss. 2 (1) (3) (4), 5 (4).* Issued: 01.07.94. Made: 24.06.94. Laid: 04.07.94. Coming into force: 01.09.94. Effect: S.I. 1993/1755; 1994/910 revoked. Territorial extent & classification: E/W. General. – 2p. – 0 11 044673 9 *£0.65*

Price/availability are liable to change without notice

EDUCATION, ENGLAND AND WALES

The Education (School Teachers' Pay and Conditions) Order 1994 No. 910. Enabling power: *School Teachers' Pay and Conditions Act 1991, ss. 2 (1) (3) (4), 5 (4).* Issued: 15.04.94. Made: 23.03.94. Laid: 25.03.94. Coming into force: 15.04.94. Effect: S.I. 1993/1755 amended. Territorial extent & classification: E/W. General. – 4p. – 0 11 043910 4 *£1.10*

The Education (Special Educational Needs) (Amendment) Regulations 1994 No. 1251. Enabling power: *Education Act 1993, s. 168 (2), sch. 9, para. 3.* Issued: 31.05.94. Made: 05.05.94. Laid: 09.05.94. Coming into force: 01.09.94. Effect: S.I. 1994/1047 amended. This S.I. is publishing simultaneously and free of charge with S.I. 1994/1047 which it amends. Territorial extent & classification: E/W. General. – 2p. – 0 11 044251 2 *£0.65*

The Education (Special Educational Needs) (Approval of Independent Schools) Regulations 1994 No. 651. Enabling power: *Education Act 1993, ss. 172 (6), 189 (2), 301 (6).* Issued: 05.04.94. Made: 09.03.94. Laid: 11.03.94. Coming into force: 01.04.94. Effect: S.I. 1991/449 revoked. Territorial extent & classification: E/W. General. – 10p. – 0 11 043651 2 *£2.40*

The Education (Special Educational Needs Code of Practice) (Appointed Day) Order 1994 No. 1414. Enabling power: *Education Act 1994, s. 158 (4).* Issued: 03.06.94. Made: 25.05.94. Laid: 05.06.94. Coming into force: 01.09.94. Effect: None. Territorial extent & classification: E/W. General. – 2p. – 0 11 044414 0 *£0.65*

The Education (Special Educational Needs) (Information) Regulations 1994 No. 1048. Enabling power: *Education Act 1980, ss. 8 (5) (7) & Education Act 1993, ss. 153 (1), 161 (5), 305 (1), sch. 11, para. 14.* Issued: 16.05.94. Made: 07.04.94. Laid: 13.04.94. Coming into force: 01.09.94. Effect: 1993 c.35 amended. Territorial extent & classification: E/W. General. –6p. – 0 11 044048 X *£1.55*

The Education (Special Educational Needs) Regulations 1994 No. 1047. Enabling power: *Education Act 1981, s. 19, sch. 1, paras. 2, 3 & Education Act 1993, ss. 166 (4), 168 (2), 172 (6), 301 (6).* Issued: 31.05.94. Made: 07.04.94. Laid: 13.04.94. Coming into force: 01.09.94. Effect: S.I. 1988/1067; 1990/1524 amended. This SI has been amended by S.I. 1994/1251 which is being issued simultaneously & free of charge with this S.I. Territorial extent & classification: E/W. General. – 24p. – 0 11 044047 1 *£4.15* Replaced by ISBN 011045913X

The Education (Special Schools Conducted by Education Associations) Regulations 1994 No. 1084. Enabling power: *Education Act 1993, ss. 228 (2) (3) (a), 301 (6).* Issued: 02.06.94. Made: 13.04.94. Laid: 18.04.94. Coming into force: 09.05.94. Effect: None. Territorial extent & classification: E/W. General. – 16p. – 0 11 044084 6 *£3.20* Replaced by ISBN 0110523083

The Education (Special Schools Conducted by Education Associations) (Amendment) Regulations 1994 No. 2848. Enabling power: *Education Act 1993, s. 228 (3) (a).* Issued: 21.11.94. Made: 03.11.94. Laid: 10.11.94. Coming into force: 01.12.94. Effect: S.I. 1994/1084 amended. This SI has been made in consequence of a defect in SI 1994/1084 and is being sent free of charge to all known recipients of that SI. Territorial extent & classification: E/W. General. – 2p. – 0 11 045848 6 *£0.65* Replaced by ISBN 0110523083

The Education (Special Schools) Regulations 1994 No. 652. Enabling power: *Education Act 1993, ss. 172 (6), 183 (2) (6), 188 (2) (4) (5) (6), 301 (6).* Issued: 31.03.94. Made: 09.03.94. Laid: 11.03.94. Coming into force: 01.04.94. Effect: S.I. 1983/1499; 1991/1450 revoked. Territorial extent & classification: E/W. General. – 10p. – 0 11 043652 0 *£2.40*

The Education (Student Loans) Regulations 1994 No. 3045. Enabling power: *Education (Student Loans) Act 1990, s. 1 (2) (7), sch. 2, para. 1, 2, 3.* Issued: 13.12.94. Made: 30.11.94. Laid: 01.12.94. Coming into force: 01.08.95. Effect: S.I. 1993/2915 revoked. Territorial extent & classification: E/W/S. General. – 12p. – 0 11 043356 4 *£2.80*

The Education (Teachers) (Amendment) Regulations 1994 No. 222. Enabling power: *Education Reform 1988, ss. 218 (1) (a) (2) (2A) (6), 232 (5).* Issued: 09.02.94. Made: 01.02.94. Laid: 07.02.94. Coming into force: 01.03.94. Effect: None. Territorial extent & classification: E/W. General. – 4p. – 0 11 043222 3 *£1.10*

The Education (Writtle Agricultural College Further Education Corporation) (Transfer to the Higher Education Sector) Order 1994 No. 2019. Enabling power: *Education Reform Act 1988, s. 122A.* Issued: 17.08.94. Made: 28.07.94. Laid: 01.08.94. Coming into force: 01.10.94. Effect: None. Territorial extent & classification: E. Local. – 2p. – 0 11 045019 1 *£0.65*

The Epsom School of Art and Design (Dissolution) Order 1994 No. 1754. Enabling power: *Further and Higher Education Act 1992, s. 27.* Issued: 29.07.94. Made: 05.07.94. Laid: 05.07.94. Coming into force: 01.08.94. Effect: None. Territorial extent & classification: E. General. – 2p. – 0 11 044754 9 *£0.65*

The Lincolnshire College of Art and Design and Lincolnshire College of Agriculture and Horticulture (Dissolution) Order 1994 No. 1830. Enabling power: *Further and Higher Education Act 1992, s. 27 & S.I. 1992/2361, regs. 3, 4.* Issued: 21.07.94. Made: 11.07.94. Laid: 11.07.94. Coming into force: 01.08.94. Effect: None. Territorial extent & classification: E. General. – 2p. – 0 11 044830 8 *£0.65*

The Margaret Danyers College (Incorporation) Order 1994 No. 2979. Enabling power: *Further and Higher Education Act 1992, ss. 16 (2), 17.* Issued: 30.11.94. Made: 23.11.94. Laid: 01.12.94. Coming into force: 01.01.95. Effect: None. Territorial extent & classification: E. Local. – 2p. – 0 11 043155 3 *£0.65*

The Portsmouth College of Art, Design and Further Education (Dissolution) Order 1994 No. 1741. Enabling power: *Further and Higher Education Act 1992, s. 89 (3).* Issued: 29.07.94. Made: 01.07.94. Laid: 04.07.94. Coming into force: 01.08.94. Effect: None. Territorial extent & classification: E. General. – 2p. – 0 11 044741 7 *£0.65*

The Pupils' Registration (Amendment) Regulations 1994 No. 2128. Enabling power: *Education Act 1944, s. 80.* Issued: 22.08.94. Made: 10.08.94. Laid: 11.08.94. Coming into force: 01.09.94. Effect: S.I. 1956/357 amended. Territorial extent & classification: E/W. General. – 4p. – 0 11 045128 7 *£1.10*

Price/availability are liable to change without notice

The Religious Education (Meetings of Local Conferences and Councils) 1994 No. 1304. Enabling power: *Education Act 1993, s. 258, 301 (1) (6)*. Issued: 25.05.94. Made: 12.05.94. Laid: 16.05.94. Coming into force: 01.09.94. Effect: None. Territorial extent & classification: E/W. General. – 4p. – 0 11 044304 7 £1.10

The Special Educational Needs Tribunal Regulations 1994 No. 1910. Enabling power: *Education Act 1993, ss. 177 (5), 178 (2), 180 (1) (2), 301 (6), 305 (1)*. Issued: 29.07.94. Made: 14.07.94. Laid: 19.07.94. Coming into force: 01.09.94. Effect: None. Territorial extent & classification: E/W. General. – 16p. – 0 11 044910 X £3.20

The Teachers (Compensation for Redundancy and Premature Retirement) (Amendment) Regulations 1994 No. 1059. Enabling power: *Superannuation Act 1972, s. 24*. Issued: 05.05.94. Made: 12.04.94. Laid: 13.04.94. Coming into force: 01.05.94. Effect: S.I. 1989/298 amended. Territorial extent & classification: E/W. General. – 4p. – 0 11 044059 5 £1.10

The Teachers' Superannuation (Additional Voluntary Contributions) Regulations 1994 No.2924. Enabling power: *Superannuation Act 1972, s. 9, 12, sch. 3*. Issued: 29.11.94. Made: 17.11.94. Laid: 21.11.94. Coming into force: 12.12.94. Effect: S.I. 1989/946 revoked. Territorial extent & classification: E/W. General. – 20p. – 0 11 043112 X £3.70

The Teachers' Superannuation (Amendment) (No. 2) Regulations 1994 No. 2774. Enabling power: *Superannuation Act 1972, ss. 9, 12, sch. 3*. Issued: 17.11.94. Made: 27.10.94. Laid: 02.11.94. Coming into force: 01.05.94. for regs.3 to 5 & 01.12.94. Effect: S.I. 1994/1058 amended. This SI has been made in consequence of a defect in SI 1994/1058 and is being sent free of charge to all known recipients of that SI. Territorial extent & classification: E/W. General. – 2p. – 0 11 045774 9 £0.65

The Teachers' Superannuation (Amendment) (No. 3) Regulations 1994 No. 2876. Enabling power: *Superannuation Act 1972, ss. 9, 12, sch. 3*. Issued: 16.11.94. Made: 08.11.94. Laid: 10.11.94. Coming into force: 01.12.94. Effect: None. Territorial extent & classification: E/W. General. – 2p. – 0 11 043041 7 £0.65

The Teachers' Superannuation (Amendment) Regulations 1994 No. 1058. Enabling power: *Superannuation Act 1972, ss. 9, 12, sch. 3*. Issued: 05.05.94. Made: 12.04.94. Laid: 13.04.94. Coming into force: 01.05.94 except for reg. 18; 01.10.94 for reg. 18. Effect: S.I. 1988/1652 amended. Territorial extent & classification: E/W. General. – 8p. – 0 11 044058 7 £1.95 Replaced by ISBN 0110430697

The Teaching As A Career Unit (Transfer of Property, Rights and Liabilities) Order 1994 No.2463. Enabling power: *Education Act 1994 s. 17, 23 (2)*. Issued: 17.10.94. Made: 21.09.94. Laid: 21.09.94. Coming into force: 13.10.94. Effect: None. Territorial extent & classification: E/W. General. – 2p. – 0 11 045463 4 £0.65

EDUCATION, SCOTLAND

The Academic Awards and Distinctions (The Royal Scottish Academy of Music and Drama) (Scotland) Order of Council 1994 No. 1125 (S. 58). Enabling power: *Further and Higher Education (Scotland) Act 1992, ss. 48 (1), 60*. Issued: 28.04.94. Made: 21.04.94. Laid: 21.04.94. Coming into force: 13.05.94. Effect: None. Territorial extent & classification: S. Local. – 2p. – 0 11 044125 7 £0.65

The Dumfries and Galloway College of Technology (Change of Name) (Scotland) Order 1994 No.2618 (S. 129). Enabling power: *Further and Higher Education (Scotland) Act 1992, s. 3 (4)*. Issued: 17.10.94. Made: 03.10.94. Laid: 17.10.94. Coming into force: 07.11.94. Effect: None. Territorial extent & classification: S. General. – 2p. – 0 11 045618 1 £0.65

The Duncan of Jordanstone College of Art (Closure) (Scotland) Order 1994 No. 1715 (S. 77). Enabling power: *Further and Higher Education (Scotland) Act 1992, ss. 47 (1) (2) (4) (6), 60* Issued: 11.07.94. Made: 29.06.94. Laid: 11.07.94. Coming into force: 01.08.94. Effect: S.I. 1979/785; 1980/125; 1988/1715; 1992/280; amended & S.I. 1975/697 revoked. Territorial extent & classification: S. Local. – 4p. – 0 11 044715 8 £1.10

The Education (Assisted Places) (Scotland) Amendment Regulations 1994 No. 1827 (S. 82). Enabling power: *Education (Scotland) Act 1980, ss. 75A (9) (1), 75B*. Issued: 18.07.94. Made: 08.07.94. Laid: 11.07.94. Coming into force: 01.08.94. Effect: S.I. 1989/1133 amended. Territorial extent & classification: S. General. – 4p. – 0 11 044827 8 £1.10

The Education (European Community Enlargement) (Scotland) Regulations 1994 No. 3148 (S. 172). Enabling power: *Education (Scotland) Act 1980, ss. 49 (3), 73 (f), 74 (1); Education (Fees and Awards) Act 1983, ss. 1, 2*. Issued: 20.12.94. Made: 07.12.94. Laid: 09.12.94. Coming into force: 01.01.95. Effect: S.I. 1983/1215; 1988/1042; 1991/1522 amended. Territorial extent & classification: S. General. – 4p. – 0 11 043433 1 £1.10

The Education (Student Loans) Regulations 1994 No. 3045. Enabling power: *Education (Student Loans) Act 1990, s. 1 (2) (7), sch. 2, para. 1, 2, 3*. Issued: 13.12.94. Made: 30.11.94. Laid: 01.12.94. Coming into force: 01.08.95. Effect: S.I. 1993/2915 revoked. Territorial extent & classification: E/W/S. General. – 12p. – 0 11 043356 4 £2.80

The Queen Margaret College, Edinburgh (Scotland) Order of Council 1994 No. 2371 (S. 114). Enabling power: *Further and Higher Education (Scotland) Act 1992, ss. 45, 60*. Issued: 20.09.94. Made: 09.09.94. Laid: 09.09.94. Coming into force: 01.10.94. Effect: S.I. 1988/1715 amended. Territorial extent & classification: S. Local. – 10p. – 0 11 045371 9 £2.40

The Self-Governing Schools (Application and Amendment of Regulations) (Scotland) Regulations 1994 No. 351 (S. 11). Enabling power: *Education (Scotland) Act 1980, ss. 2, 19 (1), 28B (1) (a) (ii) (3), 28I, 73 (c), 135 (1) & Self-Governing Schools etc. (Scotland) Act 1989, ss. 7 (7), 23 (1), 80 (1)*. Issued: 01.03.94. Made: 16.02.94. Laid: 01.03.94. Coming into force: 22.03.94. Effect: S.I. 1956/894; 1967/1199; 1975/1135; 1982/950; 1990/295, 1551, 2551; 1993/1605 amended. Territorial extent & classification: S. General. – 6p. – 0 11 043351 3 £1.55

Price/availability are liable to change without notice

The Self-Governing Schools (Change in Characteristics) (Scotland) Regulations 1994 No.478 (S. 17). Enabling power: *Self-Governing Schools etc. (Scotland) Act 1989, ss. 30 (7) (a), 80 (1),, sch. 7, paras. 1, 4 (b)*. Issued: 11.03.94. Made: 24.02.94. Laid: 11.03.94. Coming into force: 01.04.94. Effect: None. Territorial extent & classification: S. General. – 4p. – 0 11 043478 1 £1.10

The Self-Governing Schools Grant and Recovery (Scotland) Regulations 1994 No. 431 (S. 16). Enabling power: *Self-Governing Schools etc. (Scotland) Act 1989, ss. 26, 27 (5), 28, 78 (4)*. Issued: 10.03.94. Made: 23.02.94. Laid: 10.03.94. Coming into force: 01.04.94. Effect: None. Territorial extent & classification: S. General. – 20p. – 0 11 043431 5 £3.70

The Self-Governing Schools (Suspension of Proposals) (Scotland) Order 1994 No. 3149 (S. 173). Enabling power: *Self-Governing Schools etc. (Scotland) Act 1989, s. 21 (1A)*. Issued: 19.12.94. Made: 05.12.94. Laid: 14.12.94. Coming into force: 04.01.95. Effect: None. Territorial extent & classification: S. General. – 4p. – 0 11 043441 2 £1.10

The St Mary's Music School (Aided Places) Amendment Regulations 1994 No. 1826 (S. 81). Enabling power: *Education (Scotland) Act 1980, ss. 73 (f), 74 (1)*. Issued: 15.07.94. Made: 08.07.94. Laid: 11.07.94. Coming into force: 01.08.94. Effect: S.I. 1989/1134 amended. Territorial extent & classification: S. General. – 4p. – 0 11 044826 X £1.10

The Teachers' Superannuation (Scotland) Amendment Regulations 1994 No. 2699 (S. 137). Enabling power: *Superannuation Act 1972, ss. 9, 12, sch. 3*. Issued: 28.10.94. Made: 11.10.94. Laid: 28.10.94. Coming into force: 01.04.95. for reg.8, 30.11.94. all others. Effect: S.I. 1992/280 amended. Territorial extent & classification: S. General. – 8p. – 0 11 045699 8 £1.95

The Teaching Council (Scotland) Election Amendment Scheme 1994 Approval Order 1994 No.1702 (S. 76). Enabling power: *Teaching Council (Scotland) Act 1965, sch. 1, para. 1 (8)*. Issued: 11.07.94. Made: 24.06.94. Laid: 08.07.94. Coming into force: 29.07.94. Effect: SI 1989/2308 amended. Territorial extent & classification: S. General. – 4p. – 0 11 044702 6 £1.10

The University of Abertay Dundee (Scotland) Order of Council 1994 No. 1980 (S. 90). Enabling power: *Further and Higher Education (Scotland) Act 1992, ss. 45, 60*. Issued: 28.09.94. Made: 26.07.94. Laid: 26.07.94. Coming into force: 17.08.94. Effect: None. Territorial extent & classification: S. General. – 16p. – 0 11 044980 0 £3.20

ELECTRICITY

The Electricity (Class Exemptions from the Requirement for a Licence) (Amendment) (No. 2) Order 1994 No. 1683. Enabling power: *Electricity Act 1989, s.5, 111 (2)*. Issued: 05.07.94. Made: 23.06.94. Laid: 27.06.94. Coming into force: 18.07.94. Effect: S.I. 1990/193 amended. Territorial extent & classification: E/W/S. General. – 2p. – 0 11 044683 6 £0.65

The Electricity (Class Exemptions from the Requirement for a Licence) (Amendment) Order 1994 No. 1070. Enabling power: *Electricity Act 1989, ss. 5, 111 (2)*. Issued: 13.05.94. Made: 13.04.94. Laid: 14.04.94. Coming into force: 05.05.94. Effect: S.I. 1990/193 amended. Territorial extent & classification: E/W/S. General. – 6p. – 0 11 044070 6 £1.55

The Electricity (Non-Fossil Fuel Sources) (England and Wales) Order 1994 No.3259. Enabling power: *Electricity Act 1989, s. 32*. Issued: 01.02.95. Made: 15.12.94. Laid: 20.12.94. Coming into force: 21.12.94. Effect: None. Territorial extent & classification: E/W. General. – 16p. – 0 11 043937 6 £3.20 Replaced by ISBN 0110523318

The Electricity (Non-Fossil Fuel Sources) (Scotland) Order 1994 No. 3275 (S. 190). Enabling power: *Electricity Act 1989, s. 32 (1) (2)*. Issued: 11.01.95. Made: 19.12.94. Laid: 20.12.94. Coming into force: 21.12.94. Effect: None. Territorial extent & classification: S. General. – 12p. – 0 11 043838 8 £2.80

The Electricity Supply (Amendment) (No. 2) Regulations 1994 No. 3021. Enabling power: *Electricity Act 1989, s. 29*. Issued: 12.12.94. Made: 24.11.94. Laid: 30.11.94. Coming into force: 01.01.95. Effect: S.I. 1988/1057 amended. Territorial extent & classification: E/W/S. General. – 2p. – 0 11 043352 1 £0.65

The Electricity Supply (Amendment) Regulations 1994 No. 533. Enabling power: *Electricity Act 1989, s. 29, 60*. Issued: 15.03.94. Made: 28.02.94. Laid: 07.03.94. Coming into force: 01.04.94. Effect: S.I. 1988/1057; 1990/390 amended. Territorial extent & classification: E/W/S. General. – 4p. – 0 11 043533 8 £1.10

The Environmental Assessment (Scotland) Amendment Regulations 1994 No. 2012 (S. 91). Enabling power: *European Communities Act 1972, s. 2 (2) & Town and Country Planning (Scotland) Act 1972, s. 26B*. Issued: 09.08.94. Made: 19.07.94. Laid: 29.07.94. Coming into force: 19.08.94. Effect: S.I. 1988/1221; 1984 c. 54 amended. Territorial extent & classification: S. General. – 8p. – 0 11 045012 4 £1.95

ELECTROMAGNETIC COMPATIBILITY

The Electromagnetic Compatibility (Amendment) Regulations 1994 No. 3080. Enabling power: *European Communities Act 1972, s. 2 (2)*. Issued: 23.12.94. Made: 02.12.94. Laid: 05.12.94. Coming into force: 30.12.94. for regs. 1, 2, 6 (1); 01.05.95. for reg. 6 (2); 01.01.95. for remainder. Effect: S.I. 1992/2372 amended. Territorial extent & classification: GB. General. – Implements DIR 93/68 (OJ L 220/93) as amended by DIR 89/336 (L 139/89). – 8p. – 0 11 043614 8 £1.95

Price/availability are liable to change without notice

EMPLOYMENT AND TRAINING

The Agricultural Training Board (Revocation) Order 1994 No. 555. Enabling power: *Agricultural Training Board Act 1982, ss. 1 (2), 3 (1) (b) (5) (6)*. Issued: 18.03.94. Made: 07.03.94. Laid: 07.03.94. Coming into force: 01.10.94. for art. 3; 29.03.94. for all others. Effect: S.I. 1966/969 revoked. Territorial extent & classification: E/W/S. General. – 4p. – 0 11 043555 9 £1.10

The Industrial Training Levy (Construction Board) Order 1994 No. 159. Enabling power: *Industrial Training Act 1982, s. 11(1)*. Issued: 07.02.94. Made: 31.01.94. Coming into force: 01.02.94. Effect: None. Supersedes Draft ISBN 0110358651 previously published 18.11.93. Territorial extent & classification: E/W/S. General. – 6p. – 0 11 043159 6 £1.55

The Industrial Training Levy (Engineering Construction Board) Order 1994 No. 158. Enabling power: *Industrial Training Act 1982, s. 11 (1)*. Issued: 07.02.94. Made: 31.01.94. Coming into force: 01.02.94. Effect: None. Supersedes Draft ISBN 0110358805 previously published 07.12.93. Territorial extent & classification: E/W/S. General. – 6p. – 0 11 043158 8 £1.55

ENERGY CONSERVATION

The Boiler (Efficiency) (Amendment) Regulations 1994 No. 3083. Enabling power: *European Communities Act 1972, s. 2*. Issued: 09.12.94. Made: 02.12.94. Laid: 09.12.94. Coming into force: 01.01.95. Effect: S.I. 1993/3083 amended. Territorial extent & classification: GB. General. – Implements DIR 92/42 (OJ L 167/92) as amended by DIR 93/68 (OJ L 220/93). – 4p. – 0 11 043347 5 £1.10

The Energy Information (Refrigerators and Freezers) Regulations 1994 No. 3076. Enabling power: *European Communities Act 1972, s. 2 (2) (a)*. Issued: 09.12.94. Made: 02.12.94. Laid: 09.12.94. Coming into force: 01.01.95. Effect: None. Territorial extent & classification: GB. General. – Implements DIR 92/75 (OJ L 297/92) & DIR 94/2 (OJ L 45/94). – 20p. – 0 11 043327 0 £3.70

The Home Energy Efficiency Grants (Amendment) Regulations 1994 No. 637. Enabling power: *Social Security Act 1990, s. 15*. Issued: 18.03.94. Made: 08.03.94. Laid: 09.03.94. Coming into force: 01.04.94. Effect: S.I. 1992/483 amended. Territorial extent & classification: E/W. General. – 4p. – 0 11 043637 7 £1.10

ENVIRONMENTAL PROTECTION

The Environmental Protection Act 1990 (Commencement No. 14) Order 1994 No. 780 (C. 15). Enabling power: *Environmental Protection Act 1990, s. 164 (3)*. Bringing into operation various provisions of the 1990 act on 16.03.94. Issued: 21.03.94. Made: 15.03.94. Effect: None. Territorial extent & classification: E/W. General. – 4p. – 0 11 043780 2 £1.10

The Environmental Protection Act 1990 (Commencement no. 15) (Amendment) Order 1994 No.2487 (C. 49). Enabling power: *Environmental Protection Act 1990, s. 164 (3)*. Bringing various provisions of the 1990 act into operation on 20.09.94. Issued: 30.09.94. Made: 19.09.94. Effect: S.I. 1994/1096 amended. Territorial extent & classification: E/W/S. General. – 2p. – 0 11 045487 1 £0.65

The Environmental Protection Act 1990 (Commencement No. 15) (Amendment No. 2) Order 1994 No.3234 (C. 81). Enabling power: *Environmental Protection Act 1990, s. 164 (3)*. Bringing various provisions of the 1990 act into operation on 01.04.95. Issued: 22.12.94. Made: 06.12.94. Effect: S.I. 1994/1096, 2487 amended. Territorial extent & classification: E/W/S. General. – 2p. – 0 11 043705 5 £0.65

The Environmental Protection Act 1990 (Commencement No. 15) Order 1994 No. 1096 (C. 18). Enabling power: *Environmental Protection Act 1990, s. 164 (3)*. Bringing into operation various provisions of this act on 01.05.94. Issued: 20.04.94. Made: 14.04.94. Effect: None. With correction slip. Territorial extent & classification: GB. General. – 6p. – 0 11 044096 X £1.55

The Environmental Protection Act 1990 (Commencement No. 16) Order 1994 No. 2854 (C. 64). Enabling power: *Environmental Protection Act 1990, s. 164 (3)*. Bringing into operation various provisions of the 1990 act on 01.12.94. Issued: 15.11.94. Made: 06.11.94. Effect: None. Territorial extent & classification: E/W/S. General. – 10p. – 0 11 043040 9 £2.40

The Environmental Protection (Authorisation of Processes) (Determination Periods) (Amendment) Order 1994 No. 2847. Enabling power: *Environmental Protection Act 1990, sch. 1, para. 5 (3)*. Issued: 14.11.94. Made: 06.11.94. Laid: 10.11.94. Coming into force: 01.12.94. Effect: S.I. 1991/513 amended. Territorial extent & classification: E/W/S. General. – 2p. – 0 11 045847 8 £0.65

The Environmental Protection (Non-Refillable Refrigerant Containers) Regulations 1994 No.199. Enabling power: *Environmental Protection Act 1990, s. 140 (1) (2) (3) (b) to (d) (9)*. Issued: 09.02.94. Made: 31.01.94. Laid: 09.02.94. Coming into force: 02.03.94. Effect: None. Territorial extent & classification: GB. General. – 6p. – 0 11 043199 5 £1.55

The Environmental Protection (Prescribed Processes and Substances Etc.) (Amendment) (No. 2) Regulations 1994 No. 1329. Enabling power: *Environmental Protection Act 1990, s. 2, sch. 1, paras. 1 (2) (5), 2 (2)*. Issued: 26.05.94. Made: 17.05.94. Laid: 18.05.94. Coming into force: 01.06.94. Except for reg. 4 & 01.12.94. for reg. 4. Effect: S.I. 1994/1271 amended. This SI has been made in consequence of a defect in SI 1994/1271 and is being sent free of charge to all known recipients of that SI. Territorial extent & classification: E/W/S. General. – 6p. – 0 11 044329 2 £1.55

Price/availability are liable to change without notice

The Environmental Protection (Prescribed Processes and Substances Etc.) (Amendment) Regulations 1994 No. 1271. Enabling power: *Environmental Protection Act 1990, s. 2, sch. 1, paras. 1, 2, 6, 7.* Issued: 19.05.94. Made: 10.05.94. Laid: 11.05.94. Coming into force: 01.06.94 except for reg. 4 & 01.12.94 for reg. 4. Effect: S.I. 1991/472, 507 amended. Territorial extent & classification: E/W/S. General. – 20p. – 0 11 044271 7 £3.70 Replaced by ISBN 0110459180

The Environmental Protection (Waste Recycling Payments) (Amendment) Regulations 1994 No.522. Enabling power: *Environmental Protection Act 1990, s. 52 (8).* Issued: 10.03.94. Made: 01.03.94. Laid: 10.03.94. Coming into force: 01.04.94. Effect: S.I. 1992/462 amended. Territorial extent & classification: E/W/S. General. – 4p. – 0 11 043522 2 £1.10

The Household Appliances (Noise Emission) (Amendment) Regulations 1994 No. 1386. Enabling power: *European Communities Act 1972, s. 2 (2).* Issued: 03.06.94. Made: 23.05.94. Laid: 25.05.94. Coming into force: 28.06.94. Effect: S.I. 1990/161 amended. Territorial extent & classification: GB. General. – 4p. – 0 11 044386 1 £1.10

The Marketing of Gas Oil (Sulphur Content) Regulations 1994 No. 2249. Enabling power: *European Communities Act 1972, s. 2 (2).* Issued: 09.09.94. Made: 30.08.94. Laid: 01.09.94. Coming into force: 01.10.94. Effect: S.I. 1990/1096; S.R. 1991/235 revoked. Territorial extent & classification: GB. General. – 4p. – 0 11 045249 6 £1.10

The Notification of Existing Substances (Enforcement) Regulations 1994 No. 1806. Enabling power: *European Communities Act 1972, s. 2 (2).* Issued: 18.07.94. Made: 30.06.94. Laid: 08.07.94. Coming into force: 29.07.94. Effect: None. Territorial extent & classification: E/W/S. General. – 8p. – 0 11 044806 5 £1.95

The Transfrontier Shipment of Waste Regulations 1994 No. 1137. Enabling power: *European Communities Act 1972, 2 (2) & Control of Pollution (Amendment) Act 1989, ss. 2, 3, 9 (1) & Environmental Protection Act 1990, s. 74 (6).* Issued: 06.05.94. Made: 22.04.94. Laid: 25.04.94. Coming into force: 06.05.94. Effect: S.I. 1980/1709; 1991/1624; 1994/1056; S.R. 1981/252 amended & S.I. 1988/1562, 1790; S.R. 1989/115 revoked. Territorial extent & classification: GB. General. – 10p. – 0 11 044137 0 £2.40

The Waste Management Licensing Regulations 1994 No. 1056. Enabling power: *European Communities Act 1972, s. 2 (2) & Control of Pollution Act 1974, ss. 30 (4), 104 (1) & Control of Pollution (Amendment) Act 1989, ss. 1 (3), 2, 8 (2), 9 (1) & Environmental Protection Act 1990, ss. 29 (10), 33 (3), 35 (6), 36 (1), 39 (3), 40 (3), 43 (8), 45 (3), 54 (14), 64 (1) (4) (8), 74 (6), 75 (8), 156.* Issued: 18.04.94. Made: 12.04.94. Laid: 13.04.94. Coming into force: 01.05.94 except for regs. 4 & 5. 10.08.94 for regs. 4 & 5. Effect: 1972 c. 52; 1974 c. 40; 1985 c. 48; 1989 c. 29; 1990 c. 8, c. 43; 1991 c. 57; S.I. 1985/1699; 1988/819; 1991/1624; 1992/588 amended. Territorial extent & classification: E/W/S. General. – 50p. – 0 11 044056 0 £7.35

EUROPEAN COMMUNITIES

The European Communities (Definition of Treaties) (Europe Agreement Establishing an Association between the European Communities and their Member States and Romania) Order 1994 No.760. Enabling power: *European Communities Act 1972, s. 1.* Issued: 25.03.94. Made: 15.03.94. Laid: 07.02.94. Coming into force: In accord. with art. 1. Effect: None. Territorial extent & classification: GB. General. – 4p. – 0 11 043760 8 £1.10

The European Communities (Definition of Treaties) (Europe Agreement Establishing an Association between the European Communities and their Member States and the Czech Republic) Order 1994 No. 759. Enabling power: *European Communities Act 1972, s. 1.* Issued: 25.03.94. Made: 15.03.94. Laid: 07.02.94. Coming into force: In accord. with art. 1. Effect: None. Territorial extent & classification: GB. General. – 2p. – 0 11 043759 4 £0.65

The European Communities (Definition of Treaties) (Europe Agreement Establishing an Association between the European Communities and their Member States and the Republic of Bulgaria) Order 1994 No. 758. Enabling power: *European Communities Act 1972, s. 1.* Issued: 25.03.94. Made: 15.03.94. Laid: 07.02.94. Coming into force: In accord. with art. 1. Effect: None. Territorial extent & classification: GB. General. – 4p. – 0 11 043758 6 £1.10

The European Communities (Definition of Treaties) (Europe Agreement Establishing an Association between the European Communities and their Member States and the Slovak Republic) Order 1994 No. 761. Enabling power: *European Communities Act 1972, s. 1.* Issued: 25.03.94. Made: 15.03.94. Laid: 07.02.94. Coming into force: In accord. with art. 1. Effect: None. Territorial extent & classification: GB. General. – 2p. – 0 11 043761 6 £0.65

The European Communities (Designation) (No. 2) Order 1994 No. 1327. Enabling power: *European Communities Act 1972, s. 2 (2).* Issued: 01.06.94. Made: 18.05.94. Laid: 01.06.94. Coming into force: 22.06.94. Effect: None. Territorial extent & classification: GB. General. – 2p. – 0 11 044327 6 £0.65

The European Communities (Designation) (No. 3) Order 1994 No. 1887. Enabling power: *European Communities Act 1972, s. 2 (2).* Issued: 29.07.94. Made: 19.07.94. Laid: 29.07.94. Coming into force: 19.08.94. Effect: None. Territorial extent & classification: GB. General. – 2p. – 0 11 044887 1 £0.65

The European Communities (Designation) (No. 4) Order 1994 No. 2791. Enabling power: *European Communities Act 1972, s. 2 (2).* Issued: 11.11.94. Made: 02.11.94. Laid: 11.11.94. Coming into force: 05.12.94. Effect: None. Territorial extent & classification: GB. General. – 2p. – 0 11 045791 9 £0.65

The European Communities (Designation) Order 1994 No. 757. Enabling power: *European Communities Act 1972, s. 2 (2).* Issued: 25.03.94. Made: 15.03.94. Laid: 25.03.94. Coming into force: 15.04.94. Effect: None. Territorial extent & classification: GB. General. – 4p. – 0 11 043757 8 £1.10

Price/availability are liable to change without notice

The European Communities (Iron and Steel Employees Re-adaptation Benefits Scheme) (No. 2) (Scheme Termination) Regulations 1994 No. 141. Enabling power: *European Communities Act 1972, s. 2 (2).* Issued: 03.02.94. Made: 26.01.94. Laid: 27.01.94. Coming into force: 28.01.94. Effect: None. Territorial extent & classification: GB. General. – 4p. – 0 11 043141 3 *£1.10*

The Highlands and Islands Agricultural Programme Regulations 1994 No. 3096 (S. 167). Enabling power: *European Communities Act 1972, s. 2 (2).* Issued: 16.12.94. Made: 05.12.94. Laid: 09.12.94. Coming into force: 30.12.94. Effect: None. Territorial extent & classification: S. General. – Implements REG 4256/88 [OJ L374/88], lays down provisions for implementing REG 2052/88 [OJ L185/88]. – 8p. – 0 11 043377 7 *£1.95*

EUROPEAN PARLIAMENT

The European Parliamentary (United Kingdom Representatives) Pensions (Consolidation and Amendment) Order 1994 No. 1662. Enabling power: *European Parliament (Pay and Pensions) Act 1979, s. 4 (1) (2) (3) (4).* Issued: 04.07.94. Made: 21.06.94. Laid: 24.06.94. Coming into force: 15.07.94. Effect: S.I. 1980/1450; 1982/133; 1985/1116; 1992/1197 revoked. Territorial extent & classification: UK General. – 34p. – 0 11 044662 3 *£6.10*

The European Parliament (Pay and Pensions) Act 1979 (Section 3 (Amendment)) Order 1994 No.1663. Enabling power: *European Parliament (Pay and Pensions) Act 1979, s. 3A (1) (3).* Issued: 01.07.94. Made: 21.06.94. Laid: 24.06.94. Coming into force: 15.07.94. Effect: 1979 c. 50 amended. Territorial extent & classification: UK. General. – 4p. – 0 11 044663 1 *£1.10*

EXTRADITION

The European Convention on Extradition (Amendment) Order 1994 No. 3203. Enabling power: *Extradition Act 1989, s. 4 (1).* Issued: 23.12.94. Made: 14.12.94. Laid: 23.12.94. Coming into force: In accord. with art. 1. Effect: S.I. 1990/1507 amended. Territorial extent & classification: GB. General. – 2p. – 0 11 043720 9 *£0.65*

The European Convention on Extradition (Bulgaria) (Amendment) Order 1994 No. 2796. Enabling power: *Extradition Act 1989, s. 4 (1).* Issued: 14.11.94. Made: 02.11.94. Laid: 14.11.94. Coming into force: 12.12.94. Effect: S.I. 1990/1507 amended. Territorial extent & classification: U.K./CI/IOM. General. – 2p. – 0 11 045796 X *£0.65*

The Extradition (Drug Trafficking) (Certain Territories) Order 1994 No. 2794. Enabling power: *Extradition Act 1870, ss. 2, 21; Extradition Act 1989, ss. 4 (1), 22 (3), 30 (1), 37 (3).* Issued: 11.11.94. Made: 02.11.94. Laid: 14.11.94. Coming into force: In accord. with art. 1 Effect: S.I. 1991/1701 amended. Territorial extent & classification: GB. General. – 4p. – 0 11 045794 3 *£1.10*

FAMILY LAW

The Children (Allocation of Proceedings) (Amendment) (No. 2) Order 1994 No. 3138. Enabling power: *Children Act 1989, sch. 11, part 1.* Issued: 19.12.94. Made: 08.12.94. Laid: 09.12.94. Coming into force: 03.01.95. Effect: 1976 c. 36 & S.I. 1991/1677 amended. Territorial extent & classification: E/W. General. – 2p. – 0 11 043443 9 *£0.65*

The Children (Allocation of Proceedings) (Amendment) Order 1994 No. 2164 (L. 12). Enabling power: *Children Act 1989, sch. 11, pt. 1.* Issued: 24.08.94. Made: 11.08.94. Laid: 24.08.94. Coming into force: 01.11.94. Effect: S.I. 1991/1677 amended. Territorial extent & classification: E/W. General. – 2p. – 0 11 045164 3 *£0.65*

The Family Proceedings (Amendment) (No. 2) Rules 1994 No. 2165 (L. 13). Enabling power: *Matrimonial and Family Proceedings Act 1984, s. 40 (1).* Issued: 24.08.94. Made: 11.08.94. Laid: 24.08.94. Coming into force: 01.11.94. Effect: S.I. 1991/1247 amended. Territorial extent & classification: E/W. General. – 20p. – 0 11 045165 1 *£3.70*

FAMILY LAW: CHILD SUPPORT

The Child Support Act 1991 (Consequential Amendments) Order 1994 No. 731. Enabling power: *Child Support Act 1991, ss. 52 (1), 58 (7).* Issued: 21.03.94. Made: 14.03.94. Laid: 21.03.94. Coming into force: 11.04.94. Effect: 1978 c. 22; 1980 c. 43; 1989 c. 41 amended. Territorial extent & classification: E/W/S. General. – 4p. – 0 11 043731 4 *£1.10*

The Child Support (Miscellaneous Amendments and Transitional Provisions) Regulations 1994 No.227. Enabling power: *Child Support Act 1991, ss. 16, 17 (6) (b), 32 (2) (c), 35 (2) (b), 47, 51, 52 (4), sch. 1, paras. 1 (3), 4 (1), 6 (6), 8.* Issued: 07.02.94. Made: 03.02.94. Laid: 13.01.94. Coming into force: 07.02.94. Effect: S.I. 1992/1813, 1815, 1989, 3094 amended. Supersedes Draft ISBN 0110458613 previously published 21.01.94. Territorial extent & classification: E/W/S. General. – 8p. – 0 11 043227 4 *£1.95*

FAMILY PROCEEDINGS

The Family Proceedings (Amendment) (No. 3) Rules 1994 No. 2890 (L. 17). Enabling power: *Matrimonial and Family Proceedings Act 1984, s. 40 (1).* Issued: 21.11.94. Made: 25.10.94. Laid: 14.11.94. Coming into force: 06.12.94. Effect: S.I. 1991/1247 amended. Territorial extent & classification: E/W. General. – 4p. – 0 11 043077 8 *£1.10*

The Family Proceedings (Amendment) (No. 4) Rules 1994 No. 3155 (L. 21). Enabling power: *Matrimonial and Family Proceedings Act 1984, s. 40.* Issued: 22.12.94. Made: 08.12.94. Laid: 12.12.94. Coming into force: 03.01.95. Effect: S.I. 1991/1247 amended. Territorial extent & classification: E/W. General. – 92p. – 0 11 043515 X *£9.40*

Price/availability are liable to change without notice

The Family Proceedings (Amendment) Rules 1994 No. 808 (L. 4). Enabling power: *Matrimonial and Family Proceedings Act 1984, s. 40 (1)*. Issued: 25.03.94. Made: 21.03.94. Laid: 21.03.94. Coming into force: 11.04.94. Effect: S.I. 1991/1247, 21113 amended. Territorial extent & classification: E/W. General. – 8p. – 0 11 043808 6 £1.95

FEES AND CHARGES

The European Economic Interest Grouping (Fees) (Amendment) Regulations 1994 No. 2327. Enabling power: *Finance Act 1973, s. 56*. Issued: 27.09.94. Made: 06.09.94. Laid: 08.09.94. Coming into force: 01.10.94. Effect: S.I. 1989/950 amended. Territorial extent & classification: E/W/S. General. – 2p. – 0 11 045327 1 £0.65

The Seed Potatoes (Fees) (Scotland) Order 1994 No. 1859 (S. 84). Enabling power: *Finance (No. 2) Act 1987, s. 102 (4)*. Issued: 21.07.94. Made: 11.07.94. Laid: 16.06.94. Coming into force: 12.07.94. Effect: None. Territorial extent & classification: S. General. – 2p. – 0 11 044859 6 £0.65

FINANCIAL SERVICES

The Auditors (Financial Services Act 1986) Rules 1994 No. 526. Enabling power: *Financial Services Act 1986, s. 109*. Issued: 14.03.94. Made: 03.03.94. Coming into force: 01.05.94. Effect: None. Supersedes Draft ISBN 0110458532 published on 17.01.94. Territorial extent & classification: GB. General. – 2p. – 0 11 043526 5 £0.65

The Financial Services Act 1986 (Miscellaneous Exemptions) Order 1994 No. 1517. Enabling power: *Financial Services Act 1986, s. 46*. Issued: 08.07.94. Made: 08.06.94. Laid: 09.06.94. Coming into force: 01.07.94. Effect: S.I. 1988/350 amended. Territorial extent & classification: GB. General. – 2p. – 0 11 044517 1 £0.65

The Financial Services (Disclosure of Information) (Designated Authorities) (No. 8) Order 1994 No. 340. Enabling power: *Financial Services Act 1986, s. 180 (3) & Companies Act 1985, s. 449 (1B) (1C) & Companies Act 1989, s. 87 (5)*. Issued: 09.03.94. Made: 15.02.94. Laid: 17.02.94. Coming into force: 10.03.94. Effect: 1989 c.40 amended. Territorial extent & classification: E/W/S. General. – 2p. – 0 11 043340 8 £0.65

FIRE PRECAUTIONS

The Fire Precautions (Sub-surface Railway Stations) (Amendment) Regulations 1994 No.2184. Enabling power: *Fire Precautions Act 1971, ss. 12 (1) (3) (4), 37 (2) (3), 40 (1)*. Issued: 26.02.94. Made: 18.08.94. Laid: 26.08.94. Coming into force: 01.01.96. Effect: S.I. 1989/1401 amended. Territorial extent & classification: E/W/S. General. – 2p. – 0 11 045184 8 £0.65

FOOD

The Animals, Meat and Meat Products (Examination for Residues and Maximum Residue Limits) (Amendment) Regulations 1994 No. 2465. Enabling power: *Food Safety Act 1990, ss. 6 (4), 16 (1) (3), 17 (1), 48 (1)*. Issued: 29.09.94. Made: 06.09.94. Laid: 23.09.94. Coming into force: 14.10.94. Effect: S.I. 1991/2843 amended. Territorial extent & classification: E/W/S. General. – 6p. – 0 11 045465 0 £1.55

The Bovine Offal (Prohibition) (Amendment) Regulations 1994 No.2628. Enabling power: *Food Safety Act 1990, s. 16 (1) (a) (f) (3)*. Issued: 14.11.94. Made: 10.10.94. Laid: 12.10.94. Coming into force: 02.11.94. Effect: S.I. 1989/2061 amended. Territorial extent & classification: E/W. General. – 4p. – 0 11 045628 9 £1.10

The Bovine Offal (Prohibition) (Scotland) Amendment Regulations 1994 No. 2544 (S. 120). Enabling power: *Food Safety Act 1990, s. 16 (1) (a) (3)*. Issued: 12.10.94. Made: 27.09.94. Laid: 12.10.94. Coming into force: 02.11.94. Effect: S.I. 1990/112 amended. Territorial extent & classification: S. General. – 2p. – 0 11 045544 4 £0.65

The Dairy Produce Quotas (Amendment) (No. 2) Regulations 1994 No. 2919. Enabling power: *European Communities Act 1972, s. 2 (2)*. Issued: 19.12.94. Made: 15.11.94. Laid: 17.11.94. Coming into force: 08.12.94. Effect: S.I. 1994/672 amended. Territorial extent & classification: GB. General. – 2p. – 0 11 043411 0 £0.65

The Dairy Produce Quotas (Amendment) Regulations 1994 No. 2448. Enabling power: *European Communities Act 1972, s. 2 (2)*. Issued: 25.10.94. Made: 14.09.94. Laid: 16.09.94. Coming into force: 07.10.94. Effect: S.I. 1994/672 amended. Territorial extent & classification: GB. General. – 2p. – 0 11 045448 0 £0.65

The Dairy Produce Quotas (Amendment) Regulations 1994 No. 160. Enabling power: *European Communities Act 1972, s. 2 (2)*. Issued: 14.03.94. Made: 31.01.94. Laid: 01.02.94. Coming into force: 22.02.94. Effect: S.I. 1993/923 amended. With correction slip issued 11.04.94. The back page only of the original SI bore the incorrect titled, The Medicines Act 1968 (Amendment) Regulations 1993, and the incorrect heading, Medicines. Territorial extent & classification: GB. General. – 4p. – 0 11 043160 X £1.10

The Dairy Produce Quotas Regulations 1994 No. 672. Enabling power: *European Communities Act 1972, s. 2 (2)*. Issued: 25.04.94. Made: 09.03.94. Laid: 11.03.94. Coming into force: 01.04.94. Effect: S.I. 1993/923, 3234; 1994/160 revoked. Territorial extent & classification: GB. General. – 36p. – 0 11 043672 5 £6.10

The Drinking Water in Containers Regulations 1994 No. 743. Enabling power: *Food Safety Act 1990, ss. 6 (4), 17 (1), 26 (1) (3), 48 (1)*. Issued: 24.03.94. Made: 11.03.94. Laid: 15.03.94. Coming into force: 01.04.94. Effect: None. Territorial extent & classification: E/W/S. General. – 8p. – 0 11 043743 8 £1.95

The Flavourings in Food (Amendment) Regulations 1994 No. 1486. Enabling power: *Food Safety Act 1990, ss. 16 (1) (a) (e), 26 (1) (3), 48 (1)*. Issued: 13.06.94. Made: 24.05.94. Laid: 09.06.94. Coming into force: 30.06.94. Effect: S.I. 1984//1305, 1519; 1992/1971 amended. Territorial extent & classification: E/W/S. General. – 4p. – 0 11 044486 8 £1.10

The Food Labelling (Amendment) Regulations 1994 No. 804. Enabling power: *Food Safety Act 1990, ss. 6 (4), 16 (1) (e), 26 (1) (a) (3), 48 (1)*. Issued: 28.03.94. Made: 15.03.94. Laid: 28.03.94. Coming into force: 01.03.94. Effect: S.I. 1984/1305 amended. Territorial extent & classification: E/W. General. – 8p. – 0 11 043804 3 *£1.95*

The Food Labelling (Scotland) Amendment Regulations 1994 No. 960 (S. 40). Enabling power: *Food Safety Act 1990, ss. 16 (1) (e), 26 (1) (a) (3), 48 (1)*. Issued: 13.04.94. Made: 24.03.94. Laid: 13.04.94. Coming into force: 01.03.95. Effect: S.I. 1984/1519 amended. Territorial extent & classification: S. General. – 8p. – 0 11 043960 0 *£1.95*

The Materials and Articles in Contact with Food (Amendment) Regulations 1994 No. 979. Enabling power: *European Communities Act 1972, s. 2 (2)*. Issued: 12.04.94. Made: 15.03.94. Laid: 30.03.94. Coming into force: 29.04.94, for all regs. except reg. 2 (e). 01.01.94, for reg. 2 (e). Effect: S.I. 1987/1523 amended. Territorial extent & classification: E/W/S. General. –4p. – 0 11 043979 1 *£1.10*

The Meat Products (Hygiene) Regulations 1994 No. 3082. Enabling power: *Food Safety Act 1990, ss. 16 (1) (b) (c) (d) (e) (f), 17 (1), 26, 45, 48 (1), 49 (2), sch. 1, paras. 5 (1) (2) (3), 6 (1) (a), 7 (1) (2)*. Issued: 15.12.94. Made: 21.11.94. Laid: 09.12.94. Coming into force: 01.01.95. Effect: S.I. 1960/1602; 1966/791; 1970/1172; 1991/2825 amended. Territorial extent & classification: E/W/S. General. – 32p. – 0 11 043395 5 *£5.60*

The Milk and Dairies and Milk (Special Designation) (Charges) (Amendment) Regulations 1994 No. 1446. Enabling power: *Food Safety Act 1990, ss. 6 (4), 45*. Issued: 10.06.94. Made: 31.05.94. Laid: 03.06.94. Coming into force: 24.06.94. Effect: S.I. 1990/1584 amended. Territorial extent & classification: E/W. General. – 4p. – 0 11 044446 9 *£1.10*

The Poultry Meat, Farmed Game Meat and Rabbit Meat (Hygiene and Inspection) Regulations 1994 No. 1029. Enabling power: *Food Safety Act 1990 ss. 16 (1) (b) (c) (d) (f) (2) (a) (3), 17 (1), 19 (1) (b), 26, 37 (2), 48 (1), 49 (2), sch. 1, paras. 2 (1), 3 (1), 5 (1) (2) (a) (3), 6 (1) (a), 7 (1) (2) & European Communities Act 1972, s. 2 (2)*. Issued: 21.04.94. Made: 07.04.94. Laid: 07.04.94. Coming into force: 01.05.94. Effect: S.I. 1960/1602; 1966/791; 1970/1172; 1982/1727; 1983/704 (S. 61); 1985/67, 1068 (S.87); 1990/2486, 2494, 2625 (S.220); 1991/2825; 1992/2921; 1993/3247 amended & S.I. 1976/1209, 1221 (S.103); 1979/693, 768 (S.71); 1981/1168, 1169 (S.119); 1992/2036, 2061 (S.208); 1993/209, 235 (S.17) revoked Territorial extent & classification: E/W/S. General. – Give effect to DIR 71/118, 91/495, part 91/494 (L 268/91) as am. by DIR 93/121 (L 340/93). – 54p. – 0 11 044029 3 *£7.35*

The Quick-Frozen Foodstuffs (Amendment) Regulations 1994 No. 298. Enabling power: *Food Safety Act 1990, ss. 6 (4), 16 (1), 17 (1), 26 (1) (a) (2) (a) (3), 48 (1)*. Issued: 18.02.94. Made: 09.02.94. Laid: 11.02.94. Coming into force: 01.09.94. Effect: S.I. 1990/2615 amended. Territorial extent & classification: E/W/S. General. – 4p. – 0 11 043298 3 *£1.10*

The Welfare Food Amendment Regulations 1994 No. 2004. Enabling power: *Social Security Act 1988, s. 13 (3) (4) & Social Security Contributions and Benefits Act 1992, s. 175 (2) to (5)*. Issued: 04.08.94. Made: 28.07.94. Laid: 29.07.94. Coming into force: 19.08.94. Effect: S.I. 1988/536; 1992/637; 1993/1105 amended. Territorial extent & classification: E/W/S. General. – 4p. – 0 11 045004 3 *£1.10*

FOOD: FOOD SAFETY

The Conwy Mussel Fishery (Amendment) Regulations 1994 No. 275. Enabling power: *European Communities Act 1972, sch. 2, para. 2 (2)*. Issued: 07.03.94. Made: 01.02.94. Laid: 14.02.94. Coming into force: 07.03.94. Effect: None. This SI has been made in consequence of a defect in SI 1992/3164 ISBN 0110252340 and is being sent free of charge to all known recipients of that SI. Territorial extent & classification: W. General. – 2p. – 0 11 043275 4 *£0.65*

The Food Safety (Fishery Products) (Import Conditions and Miscellaneous Amendments) Regulations 1994 No. 2783. Enabling power: *Food Safety Act 1990, ss. 6 (4), 16 (1), 17 (1), 18 (1) (c), 26 (3), 48 (1), 49 (2), sch. 1, paras. 2, 5 (1) (2), 6 (1), 7 (1)*. Issued: 08.11.94. Made: 31.10.94. Laid: 31.10.94. Coming into force: 21.11.94. Effect: S.I. 1959/413; 1960/1602; 1966/791; 1970/1172; 1991/2486; 1992/1507, 1601, 2364, 3163, 3165, 3298 amended. Territorial extent & classification: E/W/S. General. – Implements remaining parts of DIR 91/493 (L 268/91) & additional health conditions in DEC 93/25, 51, 146; DIR 90/675 art. 18 (3). –24p. – 0 11 045783 8 *£4.15*

The Food Safety (Live Bivalve Molluscs and Other Shellfish) (Import Conditions and Miscellaneous Amendments) Regulations 1994 No. 2782. Enabling power: *Food Safety Act 1990, ss. 6 (4), 16 (1), 17 (1), 18 (1) (c), 26 (3), 48 (1), 49 (2), sch. 1, paras. 2 (2), 5 (1) (2), 6 (1), 7 (1)*. Issued: 08.11.94. Made: 31.10.94. Laid: 31.10.94. Coming into force: 21.11.94. Effect: S.I. 1992/3164 amended. Territorial extent & classification: E/W/S. General. –Implements remaining DIR 91/492 & DEC 93/383. – 16p. – 0 11 045782 X *£3.20*

FRIENDLY SOCIETIES

The Friendly Societies (Accounts and Related Provisions) Regulations 1994 No. 1983. Enabling power: *Friendly Societies Act 1992, ss. 70, 71, sch. 14, para. 17*. Issued: 26.08.94. Made: 20.07.94. Laid: 01.08.94. Coming into force: 01.09.94. Effect: None. With correction slip dated November 1994 Territorial extent & classification: GB. General. – 54p. – 0 11 044983 5 *£7.35*

The Friendly Societies Act 1992 (Amendment) Regulations 1994 No. 1984. Enabling power: *European Communities Act 1972, s. 2 (2)*. Issued: 26.08.94. Made: 21.07.94. Laid: 01.08.94. Coming into force: 01.09.94. Effect: 1992 c. 40; S.I. 1993/2519 amended. With correction slips dated November 1994 and February 1995. Territorial extent & classification: GB. General. –41p. – 0 11 044984 3 *£6.10*

The Friendly Societies Act 1992 (Commencement no. 8) Order 1994 No. 2543 (C. 51). Enabling power: *Friendly Societies Act 1992, s. 126 (2). Bringing into operation various provisions of the 1992 act on 01.11.94, 01.04.95*. Issued: 01.11.94. Made: 28.09.94. Effect: None. Territorial extent & classification: GB. General. –4p. – 0 11 045543 6 *£1.10*

Price/availability are liable to change without notice

The Friendly Societies (Auditors) Order 1994 No. 132. Enabling power: *Friendly Societies Act 1992, s. 79 (9)*. Issued: 10.02.94. Made: 26.01.94. Laid: 26.01.94. Coming into force: 01.05.94. Effect: None. Territorial extent & classification: GB. General. – 2p. – 0 11 043132 4 *£0.65*

The Friendly Societies (Authorisation) Regulations 1994 No. 1982. Enabling power: *Friendly Societies Act 1992, s. 121 (3), sch. 13, para. 2 (2)*. Issued: 26.08.94. Made: 20.07.94. Laid: 01.08.94. Coming into force: 01.09.94. Effect: S.I. 1993/2521 revoked. Territorial extent & classification: GB. General. – 8p. – 0 11 044982 7 *£1.95*

The Friendly Societies (General Charge and Fees) (Amendment) Regulations 1994 No.657. Enabling power: *Friendly Societies Act 1992, ss. 2 (2), 114 (2) & Friendly Societies Act 1974, s. 104 (1)*. Issued: 08.04.94. Made: 08.03.94. Laid: 09.03.94. Coming into force: 01.04.94. Effect: S.I. 1993/547 amended. Territorial extent & classification: GB. General. –6p.– 0 11 043657 1 *£1.55*

The Friendly Societies (Insurance Business) Regulations 1994 No. 1981. Enabling power: *Friendly Societies Act 1992, ss. 45 (1) (2), 46 (1) 93) (8), 48 (1) (2) (6) (7), 49 (1), 56 (1) (2) 95), 121 (3)*. Issued: 26.08.94. Made: 20.07.94. Laid: 01.08.94. Coming into force: 01.09.94. Effect: S.I. 1993/2519 amended & S.I. 1993/2520 revoked. Territorial extent & classification: GB. General. – 52p. – 0 11 044981 9 *£7.35*

GAS

The Gas (Exempt Supplies) Act 1993 (Commencement) Order 1994 No. 2568 (C. 54). Enabling power: *Gas (Exempt Supplies) Act 1993, s. 4 (2)*. Bringing into operation various provisions of the 1993 act on 31.10.94. Issued: 13.10.94. Made: 01.10.94. Effect: None. Territorial extent & classification: E/W/S. General. – 2p. – 0 11 045568 1 *£0.65*

GOVERNMENT TRADING FUNDS

The HMSO Trading Fund (Amendment) Order 1994 No. 1192. Enabling power: *Government Trading Funds Act 1973, ss. 1 (1), 6 (1)*. Issued: 31.05.94. Made: 26.04.94. Laid: 13.04.94. Coming into force: 01.05.94. Effect: S.I. 1980/456 amended. Territorial extent & classification: GB. General. – 4p. – 0 11 044192 3 *£1.10*

HARBOURS, DOCKS, PIERS AND FERRIES

The Gloucester Harbour Revision Order 1994 No. 3162. Enabling power: *Harbours Act 1964, s. 14*. Issued: 19.12.94. Made: 09.12.94. Coming into force: 23.12.94. Effect: Gloucester Harbour Revision Orders 1890 & 1963 & S.I. 1988/1040 amended & S.I. 1990/1116 revoked. Territorial extent & classification: E. Local. – 16p. – 0 11 043413 7 *£3.20*

The Lancaster Port Commission Harbour Revision Order 1994 No. 1647. Enabling power: *Harbours Act 1964, s. 14 (7)*. Issued: 27.06.94. Made: 20.06.94. Coming into force: 01.07.94. Effect: S.I. 1967/532 amended. Territorial extent & classification: E. Local. –12p.– 0 11 044647 X *£2.80*

The Lerwick Harbour Revision Order 1994 No. 1778. Enabling power: *Harbours Act 1964, s. 14 (7)*. Issued: 13.07.94. Made: 04.07.94. Coming into force: 11.07.94. Effect: 1975 c. xxv amended. Territorial extent & classification: S. Local. – 2p. – 0 11 044778 6 *£0.65*

The North Killingholme Haven Harbour Empowerment Order 1994 No. 1693. Enabling power: *Harbours Act 1964, s. 16*. Issued: 05.07.94. Made: 27.06.94. Coming into force: 08.07.94. Effect: None. Territorial extent & classification: E. Local. – 18p. – 0 11 044693 3 *£3.70*

The Portsmouth Mile End Quay (Continental Ferry Port Phase 7) Harbour Revision Order 1994 No.2733. Enabling power: *Harbours Act 1964, s. 14*. Issued: 28.10.94. Made: 20.10.94. Coming into force: 01.11.94. Effect: None. Territorial extent & classification: E. Local. – 10p. – 0 11 045733 1 *£2.40*

The Saundersfoot Harbour Revision Order 1994 No. 2253. Enabling power: *Harbours Act 1946, s. 14*. Issued: 21.09.94. Made: 18.08.94. Coming into force: 19.08.94. Effect: S.I. 1958/886 amended. Territorial extent & classification: W. Local. – 2p. – 0 11 045253 4 *£0.65*

The Shetland Islands Council Harbour Revision Order 1994 No. 2846. Enabling power: *Harbours Act 1964, s. 14*. Issued: 14.11.94. Made: 02.11.94. Coming into force: 01.12.94. Effect: 1974 c. viii amended. Territorial extent & classification: S. Local. – 2p. – 0 11 045846 X *£0.65*

The Tees and Hartlepool Harbour Revision Order 1994 No. 2064. Enabling power: *Harbours Act 1964, s. 14*. Issued: 11.08.94. Made: 29.07.94. Coming into force: 30.07.94. Effect: S.I. 1975/693 amended. Territorial extent & classification: E/W. Local. – 2p. – 0 11 045064 7 *£0.65*

The Tees and Hartlepool Port Authority (Dissolution) Order 1994 No. 818. Enabling power: *Ports Act 1991, s. 7 (1)*. Issued: 25.03.94. Made: 16.03.94. Coming into force: 31.03.94. Effect: None. Territorial extent & classification: E. Local. – 2p. – 0 11 043818 3 *£0.65*

The Ventnor Harbour Revision Order 1994 No. 2298. Enabling power: *Harbours Act 1964, s. 14 (d) (7)*. Issued: 12.09.94. Made: 09.08.94. Coming into force: 30.08.94. Effect: 1884 c. cxviii & Ventnor Pier Order 1910 revoked. Territorial extent & classification: E. Local. – 16p. – 0 11 045298 4 *£3.20*

The Wells Harbour Revision Order 1994 No. 1440. Enabling power: *Harbours Act 1964, s. 14*. Issued: 15.06.94. Made: 23.05.94. Coming into force: 28.05.94. Effect: 1835 c. lxviii; 1844 c. xciii amended. Territorial extent & classification: E. Local. – 20p. – 0 11 044440 X *£3.70*

Price/availability are liable to change without notice

HEALTH AND SAFETY

The Batteries and Accumulators (Containing Dangerous Substances) Regulations 1994 No.232. Enabling power: *European Communities Act 1972, s. 2 (2).* Issued: 14.02.94. Made: 02.02.94. Laid: 07.02.94. Coming into force: 01.03.94. For all regs. 01.08.94. For reg. 4, 6. Effect: None. Territorial extent & classification: E/W/S. General. – 6p. – 0 11 043232 0 *£1.55*

The Carriage of Dangerous Goods by Rail Regulations 1994 No. 670. Enabling power: *Health and Safety at Work etc. Act 1974, ss. 15 (1) (2) (4) (b) (5) (b) (6) (b), 82 (3) (a), sch. 3, paras. 1 (1) (2) (3), 3, 6, 12, 14, 16.* Issued: 21.03.94. Made: 09.03.94. Laid: 10.03.94. Coming into force: 01.04.94. Effect: None. Territorial extent & classification: E/W/S. General. – 16p. – 0 11 043670 9 *£3.20*

The Carriage of Dangerous Goods by Road and Rail (Classification, Packaging and Labelling) Regulations 1994 No. 669. Enabling power: *Health and Safety at Work etc. Act 1974, ss. 15 (1) (2) (4) (5) (6) (b) (9), 18 (2), 82 (3) (a), sch. 3, paras. 12 (1) (2) (3) (4), 3, 4 (1).* Issued: 25.03.94. Made: 09.03.94. Laid: 10.03.94. Coming into force: 01.04.94. Effect: S.I. 1985/2023; 1987/37, 2115; 1989/615, 1903; 1990/304; 1991/2097; 1992/742, 643, 744; 1993/1746 amended. With correction slip issued 12.04.94. Territorial extent & classification: E/W/S. General. – 36p., ill. – 0 11 043669 5 *£7.60*

The Chemicals (Hazard Information and Packaging for Supply) Regulations 1994 No. 3247. Enabling power: *European Communities Act 1972, s. 2 (2) & Health and Safety at Work etc. Act 1974, ss. 15 (1) (2) (3) (9) (a) (5) (b) (6) (b) (9), 80 (1) (4), 82 (3) (a), sch. 3, paras. 1 (1) (b) (c) (4) (5), 15, 16.* Issued: 09.01.95. Made: 20.12.94. Laid: 09.01.95. Coming into force: 31.01.95. Effect: 1912 c. civ; 1928 c. 32; 1939 c. xcvii; S.R. & O. 1929/993; S.I. 1949/2224; 1952/1689; 1960/1932; 1972/917; 1984/1902; 1987/37, 2115; 1989/1903; 1993/3050; 1994/669, 2844, 3246 amended & S.I. 1986/758; 1990/1736; 1993/1546, 1746 revoked. Territorial extent & classification: E/W/S. General. – Implements DIR 92/32 (OJ L 154/92), DIR 88/379 (OJ L 187/88), DIR 90/35 (OJ 19/90), DIR 91/410 (OJ L 228/91), DIR 91/442 (L 238/91), DIR 92/37 (OJ L 154/92), DIR 93/18 (OJ L 104/93), DIR 93/21 (OJ L 110/93), DIR 93/72 (OJ L 258/93), DIR 93/112 (OJ L 314/93). – 44p.; col. ill. – 0 11 043877 9 *£6.75*

The Construction (Design and Management) Regulations 1994 No. 3140. Enabling power: *Health and Safety at Work etc. Act 1974, ss. 15 (1) (2) (3) (a) (c) (4) (a) (6) (b) (9), 82 (3) (a), sch. 3, paras. 1 (1) (c), 6 (1), 14, 15 (1), 20, 21.* Issued: 10.01.95. Made: 19.12.94. Laid: 10.01.95. Coming into force: 31.03.95. Effect: 1961 c. 34; S.I. 1961/1580; 1965/221; 1989/1903 amended Territorial extent & classification: E/W/S. General. – Implements provisions of DIR 92/57 (OJ L 245/92). – 10p. – 0 11 043845 0 *£3.20*

The Control of Industrial Major Accident Hazards (Amendment) Regulations 1994 No.118. Enabling power: *European Communities Act 1972, 2 (2) & Health and Safety at Work etc. Act 1974, ss. 15 (1) (2), 82 (3) (a), sch. 3, paras. 1 (1) (b) (c) (2), 15 (1), 20.* Issued: 31.01.94. Made: 24.01.94. Laid: 31.01.94. Coming into force: 28.02.94. Effect: S.I. 1984/1902 amended. Territorial extent & classification: E/W/S. General. – 4p. – 0 11 043118 9 *£1.10*

The Control of Substances Hazardous to Health Regulations 1994 No. 3246. Enabling power: *European Communities Act 1972, s. 2 (2) & Health and Safety at Work etc. Act 1974, ss. 15 (1) (2) (3) (a) (b) (4) (5) (b) (6) (b) (9), 52 (2) (3), 82 (3) (a), sch. 3, paras. 1 (1) (2), 2, 3 (1), 6 (1), 8, 9, 11, 13 (1), (3), 14, 15 (1), 16.* Issued: 22.12.94. Made: 12.12.94. Laid: 22.12.94. Coming into force: 16.01.95. Effect: S.I. 1992/2966; 1993/745, 1746 amended & S.I. 1981/1011; 1988/1657; 1991/2431; 1992/2382 revoked. Territorial extent & classification: E/W/S. General. – Implements DIR 90/679. – 28p. – 0 11 043721 7 *£4.70*

The Gas Safety (Installation and Use) Regulations 1994 No. 1886. Enabling power: *Health and Safety at Work etc. Act 1974, ss. 15 (1) (2) (4) (a) (5) (6) (b), 82 (3) (a), sch. 3, paras. 1 (1) (2) (3), 4 (1), 12, 16.* Issued: 20.07.94. Made: 15.07.94. Laid: 20.07.94. Coming into force: 01.01.95, for reg. 3 (to the extent specified in reg. 1 (3)). 01.01.96, for reg. 30 (2) (3). 01.01.97, for reg. 14 (2) (5) (b). 01.01.97, for reg. 14 (4) (to the extent specified in reg. 1 (4) (b)). 31.10.94, for the remainder. Effect: S.I. 1984/1358; 1990/824 revoked. Territorial extent & classification: E/W/S. General. – 20p. – 0 11 044886 3 *£3.70*

The Health and Safety (Fees) Regulations 1994 No. 397. Enabling power: *Health and Safety at Work etc. Act 1974, ss. 43 (2) (4) (5) (6), 82 (3) (a).* Issued: 03.03.94. Made: 22.02.94. Laid: 03.03.94. Coming into force: 28.03.94. Effect: S.I. 1992/744 amended. Territorial extent & classification: E/W/S. General. – 20p. – 0 11 043397 1 *£3.70*

The Management of Health and Safety at Work (Amendment) Regulations 1994 No. 2865. Enabling power: *Health and Safety at Work etc. Act 1974, ss. 15 (1), 47 (2), sch. 3, paras. 7, 8.* Issued: 10.11.94. Made: 07.11.94. Laid: 10.11.94. Coming into force: 01.12.94. Effect: S.I. 1992/2051 amended. Territorial extent & classification: E/W/S. General. – Implements arts. 4 to 7 of DIR 92/85 [L 348/92]. – 4p. – 0 11 043021 2 *£1.10*

The Notification of Existing Substances (Enforcement) Regulations 1994 No. 1806. Enabling power: *European Communities Act 1972, s. 2 (2).* Issued: 18.07.94. Made: 30.06.94. Laid: 08.07.94. Coming into force: 29.07.94. Effect: None. Territorial extent & classification: E/W/S. General. – 8p. – 0 11 044806 5 *£1.95*

The Personal Protective Equipment (EC Directive) (Amendment) Regulations 1994 No. 2326. Enabling power: *European Communities Act 1972, s. 2 (2).* Issued: 15.09.94. Made: 05.09.94. Laid: 08.09.94. Coming into force: 01.10.94. for reg. 2; 01.01.95. for all other purposes. Effect: S.I. 1992/2932, 2966, 3139; S.R. 1993/20 amended & S.I. 1993/3074 revoked. Territorial extent & classification: GB. General. – 4p., ill. – 0 11 045326 3 *£1.10*

The Railways (Safety Case) Regulations 1994 No. 237. Enabling power: *Health and Safety at Work etc. Act 1974, ss. 15 (1) (2) (4) (a) (5) (b) (6) (b), 82 (3) (a), sch. 3, paras. 1 (1) (c), 8 (1), 9, 15 (1), 16.* Issued: 11.02.94. Made: 03.02.94. Laid: 07.02.94. Coming into force: 28.02.94. Effect: S.I. 1992/3060 amended. Territorial extent & classification: E/W/S. General. – 12p. – 0 11 043237 1 *£2.80*

Price/availability are liable to change without notice

The Railways (Safety Critical Work) Regulations 1994 No. 299. Enabling power: *Health and Safety at Work etc. Act 1974, ss. 15 (1) (2) (4) (a) (5) (b) (6) (b), 82 (3) (a), sch. 3, paras, 1 (1) (c), 6 (2), 7, 8 (1), 14.* Issued: 18.02.94. Made: 10.02.94. Laid: 18.02.94. Coming into force: 01.04.94. Effect: None. Territorial extent & classification: E/W/S. General. – 4p. – 0 11 043299 1 *£1.10*

The Simple Pressure Vessels (Safety) (Amendment) Regulations 1994 No. 3098. Enabling power: *European Communities Act 1972, s. 2 (2).* Issued: 04.01.95. Made: 05.12.94. Laid: 08.12.94. Coming into force: 01.01.95. Effect: S.I. 1991/2749; 1992/2932 amended. Territorial extent & classification: GB. General [but amendment to SI 1992/2932 does not apply to NI]. – Implements Article 2 of DIR 93/68 (the CE Marking Directive) which amends DIR 87/404. –12p. – 0 11 043756 X *£2.80*

The Supply of Machinery (Safety) (Amendment) Regulations 1994 No. 2063. Enabling power: *European Communities Act 1972, s. 2 (2).* Issued: 19.08.94. Made: 26.07.94. Laid: 09.08.94. Coming into force: 01.09.94. except for reg. 4 and sch. 2 which come into force on 01.01.95. Effect: S.I. 1992/2932, 3073 amended. Reprinted to include corrections previously printed as a correction slip, dated August 1994. Territorial extent & classification: E/W/S. General. – 16p. – 0 11 045063 9 *£3.20*

HIGH COURT OF JUSTICIARY, SCOTLAND

Act of Adjournal (Consolidation Amendment) (Miscellaneous) 1994 No. 1769 (S. 78). Enabling power: *Criminal Procedure (Scotland) Act 1975, ss. 282, 457.* Issued: 14.07.94. Made: 01.07.94. Coming into force: 01.08.94. Effect: S.I. 1988/110 amended. Territorial extent & classification: S. General. – 4p. – 0 11 044769 7 *£1.10*

The High Court of Justiciary Fees Amendment Order 1994 No. 3266 (S. 186). Enabling power: *Courts of Law Fees (Scotland) Act 1895, s. 2.* Issued: 12.01.95. Made: 08.12.94. Laid: 20.12.94. Coming into force: 01.02.95. Effect: S.I. 1984/252 amended & 1993/426 revoked. Territorial extent & classification: S. General. – 4p. – 0 11 043846 9 *£1.10*

HIGHWAYS, ENGLAND AND WALES

The Birmingham City Council (Birmingham and Fazeley Canal Bridge) Scheme 1990 Confirmation Instrument 1994 No. 564. Enabling power: *Highways Act 1980, s. 106 (3).* Issued: 10.03.94. Made: 28.02.94. Coming into force: On the date on which notice that it has been confirmed is first published in accord. with para. 1 of sch. 2 to the Highways Act 1980. Effect: None. Territorial extent & classification: E/W. Local. – 8p., ill. – 0 11 043564 8 *£1.95*

The Birmingham City Council (Birmingham and Fazeley Canal Bridge) Scheme 1992 Confirmation Instrument 1994 No. 28. Enabling power: *Highways Act 1980, ss. 106 (3), 108 (4).* Issued: 18.01.94. Made: 05.01.94. Coming into force: On the date on which notice that it has been confirmed is first published in accord. with Highways Act 1980, sch. 2, para. 1. Effect: None. Territorial extent & classification: E/W. Local. – 10p., ill. – 0 11 043028 X *£2.40*

The Buckinghamshire County Council (Marsh Drive Great Linford) (Canal Footbridge) Scheme 1993 Confirmation Instrument 1994 No. 2042. Enabling power: *Highways Act 1980, s. 106.* Issued: 08.08.94. Made: 29.07.94. Coming into force: The scheme will become operative on the date on which notice that it has been confirmed is first published in accord. with paragraph 1 of schedule 2 to the Highways Act 1980. Effect: None. Territorial extent & classification: E/W. Local. – 8p. [1 sheet folded]. – 0 11 045042 6 *£1.95*

The Cambridgeshire County Council (River Nene B1040 Dog-in-a-Doublet Bridge) Scheme 1994 Confirmation Instrument 1994 No. 3056. Enabling power: *Highways Act 1980, s. 106 (3).* Issued: 08.12.94. Made: 30.11.94. Coming into force: The scheme will become operative on the date on which notice that it has been confirmed is first published in accord. with para. 1, sch. 2 to the Highways Act 1980. Effect: None. Territorial extent & classification: E/W. Local. – 12p., ill. – 0 11 043313 0 *£2.80*

The Cheshire County Council (Trent and Mersey Canal Bridge, Wheelock) Scheme 1993 Confirmation Instrument 1994 No. 1682. Enabling power: *Highways Act 1980, s. 106 (3).* Issued: 01.07.94. Made: 15.06.94. Coming into force: The scheme will become operative on the date on which notice that it has been confirmed is first published in accord. with paragraph 1 of schedule 2 to the Highways Act 1980. Effect: None. Territorial extent & classification: E/W. Local. – 4p. – 0 11 044682 8 *£1.10*

The City Council of Sheffield (Broughton Lane Bridge) Scheme 1993 Confirmation Instrument 1994 No. 2462. Enabling power: *Highways Act 1980, s. 106 (3).* Issued: 28.09.94. Made: 15.09.94. Coming into force: The scheme will become operative on the date on which notice that it has been confirmed is first published in accordance with para. 1 of sch. 2 of the Highways Act 1980. Effect: None. Territorial extent & classification: E/W. Local. – 10p., ill. – 0 11 045462 6 *£2.40*

The City of Stoke-on-Trent (Downfields Canal Bridge) Scheme, 1993 Confirmation Instrument 1994 No. 551. Enabling power: *Highways Act 1980, s. 106 (3).* Issued: 11.03.94. Made: 01.03.94. Coming into force: On the date on which notice that it is has been confirmed is first published in accordance with para. 1 of sch. 2 to the Highways Act 1980. Effect: None. Territorial extent & classification: E/W. Local. – 4p. – 0 11 043551 6 *£1.10*

The County Council of Norfolk (Reconstruction of Three Holes Bridge) Scheme 1993 Confirmation Instrument 1994 No. 2087. Enabling power: *Highways Act 1980, s. 106 (3).* Issued: 11.08.94. Made: 29.07.94. Coming into force: The scheme will become operative on the date on which notice that it has been confirmed is first published in accordance with para. 1 of sch.2 to the Highways Act 1980. Effect: None. Territorial extent & classification: E/W. Local. – 4p. – 0 11 045087 6 *£1.10*

The County Council of Norfolk (Reconstruction of Three Holes Bridge - Temporary Bridge) Scheme 1993 Confirmation Instrument 1994 No. 2086. Enabling power: *Highways Act 1980, s. 106 (3)*. Issued: 11.08.94. Made: 29.07.94. Coming into force: The scheme will become operative on the date on which notice that it has been confirmed is first published in accordance with para. 1 of sch. 2 to the Highways Act 1980. Effect: None. Territorial extent & classification: E/W. General. – 4p. – 0 11 045086 8 £1.10

The County Council of Northumberland (Duplicate Kitty Brewster Bridge) Scheme 1994 Confirmation Instrument 1994 No. 2170. Enabling power: *Highways Act 1980, s. 106 (3)*. Issued: 25.08.94. Made: 15.08.94. Coming into force: The scheme will become operative on the date on which notice that it has been confirmed is first published in acc. with para. 1, sch. 2 of the Highways Act 1980. Effect: None. Territorial extent & classification: E/W. Local. – 10p., ill. – 0 11 045170 8 £2.40

The Dartford-Thurrock Crossing Regulations 1994 No. 2031. Enabling power: *Dartford-Thurrock Crossing Act 1988, ss. 25 (1) (2), 26, 44 (3), 46 (1)*. Issued: 11.08.94. Made: 01.08.94. Laid: 11.08.94. Coming into force: 01.09.94. Effect: S.I. 1989/2372; 1990/1598; 1991/1805; 1992/1934; 1993/1961 revoked. Territorial extent & classification: E/W. Local. –6p. – 0 11 045031 0 £1.55

The Essex County Council (Haven Road Bridge) Scheme 1993 Confirmation Instrument 1994 No. 1688. Enabling power: *Highways Act 1980, s. 106 (3)*. Issued: 05.07.94. Made: 24.06.94. Coming into force: The scheme will become operative on the date on which notice that it has been confirmed is first published in accordance with paragraph 1 of schedule 2 to the Highways Act 1980. Effect: None. Territorial extent & classification: E/W. Local. – 4p. – 0 11 044688 7 £1.10

The Highways (Assessment of Environmental Effects) Regulations 1994 No. 1002. Enabling power: *European Communities Act 1972, s. 2 (2)*. Issued: 12.04.94. Made: 30.03.94. Laid: 12.04.94. Coming into force: 11.05.94. Effect: 1980 c. 66 amended. Territorial extent & classification: E/W. General. – 2p. – 0 11 044002 1 £0.65

The Oxfordshire County Council (Shifford Island Footbridge) Scheme 1993 Confirmation Instrument 1994 No. 12. Enabling power: *Highways Act 1980, s. 106 (3)*. Issued: 17.01.94. Made: 05.01.94. Coming into force: The Sch. will become operative on the date on which notice that it has been confirmed is 1st published in acc. with sch. 2, para. 1 to Highways Act 1980. Effect: None. Territorial extent & classification: E/W. Local. – 10p., ill. – 0 11 043012 3 £2.40

The Severn Bridge (Amendment) Regulations 1994 No. 1777. Enabling power: *Severn Bridges Act 1992, s. 21 (1)*. Issued: 11.07.94. Made: 02.07.94. Laid: 11.07.94. Coming into force: 01.08.94. Effect: S.I. 1993/1595 amended. Territorial extent & classification: E/W. Local. – 2p. – 0 11 044777 8 £0.65

The Severn Bridges Tolls Order 1994 No. 3158. Enabling power: *Severn Bridges Act 1992, s. 9 (2) (b)*. Issued: 16.12.94. Made: 06.12.94. Coming into force: 01.01.95. Effect: S.I. 1993/3135 revoked. Territorial extent & classification: E/W. Local. – 2p. – 0 11 043406 4 £0.65

The York City Council (Foss Bank Bridge) Scheme 1993 Confirmation Instrument 1994 No. 2040. Enabling power: *Highways Act 1980, s. 106 (3)*. Issued: 08.08.94. Made: 01.08.94. Coming into force: The scheme will become operative on the date on which notice that it has been confirmed is first published in accordance with paragraph 1 of schedule 2 to the Highways Act 1980. Effect: None. Territorial extent & classification: E/W. Local. – 4p. – 0 11 045040 X £1.10

The York City Council (Peasholme Green Bridge) Scheme 1993 Confirmation Instrument 1994 No. 2041. Enabling power: *Highways Act 1980, s. 106 (3)*. Issued: 08.08.94. Made: 01.08.94. Coming into force: The scheme will become operative on the date on which it has been confirmed is first published in accordance with paragraph 1 of schedule 2 to the Highways Act 1980. Effect: None. Territorial extent & classification: E/W. Local. – 4p. – 0 11 045041 8 £1.10

HIGHWAYS, ENGLAND AND WALES: SPECIAL ROADS

The A1 Trunk Road (Kirk Deighton New Junction to Walshford Section and Connecting Roads) Scheme 1994 No. 2517. Enabling power: *Highways Act 1980, ss. 16, 17, 19*. Issued: 04.10.94. Made: 22.09.94. Coming into force: 21.10.94. Effect: None. Territorial extent & classification: E/W. Local. – 24p. – 0 11 045517 7 £0.65

The Dartford-Thurrock Crossing Tolls Order 1994 No. 2033. Enabling power: *Dartford-Thurrock Crossing Act 1988, s. 17 (4)*. Issued: 11.08.94. Made: 01.08.94. Coming into force: 01.09.94. Effect: S.I. 1992/1933 revoked. Territorial extent & classification: E/W. Local. – 4p. – 0 11 045033 7 £1.10

The M1 - A1 Link (Belle Isle to Bramham Crossroads Section and Connecting Roads) Scheme 1994 No. 1020. Enabling power: *Highways Act 1980, ss. 16, 17, 19, 106, 108*. Issued: 14.04.94. Made: 30.03.94. Coming into force: 29.04.94. Effect: None. Territorial extent & classification: E/W. Local. – 10p., ill. – 0 11 044020 X £2.40

The M1 Motorway (Belle Isle) Scheme 1994 No. 1021. Enabling power: *Highways Act 1980, ss. 16, 17, 19*. Issued: 13.04.94. Made: 30.03.94. Coming into force: 29.04.94. Effect: None. Territorial extent & classification: E/W. Local. – 2p. – 0 11 044021 8 £0.65

The (M1) Motorway (Lockington) Connecting Roads Scheme 1994 No. 800. Enabling power: *Highways Act 1980, ss. 16, 17, 19*. Issued: 21.03.94. Made: 14.03.94. Coming into force: 29.03.94. Effect: None. Territorial extent & classification: E/W. Local. – 2p. – 0 11 043800 0 £0.65

Price/availability are liable to change without notice

The M5 Motorway (Junction 29) and the A30 Trunk Road (Honiton to Exeter Improvement) (Slip Roads Special Roads) Scheme 1994 No. 1011. Enabling power: *Highways Act 1980, ss. 16, 17, 19.* Issued: 08.04.94. Made: 30.03.94. Coming into force: 14.04.94. Effect: None. Territorial extent & classification: E/W. Local. – 4p. – 0 11 044011 0 £1.10

The M27 South Coast Motorway (Ower-Chilworth Section) Connecting Roads Scheme 1970 (Variation) Scheme 1994 No. 2141. Enabling power: *Highways Act 1980, ss. 16, 17, 19, 326 (7) (8).* Issued: 19.08.94. Made: 12.08.94. Coming into force: 16.09.94. Effect: None. Territorial extent & classification: E/W. Local. – 2p. – 0 11 045141 4 £0.65

The M62/M1 Motorway (Lofthouse Interchange Diversion and Connecting Road) Scheme 1994 No.1023. Enabling power: *Highways Act 1980, ss. 16, 17, 19.* Issued: 13.04.94. Made: 30.03.94. Coming into force: 29.04.94. Effect: None. Territorial extent & classification: E/W. Local. – 2p. – 0 11 044023 4 £0.65

The M606 Motorway (Staygate Extension) Scheme 1994 No. 2413. Enabling power: *Highways Act 1984, ss. 16, 17, 19.* Issued: 21.09.94. Made: 09.09.94. Coming into force: 07.10.94. Effect: None. Territorial extent & classification: E/W. Local. – 2p. – 0 11 045413 8 £0.65

HIGHWAYS, ENGLAND AND WALES: TRUNK ROADS

The A1 Trunk Road (Lengths of A1 Carriageway at Micklefield and Bramham) (Detrunking) Order 1994 No. 1025. Enabling power: *Highways Act 1980, ss. 10, 12.* Issued: 13.04.94. Made: 30.03.94. Coming into force: 29.04.94. Effect: None. Territorial extent & classification: E/W. Local. – 2p. – 0 11 044025 0 £0.65

The A1 Trunk Road (Wetherby to Kirk Deighton New Junction and Connecting Roads) Order 1994 No. 2515. Enabling power: *Highways Act 1980, ss. 10, 41.* Issued: 04.10.94. Made: 22.09.94. Coming into force: 21.10.94. Effect: None. Territorial extent & classification: E/W. Local. – 4p. – 0 11 045515 0 £1.10

The A1 Trunk Road (Wetherby to Walshford) (Detrunking) Order 1994 No. 2516. Enabling power: *Highways Act 1980, ss. 10, 12.* Issued: 04.10.94. Made: 22.09.94. Coming into force: 21.10.94. Effect: None. Territorial extent & classification: E/W. Local. – 4p. – 0 11 045516 9 £1.10

The A12 Trunk Road (Lowestoft Eastern Relief Road) (Trunking and Detrunking) Order 1994 No.2651. Enabling power: *Highways Act 1980, s. 10.* Issued: 19.10.94. Made: 19.09.94. Coming into force: 24.10.94. Effect: None. Territorial extent & classification: E/W. Local. – 2p. – 0 11 045651 3 £0.65

The A18 Trunk Road (Junction 5, M180 Motorway) (Detrunking) Order 1993 No.110. Enabling power: *Highways Act 1980, ss. 10, 12.* Issued: 28.01.94. Made: 19.01.94. Coming into force: 24.02.94. Effect: None. Territorial extent & classification: E/W. Local. – 2p. – 0 11 043110 3 £0.65

The A19 Trunk Road (Portrack Roundabout) (Trunking) Order 1994 No. 2801. Enabling power: *Highways Act 1980, s. 10.* Issued: 09.11.94. Made: 02.11:94. Coming into force: 14.11.94. Effect: None. Territorial extent & classification: E/W. Local. – 2p. – 0 11 045801 X £0.65

The A23 Trunk Road (Coulsdon Inner Relief Road) (Detrunking) Order 1994 No. 1038. Enabling power: *Highways Act 1980, ss. 10, 12.* Issued: 14.04.94. Made: 06.04.94. Coming into force: 21.04.94. Effect: None. Territorial extent & classification: E/W. Local. – 2p. – 0 11 044038 2 £0.65

The A23 Trunk Road (Coulsdon Inner Relief Road, Trunk Road and Slip Roads) Order 1994 No.1037. Enabling power: *Highways Act 1980, ss. 10, 41.* Issued: 14.04.94. Made: 06.04.94. Coming into force: 21.04.94. Effect: None. Territorial extent & classification: E/W. Local. – 2p. – 0 11 044037 4 £0.65

The A30 Trunk Road (Honiton to Exeter Improvement and Slip Roads) Order 1994 No. 1009. Enabling power: *Highways Act 1980, ss. 10, 41.* Issued: 08.04.94. Made: 30.03.94. Coming into force: 14.04.94. Effect: None. Territorial extent & classification: E/W. Local. – 4p. – 0 11 044009 9 £1.10

The A30 Trunk Road (Honiton to Exeter Improvement) (Detrunking) Order 1994 No. 1010. Enabling power: *Highways Act 1980, ss. 10, 12.* Issued: 08.04.94. Made: 30.03.94. Coming into force: 14.04.94. Effect: None. Territorial extent & classification: E/W. Local. – 4p. – 0 11 044010 2 £1.10

The A47 Trunk Road (Allexton - Belton in Rutland Improvement) Order 1994 No. 2158. Enabling power: *Highways Act 1980, ss. 10, 41.* Issued: 24.08.94. Made: 09.08.94. Coming into force: 05.09.94. Effect: None. Territorial extent & classification: E/W. Local. – 2p. – 0 11 045158 9 £0.65

The A50 Trunk Road (Blythe Bridge to Queensway and Connecting Roads) (No.2) Order 1994 No.1330. Enabling power: *Highways Act 1980, ss. 10, 41.* Issued: 23.05.94. Made: 17.05.94. Coming into force: 27.05.94. Effect: None. Territorial extent & classification: E/W. Local. – 2p. – 0 11 044330 6 £0.65

The A63 Trunk Road (Selby Road Junction) Order 1994 No. 1024. Enabling power: *Highways Act 1980, ss. 10, 41.* Issued: 13.04.94. Made: 30.03.94. Coming into force: 29.04.94. Effect: None. Territorial extent & classification: E/W. Local. – 2p. – 0 11 044024 2 £0.65

The A64 Trunk Road (Bramham Crossroads) Order 1994 No. 1022. Enabling power: *Highways Act 1980, ss. 10, 41.* Issued: 13.04.94. Made: 30.03.94. Coming into force: 29.04.94. Effect: None. Territorial extent & classification: E/W. Local. – 2p. – 0 11 044022 6 £0.65

The A69 Trunk Road (Haltwhistle Bypass) Order 1994 No. 3134. Enabling power: *Highways Act 1980, ss. 10, 41.* Issued: 12.12.94. Made: 05.12.94. Coming into force: 16.12.94. Effect: None. Territorial extent & classification: E/W. Local. – 2p. – 0 11 043384 X £0.65

Price/availability are liable to change without notice

The A69 Trunk Road (Haltwhistle Town) (Detrunking) Order 1994 No. 3135. Enabling power: *Highways Act 1980, ss. 10, 12.* Issued: 12.12.94. Made: 05.12.94. Coming into force: 16.12.94. Effect: None. Territorial extent & classification: E/W. Local. – 2p. – 0 11 043385 8 £0.65

The A259 Trunk Road (A20 Castle Hill Interchange to A260 Canterbury Road Roundabout, Folkestone) Order 1994 No. 2912. Enabling power: *Highways Act 1980, s. 10.* Issued: 23.11.94. Made: 08.11.94. Coming into force: 01.04.95. Effect: None. Territorial extent & classification: E/W. Local. – 2p. – 0 11 043090 5 £0.65

The A406 Trunk Road (Golders Green Road/ Brent Street Junction Improvement, Trunk Road) 1994 No. 43. Enabling power: *Highways Act 1980, ss. 10, 41.* Issued: 18.01.94. Made: 10.01.94. Coming into force: 03.02.94. Effect: None. Territorial extent & classification: E/W. Local. – 2p. – 0 11 043043 3 £0.65

The A417 Trunk Road (Daglingworth Quarry Junction) (Detrunking) Order 1994 No. 2417. Enabling power: *Highways Act 1980, ss. 10, 12.* Issued: 20.09.94. Made: 12.09.94. Coming into force: 29.09.94. Effect: None. Territorial extent & classification: E/W. Local. – 2p. – 0 11 045417 0 £0.65

The A417 Trunk Road (Daglingworth Quarry Junction) Order 1994 No. 2416. Enabling power: *Highways Act 1980, ss. 10, 41.* Issued: 20.09.94. Made: 12.09.94. Coming into force: 29.09.94. Effect: None. Territorial extent & classification: E/W. Local. – 2p. – 0 11 045416 2 £0.65

The A417 Trunk Road (North of Stratton to Nettleton Improvement) (Detrunking) Order 1994 No.2415. Enabling power: *Highways Act 1980, ss. 10, 12.* Issued: 20.09.94. Made: 12.09.94. Coming into force: 29.09.94. Effect: None. Territorial extent & classification: E/W. Local. – 2p. – 0 11 045415 4 £0.65

The A417 Trunk Road (North of Stratton to Nettleton Improvement) Order 1994 No. 2414. Enabling power: *Highways Act 1980, ss. 10, 41.* Issued: 20.09.94. Made: 12.09.94. Coming into force: 29.09.94. Effect: None. Territorial extent & classification: E/W. Local. – 2p. – 0 11 045414 6 £0.65

The A419 Trunk Road (Latton Bypass and Slip Roads) (Detrunking) Order 1994 No. 2913. Enabling power: *Highways Act 1980, ss. 10, 12.* Issued: 23.11.94. Made: 14.11.94. Coming into force: 30.11.94. Effect: None. Territorial extent & classification: E/W. Local. – 2p. – 0 11 043088 3 £0.65

The A419 Trunk Road (Latton Bypass and Slip Roads) Order 1994 No. 2897. Enabling power: *Highways Act 1980, ss. 10, 41.* Issued: 23.11.94. Made: 14.11.94. Coming into force: 30.11.94. Effect: None. Territorial extent & classification: E/W. Local. – 2p. – 0 11 043079 4 £0.65

The A419/417 Trunk Road (Cirencester and Stratton Bypass and Slip Roads) Order 1994 No.2418. Enabling power: *Highways Act 1980, ss. 10, 41.* Issued: 20.09.94. Made: 12.09.94. Coming into force: 29.09.94. Effect: None. Territorial extent & classification: E/W. Local. – 2p. – 0 11 045418 9 £0.65

The A419/417 Trunk Road (Cirencester and Stratton Bypass and Slip Roads) (Detrunking) Order 1994 No. 2419. Enabling power: *Highways Act 1980, ss. 10, 12.* Issued: 20.09.94. Made: 12.09.94. Coming into force: 29.09.94. Effect: None. Territorial extent & classification: E/W. Local. – 2p. – 0 11 045419 7 £0.65

The A550 and A5117 Trunk Roads (Improvement between Deeside Park and Ledsham) and Connecting Roads Order 1994 No. 2405. Enabling power: *Highways Act 1980, ss. 10, 41.* Issued: 20.09.94. Made: 31.08.94. Coming into force: 30.09.94. Effect: None. Territorial extent & classification: E/W. Local. – 4p. – 0 11 045405 7 £1.10

The A550 Trunk Road (Improvement between Deeside Park and Ledsham) (Detrunking) Order 1994 No. 2406. Enabling power: *Highways Act 1980, s. 10.* Issued: 20.09.94. Made: 31.08.94. Coming into force: 30.09.94. Effect: None. Territorial extent & classification: E/W. Local. – 2p. – 0 11 045406 5 £0.65

The A564 Trunk Road (Stoke - Derby Route) (Derby Southern Bypass and Slip Road) (No.3) Order 1994 No.799. Enabling power: *Highways Act 1980, ss. 10, 41.* Issued: 21.03.94. Made: 14.03.94. Coming into force: 29.03.94. Effect: None. Territorial extent & classification: E/W. Local. – 2p. – 0 11 043799 3 £0.65

The A564 Trunk Road (Stoke - Derby Route) (Derby Southern Bypass, Derby Spur, Junctions and Slip Roads) Amendment Order 1994 No. 801. Enabling power: *Highways Act 1980, s. 10.* Issued: 21.03.94. Made: 14.03.94. Coming into force: 29.03.94. Effect: S.I. 1992/176, 179, 180 amended. Territorial extent & classification: E/W. Local. – 4p. – 0 11 043801 9 £1.10

The A564 Trunk Road (Stoke - Derby Route) (Derby Southern Bypass) (Detrunking) (No.2) Order 1994 No. 802. Enabling power: *Highways Act 1980, ss. 10, 12.* Issued: 21.03.94. Made: 14.03.94. Coming into force: 29.03.94. Effect: None. Territorial extent & classification: E/W. Local. – 2p. – 0 11 043802 7 £0.65

The A570 St. Helens-Ormskirk-Southport Trunk Road (Moor Street and St. Helens Road, Ormskirk) (Detrunking) Order 1994 No. 1719. Enabling power: *Highways Act 1980, ss. 10, 12.* Issued: 08.07.94. Made: 20.06.94. Coming into force: 11.07.94. Effect: None. Territorial extent & classification: E/W. Local. – 2p. – 0 11 044719 0 £0.65

The A628/A616 Trunk Road (Flouch Junction Improvement and Detrunking) Order 1994 No.2390. Enabling power: *Highways Act 1980, ss. 10, 12, 41.* Issued: 15.09.94. Made: 09.09.94. Coming into force: 30.09.94. Effect: None. Territorial extent & classification: E/W. Local. – 2p. – 0 11 045390 5 £0.65

The A629/A650 Trunk Road (Kildwick to Crossflatts) (Detrunking) Order 1994 No. 1088. Enabling power: *Highways Act 1980, ss. 10, 12.* Issued: 22.04.94. Made: 31.03.94. Coming into force: 29.04.94. Effect: None. Territorial extent & classification: E/W. General. – 4p. – 0 11 044088 9 £1.10

The A630 Trunk Road (Doncaster) (Detrunking) Order 1994 No. 3307. Enabling power: *Highways Act 1980, ss. 10, 12.* Issued: 06.01.95. Made: 20.12.94. Coming into force: 01.02.95. Effect: None. Territorial extent & classification: E/W. Local. – 2p. – 0 11 043878 7 £0.65

The A1033 Trunk Road (Hedon Road) (Detrunking) Order 1994 No. 2153. Enabling power: *Highways Act 1980, ss. 10, 12.* Issued: 22.08.94. Made: 08.08.94. Coming into force: 02.09.94. Effect: None. Territorial extent & classification: E/W. Local. – 2p. – 0 11 045153 8 *£0.65*

The A1033 Trunk Road (Hedon Road Improvement) Order 1994 No. 2152. Enabling power: *Highways Act 1980, ss. 10, 41.* Issued: 22.08.94. Made: 08.08.94. Coming into force: 02.09.94. Effect: None. Territorial extent & classification: E/W. Local. – 4p. – 0 11 045152 X *£1.10*

The B4260 Trunk Road (De-Trunking at Ross-on-Wye) Order 1994 No. 898. Enabling power: *Highways Act 1980, ss. 10, 12.* Issued: 28.03.94. Made: 21.03.94. Coming into force: 01.04.94. Effect: None. Territorial extent & classification: E/W. Local. – 2p. – 0 11 043898 1 *£0.65*

The Cardiff-Glan Conwy Trunk Road (A470) (Nant Crew Improvement) Order 1994 No. 2660. Enabling power: *Highways Act 1980, s. 10.* Issued: 28.10.94. Made: 10.10.94. Coming into force: 07.11.94. Effect: None. Territorial extent & classification: E/W. Local. – 2p. – 0 11 045660 2 *£0.65*

The Fishguard - Bangor Trunk Road (A487) (Pont Seiont Improvement, Caernarfon) Order 1994 No. 2215. Enabling power: *Highways Act 1980, ss. 10, 12.* Issued: 07.09.94. Made: 25.08.94. Coming into force: 08.09.94. Effect: None. Territorial extent & classification: E/W. General. – 2p. – 0 11 045215 1 *£0.65*

The London-Fishguard Trunk Road (A40) (Whitland By-pass) Order 1994 No. 1614. Enabling power: *Highways Act 1980, ss. 10, 12, 326.* Issued: 28.06.94. Made: 15.06.94. Coming into force: 06.07.94. Effect: S.I. 1939/404 amended & S.I. 1965/1410; 1985/2068 revoked. Territorial extent & classification: E. Local. – 4p. – 0 11 044614 3 *£1.10*

The London-Holyhead Trunk Road (A5) (Bangor Bypass Section) (Eastbound on Slip Road from A4087 Caernarfon Road) Order 1994 No. 1972. Enabling power: *Highways Act 1980, s. 10.* Issued: 09.08.94. Made: 15.07.94. Coming into force: 18.08.94. Effect: None. Territorial extent & classification: E/W. Local. – 2p. – 0 11 044972 X *£0.65*

The London-Holyhead Trunk Road (Gwalchmai By-Pass) (Revocation) Order 1994 No. 108. Enabling power: *Highways Act 1980, s. 10.* Issued: 08.02.94. Made: 18.01.94. Coming into force: 08.02.94. Effect: None. Territorial extent & classification: W. Local. – 2p. – 0 11 043106 5 *£0.65*

HOUSE OF LORDS

The Maximum Number of Judges Order 1994 No. 3217. Enabling power: *Administration of Justice Act 1968, s. 1 (2) & Supreme Court Act 1981, s. 2 (4).* Issued: 22.12.94. Made: 14.12.94. Laid: 16.11.94. Coming into force: 15.12.94. Effect: 1968 c. 5 & 1981 c. 54 amended. Territorial extent & classification: E/W. General. – 2p. – 0 11 043584 2 *£0.65*

HOUSING, ENGLAND AND WALES

The Castle Vale Housing Action Trust (Transfer of Property) Order 1994 No. 566. Enabling power: *Housing Act 1988, ss. 74, 75 (4).* Issued: 10.03.94. Made: 07.03.94. Laid: 10.03.94. Coming into force: 31.03.94. Effect: None. Territorial extent & classification: E/W. Local. – 4p. – 0 11 043566 4 *£1.10*

The Collective Enfranchisement and Tenants' Audit (Qualified Surveyors) Regulations 1994 No.1263. Enabling power: *Leasehold Reform, Housing and Urban Development Act 1993, ss. 13 (7) (a), 78 (5).* Issued: 17.05.94. Made: 07.05.94. Laid: 17.05.94. Coming into force: 07.06.94. Effect: None. Territorial extent & classification: E/W. General. – 2p. – 0 11 044263 6 *£0.65*

The Home Purchase Assistance (Commutation of Repayments) Order 1994 No. 548. Enabling power: *Local Government and Housing Act 1989, s. 172 (1) (2).* Issued: 11.03.94. Made: 28.02.94. Laid: 11.03.94. Coming into force: 07.04.94. Effect: Home Purchase Assistance Directions 1978 amended. Territorial extent & classification: E/W/S. General. – 4p. – 0 11 043548 6 *£1.10*

The Housing Associations (Permissible Additional Purposes) (England and Wales) Order 1994 No.2895. Enabling power: *Housing Act 1988, ss. 48 (2) (3).* Issued: 29.11.94. Made: 09.11.94. Laid: 17.11.94. Coming into force: 08.12.94. Effect: 1985 c. 69 amended. Territorial extent & classification: E/W. General. – 4p. – 0 11 043147 2 *£1.10*

The Housing (Change of Landlord) (Payment of Disposal Cost by Instalments) (Amendment No. 2) Regulations 1994 No. 2916. Enabling power: *Housing Act 1988, ss. 104 (2A), 112, 114 (1).* Issued: 25.11.94. Made: 15.11.94. Laid: 25.11.94. Coming into force: 16.12.94. Effect: S.I. 1990/1019 amended & S.I. 1994/266 revoked. Territorial extent & classification: E/W. General. – 2p. – 0 11 043092 1 *£0.65*

The Housing (Change of Landlord) (Payment of Disposal Cost by Instalments) (Amendment) Regulations 1994 No. 266. Enabling power: *Housing Act 1988, ss. 104 (2A), 111 (a), 112, 114 (1).* Issued: 15.02.94. Made: 04.02.94. Laid: 15.02.94. Coming into force: 08.03.94. Effect: S.I. 1990/1019 amended & S.I. 1993/581 revoked. Territorial extent & classification: E/W. General. – 2p. – 0 11 043266 5 *£0.65*

HOUSING, ENGLAND AND WALES

The Housing Renovation etc. Grants (Prescribed Forms and Particulars) Regulations 1994 No.565. Enabling power: *Local Government and Housing Act 1989, ss. 102 (2) (4), 137 (2), 138 (1), 190 (1)*. Issued: 17.03.94. Made: 05.03.94. Laid: 14.03.94. Coming into force: 04.04.94. Effect: S.I. 1990/1236; 1991/898; 1992/562; 1993/552, 1452 revoked. Territorial extent & classification: E/W. General. – 72p. – 0 11 043565 6 *£8.10*

The Housing Renovation etc. Grants (Prescribed Forms and Particulars) (Welsh Forms and Particulars) (Amendment) Regulations 1994 No. 435. Enabling power: *Local Government and Housing Act 1989, ss. 102 (2) (4), 138 (1), 190 (1), 191 (1)*. Issued: 16.03.94. Made: 17.02.94. Laid: 01.03.94. Coming into force: 22.03.94. Effect: S.I. 1991/80 amended. This SI has been made in consequence of a defect in SI 1991/80 and is being sent free of charge to all known recipients of that SI. Territorial extent & classification: W. General. – 2p. – 0 11 043435 8 *£0.65*

The Housing Renovation etc. Grants (Prescribed Forms and Particulars) (Welsh Forms and Particulars) (Amendment) Regulations 1994 No. 2765. Enabling power: *Local Government and Housing Act 1989, ss. 102 (2) (4), 137 (2), 138 (1), 190 (1), 191 (1)*. Issued: 17.11.94. Made: 24.10.94. Laid: 17.11.94. Coming into force: 09.12.94. Effect: S.I. 1994/693 amended. This SI is partly in the Welsh language. This SI has been made in consequence of a defect in SI 1994/693 and is being sent free of charge to all known recipients of that SI. Territorial extent & classification: W. General. – 4p. – 0 11 045765 X *£1.10*

The Housing Renovation etc. Grants (Prescribed Forms and Particulars) (Welsh Forms and Particulars) Regulations 1994 No. 693. Enabling power: *Local Government and Housing Act 1989, ss. 102 (2) (4), 137 (2), 138 (1), 190 (1)*. Issued: 27.04.94. Made: 10.03.94. Laid: 14.03.94. Coming into force: 04.04.94. Effect: S.I. 1991/180, 1403; 1992/759; 1993/715, 2078; 1994/435 revoked. This SI is partly in the Welsh language. With correction slip issued 24.05.94. Territorial extent & classification: W. General. – 76p. – 0 11 043693 8 *£8.70* Replaced by ISBN 0110430204

The Housing Renovation etc. Grants (Reduction of Grant) Regulations 1994 No. 648. Enabling power: *Local Government and Housing Act 1989, ss. 109, 137 (2)*. Issued: 16.03.94. Made: 07.03.94. Laid: 14.03.94. Coming into force: 04.04.94. Effect: S.I. 1990/1189; 1991/897; 1992/705; 1993/551 revoked. Territorial extent & classification: E/W. General. – 46p. – 0 11 043648 2 *£6.75*

The Housing (Right to Buy Delay Procedure) (Prescribed Forms) (Welsh Forms) Regulations 1994 No. 2931. Enabling power: *Housing Act 1985, s. 176 (1) (5)*. Issued: 02.12.94. Made: 09.11.94. Coming into force: 12.12.94. Effect: S.I. 1989/240 amended. Territorial extent & classification: W. General. – In English & Welsh. – 6p. – 0 11 043128 6 *£1.55*

The Housing (Right to Buy) (Prescribed Forms) (Welsh Forms) Regulations 1994 No. 2932. Enabling power: *Housing Act 1985, s. 176 (1) (5)*. Issued: 02.12.94. Made: 09.11.94. Coming into force: 12.12.94. Effect: S.I. 1988/1265 revoked. Territorial extent & classification: W. General. – In English & Welsh. – 20p. – 0 11 043137 5 *£3.70*

The Housing (Right to Buy) (Priority of Charges) Order 1994 No. 1762. Enabling power: *Housing Act 1985, s. 156 (4)*. Issued: 12.07.94. Made: 01.07.94. Coming into force: 22.07.94. Effect: S.I. 1991/2052 amended. Territorial extent & classification: E/W. General. –4p. – 0 11 044762 X *£1.10*

The Housing (Right to Manage) Regulations 1994 No. 627. Enabling power: *Housing Act 1985, ss. 27 (3) (7), 27AB*. Issued: 15.03.94. Made: 07.03.94. Laid: 11.03.94. Coming into force: 01.04.94. Effect: None. Territorial extent & classification: E/W. General. – 10p. – 0 11 043627 X *£2.40*

The Housing (Welfare Services) Order 1994 No. 42. Enabling power: *Leasehold Reform, Housing and Urban Development Act 1993, s. 128*. Issued: 21.01.94. Made: 12.01.94. Coming into force: 01.04.94. Effect: None. Territorial extent & classification: E. General. – 2p. – 0 11 043042 5 *£0.65*

The Leasehold Reform, Housing and Urban Development Act 1993 (Commencement No. 4) Order 1994 No. 935 (C. 16). Enabling power: *Leasehold Reform, Housing and Urban Development Act 1993, s. 188 (2) (3)*. Issued: 30.03.94. Made: 25.03.94. Coming into force: 01.04.94. Effect: None. Territorial extent & classification: E/W. General. – 4p. – 0 11 043935 X *£1.10*

The Mortgage Indemnities (Recognised Bodies) Order 1994 No. 1763. Enabling power: *Housing Act 1985, s. 444 (1)*. Issued: 12.07.94. Made: 01.07.94. Coming into force: 22.07.94. Effect: S.I. 1991/2053 amended. Territorial extent & classification: E/W. General. – 4p. – 0 11 044763 8 *£1.10*

The Registered Housing Associations (Accounting Requirements) (Wales) Order 1994 No.668. Enabling power: *Housing Associations Act 1985, s. 24 (1) (2) (5) (6) & Housing Act 1988, s. 55 (2)*. Issued: 08.04.94. Made: 09.03.94. Laid: 11.03.94. Coming into force: 01.04.94. Effect: S.I. 1988/395; 1989/327 amended. Territorial extent & classification: W. General. – 12p. – 0 11 043668 7 *£2.80*

The Rent Officers (Additional Functions) (Amendment No. 2) Order 1994 No. 3040. Enabling power: *Housing Act 1988, s. 121 (1) (2)*. Issued: 07.12.94. Made: 28.11.94. Laid: 07.12.94. Coming into force: 01.01.95. Effect: S.I. 1990/428 amended. Territorial extent & classification: E/W. General. – 2p. – 0 11 043272 X *£0.65*

The Rent Officers (Additional Functions) (Amendment) Order 1994 No. 568. Enabling power: *Housing Act 1988, s. 121*. Issued: 11.03.94. Made: 06.03.94. Laid: 11.03.94. Coming into force: 01.04.94. Effect: S.I. 1990/428; 1993/652 amended. Territorial extent & classification: E/W. General. – 4p. – 0 11 043568 0 *£1.10*

The Secure Tenants of Local Authorities (Compensation for Improvements) Regulations 1994 No.613. Enabling power: *Housing Act 1985, s. 99A*. Issued: 15.03.94. Made: 05.03.94. Laid: 11.03.94. Coming into force: 01.04.94. Effect: None. Territorial extent & classification: E/W/S. General. – 4p. – 0 11 043613 X *£1.10*

Price/availability are liable to change without notice

HOUSING, SCOTLAND

The Secure Tenants of Local Housing Authorities (Right to Repair) (Amendment) Regulations 1994 No. 844. Enabling power: *Housing Act 1985, s. 96 (5)*. Issued: 29.03.94. Made: 22.03.94. Laid: 23.03.94. Coming into force: 01.04.94. Effect: S.I. 1994/133 amended. This SI has been made in consequence of a defect in SI 1994/133 and is being sent free of charge to all known recipients of that SI. Territorial extent & classification: E/W. General. – 2p. – 0 11 043844 2 £0.65

The Secure Tenants of Local Housing Authorities (Right to Repair) Regulations 1994 No.133. Enabling power: *Housing Act 1985, s. 96*. Issued: 02.02.94. Made: 25.01.94. Coming into force: 01.04.94. Effect: None. Territorial extent & classification: E/W. General. – 6p. – 0 11 043133 2 £1.55 Replaced by ISBN 0110458958

The Stonebridge Housing Action Trust (Area and Constitution) Order 1994 No. 1987. Enabling power: *Housing Act 1988, s. 60, 62 (1) (a)*. Issued: 01.08.94. Made: 26.07.94. Laid: 14.06.94. Coming into force: 27.07.94. Effect: None. Supersedes Draft ISBN 0110459334 published on 15.06.94. Territorial extent & classification: E. Local. – 4p., ill. – 0 11 044987 8 £1.10

The Tower Hamlets Housing Action Trust (Transfer of Property) Order 1994 No. 695. Enabling power: *Housing Act 1988, ss. 74, 75 (4)*. Issued: 17.03.94. Made: 10.03.94. Coming into force: 31.03.94. Effect: None. Territorial extent & classification: E. Local. –4p. – 0 11 043695 4 £1.10

HOUSING, SCOTLAND

The Home Purchase Assistance (Commutation of Repayments) Order 1994 No. 548. Enabling power: *Local Government and Housing Act 1989, s. 172 (1) (2)*. Issued: 11.03.94. Made: 28.02.94. Laid: 11.03.94. Coming into force: 07.04.94. Effect: Home Purchase Assistance Directions 1978 amended. Territorial extent & classification: E/W/S. General. – 4p. – 0 11 043548 6 £1.10

The Housing Revenue Account General Fund Contribution Limits (Scotland) Order 1994 No.106 (S. 2). Enabling power: *Housing (Scotland) Act 1987, s. 204*. Issued: 27.01.94. Made: 19.01.94. Laid: 25.01.94. Coming into force: 15.02.94. Effect: None. Territorial extent & classification: S. General. – 2p. – 0 11 043108 1 £0.65

The Housing Support Grant (Scotland) Order 1994 No. 430 (S. 15). Enabling power: *Housing (Scotland) Act 1987, ss. 191, 192*. Issued: 07.03.94. Made: 22.02.94. Laid: 25.01.94. Coming into force: 01.04.94. Effect: None. Territorial extent & classification: S. General. – 6p. – 0 11 043430 7 £1.55

The Local Authorities (Recognised Bodies for Heritable Securities Indemnities) (Scotland) Amendment Order 1994 No. 3253 (S. 181). Enabling power: *Housing (Scotland) Act 1987, s. 229 (6)*. Issued: 10.01.95. Made: 13.12.94. Coming into force: 20.12.94. Effect: S.I. 1994/2030 amended. Territorial extent & classification: S. General. – 2p. – 0 11 043796 9 £0.65

The Local Authorities (Recognised Bodies for Heritable Securities Indemnities) (Scotland) Order 1994 No. 2030 (S. 92). Enabling power: *Housing (Scotland) Act 1987, s. 229 (6)*. Issued: 11.08.94. Made: 27.07.94. Coming into force: 04.08.94. Effect: None. Territorial extent & classification: S. General. – 2p. – 0 11 045030 2 £0.65

The Rent Officers (Additional Functions) (Scotland) Amendment (No.2) Order 1994 No.3108 (S.169). Enabling power: *Housing (Scotland) Act 1988, s. 70*. Issued: 16.12.94. Made: 05.12.94. Laid: 07.12.94. Coming into force: 01.01.95. Effect: S.I. 1990/396 amended. Territorial extent & classification: S. General. – 4p. – 0 11 043375 0 £1.10

The Rent Officers (Additional Functions) (Scotland) Amendment Order 1994 No. 582 (S. 25). Enabling power: *Housing (Scotland) Act 1988, s. 70 & Local Government Finance Act 1992, ss. 113, 114*. Issued: 16.03.94. Made: 03.03.94. Laid: 11.03.94. Coming into force: 01.04.94. Effect: S.I. 1990/396; 1993/646 amended. Territorial extent & classification: S. General. –4p. – 0 11 043582 6 £1.10

The Right to Purchase (Prescribed Persons) (Scotland) Amendment Order 1994 No. 2097 (S. 109). Enabling power: *Housing (Scotland) Act 1987, s. 61 (11) (w)*. Issued: 16.08.94. Made: 04.08.94. Laid: 16.08.94. Coming into force: 06.09.94. Effect: S.I. 1993/1625 amended. Territorial extent & classification: S. General. – 2p. – 0 11 045097 3 £0.65

The Secure Tenants (Compensation for Improvements) (Scotland) Regulations 1994 No.632 (S. 30). Enabling power: *Housing (Scotland) Act 1987, s. 58A, 338*. Issued: 17.03.94. Made: 07.03.94. Laid: 11.03.94. Coming into force: 01.04.94. Effect: None. With correction slip. Territorial extent & classification: S. General. – 6p. – 0 11 043632 6 £1.55

The Secure Tenants (Right to Repair) (Scotland) Regulations 1994 No. 1046 (S. 54). Enabling power: *Housing (Scotland) Act 1987, ss. 60, 338*. Issued: 20.04.94. Made: 06.04.94. Laid: 20.04.94. Coming into force: 01.10.94. Effect: None. Territorial extent & classification: S. General. – 6p. – 0 11 044046 3 £1.55

HOVERCRAFT

The Hovercraft (Fees) Regulations 1994 No. 1382. Enabling power: *S.I. 1972/674, art. 35*. Issued: 01.06.94. Made: 19.05.94. Coming into force: 01.07.94. Effect: S.I. 1992/478 amended. Territorial extent & classification: GB. General. – 4p. – 0 11 044382 9 £1.10

HUMAN FERTILISATION AND EMBRYOLOGY

The Human Fertilisation and Embryology Act 1990 (Commencement No. 5) Order 1994 No.1776 (C. 33). Enabling power: *Human Fertilisation and Embryology Act 1990, s. 49 (2)*. Bringing into operation various provisions of the 1990 act on 05.07.94. & 01.11.94. Issued: 13.07.94. Made: 04.07.94. Effect: None. With correction slip dated August 1994. Territorial extent & classification: E/W. General. – 2p. – 0 11 044776 X £0.65

Price/availability are liable to change without notice

The Parental Orders (Human Fertilisation and Embryology) Regulations 1994 No. 2767. Enabling power: *Human Fertilisation and Embryology Act 1990, s. 30 (9), 45 (1) (3).* Issued: 07.11.94. Made: 28.10.94. Coming into force: 01.11.94. Effect: None. Supersedes Draft ISBN 0110459415 issued on 11.07.94. Territorial extent & classification: E/W. General. –20p. – 0 11 045767 6 *£3.70*

The Parental Orders (Human Fertilisation and Embryology) (Scotland) Regulations 1994 No.2804 (S. 141). Enabling power: *Human Fertilisation and Embryology Act 1990, ss. 30 (9), 45.* Issued: 14.11.94. Made: 31.10.94. Laid: 12.07.94. Coming into force: 01.11.94. Effect: 1964 c. 41; 1965 c. 49; 1978 c. 28; 1984 c. 56; 1985 c. 60; 1986 c. 55; 1990 c. 37 amended. Territorial extent & classification: S. General. – 12p. – 0 11 045804 4 *£2.80*

IMMIGRATION

The Immigration (European Economic Area) Order 1994 No. 1895. Enabling power: *European Communities Act 1972, s. 2 (2).* Issued: 27.07.94. Made: 19.07.94. Coming into force: 20.07.94. Effect: None. Supersedes Draft ISBN 110458915 published 28.03.94. Territorial extent & classification: UK. General. –8p. – 0 11 044895 2 *£1.95*

INCOME TAX

The Currency Contracts and Options (Amendment of Enactments) Order 1994 No. 3233. Enabling power: *Finance Act 1994, s. 177 (6).* Issued: 16.01.95. Made: 15.12.94. Laid: 16.12.94. Coming into force: 23.03.95. Effect: 1994 c.9 amended. Territorial extent & classification: GB. General. – 2p. – 0 11 043904 X *£0.65*

The Distraint by Collectors (Fees, Costs and Charges) Regulations 1994 No. 236. Enabling power: *Taxes Management Act 1970, s. 61 (6).* Issued: 10.02.94. Made: 03.02.94. Laid: 04.02.94. Coming into force: 01.03.94. Effect: None. Territorial extent & classification: GB. General. – 4p. – 0 11 043236 3 *£1.10*

The Double Taxation Relief (Air Transport) (Saudi Arabia) Order 1994 No. 767. Enabling power: *Income and Corporation Taxes Act 1988, s. 788 (10).* Issued: 25.03.94. Made: 15.03.94. Laid: 24.11.93. Coming into force: In accord. with art. 6 of the sch. Effect: None. Supersedes Draft SI ISBN 0110358694 previously published on 24.11.93. Territorial extent & classification: GB. General. – 4p. – 0 11 043767 5 *£1.10*

The Double Taxation Relief (Taxes on Income) (Austria) Order 1994 No. 768. Enabling power: *Income and Corporation Taxes Act 1988, s. 788 (10).* Issued: 25.03.94. Made: 15.03.94. Laid: 24.11.93. Coming into force: In accord. with art. II of the sch. Effect: S.I. 1970/1947 amended. This SI supersedes Draft SI ISBN 0110358716 previously published on 24.11.93. Territorial extent & classification: GB. General. – 4p. – 0 11 043768 3 *£1.10*

The Double Taxation Relief (Taxes on Income) (Estonia) Order 1994 No. 3207. Enabling power: *Income and Corporation Taxes Act 1988, s. 788.* Issued: 21.12.94. Made: 14.12.94. Laid: 20.07.94. Coming into force: Per art. 30, the date of entry into force will in due course be published in the London, Edinburgh and Belfast Gazettes. Effect: None. Supersedes Draft ISBN 011045944x published on 20.07.94. Territorial extent & classification: GB. General. – 20p. – 0 11 043598 2 *£3.70*

The Double Taxation Relief (Taxes on Income) (Guernsey) Order 1994 No. 3209. Enabling power: *Income and Corporation Taxes Act 1988, s. 788* Issued: 21.12.94. Made: 14.12.94. Laid: 20.07.94. Coming into force: Per sch. para. 2, the date of entry into force will in due course be published in the London, Edinburgh and Belfast gazettes. Effect: S.I. 1952/1215 amended. Supersedes Draft ISBN 0110459512 published on 20.07.94. Territorial extent & classification: GB. General. – 2p. – 0 11 043588 5 *£0.65*

The Double Taxation Relief (Taxes on Income) (Indonesia) Order 1994 No. 769. Enabling power: *Income and Corporation Taxes Act 1988, s. 788 (10).* Issued: 25.03.94. Made: 15.03.94. Laid: 24.11.93. Coming into force: In accord. with art. 27 of the sch. Effect: None. Supersedes Draft SI ISBN 0110358686 previously published on 24.11.93. Territorial extent & classification: GB. General. – 16p. – 0 11 043769 1 *£3.20*

The Double Taxation Relief (Taxes on Income) (Isle of Man) Order 1994 No. 3208. Enabling power: *Income and Corporation Taxes Act 1988, s. 788.* Issued: 21.12.94. Made: 14.12.94. Laid: 20.07.94. Coming into force: Per sch. para. 4, the date of entry into force will in due course be published in the London, Edinburgh and Belfast Gazettes. Effect: S.I. 1955/1205, 1991/2880 amended. Supersedes Draft SI ISBN 0110459520 published on 20.07.94. Territorial extent & classification: GB. General. – 2p. – 0 11 043594 X *£0.65*

The Double Taxation Relief (Taxes on Income) (Jersey) Order 1994 No. 3210. Enabling power: *Income and Corporation Taxes Act 1988, s. 788.* Issued: 21.12.94. Made: 14.12.94. Laid: 20.07.94. Coming into force: In accord. with sch. para. 2, the date of entry into force will in due course be published in the London, Edinburgh and Belfast Gazettes. Effect: S.I. 1952/1216 amended. Supersedes Draft SI ISBN 0110459539 published 20.07.94. Territorial extent & classification: GB. General. – 2p. – 0 11 043585 0 *£0.65*

The Double Taxation Relief (Taxes on Income) (Kazakhstan) Order 1994 No. 3211. Enabling power: *Income and Corporation Taxes Act 1988, s. 788.* Issued: 21.12.94. Made: 14.12.94. Laid: 20.07.94. Coming into force: Per art. 29, the date of entry into force will in due course be published in the London, Edinburgh and Belfast Gazettes. Effect: None. Supersedes Draft ISBN 0110459466 published on 20.07.94. Territorial extent & classification: GB. General. – 20p. – 0 11 043593 1 *£3.70*

The Double Taxation Relief (Taxes on Income) (Mexico) Order 1994 No. 3212. Enabling power: *Income and Corporation Taxes Act 1988, s. 788.* Issued: 21.12.94. Made: 14.12.94. Laid: 20.07.94. Coming into force: Per art. 29, the date of entry into force will in due course be published in the London, Edinburgh and Belfast Gazettes. Effect: None. Supersedes Draft ISBN 0110459474 published 20.07.94. Territorial extent & classification: GB. General. – 20p. – 0 11 043557 5 *£3.70*

Price/availability are liable to change without notice

INCOME TAX

The Double Taxation Relief (Taxes on Income) (Russian Federation) Order 1994 No. 3213. Enabling power: *Income and Corporation Taxes Act 1988, s. 788.* Issued: 21.12.94. Made: 14.12.94. Laid: 20.07.94. Coming into force: Per art. 28, the date of entry into force will in due course be published in the London, Edinburgh and Belfast Gazettes. Effect: None. Supersedes Draft ISBN 0110459482 published on 20.07.94. Territorial extent & classification: GB. General. – 20p. – 0 11 043605 9 £3.70

The Double Taxation Relief (Taxes on Income) (Switzerland) Order 1994 No. 3215. Enabling power: *Income and Corporation Taxes Act 1988, s. 788.* Issued: 21.12.94. Made: 14.12.94. Laid: 20.07.94. Coming into force: Per art. IV, the date of entry into force will be published in the London, Edinburgh and Belfast Gazettes. Effect: S.I. 1978/1408; 1982/714 amended. Supersedes Draft ISBN 0110459490 published 20.07.94. Territorial extent & classification: GB. General. – 4p. – 0 11 043596 6 £1.10

The Double Taxation Relief (Taxes on Income) (United States of America Dividends) (Amendment) Regulations 1994 No. 1418. Enabling power: *Income and Corporation Taxes Act 1988, s. 791.* Issued: 03.06.94. Made: 25.05.94. Coming into force: 16.06.94. Effect: S.R. & O. 1946/1331 amended. Territorial extent & classification: GB. General. – 2p. – 0 11 044418 3 £0.65

The Double Taxation Relief (Taxes on Income) (Uzbekistan) Order 1994 No. 770. Enabling power: *Income and Corporation Taxes Act 1988, s. 788 (10).* Issued: 25.03.94. Made: 15.03.94. Laid: 24.11.93. Coming into force: In accord. with art. 29 of the sch. Effect: None. Supersedes Draft ISBN 0110358724 previously published on 24.11.93. Territorial extent & classification: GB. General. – 20p. – 0 11 043770 5 £3.70

The Double Taxation Relief (Taxes on Income) (Vietnam) Order 1994 No. 3216. Enabling power: *Income and Corporation Taxes Act 1988, s. 788.* Issued: 21.12.94. Made: 14.12.94. Laid: 20.07.94. Coming into force: Per art. 27, the date of entry into force will in due course be published in the London, Edinburgh and Belfast Gazettes. Effect: None. Supersedes Draft ISBN 0110459504 published on 20.07.94. Territorial extent & classification: GB. General. – 20p. – 0 11 043618 0 £3.70

The Exchange Gains and Losses (Alternative Method of Calculation of Gain and Loss) Regulations 1994 No. 3227. Enabling power: *Finance Act 1993, s. 164 (14), 167 (1) (4) to (6), sch. 15.* Issued: 16.01.95. Made: 15.12.94. Laid: 16.12.94. Coming into force: 23.03.95. Effect: None. Territorial extent & classification: GB. General. – 12p. – 0 11 043897 3 £2.80

The Exchange Gains and Losses (Debts of Varying Amounts) Regulations 1994 No. 3232. Enabling power: *Finance Act 1993, ss. 136 (14), 167 (1) (4) (5).* Issued: 16.01.95. Made: 15.12.94. Laid: 16.12.94. Coming into force: 23.03.95. Effect: 1993 c.34 amended. Territorial extent & classification: GB. General. – 4p. – 0 11 043891 4 £1.10

The Exchange Gains and Losses (Deferral of Gains and Losses) Regulations 1994 No.3228. Enabling power: *Finance Act 1993, ss. 143 (7), 164 (14), 167 (1).* Issued: 16.01.95. Made: 15.12.94. Laid: 16.12.94. Coming into force: 23.03.95. Effect: None. Territorial extent & classification: GB. General. – 6p. – 0 11 043892 2 £1.55

The Exchange Gains and Losses (Excess Gains and Losses) Regulations 1994 No. 3229. Enabling power: *Finance Act 1993, ss. 148, 164 (14), 167 (1).* Issued: 16.01.95. Made: 15.12.94. Laid: 16.12.94. Coming into force: 23.03.95. Effect: None. Territorial extent & classification: GB. General. – 4p. – 0 11 043893 0 £1.10

The Exchange Gains and Losses (Insurance Companies) Regulations 1994 No. 3231. Enabling power: *Finance Act 1993, ss. 167 (1), 168 (2) to (5).* Issued: 16.01.95. Made: 15.12.94. Laid: 16.12.94. Coming into force: 23.03.95. Effect: None. Territorial extent & classification: GB. General. – 4p. – 0 11 043890 6 £1.10

The Exchange Gains and Losses (Transitional Provisions) Regulations 1994 No. 3226. Enabling power: *Finance Act 1993, ss. 164 (14), 165 (4) (5), 167 (1) (4) to (6), sch. 16.* Issued: 16.01.95. Made: 15.12.94. Laid: 16.12.94. Coming into force: 23.03.95. Effect: None. Territorial extent & classification: GB. General. – 28p. – 0 11 043900 7 £4.70

The Finance Act 1989, section 152, (Appointed Day) Order 1994 No. 87 (C. 4). Enabling power: *Finance Act 1989, s. 152 (7). Bringing into operation various provisions of this act on 01.02.94.* Issued: 27.01.94. Made: 19.01.94. Effect: None. Territorial extent & classification: GB. General. – 2p. – 0 11 043087 5 £0.65

The Finance Act 1989, section 165 (2), (Appointed Day) Order 1994 No. 2508 (C. 50). Enabling power: *Finance Act 1989, s. 165 (2). Bringing various provisions of this act into operation on 20.05.95.* Issued: 04.10.94. Made: 23.09.94. Effect: None. Territorial extent & classification: GB. General. – 2p. – 0 11 045508 8 £0.65

The Finance Act 1993, section 165, (Appointed Day) Order 1994 No. 3224 (C. 79). Enabling power: *Finance Act 1993, ss. 165 (7) (b), 167 (1). Bringing into force various provisions of this act on 23.03.95.* Issued: 16.01.95. Made: 15.12.94. Effect: None. Territorial extent & classification: GB. General. – 2p. – 0 11 043906 6 £0.65

The Finance Act 1994, Chapter II of Part IV, (Appointed Day) Order 1994 No. 3225 (C. 80). Enabling power: *Finance Act 1994, s. 147 (4) (b). Bringing into force various provisions of this act on 23.03.95.* Issued: 16.01.95. Made: 15.12.94. Effect: None. Territorial extent & classification: GB. General. – 2p. – 0 11 043907 4 £0.65

The General and Special Commissioners (Amendment of Enactments) Regulations 1994 No.1813. Enabling power: *Taxes Management Act 1970, ss. 46A, 56B.* Issued: 14.07.94. Made: 06.07.94. Laid: 14.07.94. Coming into force: 01.09.94. Effect: 1970 c. 9; 1972 c. 41; 1975 c. 22; 1984 c. 43, 51; 1988 c. 1; 1988 c. 39; 1989 c. 26; 1994 c.9 & S.I. 1959/452; 1967/149; 1986/1711; 1989/421; 1990/627; 1991/851; 1992/511; 1993/415, 744; 1994/728 amended & S.I. 1987/1422 revoked. Territorial extent & classification: E/W. General. – 12p. – 0 11 044813 8 £2.80

The General Commissioners (Jurisdiction and Procedure) Regulations 1994 No. 1812. Enabling power: *Taxes Management Act 1970, ss. 46A, 56B.* Issued: 14.07.94. Made: 06.07.94. Laid: 14.07.94. Coming into force: 01.09.94. Effect: None. Territorial extent & classification: E/W. General. – 16p. – 0 11 044812 X £3.20

Price/availability are liable to change without notice

The Income Tax (Authorised Unit Trusts) (Interest Distributions) Regulations 1994 No.2318. Enabling power: *Income and Corporations Taxes Act 1988, ss. 468O (3) (4), 468P (8) (9).* Issued: 13.09.94. Made: 05.09.94. Laid: 06.09.94. Coming into force: 27.09.94. Effect: 1988 c. 1 amended. With correction slip. Territorial extent & classification: GB. General. –4p. – 0 11 045318 2 *£1.10*

The Income Tax (Building Societies) (Dividends and Interest) (Amendment) Regulations 1994 No.296. Enabling power: *Income and Corporation Taxes Act 1988, s. 477A (1).* Issued: 17.02.94. Made: 10.02.94. Laid: 11.02.94. Coming into force: 04.03.94. Effect: S.I. 1990/2231 amended. Territorial extent & classification: GB. General. – 4p. – 0 11 043296 7 *£1.10*

The Income Tax (Car Benefits) (Replacement Accessories) Regulations 1994 No. 777. Enabling power: *Income and Corporation Taxes Act 1988, s. 168E.* Issued: 05.04.94. Made: 15.03.94. Laid: 16.03.94. Coming into force: 06.04.94. Effect: None. Territorial extent & classification: GB. General. – 4p. – 0 11 043777 2 *£1.10*

The Income Tax (Cash Equivalents of Car Fuel Benefits) Order 1994 No. 3010. Enabling power: *Income and Corporation Taxes Act 1988, s. 158 (4).* Issued: 08.12.94. Made: 29.11.94. Laid: 29.11.94. Coming into force: 06.04.95. Effect: 1988 c. 1 amended. Territorial extent & classification: GB. General. – 2p. – 0 11 043294 0 *£0.65*

The Income Tax (Definition of Unit Trust Scheme) (Amendment) Regulations 1994 No.1479. Enabling power: *Income and Corporation Taxes Act 1988. s. 469 (7).* Issued: 13.06.94. Made: 03.06.94. Laid: 06.06.94. Coming into force: 27.06.94. Effect: S.I. 1992/3133 amended. Territorial extent & classification: GB. General. – 2p. – 0 11 044479 5 *£0.65*

The Income Tax (Deposit-Takers) (Interest Payments) (Amendment) Regulations 1994 No.295. Enabling power: *Income and Corporation Taxes Act 1988, s. 480B.* Issued: 17.02.94. Made: 10.02.94. Laid: 11.02.94. Coming into force: 04.03.94. Effect: S.I. 1990/2232 amended. Territorial extent & classification: GB. General. – 2p. – 0 11 043295 9 *£0.65*

The Income Tax (Employments) (Amendment) Regulations 1994 No. 775. Enabling power: *Income and Corporation Taxes Act 1988, s. 203.* Issued: 29.03.94. Made: 15.03.94. Laid: 16.03.94. Coming into force: 06.04.94. Effect: S.I. 1993/744 amended. Territorial extent & classification: GB. General. – 4p. – 0 11 043775 6 *£1.10*

The Income Tax (Employments) (Notional Payments) Regulations 1994 No. 1212. Enabling power: *Income and Corporation Taxes Act 1988, s. 203.* Issued: 16.05.94. Made: 04.05.94. Laid: 04.05.94. Coming into force: 25.05.94. Effect: S.I. 1993/744 amended. Territorial extent & classification: GB. General. – 6p. – 0 11 044212 1 *£1.55*

The Income Tax (Indexation) Order 1994 No. 3012. Enabling power: *Income and Corporation Taxes Act 1988, ss. 1 (6), 257C (3).* Issued: 08.12.94. Made: 29.11.94. Coming into force: 06.04.95. Effect: 1988 c. 1 amended. Territorial extent & classification: GB. General. –2p. – 0 11 043300 9 *£0.65*

The Income Tax (Replacement Cars) Regulations 1994 No. 778. Enabling power: *Income and Corporation Taxes Act 1988, sch. 6, para. 8.* Issued: 31.03.94. Made: 15.03.94. Laid: 16.03.94. Coming into force: 06.04.94. Effect: None. Territorial extent & classification: GB. General. – 4p. – 0 11 043778 0 *£1.10*

The Insurance Companies (Pension Business) (Transitional Provisions) (Amendment) Regulations 1994 No. 3036. Enabling power: *Income and Corporation Taxes Act 1988, sch. 19AB, paras. 4 (1) (4) (6).* Issued: 17.01.95. Made: 29.11.94. Laid: 30.11.94. Coming into force: 21.12.94. Effect: S.I. 1992/2326 amended. Territorial extent & classification: GB. General. –2p. – 0 11 043908 2 *£0.65*

The Lloyd's Underwriters (Tax) (1991-92) Regulations 1994 No. 728. Enabling power: *Income and Corporation Taxes Act 1988, s. 451 (1) (1A), sch. 19A, para. 1 (1) (3) & Finance Act 1989, s. 92 (5) (6) (7) & Taxation of Chargeable Gains Act 1992, s. 209 (2) (4) (5) (6).* Issued: 05.04.94. Made: 14.03.94. Laid: 14.03.94. Coming into force: 05.04.94. Effect: 1970 c. 9 amended. Territorial extent & classification: E/W/NI. General. – 6p. – 0 11 043728 4 *£1.55*

The Local Currency Elections Regulations 1994 No. 3230. Enabling power: *Finance Act 1993, ss. 93 (1) (6), 94 (1) (2) (3) (11), 95 (1) (2) (3).* Issued: 16.01.95. Made: 15.12.94. Laid: 16.12.94. Coming into force: 23.03.95. Effect: None. Territorial extent & classification: GB. General. – 6p. – 0 11 043905 8 *£1.55*

The Overseas Life Assurance Fund (Amendment) Order 1994 No. 3278. Enabling power: *Income and Corporation Taxes Act 1988, sch. 19AA, para. 1 (2).* Issued: 20.01.95. Made: 19.12.94. Laid: 20.12.94. Coming into force: 10.01.95. Effect: 1988 c. 1 amended. Territorial extent & classification: GB. General. – 4p. – 0 11 043915 5 *£1.10*

The Private Medical Insurance (Disentitlement to Tax Relief and Approved Benefits) Regulations 1994 No. 1518. Enabling power: *Finance Act 1989, ss. 54 (7) (8), 55 (2A), 56 (3).* Issued: 21.06.94. Made: 08.06.94. Laid: 09.06.94. Coming into force: 01.07.94. Effect: S.I. 1989/2389; 1992/1619 revoked. Territorial extent & classification: GB. General. – 6p. – 0 11 044518 X *£1.55*

The Private Medical Insurance (Tax Relief) (Amendment) Regulations 1994 No. 1527. Enabling power: *Finance Act 1989, ss. 54 (4), 57.* Issued: 24.06.94. Made: 09.06.94. Laid: 09.06.94. Coming into force: 01.07.94. Effect: S.I. 1989/2387 amended. Territorial extent & classification: GB. General. – 6p. – 0 11 044527 9 *£1.55*

The Retirement Benefits Schemes (Indexation of Earnings Cap) Order 1994 No. 3009. Enabling power: *Income and Corporation Taxes Act 1988, s. 590C (6).* Issued: 08.12.94. Made: 29.11.94. Coming into force: 06.04.95. Effect: 1988 c. 1 amended. Territorial extent & classification: GB. General. – 2p. – 0 11 043293 2 *£0.65*

The Special Commissioners (Jurisdiction and Procedure) Regulations 1994 No. 1811. Enabling power: *Taxes Management Act 1970, ss. 46A, 56B to 56D.* Issued: 14.07.94. Made: 06.07.94. Laid: 14.07.94. Coming into force: 01.09.94. Effect: None. Territorial extent & classification: E/W. General. – 16p. – 0 11 044811 1 *£3.20*

Price/availability are liable to change without notice

The Taxes (Interest Rate) (Amendment No. 2) Regulations 1994 No. 1567. Enabling power: *Finance Act 1989, s. 178 & Income and Corporation Taxes Act 1988, s. 160 (5)*. Issued: 30.06.94. Made: 14.06.94. Laid: 15.06.94. Coming into force: 06.07.94. Effect: S.I. 1989/1297 amended. Territorial extent & classification: GB. General. – 2p. – 0 11 044567 8 £0.65

The Taxes (Interest Rate) (Amendment No. 3) Regulations 1994 No. 2657. Enabling power: *Finance Act 1989, s. 178*. Issued: 24.10.94. Made: 11.10.94. Laid: 12.10.94. Coming into force: 06.11.94. Effect: None. Territorial extent & classification: GB. General. – 2p. – 0 11 045657 2 £0.65

The Taxes (Interest Rate) (Amendment) Regulations 1994 No. 1307. Enabling power: *Finance Act 1989, s. 178 & Income and Corporation Taxes Act 1988, s. 160 (5)*. Issued: 26.05.94. Made: 13.05.94. Laid: 16.05.94. Coming into force: 06.06.94. Effect: S.I. 1989/1297 amended. Territorial extent & classification: GB. General. – 2p. – 0 11 044307 1 £0.65

INDUSTRIAL AND PROVIDENT SOCIETIES

The Industrial and Provident Societies (Amendment of Fees) Regulations 1994 No. 660. Enabling power: *Industrial and Provident Societies Act 1965, ss. 70 (1), 71 (1)*. Issued: 08.04.94. Made: 08.03.94. Laid: 09.03.94. Coming into force: 01.04.94. Effect: S.I. 1965/1995 amended & S.I. 1993/549 revoked. Territorial extent & classification: GB. General. – 4p. – 0 11 043660 1 £1.10

The Industrial and Provident Societies (Credit Unions) (Amendment of Fees) Regulations 1994 No. 658. Enabling power: *Industrial and Provident Societies Act 1965, ss. 70 (1), 71 (1)*. Issued: 08.04.94. Made: 08.03.94. Laid: 09.03.94. Coming into force: 01.04.94. Effect: S.I. 1979/937 amended & S.I. 1993/548 revoked. Territorial extent & classification: GB. General. – 4p. – 0 11 043658 X £1.10

The Industrial and Provident Societies (Increase in Shareholding Limit) Order 1994 No. 341. Enabling power: *Industrial and Provident Societies Act 1975, s. 2*. Issued: 01.03.94. Made: 15.02.94. Laid: 18.02.94. Coming into force: 15.03.94. Effect: None. Territorial extent & classification: E/W/S. General. – 4p. – 0 11 043341 6 £1.10

INDUSTRIAL DEVELOPMENT

The Scottish Development Agency Dissolution Order 1994 No. 1976 (S. 89). Enabling power: *Enterprise and New Towns (Scotland) Act 1990, s. 23 (3)*. Issued: 29.07.94. Made: 20.07.94. Coming into force: 29.07.94. Effect: None. Territorial extent & classification: S. General. – 2p. – 0 11 044976 2 £0.65

INDUSTRIAL TRIBUNALS

The Industrial Tribunals (Constitution and Rules of Procedure) (Amendment) Regulations 1994 No. 536. Enabling power: *Employment Protection (Consolidation) Act 1978, ss. 128 (1), 154 (3), sch. 9, paras. 1, 1A, 1B*. Issued: 09.03.94. Made: 03.03.94. Laid: 09.03.94. Coming into force: 01.04.94. Effect: S.I. 1993/2687 amended. Territorial extent & classification: E/W. General. – 2p. – 0 11 043536 2 £0.65

The Industrial Tribunals (Constitution and Rules of Procedure) (Scotland) (Amendment) Regulations 1994 No. 538. Enabling power: *Employment Protection (Consolidation) Act 1978, ss. 128 (1), 154 (3), sch. 9, paras. 1, 1A, 1B*. Issued: 09.03.94. Made: 03.03.94. Laid: 09.03.94. Coming into force: 01.04.94. Effect: S.I. 1993/2688 amended. Territorial extent & classification: S. General. – 2p. – 0 11 043538 9 £0.65

The Industrial Tribunals Extension of Jurisdiction (England and Wales) Order 1994 No. 1623. Enabling power: *Employment (Consolidation) Act 1978, ss. 131 (1) (4A) (5) (5A), 154 (3)*. Issued: 15.07.94. Made: 11.07.94. Laid: 10.05.94. Coming into force: 12.07.94. Effect: None. Draft ISBN 0110459040 previously published 12.05.94. will be superseded by this SI. Territorial extent & classification: E/W. General. – 4p. – 0 11 044623 2 £1.10

The Industrial Tribunals Extension of Jurisdiction (Scotland) Order 1994 No. 1624. Enabling power: *Employment Protection (Consolidation) Act 1978, ss. 131 (1) (4A) (5) (5A), 154 (3)*. Issued: 15.07.94. Made: 11.07.94. Coming into force: 12.07.94. Effect: None. Draft SI ISBN 0110459032 previously published 10.05.94. will be superseded by this SI. Territorial extent & classification: S. General. – 4p. – 0 11 044624 0 £1.10

INHERITANCE TAX

The Double Taxation Relief (Taxes on Estates of Deceased Persons and Inheritances) (Switzerland) Order 1994 No. 3214. Enabling power: *Inheritance Tax Act 1984, s. 158*. Issued: 21.12.94. Made: 14.12.94. Laid: 20.07.94. Coming into force: Per art. 15. Effect: None. Supersedes Draft ISBN 0110459431 published 20.07.94. Territorial extent & classification: GB. General. – 10p. – 0 11 043716 0 £2.40

The General and Special Commissioners (Amendment of Enactments) Regulations 1994 No. 1813. Enabling power: *Taxes Management Act 1970, ss. 46A, 56B*. Issued: 14.07.94. Made: 06.07.94. Laid: 14.07.94. Coming into force: 01.09.94. Effect: 1970 c. 9; 1972 c. 41; 1975 c. 22; 1984 c. 43, 51; 1988 c. 1; 1988 c. 39; 1989 c. 26; 1994 c. 9 & S.I. 1959/452; 1967/149; 1986/1711; 1989/421; 1990/627; 1991/851; 1992/511; 1993/415, 744; 1994/728 amended & S.I. 1987/1422 revoked. Territorial extent & classification: E/W. General. – 12p. – 0 11 044813 8 £2.80

The Inheritance Tax (Indexation) Order 1994 No. 3011. Enabling power: *Inheritance Tax Act 1984, s. 8 (4)*. Issued: 08.12.94. Made: 29.11.94. Coming into force: 06.04.95. Effect: 1984 c. 51 amended. Territorial extent & classification: GB. General. – 2p. – 0 11 043297 5 £0.65

The Special Commissioners (Jurisdiction and Procedure) Regulations 1994 No. 1811. Enabling power: *Taxes Management Act 1970, ss. 46A, 56B to 56D*. Issued: 14.07.94. Made: 06.07.94. Laid: 14.07.94. Coming into force: 01.09.94. Effect: None. Territorial extent & classification: E/W. General. – 16p. – 0 11 044811 1 £3.20

The Taxes (Interest Rate) (Amendment No. 2) Regulations 1994 No. 1567. Enabling power: *Finance Act 1989, s. 178 & Income and Corporation Taxes Act 1988, s. 160 (5).* Issued: 30.06.94. Made: 14.06.94. Laid: 15.06.94. Coming into force: 06.07.94. Effect: S.I. 1989/1297 amended. Territorial extent & classification: GB. General. – 2p. – 0 11 044567 8 *£0.65*

The Taxes (Interest Rate) (Amendment No. 3) Regulations 1994 No. 2657. Enabling power: *Finance Act 1989, s. 178.* Issued: 24.10.94. Made: 11.10.94. Laid: 12.10.94. Coming into force: 06.11.94. Effect: None. Territorial extent & classification: GB. General. – 2p. – 0 11 045657 2 *£0.65*

The Taxes (Interest Rate) (Amendment) Regulations 1994 No. 1307. Enabling power: *Finance Act 1989, s. 178 & Income and Corporation Taxes Act 1988, s. 160 (5).* Issued: 26.05.94. Made: 13.05.94. Laid: 16.05.94. Coming into force: 06.06.94. Effect: S.I. 1989/1297 amended. Territorial extent & classification: GB. General. – 2p. – 0 11 044307 1 *£0.65*

INJURIES IN WAR COMPENSATION

The Injuries in War (Shore Employments) Compensation (Amendment) Scheme 1994 No. 1012. Enabling power: *Injuries in War Compensation Act 1914 (session 2), s. 1.* Issued: 12.04.94. Made: 30.03.94. Coming into force: 11.04.94. Effect: 1914 c. 18 (5 & 6 Geo. 5) amended. Territorial extent & classification: GB. General. – 2p. – 0 11 044012 9 *£0.65*

INSIDER DEALING

The Insider Dealing (Securities and Regulated Markets) Order 1994 No. 187. Enabling power: *Criminal Justice Act 1993, ss. 54 (1), 60 (1), 62 (1), 64 (3).* Issued: 09.02.94. Made: 01.02.94. Coming into force: 01.03.94. Effect: None. Supersedes Draft ISBN 0110358740 previously published on 16.12.93. With correction slip dated February 1994. Territorial extent & classification: GB. General. – 4p. – 0 11 043187 1 *£1.10*

The Traded Securities (Disclosure) Regulations 1994 No. 188. Enabling power: *European Communities Act 1972, s. 2 (2).* Issued: 09.02.94. Made: 01.02.94. Laid: 01.02.94. Coming into force: 01.03.94. Effect: None. Territorial extent & classification: GB. General. 4p. 0 11 043188 X *£1.10*

INSOLVENCY

The Civil Courts (Amendment No. 4) Order 1994 No. 2893. Enabling power: *Supreme Court Act 1981, s. 99 (1) & County Court Act 1984, ss. 2 (1), 26 & Insolvency Act 1986, ss. 117, 374.* Issued: 25.11.94. Made: 14.11.94. Laid: 14.11.94. Coming into force: 05.12.94, except for art. 5 (a). 09.01.95, for art. 5 (a). Effect: S.I. 1983/713 amended. Territorial extent & classification: E/W. General. – 2p. – 0 11 043095 6 *£0.65*

The Insolvent Partnerships Order 1994 No. 2421. Enabling power: *Insolvency Act 1986, s. 420 (1) (2) & Company Directors Disqualification Act 1986, s. 21 (2).* Issued: 10.10.94. Made: 13.09.94. Laid: 16.09.94. Coming into force: 01.12.94. Effect: 1986 c. 45, 46 amended & S.I. 1986/2142 revoked. Territorial extent & classification: E/W. General. – 140p. – 0 11 045421 9 *£12.30*

INSOLVENCY: COMPANIES

The Insolvency Fees (Amendment) Order 1994 No. 2541. Enabling power: *Insolvency Act 1986, ss. 414, 415.* Issued: 10.10.94. Made: 28.09.94. Laid: 30.09.94. Coming into force: 24.10.94. Effect: S.I. 1986/2030 amended. Territorial extent & classification: E/W. General. –4p. – 0 11 045541 X *£1.10*

The Insolvency Regulations 1994 No. 2507. Enabling power: *S.I. 1986/1925, rule 12.1 & Insolvency Act 1986, ss. 411, 412, sch. 8, para. 27, sch. 9, para. 30.* Issued: 07.10.94. Made: 26.09.94. Laid: 28.09.94. Coming into force: 24.10.94. Effect: S.I. 1986/1994; 1987/1959; 1988/1739; 1991/380 revoked. Territorial extent & classification: E/W. General. – 20p. – 0 11 045507 X *£3.70*

INSOLVENCY: INDIVIDUALS, ENGLAND AND WALES

The Insolvency Fees (Amendment) Order 1994 No. 2541. Enabling power: *Insolvency Act 1986, ss. 414, 415.* Issued: 10.10.94. Made: 28.09.94. Laid: 30.09.94. Coming into force: 24.10.94. Effect: S.I. 1986/2030 amended. Territorial extent & classification: E/W. General. –4p. – 0 11 045541 X *£1.10*

The Insolvency Regulations 1994 No. 2507. Enabling power: *S.I. 1986/1925, rule 12.1 & Insolvency Act 1986, ss. 411, 412, sch. 8, para. 27, sch. 9, para. 30.* Issued: 07.10.94. Made: 26.09.94. Laid: 28.09.94. Coming into force: 24.10.94. Effect: S.I. 1986/1994; 1987/1959; 1988/1739; 1991/380 revoked. Territorial extent & classification: E/W. General. – 20p. – 0 11 045507 X *£3.70*

INSURANCE

The Auditors (Insurance Companies Act 1982) Regulations 1994 No. 449. Enabling power: *Insurance Companies Act 1982, s. 21A (1).* Issued: 08.03.94. Made: 22.02.94. Laid: 14.01.94. (Commons) 17.01.94. (Lords) Coming into force: 01.07.94. Effect: None. Supersedes Draft ISBN 0110458648. Territorial extent & classification: GB. General. – 4p. – 0 11 043449 8 *£1.10*

The Employers' Liability (Compulsory Insurance) Exemption (Amendment) Regulations 1994 No. 520. Enabling power: *Employers' Liability (Compulsory Insurance) Act 1969, ss. 3 (1) (c), 6.* Issued: 07.03.94. Made: 02.03.94. Laid: 07.03.94. Coming into force: 01.04.94. Effect: S.I. 1971/1933 amended. Territorial extent & classification: E/W/S. General. – 2p. – 0 11 043520 6 *£0.65*

Price/availability are liable to change without notice

The Employers' Liability (Compulsory Insurance) General (Amendment) Regulations 1994 No.3301. Enabling power: *Employers' Liability (Compulsory Insurance) Act 1969, ss. 1 (2), 6.* Issued: 06.01.95. Made: 21.12.94. Laid: 22.12.94. Coming into force: 01.01.95. Effect: S.I. 1971/1117 amended. Territorial extent & classification: E/W/S. General. – 2p. – 0 11 043873 6 £0.65

The Insurance Brokers Registration Council (Code of Conduct) Approval Order 1994 No.2569. Enabling power: *Insurance Brokers (Registration) Act 1977, ss. 27 (1), 28 (1).* Issued: 13.10.94. Made: 01.10.94. Laid: 06.10.94. Coming into force: 21.11.94. Effect: S.I. 1978/1394 revoked. Territorial extent & classification: GB. General. – 6p. – 0 11 045569 X £1.55

The Insurance Brokers Registration Council (Registration and Enrolment) (Amendment) Rules Approval Order 1994 No.3069. Enabling power: *Insurance Brokers (Registration) Act 1977, ss. 27 (1), 28 (1).* Issued: 13.12.94. Made: 01.12.94. Laid: 06.12.94. Coming into force: 01.01.95. Effect: S.I. 1991/2566 revoked. Territorial extent & classification: GB. General. –2p. – 0 11 043366 1 £0.65

The Insurance Companies (Accounts and Statements) (Amendment) Regulations 1994 No.1515. Enabling power: *European Communities Act 1972 s. 2 (2) & Insurance Companies Act 1982, ss. 17, 18, 20, 21, 96 (1), 97.* Issued: 13.07.94. Made: 07.06.94. Laid: 08.06.94. Coming into force: 01.07.94. Effect: S.I. 1983/1811 amended. Territorial extent & classification: GB. General. – 16p. – 0 11 044515 5 £3.20

The Insurance Companies (Amendment No. 2) Regulations 1994 No. 3133. Enabling power: *European Communities Act 1972, s. 2 (2) & Insurance Companies Act 1982, ss. 5 (1) (a), 17, 18, 20, 21, 32 (1) (2) (3), 33 (1), 35 (1), 62 (1B), 78 (1) (2) (5), 90, 96 (1), 97.* Issued: 05.01.95. Made: 07.12.94. Laid: 08.12.94. Coming into force: 31.12.94. Effect: S.I. 1983/1811; 1994/1516 amended. Territorial extent & classification: GB. General. – Makes amendments consequential to the amendments made to the Insurance Companies Act 1982 by the Insurance Companies (Amendment) Regulations 1994 which implement the Agreement on the European Economic Area as regards the application of DIR 92/49 [OJ L228 1992] & DIR 92/96 [OJ L360 1992] to Austria, Iceland, Norway & Sweden & in the case of DIR 92/96 to Finland & other related amendments. –12p. – 0 11 043822 1 £2.40

The Insurance Companies (Amendment) Regulations 1994 No. 3132. Enabling power: *European Communities Act 1972, s. 2 (2).* Issued: 05.01.95. Made: 07.12.94. Laid: 08.12.94. Coming into force: 30.12.94. Effect: 1982 c. 50; 1987 c. 22; S.I. 1994/1696 amended. Territorial extent & classification: GB. General. – Implements the Agreement on the European Economic Area (Cm 2073) as regards the application of DIR 92/49 [OJ L228 1992] & DIR 92/96 [OJ L360 1992]. – 10p. – 0 11 043821 3 £2.40

The Insurance Companies Regulations 1994 No. 1516. Enabling power: *European Communities Act 1972, s. 2 (2) & Insurance Companies Act 1982, ss. 2 (5), 5 (1) (a), 7 (6), 9 (1) (b) (c) (7), 15 (6), 32 (1) (2) (3), 33 (1), 35 (1), 60 (1), 61 (1), 62 (1), 72 (1) (2), 74 (1) (2), 75 (2) (5), 78 (1) (2) (5) (6), 84 (1), 86, 90, 96 (1), 97.* Issued: 15.07.94. Made: 07.06.94. Laid: 08.06.94. Coming into force: 01.07.94. Effect: 1985 c. 6; S.I. 1983/224 amended & S.I. 1981/1654; 1982/675; 1983/396; 1985/1419; 1988/673; 1990/1160; 1990/1181; 1991/1999, 2511; 1992/445; 1993/1092 revoked. Territorial extent & classification: GB. General. – Consolidates S.I. 1981/1654 as amended with further amendments, principally to implement DIR 92/49 (L 228/92); 92/96 (L 360/92) - "third directives" pursuant to DIR 87/343 (L 185/87), 88/357 (L 172/88), 90/619 (L 330/90). – 101p. – 0 11 044516 3 £10.35

The Insurance Companies (Third Insurance Directives) Regulations 1994 No. 1696. Enabling power: *European Communities Act 1972, s. 2 (2).* Issued: 07.07.94. Made: 27.06.94. Laid: 24.05.94. Coming into force: 01.07.94. Effect: 1951 c. 20 (NI); 1959 c. 25 (NI); 1960 c. 2 (NI); 1974 c. 47; 1975 c. 75; 1981 c. 20; 1982 c. 50; 1984 c. 35; 1985 c. 6, 68, 69; 1986 c. 60; 1987 c. 22, 26, 38, 41; 1989 c. 40; 1990 c. 40, 41; 1991 c. 24; 1993 c. 8; S.I. 1975/1023; 1978/1358; 1981/156 (NI.3); 1984/1555; 1986/1032 (NI. 6), 1877; 1987/1388 (S. 104), 1389 (S. 105), 1850 (S. 128); 1988/645; 1992/2649, 2890; 1993/1933, 3252; S.R. 1979/195; 1992/547 amended & S.I. 1990/1207 revoked. Supersedes Draft SI ISBN 0110459389 published 16.06.94. Territorial extent & classification: GB. General. – Give effect to DIR 92/49 (L 228/92), 92/96 (L 360/92). – 80p. – 0 11 044696 8 £8.70

The Insurance (Fees) Regulations 1994 No. 643. Enabling power: *Insurance Companies Act 1982, ss. 94A, 96 (1), 97.* Issued: 05.04.94. Made: 07.03.94. Laid: 10.03.94. Coming into force: 01.04.94. Effect: S.I. 1993/601 revoked. Territorial extent & classification: GB. General. –6p. – 0 11 043643 1 £1.55

INSURANCE PREMIUM TAX

The Finance Act 1994 (Appointed Day) Order 1994 No. 1773 (C. 32). Enabling power: *Finance Act 1994, ss. 61, 74 (1). Bringing into operation various provisions of the 1994 act on 01.10.94.* Issued: 13.07.94. Made: 06.07.94. Effect: None. Territorial extent & classification: GB. General. – 2p. – 0 11 044773 5 £0.65

The Insurance Premium Tax (Prescribed Rates of Interest) Order 1994 No. 1819. Enabling power: *Finance Act 1994, s. 74 (1), sch. 7, paras. 21 (5), 22 (2).* Issued: 19.07.94. Made: 08.07.94. Laid: 11.07.94. Coming into force: 01.10.94. Effect: None. Territorial extent & classification: GB. General. – 2p. – 0 11 044819 7 £0.65

The Insurance Premium Tax Regulations 1994 No. 1774. Enabling power: *Finance Act 1994, ss. 53 (6), 54, 55 (1) to (8), 57 (15), 58 (2) (4), 62 (1) (3) to (7), 65 (1) to (3) (5) (7) to (13), 68 (1) to (11), 74 (2) (7) (8), sch. 7, paras. 1 (1) to (3), 7 (7) (8), 8 (6).* Issued: 14.07.94. Made: 06.07.94. Laid: 07.07.94. Coming into force: 01.08.94. Effect: None. Territorial extent & classification: GB. General. – 28p. – 0 11 044774 3 £4.70

The Insurance Premium Tax (Taxable Insurance Contracts) Order 1994 No. 1698. Enabling power: *Finance Act 1994, ss. 71 (1) to (4), 74 (7) (8).* Issued: 26.07.94. Made: 29.06.94. Laid: 30.06.94. Coming into force: 01.10.94. Effect: 1994 c. 9 amended. Supersedes SI of same number & ISBN published on 13.07.94. Territorial extent & classification: GB. General. –8p. – 0 11 044698 4 £1.95

Price/availability are liable to change without notice

INTELLIGENCE SERVICES

The Intelligence Services Act 1994 (Channel Islands) Order 1994 No. 2955. Enabling power: *Security Services Act 1989, s. 7 (4) & Intelligence Services Act 1994, s. 12 (4)*. Issued: 05.12.94. Made: 24.11.94. Coming into force: 15.12.94. Effect: S.I. 1990/249 revoked. Territorial extent & classification: Guernsey & Jersey. General. – 2p. – 0 11 043209 6 £0.65

The Intelligence Services Act 1994 (Commencement) Order 1994 No. 2734 (C. 60). Enabling power: *Intelligence Services Act 1994, s. 12 (2)*. Bringing into operation various provisions of the 1994 act on 02.11.94, 15.12.94. Issued: 31.10.94. Made: 15.10.94. Effect: None. Territorial extent & classification: GB. General. – 2p. – 0 11 045734 X £0.65

INTERNATIONAL IMMUNITIES AND PRIVILEGES

The European Molecular Biology Laboratory (Immunities and Privileges) Order 1994 No. 1890. Enabling power: *International Organisations Act 1968, s. 1*. Issued: 29.07.94. Made: 19.07.94. Laid: 21.06.94. Coming into force: In accord. with art. 1 (1). Effect: S.I. 1974/1254 revoked. Territorial extent & classification: GB. General. – 6p. – 0 11 044890 1 £1.55

ISLE OF MAN

The Excise Duty (Amendment of the Isle of Man Act 1979) Order 1994 No. 3041. Enabling power: *Isle of Man Act 1979, s. 1 (2)*. Issued: 08.12.94. Made: 28.11.94. Laid: 30.11.94. Coming into force: 01.01.95. Effect: 1979 c. 58 amended. Territorial extent & classification: GB. General. – 2p. – 0 11 043321 1 £0.65

JUDGMENTS

The Reciprocal Enforcement of Foreign Judgments (Australia) Order 1994 No. 1901. Enabling power: *Administration of Justice Act 1920, s. 14 (2)*. Issued: 29.07.94. Made: 19.07.94. Coming into force: In accord. with art. 1. Effect: S.I. 1984/129 amended & S.I.1955/559 revoked. Territorial extent & classification: GB. General. – 8p. – 0 11 044901 0 £1.95

JUSTICES OF THE PEACE, ENGLAND AND WALES

The Petty Sessional Divisions (Essex) Order 1994 No. 2760. Enabling power: *Justices of the Peace Act 1979, s. 3 (a) (5)*. Made: 21.10.94. Coming into force: 01.01.96. exc. sch. para. 2 shall come into force forthwith Effect: None. – *Unpublished*

The Petty Sessional Divisions (Gloucestershire) Order 1994 No. 719. Enabling power: *Justices of the Peace Act 1979, s. 23 (3) (a) (5)*. Made: 03.03.94. Coming into force: 03.03.94. for sch., para. 2 & 01.07.94 for all other purposes Effect: None. – *Unpublished*

The Petty Sessional Divisions (Hampshire) Order 1994 No. 1717. Enabling power: *Justices of the Peace Act 1979, s. 23 (3) (a) (5)*. Made: 28.06.94. Coming into force: 01.01.95. Effect: None. – *Unpublished*

The Petty Sessional Divisions (Hertfordshire) Order 1994 No. 1106. Enabling power: *Justices of the Peace Act 1979, s. 23 (3) (a) (5)*. Made: 18.04.94. Coming into force: In accord with art. 1. Effect: None. – *Unpublished*

The Petty Sessional Divisions (Lancashire) Order 1994 No. 946. Enabling power: *Justices of the Peace Act 1979, s. 23 (3) (a) (5)*. Made: 25.03.94. Coming into force: 25.03.94. for sch. 3, para.2 & 01.04.94. for all other purposes. Effect: None. – *Unpublished*

The Petty Sessional Divisions (Oxfordshire) Order 1994 No. 1208. Enabling power: *Justices of the Peace Act 1979, s. 23 (3 (a) (5)*. Made: 28.04.94. Coming into force: 28.04.94. for sch. 3, para. 2 & 01.07.94. for all other purposes. Effect: None. – *Unpublished*

The Petty Sessional Divisions (Suffolk) Order 1994 No. 480. Enabling power: *Justices of the Peace Act 1979, s. 23 (3) (a) (5)*. Made: 24.02.94. Coming into force: 24.02.94. for sch., para. 2 & 01.01.95. for all other purposes. Effect: None. – *Unpublished*

LAND CHARGES

The Land Charges (Amendment) Rules 1994 No. 287. Enabling power: *Land Charges Act 1972, ss 10 (1) (6), 16 (1), 17 (1)*. Issued: 18.02.94. Made: 28.01.94. Coming into force: 28.03.94. Effect: S.I. 1974/1286 amended. Territorial extent & classification: E/W. General. – 2p. – 0 11 043287 8 £0.65

The Land Charges Fees (Amendment) Rules 1994 No. 286. Enabling power: *Land Charges Act 1972, ss. 9 (1), 10 (2), 16 (1), 17 (1)*. Issued: 18.02.94. Made: 08.02.94. Coming into force: 28.03.94. Effect: S.I. 1990/327 amended. Territorial extent & classification: E/W. General. – 2p. – 0 11 043286 X £0.65

LAND DRAINAGE

The Alteration of Boundaries of the Newark Area and Upper Witham Internal Drainage Districts Order 1994 No. 310. Enabling power: *Land Drainage Act 1991, s. 3 (5) (7)*. Issued: 09.03.94. Made: 23.12.93. Coming into force: 09.02.94. Effect: None. Territorial extent & classification: E. Local. – 4p. – 0 11 043310 6 £1.10

The Environmental Assessment (Scotland) Amendment Regulations 1994 No. 2012 (S. 91). Enabling power: *European Communities Act 1972, s. 2 (2) & Town and Country Planning (Scotland) Act 1972, s. 26B.* Issued: 09.08.94. Made: 19.07.94. Laid: 29.07.94. Coming into force: 19.08.94. Effect: S.I. 1988/1221; 1984 c. 54 amended. Territorial extent & classification: S. General. – 8p. – 0 11 045012 4 £1.95

The National Rivers Authority (Alteration of Boundaries of the South Holland Internal Drainage District) Order 1993 No. 723. Enabling power: *Land Drainage Act 1991, s. 3 (5) (7).* Issued: 13.04.94. Made: 06.04.94. Coming into force: 07.03.94. Effect: None. Territorial extent & classification: E. Local. – 4p. – 0 11 043723 3 £1.10

The National Rivers Authority (Severn-Trent and Anglian Regional Defence Committees Areas) (Boundaries) Order 1994 No. 245. Enabling power: *Water Resources Act 1991, sch. 3, para. 1 (1) (3).* Issued: 21.02.94. Made: 01.02.94. Laid: 07.02.94. Coming into force: 01.04.94. Effect: None. Territorial extent & classification: E/W. Local. – 2p. – 0 11 043245 2 £0.65

The Reconstitution of the Buckingham Internal Drainage Board Order 1994 No. 2851. Enabling power: *Land Drainage Act 1991, s. 3 (5) (7).* Issued: 29.11.94. Made: 05.09.94. Coming into force: 01.11.94. Effect: S.I. 1960/689 amended. Territorial extent & classification: E. Local. – 4p. – 0 11 043151 0 £1.10

The Reconstitution of the Langport District Drainage Board Order 1994 No. 1411. Enabling power: *Land Drainage Act 1991, s. 3 (5) (7).* Issued: 27.06.94. Made: 30.03.94. Coming into force: 23.05.94. Effect: None. Territorial extent & classification: E. Local. –4p. – 0 11 044411 6 £1.10

LANDLORD AND TENANT, ENGLAND AND WALES

The Agricultural Holdings (Units of Production) Order 1994 No. 2183. Enabling power: *Agricultural Holdings Act 1986, sch. 6, para. 4.* Issued: 20.09.94. Made: 05.08.94. Laid: 22.08.94. Coming into force: 12.09.94. Effect: S.I. 1993/2037 revoked. Territorial extent & classification: E/W. General. – 6p. – 0 11 045183 X £1.55

The Rent Act 1977 (Forms etc.) (Welsh Forms and Particulars) (Amendment) Regulations 1994 No.725. Enabling power: *Rent Act 1977, ss. 66 (2), 67 (2), 67A (5), 73 (3), 74 (1) & Welsh Language Act 1993, s. 26 (3).* Issued: 06.04.94. Made: 10.03.94. Laid: 16.03.94. Coming into force: 06.04.94. Effect: S.I. 1993/1511 amended. This SI has been made in consequence of a defect in SI 1993/1511 & is being sent free of charge to all known recipients of the original. Territorial extent & classification: E/W. General. – 24p. – 0 11 043725 X £0.65

LAND REGISTRATION, ENGLAND AND WALES

The Land Registration Fees Order 1994 No. 1974. Enabling power: *Land Registration Act 1925, ss. 144, 145 & Public Offices Fees Act 1879, ss. 2, 3 & Finance Act 1990, s. 128.* Issued: 29.07.94. Made: 19.07.94. Coming into force: 03.10.94. Effect: S.I. 1993/3223 superseded. Territorial extent & classification: E/W. General. – 12p. – 0 11 044974 6 £2.80

The Registration (Execution of Deeds) Rules 1994 No. 1130. Enabling power: *Land Registration Act 1925, s. 144.* Issued: 29.04.94. Made: 21.04.94. Laid: 21.04.94. Coming into force: 16.05.94. Effect: S.R. & O. 1925/1093 amended. Territorial extent & classification: E/W. General. – 4p. – 0 11 044130 3 £1.10

LAND REGISTRATION, SCOTLAND

The Land Registration (Scotland) Act 1979 (Commencement No. 8) Order 1994 No. 2588 (C. 56) (S. 124). Enabling power: *Land Registration (Scotland) Act 1979, s. 30 (2). Bringing into operation various provisions of the 1979 act on 01.04.95.* Issued: 14.10.94. Made: 29.09.94. Effect: None. Territorial extent & classification: S. General. – 2p. – 0 11 045588 6 £0.65

LANDS TRIBUNAL

The Lands Tribunal for Scotland (Amendment) (Fees) Rules 1994 No. 497 (S. 19). Enabling power: *Lands Tribunal Act 1949, s. 3 (6) (12) (e).* Issued: 10.03.94. Made: 28.02.94. Coming into force: 01.04.94. Effect: S.I. 1971/218 amended & S.I. 1993/296 revoked. Territorial extent & classification: S. General. – 4p. – 0 11 043497 8 £1.10

LEGAL AID AND ADVICE, ENGLAND AND WALES

The Civil Legal Aid (Assessment of Resources) (Amendment) Regulations 1994 No. 806. Enabling power: *Legal Aid Act 1988, ss. 15 (1), 16, 34, 43.* Issued: 25.03.94. Made: 17.03.94. Laid: 21.03.94. Coming into force: 11.04.94. Effect: S.I. 1989/338 amended. Territorial extent & classification: E/W. General. – 2p. – 0 11 043806 X £0.65

The Civil Legal Aid (General) (Amendment) (No. 2) Regulations 1994 No. 1822. Enabling power: *Legal Aid Act 1988, ss. 16 (6), 34, 43.* Issued: 15.07.94. Made: 05.07.94. Laid: 11.07.94. Coming into force: 01.08.94. Effect: S.I. 1989/339 amended. Territorial extent & classification: E/W. General. – 8p. – 0 11 044822 7 £1.95

The Civil Legal Aid (General) (Amendment) Regulations 1994 No. 229. Enabling power: *Legal Aid Act 1988, ss. 31, 34, 43.* Issued: 16.02.94. Made: 02.02.94. Laid: 03.02.94. Coming into force: 25.02.94. Effect: S.I. 1989/339 amended. Territorial extent & classification: E/W. General. – 6p. – 0 11 043229 0 £1.55

The Legal Advice and Assistance (Amendment) (No. 2) Regulations 1994 No. 1823. Enabling power: *Legal Aid Act 1988, ss. 34, 43.* Issued: 15.07.94. Made: 05.07.94. Laid: 11.07.94. Coming into force: 01.08.94. Effect: S.I. 1989/340 amended. Territorial extent & classification: E/W. General. – 4p. – 0 11 044823 5 £1.10

The Legal Advice and Assistance (Amendment) Regulations 1994 No. 805. Enabling power: *Legal Aid Act 1988, ss. 34, 43*. Issued: 25.03.94. Made: 17.03.94. Laid: 21.03.94. Coming into force: 11.04.94. Effect: S.I. 1989/340 amended. Territorial extent & classification: E/W. General. – 2p. – 0 11 043805 1 £0.65

The Legal Advice and Assistance at Police Stations (Remuneration) (Amendment) (No. 2) Regulations 1994 No. 3303. Enabling power: *Legal Aid Act 1988, ss. 34, 43*. Issued: 12.01.95. Made: 19.12.94. Laid: 22.12.94. Coming into force: 01.02.95. Effect: S.I. 1989/342 amended. Territorial extent & classification: E/W. General. – 2p. – 0 11 043883 3 £0.65

The Legal Advice and Assistance at Police Stations (Remuneration) (Amendment) Regulations 1994 No. 1824. Enabling power: *Legal Aid Act 1988, ss. 34, 43*. Issued: 15.07.94. Made: 05.07.94. Laid: 11.07.94. Coming into force: 01.08.94. Effect: S.I. 1989/342 amended. Territorial extent & classification: E/W. General. – 2p. – 0 11 044824 3 £0.65

The Legal Aid in Civil Proceedings (Renumeration) Regulations 1994 No. 228. Enabling power: *Legal Aid Act 1988, ss. 31, 34, 43*. Issued: 16.02.94. Made: 02.02.94. Laid: 03.02.94. Coming into force: 25.02.94. Effect: None. Territorial extent & classification: E/W. General. – 4p. – 0 11 043228 2 £1.10

The Legal Aid in Criminal and Care Proceedings (Costs) (Amendment) (No. 2) Regulations 1994 No. 1825. Enabling power: *Legal Aid Act 1988, ss. 25 (2), 34, 43*. Issued: 15.07.94. Made: 05.07.94. Laid: 11.07.94. Coming into force: 01.08.94. Effect: S.I. 1989/343 amended. Territorial extent & classification: E/W. General. – 2p. – 0 11 044825 1 £0.65

The Legal Aid in Criminal and Care Proceedings (Costs) (Amendment) Regulations 1994 No.1477. Enabling power: *Legal Aid Act 1988, ss. 25 (2), 34, 43*. Issued: 13.06.94. Made: 03.06.94. Laid: 06.06.94. Coming into force: 29.06.94. Effect: S.I. 1989/343 amended. Territorial extent & classification: E/W. General. – 2p. – 0 11 044477 9 £0.65

The Legal Aid in Criminal and Care Proceedings (Costs) (Amendment) (No. 3) Regulations 1994 No. 2218. Enabling power: *Legal Aid Act 1988, ss. 25 (2), 34, 43*. Issued: 02.09.94. Made: 25.08.94. Laid: 02.09.94. Coming into force: 01.10.94. Effect: S.I. 1989/343 amended. With correction slip dated October 1994 Territorial extent & classification: E/W. General. –4p. – 0 11 045218 6 £1.10

The Legal Aid in Criminal and Care Proceedings (General) (Amendment) (No. 2) Regulations 1994 No. 3136. Enabling power: *Legal Aid Act 1988, s. 2, 34, 43*. Issued: 21.12.94. Made: 08.12.94. Laid: 09.12.94. Coming into force: 01.01.95. Effect: S.I. 1989/344 amended. Territorial extent & classification: E/W. General. – 4p. – 0 11 043514 1 £1.10

The Legal Aid in Criminal and Care Proceedings (General) (Amendment) Regulations 1994 No.807. Enabling power: *Legal Aid Act 1988, ss. 21 (5), 23, 34, 43*. Issued: 25.03.94. Made: 17.03.94. Laid: 21.03.94. Coming into force: 11.04.94. Effect: S.I. 1989/344 amended. Territorial extent & classification: E/W. General. – 2p. – 0 11 043807 8 £0.65

The Legal Aid in Family Proceedings (Remuneration) (Amendment) Regulations 1994 No.230. Enabling power: *Legal Aid Act 1988, ss. 31, 34, 43*. Issued: 16.02.94. Made: 02.02.94. Laid: 03.02.94. Coming into force: 25.02.94. Effect: S.I. 1991/2038 amended. Territorial extent & classification: E/W. General. – 4p. – 0 11 043230 4 £1.10

The Legal Aid (Scope) Regulations 1994 No. 2768. Enabling power: *Legal Aid Act 1988, ss. 8, 14, 43*. Issued: 07.11.94. Made: 28.10.94. Laid: 05.07.94. Coming into force: 01.11.94. Effect: 1988 c. 34 amended. Territorial extent & classification: E/W. General. –2p. – 0 11 045768 4 £0.65

LEGAL AID AND ADVICE, SCOTLAND

The Advice and Assistance (Assistance by Way of Representation) (Scotland) Amendment Regulations 1994 No. 1000 (S. 43). Enabling power: *Legal Aid (Scotland) Act 1986, ss. 9 (1) (2) (a) (c) (d) (3), 36 (1), 37 (1)*. Issued: 12.04.94. Made: 28.03.94. Laid: 11.03.94. Coming into force: 11.04.94. Effect: S.I. 1988/2290 amended. Territorial extent & classification: S. General. – 4p. – 0 11 044000 5 £1.10

The Advice and Assistance (Financial Conditions) (Scotland) Regulations 1994 No. 997 (S. 41). Enabling power: *Legal Aid (Scotland) Act 1986, ss. 11 (2), 36 (1) (2) (b), 37 (1)*. Issued: 12.04.94. Made: 28.03.94. Laid: 11.03.94. Coming into force: 11.04.94. Effect: S.I. 1993/971 revoked. Territorial extent & classification: S. General. – 2p. – 0 11 043997 X £0.65

The Advice and Assistance (Scotland) Amendment Regulations 1994 No. 1061 (S.57). Enabling power: *Legal Aid (Scotland) Act 1986, ss. 12 (3), 36 (1) (2a), 37 (1) (3), 42*. Issued: 22.04.94. Made: 12.04.94. Laid: 14.04.94. Coming into force: 05.05.94. Effect: S.I. 1987/382 amended. Territorial extent & classification: S. General. – 4p. – 0 11 044061 7 £1.10

The Civil Legal Aid (Financial Conditions) (Scotland) Regulations 1994 No. 998 (S. 42). Enabling power: *Legal Aid (Scotland) Act 1986, ss. 36 (1) (2) (b), 37 (1)*. Issued: 12.04.94. Made: 28.03.94. Laid: 11.03.94. Coming into force: 11.04.94. Effect: S.I. 1992/1586: 1993/1970 amended. Territorial extent & classification: S. General. – 2p. – 0 11 043998 8 £0.65

The Civil Legal Aid (Scotland) Amendment Regulations 1994 No. 1049 (S. 55). Enabling power: *Legal Aid (Scotland) Act 1986, ss. 17 (2B), 36 (1) (2) (a) (d) (h) (3) (e), 37 (1)*. Issued: 21.04.94. Made: 08.04.94. Laid: 14.04.94. Coming into force: 05.05.94. Effect: S.I. 1987/381; 1988/1171, 1891; 1990/631; 1992/753; 1993/535 amended. Territorial extent & classification: S. General. – 6p. – 0 11 044049 8 £1.55

Price/availability are liable to change without notice

The Civil Legal Aid (Scotland) (Fees) Amendment (No. 2) Regulations 1994 No. 1233 (S. 64). Enabling power: *Legal Aid (Scotland) Act 1986 ss. 33 (2) (a), 36 (1) (2) (a)*. Issued: 13.05.94. Made: 05.05.94. Laid: 06.05.94. Coming into force: 27.05.94. Effect: S.I. 1989/1490 amended. Territorial extent & classification: S. General. – 2p. – 0 11 044233 4 *£0.65*

The Civil Legal Aid (Scotland) (Fees) Amendment Regulations 1994 No. 1015 (S. 47). Enabling power: *Legal Aid (Scotland) Act 1986, ss. 33 (2) (a) (3), 36 (1) (2) (a)*. Issued: 15.04.94. Made: 31.03.94. Laid: 14.04.94. Coming into force: 05.05.94. Effect: S.I. 1989/1490; 1991/565; 1992/372 amended & S.I. 1990/1036; 1993/531 revoked. Territorial extent & classification: S. General. – 24p. – 0 11 044015 3 *£2.80*

The Criminal Legal Aid (Scotland) Amendment Regulations 1994 No. 1050 (S. 56). Enabling power: *Legal Aid (Scotland) Act 1986, s. 36 (1) (2) (a) (c)*. Issued: 21.04.94. Made: 08.04.94. Laid: 14.04.94. Coming into force: 05.05.94. Effect: S.I. 1987/307; 1988/1126 amended & S.I. 1993/532 revoked. Territorial extent & classification: S. General. – 4p. – 0 11 044050 1 *£1.10*

The Criminal Legal Aid (Scotland) (Fees) Amendment Regulations 1994 No. 1019 (S. 51). Enabling power: *Legal Aid (Scotland) Act 1986, s. 33 (2) (a) (3), 36 (1) (2) (a)*. Issued: 18.04.94. Made: 31.03.94. Laid: 14.04.94. Coming into force: 05.05.94. Effect: S.I. 1989/1491 amended & S.I. 1993/530 revoked. This SI has been printed to correct defects in SI 1993/530 & is being issued free of charge to all known recipients of that SI. Territorial extent & classification: S. General. – 2p. – 0 11 044019 6 *£0.65*

The Criminal Legal Aid (Scotland) (Prescribed Proceedings) Regulations 1994 No. 1001 (S. 44). Enabling power: *Legal Aid (Scotland) Act 1986, ss. 21 (2), 36 (1), 37 (1)*. Issued: 12.04.94. Made: 28.03.94. Laid: 11.03.94. Coming into force: 11.04.94. Effect: None. Territorial extent & classification: S. General. – 2p. – 0 11 044001 3 *£0.65*

The Legal Aid in Contempt of Court Proceedings (Scotland) Amendment Regulations 1994 No.1016 (S. 48). Enabling power: *Legal Aid (Scotland) Act 1986, s. 36 (1) (2) (a)*. Issued: 18.04.94. Made: 31.03.94. Laid: 14.04.94. Coming into force: 05.05.94. Effect: S.I. 1992/1227 amended & S.I. 1993/528 revoked. This SI has been printed to correct defects in SI 1993/528 & is being issued free of charge to all known recipients of that SI. Territorial extent & classification: S. General. – 2p. – 0 11 044016 1 *£0.65*

The Legal Aid in Contempt of Court Proceedings (Scotland) (Fees) Amendment Regulations 1994 No. 1018 (S. 50). Enabling power: *Legal Aid (Scotland) Act 1986, s. 33 (2) (a) (3), 36 (1) (2) (a)*. Issued: 18.04.94. Made: 31.03.93. Laid: 14.04.94. Coming into force: 05.05.94. Effect: S.I. 1992/1228 amended & S.I. 1993/529 revoked. This SI has been printed to correct defects in SI 1993/529 and is being issued free of charge to all known recipients of that SI. Territorial extent & classification: S. General. – 2p. – 0 11 044018 8 *£0.65*

The Legal Aid (Scotland) (Children) Amendment Regulations 1994 No. 1017 (S. 49). Enabling power: *Legal Aid (Scotland) Act 1986, s.36 (1) (2) (a)*. Issued: 14.04.94. Made: 31.03.94. Laid: 14.04.94. Coming into force: 05.05.94. Effect: S.I. 1987/384; 1993/534 amended. This SI has been made in consequence of a defect in SI 1993/534 (S.71) & is being sent free of charge to all known recipients of the original. Territorial extent & classification: S. General. – 2p. – 0 11 044017 X *£0.65*

LEGAL PROFESSION

The Solicitors (Disciplinary Proceedings) Rules 1994 No. 288. Enabling power: *Solicitors Act 1974, s. 46*. Issued: 17.02.94. Made: 21.01.94. Coming into force: 01.03.94. Effect: S.I. 1985/226 amended. Territorial extent & classification: E/W. General. – 20p. – 0 11 043288 6 *£3.70*

LEGAL SERVICES

The Commissioners for Oaths (Prescribed Bodies) Regulations 1994 No. 1380. Enabling power: *Courts and Legal Services Act 1990, ss. 113 (1) (6), 119 (1)*. Issued: 01.06.94. Made: 23.05.94. Laid: 25.05.94. Coming into force: 17.06.94. Effect: None. Territorial extent & classification: E/W. General. – 2p. – 0 11 044380 2 *£0.65*

LOCAL GOVERNMENT, ENGLAND AND WALES

The Accounts and Audit (Amendment) Regulations 1994 No. 3018. Enabling power: *Local Government Finance Act 1982, s. 23*. Issued: 05.12.94. Made: 29.11.94. Laid: 01.12.94. Coming into force: 22.12.94. Effect: S.I. 1983/1761 amended. Territorial extent & classification: E/W. General. – 4p. – 0 11 043270 3 *£1.10*

The Isle of Wight (Structural Change) Order 1994 No. 1210. Enabling power: *Local Government Act 1992, ss. 17, 26*. Issued: 06.05.94. Made: 30.04.94. Laid: 22.03.94. Coming into force: 01.05.94. Effect: None. Supersedes Draft ISBN 0110458893 previously published on 23.03.94. Territorial extent & classification: E. General. – 8p. – 0 11 044210 5 *£1.95*

The Local Authorities (Armorial Bearings) Order 1994 No. 1888. Enabling power: *Local Government Act 1972, s. 247*. Issued: 27.07.94. Made: 19.07.94. Coming into force: 20.07.94. Effect: None. Territorial extent & classification: E/W. Local. – 2p. – 0 11 044888 X *£0.65*

The Local Authorities (Capital Finance) (Amendment) Regulations 1994 No. 553. Enabling power: *Local Government and Housing Act 1989, s. 190 (1), sch. 3, para. 15 (1) (a)*. Issued: 11.03.94. Made: 04.03.94. Laid: 11.03.94. Coming into force: 01.04.94. Effect: S.I. 1990/432 amended. Territorial extent & classification: GB. General. – 2p. – 0 11 043553 2 *£0.65*

The Local Authorities (Capital Finance) (Rate of Discount for 1994/95) Regulations 1994 No.560. Enabling power: *Local Government and Housing Act 1989, s. 49 (2)*. Issued: 11.03.94. Made: 06.03.94. Laid: 11.03.94. Coming into force: 01.04.94. Effect: None. Territorial extent & classification: E/W. General. – 2p. – 0 11 043560 5 *£0.65*

Price/availability are liable to change without notice

The Local Authorities (Charges for Land Searches) Regulations 1994 No. 1885. Enabling power: *Local Government and Housing Act 1989, ss. 150, 152 (5).* Issued: 04.05.94. Made: 12.07.94. Coming into force: 13.07.94. Effect: None. Supersedes Draft ISBN 0110459008. Territorial extent & classification: E/W. General. – 2p. – 0 11 044885 5 *£0.65*

The Local Authorities (Goods and Services) (Public Bodies) (No. 2) Order 1994 No.1389. Enabling power: *Local Authorities (Goods and Services) Act 1970, s. 1 (5) (6).* Issued: 01.06.94. Made: 21.05.94. Laid: 01.06.94. Coming into force: 30.06.94. Effect: None. Territorial extent & classification: E/W. General. – 2p. – 0 11 044389 6 *£0.65*

The Local Authorities (Goods and Services) (Public Bodies) Order 1994 No. 37. Enabling power: *Local Authorities (Goods and Services) Act 1970, s. 1 (5) (6).* Issued: 03.02.94. Made: 17.01.94. Laid: 18.01.94. Coming into force: 08.02.94. Effect: None. Territorial extent & classification: W. General. – 2p. – 0 11 043037 9 *£0.65*

The Local Authorities (Members' Allowances) (Amendment) Regulations 1994 No. 615. Enabling power: *Local Government Act 1972, ss. 173, 175 (1A), 270 (1) & Local Government Act 1989, ss. 18, 190 (1).* Issued: 15.03.94. Made: 07.03.94. Laid: 11.03.94. Coming into force: 01.04.94. Effect: S.I. 1991/351 amended & S.I. 1993/545 revoked. Territorial extent & classification: E/W/S. General. – 4p. – 0 11 043615 6 *£1.10*

The Local Government Act 1988 (Competition) (Construction and Property Services) (England) Regulations 1994 No. 3166. Enabling power: *Local Government Act 1988, ss. 6 (3), 15 (6).* Issued: 19.12.94. Made: 12.12.94. Laid: 19.12.94. Coming into force: 09.01.95. Effect: None. Territorial extent & classification: E/W. General. – 4p. – 0 11 043434 X *£1.10*

The Local Government Act 1988 (Competition) (Defined Activities) (Construction and Property Services) Order 1994 No. 2888. Enabling power: *Local Government Act 1988, ss. 2 (3), 15 (7) (8).* Issued: 22.11.94. Made: 10.11.94. Coming into force: 11.11.94. Effect: None. Supersedes Draft ISBN 0110459571 published on 30.08.94. Territorial extent & classification: E/W/S. General. – 4p. – 0 11 043075 1 *£1.10*

The Local Government Act 1988 (Competition) (Defined Activities) (Housing Management) Order 1994 No. 1671. Enabling power: *Local Government Act 1988, ss. 2 (3), 15 (7) (8).* Issued: 30.06.94. Made: 22.06.94. Laid: 11.05.94. Coming into force: 23.06.94. Effect: 1988 c. 9 amended. Territorial extent & classification: E/W/S. General. – 4p. – 0 11 044671 2 *£1.10*

The Local Government Act 1988 (Competition) (Defined Activities) Order 1994 No. 2884. Enabling power: *Local Government Act 1988, s. 2 (3), 15 (7) (8).* Issued: 22.11.94. Made: 09.11.94. Laid: 14.06.94. Coming into force: 10.11.94. Effect: 1988 c. 9 amended. Territorial extent & classification: E/W/S. General. – 6p. – 0 11 043068 9 *£1.55*

The Local Government Act 1988 (Competition) (Housing Management) (England) Regulations 1994 No. 2297. Enabling power: *Local Government Act 1988, ss. 6 (3), 15 (6) (7).* Issued: 13.09.94. Made: 30.08.94. Laid: 13.09.94. Coming into force: 04.10.94. Effect: None. Territorial extent & classification: E. General. – 6p. – 0 11 045297 6 *£1.55*

The Local Government Act 1988 (Competition) (Legal Services) (England) Regulations 1994 No.3164. Enabling power: *Local Government Act 1988, ss. 6 (3), 15 (6).* Issued: 19.12.94. Made: 12.12.94. Laid: 19.12.94. Coming into force: 09.01.95. Effect: None. Territorial extent & classification: E/W. General. – 4p. – 0 11 043420 X *£1.10*

The Local Government Act 1988 (Defined Activities) (Competition) (Supervision of Parking, Management of Vehicles and Security Work) (England) Regulations 1994 No. 3165. Enabling power: *Local Government Act 1988, ss. 6 (3), 8 (1), 15 (6) (7).* Issued: 19.12.94. Made: 12.12.94. Laid: 19.12.94. Coming into force: 09.01.95. Effect: None. Territorial extent & classification: E/W. General. – 4p. – 0 11 043437 4 *£1.10*

The Local Government Act 1988 (Defined Activities) (Exemption) (Brighton Borough Council and East Yorkshire Borough Council) Order 1994 No. 1167. Enabling power: *Local Government Act 1988, ss. 2 (9), 15 (5).* Issued: 03.05.94. Made: 23.04.94. Laid: 03.05.94. Coming into force: 24.05.94. Effect: None. Territorial extent & classification: E/W. Local. – 4p. – 0 11 044167 2 *£1.10*

The Local Government Act 1988 (Defined Activities) (Exemption) (Broxtowe Borough Council and Harrogate Borough Council) Order 1994 No. 902. Enabling power: *Local Government Act 1988, ss. 2 (9), 15 (5).* Issued: 30.03.94. Made: 23.03.94. Laid: 30.03.94. Coming into force: 20.04.94. Effect: None. Territorial extent & classification: E/W. Local. – 2p. – 0 11 043902 3 *£0.65*

The Local Government Act 1988 (Defined Activities) (Exemption) (England) Order 1994 No.569. Enabling power: *Local Government Act 1988, ss. 2 (9), 15 (5).* Issued: 10.03.94. Made: 07.03.94. Laid: 10.03.94. Coming into force: 31.03.94. Effect: None. Territorial extent & classification: E/W. General. – 2p. – 0 11 043569 9 *£0.65*

The Local Government Act 1988 (Defined Activities) (Exemption) (Gateshead Borough Council) Order 1994 No. 2744. Enabling power: *Local Government Act 1988, ss. 2 (9), 15 (5).* Issued: 02.11.94. Made: 25.10.94. Laid: 02.11.94. Coming into force: 23.11.94. Effect: None. Territorial extent & classification: E/W. Local. – 2p. – 0 11 045744 7 *£0.65*

The Local Government Act 1988 (Defined Activities) (Exemption) (Gillingham Borough Council) Order 1994 No. 2154. Enabling power: *Local Government Act 1988, ss. 2 (9), 15 (5).* Issued: 24.08.94. Made: 15.08.94. Laid: 24.08.94. Coming into force: 14.09.94. Effect: None. Territorial extent & classification: E/W. Local. – 2p. – 0 11 045154 6 *£0.65*

The Local Government Act 1988 (Defined Activities) (Exemption) (Harlow District Council) Order 1994 No.15. Enabling power: *Local Government Act 1988, ss. 2 (9), 15 (5).* Issued: 14.01.94. Made: 10.01.94. Laid: 14.01.94. Coming into force: 04.02.94. Effect: None. Territorial extent & classification: E/W. Local. – 2p. – 0 11 043015 8 *£0.65*

Price/availability are liable to change without notice

LOCAL GOVERNMENT, ENGLAND AND WALES

The Local Government Act 1988 (Defined Activities) (Exemption) (Hastings Borough Council, Worthing Borough Council and Barnet London Borough Council) Order 1994 No. 3161. Enabling power: *Local Government Act 1988, ss. 2 (9), 15 (5)*. Issued: 14.12.94. Made: 08.12.94. Laid: 14.12.94. Coming into force: 04.01.95. Effect: None. With correction slip issued 10.01.95. Territorial extent & classification: E/W. Local. – 2p. – 0 11 043396 3 *£0.65*

The Local Government Act 1988 (Defined Activities) (Exemption) (South Norfolk District Council) Order 1994 No. 3189. Enabling power: *Local Government Act 1988, ss. 2 (9), 15 (5)*. Issued: 20.12.94. Made: 12.12.94. Laid: 20.12.94. Coming into force: 10.01.95. Effect: None. Territorial extent & classification: E/W. Local. – 2p. – 0 11 043467 6 *£0.65*

The Local Government Act 1988 (Defined Activities) (Exemption) (Southwark London Borough Council) Order 1994 No. 3190. Enabling power: *Local Government Act 1988, ss. 2 (9), 15 (5)*. Issued: 20.12.94. Made: 12.12.94. Laid: 20.12.94. Coming into force: 01.08.95. Effect: None. Territorial extent & classification: E/W. Local. – 2p. – 0 11 043466 8 *£0.65*

The Local Government Act 1988 (Defined Activities) (Exemption) (Tower Hamlets London Borough Council) Order 1994 No. 2196. Enabling power: *Local Government Act 1988, ss. 2 (9), 15 (5)*. Issued: 31.08.94. Made: 22.08.94. Laid: 31.08.94. Coming into force: 21.09.94. Effect: None. Territorial extent & classification: E/W. General. – 4p. – 0 11 045196 1 *£1.10*

The Local Government Act 1988 (Defined Activities) (Exemptions) (England & Wales) Order 1994 No. 2296. Enabling power: *Local Government Act 1988, ss. 2 (9), 15 (5)*. Issued: 13.09.94. Made: 01.09.94. Laid: 13.09.94. Coming into force: 04.10.94. Effect: S.I. 1988/1372, 1469 amended. Territorial extent & classification: E/W. General. – 2p. – 0 11 045296 8 *£0.65*

The Local Government Act 1988 (Defined Activities) (Exemptions) (Wales) Order 1994 No. 339. Enabling power: *:Local Government Act 1988, ss. 2 (9), 15 (5) (7)*. Issued: 05.04.94. Made: 14.02.94. Laid: 21.02.94. Coming into force: 01.04.94. Effect: None. Territorial extent & classification: W. General. – 4p. – 0 11 043339 4 *£1.10*

The Local Government Act 1992 (Commencement No. 4) Order 1994 No. 1445 (C. 25). Enabling power: *Local Government Act 1992, s. 30 (3). Bringing into operation various provisions of this Act on 13.06.94.* Issued: 08.06.94. Made: 01.06.94. Effect: None. Territorial extent & classification: E/W/S. General. – 2p. – 0 11 044445 0 *£0.65*

The Local Government Changes for England (Calculation of Council Tax Base) Regulations 1994 No. 2826. Enabling power: *Local Government Act 1992, ss. 19 (1) (2), 26 (3) (4)*. Issued: 14.11.94. Made: 05.11.94. Laid: 08.11.94. Coming into force: 29.11.94. Effect: S.I. 1992/612, 2904 amended. Territorial extent & classification: E. General. – 4p. – 0 11 045826 5 *£1.10*

The Local Government Changes for England (Collection Fund Surpluses and Deficits) Regulations 1994 No. 3115. Enabling power: *Local Government Act 1992, ss. 19 (1) (2), 26 (3) (4)*. Issued: 13.12.94. Made: 07.12.94. Laid: 08.12.94. Coming into force: 29.12.94. Effect: S.I. 1992/2428 amended. Territorial extent & classification: E/W. General. – 4p. – 0 11 043383 1 *£1.10*

The Local Government Changes for England (Direct Labour and Service Organisations) Regulations 1994 No. 3167. Enabling power: *Local Government Act 1992, ss. 19, 26 (4)*. Issued: 19.12.94. Made: 12.12.94. Laid: 19.12.94. Coming into force: 09.01.95. Effect: 1980 c.65 amended. Territorial extent & classification: E/W. General. – 8p. – 0 11 043445 5 *£1.95*

The Local Government Changes for England (Finance, Miscellaneous Provisions) Regulations 1994 No. 3223. Enabling power: *Local Government Act 1992, ss. 19 (1) (2), 26 (3) to (5)*. Issued: 06.01.95. Made: 14.12.94. Laid: 15.12.94. Coming into force: 30.12.94. Effect: S.I. 1991/185; 1992/2903, 3239 amended. Territorial extent & classification: E/W. General. – 4p. – 0 11 043840 X *£1.10*

The Local Government Changes for England (Finance) Regulations 1994 No. 2825. Enabling power: *Local Government Act 1992, ss. 19 (1) (2), 26 (3) to (5)*. Issued: 14.11.94. Made: 04.11.94. Coming into force: 28.11.94. Effect: 1972 c. 70; 1988 c. 41; 1989 c. 42; 1992 c. 19 amended. With correction slip date January 1995. Territorial extent & classification: E. General. – 20p. – 0 11 045825 7 *£3.70*

The Local Government Changes for England (Non-Domestic Rating) (Contributions) Regulations 1994 No. 3054. Enabling power: *Local Government Act 1992, ss. 19 (1), 26 (3) (4)*. Issued: 07.12.94. Made: 30.11.94. Laid: 07.12.94. Coming into force: 28.12.94. Effect: S.I. 1992/3082 amended. Territorial extent & classification: E. General. – 4p. – 0 11 043289 4 *£1.10*

The Local Government Changes for England Regulations 1994 No. 867. Enabling power: *Local Government Act 1992, ss. 19, 26*. Issued: 25.03.94. Made: 22.03.94. Laid: 22.03.94. Coming into force: 12.04.94. Effect: None. With correction slip dated May 1994. Territorial extent & classification: E/W. General. – 16p. – 0 11 043867 1 *£3.20*

The Local Government (Committees) (Devon and Cornwall) Regulations 1994 No. 961. Enabling power: *Local Government and Housing Act 1989, ss. 13 (4) (g), 190 (1)*. Issued: 04.04.94. Made: 28.03.94. Laid: 07.04.94. Coming into force: 28.04.94. Effect: None. Territorial extent & classification: E. General. – 2p. – 0 11 043961 9 *£0.65*

The Local Government (Compensation for Redundancy) Regulations 1994 No. 3025. Enabling power: *Superannuation Act 1972, s. 24*. Issued: 05.12.94. Made: 28.11.94. Laid: 05.12.94. Coming into force: 28.12.94, 01.04.80. Effect: S.I. 1982/1009 amended. N.B. Part 4 of the Regs. is made retrospective to 01.04.80. Territorial extent & classification: E/W. General. –8p. – 0 11 043254 1 *£1.95*

Price/availability are liable to change without notice

The Local Government (Direct Labour Organisations) (Competition) (Amendment) (England) Regulations 1994 No. 1439. Enabling power: *Local Government, Planning and Land Act 1980, ss. 7 (1) (b) (4) (6), 9 (3), 23 (1).* Issued: 10.06.94. Made: 26.05.94. Laid: 10.06.94. Coming into force: 01.04.95. Effect: S.I. 1989/1588 amended. Territorial extent & classification: E. General. – 2p. – 0 11 044439 6 *£0.65*

The Local Government (Direct Labour Organisations) (Competition) (Exemption) (England) Regulations 1994 No. 567. Enabling power: *Local Government, Planning and Land Act 1980, ss. 7 (4) (b), 23 (1).* Issued: 10.03.94. Made: 07.03.94. Laid: 10.03.94. Coming into force: 31.03.94. Effect: None. Territorial extent & classification: E/W. General. – 2p. – 0 11 043567 2 *£0.65*

The Local Government (Magistrates' Courts etc.) (Amendment) Order 1994 No. 2812. Enabling power: *Local Government Act 1985, s. 101.* Issued: 17.11.94. Made: 02.11.94. Laid: 03.11.94. Coming into force: 28.11.94. Effect: SI 1985/1383 amended. Territorial extent & classification: E/W. General. – 2p. – 0 11 045812 5 *£0.65*

The Local Government, Planning and Land Act 1980 (Competition) (Wales) Regulations 1994 No.338. Enabling power: *Local Government, Planning and Land Act 1980, ss. 7 (2) (4) (a) (b) (6), 9 (3) (a), 23 (1).* Issued: 05.04.94. Made: 14.02.94. Laid: 21.02.94. Coming into force: 01.04.94. Effect: None. Territorial extent & classification: W. General. – 4p. – 0 11 043338 6 *£1.10*

The Local Government (Publication of Manpower Information) (England) (Revocation) Regulations 1994 No. 2422. Enabling power: *Local Government, Planning and Land Act 1980, s. 3 (2) (4) (7).* Issued: 23.09.94. Made: 14.09.94. Laid: 23.09.94. Coming into force: 14.10.94. Effect: S.I. 1983/8 revoked. Territorial extent & classification: E. General. – 2p. – 0 11 045422 7 *£0.65*

The Local Government (Publication of Manpower Information) (Wales) (Revocation) Regulations 1994 No. 2677. Enabling power: *Local Government Planning and Land Act 1980, s. 3 (2) (4) (7).* Issued: 18.11.94. Made: 17.10.94. Laid: 18.10.94. Coming into force: 09.11.94. Effect: S.I. 1983/615 revoked. Territorial extent & classification: W. General. – 2p. – 0 11 045677 7 *£0.65*

The Local Government Superannuation (Amendment) Regulations 1994 No. 3026. Enabling power: *Superannuation Act 1972, s. 12 (6).* Issued: 07.12.94. Made: 29.11.94. Laid: 07.12.94. Coming into force: 28.12.94. Effect: S.I. 1986/24 amended. Territorial extent & classification: E/W. General. – 6p. – 0 11 043256 8 *£1.55*

The Local Government (Wales) Act 1994 (Commencement No. 1) Order 1994 No. 2109 (C. 40). Enabling power: *Local Government (Wales) Act 1994, s. 66 (3). Bringing into into operation various provisions of the 1994 act on 15.08.94.* Issued: 22.08.94. Made: 06.08.94. Effect: None. Territorial extent & classification: E/W. General. – 2p. – 0 11 045109 0 *£0.65*

The Welsh Principal Councils (Day of Election) Order 1994 No. 2843. Enabling power: *Local Government Act 1972, sch. 5, para. 1.* Issued: 14.11.94. Made: 06.11.94. Coming into force: In accord. with art. 1. Effect: None. Territorial extent & classification: E/W. General. – 2p. – 0 11 045843 5 *£0.65*

LOCAL GOVERNMENT, ENGLAND AND WALES: CHANGES IN LOCAL GOVERNMENT AREAS

The Berkshire, Buckinghamshire and Surrey (County Boundaries) Order 1994 No. 330. Enabling power: *Local Government Act 1972, ss. 51 (2), 67 (4) (5).* Issued: 23.02.94. Made: 15.02.94. Laid: 23.02.94. Coming into force: 01.12.94. for the purposes referred to in art. 1 (2). 01.04.95. for all other purposes. Effect: None. Territorial extent & classification: E/W. Local. – 4p., ill. – 0 11 043330 0 *£1.10*

The Cardiff And Vale of Glamorgan (Areas) Order 1994 No. 130. Enabling power: *Local Government Act 1972, ss. 58 (2), 67 (4).* Issued: 01.03.94. Made: 26.01.94. Laid: 04.02.94. Coming into force: 01.03.94, for the purposes described in art. 1 (2). 01.04.94, for all other purposes. Effect: None. Territorial extent & classification: W. Local. – 6p., ill. – 0 11 043130 8 *£1.55*

The Chorley (Parishes) Order 1994 No. 67. Enabling power: *Local Government Act 1972, s. 51 (2).* Made: 13.01.94. Coming into force: 19.01.94, 01.04.94. Effect: None. – *Unpublished*

The City of Worcester (Parishes) Order 1994 No. 218. Enabling power: *Local Government Act 1972, s. 51 (2).* Made: 28.01.94. Coming into force: 01.02.94.for purposes of art. 1 (2). & 01.04.94.for all other purposes. Effect: None. – *Unpublished*

The Derwentside (Parishes) Order 1994 No. 1720. Enabling power: *Local Government Act 1972, ss. 51 (2), 67 (4) (5).* Made: 28.06.94. Coming into force: 01.12.94. for the purposes of art. 1 (2) & 01.04.95. for all other purposes. Effect: None. – *Unpublished*

The Greater London and Surrey (County and London Borough Boundaries) Order 1994 No.331. Enabling power: *Local Government Act 1972, ss. 51 (2), 67 (4).* Issued: 23.02.94. Made: 15.02.94. Laid: 23.02.94. Coming into force: 01.12.94 for the purposes referred to in art. 1 (2); 01.04.95 for all other purposes. Effect: None. Territorial extent & classification: E/W. Local. – 10p., ill. – 0 11 043319 2 *£2.40*

The Ogwr (Ogwr Valley and Garw Valley Communities) Order 1994 No. 3168. Enabling power: *Local Government Act 1972, s. 58 (2).* Issued: 12.01.95. Made: 12.12.94. Coming into force: 01.03.95. for purposes described in art. 1 (2). 01.04.95. for all other purposes. Effect: None. Territorial extent & classification: E/W. Local. – 4p.; ill. – 0 11 043885 X *£1.10*

The Rochford (Parishes) Order 1994 No. 219. Enabling power: *Local Government Act 1972, s. 51 (2).* Made: 28.01.94. Coming into force: 01.02.94.for purposes of art. 1 (2). & 01.04.94.for all other purposes Effect: None. – *Unpublished*

The Rotherham (Parishes) Order 1994 No. 66. Enabling power: *Local Government Act 1972, ss. 51 (2), 67 (4) (5).* Made: 13.01.94. Coming into force: 19.01.94, 01.04.94. Effect: None. – *Unpublished*

The Vale of Glamorgan (Barry and Dinas Powys Communities) Order 1994 No. 142. Enabling power: *Local Government Act 1972, s. 58 (2).* Issued: 03.02.94. Made: 26.01.94. Coming into force: 01.03.94, for the purposes described in art. 1 (2). 01.04.94, for all other purposes. Effect: None. Territorial extent & classification: W. Local. – 4p., ill. – 0 11 043142 1 £1.10

The Warrington (Parishes) Order 1994 No. 557. Enabling power: *Local Government Act 1972, ss. 51 (2), 67 (4) (5).* Made: 22.02.94. Coming into force: 23.02.94. for art. 1 (2) & 02.04.94. for all other purposes. Effect: None. – *Unpublished*

LOCAL GOVERNMENT, ENGLAND AND WALES: FINANCE

The Local Authorities (Alteration of Requisite Calculations and Funds) Regulations 1994 No.246. Enabling power: *Local Government Finance Act 1988, ss. 99 (1) to (3), 140 (4), 143 (1), 146 (6) & Local Government Finance Act 1992, ss. 32 (9), 33 (4), 43 (7), 44 (4), 113 (1).* Issued: 10.02.94. Made: 07.02.94. Laid: 07.02.94. Coming into force: 08.02.94. Effect: 1992 c.14; S.I. 1992/2428; 1993/401 amended & S.I. 1992/2429 revoked. Territorial extent & classification: E/W. General. – 4p. – 0 11 043246 0 £1.10

The Local Authorities (Funds) (Wales) (Amendment) Regulations 1994 No. 2964. Enabling power: *Local Government Finance Act 1988, ss. 99 (1) (2) (4), 140 (4), 143 (1), 146 (6).* Issued: 21.12.94. Made: 22.11.94. Laid: 24.11.94. Coming into force: 15.12.94. Effect: S.I. 1992/2929 amended. Territorial extent & classification: W. General. – 2p. – 0 11 043516 8 £0.65

LOCAL GOVERNMENT, ENGLAND AND WALES: WALES

The Local Government Reorganisation (Wales) (Transitional Provisions) Order 1994 No.3124. Enabling power: *Local Government (Wales) Act 1994, s. 54 (1) (2) (e).* Issued: 16.12.94. Made: 02.12.94. Laid: 09.12.94. Coming into force: 03.01.95. Effect: S.I. 1991/351 amended. Territorial extent & classification: W. General. – 2p. – 0 11 043409 9 £0.65

The Local Government (Wales) Act 1994 (Commencement No. 2) Order 1994 No. 2790 (C. 62). Enabling power: *Local Government (Wales) Act 1994, ss. 63 (5), 66 (3). Bringing into operation various provisions of the 1994 act on 24.10.94.* Issued: 09.11.94. Made: 19.10.94. Effect: None. Territorial extent & classification: W. General. – 4p. – 0 11 045790 0 £1.10

LOCAL GOVERNMENT, SCOTLAND

The Local Government Act 1988 (Competition) (Defined Activities) (Housing Management) Order 1994 No. 1671. Enabling power: *Local Government Act 1988, ss. 2 (3), 15 (7) (8).* Issued: 30.06.94. Made: 22.06.94. Laid: 11.05.94. Coming into force: 23.06.94. Effect: 1988 c. 9 amended. Territorial extent & classification: E/W/S. General. – 4p. – 0 11 044671 2 £1.10

The Local Government Act 1988 (Competition) (Defined Activities) (Construction and Property Services) Order 1994 No. 2888. Enabling power: *Local Government Act 1988, ss. 2 (3), 15 (7) (8).* Issued: 22.11.94. Made: 10.11.94. Coming into force: 11.11.94. Effect: None. Supersedes Draft ISBN 0110459571 published on 30.08.94. Territorial extent & classification: E/W/S. General. – 4p. – 0 11 043075 1 £1.10

The Local Government Act 1988 (Competition) (Defined Activities) Order 1994 No. 2884. Enabling power: *Local Government Act 1988, s. 2 (3), 15 (7) (8).* Issued: 22.11.94. Made: 09.11.94. Laid: 14.06.94. Coming into force: 10.11.94. Effect: 1988 c. 9 amended. Territorial extent & classification: E/W/S. General. – 6p. – 0 11 043068 9 £1.55

The Local Government Act 1988 (Defined Activities) (Exemption) (Livingston Development Corporation) Order 1994 No. 3084 (S. 164). Enabling power: *Local Government Act 1988, ss. 2 (9), 15 (5).* Issued: 16.12.94. Made: 05.12.94. Laid: 09.12.94. Coming into force: 31.12.94. Effect: None. Territorial extent & classification: S. General. – 2p. – 0 11 043376 9 £0.65

The Local Government Act 1988 (Supervision of Parking) (Exemption) (Scotland) Order 1994 No.3107 (S. 168). Enabling power: *Local Government Act 1988, ss. 2 (9), 15 (5).* Issued: 16.12.94. Made: 06.12.94. Laid: 09.12.94. Coming into force: 31.12.94. Effect: None. Territorial extent & classification: S. General. – 2p. – 0 11 043374 2 £0.65

The Local Government Act 1992 (Commencement No. 4) Order 1994 No. 1445 (C. 25). Enabling power: *Local Government Act 1992, s. 30 (3). Bringing into operation various provisions of this Act on 13.06.94.* Issued: 08.06.94. Made: 01.06.94. Effect: None. Territorial extent & classification: E/W/S. General. – 2p. – 0 11 044445 0 £0.65

The Local Government (Compensation for Redundancy) (Scotland) Regulations 1994 No.3068 (S. 162). Enabling power: *Superannuation Act 1972, s. 24.* Issued: 13.12.94. Made: 01.12.94. Laid: 05.12.94. Coming into force: 28.12.94. Effect: S.I. 1979/785 amended. Territorial extent & classification: S. General. – 6p. – 0 11 043303 3 £1.55

The Local Government etc. (Allowances) (Scotland) Amendment Regulations 1994 No. 630 (S. 29). Enabling power: *Local Government (Scotland) Act 1973, ss. 45, 47 49A, 235 (1) & Local Government and Housing Act 1989, ss. 18, 190 (1).* Issued: 17.03.94. Made: 08.03.94. Laid: 11.03.94. Coming into force: 01.04.94. Effect: S.I. 1991/397 amended. Territorial extent & classification: S. General. – 4p. – 0 11 043630 X £1.10

The Local Government etc. (Scotland) Act 1994 (Commencement No. 1) Order 1994 No.2850 (C. 63) (S. 145). Enabling power: *Local Government etc. (Scotland) Act 1994, ss. 182 (2), 184 (2). Bringing into operation the 1994 act on 01.11.94, 04.01.95, 06.01.96.* Issued: 15.11.94. Made: 07.11.94. Effect: 18 & 19 Vict. c. 68; 10 & 11 Geo. 6, c. 41; 1968 c. 47; 1973 c. 65; 1974 c. 40; 1980 c. 45; 1982 c. 45 amended. Territorial extent & classification: S. General. – 8p. – 0 11 045850 8 £1.95

The Local Government Finance (Scotland) Order 1994 No. 528 (S. 22). Enabling power: *Local Government Finance (Scotland) Act 1992, sch. 12, paras. 1, 9 (4).* Issued: 16.03.94. Made: 17.02.94. Laid: 17.02.94. Coming into force: 01.03.94. Effect: S.I. 1993/341 revoked. Territorial extent & classification: S. General. 6p. 0 11 043528 1 £1.55

The Local Government Staff Commission (Scotland) Order 1994 No. 2958 (S. 148). Enabling power: *Local Government etc. (Scotland) Act 1994, ss. 12 (1) (2) (3), 12.* Issued: 29.11.94. Made: 22.11.94. Laid: 23.11.94. Coming into force: 25.11.94. Effect: None. Territorial extent & classification: S. General. – 6p. – 0 11 043148 0 £1.55

The Local Government (Transitional Election Arrangements) (Scotland) Order 1994 No.3255 (S. 183). Enabling power: *Local Government etc. (Scotland) Act 1994, s. 18 (1) (2).* Issued: 09.01.95. Made: 13.12.94. Laid: 16.12.94. Coming into force: 06.01.95. Effect: 1983 c. 2; S.I. 1986/1111, 2213 amended. Territorial extent & classification: S. General. – 12p. – 0 11 043793 4 £2.80

The Lothian Region (Electoral Arrangements) Amendment Order 1994 No. 259 (S. 9). Enabling power: *Local Government (Scotland) Act 1973, s. 17 (2).* Issued: 15.02.94. Made: 04.02.94. Coming into force: In accord. with art. 1 (2). Effect: S.I. 1993/1191 amended. Territorial extent & classification: S. Local. – 4p. – 0 11 043259 2 £1.10

The Revenue Support Grant (Scotland) Order 1994 No. 529 (S. 23). Enabling power: *Abolition of Domestic Rates Etc. (Scotland) Act 1987, sch. 4, para. 1.* Issued: 15.03.94. Made: 17.02.94. Laid: 17.02.94. Coming into force: 01.03.94. Effect: S.I. 1992/1629; 1993/322 revoked. Territorial extent & classification: S. General. – 4p. – 0 11 043529 X £1.95

The Urban Waste Water Treatment (Scotland) Regulations 1994 No. 2842 (S. 144). Enabling power: *European Communities Act 1972, s. 2 (2).* Issued: 15.11.94. Made: 31.10.94. Laid: 09.11.94. Coming into force: 30.11.94. Effect: None. With correction slip, dated December 1994. Territorial extent & classification: S. General. – Implements, as respects Scotland, DIR 91/271 [L 135/91]. – 16p. – 0 11 045842 7 £3.20

LONDON GOVERNMENT

The London Residuary Body (Pits at Stone) Order 1994 No. 3104. Enabling power: *Local Government Act 1985, ss. 67 (3), 100 (2) (4), 101.* Issued: 09.12.94. Made: 06.12.94. Laid: 09.12.94. Coming into force: 31.12.94. Effect: None. About pits located at Stone (Kent). Territorial extent & classification: E/W. General. – 4p. – 0 11 043364 5 £1.10

MAGISTRATES' COURTS

The Backing of Warrants (Republic of Ireland) (Rule of Speciality) Order 1994 No.1952. Enabling power: *Backing of Warrants (Republic of Ireland) Act 1965, ss. 2 (5), 6A, 6B, 6C.* Issued: 28.07.94. Made: 20.07.94. Laid: 28.07.94. Coming into force: 22.08.94. Effect: None. Territorial extent & classification: UK/CI/IOM. General. – 4p. – 0 11 044952 5 £1.10

The Family Proceedings Courts (Children Act 1989) (Amendment) (No. 2) Rules 1994 No.3156 (L. 22). Enabling power: *Magistrates' Court Act 1980, s. 144.* Issued: 21.12.94. Made: 08.12.94. Laid: 12.12.94. Coming into force: 03.01.95. Effect: S.I. 1991/1395 amended. Territorial extent & classification: E/W. General. – [98]p. – 0 11 043616 4 £10.35

The Family Proceedings Courts (Children Act 1989) (Amendment) Rules 1994 No.2166 (L.14). Enabling power: *Magistrates' Courts Act 1980, s. 144.* Issued: 24.08.94. Made: 11.08.94. Laid: 24.08.94. Coming into force: 01.11.94. Effect: S.I. 1991/1395 amended. Territorial extent & classification: E/W. General. – 20p. – 0 11 045166 X £3.70

The Family Proceedings Courts (Miscellaneous Amendments) Rules 1994 No. 809 (L. 5). Enabling power: *Magistrates' Courts Act 1980, s. 144.* Issued: 25.03.94. Made: 21.03.94. Laid: 21.03.94. Coming into force: 11.04.94. Effect: S.I. 1991/1395, 1991 amended. Territorial extent & classification: E/W. General. – 6p. – 0 11 043809 4 £1.55

The Licensing (Fees) (Amendment) Order 1994 No. 3103. Enabling power: *Licensing Act 1964, ss. 29 (1), 198 (2).* Issued: 21.12.94. Made: 05.12.94. Laid: 09.12.94. Coming into force: 03.01.95. Effect: S.I. 1978/1644 amended. Territorial extent & classification: E/W. General. – 2p. – 0 11 043509 5 £0.65

The Magistrates' Courts Committees (Constitution) Regulations 1994 No. 2811. Enabling power: *Justices of the Peace Act 1979, s. 21.* Issued: 17.11.94. Made: 02.11.94. Laid: 03.11.94. Coming into force: 28.11.94. Effect: SI 1973/1522; 1980/1258; 1992/2047 revoked. Territorial extent & classification: E/W. General. – 8p. – 0 11 045811 7 £1.95

The Magistrates' Courts Fees (Amendment) Order 1994 No. 3250 (L. 23). Enabling power: *Magistrates' Courts Act 1980, s. 137 (4).* Issued: 22.12.94. Made: 15.12.94. Laid: 20.10.94. Coming into force: 01.02.95. Effect: 1980 c.43 amended. Territorial extent & classification: E/W. General. – 2p. – 0 11 043722 5 £0.65

The Police and Magistrates' Courts Act 1994 (Commencement No. 3) and Transitional Provisions) Order 1994 No. 2594 (C. 55). Enabling power: *Police and Magistrates' Courts Act 1994, s. 94 (2) (4) (5) (7). Bringing into operation various provisions of the 1994 act on 01.11.94.* Issued: 17.10.94. Made: 08.10.94. Laid: 10.10.94. Effect: None. Territorial extent & classification: E/W. General. – 4p. – 0 11 045594 0 £1.10

Price/availability are liable to change without notice

MAGISTRATES' COURTS: PROCEDURE

The Magistrates' Courts (Bail) (Amendment) Rules 1994 No. 1481 (L. 10). Enabling power: *Magistrates' Courts Act 1980, s. 144.* Issued: 13.06.94. Made: 26.05.94. Laid: 06.06.94. Coming into force: 27.06.94. Effect: S.I. 1970/231; 1981/552, 553 amended. Territorial extent & classification: E/W. General. – 8p. – 0 11 044481 7 £1.95

The Magistrate's Courts (Miscellaneous Amendments) Rules 1994 No. 3154 (L. 20). Enabling power: *Magistrate's Courts Act 1980, s. 144.* Issued: 20.12.94. Made: 08.12.94. Laid: 12.12.94. Coming into force: 03.02.95. Effect: S.I. 1981/552; 1991/1923 amended. Territorial extent & classification: E/W. General. – 4p. – 0 11 043513 3 £1.10

MAINTENANCE OF DEPENDANTS

The Reciprocal Enforcement of Maintenance Orders (Hague Convention Countries) (Variation) Order 1994 No. 1902. Enabling power: *Maintenance Orders (Reciprocal Enforcement) Act 1972, ss. 40, 45 (1).* Issued: 29.07.94. Made: 19.07.94. Coming into force: 01.09.94. Effect: S.I. 1993/593 amended. Territorial extent & classification: GB. General. – 2p. – 0 11 044902 9 £0.65

MARINE POLLUTION

The Food and Environment Protection Act 1985 (Isle of Man) (Revocation) Order 1994 No.3205. Enabling power: *Food and Environment Protection Act 1985, s. 26 (1) (2).* Issued: 22.12.94. Made: 14.12.94. Coming into force: 01.01.95. Effect: S.I. 1987/666 revoked. Territorial extent & classification: IOM. General. – 2p. – 0 11 043719 5 £0.65

The Merchant Shipping (BCH Code) (Amendment) Regulations 1994 No. 2084. Enabling power: *S.I. 1987/470, art. 3.* Issued: 11.08.94. Made: 04.08.94. Laid: 11.08.94. Coming into force: 01.09.94. Effect: S.I. 1987/550 amended. Territorial extent & classification: GB. General. – 4p. – 0 11 045084 1 £1.10

The Merchant Shipping (Control of Pollution by Noxious Liquid Substances in Bulk) (Amendment) Regulations 1994 No. 2083. Enabling power: *S.I. 1987/470, art. 3.* Issued: 11.08.94. Made: 04.08.94. Laid: 11.08.94. Coming into force: 01.09.94. Effect: S.I. 1987/551 amended. Territorial extent & classification: GB. General. – 4p. – 0 11 045083 3 £1.10

The Merchant Shipping (IBC Code) (Amendment) Regulations 1994 No. 2082. Enabling power: *Merchant Shipping Act 1979, ss. 21 (1) (a) (b) (3) (4) (5) (6), 22 (1) & S.I. 1987/470 art. 3.* Issued: 11.08.94. Made: 04.08.94. Laid: 11.08.94. Coming into force: 01.09.94. Effect: S.I. 1987/549 amended. Territorial extent & classification: GB. General. – 4p. – 0 11 045082 5 £1.10

The Merchant Shipping (Prevention of Oil Pollution) (Amendment) Regulations 1994 No.2085. Enabling power: *S.I. 1983/1106, art. 3.* Issued: 11.08.94. Made: 04.08.94. Laid: 11.08.94. Coming into force: 01.09.94. Effect: S.I. 1983/1398 amended. Territorial extent & classification: GB. General. – 4p. – 0 11 045085 X £1.10

The Merchant Shipping (Reporting Requirements for Ships Carrying Dangerous or Polluting Goods) Regulations 1994 No. 3245. Enabling power: *Merchant Shipping Act 1979, ss. 21 (1) (a) (b) (3) to (6), 22 (1) & S.I. 1987/470, art. 3 & 1990/2595, art. 3.* Issued: 21.12.94. Made: 14.12.94. Laid: 21.12.94. Coming into force: 11.01.95. Effect: S.I. 1990/2605 amended & S.I. 1987/586 revoked. Territorial extent & classification: GB. General. – 6p. – 0 11 043713 6 £1.55

The Merchant Shipping (Sterling Equivalents) (Revocation) Order 1994 No. 2788. Enabling power: *Merchant Shipping Act 1974, s. 1 (7).* Issued: 08.11.94. Made: 02.11.94. Coming into force: 22.11.94. Effect: S.I. 1989/1882 revoked. Territorial extent & classification: GB. General. – 2p. – 0 11 045788 9 £0.65

MARRIAGE

The Marriage Act 1994 (Commencement No. 1) Order 1994 No. 3116 (C. 73). Enabling power: *Marriage Act 1994, s. 3 (2). Bringing into operation various provisions of the 1994 act on 01.01.95.* Issued: 13.12.94. Made: 07.12.94. Effect: None. Territorial extent & classification: E/W. General. – 2p. – 0 11 043367 X £0.65

MEDICAL PROFESSION

The General Medical Council (Constitution of Fitness to Practise Committees) (Amendment No. 2) Rules Order of Council 1994 No. 3171. Enabling power: *Medical Act 1983, sch. 1, paras. 20, 21, 22.* Issued: 11.01.95. Made: 12.12.94. Laid: 13.12.94. Coming into force: 03.01.95. Effect: S.I. 1986/1390 amended. Territorial extent & classification: GB. General. – 4p. – 0 11 043882 5 £1.10

The General Medical Council (Constitution of Fitness to Practise Committees) (Amendment) Rules Order of Council 1994 No. 2022. Enabling power: *Medical Act 1983, sch. 1, paras. 21, 22.* Issued: 08.08.94. Made: 29.07.94. Laid: 01.08.94. Coming into force: 22.08.94. Effect: S.I. 1986/1390; 1987/1120 amended. Territorial extent & classification: GB. General. – 4p. – 0 11 045022 1 £1.10

The General Medical Council Preliminary Proceedings Committee and Professional Conduct Committee (Procedure) (Amendment) Rules Order of Council 1994 No. 3298. Enabling power: *Medical Act 1983, sch. 4, para. 1, 5.* Issued: 12.01.95. Made: 21.12.94. Laid: 29.12.94. Coming into force: 19.01.95. Effect: S.I. 1988/2255 amended. Territorial extent & classification: GB. General. – 4p. – 0 11 043887 6 £1.10

The Vocational Training for General Medical Practice (European Requirements) Regulations 1994 No. 3130. Enabling power: *European Communities Act 1972, s. 2 (2) & National Health Service Act 1977, ss. 15 (1), 29, 32, 126 (4) & National Health Service (Scotland) Act 1978, ss. 19, 22, 105 (7).* Issued: 03.01.95. Made: 08.12.94. Laid: 09.12.94. Coming into force: 01.01.95. Effect: None. Territorial extent & classification: GB. General. – These regulations arise out of Title IV of DIR 93/16 of 5 April 1993. – 12p. – 0 11 043742 X *£2.40*

MEDICINES

The Marketing Authorisations for Veterinary Medicinal Products Regulations 1994 No.3142. Enabling power: *European Communities Act s. 2 (2).* Issued: 02.02.95. Made: 05.12.94. Laid: 09.12.94. Coming into force: 01.01.95. Effect: S.R. 1970/240; 1977/359; 1992/39; 1994/199; S.I. 1971/1326; 1972/2076; 1976/1726; 1978/40; 1980/14, 1923, 1924; 1981/1011; 1982/207, 234; 1985/71, 1542; 1986/228, 1510; 1988/1009, 1771; 1989/2325; 1990/566; 1991/1392, 1506, 2843; 1992/33, 1520; 1993/3250; 1994/2328, 2852, 2986, 2987 amended & S.I. 1983/1727; 1993/2398; 1994/2157 revoked. Territorial extent & classification: E/W/S. General. – Implements DIR 81/851 [OJ L317/81]; 81/852 OJ L317/81]; 90/676 [OJ L373/90]; 90/677 [OJ L373/90]; 91/412 OJ L228/91]; 92/18 [OJ L97/92]; 92/74 [OJ L297/92]; 93/40 [OJ L214/93] and REG 2309/93 [OJ L214/93]. –20p. – 0 11 043940 6 *£3.70*

The Medical Devices (Consequential Amendments - Medicines) Regulations 1994 No. 3119. Enabling power: *European Communities Act 1972, s. 2 (2).* Issued: 14.12.94. Made: 07.12.94. Laid: 08.12.94. Coming into force: 01.01.95. Effect: 1968 c. 67 & S.I. 1971/1267; 1975/533; 1976/968 amended. Territorial extent & classification: GB. General. – Implements DIR 93/42 [OJ L169/93]. –4p. – 0 11 043382 3 *£1.10*

The Medicinal Products: Prescription by Nurses etc. Act 1992 (Commencement No. 1) Order 1994 No. 2408 (C. 48). Enabling power: *Medicinal Products: Prescription by Nurses etc. Act 1992, s. 6 (2).* Bringing various provisions of the 1992 act into operation on 03.10.94. Issued: 20.09.94. Made: 12.09.94. Effect: None. Territorial extent & classification: E/W/S. General. – 2p. – 0 11 045408 1 *£0.65*

The Medicines Act 1968 (Amendment) (No. 2) Regulations 1994 No. 276. Enabling power: *European Communities Act 1972, s. 2 (2).* Issued: 15.02.94. Made: 09.02.94. Laid: 10.02.94. Coming into force: 13.02.94. Effect: S.I. 1994/101 amended. This SI has been made in consequence of a defect in SI 1994/101 issued 27.01.94. & is being issued free of charge to all known recipients of that SI. Territorial extent & classification: E/W. General. – 4p. – 0 11 043276 2 *£1.10*

The Medicines Act 1968 (Amendment) Regulations 1994 No. 101. Enabling power: *European Communities Act 1972, s. 2 (2).* Issued: 27.01.94. Made: 20.12.93. Laid: 24.01.94. Coming into force: 14.02.94. Effect: 1968 c. 67 amended. Territorial extent & classification: E/W. General. – 4p. – 0 11 043101 4 *£1.10*

The Medicines (Advertising) Regulations 1994 No. 1932. Enabling power: *European Communities Act 1972, s. 2 (2) & Medicines Act 1968, ss. 61, 66 (1) (i) (j), 95 (1) (2) (3) (4) (5) (6), 129 (5).* Issued: 25.07.94. Made: 18.07.94. Laid: 19.07.94. Coming into force: 09.08.94. Effect: S.I. 1975/1326; 1978/41 amended & S.I. 1978/1020 revoked. Territorial extent & classification: GB. General. – 20p. – 0 11 044932 0 *£3.70*

The Medicines (Advisory Board on the Registration of Homoeopathic Products) Order 1994 No.102. Enabling power: *Medicines Act 1968, s. 4.* Issued: 27.01.94. Made: 23.12.93. Coming into force: 14.02.94. Effect: None. Territorial extent & classification: E/W. General. – 4p. – 0 11 043102 2 *£1.10*

The Medicines (Child Safety) Amendment Regulations 1994 No. 1402. Enabling power: *Medicines Act 1968, ss. 87 (1), 91 (3), 129 (5).* Issued: 01.06.94. Made: 24.05.94. Laid: 25.05.94. Coming into force: 15.06.94. Effect: S.I. 1975/2000 amended. Territorial extent & classification: GB. General. – 4p. – 0 11 044402 7 *£1.10*

The Medicines (Committee on Dental and Surgical Materials) (Revocation) Order 1994 No.3120. Enabling power: *Medicines Act 1968, s. 4, 129 (4).* Issued: 14.12.94. Made: 07.12.94. Coming into force: 01.01.95. Effect: S.I. 1975/1473; 1979/1535 revoked. Territorial extent & classification: GB. General. – Concerns the implementation of DIR 93/42 [OJ L169/93]. –4p. – 0 11 043381 5 *£1.10*

The Medicines (Control of Substances for Manufacture and Exportation of Specified Products for Human Use) Amendment Order 1994 No. 787. Enabling power: *Medicines Act 1968, ss. 49, 129 (4).* Issued: 23.03.94. Made: 16.03.94. Laid: 17.03.94. Coming into force: 11.04.94. Effect: S.I. 1971/1200; 1985/1403 amended & S.I. 1971/1198 revoked. Territorial extent & classification: GB. General. – 4p. – 0 11 043787 X *£1.10*

The Medicines (Fees Relating to Medicinal Products for Animal Use) Regulations 1994 No.1554. Enabling power: *Medicines Act 1971, s. 1 (1) (2).* Issued: 08.07.94. Made: 12.06.94. Laid: 13.06.94. Coming into force: 04.07.94. Effect: S.I. 1992/694 revoked. Territorial extent & classification: GB. General. – 16p. – 0 11 044554 6 *£3.20*

The Medicines for Human Use (Marketing Authorisations Etc.) Regulations 1994 No. 3144. Enabling power: *European Communities Act 1972, s. 2 (2).* Issued: 14.12.94. Made: 08.12.94. Laid: 09.12.94. Coming into force: 01.01.95. Effect: 1968 c. 29, c. 67; S.I. 1975/762, 2000; 1976/1726; 1977/655, 1038, 2168; 1978/40; 1980/14, 1923, 1924; 1981/1011; 1984/1305; 1985/71; 1986/144; 1988/1771; 1990/566; 1991/1506; 1993/2538; 3250; 1994/743, 1932, 2328, 2987 amended. Territorial extent & classification: GB. General. – Implements DIR 65/65 [OJ L22/65], 75/318 [OJ L147/75], 75/319 [OJ L147/75](ch. I to II/V to VI) & any reg. adopted by the Commission under art. 15 of that directive, 89/342 [OJ L142/89], 89/343 [OJ L142/89], 89/381 [OJ L181/89], 92/26 [OJ L113/92], 92/27 [OJ L113/92], 92/73 [OJ L297/92], & Reg. (EEC) no. 2309/93 [OJ L214/93] & any reg. adopted by the Commission under art. 15.4 or 22.1 of that reg. – 24p. – 0 11 043394 7 *£4.15*

Price/availability are liable to change without notice

The Medicines (Homoeopathic Medicinal Products for Human Use) Amendment Regulations 1994 No.899. Enabling power: *European Communities Act 1972, s. 2 (2)*. Issued: 30.03.94. Made: 24.03.94. Laid: 30.03.94. Coming into force: 20.04.94. Effect: S.I. 1994/105 amended. This SI has been made in consequence of a defect in SI 1994/105 and is being sent free of charge to all known recipients of that SI. Territorial extent & classification: E/W. General. – 4p. – 0 11 043899 X *£1.10*

The Medicines (Homoeopathic Medicinal Products for Human Use) Regulations 1994 No.105. Enabling power: *European Communities Act 1972, s. 2 (2)*. Issued: 27.01.94. Made: 19.01.94. Laid: 24.01.94. Coming into force: 14.02.94. Effect: None. Territorial extent & classification: E/W. General. – 12p. – 0 11 043105 7 *£2.80* Replaced by ISBN 011045894X

The Medicines (Labelling and Leaflets) Amendment Regulations 1994 No. 104. Enabling power: *Medicines Act 1968, ss. 85 (1), 86 (1), 91 (3)*. Issued: 27.01.94. Made: 19.01.94. Laid: 24.01.94. Coming into force: 14.02.94. Effect: S.I. 1976/1726; 1977/1055 amended. Territorial extent & classification: GB. General. – 6p. – 0 11 043104 9 *£1.55*

The Medicines (Medicated Animal Feeding Stuffs) (Amendment) Regulations 1994 No. 1531. Enabling power: *Medicines Act 1968, ss. 40, 129 (1) (5)*. Issued: 08.07.94. Made: 09.06.94. Laid: 10.06.94. Coming into force: 01.07.94. Effect: S.I. 1992/1520 amended. Territorial extent & classification: GB. General. – 6p. – 0 11 044531 7 *£1.55*

The Medicines (Monitoring of Advertising) Regulations 1994 No. 1933. Enabling power: *European Communities Act 1972, s. 2 (2)*. Issued: 25.07.94. Made: 18.07.94. Laid: 19.07.94. Coming into force: 09.08.94. Effect: None. Territorial extent & classification: GB. General. – 6p. – 0 11 044933 9 *£1.55*

The Medicines (Pharmacies) (Applications for Registration and Fees) Amendment Regulations 1994 No. 2936. Enabling power: *Medicines Act 1968, ss. 75 (1), 76 (1) (2) (6), 129 (5)*. Issued: 28.11.94. Made: 18.11.94. Laid: 28.11.94. Coming into force: 01.01.95. Effect: S.I. 1973/1822 amended & S.I. 1993/2902 revoked. Territorial extent & classification: GB. General. – 2p. – 0 11 043124 3 *£0.65*

The Medicines (Pharmacy and General Sale - Exemption) Order 1994 No. 2409. Enabling power: *Medicines Act 1968, ss. 57 (1) (2), 129 (4)*. Issued: 19.09.94. Made: 07.09.94. Laid: 13.09.94. Coming into force: 12.10.94. Effect: S.I. 1980/1924 amended. Territorial extent & classification: GB. General. – 4p. – 0 11 045409 X *£1.10*

The Medicines (Products for Human Use - Fees) Amendment Regulations 1994 No. 696. Enabling power: *Medicines Act 1971, s. 1 (1) (2)*. Issued: 17.03.94. Made: 10.03.94. Laid: 11.03.94. Coming into force: 01.04.94. Effect: S.I. 1991/1474 amended. Territorial extent & classification: GB. General. – 8p. – 0 11 043696 2 *£1.95*

The Medicines (Products Other Than Veterinary Drugs) (General Sale List) (Amendment) Order 1994 No. 2410. Enabling power: *Medicines Act 1968, ss. 51, 129 (4)*. Issued: 19.09.94. Made: 07.09.94. Coming into force: 12.10.94. Effect: S.I. 1984/769 amended. Territorial extent & classification: GB. General. – 8p. – 0 11 045410 3 *£1.95*

The Medicines (Products Other Than Veterinary Drugs) (Prescription Only) Amendment (No. 2) Order 1994 No. 3016. Enabling power: *Medicines Act 1968, ss. 58 (1) (4) (5), 129 (4)*. Issued: 05.12.94. Made: 25.11.94. Laid: 05.12.94. Coming into force: 30.12.94. Effect: S.I. 1983/1212 amended. Territorial extent & classification: GB. General. – 4p. – 0 11 043251 7 *£1.10*

The Medicines (Products Other Than Veterinary Drugs) (Prescription Only) Amendment (No. 3) Order 1994 No. 3050. Enabling power: *Medicines Act 1968, ss. 58 (1), 129 (4)*. Issued: 07.12.94. Made: 29.11.94. Laid: 07.12.94. Coming into force: 31.12.94. Effect: S.I. 1983/1212 amended. Territorial extent & classification: GB. General. – 4p. – 0 11 043283 5 *£1.10*

The Medicines (Products Other than Veterinary Drugs) (Prescription Only) Amendment Order 1994 No. 558. Enabling power: *Medicines Act 1986, ss. 58 (1) (4) (5), 129 (4)*. Issued: 14.03.94. Made: 07.03.94. Laid: 08.03.94. Coming into force: 29.03.94. Effect: S.I. 1983/1212; 1993/3256 amended. This SI has been made in consequence of a defect in SI 1993/3256 and is being sent free of charge to all known recipients of that SI. Territorial extent & classification: GB. General. – 4p. – 0 11 043558 3 *£1.10*

The Medicines (Restrictions on the Administration of Veterinary Medicinal Products) Regulations 1994 No. 2987. Enabling power: *European Communities Act 1972, s. 2 (2)*. Issued: 02.12.94. Made: 21.11.94. Laid: 02.12.94. Coming into force: 31.12.94. Effect: 1968 c. 67; S.I. 1991/2843 amended & S.I. 1983/1732 revoked. Territorial extent & classification: GB. General. – Partially implements DIR 81/851 (OJ L 317/81) as amended by DIR 90/676 (OJ L 373/90) & DIR 92/74 (OJ L 297/92). – 6p. – 0 11 043193 6 *£1.55*

The Medicines (Sale or Supply) (Miscellaneous Provisions) Amendment Regulations 1994 No.2411. Enabling power: *Medicines Act 1968, ss. 53 (4), 129 (1) (5)*. Issued: 19.09.94. Made: 08.09.94. Laid: 13.09.94. Coming into force: 12.10.94. Effect: S.I. 1980/1923 amended. Territorial extent & classification: GB. General. – 4p. – 0 11 045411 1 *£1.10*

The Medicines (Standard Provisions for Licences and Certificates) Amendment Regulations 1994 No. 103. Enabling power: *Medicines Act 1968, ss. 47 (1), 129 (5)*. Issued: 27.01.94. Made: 23.12.93. Laid: 24.01.94. Coming into force: 14.02.94. Effect: S.I. 1971/972 amended. Territorial extent & classification: GB. General. – 4p. – 0 11 043103 0 *£1.10*

The Medicines (Standard Provisions for Manufacturer's Licences for Veterinary Medicinal Products) Regulations 1994 No.2852. Enabling power: *Medicines Act 1968, ss. 47 (1), 129 (5)*. Issued: 14.11.94. Made: 26.10.94. Laid: 08.11.94. Coming into force: 01.12.94. Effect: S.I. 1971/972 amended. Territorial extent & classification: GB. General. – 4p. – 0 11 043038 7 *£1.10*

The Medicines (Veterinary Drugs) (Pharmacy and Merchants' List) (Amendment No. 2) Order 1994 No. 3169. Enabling power: *Medicines Act 1968, ss. 57 (1) (2) (2A), 129 (4).* Issued: 16.02.95. Made: 12.12.94. Laid: 13.12.94. Coming into force: 03.01.95. Effect: S.I. 1992/33 amended. Territorial extent & classification: GB. General. – 20p. – 0 11 043942 2 £3.70

The Medicines (Veterinary Drugs) (Pharmacy and Merchants' List) (Amendment) Order 1994 No.599. Enabling power: *Medicines Act 1968, ss. 57 (1) (2), 129 (4).* Issued: 24.03.94. Made: 07.03.94. Laid: 10.03.94. Coming into force: 01.04.94. Effect: S.I. 1992/33 amended. Territorial extent & classification: GB. General. – 16p. – 0 11 043599 0 £3.20

The Medicines (Veterinary Drugs) (Renewal Applications for Licences and Animal Test Certificates) Regulations 1994 No. 3143. Enabling power: *Medicines Act 1968, ss. 18 (1), 36 (1), 129 (1).* Issued: 27.01.95. Made: 07.12.94. Laid: 09.12.94. Coming into force: 01.01.95. Effect: S.I. 1993/1227 revoked. Territorial extent & classification: GB. General. – 4p. – 0 11 052315 6 £1.10

The Medicines (Veterinary Medicinal Products) (Applications for Product Licences) (Amendment) Regulations 1994 No. 2157. Enabling power: *Medicines Act 1968, s. 18, 129 (1) (4) & European Communities Act 1972, s. 2 (2).* Issued: 25.08.94. Made: 03.08.94. Laid: 18.08.94. Coming into force: 08.09.94. Effect: S.I. 1993/2398 amended. Territorial extent & classification: GB. General. – 4p. – 0 11 045157 0 £1.10

The Medicines (Veterinary Medicinal Products) (Veterinary Surgeons from Other EEA States) Regulations 1994 No. 2986. Enabling power: *European Communities Act 1972, s. 2 (2).* Issued: 02.12.94. Made: 21.11.94. Laid: 02.12.94. Coming into force: 31.12.94. Effect: 1968 c. 67 amended. Territorial extent & classification: GB. General. – Partially implements DIR 81/851 (OJ L 317/81) as amended by DIR 90/676 (OJ L 373/90). – 4p. – 0 11 043191 X £1.10

MENTAL HEALTH

The Court of Protection (Enduring Powers of Attorney) Rules 1994 No. 3047. Enabling power: *Mental Health Act 1983, ss. 106, 108.* Issued: 09.12.94. Made: 29.11.94. Laid: 01.12.94. Coming into force: 22.12.94. Effect: SI 1986/127; 1990/864 revoked. Territorial extent & classification: E/W. General. – 26p. – 0 11 043333 5 £4.70

The Court of Protection Rules 1994 No. 3046. Enabling power: *Mental Health Act 1983, ss. 106, 107, 108.* Issued: 09.12.94. Made: 29.11.94. Laid: 01.12.94. Coming into force: 22.12.94. Effect: SI 1984/2035; 1992/1899 revoked. Territorial extent & classification: E/W. General. – 34p. – 0 11 043332 7 £6.10

The Mental Health (Class of Nurse) (Scotland) Order 1994 No. 1675 (S. 74). Enabling power: *Mental Health (Scotland) Act 1984, s. 25 (2) (6).* Issued: 04.07.94. Made: 14.06.94. Coming into force: 05.07.94. Effect: S.I. 1984/1095 revoked. Territorial extent & classification: S. General. – 2p. – 0 11 044675 5 £0.65

MERCHANT SHIPPING

The Merchant Shipping (Accident Reporting and Investigation) Regulations 1994 No.2013. Enabling power: *Merchant Shipping Act 1979, s. 21 (1) (a) & Merchant Shipping Act 1988, ss. 33, 53.* Issued: 05.08.94. Made: 28.07.94. Laid: 05.08.94. Coming into force: 26.08.94. Effect: S.I. 1985/855; 1989/1172 revoked. Territorial extent & classification: GB. General. – 8p. – 0 11 045013 2 £1.95

The Merchant Shipping Act 1979 (Commencement No. 14) Order 1994 No. 2789 (C. 61). Enabling power: *Merchant Shipping Act 1979, s. 52 (2). Bringing into operation various provisions of the 1979 Act on 22.11.94.* Issued: 08.11.94. Made: 02.11.94. Effect: None. Territorial extent & classification: GB. General. – 4p. – 0 11 045789 7 £1.10

The Merchant Shipping Act 1988 (Commencement No. 4) Order 1994 No. 1201 (C. 19). Enabling power: *Merchant Shipping Act 1988, s. 58 (2). Bringing into operation various provisions of this act on 01.06.94.* Issued: 23.05.94. Made: 28.04.94. Effect: None. Territorial extent & classification: GB. General. – 4p. – 0 11 044201 6 £1.10

The Merchant Shipping (Fees) (Amendment) Regulations 1994 No. 502. Enabling power: *Merchant Shipping (Safety Convention) Act 1949, s.33; Merchant Shipping (Load Lines) Act 1967, s.26; Anchors and Chain Cables Act 1967, s. 1(1)(d); Fishing Vessels (Safety Provisions) Act 1970, s.6; Merchant Shipping Act 1970, s.84; Merchant Shipping Act 1974, s.17, sch.5; Merchant Shipping Act 1979, s.21(1)(3)(r); S.I. 1983/1398, art.3(1)(a); S.I. 1987/470 & Merchant Shipping (Registration etc.) Act 1993, s.3(i).* Issued: 08.03.94. Made: 01.03.94. Laid: 08.03.94. Coming into force: 21.03.94. Effect: S.I. 1991/784 amended. With correction slip. Territorial extent & classification: GB. General. – 6p. – 0 11 043502 8 £1.55

The Merchant Shipping (Liability of Shipowners and Others) (Rate of Interest) Order 1994 No.3049. Enabling power: *Merchant Shipping Act 1979, sch. 4, pt. 2, para. 8 (1).* Issued: 08.12.94. Made: 29.11.94. Laid: 08.12.94. Coming into force: 01.01.95. Effect: S.I. 1986/1932 revoked. Territorial extent & classification: GB. General. – 2p. – 0 11 043274 6 £0.65

The Merchant Shipping (Modification of Enactments) (Bareboat Charter Ships) Order 1994 No.774. Enabling power: *Merchant Shipping (Registration, etc.) Act 1993, s. 7 (8).* Issued: 24.03.94. Made: 15.03.94. Laid: 18.03.94. Coming into force: 21.03.94. Effect: None. Territorial extent & classification: GB. General. – 2p. – 0 11 043774 8 £0.65

The Merchant Shipping (Registration of Ships) (Amendment) Regulations 1994 No. 541. Enabling power: *Merchant Shipping (Registration, etc.) Act 1993, ss. 2, 3, 7 (5) & sch.* Issued: 11.03.94. Made: 04.03.94. Laid: 11.03.94. Coming into force: 21.03.94. Effect: S.I. 1993/3138 amended. This SI has been made in consequence of a defect in SI 1993/3138 and is being sent free of charge to all known recipients of that SI. Territorial extent & classification: GB. General. – 4p. – 0 11 043541 9 £1.10

Price/availability are liable to change without notice

The Merchant Shipping (Salvage and Pollution) Act 1994 (Commencement No. 1) Order 1994 No.1988 (C. 37). Enabling power: *Merchange Shipping (Salvage and Pollution) Act 1994, s. 10 (4)*. Bringing into operation various provisions of the 1994 act on 28.07.94; 01.10.94. Issued: 03.08.94. Made: 26.07.94. Effect: None. Territorial extent & classification: GB. General. – 4p. – 0 11 044988 6 *£1.10*

MERCHANT SHIPPING: MASTERS AND SEAMEN

The Merchant Shipping (Seamen's Wages and Accounts) (Amendment) Regulations 1994 No.791. Enabling power: *Merchant Shipping Act 1970, s. 9*. Issued: 23.03.94. Made: 16.03.94. Laid: 23.03.94. Coming into force: 13.04.94. Effect: S.I. 1972/1700 amended. Territorial extent & classification: GB. General. – 2p. – 0 11 043791 8 *£0.65*

MERCHANT SHIPPING: SAFETY

The Merchant Shipping (Gas Carriers) Regulations 1994 No. 2464. Enabling power: *Merchant Shipping Act 1979, ss. 21 (1) (b) (3) to (6), 22 (1)*. Issued: 29.09.94. Made: 19.09.94. Laid: 29.09.94. Coming into force: 01.10.94. Effect: S.I. 1986/1073 revoked. Territorial extent & classification: GB. General. – 8p. – 0 11 045464 2 *£1.95*

The Merchant Shipping (IBC Code) (Amendment) Regulations 1994 No. 2082. Enabling power: *Merchant Shipping Act 1979, ss. 21 (1) (a) (b) (3) (4) (5) (6), 22 (1) & S.I. 1987/470 art. 3*. Issued: 11.08.94. Made: 04.08.94. Laid: 11.08.94. Coming into force: 01.09.94. Effect: S.I. 1987/549 amended. Territorial extent & classification: GB. General. – 4p. – 0 11 045082 5 *£1.10*

The Merchant Shipping (Radio) (Fishing Vessels) (Amendment) Rules 1994 No. 1104. Enabling power: *Merchant Shipping (Safety Convention) Act 1949, s. 3*. Issued: 27.04.94. Made: 19.04.94. Laid: 20.04.94. Coming into force: 30.04.94. Effect: S.I. 1974/1919 amended. Territorial extent & classification: GB. General. – 4p. – 0 11 044104 4 *£1.10*

The Merchant Shipping (Reporting Requirements for Ships Carrying Dangerous or Polluting Goods) Regulations 1994 No. 3245. Enabling power: *Merchant Shipping Act 1979, ss. 21 (1) (a) (b) (3) to (6), 22 (1) & S.I. 1987/470, art. 3 & 1990/2595, art. 3*. Issued: 21.12.94. Made: 14.12.94. Laid: 21.12.94. Coming into force: 11.01.95. Effect: S.I. 1990/2605 amended & S.I. 1987/586 revoked. Territorial extent & classification: GB. General. – 6p. – 0 11 043713 6 *£1.55*

The Merchant Shipping (Ro-Ro Passenger Ship Survivability) (No. 2) Regulations 1994 No.1383. Enabling power: *Merchant Shipping Act 1979, ss. 21 (1) (a) (c) (3) to (6), 22 (1)*. Issued: 01.06.94. Laid: 28.03.94. Made: 18.05.94. Coming into force: 19.05.94. Effect: S.I. 1994/422 revoked. Supersedes Draft ISBN 0110458966 published on 05.04.94 & being issued free of charge to all known recipients of that SI. Territorial extent & classification: GB. General. – 4p. – 0 11 044383 7 *£1.10*

The Merchant Shipping (Ro-Ro Passenger Ship Survivability) Regulations 1994 No. 422. Enabling power: *Merchant Shipping Act 1979, ss. 21 (1) (a) (b) (3) to (6), 22 (1)*. Issued: 04.03.94. Made: 25.02.94. Laid: 04.03.94. Coming into force: 25.02.94. Effect: S.I. 1980/535; 1984/1216 amended. Territorial extent & classification: GB. General. – 4p. – 0 11 043422 6 *£1.10*

The Merchant Shipping (Safety Officials and Reporting of Accidents and Dangerous Occurrences) (Amendment) Regulations 1994 No. 2014. Enabling power: *Merchant Shipping Act 1979, s. 21 (1) (a) (3) to (6), 22 (1) (a)*. Issued: 05.08.94. Made: 28.07.94. Laid: 05.08.94. Coming into force: 26.08.94. Effect: S.I. 1982/876 amended. Territorial extent & classification: GB. General. – 2p. – 0 11 045014 0 *£0.65*

The Merchant Shipping (Salvage and Pollution) Act 1994 (Commencement No. 2) Order 1994 No.2971 (C. 68). Enabling power: *Merchant Shipping (Salvage and Pollution) Act 1994, s. 10 (4)*. Bringing into operation various provisions of the 1994 act on 01.01.95. Issued: 30.11.94. Made: 22.11.94. Effect: None. Territorial extent & classification: GB. General. – 4p. – 0 11 043152 9 *£1.10*

METROPOLITAN AND CITY POLICE DISTRICTS: CABS

The London Cab Order 1994 No. 1087. Enabling power: *Metropolitan Public Carriage Act 1869, s. 9 & London Cab and Stage Carriage Act 1907, s. 1 & London Cab Act 1968, s. 1*. Issued: 21.04.94. Made: 31.03.94. Coming into force: 23.04.94. Effect: S.R.& O. 1934/1346 amended. Territorial extent & classification: E. Local. – 2p. – 0 11 044087 0 *£0.65*

MONOPOLIES AND MERGERS

The Fair Trading Act (Amendment) (Merger Prenotification) Regulations 1994 No. 1934. Enabling power: *Fair Trading Act 1973, s. 75F (1) (2)*. Issued: 01.08.94. Made: 18.07.94. Laid: 14.06.94. Coming into force: 18.08.94. Effect: 1973 c. 41; S.I. 1990/501 amended. Supersedes Draft ISBN 0110459377 published on 22.06.94. Territorial extent & classification: GB. General. – 2p. – 0 11 044934 7 *£0.65*

The Merger References (Increase in Value of Assets) Order 1994 No. 72. Enabling power: *Fair Trading Act 1973, s. 64 (7)*. Issued: 26.01.94. Made: 11.01.94. Laid: 19.01.94. Coming into force: 09.02.94. Effect: 1973 c.41 amended. Territorial extent & classification: GB. General. – 2p. – 0 11 043072 7 *£0.65*

The Merger Reference (Thomas Cook Group Limited and Barclays Bank plc) (No. 2) Order 1994 No.2953. Enabling power: *Fair Trading Act 1973, s. 74*. Issued: 06.01.95. Made: 22.11.94. Laid: 22.11.94. Coming into force: 23.11.94. Effect: S.I. 1994/2877 revoked. Territorial extent & classification: GB. General. – 4p. – 0 11 043865 5 *£1.10*

Price/availability are liable to change without notice

The Merger Reference (Thomas Cook Group Limited and Barclays Bank plc) Order 1994 No.2877. Enabling power: *Fair Trading Act 1973, s. 74*. Issued: 06.01.95. Made: 09.11.94. Laid: 10.11.94. Coming into force: 10.11.94. Effect: None. Territorial extent & classification: GB. General. – 2p. – 0 11 043847 7 £0.65

The Monopoly References (Alteration of Exclusions) Order 1994 No. 1922. Enabling power: *Fair Trading Act 1973, s. 50 (5)*. Issued: 18.08.94. Made: 14.07.94. Laid: 19.07.94. Coming into force: 31.10.94. Effect: 1973 c. 41 amended. Territorial extent & classification: GB. General. – 2p. – 0 11 044922 3 £0.65

NATIONAL ASSISTANCE SERVICES

The National Assistance (Assessment of Resources) (Amendment No. 2) Regulations 1994 No.2386. Enabling power: *National Assistance Act 1948, s. 22 (5)*. Issued: 19.09.94. Made: 09.09.94. Laid: 12.09.94. Coming into force: 03.10.94. Effect: S.I. 1992/2977; 1994/825 amended. This SI has been made in consequence of a defect in SI 1994/825 and is being sent free of charge to all known recipients of that SI. Territorial extent & classification: E/W. General. – 2p. – 0 11 045386 7 £0.65

The National Assistance (Assessment of Resources) (Amendment) Regulations 1994 No.825. Enabling power: *National Assistance Act 1948, s. 22 (5)*. Issued: 25.03.94. Made: 21.03.94. Laid: 21.03.94. Coming into force: 11.04.94. Effect: S.I. 1992/2977 amended. With correction slip. Territorial extent & classification: E/W. General. – 4p. – 0 11 043825 6 £1.10 Replaced by ISBN 011045958X

The National Assistance (Sums for Personal Requirements) Regulations 1994 No. 826. Enabling power: *National Assistance Act 1948, ss. 22 (4), 35 (1), 64 (1)*. Issued: 25.03.94. Made: 21.03.94. Laid: 21.03.94. Coming into force: 11.04.94. Effect: S.I. 1993/462 revoked. Territorial extent & classification: E/W. General. – 4p. – 0 11 043826 4 £1.10

NATIONAL DEBT

The National Savings Stock Register (Amendment) Regulations 1994 No. 3277. Enabling power: *National Debt Act 1972, s. 3*. Issued: 20.01.95. Made: 19.12.94. Laid: 20.12.94. Coming into force: 01.02.95. Effect: S.I. 1976/2012 amended. Territorial extent & classification: GB. General. – 4p. – 0 11 043916 3 £1.10

The Savings Certificates (Amendment) Regulations 1994 No. 343. Enabling power: *National Debt Act 1972, s. 11*. Issued: 28.02.94. Made: 17.02.94. Laid: 18.02.94. Coming into force: 11.03.94. Effect: S.I. 1991/1031 amended. Territorial extent & classification: GB. General. – 4p. – 0 11 043343 2 £1.10

NATIONAL HEALTH SERVICE, ENGLAND AND WALES

The Addenbrooke's National Health Service Trust (Transfer of Trust Property) Order 1994 No.2687. Enabling power: *National Health Service Act 1977, s. 92 (1)*. Issued: 26.10.94. Made: 18.10.94. Laid: 26.10.94. Coming into force: 16.11.94. Effect: None. Territorial extent & classification: E/W. General. – 2p. – 0 11 045687 4 £0.65

The Aintree Hospitals National Health Service Trust (Transfer of Trust Property) (No. 2) Order 1994 No. 2988. Enabling power: *National Health Service Act 1977, s. 92 (1)*. Issued: 01.12.94. Made: 24.11.94. Laid: 01.12.94. Coming into force: 22.12.94. Effect: None. Territorial extent & classification: E/W. General. – 2p. – 0 11 043206 1 £0.65

The Aintree Hospitals National Health Service Trust (Transfer of Trust Property) Order 1994 No. 2521. Enabling power: *National Health Service Act 1977, s. 92 (1)*. Issued: 06.01.94. Made: 27.09.94. Laid: 06.10.94. Coming into force: 27.10.94. Effect: None. Territorial extent & classification: E/W. General. – 2p. – 0 11 045521 5 £0.65

The Airedale National Health Service Trust (Transfer of Trust Property) Order 1994 No.1309. Enabling power: *National Health Service Act 1977, s. 92 (1)*. Issued: 23.05.94. Made: 16.05.94. Laid: 23.05.94. Coming into force: 13.06.94. Effect: None. Territorial extent & classification: E/W. General. – 2p. – 0 11 044309 8 £0.65

The Alexandra Health Care National Health Service Trust (Establishment) Order 1994 No.169. Enabling power: *National Health Service and Community Care Act 1990, s. 5 (1), sch. 2, paras. 1, 3, 4, 5, 6 (2) (d)*. Issued: 09.02.94. Made: 28.01.94. Coming into force: 08.02.94. Effect: None. Territorial extent & classification: E/W. General. – 4p. – 0 11 043169 3 £1.10

The Allington National Health Service Trust (Transfer of Trust Property) Order 1994 No.2335. Enabling power: *National Health Service Act 1977, s. 92 (1)*. Issued: 14.09.94. Made: 07.09.94. Laid: 14.09.94. Coming into force: 05.10.94. Effect: None. Territorial extent & classification: E/W. General. – 2p. – 0 11 045335 2 £0.65

The Andover District Community Health Care National Health Service Trust (Transfer of Trust Property) Order 1994 No. 624. Enabling power: *National Health Service Act 1977, s. 92 (1)*. Issued: 18.03.94. Made: 08.03.94. Laid: 09.03.94. Coming into force: 30.03.94. Effect: None. Territorial extent & classification: E/W. General. – 2p. – 0 11 043624 5 £0.65

The Anglian Harbours National Health Service Trust (Transfer of Trust Property) Order 1994 No.22. Enabling power: *National Health Service Act 1977, s. 92 (1)*. Issued: 18.01.94. Made: 11.01.94. Laid: 18.01.94. Coming into force: 08.02.94. Effect: None. Territorial extent & classification: E/W. General. – 2p. – 0 11 043022 0 £0.65

The Ashford Hospitals National Health Service Trust (Establishment) Amendment Order 1994 No.1555. Enabling power: *National Health Service Act 1977, s. 126 (3) & National Health Service and Community Care Act 1990, s. 5 (1)*. Issued: 20.06.94. Made: 10.06.94. Coming into force: 20.06.94. Effect: S.I. 1991/2319 amended. Territorial extent & classification: E/W. General. – 2p. – 0 11 044555 4 £0.65

Price/availability are liable to change without notice

The Ashford Hospital National Health Service Trust (Transfer of Trust Property) Order 1994 No. 1053. Enabling power: *National Health Service Act 1977, s. 92 (1)*. Issued: 19.04.94. Made: 12.04.94. Laid: 19.04.94. Coming into force: 10.05.94. Effect: None. Territorial extent & classification: E/W. General. – 2p. – 0 11 044053 6 *£0.65*

The Authorities for London Post-Graduate Teaching Hospitals (Abolition) Order 1994 No.1831. Enabling power: *National Health Service Act 1977, ss. 11, 126 (3) (4) & National Health Service and Community Care Act 1990, s. 5 (10)*. Issued: 18.07.94. Made: 11.07.94. Laid: 11.07.94. Coming into force: 01.08.94. Effect: None. Territorial extent & classification: E/W. General. – 4p. – 0 11 044831 6 *£1.10*

The Avalon, Somerset, National Health Service Trust (Transfer of Trust Property) Order 1994 No. 481. Enabling power: *National Health Service Act 1977, s. 92 (1)*. Issued: 09.03.94. Made: 01.03.94. Laid: 02.03.94. Coming into force: 23.03.94. Effect: None. Territorial extent & classification: E/W. General. – 2p. – 0 11 043481 1 *£0.65*

The Avon Ambulance Service National Health Service Trust (Transfer of Trust Property) Order 1994 No. 1310. Enabling power: *National Health Service Act 1977, s. 92 (1)*. Issued: 23.05.94. Made: 16.05.94. Laid: 23.05.94. Coming into force: 13.06.94. Effect: None. Territorial extent & classification: E/W. General. – 2p. – 0 11 044310 1 *£0.65*

The Aylesbury Vale Community Healthcare National Health Service Trust (Transfer of Trust Property) Order 1994 No. 1913. Enabling power: *National Health Service Act 1977, s. 92 (1)*. Issued: 25.07.94. Made: 15.07.94. Laid: 19.07.94. Coming into force: 09.08.94. Effect: None. Territorial extent & classification: E/W. General. – 2p. – 0 11 044913 4 *£0.65*

The Barnet Community Healthcare National Health Service Trust (Transfer of Trust Property) Order 1994 No. 1311. Enabling power: *National Health Service Act 1977, s. 92 (1)*. Issued: 23.05.94. Made: 16.05.94. Laid: 23.05.94. Coming into force: 13.06.94. Effect: None. Territorial extent & classification: E/W. General. – 2p. – 0 11 044311 X *£0.65*

The Barnsley District General Hospital National Health Service Trust (Transfer of Trust Property) Order 1994 No. 484. Enabling power: *National Health Service Act 1977, s. 92 (1)*. Issued: 09.03.94. Made: 01.03.94. Laid: 02.03.94. Coming into force: 23.03.94. Effect: None. Territorial extent & classification: E/W. General. – 2p. – 0 11 043484 6 *£0.65*

The Basildon and Thurrock General Hospitals National Health Service Trust (Transfer of Trust Property) Order 1994 No. 2363. Enabling power: *National Health Service Act 1977, s. 92 (1)*. Issued: 15.09.94. Made: 08.09.94. Laid: 15.09.94. Coming into force: 06.10.94. Effect: None. Territorial extent & classification: E/W. General. – 2p. – 0 11 045363 8 *£0.65*

The Bedford and Shires Health and Care National Health Service Trust (Transfer of Trust Property) Order 1994 No. 663. Enabling power: *National Health Service Act 1977, s. 92 (1)*. Issued: 18.03.94. Made: 08.03.94. Laid: 10.03.94. Coming into force: 31.03.94. Effect: None. Territorial extent & classification: E/W. General. – 2p. – 0 11 043663 6 *£0.65*

The Bedford Hospital National Health Service Trust (Transfer of Trust Property) Order 1994 No. 662. Enabling power: *National Health Service Act 1977, s. 92 (1)*. Issued: 18.03.94. Made: 08.03.94. Laid: 10.03.94. Coming into force: 31.03.94. Effect: None. Territorial extent & classification: E/W. General. – 2p. – 0 11 043662 8 *£0.65*

The Bedfordshire and Hertfordshire Ambulance and Paramedic Service National Health Service Trust (Transfer of Trust Property) Order 1994 No. 661. Enabling power: *National Health Service Act 1977, s. 92 (1)*. Issued: 18.03.94. Made: 08.03.94. Laid: 10.03.94. Coming into force: 31.03.94. Effect: None. Territorial extent & classification: E/W. General. – 2p. – 0 11 043661 X *£0.65*

The Bedfordshire and Hertfordshire Ambulance and Paramedic Service National Health Service Trust (Transfer of Trust Property) Order 1994 No. 1343. Enabling power: *National Health Service Act 1977, s. 92 (1)*. Issued: 25.05.94. Made: 18.05.94. Laid: 25.05.94. Coming into force: 15.06.94. Effect: None. Territorial extent & classification: E/W. General. – 2p. – 0 11 044343 8 *£0.65*

The Bethlem and Maudsley National Health Service Trust (Establishment) Order 1994 No.404. Enabling power: *National Health Service and Community Care Act 1990, s. 5 (1), sch. 2, paras. 1, 3, 4, 5, 6 (2) (d)*. Issued: 03.03.94. Made: 23.02.94. Coming into force: 21.03.94. Effect: None. Territorial extent & classification: E/W. General. – 4p. – 0 11 043404 8 *£1.10*

The Bexley Community Health National Health Service Trust (Establishment) Order 1994 No.183. Enabling power: *National Health Service and Community Care Act 1990, s. 5 (1), sch. 2, paras. 1, 3, 4, 5, 6 (2) (d)*. Issued: 09.02.94. Made: 28.01.94. Coming into force: 08.02.94. Effect: None. Territorial extent & classification: E/W. General. – 4p. – 0 11 043183 9 *£1.10*

The Bexley Community Health National Health Service Trust (Transfer of Trust Property) Order 1994 No. 2336. Enabling power: *National Health Service Act 1977, s. 92 (1)*. Issued: 14.09.94. Made: 07.09.94. Laid: 14.09.94. Coming into force: 05.10.94. Effect: None. Territorial extent & classification: E/W. General. – 2p. – 0 11 045336 0 *£0.65*

The Birmingham Children's Hospital National Health Service Trust (Establishment) Order 1994 No. 3182. Enabling power: *National Health Service and Community Care Act 1990, s. 5 (1), sch. 2, paras. 1, 3, 4, 5, 6 (2) (d)*. Issued: 20.12.94. Made: 12.12.94. Coming into force: 22.12.94. Effect: None. Territorial extent & classification: E/W. General. – 4p. – 0 11 043461 7 *£1.10*

The Blackburn, Hyndburn and Ribble Valley Health Care National Health Service Trust (Transfer of Trust Property) Order 1994 No. 1559. Enabling power: *National Health Service Act 1977, s. 92 (1)*. Issued: 21.06.94. Made: 14.06.94. Laid: 21.06.94. Coming into force: 12.07.94. Effect: None. Territorial extent & classification: E/W. General. – 2p. – 0 11 044559 7 *£0.65*

The Black Country Mental Health National Health Service Trust (Establishment) Order 1994 No.3177. Enabling power: *National Health Service and Community Care Act 1990, s. 5 (1), sch. 2, paras. 1, 3, 4, 5, 6 (2) (d)*. Issued: 20.12.94. Made: 12.12.94. Coming into force: 22.12.94. Effect: None. Territorial extent & classification: E/W. General. – 4p. – 0 11 043459 5 *£1.10*

The Blackpool Victoria Hospital National Health Service Trust (Transfer of Trust Property) Order 1994 No. 2950. Enabling power: *National Health Service Act 1977, s. 92 (1)*. Issued: 28.11.94. Made: 22.11.94. Laid: 28.11.94. Coming into force: 19.12.94. Effect: None. Territorial extent & classification: E/W. General. – 2p. – 0 11 043140 5 *£0.65*

The Blackpool, Wyre and Fylde Community National Health Service Trust (Transfer of Trust Property) Order 1994 No. 2951. Enabling power: *National Health Service Act 1977, s. 92 (1)*. Issued: 28.11.94. Made: 22.11.94. Laid: 28.11.94. Coming into force: 19.12.94. Effect: None. Territorial extent & classification: E/W. General. – 2p. – 0 11 043138 3 *£0.65*

The Bournewood Community and Mental Health National Health Service Trust (Establishment) Order 1994 No. 3173. Enabling power: *National Health Service and Community Care Act 1990, s. 5 (1), sch. 2, paras. 1, 3, 4, 5, 6 (2) (d)*. Issued: 20.12.94. Made: 12.12.94. Coming into force: 22.12.94. Effect: None. Territorial extent & classification: E/W. General. – 2p. – 0 11 043465 X *£0.65*

The Bridgend and District National Health Service Trust (Transfer of Trust Property) Order 1994 No. 2412. Enabling power: *National Health Service Act 1977, s. 92 (1)*. Issued: 29.09.94. Made: 13.09.94. Laid: 14.09.94. Coming into force: 05.10.94. Effect: None. Territorial extent & classification: W. General. – 2p. – 0 11 045412 X *£0.65*

The Brighton Health Care National Health Service Trust (Transfer of Trust Property) Order 1994 No. 23. Enabling power: *National Health Service Act 1977, s. 92 (1)*. Issued: 18.01.94. Made: 11.01.94. Laid: 18.01.94. Coming into force: 08.02.94. Effect: None. Territorial extent & classification: E/W. General. – 2p. – 0 11 043023 9 *£0.65*

The Bromley Hospitals National Health Service Trust (Transfer of Trust Property) Order 1994 No. 1572. Enabling power: *National Health Service Act 1977, s. 92 (1)*. Issued: 22.06.94. Made: 14.06.94. Laid: 22.06.94. Coming into force: 13.07.94. Effect: None. Territorial extent & classification: E/W. General. – 2p. – 0 11 044572 4 *£0.65*

The Burnley Health Care National Health Service Trust (Transfer of Trust Property) Order 1994 No. 24. Enabling power: *National Health Service Act 1977, s. 92 (1)*. Issued: 18.01.94. Made: 11.01.94. Laid: 18.01.94. Coming into force: 08.02.94. Effect: None. Territorial extent & classification: E/W. General. – 2p. – 0 11 043024 7 *£0.65*

The Calderdale Healthcare National Health Service Trust (Transfer of Trust Property) Order 1994 No. 2366. Enabling power: *National Health Service Act 1977, s. 92 (1)*. Issued: 15.09.94. Made: 08.09.94. Laid: 15.09.94. Coming into force: 06.10.94. Effect: None. Territorial extent & classification: E/W. General. – 2p. – 0 11 045366 2 *£0.65*

The Calderstones National Health Service Trust (Transfer of Trust Property) Order 1994 No.51. Enabling power: *National Health Service Act 1977, s. 92 (1)*. Issued: 20.01.94. Made: 13.01.94. Laid: 20.01.94. Coming into force: 10.02.94. Effect: None. Territorial extent & classification: E/W. General. – 2p. – 0 11 043051 4 *£0.65*

The Canterbury and Thanet Community Health Care National Health Service Trust (Transfer of Trust Property) Order 1994 No. 620. Enabling power: *National Health Service Act 1977, s. 92 (1)*. Issued: 17.03.94. Made: 08.03.94. Laid: 09.03.94. Coming into force: 30.03.94. Effect: None. Territorial extent & classification: E/W. General. – 2p. – 0 11 043620 2 *£0.65*

The Central Manchester National Health Service Trust (Transfer of Trust Property) Order 1994 No. 318. Enabling power: *National Health Service Act 1977, s. 92 (1)*. Issued: 22.02.94. Made: 14.02.94. Laid: 22.02.94. Coming into force: 15.03.94. Effect: None. Territorial extent & classification: E/W. General. – 2p. – 0 11 043318 1 *£0.65*

The Central Middlesex Hospital National Health Service Trust (Transfer of Trust Property) Order 1994 No. 359. Enabling power: *National Health Service Act 1977, s. 92 (1)*. Issued: 28.02.94. Made: 21.02.94. Laid: 28.02.94. Coming into force: 21.03.94. Effect: None. Territorial extent & classification: E/W. General. – 2p. – 0 11 043359 9 *£0.65*

The Chase Farm Hospitals National Health Service Trust (Transfer of Trust Property) Order 1994 No. 1312. Enabling power: *National Health Service Act 1977, s. 92 (1)*. Issued: 23.05.94. Made: 16.05.94. Laid: 23.05.94. Coming into force: 13.06.94. Effect: None. Territorial extent & classification: E/W. General. – 2p. – 0 11 044312 8 *£0.65*

The Chelsea and Westminster Healthcare National Health Service Trust (Establishment) Order 1994 No. 855. Enabling power: *National Health Service and Community Care Act 1990, s. 5 (1), sch. 2, paras. 1, 3, 4, 5, 6 (2) (d)*. Issued: 28.03.94. Made: 21.03.94. Coming into force: 31.03.94. Effect: None. Territorial extent & classification: E/W. General. – 4p. – 0 11 043855 8 *£1.10*

The Chesterfield and North Derbyshire Royal Hospital National Health Service Trust (Establishment) (Amendment) Order 1994 No. 2522. Enabling power: *National Health Service Act 1977, s. 92 (1)*. Issued: 06.01.94. Made: 27.09.94. Coming into force: 07.10.94. Effect: S.I. 1992/2474 amended. Territorial extent & classification: E/W. General. – 2p. – 0 11 045522 3 *£0.65*

The Chorley and South Ribble National Health Service Trust (Transfer of Trust Property) Order 1994 No. 1313. Enabling power: *National Health Service Act 1977, s. 92 (1)*. Issued: 23.05.94. Made: 16.05.94. Laid: 23.05.94. Coming into force: 13.06.94. Effect: None. Territorial extent & classification: E/W. General. – 2p. – 0 11 044313 6 *£0.65*

The Churchill John Radcliffe National Health Service Trust (Change of Name) Order 1994 No. 482. Enabling power: *National Health Service Act 1977, s. 126 (3) (4) & National Health Service and Community Care Act 1990, s. 5 (1)*. Issued: 09.03.94. Made: 01.03.94. Coming into force: 11.03.94. Effect: S.I. 1993/2544 amended. Territorial extent & classification: E/W. General. – 2p. – 0 11 043482 X *£0.65*

The Cleveland Ambulance National Health Service Trust (Transfer of Trust Property) Order 1994 No. 25. Enabling power: *National Health Service Act 1977, s. 92 (1)*. Issued: 18.01.94. Made: 11.01.94. Laid: 18.01.94. Coming into force: 08.02.94. Effect: None. Territorial extent & classification: E/W. General. – 2p. – 0 11 043025 5 *£0.65*

The CommuniCare National Health Service Trust (Transfer of Trust Property) Order 1994 No. 1560. Enabling power: *National Health Service Act 1977, s. 92 (1)*. Issued: 21.06.94. Made: 14.06.94. Laid: 21.06.94. Coming into force: 12.07.94. Effect: None. Territorial extent & classification: E/W. General. – 2p. – 0 11 044560 0 *£0.65*

The Community Health Care: North Durham National Health Service Trust (Establishment) Amendment Order 1994 No. 194. Enabling power: *National Health Service Act 1977, s. 126 (3) & National Health Service and Community Care Act 1990, s. 5 (1)*. Issued: 09.02.94. Made: 31.01.94. Coming into force: 10.02.94. Effect: S.I. 1993/2612 amended. Territorial extent & classification: E/W. General. – 2p. – 0 11 043194 4 *£0.65*

The Community Health Care Service (North Derbyshire) National Health Service Trust (Transfer of Trust Property) Order 1994 No. 2695. Enabling power: *National Health Service Act 1977, s. 92 (1)*. Issued: 26.10.94. Made: 18.10.94. Laid: 26.10.94. Coming into force: 16.11.94. Effect: None. Territorial extent & classification: E/W. General. – 2p. – 0 11 045695 5 *£0.65*

The Community Health Services, Southern Derbyshire National Health Service Trust (Transfer of Trust Property) Order 1994 No. 1314. Enabling power: *National Health Service Act 1977, s. 92 (1)*. Issued: 23.05.94. Made: 16.05.94. Laid: 23.05.94. Coming into force: 13.06.94. Effect: None. Territorial extent & classification: E/W. General. – 2p. – 0 11 044314 4 *£0.65*

The Cornwall and Isles of Scilly Learning Disabilities National Health Service Trust (Transfer of Trust Property) Order 1994 No. 29. Enabling power: *National Health Service Act 1977, s. 92 (1)*. Issued: 19.01.94. Made: 12.01.94. Laid: 19.01.94. Coming into force: 09.02.94. Effect: None. Territorial extent & classification: E/W. General. – 2p. – 0 11 043029 8 *£0.65*

The Cornwall Healthcare National Health Service Trust (Transfer of Trust Property) Order 1994 No. 1315. Enabling power: *National Health Service Act 1977, s. 92 (1)*. Issued: 23.05.94. Made: 16.05.94. Laid: 23.05.94. Coming into force: 13.06.94. Effect: None. Territorial extent & classification: E/W. General. – 2p. – 0 11 044315 2 *£0.65*

The Cornwall Healthcare National Health Service Trust (Transfer of Trust Property) Order 1994 No. 2368. Enabling power: *National Health Service Act 1977, s. 92 (1)*. Issued: 15.09.94. Made: 08.09.94. Laid: 15.09.94. Coming into force: 06.10.94. Effect: None. Territorial extent & classification: E/W. General. – 2p. – 0 11 045368 9 *£0.65*

The Cornwall Healthcare National Health Service Trust (Transfer of Trust Property) (No.2) Order 1994 No. 1388. Enabling power: *National Health Service Act 1977, s. 92 (1)*. Issued: 01.06.94. Made: 24.05.94. Laid: 25.05.94. Coming into force: 15.06.94. Effect: None. With correction slip dated June 1994. Territorial extent & classification: E/W. General. – 2p. – 0 11 044388 8 *£0.65*

The Countess of Chester Hospital National Health Service Trust (Transfer of Trust Property) Order 1994 No. 1301. Enabling power: *National Health Service Act 1977, s. 92 (1)*. Issued: 19.05.94. Made: 12.05.94. Laid: 19.05.94. Coming into force: 09.06.94. Effect: None. Territorial extent & classification: E/W. General. – 2p. – 0 11 044301 2 *£0.65*

The Coventry Healthcare National Health Service Trust (Establishment) Order 1994 No. 170. Enabling power: *National Health Service and Community Care Act 1990, s. 5 (1), sch. 2, paras. 1, 3, 4, 5, 6 (2) (d)*. Issued: 09.02.94. Made: 28.01.94. Coming into force: 08.02.94. Effect: None. Territorial extent & classification: E/W. General. – 4p. – 0 11 043170 7 *£1.10*

The Crawley Horsham National Health Service Trust (Transfer of Trust Property) Order 1994 No. 2688. Enabling power: *National Health Service Act 1977, s. 92 (1)*. Issued: 26.10.94. Made: 18.10.94. Laid: 26.10.94. Coming into force: 16.11.94. Effect: None. Territorial extent & classification: E/W. General. – 2p. – 0 11 045688 2 *£0.65*

The Dacorum and St Albans Community National Health Service Trust Dissolution Order 1994 No. 862. Enabling power: *National Health Service Act 1977, s. 126 (3) & National Health Service and Community Care Act 1990, s. 5 (1), sch. 2, para. 29 (1)*. Issued: 28.03.94. Made: 21.03.94. Coming into force: 01.04.94. Effect: S.I. 1991/2336 revoked. Territorial extent & classification: E/W. General. – 2p. – 0 11 043862 0 *£0.65*

Price/availability are liable to change without notice

The Derby City General Hospital National Health Service Trust (Transfer of Trust Property) Order 1994 No. 1317. Enabling power: *National Health Service Act 1977, s. 92 (1).* Issued: 23.05.94. Made: 16.05.94. Laid: 23.05.94. Coming into force: 13.06.94. Effect: None. Territorial extent & classification: E/W. General. – 2p. – 0 11 044317 9 *£0.65*

The Doncaster Healthcare National Health Service Trust (Transfer of Trust Property) Order 1994 No. 30. Enabling power: *National Health Service Act 1977, s. 92 (1).* Issued: 19.01.94. Made: 12.01.94. Laid: 19.01.94. Coming into force: 09.02.94. Effect: None. Territorial extent & classification: E/W. General. – 2p. – 0 11 043030 1 *£0.65*

The Dorset Ambulance National Health Service Trust (Transfer of Trust Property) Order 1994 No. 896. Enabling power: *National Health Service Act 1977, s. 92 (1).* Issued: 29.03.94. Made: 23.03.94. Laid: 29.03.94. Coming into force: 19.04.94. Effect: None. Territorial extent & classification: E/W. General. – 2p. – 0 11 043896 5 *£0.65*

The Dorset Community National Health Service Trust (Establishment) Order 1994 No.167. Enabling power: *National Health Service and Community Care Act 1990, s. 5 (1), sch. 2, paras. 1, 3, 4, 5, 6 (2) (d).* Issued: 09.02.94. Made: 28.01.94. Coming into force: 08.02.94. Effect: None. Territorial extent & classification: E/W. General. – 4p. – 0 11 043167 7 *£1.10*

The Dudley Group of Hospitals National Health Service Trust (Establishment) Order 1994 No.168. Enabling power: *National Health Service and Community Care Act 1990, s. 5 (1), sch. 2, paras. 1, 3, 4, 5, 6 (2) (d).* Issued: 09.02.94. Made: 28.01.94. Coming into force: 08.02.94. Effect: None. Territorial extent & classification: E/W. General. – 4p. – 0 11 043168 5 *£1.10*

The Dudley Priority Health National Health Service Trust (Establishment) Order 1994 No.162. Enabling power: *National Health Service and Community Care Act 1990, s. 5 (1), sch. 2, paras. 1, 3, 4, 5, 6 (2) (d).* Issued: 09.02.94. Made: 28.01.94. Coming into force: 08.02.94. Effect: None. Territorial extent & classification: E/W. General. – 4p. – 0 11 043162 6 *£1.10*

The Durham County Ambulance Service National Health Service Trust (Transfer of Trust Property) Order 1994 No. 1318. Enabling power: *National Health Service Act 1977, s. 92 (1).* Issued: 23.05.94. Made: 16.05.94. Laid: 23.05.94. Coming into force: 13.06.94. Effect: None. Territorial extent & classification: E/W. General. – 2p. – 0 11 044318 7 *£0.65*

The Ealing Hospital National Health Service Trust (Transfer of Trust Property) Order 1994 No.2340. Enabling power: *National Health Service Act 1977, s. 92 (1).* Issued: 14.09.94. Made: 07.09.94. Laid: 14.09.94. Coming into force: 05.10.94. Effect: None. Territorial extent & classification: E/W. General. – 2p. – 0 11 045340 9 *£0.65*

The East Anglian Ambulance National Health Service Trust (Transfer of Trust Property) Order 1994 No. 2689. Enabling power: *National Health Service Act 1977, s. 92 (1).* Issued: 26.10.94. Made: 18.10.94. Laid: 26.10.94. Coming into force: 16.11.94. Effect: None. Territorial extent & classification: E/W. General. – 2p. – 0 11 045689 0 *£0.65*

The East Berkshire Community Health National Health Service Trust (Transfer of Trust Property) Order 1994 No. 990. Enabling power: *National Health Service Act 1977, s. 92 (1).* Issued: 08.04.94. Made: 30.03.94. Laid: 07.04.94. Coming into force: 28.04.94. Effect: None. Territorial extent & classification: E/W. General. – 2p. – 0 11 043990 2 *£0.65*

The East Berkshire National Health Service Trust for People with Learning Disabilities (Transfer of Trust Property) Order 1994 No. 992. Enabling power: *National Health Service Act 1977, s. 92 (1).* Issued: 08.04.94. Made: 30.03.94. Laid: 07.04.94. Coming into force: 28.04.94. Effect: None. Territorial extent & classification: E/W. General. – 2p. – 0 11 043992 9 *£0.65*

The East Birmingham Hospital National Health Service Trust (Establishment) Amendment Order 1994 No. 2690. Enabling power: *National Health Service Act 1977, s. 126 (3) & National Health Service and Community Care Act 1990, s. 5 (1).* Issued: 26.10.94. Made: 18.10.94. Coming into force: 28.10.94. Effect: S.I. 1991/2342 amended. Territorial extent & classification: E/W. General. – 2p. – 0 11 045690 4 *£0.65*

The Eastbourne and County Healthcare National Health Service Trust (Transfer of Trust Property) Order 1994 No. 666. Enabling power: *National Health Service Act 1977, s. 92 (1).* Issued: 18.03.94. Made: 08.03.94. Laid: 10.03.94. Coming into force: 31.03.94. Effect: None. Territorial extent & classification: E/W. General. – 2p. – 0 11 043666 0 *£0.65*

The East Cheshire National Health Service Trust (Transfer of Trust Property) Order 1994 No.986. Enabling power: *National Health Service Act 1977, s. 92 (1).* Issued: 08.04.94. Made: 30.03.94. Laid: 07.04.94. Coming into force: 28.04.94. Effect: None. Territorial extent & classification: E/W. General. – 2p. – 0 11 043986 4 *£0.65*

The East Glamorgan National Health Service Trust (Establishment) Order 1994 No. 316. Enabling power: *National Health Service and Community Care Act 1990, s. 5 (1), sch. 2, paras. 1, 3, 4, 5, 6 (2) (d).* Issued: 07.03.94. Made: 14.02.94. Coming into force: 07.03.94. Effect: None. Territorial extent & classification: W. General. – 4p. – 0 11 043316 5 *£1.10*

The East Hertfordshire National Health Service Trust (Transfer of Trust Property) Order 1994 No. 1300. Enabling power: *National Health Service Act 1977, s. 92 (1).* Issued: 19.05.94. Made: 12.05.94. Laid: 19.05.94. Coming into force: 09.06.94. Effect: None. Territorial extent & classification: E/W. General. – 2p. – 0 11 044300 4 *£0.65*

Price/availability are liable to change without notice

NATIONAL HEALTH SERVICE, ENGLAND AND WALES

The East Suffolk Health Services National Health Service Trust (Transfer of Trust Property) Order 1994 No. 2338. Enabling power: *National Health Service Act 1977, s. 92 (1)*. Issued: 14.09.94. Made: 07.09.94. Laid: 14.09.94. Coming into force: 05.10.94. Effect: None. Territorial extent & classification: E/W. General. – 2p. – 0 11 045338 7 £0.65

The East Surrey Hospital and Community Healthcare National Health Service Trust (Transfer of Trust Property) Order 1994 No. 993. Enabling power: *National Health Service Act 1977, s. 92 (1)*. Issued: 08.04.94. Made: 30.03.94. Laid: 07.04.94. Coming into force: 28.04.94. Effect: None. Territorial extent & classification: E/W. General. – 2p. – 0 11 043993 7 £0.65

The East Surrey Learning Disability and Mental Health Service National Health Service Trust (Establishment) Order 1994 No. 181. Enabling power: *National Health Service and Community Care Act 1990, s. 5 (1), sch. 2, paras. 1, 3, 4, 5, 6 (2) (d)*. Issued: 09.02.94. Made: 28.01.94. Coming into force: 08.02.94. Effect: None. Territorial extent & classification: E/W. General. – 4p. – 0 11 043181 2 £1.10

The East Sussex Health Authority (Transfer of Trust Property) Order 1994 No. 1316. Enabling power: *National Health Service Act 1977, s. 92 (1)*. Issued: 23.05.94. Made: 16.05.94. Laid: 23.05.94. Coming into force: 13.06.94. Effect: None. Territorial extent & classification: E/W. General. – 2p. – 0 11 044316 0 £0.65

The East Yorkshire Hospitals National Health Service Trust (Transfer of Trust Property) Order 1994 No. 1914. Enabling power: *National Health Service Act 1977, s. 92 (1)*. Issued: 25.07.94. Made: 15.07.94. Laid: 19.07.94. Coming into force: 09.08.94. Effect: None. Territorial extent & classification: E/W. General. – 2p. – 0 11 044914 2 £0.65

The Enfield Community Care National Health Service Trust (Transfer of Trust Property) Order 1994 No. 1915. Enabling power: *National Health Service Act 1977, s. 92 (1)*. Issued: 25.07.94. Made: 15.07.94. Laid: 19.07.94. Coming into force: 09.08.94. Effect: None. Territorial extent & classification: E/W. General. – 2p. – 0 11 044915 0 £0.65

The Essex and Herts Community National Health Service Trust (Establishment) Order 1994 No. 3180. Enabling power: *National Health Service and Community Care Act 1990, s. 5 (1), sch. 2, paras. 1, 3, 4, 5, 6 (2) (d)*. Issued: 20.12.94. Made: 12.12.94. Coming into force: 22.12.94. Effect: None. Territorial extent & classification: E/W. General. – 4p. – 0 11 043446 3 £1.10

The Essex Rivers Healthcare National Health Service Trust (Transfer of Trust Property) Order 1994 No. 281. Enabling power: *National Health Service Act 1977, s. 92 (1)*. Issued: 16.02.94. Made: 09.02.94. Laid: 16.02.94. Coming into force: 09.03.94. Effect: None. Territorial extent & classification: E/W. General. – 2p. – 0 11 043281 9 £0.65

The Exeter and North Devon Health Authority (Transfer of Trust Property) Order 1994 No. 1319. Enabling power: *National Health Service Act 1977, s. 92 (1)*. Issued: 23.05.94. Made: 16.05.94. Laid: 23.05.94. Coming into force: 13.06.94. Effect: None. Territorial extent & classification: E/W. General. – 2p. – 0 11 044319 5 £0.65

The Forest Healthcare National Health Service Trust (Transfer of Trust Property) Order 1994 No. 31. Enabling power: *National Health Service Act 1977, s. 92 (1)*. Issued: 19.01.94. Made: 12.01.94. Laid: 19.01.94. Coming into force: 09.02.94. Effect: None. Territorial extent & classification: E/W. General. – 2p. – 0 11 043031 X £0.65

The Fosse Health, Leicestershire Community National Health Service Trust (Transfer of Trust Property) Order 1994 No. 1320. Enabling power: *National Health Service Act 1977, s. 92 (1)*. Issued: 23.05.94. Made: 16.05.94. Laid: 23.05.94. Coming into force: 13.06.94. Effect: None. Territorial extent & classification: E/W. General. – 2p. – 0 11 044320 9 £0.65

The Fosse Health, Leicestershire Community National Health Service Trust (Establishment) Order 1994 No. 3185. Enabling power: *National Health Service and Community Care Act 1990, s. 5 (1), sch. 2, paras. 1, 3, 4, 5, 6 (2) (d)*. Issued: 20.12.94. Made: 12.12.94. Coming into force: 01.04.95. Effect: None. Territorial extent & classification: E/W. General. – 2p. – 0 11 043448 X £0.65

The Freeman Group of Hospitals National Health Service Trust (Transfer of Trust Property) Order 1994 No. 32. Enabling power: *National Health Service Act 1977, s. 92 (1)*. Issued: 19.01.94. Made: 12.01.94. Laid: 19.01.94. Coming into force: 09.02.94. Effect: None. Territorial extent & classification: E/W. General. – 2p. – 0 11 043032 8 £0.65

The Frenchay Healthcare National Health Service Trust (Transfer of Trust Property) Order 1994 No. 33. Enabling power: *National Health Service Act 1977, s. 92 (1)*. Issued: 19.01.94. Made: 12.01.94. Laid: 19.01.94. Coming into force: 09.02.94. Effect: None. Territorial extent & classification: E/W. General. – 2p. – 0 11 043033 6 £0.65

The Frimley Park Hospital National Health Service Trust (Transfer of Trust Property) Order 1994 No. 59. Enabling power: *National Health Service Act 1977, s. 92 (1)*. Issued: 21.01.94. Made: 14.01.94. Laid: 21.01.94. Coming into force: 11.02.94. Effect: None. Territorial extent & classification: E/W. General. – 2p. – 0 11 043059 X £0.65

The Furness Hospitals National Health Service Trust (Establishment) Order 1994 No. 179. Enabling power: *National Health Service and Community Care Act 1990, s. 5 (1), sch. 2, paras. 1, 3, 4, 5, 6 (2) (d)*. Issued: 09.02.94. Made: 28.01.94. Coming into force: 08.02.94. Effect: None. Territorial extent & classification: E/W. General. – 4p. – 0 11 043179 0 £1.10

Price/availability are liable to change without notice

The Gateshead Community Health National Health Service Trust Dissolution Order 1994 No.827. Enabling power: *National Health Service Act 1977, s. 126 (3) & National Health Service and Community Care Act 1990, s. 5 (1), sch. 2, para. 29 (1)*. Issued: 28.03.94. Made: 18.03.94. Coming into force: 01.04.94. Effect: S.I. 1991/2351 revoked. Territorial extent & classification: E/W. General. – 2p. – 0 11 043827 2 £0.65

The Gateshead Healthcare National Health Service Trust (Establishment) Order 1994 No.196. Enabling power: *National Health Service and Community Care Act 1990, s. 5 (1), sch. 2, paras. 1, 3, 4, 5, 6 (2) (d)*. Issued: 09.02.94. Made: 31.01.94. Coming into force: 01.04.94. Effect: None. Territorial extent & classification: E/W. General. – 4p. – 0 11 043196 0 £1.10

The Glenfield Hospital National Health Service Trust (Transfer of Trust Property) Order 1994 No. 1917. Enabling power: *National Health Service Act 1977, s. 92 (1)*. Issued: 25.07.94. Made: 15.07.94. Laid: 19.07.94. Coming into force: 09.08.94. Effect: None. Territorial extent & classification: E/W. General. – 2p. – 0 11 044917 7 £0.65

The Gloucestershire Ambulance Service National Health Service Trust (Transfer of Trust Property) Order 1994 No. 1571. Enabling power: *National Health Service Act 1977, s. 92 (1)*. Issued: 22.06.94. Made: 14.06.94. Laid: 22.06.94. Coming into force: 13.07.94. Effect: None. Territorial extent & classification: E/W. General. – 2p. – 0 11 044571 6 £0.65

The Good Hope Hospital National Health Service Trust (Transfer of Trust Property) Order 1994 No. 280. Enabling power: *National Health Service Act 1977, s. 92 (1)*. Issued: 16.02.94. Made: 09.02.94. Laid: 16.02.94. Coming into force: 09.03.94. Effect: None. Territorial extent & classification: E/W. General. – 2p. – 0 11 043280 0 £0.65

The Grantham and District Hospital National Health Service Trust (Establishment) Order 1994 No. 3175. Enabling power: *National Health Service and Community Care Act 1990, s. 5 (1), sch. 2, paras. 1, 3, 4, 5, 6 (2) (d)*. Issued: 20.12.94. Made: 12.12.94. Coming into force: 22.12.94. Effect: None. Territorial extent & classification: E/W. General. – 4p. – 0 11 043463 3 £1.10

The Great Ormond Street Hospital for Children National Health Service Trust (Establishment) Order 1994 No. 400. Enabling power: *National Health Service and Community Care Act 1990, s. 5 (1), sch. 2, paras. 1, 3, 4, 5, 6 (2) (d)*. Issued: 03.03.94. Made: 23.02.94. Coming into force: 21.03.94. Effect: None. Territorial extent & classification: E/W. General. – 4p. – 0 11 043400 5 £1.10

The Grimsby Health National Health Service Trust (Transfer of Trust Property) Order 1994 No.1299. Enabling power: *National Health Service Act 1977, s. 92 (1)*. Issued: 19.05.94. Made: 12.05.94. Laid: 19.05.94. Coming into force: 09.06.94. Effect: None. Territorial extent & classification: E/W. General. – 2p. – 0 11 044299 7 £0.65

The Halton General Hospital National Health Service Trust (Transfer of Trust Property) Order 1994 No. 1211. Enabling power: *National Health Service Act 1977, s. 92 (1)*. Issued: 10.05.94. Made: 03.05.94. Laid: 10.05.94. Coming into force: 31.05.94. Effect: None. Territorial extent & classification: E/W. General. – 2p. – 0 11 044211 3 £0.65

The Hammersmith Hospitals National Health Service Trust (Establishment) Order 1994 No.853. Enabling power: *National Health Service and Community Care Act 1990, s. 5 (1), sch. 2, paras. 1, 3, 4, 5, 6 (2) (d)*. Issued: 28.03.94. Made: 21.03.94. Coming into force: 31.03.94. Effect: None. Territorial extent & classification: E/W. General. – 4p. – 0 11 043853 1 £1.10

The Hampshire Ambulance Service National Health Service Trust (Transfer of Trust Property) Order 1994 No. 664. Enabling power: *National Health Service Act 1977, s. 92 (1)*. Issued: 18.03.94. Made: 08.03.94. Laid: 10.03.94. Coming into force: 31.03.94. Effect: None. Territorial extent & classification: E/W. General. – 2p. – 0 11 043664 4 £0.65

The Harrow and Hillingdon Healthcare National Health Service Trust (Establishment) Order 1994 No. 848. Enabling power: *National Health Service and Community Care Act 1990, s. 5 (1), sch. 2, paras. 1, 3, 4, 5, 6 (2) (d)*. Issued: 28.03.94. Made: 21.03.94. Coming into force: 01.04.94. Effect: None. Territorial extent & classification: E/W. General. – 4p. – 0 11 043848 5 £1.10

The Harrow and Hillingdon Healthcare National Health Service Trust (Transfer of Trust Property) (No. 2) Order 1994 No. 2708. Enabling power: *National Health Service Act 1977, s. 92 (1)*. Issued: 27.10.94. Made: 19.10.94. Laid: 27.10.94. Coming into force: 17.11.94. Effect: None. Territorial extent & classification: E/W. General. – 2p. – 0 11 045708 0 £0.65

The Harrow and Hillingdon Healthcare National Health Service Trust (Transfer of Trust Property) Order 1994 No. 1561. Enabling power: *National Health Service Act 1977, s. 92 (1)*. Issued: 21.06.94. Made: 14.06.94. Laid: 21.06.94. Coming into force: 12.07.94. Effect: None. Territorial extent & classification: E/W. General. – 2p. – 0 11 044561 9 £0.65

The Harrow Community Health Services National Health Service Trust Dissolution Order 1994 No.858. Enabling power: *National Health Service Act 1977, s. 126 (3) & National Health Service and Community Care Act 1990, s. 5 (1), sch. 2, para. 29 (1)*. Issued: 28.03.94. Made: 21.03.94. Coming into force: 01.04.94. Effect: S.I. 1991/2355 revoked. Territorial extent & classification: E/W. General. – 2p. – 0 11 043858 2 £0.65

The Hartlepool and Peterlee Hospitals National Health Service Trust (Transfer of Trust Property) Order 1994 No. 2990. Enabling power: *National Health Service Act 1977, s. 92 (1)*. Issued: 01.12.94. Made: 24.11.94. Laid: 01.12.94. Coming into force: 22.12.94. Effect: None. Territorial extent & classification: E/W. General. – 2p. – 0 11 043207 X £0.65

NATIONAL HEALTH SERVICE, ENGLAND AND WALES

The Hartlepool Community Care National Health Service Trust (Transfer of Trust Property) Order 1994 No. 2989. Enabling power: *National Health Service Act 1977, s. 92 (1)*. Issued: 01.12.94. Made: 24.11.94. Laid: 01.12.94. Coming into force: 22.12.94. Effect: None. Territorial extent & classification: E/W. General. – 2p. – 0 11 043205 3 £0.65

The Health Service Commissioner for England (National Blood Authority) Order 1994 No.2954. Enabling power: *Health Service Commissioners Act 1993, s. 2 (5)*. Issued: 06.12.94. Made: 24.11.94. Laid: 06.12.94. Coming into force: 01.01.95. Effect: None. Territorial extent & classification: E/W. General. – 2p. – 0 11 043210 X £0.65

The Heatherwood and Wexham Park Hospitals' National Health Service Trust (Transfer of Trust Property) Order 1994 No. 991. Enabling power: *National Health Service Act 1977, s. 92 (1)*. Issued: 08.04.94. Made: 30.03.94. Laid: 07.04.94. Coming into force: 28.04.94. Effect: None. Territorial extent & classification: E/W. General. – 2p. – 0 11 043991 0 £0.65

The Heathlands Mental Health National Health Service Trust (Establishment) Order 1994 No.184. Enabling power: *National Health Service and Community Care Act 1990, s. 5 (1), sch. 2, paras. 1, 3, 4, 5, 6 (2) (d)*. Issued: 09.02.94. Made: 28.01.94. Coming into force: 08.02.94. Effect: None. Territorial extent & classification: E/W. General. – 4p. – 0 11 043184 7 £1.10

The Hereford and Worcester Ambulance Service National Health Service Trust (Transfer of Trust Property) Order 1994 No. 1333. Enabling power: *National Health Service Act 1977, s. 92(1)*. Issued: 25.05.94. Made: 18.05.94. Laid: 25.05.94. Coming into force: 15.06.94. Effect: None Territorial extent & classification: E/W. General. – 2p. – 0 11 044333 0 £0.65

The Hillingdon Community Health National Health Service Trust Dissolution Order 1994 No.863. Enabling power: *National Health Service Act 1977, s. 126 (3) & National Health Service and Community Care Act 1990, s. 5 (1), sch. 2, para. 29 (1)*. Issued: 28.03.94. Made: 21.03.94. Coming into force: 01.04.94. Effect: S.I. 1991/2359 revoked. Territorial extent & classification: E/W. General. – 2p. – 0 11 043863 9 £0.65

The Hillingdon Hospital National Health Service Trust (Transfer of Trust Property) Order 1994 No. 623. Enabling power: *National Health Service Act 1977, s. 92 (1)*. Issued: 17.03.94. Made: 08.03.94. Laid: 09.03.94. Coming into force: 30.03.94. Effect: None. Territorial extent & classification: E/W. General. – 2p. – 0 11 043623 7 £0.65

The Hinchingbrooke Health Care National Health Service Trust (Transfer of Trust Property) Order 1994 No. 2691. Enabling power: *National Health Service Act 1977, s. 92 (1)*. Issued: 26.10.94. Made: 18.10.94. Laid: 26.10.94. Coming into force: 16.11.94. Effect: None. Territorial extent & classification: E/W. General. – 2p. – 0 11 045691 2 £0.65

The Homerton Hospital National Health Service Trust (Establishment) Order 1994 No.3181. Enabling power: *National Health Service and Community Care Act 1990, s. 5 (1), sch. 2, paras. 1, 3, 4, 5, 6 (2) (d)*. Issued: 20.12.94. Made: 12.12.94. Coming into force: 24.12.94. Effect: None. Territorial extent & classification: E/W. General. – 4p. – 0 11 043462 5 £1.10

The Homewood National Health Service Trust (Transfer of Trust Property) Order 1994 No.60. Enabling power: *National Health Service Act 1977, s. 92 (1)*. Issued: 21.01.94. Made: 14.01.94. Laid: 21.01.94. Coming into force: 11.02.94. Effect: None. Territorial extent & classification: E/W. General. – 2p. – 0 11 043060 3 £0.65

The Huddersfield Health Care Services National Health Service Trust (Transfer of Trust Property) Order 1994 No. 494. Enabling power: *National Health Service Act 1977, s. 92 (1)*. Issued: 09.03.94. Made: 02.03.94. Laid: 03.03.94. Coming into force: 24.03.94. Effect: None. Territorial extent & classification: E/W. General. – 2p. – 0 11 043494 3 £0.65

The Humberside Ambulance Service National Health Service Trust (Transfer of Trust Property) Order 1994 No. 489. Enabling power: *National Health Service Act 1977, s. 92 (1)*. Issued: 09.03.94. Made: 02.03.94. Laid: 03.03.94. Coming into force: 24.03.94. Effect: None. Territorial extent & classification: E/W. General. – 2p. – 0 11 043489 7 £0.65

The Ipswich Hospital National Health Service Trust (Transfer of Trust Property) Order 1994 No.2339. Enabling power: *National Health Service Act 1977, s. 92 (1)*. Issued: 14.09.94. Made: 07.09.94. Laid: 14.09.94. Coming into force: 05.10.94. Effect: None. Territorial extent & classification: E/W. General. – 2p. – 0 11 045339 5 £0.65

The Isles of Scilly (National Health Service) Order 1994 No. 2773. Enabling power: *National Health Service and Community Care Act 1990, s. 67 (6)*. Issued: 04.11.94. Made: 28.10.94. Coming into force: 08.11.94. Effect: None. Territorial extent & classification: E/W. General. – 2p. – 0 11 045773 0 £0.65

The James Paget Hospital National Health Service Trust (Transfer of Trust Property) Order 1994 No. 34. Enabling power: *National Health Service Act 1977, s. 92 (1)*. Issued: 19.01.94. Made: 12.01.94. Laid: 19.01.94. Coming into force: 09.02.94. Effect: None. Territorial extent & classification: E/W. General. – 2p. – 0 11 043034 4 £0.65

The Kent and Canterbury Hospitals National Health Service Trust (Transfer of Trust Property) Order 1994 No. 665. Enabling power: *National Health Service Act 1977, s. 92 (1)*. Issued: 18.03.94. Made: 08.03.94. Laid: 10.03.94. Coming into force: 31.03.94. Effect: None. Territorial extent & classification: E/W. General. – 2p. – 0 11 043665 2 £0.65

The Kent and Sussex Weald National Health Service Trust (Establishment) Order 1994 No.163. Enabling power: *National Health Service and Community Care Act 1990, s. 5 (1), sch. 2, paras. 1, 3, 4, 5, 6 (2) (d)*. Issued: 09.02.94. Made: 28.01.94. Coming into force: 08.02.94. Effect: None. Territorial extent & classification: E/W. General. – 4p. – 0 11 043163 4 £1.10

The Kingston and District Community National Health Service Trust (Transfer of Trust Property) Order 1994 No. 2692. Enabling power: *National Health Service Act 1977, s. 92 (1)*. Issued: 26.10.94. Made: 18.10.94. Laid: 26.10.94. Coming into force: 16.11.94. Effect: None. Territorial extent & classification: E/W. General. – 2p. – 0 11 045692 0 £0.65

The Leeds Community and Mental Health Services Teaching National Health Service Trust (Transfer of Trust Property) Order 1994 No. 1562. Enabling power: *National Health Service Act 1977, s. 92 (1)*. Issued: 21.06.94. Made: 14.06.94. Laid: 21.06.94. Coming into force: 12.07.94. Effect: None. Territorial extent & classification: E/W. General. – 2p. – 0 11 044562 7 £0.65

The Leicester General Hospital National Health Service Trust (Transfer of Trust Property) Order 1994 No. 1916. Enabling power: *National Health Service Act 1977, s. 92 (1)*. Issued: 25.07.94. Made: 15.07.94. Laid: 19.07.94. Coming into force: 09.08.94. Effect: None. Territorial extent & classification: E/W. General. – 2p. – 0 11 044916 9 £0.65

The Leicester Royal Infirmary National Health Service Trust (Transfer of Trust Property) Order 1994 No. 1918. Enabling power: *National Health Service Act 1977, s. 92 (1)*. Issued: 25.07.94. Made: 15.07.94. Laid: 19.07.94. Coming into force: 09.08.94. Effect: None. Territorial extent & classification: E/W. General. – 2p. – 0 11 044918 5 £0.65

The Lincoln District Healthcare National Health Service Trust (Transfer of Trust Property) Order 1994 No. 2693. Enabling power: *National Health Service Act 1977, s. 92 (1)*. Issued: 26.10.94. Made: 18.10.94. Laid: 26.10.94. Coming into force: 16.11.94. Effect: None. Territorial extent & classification: E/W. General. – 2p. – 0 11 045693 9 £0.65

The Liverpool Obstetric and Gynaecology Services National Health Service Trust (Change of Name) Order 1994 No. 2784. Enabling power: *National Health Service Act 1977, s. 126 (3) (4) & National Health Service and Community Care Act 1990, s. 5 (1)*. Issued: 07.11.94. Made: 01.11.94. Coming into force: 11.11.94. Effect: S.I. 1991/2366 amended. Territorial extent & classification: E/W. General. – 2p. – 0 11 045784 6 £0.65

The Louth and District Healthcare National Health Service Trust (Transfer of Trust Property) Order 1994 No. 2694. Enabling power: *National Health Service Act 1977, s. 92 (1)*. Issued: 26.10.94. Made: 18.10.94. Laid: 26.10.94. Coming into force: 16.11.94. Effect: None. Territorial extent & classification: E/W. General. – 2p. – 0 11 045694 7 £0.65

The Luton and Dunstable Hospital Trust National Health Service Trust (Transfer of Trust Property) Order 1994 No. 486. Enabling power: *National Health Service Act 1977, s. 92 (1)*. Issued: 09.03.94. Made: 01.03.94. Laid: 02.03.94. Coming into force: 23.03.94. Effect: None. Territorial extent & classification: E/W. General. – 2p. – 0 11 043486 2 £0.65

The Maidstone Priority Care National Health Service Trust (Transfer of Trust Property) Order 1994 No. 1563. Enabling power: *National Health Service Act 1977, s. 92 (1)*. Issued: 21.06.94. Made: 14.06.94. Laid: 21.06.94. Coming into force: 12.07.94. Effect: None. Territorial extent & classification: E/W. General. – 2p. – 0 11 044563 5 £0.65

The Manchester Children's Hospitals National Health Service Trust (Establishment) Order 1994 No. 3174. Enabling power: *National Health Service and Community Care Act 1990, s. 5 (1), sch. 2, paras. 1, 3, 4, 5, 6 (2) (d)*. Issued: 20.12.94. Made: 12.12.94. Coming into force: 22.12.94. Effect: None. Territorial extent & classification: E/W. General. – 4p. – 0 11 043464 1 £1.10

The Mancunian Community Health National Health Service Trust (Establishment) Order 1994 No.185. Enabling power: *National Health Service and Community Care Act 1990, s. 5 (1), sch. 2, paras. 1, 3, 4, 5, 6 (2) (d)*. Issued: 09.02.94. Made: 28.01.94. Coming into force: 08.02.94. Effect: None. Territorial extent & classification: E/W. General. – 4p. – 0 11 043185 5 £1.10

The Mancunian Community Health National Health Service Trust Dissolution Order 1994 No.828. Enabling power: *National Health Service Act 1977, s. 126 (3) & National Health Service and Community Care Act 1990, s. 5 (1), sch. 2, para. 29 (1)*. Issued: 28.03.94. Made: 18.03.94. Coming into force: 01.04.94. Effect: S.I. 1992/2586 revoked. Territorial extent & classification: E/W. General. – 2p. – 0 11 043828 0 £0.65

The Mancunian Community Health National Health Service Trust (Transfer of Trust Property) Order 1994 No. 622. Enabling power: *National Health Service Act 1977, s. 92 (1)*. Issued: 17.03.94. Made: 08.03.94. Laid: 09.03.94. Coming into force: 30.03.94. Effect: None. Territorial extent & classification: E/W. General. – 2p. – 0 11 043622 9 £0.65

The Medicinal Products: Prescription by Nurses etc. Act 1992 (Commencement No. 1) Order 1994 No. 2408 (C. 48). Enabling power: *Medicinal Products: Prescription by Nurses etc. Act 1992, s. 6 (2)*. Bringing various provisions of the 1992 act into operation on 03.10.94. Issued: 20.09.94. Made: 12.09.94. Effect: None. Territorial extent & classification: E/W/S. General. – 2p. – 0 11 045408 1 £0.65

The Merton and Sutton Community National Health Service Trust (Transfer of Trust Property) Order 1994 No. 485. Enabling power: *National Health Service Act 1977, s. 92 (1)*. Issued: 09.03.94. Made: 01.03.94. Laid: 02.03.94. Coming into force: 23.03.94. Effect: None. Territorial extent & classification: E/W. General. – 2p. – 0 11 043485 4 £0.65

The Microbiological Research Authority (Establishment and Constitution) Order 1994 No.603. Enabling power: *National Health Service Act 1977, ss. 11 (1) (2) (4), 126 (4), sch. 5, para. 9 (7) (b)*. Issued: 15.03.94. Made: 08.03.94. Laid: 08.03.94. Coming into force: 01.04.94. Effect: None. Territorial extent & classification: E/W. General. – 4p. – 0 11 043603 2 £1.10

Price/availability are liable to change without notice

The Microbiological Research Authority Regulations 1994 No. 602. Enabling power: *National Health Service Act 1977, s. 126 (4), sch. 5, para. 12, 16*. Issued: 15.03.94. Made: 08.03.94. Laid: 08.03.94. Coming into force: 01.04.94. Effect: None. Territorial extent & classification: E/W. General. – 4p. – 0 11 043602 4 *£1.10*

The Mid Anglia Community Health National Health Service Trust (Transfer of Trust Property) Order 1994 No. 2341. Enabling power: *National Health Service Act 1977, s. 92 (1)*. Issued: 14.09.94. Made: 07.09.94. Laid: 14.09.94. Coming into force: 05.10.94. Effect: None. Territorial extent & classification: E/W. General. – 2p. – 0 11 045341 7 *£0.65*

The Mid Essex Community Health National Health Service Trust (Dissolution) Order 1994 No.745. Enabling power: *National Health Service Act 1977, s. 126 (3) & National Health Service and Community Care Act 1990, s. 5 (1), sch. 2, para. 29 (1)*. Issued: 21.03.94. Made: 14.03.94. Coming into force: 24.03.94, for the purposes of art. 3; 01.04.94, for all other purposes. Effect: S.I. 1992/2514; 1993/3140 revoked. Territorial extent & classification: E/W. General. Supersedes S.I. 1993/3140 ISBN 011341627 issued 23.12.93. & is being issued free of charge to all known recipients of the original. – 2p. – 0 11 043745 4 *£0.65*

The Mid Essex Community Health National Health Service Trust (Transfer of Trust Property) Order 1994 No. 224. Enabling power: *National Health Service Act 1977, s. 92 (1)*. Issued: 10.02.94. Made: 03.02.94. Laid: 10.02.94. Coming into force: 03.03.94. Effect: None. Territorial extent & classification: E/W. General. – 2p. – 0 11 043224 X *£0.65*

The Mid Kent Healthcare National Health Service Trust (Transfer of Trust Property) Order 1994 No. 1573. Enabling power: *National Health Service Act 1977, s. 92 (1)*. Issued: 22.06.94. Made: 14.06.94. Laid: 22.06.94. Coming into force: 13.07.94. Effect: None. Territorial extent & classification: E/W. General. – 2p. – 0 11 044573 2 *£0.65*

The Mid-Staffordshire General Hospitals National Health Service Trust (Transfer of Trust Property) Order 1994 No. 488. Enabling power: *National Health Service Act 1977, s. 92 (1)*. Issued: 09.03.94. Made: 01.03.94. Laid: 02.03.94. Coming into force: 23.03.94. Effect: None. Territorial extent & classification: E/W. General. – 2p. – 0 11 043488 9 *£0.65*

The Mid-Sussex National Health Service Trust (Establishment) Order 1994 No. 165. Enabling power: *National Health Service and Community Care Act 1990, s. 5 (1), sch. 2, paras. 1, 3, 4, 5, 6 (2) (d)*. Issued: 09.02.94. Made: 28.01.94. Coming into force: 08.02.94. Effect: None. Territorial extent & classification: E/W. General. – 4p. – 0 11 043165 0 *£1.10*

The Milton Keynes Community Health National Health Service Trust (Transfer of Trust Property) Order 1994 No. 1919. Enabling power: *National Health Service Act 1977, s. 92 (1)*. Issued: 25.07.94. Made: 15.07.94. Laid: 19.07.94. Coming into force: 09.08.94. Effect: None. Territorial extent & classification: E/W. General. – 2p. – 0 11 044919 3 *£0.65*

The Milton Keynes General National Health Service Trust (Transfer of Trust Property) Order 1994 No. 1920. Enabling power: *National Health Service Act 1977, s. 92 (1)*. Issued: 25.07.94. Made: 15.07.94. Laid: 19.07.94. Coming into force: 09.08.94. Effect: None. Territorial extent & classification: E/W. General. – 2p. – 0 11 044920 7 *£0.65*

The Moorfields Eye Hospital National Health Service Trust (Establishment) Order 1994 No.403. Enabling power: *National Health Service and Community Care Act 1990, s. 5 (1), sch. 2, paras. 1, 3, 4, 5, 6 (2) (d)*. Issued: 03.03.94. Made: 23.02.94. Coming into force: 21.03.94. Effect: None. Territorial extent & classification: E/W. General. – 4p. – 0 11 043403 X *£1.10*

The Morriston Hospital National Health Service Trust (Establishment) Order 1994 No.317. Enabling power: *National Health Service and Community Care Act 1990, s. 5 (1), sch. 2, paras. 1, 3, 4, 5, 6 (2) (d)*. Issued: 07.03.94. Made: 14.02.94. Coming into force: 07.03.94. Effect: None. Territorial extent & classification: W. General. – 4p. – 0 11 043317 3 *£1.10*

The Mount Vernon and Watford Hospitals National Health Service Trust (Establishment) Order 1994 No. 852. Enabling power: *National Health Service and Community Care Act 1990, s. 5 (1), sch. 2, paras. 1, 3, 4, 5, 6 (2) (d)*. Issued: 28.03.94. Made: 21.03.94. Coming into force: 31.03.94. Effect: None. Territorial extent & classification: E/W. General. – 4p. – 0 11 043852 3 *£1.10*

The Mount Vernon Hospital National Health Service Trust Dissolution Order 1994 No.860. Enabling power: *National Health Service Act 1977, s. 126 (3) & National Health Service and Community Care Act 1990, s. 5 (1), sch. 2, para. 29 (1)*. Issued: 28.03.94. Made: 21.03.94. Coming into force: 01.04.94. Effect: S.I. 1990/2427 revoked. Territorial extent & classification: E/W. General. – 2p. – 0 11 043860 4 *£0.65*

The Mount Vernon Hospital National Health Service Trust (Transfer of Trust Property) Order 1994 No. 679. Enabling power: *National Health Service Act 1977, s. 92 (1)*. Issued: 18.03.94. Made: 10.03.94. Laid: 10.03.94. Coming into force: 31.03.94. Effect: None. Territorial extent & classification: E/W. General. – 2p. – 0 11 043679 2 *£0.65*

The National Blood Authority (Establishment and Constitution) Amendment Order 1994 No.589. Enabling power: *National Health Service Act 1977, ss. 11 (1) (992), 126 (3)*. Issued: 14.03.94. Made: 08.03.94. Laid: 08.03.94. Coming into force: 01.04.94. Effect: S.I. 1993/585 amended. Territorial extent & classification: E/W. General. – 2p. – 0 11 043589 3 *£0.65*

Price/availability are liable to change without notice

NATIONAL HEALTH SERVICE, ENGLAND AND WALES

The National Board for Nursing, Midwifery and Health Visiting for England (Constitution and Administration) Amendment Order 1994 No. 586. Enabling power: *Nurses, Midwives and Health Visitors Act 1979, ss. 6 (1) (da)*. Issued: 14.03.94. Made: 08.03.94. Laid: 08.03.94. Coming into force: 01.04.94. Effect: S.I. 1993/629 amended. Territorial extent & classification: E/W. General. – 2p. – 0 11 043586 9 £0.65

The National Health Service Act 1977 (Composition of Medical Practices Committee) Modification Order 1994 No. 545. Enabling power: *Naitonal Health Service Act 1977, s. 7 (1A)*. Issued: 11.03.94. Made: 04.03.94. Laid: 07.03.94. Coming into force: 01.04.94. Effect: 1977 c. 49 amended. Territorial extent & classification: E/W. General. – 2p. – 0 11 043545 1 £0.65

The National Health Service (Charges for Drugs and Appliances) Amendment Regulations 1994 No. 690. Enabling power: *National Health Service Act 1977, ss. 77, 126 (4)*. Issued: 16.03.94. Made: 10.03.94. Laid: 10.03.94. Coming into force: 01.04.94. Effect: S.I. 1989/419 amended. Territorial extent & classification: E/W. General. – 4p. – 0 11 043669 0 3 £1.10

The National Health Service (Charges to Overseas Visitors) (Amendment) Regulations 1994 No. 1535. Enabling power: *National Health Service Act 1977, s. 121*. Issued: 16.06.94. Made: 09.06.94. Laid: 10.06.94. Coming into force: 01.07.94. Effect: S.I. 1989/306 amended. Territorial extent & classification: E/W. General. – 4p. – 0 11 044535 X £1.10

The National Health Service (Dental Charges) Amendment Regulations 1994 No. 530. Enabling power: *National Health Service Act 1977, s. 79A, sch. 12, paras. 3 (2) (3)*. Issued: 10.03.94. Made: 04.03.94. Laid: 07.03.94. Coming into force: 01.04.94. Effect: S.I. 1989/394 amended. Territorial extent & classification: E/W. General. – 2p. – 0 11 043530 3 £0.65

The National Health Service (Determination of Districts) (No. 2) Order 1994 No. 1261. Enabling power: *National Health Service Act 1977, ss. 8 (1) (2) (4), 126 (4)*. Issued: 17.05.94. Made: 10.05.94. Laid: 11.05.94. Coming into force: 01.06.94. Effect: S.I. 1981/1837 amended. Territorial extent & classification: E/W. General. – 4p. – 0 11 044261 X £1.10

The National Health Service (Determination of Districts) (No. 3) Order 1994 No. 2289. Enabling power: *National Health Service Act 1977, ss. 8 (1) (2) (4)*. Issued: 12.09.94. Made: 05.09.94. Laid: 06.09.94. Coming into force: 01.10.94. Effect: S.I. 1981/1837 amended. Territorial extent & classification: E/W. General. – 4p. – 0 11 045289 5 £1.10

The National Health Service (Determination of Districts) Order 1994 No. 681. Enabling power: *National Health Service Act 1977, ss. 8 (1) (2) (4), 126 (4)*. Issued: 16.03.94. Made: 10.03.94. Laid: 10.03.94. Coming into force: 01.04.94. Effect: None. Territorial extent & classification: E/W. General. – 24p. – 0 11 043681 4 £4.15

The National Health Service (Determination of Regions) Order 1994 No. 683. Enabling power: *National Health Service Act 1977, ss. 8 (1) (2) (4), 126 (3) (4)*. Issued: 16.03.94. Made: 10.03.94. Laid: 10.03.94. Coming into force: 01.04.94. Effect: S.I. 1990/1755 amended & S.I. 1981/1836; 1982/343; 1993/571 revoked. Territorial extent & classification: E/W. General. – 12p. – 0 11 043683 0 £2.80

The National Health Service (District Health Authorities) (No. 2) Order 1994 No. 1260. Enabling power: *National Health Service Act 1977, ss. 8 (1) (b) (1A) (c), 126 (3)*. Issued: 17.05.94. Made: 10.05.94. Laid: 11.05.94. Coming into force: 01.06.94. Effect: S.I. 1990/1756 amended. Territorial extent & classification: E/W. General. – 2p. – 0 11 044260 1 £0.65

The National Health Service (District Health Authorities) (No. 3) Order 1994 No. 2288. Enabling power: *National Health Service Act 1977, ss. 8 (1) (b) (1A) (c), 126 (3)*. Issued: 12.09.94. Made: 05.09.94. Laid: 06.09.94. Coming into force: 01.10.94. Effect: S.I. 1990/1756 amended. Territorial extent & classification: E/W. General. – 2p. – 0 11 045288 7 £0.65

The National Health Service (District Health Authorities) Order 1994 No. 680. Enabling power: *National Health Service Act 1977, ss. 8 (1) (b) (1A) (c), 126 (3)*. Issued: 16.03.94. Made: 10.03.94. Laid: 10.03.94. Coming into force: 01.04.94. Effect: S.I. 1990/1756 amended. Territorial extent & classification: E/W. General. – 8p. – 0 11 043680 6 £1.95

The National Health Service Functions (Directions to Authorities and Administration Arrangements) Amendment Regulations 1994 No. 590. Enabling power: *National Health Service Act 1977, ss. 13, 14 (2), 17 (1), 18 (1), 126 (4) (5)*. Issued: 18.03.94. Made: 11.03.94. Laid: 11.03.94. Coming into force: 01.04.94. Effect: S.I. 1991/554 amended. Territorial extent & classification: E/W. General. – 2p. – 0 11 043590 7 £0.65

The National Health Service (Functions of Family Health Services Authorities in London) Regulations 1994 No. 284. Enabling power: *National Health Service Act 1977, ss. 15 (1) (b), 16, 17, 126 (4) (5)*. Issued: 16.02.94. Made: 08.02.94. Laid: 10.02.94. Coming into force: 03.03.94. Effect: None. Territorial extent & classification: E/W. General. – 4p. – 0 11 043284 3 £1.10

The National Health Service (Fund-holding Practices) Amendment Regulations 1994 No. 640. Enabling power: *National Health Service Act 1977, s. 126 (4) (5) & National Health Service and Community Care Act 1990, ss. 14 (6), 15 (7), 16 (2)*. Issued: 15.03.94. Made: 09.03.94. Laid: 09.03.94. Coming into force: 01.04.94. Effect: S.I. 1993/567 amended. Territorial extent & classification: E/W. General. – 2p. – 0 11 043640 7 £0.65

The National Health Service (General Medical Services) Amendment (No. 2) Regulations 1994 No. 2620. Enabling power: *National Health Service Act 1977, ss. 29, 126 (4)*. Issued: 13.10.94. Made: 10.10.94. Laid: 11.10.94. Coming into force: 01.11.94. Effect: S.I. 1992/635 amended. Territorial extent & classification: E/W. General. – 6p. – 0 11 045620 3 £1.55

Price/availability are liable to change without notice

NATIONAL HEALTH SERVICE, ENGLAND AND WALES

The National Health Service (General Medical Services) Amendment Regulations 1994 No.633. Enabling power: *National Health Service Act 1977, ss. 15 (1), 29, 30 (1), 33 (2A), 126 (4).* Issued: 18.03.94. Made: 09.03.94. Laid: 09.03.94. Coming into force: 01.04.94. Effect: S.I. 1992/635 amended. Territorial extent & classification: E/W. General. – 4p. – 0 11 043633 4 £1.10

The National Health Service (Optical Charges and Payments) Amendment (No. 2) Regulations 1994 No. 495. Enabling power: *National Health Service Act 1977, s. 126 (4), sch. 12, para. 2A.* Issued: 09.03.94. Made: 02.03.94. Laid: 03.03.94. Coming into force: 01.04.94. Effect: S.I. 1989/396 amended. Territorial extent & classification: E/W. General. – 4p. – 0 11 043495 1 £1.10

The National Health Service (Optical Charges and Payments) Amendment (No. 3) Regulations 1994 No. 2619. Enabling power: *National Health Service Act 1977, s. 126 (4), sch. 12, para. 2A.* Issued: 14.10.94. Made: 10.10.94. Laid: 11.10.94. Coming into force: 01.11.94. Effect: S.I. 1989/396 amended. Territorial extent & classification: E/W. General. – 2p. – 0 11 045619 X £0.65

The National Health Service (Optical Charges and Payments) Amendment Regulations 1994 No.131. Enabling power: *National Health Service Act 1977, s. 126 (4), sch. 12, para. 2A.* Issued: 01.02.94. Made: 26.01.94. Laid: 31.01.94. Coming into force: 21.02.94. Effect: S.I. 1989/396 amended. Territorial extent & classification: E/W. General. – 2p. – 0 11 043131 6 £0.65

The National Health Service (Pharmaceutical Services and Charges for Drugs and Appliances) Amendment Regulations 1994 No. 2402. Enabling power: *National Health Service Act 1977, ss. 41, 42, 43, 77, 126 (4).* Issued: 20.09.94. Made: 12.09.94. Laid: 12.09.94. Coming into force: 03.10.94. Effect: S.I. 1989/419; 1992/662 amended. Territorial extent & classification: E/W. General. – 4p. – 0 11 045402 2 £1.10

The National Health Service (Regional and District Health Authorities) (Miscellaneous Amendments) Regulations 1994 No. 682. Enabling power: *National Health Service Act 1977, ss. 13, 16, 17, 18, 42, 126 (4) & National Health Service and Community Care Act 1990, sch. 1, para. 2 (3).* Issued: 16.03.94. Made: 10.03.94. Laid: 10.03.94. Coming into force: 01.04.94. Effect: S.I. 1990/1331; 1992/660 amended. Territorial extent & classification: E/W. General. – 4p. – 0 11 043682 2 £1.10

The National Health Service (Regional Health Authorities) Order 1994 No. 684. Enabling power: *National Health Service Act 1977, ss. 8 (1) (a) (1A) (a), 126 (3).* Issued: 16.03.94. Made: 10.03.94. Laid: 10.03.94. Coming into force: 01.04.94. Effect: S.I. 1975/1100 revoked. Territorial extent & classification: E/W. General. – 4p. – 0 11 043684 9 £1.10

The National Health Service (Service Committees and Tribunal) Amendment Regulations 1994 No.634. Enabling power: *National Health Service Act 1977, ss. 29, 36, 39, 42, 126.* Issued: 18.03.94. Made: 09.03.94. Laid: 09.03.94. Coming into force: 01.04.94. Effect: S.I. 1992/664 amended. Territorial extent & classification: E/W. General. – 4p. – 0 11 043634 2 £1.10

The National Health Service Trusts (Originating Capital Debt) Order 1994 No. 405. Enabling power: *National Health Service and Community Care Act 1990, s. 9 (1) (4).* Issued: 03.03.94. Made: 23.02.94. Coming into force: 14.03.94. Effect: None. Territorial extent & classification: E/W. General. – 6p. – 0 11 043405 6 £1.55

The Newcastle City Health National Health Service Trust (Establishment) Order 1994 No.851. Enabling power: *National Health Service and Community Care Act 1990, s. 5 (1), sch. 2, paras. 1, 3, 4, 5, 6 (2) (d).* Issued: 28.03.94. Made: 21.03.94. Coming into force: 31.03.94. Effect: None. Territorial extent & classification: E/W. General. – 4p. – 0 11 043851 5 £1.10

The Newcastle Mental Health National Health Service Trust Dissolution Order 1994 No.861. Enabling power: *National Health Service Act 1977, s. 126 (3) & National Health Service and Community Care Act 1990, s. 5 (1), sch. 2, para. 29 (1).* Issued: 28.03.94. Made: 21.03.94. Coming into force: 01.04.94. Effect: S.I. 1990/2428 revoked. Territorial extent & classification: E/W. General. – 2p. – 0 11 043861 2 £0.65

The Newham Healthcare National Health Service Trust (Establishment) Order 1994 No.308. Enabling power: *National Health Service and Community Care Act 1990, s. 5 (1), sch. 2, paras., 1, 3, 4, 5, 6 (2) (d).* Issued: 21.02.94. Made: 11.02.94. Coming into force: 21.02.94. Effect: None. Territorial extent & classification: E/W. General. – 4p. – 0 11 043308 4 £1.10

The New Possibilities National Health Service Trust (Transfer of Trust Property) Order 1994 No.278. Enabling power: *National Health Service Act 1977, s. 92 (1).* Issued: 16.02.94. Made: 09.02.94. Laid: 16.02.94. Coming into force: 09.03.94. Effect: None. Territorial extent & classification: E/W. General. – 2p. – 0 11 043278 9 £0.65

The Norfolk and Norwich Health Care National Health Service Trust (Establishment) Order 1994 No. 176. Enabling power: *National Health Service and Community Care Act 1990, s. 5 (1), sch. 2, paras. 1, 3, 4, 5, 6 (2) (d).* Issued: 09.02.94. Made: 28.01.94. Coming into force: 08.02.94. Effect: None. Territorial extent & classification: E/W. General. – 4p. – 0 11 043176 6 £1.10

The North East Essex Mental Health National Health Service Trust (Transfer of Trust Property) Order 1994 No. 988. Enabling power: *National Health Service Act 1977, s. 92 (1).* Issued: 08.04.94. Made: 30.03.94. Laid: 07.04.94. Coming into force: 28.04.94. Effect: None. Territorial extent & classification: E/W. General. – 2p. – 0 11 043988 0 £0.65

The Northern Birmingham Mental Health National Health Service Trust (Establishment) Order 1994 No. 173. Enabling power: *National Health Service and Community Care Act 1990, s. 5 (1), sch. 2, paras. 1, 3, 4, 5, 6 (2) (d).* Issued: 09.02.94. Made: 28.01.94. Coming into force: 08.02.94. Effect: None. Territorial extent & classification: E/W. General. – 4p. – 0 11 043173 1 £1.10

The Northgate and Prudhoe National Health Service Trust (Establishment) Order 1994 No.198. Enabling power: *National Health Service and Community Care Act 1990, s. 5 (1), sch. 2, paras. 1, 3, 4, 5, 6 (2) (d).* Issued: 09.02.94. Made: 31.01.94. Coming into force: 01.04.94. Effect: None. Territorial extent & classification: E/W. General.–4p.–0 11 043198 7 *£1.10*

The Northgate National Health Service Trust Dissolution Order 1994 No. 829. Enabling power: *National Health Service Act 1977, s. 126 (3) & National Health Service and Community Care Act 1990, s. 5 (1), sch. 2, para. 29 (1).* Issued: 28.03.94. Made: 18.03.94. Coming into force: 01.04.94. Effect: S.I. 1991/2379 revoked. Territorial extent & classification: E/W. General.–2p.–0 11 043829 9 *£0.65*

The North Hampshire Hospitals National Health Service Trust (Establishment) Order 1994 No.178. Enabling power: *National Health Service and Community Care Act 1990, s. 5 (1), sch. 2, paras. 1, 3, 4, 5, 6 (2) (d).* Issued: 09.02.94. Made: 28.01.94. Coming into force: 08.02.94. Effect: None. Territorial extent & classification: E/W. General.–4p.–0 11 043178 2 *£1.10*

The North Hertfordshire National Health Service Trust (Transfer of Trust Property) Order 1994 No. 35. Enabling power: *National Health Service Act 1977, s. 92 (1).* Issued: 19.01.94. Made: 12.01.94. Laid: 19.01.94. Coming into force: 09.02.94. Effect: None. Territorial extent & classification: E/W. General.–2p.–0 11 043035 2 *£0.65*

The North Kent Healthcare National Health Service Trust (Establishment) Amendment Order 1994 No. 797. Enabling power: *National Health Service Act 1977, s. 5 (1) & National Health Service and Community Care Act 1990, s. 5 (1).* Issued: 24.03.94. Made: 17.03.94. Coming into force: 01.04.94. Effect: S.I. 1993/2639 amended. This SI has been made in consequence of a defect in SI 1993/2639 and is being sent free of charge to all known recipients of that SI. Territorial extent & classification: E/W. General.–2p.–0 11 043797 7 *£0.65*

The North Staffordshire Hospital Centre National Health Service Trust (Transfer of Trust Property) Order 1994 No. 2337. Enabling power: *National Health Service Act 1977, s. 92 (1).* Issued: 14.09.94. Made: 07.09.94. Laid: 14.09.94. Coming into force: 05.10.94. Effect: None. Territorial extent & classification: E/W. General. – 2p. – 0 11 045337 9 *£0.65*

The North Warwickshire National Health Service Trust (Transfer of Trust Property) Order 1994 No. 987. Enabling power: *National Health Service Act 1977, s. 92 (1).* Issued: 08.04.94. Made: 30.03.94. Laid: 07.04.94. Coming into force: 28.04.94. Effect: None. Territorial extent & classification: E/W. General.–2p.–0 11 043987 2 *£0.65*

The North West Anglia Health Care National Health Service Trust (Transfer of Trust Property) Order 1994 No. 1576. Enabling power: *National Health Service Act 1977, s. 92 (1).* Issued: 22.06.94. Made: 14.06.94. Laid: 22.06.94. Coming into force: 13.07.94. Effect: None. Territorial extent & classification: E/W. General.–2p.–0 11 044576 7 *£0.65*

The North West London Mental Health National Health Service Trust (Transfer of Trust Property) Order 1994 No. 358. Enabling power: *National Health Service Act 1977, s. 92 (1).* Issued: 28.02.94. Made: 21.02.94. Laid: 28.02.94. Coming into force: 21.03.94. Effect: None. Territorial extent & classification: E/W. General. – 2p. – 0 11 043358 0 *£0.65*

The Northwick Park and St. Mark's National Health Service Trust (Transfer of Trust Property) Order 1994 No. 2696. Enabling power: *National Health Service Act 1977, s. 92 (1).* Issued: 26.10.94. Made: 18.10.94. Laid: 26.10.94. Coming into force: 16.11.94. Effect: None. Territorial extent & classification: E/W. General.–2p.–0 11 045696 3 *£0.65*

The Northwick Park Hospital National Health Service Trust (Change of Name) Order 1994 No.195. Enabling power: *National Health Service Act 1977, s. 126 (3) (4) & National Health Service and Community Care Act 1990, s. 5 (1).* Issued: 09.02.94. Made: 31.01.94. Coming into force: 10.02.94. Effect: S.I. 1992/2537 amended. Territorial extent & classification: E/W. General.–2p.–0 11 043195 2 *£0.65*

The North Yorkshire Ambulance Service National Health Service Trust (Transfer of Trust Property) Order 1994 No. 490. Enabling power: *National Health Service Act 1977, s. 92 (1).* Issued: 09.03.94. Made: 02.03.94. Laid: 03.03.94. Coming into force: 24.03.94. Effect: None. Territorial extent & classification: E/W. General. – 2p. – 0 11 043490 0 *£0.65*

The Nottingham City Hospital National Health Service Trust (Transfer of Trust Property) Order 1994 No. 2334. Enabling power: *National Health Service Act 1977, s. 92 (1).* Issued: 14.09.94. Made: 07.09.94. Laid: 14.09.94. Coming into force: 05.10.94. Effect: None. Territorial extent & classification: E/W. General.–2p.–0 11 045334 4 *£0.65*

The Nottingham Community Health National Health Service Trust (Transfer of Trust Property) Order 1994 No. 2332. Enabling power: *National Health Service Act 1977, s. 92 (1).* Issued: 14.09.94. Made: 07.09.94. Laid: 14.09.94. Coming into force: 05.10.94. Effect: None. Territorial extent & classification: E/W. General. – 2p. – 0 11 045332 8 *£0.65*

The Nottingham Healthcare National Health Service Trust (Transfer of Trust Property) Order 1994 No. 2333. Enabling power: *National Health Service Act 1977, s. 92 (1).* Issued: 14.09.94. Made: 07.09.94. Laid: 14.09.94. Coming into force: 05.10.94. Effect: None. Territorial extent & classification: E/W. General.–2p.–0 11 045333 6 *£0.65*

The Nottinghamshire Ambulance Service National Health Service Trust (Transfer of Trust Property) Order 1994 No. 2342. Enabling power: *National Health Service Act 1977, s. 92 (1).* Issued: 14.09.94. Made: 07.09.94. Laid: 14.09.94. Coming into force: 05.10.94. Effect: None. Territorial extent & classification: E/W. General. – 2p. – 0 11 045342 5 *£0.65*

Price/availability are liable to change without notice

The Nuffield Orthopaedic Centre National Health Service Trust (Transfer of Trust Property) Order 1994 No. 223. Enabling power: *National Health Service Act 1977, s. 92 (1)*. Issued: 10.02.94. Made: 03.02.94. Laid: 10.02.94. Coming into force: 03.03.94. Effect: None. Territorial extent & classification: E/W. General. – 2p. – 0 11 043223 1 £0.65

The Papworth Hospital National Health Service Trust (Transfer of Trust Property) (No. 2) Order 1994 No. 2709. Enabling power: *National Health Service Act 1977, s. 92 (1)*. Issued: 27.10.94. Made: 19.10.94. Laid: 27.10.94. Coming into force: 17.11.94. Effect: None. Territorial extent & classification: E/W. General. – 2p. – 0 11 045709 9 £0.65

The Papworth Hospital National Health Service Trust (Transfer of Trust Property) Order 1994 No. 2697. Enabling power: *National Health Service Act 1977, s. 92 (1)*. Issued: 26.10.94. Made: 18.10.94. Laid: 26.10.94. Coming into force: 16.11.94. Effect: None. Territorial extent & classification: E/W. General. – 2p. – 0 11 045697 1 £0.65

The Parkside National Health Service Trust (Transfer of Trust Property) (No. 2) Order 1994 No. 2952. Enabling power: *National Health Service Act 1977, s. 92 (1)*. Issued: 28.11.94. Made: 22.11.94. Laid: 28.11.94. Coming into force: 19.12.94. Effect: None. Territorial extent & classification: E/W. General. – 2p. – 0 11 043136 7 £0.65

The Parkside National Health Service Trust (Transfer of Trust Property) Order 1994 No. 360. Enabling power: *National Health Service Act 1977, s. 92 (1)*. Issued: 28.02.94. Made: 21.02.94. Laid: 28.02.94. Coming into force: 21.03.94. Effect: None. Territorial extent & classification: E/W. General. – 2p. – 0 11 043360 2 £0.65

The Pathfinder National Health Service Trust (Establishment) Order 1994 No. 3178. Enabling power: *National Health Service and Community Care Act 1990, s. 5 (1), sch. 2, paras. 1, 3, 4, 5, 6 (2) (d)*. Issued: 20.12.94. Made: 12.12.94. Coming into force: 22.12.94. Effect: None. Territorial extent & classification: E/W. General. – 4p. – 0 11 043457 9 £1.10

The Peterborough Hospitals National Health Service Trust (Transfer of Trust Property) Order 1994 No. 1564. Enabling power: *National Health Service Act 1977, s. 92 (1)*. Issued: 21.06.94. Made: 14.06.94. Laid: 21.06.94. Coming into force: 12.07.94. Effect: None. Territorial extent & classification: E/W. General. – 2p. – 0 11 044564 3 £0.65

The Phoenix National Health Service Trust (Transfer of Trust Property) (No. 2) Order 1994 No. 61. Enabling power: *National Health Service Act 1977, s. 92 (1)*. Issued: 21.01.94. Made: 14.01.94. Laid: 21.01.94. Coming into force: 11.02.94. Effect: None. Territorial extent & classification: E/W. General. – 2p. – 0 11 043061 1 £0.65

The Phoenix National Health Service Trust (Transfer of Trust Property) Order 1994 No. 52. Enabling power: *National Health Service Act 1977, s. 92 (1)*. Issued: 20.01.94. Made: 13.01.94. Laid: 20.01.94. Coming into force: 10.02.94. Effect: None. Territorial extent & classification: E/W. General. – 2p. – 0 11 043052 2 £0.65

The Pinderfields Hospitals National Health Service Trust (Transfer of Trust Property) Order 1994 No. 2258. Enabling power: *National Health Service Act 1977, s. 92 (1)*. Issued: 08.09.94. Made: 01.09.94. Laid: 08.09.94. Coming into force: 29.09.94. Effect: None. Territorial extent & classification: E/W. General. – 2p. – 0 11 045258 5 £0.65

The Plymouth Community Services National Health Service Trust (Transfer of Trust Property) Order 1994 No. 26. Enabling power: *National Health Service Act 1977, s. 92 (1)*. Issued: 18.01.94. Made: 11.01.94. Laid: 18.01.94. Coming into force: 08.02.94. Effect: None. Territorial extent & classification: E/W. General. – 2p. – 0 11 043026 3 £0.65

The Pontefract Hospitals National Health Service Trust (Transfer of Trust Property) Order 1994 No. 2255. Enabling power: *National Health Service Act 1977, s. 92 (1)*. Issued: 08.09.94. Made: 01.09.94. Laid: 08.09.94. Coming into force: 29.09.94. Effect: None. Territorial extent & classification: E/W. General. – 2p. – 0 11 045255 0 £0.65

The Premier Health National Health Service Trust Dissolution Order 1994 No. 832. Enabling power: *National Health Service Act 1977, s. 126 (3) & National Health Service and Community Care Act 1990, s. 5 (1), sch. 2, para. 29 (1)*. Issued: 28.03.94. Made: 18.03.94. Coming into force: 01.04.94. Effect: S.I. 1991/2388 revoked. Territorial extent & classification: E/W. General. – 2p. – 0 11 043832 9 £0.65

The Premier Health National Health Service Trust (Establishment) Order 1994 No. 197. Enabling power: *National Health Service and Community Care Act 1990, s. 5 (1), sch. 2, paras. 1, 3, 4, 5, 6 (2) (d)*. Issued: 09.02.94. Made: 31.01.94. Coming into force: 01.04.94. Effect: None. Territorial extent & classification: E/W. General. – 4p. – 0 11 043197 9 £1.10

The Princess Alexandra Hospital National Health Service Trust (Establishment) Order 1994 No. 3179. Enabling power: *National Health Service and Community Care Act 1990, s. 5 (1), sch. 2, paras. 1, 3, 4, 5, 6 (2) (d)*. Issued: 20.12.94. Made: 12.12.94. Coming into force: 22.12.94. Effect: None. With correction slip dated January 1995. Territorial extent & classification: E/W. General. – 4p. – 0 11 043456 0 £1.10

The Queen Mary's Sidcup National Health Service Trust (Transfer of Trust Property) Order 1994 No. 2369. Enabling power: *National Health Service Act 1977, s. 92 (1)*. Issued: 15.09.94. Made: 08.09.94. Laid: 15.09.94. Coming into force: 06.10.94. Effect: None. Territorial extent & classification: E/W. General. – 2p. – 0 11 045369 7 £0.65

The Redbridge Health Care National Health Service Trust (Transfer of Trust Property) Order 1994 No. 2357. Enabling power: *National Health Service Act 1977, s. 92 (1)*. Issued: 15.09.94. Made: 08.09.94. Laid: 15.09.94. Coming into force: 06.10.94. Effect: None. Territorial extent & classification: E/W. General. – 2p. – 0 11 045357 3 £0.65

The Regional and District Health Authorities (Membership and Procedure) Amendment Regulations 1994 No. 1262. Enabling power: *National Health Service Act 1977, s. 128 (1) & National Health Service and Community Care Act 1990, sch. 1, para. 2 (3)*. Issued: 17.05.94. Made: 10.05.94. Laid: 11.05.94. Coming into force: 01.06.94. Effect: S.I. 1990/1331 amended. Territorial extent & classification: E/W. General. – 2p. – 0 11 044262 8 £0.65

The Richmond, Twickenham and Roehampton Healthcare National Health Service Trust (Transfer of Trust Property) Order 1994 No. 279. Enabling power: *National Health Service Act 1977, s. 92 (1)*. Issued: 16.02.94. Made: 09.02.94. Laid: 16.02.94. Coming into force: 09.03.94. Effect: None. Territorial extent & classification: E/W. General. – 2p. – 0 11 043279 7 £0.65

The Robert Jones and Agnes Hunt Orthopaedic and District Hospital National Health Service Trust (Transfer of Trust Property) Order 1994 No. 2364. Enabling power: *National Health Service Act 1977, s. 92 (1)*. Issued: 15.09.94. Made: 08.09.94. Laid: 15.09.94. Coming into force: 06.10.94. Effect: None. Territorial extent & classification: E/W. General. – 2p. – 0 11 045364 6 £0.65

The Rotherham General Hospital's National Health Service Trust (Transfer of Trust Property) Order 1994 No. 2365. Enabling power: *National Health Service Act 1977, s. 92 (1)*. Issued: 15.09.94. Made: 08.09.94. Laid: 15.09.94. Coming into force: 06.10.94. Effect: None. Territorial extent & classification: E/W. General. – 2p. – 0 11 045365 4 £0.65

The Rotherham Priority Health Services National Health Service Trust (Transfer of Trust Property) Order 1994 No. 2360. Enabling power: *National Health Service Act 1977, s. 92 (1)*. Issued: 15.09.94. Made: 08.09.94. Laid: 15.09.94. Coming into force: 06.10.94. Effect: None. Territorial extent & classification: E/W. General. – 2p. – 0 11 045360 3 £0.65

The Royal Berkshire Ambulance National Health Service Trust (Transfer of Trust Property) Order 1994 No. 1298. Enabling power: *National Health Service Act 1977, s. 92 (1)*. Issued: 19.05.94. Made: 12.05.94. Laid: 19.05.94. Coming into force: 09.06.94. Effect: None. Territorial extent & classification: E/W. General. – 2p. – 0 11 044298 9 £0.65

The Royal Berkshire and Battle Hospitals National Health Service Trust (Transfer of Trust Property) Order 1994 No. 1297. Enabling power: *National Health Service Act 1977, s. 92 (1)*. Issued: 19.05.94. Made: 12.05.94. Laid: 19.05.94. Coming into force: 09.06.94. Effect: None. Territorial extent & classification: E/W. General. – 2p. – 0 11 044297 0 £0.65

The Royal Brompton Hospital National Health Service Trust (Establishment) Order 1994 No. 402. Enabling power: *National Health Service and Community Care Act 1990, s. 5 (1), sch. 2, paras. 1, 3, 4, 5, 6 (2) (d)*. Issued: 03.03.94. Made: 23.02.94. Coming into force: 21.03.94. Effect: None. Territorial extent & classification: E/W. General. – 4p. – 0 11 043402 1 £1.10

The Royal Cornwall Hospitals National Health Service Trust (Transfer of Trust Property) Order 1994 No. 1296. Enabling power: *National Health Service Act 1977, s. 92 (1)*. Issued: 19.05.94. Made: 12.05.94. Laid: 19.05.94. Coming into force: 09.06.94. Effect: None. Territorial extent & classification: E/W. General. – 2p. – 0 11 044296 2 £0.65

The Royal Devon and Exeter Healthcare National Health Service Trust (Transfer of Trust Property) Order 1994 No. 487. Enabling power: *National Health Service Act 1977, s. 92 (1)*. Issued: 09.03.94. Made: 01.03.94. Laid: 02.03.94. Coming into force: 23.03.94. Effect: None. Territorial extent & classification: E/W. General. – 2p. – 0 11 043487 0 £0.65

The Royal Hospital of St Bartholomew, the Royal London Hospital and London Chest Hospital National Health Service Trust (Establishment) Order 1994 No. 307. Enabling power: *National Health Service and Community Care Act 1990, s. 5 (1), sch. 2, paras., 1, 3, 4, 5, 6 (2) (d)*. Issued: 21.02.94. Made: 11.02.94. Coming into force: 21.02.94. Effect: None. Territorial extent & classification: E/W. General. – 4p. – 0 11 043307 6 £1.10

The Royal Hull Hospitals National Health Service Trust (Transfer of Trust Property) Order 1994 No. 493. Enabling power: *National Health Service Act 1977, s. 92 (1)*. Issued: 09.03.94. Made: 02.03.94. Laid: 03.03.94. Coming into force: 24.03.94. Effect: None. Territorial extent & classification: E/W. General. – 2p. – 0 11 043493 5 £0.65

The Royal Liverpool and Broadgreen University Hospitals National Health Service Trust (Establishment) Order 1994 No. 3184. Enabling power: *National Health Service and Community Care Act 1990, s. 5 (1), sch. 2, paras. 1, 3, 4, 5, 6 (2) (d)*. Issued: 20.12.94. Made: 12.12.94. Coming into force: 01.04.95. Effect: None. Territorial extent & classification: E/W. General. – 2p. – 0 11 043455 2 £0.65

The Royal London Hospital and Associated Community Services National Health Service Trust Dissolution Order 1994 No. 830. Enabling power: *National Health Service Act 1977, s. 126 (3) & National Health Service and Community Care Act 1990, s. 5 (1), sch. 2, para. 29 (1)*. Issued: 28.03.94. Made: 18.03.94. Coming into force: 01.04.94. Effect: S.I. 1990/2438 revoked. Territorial extent & classification: E/W. General. – 2p. – 0 11 043830 2 £0.65

The Royal Marsden National Health Service Trust (Establishment) Order 1994 No. 401. Enabling power: *National Health Service and Community Care Act 1990, s. 5 (1), sch. 2, paras. 1, 3, 4, 5, 6 (2) (d)*. Issued: 03.03.94. Made: 23.02.94. Coming into force: 21.03.94. Effect: None. Territorial extent & classification: E/W. General. – 4p. – 0 11 043401 3 £1.10

The Royal Shrewsbury Hospitals National Health Service Trust (Transfer of Trust Property) Order 1994 No. 2358. Enabling power: *National Health Service Act 1977, s. 92 (1)*. Issued: 15.09.94. Made: 08.09.94. Laid: 15.09.94. Coming into force: 06.10.94. Effect: None. Territorial extent & classification: E/W. General. – 2p. – 0 11 045358 1 £0.65

NATIONAL HEALTH SERVICE, ENGLAND AND WALES

The Royal Victoria Infirmary and Associated Hospitals National Health Service Trust Dissolution Order 1994 No. 859. Enabling power: *National Health Service Act 1977, s. 126 (3) & National Health Service and Community Care Act 1990, s. 5 (1), sch. 2, para. 29 (1).* Issued: 28.03.94. Made: 21.03.94. Coming into force: 01.04.94. Effect: S.I. 1991/2393 revoked. Territorial extent & classification: E/W. General. – 2p. – 0 11 043859 0 £0.65

The Royal Victoria Infirmary and Associated Hospitals National Health Service Trust (Establishment) Order 1994 No. 849. Enabling power: *National Health Service and Community Care Act 1990, s. 5 (1), sch. 2, paras. 1, 3, 4, 5, 6 (2) (d).* Issued: 28.03.94. Made: 21.03.94. Coming into force: 31.03.94. Effect: None. Territorial extent & classification: E/W. General. – 4p. – 0 11 043849 3 £1.10

The Royal West Sussex National Health Service Trust (Establishment) Order 1994 No.166. Enabling power: *National Health Service and Community Care Act 1990, s. 5 (1), sch. 2, paras. 1, 3, 4, 5, 6 (2) (d).* Issued: 09.02.94. Made: 28.01.94. Coming into force: 08.02.94. Effect: None. Territorial extent & classification: E/W. General. – 4p. – 0 11 043166 9 £1.10

The Rugby National Health Service Trust (Transfer of Trust Property) Order 1994 No.53. Enabling power: *National Health Service Act 1977, s. 92 (1).* Issued: 20.01.94. Made: 13.01.94. Laid: 20.01.94. Coming into force: 10.02.94. Effect: None. Territorial extent & classification: E/W. General. – 2p. – 0 11 043053 0 £0.65

The Salford Hospitals National Health Service Trust (Change of Name) Order 1994 No.1269. Enabling power: *National Health Service Act 1977, s. 126 (3) (4) & National Health Service and Community Care Act 1990, s. 5 (1).* Issued: 19.05.94. Made: 10.05.94. Coming into force: 20.05.94. Effect: S.I. 1994/164 amended. Territorial extent & classification: E/W. General. – 2p. – 0 11 044269 5 £0.65

The Salford Hospitals National Health Service Trust (Establishment) Order 1994 No.164. Enabling power: *National Health Service and Community Care Act 1990, s. 5 (1), sch. 2, paras. 1, 3, 4, 5, 6 (2) (d).* Issued: 09.02.94. Made: 28.01.94. Coming into force: 08.02.94. Effect: None. Territorial extent & classification: E/W. General. – 4p. – 0 11 043164 2 £1.10

The Sandwell Healthcare National Health Service Trust (Establishment) Order 1994 No.172. Enabling power: *National Health Service and Community Care Act 1990, s. 5 (1), sch. 2, paras. 1, 3, 4, 5, 6 (2) (d).* Issued: 09.02.94. Made: 28.01.94. Coming into force: 08.02.94. Effect: None. Territorial extent & classification: E/W. General. – 4p. – 0 11 043172 3 £1.10

The Scunthorpe and Goole Hospitals National Health Service Trust (Transfer of Trust Property) Order 1994 No. 1335. Enabling power: *National Health Service Act 1977, s. 92 (1).* Issued: 25.05.94. Made: 18.05.94. Laid: 25.05.94. Coming into force: 15.06.94. Effect: None. Territorial extent & classification: E/W. General. – 2p. – 0 11 044335 7 £0.65

The Scunthorpe Community Health Care National Health Service Trust (Transfer of Trust Property) Order 1994 No. 1334. Enabling power: *National Health Service Act 1977, s. 92 (1).* Issued: 25.05.94. Made: 18.05.94. Laid: 25.05.94. Coming into force: 15.06.94. Effect: None. Territorial extent & classification: E/W. General. – 2p. – 0 11 044334 9 £0.65

The Shropshire's Community Health Service National Health Service Trust (Transfer of Trust Property) Order 1994 No. 2257. Enabling power: *National Health Service Act 1977, s. 92 (1).* Issued: 08.09.94. Made: 01.09.94. Laid: 08.09.94. Coming into force: 29.09.94. Effect: None. Territorial extent & classification: E/W. General. – 2p. – 0 11 045257 7 £0.65

The Shropshire's Mental Health National Health Service Trust (Transfer of Trust Property) Order 1994 No. 1574. Enabling power: *National Health Service Act 1977, s. 92 (1).* Issued: 22.06.94. Made: 14.06.94. Laid: 22.06.94. Coming into force: 13.07.94. Effect: None. Territorial extent & classification: E/W. General. – 2p. – 0 11 044574 0 £0.65

The Southampton University Hospitals National Health Service Trust (Transfer of Trust Property) Order 1994 No. 491. Enabling power: *National Health Service Act 1977, s. 92 (1).* Issued: 09.03.94. Made: 02.03.94. Laid: 03.03.94. Coming into force: 24.03.94. Effect: None. Territorial extent & classification: E/W. General. – 2p. – 0 11 043491 9 £0.65

The South Bedfordshire Community Health Care National Health Service Trust (Transfer of Trust Property) Order 1994 No. 483. Enabling power: *National Health Service Act 1977, s. 92 (1).* Issued: 09.03.94. Made: 01.03.94. Laid: 02.03.94. Coming into force: 23.03.94. Effect: None. Territorial extent & classification: E/W. General. – 2p. – 0 11 043483 8 £0.65

The South Birmingham Community Health National Health Service Trust (Change of Name) Order 1994 No. 798. Enabling power: *National Health Service Act 1977, s. 126 (3) (4) & National Health Serivce and Community Care Act 1990, s. 5 (1).* Issued: 23.03.94. Made: 17.03.94. Coming into force: 01.04.94. Effect: None. Territorial extent & classification: E/W. General. – 2p. – 0 11 043798 5 £0.65

The South Birmingham Mental National Health Service Trust (Establishment) Order 1994 No.171. Enabling power: *National Health Service and Community Care Act 1990, s. 5 (1), sch. 2, paras. 1, 3, 4, 5, 6 (2) (d).* Issued: 09.02.94. Made: 28.01.94. Coming into force: 08.02.94. Effect: None. Territorial extent & classification: E/W. General. – 4p. – 0 11 043171 5 £1.10

The South Downs Health National Health Service Trust (Transfer of Trust Property) Order 1994 No. 27. Enabling power: *National Health Service Act 1977, s. 92 (1).* Issued: 18.01.94. Made: 11.01.94. Laid: 18.01.94. Coming into force: 08.02.94. Effect: None. Territorial extent & classification: E/W. General. – 2p. – 0 11 043027 1 £0.65

Price/availability are liable to change without notice

The South East London Mental Health National Health Service Trust (Change of Name and Miscellaneous Amendments) Order 1994 No. 856. Enabling power: *National Health Service Act 1977, s. 126 (3) (4) & National Health Service and Community Care 1990, s. 5 (1)*. Issued: 28.03.94. Made: 21.03.94. Coming into force: 01.04.94. Effect: S.I. 1993/2633 amended. This SI has been made in consequence of a defect in SI 1993/2633 and is being sent free of charge to all known recipients of that SI. Territorial extent & classification: E/W. General. – 2p. – 0 11 043856 6 *£0.65*

The Southend Community Care Services National Health Service Trust (Transfer of Trust Property) Order 1994 No. 995. Enabling power: *National Health Service Act 1977, s. 92 (1)*. Issued: 08.04.94. Made: 30.03.94. Laid: 07.04.94. Coming into force: 28.04.94. Effect: None. Territorial extent & classification: E/W. General. – 2p. – 0 11 043995 3 *£0.65*

The Southend Health Care Services National Health Service Trust (Transfer of Trust Property) Order 1994 No. 994. Enabling power: *National Health Service Act 1977, s. 92 (1)*. Issued: 08.04.94. Made: 30.03.94. Laid: 07.04.94. Coming into force: 28.04.94. Effect: None. Territorial extent & classification: E/W. General. – 2p. – 0 11 043994 5 *£0.65*

The Southern Derbyshire Mental Health National Health Service Trust (Transfer of Trust Property) Order 1994 No. 1336. Enabling power: *National Health Service Act 1977, s. 92 (1)*. Issued: 25.05.94. Made: 18.05.94. Laid: 25.05.94. Coming into force: 15.06.94. Effect: None. Territorial extent & classification: E/W. General. – 2p. – 0 11 044336 5 *£0.65*

The South Kent Hospitals National Health Service Trust (Establishment) Order 1994 No.175. Enabling power: *National Health Service and Community Care Act 1990, s. 5 (1), sch. 2, paras. 1, 3, 4, 5, 6 (2) (d)*. Issued: 09.02.94. Made: 28.01.94. Coming into force: 08.02.94. Effect: None. Territorial extent & classification: E/W. General. – 4p. – 0 11 043175 8 *£1.10*

The South Lincolnshire Community and Mental Health Services National Health Service Trust (Transfer of Trust Property) Order 1994 No. 2991. Enabling power: *National Health Service Act 1977, s. 92 (1)*. Issued: 01.12.94. Made: 24.11.94. Laid: 01.12.94. Coming into force: 22.12.94. Effect: None. Territorial extent & classification: E/W. General. – 2p. – 0 11 043204 5 *£0.65*

The South Manchester University Hospitals National Health Service Trust (Establishment) Order 1994 No. 161. Enabling power: *National Health Service and Community Care Act 1990, s. 5 (1), sch. 2, paras. 1, 3, 4, 5, 6 (2) (d)*. Issued: 09.02.94. Made: 28.01.94. Coming into force: 08.02.94. Effect: None. Territorial extent & classification: E/W. General. – 4p. – 0 11 043161 8 *£1.10*

The South Tees Acute Hospitals National Health Service Trust (Transfer of Trust Property) Order 1994 No. 54. Enabling power: *National Health Service Act 1977, s. 92 (1)*. Issued: 20.01.94. Made: 13.01.94. Laid: 20.01.94. Coming into force: 10.02.94. Effect: None. Territorial extent & classification: E/W. General. – 2p. – 0 11 043054 9 *£0.65*

The South Tees Community and Mental Health National Health Service Trust (Transfer of Trust Property) Order 1994 No. 625. Enabling power: *National Health Service Act 1977, s. 92 (1)*. Issued: 17.03.94. Made: 08.03.94. Laid: 09.03.94. Coming into force: 30.03.94. Effect: None. Territorial extent & classification: E/W. General. – 2p. – 0 11 043625 3 *£0.65*

The South Warwickshire General Hospitals National Health Service Trust (Transfer of Trust Property) Order 1994 No. 2362. Enabling power: *National Health Service Act 1977, s. 92 (1)*. Issued: 15.09.94. Made: 08.09.94. Laid: 15.09.94. Coming into force: 06.10.94. Effect: None. Territorial extent & classification: E/W. General. – 2p. – 0 11 045362 X *£0.65*

The South Warwickshire Health Care National Health Service Trust (Transfer of Trust Property) Order 1994 No. 1338. Enabling power: *National Health Service Act 1977, s. 92 (1)*. Issued: 25.05.94. Made: 18.05.94. Laid: 25.05.94. Coming into force: 15.06.94. Effect: None. Territorial extent & classification: E/W. General. – 2p. – 0 11 044338 1 *£0.65*

The South West Durham Mental Health National Health Service Trust (Transfer of Trust Property) Order 1994 No. 1921. Enabling power: *National Health Service Act 1977, s. 92 (1)*. Issued: 25.07.94. Made: 15.07.94. Laid: 19.07.94. Coming into force: 09.08.94. Effect: None. Territorial extent & classification: E/W. General. – 2p. – 0 11 044921 5 *£0.65*

The South Western Regional Health Authority (Transfer of Trust Property) Order 1994 No.225. Enabling power: *National Health Service Act 1977, s. 92 (1)*. Issued: 10.02.94. Made: 03.02.94. Laid: 10.02.94. Coming into force: 03.03.94. Effect: None. Territorial extent & classification: E/W. General. 2p. 0 11 043225 8 *£0.65*

The South Yorkshire Metropolitan Ambulance and Paramedic Service National Health Service Trust (Transfer of Trust Property) Order 1994 No. 492. Enabling power: *National Health Service Act 1977, s. 92 (1)*. Issued: 09.03.94. Made: 02.03.94. Laid: 03.03.94. Coming into force: 24.03.94. Effect: None. Territorial extent & classification: E/W. General. – 2p. – 0 11 043492 7 *£0.65*

The St Albans and Hemel Hempstead National Health Service Trust (Establishment) Order 1994 No. 177. Enabling power: *National Health Service and Community Care Act 1990, s. 5 (1), sch. 2, paras. 1, 3, 4, 5, 6 (2) (d)*. Issued: 09.02.94. Made: 28.01.94. Coming into force: 08.02.94. Effect: None. Territorial extent & classification: E/W. General. – 4p. – 0 11 043177 4 *£1.10*

The St. George's Healthcare National Health Service Trust (Transfer of Trust Property) Order 1994 No. 2698. Enabling power: *National Health Service Act 1977, s. 92 (1).* Issued: 26.10.94. Made: 18.10.94. Laid: 26.10.94. Coming into force: 16.11.94. Effect: None. Territorial extent & classification: E/W. General. – 2p. – 0 11 045698 X £0.65

The St Helens and Knowsley Community Health National Health Service Trust (Transfer of Trust Property) Order 1994 No. 62. Enabling power: *National Health Service Act 1977, s. 92 (1).* Issued: 21.01.94. Made: 14.01.94. Laid: 21.01.94. Coming into force: 11.02.94. Effect: None. Territorial extent & classification: E/W. General. – 2p. – 0 11 043062 X £0.65

The St. James's and Seacroft University Hospitals National Health Service Trust (Establishment) Order 1994 No. 3183. Enabling power: *National Health Service and Community Care Act 1990, s. 5 (1), sch. 2, paras. 1, 3, 4, 5, 6 (2) (d).* Issued: 20.12.94. Made: 12.12.94. Coming into force: 01.04.95. Effect: None. Territorial extent & classification: E/W. General. – 4p. – 0 11 043458 7 £1.10

The Surrey Ambulance National Health Service Trust (Change of Name) Order 1994 No.1268. Enabling power: *National Health Service Act 1977, s. 126 (3) (4) & National Health Service and Commuity Care Act 1990, s. 5 (1).* Issued: 19.05.94. Made: 10.05.94. Coming into force: 20.05.94. Effect: S.I. 1994/182 amended. Territorial extent & classification: E/W. General. – 2p. – 0 11 044268 7 £0.65

The Surrey Ambulance National Health Service Trust (Establishment) Order 1994 No.182. Enabling power: *National Health Service and Community Care Act 1990, s. 5 (1), sch. 2, paras. 1, 3, 4, 5, 6 (2) (d).* Issued: 09.02.94. Made: 28.01.94. Coming into force: 08.02.94. Effect: None. Territorial extent & classification: E/W. General. – 4p. – 0 11 043182 0 £1.10

The Sussex Ambulance Service National Health Service Trust (Establishment) Order 1994 No.3176. Enabling power: *National Health Service and Community Care Act 1990, s. 5 (1), sch. 2, paras. 1, 3, 4, 5, 6 (2) (d).* Issued: 20.12.94. Made: 12.12.94. Coming into force: 22.12.94. Effect: None. Territorial extent & classification: E/W. General. – 4p. – 0 11 043460 9 £1.10

The Swansea National Health Service Trust (Transfer of Trust Property) Order 1994 No.945. Enabling power: *National Health Service Act 1977, s. 92 (1).* Issued: 13.04.94. Made: 24.03.94. Laid: 29.03.94. Coming into force: 13.04.94. Effect: None. Territorial extent & classification: W. General. – 2p. – 0 11 043945 7 £0.65

The Tavistock and Portman National Health Service Trust (Establishment) Order 1994 No.309. Enabling power: *National Health Service and Community Care Act 1990, s. 5 (1), sch. 2, paras., 1, 3, 4, 5, 6 (2) (d).* Issued: 21.02.94. Made: 11.02.94. Coming into force: 21.02.94. Effect: None. Territorial extent & classification: E/W. General. – 4p. – 0 11 043309 2 £1.10

The Thameside Community Health Care National Health Service Trust (Transfer of Trust Property) Order 1994 No. 2367. Enabling power: *National Health Service Act 1977, s. 92 (1).* Issued: 15.09.94. Made: 08.09.94. Laid: 15.09.94. Coming into force: 06.10.94. Effect: None. Territorial extent & classification: E/W. General. – 2p. – 0 11 045367 0 £0.65

The Thameslink Healthcare Services National Health Service Trust (Transfer of Trust Property) Order 1994 No. 1337. Enabling power: *National Health Service Act 1977, s. 92 (1).* Issued: 25.05.94. Made: 18.05.94. Laid: 25.05.94. Coming into force: 15.06.94. Effect: None. Territorial extent & classification: E/W. General. – 2p. – 0 11 044337 3 £0.65

The Thanet Health Care National Health Service Trust (Transfer of Trust Property) Order 1994 No. 619. Enabling power: *National Health Service Act 1977, s. 92 (1).* Issued: 17.03.94. Made: 08.03.94. Laid: 09.03.94. Coming into force: 30.03.94. Effect: None. Territorial extent & classification: E/W. General. – 2p. – 0 11 043619 9 £0.65

The Trafford Healthcare National Health Service Trust (Establishment) Order 1994 No.180. Enabling power: *National Health Service and Community Care Act 1990, s. 5 (1), sch. 2, paras. 1, 3, 4, 5, 6 (2) (d).* Issued: 09.02.94. Made: 28.01.94. Coming into force: 08.02.94. Effect: None. Territorial extent & classification: E/W. General. – 4p. – 0 11 043180 4 £1.10

The Two Shires Ambulance National Health Service Trust (Transfer of Trust Property) Order 1994 No. 989. Enabling power: *National Health Service Act 1977, s. 92 (1).* Issued: 08.04.94. Made: 30.03.94. Laid: 07.04.94. Coming into force: 28.04.94. Effect: None. Territorial extent & classification: E/W. General. – 2p. – 0 11 043989 9 £0.65

The Two Shires Ambulance National Health Service Trust (Transfer of Trust Property) (No. 2) Order 1994 No. 1294. Enabling power: *National Health Service Act 1977, s. 92 (1).* Issued: 19.05.94. Made: 12.05.94. Laid: 19.05.94. Coming into force: 09.06.94. Effect: None. Territorial extent & classification: E/W. General. – 2p. – 0 11 044294 6 £0.65

The United Leeds Teaching Hospitals National Health Service Trust (Establishment) Order 1994 No. 3186. Enabling power: *National Health Service and Community Care Act 1990, s. 5 (1), sch. 2, paras. 1, 3, 4, 5, 6 (2) (d).* Issued: 20.12.94. Made: 12.12.94. Coming into force: 01.04.95. Effect: None. Territorial extent & classification: E/W. General. – 2p. – 0 11 043444 7 £0.65

The United Leeds Teaching Hospitals National Health Service Trust (Transfer of Trust Property) Order 1994 No. 1054. Enabling power: *National Health Service Act 1977, s. 92 (1).* Issued: 19.04.94. Made: 12.04.94. Laid: 19.04.94. Coming into force: 10.05.94. Effect: None. Territorial extent & classification: E/W. General. – 2p. – 0 11 044054 4 £0.65

Price/availability are liable to change without notice

The University College London Hospitals National Health Service Trust (Establishment) Order 1994 No. 850.
Enabling power: *National Health Service and Community Care Act 1990, s. 5 (1), sch. 2, paras. 1, 3, 4, 5, 6 (2) (d)*. Issued: 28.03.94. Made: 21.03.94. Coming into force: 31.03.94. Effect: None. Territorial extent & classification: E/W. General. – 4p. – 0 11 043850 7 *£1.10*

The Vocational Training for General Medical Practice (European Requirements) Regulations 1994 No. 3130.
Enabling power: *European Communities Act 1972, s. 2 (2) & National Health Service Act 1977, ss. 15 (1), 29, 32, 126 (4) & National Health Service (Scotland) Act 1978, ss. 19, 22, 105 (7)*. Issued: 03.01.95. Made: 08.12.94. Laid: 09.12.94. Coming into force: 01.01.95. Effect: None. Territorial extent & classification: GB. General. – These regulations arise out of Title IV of DIR 93/16 of 5 April 1993. – 12p. – 0 11 043742 X *£2.40*

The Wakefield and Pontefract Community Health National Health Service Trust (Transfer of Trust Property) Order 1994 No. 2256. Enabling power: *National Health Service Act 1977, s. 92 (1)*. Issued: 08.09.94. Made: 01.09.94. Laid: 08.09.94. Coming into force: 29.09.94. Effect: None. Territorial extent & classification: E/W. General. – 2p. – 0 11 045256 9 *£0.65*

The Walsall Community Health National Health Service Trust (Transfer of Trust Property) Order 1994 No. 226.
Enabling power: *National Health Service Act 1977, s. 92 (1)*. Issued: 10.02.94. Made: 03.02.94. Laid: 10.02.94. Coming into force: 03.03.94. Effect: None. Territorial extent & classification: E/W. General. – 2p. – 0 11 043226 6 *£0.65*

The Warrington Community Health Care National Health Service Trust (Transfer of Trust Property) Order 1994 No. 1206. Enabling power: *National Health Service Act 1977, s. 92 (1)*. Issued: 09.05.94. Made: 03.05.94. Laid: 09.05.94. Coming into force: 30.05.94. Effect: None. Territorial extent & classification: E/W. General. – 2p. – 0 11 044206 7 *£0.65*

The Warrington Hospital National Health Service Trust (Transfer of Trust Property) Order 1994 No. 1205.
Enabling power: *National Health Service Act 1977, s. 92 (1)*. Issued: 09.05.94. Made: 03.05.94. Laid: 09.05.94. Coming into force: 30.05.94. Effect: None. Territorial extent & classification: E/W. General. – 2p. – 0 11 044205 9 *£0.65*

The Weald of Kent Community National Health Service Trust (Establishment) Order 1994 No. 174. Enabling power: *National Health Service and Community Care Act 1990, s. 5 (1), sch. 2, paras. 1, 3, 4, 5, 6 (2) (d)*. Issued: 09.02.94. Made: 28.01.94. Coming into force: 08.02.94. Effect: None. Territorial extent & classification: E/W. General. 4p. – 0 11 043174 X *£1.10*

The Wellhouse National Health Service Trust (Transfer of Trust Property) Order 1994 No. 1575. Enabling power: *National Health Service Act 1977, s. 92 (1)*. Issued: 22.06.94. Made: 14.06.94. Laid: 22.06.94. Coming into force: 13.07.94. Effect: None. Territorial extent & classification: E/W. General. – 2p. – 0 11 044575 9 *£0.65*

The West Berkshire Priority Care Service National Health Service Trust (Transfer of Trust Property) Order 1994 No. 1295. Enabling power: *National Health Service Act 1977, s. 92 (1)*. Issued: 19.05.94. Made: 12.05.94. Laid: 19.05.94. Coming into force: 09.06.94. Effect: None. Territorial extent & classification: E/W. General. – 2p. – 0 11 044295 4 *£0.65*

The Westcountry Ambulance Service National Health Service Trust (Transfer of Trust Property) Order 1994 No. 1086. Enabling power: *National Health Service Act 1977, s. 92 (1)*. Issued: 21.04.94. Made: 14.04.94. Laid: 21.04.94. Coming into force: 12.05.94. Effect: None. Territorial extent & classification: E/W. General. – 2p. – 0 11 044086 2 *£0.65*

The Westcountry Ambulance Service National Health Service Trust (Transfer of Trust Property) Order 1994 No. 36. Enabling power: *National Health Service Act 1977, s. 92 (1)*. Issued: 19.01.94. Made: 12.01.94. Laid: 19.01.94. Coming into force: 09.02.94. Effect: None. With correction slip, dated February 1994. Territorial extent & classification: E/W. General. – 2p. – 0 11 043036 0 *£0.65*

The West Cumbria Health Care National Health Service Trust (Transfer of Trust Property) Order 1994 No. 2361. Enabling power: *National Health Service Act 1977, s. 92 (1)*. Issued: 15.09.94. Made: 08.09.94. Laid: 15.09.94. Coming into force: 06.10.94. Effect: None. Territorial extent & classification: E/W. General. – 2p. – 0 11 045361 1 *£0.65*

The West Dorset Community Health National Health Service Trust Dissolution Order 1994 No. 833. Enabling power: *National Health Service Act 1977, s. 126 (3) & National Health Service and Community Care Act 1990, s. 5 (1), sch. 2, para. 29 (1)*. Issued: 28.03.94. Made: 18.03.94. Coming into force: 01.04.94. Effect: S.I. 1990/2452 revoked. Territorial extent & classification: E/W. General. – 2p. – 0 11 043833 7 *£0.65*

The West Dorset Mental Health National Health Service Trust Dissolution Order 1994 No. 831. Enabling power: *National Health Service Act 1977, s. 126 (3) & National Health Service and Community Care Act 1990, s. 5 (1), sch. 2, para. 29 (1)*. Issued: 28.03.94. Made: 18.03.94. Coming into force: 01.04.94. Effect: S.I. 1990/2454 revoked. Territorial extent & classification: E/W. General. – 2p. – 0 11 043831 0 *£0.65*

The West Herts Community Health National Health Service Trust (Establishment) Order 1994 No. 854. Enabling power: *National Health Service and Community Care Act 1990, s. 5 (1), sch. 2, paras. 1, 3, 4, 5, 6 (2) (d)*. Issued: 28.03.94. Made: 21.03.94. Coming into force: 31.03.94. Effect: None. Territorial extent & classification: E/W. General. – 4p. – 0 11 043854 X *£1.10*

The West Lindsey National Health Service Trust (Establishment) Amendment Order 1994 No. 1534. Enabling power: *National Health Service Act 1977, s. 126 (3) & National Health Service and Community Care Act 1990, s. 5 (1)*. Issued: 16.06.94. Made: 09.06.94. Coming into force: 20.06.94. Effect: S.I. 1992/2471 amended. Territorial extent & classification: E/W. General. – 2p. – 0 11 044534 1 *£0.65*

Price/availability are liable to change without notice

The West Lindsey National Health Service Trust (Transfer of Trust Property) Order 1994 No.621. Enabling power: *National Health Service Act 1977, s. 92 (1).* Issued: 17.03.94. Made: 08.03.94. Laid: 09.03.94. Coming into force: 30.03.94. Effect: None. Territorial extent & classification: E/W. General. – 2p. – 0 11 043621 0 *£0.65*

The West London Healthcare National Health Service Trust (Transfer of Trust Property) Order 1994 No. 1339. Enabling power: *National Health Service Act 1977, s. 92 (1).* Issued: 25.05.94. Made: 18.05.94. Laid: 25.05.94. Coming into force: 15.06.94. Effect: None. Territorial extent & classification: E/W. General. – 2p. – 0 11 044339 X *£0.65*

The West Middlesex University Hospital National Health Service Trust (Transfer of Trust Property) Order 1994 No. 1340. Enabling power: *National Health Service Act 1977, s. 92 (1).* Issued: 25.05.94. Made: 18.05.94. Laid: 25.05.94. Coming into force: 15.06.94. Effect: None. Territorial extent & classification: E/W. General. – 2p. – 0 11 044340 3 *£0.65*

The West Suffolk Hospitals National Health Service Trust (Transfer of Trust Property) Order 1994 No. 2370. Enabling power: *National Health Service Act 1977, s. 92 (1).* Issued: 15.09.94. Made: 08.09.94. Laid: 15.09.94. Coming into force: 06.10.94. Effect: None. Territorial extent & classification: E/W. General. – 2p. – 0 11 045370 0 *£0.65*

The Wiltshire Ambulance Service National Health Service Trust (Transfer of Trust Property) Order 1994 No. 1332. Enabling power: *National Health Service Act 1977, s. 92 (1).* Issued: 25.05.94. Made: 18.05.94. Laid: 25.05.94. Coming into force: 15.06.94. Effect: None. Territorial extent & classification: E/W. General. – 2p. – 0 11 044332 2 *£0.65*

The Wolverhampton Health Care National Health Service Trust (Establishment) Order 1994 No.3197. Enabling power: *National Health Service and Community Care Act 1990, s. 5 (1), sch. 2, paras. 1, 3, 4, 5, 6 (2) (d).* Issued: 21.12.94. Made: 13.12.94. Coming into force: 23.12.94. Effect: None. Territorial extent & classification: E/W. General. – 4p. – 0 11 043519 2 *£1.10*

The Worcester Royal Infirmary National Health Service Trust (Transfer of Trust Property) Order 1994 No. 1341. Enabling power: *National Health Service Act 1977, s. 92 (1).* Issued: 25.05.94. Made: 18.05.94. Laid: 25.05.94. Coming into force: 15.06.94. Effect: None. Territorial extent & classification: E/W. General. – 2p. – 0 11 044341 1 *£0.65*

The Worthing Priority Care National Health Service Trust (Transfer of Trust Property) Order 1994 No. 2359. Enabling power: *National Health Service Act 1977, s. 92 (1).* Issued: 15.09.94. Made: 08.09.94. Laid: 15.09.94. Coming into force: 06.10.94. Effect: None. Territorial extent & classification: E/W. General. – 2p. – 0 11 045359 X *£0.65*

The York Health Services National Health Service Trust (Transfer of Trust Property) Order 1994 No. 55. Enabling power: *National Health Service Act 1977, s. 92 (1).* Issued: 20.01.94. Made: 13.01.94. Laid: 20.01.94. Coming into force: 10.02.94. Effect: None. Territorial extent & classification: E/W. General. – 2p. – 0 11 043055 7 *£0.65*

NATIONAL HEALTH SERVICE, SCOTLAND

The Argyll and Bute National Health Service Trust (Establishment) Order 1994 No. 2996 (S. 151). Enabling power: *National Health Service (Scotland) Act 1978, ss. 12A (1) (4), sch. 7A, paras. 1, 3, 4, 5, 6 (2) (d).* Issued: 08.12.94. Made: 25.11.94. Coming into force: 29.11.94. Effect: None. Territorial extent & classification: S. General. – 4p. – 0 11 043217 7 *£1.10*

The Borders Community Health Services National Health Service Trust (Establishment) Order 1994 No. 2997 (S. 152). Enabling power: *National Health Service (Scotland) Act 1978, ss. 12A (1) (4), sch. 7A, paras. 1, 3, 4, 5, 6 (2) (d).* Issued: 08.12.94. Made: 25.11.94. Coming into force: 29.11.94. Effect: None. Territorial extent & classification: S. General. – 4p. – 0 11 043218 5 *£1.10*

The Borders General Hospital National Health Service Trust (Establishment) Order 1994 No.2998 (S. 153). Enabling power: *National Health Service (Scotland) Act 1978, ss. 12A (1) (4), sch. 7A, paras. 1, 3, 4, 5, 6 (2) (d).* Issued: 08.12.94. Made: 25.11.94. Coming into force: 29.11.94. Effect: None. Territorial extent & classification: S. General. – 4p. – 0 11 043219 3 *£1.10*

The Central Scotland Healthcare National Health Service Trust (Appointment of Trustees) Order 1994 No. 2485 (S. 117). Enabling power: *National Health Service (Scotland) Act 1978, s. 12G (2).* Issued: 30.09.94. Made: 15.09.94. Coming into force: 01.10.94. Effect: None. Territorial extent & classification: S. General. – 2p. – 0 11 045485 5 *£0.65*

The Central Scotland Healthcare National Health Service Trust (Establishment) Order 1994 No.1607 (S. 71). Enabling power: *National Health Service (Scotland) Act 1978, ss. 12A (1) (4), sch. 7A, paras. 1, 3, 4, 5, 6 (2) (d).* Issued: 24.06.94. Made: 14.06.94. Coming into force: 17.06.94. Effect: None. Territorial extent & classification: S. General. – 4p. – 0 11 044607 0 *£1.10*

The Dumfries and Galloway Community Health National Health Service Trust (Establishment) Order 1994 No. 2999 (S. 154). Enabling power: *National Health Service (Scotland) Act 1978, ss. 12A (1) (4), sch. 7A, paras. 1, 3, 4, 5, 6 (2) (d).* Issued: 08.12.94. Made: 25.11.94. Coming into force: 29.11.94. Effect: None. Territorial extent & classification: S. General. – 4p. – 0 11 043220 7 *£1.10*

NATIONAL HEALTH SERVICE, SCOTLAND

The Glasgow Community and Mental Health Services National Health Service Trust (Change of Name) (Establishment) Amendment Order 1994 No. 107 (S. 3). Enabling power: *National Health Service (Scotland) Act 1978, s. 12A (1), sch. 7A, paras. 1, 3 (1) (a)*. Issued: 27.01.94. Made: 18.01.94. Coming into force: 24.01.94. Effect: S.I. 1993/2935 amended. This S.I. has been made in consequence of a defect in SI 1993/2935 (S.269) & is being issued free of charge to all known recipients of that SI. Territorial extent & classification: S. General. – 2p. – 0 11 043107 3 £0.65

The Glasgow Dental Hospital and School National Health Service Trust (Establishment) Order 1994 No. 2995 (S. 150). Enabling power: *National Health Service (Scotland) Act 1978, ss. 12A (1) (4), sch. 7A, paras. 1, 3, 4, 5, 6 (2) (d)*. Issued: 08.12.94. Made: 25.11.94. Coming into force: 29.11.94. Effect: None. Territorial extent & classification: S. General. – 4p. – 0 11 043216 9 £1.10

The Lanarkshire Healthcare National Health Service Trust (Establishment) Order 1994 No.3000 (S. 155). Enabling power: *National Health Service (Scotland) Act 1978, ss. 12A (1) (4), sch. 7A, paras. 1, 3, 4, 5, 6 (2) (d)*. Issued: 08.12.94. Made: 25.11.94. Coming into force: 29.11.94. Effect: None. Territorial extent & classification: S. General. – 4p. – 0 11 043231 2 £1.10

The Lomond Healthcare National Health Service Trust (Establishment) Order 1994 No.3001 (S. 156). Enabling power: *National Health Service (Scotland) Act 1978, ss. 12A (1) (4), sch. 7A, paras. 1, 3, 4, 5, 6 (2) (d)*. Issued: 08.12.94. Made: 25.11.94. Coming into force: 29.11.94. Effect: None. Territorial extent & classification: S. General. – 4p. – 0 11 043235 5 £1.10

The National Health Service and Community Care Act 1990 (Commencement No. 11) (Scotland) Order 1990 No. 2658 (C. 57) (S. 136). Enabling power: *National Health Service and Community Care Act 1990, s. 67 (2)*. Bringing into operation various provisions of the 1990 act on 24.10.94., 01.12.94., 01.04.95. Issued: 20.10.94. Made: 10.10.94. Effect: None. Territorial extent & classification: S. General. – 4p. – 0 11 045658 0 £1.10

The National Health Service (Charges for Drugs and Appliances) (Scotland) Amendment Regulations 1994 No. 697 (S. 34). Enabling power: *National Health Service (Scotland) Act 1978, ss. 19, 27, 69, 75 (a), 105 (7), 108 (1)*. Issued: 18.03.94. Made: 10.03.94. Laid: 11.03.94. Coming into force: 01.04.94. Effect: S.I. 1989/326 amended. Territorial extent & classification: S. General. – 4p. – 0 11 043697 0 £1.10

The National Health Service (Charges to Overseas Visitors) (Scotland) Amendment Regulations 1994 No. 1770 (S. 79). Enabling power: *National Health Service (Scotland) Act 1978, ss. 98, 105 (7), 108 (1)*. Issued: 14.07.94. Made: 30.06.94. Laid: 13.07.94. Coming into force: 03.08.94. Effect: S.I. 1989/364 amended. Territorial extent & classification: S. General. – 4p. – 0 11 044770 0 £1.10

The National Health Service (Dental Charges) (Scotland) Amendment Regulations 1994 No.636 (S. 32). Enabling power: *National Health Service (Scotland) Act 1978, ss. 70 (1A), 71 (1) 71A, 105 (7), 108 (1), sch. 11, para. 3 (3)*. Issued: 17.03.94. Made: 04.03.94. Laid: 10.03.94. Coming into force: 01.04.94. Effect: S.I. 1989/363 amended. Territorial extent & classification: S. General. – 2p. – 0 11 043636 9 £0.65

The National Health Service (General Medical and Pharmaceutical Services) (Scotland) Amendment Regulations 1994 No. 884 (S.36). Enabling power: *National Health Service (Scotland) Act 1978, ss. 19, 27, 105 (7), 108 (1)*. Issued: 29.03.94. Made: 22.03.94. Laid: 25.03.94. Coming into force: 15.04.94. Effect: S.I. 1974/506 amended. Territorial extent & classification: S. General. – 4p. – 0 11 043884 1 £1.10

The National Health Service (General Medical and Pharmaceutical Services) (Scotland) Amendment (No. 2) Regulations 1994 No. 2624 (S. 133). Enabling power: *National Health Service (Scotland) Act 1978, ss. 19. 27, 108 (1)*. Issued: 19.10.94. Made: 11.10.94. Laid: 11.10.94. Coming into force: 01.11.94. Effect: S.I. 1974/506 amended. Territorial extent & classification: S. General. – 4p. – 0 11 045624 6 £1.10

The National Health Service (Optical Charges and Payments) (Scotland) Amendment (No. 2) Regulations 1994 No. 635 (S. 31). Enabling power: *National Health Service (Scotland) Act 1978, ss. 26, 70 (1), 73 (a) (c), 74 (a) (c), 105 (7), 108 (1), sch. 11, paras. 2, 2A*. Issued: 17.03.94. Made: 04.03.94. Laid: 10.03.94. Coming into force: 01.04.94. Effect: S.I. 1989/392 amended. Territorial extent & classification: S. General. – 4p. – 0 11 043635 0 £1.10

The National Health Service (Optical Charges and Payments) (Scotland) Amendment (No. 3) Regulations 1994 No. 2587 (S. 123). Enabling power: *National Health Service (Scotland) Act 1978, ss. 70 (1), 105 (7), 108 (1), sch. 11, paras. 2, 2A*. Issued: 14.10.94. Made: 04.10.94. Laid: 10.10.94. Coming into force: 01.11.94. Effect: S.I. 1989/392 amended. Territorial extent & classification: S. General. – 2p. – 0 11 045587 8 £0.65

The National Health Service (Optical Charges and Payments) (Scotland) Amendment Regulations 1994 No. 145 (S. 5). Enabling power: *National Health Service (Scotland) Act 1978, ss. 70 (1), 105 (7), 108 (1), sch. 11, para. 2A*. Issued: 03.02.94. Made: 26.01.94. Laid: 31.01.94. Coming into force: 21.02.94. Effect: S.I. 1989/392 amended. Territorial extent & classification: S. General. – 2p. – 0 11 043145 6 £0.65

The National Health Service (Service Committees and Tribunal) (Scotland) Amendment Regulations 1994 No. 3038 (S. 157). Enabling power: *National Health Service (Scotland) Act 1978, ss. 19 (2), 25 (2) 26 (2), 27 (2), 105 (7), 108 (1)*. Issued: 09.12.94. Made: 25.11.94. Laid: 09.12.94. Coming into force: 01.01.95. Effect: S.I. 1992/434 amended. Territorial extent & classification: S. General. – 4p. – 0 11 043320 3 £1.10

The National Health Service Trusts (Appointment of Trustees) (Scotland) Order 1994 No.510 (S. 21). Enabling power: *National Health Service (Scotland) Act 1978, s. 12G (2)*. Issued: 11.03.94. Made: 01.03.94. Coming into force: 01.04.94. Effect: None. Territorial extent & classification: S. General. – 2p. – 0 11 043510 9 £0.65

The National Health Service Trusts (Apppointment of Trustees) (Scotland) (No. 2) Order 1994 No. 3254 (S. 182). Enabling power: *National Health Service (Scotland) Act 1978, s. 12G (2)*. Issued: 09.01.95. Made: 13.12.94. Coming into force: 01.04.95. Effect: None. Territorial extent & classification: S. General. – 2p. – 0 11 043789 6 £0.65

Price/availability are liable to change without notice

The National Health Service Trusts (Membership and Procedure) (Scotland) Amendment Regulations 1994 No. 1408 (S. 66). Enabling power: *National Health Service (Scotland) Act 1978, ss. 12A (5), 105 (7), 108 (1)*. Issued: 02.06.94. Made: 23.05.94. Laid: 26.05.94. Coming into force: 16.06.94. Effect: S.I. 1991/535 amended. Territorial extent & classification: S. General. – 2p. – 0 11 044408 6 *£0.65*

The National Health Service Trusts (Originating Capital Debt) (Scotland) Order 1994 No. 496 (S. 18). Enabling power: *National Health Service (Scotland) Act 1978, s, 12E (1) (4)*. Issued: 09.03.94. Made: 25.02.94. Coming into force: 09.03.94. Effect: None. Territorial extent & classification: S. General. – 2p. – 0 11 043496 X *£0.65*

The Royal Scottish National Hospital and Community National Health Service Trust (Dissolution) Order 1994 No. 2484 (S. 116). Enabling power: *National Health Service (Scotland) Act 1978, s. 105 (6), sch. 7A, para. 25 (1)*. Issued: 30.09.94. Made: 15.09.94. Coming into force: 01.10.94. Effect: S.I. 1992/2338 revoked. Territorial extent & classification: S. General. – 2p. – 0 11 045484 7 *£0.65*

The Scottish Ambulance Service National Health Service Trust (Establishment) Order 1994 No. 2994 (S. 149). Enabling power: *National Health Service (Scotland) Act 1978, ss. 12A (1) (4), sch. 7A, paras. 1, 3, 4, 5, 6 (2) (d)*. Issued: 08.12.94. Made: 25.11.94. Coming into force: 29.11.94. Effect: None. Territorial extent & classification: S. General. – 4p. – 0 11 043215 0 *£1.10*

The Vocational Training for General Medical Practice (European Requirements) Regulations 1994 No. 3130. Enabling power: *European Communities Act 1972, s. 2 (2) & National Health Service Act 1977, ss. 15 (1), 29, 32, 126 (4) & National Health Service (Scotland) Act 1978, ss. 19, 22, 105 (7)*. Issued: 03.01.95. Made: 08.12.94. Laid: 09.12.94. Coming into force: 01.01.95. Effect: None. Territorial extent & classification: GB. General. – These regulations arise out of Title IV of DIR 93/16 of 5 April 1993. – 12p. – 0 11 043742 X *£2.40*

NATIONAL LOTTERY

The National Lottery etc. Act 1993 (Amendment of Section 23) Order 1994 No. 1342. Enabling power: *National Lottery etc. Act 1993, s. 29*. Issued: 26.05.94. Made: 17.05.94. Laid: 20.05.94. Coming into force: 13.06.94. Effect: 1993 c. 39 amended. Territorial extent & classification: GB. General. – 2p. – 0 11 044342 X *£0.65*

The National Lottery etc. Act 1993 (Commencement No. 2 and Transitional Provisions) Order 1994 No. 1055 (C. 16). Enabling power: *National Lottery etc. Act 1993, s. 60 (5)*. Bringing into operation various provisions of this act on 03.05.94, 03.10.94. Issued: 20.04.94. Made: 10.04.94. Effect: None. Territorial extent & classification: E/W/S. General. – 4p. – 0 11 044055 2 *£1.10*

The National Lottery etc. Act 1993 (Commencement No. 3) Order 1994 No. 2659 (C. 58). Enabling power: *National Lottery etc. Act 1993, s. 65*. Bringing into operation various provisions of the 1993 act on 14.11.94. Issued: 19.10.94. Made: 10.10.94. Effect: None. Territorial extent & classification: E/W/S. General. – 2p. – 0 11 045659 9 *£0.65*

The National Lottery (Licence Fees) Order 1994 No. 1200. Enabling power: *National Lottery etc. Act 1993, ss. 7 (5), 60 (4)*. Issued: 10.05.94. Made: 28.04.94. Laid: 03.05.94. Coming into force: 24.05.94. Effect: None. Territorial extent & classification: GB. General. – 2p. – 0 11 044200 8 *£0.65*

The National Lottery Regulations 1994 No. 189. Enabling power: *National Lottery, etc. Act 1993, s. 12*. Issued: 09.02.94. Made: 31.01.94. Laid: 09.02.94. Coming into force: 01.04.94. Effect: None. Territorial extent & classification: GB. General. – 4p. – 0 11 043189 8 *£1.10*

The National Lottery (Revocation of Licences) Procedure Regulations 1994 No. 1170. Enabling power: *National Lottery etc. Act 1993, s. 60 (5), sch. 3, paras. 8, 10*. Issued: 04.05.94. Made: 25.04.94. Laid: 26.04.94. Coming into force: 19.05.94. Effect: None. With correction slip. Territorial extent & classification: E/W/S. Local. – 6p. – 0 11 044170 2 *£1.55*

NEW TOWNS

The New Town (East Kilbride) Winding Up (Variation) Order 1994 No. 200 (S. 6). Enabling power: *New Towns (Scotland) Act 1968, s. 36 (1) (3) (4)*. Issued: 10.02.94. Made: 31.01.94. Coming into force: 01.03.94. Effect: S.I. 1992/355 amended & S.I. 1965/2118 revoked. Territorial extent & classification: S. Local. – 2p. – 0 11 043200 2 *£0.65*

NEW TOWNS, ENGLAND AND WALES

The Development Board for Rural Wales (Transfer of Housing Stock) (Amendment) Regulations 1994 No. 1005. Enabling power: *Local Government and Housing Act 1989, ss. 172, 190 (1)*. Issued: 12.04.94. Made: 28.03.94. Laid: 12.04.94. Coming into force: 03.05.94. Effect: S.I. 1993/1808 amended. This SI has been made in consequence of a defect in SI 1993/1808 and is free of charge to all known recipients of that SI. Territorial extent & classification: W. General. –4p. – 0 11 044005 6 *£1.10*

NORTHERN IRELAND

The Agriculture (Miscellaneous Provisions) (Northern Ireland) Order 1994 No. 1891 (NI. 6). Enabling power: *Northern Ireland Act 1974, sch. 1, para. 1*. Issued: 10.08.94. Made: 19.07.94. Effect: 1964 c. 25 (NI); 1972 c. 4 (NI), c. 7 (NI); 1975 c. 25; S.I. 1973 NI 1; 1975 NI 17; 1977 NI 12; 1981 NI 22 amended. Supersedes Draft ISBN 0110459059 published on 24.05.94. Territorial extent & classification: NI. General. – 16p. – 0 11 044891 X *£3.20*

Price/availability are liable to change without notice

The Airports (Northern Ireland) Order 1994 No. 426 (NI. 1). Enabling power: *Northern Ireland Act 1974, sch. 1, para. 1.* Issued: 28.03.94. Made: 24.02.94. Coming into force: In accord. with art.1 (2) (3). Effect: 1970 c.18; 1973 c.41; 1974 c.39; 1975 c.25; 1976 c.34; 1979 c.38; 1980 c.21; 1982 c.60; 1986 c.31; 1987 c.43; S.I. 1973 NI21; 1976 NI6; 1982 NI9; 1983 NI18; 1987 NI20; 1989 NI12; 1991 NI11; 1992 NI1, NI5 amended & 1971 c. 15 (NI) revoked. Supersedes Draft ISBN 0110358767 previously published on 09.12.93. Territorial extent & classification: NI.General. – 84p. – 0 11 043426 9 £8.70

The Appropriation (No. 2) (Northern Ireland) Order 1994 No. 1892 (NI. 7). Enabling power: *Northern Ireland Act 1974, sch. 1, para. 1.* Issued: 01.08.94. Made: 19.07.94. Coming into force: 19.07.94. Effect: None. Territorial extent & classification: NI. General. Supersedes Draft ISBN 0 11 045909 1 published on 25.05.94. – 8p. – 0 11 044892 8 £1.95

The Appropriation (Northern Ireland) Order 1994 No. 762 (NI. 3). Enabling power: *Northern Ireland Act 1974, sch. 1, para. 1.* Issued: 28.03.94. Made: 15.03.94. Coming into force: 15.03.94. Effect: None. Territorial extent & classification: NI. General. – 16p. – 0 11 043762 4 £3.20

The Betting and Lotteries (Northern Ireland) Order 1994 No. 1893 (NI. 8). Enabling power: *Northern Ireland Act 1974, sch. 1, para. 1.* Issued: 02.08.94. Made: 19.07.94. Coming into force: In accord. with art. 1 (2). Effect: S.I. 1985 NI 11 amended. Supersedes draft SI ISBN 0110459067 published 24.05.94. Territorial extent & classification: NI. General. – 8p. – 0 11 044893 6 £1.95

The Civil Service (Management Functions) (Northern Ireland) Order 1994 No. 1894 (NI. 9). Enabling power: *Northern Ireland Act 1974, sch. 1, para. 1.* Issued: 02.08.94. Made: 19.07.94. Coming into force: 20.09.94. Effect: None. Supersedes Draft ISBN 0110458621 published 08.02.94. Territorial extent & classification: NI. General. – 4p. – 0 11 044894 4 £1.10

The Criminal Justice (Northern Ireland) Order 1994 No. 2795 (NI. 15). Enabling power: *Northern Ireland Act 1974, sch. 1, para. 1.* Issued: 23.11.94. Made: 02.11.94. Coming into force: In accord. with art. 1 (2). Effect: 1945 c. 15 (NI); 1950 c. 7; 1952 c. 5 (NI); 1953 c. 3; 1954 c. 33; 1959 c. 15; 1966 c. 17 (NI); 1968 c. 34 (NI); 1971 c. 38; 1980 c. 47; 1981 c. 49; 1984 c. 12; 1986 c. 35; 1988 c. 48; 1990 c. 42; 1991 c. 24, 62; 1976 NI 4; 1977 NI 16; 1978 NI 5; 1980 NI 3; 1981 NI 7, 26; 1984 NI 3; 1986 NI 15; 1989 NI 15, 19; 1990 NI 17, 42 amended. Supersedes Draft ISBN 0110459148 published on 14.06.94. Territorial extent & classification: NI. General. – 32p. – 0 11 045795 1 £5.60

The Firearms (Amendment) (Northern Ireland) Order 1994 No. 3204 (NI. 17). Enabling power: *Northern Ireland Act 1974, sch. 1, para. 1.* Issued: 09.01.95. Made: 14.12.94. Laid: 23.12.94. Coming into force: 15.02.95. Effect: SI 1981 NI 2 amended. Territorial extent & classification: NI. General. – 4p. – 0 11 043735 7 £1.10

The Health and Personal Social Services (Northern Ireland) Order 1994 No. 429 (NI. 2). Enabling power: *Northern Ireland Act 1974, sch. 1, para. 1.* Issued: 14.03.94. Made: 24.02.94. Coming into force: 01.03.94, 01.04.94. Effect: 1968 c. 34; 1972 (NI. 14); 1979 c. 36; 1989 c. 10; 1992 c. 7 1976 (NI. 22); 1986 (NI. 3), (NI. 4); 1987 (NI. 22); 1991 (NI. 1), (NI. 14) amended. Supersedes Draft ISBN 0110358759 published on 09.12.93. Territorial extent & classification: NI/General. – 24p. – 0 11 043429 3 £4.15

The Litter (Northern Ireland) Order 1994 No. 1896 (NI. 10). Enabling power: *Northern Ireland Act 1974, sch. 1, para. 1.* Issued: 10.08.94. Made: 19.07.94. Effect: SI 1978 NI 19, 1983 NI 8, 1985 NI 15 amended. Supersedes Draft ISBN 0110459016 published 13.05.94. Territorial extent & classification: NI. General. – 26p. – 0 11 044896 0 £4.70

The Local Elections (Variation of Limits of Candidates' Election Expenses) (Northern Ireland) Order 1994 No. 763. Enabling power: *Northern Ireland Constitution Act 1973, s. 38 (1) (a) (4).* Issued: 25.03.94. Made: 15.03.94. Coming into force: 16.03.94. Effect: 1962 c. 14 (NI) amended & S.I. 1993/941 revoked. Supersedes Draft ISBN 0110458818 published 17/02/94. Territorial extent & classification: NI. General. – 2p. – 0 11 043763 2 £0.65

The Northern Ireland Act 1974 (Interim Period Extension) Order 1994 No. 1772. Enabling power: *Northern Ireland Act 1974, s. 1 (4).* Issued: 12.07.94. Made: 04.07.94. Coming into force: 04.07.94. Effect: None. Supersedes Draft ISBN 0110459172 published on 01.06.94. Territorial extent & classification: NI. General. – 2p. – 0 11 044772 7 £0.65

The Northern Ireland (Emergency and Prevention of Terrorism Provisions) (Continuance) Order 1994 No. 1569. Enabling power: *Northern Ireland (Emergency Provisions) Act 1991, s. 69 (3) (a) & Prevention of Terrorism (Temporary Provisions) Act 1989, s. 27 (11) (a).* Issued: 22.06.94. Made: 13.06.94. Coming into force: 16.06.94. Effect: None. Supersedes Draft ISBN 0110458982 published 20.04.94. Territorial extent & classification: NI. General. – 2p. – 0 11 044569 4 £0.65

The Northern Ireland (Emergency Provisions) Act 1991 (Guernsey) Order 1994 No. 764. Enabling power: *Northern Ireland (Emergency Provisions) Act 1991, s. 71 (3).* Issued: 25.03.94. Made: 15.03.94. Coming into force: 15.04.94. Effect: None. Territorial extent & classification: Guernsey. General. – 4p. – 0 11 043764 0 £1.10

The Police and Magistrates' Courts Act 1994 (Commencement No. 2) Order 1994 No. 2151 (C. 44). Enabling power: *Police and Magistrates' Courts Act 1994, s. 94 (1) (4). Bringing into operation various provisions of this Act on 23.08.94.* Issued: 22.08.94. Made: 15.08.94. Effect: None. Territorial extent & classification: NI. General. – 2p. – 0 11 045151 1 £0.65

The Ports (Northern Ireland Consequential Provisions) Order 1994 No. 2810 Enabling power: *Northern Ireland Constitution Act 1973, s. 38 (2).* Issued: 23.11.94. Made: 02.11.94. Coming into force: In accord. with art. 1 (2). Effect: None. Supersedes Draft ISBN 0110458524 published on 19.01.94. Territorial extent & classification: GB. General. – 2p. – 0 11 045810 9 £0.65

Price/availability are liable to change without notice

The Ports (Northern Ireland) Order 1994 No. 2809. Enabling power: *Northern Ireland Act 1974, sch. 1, para. 1.* Issued: 23.11.94. Made: 02.11.94. Coming into force: 03.01.95. Effect: None. Supersedes Draft ISBN 0110458516 issued on 19.01.94. Territorial extent & classification: NI. General. –32p. – 0 11 045809 5 £5.60

The Rates (Amendment) (Northern Ireland) Order 1994 No. 1897 (NI. 11). Enabling power: *Northern Ireland Act 1974, sch. 1, para. 1.* Issued: 02.08.94. Made: 19.07.94. Coming into force: 19.09.94. Effect: S.I. 1972 NI 22; 1977 NI 28; 1979 NI 4 amended. Supersedes Draft ISBN 0110459199 published 14.06.94. Territorial extent & classification: NI. General. –8p. – 0 11 044897 9 £1.95

The Remand (Temporary Provisions) (Northern Ireland) Order 1994 No. 1993 (NI. 14). Enabling power: *Northern Ireland Act 1974, sch. 1, para. 1.* Issued: 15.08.94. Made: 27.07.94. Laid: 27.07.94. Coming into force: 27.07.94. Effect: None. Territorial extent & classification: NI. General. – 4p. – 0 11 044993 2 £1.10

The Road Vehicles (Registration and Licensing) (Amendment) (No. 2) Regulations (Northern Ireland) 1994 No. 3297. Enabling power: *Vehicle Excise and Registration Act 1994, ss. 7 (6), 14 (4) 23 (5) (b), 57.* Issued: 09.01.95. Made: 20.12.94. Laid: 09.01.95. Coming into force: 30.01.95. Effect: S.R. & O. 1973/490 amended. Territorial extent & classification: NI. General. – 4p. – 0 11 043864 7 £1.10

The Road Vehicles (Registration and Licensing) (Amendment) Regulations (Northern Ireland) 1994 No. 2735. Enabling power: *Vehicle Excise and Registration Act 1994, ss. 22 (1) (c), 57 (3).* Issued: 31.10.94. Made: 23.10.94. Laid: 31.10.94. Coming into force: 01.12.94. Effect: S.R. & O. (NI) 1973/490 amended. Territorial extent & classification: NI. General. – 2p. – 0 11 045735 8 £0.65

The Social Security (Contributions) (Northern Ireland) Order 1994 No. 765 (NI. 4). Enabling power: *Northern Ireland Act 1974, sch. 1, para. 1.* Issued: 28.03.94. Made: 15.03.94. Laid: 17.03.94. Coming into force: In accord. with art. 1 (2). Effect: 1992 c.7, c.8 amended. Territorial extent & classification: NI. General. – 4p. – 0 11 043765 9 £1.10

The Social Security (Incapacity for Work) (Northern Ireland) Order 1994 No. 1898 (NI. 12). Enabling power: *Northern Ireland Act 1974, sch. 1, para. 1.* Issued: 05.08.94. Made: 19.07.94. Laid: 29.07.94. Coming into force: As appointed under art. 1 (2). Effect: 1965 c. 19; 1992 c. 7, c. 8; 1993 c. 49 amended. Territorial extent & classification: NI. General. – 52p. – 0 11 044898 7 £7.35

The Statutory Sick Pay (Northern Ireland) Order 1994 No. 766 (NI. 5). Enabling power: *Northern Ireland Act 1974, sch. 1, para. 1.* Issued: 28.03.94. Made: 15.03.94. Laid: 17.03.94. Coming into force: In accord. with art. 1 (2). Effect: 1992 c.7, c.8 amended. Territorial extent & classification: NI. General. – 4p. – 0 11 043766 7 £1.10

The Vehicle Licences (Duration of First Licences and Rate of Duty) (Amendment) Order 1994 No. 3095. Enabling power: *Vehicles Excise and Registration Act 1994, ss. 3 (3), 4 (4) (5).* Issued: 13.12.94. Made: 05.12.94. Laid: 07.12.94. Coming into force: 01.01.95. Effect: S.I. 1986/1428 amended & S.I. 1986/1427 revoked. Territorial extent & classification: GB. General. – 2p. – 0 11 043365 3 £0.65

The Wills and Administration Proceedings (Northern Ireland) Order 1994 No. 1899 (NI. 13). Enabling power: *Northern Ireland Act 1974, sch. 1, para. 1.* Issued: 10.08.94. Made: 19.07.94. Effect: 1837 c. 26, 1969 c. 28 (NI), 1977 NI 17, 1979 NI 14, 1986 NI 4, 1987 NI 22 amended & 1852 c. 24, 1954 c. 20 (NI) revoked. Supersedes draft SI ISBN 110459024 published on 13.05.94. Territorial extent & classification: NI. General. – 20p. – 0 11 044899 5 £3.70

OATHS

The Commissioners for Oaths (Prescribed Bodies) Regulations 1994 No. 1380. Enabling power: *Courts and Legal Services Act 1990, ss. 113 (1) (6), 119 (1).* Issued: 01.06.94. Made: 23.05.94. Laid: 25.05.94. Coming into force: 17.06.94. Effect: None. Territorial extent & classification: E/W. General. – 2p. – 0 11 044380 2 £0.65

OFFICIAL SECRETS

The Official Secrets (Prohibited Places) Order 1994 No. 968. Enabling power: *Official Secrets Act 1911, s. 3 (c).* Issued: 07.04.94. Made: 28.03.94. Coming into force: 01.04.94. Effect: S.I. 1975/182; 1993/863 revoked. Territorial extent & classification: GB. General. – 2p. – 0 11 043968 6 £0.65

OFFSHORE INSTALLATIONS

The Offshore Installations (Safety Zones) (No. 2) Order 1994 No. 1836. Enabling power: *Petroleum Act 1987, s. 22 (1) (2).* Issued: 18.07.94. Made: 11.07.94. Coming into force: 09.08.94. Effect: None. Territorial extent & classification: E/W/S. General. – 4p. – 0 11 044836 7 £1.10

The Offshore Installations (Safety Zones) Order 1994 No. 372. Enabling power: *Petroleum Act 1987, s. 22 (1) (2).* Issued: 28.02.94. Made: 16.02.94. Coming into force: 21.03.94. Effect: None. Territorial extent & classification: E/W/S. General. – 2p. – 0 11 043372 6 £0.65

OPEN SPACES

The Hyde Park and The Regent's Park (Vehicle Parking) Regulations 1994 No. 432. Enabling power: *Parks Regulation (Amendment) Act 1926, s. 2 (1), & Road Traffic Regulation Act 1984, s. 62.* Issued: 04.03.94. Made: 24.02.94. Coming into force: 01.03.94. Effect: None. Supersedes Draft ISBN 0110458583 previously published on 20.01.94. Territorial extent & classification: E. General. – 4p. – 0 11 043432 3 £1.10

OPTICIANS

The General Optical Council (Companies Committee Rules) Order of Council 1994 No.2579. Enabling power: *Opticians Act 1989, s. 3 (2).* Issued: 12.10.94. Made: 04.10.94. Coming into force: 01.11.94. Effect: S.I. 1959/955; 1971/1525 revoked. Territorial extent & classification: GB. General. – 4p. – 0 11 045579 7 *£1.10*

The General Optical Council (Maximum Penalty) Order of Council 1994 No. 3327. Enabling power: *Opticians Act 1989, s. 16 (3).* Issued: 13.01.95. Made: 29.12.94. Laid: 06.01.95. Coming into force: 27.01.95. Effect: 1989 c. 44 amended. Territorial extent & classification: GB. General. – 2p. – 0 11 043889 2 *£0.65*

The General Optical Council (Registration and Enrolment (Amendment) Rules) Order of Council 1994 No. 729. Enabling power: *Opticians Act 1989, s. 10.* Issued: 22.03.94. Made: 11.03.94. Coming into force: 01.04.94. Effect: S.I. 1997/176 amended & S.I. 1993/483 revoked. Territorial extent & classification: GB. General. – 2p. – 0 11 043729 2 *£0.65*

The General Optical Council (Testing of Sight by Persons Training as Ophthalmic Opticians Rules) Order of Council 1994 No. 70. Enabling power: *Opticians Act 1989, s. 24 (3).* Issued: 24.01.94. Made: 17.01.94. Coming into force: 17.01.94. Effect: S.I. 1974/1329 revoked. Territorial extent & classification: GB. General. – 4p. – 0 11 043070 0 *£1.10*

OVERSEAS DEVELOPMENT AND CO-OPERATION

The Commonwealth Development Corporation (Additional Enterprises) Order 1994 No. 2880. Enabling power: *Commonwealth Development Corporation Act 1978, s. 3 (3) (4).* Issued: 17.11.94. Made: 09.11.94. Laid: 11.11.94. Coming into force: 02.12.94. Effect: SI 1987/1253; 1989/2364 revoked. Territorial extent & classification: GB. General. – 4p. – 0 11 043066 2 *£1.10*

PARLIAMENT

The Ministerial and other Salaries Order 1994 No. 3206. Enabling power: *Ministerial and other Salaries Act 1975, s. 1 (4).* Issued: 21.12.94. Made: 14.12.94. Coming into force: 01.01.95. Effect: S.I. 1993/3166 revoked. Territorial extent & classification: GB. General. –4p. – 0 11 043597 4 *£1.10*

Parliament: resolution of the House of Commons, dated 4th March 1994, passed in pursuance of the House of Commons Members' Fund Act 1948, s.3 (11 & 12 Geo. 6 c.36) & the House of Commons Members' Fund and Parliamentary Pensions Act 1981, s.2 (1981 c.7) No. 631. Enabling power: *House of Commons Members' Fund Act 1948, s. 3 & House of Commons Members' Fund and Parliamentary Pensions Act 1981, s. 2.* Issued: 28.03.94. Made: 04.03.94. Coming into force: 01.04.94. Effect: 1939 c. 49 amended. Territorial extent & classification: GB. General. – 2p. – 0 11 043631 8 *£0.65*

PARTNERSHIP

The Partnerships (Unrestricted Size) No. 11 Regulations 1994 No. 644. Enabling power: *Companies Act 1985, ss. 716 (2) (d), 744.* Issued: 25.03.94. Made: 07.03.94. Coming into force: 29.03.94. Effect: S.I. 1968/1222 amended. Territorial extent & classification: E/W/S. General. – 2p. – 0 11 043644 X *£0.65*

PATENTS

The Patent Agents (Mixed Partnerships and Bodies Corporate) Rules 1994 No. 362. Enabling power: *Copyright, Designs and Patents Act 1988, ss. 279 (1) (2) (a) (2) (b) (i).* Issued: 10.03.94. Made: 17.02.94. Laid: 03.03.94. Coming into force: 24.03.94. Effect: None. Territorial extent & classification: GB. General. – 2p. – 0 11 043362 9 *£0.65*

The Patents (Convention Countries) Order 1994 No. 3220. Enabling power: *Patents Act 1977, s. 90 (1), 124 (3).* Issued: 23.12.94. Made: 14.12.94. Laid: 23.12.94. Coming into force: 13.01.95. Effect: S.R. & O. 1901/1799; 1938/767, 768; 1946/170; S.I. 1948/104, 872, 1006; 1949/2338; 1950/522, 1653; 1952/2107; 1953/394, 971, 1899; 1956/1003; 1957/600; 1958/263, 1053, 1054; 1960/201, 437, 1651; 1958; 1962/1083; 1963/366, 1326, 1487, 1757, 1919, 2082; 1964/265, 692, 998, 1196; 1965/977, 1123, 1711, 1304, 2013; 1966/80, 81, 396; 1967/158, 481, 1492, 1681, 1682; 1969/865; 1972/972; 1973/773; 1974/2146; 1975/2195; 1976/1785; 1977/1633, 1634, 2161; 1978/187; 1982/162; 1983/1709; 1984/367, 1694; 1985/173, 456, 457; 1988/1856; 1992/2672; 1993/1258 revoked. Territorial extent & classification: GB/IOM. General. – 6p. – 0 11 043739 X *£1.55*

The Patents County Court (Designation and Jurisdiction) Order 1994 No. 1609. Enabling power: *Copyright, Designs and Patents Act 1988, s. 287.* Issued: 30.06.94. Made: 17.06.94. Coming into force: 11.07.94. Effect: S.I. 1990/1496 revoked. Territorial extent & classification: E/W. General. – 2p. – 0 11 044609 7 *£0.65*

PENSIONS

The Guaranteed Minimum Pensions Increase Order 1994 No. 500. Enabling power: *Pensions Schemes Act 1993, s. 109.* Issued: 08.03.94. Made: 01.03.94. Laid: 10.02.94. Coming into force: 06.04.94. Effect: None. Supersedes Draft ISBN 0110458672. Territorial extent & classification: E/W/S. General. – 2p. – 0 11 043500 1 *£0.65*

The Home Guard (Amendment) Order 1994 No. 771. Enabling power: *Social Security (Miscellaneous Provisions) Act 1977, s. 12 (1) (3).* Issued: 25.03.94. Made: 15.03.94. Laid: 25.03.94. Coming into force: 28.03.94. Effect: Cmnd. 2563; Cmnd. 2564 amended. Territorial extent & classification: GB. General. – 2p. – 0 11 043771 3 *£0.65*

Price/availability are liable to change without notice

PENSIONS

The Local Government Superannuation (Greater Manchester Buses Limited) Regulations 1994 No.948. Enabling power: *Superannuation Act 1972, ss. 7, 12.* Issued: 13.04.94. Made: 25.03.94. Laid: 28.03.94. Coming into force: 29.03.94. Effect: 1971 c. 11; S.I. 1974/1740; 1986/24 amended. Territorial extent & classification: E. General. – 4p. – 0 11 043948 1 *£1.10*

The Local Government Superannuation (Greater Manchester Buses North Limited) Regulations 1994 No. 963. Enabling power: *Superannuation Act 1972, s. 7.* Issued: 13.04.94. Made: 28.03.94. Laid: 29.03.94. Coming into force: 30.03.94. Effect: S.I. 1993/3043 amended. Territorial extent & classification: E. General. – 2p. – 0 11 043963 5 *£0.65*

The Local Government Superannuation (Investments) Regulations 1994 No. 1909. Enabling power: *Superannuation Act 1972, s. 7.* Issued: 27.07.94. Made: 19.07.94. Laid: 27.07.94. Coming into force: 17.08.94. Effect: S.I. 1986/24 amended. Territorial extent & classification: E/W. General. – 2p. – 0 11 044909 6 *£0.65*

The Local Government Superannuation (Local Government Reorganisation in England) Regulations 1994 No. 3221. Enabling power: *Superannuation Act 1972, s. 7.* Issued: 21.12.94. Made: 14.12.94. Laid: 16.12.94. Coming into force: 06.01.95. Effect: S.I. 1986/24 amended. Territorial extent & classification: E. General. – 4p. – 0 11 043550 8 *£1.10*

The Local Government Superannuation (Scotland) Amendment Regulations 1994 No. 531 (S. 24). Enabling power: *Superannuation Act 1972, ss. 7, 12.* Issued: 14.03.94. Made: 02.03.94. Laid: 11.03.94. Coming into force: 01.04.94. Effect: S.I. 1987/1850 amended. Territorial extent & classification: S. General. – 4p. – 0 11 043531 1 *£1.10*

The Naval, Military and Air Forces etc. (Disablement and Death) Service Pensions Amendment (No. 2) Order 1994 No. 1906. Enabling power: *Social Security (Miscellaneous Provisions) Act 1977, ss. 12 (1), 24 (3).* Issued: 29.07.94. Made: 19.07.94. Laid: 29.07.94. Coming into force: 03.10.94. Effect: S.I. 1983/883 amended. Territorial extent & classification: GB. General. – 2p. – 0 11 044906 1 *£0.65*

The Naval, Military and Air Force etc. (Disablement and Death) Service Pensions Amendment Order 1994 No. 772. Enabling power: *Social Security (Miscellaneous Provisions) Act 1977, ss. 12 (1), 24 (3).* Issued: 25.03.94. Made: 15.03.94. Laid: 25.03.94. Coming into force: 28.03.94. for the purposes of arts. 1, 4, 5 (3). 11.04.94. for all other purposes. Effect: S.I. 1983/883 amended. Territorial extent & classification: GB. General. – 20p. – 0 11 043772 1 *£3.70*

The Occupational and Personal Pension Schemes (Consequential Amendments) Regulations 1994 No.1062. Enabling power: *Pension Schemes Act 1993, ss. 6, 7(1)(6)(7), 8(3), 9 (2)(3)(5), 10(2)(3), 11(5), 12(3), 19, 20(1)(2)(3), 21, 22, 23(1)(7), 24(3), 26, 27(3), 28(2)(3)(4)(5), 29, 30(1), 32, 34(1)(8), 35(6), 36(6), 39, 43(1)(3)(4), 44, 45(3), 48(2)(4), 50(4)(5), 51(4), 55(2)(3)(5), 56(1)(2), 57(1)(2)(4), 59(2)(3), 60(7), 61(5), 62(2), 63(2), 71(6), 73(1)(4), 75(1)(7), 77(5)(6), 82, 88(1), 95(2)to(6), 97, 98(1)(2), 111, 112(1), 113(1)(3)(4), 114, 116, 117, 118(3)(4), 119(3), 135(1), 136(1), 138(7), 144(5), 146(4)(6), 153(1)(2)(3)(5)(6), 154, 156, 160(1), 163(2)(4)(5)(6), 165(6), 172(4), 178, 181(1)(2)(3)(4), 182(2)(3), 183(1)(3), sch. 1,para.10(1)(2)(4), sch. 2, sch. 3, para. 5(2), sch. 6, para. 17.* Issued: 21.04.94. Made: 12.04.94. Laid: 21.04.94. Coming into force: 12.05.94. Effect: S.I. 1973/1776; 1976/142, 185; 1984/380; 1985/1323, 1929, 1931; 1986/1046, 1718; 1987/1101, 1102, 1103, 1106, 1108, 1110, 1111, 1112, 1113, 1117, 1118; 1988/137, 2238; 1990/1140, 1143, 2021, 2075, 2277, 2278; 1991/166, 167, 168, 588; 1992/246 amended. With correction slip dated July 1994. Territorial extent & classification: E/W/S. General. – 24p. – 0 11 044062 5 *£4.15*

The Occupational Pension Schemes (Deficiency on Winding Up etc.) Regulations 1994 No.895. Enabling power: *Pensions Schemes Act 1993, ss. 144 (5), 153 (5) (a) (b), 181 (1), 182 (2) (3), 183 (3).* Issued: 29.03.94. Made: 23.03.94. Laid: 29.03.94. Coming into force: 19.04.94. Effect: S.I. 1992/1555 revoked. Territorial extent & classification: E/W/S. General. –4p. – 0 11 043895 7 *£1.10*

The Occupational Pensions (Revaluation) Order 1994 No. 2891. Enabling power: *Pensions Schemes Act 1993, s. 2(1), sch. 3.* Issued: 18.11.94. Made: 11.11.94. Laid: 18.11.94. Coming into force: 01.01.95. Effect: None. Territorial extent & classification: E/W/S. General. – 2p. – 0 11 043074 3 *£0.65*

The Pension Schemes Act 1993 (Commencement No. 1) Order 1994 No. 86 (C. 3). Enabling power: *Pension Schemes Act 1993, s. 193 (2) (3). Bringing into operation various provisions of the act on 19.01.94.* Issued: 26.01.94. Made: 19.01.94. Effect: None. Territorial extent & classification: E/W/S. General. – 2p. – 0 11 043086 7 *£0.65*

The Pensions Increase (Review) Order 1994 No. 776. Enabling power: *Social Security Pensions Act 1975, ss. 59 (1) (2) (5)) (5ZA).* Issued: 23.03.94. Made: 15.03.94. Laid: 16.03.94. Coming into force: 11.04.94. Effect: None. Territorial extent & classification: GB. General. – 4p. – 0 11 043776 4 *£1.10*

The Personal Injuries (Civilians) Amendment (No. 2) Scheme 1994 No. 2021. Enabling power: *Personal Injuries (Emergency Provisions) Act 1939, ss. 1, 2.* Issued: 05.08.94. Made: 29.07.94. Laid: 05.08.94. Coming into force: 03.10.94. Effect: S.I. 1983/686 amended. Territorial extent & classification: E/W/S. General. – 4p. – 0 11 045021 3 *£1.10*

The Personal Injuries (Civilians) Amendment Scheme 1994 No. 715. Enabling power: *Personal Injuries (Emergency Provisions) Act 1939, s. 1, 2.* Issued: 21.03.94. Made: 17.03.94. Laid: 21.03.94. Coming into force: 11.04.94. Effect: S.I. 1983/686 amended. Territorial extent & classification: E/W/S. General. – 8p. – 0 11 043715 2 *£1.95*

The Protected Rights (Transfer Payment) Amendment Regulations 1994 No. 1751. Enabling power: *Pension Schemes Act 1993, ss. 28 (2) (b), 182 (2) (3).* Issued: 08.07.94. Made: 04.07.94. Laid: 08.07.94. Coming into force: 29.07.94. Effect: S.I. 1987/1118 amended. Territorial extent & classification: E/W/S. General. – 2p. – 0 11 044751 4 *£0.65*

Price/availability are liable to change without notice

The Superannuation (Children's Pensions) (Earnings Limit) Order 1994 No. 350. Enabling power: *Judical Pensions Act 1981, s. 21 (5)*. Issued: 28.02.94. Made: 18.02.94. Laid: 21.02.94. Coming into force: 11.04.94. Effect: 1981 c. 20 amended & S.I. 1993/220 revoked. Territorial extent & classification: GB. General. – 2p. – 0 11 043350 5 *£0.65*

The Ulster Defence Regiment (Amendment) Order 1994 No. 773. Enabling power: *Social Security (Miscellaneous Provisions) Act 1977, s. 12 (1) (3)*. Issued: 25.03.94. Made: 15.03.94. Laid: 25.03.94. Coming into force: 28.03.94. Effect: Cmnd. 4567 amended. Territorial extent & classification: GB. General. – 2p. – 0 11 043773 X *£0.65*

PIPE-LINES

The Lazy Acres Natural Gas Pipe-Lines Order 1994 No. 1994. Enabling power: *Pipe-lines Act 1962, s. 7 (2)*. Issued: 25.08.94. Made: 26.07.94. Laid: 02.08.94. Coming into force: 01.09.94. Effect: None. Territorial extent & classification: E. Local. – 4p., ill. – 0 11 044944 4 *£1.10*

PLANT BREEDERS' RIGHTS

The Plant Breeders' Rights (Fees) (Amendment) Regulations 1994 No. 675. Enabling power: *Plant Varieties and Seeds Act 1964, ss. 9 (1), 36*. Issued: 25.03.94. Made: 09.03.94. Laid: 11.03.94. Coming into force: 01.04.94. Effect: S.I. 1990/618 amended & S.I. 1993/430 revoked. Territorial extent & classification: GB. General. – 6p. – 0 11 043675 X *£1.55*

PLANT HEALTH

The Plant Health Fees (Scotland) Order 1994 No. 1441 (S. 67). Enabling power: *Plant Health Act 1967, ss. 1 (2) (b), 2, 3 (1), 4A & Finance Act 1973. s. 56*. Issued: 08.06.94. Made: 24.05.94. Laid: 02.06.94. Coming into force: 23.06.94. Effect: S.I. 1993/1477, 2344 revoked. Territorial extent & classification: S. General. – 4p. – 0 11 044441 8 *£1.10*

The Plant Health (Forestry) (Great Britain) (Amendment) Order 1994 No. 3094. Enabling power: *Plant Health Act 1967, ss. 2, 3*. Issued: 14.12.94. Made: 01.12.94. Laid: 08.12.94. Coming into force: 29.12.94. Effect: S.I. 1993/1283 amended. Territorial extent & classification: E/W/S. General. – Implements DIR 77/93; 93/51 [OJ L205/93]. – 12p. – 0 11 043369 6 *£2.80*

The Treatment of Spruce Bark (Amendment) Order 1994 No. 3093. Enabling power: *Plant Health Act 1967, ss. 2, 3*. Issued: 14.12.94. Made: 01.12.94. Laid: 08.12.94. Coming into force: 29.12.94. Effect: S.I. 1993/1282 amended. Territorial extent & classification: E/W. General. – 4p. – 0 11 043370 X *£1.10*

POLICE

The Metropolitan Police Force (Compensation for Loss of Office) Regulations 1994 No. 1730. Enabling power: *Superannuation Act 1972, s. 24*. Issued: 08.07.94. Made: 28.06.94. Laid: 08.07.94. Coming into force: 01.08.94. Effect: None. Territorial extent & classification: E/W. General. – 4p. – 0 11 044730 1 *£1.10*

The Ministry of Defence Police (Police Committee) (Amendment) Regulations 1994 No. 1102. Enabling power: *Ministry of Defence Police Act 1987, s. 1 (5)*. Issued: 25.04.94. Made: 12.04.94. Laid: 19.04.94. Coming into force: 12.05.94. Effect: S.I. 1988/1098 amended. Territorial extent & classification: GB. General. – 2p. – 0 11 044102 8 *£0.65*

The Police (Amendment) (No. 2) Regulations 1994 No. 2195. Enabling power: *Police Act 1964, s. 33*. Issued: 26.08.94. Made: 23.08.94. Laid: 24.08.94. Coming into force: 01.09.94. Effect: S.I. 1987/851 amended. Territorial extent & classification: E/W. General. – 8p. – 0 11 045195 3 *£1.95*

The Police (Amendment) (No. 3) Regulations 1994 No. 2331. Enabling power: *Police Act 1964, s. 33*. Issued: 16.09.94. Made: 06.09.94. Laid: 09.09.94. Coming into force: 30.09.94. Effect: S.I. 1987/851; 1994/2195 amended. Territorial extent & classification: E/W. General. – 8p. – 0 11 045331 X *£1.95* Replaced by ISBN 0110432134

The Police (Amendment) (No. 4) Regulations 1994 No. 2993. Enabling power: *Police Act 1964, s. 33*. Issued: 02.12.94. Made: 24.11.94. Laid: 30.11.94. Coming into force: 21.12.94. Effect: S.I. 1987/851 amended. This SI has been made in consequence of a defect in SI 1994/2331 and is being sent free of charge to all known recipients of that SI. Territorial extent & classification: E/W. General. – 4p. – 0 11 043212 6 *£1.10*

The Police (Amendment) Regulations 1994 No. 1308. Enabling power: *Police Act 1964, s. 33*. Issued: 24.05.94. Made: 15.05.94. Laid: 18.05.94. Coming into force: 08.06.94. Effect: S.I. 1987/851 amended. Territorial extent & classification: E/W. General. – 4p. – 0 11 044308 X *£1.10*

The Police and Magistrates' Courts Act 1994 (Commencement No. 1 and Transitional Provisions) Order 1994 No. 2025 (C. 38). Enabling power: *Police and Magistrates' Courts Act 1994, s. 94 (1) (4) (5) (6)*. Bringing into operation various provisions on 08.08.94. Issued: 05.08.94. Made: 01.08.94. Laid: 05.08.94. Effect: None. Territorial extent & classification: E/W. General. – 6p. – 0 11 045025 6 *£1.55*

The Police and Magistrates' Courts Act 1994 (Commencement No. 4 and Transitional Provisions) (Scotland) Order 1994 No. 3075 (C. 72) (S.163). Enabling power: *Police and Magistrates' Courts Act 1994, s. 94 (1) (4) (5)*. Bringing into operation various provisions of this Act on 01.01.95. Issued: 12.12.94. Made: 02.12.94. Laid: 09.12.94. Effect: None. Territorial extent & classification: S. General. – 4p. – 0 11 043346 7 *£1.10*

Price/availability are liable to change without notice

The Police and Magistrates' Courts Act 1994 (Commencement No. 5 and Transitional Provisions) Order 1994 No. 3262 (C. 83). Enabling power: *Police and Magistrates' Courts Act 1994, s. 94 (1) (4) (5) (6).* Bringing various provisions of the 1994 act into operation on 31.12.94. for arts. 1 to 3 & 15.01.95. for remainder of the order. Issued: 22.12.94. Made: 14.12.94. Laid: 22.12.94. Effect: None. Territorial extent & classification: E/W. General. – 12p. – 0 11 043751 9 *£2.80* Replaced by ISBN 0110551699

The Police Authorities (Selection Panel) Regulations 1994 No. 2023. Enabling power: *Police Act 1964, sch. 1C, para. 11.* Issued: 05.08.94. Made: 01.08.94. Laid: 05.08.94. Coming into force: In accord. with reg. 1 (2) (3). Effect: None. Territorial extent & classification: E/W. General. – 6p. – 0 11 045023 X *£1.55*

The Police Cadets (Scotland) Amendment Regulations 1994 No. 2096 (S. 108). Enabling power: *Police (Scotland) Act 1967, s. 27.* Issued: 18.08.94. Made: 03.08.94. Laid: 10.08.94. Coming into force: 31.08.94. Effect: S.I. 1968/208 amended & SI 1992/3047 revoked. Territorial extent & classification: S. General. – 2p. – 0 11 045096 5 *£0.65*

The Police (Number of Members of Police Authorities) Order 1994 No. 2024. Enabling power: *Police Act 1964, s. 3A (2).* Issued: 05.08.94. Made: 01.08.94. Laid: 05.08.94. Coming into force: In acc. with art. 1 (2). Effect: None. Territorial extent & classification: E/W. General. – 2p. – 0 11 045024 8 *£0.65*

The Police Pensions (Amendment) Regulations 1994 No. 641. Enabling power: *Police Pensions Act 1976, s. 1.* Issued: 16.03.94. Made: 08.03.94. Laid: 10.03.94. Coming into force: 01.04.94. Effect: S.I. 1987/257 amended. Territorial extent & classification: E/W/S. General. – 6p. – 0 11 043641 5 *£1.55*

The Police (Promotion) (Scotland) Amendment Regulations 1994 No. 1953 (S. 88). Enabling power: *Police (Scotland) Act 1967, s. 26 (1) (1A) (2) (a) (6).* Issued: 29.07.94. Made: 20.07.94. Laid: 25.07.94. Coming into force: 14.08.94. Effect: S.I. 1968/717 amended. Territorial extent & classification: S. General. – 2p. – 0 11 044953 3 *£0.65*

The Police (Scotland) Amendment (No. 2) Regulations 1994 No. 2231 (S. 111). Enabling power: *Police (Scotland) Act 1967, s. 26.* Issued: 07.09.94. Made: 26.08.94. Laid: 30.08.94. Coming into force: 01.09.94. Effect: S.I. 1976/1073 amended. Territorial extent & classification: S. General. – 8p. – 0 11 045231 3 *£1.95*

The Police (Scotland) Amendment Regulations 1994 No. 2095 (S. 107). Enabling power: *Police (Scotland) Act 1967, s. 26.* Issued: 18.08.94. Made: 03.08.94. Laid: 10.08.94. Coming into force: 31.08.94. Effect: S.I. 1976/1073; 1992/3170; 1993/3081 amended. Territorial extent & classification: S. General. – 4p. – 0 11 045095 7 *£1.10*

The Police (Secretary of State's Objectives) Order 1994 No. 2678. Enabling power: *Police Act 1994, s. 28A.* Issued: 20.10.94. Made: 15.10.94. Laid: 20.10.94. Coming into force: 01.11.94. Effect: None. Territorial extent & classification: E/W. General. – 2p. – 0 11 045678 5 *£0.65*

The Police (Special Constables) (Scotland) Amendment Regulations 1994 No. 3039 (S. 158). Enabling power: *Police (Scotland) Act 1967, s. 26.* Issued: 09.12.94. Made: 28.11.94. Laid: 09.12.94. Coming into force: 01.01.95. Effect: S.I. 1966/97 amended. Territorial extent & classification: S. General. – 2p. – 0 11 043324 6 *£0.65*

The Welsh Language (Names for Police Authorities in Wales) Order 1994 No. 2736. Enabling power: *Welsh Language Act 1993, ss. 25, 27 (4) (b).* Issued: 01.11.94. Made: 24.10.94. Laid: 27.10.94. Coming into force: 21.11.94. Effect: None. Territorial extent & classification: E/W/S. General. – 2p. – 0 11 045736 6 *£0.65*

PORT HEALTH AUTHORITIES, ENGLAND AND WALES

The New Shoreham Port Health Authority (Revocation) Order 1994 No. 2878. Enabling power: *Public Health (Control of Disease) Act 1984, ss. 2, 4.* Made: 07.11.94. Coming into force: 08.11.94. Effect: SR & O 1894/837; 1895/796; 1898/1136; 1901/399; 1938/423 and revoked S.I. 1950/1386 amended. – *Unpublished*

POWERS OF ATTORNEY

The Court of Protection (Enduring Powers of Attorney) Rules 1994 No. 3047. Enabling power: *Mental Health Act 1983, ss. 106, 108.* Issued: 09.12.94. Made: 29.11.94. Laid: 01.12.94. Coming into force: 22.12.94. Effect: SI 1986/127; 1990/864 revoked. Territorial extent & classification: E/W. General. – 26p. – 0 11 043333 5 *£4.70*

PREVENTION AND SUPPRESSION OF TERRORISM

The Prevention of Terrorism (Temporary Provisions) Act 1989 (Continuance) Order 1994 No. 835. Enabling power: *Prevention of Terrorism (Temporary Provisions) Act 1989, s. 27 (6) (a).* Issued: 30.03.94. Made: 19.03.94. Coming into force: 22.03.94. Effect: None. Supersedes Draft ISBN 0110458788 previously published on 17.02.94. Territorial extent & classification: GB. General. – 2p. – 0 11 043835 3 *£0.65*

The Suppression of Terrorism Act 1978 (Designation of Countries) Order 1994 No. 2978. Enabling power: *Suppression of Terrorism Act 1978, s. 8.* Issued: 30.11.94. Made: 22.11.94. Laid: 28.11.94. Coming into force: 19.12.94. Effect: None. Territorial extent & classification: GB. General. – 2p. – 0 11 043154 5 *£0.65*

PRICES

The Price Marking (Amendment) Order 1994 No. 1853. Enabling power: *Prices Act 1974, s. 4.* Issued: 28.07.94. Made: 13.07.94. Laid: 19.07.94. Coming into force: Immediately after the Units of Measurement Regulations 1994 come into force, in accord. with art. 1. Effect: S.I. 1976/796; 1991/1382 amended. With correction slip dated January 1995. Territorial extent & classification: E/W/S. General. – Amendments made by Council DIR 89/617/EEC (OJ No. L357, 7.12.89, p. 28) to Council DIR 80/181/EEC (OJ No. L39, 15.2.80, p. 40). –6p. – 0 11 044853 7 *£1.55*

Price/availability are liable to change without notice

PRISONS

The Criminal Justice Act 1991 (Suspension of Prisoner Custody Officer Certificate) (Amendment) Regulations 1994 No. 3193. Enabling power: *Criminal Justice Act 1991, sch. 10, para. 3 (2)*. Issued: 20.12.94. Made: 10.12.94. Laid: 16.12.94. Coming into force: 09.01.95. Effect: S.I. 1992/727 amended. Territorial extent & classification: E/W. General. – 2p. – 0 11 043479 X £0.65

The Prison (Amendment) Rules 1994 No. 3195. Enabling power: *Prison Act 1952, s. 47*. Issued: 20.12.94. Made: 10.12.94. Laid: 16.12.94. Coming into force: 09.01.95. Effect: S.I. 1964/388 amended. Territorial extent & classification: E/W. General. – 4p. – 0 11 043480 3 £1.10

The Prisons and Young Offenders Institutions (Scotland) Rules 1994 No. 1931 (S. 85). Enabling power: *Prisons (Scotland) Act 1989, s. 39*. Issued: 01.08.94. Made: 15.07.94. Laid: 19.07.94. Coming into force: 01.11.94. for all purposes except those specified in rule 1 (3) (5): 01.10.94. for purposes specified in rule 1 (3): 01.01.95. for purposes specified in rule 1 (5). Effect: S.I. 1952/565; 1954/240; 1956/671; 1965/195; 1966/1551, 1552; 1970/2013; 1979/1630; 1981/1222, 1223; 1984/2058; 1987/2231; 1988/537; 1993/2227, 2228 revoked. Territorial extent & classification: S. General. – 64p. – 0 11 044931 2 £8.05

PROBATION

The Combined Probation Areas (Buckinghamshire) Order 1994 No. 473. Enabling power: *Probation Service Act 1993, s. 2*. Issued: 08.03.94. Made: 27.02.94. Coming into force: 01.04.94. Effect: S.I. 1986/1713 amended. Territorial extent & classification: E/W. Local. – 2p. – 0 11 043473 0 £0.65

The Combined Probation Areas (Derbyshire) Order 1994 No. 3313. Enabling power: *Probation Service Act 1993, s. 2*. Issued: 10.01.95. Made: 23.12.94. Coming into force: 01.01.95. Effect: S.I. 1986/1713 amended. Territorial extent & classification: E/W. Local. – 2p. – 0 11 043879 5 £0.65

The Combined Probation Areas (Gloucestershire) Order 1994 No. 1542. Enabling power: *Probation Services Act 1993, s. 2*. Issued: 17.06.94. Made: 08.06.94. Coming into force: 01.07.94. Effect: S.I. 1986/1713 amended. Territorial extent & classification: E/W. Local. – 2p. – 0 11 044542 2 £0.65

The Combined Probation Areas (Greater Manchester) Order 1994 No. 471. Enabling power: *Probation Service Act 1993, s. 2*. Issued: 08.03.94. Made: 27.02.94. Coming into force: 01.04.94. Effect: S.I. 1986/1713 amended. Territorial extent & classification: E/W. Local. – 2p. – 0 11 043471 4 £0.65

The Combined Probation Areas (Hertfordshire) Order 1994 No. 3314. Enabling power: *Probation Service Act 1993, s. 2*. Issued: 10.01.95. Made: 23.12.94. Coming into force: 01.01.95. Effect: S.I. 1986/1713 amended. Territorial extent & classification: E/W. Local. – 2p. – 0 11 043880 9 £0.65

The Combined Probation Areas (Lancashire) Order 1994 No. 969. Enabling power: *Probation Service Act 1993, s. 2*. Issued: 08.04.94. Made: 29.03.94. Coming into force: 01.04.94. Effect: S.I. 1986/1713 amended. Territorial extent & classification: E/W. Local. – 2p. – 0 11 043969 4 £0.65

The Combined Probation Areas (Oxfordshire) Order 1994 No. 1543. Enabling power: *Probation Services Act 1993, s. 2*. Issued: 17.06.94. Made: 08.06.94. Coming into force: 01.07.94. Effect: S.I. 1986/1713 amended. Territorial extent & classification: E/W. Local. – 2p. – 0 11 044543 0 £0.65

The Combined Probation Areas (Suffolk) Order 1994 No. 3315. Enabling power: *Probation Service Act 1993, s. 2*. Issued: 10.01.95. Made: 23.12.94. Coming into force: 01.01.95. Effect: S.I. 1986/1713 amended. Territorial extent & classification: E/W. Local. – 2p. – 0 11 043881 7 £0.65

The Probation (Amendment) Rules 1994 No. 1228. Enabling power: *Probation Service Act 1993, ss. 9, 25 (1) (d)*. Issued: 12.05.94. Made: 02.05.94. Laid: 12.05.94. Coming into force: 13.06.94. Effect: S.I. 1984/647 amended. Territorial extent & classification: E/W. General. – 2p. – 0 11 044228 8 £0.65

PROTECTION OF WRECKS

The Protection of Wrecks (Designation No. 1) Order 1994 No. 1842. Enabling power: *Protection of Wrecks Act 1973, s. 1 (1) (2) (4)*. Issued: 12.09.94. Made: 12.07.94. Laid: 13.07.94. Coming into force: 14.07.94. Effect: None. Territorial extent & classification: E. General. – 2p. – 0 11 044842 1 £0.65

The Protection of Wrecks (MV Braer) (Revocation) Order 1994 No. 2372. Enabling power: *Protection of Wrecks Act 1993, ss. 2 (1) (2), 3 (2)*. Issued: 16.09.94. Made: 09.09.94. Laid: 16.09.94. Coming into force: 07.10.94. Effect: S.I 1993/199 revoked. Territorial extent & classification: S. Local. – 2p. – 0 11 045372 7 £0.65

PUBLIC HEALTH, ENGLAND AND WALES

The Gipsy Encampments (District of Wychavon) Order 1994 No. 1189. Enabling power: *Caravan Sites Act 1968, s. 12 (2)*. Issued: 06.05.94. Made: 27.04.94. Laid: 28.04.94. Coming into force: 19.05.94. Effect: None. Territorial extent & classification: E/W. Local. – 2p. – 0 11 044189 3 £0.65

The Gipsy Encampments (Rushmoor and Hart) Order 1994 No. 2026. Enabling power: *Caravan Sites Act 1968, s. 12 (2)*. Issued: 09.08.94. Made: 01.08.94. Laid: 09.08.94. Coming into force: 30.08.94. Effect: None. Territorial extent & classification: E/W. General. – 2p. – 0 11 045026 4 £0.65

The Motor Fuel (Composition and Content) Regulations 1994 No. 2295. Enabling power: *Clean Air Act 1993, ss. 30 (1) (3), 63 (1)*. Issued: 08.09.94. Made: 02.09.94. Laid: 08.09.94. Coming into force: 01.10.94. Effect: S.I. 1976/1989; 1981/1523; 1985/1728; 1989/547; 1990/1097 revoked. Territorial extent & classification: GB. General. – 12p. – 0 11 045295 X £2.80

Price/availability are liable to change without notice

The Public Health (International Trains) Regulations 1994 No. 311. Enabling power: *Public Health (Control of Disease) Act 1984, s. 13*. Issued: 18.02.94. Made: 14.02.94. Laid: 15.02.94. Coming into force: 08.03.94. Effect: None. Territorial extent & classification: E/W. General. – 6p. – 0 11 043311 4 *£1.55*

PUBLIC HEALTH, ENGLAND AND WALES: CONTAMINATION OF FOOD

The Food Protection (Emergency Prohibitions) (Oil and Chemical Pollution of Fish) (No.2) Order 1993 (Partial Revocation No. 3) Order 1994 No. 2555. Enabling power: *Food and Environment Protection Act 1985, s. 1 (1) (2), 24 (1) (3)*. Issued: 11.10.94. Made: 30.09.94. Laid: 03.10.94. Coming into force: 01.10.94. Effect: S.I. 1993/143 amended. Territorial extent & classification: GB. General. – 2p. – 0 11 045555 X *£0.65*

The Food Protection (Emergency Prohibitions) (Paralytic Shellfish Poisoning) (No. 2) Order 1994 No. 1977. Enabling power: *Food and Environment Protection Act 1985, s. 1 (1) (2), 24 (1) (3)*. Issued: 03.08.94. Made: 22.07.94. Laid: 26.07.94. Coming into force: 22.07.94. Effect: None. Territorial extent & classification: GB. General. – 4p. – 0 11 044977 0 *£1.10*

The Food Protection (Emergency Prohibitions) (Paralytic Shellfish Poisoning) (No. 2) Order 1994 Revocation Order 1994 No. 2144. Enabling power: *Food and Environment Protection Act 1985, s. 1 (1) (2), 24 (1)*. Issued: 23.08.94. Made: 12.08.94. Laid: 16.08.94. Coming into force: 12.08.94. Effect: S.I. 1994/1977 revoked. Territorial extent & classification: GB. General. – 2p. – 0 11 045144 9 *£0.65*

The Food Protection (Emergency Prohibitions) (Paralytic Shellfish Poisoning) (No. 3) Order 1994 No. 2029. Enabling power: *Food and Environment Protection Act 1985, s. 1 (1) (2), 24 (1) (3)*. Issued: 11.08.94. Made: 29.07.94. Laid: 02.08.94. Coming into force: 29.07.94. In accord.with art. 1 (1). Effect: None. Territorial extent & classification: GB. General. –4p. – 0 11 045029 9 *£1.10*

The Food Protection (Emergency Prohibitions) (Paralytic Shellfish Poisoning) Order 1994 No.1950. Enabling power: *Food and Environment Protection Act 1985, ss. 1 (1) (2), 24 (1) (3)*. Issued: 29.07.94. Made: 20.07.94. Laid: 21.07.94. Coming into force: 20.07.94. Effect: None. Territorial extent & classification: GB. General. – 4p. – 0 11 044950 9 *£1.10*

The Food Protection (Emergency Prohibitions) (Paralytic Shellfish Poisoning) Orders 1994 Revocation Order 1994 No. 2193. Enabling power: *Food and Environment Protection Act 1985, ss. 1 (1) (2), 24 (1)*. Issued: 30.08.94. Made: 19.08.94. Laid: 23.08.94. Coming into force: 19.08.94. Effect: S.I. 1994/1950, 2029 revoked. Territorial extent & classification: GB. General. – 2p. – 0 11 045193 7 *£0.65*

The Food Protection (Emergency Prohibitions) (Radioactivity in Sheep) Partial Revocation Order 1994 No. 50. Enabling power: *Food and Environment Protection Act 1985, ss. 1 (1) (2), 24 (1) (3)*. Issued: 20.01.94. Made: 13.01.94. Laid: 18.01.94. Coming into force: 19.01.94. Effect: S.I. 1991/20 amended. Territorial extent & classification: S. General. – 6p. – 0 11 043050 6 *£1.55*

The Food Protection (Emergency Prohibitions) (Radioactivity in Sheep) (England) (Partial Revocation) Order 1994 No. 65. Enabling power: *Food and Environment Protection Act 1985, ss. 1 (1) (2), 24 (1) (3)*. Issued: 04.02.94. Made: 10.01.94. Laid: 17.01.94. Coming into force: 19.01.94. Effect: S.I. 1991/6 amended. Territorial extent & classification: E. General. –6p. – 0 11 043065 4 *£1.55*

The Food Protection (Emergency Prohibitions) (Radioactivity in Sheep) (Wales) (Partial Revocation) Order 1994 No. 63. Enabling power: *Food and Environment Protection Act 1985, s. 1 (1) (a)*. Issued: 01.02.94. Made: 11.01.94. Laid: 17.01.94. Coming into force: 19.01.94. Effect: None. Territorial extent & classification: W. General. – 4p. – 0 11 043063 8 *£1.10*

PUBLIC HEALTH, NORTHERN IRELAND

The Motor Fuel (Composition and Content) Regulations 1994 No. 2295. Enabling power: *Clean Air Act 1993, ss. 30 (1) (3), 63 (1)*. Issued: 08.09.94. Made: 02.09.94. Laid: 08.09.94. Coming into force: 01.10.94. Effect: S.I. 1976/1989; 1981/1523; 1985/1728; 1989/547; 1990/1097 revoked. Territorial extent & classification: GB. General. – 12p. – 0 11 045295 X *£2.80*

PUBLIC HEALTH, NORTHERN IRELAND: CONTAMINATION OF FOOD

The Food Protection (Emergency Prohibitions) (Oil and Chemical Pollution of Fish) (No.2) Order 1993 (Partial Revocation No. 3) Order 1994 No. 2555. Enabling power: *Food and Environment Protection Act 1985, s. 1 (1) (2), 24 (1) (3)*. Issued: 11.10.94. Made: 30.09.94. Laid: 03.10.94. Coming into force: 01.10.94. Effect: S.I. 1993/143 amended. Territorial extent & classification: GB. General. – 2p. – 0 11 045555 X *£0.65*

The Food Protection (Emergency Prohibitions) (Paralytic Shellfish Poisoning) (No. 2) Order 1994 No. 1977. Enabling power: *Food and Environment Protection Act 1985, s. 1 (1) (2), 24 (1) (3)*. Issued: 03.08.94. Made: 22.07.94. Laid: 26.07.94. Coming into force: 22.07.94. Effect: None. Territorial extent & classification: GB. General. – 4p. – 0 11 044977 0 *£1.10*

The Food Protection (Emergency Prohibitions) (Paralytic Shellfish Poisoning) (No. 2) Order 1994 Revocation Order 1994 No. 2144. Enabling power: *Food and Environment Protection Act 1985, s. 1 (1) (2), 24 (1)*. Issued: 23.08.94. Made: 12.08.94. Laid: 16.08.94. Coming into force: 12.08.94. Effect: S.I. 1994/1977 revoked. Territorial extent & classification: GB. General. – 2p. – 0 11 045144 9 *£0.65*

Price/availability are liable to change without notice

The Food Protection (Emergency Prohibitions) (Paralytic Shellfish Poisoning) (No. 3) Order 1994 No. 2029. Enabling power: *Food and Environment Protection Act 1985, s. 1 (1) (2), 24 (1) (3)*. Issued: 11.08.94. Made: 29.07.94. Laid: 02.08.94. Coming into force: 29.07.94. In accord.with art. 1 (1). Effect: None. Territorial extent & classification: GB. General. –4p. – 0 11 045029 9 *£1.10*

The Food Protection (Emergency Prohibitions) (Paralytic Shellfish Poisoning) Order 1994 No.1950. Enabling power: *Food and Environment Protection Act 1985, ss. 1 (1) (2), 24 (1) (3)*. Issued: 29.07.94. Made: 20.07.94. Laid: 21.07.94. Coming into force: 20.07.94. Effect: None. Territorial extent & classification: GB. General. – 4p. – 0 11 044950 9 *£1.10*

The Food Protection (Emergency Prohibitions) (Paralytic Shellfish Poisoning) Orders 1994 Revocation Order 1994 No. 2193. Enabling power: *Food and Environment Protection Act 1985, ss. 1 (1) (2), 24 (1)*. Issued: 30.08.94. Made: 19.08.94. Laid: 23.08.94. Coming into force: 19.08.94. Effect: S.I. 1994/1950, 2029 revoked. Territorial extent & classification: GB. General. – 2p. – 0 11 045193 7 *£0.65*

The Food Protection (Emergency Prohibitions) (Radioactivity in Sheep) Partial Revocation Order 1994 No. 50. Enabling power: *Food and Environment Protection Act 1985, ss. 1 (1) (2), 24 (1) (3)*. Issued: 20.01.94. Made: 13.01.94. Laid: 18.01.94. Coming into force: 19.01.94. Effect: S.I. 1991/20 amended. Territorial extent & classification: S. General. –6p. – 0 11 043050 6 *£1.55*

The Food Protection (Emergency Prohibitions) (Radioactivity in Sheep) (Wales) (Partial Revocation) Order 1994 No. 63. Enabling power: *Food and Environment Protection Act 1985, s. 1 (1) (a)*. Issued: 01.02.94. Made: 11.01.94. Laid: 17.01.94. Coming into force: 19.01.94. Effect: None. Territorial extent & classification: W. General. – 4p. – 0 11 043063 8 *£1.10*

The Food Protection (Emergency Prohibitions) (Radioactivity in Sheep) (England) (Partial Revocation) Order 1994 No. 65. Enabling power: *Food and Environment Protection Act 1985, ss. 1 (1) (2), 24 (1) (3)*. Issued: 04.02.94. Made: 10.01.94. Laid: 17.01.94. Coming into force: 19.01.94. Effect: S.I. 1991/6 amended. Territorial extent & classification: E. General. –6p. – 0 11 043065 4 *£1.55*

PUBLIC HEALTH, SCOTLAND

The Motor Fuel (Composition and Content) Regulations 1994 No. 2295. Enabling power: *Clean Air Act 1993, ss. 30 (1) (3), 63 (1)*. Issued: 08.09.94. Made: 02.09.94. Laid: 08.09.94. Coming into force: 01.10.94. Effect: S.I. 1976/1989; 1981/1523; 1985/1728; 1989/547; 1990/1097 revoked. Territorial extent & classification: GB. General. – 12p. – 0 11 045295 X *£2.80*

The Urban Waste Water Treatment (Scotland) Regulations 1994 No. 2842 (S. 144). Enabling power: *European Communities Act 1972, s. 2 (2)*. Issued: 15.11.94. Made: 31.10.94. Laid: 09.11.94. Coming into force: 30.11.94. Effect: None. With correction slip, dated December 1994. Territorial extent & classification: S. General. – Implements, as respects Scotland, DIR 91/271 [L 135/91]. – 16p. – 0 11 045842 7 *£3.20*

PUBLIC HEALTH, SCOTLAND: CONTAMINATION OF FOOD

The Food Protection (Emergency Prohibitions) (Oil and Chemical Pollution of Fish) (No.2) Order 1993 (Partial Revocation No. 3) Order 1994 No. 2555. Enabling power: *Food and Environment Protection Act 1985, s. 1 (1) (2), 24 (1) (3)*. Issued: 11.10.94. Made: 30.09.94. Laid: 03.10.94. Coming into force: 01.10.94. Effect: S.I. 1993/143 amended. Territorial extent & classification: GB. General. – 2p. – 0 11 045555 X *£0.65*

The Food Protection (Emergency Prohibitions) (Paralytic Shellfish Poisoning) (No. 2) Order 1994 No. 1977. Enabling power: *Food and Environment Protection Act 1985, s. 1 (1) (2), 24 (1) (3)*. Issued: 03.08.94. Made: 22.07.94. Laid: 26.07.94. Coming into force: 22.07.94. Effect: None. Territorial extent & classification: GB. General. – 4p. – 0 11 044977 0 *£1.10*

The Food Protection (Emergency Prohibitions) (Paralytic Shellfish Poisoning) (No. 2) Order 1994 Revocation Order 1994 No. 2144. Enabling power: *Food and Environment Protection Act 1985, s. 1 (1) (2), 24 (1)*. Issued: 23.08.94. Made: 12.08.94. Laid: 16.08.94. Coming into force: 12.08.94. Effect: S.I. 1994/1977 revoked. Territorial extent & classification: GB. General. – 2p. – 0 11 045144 9 *£0.65*

The Food Protection (Emergency Prohibitions) (Paralytic Shellfish Poisoning) (No. 3) Order 1994 No. 2029. Enabling power: *Food and Environment Protection Act 1985, s. 1 (1) (2), 24 (1) (3)*. Issued: 11.08.94. Made: 29.07.94. Laid: 02.08.94. Coming into force: 29.07.94. In accord.with art. 1 (1). Effect: None. Territorial extent & classification: GB. General. –4p. – 0 11 045029 9 *£1.10*

The Food Protection (Emergency Prohibitions) (Paralytic Shellfish Poisoning) Order 1994 No.1950. Enabling power: *Food and Environment Protection Act 1985, ss. 1 (1) (2), 24 (1) (3)*. Issued: 29.07.94. Made: 20.07.94. Laid: 21.07.94. Coming into force: 20.07.94. Effect: None. Territorial extent & classification: GB. General. – 4p. – 0 11 044950 9 *£1.10*

The Food Protection (Emergency Prohibitions) (Paralytic Shellfish Poisoning) Orders 1994 Revocation Order 1994 No. 2193. Enabling power: *Food and Environment Protection Act 1985, ss. 1 (1) (2), 24 (1)*. Issued: 30.08.94. Made: 19.08.94. Laid: 23.08.94. Coming into force: 19.08.94. Effect: S.I. 1994/1950, 2029 revoked. Territorial extent & classification: GB. General. – 2p. – 0 11 045193 7 *£0.65*

The Food Protection (Emergency Prohibitions) (Radioactivity in Sheep) Partial Revocation Order 1994 No. 50. Enabling power: *Food and Environment Protection Act 1985, ss. 1 (1) (2), 24 (1) (3)*. Issued: 20.01.94. Made: 13.01.94. Laid: 18.01.94. Coming into force: 19.01.94. Effect: S.I. 1991/20 amended. Territorial extent & classification: S. General. –6p. – 0 11 043050 6 *£1.55*

Price/availability are liable to change without notice

The Food Protection (Emergency Prohibitions) (Radioactivity in Sheep) (Wales) (Partial Revocation) Order 1994 No. 63. Enabling power: *Food and Environment Protection Act 1985, s. 1 (1) (a)*. Issued: 01.02.94. Made: 11.01.94. Laid: 17.01.94. Coming into force: 19.01.94. Effect: None. Territorial extent & classification: W. General. – 4p. – 0 11 043063 8 £1.10

The Food Protection (Emergency Prohibitions) (Radioactivity in Sheep) (England) (Partial Revocation) Order 1994 No. 65. Enabling power: *Food and Environment Protection Act 1985, ss. 1 (1) (2), 24 (1) (3)*. Issued: 04.02.94. Made: 10.01.94. Laid: 17.01.94. Coming into force: 19.01.94. Effect: S.I. 1991/6 amended. Territorial extent & classification: E. General. –6p. – 0 11 043065 4 £1.55

PUBLIC PASSENGER TRANSPORT

The British Railways (Penalty Fares) Act 1989 (Revocation of Activating Orders) Order 1994 No. 577. Enabling power: *British Railways (Penalty Fares) Act 1989, s. 3*. Issued: 28.03.94. Made: 07.03.94. Coming into force: 01.04.94. Effect: S.I. 1992/2323, 2324, 2589, 2945; 1993/115, 780, 781, 2814 revoked. Territorial extent & classification: E. General. – 4p. – 0 11 043577 X £1.10

The Deregulation and Contracting Out Act 1994 (Commencement No. 2) Order 1994 No.3188 (C. 76). Enabling power: *Deregulation and Contracting Out Act 1994, s. 82 (4)*. Bringing various provisions of the 1994 act into operation on 03.01.95. and 01.04.95. Issued: 22.12.94. Made: 09.12.94. Effect: None. Territorial extent & classification: GB. General. –4p. – 0 11 043736 5 £1.10

The London Regional Transport (Penalty Fares) Act 1992 (Activating No. 1) Order 1994 No.702. Enabling power: *London Regional Transport (Penalty Fares) Act 1992, s. 3*. Issued: 28.03.94. Made: 10.03.94. Coming into force: 03.04.94. Effect: None. Territorial extent & classification: E. General. – 2p. – 0 11 043702 0 £0.65

The South Yorkshire Light Rail Transit (Penalty Fares) (Activating) Order 1994 No.1328. Enabling power: *South Yorkshire Light Rail Transit Act 1989, s. 17 (2)*. Issued: 20.05.94. Made: 16.05.94. Coming into force: 30.05.94. Effect: None. Territorial extent & classification: E. Local. – 2p. – 0 11 044328 4 £0.65

PUBLIC PASSENGER VEHICLES

The Public Service Vehicles (Registration of Local Services) (Amendment) Regulations 1994 No.3271. Enabling power: *Public Passenger Vehicles Act 1981, s. 60 & Transport Act 1985, ss. 6 (9) (a), 134 (1)*. Issued: 09.01.95. Made: 07.12.94. Laid: 09.01.95. Coming into force: 01.02.95. Effect: S.I. 1986/1671 amended. Territorial extent & classification: E/W/S. General. – 2p. – 0 11 043753 5 £0.65

The Public Service Vehicles (Traffic Regulation Conditions) (Amendment) Regulations 1994 No.3272. Enabling power: *Public Passenger Vehicles Act 1981, s. 60 & Transport Act 1985, ss. 7 (6) (d), 134 (1)*. Issued: 09.01.95. Made: 17.12.94. Laid: 09.01.95. Coming into force: 01.02.95. Effect: S.I. 1986/1030 amended. Territorial extent & classification: E/W/S. General. – 2p. – 0 11 043754 3 £0.65

PUBLIC RECORDS

The Public Record Office (Fees) Regulations 1994 No. 2353. Enabling power: *Public Records Act 1958, s. 2 (5)*. Issued: 16.09.94. Made: 06.09.94. Coming into force: 01.10.94. Effect: S.I. 1992/3072 revoked. Territorial extent & classification: E/W. General. –6p. – 0 11 045353 0 £1.55

RACE RELATIONS

The Race Relations (Interest on Awards) Regulations 1994 No. 1748. Enabling power: *Race Relations Act 1976, s. 56 (5) (6)*. Issued: 08.07.94. Made: 04.07.94. Laid: 08.07.94. Coming into force: 01.08.94. Effect: None. Territorial extent & classification: E/W/S. General. – 4p. – 0 11 044748 4 £1.10

The Race Relations (Prescribed Public Bodies) (No. 2) Regulations 1994 No. 1986. Enabling power: *Race Relations Act 1976, s. 75 (5) (a)*. Issued: 03.08.94. Made: 19.07.94. Laid: 26.07.94. Coming into force: 08.11.94. Effect: S.I. 1994/109 revoked. Territorial extent & classification: GB. General. – 4p. – 0 11 044986 X £1.10

The Race Relations (Prescribed Public Bodies) Regulations 1994 No. 109. Enabling power: *Race Relations Act 1976, s. 75 (5) (a)*. Issued: 31.01.94. Made: 17.01.94. Laid: 25.01.94. Coming into force: 17.02.94. Effect: S.I. 1984/218; 1985/1309; 1985/1757 revoked. Territorial extent & classification: GB. General. – 4p. – 0 11 043109 X £1.10

RAILWAYS

The Railways Act 1993 (Consequential Modifications) (No. 3) Order 1994 No. 2229. Enabling power: *Railways Act 1993, s. 153*. Issued: 09.09.94. Made: 30.08.94. Laid: 09.09.94. Coming into force: 01.10.94. Effect: 1871 c. 78 (34 & 35 Vict.); S.I. 1994/857 amended. Territorial extent & classification: GB. General. – 4p. – 0 11 045229 1 £1.10

RATING AND VALUATION

The Alcan Aluminium UK Ltd. (Rateable Values) (Scotland) Order 1994 No. 2068 (S. 93). Enabling power: *Local Government (Scotland) Act 1975, ss. 6, 35, 37 (1)*. Issued: 24.08.94. Made: 29.06.94. Laid: 14.06.94. Coming into force: 30.07.94. Effect: 1956 c. 60; 1975 c. 30 amended & S.I. 1993/1644 revoked. Supersedes draft SI ISBN 0110459202 published on 14.06.94. Territorial extent & classification: S. General. – 4p. – 0 11 045068 X £1.10

Price/availability are liable to change without notice

The British Gas plc (Rateable Values) Order 1994 No. 3283. Enabling power: *Local Government Finance Act 1988, ss. 140 (4), 143 (1) (2), sch. 6, paras. 3 (1) (2)*. Issued: 23.12.94. Made: 20.12.94. Laid: 05.12.94. Coming into force: 21.12.94. Effect: S.I. 1989/2471 revoked with effect from 01.04.95. Supersedes Draft ISBN 0110459776 published on 07.12.94. Territorial extent & classification: E/W. General. – 4p. – 0 11 043788 8 *£1.10*

The British Gas plc (Rateable Values) (Scotland) Order 1994 No. 2069 (S. 94). Enabling power: *Local Government (Scotland) Act 1975, ss. 6, 35, 37 (1)*. Issued: 24.08.94. Made: 29.06.94. Laid: 14.06.94. Coming into force: 30.07.94. Effect: 1956 c. 60; 1975 c. 30 amended & S.I. 1993/879 revoked. Supersedes Draft ISBN 0110459326 published on 14.06.94. Territorial extent & classification: S. General. – 6p. – 0 11 045069 8 *£1.55*

The British Telecommunications plc. (Rateable Values) (Scotland) Order 1994 No. 2071 (S. 96). Enabling power: *Local Government (Scotland) Act 1975, ss. 6, 35, 37 (1)*. Issued: 24.08.94. Made: 29.06.94. Laid: 14.06.94. Coming into force: 30.07.94. Effect: 1956 c. 60; 1975 c. 30 amended & S.I. 1993/881 revoked. Supersedes draft SI ISBN 0110459245 published on 14.06.94. Territorial extent & classification: S. General. – 6p. – 0 11 045071 X *£1.55*

The British Waterways Board and Telecommunications Industry (Rateable Values) Revocation Order 1994 No. 3281. Enabling power: *Local Government Finance Act 1988, ss. 140 (4), 143 (1) (2), sch. 6, para. 3 (2)*. Issued: 23.12.94. Made: 20.12.94. Laid: 05.12.94. Coming into force: 21.12.94. Effect: S.I. 1991/2924 amended & S.I. 1989/2472, 2478; 1994/903 revoked with effect from 01.04.95. Supersedes Draft ISBN 0110459741 published on 05.12.94. Territorial extent & classification: E/W. General. – 4p. – 0 11 043790 X *£1.10*

The Caledonian MacBrayne Limited (Rateable Values) (Scotland) Order 1994 No. 2080 (S. 105). Enabling power: *Local Government (Scotland) Act 1975, ss. 6, 35, 37 (1)*. Issued: 24.08.94. Made: 29.06.94. Laid: 14.06.94. Coming into force: 30.07.94. Effect: 1956 c. 60; 1975 c. 30 amended & S.I. 1993/1646 revoked. Supersedes draft SI ISBN 0110459318 published on 14.06.94. Territorial extent & classification: S. General. – 4p. – 0 11 045080 9 *£1.10*

The Central Rating Lists Regulations 1994 No. 3121. Enabling power: *Local Government Finance Act 1988, ss. 53 (1) (2) (4) (5), 140 (4), 143 (1) (2)*. Issued: 14.12.94. Made: 07.12.94. Laid: 09.12.94. Coming into force: 30.12.94. Effect: S.I. 1989/1060; 1991/723; 1994/3123 amended & S.I. 1989/2263; 1990/502, 1566; 1993/166 revoked with effect from: 01.04.95. S.I 1989/2263 is amended retrospectively from March & July 1994 [see regs 3 & 4] but after 1st April 1995 the whole Regulations are revoked. Territorial extent & classification: E/W. General. – 10p. – 0 11 043387 4 *£2.40*

The Docks and Harbours (Rateable Values) (Amendment) Order 1994 No. 3280. Enabling power: *Local Government Finance Act 1988, ss. 140 (4), 143 (1) (2), sch. 6, para. 3 (1)*. Issued: 23.12.94. Made: 20.12.94. Laid: 05.12.94. Coming into force: 21.12.94. Effect: S.I. 1989/2473 amended. Supersedes Draft ISBN 011045975X published on 05.12.94. Territorial extent & classification: E/W. General. – 4p. – 0 11 043792 6 *£1.10*

The Electricity Generators (Rateable Values) (Scotland) Order 1994 No. 2072 (S. 97). Enabling power: *Local Government (Scotland) Act 1975, ss. 6, 35, 37 (1)*. Issued: 24.08.94. Made: 29.06.94. Laid: 14.06.94. Coming into force: 30.07.94. Effect: 1956 c. 60; 1975 c. 30 amended & S.I. 1993/874 revoked. Supersedes draft SI ISBN 011045930x published on 14.06.94. Territorial extent & classification: S. General. – 6p. – 0 11 045072 8 *£1.55*

The Electricity Supply Industry (Rateable Values) Order 1994 No. 3282. Enabling power: *Local Government Finance Act 1988, ss. 140 (4), 143 (1) (2), sch. 6, paras. 3 (1) (2)*. Issued: 23.12.94. Made: 20.12.94. Laid: 05.12.94. Coming into force: 21.12.94. Effect: S.I. 1989/2474, 2475; 1990/804; 1991/959 revoked with effect from 01.04.95. Supersedes Draft ISBN 0110459792 previously published on 12.12.94. Territorial extent & classification: E/W. General. – 6p. – 0 11 043795 0 *£1.55*

The Football Grounds (Rateable Values) (Scotland) Order 1994 No. 911 (S. 37). Enabling power: *Local Government (Scotland) Act 1975, ss. 6, 35, 37 (1)*. Issued: 31.03.94. Made: 23.03.94. Laid: 24.02.94. Coming into force: 24.03.94. Effect: 1956 c. 60; 1975 c. 30 amended. Territorial extent & classification: S. General. – 4p. – 0 11 043911 2 *£1.10*

The Forth Ports plc (Rateable Values) (Scotland) Order 1994 No. 2081 (S. 106). Enabling power: *Local Government (Scotland) Act 1975, ss. 6, 35, 37 (1)*. Issued: 24.08.94. Made: 29.06.94. Laid: 14.06.94. Coming into force: 30.07.94. Effect: 1956 c. 60; 1975 c. 30 amended & S.I. 1993/1645 revoked. Supersedes Draft ISBN 0110459229 published on 14.06.94. Territorial extent & classification: S. General. – 4p. – 0 11 045081 7 *£1.10*

The Glasgow Underground (Rateable Values) (Scotland) Order 1994 No. 2073 (S. 98). Enabling power: *Local Government (Scotland) Act 1975, ss. 6, 35, 37 (1)*. Issued: 24.08.94. Made: 29.06.94. Laid: 14.06.94. Coming into force: 30.07.94. Effect: 1956 c. 60; 1975 c. 30 amended & S.I. 1993/882 revoked. Supersedes Draft ISBN 011045930x published on 14.06.94. Territorial extent & classification: S. General. – 4p. – 0 11 045073 6 *£1.10*

The Industrial and Freight Transport (Rateable Values) (Scotland) Order 1994 No. 913 (S. 39). Enabling power: *Local Government (Scotland) Act 1975, ss. 6, 35, 37 (1)*. Issued: 31.03.94. Made: 23.03.94. Laid: 24.02.94. Coming into force: 01.04.94. Effect: 1956 c. 60; 1975 c. 30 amended & S.I. 1993/876 revoked. Territorial extent & classification: S. General. – 4p. – 0 11 043913 9 *£1.10*

The Local Government etc. (Scotland) Act 1994 (Commencement No. 2) Order 1994 No. 3150 (C. 74) (S. 174). Enabling power: *Local Government etc. (Scotland) Act 1994, s. 184. Bringing into operation various provisions of the 1994 act on 31.12.94. & 04.01.95. & 01.04.95.* Issued: 20.12.94. Made: 07.12.94. Effect: S.I. 1994/2850 amended. Territorial extent & classification: S. General. – 6p. – 0 11 043414 5 *£1.55*

The Local Government Finance Act 1992 (Commencement No. 9 and Transitional Provision) Order 1994 No. 3152 (C. 75) (S. 176). Enabling power: *Local Government Finance Act 1992, ss. 113 (2), 119 (2)*. Issued: 19.12.94. Made: 07.12.94. Coming into force: 31.03.95. for s. 110 (2) (3) & 01.04.95. for sch. 13, para. (1). Effect: None. Territorial extent & classification: S. General. – 4p. – 0 11 043418 8 *£1.10*

The Lochaber Power Company (Rateable Values) (Scotland) Order 1994 No. 2074 (S. 99). Enabling power: *Local Government (Scotland) Act 1975, ss. 6, 35, 37 (1).* Issued: 24.08.94. Made: 29.06.94. Laid: 14.06.94. Coming into force: 30.07.94. Effect: 1956 c. 60; 1975 c. 30 amended & S.I. 1993/883 revoked. Supersedes draft SI ISBN 0110459210 published on 14.06.94. Territorial extent & classification: S. General. – 4p. – 0 11 045074 4 *£1.10*

The Mercury Communications Ltd. (Rateable Values) (Scotland) Order 1994 No. 2075 (S. 100). Enabling power: *Local Government (Scotland) Act 1975, ss. 6, 35, 37 (1).* Issued: 24.08.94. Made: 29.06.94. Laid: 14.06.94. Coming into force: 30.07.94. Effect: 1956 c. 60; 1975 c. 30 amended & S.I. 1993/884 revoked. Supersedes draft SI ISBN 0110459296 published on 14.06.94. Territorial extent & classification: S. General. – 6p. – 0 11 045075 2 *£1.55*

The Mines and Quarries (Rateable Values) (Scotland) Order 1994 No. 912 (S. 38). Enabling power: *Local Government (Scotland) Act 1975, ss. 6, 35, 37 (1).* Issued: 31.03.94. Made: 23.03.94. Laid: 24.02.94. Coming into force: 01.04.94. Effect: 1956 c. 60; 1975 c. 30 amended & S.I. 1993/885 revoked. Territorial extent & classification: S. General. – 4p. – 0 11 043912 0 *£1.10*

The Non-Domestic Rates (Scotland) Order 1994 No. 64 (S. 1). Enabling power: *Local Government (Scotland) Act 1975, ss. 7A (1), 37 (1).* Issued: 24.01.94. Made: 12.01.94. Laid: 24.01.94. Coming into force: 14.02.94. Effect: None. Territorial extent & classification: S. General. – 4p. – 0 11 043064 6 *£1.10*

The Non-domestic Rating (Alteration of Lists and Appeals) (Amendment) Regulations 1994 No. 1809. Enabling power: *Local Government Finance Act 1988, s. 55 (2) (6),* Issued: 15.07.94. Made: 07.07.94. Laid: 08.07.94. Coming into force: 09.07.94. Effect: S.I. 1993/291 amended. Territorial extent & classification: E/W. General. – 4p. – 0 11 044809 X *£1.10*

The Non-Domestic Rating (Chargeable Amounts) Regulations 1994 No. 3279. Enabling power: *Local Government Finance Act 1988, ss. 58, 143 (1) (2).* Issued: 23.12.94. Made: 20.12.94. Laid: 12.12.94. Coming into force: 21.12.94. Effect: None. Supersedes Draft ISBN 0110433734 published on 12.12.94. Territorial extent & classification: E/W. General. – 32p. – 0 11 043783 7 *£5.60* Replaced by ISBN 0110527992

The Non-Domestic Rating Contributions (England) (Amendment No. 2) Regulations 1994 No. 1431. Enabling power: *Local Government Finance Act 1988, ss. 104 (4), 143 (1), sch. 8, para. 6 (5) (6).* Issued: 24.06.94. Made: 26.05.94. Laid: 27.05.94. Coming into force: 28.05.94. Effect: S.I. 1992/3082 amended. With correction slip dated June 1994. Territorial extent & classification: E. General. – 4p. – 0 11 044431 0 *£1.10*

The Non-Domestic Rating Contributions (England) (Amendment No. 3) Regulations 1994 No. 3139. Enabling power: *Local Government Finance Act 1988, ss. 140 (4), 143 (1) (2), sch. 8, para. 4, 6.* Issued: 21.12.94. Made: 08.12.94. Laid: 09.12.94. Coming into force: 31.12.94. Effect: S.I. 1992/3082 amended. Territorial extent & classification: E/W. General. – 4p. – 0 11 043688 1 *£1.10*

The Non-Domestic Rating Contributions (England) (Amendment) Regulations 1994 No. 421. Enabling power: *Local Government Finance Act 1988, ss. 140 (4), 143 (1), 146 (6), sch. 8, para. 6 (5) (6).* Issued: 04.03.94. Made: 24.02.94. Laid: 25.02.94. Coming into force: 26.02.94. Effect: S.I. 1992/3082 amended. Territorial extent & classification: E/W. General. – 2p. – 0 11 043421 8 *£0.65*

The Non-Domestic Rating Contributions (Scotland) Amendment Regulations 1994 No. 3146 (S. 170). Enabling power: *Local Government Finance Act 1992, ss. 113 (2), 116 (1), sch. 12, paras. 10, 11 (5) (a), 12.* Issued: 19.12.94. Made: 07.12.94. Laid: 09.12.94. Coming into force: 31.12.94. Effect: S.I. 1992/3061 amended. Territorial extent & classification: S. General. – 4p. – 0 11 043416 1 *£1.10*

The Non-Domestic Rating Contributions (Wales) (Amendment) (No. 2) Regulations 1994 No. 1742. Enabling power: *Local Government Finance Act 1988, ss. 140 (4), 143 (1), sch. 8, paras. 6 (5) (6).* Issued: 18.07.94. Made: 22.06.94. Laid: 07.07.94. Coming into force: 28.07.94. Effect: S.I. 1992/3238 amended. Territorial extent & classification: W. General. – 4p. – 0 11 044742 5 *£1.10*

The Non-Domestic Rating Contributions (Wales) (Amendment) (No. 3) Regulations 1994 No. 3125. Enabling power: *Local Government Finance Act 1988, ss. 140 (4), 143 (1) (2), 146 (6), sch. 8, paras. 4, 6.* Issued: 12.01.95. Made: 08.12.94. Laid: 09.12.94. Coming into force: 31.12.94. Effect: S.I. 1992/3238 amended. Territorial extent & classification: W. General. –4p. – 0 11 043886 8 *£1.10*

The Non-Domestic Rating Contributions (Wales) (Amendment) Regulations 1994 No. 547. Enabling power: *Local Government Finance Act 1988, ss. 140 (4), 143 91), 146 (6), sch. 8, para. 6 (5) (6).* Issued: 05.04.94. Made: 07.03.94. Laid: 10.03.94. Coming into force: 31.03.94. Effect: S.I. 1992/3238 amended. Territorial extent & classification: W. General. – 2p. – 0 11 043547 8 *£0.65*

The Non-Domestic Rating (Demand Notices) (Wales) (Amendment) Regulations 1994 No. 415. Enabling power: *Welsh Language Act 1993, s. 26 & Local Government Finance Act 1988, ss. 140 (4), 143 (1) (2), 146 (6), sch. 9, paras. 1, 2 (2) (h).* Issued: 01.03.94. Made: 25.02.94. Laid: 28.02.94. Coming into force: 01.03.94. Effect: S.I. 1993/252 amended. Territorial extent & classification: W. General. – 2p. – 0 11 043415 3 *£0.65*

The Non-Domestic Rating (Miscellaneous Provisions) (No. 2) (Amendment) Regulations 1994 No. 3122. Enabling power: *Local Government Finance Act 1988, ss. 64 (3), 143 (1), sch. 6, para. 2 (8).* Issued: 14.12.94. Made: 07.12.94. Laid: 09.12.94. Coming into force: 30.12.94. Effect: S.I. 1989/2303 amended. Territorial extent & classification: E/W. General. – 4p. – 0 11 043389 0 *£1.10*

The Non-Domestic Rating (Railways) and Central Rating Lists (Amendment) Regulations 1994 No. 834. Enabling power: *Local Government Finance Act 1988, ss. 53 (1) (4), 64 (3), 65 (4), 140 (4), 143 (1).* Issued: 24.03.94. Made: 21.03.94. Laid: 21.03.94. Coming into force: 01.04.94. Effect: S.I. 1989/2263 amended. With correction slip [dated June 1994]. Territorial extent & classification: E/W. General. – 4p. – 0 11 043834 5 *£1.10*

Price/availability are liable to change without notice

The Non-Domestic Rating (Railways, Telecommunications and Canals) Regulations 1994 No.3123. Enabling power: *Local Government Finance Act 1988, ss. 64 (3), 65 (4), 143 (1) (2).* Issued: 14.12.94. Made: 07.12.94. Laid: 09.12.94. Coming into force: 30.12.94. Effect: S.I. 1994/834 revoked with effect from 1st April 1995. Territorial extent & classification: E/W. General. – 6p. – 0 11 043388 2 *£1.55*

The Non-Domestic Rating (Unoccupied Property) (Scotland) Regulations 1994 No. 3200 (S. 180). Enabling power: *Local Government (Scotland) Act 1966, ss. 24 (2), 24A (4).* Issued: 21.12.94. Made: 12.12.94. Laid: 21.12.94. Coming into force: 01.04.95. Effect: None. Territorial extent & classification: S. General. – 4p. – 0 11 043521 4 *£1.10*

The Railways (Rateable Values) (Amendment) Order 1994 No. 999. Enabling power: *Local Government Finance Act 1988, ss. 140 (4), 143 (1), sch. 6, para. 3 (2).* Issued: 08.04.94. Made: 30.03.94. Laid: 14.03.94. Coming into force: 01.04.94. Effect: S.I. 1989/2477 amended. Supersedes Draft ISBN 0110458885 issued 18.03.94. Territorial extent & classification: E/W. General. – 2p. – 0 11 043999 6 *£0.65*

The Railways (Rateable Values) Order 1994 No. 3284. Enabling power: *Local Government Finance Act 1988, ss. 140 (4), 143 (1) (2), sch. 6, para. 3 (2).* Issued: 23.12.94. Made: 20.12.94. Laid: 05.12.94. Coming into force: 21.12.94. Effect: S.I. 1989/2477; 1994/999 revoked with effect from 01.04.95. Supersedes Draft SI ISBN 0110459717 published 05.12.94. Territorial extent & classification: E/W. General. – 6p. – 0 11 043786 1 *£1.55*

The Railways (Rateable Values) (Scotland) Order 1994 No. 2070 (S.95). Enabling power: *Local Government (Scotland) Act 1975, ss. 6, 35, 37 (1).* Issued: 24.08.94. Made: 29.07.94. Laid: 14.06.94. Coming into force: 30.07.94. Effect: 1956 c. 60; 1975 c. 30 amended & SI 1993/880 revoked. Territorial extent & classification: S. General. – 8p. – 0 11 045070 1 *£1.95*

The Scottish Hydro-Electric plc (Rateable Values) (Scotland) Order 1994 No. 2076 (S. 101). Enabling power: *Local Government (Scotland) Act 1975, ss. 6, 35, 37 (1).* Issued: 24.08.94. Made: 29.06.94. Laid: 14.06.94. Coming into force: 30.07.94. Effect: 1956 c. 60; 1975 c. 30 amended & S.I. 1993/875 revoked. Supersedes draft SI ISBN 011045927x published on 14.06.94. Territorial extent & classification: S. General. – 6p. – 0 11 045076 0 *£1.55*

The Scottish Nuclear Limited (Rateable Values) (Scotland) Order 1994 No. 2077 (S. 102). Enabling power: *Local Government (Scotland) Act 1975, ss. 6, 35, 37 (1).* Issued: 24.08.94. Made: 29.06.94. Laid: 14.06.94. Coming into force: 30.07.94. Effect: 1956 c. 60; 1975 c. 30 amended & S.I. 1993/877 revoked. Supersedes draft SI ISBN 0110459261 published on 14.06.94. Territorial extent & classification: S. General. – 4p. – 0 11 045077 9 *£1.10*

The Scottish Power plc (Rateable Values) (Scotland) Order 1994 No. 2078 (S. 103). Enabling power: *Local Government (Scotland) Act 1975, ss. 6, 35, 37 (1).* Issued: 24.08.94. Made: 29.07.94. Laid: 14.06.94. Coming into force: 30.07.94. Effect: 1956 c. 60; 1975 c. 30 amended & S.I. 1993/878 revoked. Supersedes draft SI ISBN 0110459288 published on 14.06.94. Territorial extent & classification: S. General. – 6p. – 0 11 045078 7 *£1.55*

The Telecommunications Industry (Rateable Values) (Amendment) Order 1994 No. 903. Enabling power: *Local Government Finance Act 1988, s. 143 (1), sch. 6, para. 3 (2).* Issued: 29.03.94. Made: 23.03.94. Laid: 18.02.94. Coming into force: 01.04.94. Effect: S.I. 1989/2478 amended. Supersedes Draft ISBN 0110458834 previously published on 18.02.94. Territorial extent & classification: E/W. General. – 2p. – 0 11 043903 1 *£0.65*

The Valuation for Rating (Decapitalisation Rate) (Scotland) Regulations 1994 No. 3256 (S. 184). Enabling power: *Valuation and Rating (Scotland) Act 1956, s. 6 (8A).* Issued: 04.01.95. Made: 14.12.94. Laid: 04.01.95. Coming into force: 25.01.95. Effect: S.I. 1990/505 amended. Territorial extent & classification: S. General. – 4p. – 0 11 043785 3 *£1.10*

The Valuation for Rating (Plant and Machinery) Regulations 1994 No. 2680. Enabling power: *Local Government Finance Act 1988, s. 143 (2), sch. 6, para. 2 (8).* Issued: 21.10.94. Made: 16.10.94. Laid: 21.10.94. Coming into force: 01.04.95. Effect: S.I. 1989/441 revoked. Territorial extent & classification: E/W. General. – 6p. – 0 11 045680 7 *£1.55*

The Valuation for Rating (Plant and Machinery) (Scotland) Regulations 1994 No. 3199 (S. 179). Enabling power: *Lands Valuation (Scotland) Act 1854, s. 42.* Issued: 21.12.94. Made: 12.12.94. Laid: 21.12.94. Coming into force: 01.04.95. Effect: None. Territorial extent & classification: S. General. – 8p. – 0 11 043518 4 *£1.95*

The Water Undertakers (Rateable Values) Order 1994 No. 3285. Enabling power: *Local Government Finance Act 1988, ss. 140 (4), 143 (1) (2), sch. 6, s. 3 (2).* Issued: 23.12.94. Made: 20.12.94. Laid: 05.12.94. Coming into force: 21.12.94. Effect: S.I. 1991/2924 amended & S.I. 1989/2479; 1993/772 revoked with effect from 1st April 1995. Supersedes Draft ISBN 0110459725. Territorial extent & classification: E/W. General. – 6p. – 0 11 043794 2 *£1.55*

The Water Undertakings (Rateable Values) (Scotland) Order 1994 No. 2079 (S. 104). Enabling power: *Local Government (Scotland) Act 1975, ss. 6, 35, 37 (1).* Issued: 24.08.94. Made: 29.06.94. Laid: 14.06.94. Coming into force: 30.07.94. Effect: 1956 c. 60; 1975 c. 30 amended & S.I. 1993/886 revoked. Supersedes draft SI ISBN 0110459237 published on 14.06.94. Territorial extent & classification: S. General. – 6p. – 0 11 045079 5 *£1.55*

REGISTRATION OF BIRTHS, DEATHS, MARRIAGES, ETC

The Parental Order Register (Form of Entry) (Scotland) Regulations 1994 No. 3147 (S. 171). Enabling power: *Adoption (Scotland) Act 1978, sch. 1, para. 1 (1).* Issued: 20.12.94. Made: 05.12.94. Laid: 09.12.94. Coming into force: 01.01.95. Effect: None. Territorial extent & classification: S. General. – 4p. – 0 11 043419 6 *£1.10*

The Registration of Births, Still-Births, Deaths and Marriages (Prescription of Forms) (Scotland) Amendment Regulations 1994 No. 3151 (S. 175). Enabling power: *Registration of Births, Deaths and Marriages (Scotland) Act 1965, ss. 40 (2), 43 (4) (5), 54 (1) (b), 56.* Issued: 20.12.94. Made: 05.12.94. Coming into force: 01.01.95. Effect: S.I. 1965/1839; 1971/1158 amended. Territorial extent & classification: S. General. – 8p. – 0 11 043439 0 *£1.95*

Price/availability are liable to change without notice

REGISTRATION OF BIRTHS, DEATHS, MARRIAGES, ETC.: ENGLAND AND WALES

The Forms of Entry for Parental Orders Regulations 1994 No. 2981. Enabling power: *Adoption Act 1976, s. 67 (5), sch. 1, para. 1 (1)*. Issued: 01.12.94. Made: 23.11.94. Laid: 24.11.94. Coming into force: 15.12.94. Effect: None. Territorial extent & classification: E/W. General. – 4p. – 0 11 043190 1 *£1.10*

The Registration of Births and Deaths (Amendment) Regulations 1994 No. 1948. Enabling power: *Births and Deaths Registration Act 1953, ss. 1 (1), 5, 9 (5), 10, 10A, 11 (1) (b), 12, 14 (1), 29 (2), 39, 41 & Registration Service Act 1953, s. 20 (a), 21 (1)*. Issued: 23.08.94. Made: 20.07.94. Coming into force: 01.04.95. Effect: S.I. 1987/2088 amended. N.B. Corrected reprint with same no. & ISBN (previously issued 27.07.94). Territorial extent & classification: E/W. General. – 10p. – 0 11 044948 7 *£2.40*

The Registration of Births, Deaths and Marriages (Fees) Order 1994 No. 3257. Enabling power: *Public Expenditure and Receipts Act 1968, s. 5 (1) (2), sch. 3, paras. 1, 2*. Issued: 23.12.94. Made: 16.12.94. Laid: 19.12.94. Coming into force: 01.02.95. for arts. 1 & 2 & (for some purposes) art.4; 01.04.95. for the remainder. Effect: S.I. 1993/1116 revoked. Territorial extent & classification: E/W. General. – 6p. – 0 11 043746 2 *£1.55*

REPRESENTATION OF THE PEOPLE

The European Parliamentary Elections Act 1993 (Commencement) Order 1994 No. 1089 (C. 17). Enabling power: *European Parliamentary Elections Act 1993, s. 3 (3)*. Bringing into operation various provisions of this act on 01.05.94. Issued: 22.04.94. Made: 15.04.94. Effect: None. Territorial extent & classification: E/W. General. – 2p. – 0 11 044089 7 *£0.65*

The European Parliamentary Elections (Amendment) Regulations 1994 No. 748. Enabling power: *European Parliamentary Elections Act 1978, sch. 1, para. 2*. Issued: 17.02.94. Made: 13.03.94. Coming into force: 14.03.94. Effect: S.I. 1986/2209 amended. Supersedes Draft ISBN 0110458761 published on 17.02.94. Territorial extent & classification: E/W. General. – 2p. – 0 11 043748 9 *£0.65*

The European Parliamentary Elections (Changes to the Franchise and Qualification of Representatives) Regulations 1994 No. 342. Enabling power: *European Communities Act 1972, sch. 2, para. 2 (2)*. Issued: 22.02.94. Made: 16.02.94. Coming into force: 17.02.94. In accordance with reg. 1 (2) (3). Effect: 1978 c.10; & S.I. 1986/1081, 1091, 1111, 2209, 2250 amended. Supersedes Draft ISBN 0110458680 previously published 02.02.94. Territorial extent & classification: GB. General. – 24p. – 0 11 043342 4 *£4.15*

The European Parliamentary Elections (Day of Election) Order 1994 No. 83. Enabling power: *European Parliamentary Elections Act 1978, sch. 1, para. 3 (1)*. Issued: 27.01.94. Made: 18.01.94. Laid: 27.01.94. Coming into force: 01.03.94. Effect: None. Territorial extent & classification: GB. General. – 2p. – 0 11 043083 2 *£0.65*

The European Parliamentary Elections (Northern Ireland) (Amendment) Regulations 1994 No. 782. Enabling power: *European Parliamentary Elections Act 1978, sch. 1, para. 2*. Issued: 23.03.94. Made: 14.03.94. Coming into force: 15.03.94. Effect: S.I. 1986/2250; 1989/502 amended. Supersedes Draft ISBN 0110458826 published on 17.02.94. Territorial extent & classification: NI. General. – 2p. – 0 11 043782 9 *£0.65*

The European Parliamentary Elections (Returning Officer's Charges) (Northern Ireland) Order 1994 No. 1412. Enabling power: *Representation of the People Act 1983, s. 29 (3)*. Issued: 02.06.94. Made: 24.05.94. Coming into force: 01.06.94. Effect: S.I. 1989/996 revoked. Territorial extent & classification: NI. General. – 4p. – 0 11 044412 4 *£1.10*

The European Parliamentary Elections (Returning Officers' Charges) Order 1994 No. 1379. Enabling power: *Representation of the People Act 1983, s. 29 (3)*. Issued: 31.05.94. Made: 18.05.94. Coming into force: 01.06.94. Effect: None. Territorial extent & classification: E/W/S. General. – 6p. – 0 11 044379 9 *£1.55*

The European Parliamentary Elections (Returning Officers) (England and Wales) Order 1994 No. 894. Enabling power: *European Parliamentary Elections Act 1978, s. 9 (2), sch. 1, para. 4 (1)*. Issued: 30.03.94. Made: 21.03.94. Coming into force: In accord. with art. 1 (2) (3). Effect: None. Territorial extent & classification: E/W. General. – 4p. – 0 11 043894 9 *£1.10*

The Local Government (Transitional Election Arrangements) (Scotland) Order 1994 No. 3255 (S. 183). Enabling power: *Local Government etc. (Scotland) Act 1994, s. 18 (1) (2)*. Issued: 09.01.95. Made: 13.12.94. Laid: 16.12.94. Coming into force: 06.01.95. Effect: 1983 c. 2; S.I. 1986/1111, 2213 amended. Territorial extent & classification: S. General. – 12p. – 0 11 043793 4 *£2.80*

The Parliamentary Elections (Returning Officer's Charges) (Northern Ireland) Order 1994 No. 1413. Enabling power: *Representation of the People Act 1983, s. 29 (3) (4)*. Issued: 02.06.94. Made: 24.05.94. Coming into force: 01.06.94. Effect: S.I. 1992/730 revoked. Territorial extent & classification: NI. General. – 4p. – 0 11 044413 2 *£1.10*

The Parliamentary Elections (Returning Officers' Charges) Order 1994 No. 1044. Enabling power: *Representation of the People Act 1983, s. 29 (3) (4)*. Issued: 14.04.94. Made: 31.03.94. Coming into force: 08.04.94. Effect: S.I. 1992/717 revoked. Territorial extent & classification: E/W/S. General. – 4p. – 0 11 044044 7 *£1.10*

The Representation of the People (Variation of Limits of Candidates' Election Expenses) Order 1994 No. 747. Enabling power: *Representation of the People Act 1983, ss. 76A (1), 197 (3)*. Issued: 23.03.94. Made: 13.03.94. Coming into force: 14.03.94. Effect: 1983 c. 2 amended & S.I. 1992/706 revoked. Supersedes Draft ISBN 0110458753 published on 17/02/94. Territorial extent & classification: E/W. General. – 2p. – 0 11 043747 0 *£0.65*

REPRESENTATION OF THE PEOPLE: EUROPEAN PARLIAMENTARY ELECTIONS

The European Parliamentary Constituencies (England) Order 1994 No. 427. Enabling power: *European Parliamentary Elections Act 1993, sch. pt. II, para. 8 (5)*. Issued: 04.03.94. Made: 24.02.94. Coming into force: In accordance with art. 1 (2). Effect: None. Supersedes Draft ISBN 0110458567 previously published on 20.01.94. With correction slip dated June 1994. Territorial extent & classification: E. General. – 16p. – 0 11 043427 7 *£3.20*

The European Parliamentary Constituencies (Wales) Order 1994 No. 428. Enabling power: *European Parliamentary Elections Act 1993, sch. pt. II, para. 8 (5)*. Issued: 04.03.94. Made: 24.02.94. Coming into force: In accordance with art. 1 (2). Effect: None. Supersedes Draft ISBN 0110458575 previously published on 20.01.94. Territorial extent & classification: W. General. – 4p. – 0 11 043428 5 *£1.10*

RESTRICTIVE TRADE PRACTICES

The Registration of Restrictive Trading Agreements (EEC Documents) (Revocation) Regulations 1994 No. 1095. Enabling power: *Restrictive Trade Practices Act 1976, s. 27 (1), 42*. Issued: 28.04.94. Made: 30.03.94. Laid: 20.04.94. Coming into force: 01.06.94. Effect: S.I. 1973/950 revoked. Territorial extent & classification: GB. General. – 2p. – 0 11 044095 1 *£0.65*

RIGHTS IN PERFORMANCES

The Performances (Reciprocal Protection) (Convention Countries) Order 1994 No. 264. Enabling power: *Copyright, Designs and Patents Act 1988, s. 208 (1) (a)*. Issued: 18.02.94. Made: 08.02.94. Laid: 18.02.94. Coming into force: 11.03.94. Effect: S.I. 1993/943 revoked. Territorial extent & classification: GB. General. – 4p. – 0 11 043264 9 *£1.10*

RIVER, ENGLAND AND WALES

The Diseases of Fish (Control) Regulations 1994 No. 1447. Enabling power: *European Communities Act 1972, s. 2 (2)*. Issued: 10.06.94. Made: 26.05.94. Laid: 10.06.94. Coming into force: 01.07.94. Effect: None. Territorial extent & classification: E/W/S. General. – 10p. – 0 11 044447 7 *£2.40*

The Fish Health (Amendment) Regulations 1994 No. 1448. Enabling power: *European Communities Act 1972, s. 2 (2)*. Issued: 10.06.94. Made: 26.05.94. Laid: 10.06.94. Coming into force: 01.07.94. Effect: S.I. 1992/3300 amended. Territorial extent & classification: E/W/S. General. – 6p. – 0 11 044448 5 *£1.55*

RIVER, SCOTLAND

The Diseases of Fish (Control) Regulations 1994 No. 1447. Enabling power: *European Communities Act 1972, s. 2 (2)*. Issued: 10.06.94. Made: 26.05.94. Laid: 10.06.94. Coming into force: 01.07.94. Effect: None. Territorial extent & classification: E/W/S. General. – 10p. – 0 11 044447 7 *£2.40*

The Fish Health (Amendment) Regulations 1994 No. 1448. Enabling power: *European Communities Act 1972, s. 2 (2)*. Issued: 10.06.94. Made: 26.05.94. Laid: 10.06.94. Coming into force: 01.07.94. Effect: S.I. 1992/3300 amended. Territorial extent & classification: E/W/S. General. – 6p. – 0 11 044448 5 *£1.55*

The Salmon (Definition of Methods of Net Fishing and Construction of Nets) (Scotland) Amendment Regulations 1994 No. 111 (S. 4). Enabling power: *Salmon Act 1986, s. 3 (2) (d)*. Issued: 31.01.94. Made: 19.01.94. Laid: 31.01.94. Coming into force: 20.02.94. Effect: S.I. 1992/1974 amended. Territorial extent & classification: S. General. – 4p. – 0 11 043111 1 *£1.10*

The Salmon (Fish Passes and Screens) (Scotland) Regulations 1994 No. 2524 (S. 119). Enabling power: *Salmon Act 1986, s. 3 (2) (c) (f) (4) (5), 10 (2)*. Issued: 06.10.94. Made: 23.09.94. Laid: 06.10.94. Coming into force: 01.01.98. for reg. 1 (2) (a); 01.01.2000 for reg. 1 (2) (b); 01.01.95. for all others Effect: The regulations with respect to the construction & use of mill dams or lades, or water wheels made by the Commissioners, by byelaw dated 29th April & 19th July 1865, under s. 6 (6) of the Salmon Fisheries (Scotland) Act 1862 are hereby revoked. Territorial extent & classification: S. General. – 4p. – 0 11 045524 X *£1.10*

RIVER, SCOTLAND: SALMON AND FRESHWATER FISHERIES

The North West Sutherland Protection Order 1994 No. 3302 (S. 194). Enabling power: *Freshwater and Salmon Fisheries (Scotland) Act 1976, s. 1*. Issued: 12.01.95. Made: 20.12.94. Coming into force: 15.03.95. Effect: None. Territorial extent & classification: S. Local. – 4p. – 0 11 043869 8 *£1.10*

The River Clyde Catchment Area (Part) Protection Order 1994 No. 1949 (S. 87). Enabling power: *Freshwater and Salmon Fisheries (Scotland) Act 1976, s. 1, sch. 1*. Issued: 29.07.94. Made: 18.07.94. Coming into force: 07.10.94. Effect: None. Territorial extent & classification: S. Local. – 4p., ill. – 0 11 044949 5 *£1.10*

The River Lunan Catchment Area Protection (Renewal) Order 1991 Variation Order 1994 No. 2622 (S. 131). Enabling power: *Freshwater and Salmon Fisheries (Scotland) Act 1976, s. 1 (10)*. Issued: 18.10.94. Made: 06.10.94. Coming into force: 07.10.94. Effect: S.I. 1991/2236 amended. Territorial extent & classification: S. Local. – 4p.; ill. – 0 11 045622 X *£1.10*

Price/availability are liable to change without notice

The Rivers Tweed and Eye Protection (Renewal) Order 1991 Variation Order 1994 No.2621 (S. 130). Enabling power: *Freshwater and Salmon Fisheries (Scotland) Act 1976, s. 1 (10).* Issued: 18.10.94. Made: 06.10.94. Coming into force: 07.10.94. Effect: S.I. 1991/2234 amended. Territorial extent & classification: S. Local. – 4p.; ill. – 0 11 045621 1 £1.10

The River Tummel Catchment Area Protection (Renewal) Order 1991 Variation Order 1994 No.2623 (S. 132). Enabling power: *Freshwater and Salmon Fisheries (Scotland) Act 1976, s. 1 (10).* Issued: 18.10.94. Made: 06.10.94. Coming into force: 07.10.94. Effect: S.I. 1991/2235 amended. Territorial extent & classification: S. Local. – 4p.; ill. – 0 11 045623 8 £1.10

ROADS AND BRIDGES, SCOTLAND

The (A7) Edinburgh-Carlisle Trunk Road (Binks-Castleweary Diversion) Order 1994 No.2232. Enabling power: *Roads (Scotland) Act 1984, ss. 5 (2), 143 (1).* Made: 25.08.94. Coming into force: 08.09.94. Effect: None. – *Unpublished*

The (A7) Edinburgh-Carlisle Trunk Road (Binks-Castleweary Diversion Side Roads) Order 1994 No. 2233. Enabling power: *Roads (Scotland) Act 1984, s. 12 (1).* Made: 25.08.94. Coming into force: 08.09.94. Effect: None. – *Unpublished*

The A74(M) Special Road (Lockerbie) (Temporary Prohibition of Traffic) Order 1994 No.2407. Enabling power: *Roads (Scotland) Act 1984, s. 62 (1).* Made: 09.09.94. Coming into force: 21.09.94. Effect: None. – *Unpublished*

The (A80) Glasgow-Stirling Trunk Road (Crow Wood Roundabout to Muirhead) (Redetermination of Means of Exercise of Public Right of Passage) Order 1994 No. 1621. Enabling power: *Roads (Scotland) Act 1984, ss. 2 (1), 152 (2).* Made: 17.06.94. Coming into force: 29.06.94. Effect: None. – *Unpublished*

The (A82) Glasgow-Inverness Trunk Road (Kilbowie Roundabout Improvement Side Roads) Order 1994 No. 1860. Enabling power: *Road Traffic Regulation Act 1984, s. 12 (1).* Made: 12.07.94. Coming into force: 27.07.94. Effect: None. – *Unpublished*

The Edinburgh-Berwick Upon Tweed Trunk Road (A1) Old Craighall Roundabout to East of Haddington (De-trunking) 1994 No. 1374. Enabling power: *Roads (Scotland) Act 1984, ss. 5 (2), 143 (1).* Made: 17.05.94. Coming into force: 27.05.94. Effect: None. – *Unpublished*

The Edinburgh-Berwick Upon Tweed Trunk Road (A1) Old Craighall Roundabout to East of Haddington (Side Roads) 1994 No. 1373. Enabling power: *Roads (Scotland) Act 1984, ss. 9 (1) (c), 70 (1), 143 (1).* Made: 17.05.94. Coming into force: 27.05.94. Effect: None. – *Unpublished*

The Environmental Assessment (Scotland) Amendment Regulations 1994 No. 2012 (S. 91). Enabling power: *European Communities Act 1972, s. 2 (2) & Town and Country Planning (Scotland) Act 1972, s. 26B.* Issued: 09.08.94. Made: 19.07.94. Laid: 29.07.94. Coming into force: 19.08.94. Effect: S.I. 1988/1221; 1984 c. 54 amended. Territorial extent & classification: S. General. – 8p. – 0 11 045012 4 £1.95

The Glasgow - Carlisle Trunk Road A74(M) (Middlegill-Beattock De-Trunking) Order 1994 No.2611. Enabling power: *Roads (Scotland) Act s. 5 (2), 143 (1).* Made: 06.10.94. Coming into force: 21.10.94. Effect: None. – *Unpublished*

The Roads (Traffic Calming) (Scotland) Regulations 1994 No. 2488 (S. 118). Enabling power: *Roads (Scotland) Act 1984, ss. 39B, 143 (1) (A).* Issued: 10.10.94. Made: 20.09.94. Laid: 10.10.94. Coming into force: 31.10.94. Effect: None. Territorial extent & classification: S. General. – 6p., ill. – 0 11 045488 X £1.55

ROADS AND BRIDGES, SCOTLAND: SPECIAL ROADS

The Edinburgh-Berwick Upon Tweed Trunk Road (A1) Old Craighall Roundabout to East of Haddington Special Road Scheme 1994 No. 1371. Enabling power: *Roads (Scotland) Act 1984, ss. 7, 8, 10 (1), 143 (1).* Made: 17.05.94. Coming into force: 27.05.94. Effect: None. – *Unpublished*

The Edinburgh-Berwick Upon Tweed Trunk Road (A1) Old Craighall Roundabout to East of Haddington Special Road Scheme (No 2) 1994 No. 1372. Enabling power: *Roads (Scotland) Act 1984, ss. 7, 8, 10 (1), 143 (1).* Made: 17.05.94. Coming into force: 27.05.94. Effect: None. – *Unpublished*

The Edinburgh-Berwick Upon Tweed Trunk Road (A1) Old Craighall Roundabout to East of Tranent Appropriation Order 1994 No. 1375. Enabling power: *Roads (Scotland) Act 1984, ss. 9 (1) (a), 143 (1).* Made: 17.05.94. Coming into force: 27.05.94. Effect: None. – *Unpublished*

The Glasgow - Carlisle Special Road A74 (M) (Ecclefechan to Kirkpatrick-Fleming) Side Roads (Variation) Order 1994 No. 2545. Enabling power: *Roads (Scotland) Act 1984, s. 9 (1) (c).* Made: 28.09.94. Coming into force: 07.10.94. Effect: S.I. 1992/2169 amended. – *Unpublished*

The Glasgow - Carlisle Special Road A74 (M) (Ecclefechan to Kirkpatrick-Fleming) Special Road (Variation) Order 1994 No. 2546. Enabling power: *Roads (Scotland) Act 1984, s. 7.* Made: 28.09.94. Coming into force: 07.10.94. Effect: S.I. 1992/2168 amended. – *Unpublished*

The Glasgow-Carlisle Special Road A74(M) (Harthope-Middlegill) Appropriation Order 1994 No.4. Enabling power: *Roads (Scotland) Act 1984, ss. 9 (1) (a), 143 (1).* Made: 05.01.94. Coming into force: 21.01.94. Effect: None. – *Unpublished*

The Glasgow-Carlisle Special Road A74(M) Harthope-Middlegill (Side Roads) (No. 2) Order 1994 No. 6. Enabling power: *Roads (Scotland) Act 1984, ss. 9 (1) (c) (ii), 143 (1)*. Made: 05.01.94. Coming into force: 21.01.94. Effect: None. – *Unpublished*

The Glasgow-Carlisle Special Road A74(M) Harthope-Middlegill (Side Roads) Order 1994 No.5. Enabling power: *Roads (Scotland) Act 1984, s. 9 (1) (c)*. Made: 05.01.94. Coming into force: 21.01.94. Effect: None. – *Unpublished*

The Glasgow-Carlisle Special Road A74(M) (Harthope-Middlegill Special Road) Scheme 1994 No.3. Enabling power: *Roads (Scotland) Act 1984, s. 7*. Made: 05.01.94. Coming into force: 21.01.94. Effect: None. – *Unpublished*

The Glasgow-Carlisle Special Road A74(M) (Middlegill-Beattock) Appropriation Order 1994 No.2610. Enabling power: *Roads (Scotland) Act 1984, s. 9 (1) (a), 143 (1)*. Made: 06.10.94. Coming into force: 21.10.94. Effect: None. – *Unpublished*

The Glasgow-Carlisle Special Road A74(M) (Middlegill-Beattock Special Road) Scheme 1994 No.2612. Enabling power: *Roads (Scotland) Acts. 8, 10 (1), 143 (1)*. Made: 06.10.94. Coming into force: 21.10.94. Effect: None. – *Unpublished*

The Glasgow-Carlisle Special Road A74(M) Middlegill-Beattock (Side Roads) Order 1994 No.2609. Enabling power: *Roads (Scotland) Act 1984, s. 70 (1), 143 (1)*. Made: 06.10.94. Coming into force: 21.10.94. Effect: None. – *Unpublished*

ROAD TRAFFIC

The A1 Trunk Road (Haringey) (Bus Lanes) Red Route Traffic Order 1993 Variation Order 1994 No. 3005. Enabling power: *Road Traffic Regulation Act 1984, ss. 6, 124 (1) (d)*. Issued: 05.12.94. Made: 15.11.94. Coming into force: 12.12.94. Effect: S.I. 1993/897 amended. Territorial extent & classification: E. Local. – 2p. – 0 11 043253 3 *£0.65*

The A1 Trunk Road (Haringey) Red Route Traffic Order 1993 Variation Order 1994 No.3004. Enabling power: *Road Traffic Regulation Act 1984, ss. 6, 124 (1) (d)*. Issued: 05.12.94. Made: 15.11.94. Coming into force: 12.12.94. Effect: S.I. 1993/896 amended. Territorial extent & classification: E. Local. – 2p. – 0 11 043248 7 *£0.65*

The A1 Trunk Road (Islington) (Bus Lanes) Red Route Traffic Order 1993 Variation Order 1994 No. 3007. Enabling power: *Road Traffic Regulation Act 1984, ss. 6, 124 (1) (d)*. Issued: 05.12.94. Made: 15.11.94. Coming into force: 12.12.94. Effect: S.I. 1993/178 amended. Territorial extent & classification: E. Local. – 2p. – 0 11 043252 5 *£0.65*

The A1 Trunk Road (Islington) Red Route Traffic Order 1993 Variation Order 1994 No.3006. Enabling power: *Road Traffic Regulation Act 1984, ss. 6, 124 (1) (d)*. Issued: 05.12.94. Made: 15.11.94. Coming into force: 12.12.94. Effect: S.I. 1993/891 amended. Territorial extent & classification: E. Local. – 2p. – 0 11 043250 9 *£0.65*

The A4 Trunk Road (Bath Road and Colnbrook Bypass, Hillingdon) (50 Mph Speed Limit) Order 1994 No. 2948. Enabling power: *Road Traffic Regulation Act 1984, s. 84 (1) (a) (2)*. Issued: 29.11.94. Made: 21.11.94. Coming into force: 01.12.94. Effect: None. Territorial extent & classification: E. Local. – 2p. – 0 11 043146 4 *£0.65*

The A4 Trunk Road (Great West Road, Hounslow) (Prescribed Routes) Order 1994 No. 2486. Enabling power: *Road Traffic Regulation Act 1984, s. 6 (1) (3)*. Issued: 30.09.94. Made: 19.09.94. Coming into force: 30.09.94. Effect: None. Territorial extent & classification: E. Local. – 2p. – 0 11 045486 3 *£0.65*

The A13 Trunk Road (Tower Hamlets) (Bus Lanes) Traffic Order 1994 No. 2887. Enabling power: *Road Traffic Regulation Act 1984, s. 6 (1) (3), sch. 9, Part IV*. Issued: 17.11.94. Made: 07.11.94. Coming into force: 14.11.94. Effect: The Tower Hamlets (Bus Lanes) (No. 2) Traffic Order 1985 amended & The Tower Hamlets (Bus Lanes) (No. 1) Traffic Order 1985 revoked. Territorial extent & classification: E. Local. – 4p. – 0 11 043067 0 *£1.10*

The A20 Trunk Road (Sidcup Road, Greenwich) (Prohibition of Use of Gaps in Central Reservation) Order 1994 No. 1780. Enabling power: *Road Traffic Regulation Act 1984, s. 6 (1) (3)*. Issued: 14.07.94. Made: 04.07.94. Coming into force: 11.07.94. Effect: None. Territorial extent & classification: E. General. – 2p. – 0 11 044780 8 *£0.65*

The A23 Trunk Road (Brighton Road, Croydon) (Prohibition of Right Turn and U-Turn) Order 1994 No. 134. Enabling power: *Road Traffic Regulation Act 1984, s. 6 (1) (3)*. Issued: 03.02.94. Made: 24.01.94. Coming into force: 29.01.94. Effect: None. Territorial extent & classification: E. Local. – 2p. – 0 11 043134 0 *£0.65*

The A23 Trunk Road (Purley Way, Croydon) (Box Junction) Order 1994 No. 1566. Enabling power: *Road Traffic Regulation Act 1984, ss. 6 (1) (3), 7 (1)*. Issued: 22.06.94. Made: 06.06.94. Coming into force: 11.06.94. Effect: None. Territorial extent & classification: E. Local. – 2p. – 0 11 044566 X *£0.65*

The A23 Trunk Road (Streatham High Road, Lambeth) (Prohibition of Right Turn) Order 1994 No.2282. Enabling power: *Road Traffic Regulation Act 1984, s. 6 (1) (3)*. Issued: 09.09.94. Made: 26.08.94. Coming into force: 03.09.94. Effect: None. Territorial extent & classification: E/W. Local. – 2p. – 0 11 045282 8 *£0.65*

The Aberdeen-Fraserburgh Trunk Road (A956) (Ellon Road, Aberdeen) (Prohibition of Waiting and Loading) Order 1994 No. 1677. Enabling power: *Road Traffic Regulation Act 1984, s. 1 (1)*. Made: 20.06.94. Coming into force: 01.08.94. Effect: S.I. 1981/1585 revoked. – *Unpublished*

The Aberdeen-Fraserburgh Trunk Road (A956) (Ellon Road, Aberdeen) (Prohibition of Specified Turns) Order 1994 No. 1678. Enabling power: *Road Traffic Regulation Act 1984, s. 1 (1)*. Made: 20.06.94. Coming into force: 01.08.94. Effect: None. – *Unpublished*

Price/availability are liable to change without notice

The Cycle Racing on Highways (Tour de France 1994) Regulations 1994 No. 1226. Enabling power: *Road Traffic Act 1988, s. 31 (2) (3)*. Issued: 10.05.94. Made: 28.04.94. Laid: 10.05.94. Coming into force: 01.06.94. Effect: S.I. 1960/250 amended. Territorial extent & classification: E. General. – 2p. – 0 11 044226 1 £0.65

The Deregulation and Contracting Out Act 1994 (Commencement No. 2) Order 1994 No.3188 (C. 76). Enabling power: *Deregulation and Contracting Out Act 1994, s. 82 (4)*. Bringing various provisions of the 1994 act into operation on 03.01.95. and 01.04.95. Issued: 22.12.94. Made: 09.12.94. Effect: None. Territorial extent & classification: GB. General. – 4p. – 0 11 043736 5 £1.10

The Driving Licences (Designation of Relevant External Law) Order 1994 No. 116. Enabling power: *Road Traffic Act 1988, ss. 88 (8), 89 (2) (b) (c)*. Issued: 02.02.94. Made: 22.01.94. Coming into force: 12.02.94. Effect: None. Territorial extent & classification: E/W/S. General. – 2p. – 0 11 043116 2 £0.65

The Goods Vehicles (Operators' Licences, Qualifications and Fees) (Amendment) Regulations 1994 No. 1209. Enabling power: *Transport Act 1968, ss. 89 (1), 91 (1) & S.I. 1988/643*. Issued: 10.05.94. Made: 25.04.94. Laid: 05.05.94. Coming into force: 01.06.94. Effect: S.I. 1984/176 amended. Territorial extent & classification: GB. General. – 2p. – 0 11 044209 1 £0.65

The Goods Vehicles (Plating and Testing) (Amendment) Regulations 1994 No. 328. Enabling power: *Road Traffic Act 1988, ss. 49, 51 (1)*. Issued: 24.03.94. Made: 24.02.94. Laid: 25.02.94. Coming into force: 24.03.94. Effect: S.I. 1988/1478 amended. Territorial extent & classification: E/W/S. General. – 4p. – 0 11 043328 9 £1.10

The London North Circular Trunk Road (A406) (Barnet, Brent and Ealing) (Speed Limits) Order 1994 No. 2787. Enabling power: *Road Traffic Regulation Act 1984, ss. 82 (2), 83 (1), 84 (1) (a) (2), sch. 9, part IV*. Issued: 08.11.94. Made: 31.10.94. Coming into force: 05.11.94. Effect: S.I. 1958/301 amended & S.I. 1964/510; 1977/882; 1979/872, 873 revoked. Territorial extent & classification: E. Local. – 6p. – 0 11 045787 0 £1.55

The Motor Cars (Driving Instruction) (Amendment) Regulations 1994 No. 554. Enabling power: *Road Traffic Act 1988, ss. 125 (3), 132, 141 & S.I. 1988/643*. Issued: 10.03.94. Made: 04.03.94. Laid: 10.03.94. Coming into force: 01.04.94. Effect: S.I. 1989/2057 amended. Territorial extent & classification: E/W/S. General. – 2p. – 0 11 043554 0 £0.65

The Motor Vehicles (Competitions and Trials) (Scotland) Amendment Regulations 1994 No.2653 (S. 135). Enabling power: *Road Traffic Act 1988, s. 13 (2) (3) (b)*. Issued: 20.10.94. Made: 10.10.94. Laid: 20.10.94. Coming into force: 10.11.94. Effect: S.I. 1976/2019 amended. Territorial extent & classification: S. General. – 2p. – 0 11 045653 X £0.65

The Motor Vehicles (Driving Licences) (Amendment) (No. 2) Regulations 1994 No. 1862. Enabling power: *Road Traffic Act 1988, ss. 92 (2), 105 (1) (3), 108 (1)*. Issued: 20.07.94. Made: 12.07.94. Laid: 15.07.94. Coming into force: 05.08.94. Effect: S.I. 1987/1378 amended. With correction slip dated August 1994. Territorial extent & classification: E/W/S. General. – 2p. – 0 11 044862 6 £0.65

The Motor Vehicles (Driving Licences) (Amendment) Regulations 1994 No. 638. Enabling power: *Road Traffic Act 1988, ss. 89 (3) (4) (b), 105 (1) (3) (4), 108 (1), 192 (1)*. Issued: 23.03.94. Made: 08.03.94. Laid: 09.03.94. Coming into force: 01.04.94. Effect: S.I. 1987/1378 amended. Territorial extent & classification: E/W/S. General. – 4p. – 0 11 043638 5 £1.10

The Motor Vehicles (Driving Licences) (Large Goods and Passenger-Carrying Vehicles) (Amendment) Regulations 1994 No. 639. Enabling power: *Road Traffic Act 1988, ss. 89 (3) (4) (b), 105 (1) (3) (4), 108 (1)), 192 (1)*. 7 Issued: 23.03.94. Made: 08.03.94. Laid: 09.03.94. Coming into force: 01.04.94. Effect: S.I. 1990/2612 amended. Territorial extent & classification: E/W/S. General. – 2p. – 0 11 043639 3 £0.65

The Motor Vehicles (EC Type Approval) (Amendment) (No. 2) Regulations 1994 No. 1570. Enabling power: *European Communities Act 1972, s. 2 (2)*. Issued: 24.06.94. Made: 15.06.94. Laid: 24.06.94. Coming into force: 15.07.94. Effect: S.I. 1992/3107 amended. Territorial extent & classification: GB. General. – 2p. – 0 11 044570 8 £0.65

The Motor Vehicles (EC Type Approval) (Amendment) Regulations 1994 No. 617. Enabling power: *European Communities Act 1972, s. 2 (2)*. Issued: 23.03.94. Made: 08.03.94. Laid: 09.03.94. Coming into force: 31.03.94. Effect: S.I. 1992/3107 amended. Territorial extent & classification: GB. General. – 2p. – 0 11 043617 2 £0.65

The Motor Vehicles (Tests) (Amendment) Regulations 1994 No. 2136. Enabling power: *Road Traffic Act 1988, ss. 45, 46 & S.I. 1988/643*. Issued: 22.08.94. Made: 14.08.94. Laid: 15.08.94. Coming into force: 05.09.94. Effect: S.I. 1981/1694 amended. Territorial extent & classification: E/W/S. General. – 2p. – 0 11 045136 8 £0.65

The Motor Vehicles (Type Approval and Approval Marks) (Fees) Regulations 1994 No.1265. Enabling power: *Road Traffic Act 1988, s. 61 (1) (2) & Finance Act 1973, s. 56 (1) (2)*. Issued: 08.06.94. Made: 09.05.94. Laid: 11.05.94. Coming into force: 01.06.94. Effect: S.I. 1993/630, 2903 revoked. Territorial extent & classification: GB. General. – 56p. – 0 11 044265 2 £7.35

The Motor Vehicles (Type Approval for Goods Vehicles) (Great Britain) (Amendment) Regulations 1994 No. 2191. Enabling power: *Road Traffic Act 1988, ss. 54 (1), 61*. Issued: 30.08.94. Made: 20.08.94. Laid: 30.08.94. Coming into force: 01.10.94. Effect: S.I. 1982/1271 amended. Territorial extent & classification: E/W/S. General. – 4p. – 0 11 045191 0 £1.10

The Motor Vehicles (Type Approval) (Great Britain) (Amendment) Regulations 1994 No.2190. Enabling power: *Road Traffic Act 1988, ss. 54 (1), 61, 63*. Issued: 30.08.94. Made: 20.08.94. Laid: 30.08.94. Coming into force: 01.10.94. Effect: S.I. 1984/981 amended. Territorial extent & classification: E/W/S. General. – 4p. – 0 11 045190 2 £1.10

The Passenger and Goods Vehicles (Recording Equipment) Regulations 1994 No. 1838. Enabling power: *European Communities Act 1972, s. 2 (2)*. Issued: 19.07.94. Made: 11.07.94. Laid: 19.07.94. Coming into force: 09.08.94. Effect: 1968 c. 73; S.I. 1979/1746 amended. Territorial extent & classification: E/W/S. General. – 2p. – 0 11 044838 3 *£0.65*

The Removal and Disposal of Vehicles (Amendment) Regulations 1994 No. 1503. Enabling power: *Road Traffic Act 1991, s. 99 (1)*. Issued: 13.06.94. Made: 04.06.94. Laid: 13.06.94. Coming into force: 04.07.94. Effect: S.I. 1986/183 amended. Territorial extent & classification: E/W/S. General. – 2p. – 0 11 044503 1 *£0.65*

The Retention of Registration Marks (Amendment) Regulations 1994 No. 2976. Enabling power: *Vehicle Excise and Registration Act 1994, s. 26*. Issued: 12.12.94. Made: 24.11.94. Laid: 24.11.94. Coming into force: 16.12.94. Effect: S.I 1992/510 amended. Territorial extent & classification: E/W/S. General. – 4p. – 0 11 043345 9 *£1.10*

The Road Traffic Act 1991 (Commencement No. 10 and Transitional Provisions) Order 1994 No.81 (C. 2). Enabling power: *Road Traffic Act 1991, s. 84*. Bringing into operation various provisions of the 1991 act on 05.04.94. Issued: 04.02.94. Made: 18.01.94. Effect: S.I. 1993/3238 amended Territorial extent & classification: E. General. – 6p. – 0 11 043081 6 *£1.55*

The Road Traffic Act 1991 (Commencement No. 11 and Transitional Provisions) Order 1994 No.1482 (C. 26). Enabling power: *Road Traffic Act 1991, s. 84*. Bringing various provisions of the 1991 act into operation on 04.07.94. Issued: 10.06.94. Made: 03.06.94. Effect: None. With correction slip dated July 1994. Territorial extent & classification: E. General. – 6p. – 0 11 044482 5 *£1.55*

The Road Traffic Act 1991 (Commencement No. 12 and Transitional Provisions) Order 1994 No.1484 (C. 27). Enabling power: *Road Traffic Act 1991, s. 84*. Bringing various provisions of the 1991 act into operation on 04.07.94. Issued: 10.06.94. Made: 03.06.94. Effect: None. With correction slip dated July 1994. Territorial extent & classification: E. General. – 6p. – 0 11 044484 1 *£1.55*

The Road Traffic (Special Parking Area) (City of London) Order 1994 No. 1491. Enabling power: *Road Traffic Act 1991, s. 76 (1), 77 (6)*. Issued: 13.06.94. Made: 06.06.94. Laid: 13.06.94. Coming into force: 04.07.94. Effect: None. Territorial extent & classification: E. General. – 6p. – 0 11 044491 4 *£1.55*

The Road Traffic (Special Parking Area) (City of Westminster) Order 1994 No. 1504. Enabling power: *Road Traffic Act 1991, s. 76 (1), 77 (6)*. Issued: 13.06.94. Made: 06.06.94. Laid: 13.06.94. Coming into force: 04.07.94. Effect: None. Territorial extent & classification: E. General. – 24p. – 0 11 044504 X *£4.15*

The Road Traffic (Special Parking Area) (London Borough of Barking and Dagenham) Order 1994 No. 1488. Enabling power: *Road Traffic Act 1991, s. 76 (1), 77 (6)*. Issued: 13.06.94. Made: 06.06.94. Laid: 13.06.94. Coming into force: 04.07.94. Effect: None. Territorial extent & classification: E. General. – 6p. – 0 11 044488 4 *£1.55*

The Road Traffic (Special Parking Area) (London Borough of Barnet) Order 1994 No.1505. Enabling power: *Road Traffic Act 1991, s. 76 (1), 77 (6)*. Issued: 13.06.94. Made: 06.06.94. Laid: 13.06.94. Coming into force: 04.07.94. Effect: None. Territorial extent & classification: E. General. – 8p., ill. – 0 11 044505 8 *£1.95*

The Road Traffic (Special Parking Area) (London Borough of Bexley) Order 1994 No.1487. Enabling power: *Road Traffic Act 1991, s. 76 (1), 77 (6)*. Issued: 13.06.94. Made: 06.06.94. Laid: 13.06.94. Coming into force: 04.07.94. Effect: None. Territorial extent & classification: E. General. – 4p. – 0 11 044487 6 *£1.10*

The Road Traffic (Special Parking Area) (London Borough of Brent) Order 1994 No. 1502. Enabling power: *Road Traffic Act 1991, s. 76 (1), 77 (6)*. Issued: 13.06.94. Made: 06.06.94. Laid: 13.06.94. Coming into force: 04.07.94. Effect: None. Territorial extent & classification: E. General. – 6p. – 0 11 044502 3 *£1.55*

The Road Traffic (Special Parking Area) (London Borough of Croydon) Order 1994 No.1490. Enabling power: *Road Traffic Act 1991, s. 76 (1), 77 (6)*. Issued: 13.06.94. Made: 06.06.94. Laid: 13.06.94. Coming into force: 04.07.94. Effect: None. Territorial extent & classification: E. General. – 16p. – 0 11 044490 6 *£3.20*

The Road Traffic (Special Parking Area) (London Borough of Ealing) Order 1994 No.1489. Enabling power: *Road Traffic Act 1991, s. 76 (1), 77 (6)*. Issued: 13.06.94. Made: 06.06.94. Laid: 13.06.94. Coming into force: 04.07.94. Effect: None. Territorial extent & classification: E. General. – 8p. – 0 11 044489 2 *£1.95*

The Road Traffic (Special Parking Area) (London Borough of Enfield) Order 1994 No.1496. Enabling power: *Road Traffic Act 1991, s. 76 (1), 77 (6)*. Issued: 13.06.94. Made: 06.06.94. Laid: 13.06.94. Coming into force: 04.07.94. Effect: None. Territorial extent & classification: E. General. – 10p. – 0 11 044496 5 *£2.40*

The Road Traffic (Special Parking Area) (London Borough of Greenwich) Order 1994 No.1495. Enabling power: *Road Traffic Act 1991, s. 76 (1), 77 (6)*. Issued: 13.06.94. Made: 06.06.94. Laid: 13.06.94. Coming into force: 04.07.94. Effect: None. Territorial extent & classification: E. General. – 10p. 0 11 044495 7 *£2.40*

The Road Traffic (Special Parking Area) (London Borough of Haringey) Order 1994 No.1492. Enabling power: *Road Traffic Act 1991, s. 76 (1), 77 (6)*. Issued: 13.06.94. Made: 06.06.94. Laid: 13.06.94. Coming into force: 04.07.94. Effect: None. Territorial extent & classification: E. General. – 16p. – 0 11 044492 2 *£3.20*

The Road Traffic (Special Parking Area) (London Borough of Harrow) Order 1994 No.1493. Enabling power: *Road Traffic Act 1991, s. 76 (1), 77 (6)*. Issued: 13.06.94. Made: 06.06.94. Laid: 13.06.94. Coming into force: 04.07.94. Effect: None. Territorial extent & classification: E. General. – 4p. – 0 11 044493 0 *£1.10*

The Road Traffic (Special Parking Area) (London Borough of Havering) Order 1994 No.1494. Enabling power: *Road Traffic Act 1991, s. 76 (1), 77 (6)*. Issued: 13.06.94. Made: 06.06.94. Laid: 13.06.94. Coming into force: 04.07.94. Effect: None. Territorial extent & classification: E. General. – 8p. – 0 11 044494 9 *£1.95*

Price/availability are liable to change without notice

The Road Traffic (Special Parking Area) (London Borough of Hillingdon) Order 1994 No. 1500. Enabling power: *Road Traffic Act 1991, s. 76 (1), 77 (6)*. Issued: 13.06.94. Made: 06.06.94. Laid: 13.06.94. Coming into force: 04.07.94. Effect: None. Territorial extent & classification: E. General. – 6p. – 0 11 044500 7 *£1.55*

The Road Traffic (Special Parking Area) (London Borough of Islington) Order 1994 No. 1499. Enabling power: *Road Traffic Act 1991, s. 76 (1), 77 (6)*. Issued: 13.06.94. Made: 06.06.94. Laid: 13.06.94. Coming into force: 04.07.94. Effect: None. With correction slip dated July 1994. Territorial extent & classification: E. General. – 16p. – 0 11 044499 X *£3.20*

The Road Traffic (Special Parking Area) (London Borough of Kingston upon Thames) Order 1994 No. 1497. Enabling power: *Road Traffic Act 1991, s. 76 (1), 77 (6)*. Issued: 13.06.94. Made: 06.06.94. Laid: 13.06.94. Coming into force: 04.07.94. Effect: None. Territorial extent & classification: E. General. – 8p. – 0 11 044497 3 *£1.95*

The Road Traffic (Special Parking Area) (London Borough of Lambeth) Order 1994 No. 1508. Enabling power: *Road Traffic Act 1991, s. 76 (1), 77 (6)*. Issued: 13.06.94. Made: 06.06.94. Laid: 13.06.94. Coming into force: 04.07.94. Effect: None. Territorial extent & classification: E. General. – 12p. – 0 11 044508 2 *£2.80*

The Road Traffic (Special Parking Area) (London Borough of Merton) Order 1994 No. 1510. Enabling power: *Road Traffic Act 1991, s. 76 (1), 77 (6)*. Issued: 13.06.94. Made: 06.06.94. Laid: 13.06.94. Coming into force: 04.07.94. Effect: None. Territorial extent & classification: E. General. – 6p., ill. – 0 11 044510 4 *£1.55*

The Road Traffic (Special Parking Area) (London Borough of Newham) Order 1994 No. 1506. Enabling power: *Road Traffic Act 1991, s. 76 (1), 77 (6)*. Issued: 13.06.94. Made: 06.06.94. Laid: 13.06.94. Coming into force: 04.07.94. Effect: None. Territorial extent & classification: E. General. – 8p. – 0 11 044506 6 *£1.95*

The Road Traffic (Special Parking Area) (London Borough of Redbridge) Order 1994 No. 1509. Enabling power: *Road Traffic Act 1991, s. 76 (1), 77 (6)*. Issued: 13.06.94. Made: 06.06.94. Laid: 13.06.94. Coming into force: 04.07.94. Effect: None. Territorial extent & classification: E. General. – 8p. – 0 11 044509 0 *£1.95*

The Road Traffic (Special Parking Area) (London Borough of Sutton) Order 1994 No. 1507. Enabling power: *Road Traffic Act 1991, s. 76 (1), 77 (6)*. Issued: 13.06.94. Made: 06.06.94. Laid: 13.06.94. Coming into force: 04.07.94. Effect: None. Territorial extent & classification: E. General. – 12p. – 0 11 044507 4 *£2.80*

The Road Traffic (Special Parking Area) (London Borough of Tower Hamlets) Order 1994 No. 1613. Enabling power: *Road Traffic Act 1991, s. 76 (1), 77 (6)*. Issued: 24.06.94. Made: 20.06.94. Laid: 20.06.94. Coming into force: 04.07.94. Effect: None. Territorial extent & classification: E. General. – 16p. – 0 11 044613 5 *£3.20*

The Road Traffic (Special Parking Area) (London Borough of Waltham Forest) Order 1994 No. 1501. Enabling power: *Road Traffic Act 1991, s. 76 (1), 77 (6)*. Issued: 13.06.94. Made: 06.06.94. Laid: 13.06.94. Coming into force: 04.07.94. Effect: None. With correction slip dated July 1994. Territorial extent & classification: E. General. – 8p. – 0 11 044501 5 *£1.95*

The Road Traffic (Special Parking Area) (Royal Borough of Kensington and Chelsea) Order 1994 No. 1498. Enabling power: *Road Traffic Act 1991, s. 76 (1), 77 (6)*. Issued: 13.06.94. Made: 06.06.94. Laid: 13.06.94. Coming into force: 04.07.94. Effect: None. Territorial extent & classification: E. General. – 16p. – 0 11 044498 1 *£3.20*

The Road Traffic (Special Parking Areas) (London Borough of Barnet) (Amendment) Order 1994 No. 2785. Enabling power: *Road Traffic Act 1991, s. 76 (1), 77 (6)*. Issued: 07.11.94. Made: 01.11.94. Laid: 07.11.94. Coming into force: 28.11.94. Effect: S.I. 1994/1505 amended. Territorial extent & classification: E. General. – 6p. – 0 11 045785 4 *£1.55*

The Road Traffic (Special Parking Areas) (London Borough of Richmond on Thames) (Amendment) Order 1994 No. 1377. Enabling power: *Road Traffic Act 1991, ss. 76 (1), 77 (6)*. Issued: 26.05.94. Made: 19.05.94. Laid: 26.05.94. Coming into force: 17.06.94. Effect: S.I. 1993/3239 amended. Territorial extent & classification: E. General. – 4p. – 0 11 044377 2 *£1.10*

The Road Traffic (Special Parking Areas) (London Borough of Wandsworth) (Amendment) Order 1994 No. 2786. Enabling power: *Road Traffic Act 1991, s. 76 (1), 77 (6)*. Issued: 07.11.94. Made: 01.11.94. Laid: 07.11.94. Coming into force: 28.11.94. Effect: S.I. 1994/1474 amended. Territorial extent & classification: E. General. – 24p. – 0 11 045786 2 *£4.15*

The Road Traffic (Special Parking Areas) (London Boroughs of Bromley, Hammersmith and Fulham and Lewisham) (Amendment No. 2) Order 1994 No. 1376. Enabling power: *Road Traffic Act 1991, ss. 76 (1), 77 (6)*. Issued: 26.05.94. Made: 19.05.94. Laid: 26.05.94. Coming into force: 17.06.94. Effect: S.I. 1993/2237 amended. Territorial extent & classification: E. General. – 4p. – 0 11 044376 4 *£1.10*

The Road Traffic (Special Parking Areas) (London Boroughs of Bromley, Hammersmith and Fulham and Lewisham) (Amendment) Order 1994 No. 689. Enabling power: *Road Traffic Act 1991, s. 76 (1), 77 (6)*. Issued: 22.03.94. Made: 10.03.94. Laid: 10.03.94. Coming into force: 01.04.94. Effect: S.I. 1993/2237 amended. Territorial extent & classification: E. General. –4p. – 0 11 043689 X *£1.10*

The Road Traffic (Special Parking Areas) (London Boroughs of Camden, Hackney and Hounslow) (Amendment) Order 1994 No. 1378. Enabling power: *Road Traffic Act 1991, ss. 76 (1), 77 (6)*. Issued: 26.05.94. Made: 19.05.94. Laid: 26.05.94. Coming into force: 17.06.94. Effect: S.I. 1993/2804 amended Territorial extent & classification: E. General. – 4p. – 0 11 044378 0 *£1.10*

The Road Traffic (Special Parking Areas) (London Boroughs of Richmond upon Thames and Southwark) (Amendment) Order 1994 No. 82. Enabling power: *Road Traffic Act 1991, ss. 76 (1), 77 (6)*. Issued: 04.02.94. Made: 18.01.94. Laid: 19.01.94. Coming into force: 30.01.94. Effect: S.I. 1993/3239 amended. Territorial extent & classification: E. General. – 2p. – 0 11 043082 4 *£0.65*

Price/availability are liable to change without notice

The Road Vehicles (Construction and Use) (Amendment) (No. 2) Regulations 1994 No.329. Enabling power: *Road Traffic Act 1988, ss. 41 (1) (2) (5).* Issued: 24.03.94. Made: 24.02.94. Laid: 25.02.94. Coming into force: 24.03.94. Effect: S.I. 1986/1078 amended. Territorial extent & classification: E/W/S. General. – 10p. – 0 11 043329 7 £2.40

The Road Vehicles (Construction and Use) (Amendment) (No. 3) Regulations 1994 No.2192. Enabling power: *Road Traffic Act 1988, ss. 41 (1) (2) (5).* Issued: 30.08.94. Made: 20.08.94. Laid: 30.08.94. Coming into force: 01.10.94. Effect: S.I. 1986/1078 amended. Territorial extent & classification: E/W/S. General. – 4p. – 0 11 045192 9 £1.10

The Road Vehicles (Construction and Use) (Amendment) (No. 4) Regulations 1994 No.3270. Enabling power: *Road Traffic Act 1988, s. 41 (1) (2) (5) & European Communities Act 1972, s. 2 (2).* Issued: 09.01.95. Made: 17.12.94. Laid: 09.01.95. Coming into force: 01.02.95. Effect: S.I. 1986/1078 amended. With correction slip, dated May 1995. Territorial extent & classification: E/W/S. General. – 4p. – 0 11 043752 7 £1.10

The Road Vehicles (Construction and Use) (Amendment) Regulations 1994 No. 14. Enabling power: *Road Traffic Act 1988, ss. 41 (1) (2) (5).* Issued: 19.01.94. Made: 10.12.93. Laid: 19.01.94. Coming into force: 01.07.94. Effect: S.I. 1986/1078 amended. Territorial extent & classification: E/W/S. General. – 8p. – 0 11 043014 X £1.95

The Road Vehicles Lighting (Amendment) Regulations 1994 No. 2280. Enabling power: *Road Traffic Act 1988, s. 41 (1) (2) (5).* Issued: 09.09.94. Made: 01.09.94. Laid: 09.09.94. Coming into force: 01.10.94. for all other than reg.6; 01.04.95. for reg. 6. Effect: S.I. 1989/1796 amended. Territorial extent & classification: E/W/S. General. – 16p., ill. – 0 11 045280 1 £3.20

The Road Vehicles (Registration and Licensing) (Amendment) (No. 2) Regulations 1994 No.1911. Enabling power: *Vehicles (Excise) Act 1971, ss. 16 (2) (3) (8), 37 (1) (2).* Issued: 10.08.94. Made: 15.07.94. Laid: 10.08.94. Coming into force: 31.08.94. Effect: S.I. 1971/450 amended. Territorial extent & classification: E/W/S. General. – 4p. – 0 11 044911 8 £1.10

The Road Vehicles (Registration and Licensing) (Amendment) (No. 2) Regulations (Northern Ireland) 1994 No. 3297. Enabling power: *Vehicle Excise and Registration Act 1994, ss. 7 (6), 14 (4) 23 (5) (b), 57.* Issued: 09.01.95. Made: 20.12.94. Laid: 09.01.95. Coming into force: 30.01.95. Effect: S.R. & O. (NI) 1973/490 amended. Territorial extent & classification: NI. General. – 4p. – 0 11 043864 7 £1.10

The Road Vehicles (Registration and Licensing) (Amendment) (No. 3) Regulations 1994 No.3296. Enabling power: *Vehicle Excise and Registration Act 1994, ss. 7 (6), 14 (4) 23 (5) (b), 57.* Issued: 09.01.95. Made: 20.12.94. Laid: 09.01.95. Coming into force: 30.01.95. Effect: S.I. 1971/450 amended. Territorial extent & classification: E/W/S. General. – 4p. – 0 11 043843 4 £1.10

The Road Vehicles (Registration and Licensing) (Amendment) Regulations 1994 No. 1364. Enabling power: *Vehicles (Excise) Act 1971, s. 23 (1) (b).* Issued: 09.06.94. Made: 19.05.94. Laid: 20.05.94. Coming into force: 10.06.94. Effect: S.I. 1971/450 amended. With correction slip dated June 1994 Territorial extent & classification: GB. General. – 2p. – 0 11 044364 0 £0.65

The Sale of Registration Marks (Amendment) Regulations 1994 No. 2977. Enabling power: *Vehicle Excise and Registration Act 1994, s. 27.* Issued: 12.12.94. Made: 24.11.94. Laid: 24,11,94. Coming into force: 16.12.94. Effect: S.I 1989/1938 amended. Territorial extent & classification: E/W/S. General. – 4p. – 0 11 043335 1 £1.10

The Traffic Signs Regulations and General Directions 1994 No. 1519. Enabling power: *Road Traffic Regulation Act 1984, s. 64 & Road Traffic Act 1988, s. 36(5)* Issued: 22.07.94. Made: 26.04.94. Laid: 22.07.94. Coming into force: 12.08.94. Effect: S.I. 1969/1487; 1977/952; 1981/859(+), 1982/1879(+), 1880(+); 1983/1086(+), 1088(+); 1984/966(+); 1986/1859: 1987/1706; 1989/2139: 1990/704 revoked. [+ = These regulations are revoked except that for the purposes of The Traffic Signs (Welsh and English Language Provisions) Regulations 1985, SI 1985/713, the revocations shall have no effect] Territorial extent & classification: E/W/S. General. –368p. – 0 11 044519 8 £24.50

The Vehicle Licences (Duration of First Licences and Rate of Duty) (Amendment) Order 1994 No.3095. Enabling power: *Vehicles Excise and Registration Act 1994, ss. 3 (3), 4 (4) (5).* Issued: 13.12.94. Made: 05.12.94. Laid: 07.12.94. Coming into force: 01.01.95. Effect: S.I. 1986/1428 amended & S.I. 1986/1427 revoked. Territorial extent & classification: GB. General. – 2p. – 0 11 043365 3 £0.65

ROAD TRAFFIC: SPECIAL ROADS

The M1 Motorway (Junction 1, Barnet) (Speed Limit) Regulations 1994 No. 2461. Enabling power: *Road Traffic Regulation Act 1984, s. 17 (2) (3).* Issued: 29.09.94. Made: 19.09.94. Laid: 20.09.94. Coming into force: 27.09.94. Effect: None. Territorial extent & classification: E. Local. – 4p. – 0 11 045461 8 £1.10

The M4 Motorway (Heathrow Airport Spur) (Speed Limit) Regulations 1994 No. 2129. Enabling power: *Road Traffic Act 1984, s. 17 (2) (3).* Issued: 19.08.94. Made: 09.08.94. Laid: 19.08.94. Coming into force: 01.10.94. Effect: None. Territorial extent & classification: E. General. – 2p. – 0 11 045129 5 £0.65

ROAD TRAFFIC: SPEED LIMITS

The A1 and A428 Trunk Roads (Bedfordshire) (De-restriction) Order 1994 No. 2937. Enabling power: *Road Traffic Regulation Act 1984, ss. 82 (2), 83 (1).* Made: 15.11.94. Coming into force: 17.11.94. Effect: County Council of Bedfordshire (Built-up Areas) Order, 1935; Order No. 3, 1935; Trunk Roads (Built-up Areas) (No. 7) Order 1960; S.I. 1988/518 amended & S.I. 1984/1532, 2052; 1987/2163; 1990/1251, 1613 revoked. – *Unpublished*

Price/availability are liable to change without notice

112 ROAD TRAFFIC: SPEED LIMITS

The A1 Trunk Road (Lobley Hill - Northside Overbridge) (De-restriction) Order 1994 No.2395. Enabling power: *Road Traffic Regulation Act 1984, s. 82 (2), 83 (1)*. Made: 01.09.94. Coming into force: 04.09.94. Effect: None. – *Unpublished*

The A3 Trunk Road (Bramshott to Hindhead) (50 Miles Per Hour Speed Limit) Order 1994 No.2350. Enabling power: *Road Traffic Regulation Act 1984, s. 84 (1) (a) (2)*. Made: 05.09.94. Coming into force: 24.10.94. Effect: None. – *Unpublished*

The A3 Trunk Road (Liphook-Petersfield Bypass) (Derestriction) Order 1994 No. 2345. Enabling power: *Road Traffic Regulation Act 1984, ss. 82 (2), 83 (1)*. Made: 05.09.94. Coming into force: 19.09.94. Effect: None. – *Unpublished*

The A4 Trunk Road (Bath Road, Keynsham) (De-Restriction) Order 1994 No. 217. Enabling power: *Road Traffic Regulation Act 1984, ss. 82 (2), 83 (1)*. Made: 28.01.94. Coming into force: 01.02.94. Effect: None. – *Unpublished*

The A5 Trunk Road (Holyhead, Gwynedd) (De-restriction) Order 1994 No. 1384. Enabling power: *Road Traffic Regulation Act 1984, ss. 82 (1), 83 (1)*. Made: 04.05.94. Coming into force: 16.05.94. Effect: None. – *Unpublished*

The A5 Trunk Road (Valley, Gwynedd) (Variable Speed Limit) Order 1994 No. 1252. Enabling power: *Road Traffic Regulation Act 1984, ss. 84 (1), (1A), (2) & sch. 9, para. 27*. Made: 04.05.94. Coming into force: 11.05.94. Effect: S.I. 1994/40 amended. – *Unpublished*

The A6 Trunk Road (Barton-le-Clay and Streatley, Bedfordshire) (De-restriction) Order 1994 No. 2729. Enabling power: *Road Traffic Regulation Act 1984, ss. 82 (2), 83 (1)*. Made: 18.10.94. Coming into force: 20.10.94. Effect: S.I. 1984/2054 amended & S.I. 1991/10084 revoked. – *Unpublished*

The A6 Trunk Road (Bedfordshire) (De-Restriction) Order 1994 No. 2445. Enabling power: *Road Traffic Regulation Act 1984, ss. 82 (2), 83 (1)*. Made: 26.08.94. Coming into force: 01.09.94. Effect: Bedfordshire County Council (De-Restriction) (No. 3) Order 1962 revoked & S.I. 1984/2054 amended. – *Unpublished*

The A6 Trunk Road (Desborough Road, Rothwell, Northamptonshire) (40 MPH Speed Limit) Order 1994 No. 2526. Enabling power: *Road Traffic Regulation Act 1984, s. 84 (1) (2)*. Made: 20.09.94. Coming into force: 03.10.94. Effect: None. – *Unpublished*

The A6 Trunk Road (Houghton Conquest/Haynes, Bedfordshire) (De-Restriction) Order 1994 No.2633. Enabling power: *Road Traffic Regulation Act 1984, s. 82 (2), 83 (1)*. Made: 04.10.94. Coming into force: 06.10.94. Effect: None. – *Unpublished*

The A10 Trunk Road (Melbourn) (De-restriction) Order 1994 No. 1875. Enabling power: *Road Traffic Regulation Act 1984, ss. 82 (2), 83 (1)*. Made: 25.05.94. Coming into force: 28.05.94. Effect: None. – *Unpublished*

The A11 Trunk Road (Hethersett) (De-restriction) Order 1994 No. 1880. Enabling power: *Road Traffic Regulation Act 1984, ss. 82 (2), 83 (1)*. Made: 25.05.94. Coming into force: 28.05.94. Effect: None. – *Unpublished*

The A12 Trunk Road (Marlesford to Benhall) (50 MPH Speed Limit) Order 1994 No. 1967. Enabling power: *Road Traffic Regulation Act 1984, s. 84 (1) (a) (2)*. Made: 20.07.94. Coming into force: 05.09.94. Effect: None. – *Unpublished*

The A12 Trunk Road (Mountnessing) (De-restriction) Order 1994 No. 1878. Enabling power: *Road Traffic Regulation Act 1984, ss. 82 (2), 83 (1)*. Made: 25.05.94. Coming into force: 28.05.94. Effect: None. – *Unpublished*

The A12 Trunk Road (Rivenhall) (De-restriction) Order 1994 No. 1865. Enabling power: *Road Traffic Regulation Act 1984, ss. 82 (2), 83 (1)*. Made: 25.05.94. Coming into force: 28.05.94. Effect: None. – *Unpublished*

The A14 Trunk Road (Catthorpe Interchange, Leicestershire) (De-Restriction) Order 1994 No.2513. Enabling power: *Road Traffic Regulation Act 1984, s. 82 (2), 83 (1)*. Made: 16.09.94. Coming into force: 30.09.94. Effect: None. – *Unpublished*

The A23 and A27 Trunk Roads (Patcham and Coldean) (40 and 50 Miles Per Hour Speed Limits) Order 1994 No. 1577. Enabling power: *Road Traffic Regulation Act 1984, s. 84 (1) (a) (2)*. Made: 14.06.94. Coming into force: 27.06.94. Effect: None. – *Unpublished*

The A27 Trunk Road (Falmer to Hove) (Derestriction) Order 1994 No. 1602. Enabling power: *Road Traffic Regulation Act 1984, ss. 82 (2), 83 (1)*. Made: 14.06.94. Coming into force: 28.06.94. Effect: None. – *Unpublished*

The A36 Trunk Road (Stapleford, Wiltshire) (40 MPH Speed Limit) Order 1994 No. 1877. Enabling power: *Road Traffic Regulation Act 1984, ss. 84 (1) (a) (2)*. Made: 06.07.94. Coming into force: 12.07.94. Effect: None. – *Unpublished*

The A40 Trunk Road (Haverfordwest Bypass, Dyfed) (De-restriction) Order 1994 No. 1745. Enabling power: *Road Traffic Regulation Act 1984, ss. 82 (2), 83 (1)*. Made: 27.06.94. Coming into force: 08.07.94. Effect: None. – *Unpublished*

The A40 Trunk Road (Hillingdon) (De-Restriction) Order 1994 No. 2219. Enabling power: *Road Traffic Regulation Act 1984, ss. 82 (2), 83 (1)*. Made: 25.08.94. Coming into force: 26.08.94. Effect: None. – *Unpublished*

The A43 Trunk Road (Blisworth and Milton Malsor Bypass) (De-Restriction) Order 1994 No.1350. Enabling power: *Road Traffic Regulation Act 1984, ss. 82 (2), 83 (1)*. Made: 06.05.94. Coming into force: 20.05.94. Effect: None. – *Unpublished*

The A43 Trunk Road (Holcot-Sywell Junction, Northamptonshire) (De-restriction) Order 1994 No.1689. Enabling power: *Road Traffic Regulation Act 1984, ss. 82 (2), 83 (1)*. Made: 24.06.94. Coming into force: 25.06.94. Effect: None. – *Unpublished*

Price/availability are liable to change without notice

The A43 Trunk Road (Stamford Road, Northamptonshire) (50 MPH Speed Limit) Order 1994 No.1458. Enabling power: *Road Traffic Regulation Act 1984, s. 84 (1) (2)*. Made: 24.05.94. Coming into force: 03.06.94. Effect: None. – *Unpublished*

The A43 Trunk Road (Stamford Road, Northamptonshire) (De-Restriction) Order 1994 No.1459. Enabling power: *Road Traffic Regulation Act 1984, ss. 82 (2), 83 (1)*. Made: 24.05.94. Coming into force: 03.06.94. Effect: None. – *Unpublished*

The A45 Trunk Road (Daventry Road, Dunchurch) (De-Restriction) Order 1994 No. 1526. Enabling power: *Road Traffic Regulation Act 1984, ss. 82 (2), 83 (1)*. Made: 02.06.94. Coming into force: 06.06.94. Effect: None. – *Unpublished*

The A47 Trunk Road (Wisbech Road, Thorney, Cambridgeshire) (Variable Speed Limit) Order 1994 No. 2963. Enabling power: *Road Traffic Regulation Act 1984, s. 84 (1) (c) (1A) (2)*. Made: 17.11.94. Coming into force: 24.11.94. Effect: None. – *Unpublished*

The A49 Trunk Road (Weaverham Diversion, Weaverham) (De-Restriction) Order 1994 No.1357. Enabling power: *Road Traffic Regulation Act 1984, ss. 82 (2), 83 (1)*. Made: 15.02.94. Coming into force: 11.03.94. Effect: None. – *Unpublished*

The A54 and A556 Trunk Roads (Chester Road, Vale Royal, Cheshire) (De-Restriction) Order 1994 No. 1099. Enabling power: *Road Traffic Regulation Act 1984, ss. 82 (2), 83 (1)*. Made: 07.02.94. Coming into force: 23.02.94. Effect: None. – *Unpublished*

The A54 and A556 Trunk Roads (Chester Road, Vale Royal, Cheshire) (De-Restriction) Order 1994 No. 1184. Enabling power: *Road Traffic Regulation Act 1984, ss. 82 (2), 83 (1)*. Made: 07.02.94. Coming into force: 23.02.94. Effect: None. – *Unpublished*

The A54 Trunk Road (Chester Road, Tarvin and Kelsall, Chester) (De-Restriction) Order 1994 No. 2312. Enabling power: *Road Traffic Regulation Act 1984, ss. 82 (2), 83 (1)*. Made: 16.06.94. Coming into force: 08.07.94. Effect: None. – *Unpublished*

The A55 Trunk Road (Abergwyngregyn, Gwynedd) (De-Restriction) Order 1994 No. 3087. Enabling power: *Road Traffic Regulation Act 1984, ss. 82 (2), 83 (1)*. Made: 02.11.94. Coming into force: 14.11.94. Effect: None. – *Unpublished*

The A55 Trunk Road (Abergwyngregyn, Gwynedd) (Restricted Roads) Order 1994 No. 3126. Enabling power: *Road Traffic Regulation Act 1984, ss. 82 (2), 83 (1)*. Made: 01.12.94. Coming into force: 05.12.94. Effect: S.I. 1963/1227 revoked. – *Unpublished*

The A55 Trunk Road (Penmaenbach - Dwygyfylchi, Gwynedd) (De-restriction and 50 MPH Speed Limit) Order 1994 No. 1664. Enabling power: *Road Traffic Regulation Act 1984, ss. 82 (2), 84 (1) (2)*. Made: 13.06.94. Coming into force: 24.06.94. Effect: None. – *Unpublished*

The A55 Trunk Road (Pen-y-Clip Section, Gwynedd) (De-Restriction) Order 1994 No. 790. Enabling power: *Road Traffic Regulation Act 1984 ss. 82 (2), 83 (1)*. Made: 11.03.94. Coming into force: 19.03.94. Effect: None. – *Unpublished*

The A59 Trunk Road (Liverpool Road, Howick) (Variable Speed Limit) Order 1994 No.1469. Enabling power: *Road Traffic Regulation Act 1984, s. 84 (1) (c) (1A) (2)*. Made: 16.07.94. Coming into force: 29.07.94. Effect: None. – *Unpublished*

The A59 Trunk Road (Mellor Brook Bypass) (De-Restriction) Order 1994 No. 1100. Enabling power: *Road Traffic Regulation Act 1984, ss. 82 (2), 83 (1)*. Made: 14.01.94. Coming into force: 28.01.94. Effect: None. – *Unpublished*

The A59 Trunk Road Whalley - Clitheroe Bypass (Chatburn) De-Restriction Order 1993 No.1133. Enabling power: *Road Traffic Regulation Act 1984, ss. 82 (2), 83 (1)*. Made: 14.10.93. Coming into force: 28.10.93. Effect: None. – *Unpublished*

The A63 and A6120 Trunk Road (Austhorpe, Leeds) (40 MPH Speed Limit) Order 1994 No.2505. Enabling power: *Road Traffic Regulation Act 1984, s. 84 (1) (a) (2)*. Made: 15.09.94. Coming into force: 19.09.94. Effect: None. – *Unpublished*

The A63 Trunk Road (Monk Fryston) (40 MPH Speed Limit) (No. 2) Order 1994 No. 353. Enabling power: *Road Traffic Regulation Act 1984, s. 84 (1) (a) (2)*. Made: 24.01.94. Coming into force: 31.01.94. Effect: None. – *Unpublished*

The A65 Skipton - Kendal Trunk Road (Cowan Bridge) (40 MPH Speed Limit) Order 1994 No.3110. Enabling power: *Road Traffic Regulation Act 1984, s. 84 (1) (a) (2)*. Made: 21.09.94. Coming into force: 04.10.94. Effect: None. – *Unpublished*

The A65 Trunk Road (New Road, Ingleton) (40 MPH Speed Limit and Derestriction) Order 1994 No.881. Enabling power: *Road Traffic Regulation Act 1984, ss. 82 (2), 83 (1), 84 (1) (a) (2)*. Made: 11.03.94. Coming into force: 14.03.94. Effect: None. – *Unpublished*

The A87 Trunk Road Invergarry-Kyle of Lochalsh (Inverinate) (40 MPH Speed Limits) Order 1994 No. 1694. Enabling power: *Road Traffic Regulation Act 1984, s. 84 (1) 92)*. Made: 24.06.94. Coming into force: 07.07.94. Effect: None. – *Unpublished*

Price/availability are liable to change without notice

The A96 Aberdeen-Inverness Trunk Road (Nairn) (Restricted Road and 40 MPH Speed Limit) Order 1994 No. 812. Enabling power: *Road Traffic Regulation Act 1984 ss. 82 (2), 83 (1), 84 (1) (2)*. Made: 14.03.94. Coming into force: 24.03.94. Effect: None. – *Unpublished*

The A96 Trunk Road (Kintore) (Variable Speed Limit) Order 1994 No. 3252. Enabling power: *Road Traffic Regulation Act 1984, ss. 84 (1) (1A) (2), 121A, 124 (1) (d) & sch. 9, Part IV, para.27 (1)*. Made: 13.12.94. Coming into force: 28.12.94. Effect: None. – *Unpublished*

The A134 Trunk Road (Stradsett) (De-restriction) Order 1994 No. 1879. Enabling power: *Road Traffic Regulation Act 1984, ss. 82 (2), 83 (1)*. Made: 25.05.94. Coming into force: 28.05.94. Effect: None. – *Unpublished*

The A167 Trunk Road (Chester-Le-Street, County of Durham) (50 Miles Per Hour Speed Limit) Order 1994 No. 446. Enabling power: *Road Traffic Regulation Act 1984, ss. 84 (1) (a) (2)*. Made: 14.02.94. Coming into force: 21.02.94. Effect: None. – *Unpublished*

The A259 Trunk Road (Ferry Hill and Tanyard Lane, Winchelsea) (Restricted Roads) Order 1994 No. 1552. Enabling power: *Road Traffic Regulation Act 1984, s. 14 (1) (a)*. Made: 06.06.94. Coming into force: 20.06.94. Effect: None. – *Unpublished*

The A282 Trunk Road (Dartford-Thurrock Crossing and Approach Roads) (Speed Limits) Order 1994 No. 2046. Enabling power: *Road Traffic Regulation Act 1984, s. 84 (1) (a) (2)*. Made: 01.08.94. Coming into force: 15.08.94. Effect: None. – *Unpublished*

The A303 Trunk Road (Winterbourne Stoke, Wiltshire) (40 MPH Speed Limit) Order 1994 No.3326. Enabling power: *Road Traffic Regulation Act 1984, s. 84 (1) (a) (2), sch. 9, Part IV*. Made: 21.12.94. Coming into force: 23.12.94. Effect: S.I. 1989/961 revoked. – *Unpublished*

The A339 Trunk Road (North of Headley) (Derestriction) Order 1994 No. 2861. Enabling power: *Road Traffic Regulation Act 1984, ss. 82 (2), 83 (1)*. Made: 07.11.94. Coming into force: 21.11.94. Effect: None. – *Unpublished*

The A414 Trunk Road (Two Waters Link) (40 MPH Speed Limit) Order 1994 No. 2225. Enabling power: *Road Traffic Regulation Act 1984, s. 84 (1) (a) (2)*. Made: 23.08.94. Coming into force: 26.08.94. Effect: None. – *Unpublished*

The A420 Trunk Road (Kingston Bagpuize with Southmoor Bypass) (De-Restriction) Order 1994 No.208. Enabling power: *Road Traffic Regulation Act 1984, ss. 82 (2), 83 (1)*. Made: 31.01.94. Coming into force: 28.02.94. Effect: None. – *Unpublished*

The A465 Trunk Road (Tredegar-Dowlais Top, Gwent and Mid Glamorgan) (De-Restriction) Order 1994 No. 2828. Enabling power: *Road Traffic Regulation Act 1984, ss. 82 (2), 83 (1)*. Made: 27.10.94. Coming into force: 04.11.94. Effect: None. – *Unpublished*

The A466 Trunk Road (Wye Valley Link Road, Chepstow, Gwent) (De-Restriction) Order 1994 No.2236. Enabling power: *Road Traffic Regulation Act 1984, ss. 82 (2), 83 (1)*. Made: 11.08.94. Coming into force: 20.08.94. Effect: None. – *Unpublished*

The A470 Trunk Road (Cwmbach, Powys) (40 MPH Speed Limit) Order 1994 No. 1168. Enabling power: *Road Traffic Regulation Act 1984, s. 84 (1) (2)*. Made: 20.04.94. Coming into force: 16.05.94. Effect: None. – *Unpublished*

The A483 Trunk Road (Crossgates, Near Llandrindod Wells, Powys) (De-restriction) Order 1994 No. 1979. Enabling power: *Road Traffic Regulation Act 1984, ss. 82 (2), 83 (1)*. Made: 11.07.94. Coming into force: 25.07.94. Effect: None. – *Unpublished*

The A483 Trunk Road (Howey, Near Llandrindod Wells, Powys) (50 MPH Speed Limit) Order 1994 No. 1169. Enabling power: *Road Traffic Regulation Act 1984, s. 84 (1) (2)*. Made: 20.04.94. Coming into force: 16.05.94. Effect: None. – *Unpublished*

The A487 Trunk Road (Caernarfon, Gywnedd) (Restricted Roads and 40 MPH Speed Limit) Order 1994 No. 3330. Enabling power: *Road Traffic Regulation Act 1984, ss. 82 (2), 83 (1), 84 (1) (2), 124, sch.9, para. 27*. Made: 30.12.94. Coming into force: 14.01.95. Effect: S.I. 1981/187 revoked. – *Unpublished*

The A487 Trunk Road (Port Dinorwic By-Pass, Gwynedd) (De-restriction) Order 1994 No.796. Enabling power: *Road Traffic Regulation Act 1984 ss. 82 (2), 83 (1)*. Made: 09.03.94. Coming into force: 28.03.94. Effect: None. – *Unpublished*

The A500 Trunk Road (M6 Junction 16 to A34 at Talke) (De-Restriction) Order 1994 No.2745. Enabling power: *Road Traffic Regulation Act 1984, ss. 82 (2), 83 (1)*. Made: 11.07.94. Coming into force: 17.07.94. Effect: None. – *Unpublished*

The A500 Trunk Road (Nantwich Bypass) (De-restriction) Order 1993 No. 1397. Enabling power: *Road Traffic Regulation Act 1984, ss. 82 (2), 83 (1)*. Made: 06.07.93. Coming into force: 30.07.93. Effect: None. – *Unpublished*

The A523 Trunk Road (London Road, Sutton, Macclesfield) (50 MPH Speed Limit) Order 1994 No.2883. Enabling power: *Road Traffic Regulation Act 1984, ss. 84 (1) (a) (2)*. Made: 15.08.94. Coming into force: 01.09.94. Effect: None. – *Unpublished*

The A570 Trunk Road (Southport Road, Ormskirk) (40 Miles Per Hour Speed Limit) Order 1994 No.1401. Enabling power: *Road Traffic Regulation Act 1984, s. 84 (1) (a) (2)*. Made: 25.02.94. Coming into force: 10.03.94. Effect: None. – *Unpublished*

The A580 Trunk Road (East Lancashire Road, Wigan) (De-Restriction) Order 1994 No.1145. Enabling power: *Road Traffic Regulation Act 1984, ss. 82 (2), 83 (1)*. Made: 09.02.94. Coming into force: 03.03.94. Effect: None. – *Unpublished*

Price/availability are liable to change without notice

The A585 Trunk Road (Copse Road Diversion, Fleetwood) (De-Restriction) Order 1993 No.1144. Enabling power: *Road Traffic Regulation Act 1984, ss. 82 (2), 83 (1)*. Made: 14.10.93. Coming into force: 18.11.93. Effect: None. – *Unpublished*

The A646 Trunk Road (Burnley Road, Cliviger) (De-Restriction) Order 1993 No. 1240. Enabling power: *Road Traffic Regulation Act 1984, ss. 82 (2), 83 (1)*. Made: 01.07.93. Coming into force: 23.07.93. Effect: None. – *Unpublished*

The A646 Trunk Road (Burnley Road, Cliviger) (Variable Speed Limit) Order 1993 No.1728. Enabling power: *Road Traffic Regulation Act 1984, s. 84 (1) (c) (1A) (2)*. Made: 16.07.94. Coming into force: 29.07.94. Effect: None. – *Unpublished*

The A646 Trunk Road (Burnley Road, Friendly to Luddendenfoot) (50 MPH Speed Limit) Order 1994 No. 975. Enabling power: *Road Traffic Regulation Act 1984, s. 84 (1) (a) (2)*. Made: 25.03.94. Coming into force: 31.03.94. Effect: None. – *Unpublished*

The A646 Trunk Road (Burnley Road, Mythlmroyd and Luddendenfoot) (Various Speed Limits) Order 1994 No. 1705. Enabling power: *Road Traffic Regulation Act 1984, s. 82 (2), 83 (1), 84 (1) (a) (2)*. Made: 23.06.94. Coming into force: 30.06.94. Effect: None. – *Unpublished*

The A646 Trunk Road (Burnley Road, Todmorden) (Variable Speed Limit) Order 1994 No.2665. Enabling power: *Road Traffic Regulation Act 1984, s. 84 (1) (a) (c) (1A) (2)*. Made: 12.09.94. Coming into force: 19.09.94. Effect: See schedule. – *Unpublished*

The A985 Trunk Road Kincardine-Rosyth (Crombie) (40 MPH Speed Limit) Order 1994 No.1485. Enabling power: *Road Traffic Regulation Act 1984, s. 84 (1) (2)*. Made: 02.06.94. Coming into force: 11.06.94. Effect: None. – *Unpublished*

The A5092 Trunk Road (Greenodd to Penny Bridge) (40 Miles Per Hour Speed Limit) Order 1994 No. 2661. Enabling power: *Road Traffic Regulation Act 1984, s. 84 (1) (a) (2)*. Made: 16.09.94. Coming into force: 19.09.94. Effect: None. – *Unpublished*

The A6119 Trunk Road (Brownhill Drive, Blackburn) (40 MPH Speed Limit) Order 1994 No.2117. Enabling power: *Road Traffic Regulation Act 1984, s. 84 (1) (a) (2) (a)*. Made: 23.05.94. Coming into force: 24.06.94. Effect: None. – *Unpublished*

The Aberdeen-Fraserburgh Trunk Road (A956/A92/A952) (Stirling Village, Boddam) (40 MPH Speed Limit) Order 1994 No. 550. Enabling power: *Road Traffic Regulation Act 1984, ss. 84 (1) (2)*. Made: 01.03.94. Coming into force: 10.03.94. Effect: None. – *Unpublished*

The Aberdeen-Inverness Trunk Road (A96) (Fochabers and Mosstodloch) (40 MPH Speed Limit) Order 1994 No. 2311. Enabling power: *Road Traffic Regulation Act 1984, ss. 82 (2), 83 (1), 124 (1) (d)*. Made: 01.09.94. Coming into force: 01.10.94. Effect: S.I. 1977/1930 revoked. – *Unpublished*

The Fraserburgh-Fochabers (A98) and Aberdeen-Inverness (A96) Trunk Roads (A96) (Fochabers) (30 MPH Speed Limit) Order 1994 No. 2344. Enabling power: *Road Traffic Regulation Act 1984, ss. 82 (2), 83 (1), 124 (1) (d)*. Made: 01.09.94. Coming into force: 01.10.94. Effect: S.I. 1984/1607 amended. – *Unpublished*

The M9/A9/A882 Trunk Road (Scrabster) (40 MPH Speed Limit) Order 1994 No. 2923. Enabling power: *Road Traffic Regulation Act 1984, ss. 84 (1), 84 (2)*. Made: 14.11.94. Coming into force: 30.11.94. Effect: None. – *Unpublished*

The Trunk Road A523/A52 (Leek/Ashbourne Road) (De-Restriction) Order 1994 No. 1249. Enabling power: *Road Traffic Regulation Act 1984, ss. 82 (2), 83 (1)*. Made: 16.03.94. Coming into force: 18.03.94. Effect: None. – *Unpublished*

The Trunk Roads (40 MPH Speed Limit) (No. 9) Order 1967 Amendment Order 1994 No. 114. Enabling power: *Road Traffic Regulation Act 1984, s. 84 (1) (a) (2)*. Made: 12.01.94. Coming into force: 17.01.94. Effect: Trunk Roads (40 MPH Speed Limit) (No. 9) Order 1967 amended. – *Unpublished*

The Trunk Roads (40 MPH Speed Limit) (Dunbartonshire) (Consolidation) (Variation) Order 1994 No. 1829. Enabling power: *Road Traffic Regulation Act 1984, ss. 84 (1) (2), 124 (1) (d)*. Made: 08.07.94. Coming into force: 05.08.94. Effect: None. – *Unpublished*

The Trunk Roads (Restricted Roads) (Scotland) (Variation) Order 1994 No.1306. Enabling power: *Road Traffic Regulation Act 1984, ss. 82 (2), 83 (1), 124 (1) (d)*. Made: 12.05.94. Coming into force: 21.05.94. Effect: S.I. 1971/696 amended. – *Unpublished*

ROAD TRAFFIC: TRAFFIC REGULATION

The A1 and A52 Trunk Roads (Southbound Slip Road, Barrowby, Lincolnshire) (Temporary Prohibition of Traffic) Order 1994 No. 2498. Enabling power: *Road Traffic Regulation Act 1984, s. 14 (1) (a)*. Made: 19.09.94. Coming into force: 01.10.94. Effect: None. – *Unpublished*

The A1 and A57 Trunk Roads (Markham Moor, Bassetlaw) (Prohibition of Right and Left Turns) Order 1994 No. 915. Enabling power: *Road Traffic Regulation Act 1984, ss. 1 (1), 2 (1) (2), 3 (2)*. Made: 17.03.94. Coming into force: 04.04.94. Effect: None. – *Unpublished*

The A1 and A604 Trunk Roads (Alconbury, Cambridgeshire) (Temporary Prohibition and Restriction of Traffic) Order 1994 No. 1655. Enabling power: *Road Traffic Regulation Act 1984, s. 14 (1) (a) (5) (b)*. Made: 17.06.94. Coming into force: 24.06.94. Effect: None. – *Unpublished*

Price/availability are liable to change without notice

The A1 (M) Motorway (Junctions 4 - 6, Hertfordshire) (Temporary Prohibition and Restriction of Traffic) Order 1994 No. 2530. Enabling power: *Road Traffic Regulation Act 1984, s. 14 (1) (a)*. Made: 26.09.94. Coming into force: 03.10.94. Effect: None. – *Unpublished*

The A1 Motorway (Aycliffe Interchange) (Temporary Prohibition of Traffic) Order 1994 No. 2561. Enabling power: *Road Traffic Regulation Act 1984, s. 14 (1) (a)*. Made: 29.09.94. Coming into force: 01.10.94. Effect: None. – *Unpublished*

The A1 Trunk Road (40 MPH Speed Limit, Causey Park - Long Horsley) (Temporary Restriction of Traffic) Order 1994 No. 1582. Enabling power: *Road Traffic Regulation Act 1984, s. 14 (1) (a)*. Made: 02.06.94. Coming into force: 04.06.94. Effect: None. – *Unpublished*

The A1 Trunk Road (A1/A645 Junction) (Temporary Prohibition of Traffic) Order 1994 No. 1587. Enabling power: *Road Traffic Regulation Act 1984, s. 14 (1) (a)*. Made: 02.06.94. Coming into force: 04.06.94. Effect: None. – *Unpublished*

The A1 Trunk Road and Slip Roads (Newark-on-Trent, Nottinghamshire) (Temporary Prohibition of Traffic) Order 1994 No. 2650. Enabling power: *Road Traffic Regulation Act 1984, s. 14 (1) (a)* Made: 05.10.94. Coming into force: 08.10.94. Effect: None. – *Unpublished*

The A1 Trunk Road and Slip Roads (Woolfox to South Witham, Leicestershire) (Temporary Prohibition and Restriction of Traffic) Order 1994 No. 720. Enabling power: *Road Traffic Regulation Act 1984, s. 14 (1) (a)*. Made: 03.03.94. Coming into force: 12.03.94. Effect: None. – *Unpublished*

The A1 Trunk Road (B1288 Northside Overbridge to Blaydon Bridge) (Temporary 50 Miles Per Hour Speed Restriction) Order 1994 No. 1239. Enabling power: *Road Traffic Regulation Act 1984, s. 14 (1) (a)*. Made: 29.04.94. Coming into force: 02.05.94. Effect: None. – *Unpublished*

The A1 Trunk Road (Brotherton - Ferrybridge) (Southbound Carriageway) (Temporary 50 Miles Per Hour Speed Restriction) Order 1994 No. 1684. Enabling power: *Road Traffic Regulation Act 1984, s. 14 (1) (a)*. Made: 22.06.94. Coming into force: 23.06.94. Effect: None. – *Unpublished*

The A1 Trunk Road (Burneston Hargill) (Prohibition of Use of Gap in Central Reservation) Order 1994 No. 146. Enabling power: *Road Traffic Regulation Act 1984, ss. 1 (1), 2 (1) (2)*. Made: 20.01.94. Coming into force: 29.01.94. Effect: None. – *Unpublished*

The A1 Trunk Road (Carlton-on-Trent and Tuxford, Nottinghamshire) (Temporary Prohibition and Restriction of Traffic) Order 1994 No. 552. Enabling power: *Road Traffic Regulation Act 1984, s. 14 (1) (a)*. Made: 23.02.94. Coming into force: 03.03.94. Effect: None. – *Unpublished*

The A1 Trunk Road (Carlton-on-Trent and Tuxford, Nottinghamshire) (Temporary Prohibition and Restriction of Traffic) Order 1994 No. 1962. Enabling power: *Road Traffic Regulation Act 1984, ss. 3 (2), 14 (1) (a), (5) (b) (6)*. Made: 13.07.94. Coming into force: 16.07.94. Effect: None. – *Unpublished*

The A1 Trunk Road (Dish Hill Flyover - Fairburn, Northbound Carriageway and Various Slip Roads) (Temporary Prohibition of Traffic) Order 1994 No. 75. Enabling power: *Road Traffic Regulation Act 1984, ss. 14 (1) (a)*. Made: 14.01.94. Coming into force: 14.01.94. Effect: None. – *Unpublished*

The A1 Trunk Road (Ducketts Hill Layby - North of Scurragh House Lane Junction) (Temporary Restriction and Prohibition or Traffic) Order 1994 No. 444. Enabling power: *Road Traffic Regulation Act 1984, s. 14 (1) (a)*. Made: 23.02.94. Coming into force: 28.02.94. Effect: None. – *Unpublished*

The A1 Trunk Road (East Appleton Junction - Angleham House Junction) (Temporary Restriction and Prohibition of Traffic) Order 1994 No. 2262. Enabling power: *Road Traffic Regulation Act 1984, s. 14 (1) (a)*. Made: 26.08.94. Coming into force: 29.08.94. Effect: None. – *Unpublished*

The A1 Trunk Road (Falloden Way, Littleton Road and Aylmer road, Barnet and Haringey) (Temporary Prohibition of Traffic and Speed Restriction) Order 1994 No. 2668. Enabling power: *Road Traffic Regulation Act 1984, s. 14 (1) (4) (5) (7)*. Made: 10.10.94. Coming into force: 17.10.94. Effect: None. – *Unpublished*

The A1 Trunk Road (Five Lanes End to Top Farm, Nottinghamshire) (Prohibition of Use of Gaps in Central Reservation) Order 1994 No. 1216. Enabling power: *Road Traffic Regulation Act 1984, ss. 1 (1), 2 (1) (2)*. Made: 22.04.94. Coming into force: 06.05.94. Effect: None. – *Unpublished*

The A1 Trunk Road (Girtford, Bedfordshire) (Temporary Restriction of Traffic) Order 1994 No. 1474. Enabling power: *Road Traffic Regulation Act 1984, s. 14 (1) (a)*. Made: 31.05.94. Coming into force: 02.06.94. Effect: None. – *Unpublished*

The A1 Trunk Road (Great North Road, Colsterworth and North Witham, Lincolnshire) (Temporary Prohibition and Restriction of Traffic) Order 1994 No. 1578. Enabling power: *Road Traffic Regulation Act 1984, s. 14 (1) (a)*. Made: 27.05.94. Coming into force: 04.06.94. Effect: None. – *Unpublished*

The A1 Trunk Road (Leases Hall - East Appleton Junction) (Temporary Restriction and Prohibition of Traffic) Order 1994 No. 1470. Enabling power: *Road Traffic Regulation Act 1984, s. 14 (1) (a)*. Made: 01.06.94. Coming into force: 03.06.94. Effect: None. – *Unpublished*

The A1 Trunk Road (Little Paxton, Cambridgeshire) (Temporary Prohibition and Restriction of Traffic) Order 1994 No. 2639. Enabling power: *Road Traffic Regulation Act 1984, s. 14 (1) (a)*. Made: 10.10.94. Coming into force: 17.10.94. Effect: None. – *Unpublished*

Price/availability are liable to change without notice

The A1 Trunk Road (Little Ponton, Lincolnshire) (Temporary Prohibition of Traffic) Order 1994 No. 2267. Enabling power: *Road Traffic Regulation Act 1984, s. 14 (1) (a)*. Made: 25.08.94. Coming into force: 03.09.94. Effect: None. – *Unpublished*

The A1 Trunk Road (Long Bennington Bypass, Lincolnshire) (Temporary Prohibition and Restriction of Traffic) Order 1994 No. 1581. Enabling power: *Road Traffic Regulation Act 1984, s. 14 (1)*. Made: 10.06.94. Coming into force: 25.06.94. Effect: None. – *Unpublished*

The A1 Trunk Road (Micklefield - Selby Fork Interchange) (Temporary Restriction and Prohibition of Traffic) (No. 2) Order 1994 No. 2241. Enabling power: *Road Traffic Regulation Act 1984, s. 14 (1) (a)*. Made: 24.08.94. Coming into force: 28.08.94. Effect: None. – *Unpublished*

The A1 Trunk Road (Northway Culvert, Stotfold, Bedfordshire) (Temporary Restriction and Prohibition of Traffic) Order 1994 No. 1114. Enabling power: *Road Traffic Regulation Act 1984, s. 14 (1) (a) (5) (b)*. Made: 12.04.94. Coming into force: 15.04.94. Effect: None. – *Unpublished*

The A1 Trunk Road (Ossington Lane Bridge, Near Sutton on Trent, Nottinghamshire) (Temporary 50 Miles per Hour Speed Restriction) Order 1994 No. 2707. Enabling power: *Road Traffic Regulation Act 1984, s. 14 (1) (a)*. Made: 13.10.94. Coming into force: 22.10.94. Effect: None. – *Unpublished*

The A1 Trunk Road (Overbridge and Southbound Entry Slip Road, Cromwell, Nottinghamshire) (Temporary Prohibition of Traffic) Order 1994 No. 1565. Enabling power: *Road Traffic Regulation Act 1984, s. 14 (1) (a)*. Made: 29.06.94. Coming into force: 09.07.94. Effect: None. – *Unpublished*

The A1 Trunk Road (Selby Fork Interchange) (Temporary Prohibition of Traffic) Order 1994 No. 1097. Enabling power: *Road Traffic Regulation Act 1984, s. 14 (1) (a)*. Made: 14.04.94. Coming into force: 17.04.94. Effect: None. – *Unpublished*

The A1 Trunk Road (Slip Road - Eighton Lodge Interchange) (Temporary Prohibition of Traffic) Order 1994 No. 1121. Enabling power: *Road Traffic Regulation Act 1984, s. 14 (1) (a)*. Made: 07.04.94. Coming into force: 09.04.94. Effect: None. – *Unpublished*

The A1 Trunk Road (Southoe to Little Paxton, Cambridgeshire) (Temporary Restriction of Traffic) Order 1994 No. 1430. Enabling power: *Road Traffic Regulation Act 1984, s. 14 (1) (a)*. Made: 20.05.94. Coming into force: 27.05.94. Effect: None. – *Unpublished*

The A1 Trunk Road (Southoe to Little Paxton, Cambridgeshire) (Temporary Restriction of Traffic) Order 1994 No. 2392. Enabling power: *Road Traffic Regulation Act 1984, s. 14 (1) (a)*. Made: 05.09.94. Coming into force: 12.09.94. Effect: None. – *Unpublished*

The A1 Trunk Road (Stannington South Junction - Seaton Burn Junction) (Temporary Prohibition and 50 Miles per Hour Speed Restriction) Order 1994 No. 2769. Enabling power: *Road Traffic Regulation Act 1984, s. 14 (1) (a)*. Made: 20.10.94. Coming into force: 22.10.94. Effect: None. – *Unpublished*

The A1 Trunk Road (Stannington South Junction - Seaton Burn Junction) (Temporary Prohibition and 50 Miles Per Hour Speed Restriction) Order 1994 Amendment Order 1994 No. 3287. Enabling power: *Road Traffic Regulation Act 1984, s. 14 (1) (a)*. Made: 02.12.94. Coming into force: 05.12.94. Effect: None. – *Unpublished*

The A1 Trunk Road (Swalwell Roundabout Southbound Entry Slip Road) (Temporary Prohibition of Traffic) Order 1994 No. 2441. Enabling power: *Road Traffic Regulation Act 1984, s. 14 (1) (a)*. Made: 09.09.94. Coming into force: 11.09.94. Effect: None. – *Unpublished*

The A1 Trunk Road (Tempsford Bridge, Bedfordshire) (Temporary Restriction and Prohibition of Traffic) Order 1994 No. 940. Enabling power: *Road Traffic Regulation Act 1984, s. 14 (1) (a) (5)*. Made: 07.03.94. Coming into force: 11.03.94. Effect: None. – *Unpublished*

The A1 Trunk Road (Various Lengths Between Stamford and Norman Cross) (Temporary Prohibition and Restriction of Traffic) Order 1994 No. 2120. Enabling power: *Road Traffic Regulation Act 1984, ss. 3 (2), 14 (1) (a) (5) (b) (6)*. Made: 08.08.94. Coming into force: 15.08.94. Effect: None. – *Unpublished*

The A1 Trunk Road (Wideopen/Seaton Burn Bypass) (Temporary 50 Miles Per Hour Speed Restriction) Order 1994 No. 2308. Enabling power: *Road Traffic Regulation Act 1984, s. 14 (1) (a)*. Made: 26.08.94. Coming into force: 28.08.94. Effect: None. – *Unpublished*

The A1 Trunk Road (Wyboston Footbridge, Wyboston, Bedfordshire) (Temporary 50 Miles Per Hour Speed Restriction) Order 1994 No. 1657. Enabling power: *Road Traffic Regulation Act 1984, s. 14 (1) (a)*. Made: 13.06.94. Coming into force: 17.06.94. Effect: None. – *Unpublished*

The A1(M) (Junction 1) and M25 (Junction 23) Motorways and the A1 Trunk Road (South Mimms, Hertfordshire) (Temporary Prohibition of Traffic) Order 1994 No. 982. Enabling power: *Road Traffic Regulation Act 1984, s. 14 (1) (a)*. Made: 28.03.94. Coming into force: 05.04.94. Effect: None. – *Unpublished*

The A1(M) Motorway (Blyth Roundabout) (Temporary Restriction and Prohibition of Traffic) Order 1994 No. 77. Enabling power: *Road Traffic Regulation Act 1984, ss. 14 (1) (a)*. Made: 11.01.94. Coming into force: 13.01.94. Effect: None. – *Unpublished*

The A1(M) Motorway (Bowburn Interchange) (Temporary Prohibition of Traffic) Order 1994 No. 2381. Enabling power: *Road Traffic Regulation Act 1984, s. 14 (1) (a)*. Made: 01.09.94. Coming into force: 03.09.94. Effect: None. – *Unpublished*

Price/availability are liable to change without notice

ROAD TRAFFIC: TRAFFIC REGULATION

The A1(M) Motorway (Bowburn Interchange to Bradbury Interchange) (Temporary Restriction of Traffic) Order 1994 No. 2440. Enabling power: *Road Traffic Regulation Act 1984, s. 14 (1) (a) (7).* Made: 08.09.94. Coming into force: 10.09.94. Effect: None. – *Unpublished*

The A1(M) Motorway (Burtree Interchange - Barton Interchange) (Temporary Restriction and Prohibition of Traffic) Order 1994 No. 2439. Enabling power: *Road Traffic Regulation Act 1984, s. 14 (1) (a) (7).* Made: 08.09.94. Coming into force: 10.09.94. Effect: None. – *Unpublished*

The A1(M) Motorway (Hatfield Tunnel, Hertfordshire) (Temporary Prohibition of Traffic) No. 2 Order 1994 No. 3325. Enabling power: *Road Traffic Regulation Act 1984, s. 14 (1) (a).* Made: 19.12.94. Coming into force: 03.01.95. Effect: None. – *Unpublished*

The A1(M) Motorway (Hatfield Tunnel, Hertfordshire) (Temporary Prohibition of Traffic) Order 1994 No. 290. Enabling power: *Road Traffic Regulation Act 1984, s. 14 (1) (a).* Made: 14.01.94. Coming into force: 27.01.94. Effect: None. – *Unpublished*

The A1(M) Motorway (Junction 2, Hertfordshire) (Slip Roads) (Temporary Prohibition of Traffic) Order 1994 No. 2832. Enabling power: *Road Traffic Regulation Act 1984, s. 14 (1) (a).* Made: 31.10.94. Coming into force: 07.11.94. Effect: None. – *Unpublished*

The A1(M) Motorway (Junction 2, Hertfordshire) (Temporary Prohibition of Traffic) Order 1994 No. 8. Enabling power: *Road Traffic Regulation Act 1984, s. 14 (1) (a).* Made: 04.01.94. Coming into force: 10.01.94. Effect: None. – *Unpublished*

The A1(M) Motorway (Junction 6-7, Hertfordshire) (Temporary Prohibition of Traffic) Order 1994 No. 2754. Enabling power: *Road Traffic Regulation Act 1984, s. 14 (1) (a).* Made: 24.10.94. Coming into force: 31.10.94. Effect: None. – *Unpublished*

The A1(M) Motorway (Junction 10) (Hertfordshire and Bedfordshire) (Temporary Prohibition and Restriction of Traffic) Order 1994 No. 99. Enabling power: *Road Traffic Regulation Act 1984, s. 14 (1) (a).* Made: 17.01.94. Coming into force: 24.01.94. Effect: None. – *Unpublished*

The A1(M) Motorway (Junction 37, Marr), Northbound Exit Slip Road) (Temporary Prohibition of Traffic) Order 1994 No. 1280. Enabling power: *Road Traffic Regulation Act 1984, s. 14 (1) (a).* Made: 05.05.94. Coming into force: 08.05.94. Effect: None. – *Unpublished*

The A1(M) Motorway (Junctions 1 - 4, Hertfordshire) (Temporary Prohibition of Traffic) Order 1994 No. 2224. Enabling power: *Road Traffic Regulation Act 1984, s. 14 (1) (a).* Made: 22.08.94. Coming into force: 30.08.94. Effect: None. – *Unpublished*

The A1(M) Motorway (Junctions 3 - 4, Hertfordshire) (Temporary Prohibition of Traffic) Order 1994 No. 386. Enabling power: *Road Traffic Regulation Act 1984, s. 14 (1) (a).* Made: 21.02.94. Coming into force: 28.02.94. Effect: None. – *Unpublished*

The A1(M) Motorway (Junctions 4 - 2, Hertfordshire) (Temporary Prohibition and Restriction of Traffic) Order 1994 No. 273. Enabling power: *Road Traffic Regulation Act 1984, s. 14 (1) (a).* Made: 07.02.94. Coming into force: 14.02.94. Effect: None. – *Unpublished*

The A1(M) Motorway (Junctions 7-8, Hertfordshire) (Temporary Prohibition of Traffic) Order 1994 No. 2574. Enabling power: *Road Traffic Regulation Act 1984, s. 14 (1) (a).* Made: 03.10.94. Coming into force: 08.10.94. Effect: None. – *Unpublished*

The A1(M) Motorway (Junctions 7-8, Hertfordshire) (Temporary Prohibition of Traffic) Order 1994 No. 2246. Enabling power: *Road Traffic Regulation Act 1984, s. 14 (1) (b).* Made: 19.08.94. Coming into force: 26.08.94. Effect: None. – *Unpublished*

The A1(M) Motorway (Junctions 9 - 10, Hertfordshire and Bedfordshire) (Temporary Prohibition of Traffic) Order 1994 No. 2435. Enabling power: *Road Traffic Regulation Act 1984, s. 14 (1) (a).* Made: 12.09.94. Coming into force: 19.09.94. Effect: None. – *Unpublished*

The A1(M) Motorway (Marr - Redhouse) (Temporary Restriction of Traffic) Order 1994 No. 1472. Enabling power: *Road Traffic Regulation Act 1984, s. 14 (1) (a) (7).* Made: 31.05.94. Coming into force: 01.06.94. Effect: None. – *Unpublished*

The A1(M) Motorway (Marr - Wadworth) (Temporary Restriction and Prohibition of Traffic) Order 1994 No. 2938. Enabling power: *Road Traffic Regulation Act 1984, s. 14 (1) (a).* Made: 16.11.94. Coming into force: 19.11.94. Effect: None. – *Unpublished*

The A1(M) Motorway (Redhouse - Wadworth, Slip Roads) (Temporary 30 Miles Per Speed Restriction) Order 1994 No. 2723. Enabling power: *Road Traffic Regulation Act 1984, s. 14 (1) (a) (7).* Made: 19.10.94. Coming into force: 21.10.94. Effect: None. – *Unpublished*

The A1(M) Motorway (Sprotborough - Marr) (Temporary Restriction and Prohibition of Traffic) Order 1994 No. 1467. Enabling power: *Road Traffic Regulation Act 1984, s. 14 (1) (a).* Made: 27.05.94. Coming into force: 31.05.94. Effect: None. – *Unpublished*

The A2 Trunk Road (Bean) (Temporary Prohibition of Traffic) Order 1994 No. 388. Enabling power: *Road Traffic Regulation Act 1984, s. 14 (1) (a).* Made: 21.02.94. Coming into force: 26.02.94. Effect: None. – *Unpublished*

The A2 Trunk Road (Canterbury Bypass) (Temporary Restriction of Traffic) Order 1994 No. 1034. Enabling power: *Road Traffic Regulation Act 1984, s. 14 (1) (a).* Made: 05.04.94. Coming into force: 09.04.94. Effect: None. – *Unpublished*

ROAD TRAFFIC: TRAFFIC REGULATION

The A2 Trunk Road (Dunkirk) (Temporary Restriction and Prohibition of Traffic) Order 1994 No.123. Enabling power: *Road Traffic Regulation Act 1984, s. 14 (1) (a)*. Made: 24.01.94. Coming into force: 29.01.94. Effect: None. –*Unpublished*

The A2 Trunk Road (Eastern Docks Roundabout to Guston Roundabout) (Temporary Prohibition of Traffic) Order 1994 No. 2428. Enabling power: *Road Traffic Regulation Act 1984, s. 14 (1) (a)*. Made: 12.09.94. Coming into force: 17.09.94. Effect: None. –*Unpublished*

The A2 Trunk Road (Jubilee Way) (Temporary Prohibition of Traffic) Order 1994 No.732. Enabling power: *Road Traffic Regulation Act 1984 s. 14 (1) (a)*. Made: 28.02.94. Coming into force: 05.03.94. Effect: None. –*Unpublished*

The A2 Trunk Road (Patrixbourne) (Temporary Prohibition of Traffic) Order 1994 No.1788. Enabling power: *Road Traffic Regulation Act 1984, s. 14 (1) (a)*. Made: 04.07.94. Coming into force: 09.07.94. Effect: None. – *Unpublished*

The A2 Trunk Road (Rochester Way Relief Road) and the London South Circular Trunk Road (A205) (Westhorne Avenue, Greenwich) (Temporary Speed Restriction) Order 1994 No. 2703. Enabling power: *Road Traffic Regulation Act 1984, s. 14 (1) (4)*. Made: 17.10.94. Coming into force: 24.10.94. Effect: None. –*Unpublished*

The A2 Trunk Road (Rochester Way Relief Road, Greenwich and Bexley) (Temporary Prohibition of Traffic) (No. 2) Order 1994 No. 2283. Enabling power: *Road Traffic Regulation Act 1984, s. 14 (1) (4)*. Made: 26.08.94. Coming into force: 02.09.94. Effect: None. –*Unpublished*

The A2 Trunk Road (Rochester Way Relief Road, Greenwich and Bexley) (Temporary Prohibition of Traffic) Order 1994 No. 1238. Enabling power: *Road Traffic Regulation Act 1984, s. 14 (1) (4)*. Made: 03.05.94. Coming into force: 07.05.94. Effect: None. –*Unpublished*

The A3 Trunk Road (B366, Redhill Road) (Temporary Prohibition of Traffic) Order 1994 No.1451. Enabling power: *Road Traffic Regulation Act 1984, s. 14 (1) (b)*. Made: 31.05.94. Coming into force: 14.06.94. Effect: None. –*Unpublished*

The A3 Trunk Road (Berelands Interchange) (Temporary Prohibition of Traffic) Order 1994 No.737. Enabling power: *Road Traffic Regulation Act 1984 s. 14 (1) (a)*. Made: 07.03.94. Coming into force: 12.03.94. Effect: None. –*Unpublished*

The A3 Trunk Road (Beverley Way, Merton) (Prohibition of Left Turn) Experimental Traffic Order 1994 No. 333. Enabling power: *Road Traffic Regulation Act 1984, ss. 9 (1), 10 (2)*. Made: 14.02.94. Coming into force: 28.02.94. Effect: None. –*Unpublished*

The A3 Trunk Road (Beverley Way, Merton) (Temporary Prohibition of Traffic) Order 1994 No.2203. Enabling power: *Road Traffic Regulation Act 1984, s. 14 (1) (4)*. Made: 15.08.94. Coming into force: 22.08.94. Effect: None. –*Unpublished*

The A3 Trunk Road (Beverley Way, Merton) (Temporary Restriction of Traffic) Order 1994 No.216. Enabling power: *Road Traffic Regulation Act 1984, s. 14 (1) (4)*. Made: 31.01.94. Coming into force: 07.02.94. Effect: None. –*Unpublished*

The A3 Trunk Road (Bramshott) (Closure of a Gap in the Central Reservation) Order 1994 No.2347. Enabling power: *Road Traffic Regulation Act 1984, ss. 1 (1), 2 (1) (2)*. Made: 05.09.94. Coming into force: 03.10.94. Effect: None. –*Unpublished*

The A3 Trunk Road (Bramshott) (Restriction of Use of Gaps in the Central Reservation) Order 1994 No. 2346. Enabling power: *Road Traffic Regulation Act 1984, ss. 1 (1), 2 (1) (2)*. Made: 05.09.94. Coming into force: 03.10.94. Effect: None. –*Unpublished*

The A3 Trunk Road (Copsem to Painshill) (Temporary Restriction and Prohibition of Traffic and Pedestrians) Order 1994 No. 1789. Enabling power: *Road Traffic Regulation Act 1984, s. 14 (1) (a)*. Made: 04.07.94. Coming into force: 09.07.94. Effect: None. –*Unpublished*

The A3 Trunk Road (Guildford Bypass - Hog's Back Junction) (Temporary Restriction and Prohibition of Traffic) (No. 2) Order 1994 No. 2429. Enabling power: *Road Traffic Regulation Act 1984, s. 14 (1) (b)*. Made: 12.09.94. Coming into force: 17.09.94. Effect: S.I. 1994/2121 revoked. –*Unpublished*

The A3 Trunk Road (Guildford Bypass - Hog's Back Junction) (Temporary Restriction and Prohibition of Traffic) Order 1994 No. 2121. Enabling power: *Road Traffic Regulation Act 1984, s. 14 (1) (a), 5 (b)*. Made: 08.08.94. Coming into force: 10.08.94. Effect: None. –*Unpublished*

The A3 Trunk Road (Guildford Bypass) (Temporary Prohibition of Traffic) Order 1994 No.972. Enabling power: *Road Traffic Regulation Act 1984, s. 14 (1) (a)*. Made: 28.03.94. Coming into force: 02.04.94. Effect: None. –*Unpublished*

The A3 Trunk Road (Hindhead to Bramshott) (Temporary Restriction and Prohibition of Traffic) Order 1994 No. 2527. Enabling power: *Road Traffic Regulation Act 1984, s. 14 (1) (a)*. Made: 26.09.94. Coming into force: 01.10.94. Effect: None. –*Unpublished*

The A3 Trunk Road (Hog's Back Junction, Guildford) (One Way Traffic) Order 1994 No.2475. Enabling power: *Road Traffic Regulation Act 1984, ss. 1 (1), 2 (1) (2)*. Made: 19.09.94. Coming into force: 03.10.94. Effect: None. – *Unpublished*

ROAD TRAFFIC: TRAFFIC REGULATION

The A3 Trunk Road (Hog's Back Junction) Southbound Exit Slip Road (Temporary Prohibition of Traffic) Order 1994 No. 3035. Enabling power: *Road Traffic Regulation Act 1984, s. 14 (1) (a)*. Made: 28.11.94. Coming into force: 02.12.94. Effect: None. – *Unpublished*

The A3 Trunk Road (Hook to Bramshott) (24 Hours Clearway) Order 1994 No. 2942. Enabling power: *Road Traffic Regulation Act 1984, ss. 1 (1), 2 (1) (2), 4 (1), 6 (1) (3), 7 (1), sch. 9, para. 27 (1)*. Made: 21.11.94. Coming into force: 05.12.94. Effect: S.I. 1963/1172; 1965/740; 1993/2075 amended & S.I. 1968/1949; 1969/112; 1973/930; 1976/1010; 1977/1432, 1487; 1980/131 revoked. – *Unpublished*

The A3 Trunk Road (Kingston By-Pass, Kingston Upon Thames and Merton) (Temporary Prohibition of Traffic) Order 1994 No. 383. Enabling power: *Road Traffic Regulation Act 1984, s. 14 (1) (4)*. Made: 21.02.94. Coming into force: 01.03.94. Effect: None. – *Unpublished*

The A3 Trunk Road (Kingston By-Pass, Kingston Upon Thames and Merton) (Temporary Prohibition of Traffic) Order 1994 No. 2374. Enabling power: *Road Traffic Regulation Act 1984, s. 14 (1) (4) (7)*. Made: 26.08.94. Coming into force: 07.09.94. Effect: None. – *Unpublished*

The A3 Trunk Road (Kingston Upon Thames and Surrey) (Temporary Prohibition of Traffic) Order 1994 No. 2443. Enabling power: *Road Traffic Regulation Act 1984, s. 14 (1) 94)*. Made: 14.09.94. Coming into force: 21.09.94. Effect: None. – *Unpublished*

The A3 Trunk Road (Milford Bypass) (Temporary Prohibition of Traffic) Order 1994 No. 1347. Enabling power: *Road Traffic Regulation Act 1984, s. 14 (1) (a)*. Made: 16.05.94. Coming into force: 21.05.94. Effect: None. – *Unpublished*

The A3 Trunk Road (Robin Hood Way and Beverley Way, Kingston upon Thames) (Temporary Prohibition of Traffic) Order 1994 No. 90. Enabling power: *Road Traffic Regulation Act 1984, s. 14 (1) (4) (5) (7)*. Made: 17.01.94. Coming into force: 24.01.94. Effect: None. – *Unpublished*

The A3 Trunk Road (Tibbet's Corner Underpass, Wandsworth) (Temporary Prohibition of Traffic) Order 1994 No. 2822. Enabling power: *Road Traffic Regulation Act 1984, s. 14 (1) (4)*. Made: 31.10.94. Coming into force: 05.11.94. Effect: None. – *Unpublished*

The A3 (M) Motorway (Marker Posts 2.10 - 8.80) (Temporary Restriction and Prohibition of Traffic) Order 1994 No. 1600. Enabling power: *Road Traffic Regulation Act 1984, s. 14 (1) (a) (7)*. Made: 13.06.94. Coming into force: 18.06.94. Effect: None. – *Unpublished*

The A4 Trunk Road (Bath Road, Hillingdon and Hounslow) (Temporary Restriction of Traffic) Order 1994 No. 1076. Enabling power: *Road Traffic Regulation Act 1984, s. 14 (1) (4) (7)*. Made: 11.04.94. Coming into force: 18.04.94. Effect: None. – *Unpublished*

0@TS D = **The A4 Trunk Road (Great West Road, Hounslow) (Temporary Restriction of Traffic) (No. 2) Order 1994 No. 2704.** Enabling power: *Road Traffic Regulation Act 1984, s. 14 (1) (4)*. **Made: 17.10.94. Coming into force: 22.10.94. Effect: None.** – *Unpublished*

The A4 Trunk Road (Great West Road, Hounslow) (Temporary Restriction of Traffic) Order 1994 No. 2467. Enabling power: *Road Traffic Regulation Act 1984, s. 14 (1) (4)*. Made: 19.09.94. Coming into force: 30.09.94. Effect: None. – *Unpublished*

The A4 Trunk Road (Hammersmith Flyover, Hammersmith and Fulham) (Temporary Prohibition of Traffic) Order 1994 No. 1707. Enabling power: *Road Traffic Regulation Act 1984, s. 14 (1) (4) (5) (7)*. Made: 27.06.94. Coming into force: 05.07.94. Effect: None. – *Unpublished*

The A4 Trunk Road (Hogarth Roundabout, Hounslow) (Temporary Prohibition of Traffic) Order 1994 No. 2049. Enabling power: *Road Traffic Regulation Act 1984, s. 14 (1) (4)*. Made: 01.08.94. Coming into force: 07.08.94. Effect: None. – *Unpublished*

The A5 and A483 Trunk Roads (Oswestry Bypass) (Temporary 30 Miles Per Hour Speed Restriction) Order 1994 No. 883. Enabling power: *Road Traffic Regulation Act 1984, s. 14 (1) (a)*. Made: 18.03.94. Coming into force: 19.03.94. Effect: None. – *Unpublished*

The A5 Trunk Road (A460 (Longford Island) to M6 Junction 12) (Temporary Restriction of Traffic) Order 1994 No. 18. Enabling power: *Road Traffic Regulation Act 1984, s. 14 (1) (a)*. Made: 07.01.94. Coming into force: 08.01.94. Effect: None. – *Unpublished*

The A5 Trunk Road (Anglesey, Gwynedd) (Temporary 30 MPH Speed Limit and Prohibition of Pedestrians) (No.2) Order 1994 No. 900. Enabling power: *Road Traffic Regulation Act 1984, s. 14 (1)*. Made: 11.03.94. Coming into force: 14.03.94. Effect: None. – *Unpublished*

The A5 Trunk Road (Anglesey, Gwynedd) (Temporary Traffic Restrictions) Order 1994 No.149. Enabling power: *Road Traffic Regulation Act 1984, s. 14 (1)*. Made: 14.01.94. Coming into force: 17.02.94. Effect: None. – *Unpublished*

The A5 Trunk Road (Caergeiliog, Anglesey, Gwynedd) (Temporary Traffic Restrictions) Order 1994 No. 3091. Enabling power: *Road Traffic Regulation Act 1984, s. 14 (1) (4)*. Made: 17.11.94. Coming into force: 21.11.94. Effect: None. – *Unpublished*

The A5 Trunk Road (Glyn Bends Dinmael, Clwyd) (Temporary 40 Miles Per Hour Speed Restriction) Order 1994 No. 1198. Enabling power: *Road Traffic Regulation Act 1984, s. 14 (1)*. Made: 22.04.94. Coming into force: 09.05.94. Effect: None. – *Unpublished*

The A5 Trunk Road (Glyn Bends, Tynant-Dinmael, Clwyd) (Temporary Prohibition of Vehicles and Pedestrians) Order 1994 No. 1272. Enabling power: *Road Traffic Regulation Act 1984, s. 14 (1)*. Made: 06.05.94. Coming into force: 09.05.94. Effect: None. – *Unpublished*

The A5 Trunk Road (Llangristiolus, Anglesey, Gwynedd) (Temporary 30 MPH Speed Limit and Prohibition of Pedestrians) Order 1994 No. 2238. Enabling power: *Road Traffic Regulation Act 1984, s. 14 (1) (4)*. Made: 25.08.94. Coming into force: 05.09.94. Effect: None. – *Unpublished*

The A5 Trunk Road (Milton Keynes, Buckinghamshire) (Temporary Prohibition of Traffic) Order 1994 No. 1781. Enabling power: *Road Traffic Regulation Act 1984, s. 14 (1) (a)*. Made: 04.07.94. Coming into force: 11.07.94. Effect: None. – *Unpublished*

The A5 Trunk Road (Muckley Corner to Newtown) (Temporary Restriction of Traffic) Order 1994 No. 1285. Enabling power: *Road Traffic Regulation Act 1984, s. 14 (1) (a)*. Made: 29.04.94. Coming into force: 30.04.94. Effect: None. – *Unpublished*

The A5 Trunk Road (Valley, Gwynedd) (Variable Speed Limit) Order 1994 No. 40. Enabling power: *Road Traffic Regulation Act 1984, ss. 84 (1) (1A) (2), 124, sch. 9, para. 27*. Made: 04.01.94. Coming into force: 31.01.94. Effect: None. – *Unpublished*

The A5 Trunk Road (Watling Street, Hinckley, Leicestershire) (Temporary Prohibition of Traffic) Order 1994 No. 2859. Enabling power: *Road Traffic Regulation Act 1984, s. 14 (1) (a)*. Made: 19.10.94. Coming into force: 02.11.94. Effect: None. – *Unpublished*

The A5 Trunk Road (Wibtoft, Leicestershire) (Temporary Prohibition of Traffic) Order 1994 No.346. Enabling power: *Road Traffic Regulation Act 1984, s. 14 (1) (a)*. Made: 16.02.94. Coming into force: 24.02.94. Effect: None. – *Unpublished*

The A6 Trunk Road (Bakewell Road, Devonshire Arms to Topley Pike, Derbyshire) (Temporary Prohibition of Traffic) Order 1994 No. 3241. Enabling power: *Road Traffic Regulation Act 1984, s. 14 (1) (a)*. Made: 06.12.94. Coming into force: 09.12.94. Effect: None. – *Unpublished*

The A6 Trunk Road (Buxton Road/Hazel Grove/High Lane) Stockport (Temporary 30 Miles Per Hour Speed Restriction) Order 1994 No. 1275. Enabling power: *Road Traffic Regulation Act 1984, s. 14 (1) (a)*. Made: 29.04.94. Coming into force: 02.05.94. Effect: None. – *Unpublished*

The A6 Trunk Road (Dove Holes, Near Buxton, Derbyshire) (Temporary Prohibition of Traffic) Order 1994 No. 2373. Enabling power: *Road Traffic Regulation Act 1984, s. 14 (1) (a)*. Made: 02.09.94. Coming into force: 14.09.94. Effect: None. – *Unpublished*

The A6 Trunk Road (Fillingate Junction, Wanlip, Leicestershire) (Temporary Prohibition of Traffic) Order 1994 No. 1580. Enabling power: *Road Traffic Regulation Act 1984, s. 14 (1) (a)*. Made: 27.05.94. Coming into force: 04.06.94. Effect: None. – *Unpublished*

The A6 Trunk Road (Kegworth to Hathern, Leicestershire) (Prohibition of Use of Gaps in Central Reservation) Order 1994 No. 914. Enabling power: *Road Traffic Regulation Act 1984, ss. 1 (1), 2 (1) (2)*. Made: 17.03.94. Coming into force: 25.03.94. Effect: None. – *Unpublished*

The A6 Trunk Road (Kibworth Harcourt, Leicestershire) (Temporary Prohibition of Traffic) Order 1994 No. 2860. Enabling power: *Road Traffic Regulation Act 1984, s. 14 (1) (a)*. Made: 21.10.94. Coming into force: 05.11.94. Effect: None. – *Unpublished*

The A6 Trunk Road (Leicester Road/Harborough Road, Oadby, Leicestershire) (Temporary Prohibition of Traffic) Order 1994 No. 283. Enabling power: *Road Traffic Regulation Act 1984, s. 14 (1) (a)*. Made: 26.01.94. Coming into force: 28.01.94. Effect: None. – *Unpublished*

The A6 Trunk Road (Leicester Road Railway Bridge, Loughborough, Leicestershire) (Temporary Prohibition and Restriction of Traffic) Order 1994 No. 1246. Enabling power: *Road Traffic Regulation Act 1984, s. 14 (1) (a)*. Made: 03.05.94. Coming into force: 07.05.94. Effect: None. – *Unpublished*

The A6 Trunk Road (Leicester Road Railway Bridge, Loughborough, Leicestershire) (Temporary Prohibition of Traffic) Order 1994 No. 1963. Enabling power: *Road Traffic Regulation Act 1984, s. 14 (1) (a)*. Made: 14.07.94. Coming into force: 16.07.94. Effect: None. – *Unpublished*

The A6 Trunk Road (Lockington, Leicestershire) (Temporary Prohibition of Traffic) Order 1994 No. 2431. Enabling power: *Road Traffic Regulation Act 1984, s. 14 (1) (a) (5) (b)*. Made: 07.09.94. Coming into force: 09.09.94. Effect: None. – *Unpublished*

The A6 Trunk Road (London Road, Hazel Grove) (Box Junction) Order 1994 No. 1804. Enabling power: *Road Traffic Regulation Act 1984, ss. 1 (1), 2 (1) (2), 4 (1)*. Made: 07.02.94. Coming into force: 24.02.94. Effect: None. – *Unpublished*

The A6 Trunk Road (London Road, Near Hemington, Leicestershire) (Temporary Prohibition of Traffic) Order 1994 No. 1592. Enabling power: *Road Traffic Regulation Act 1984, s. 14 (1) (a)*. Made: 01.06.94. Coming into force: 04.06.94. Effect: None. – *Unpublished*

The A6 Trunk Road (Ranch Corner, Matlock Road, Derbyshire) (Temporary Restriction of Traffic) Order 1994 No. 203. Enabling power: *Road Traffic Regulation Act 1984, s. 14 (1) (a)*. Made: 27.01.94. Coming into force: 29.01.94. Effect: None. – *Unpublished*

The A6 Trunk Road (Wanlip, Leicestershire) (Temporary Prohibition and Restriction of Traffic) Order 1994 No. 1098. Enabling power: *Road Traffic Regulation Act 1984, s. 14 (1) (a)*. Made: 07.04.94. Coming into force: 09.04.94. Effect: None. – *Unpublished*

The A7 Trunk Road (Gilmerton Road Roundabout to Melville Dykes Road Roundabout) (Temporary Prohibition of Traffic) Order 1994 No. 2447. Enabling power: *Road Traffic Regulation Act 1984, s. 14 (1) (b) (4)*. Made: 16.09.94. Coming into force: 25.09.94. Effect: None. – *Unpublished*

The A7 Trunk Road (Highmill Bridge) (Langholm) (Dumfries and Galloway Region) (Temporary 10 MPH Speed Limit) Order 1994 No. 2294. Enabling power: *Road Traffic Regulation Act 1984, s. 14 (1) (a) (4) (a), 121A*. Made: 01.09.94. Coming into force: 11.09.94. Effect: None. – *Unpublished*

The A7, A75 and A76 Trunk Roads (Dumfries and Galloway Region) (Temporary 10 MPH Speed Limit) Order 1994 No. 2015. Enabling power: *Road Traffic Regulation Act 1984, s. 14 (1) (a) (4) (a), 121A*. Made: 28.07.94. Coming into force: 08.08.94. Effect: None. – *Unpublished*

The A8 Trunk Road (Chapelhall Junction Slip Roads) (Temporary Prohibition of Traffic) Order 1994 No. 1611. Enabling power: *Road Traffic Regulation Act 1984, s. 14 (1) (a) (4)*. Made: 17.06.94. Coming into force: 26.06.94. Effect: None. – *Unpublished*

The A8 Trunk Road/M8 Motorway (Langbank to West Ferry Interchange) (Temporary Prohibition of Traffic and Temporary Prohibition of Specified Turns) Order 1994 No. 1622. Enabling power: *Road Traffic Regulation Act 1984, s. 14 (1) (4)*. Made: 17.06.94. Coming into force: 26.06.94. Effect: None. – *Unpublished*

The A8 Trunk Road/M8 Motorway (Langbank to West Ferry Interchange) (Temporary Prohibition of Traffic and Temporary Prohibition of Specified Turns) (No 2) Order 1994 No. 2140. Enabling power: *Road Traffic Regulation Act 1984, s. 14 (1) (4)*. Made: 12.08.94. Coming into force: 22.08.94. Effect: None. – *Unpublished*

The A9 Trunk Road Edinburgh-Thurso (Dalrachney Road, Carrbridge) (Prohibition of Specified Turns) Order 1994 No. 1173. Enabling power: *Road Traffic Regulation Act 1984, ss. 1 (1), 2 (1) (2), 121A*. Made: 22.04.94. Coming into force: 01.05.94. Effect: None. – *Unpublished*

The A10 Trunk Road (Foxton Level Crossing, Cambridgeshire) (Temporary Prohibition of Traffic) Order 1994 No. 2270. Enabling power: *Road Traffic Regulation Act 1984, s. 14 (1) (a)*. Made: 29.06.94. Coming into force: 01.07.94. Effect: None. – *Unpublished*

The A10 Trunk Road (Great Cambridge Road, Enfield) (Temporary Restriction of Traffic) Order 1994 No. 148. Enabling power: *Road Traffic Regulation Act 1984, s. 14 (1) (4) (5) (7)*. Made: 27.01.94. Coming into force: 04.02.94. Effect: None. – *Unpublished*

The A10 Trunk Road (Hoddesden Bypass, Hertfordshire) (Temporary Prohibition of Traffic) Order 1994 No. 753. Enabling power: *Road Traffic Regulation Act 1984 s. 14 (1) (a)*. Made: 04.03.94. Coming into force: 11.03.94. Effect: None. – *Unpublished*

The A10 Trunk Road (Puckeridge to Royston, Hertfordshire) (Temporary Prohibition of Traffic) Order 1994 No. 754. Enabling power: *Road Traffic Regulation Act 1984 s. 14 (1) (a)*. Made: 04.03.94. Coming into force: 11.03.94. Effect: None. – *Unpublished*

The A10 Trunk Road (Reed, Hertfordshire) (Temporary Restriction of Traffic) Order 1994 No.2001. Enabling power: *Road Traffic Regulation Act 1984, s. 14 (1) (a) (5) (b)*. Made: 25.07.94. Coming into force: 01.08.94. Effect: None. – *Unpublished*

The A10 Trunk Road (Rush Green Interchange, Hertfordshire) (Temporary Prohibition of Traffic) Order 1994 No. 269. Enabling power: *Road Traffic Regulation Act 1984, s. 14 (1) (a)*. Made: 07.02.94. Coming into force: 14.02.94. Effect: None. – *Unpublished*

The A10 Trunk Road (Thundridge, Hertfordshire) (Temporary Prohibition and Restriction of Traffic) Order 1994 No. 2118. Enabling power: *Road Traffic Regulation Act 1984, s. 14 (1) (a) (5) (b)*. Made: 08.08.94. Coming into force: 15.08.94. Effect: None. – *Unpublished*

The A10 Trunk Road (Thundridge, Hertfordshire) (Temporary Restriction of Traffic) Order 1994 No. 741. Enabling power: *Road Traffic Regulation Act 1984, s. 14 (1) (a)*. Made: 03.03.94. Coming into force: 06.03.94. Effect: None. – *Unpublished*

The A10 Trunk Road (Ware Bypass, Hertfordshire) (Temporary Prohibition of Traffic) Order 1994 No. 755. Enabling power: *Road Traffic Regulation Act 1984 s. 14 (1) (a)*. Made: 07.03.94. Coming into force: 14.03.94. Effect: None. – *Unpublished*

The A10 Trunk Road (Ware Bypass, Hertfordshire) (Temporary Prohibition of Traffic) Order 1994 No. 888. Enabling power: *Road Traffic Regulation Act 1984, s. 14 (1) (a)*. Made: 21.03.94. Coming into force: 28.03.94. Effect: None. – *Unpublished*

The A11 and A14 Trunk Roads (Heath Road Bridge, Newmarket, Cambridgeshire and Suffolk) (Temporary Prohibition and Restriction of Traffic) Order 1994 No. 2753. Enabling power: *Road Traffic Regulation Act 1984, s. 14 (1) (a)*. Made: 24.10.94. Coming into force: 31.10.94. Effect: None. – *Unpublished*

The A11 Trunk Road (Besthorpe-Wymondham Improvement) (Temporary 40 Miles Per Hour Speed Restriction) Order 1994 No. 2667. Enabling power: *Road Traffic Regulation Act 1984, s. 14 (1) (a)*. Made: 05.10.94. Coming into force: 05.10.94. Effect: None. –*Unpublished*

The A11 Trunk Road (Fiveways Roundabout to Elveden, Suffolk) (Temporary 10 Miles Per Hour Speed Restriction) Order 1994 No. 2278. Enabling power: *Road Traffic Regulation Act 1984, s. 14 (1) (a)*. Made: 30.08.94. Coming into force: 05.09.94. Effect: None. –*Unpublished*

The A11 Trunk Road (London to Norwich) (Barton Mills, Suffolk) (Temporary Restriction of Traffic) Order 1994 No. 1113. Enabling power: *Road Traffic Regulation Act 1984, s. 14 (1) (a)*. Made: 25.03.94. Coming into force: 28.03.94. Effect: None. –*Unpublished*

The A11 Trunk Road (Stump Cross to Four Went Ways Improvement) (Temporary Restriction of Traffic) Order 1994 No. 1704. Enabling power: *Road Traffic Regulation Act 1984, s. 14 (1) (a)*. Made: 23.06.94. Coming into force: 25.06.94. Effect: None. –*Unpublished*

The A11 Trunk Road (Thetford, Norfolk) (Temporary 40 Miles Per Hour Speed Restriction) Order 1994 No. 1128. Enabling power: *Road Traffic Regulation Act 1984, s. 14 (1) (a)*. Made: 19.04.94. Coming into force: 26.04.94. Effect: None. –*Unpublished*

The A11 Trunk Road (Wymondham Bypass, Wymondham, Norfolk) (Temporary Prohibition of Traffic) Order 1994 No. 1030. Enabling power: *Road Traffic Regulation Act 1984, s. 14 (1) (a) (5) (b) (7)*. Made: 07.03.94. Coming into force: 10.03.94. Effect: None. –*Unpublished*

The A12 Trunk Road (A12/A45 Copdock Mill Interchange, Ipswich, Suffolk) (Temporary Restriction of Traffic) Order 1994 No. 941. Enabling power: *Road Traffic Regulation Act 1984, s. 14 (1) (a)*. Made: 04.03.94. Coming into force: 09.03.94. Effect: None. –*Unpublished*

The A12 Trunk Road (A12/M25 Brook Street Interchange, Essex) (Temporary Prohibition of Traffic) Order 1994 No. 2452. Enabling power: *Road Traffic Regulation Act 1984, s. 14 (1) (a)*. Made: 09.09.94. Coming into force: 09.09.94. Effect: None. –*Unpublished*

The A12 Trunk Road (Bentley and Capel St Mary Interchanges, Suffolk) (Temporary Prohibition and Restriction of Traffic) Order 1994 No. 2244. Enabling power: *Road Traffic Regulation Act 1984, s. 14 (1) (a)*. Made: 22.08.94. Coming into force: 29.08.94. Effect: None. –*Unpublished*

The A12 Trunk Road (Blythburgh, Suffolk) (Temporary Prohibition and Restriction of Traffic) Order 1994 No. 2836. Enabling power: *Road Traffic Regulation A 1984, s. 14 (1) (a)*. Made: 31.10.94. Coming into force: 07.11.94. Effect: None. –*Unpublished*

The A12 Trunk Road (Boreham Interchange Northbound Access Slip Road, Essex) (Temporary Prohibition of Traffic) Order 1994 No. 2277. Enabling power: *Road Traffic Regulation Act 1984, s. 14 (1) (a)*. Made: 30.08.94. Coming into force: 05.09.94. Effect: None. –*Unpublished*

The A12 Trunk Road (Boxted Road Bridge to Spring Lane, Colchester, Essex) (Temporary Restriction of Traffic) Order 1994 No. 79. Enabling power: *Road Traffic Regulation Act 1984, ss. 14 (1) (a)*. Made: 17.01.94. Coming into force: 24.01.94. Effect: None. –*Unpublished*

The A12 Trunk Road (Brook Street Interchange, Essex) (Temporary Prohibition of Traffic) Order 1994 No. 1668. Enabling power: *Road Traffic Regulation Act 1984, s. 14 (1) (a)*. Made: 20.06.94. Coming into force: 27.06.94. Effect: None. –*Unpublished*

The A12 Trunk Road (Brook Street Interchange to Maryland Interchange, Brentwood, Essex) (Temporary Prohibition of Traffic) Order 1994 No. 1965. Enabling power: *Road Traffic Regulation Act 1984, s. 14 (1) (a)*. Made: 11.07.94. Coming into force: 18.07.94. Effect: None. –*Unpublished*

The A12 Trunk Road (Capel St Mary to Four Sisters Interchange, Suffolk) (Temporary Prohibition and Restriction of Traffic) Order 1994 No. 1670. Enabling power: *Road Traffic Regulation Act 1984, s. 14 (1) (a)*. Made: 20.06.94. Coming into force: 27.06.94. Effect: None. –*Unpublished*

The A12 Trunk Road (Copdock to Washbrook Bypass) (Temporary Restriction and Prohibition of Traffic) Order 1994 No. 2685. Enabling power: *Road Traffic Regulation Act 1984, s. 14 (1) (a)*. Made: 10.10.94. Coming into force: 13.10.94. Effect: None. –*Unpublished*

The A12 Trunk Road (Crown Interchange, Essex - Stratford St Mary, Suffolk) (Temporary Prohibition and Restriction of Traffic) Order 1994 No. 2272. Enabling power: *Road Traffic Regulation Act 1984, s. 14 (1) (a)*. Made: 30.08.94. Coming into force: 05.09.94. Effect: None. –*Unpublished*

The A12 Trunk Road (Crown Interchange, Essex) (Temporary Prohibition of Traffic) Order 1994 No. 519. Enabling power: *Road Traffic Regulation Act 1984, s. 14 (1) (a)*. Made: 28.02.94. Coming into force: 07.03.94. Effect: None. –*Unpublished*

The A12 Trunk Road (Darsham Level Crossing, Suffolk) (Temporary Prohibition of Traffic) Order 1994 No. 1835. Enabling power: *Road Traffic Regulation Act 1984, s. 14 (1) (a)*. Made: 01.07.94. Coming into force: 08.07.94. Effect: None. –*Unpublished*

The A12 Trunk Road (Darsham, Suffolk) (Temporary 10 Miles Per Hour Speed Restriction) Order 1994 No. 1415. Enabling power: *Road Traffic Regulation Act 1984, s. 14 (1) (a)*. Made: 23.05.94. Coming into force: 31.05.94. Effect: None. –*Unpublished*

ROAD TRAFFIC: TRAFFIC REGULATION

The A12 Trunk Road (Feering to Marks Tey, Essex) (Temporary 10 Miles Per Hour and 40 Miles Per Hour Speed Restriction) Order 1994 No. 1669. Enabling power: *Road Traffic Regulation Act 1984, s. 14 (1) (a)*. Made: 20.06.94. Coming into force: 27.06.94. Effect: None. – *Unpublished*

The A12 Trunk Road (London to Great Yarmouth) (Bascule Bridge, Lowestoft) (Temporary Prohibition of Traffic) Order 1994 No. 44. Enabling power: *Road Traffic Regulation Act 1984, s. 14 (1) (a)*. Made: 10.01.94. Coming into force: 20.01.94. Effect: None. – *Unpublished*

The A12 Trunk Road (London to Great Yarmouth) (Bascule Bridge, Lowestoft) (Temporary Prohibition of Traffic) Order 1994 No. 509. Enabling power: *Road Traffic Regulation Act 1984, s. 14 (1) (a)*. Made: 28.02.94. Coming into force: 10.03.94. Effect: None. – *Unpublished*

The A12 Trunk Road (Mountnessing Bypass and Brook Street Interchange, Essex) (Temporary Prohibition of Traffic) Order 1994 No. 746. Enabling power: *Road Traffic Regulation Act 1984 s. 14 (1) (a)*. Made: 22.02.94. Coming into force: 26.02.94. Effect: None. – *Unpublished*

The A12 Trunk Road (Mountnessing to Margaretting, Essex) (Temporary Prohibition of Traffic) Order 1994 No. 1537. Enabling power: *Road Traffic Regulation Act 1984, s. 14 (1) (a)*. Made: 06.06.94. Coming into force: 13.06.94. Effect: None. – *Unpublished*

The A12 Trunk Road (Pakefield and Lowestoft, Suffolk) (Temporary Prohibition and Restriction of Traffic) Order 1994 No. 321. Enabling power: *Road Traffic Regulation Act 1984, s. 14 (1) (a) (5) (b) (7)*. Made: 14.02.94. Coming into force: 21.02.94. Effect: None. – *Unpublished*

The A12 Trunk Road (Spring Lane to Crown Interchange, Colchester, Essex) (Temporary Prohibition and Restriction of Traffic) No. 2 Order 1994 No. 2746. Enabling power: *Road Traffic Regulation Act 1984, s. 14 (1) (a)*. Made: 24.10.94. Coming into force: 01.11.94. Effect: S.I. 1994/2210 revoked. – *Unpublished*

The A12 Trunk Road (Spring Lane to Crown Interchange, Colchester, Essex) (Temporary Prohibition and Restriction of Traffic) Order 1994 No. 2210. Enabling power: *Road Traffic Regulation Act 1984, s. 14 (1) (a)*. Made: 15.08.94. Coming into force: 22.08.94. Effect: None. – *Unpublished*

The A12 Trunk Road (Wangford Bypass, Suffolk) (Temporary Restriction of Traffic) Order 1994 No. 3331. Enabling power: *Road Traffic Regulation Act 1984, s. 14 (1) (a)*. Made: 28.12.94. Coming into force: 03.01.95. Effect: None. – *Unpublished*

The A12 Trunk Road (Western Bypass, Great Yarmouth) (Temporary Prohibition of Traffic) Order 1994 No. 2918. Enabling power: *Road Traffic Regulation Act 1984, s. 14 (1) (a)*. Made: 14.11.94. Coming into force: 21.11.94. Effect: None. – *Unpublished*

The A12 Trunk Road (Witham Pass) (Temporary 50 MPH Speed Restriction and Prohibition of Traffic) Order 1994 No. 2176. Enabling power: *Road Traffic Regulation Act 1984, s. 14 (1) (a)*. Made: 11.08.94. Coming into force: 20.08.94. Effect: None. – *Unpublished*

The A12/A127 Trunk Road (Gallows Corner Flyover, Havering) (Temporary Prohibition of Traffic) Order 1994 No. 2747. Enabling power: *Road Traffic Regulation Act 1984, s. 14 (1) (4)*. Made: 24.10.94. Coming into force: 03.11.94. Effect: None. – *Unpublished*

The A13 Trunk Road (A406 Interchange Underpass, Newham) (Temporary Prohibition of Traffic) Order 1994 No. 289. Enabling power: *Road Traffic Regulation Act 1984, s. 14 (1) (4)*. Made: 08.02.94. Coming into force: 13.02.94. Effect: None. – *Unpublished*

The A13 Trunk Road (Beckton and Canning Town Flyovers, Newham) (Temporary Prohibition of Traffic) Order 1994 No. 2050. Enabling power: *Road Traffic Regulation Act 1984, s. 14 (1) (4)*. Made: 01.08.94. Coming into force: 07.08.94. Effect: None. – *Unpublished*

The A13 Trunk Road (Commercial Road, Tower Hamlets) (Temporary Restriction of Traffic) Order 1994 No. 17. Enabling power: *Road Traffic Regulation Act 1984, s. 14 (1) (4)*. Made: 04.01.94. Coming into force: 10.01.94. Effect: None. – *Unpublished*

The A13 Trunk Road (Mardyke Roundabout, Essex) (Temporary Restriction of Traffic) Order 1994 No. 356. Enabling power: *Road Traffic Regulation Act 1984, s. 14 (1) (a)*. Made: 14.02.94. Coming into force: 21.02.94. Effect: None. – *Unpublished*

The A13 Trunk Road (Movers Lane and Lodge Avenue Flyovers, Barking and Dagenham) (Temporary Prohibition of Traffic) Order 1994 No. 1463. Enabling power: *Road Traffic Regulation Act 1984, s. 14 (1) (4)*. Made: 26.05.94. Coming into force: 04.06.94. Effect: None. – *Unpublished*

The A13 Trunk Road (New Road, Havering) (Temporary Prohibition of Traffic and Speed Restriction) (No. 2) Order 1994 No. 2748. Enabling power: *Road Traffic Regulation Act 1984, s. 14 (1) (4) (7)*. Made: 24.10.94. Coming into force: 29.10.94. Effect: None. – *Unpublished*

The A13 Trunk Road (New Road, Havering) (Temporary Prohibition of Traffic and Speed Restriction) Order 1994 No. 2284. Enabling power: *Road Traffic Regulation Act 1984, s. 14 (1) (4) (7)*. Made: 26.08.94. Coming into force: 03.09.94. Effect: None. – *Unpublished*

The A13 Trunk Road (North Stifford and Baker Street Interchanges, Essex) (Temporary Prohibition of Traffic) Order 1994 No. 1713. Enabling power: *Road Traffic Regulation Act 1984, s. 14 (1) (a)*. Made: 20.06.94. Coming into force: 27.06.94. Effect: None. – *Unpublished*

Price/availability are liable to change without notice

The A13 Trunk Road (Purfleet, Essex) (Temporary Restriction of Traffic) Order 1994 No. 2243. Enabling power: *Road Traffic Regulation Act 1984, s. 14 (1) (a)*. Made: 22.08.94. Coming into force: 30.08.94. Effect: None. – *Unpublished*

The A13 Trunk Road (Ripple Road and New Road, Barking and Dagenham) (Temporary Restriction of Traffic) Order 1994 No. 1964. Enabling power: *Road Traffic Regulation Act 1984, s. 14 (1) (a) (7)*. Made: 22.07.94. Coming into force: 30.07.94. Effect: None. – *Unpublished*

The A13 Trunk Road (Ripple Road, Barking and Dagenham) (Temporary Restriction of Traffic) Order 1994 No. 996. Enabling power: *Road Traffic Regulation Act 1984, s. 14 (1) (4)*. Made: 30.03.94. Coming into force: 09.04.94. Effect: None. – *Unpublished*

The A13 Trunk Road (Ripple Road, Barking and Dagenham) (Temporary Restriction of Traffic) (No. 2) Order 1994 No. 1359. Enabling power: *Road Traffic Regulation Act 1984, s. 14 (1) (4)*. Made: 16.05.94. Coming into force: 20.05.94. Effect: None. – *Unpublished*

The A13 Trunk Road (Ripple Road, Barking and Dagenham) (Temporary Restriction of Traffic) (No. 3) Order 1994 No. 1461. Enabling power: *Road Traffic Regulation Act 1984, s. 14 (1) (4)*. Made: 26.05.94. Coming into force: 04.06.94. Effect: None. – *Unpublished*

The A13 Trunk Road (Sandy Lane, Wennington, Essex) (Temporary Prohibition and Restriction of Traffic) Order 1994 No. 2682. Enabling power: *Road Traffic Regulation Act 1984, s. 14 (1) (a), 15 (2)*. Made: 14.10.94. Coming into force: 22.10.94. Effect: None. – *Unpublished*

The A14 Trunk Road (A1 and B1514 Interchanges, Brampton, Cambridgeshire) (Temporary Prohibition of Traffic) Order 1994 No. 2934. Enabling power: *Road Traffic Regulation Act 1984, s.14 (1) (a)*. Made: 17.11.94. Coming into force: 18.11.94. Effect: None. – *Unpublished*

The A14 Trunk Road (A141 Interchange Slip Road, Cambridgeshire) (Temporary Prohibition of Traffic) Order 1994 No. 1834. Enabling power: *Road Traffic Regulation Act 1984, s. 14 (1) (a)*. Made: 05.07.94. Coming into force: 08.07.94. Effect: None. – *Unpublished*

The A14 Trunk Road (Brampton, Cambridgeshire) (Temporary Prohibition and 10 Miles per Hour and 40 Miles Per Hour Speed Restriction) Order 1994 No. 2430. Enabling power: *Road Traffic Regulation Act 1984, s. 14 (1) (a)*. Made: 08.09.94. Coming into force: 09.09.94. Effect: None. – *Unpublished*

The A14 Trunk Road (Brington to Barham, Cambridgeshire) (Temporary Prohibition and Restriction of Traffic) Order 1994 No. 1175. Enabling power: *Road Traffic Regulation Act 1984, s. 14 (1) (a)*. Made: 19.04.94. Coming into force: 26.04.94. Effect: None. – *Unpublished*

The A14 Trunk Road (Catthorpe Interchange, Leicestershire and Rothwell Interchange, Northamptonshire) and Slip Roads (24 Hour Clearway) Order 1994 No. 2514. Enabling power: *Road Traffic Regulation Act 1984, ss. 1 (1) (2), 2 (1) (2), 3 (2), 4 (1)*. Made: 16.09.94. Coming into force: 30.09.94. Effect: None. – *Unpublished*

The A14 Trunk Road (Cow Lane and Rusts Lane Interchanges, Cambridgeshire) (Temporary Restriction and Prohibition of Traffic) Order 1994 No. 2469. Enabling power: *Road Traffic Regulation Act 1984, s. 14 (1) (a), 5 (b)*. Made: 19.09.94. Coming into force: 26.09.94. Effect: None. – *Unpublished*

The A14 Trunk Road (Cranford St John and Thrapston, Northamptonshire) (Temporary Prohibition of Traffic) Order 1994 No. 367. Enabling power: *Road Traffic Regulation Act 1984, s. 14 (1) (a)*. Made: 17.02.94. Coming into force: 24.02.94. Effect: None. – *Unpublished*

The A14 Trunk Road (Kettering Bypass, Northamptonshire) (Temporary Prohibition of Traffic) Order 1994 No. 2499. Enabling power: *Road Traffic Regulation Act 1984, s. 14 (1) (a)*. Made: 19.09.94. Coming into force: 22.09.94. Effect: None. – *Unpublished*

The A14 Trunk Road (Milton Interchange, Cambridgeshire) (Eastbound Entry Slip Road) (Temporary Prohibition of Traffic) Order 1994 No. 2670. Enabling power: *Road Traffic Regulation Act 1984, s. 14 (1) (a)*. Made: 10.10.94. Coming into force: 17.10.94. Effect: None. – *Unpublished*

The A14 Trunk Road (Risby - Beyton, Suffolk) (Temporary Prohibition and Restriction of Traffic) Order 1994 No. 2755. Enabling power: *Road Traffic Regulation Act 1984, s. 14 (1) (a)*. Made: 24.10.94. Coming into force: 31.10.94. Effect: None. – *Unpublished*

The A14 Trunk Road (Stowmarket Bypass) (Temporary Restriction and Prohibition of Traffic) Order 1994 No. 2683. Enabling power: *Road Traffic Regulation Act 1984, s. 14 (1) (a)*. Made: 30.09.94. Coming into force: 03.10.94. Effect: None. – *Unpublished*

The A14 Trunk Road (St Saviours Interchange, Bury St Edmunds, Suffolk) (Slip Roads) (Temporary Prohibition of Traffic) Order 1994 No. 2279. Enabling power: *Road Traffic Regulation Act 1984, s. 14 (1) (a)*. Made: 30.08.94. Coming into force: 05.09.94. Effect: None. – *Unpublished*

The A14 Trunk Road (Various Lengths Between Alconbury and Fen Ditton, Cambridgeshire) (Temporary Prohibition and Restriction of Traffic) Order 1994 No. 3316. Enabling power: *Road Traffic Regulation Act 1984, s. 14 (1) (a)*. Made: 28.12.94. Coming into force: 03.01.95. Effect: None. – *Unpublished*

The A15 Trunk Road (Barton Interchange - Bonby Lodge Interchange and Slip Roads) (Temporary Prohibition of Traffic) Order 1994 No. 231. Enabling power: *Road Traffic Regulation Act 1984, s. 14 (1) (a)*. Made: 28.01.94. Coming into force: 29.01.94. Effect: None. – *Unpublished*

Price/availability are liable to change without notice

The A15 Trunk Road (Barton Interchange - Bonby Lodge Interchange and Slip Roads) (Temporary Prohibition of Traffic) Order 1994 No. 2725. Enabling power: *Road Traffic Regulation Act 1984, s. 14 (1) (a)*. Made: 18.10.94. Coming into force: 20.10.94. Effect: None. – *Unpublished*

The A15 Trunk Road (Ermine Street, Hackthorn and Spridlington, Lincolnshire) (Temporary 10 Miles Per Hour Speed Restriction) Order 1994 No. 2269. Enabling power: *Road Traffic Regulation Act 1984, s. 14 (1) (a)*. Made: 24.08.94. Coming into force: 03.09.94. Effect: None. – *Unpublished*

The A15 Trunk Road (Ermine Street, Scampton, Lincolnshire) (Prohibition and Restriction of Waiting) Order 1994 No. 1452. Enabling power: *Road Traffic Regulation Act 1984, ss. 1 (1), 2 (1) (2), 4 (1)*. Made: 28.04.94. Coming into force: 22.06.94. Effect: None. – *Unpublished*

The A16 Trunk Road (Brazenose Lane, Stamford, Lincolnshire) (Temporary Prohibition of Traffic) Order 1994 No. 314. Enabling power: *Road Traffic Regulation Act 1984, s. 14 (1) (a)*. Made: 10.02.94. Coming into force: 19.02.94. Effect: None. – *Unpublished*

The A16 Trunk Road (High Ferry Level Crossing, Lincolnshire) (Temporary Prohibition of Traffic) Order 1994 No. 1457. Enabling power: *Road Traffic Regulation Act 1984, s. 14 (1) (a)*. Made: 30.05.94. Coming into force: 09.06.94. Effect: None. – *Unpublished*

The A16 Trunk Road (Littleworth Drove, Spalding, Lincolnshire) (Temporary 40 Miles Per Hour Speed Restriction) Order 1994 No. 2268. Enabling power: *Road Traffic Regulation Act 1984, s. 14 (1) (4)*. Made: 19.08.94. Coming into force: 04.09.94. Effect: None. – *Unpublished*

The A16 Trunk Road (Littleworth Station Level Crossing, Lincolnshire) (Temporary Prohibition of Traffic) Order 1994 No. 1620. Enabling power: *Road Traffic Regulation Act 1984, s. 14 (1) (a)*. Made: 10.06.94. Coming into force: 16.06.94. Effect: None. – *Unpublished*

The A16 Trunk Road (London Road, Spalding, Lincolnshire) (Prohibition of Waiting) Order 1994 No. 2684. Enabling power: *Road Traffic Regulation Act 1984, ss. 1 (1) (2), 2 (1) (2)*. Made: 06.10.94. Coming into force: 24.10.94. Effect: None. – *Unpublished*

The A16 Trunk Road (Lough Bypass and Grimsby Road, Louth, Lincolnshire) (Temporary 40 Miles Per Hour Speed Restriction) Order 1994 No. 3318. Enabling power: *Road Traffic Regulation Act 1984, s. 14 (1) (a)*. Made: 29.12.94. Coming into force: 07.01.95. Effect: None. – *Unpublished*

The A16 Trunk Road (Main Road, Sibsey, Lincolnshire) (Temporary Prohibition of Traffic) Order 1994 No. 836. Enabling power: *Road Traffic Regulation Act 1984, s. 14 (1) (a)*. Made: 11.03.94. Coming into force: 18.03.94. Effect: None. – *Unpublished*

The A16 Trunk Road (Main Road, Tallington, Lincolnshire) (Temporary 10 Miles Per Hour Speed Restriction) Order 1994 No. 2525. Enabling power: *Road Traffic Regulation Act 1984, s. 14 (1) (a)*. Made: 19.09.94. Coming into force: 24.09.94. Effect: None. – *Unpublished*

The A16 Trunk Road (Pinchbeck Road/Spalding Road, Spalding, Lincolnshire) (Temporary Restriction of Traffic) Order 1994 No. 1725. Enabling power: *Road Traffic Regulation Act 1984, s. 14 (1)*. Made: 21.06.94. Coming into force: 25.06.94. Effect: None. – *Unpublished*

The A16 Trunk Road (Spalding Road, Sutterton, Lincolnshire) (Temporary 40 Miles Per Hour Restriction) Order 1994 No. 614. Enabling power: *Road Traffic Regulation Act 1984, s. 14 (1) (a)*. Made: 28.02.94. Coming into force: 07.03.94. Effect: None. – *Unpublished*

The A16 Trunk Road (Spilsby Bypass, Lincolnshire) (Temporary Prohibition of Traffic) Order 1994 No. 2500. Enabling power: *Road Traffic Regulation Act 1984, s. 14 (1) (a)*. Made: 09.09.94. Coming into force: 17.09.94. Effect: None. – *Unpublished*

The A16 Trunk Road (Town Bridge, Stamford, Lincolnshire) (Temporary Restriction of Traffic) Order 1994 No. 2437. Enabling power: *Road Traffic Regulation Act 1984, s. 14 (1) (a)*. Made: 09.09.94. Coming into force: 10.09.94. Effect: None. – *Unpublished*

The A17 Trunk Road (Heckington Bypass and Boston Road, Lincolnshire) (Temporary 10 Miles Per Hour Speed Restriction) Order 1994 No. 1926. Enabling power: *Road Traffic Regulation Act 1984, s. 14 (1) (a)*. Made: 08.07.94. Coming into force: 16.07.94. Effect: None. – *Unpublished*

The A17 Trunk Road (Leadenham, Lincolnshire) (Temporary Prohibition and Restriction of Traffic) Order 1994 No. 3319. Enabling power: *Road Traffic Regulation Act 1984, s. 14 (1) (a)*. Made: 29.12.94. Coming into force: 07.01.95. Effect: None. – *Unpublished*

The A17 Trunk Road (Main Road, Swineshead, Lincolnshire) (Temporary Restriction of Traffic) Order 1994 No. 258. Enabling power: *Road Traffic Regulation Act 1984, s. 14 (1) (a)*. Made: 27.01.94. Coming into force: 05.02.94. Effect: None. – *Unpublished*

The A17 Trunk Road (Sleaford Road, Leadenham and Fubeck, and Windmill Hill, North Rauceby, Lincolnshire) (Temporary 10 Miles Per Hour Speed Restriction) Order 1994 No. 434. Enabling power: *Road Traffic Regulation Act 1984, s. 14 (1) (a)*. Made: 22.02.94. Coming into force: 05.03.94. Effect: None. – *Unpublished*

The A17 Trunk Road (Swineshead Level Crossing, Lincolnshire) (Temporary Prohibition of Traffic) Order 1994 No. 842. Enabling power: *Road Traffic Regulation Act 1984, s. 14 (1) (a)*. Made: 11.03.94. Coming into force: 24.03.94. Effect: None. – *Unpublished*

The A17 Trunk Road (Swineshead Level Crossing, Lincolnshire) (Temporary Prohibition of Traffic) (No. 2) Order 1994 No. 1726. Enabling power: *Road Traffic Regulation Act 1984, s. 14 (1) (a)*. Made: 27.06.94. Coming into force: 07.07.94. Effect: None. – *Unpublished*

The A19 Trunk Road (A19/A64 Junction, Fulford Interchange) (Dedicated Right Turn) Experimental Order 1994 No. 2054. Enabling power: *Road Traffic Regulation Act 1984, s. 9 (1) (3), 10 (2)*. Made: 27.07.94. Coming into force: 10.08.94. Effect: None. – *Unpublished*

The A19 Trunk Road (A66 Junction - Tees Viaduct) (Temporary Prohibition of Traffic) Order 1994 No. 98. Enabling power: *Road Traffic Regulation Act 1984, s. 14 (1) (a)*. Made: 14.01.94. Coming into force: 21.01.94. Effect: S.I. 1992/1925 revoked. – *Unpublished*

The A19 Trunk Road (A66 Stockton Road Interchange, Slip roads) (Temporary Prohibition of Traffic) Order 1994 No. 1237. Enabling power: *Road Traffic Regulation Act 1984, s. 14 (1) (a)*. Made: 28.04.94. Coming into force: 30.04.94. Effect: None. – *Unpublished*

The A19 Trunk Road (A139 Overbridge to Thames Road Overbridge) (Temporary Prohibition and 50 Miles Per Hour Speed Restriction) Order 1994 No. 2114. Enabling power: *Road Traffic Regulation Act 1984, s. 14 (1) (a)*. Made: 04.08.94. Coming into force: 07.08.94. Effect: None. – *Unpublished*

The A19 Trunk Road (A689 Wolviston Interchange) (Temporary Prohibition of Traffic) Order 1994 No. 2737. Enabling power: *Road Traffic Regulation Act 1984, s. 14 (1) (a)*. Made: 18.10.94. Coming into force: 20.10.94. Effect: None. – *Unpublished*

The A19 Trunk Road (B1280 to A690 Interchange) (Temporary Prohibition of Traffic) Order 1994 No. 1286. Enabling power: *Road Traffic Regulation Act 1984, s. 14 (1) (a) (5) (b) (7)*. Made: 05.05.94. Coming into force: 07.05.94. Effect: None. – *Unpublished*

The A19 Trunk Road (Easington) (No Right Turn Through Gap in Central Reservation) Order 1994 No. 2056. Enabling power: *Road Traffic Regulation Act 1984, ss. 1 (1), 2 (1) (2)*. Made: 22.07.94. Coming into force: 28.07.94. Effect: None. – *Unpublished*

The A19 Trunk Road (Easington) (Prohibition of Use of Gap in Central Reservation) Order 1994 No. 2982. Enabling power: *Road Traffic Regulation Act 1984, ss. 1 (1), 2 (1) (2)*. Made: 16.11.94. Coming into force: 18.11.94. Effect: None. – *Unpublished*

The A19 Trunk Road (Eden Vale) (Restriction of Use of Gap in Central Reservation) Order 1994 No. 1360. Enabling power: *Road Traffic Regulation Act 1984, ss. 1 (1), 2 (1) (2)*. Made: 13.05.94. Coming into force: 20.05.94. Effect: None. – *Unpublished*

The A19 Trunk Road (Escrick Village) (Temporary 40 and 10 Miles Per Hour Speed Restriction) Order 1994 No. 413. Enabling power: *Road Traffic Regulation Act 1984, s. 14 (1) (a)*. Made: 18.02.94. Coming into force: 19.02.94. Effect: None. – *Unpublished*

The A19 Trunk Road (Fisher Lane Roundabout to Moor Farm Roundabout) (Temporary Restriction of Traffic) Order 1994 No. 2858. Enabling power: *Road Traffic Regulation Act 1984, s. 14 (1) (a)*. Made: 03.11.94. Coming into force: 06.11.94. Effect: None. – *Unpublished*

The A19 Trunk Road (Haverton Hill Interchange Northbound Exit and Southbound Entry Slip Roads) (Temporary 40 Miles Per Hour Speed Restriction) Order 1994 No. 2817. Enabling power: *Road Traffic Regulation Act 1984, s. 14 (1) (a), 15 (2)*. Made: 27.10.94. Coming into force: 31.10.94. Effect: None. – *Unpublished*

The A19 Trunk Road (Knayton and Borrowby Bypass) (Temporary Restriction and Prohibition of Traffic) Order 1994 No. 2560. Enabling power: *Road Traffic Regulation Act 1984, s. 14 (1) (a)*. Made: 27.09.94. Coming into force: 29.09.94. Effect: None. – *Unpublished*

The A19 Trunk Road (Mandale Interchange and Crathorne Interchange) (Temporary Prohibition of Traffic) Order 1994 No. 443. Enabling power: *Road Traffic Regulation Act 1984, s. 14 (1) (a)*. Made: 27.01.94. Coming into force: 29.01.94. Effect: None. – *Unpublished*

The A19 Trunk Road (New Street, Selby) (Temporary Prohibition of Traffic) Order 1994 No.1687. Enabling power: *Road Traffic Regulation Act 1984, s. 14 (1) (a)*. Made: 22.06.94. Coming into force: 24.06.94. Effect: None. – *Unpublished*

The A19 Trunk Road (Sheraton to Peterlee Interchanges) (Temporary 50 Miles Per Hour Speed Restriction) Order 1994 No. 255. Enabling power: *Road Traffic Regulation Act 1984, s. 14 (1) (a)*. Made: 27.01.94. Coming into force: 29.01.94. Effect: None. – *Unpublished*

The A19 Trunk Road (Sheraton to Peterlee Interchange) (Temporary Prohibition and Restriction of Traffic) Order 1994 No. 1353. Enabling power: *Road Traffic Regulation Act 1984, s. 14 (1) (a)*. Made: 11.05.94. Coming into force: 15.05.94. Effect: None. – *Unpublished*

The A19 Trunk Road (Slip Road, Herrington Interchange) (Temporary Prohibition of Traffic) Order 1994 No. 1120. Enabling power: *Road Traffic Regulation Act 1984, s. 14 (1) (a)*. Made: 07.04.94. Coming into force: 09.04.94. Effect: None. – *Unpublished*

The A19 Trunk Road (Slip Road - Peterlee Interchange) (Temporary Prohibition of Traffic) Order 1994 No. 1094. Enabling power: *Road Traffic Regulation Act 1984, s. 14 (1) (a)*. Made: 07.04.94. Coming into force: 09.04.94. Effect: None. – *Unpublished*

The A19 Trunk Road (Slip Roads, Easington Interchange) (Temporary Prohibition of Traffic) Order 1994 No. 1080. Enabling power: *Road Traffic Regulation Act 1984, s. 14 (1) (a)*. Made: 07.04.94. Coming into force: 09.04.94. Effect: None. – *Unpublished*

The A19 Trunk Road (Stainsby Grange-Redhill Overbridge) (Temporary Prohibition and Restriction) Order 1994 No. 2631. Enabling power: *Road Traffic Regulation Act 1984, s. 14 (1) (a)*. Made: 29.09.94. Coming into force: 01.10.94. Effect: None. – *Unpublished*

The A19 Trunk Road (Tees Viaduct) (Temporary Prohibition of Traffic) Order 1994 No.2473. Enabling power: *Road Traffic Regulation Act 1984, s. 14 (1) (a)*. Made: 15.09.94. Coming into force: 16.09.94. Effect: None. – *Unpublished*

The A19 Trunk Road (Wellfield Interchange) (Temporary Prohibition of Traffic) Order 1994 No.257. Enabling power: *Road Traffic Regulation Act 1984, s. 14 (1) (a)*. Made: 04.02.94. Coming into force: 06.02.94. Effect: None. – *Unpublished*

The A20 Trunk Road (Court Wood to South Military Road) (Temporary Prohibition of Traffic) Order 1994 No. 1598. Enabling power: *Road Traffic Regulation Act 1984, s. 14 (1) (a)*. Made: 13.06.94. Coming into force: 18.06.94. Effect: None. – *Unpublished*

The A20 Trunk Road (Sidcup By Pass, Bexley) (Temporary Prohibition of Traffic) Order 1994 No.3109. Enabling power: *Road Traffic Regulation Act 1984, s. 14 (1) (4) (5) (7)*. Made: 05.12.94. Coming into force: 10.12.94. Effect: None. – *Unpublished*

The A20 Trunk Road (Sidcup Road, Greenwich) (Temporary Restriction of Traffic) Order 1994 No.2383. Enabling power: *Road Traffic Regulation Act 1984, s. 14 (1) (4)*. Made: 05.09.94. Coming into force: 12.09.94. Effect: None. – *Unpublished*

The A21 Trunk Road (Flimwell Bypass) (Temporary Restriction and Prohibition of Traffic) Order 1994 No. 2276. Enabling power: *Road Traffic Regulation Act 1984, s. 14 (1) (a) (7)*. Made: 30.08.94. Coming into force: 03.09.94. Effect: None. – *Unpublished*

The A21 Trunk Road (Flimwell) (Temporary 40 Miles Per Hour Speed Restriction) Order 1994 No.1787. Enabling power: *Road Traffic Regulation Act 1984, s. 14 (1) (a)*. Made: 04.07.94. Coming into force: 09.07.94. Effect: None. – *Unpublished*

The A21 Trunk Road (North of Lamberhurst) (Temporary Prohibition of Traffic) Order 1994 No.2274. Enabling power: *Road Traffic Regulation Act 1984, s. 14 (1) (a)*. Made: 30.08.94. Coming into force: 03.09.94. Effect: None. – *Unpublished*

The A21 Trunk Road (Somerhill Park Link) (Temporary 50 Miles Per Hour Speed Restriction) Order 1994 No. 2821. Enabling power: *Road Traffic Regulation Act 1984, s. 14 (1) (a)*. Made: 31.10.94. Coming into force: 05.11.94. Effect: None. – *Unpublished*

The A21 Trunk Road (Tonbridge Bypass North) (Temporary Restriction and Prohibition of Traffic) Order 1994 No. 2113. Enabling power: *Road Traffic Regulation Act 1984, s. 14 (1) (a)*. Made: 08.08.94. Coming into force: 20.08.94. Effect: None. – *Unpublished*

The A23 Trunk Road (Brighton Road, Croydon) (Temporary Restriction of Traffic) Order 1994 No.2875. Enabling power: *Road Traffic Regulation Act 1984, s. 14 (1) (4) (5) (7)*. Made: 07.11.94. Coming into force: 14.11.94. Effect: None. – *Unpublished*

The A23 Trunk Road (Lombard Roundabout, Croydon) (Temporary Restriction of Traffic) Order 1994 No. 2285. Enabling power: *Road Traffic Regulation Act 1984, s. 14 (1) (4)*. Made: 26.08.94. Coming into force: 02.09.94. Effect: None. – *Unpublished*

The A23 Trunk Road (London Road, Croydon) (Temporary Restriction of Traffic) (No. 2) Order 1994 No. 2823. Enabling power: *Road Traffic Regulation Act 1984, s. 14 (1) (4)*. Made: 31.10.94. Coming into force: 05.11.94. Effect: None. – *Unpublished*

The A23 Trunk Road (London Road, Croydon) (Temporary Restriction of Traffic) Order 1994 No.274. Enabling power: *Road Traffic Regulation Act 1984, s. 14 (1) (4)*. Made: 07.02.94. Coming into force: 14.02.94. Effect: None. – *Unpublished*

The A23 Trunk Road (Muddleswood to Patcham) (Temporary 50 Miles Per Hour Speed Restriction) Order 1994 No. 1026. Enabling power: *Road Traffic Regulation Act 1984, s. 14 (1) (a)*. Made: 05.04.94. Coming into force: 09.04.94. Effect: None. – *Unpublished*

The A23 Trunk Road (Orchard Way Service Road) (Temporary Prohibition of Traffic) Order 1994 No. 2751. Enabling power: *Road Traffic Regulation Act 1984, s. 14 (1) (b)*. Made: 24.10.94. Coming into force: 01.11.94. Effect: None. – *Unpublished*

The A23 Trunk Road (Purley Way, Croydon) (Temporary Restriction of Traffic) Order 1994 No.2874. Enabling power: *Road Traffic Regulation Act 1984, s. 14 (1) (4)*. Made: 07.11.94. Coming into force: 14.11.94. Effect: None. – *Unpublished*

The A23 Trunk Road (Streatham High Road, Lambeth) (Temporary Restriction of Traffic) (No. 2) Order 1994 No. 2669. Enabling power: *Road Traffic Regulation Act 1984, s. 14 (1) (4)*. Made: 10.10.94. Coming into force: 17.10.94. Effect: None. – *Unpublished*

The A23 Trunk Road (Streatham High Road, Lambeth) (Temporary Restriction of Traffic) Order 1994 No. 1866. Enabling power: *Road Traffic Regulation Act 1984, s. 14 (1) (4) (5) (7)*. Made: 11.07.94. Coming into force: 17.07.94. Effect: None. – *Unpublished*

The A23 Trunk Road (Streatham Hill, Lambeth) (Temporary Restriction of Traffic) Order 1994 No. 2130. Enabling power: *Road Traffic Regulation Act 1984, s. 14 (1) (4)*. Made: 08.08.94. Coming into force: 15.08.94. Effect: None. – *Unpublished*

The A23 Trunk Road (Thornton Road, Croydon) (Temporary Restriction of Traffic) Order 1994 No.1590. Enabling power: *Road Traffic Regulation Act 1984, s. 14 (1) (a) (4)*. Made: 06.06.94. Coming into force: 13.06.94. Effect: None. – *Unpublished*

The A27 Trunk Road (Arundel to Fishbourne Roundabout) (24 Hours Clearway) Order 1994 No.389. Enabling power: *Road Traffic Regulation Act 1984, ss. 1 (1), 2 (1), (2), 4 (1)*. Made: 21.02.94. Coming into force: 21.03.94. Effect: None. – *Unpublished*

The A27 Trunk Road (Beddingham Level Crossing) (Temporary Prohibition of Traffic) (No. 2) Order 1994 No. 1456. Enabling power: *Road Traffic Regulation Act 1984, s. 14 (1) (a) (5) (b) (7)*. Made: 31.05.94. Coming into force: 04.06.94. Effect: None. – *Unpublished*

The A27 Trunk Road (Beddingham Level Crossing) (Temporary Prohibition of Traffic) Order 1994 No. 209. Enabling power: *Road Traffic Regulation Act 1984, s. 14 (1) (a) (5) (b) (7)*. Made: 31.01.94. Coming into force: 05.02.94. Effect: None. – *Unpublished*

The A27 Trunk Road (Beddingham Level Crossing) (Temporary Prohibition of Traffic) (No. 3) Order 1994 No. 2211. Enabling power: *Road Traffic Regulation Act 1984, s. 14 (1) (4) (5) (b) (7)*. Made: 22.08.94. Coming into force: 27.08.94. Effect: None. – *Unpublished*

The A27 Trunk Road (Beddingham Level Crossing) (Temporary Prohibition of Traffic) (No. 4) Order 1994 No. 3111. Enabling power: *Road Traffic Regulation Act 1984, s. 14 (1) (a) (5) (b) (7)*. Made: 05.12.94. Coming into force: 10.12.94. Effect: None. – *Unpublished*

The A27 Trunk Road (Chichester Bypass) (Temporary Restriction of Traffic) Order 1994 No.2962. Enabling power: *Road Traffic Regulation Act 1984, s. 14 (1) (a)*. Made: 21.11.94. Coming into force: 26.11.94. Effect: None. – *Unpublished*

The A27 Trunk Road (Falmer to Ashcombe Roundabout) (Temporary Restriction and Prohibition of Traffic) Order 1994 No. 973. Enabling power: *Road Traffic Regulation Act 1984, s. 14 (1) (a)*. Made: 28.03.94. Coming into force: 02.03.94. Effect: None. – *Unpublished*

The A27 Trunk Road (Langstone Roundabout) Westbound Exit Slip Road (Temporary Prohibition of Traffic) Order 1994 No. 2348. Enabling power: *Road Traffic Regulation Act 1984, s. 14 (1) (a)*. Made: 05.09.94. Coming into force: 10.09.94. Effect: None. – *Unpublished*

The A27 Trunk Road (Patching) (Temporary Restriction of Traffic) Order 1994 No. 976. Enabling power: *Road Traffic Regulation Act 1984, s. 14 (1) (a)*. Made: 28.03.94. Coming into force: 02.03.94. Effect: None. – *Unpublished*

The A27 Trunk Road (Patching) (Temporary Restriction of Traffic) (No. 2) Order 1994 No.1453. Enabling power: *Road Traffic Regulation Act 1984, s. 14 (1) (a)*. Made: 31.05.94. Coming into force: 04.06.94. Effect: S.I. 1994/976 revoked. – *Unpublished*

The A27 Trunk Road (Tangmere Roundabout to Fontwell Roundabout) (Prohibition of Use of Central Reservation) Order 1994 No. 2702. Enabling power: *Road Traffic Regulation Act 1984, ss. 1 (1), 2 (1) (2)*. Made: 17.10.94. Coming into force: 07.11.94. Effect: None. – *Unpublished*

The A27 Trunk Road (Tangmere to Fontwell) (Temporary 50 Miles Per Hour Speed Restriction) Order 1994 No. 2970. Enabling power: *Road Traffic Regulation Act 1984, s. 14 (1) (a)*. Made: 21.11.94. Coming into force: 26.11.94. Effect: None. – *Unpublished*

The A27 Trunk Road (Wade Court Bridge) (Temporary Restriction and Prohibition of Traffic) Order 1994 No. 121. Enabling power: *Road Traffic Regulation Act 1984, s. 14 (1) (a)*. Made: 24.01.94. Coming into force: 29.01.94. Effect: None. – *Unpublished*

The A30 Trunk Road and the M25 Motorway (Staines) (Temporary Restriction and Prohibition of Traffic) Order 1993 Amendment Order 1993 No. 733. Enabling power: *Road Traffic Regulation Act 1984 s. 14 (1) (a)*. Made: 10.03.94. Coming into force: 11.03.94. Effect: S.I. 1993/2426 amended. – *Unpublished*

The A30 Trunk Road (Blackhorse Lane) (Temporary 40 Miles Per Hour Speed Restriction) Order 1994 No. 3114. Enabling power: *Road Traffic Regulation Act 1984, s. 14 (1) (a)*. Made: 17.11.94. Coming into force: 21.11.94. Effect: None. – *Unpublished*

The A30 Trunk Road (Great South West Road, Hounslow) (Temporary Restriction of Traffic) Order 1994 No. 2468. Enabling power: *Road Traffic Regulation Act 1984, s. 14 (1) (4)*. Made: 19.09.94. Coming into force: 28.09.94. Effect: None. – *Unpublished*

The A30 Trunk Road (Indian Queens/Fraddon) (Temporary Restriction of Traffic) Order 1994 No.2739. Enabling power: *Road Traffic Regulation Act 1984, s. 14 (1) (a)*. Made: 19.10.94. Coming into force: 24.10.94. Effect: None. – *Unpublished*

The A30 Trunk Road (Little Silver to Shillingford Road) (Temporary Restriction of Traffic) Order 1994 No. 2772. Enabling power: *Road Traffic Regulation Act 1984, s. 14 (1) (a)*. Made: 21.10.94. Coming into force: 25.10.94. Effect: None. – *Unpublished*

The A30 Trunk Road (Shallowater Hill) (Temporary Restriction of Traffic) Order 1994 No.21. Enabling power: *Road Traffic Regulation Act 1984, s. 14 (1) (a)*. Made: 05.01.94. Coming into force: 07.01.94. Effect: S.I. 1993/2785 revoked. – *Unpublished*

The A31 Trunk Road (Ashley Heath Roundabout - Woolsbridge Roundabout) (Temporary Prohibition of Traffic) Order 1994 No. 207. Enabling power: *Road Traffic Regulation Act 1984, s. 14 (1) (a)*. Made: 27.01.94. Coming into force: 29.01.94. Effect: None. – *Unpublished*

The A31 Trunk Road (Ashley Heath Roundabout - Woolsbridge Roundabout) (Temporary Restriction and Prohibition of Traffic) (No 2) Order 1994 No. 1225. Enabling power: *Road Traffic Regulation Act 1984, s. 14 (1) (a)*. Made: 28.04.94. Coming into force: 30.04.94. Effect: None. – *Unpublished*

The A31 Trunk Road (Bere Regis - World's End) (Temporary Restriction and Prohibition of Traffic) Order 1994 No. 2728. Enabling power: *Road Traffic Regulation Act 1984, s. 14 (1) (a)*. Made: 17.10.94. Coming into force: 19.10.94. Effect: None. – *Unpublished*

The A31 Trunk Road (Roundhouse Roundabout-Winterborne Zelston) (Temporary 40 Miles Per Hour Speed Restriction) Order 1994 No. 293. Enabling power: *Road Traffic Regulation Act 1984, s. 14 (1) (4)*. Made: 03.02.94. Coming into force: 05.02.94. Effect: None. – *Unpublished*

The A31 Trunk Road (Verwood Road Junction) Eastbound Exit Slip Road (Temporary Prohibition of Traffic) Order 1994 No. 1160. Enabling power: *Road Traffic Regulation Act 1984, s. 14 (1) (a)*. Made: 14.04.94. Coming into force: 16.04.94. Effect: None. – *Unpublished*

The A33 Trunk Road (Compton) (Temporary Prohibition of Traffic) Order 1994 No. 13. Enabling power: *Road Traffic Regulation Act 1984, s. 14 (1) (a)*. Made: 04.01.94. Coming into force: 08.01.94. Effect: None. – *Unpublished*

The A33 Trunk Road (Hockley Traffic Lights) (Temporary Restriction of Traffic) Order 1994 No.1790. Enabling power: *Road Traffic Regulation Act 1984, s. 14 (1) (a)*. Made: 04.07.94. Coming into force: 09.07.94. Effect: None. – *Unpublished*

The A33 Trunk Road (Poles Lane Bridge to Shepherds Lane Bridge) (Temporary Restriction of Traffic) Order 1994 No. 2571. Enabling power: *Road Traffic Regulation Act 1984, s. 14 (1) (a)*. Made: 03.10.94. Coming into force: 10.10.94. Effect: None. – *Unpublished*

The A33 Trunk Road (Shawford Slip Roads) (Temporary Restriction of Traffic) Order 1994 No.387. Enabling power: *Road Traffic Regulation Act 1984, s. 14 (1) (a)*. Made: 21.02.94. Coming into force: 26.02.94. Effect: None. – *Unpublished*

The A34 Trunk Road (Abingdon Bypass) (Temporary Prohibition and Restriction of Traffic) Order 1994 No. 2123. Enabling power: *Road Traffic Regulation Act 1984, s. 14 (1) (a)*. Made: 08.08.94. Coming into force: 13.08.94. Effect: None. – *Unpublished*

The A34 Trunk Road (Aston-By-Stone) (Temporary Restriction of Traffic) Order 1994 No.1956. Enabling power: *Road Traffic Regulation Act 1984, s. 14 (1) (a)*. Made: 15.07.94. Coming into force: 16.07.94. Effect: None. – *Unpublished*

The A34 Trunk Road (Beedon to East Ilsley) (Temporary Restriction and Prohibition of Traffic) Order 1994 No. 1278. Enabling power: *Road Traffic Regulation Act 1984, s. 14 (1) (a)*. Made: 09.05.94. Coming into force: 14.05.94. Effect: None. – *Unpublished*

The A34 Trunk Road (Burghclere) (Temporary Restriction and Prohibition of Traffic) Order 1994 No. 2213. Enabling power: *Road Traffic Regulation Act 1984, s. 14 (1) (a)*. Made: 22.08.94. Coming into force: 27.08.94. Effect: None. – *Unpublished*

The A34 Trunk Road (Chieveley) (Temporary Restriction of Traffic) Order 1994 No. 1595. Enabling power: *Road Traffic Regulation Act 1984, s. 14 (1) (a)*. Made: 13.06.94. Coming into force: 18.06.94. Effect: None. – *Unpublished*

The A34 Trunk Road (Chieveley to Donnington) (Temporary Prohibition of Traffic) Order 1994 No. 738. Enabling power: *Road Traffic Regulation Act 1984 s. 14 (1) (a)*. Made: 07.03.94. Coming into force: 12.03.94. Effect: None. – *Unpublished*

The A34 Trunk Road (Marker Posts 3.05 - 6.45) (Temporary Restriction and Prohibition of Traffic) Order 1994 No. 442. Enabling power: *Road Traffic Regulation Act 1984, s. 14 (1) (a)*. Made: 24.02.94. Coming into force: 25.02.94. Effect: None. – *Unpublished*

The A34 Trunk Road (Marker Posts 13.30 - 18.80) (Temporary Restriction of Traffic) Order 1994 No. 93. Enabling power: *Road Traffic Regulation Act 1984, s. 14 (1) (a)*. Made: 17.01.94. Coming into force: 22.01.94. Effect: None. – *Unpublished*

The A34 Trunk Road (Walsall Road) (Temporary Restriction of Traffic) Order 1994 No.1800. Enabling power: *Road Traffic Regulation Act 1984, s. 14 (1) (a)*. Made: 01.07.94. Coming into force: 02.07.94. Effect: None. – *Unpublished*

The A36 Trunk Road (Alderbury Bypass) (Temporary Restriction and Prohibition of Traffic) Order 1994 No. 1460. Enabling power: *Road Traffic Regulation Act 1984, s. 14 (1) (a)*. Made: 24.05.94. Coming into force: 27.05.94. Effect: None. – *Unpublished*

The A36 Trunk Road (Landford) (Temporary 40 Miles Per Hour Speed Restriction) Order 1994 No.291. Enabling power: *Road Traffic Regulation Act 1984, s. 14 (1) (a)*. Made: 08.02.94. Coming into force: 11.02.94. Effect: None. – *Unpublished*

The A36 Trunk Road (Ower Link) (24 Hours Clearway) Order 1994 No. 2750. Enabling power: *Road Traffic Regulation Act 1984, ss. 1 (1), 2 (1) (2), 4 (1).* Made: 24.10.94. Coming into force: 01.11.94. Effect: None. – *Unpublished*

The A36 Trunk Road (Plaitford to West Wellow) (Temporary 10 Miles Per Hour Speed Restriction) Order 1994 No. 1599. Enabling power: *Road Traffic Regulation Act 1984, s. 14 (1) (a).* Made: 13.06.94. Coming into force: 18.06.94. Effect: None. – *Unpublished*

The A36 Trunk Road (Wylye Bypass, Wiltshire) (Temporary 50 Miles Per Hour Speed Restriction) Order 1994 No. 243. Enabling power: *Road Traffic Regulation Act 1984, s. 14 (1).* Made: 02.02.94. Coming into force: 05.02.94. Effect: None. – *Unpublished*

The A38 Trunk Road (Abbey Hill, Derbyshire) (Temporary 50 Miles Per Hour Speed Restriction) Order 1994 No. 19. Enabling power: *Road Traffic Regulation Act 1984, s. 14 (1) (a).* Made: 05.01.94. Coming into force: 08.01.94. Effect: None. – *Unpublished*

The A38 Trunk Road (Alfreton and South Normanton Bypass, Derbyshire) (Temporary Prohibition of Traffic) Order 1994 No. 1579. Enabling power: *Road Traffic Regulation Act 1984, s. 14 (1) (a).* Made: 27.05.94. Coming into force: 10.06.94. Effect: None. – *Unpublished*

The A38 Trunk Road (Alfreton, Ripley, Derbyshire) (Temporary Prohibition of Traffic) Order 1994 No. 45. Enabling power: *Road Traffic Regulation Act 1984, s. 14 (1) (a).* Made: 05.01.94. Coming into force: 13.01.94. Effect: None. – *Unpublished*

The A38 Trunk Road and Connecting Roads (Kingsway, Derby, Derbyshire) (Temporary Prohibition and Restriction of Traffic) Order 1994 No. 2480. Enabling power: *Road Traffic Regulation Act 1984, s. 14 (1) (a).* Made: 16.09.94. Coming into force: 27.09.94. Effect: None. – *Unpublished*

The A38 Trunk Road (Barton Turn to Branston Interchange) (Temporary Restriction of Traffic) Order 1994 No. 1132. Enabling power: *Road Traffic Regulation Act 1984, s. 14 (1) (a).* Made: 05.04.94. Coming into force: 06.04.94. Effect: None. – *Unpublished*

The A38 Trunk Road (Birchwood Lane Bridge, Near Alfreton, Derbyshire) (Temporary Prohibition and Restriction of Traffic) Order 1994 No. 2779. Enabling power: *Road Traffic Regulation Act 1984, s. 14 (1) (a).* Made: 24.10.94. Coming into force: 31.10.94. Effect: None. – *Unpublished*

The A38 Trunk Road (Claymills Junction Bridge) (Temporary 30 Miles Per Hour Speed Restriction) Order 1994 No. 335. Enabling power: *Road Traffic Regulation Act 1984, s. 14 (1) (a).* Made: 04.02.94. Coming into force: 05.02.94. Effect: None. – *Unpublished*

The A38 Trunk Road (Exeter - Plymouth Slip Roads, Devonshire) (Temporary Prohibition of Traffic) Order 1994 No. 3320. Enabling power: *Road Traffic Regulation Act 1984, s. 14 (1) (a).* Made: 21.12.94. Coming into force: 29.12.94. Effect: None. – *Unpublished*

The A38 Trunk Road (Exeter to Plymouth) (Temporary Restriction of Traffic) Order 1994 No.3321. Enabling power: *Road Traffic Regulation Act 1984, s. 14 (1) (a).* Made: 21.12.94. Coming into force: 29.12.94. Effect: None. – *Unpublished*

The A38 Trunk Road (Fernhill Heath Railway Bridge) (Temporary Restriction of Traffic) Order 1994 No. 1545. Enabling power: *Road Traffic Regulation Act 1984, s. 14 (1) (b).* Made: 02.06.94. Coming into force: 03.06.94. Effect: None. – *Unpublished*

The A38 Trunk Road (Forder Valley - March Mills Link Road) (Temporary Prohibition of Traffic) Order 1994 No. 455. Enabling power: *Road Traffic Regulation Act 1984, s. 14 (1) (a).* Made: 23.02.94. Coming into force: 25.02.94. Effect: None. – *Unpublished*

The A38 Trunk Road (Haldon Hill) (Temporary Restriction and Prohibition of Traffic) Order 1994 No. 2180. Enabling power: *Road Traffic Regulation Act 1984, s. 14 (1) (a).* Made: 03.08.94. Coming into force: 08.08.94. Effect: None. – *Unpublished*

The A38 Trunk Road (Little Eaton Bypass, Derbyshire) (Temporary Prohibition and Restriction of Traffic) Order 1994 No. 1066. Enabling power: *Road Traffic Regulation Act 1984, s. 14 (1) (a).* Made: 07.04.94. Coming into force: 09.04.94. Effect: None. – *Unpublished*

The A38 Trunk Road (Monks Bridge, Derbyshire) (Temporary Prohibition of Traffic) Order 1994 No. 457. Enabling power: *Road Traffic Regulation Act 1984, s. 14 (1) (a).* Made: 22.02.94. Coming into force: 26.02.94. Effect: None. – *Unpublished*

The A38 Trunk Road (Nix's Hill Bridge, Near Alfreton, Derbyshire) (Temporary Prohibition and Restriction of Traffic) Order 1994 No. 3145. Enabling power: *Road Traffic Regulation Act 1984, s. 14 (1) (a).* Made: 23.12.94. Coming into force: 05.01.95. Effect: None. – *Unpublished*

The A38 Trunk Road (Trerulefoot Roundabout S. Hellier to Heskyn Junction S. Hellier) (Temporary Prohibition of Traffic) Order 1994 No. 2391. Enabling power: *Road Traffic Regulation Act 1984, s. 14 (1) (a).* Made: 30.06.94. Coming into force: 04.07.94. Effect: None. – *Unpublished*

The A38 Trunk Road (Trethawle - Tinkers Lake) (Temporary Prohibition of Traffic) Order 1994 No. 616. Enabling power: *Road Traffic Regulation Act 1984, s. 14 (1) (a).* Made: 03.03.94. Coming into force: 05.03.94. Effect: None. – *Unpublished*

132 ROAD TRAFFIC: TRAFFIC REGULATION

The A38 Trunk Road (Voss Farm Bridge) (Temporary Prohibition of Traffic) Order 1994 No.2598. Enabling power: *Road Traffic Regulation Act 1984, s. 14 (1) (a) (b)*. Made: 09.09.94. Coming into force: 16.09.94. Effect: None. – *Unpublished*

The A38 Trunk Road (Wrangaton to Lower Dean) (Temporary Restriction and Prohibition of Traffic) Order 1994 No. 2641. Enabling power: *Road Traffic Regulation Act 1984, s. 14 (1) (a)*. Made: 30.09.94. Coming into force: 03.10.94. Effect: None. – *Unpublished*

The A39 Trunk Road (Camelford) (Temporary Prohibition of Traffic) (No. 2) Order 1994 No.302. Enabling power: *Road Traffic Regulation Act 1984, s. 14 (1) (a)*. Made: 09.02.94. Coming into force: 11.02.94. Effect: None. – *Unpublished*

The A39 Trunk Road (Fore Street, Camelford) (Temporary Prohibition of Traffic) Order 1994 No.1846. Enabling power: *Road Traffic Regulation Act 1984, s. 14 (1) (a)*. Made: 13.04.94. Coming into force: 15.04.94. Effect: None. – *Unpublished*

The A39 Trunk Road (Old River Camel Bridge, Wadebridge) (Temporary Prohibition of Traffic) Order 1994 No. 294. Enabling power: *Road Traffic Regulation Act 1984, s. 14 (1) (a)*. Made: 02.02.94. Coming into force: 04.02.94. Effect: None. – *Unpublished*

The A39 Trunk Road (Wadebridge) (Various Restrictions) Order 1994 No. 967. Enabling power: *Road Traffic Regulation Act 1984, ss. 1 (1), 2 (1) (2) (4) & sch. 9, pt. IV*. Made: 09.03.94. Coming into force: 11.03.94. Effect: None. – *Unpublished*

The A40 and A483 Trunk Roads (Various Roads, Llandeilo, Dyfed) (Prohibition and Restriction of Waiting) Order 1994 No. 2807. Enabling power: *Road Traffic Regulation Act 1984, ss. 1 (1), 2 (1) (2), 4 (2), 124*. Made: 20.10.94. Coming into force: 31.10.94. Effect: S.I. 1989/891 revoked. – *Unpublished*

The A40 Trunk Road (Churchdown Footbridge) (Temporary Prohibition of Traffic) Order 1994 No.2911. Enabling power: *Road Traffic Regulation Act 1984, s. 14 (1) (a)*. Made: 14.11.94. Coming into force: 21.11.94. Effect: None. – *Unpublished*

The A40 Trunk Road (Denham Interchange, Buckinghamshire) (Temporary Prohibition of Traffic) Order 1994 No. 1027. Enabling power: *Road Traffic Regulation Act 1984, s. 14 (1) (a)*. Made: 05.04.94. Coming into force: 09.04.94. Effect: None. – *Unpublished*

The A40 Trunk Road (Dowdeswell Reservoir) (Temporary 40 Miles Per Hour Speed Restriction) Order 1994 No. 1045. Enabling power: *Road Traffic Regulation Act 1984, s. 14 (1) (a)*. Made: 09.03.94. Coming into force: 11.03.94. Effect: None. – *Unpublished*

The A40 Trunk Road (Forest Hill) (Prohibition of Use of Gaps in the Central Reservation) Order 1994 No. 2863. Enabling power: *Road Traffic Regulation Act 1984, ss. 1 (1), 2 (1) (2)*. Made: 07.11.94. Coming into force: 12.11.94. Effect: None. – *Unpublished*

The A40 Trunk Road (Glangrwyney Bridge, Powys) (Temporary Prohibition of Vehicles) Order 1994 No. 2356. Enabling power: *Road Traffic Regulation Act 1984, s. 14 (1) (4)*. Made: 07.10.94. Coming into force: 09.10.94. Effect: None. – *Unpublished*

The A40 Trunk Road (Glangrwyney Village, Powys) (Temporary Prohibition of Vehicles) Order 1994 No. 1040. Enabling power: *Road Traffic Regulation Act 1984, s. 14 (1)*. Made: 25.03.94. Coming into force: 27.03.94. Effect: None. – *Unpublished*

The A40 Trunk Road (Hanger Lane Underpass, Ealing) (Temporary Prohibition of Traffic) (No. 2) Order 1994 No. 1959. Enabling power: *Road Traffic Regulation Act 1984, s. 14 (1) (4)*. Made: 18.07.94. Coming into force: 25.07.94. Effect: None. – *Unpublished*

The A40 Trunk Road (Hanger Lane Underpass, Ealing) (Temporary Prohibition of Traffic) Order 1994 No. 1358. Enabling power: *Road Traffic Regulation Act 1984, s. 14 (1) (4)*. Made: 16.05.94. Coming into force: 23.05.94. Effect: None. – *Unpublished*

The A40 Trunk Road (New Manor Farm, Oxford Northern Bypass) (Closure of a Gap in the Central Reservation) Order 1994 No. 2273. Enabling power: *Road Traffic Regulation Act 1984, ss. 1 (1), 2 (1) (2)*. Made: 30.08.94. Coming into force: 19.09.94. Effect: None. – *Unpublished*

The A40 Trunk Road (Old Bath Road, Cheltenham) (Temporary Prohibition of Traffic) Order 1994 No. 1122. Enabling power: *Road Traffic Regulation Act 1984, s. 14 (1) (a) (7)*. Made: 30.03.94. Coming into force: 01.04.94. Effect: None. – *Unpublished*

The A40 Trunk Road (Raglan-Abergavenny, Gwent) (Temporary Prohibition of Vehicles and 50 MPH Speed Limit) Order 1994 No. 2135. Enabling power: *Road Traffic Regulation Act 1984, s. 14 (1)*. Made: 05.08.94. Coming into force: 08.08.94. Effect: None. – *Unpublished*

The A40 Trunk Road (Raglan Junction, Gwent) (Temporary 30 MPH Speed Limit) Order 1994 No.2125. Enabling power: *Road Traffic Regulation Act 1984, s. 14 (1) (4)*. Made: 29.07.94. Coming into force: 01.08.94. Effect: None. – *Unpublished*

The A40 Trunk Road (Shipton Hill) (Temporary Restriction of Traffic) Order 1994 No.618. Enabling power: *Road Traffic Regulation Act 1984, s. 14 (1) (a)*. Made: 03.03.94. Coming into force: 05.03.94. Effect: None. – *Unpublished*

The A40 Trunk Road (Suffolk Road) (Temporary Prohibition of Traffic) Order 1994 No.2427. Enabling power: *Road Traffic Regulation Act 1984, s. 14 (1) (a)*. Made: 31.08.94. Coming into force: 03.09.94. Effect: None. – *Unpublished*

The A40 Trunk Road (Westal Green, Cheltenham) (Temporary Restriction of Traffic) Order 1994 No. 2393. Enabling power: *Road Traffic Regulation Act 1984, s. 14 (1) (a)*. Made: 01.09.94. Coming into force: 03.09.94. Effect: None. – *Unpublished*

The A40 Trunk Road (Western Avenue, Ealing) (Temporary Prohibition of Traffic) Order 1994 No.2202. Enabling power: *Road Traffic Regulation Act 1984, s. 14 (1) (4)*. Made: 15.08.94. Coming into force: 22.08.94. Effect: None. – *Unpublished*

The A40 Trunk Road (Western Avenue, Hillingdon) (Temporary Prohibition of Traffic) Order 1994 No. 917. Enabling power: *Road Traffic Regulation Act 1984, s. 14 (1) (4) (7)*. Made: 21.03.94. Coming into force: 28.03.94. Effect: None. – *Unpublished*

The A40 Trunk Road (Western Avenue, Hillingdon) (Temporary Prohibition of Traffic) (No. 2) Order 1994 No. 2466. Enabling power: *Road Traffic Regulation Act 1984, s. 14 (1) (4) (7)*. Made: 19.09.94. Coming into force: 24.09.94. Effect: None. – *Unpublished*

The A40 Trunk Road (Western Avenue, Hillingdon) (Temporary Prohibition of Traffic) Order 1994 No. 1629. Enabling power: *Road Traffic Regulation Act 1984, s. 14 (1) (4)*. Made: 17.06.94. Coming into force: 24.06.94. Effect: None. – *Unpublished*

The A40 Trunk Road (Whitchurch to Ross-on-Wye) (Prohibition of Vehicles Over 7.5 Tonnes in Pencraig Layby) Order 1994 No. 1658. Enabling power: *Road Traffic Regulation Act 1984, ss. 1 (1), 2 (1) (2), 4 (1)*. Made: 26.05.94. Coming into force: 01.06.94. Effect: None. – *Unpublished*

The A40 Trunk Road (Witney Bypass) (Temporary Restriction and Prohibition of Traffic) Order 1994 No. 2637. Enabling power: *Road Traffic Regulation Act 1984, s. 14 (1) (a)*. Made: 10.10.94. Coming into force: 15.10.94. Effect: None. – *Unpublished*

The A40/A449 Trunk Road (Coldra-Monmouth, Gwent) (Temporary Traffic Restrictions) Order 1994 No. 9. Enabling power: *Road Traffic Regulations Act 1984, s. 14 (1)*. Made: 22.12.93. Coming into force: 04.01.94. Effect: None. – *Unpublished*

The A40(M) and A501 Trunk Roads (Westway and Marylebone Flyover) (Temporary Prohibition of Traffic) (No. 2) Order 1994 No. 2384. Enabling power: *Road Traffic Regulation Act 1984, s. 14 (1) (4) (5) (7)*. Made: 05.09.94. Coming into force: 11.09.94. Effect: None. – *Unpublished*

The A40(M) and A501 Trunk Roads (Westway and Marylebone Flyover) (Temporary Prohibition of Traffic) Order 1994 No. 1630. Enabling power: *Road Traffic Regulation Act 1984, s. 14 (1) (4) (5) (7)*. Made: 20.06.94. Coming into force: 26.06.94. Effect: None. – *Unpublished*

The A41 Trunk Road (A41 Ring Road) (Temporary Restriction and Prohibition of Traffic) Order 1994 No. 2539. Enabling power: *Road Traffic Regulation Act 1984, s. 14 (1) (a)*. Made: 09.09.94. Coming into force: 11.09.94. Effect: None. – *Unpublished*

The A41 Trunk Road (Aylesbury, Buckinghamshire) (24 Hours Clearway) Order 1994 No.2840. Enabling power: *Road Traffic Regulation Act 1984, ss. 1 (1), 2 (1) (2), 4 (1)*. Made: 01.11.94. Coming into force: 07.11.94. Effect: None. – *Unpublished*

The A41 Trunk Road (Berkhamstead Bypass) (Eastbound On-Slip Road) (Temporary Prohibition of Traffic) Order 1994 No. 127. Enabling power: *Road Traffic Regulation Act 1984, s. 14 (1) (a)*. Made: 24.01.94. Coming into force: 26.01.94. Effect: None. – *Unpublished*

The A41 Trunk Road (Brent Cross Flyover, Barnet) (Temporary Prohibition of Traffic) Order 1994 No. 2131. Enabling power: *Road Traffic Regulation Act 1984, s. 14 (1) (4) (5) (7)*. Made: 08.08.94. Coming into force: 15.08.94. Effect: None. – *Unpublished*

The A41 Trunk Road (Finchley Road, Westminster) (Temporary Restriction of Traffic) Order 1994 No. 1961. Enabling power: *Road Traffic Regulation Act 1984, s. 14 (1) (4)*. Made: 18.07.94. Coming into force: 25.07.94. Effect: None. – *Unpublished*

The A41 Trunk Road (Kings Langley and Berkhamsted Bypasses) (Temporary Prohibition of Traffic) Order 1994 No. 2171. Enabling power: *Road Traffic Regulation Act 1984, s. 14 (1) (a)*. Made: 22.07.94. Coming into force: 22.07.94. Effect: None. – *Unpublished*

The A41 Trunk Road (Kings Langley/Berkhamsted/Tring Bypass, Hertfordshire) (Temporary Prohibition of Traffic) Order 1994 No. 368. Enabling power: *Road Traffic Regulation Act 1984, s. 14 (1) (a)*. Made: 18.02.94. Coming into force: 26.02.94. Effect: None. – *Unpublished*

The A41 Trunk Road (Kings Langley - Tring, Hertfordshire) (Slip Roads) (Temporary Prohibition of Traffic) Order 1994 No. 2833. Enabling power: *Road Traffic Regulation Act 1984, s. 14 (1) (a)*. Made: 31.10.94. Coming into force: 07.11.94. Effect: None. – *Unpublished*

The A41 Trunk Road (New Ferry/Rock Ferry Bypass) Wirral (Temporary Restriction and Prohibition of Traffic) Order 1994 No. 1143. Enabling power: *Road Traffic Regulation Act 1984, s. 14 (1) (a)*. Made: 25.03.94. Coming into force: 27.03.94. Effect: None. – *Unpublished*

The A41 Trunk Road (South of Prees Island) (Temporary 30 Miles per Hour Speed Restriction) Order 1994 No. 1548. Enabling power: *Road Traffic Regulation Act 1984, s. 14 (1) (a)* Made: 13.05.94. Coming into force: 14.05.94. Effect: None. – *Unpublished*

The A41 Trunk Road (Various Roads, Aylesbury) (Prohibition and Restriction of Waiting) Order 1994 No. 2831. Enabling power: *Road Traffic Regulation Act 1984, ss. 1 (1), 2 (1) (2), 3 (2), 4 (2).* Made: 01.11.94. Coming into force: 07.11.94. Effect: S.I. 1978/249 amended & s.I. 1977/726; 1979/1162 revoked. – *Unpublished*

The A41 Trunk Road (Whitchurch Road) Chowley, Cheshire (Temporary 30 MPH Speed Restriction) Order 1994 No. 824. Enabling power: *Road Traffic Regulation Act 1984, s. 14 (1) (a).* Made: 06.01.94. Coming into force: 09.01.94. Effect: None. – *Unpublished*

The A41 Trunk Road (Whitchurch Road) Christleton (Temporary 10 Miles Per Hour Speed Restriction) Order 1994 No. 2302. Enabling power: *Road Traffic Regulation Act 1984, s. 14 (1) (a).* Made: 23.08.94. Coming into force: 09.09.94. Effect: None. – *Unpublished*

The A41 Trunk Road (Whitchurch Road, Hampton Heath, Cheshire) (Temporary Prohibition and Restriction of Traffic) Order 1994 No. 390. Enabling power: *Road Traffic Regulation Act 1984, s. 14 (1) (a).* Made: 17.01.94. Coming into force: 23.01.94. Effect: None. – *Unpublished*

The A41/A49 Trunk Roads (Whitchurch Bypass) (Clearway) Order 1993 No. 155. Enabling power: *Road Traffic Regulation Act 1984, ss. 1 (1), 2 (1) (2), 4 (1).* Made: 17.11.93. Coming into force: 17.12.93. Effect: None. – *Unpublished*

The A43 Trunk Road (Blisworth and Milton Malsor Bypass) (24 Hour Clearway) Order 1994 No. 1351. Enabling power: *Road Traffic Regulation Act 1984, ss. 1 (1), 2 (1) (2), 3 (2), 4 (1).* Made: 06.05.94. Coming into force: 20.05.94. Effect: S.I. 1968/1709 revoked. – *Unpublished*

The A43 Trunk Road (Blisworth and Milton Malsor Bypass) (One-Way Traffic) Order 1994 No. 1349. Enabling power: *Road Traffic Regulation Act 1984, ss. 1 (1), 2 (1) (2).* Made: 06.05.94. Coming into force: 20.05.94. Effect: None. – *Unpublished*

The A43 Trunk Road (Stamford Road, Northamptonshire) (Temporary Restriction of Traffic) Order 1994 No. 315. Enabling power: *Road Traffic Regulation Act 1984, s. 14 (1) (a).* Made: 11.02.94. Coming into force: 19.02.94. Effect: None. – *Unpublished*

The A43 Trunk Road (Stamford Road, Northamptonshire) (Temporary Restriction of Traffic) Order 1994 Amendment Order 1994 No. 1031. Enabling power: *Road Traffic Regulation Act 1984, s. 14 (1) (a).* Made: 23.03.94. Coming into force: 25.03.94. Effect: None. – *Unpublished*

The A45 Trunk Road (Birmingham Road) (Temporary 40 Miles per Hour Speed Restriction) Order 1994 No. 100. Enabling power: *Road Traffic Regulation Act 1984, s. 14 (1) (a).* Made: 14.01.94. Coming into force: 15.01.94. Effect: None. – *Unpublished*

The A45 Trunk Road (Cambridge Northern Bypass, Cambridgeshire) (Temporary Prohibition and Restriction of Traffic) Order 1994 No. 374. Enabling power: *Road Traffic Regulation Act 1984, s. 14 (1) (a).* Made: 18.02.94. Coming into force: 25.02.94. Effect: None. – *Unpublished*

The A45 Trunk Road (Caxton - Eltisley, Cambridgeshire) (Temporary Prohibition of Traffic) Order 1994 No. 1783. Enabling power: *Road Traffic Regulation Act 1984, s. 14 (1) (a).* Made: 04.07.94. Coming into force: 11.07.94. Effect: None. – *Unpublished*

The A45 Trunk Road (Coventry Road Stonebridge) (Temporary 40 Miles Per Hour Speed Restriction) Order 1994 No. 966. Enabling power: *Road Traffic Regulation Act 1984, s. 14 (1) (a).* Made: 23.03.94. Coming into force: 24.03.94. Effect: None. – *Unpublished*

The A45 Trunk Road (Coventry) Temporary Restriction of Traffic) Order 1994 No. 847. Enabling power: *Road Traffic Regulation Act 1984, s. 14 (1) (a).* Made: 11.03.94. Coming into force: 12.03.94. Effect: None. – *Unpublished*

The A45 Trunk Road (Fishponds Way, Suffolk) (Temporary Restriction of Traffic) Order 1994 No. 1417. Enabling power: *Road Traffic Regulation Act 1984, s. 14 (1) (a).* Made: 23.05.94. Coming into force: 31.05.94. Effect: None. – *Unpublished*

The A45 Trunk Road (Ipswich Western Bypass, Ipswich, Suffolk) (Temporary Restriction of Traffic) Order 1994 No. 942. Enabling power: *Road Traffic Regulation Act 1984, s. 14 (1) (a).* Made: 04.03.94. Coming into force: 09.03.94. Effect: None. – *Unpublished*

The A45 Trunk Road (London Road, Stretton-on-Dunsmore) (Prohibition of Use of Gap in the Central Reservation) Order 1994 No. 3239. Enabling power: *Road Traffic Regulation Act 1984, ss. 1 (1), 2 (1) (2).* Made: 08.12.94. Coming into force: 12.12.94. Effect: None. – *Unpublished*

The A45 Trunk Road (Orwell Bridge, Ipswich Southern Bypass, Ipswich, Suffolk) (Temporary Restriction of Traffic) Order 1994 No. 140. Enabling power: *Road Traffic Regulation Act 1984, ss. 14 (1) (a).* Made: 20.01.94. Coming into force: 02.02.94. Effect: None. – *Unpublished*

The A45 Trunk Road (Orwell Bridge, Ipswich Southern Bypass, Ipswich, Suffolk) (Temporary Restriction of Traffic) Order 1994 No. 1218. Enabling power: *Road Traffic Regulation Act 1984, s. 14 (1) (a).* Made: 11.04.94. Coming into force: 14.04.94. Effect: None. – *Unpublished*

The A45 Trunk Road (Packington Junction) (Temporary 40 Miles Per Hour Speed Restriction) Order 1994 No. 1723. Enabling power: *Road Traffic Regulation Act 1984, s. 14 (1) (a).* Made: 02.06.94. Coming into force: 05.06.94. Effect: None. – *Unpublished*

The A45 Trunk Road (Risby, Suffolk) (Temporary Prohibition and Restriction of Traffic) Order 1994 No. 320. Enabling power: *Road Traffic Regulation Act 1984, s. 14 (1) (a)*. Made: 14.02.94. Coming into force: 21.02.94. Effect: None. – *Unpublished*

The A45 Trunk Road (Stonebridge Highway) (Temporary 40 Miles Per Hour Speed Restriction) Order 1994 No. 2470. Enabling power: *Road Traffic Regulation Act 1984, s. 14 (1) (a)*. Made: 16.09.94. Coming into force: 17.09.94. Effect: None. – *Unpublished*

The A45 Trunk Road (Stonebridge Improvement) (Temporary Restriction of Traffic) Order 1994 No. 2455. Enabling power: *Road Traffic Regulation Act 1984, s. 14 (1) (a)*. Made: 14.09.94. Coming into force: 15.09.94. Effect: None. – *Unpublished*

The A45 Trunk Road (Stowmarket Bypass) (Temporary Restriction of Traffic) Order 1994 No.2053. Enabling power: *Road Traffic Regulation Act 1984, s. 14 (1) (a)*. Made: 25.07.94. Coming into force: 01.08.94. Effect: None. – *Unpublished*

The A45 Trunk Road (Whitehouse Interchange Slip Roads, Suffolk) (Temporary Prohibition of Traffic) Order 1994 No. 212. Enabling power: *Road Traffic Regulation Act 1984, s. 14 (1) (a)*. Made: 31.01.94. Coming into force: 07.02.94. Effect: None. – *Unpublished*

The A46 Trunk Road (Farndon, Nottinghamshire) (Temporary Restriction of Traffic) Order 1994 No. 113. Enabling power: *Road Traffic Regulation Act 1984, s. 14 (1) (a)*. Made: 20.01.94. Coming into force: 28.01.94. Effect: None. – *Unpublished*

The A46 Trunk Road (Gloucester Road, Tadwick (Temporary Prohibition of Traffic) Order 1994 No. 598. Enabling power: *Road Traffic Regulation Act 1984, s. 14 (1) (a)*. Made: 02.03.94. Coming into force: 04.03.94. Effect: None. – *Unpublished*

The A46 Trunk Road (Near Syston, Leicestershire) (Temporary Prohibition and Restriction of Traffic) Order 1994 No. 1356. Enabling power: *Road Traffic Regulation Act 1984, s. 14 (1) (a)*. Made: 10.05.94. Coming into force: 13.05.94. Effect: S.I. 1993/2081 revoked. – *Unpublished*

The A46 Trunk Road (Saxondale Roundabout, Widmerpool, Nottinghamshire) (Temporary Prohibition of Traffic) Order 1994 No. 459. Enabling power: *Road Traffic Regulation Act 1984, s. 14 (1) (a)*. Made: 24.02.94. Coming into force: 03.03.94. Effect: None. – *Unpublished*

The A46 Trunk Road (Swainswick, Avon) (Temporary 40 Miles Per Hour Speed Restriction) Order 1994 No. 1547. Enabling power: *Road Traffic Regulation Act 1984, s. 14 (1) (a)*. Made: 08.06.94. Coming into force: 10.06.94. Effect: None. – *Unpublished*

The A46 Trunk Road (Swainswick, Avon) (Temporary Box Junction) Order 1994 No. 2000. Enabling power: *Road Traffic Regulation Act 1984, s. 14 (1) (a)*. Made: 25.07.94. Coming into force: 27.07.94. Effect: None. – *Unpublished*

The A46 Trunk Road (Thurmaston Roundabout, Widmerpool Interchange, Leicestershire and Nottinghamshire) (Temporary Prohibition of Traffic) Order 1994 No. 2147. Enabling power: *Road Traffic Regulation Act 1984, s. 14 (1) (a)*. Made: 06.08.94. Coming into force: 09.08.94. Effect: None. – *Unpublished*

The A46 Trunk Road (Warwick Bypass) (Temporary Restriction of Traffic) Order 1994 No.1955. Enabling power: *Road Traffic Regulation Act 1984, s. 14 (1) (a)*. Made: 14.07.94. Coming into force: 15.07.94. Effect: None. – *Unpublished*

The A46 Trunk Road (Widmerpool Interchange, Nottinghamshire) (Temporary Prohibition and Restriction of Traffic) Order 1994 No. 1591. Enabling power: *Road Traffic Regulation Act 1984, ss. 3 (2), 14 (1) (a) (5) (b) (6)*. Made: 09.06.94. Coming into force: 18.06.94. Effect: None. – *Unpublished*

The A47 Trunk Road (A47/A1122 Junction, Swaffham) (Temporary 40 Miles Per Hour Speed Restriction) Order 1994 No. 2208. Enabling power: *Road Traffic Regulation Act 1984, s. 14 (1) (a)*. Made: 29.07.94. Coming into force: 05.08.94. Effect: None. – *Unpublished*

The A47 Trunk Road (Birmingham to Great Yarmouth) (Soke Parkway, Peterborough, Cambridgeshire) (Temporary Restriction and Prohibition of Traffic) Order 1994 No. 38. Enabling power: *Road Traffic Regulation Act 1984, ss. 14 (1) (a)*. Made: 17.01.94. Coming into force: 20.01.94. Effect: None. – *Unpublished*

The A47 Trunk Road (C258 Church Road, Great Plumstead) (Prohibition of Use of Gap in Central Reservation) Order 1994 No. 411. Enabling power: *Road Traffic Regulation Act 1984, s. 14 (1) (a)*. Made: 11.02.94. Coming into force: 28.02.94. Effect: None. – *Unpublished*

The A47 Trunk Road (East Norton Bypass, Harborough, Leicestershire) (Temporary Prohibition of Traffic) Order 1994 No. 2608. Enabling power: *Road Traffic Regulation Act 1984, s. 14 (1) (a)*. Made: 03.10.94. Coming into force: 08.10.94. Effect: None. – *Unpublished*

The A47 Trunk Road (Great Plumstead) (Temporary 30 Miles Per Hour Speed Restriction) Order 1994 No. 419. Enabling power: *Road Traffic Regulation Act 1984, s. 14 (1) (a)*. Made: 21.02.94. Coming into force: 25.02.94. Effect: None. – *Unpublished*

The A47 Trunk Road, (Hockering, Norfolk) (Temporary Restriction of Traffic) Order 1994 No.1362. Enabling power: *Road Traffic Regulation Act 1984, s. 14 (1) (a)*. Made: 16.05.94. Coming into force: 22.05.94. Effect: None. – *Unpublished*

The A47 Trunk Road (Nab Lane Subway, Peterborough) (Temporary Restriction and Prohibition of Traffic) Order 1994 No. 2730. Enabling power: *Road Traffic Regulation Act 1984, s. 14 (1) (a)*. Made: 17.10.94. Coming into force: 21.10.94. Effect: None. – *Unpublished*

The A47 Trunk Road, (Necton, Norfolk) (Temporary 40 Miles Per Hour Speed Restriction) Order 1994 No. 1283. Enabling power: *Road Traffic Regulation Act 1984, s. 14 (1) (a)*. Made: 09.05.94. Coming into force: 16.05.94. Effect: None. – *Unpublished*

The A47 Trunk Road (Norwich Road, West Bilney, Norfolk) (Temporary 40 Miles Per Hour Speed Restriction) Order 1994 No. 2385. Enabling power: *Road Traffic Regulation Act 1984, s. 14 (1) (a)*. Made: 05.09.94. Coming into force: 12.09.94. Effect: None. – *Unpublished*

The A47 Trunk Road (Soke Parkway, Peterborough, Cambridgeshire) (Slip Roads) (Temporary Prohibition of Traffic) Order 1994 No. 2051. Enabling power: *Road Traffic Regulation Act 1984, s. 14 (1) (a)*. Made: 01.08.94. Coming into force: 08.08.94. Effect: None. – *Unpublished*

The A47 Trunk Road (Soke Parkway, Peterborough, Cambridgeshire) (Temporary Prohibition and Restriction of Traffic) Order 1994 No. 272. Enabling power: *Road Traffic Regulation Act 1984, s. 14 (1) (a)*. Made: 07.02.94. Coming into force: 14.02.94. Effect: None. – *Unpublished*

The A47 Trunk Road (Southorpe and Thornaugh, Cambridgeshire) (Temporary Prohibition of Traffic) Order 1994 No. 213. Enabling power: *Road Traffic Regulation Act 1984, s. 14 (1) (a)*. Made: 31.01.94. Coming into force: 07.02.94. Effect: None. – *Unpublished*

The A47 Trunk Road (Swaffham Bypass, Swaffham, Norfolk) (Temporary Prohibition of Traffic) Order 1994 No. 511. Enabling power: *Road Traffic Regulation Act 1984, s. 14 (1) (a)*. Made: 21.02.94. Coming into force: 23.02.94. Effect: None. – *Unpublished*

The A47 Trunk Road (The Causeway, Eye, Cambridgeshire) (Temporary 30 Miles Per Hour Speed Restriction) Order 1994 No. 271. Enabling power: *Road Traffic Regulation Act 1984, s. 14 (1) (a)*. Made: 07.02.94. Coming into force: 14.02.94. Effect: None. – *Unpublished*

The A47 Trunk Road (Thorney, Cambridgeshire) (Prohibition and Restriction of Waiting) Order 1994 No. 2819. Enabling power: *Road Traffic Regulation Act 1984, ss. 1 (1), 2 (1) (2), 3 (2), 4 (1) (2)*. Made: 27.10.94. Coming into force: 03.11.94. Effect: None. – *Unpublished*

The A47 Trunk Road (Walpole Highway and Tilney High End) (Temporary 30 Miles Per Hour and 40 Miles Per Hour Speed Restriction) Order 1994 No. 1220. Enabling power: *Road Traffic Regulation Act 1984, ss. 14 (1) (a), 15 (2) (a)*. Made: 28.04.94. Coming into force: 02.05.94. Effect: None. – *Unpublished*

The A47 Trunk Road (Walpole Highway and Tilney High End) (Temporary 30 Miles Per Hour and 40 Miles Per Hour Speed Restriction) Order 1994 Amendment Order 1994 No. 2382. Enabling power: *Road Traffic Regulation Act 1984, ss. 14 (1) (a), 15 (2) (a)*. Made: 26.08.94. Coming into force: 29.08.94. Effect: None. – *Unpublished*

The A47 Trunk Road (West Bilney to East Winch, Norfolk) (Temporary 40 Miles Per Hour Speed Restriction) Order 1994 No. 815. Enabling power: *Road Traffic Regulation Act 1984, s. 14 (1) (a)*. Made: 14.03.94. Coming into force: 20.03.94. Effect: None. – *Unpublished*

The A47 Trunk Road (Western Bypass, Great Yarmouth) (Temporary Prohibition of Traffic) Order 1994 No. 887. Enabling power: *Road Traffic Regulation Act 1984, s. 14 (1) (a) (7)*. Made: 14.03.94. Coming into force: 18.03.94. Effect: None. – *Unpublished*

The A48 Trunk Road (Blakeney and Newnham) (Temporary Prohibition of Traffic) Order 1994 No. 908. Enabling power: *Road Traffic Regulation Act 1984, s. 14 (1) (a)*. Made: 23.02.94. Coming into force: 25.02.94. Effect: None. – *Unpublished*

The A48 Trunk Road (Briton Ferry Roundabout - Earlswood Roundabout, West Glamorgan) (Temporary Prohibition of Vehicles) Order 1994 No. 1604. Enabling power: *Road Traffic Regulation Act 1984, s. 14 (1)*. Made: 03.06.94. Coming into force: 04.06.94. Effect: None. – *Unpublished*

The A49 Trunk Road (Tarporley Road) Cuddington (Temporary 10 Miles Per Hour Speed Restriction) Order 1994 No. 2316. Enabling power: *Road Traffic Regulation Act 1984, s. 14 (1) (a)*. Made: 23.08.94. Coming into force: 09.09.94. Effect: None. – *Unpublished*

The A49 Trunk Road (Warrington Road) Acton Bridge to Dones Green, Cheshire (Temporary Prohibition of Traffic) Order 1994 No. 817. Enabling power: *Road Traffic Regulation Act 1984, s. 14 (1) (a)*. Made: 28.01.94. Coming into force: 31.01.94. Effect: None. – *Unpublished*

The A49 Trunk Road (Whitchurch Road) at Spurstow, Cheshire (Temporary 10 Miles Per Hour Speed Restriction) Order 1994 No. 379. Enabling power: *Road Traffic Regulation Act 1984, s. 14 (1) (a)*. Made: 04.02.94. Coming into force: 06.02.94. Effect: None. – *Unpublished*

The A50 Trunk Road (Doveridge, Derbyshire) (Temporary Prohibition and Restriction of Traffic) Order 1994 No. 2146. Enabling power: *Road Traffic Regulation Act 1984, s. 14 (1) (a)*. Made: 08.08.94. Coming into force: 13.08.94. Effect: None. – *Unpublished*

The A50 Trunk Road (Sudbury Bypass, Derbyshire) (Temporary Prohibition and Restriction of Traffic) Order 1994 No. 2882. Enabling power: *Road Traffic Regulation Act 1984, s. 14 (1) (a)*. Made: 08.11.94. Coming into force: 13.11.94. Effect: None. – *Unpublished*

The A51 and A55 Trunk Roads (Roundabout Junction) Littleton (Temporary 10 Miles Per Hour Speed Restriction) Order 1994 No. 2323. Enabling power: *Road Traffic Regulation Act 1984, s. 14 (1) (a)*. Made: 23.08.94. Coming into force: 10.09.94. Effect: None. – *Unpublished*

The A51 Trunk Road (Chester Road, Hurleston) (Temporary 30 Miles Per Hour Speed Restriction) Order 1994 No. 2756. Enabling power: *Road Traffic Regulation Act 1984, s. 14 (1) (a)*. Made: 21.09.94. Coming into force: 22.09.94. Effect: None. – *Unpublished*

The A51 Trunk Road (Chester Road) Nantwich (Temporary Prohibition of Traffic) Order 1994 No.2720. Enabling power: *Road Traffic Regulation Act 1984, s. 14 (1) (a)*. Made: 10.10.94. Coming into force: 11.10.94. Effect: None. – *Unpublished*

The A51 Trunk Road (Nantwich Road) (Temporary 30 Miles Per Hour Speed Restriction) Order 1994 No. 2856. Enabling power: *Road Traffic Regulation Act 1984, s. 14 (1) (a)*. Made: 13.10.94. Coming into force: 06.11.94. Effect: None. – *Unpublished*

The A52 Trunk Road (Birdsgrove Lane to Stanton Lane) (Temporary 10 Miles Per Hour and 40 Miles Per Hour Speed Restriction) Order 1994 No. 2471. Enabling power: *Road Traffic Regulation Act 1984, s. 14 (1) (a)*. Made: 16.09.94. Coming into force: 17.09.94. Effect: None. – *Unpublished*

The A52 Trunk Road (Clifton Boulevard, Nottingham, Nottinghamshire) (Temporary Restriction of Traffic) Order 1994 No. 2538. Enabling power: *Road Traffic Regulation Act 1984, s. 14 (1) (a)*. Made: 23.09.94. Coming into force: 29.09.94. Effect: None. – *Unpublished*

The A52 Trunk Road (Elton, Nottinghamshire) (Temporary Speed Restriction) Order 1994 No.347. Enabling power: *Road Traffic Regulation Act 1984, s. 14 (1) (a)*. Made: 16.02.94. Coming into force: 21.02.94. Effect: None. – *Unpublished*

The A52 Trunk Road (Radcliffe on Trent, Nottinghamshire) (Prohibition of Use of Gap in Central Reservation) Order 1994 No. 1215. Enabling power: *Road Traffic Regulation Act 1984, ss. 1 (1), 2 (1) (2)*. Made: 22.04.94. Coming into force: 06.05.94. Effect: None. – *Unpublished*

The A52 Trunk Road (Spondon, Derbyshire) (Temporary Prohibition of Traffic) Order 1994 No.303. Enabling power: *Road Traffic Regulation Act 1984, s. 14 (1) (a)*. Made: 09.02.94. Coming into force: 12.02.94. Effect: None. – *Unpublished*

The A52, A453 and the A60 Trunk Roads (Nottingham Knight Roundabout, Dunkirk Roundabout, Nottinghamshire) (Temporary Prohibition and Restriction of Traffic) Order 1994 No. 2606. Enabling power: *Road Traffic Regulation Act 1984, ss. 3 (2), 14 (1) (a) (5) (b) (6)*. Made: 28.09.94. Coming into force: 08.10.94. Effect: None. – *Unpublished*

The A55 and A494 Trunk Roads (Ewloe, Clwyd) (Prohibition of Cyclists) Order 1994 No.2808. Enabling power: *Road Traffic Regulation Act 1984, ss. 1 (1), 2 (1) (2)*. Made: 25.10.94. Coming into force: 07.11.94. Effect: None. – *Unpublished*

The A55 Chester - Bangor Trunk Road (Holywell - Glan Conwy, Clwyd and Gwynedd) (Temporary 40 MPH Speed Limit) Order 1994 No. 1305. Enabling power: *Road Traffic Regulation Act 1984, s. 14 (1) (7)*. Made: 10.05.94. Coming into force: 10.05.94. Effect: None. – *Unpublished*

The A55 Trunk Road (Abergwyngregyn, Gwynedd) (Clearway) Order 1994 No. 3127. Enabling power: *Road Traffic Regulation Act 1984, ss. 1 (1), 2 (1) (2)*. Made: 01.12.94. Coming into force: 05.12.94. Effect: None. – *Unpublished*

The A55 Trunk Road (Abergwyngregyn, Gwynedd) (Closure of Central Reservation Crossing) Order 1994 No. 1973. Enabling power: *Road Traffic Regulation Act 1984, ss. 1 (1), 2 (1)*. Made: 03.10.94. Coming into force: 10.10.94. Effect: None. – *Unpublished*

The A55 Trunk Road (Abergwyngregyn, Gwynedd) (One Way Traffic) Order 1994 No. 3090. Enabling power: *Road Traffic Regulation Act 1984, ss. 1 (1), 2 (1) (2)*. Made: 31.10.94. Coming into force: 07.11.94. Effect: None. – *Unpublished*

The A55 Trunk Road (Brookside Junction, Northop Hall, Clwyd) (Temporary 50 MPH Speed Limit) Order 1994 No. 220. Enabling power: *Road Traffic Regulation Act 1984, s. 14 (1)*. Made: 28.01.94. Coming into force: 31.01.94. Effect: None. – *Unpublished*

The A55 Trunk Road (Burntwood, Clwyd) (Temporary Prohibition of Vehicles) Order 1994 No.10. Enabling power: *Road Traffic Regulations Act 1984, s. 14 (1)*. Made: 22.12.93. Coming into force: 14.01.94. Effect: None. – *Unpublished*

The A55 Trunk Road (Bus Stop and Turning Lay-bys, Abergwyngregyn, Gwynedd) (Traffic Restrictions) Order 1994 No. 3299. Enabling power: *Road Traffic Regulation Act 1984, ss. 1 (1), 2 (1) (2)*. Made: 14.12.94. Coming into force: 23.12.94. Effect: None. – *Unpublished*

The A55 Trunk Road (Chester Southerly Bypass) Cheshire/Clwyd Boundary (Temporary Prohibition and Restriction of Traffic) Order 1994 No. 872. Enabling power: *Road Traffic Regulation Act 1984, s. 14 (1) (a)*. Made: 02.03.94. Coming into force: 04.03.94. Effect: None. – *Unpublished*

The A55 Trunk Road (Conwy Crossing Tunnel, Gwynedd) (Temporary Prohibition of Vehicles) Order 1994 No. 190. Enabling power: *Road Traffic Regulation Act 1984, s. 14 (1) (7)*. Made: 24.01.94. Coming into force: 24.01.94. Effect: None. – *Unpublished*

Price/availability are liable to change without notice

The A55 Trunk Road (Eastbound Carriageway, Penmaenbach Headland, Gwynedd) (Temporary Prohibition of Vehicles) Order 1994 No. 705. Enabling power: *Road Traffic Regulation Act 1984, ss. 14 (1) (7)*. Made: 28.02.94. Coming into force: 28.02.94. Effect: None. – *Unpublished*

The A55 Trunk Road (Eastbound Carriageway, Pen-Y-Clip Section, Gwynedd) (Prohibition of Pedestrians) Order 1994 No. 378. Enabling power: *Road Traffic Regulation Act 1984, ss. 1 (1), 2 (1) (3)*. Made: 17.02.94. Coming into force: 28.02.94. Effect: None. – *Unpublished*

The A55 Trunk Road (Llanfairfechan, Gwynedd) (Temporary Closure of Central Reservation Crossing) Order 1994 No. 2548. Enabling power: *Road Traffic Regulation Act 1984, s. 14 (1) (4) (7)*. Made: 26.09.94. Coming into force: 26.09.94. Effect: None. – *Unpublished*

The A55 Trunk Road (Nant-y-Faenol Lane, St. Asaph, Clwyd) (Prohibition of Left-Hand Turn) Order 1994 No. 1971. Enabling power: *Road Traffic Regulation Act 1984, ss. 1 (1), 2 (1) (2)*. Made: 04.07.94. Coming into force: 18.07.94. Effect: None. – *Unpublished*

The A55 Trunk Road (Northop, Clwyd) (Temporary Prohibition of Vehicles) Order 1994 No.3329. Enabling power: *Road Traffic Regulation Act 1984, s. 14 (1) (4)*. Made: 30.12.94. Coming into force: 08.01.95. Effect: None. – *Unpublished*

The A55 Trunk Road (Old Telford Road, Pen-y-Clip Section, Gwynedd) (Prohibition of Motor Vehicles and Pedestrians) Order 1994 No. 191. Enabling power: *Road Traffic Regulation Act 1984, ss. 1 (1), 2 (1) (3)*. Made: 20.01.94. Coming into force: 14.02.94. Effect: None. – *Unpublished*

The A55 Trunk Road (Penmaenbach, Gwynedd) (Temporary Traffic Restrictions) Order 1994 No.2477. Enabling power: *Road Traffic Regulation Act 1984, s. 14 (1) (4) (7)*. Made: 16.09.94. Coming into force: 27.09.94. Effect: None. – *Unpublished*

The A55 Trunk Road (Penmaenbach Tunnel, Gwynedd) (Closure of Central Reservation Crossings) Order 1994 No. 3088. Enabling power: *Road Traffic Regulation Act 1984, ss. 1 (1), 2 (1) (2), 124, sch. 9, para. 27*. Made: 02.11.94. Coming into force: 14.12.94. Effect: S.I. 1989/53 revoked. – *Unpublished*

The A55 Trunk Road (Penmaenbach Tunnel, Gwynedd) (Temporary Prohibition of U-Turns) Order 1994 No. 2512. Enabling power: *Road Traffic Regulation Act 1984, s. 14 (1) (4)*. Made: 19.09.94. Coming into force: 26.09.94. Effect: None. – *Unpublished*

The A55 Trunk Road (Penmaenbach Tunnel, Gwynedd) (Temporary Traffic Restrictions) Order 1994 No. 39. Enabling power: *Road Traffic Regulation Act 1984, s. 14 (1) (7)*. Made: 05.01.94. Coming into force: 10.01.94. Effect: None. – *Unpublished*

The A55 Trunk Road (Penmaenbach Tunnel, Gwynedd) (Temporary Traffic Restrictions) Variation Order 1994 No. 1833. Enabling power: *Road Traffic Regulation Act 1984, s. 14 (1), 124, sch. 9, para. 27*. Made: 25.05.94. Coming into force: 30.05.94. Effect: S.I. 1994/39 amended. – *Unpublished*

The A55 Trunk Road (Penmaenmawr West Junction, Pen-Y-Clip Tunnel, Gwynedd) (Temporary Prohibition of Vehicles) Order 1994 No. 2829. Enabling power: *Road Traffic Regulation Act 1984, s. 14 (1) (4)* Made: 28.10.94. Coming into force: 01.11.94. Effect: None. – *Unpublished*

The A55 Trunk Road (Pen-y-Clip, Gwynedd) (Temporary Traffic Restrictions) Order 1994 No.3089. Enabling power: *Road Traffic Regulation Act 1984, s. 14 (1) (4) (7)*. Made: 02.11.94. Coming into force: 02.11.94. Effect: None. – *Unpublished*

The A55 Trunk Road (Pen-y-Clip Section, Gwynedd) (One-Way Traffic) Order 1994 No.192. Enabling power: *Road Traffic Regulation Act 1984, ss. 1 (1), 2 (1) (2)*. Made: 24.01.94. Coming into force: 14.02.94. Effect: None. – *Unpublished*

The A55 Trunk Road (Pen-Y-Clip Tunnel, Gwynedd) (Temporary Traffic Restrictions) Order 1994 No. 448. Enabling power: *Road Traffic Regulation Act 1984, ss. 14 (1) (7)*. Made: 18.02.94. Coming into force: 21.02.94. Effect: None. – *Unpublished*

The A55 Trunk Road (Rhuallt, Clwyd) (Temporary 50 MPH Speed Limit) Order 1994 No.793. Enabling power: *Road Traffic Regulation Act 1984 s. 14 (1)*. Made: 11.03.94. Coming into force: 14.03.94. Effect: None. – *Unpublished*

The A56 Trunk Road (Haslingden Bypass) Rossendale (Temporary Prohibition of Traffic) Order 1994 No.2721. Enabling power: *Road Traffic Regulation Act 1984, s. 14 (1) (a)*. Made: 05.10.94. Coming into force: 16.10.94. Effect: None. – *Unpublished*

The A57 Trunk Road (Manchester Rd., Denton) (Box Junction) Order 1994 No. 3027. Enabling power: *Road Traffic Regulation Act 1984, ss. 1 (1), 2 (1) (2), 4 (1)*. Made: 07.07.94. Coming into force: 08.08.94. Effect: None. – *Unpublished*

The A57 Trunk Road (Newton On Trent Bypass, Lincolnshire) (De-Restriction) Order 1994 No.1214. Enabling power: *Road Traffic Regulation Act 1984, ss. 82 (2), 83 (1)*. Made: 25.04.94. Coming into force: 09.06.94. Effect: None. – *Unpublished*

The A57 Trunk Road (Retford Road Bridge) (Temporary Restriction of Traffic) Order 1994 No.2309. Enabling power: *Road Traffic Regulation Act 1984, s. 14 (1) (a)*. Made: 31.08.94. Coming into force: 02.09.94. Effect: None. – *Unpublished*

The A59 Trunk Road (Liverpool Road) Aughton (24 Clearway) Order 1994 No. 3028. Enabling power: *Road Traffic Regulation Act 1984, ss. 1(1), 2(1)(2), 3(2), 4(1).* Made: 17.08.94. Coming into force: 29.09.94. Effect: None. *– Unpublished*

The A59 Trunk Road (Liverpool Road, Penwortham) (Prohibition of Waiting) Order 1994 No.2301. Enabling power: *Road Traffic Regulation Act 1984, ss. 1(1), 2(1)(2), 3(2), 4(1).* Made: 14.06.94. Coming into force: 08.07.94. Effect: None. *– Unpublished*

The A59 Trunk Road (Liverpool Road, Penwortham) (Temporary Prohibition of 'U'Turns) Order 1994 No. 2645. Enabling power: *Road Traffic Regulation Act 1984, s. 14 (1).* Made: 30.09.94. Coming into force: 30.09.94. Effect: None. *– Unpublished*

The A59 Trunk Road (Longsight Road/Whalley Clitheroe Bypass) Northcote Road to Bramley Meade Roundabout (Temporary Prohibition of Traffic) Order 1994 No. 2857. Enabling power: *Road Traffic Regulation Act 1984, s. 14(1)(a).* Made: 14.10.94. Coming into force: 16.10.94. Effect: None. *– Unpublished*

The A59 Trunk Road (Longton Bypass) (Closure of Gaps in Central Reservation) Order 1994 No.1129. Enabling power: *Road Traffic Regulation Act 1984, ss. 1(1), 2(1)(2).* Made: 14.01.94. Coming into force: 28.01.94. Effect: None. *– Unpublished*

The A59 Trunk Road (Longton Bypass, South Ribble) (Temporary Restriction of Traffic) Order 1994 No. 1148. Enabling power: *Road Traffic Regulation Act 1984, s. 14(1)(a).* Made: 15.04.94. Coming into force: 17.04.94. Effect: None. *– Unpublished*

The A59 Trunk Road (Northway) at Sefton (Temporary 20 Miles Per Hour Speed Restriction) Order 1993 No. 376. Enabling power: *Road Traffic Regulation Act 1984, s. 14(1)(a).* Made: 24.11.93. Coming into force: 28.11.93. Effect: None. *– Unpublished*

The A59 Trunk Road (Northway, Aughton) (Temporary 60 MPH Speed Restriction) Order 1994 No.2928. Enabling power: *Road Traffic Regulation Act 1984, s. 14(1)(b).* Made: 08.11.94. Coming into force: 11.11.94. Effect: None. *– Unpublished*

The A59 Trunk Road (Northway) Aughton, West Lancashire (Temporary Restriction of Traffic) Order 1994 No. 597. Enabling power: *Road Traffic Regulation Act 1984, s. 14(1)(a).* Made: 24.02.94. Coming into force: 27.02.94. Effect: None. *– Unpublished*

The A59 Trunk Road (Preston New Road, Service Road) (Prohibition of Waiting and One-way Traffic) Order 1994 No. 2941. Enabling power: *Road Traffic Regulation Act 1984, ss. 1(1), 2(1)(2), 3(2), 4(1).* Made: 01.08.94. Coming into force: 31.08.94. Effect: None. *– Unpublished*

The A59 Trunk Road (Skipton Bypass - Low Lodge) (Temporary Restriction and Prohibition of Traffic) Order 1994 No. 2672. Enabling power: *Road Traffic Regulation Act 1984, s. 14(1)(a).* Made: 13.10.94. Coming into force: 15.10.94. Effect: None. *– Unpublished*

The A61 Trunk Road (Alfreton Hill, Alfreton, Derbyshire) Temporary Prohibition and Restriction of Traffic) Order 1994 No. 843. Enabling power: *Road Traffic Regulation Act 1984, s. 14(1)(a).* Made: 15.03.94. Coming into force: 19.03.94. Effect: None. *– Unpublished*

The A61 Trunk Road and Slip Roads (Chesterfield, Derbyshire) (Temporary Prohibition and Restriction of Traffic) Order 1994 No. 2607. Enabling power: *Road Traffic Regulation Act 1984, s. 14(1)(a).* Made: 29.09.94. Coming into force: 30.09.94. Effect: None. *– Unpublished*

The A61 Trunk Road (Dronfield Bypass, Derbyshire) (Temporary Restriction of Traffic) Order 1994 No. 364. Enabling power: *Road Traffic Regulation Act 1984, s. 14(1)(a).* Made: 18.02.94. Coming into force: 26.02.94. Effect: None. *– Unpublished*

The A63 Trunk Road (Barrowby Road) (Temporary Prohibition of Use of Gap in Central Reservation) Order 1994 No. 1247. Enabling power: *Road Traffic Regulation Act 1984, s. 14(1)(a).* Made: 29.04.94. Coming into force: 30.04.94. Effect: None. *– Unpublished*

The A63 Trunk Road (Long's Corner Roundabout - Barnhill Junction, Howden) (Temporary Prohibition of Traffic) Order 1994 No. 408. Enabling power: *Road Traffic Regulation Act 1984, s. 14(1)(a).* Made: 04.02.94. Coming into force: 07.02.94. Effect: None. *– Unpublished*

The A63 Trunk Road (Mount Pleasant Roundabout - Great Union Street Roundabout) (Temporary Prohibition of Traffic) Order 1994 No. 2780. Enabling power: *Road Traffic Regulation Act 1984, s. 14(1)(a).* Made: 26.10.94. Coming into force: 28.10.94. Effect: None. *– Unpublished*

The A63 Trunk Road (Mytongate Roundabout, Hull) (Temporary Prohibition of Traffic) Order 1994 No. 416. Enabling power: *Road Traffic Regulation Act 1984, s. 14(1)(a).* Made: 11.02.94. Coming into force: 28.02.94. Effect: None. *– Unpublished*

The A63 Trunk Road (Mytongate Roundabout, Hull) (Temporary Prohibition of Traffic) (No.2) Order 1994 No. 1939. Enabling power: *Road Traffic Regulation Act 1984, s. 14(1)(a).* Made: 21.06.94. Coming into force: 25.06.94. Effect: None. *– Unpublished*

The A63 Trunk Road (Mytongate Roundabout - Market Place, Hull) (Temporary Prohibition of Traffic) Order 1994 No. 2264. Enabling power: *Road Traffic Regulation Act 1984, s. 14(1)(a)(5)(b).* Made: 25.08.94. Coming into force: 29.08.94. Effect: None. *– Unpublished*

Price/availability are liable to change without notice

The A63 Trunk Road (Osgodby Railway Bridge) (Temporary 40 Miles Per Hour Speed Restriction) Order 1994 No. 2837. Enabling power: *Road Traffic Regulation Act 1984, s. 14 (1) (a)*. Made: 28.10.94. Coming into force: 30.10.94. Effect: None. – *Unpublished*

The A63 Trunk Road (School Lane and Austhorpe Grove Junction) (Temporary Restriction of Gap in Central Reservation) Order 1993 No. 244. Enabling power: *Road Traffic Regulation Act 1984, s. 14 (1) (a)*. Made: 01.12.93. Coming into force: 31.12.93. Effect: None. – *Unpublished*

The A63 Trunk Road (Selby Road, Colton) (Temporary Restriction of Traffic and Prohibition of Use of Gap in Central Reservation) Order 1994 No. 1940. Enabling power: *Road Traffic Regulation Act 1984, s. 14 (1) (a)*. Made: 21.06.94. Coming into force: 23.06.94. Effect: None. – *Unpublished*

The A63 Trunk Road (Selby Road, Leeds) (School Lane and Bullerthorpe Lane Junctions) (Prohibition of Use of Gaps in Central Reservation) Order 1994 No. 2497. Enabling power: *Road Traffic Regulation Act 1984, ss. 1 (1), 2 (1) (2)*. Made: 15.09.94. Coming into force: 19.09.94. Effect: None. – *Unpublished*

The A63 Trunk Road (Thorpe Willoughby Railway Crossing) (Temporary Prohibition of Traffic) Order 1994 No. 1714. Enabling power: *Road Traffic Regulation Act 1984, s. 14 (1) (a)*. Made: 27.06.94. Coming into force: 30.06.94. Effect: None. – *Unpublished*

The A64 Trunk Road (Copmanthorpe - Fulford Interchange) (Temporary Restriction and Prohibition of Traffic) Order 1994 No. 2394. Enabling power: *Road Traffic Regulation Act 1984, s. 14 (1) (a)*. Made: 01.09.94. Coming into force: 03.09.94. Effect: None. – *Unpublished*

The A64 Trunk Road (Grimston Bar Interchange - Fulford) (Temporary Restriction and Prohibition of Traffic) Order 1994 No. 78. Enabling power: *Road Traffic Regulation Act 1984, ss. 14 (1) (a)*. Made: 14.01.94. Coming into force: 16.01.94. Effect: None. – *Unpublished*

The A64 Trunk Road (Grimston Bar Interchange, Westbound Entry Slip Road) (Temporary Prohibition of Traffic) Order 1994 No. 880. Enabling power: *Road Traffic Regulation Act 1984, s. 14 (1) (a)*. Made: 11.03.94. Coming into force: 12.03.94. Effect: None. – *Unpublished*

The A64 Trunk Road (Marrs Farm to Scagglesthorpe Junction) (Temporary Prohibition of "U" Turns) Order 1994 No. 1112. Enabling power: *Road Traffic Regulation Act 1984, s. 14 (1) (a)*. Made: 15.04.94. Coming into force: 17.04.94. Effect: None. – *Unpublished*

The A64 Trunk Road (Potter Brompton Layby, Western End) (Prohibition of Entry) Order 1994 No. 1801. Enabling power: *Road Traffic Regulation Act 1984, ss. 1 (1), 2 (1) (2)*. Made: 01.07.94. Coming into force: 11.07.94. Effect: None. – *Unpublished*

The A64 Trunk Road (York Road, Kiddal tdo Bramham) (Temporary 30 Miles Per Hour Speed Restriction) Order 1994 No. 2664. Enabling power: *Road Traffic Regulation Act 1984, s. 14 (1) (a)*. Made: 15.09.94. Coming into force: 18.09.94. Effect: None. – *Unpublished*

The A65 Trunk Road (10 MPH Speed Limit Spital Bridge) (Temporary Restriction of Traffic) Order 1994 No. 1858. Enabling power: *Road Traffic Regulation Act 1984, s. 14 (1) (a)*. Made: 07.04.94. Coming into force: 10.04.94. Effect: None. – *Unpublished*

The A65 Trunk Road (A59 Harrogate Road Roundabout, Skibeden - Ellenber Farm) (Temporary 10 Miles Per Hour and 40 Miles Per Hour Speed Restriction) Order 1994 No. 2454. Enabling power: *Road Traffic Regulation Act 1984, s. 14 (1) (a)*. Made: 15.09.94. Coming into force: 17.09.94. Effect: None. – *Unpublished*

The A65 Trunk Road (Boxtree and Stanley Bridge) (Temporary Prohibition and 10 Miles per Hour and 40 Miles Per Hour Speed Restriction) Order 1994 No. 2423. Enabling power: *Road Traffic Regulation Act 1984, s. 14 (1) (a)*. Made: 01.09.94. Coming into force: 03.09.94. Effect: None. – *Unpublished*

The A65 Trunk Road (Greta Bridge - Bradford House Junction, Ingleton) (Temporary 40 Miles per Hour Speed Restriction) Order 1994 No. 97. Enabling power: *Road Traffic Regulation Act 1984, s. 14 (1) (a)*. Made: 11.01.94. Coming into force: 13.01.94. Effect: None. – *Unpublished*

The A65 Trunk Road (Harden Bridge - Rawlingshaw) (Temporary Restriction and Prohibition of Traffic) Order 1994 No. 355. Enabling power: *Road Traffic Regulation Act 1984, s. 14 (1) (a)*. Made: 04.02.94. Coming into force: 06.02.94. Effect: None. – *Unpublished*

The A65 Trunk Road (Hellifield Railway Bridge) (Temporary Prohibition of Traffic) Order 1994 No. 2671. Enabling power: *Road Traffic Regulation Act 1984, s. 14 (1) (a)*. Made: 13.10.94. Coming into force: 15.10.94. Effect: None. – *Unpublished*

The A65 Trunk Road (Ilkley Road, Burley in Wharfedale) (Temporary 20 Miles Per Hour Speed Restriction) Order 1994 No. 1954. Enabling power: *Road Traffic Regulation Act 1984, s. 14 (1) (a)*. Made: 15.07.94. Coming into force: 16.07.94. Effect: None. – *Unpublished*

The A65 Trunk Road (Skipton Road, Addingham) (Temporary 30 Miles Per Hour Speed Restriction) Order 1994 No. 3074. Enabling power: *Road Traffic Regulation Act 1984, s. 14 (1) (a)*. Made: 01.12.94. Coming into force: 04.12.94. Effect: None. – *Unpublished*

The A65 Trunk Road (Skipton Road, Ilkley) (Temporary 10 Miles Per Hour and 40 Miles Per Hour Speed Restriction) Order 1994 No. 2007. Enabling power: *Road Traffic Regulation Act 1984, s. 14 (1) (a)*. Made: 28.07.94. Coming into force: 30.07.94. Effect: None. – *Unpublished*

The A65 Trunk Road (Skir Beck Farm - Long Preston) (Temporary Restriction and Prohibition of Traffic) Order 1994 No. 2727. Enabling power: *Road Traffic Regulation Act 1984, s. 14 (1) (a)*. Made: 19.10.94. Coming into force: 21.10.94. Effect: None. – *Unpublished*

The A66 Trunk Road (Bowes-Cumbrian County Boundary) (Temporary Restriction of Traffic) Order 1994 No. 1067. Enabling power: *Road Traffic Regulation Act 1984, s. 14 (1)*. Made: 08.04.94. Coming into force: 10.04.94. Effect: None. – *Unpublished*

The A66 Trunk Road (Braithwaite to Woodend Brow) (Temporary Prohibition and Restriction of Traffic) Order 1994 No. 1081. Enabling power: *Road Traffic Regulation Act 1984, s. 14 (1) (a) (5) (b)*. Made: 06.04.94. Coming into force: 08.04.94. Effect: None. – *Unpublished*

The A66 Trunk Road (Brougham Junction to Winderwath Junction) (Temporary Prohibition and 10 Miles per Hour and 40 Miles Per Hour Speed Restriction) Order 1994 No. 2442. Enabling power: *Road Traffic Regulation Act 1984, s. 14 (1) (a)*. Made: 08.09.94. Coming into force: 10.09.94. Effect: None. – *Unpublished*

The A66 Trunk Road (Cockermouth Bypass) (Temporary 30 Miles per Hour Speed Restriction) Order 1994 No. 128. Enabling power: *Road Traffic Regulation Act 1984, s. 14 (1) (a)*. Made: 20.01.94. Coming into force: 29.01.94. Effect: None. – *Unpublished*

The A66 Trunk Road (County of Cumbria) (Lay-Bys Restriction of Waiting) Order 1994 No.3288. Enabling power: *Road Traffic Regulation Act 1984, ss. 1 (1), 2 (1) (2), 4 (1)*. Made: 14.12.94. Coming into force: 16.12.94. Effect: None. – *Unpublished*

The A66 Trunk Road (Culgaith Road Junction) (Temporary 40 Miles Per Hour Speed Restriction) Order 1994 No. 3052. Enabling power: *Road Traffic Regulation Act 1984, s. 14 (1) (a)*. Made: 23.11.94. Coming into force: 27.11.94. Effect: None. – *Unpublished*

The A66 Trunk Road (Elton Interchange) (Temporary Prohibition of Traffic) Order 1994 No.722. Enabling power: *Road Traffic Regulation Act 1984 s. 14 (1) (a)*. Made: 01.03.94. Coming into force: 03.03.94. Effect: None. – *Unpublished*

The A66 Trunk Road (Elton Interchange) (Temporary Prohibition of Traffic) Order 1994 No.2088. Enabling power: *Road Traffic Regulation Act 1984, s. 14 (1) (a)*. Made: 02.08.94. Coming into force: 04.08.94. Effect: None. – *Unpublished*

The A66 Trunk Road (Fitz Cottage to Brigham) (Temporary 40 Miles Per Hour Speed Restriction) Order 1994 No. 1937. Enabling power: *Road Traffic Regulation Act 1984, s. 14 (1) (a)*. Made: 14.07.94. Coming into force: 15.07.94. Effect: None. – *Unpublished*

The A66 Trunk Road (Glendermackin, Troutbeck Climbing Lane) (Temporary Restriction of Traffic) Order 1994 No. 153. Enabling power: *Road Traffic Regulation Act 1984, s. 14 (1) (a)*. Made: 24.01.93. Coming into force: 04.02.94. Effect: None. – *Unpublished*

The A66 Trunk Road (Great Clifton, Naddle Beck and Smithy Green) (Temporary Prohibition and Restriction of Traffic) Order 1994 No. 1849. Enabling power: *Road Traffic Regulation Act 1984, s. 14 (1) (a)*. Made: 06.07.94. Coming into force: 10.07.94. Effect: None. – *Unpublished*

The A66 Trunk Road (Kempley Bank - Countess Pillar) (Temporary Restriction of Traffic) Order 1994 No. 373. Enabling power: *Road Traffic Regulation Act 1984, s. 14 (1) (a)*. Made: 17.02.94. Coming into force: 26.02.94. Effect: None. – *Unpublished*

The A66 Trunk Road (Kempley Bank to Countess Pillar Improvement) (Prohibition of Right Turn) Order 1994 No. 1691. Enabling power: *Road Traffic Regulation Act 1984, ss. 1 (1), 2 (1) (2)*. Made: 23.06.94. Coming into force: 01.07.94. Effect: None. – *Unpublished*

The A66 Trunk Road (Keswick Bypass) (Temporary Prohibition and 40 Miles Per Hour and 10 Miles Per Hour Speed Restrictions) Order 1994 No. 2472. Enabling power: *Road Traffic Regulation Act 1984, s. 14 (1) (a)*. Made: 14.09.94. Coming into force: 17.09.94. Effect: None. – *Unpublished*

The A66 Trunk Road (Penruddock) (Temporary 10 Miles Per Hour Speed Restriction) Order 1994 No. 1686. Enabling power: *Road Traffic Regulation Act 1984, s. 14 (1) (a)*. Made: 17.06.94. Coming into force: 30.06.94. Effect: None. – *Unpublished*

The A66 Trunk Road (Teesside Park Interchange) (Temporary Prohibition of Traffic) Order 1994 No. 1584. Enabling power: *Road Traffic Regulation Act 1984, s. 14 (1) (a)*. Made: 09.06.94. Coming into force: 12.06.94. Effect: None. – *Unpublished*

The A66 Trunk Road (Thornaby Road Interchange) (Temporary Prohibition of Traffic) Order 1994 No. 1927. Enabling power: *Road Traffic Regulation Act 1984, s. 14 (1) (a)*. Made: 12.07.94. Coming into force: 15.07.94. Effect: None. – *Unpublished*

The A66 Trunk Road (Warcop Junction - Musgrave Bridge) (Temporary 10 Miles Per Hour and 40 Miles Per Hour Speed Restriction) Order 1994 No. 1523. Enabling power: *Road Traffic Regulation Act 1984, s. 14 (1) (a)*. Made: 02.06.94. Coming into force: 05.06.94. Effect: None. – *Unpublished*

The (A68) Edinburgh-Newcastle Upon Tyne Trunk Road (Dalkeith) (Temporary One-Way Traffic and Prohibition of Waiting) Order 1994 No. 285. Enabling power: *Road Traffic Regulation Act 1984, s. 14 (1) (a) (4) (a) (5)*. Made: 03.02.94. Coming into force: 21.02.94. Effect: None. – *Unpublished*

142 ROAD TRAFFIC: TRAFFIC REGULATION

The A69 Trunk Road (40 MPH Speed Limit West of Haydon Bridge) (Temporary Restriction of Traffic) Order 1994 No. 1856. Enabling power: *Road Traffic Regulation Act 1984, s. 14 (1) (a)*. Made: 07.07.94. Coming into force: 10.07.94. Effect: None. – *Unpublished*

The A69 Trunk Road (Byegill Farm) (Temporary 10 Miles Per Hour Speed Restriction) Order 1994 No. 1685. Enabling power: *Road Traffic Regulation Act 1984, s. 14 (1) (a)*. Made: 17.06.94. Coming into force: 30.06.94. Effect: None. – *Unpublished*

The A69 Trunk Road (Constantius Bridge to Kingshaw Green Railway Bridge) (Temporary Prohibition and Restriction of Traffic) Order 1994 No. 458. Enabling power: *Road Traffic Regulation Act 1984, s. 14 (1)*. Made: 25.02.94. Coming into force: 28.02.94. Effect: None. – *Unpublished*

The A69 Trunk Road (Cross Bank, Haltwhistle) (Temporary 10 Miles Per Hour Speed Restriction) Order 1994 No. 591. Enabling power: *Road Traffic Regulation Act 1984, s. 14 (1) (a)*. Made: 03.03.94. Coming into force: 06.03.94. Effect: None. – *Unpublished*

The A69 Trunk Road (East of Bush Cottage) (Temporary 40 Miles Per Hour Speed Restriction) Order 1994 No. 2380. Enabling power: *Road Traffic Regulation Act 1984, s. 14 (1) (a)*. Made: 01.09.94. Coming into force: 04.09.94. Effect: None. – *Unpublished*

The A69 Trunk Road (Hayton) (Temporary Prohibition and Restriction of Traffic) Order 1994 No.2133. Enabling power: *Road Traffic Regulation Act 1984, s. 14 (1) (a) (5)*. Made: 05.08.94. Coming into force: 06.08.94. Effect: None. – *Unpublished*

The A69 Trunk Road (Rosehill Interchange) (Temporary 30 Miles Per Hour Speed Restriction) Order 1994 No. 2115. Enabling power: *Road Traffic Regulation Act 1984, s. 14 (1) (a)*. Made: 04.08.94. Coming into force: 07.08.94. Effect: None. – *Unpublished*

The A69 Trunk Road (Scotby Junction to Wetheral Plains) (Temporary Prohibition and Restriction of Traffic) Order 1994 No. 2089. Enabling power: *Road Traffic Regulation Act 1984, s. 14 (1) (a)*. Made: 01.08.94. Coming into force: 03.08.94. Effect: None. – *Unpublished*

The A69 Trunk Road (Wetheral Plains to Algionby and Broomriggs) (Temporary 10 Miles Per Hour and 40 Miles Per Hour Speed Restriction) Order 1994 No. 1525. Enabling power: *Road Traffic Regulation Act 1984, s. 14 (1) (a)*. Made: 03.06.94. Coming into force: 11.06.94. Effect: None. – *Unpublished*

The A69 Trunk Road (Wetheral Plains, Warwick Bridge, Burnrigg Junction) (Temporary Prohibition and Restriction of Traffic) Order 1994 No. 2062. Enabling power: *Road Traffic Regulation Act 1984, s. 14 (1) (a)*. Made: 01.08.94. Coming into force: 03.08.94. Effect: None. – *Unpublished*

The (A73) Trunk Road (Roberton Bridge) (Temporary Prohibition of Traffic) (No. 2) Order 1994 No. 2186. Enabling power: *Road Traffic Regulation Act 1984, s. 14 (1) (a) (4)*. Made: 19.08.94. Coming into force: 27.08.94. Effect: None. – *Unpublished*

The (A73) Trunk Road (Roberton Bridge) (Temporary Prohibition of Traffic) Order 1994 No.1387. Enabling power: *Road Traffic Regulation Act 1984, s. 14 (1) (a) (4)*. Made: 20.05.94. Coming into force: 02.06.94. Effect: None. – *Unpublished*

The A74M Motorway (Gretna Bypass) (Temporary Restriction of Traffic) Order 1994 No.301. Enabling power: *Road Traffic Regulation Act 1984, s. 14 (1) (a)*. Made: 03.02.94. Coming into force: 11.02.94. Effect: None. – *Unpublished*

The A74 Trunk Road (Carlisle-Gretna) (Temporary Prohibition and Restriction of Traffic) Order 1994 No. 300. Enabling power: *Road Traffic Regulation Act 1984, s. 14 (1) (a)*. Made: 03.02.94. Coming into force: 11.02.94. Effect: None. – *Unpublished*

The (A74) Trunk Road Glasgow-Carlisle (Muirhouse) (Temporary Prohibition of Traffic) Order 1994 No. 584. Enabling power: *Road Traffic Regulation Act 1984, s. 14 (1)*. Made: 04.03.94. Coming into force: 05.03.94. Effect: None. – *Unpublished*

The A74 Trunk Road (River Sark to Guards Mill Section) (Temporary 50 Miles Per Hour Speed Restriction) Order 1994 No. 1221. Enabling power: *Road Traffic Regulation Act 1984, s. 14 (1) (a)*. Made: 27.04.94. Coming into force: 05.05.94. Effect: None. – *Unpublished*

The A77 Trunk Road (Turnberry) (Temporary Prohibition of Waiting and Loading) Order 1994 No.1703. Enabling power: *Roads (Scotland) Act 1984, s. 62*. Made: 27.06.94. Coming into force: 11.07.94. Effect: None. – *Unpublished*

The (A82) Glasgow-Inverness Trunk Road/ (A898) Erskine Bridge Trunk Road (Dalnottar Interchange Slip Road) (Temporary Prohibition of Traffic) Order 1994 No. 583. Enabling power: *Road Traffic Regulation Act 1984, ss. 14 (1) (a) (4)*. Made: 25.02.94. Coming into force: 07.03.94. Effect: None. – *Unpublished*

The (A90/M90) Trunk Road (Inverkeithing-Perth-Dundee-Aberdeen) (Barnhill Interchange and Walnut Grove Junction) (Temporary Prohibition of Traffic and Temporary Prohibition of Specified Turns) Order 1994 No. 1254. Enabling power: *Road Traffic Regulation Act 1984, s. 14 (1) (a) (4) (a)*. Made: 05.05.94. Coming into force: 07.05.94. Effect: None. – *Unpublished*

The A91 Arlary-St Andrews Trunk Road (Cupar) (Prohibition of Waiting and Loading) Order 1994 No. 1752. Enabling power: *Road Traffic Regulation Act 1984, s. 1 (1)*. Made: 01.07.94. Coming into force: 11.07.94. Effect: S.I. 1972/1491 revoked. – *Unpublished*

The A92/A914 Trunk Road (Preston Roundabout to Markinch Road Junction) (Temporary Prohibition of Traffic) Order 1994 No. 1541. Enabling power: *Road Traffic Regulation Act 1984, s. 14 (1) (a) (4)*. Made: 09.06.94. Coming into force: 20.06.94. Effect: None. – *Unpublished*

The A92/A914 Trunk Road (Preston Roundabout to Markinch Road Junction) (Temporary Prohibition of Traffic) (No. 2) Order 1994 No. 1839. Enabling power: *Road Traffic Regulation Act 1984, s. 14 (1) (a) (4)*. Made: 08.07.94. Coming into force: 19.07.94. Effect: None. – *Unpublished*

The A98 Fraserburgh-Fochabers Trunk Road (Castle Street, Banff) (Prohibition of Waiting) Order 1994 No. 1108. Enabling power: *Road Traffic Regulation Act 1984, ss. 1 (1), 2 (1) (2), 121A (1)*. Made: 18.04.94. Coming into force: 02.05.94. Effect: None. – *Unpublished*

The A102 Trunk Road (Blackwall Tunnel Approach Roads, Tower Hamlets) (Temporary Prohibition of Traffic) (No. 2) Order 1994 No. 2048. Enabling power: *Road Traffic Regulation Act 1984, s. 14 (1) (4) (5) (7)*. Made: 01.08.94. Coming into force: 06.08.94. Effect: None. – *Unpublished*

The A102 Trunk Road (Blackwall Tunnel Approach Roads, Tower Hamlets) (Temporary Prohibition of Traffic) Order 1994 No. 1476. Enabling power: *Road Traffic Regulation Act 1984, s. 14 (1) (a) (4) (5) (7)*. Made: 01.06.94. Coming into force: 05.06.94. Effect: None. – *Unpublished*

The A102 Trunk Road (Blackwall Tunnel Approach, Tower Hamlets) (Temporary Prohibition of Traffic) (No. 2) Order 1994 No. 513. Enabling power: *Road Traffic Regulation Act 1984, ss. 14 (1) (4)*. Made: 28.02.94. Coming into force: 05.03.94. Effect: None. – *Unpublished*

The A102 Trunk Road (Blackwall Tunnel Approach, Tower Hamlets) (Temporary Prohibition of Traffic) Order 1994 No. 56. Enabling power: *Road Traffic Regulation Act 1984, s. 14 (1) (4)*. Made: 11.01.94. Coming into force: 16.01.94. Effect: None. – *Unpublished*

The A102 Trunk Road (Blackwall Tunnel Approach, Tower Hamlets) (Temporary Prohibition of Traffic) (No. 3) Order 1994 No. 3306. Enabling power: *Road Traffic Regulation Act 1984, s. 14 (1) (4) (5) (7)*. Made: 19.12.94. Coming into force: 06.01.95. Effect: None. – *Unpublished*

The A102 Trunk Road (Blackwall Tunnel Northern Approach, Tower Hamlets) (Temporary Prohibition of Traffic) Order 1994 No. 57. Enabling power: *Road Traffic Regulation Act 1984, s. 14 (1) (4)*. Made: 11.01.94. Coming into force: 15.01.94. Effect: None. – *Unpublished*

The A102 Trunk Road (Blackwall Tunnel Northern Approach, Tower Hamlets) (Temporary Prohibition of Traffic) (No. 3) Order 1994 No. 3305. Enabling power: *Road Traffic Regulation Act 1984, s. 14 (1) (4)*. Made: 19.12.94. Coming into force: 07.01.95. Effect: None. – *Unpublished*

The A102 Trunk Road (Blackwall Tunnels, Greenwich and Tower Hamlets) (Temporary Prohibition of Traffic) Order 1994 No. 3030. Enabling power: *Road Traffic Regulation Act 1984, s. 14 (1) (4)*. Made: 28.11.94. Coming into force: 06.12.94. Effect: None. – *Unpublished*

The A102 Trunk Road (Blackwell Tunnel Approach Roads, Tower Hamlets) (Temporary Prohibition of Traffic) (No. 3) Order 1994 No. 2873. Enabling power: *Road Traffic Regulation Act 1984, s. 14 (1) (4)*. Made: 07.11.94. Coming into force: 12.11.94. Effect: None. – *Unpublished*

The A102 Trunk Road (Blackwell Tunnel Northern Approach, Tower Hamlets) (Temporary Prohibition of Traffic) (No. 2) Order 1994 No. 384. Enabling power: *Road Traffic Regulation Act 1984, s. 14 (1) (4) (5) (7)*. Made: 22.02.94. Coming into force: 01.03.94. Effect: None. – *Unpublished*

The A127 Trunk Road (A127/A129 Interchange, Rayleigh Weir, Essex) (Temporary Prohibition of Traffic) Order 1994 No. 1654. Enabling power: *Road Traffic Regulation Act 1984, s. 14 (1) (a)*. Made: 10.06.94. Coming into force: 14.06.94. Effect: None. – *Unpublished*

The A127 Trunk Road (Basildon, Essex) (Temporary Prohibition and Restriction of Traffic) Order 1994 No. 324. Enabling power: *Road Traffic Regulation Act 1984, s. 14 (1) (a)*. Made: 14.02.94. Coming into force: 21.02.94. Effect: None. – *Unpublished*

The A127 Trunk Road (Basildon Flyover - A176 Interchange, Essex) (Temporary 40 Miles Per Hour Speed Restriction of Traffic) Order 1994 No. 594. Enabling power: *Road Traffic Regulation Act 1984, s. 14 (1) (a)*. Made: 01.03.94. Coming into force: 08.03.94. Effect: None. – *Unpublished*

The A127 Trunk Road (Essex) (Temporary Prohibition and Restriction of Traffic) Order 1994 No.2438. Enabling power: *Road Traffic Regulation Act 1984, s. 14 (1) (a)*. Made: 12.09.94. Coming into force: 19.09.94. Effect: None. – *Unpublished*

The A127 Trunk Road (Fairglen to Nevendon, Essex) (Temporary Prohibition and Restriction of Traffic) Order 1994 No. 2271. Enabling power: *Road Traffic Regulation Act 1984, s. 14 (1) (a)*. Made: 30.08.94. Coming into force: 05.09.94. Effect: None. – *Unpublished*

The A127 Trunk Road (Halfway House Interchange, Essex) (Temporary Prohibition and Restriction of Traffic) Order 1994 No. 2777. Enabling power: *Road Traffic Regulation Act 1984, s. 14 (1) (a)*. Made: 24.10.94. Coming into force: 31.10.94. Effect: None. – *Unpublished*

The A134 Trunk Road (Thetford Road, Northwold, Norfolk) (Temporary 40 Miles Per Hour Speed Restriction) Order 1994 No. 2778. Enabling power: *Road Traffic Regulation Act 1984, s. 14 (1) (a)*. Made: 24.10.94. Coming into force: 31.10.94. Effect: None. – *Unpublished*

Price/availability are liable to change without notice

The A134 Trunk Road (Wereham) (Temporary 10 Miles Per Hour Speed Restriction) Order 1994 No.2207. Enabling power: *Road Traffic Regulation Act 1984, s. 14 (1) (a)*. Made: 01.06.94. Coming into force: 08.06.94. Effect: None. – *Unpublished*

The A140 Trunk Road (Creeting St Mary Culvert, Suffolk) (Temporary Restriction and Prohibition of Traffic) Order 1994 No. 2906. Enabling power: *Road Traffic Regulation Act 1984, s. 14 (1) (a)*. Made: 09.11.94. Coming into force: 11.11.94. Effect: None. – *Unpublished*

The A160 Trunk Road (Habrough Roundabout - Manby Road Roundabout) (Temporary Prohibition of Traffic) Order 1994 No. 460. Enabling power: *Road Traffic Regulation Act 1984, s. 14 (1) (a)*. Made: 24.02.94. Coming into force: 26.02.94. Effect: None. – *Unpublished*

The A167 Trunk Road (Cock O' the North to Browney Bridge) (Temporary Prohibition and Restriction of Traffic) Order 1994 No. 1583. Enabling power: *Road Traffic Regulation Act 1984, s. 14 (1) (a)*. Made: 02.06.94. Coming into force: 05.06.94. Effect: None. – *Unpublished*

The A167 Trunk Road (Croxdale Station Lay By) (Temporary Prohibition of Traffic) Order 1994 No. 3244. Enabling power: *Road Traffic Regulation Act 1984, s. 14 (1) (a)*. Made: 08.12.94. Coming into force: 10.12.94. Effect: None. – *Unpublished*

The A167 Trunk Road (Croxdale to Thinford) (Temporary Prohibition and Restriction of Traffic) Order 1994 No. 1942. Enabling power: *Road Traffic Regulation Act 1984, s. 14 (1) (a)*. Made: 15.07.94. Coming into force: 17.07.94. Effect: None. – *Unpublished*

The A167 Trunk Road (Hermitage to Ropery Lane) (Temporary Prohibition of Traffic) Order 1994 No. 2635. Enabling power: *Road Traffic Regulation Act 1984, s. 14 (1) (a)*. Made: 06.10.94. Coming into force: 08.10.94. Effect: None. – *Unpublished*

The A167 Trunk Road (Park Road South, Chester-Le-Street) (Prohibition of Entry) Order 1994 No. 152. Enabling power: *Road Traffic Regulation Act 1984, ss. 1 (1), 2 (1) (2)*. Made: 25.01.94. Coming into force: 28.01.94. Effect: None. – *Unpublished*

The A167 Trunk Road (Picktree Lane Roundabout) (Temporary Prohibition of Traffic) Order 1994 No. 1074. Enabling power: *Road Traffic Regulation Act 1984, s. 14 (1) (a)*. Made: 07.04.94. Coming into force: 09.04.94. Effect: None. – *Unpublished*

The A168 Trunk Road (Topcliffe Bypass) (Temporary Restriction and Prohibition of Traffic) Order 1994 No. 96. Enabling power: *Road Traffic Regulation Act 1984, s. 14 (1) (a)*. Made: 14.01.94. Coming into force: 15.01.94. Effect: None. – *Unpublished*

The A174 Trunk Road (A171 and A172 Junctions, Parkway) (Temporary Prohibition and Restriction of Traffic) Order 1994 No. 974. Enabling power: *Road Traffic Regulation Act 1984, s. 14 (1) (a)*. Made: 11.03.94. Coming into force: 13.03.94. Effect: None. – *Unpublished*

The A174 Trunk Road (Parkway, Stokesley Road) (Temporary Prohibition of Traffic) Order 1994 No. 2557. Enabling power: *Road Traffic Regulation Act 1984, s. 14 (1) (a)*. Made: 28.09.94. Coming into force: 30.09.94. Effect: None. – *Unpublished*

The A174 Trunk Road (Stainton Interchange) (Temporary Prohibition of Traffic) Order 1994 No.2148. Enabling power: *Road Traffic Regulation Act 1984, s. 14 (1) (a)*. Made: 11.08.94. Coming into force: 12.08.94. Effect: None. – *Unpublished*

The A180 Trunk Road (Stallingborough Interchange, Westbound Exit Slip Road) (Temporary Prohibition of Traffic) Order 1994 No. 2504. Enabling power: *Road Traffic Regulation Act 1984, s. 14 (1) (a)*. Made: 16.09.94. Coming into force: 21.09.94. Effect: None. – *Unpublished*

The A194(M) Motorway (Birtley to Whitemare Pool Roundabout) (Temporary Restriction of Traffic) Order 1994 No. 2815. Enabling power: *Road Traffic Regulation Act 1984, s. 14 (1) (a) (7)*. Made: 27.10.94. Coming into force: 29.10.94. Effect: None. – *Unpublished*

The A194(M) Motorway (Follingsby and Havannah Interchanges) (Temporary Prohibition of Traffic) Order 1994 No. 1090. Enabling power: *Road Traffic Regulation Act 1984, s. 14 (1) (a)*. Made: 07.04.94. Coming into force: 09.04.94. Effect: None. – *Unpublished*

The A194(M) Motorway (Whitemare Pool Roundabout) (Temporary Prohibition of Traffic) Order 1994 No. 2433. Enabling power: *Road Traffic Regulation Act 1984, s. 14 (1) (a)*. Made: 08.09.94. Coming into force: 10.09.94. Effect: None. – *Unpublished*

The A249 Trunk Road (Brielle Way) (Temporary Prohibition of Traffic) Order 1994 No.2870. Enabling power: *Road Traffic Regulation Act 1984, s. 14 (1) (a)*. Made: 07.11.94. Coming into force: 12.11.94. Effect: None. – *Unpublished*

The A249 Trunk Road (Kingsferry Bridge) (Temporary Prohibition of Traffic) Order 1994 No.2375. Enabling power: *Road Traffic Regulation Act 1984, s. 14 (1) (a)*. Made: 05.09.94. Coming into force: 10.09.94. Effect: None. – *Unpublished*

The A249 Trunk Road (Queenborough Bypass) (Temporary Restriction and Prohibition of Traffic) (No. 2) Order 1994 No. 1653. Enabling power: *Road Traffic Regulation Act 1984, s. 14 (1) (a)*. Made: 20.06.94. Coming into force: 27.06.94. Effect: S.I. 1994/890 revoked. – *Unpublished*

Price/availability are liable to change without notice

The A249 Trunk Road (Queenborough Bypass) (Temporary Restriction and Prohibition of Traffic) Order 1994 No. 890. Enabling power: *Road Traffic Regulation Act 1984, s. 14 (1) (a)*. Made: 21.03.94. Coming into force: 26.03.94. Effect: None.–*Unpublished*

The A249 Trunk Road (Stockbury Roundabout to Kingsferry Bridge) (Temporary 40 Miles Per Hour Speed Restriction) (No. 2) Order 1994 No. 2869. Enabling power: *Road Traffic Regulation Act 1984, s. 14 (1) (a)*. Made: 07.11.94. Coming into force: 12.11.94. Effect: S.I. 1994/2122 revoked.–*Unpublished*

The A249 Trunk Road (Stockbury Roundabout to Kingsferry Bridge) (Temporary 40 Miles Per Hour Speed Restriction) Order 1994 No. 2122. Enabling power: *Road Traffic Regulation Act 1984, s. 14 (1) (a)*. Made: 08.08.94. Coming into force: 13.08.94. Effect: None.–*Unpublished*

The A259 Trunk Road (Dymchurch Road) (Temporary 30 Miles Per Hour Speed Restriction) Order 1994 No. 2960. Enabling power: *Road Traffic Regulation Act 1984, s. 14 (1) (a)*. Made: 21.11.94. Coming into force: 26.11.94. Effect: None.–*Unpublished*

The A259 Trunk Road (Dymchurch Road) (Temporary Restriction of Traffic) Order 1994 No.47. Enabling power: *Road Traffic Regulation Act 1984, s. 14 (1) (a)*. Made: 10.01.94. Coming into force: 15.01.94. Effect: None. –*Unpublished*

The A259 Trunk Road (East Guldeford to Kent Ditch) (Temporary Prohibition of Traffic) Order 1994 No.2961. Enabling power: *Road Traffic Regulation Act 1984, s. 14 (1) (a)*. Made: 14.11.94. Coming into force: 19.11.94. Effect: None.–*Unpublished*

The A259 Trunk Road (Guestling Thorn) (Temporary Prohibition of Traffic) Order 1994 No.517. Enabling power: *Road Traffic Regulation Act 1984, s. 14 (1) (a)*. Made: 28.02.94. Coming into force: 05.03.94. Effect: None. –*Unpublished*

The A259 Trunk Road (Guldeford Lane) (Temporary Speed Restrictions) Order 1994 No.418. Enabling power: *Road Traffic Regulation Act 1984, s. 14 (1) (a)*. Made: 21.02.94. Coming into force: 26.02.94. Effect: None. – *Unpublished*

The A259 Trunk Road (Hythe Road) (Temporary 30 Miles Per Hour Speed Restriction) Order 1994 No. 1355. Enabling power: *Road Traffic Regulation Act 1984, s. 14 (1) (a)*. Made: 16.05.94. Coming into force: 21.05.94. Effect: None.–*Unpublished*

The A259 Trunk Road (King Offa Way-De La Warr Road) (Temporary Restriction of Traffic) Order 1994 No. 124. Enabling power: *Road Traffic Regulation Act 1984, s. 14 (1) (a)*. Made: 24.01.94. Coming into force: 29.01.94. Effect: None.–*Unpublished*

The A282 Trunk Road (Dartford-Thurrock Crossing) (Temporary Restriction of Traffic) Order 1994 No. 1033. Enabling power: *Road Traffic Regulation Act 1984, s. 14 (1) (b)*.Made: 05.04.94. Coming into force: 09.04.94. Effect: None.–*Unpublished*

The A282 Trunk Road (Dartford Tunnels and Approaches (One Way Traffic and Weight Restriction) Order 1994 No. 515. Enabling power: *Road Traffic Regulation Act 1984, ss. 1 (1), (2) (1) (2)*. Made: 28.02.94. Coming into force: 14.03.94. Effect: None.–*Unpublished*

The A282 Trunk Road (Dartford Tunnels) (Temporary Restriction of Traffic) Order 1994 No.2537. Enabling power: *Road Traffic Regulation Act 1984, s. 14 (1) (b) (7)*. Made: 26.09.94. Coming into force: 03.10.94. Effect: None.–*Unpublished*

The A303 Trunk Road (Andover to Barnsbury) (Temporary 50 Miles Per Hour Speed Restriction) Order 1994 No. 2573. Enabling power: *Road Traffic Regulation Act 1984, s. 14 (1) (a)*. Made: 03.10.94. Coming into force: 08.10.94. Effect: None.–*Unpublished*

The A303 Trunk Road (Barton Stacey) (Prohibition of Use of Gaps in the Central Reservation) Order 1994 No. 211. Enabling power: *Road Traffic Regulation Act 1984, ss. 1 (1), 2 (1) (2)*. Made: 31.01.94. Coming into force: 14.02.94. Effect: None.–*Unpublished*

The A303 Trunk Road (Barton Stacey) (Temporary Prohibition of Traffic) Order 1994 No.1177. Enabling power: *Road Traffic Regulation Act 1984, s. 14 (1) (a)*. Made: 25.04.94. Coming into force: 30.04.94. Effect: None. –*Unpublished*

The A303 Trunk Road (Barton Stacey) (Temporary Restriction of Traffic) Order 1994 No.1279. Enabling power: *Road Traffic Regulation Act 1984, s. 14 (1) (a)*. Made: 09.05.94. Coming into force: 14.05.94. Effect: None. – *Unpublished*

The A303 Trunk Road (Blackford Junction - Yarlington Junction) (Temporary Prohibition of Traffic) Order 1994 No. 69. Enabling power: *Road Traffic Regulation Act 1984, ss. 14 (1) (b)*. Made: 13.01.94. Coming into force: 15.01.94. Effect: None.–*Unpublished*

The A303 Trunk Road (Harewood Forest to Bransbury) (Temporary Restriction of Traffic) Order 1994 No. 91. Enabling power: *Road Traffic Regulation Act 1984, s. 14 (1) (a)*. Made: 17.01.94. Coming into force: 22.01.94. Effect: None.–*Unpublished*

The A303 Trunk Road (Hunton Down) (Closure of A Gap in the Central Reservation) Order 1994 No. 151. Enabling power: *Road Traffic Regulation Act 1984, ss. 1 (1), 2 (1) (2)*. Made: 27.01.94. Coming into force: 08.02.94. Effect: None.–*Unpublished*

The A303 Trunk Road (Ilchester Bypass) (Temporary Restriction of Traffic) Order 1994 No.649. Enabling power: *Road Traffic Regulation Act 1984, s. 14 (1) (a)*. Made: 03.03.94. Coming into force: 05.03.94. Effect: None. –*Unpublished*

The A303 Trunk Road (Ilchester Bypass) (Temporary Restriction and Prohibition of Traffic) Order 1994 No. 2662. Enabling power: *Road Traffic Regulation Act 1984, s. 14 (1) (a)*. Made: 29.09.94. Coming into force: 01.10.94. Effect: None. –*Unpublished*

The A303 Trunk Road (Marsh Bypass) (Temporary Restriction of Traffic) Order 1994 No.313. Enabling power: *Road Traffic Regulation Act 1984, s. 14 (1) (a)*. Made: 10.02.94. Coming into force: 12.02.94. Effect: None. – *Unpublished*

The A303 Trunk Road (Tidbury Farm) (Prohibition of Use of a Gap in Central Reservation) Order 1994 No. 1996. Enabling power: *Road Traffic Regulation Act 1984, ss. 1 (1), 2 (1) (2)*. Made: 25.07.94. Coming into force: 17.08.94. Effect: None. –*Unpublished*

The A316 Trunk Road (Country Way, Hounslow) (Temporary Prohibition of Traffic) Order 1994 No.2980. Enabling power: *Road Traffic Regulation Act 1984, s. 14 (1) (4)*. Made: 14.11.94. Coming into force: 21.11.94. Effect: None. –*Unpublished*

The A316 Trunk Road (Great Chertsey Road, Hounslow and Richmond) (Temporary Restriction of Traffic) Order 1994 No. 1869. Enabling power: *Road Traffic Regulation Act 1984, s. 14 (1) (4)*. Made: 11.07.94. Coming into force: 18.07.94. Effect: None. –*Unpublished*

The A316 Trunk Road (Hogarth Car Bridge, Hounslow) (Temporary Prohibition of Traffic) Order 1994 No. 965. Enabling power: *Road Traffic Regulation Act 1984, s. 14 (1) (4)*. Made: 25.03.94. Coming into force: 10.04.94. Effect: None. –*Unpublished*

The A316 Trunk Road (Richmond Upon Thames and Hounslow) (Temporary 30 MPH Speed Restriction) Order 1994 No. 2529. Enabling power: *Road Traffic Regulation Act 1984, s. 14 (1) (a) (4)*. Made: 26.09.94. Coming into force: 03.10.94. Effect: None. –*Unpublished*

The A339 Trunk Road (Basingstoke Northern Bypass) (Temporary Prohibition of Traffic) Order 1994 No. 92. Enabling power: *Road Traffic Regulation Act 1984, s. 14 (1) (a)*. Made: 17.01.94. Coming into force: 22.01.94. Effect: None. –*Unpublished*

The A339 Trunk Road (Kingsclere) (Temporary Restriction and Prohibition of Traffic) Order 1994 No. 1709. Enabling power: *Road Traffic Regulation Act 1984, s. 14 (1) (a)*. Made: 27.06.94. Coming into force: 02.07.94. Effect: None. –*Unpublished*

The A339 Trunk Road (Sandford Springs Service Road) (One Way Traffic) Order 1994 No.3289. Enabling power: *Road Traffic Regulation Act 1984, ss. 1 (1), 2 (1) (2)*. Made: 19.12.94. Coming into force: 28.12.94. Effect: None. –*Unpublished*

The A404 Trunk Road (Bisham) (Temporary Closure of Laybys) Order 1994 No. 873. Enabling power: *Road Traffic Regulation Act 1984, s. 14 (1) (a)*. Made: 14.03.94. Coming into force: 19.03.94. Effect: None. –*Unpublished*

The A404 Trunk Road (Maidenhead Thicket to Handy Cross) (24 Hours Clearway) Order 1994 No.736. Enabling power: *Road Traffic Regulation Act 1984 ss. 1 (1), 2 (1) (2), 4 (1)*. Made: 04.03.94. Coming into force: 29.03.94. Effect: None. –*Unpublished*

The A405 Trunk Road (Bricket Wood, Hertfordshire) (Temporary Prohibition of Traffic) Order 1994 No. 512. Enabling power: *Road Traffic Regulation Act 1984, s. 14 (1) (a)*. Made: 07.02.94. Coming into force: 08.03.94. Effect: None. –*Unpublished*

The A405 Trunk Road (Horseshoe Lane/St Albans Road Junction to Leavesden Interchange, Watford) (Temporary Restriction of Traffic) Order 1994 No. 2603. Enabling power: *Road Traffic Regulation Act 1984, s. 14 (1) (a)*. Made: 04.10.94. Coming into force: 10.10.94. Effect: None. –*Unpublished*

The A405 Trunk Road (Kingsway North Orbital Road, Watford, Hertfordshire) (Temporary Prohibition and Restriction of Traffic) Order 1994 No. 1782. Enabling power: *Road Traffic Regulation Act 1984, s. 14 (1) (a) (5) (b)*. Made: 04.07.94. Coming into force: 11.07.94. Effect: None. –*Unpublished*

The A405 Trunk Road (St Albans Road, Watford) (Temporary Restriction of Traffic) Order 1994 No. 1711. Enabling power: *Road Traffic Regulation Act 1984, s. 14 (1) (b)*. Made: 27.06.94. Coming into force: 04.07.94. Effect: None. –*Unpublished*

The A405 Trunk Road (St Albans Road, Watford) (Temporary Restriction of Traffic) Order 1994 No. 2200. Enabling power: *Road Traffic Regulation Act 1984, s. 14 (1) (a) (b)*. Made: 16.08.94. Coming into force: 23.08.94. Effect: None. –*Unpublished*

The A406 Trunk Road (Staples Corner Flyover, Barnet and Brent) (Temporary Prohibition of Traffic) Order 1994 No. 1867. Enabling power: *Road Traffic Regulation Act 1984, s. 14 (1) (4)*. Made: 11.07.94. Coming into force: 18.07.94. Effect: None. –*Unpublished*

The A414 Trunk Road (A1 (M) Motorway Junction 3 - Colney Heath, Hertfordshire) (Temporary Prohibition and Restriction of Traffic) Order 1994 No. 2700. Enabling power: *Road Traffic Regulation Act 1984, s. 14 (1) (a) (5) (b)*. Made: 10.10.94. Coming into force: 17.10.94. Effect: None. –*Unpublished*

The A414 Trunk Road (Eastbound Exit Slip Road to Napsbury Lane, St Albans) (Temporary Prohibition of Traffic) Order 1994 No. 508. Enabling power: *Road Traffic Regulation Act 1984, s. 14 (1) (a)*. Made: 28.02.94. Coming into force: 01.03.94. Effect: None. –*Unpublished*

Price/availability are liable to change without notice

The A414 Trunk Road (London Road Junction) (Left Turn Only, Right Turn Only, Ahead Only) Order 1994 No. 2197. Enabling power: *Road Traffic Regulation Act 1984, s. 1 (1), 2 (1) (2)*. Made: 16.08.94. Coming into force: 20.08.94. Effect: None. – *Unpublished*

The A417 Trunk Road (Barnwood Bypass) (Temporary Prohibition of Traffic) Order 1994 No.2559. Enabling power: *Road Traffic Regulation Act 1984, s. 14 (1) (a) (7) (5) (b)*. Made: 03.08.94. Coming into force: 05.08.94. Effect: None. – *Unpublished*

The A417 Trunk Road (Brockworth Bypass) (Temporary 40 Miles Per Hour and 50 Miles Per Hour Speed Restriction) Order 1994 No. 1123. Enabling power: *Road Traffic Regulation Act 1984, s. 14 (1) (a) 15 (2)*. Made: 30.03.94. Coming into force: 01.04.94. Effect: None. – *Unpublished*

The A417 Trunk Road (Crickley Hill) (Temporary Prohibition of Traffic) Order 1994 No.1928. Enabling power: *Road Traffic Regulation Act 1984, s. 14 (1) (a)*. Made: 07.07.94. Coming into force: 15.07.94. Effect: None. – *Unpublished*

The A417 Trunk Road (New Mills Footbridge) (Temporary Prohibition of Traffic) Order 1994 No.2910. Enabling power: *Road Traffic Regulation Act 1984, s. 14 (1) (a)*. Made: 14.11.94. Coming into force: 21.11.94. Effect: None. – *Unpublished*

The A419 Trunk Road (Cirencester Bypass) (Temporary Prohibition of Traffic) Order 1994 No.2824. Enabling power: *Road Traffic Regulation Act 1984, s. 14 (1) (a)*. Made: 19.10.94. Coming into force: 24.10.94. Effect: None. – *Unpublished*

The A419 Trunk Road (Junction 15 - Commonhead Roundabout) (Temporary Restriction and Prohibition of Traffic) Order 1994 No. 1069. Enabling power: *Road Traffic Regulation Act 1984, s. 14 (1) (a)*. Made: 30.03.94. Coming into force: 01.04.94. Effect: None. – *Unpublished*

The A419 Trunk Road (Stratton St Margaret Bypass) (Temporary Restriction and Prohibition of Traffic) Order 1994 No. 7. Enabling power: *Road Traffic Regulation Act 1984, s. 14 (1) (a)*. Made: 05.01.94. Coming into force: 07.01.94. Effect: None. – *Unpublished*

The A420 Trunk Road (Bessels Leigh to Tubney) (Temporary 40 Miles Per Hour Speed Restriction) Order 1994 No. 516. Enabling power: *Road Traffic Regulation Act 1984, s. 14 (1) (a)*. Made: 28.02.94. Coming into force: 05.03.94. Effect: None. – *Unpublished*

The A420 Trunk Road (Faringdon Bypass) (Temporary 10 Miles Per Hour and 40 Miles Per Hour Speed Restriction) Order 1994 No. 2482. Enabling power: *Road Traffic Regulation Act 1984, s. 14 (1) (a)*. Made: 19.09.94. Coming into force: 24.09.94. Effect: None. – *Unpublished*

The A423 Trunk Road (Banbury to Southam) (Temporary 10 Miles Per Hour and 40 Miles Per Hour Speed Restriction) Order 1994 No. 877. Enabling power: *Road Traffic Regulation Act 1984, s. 14 (1) (a)*. Made: 14.03.94. Coming into force: 19.03.94. Effect: None. – *Unpublished*

The A428 Trunk Road (St Neots Bypass and Tithe Farm Roundabout, Cambridgeshire and Bedfordshire) (Temporary Prohibition and Restriction of Traffic) Order 1994 No. 2174. Enabling power: *Road Traffic Regulation Act 1984, s. 14 (1) (a) (5) (b)*. Made: 15.08.94. Coming into force: 22.08.94. Effect: None. – *Unpublished*

The A435 Trunk Road (Evesham Bypass) (Temporary 40 Miles Per Hour Speed Restriction) Order 1994 No. 2090. Enabling power: *Road Traffic Regulation Act 1984, s. 14 (1) (a)*. Made: 30.07.94. Coming into force: 31.07.94. Effect: None. – *Unpublished*

The A435 Trunk Road (Evesham Road, Harvington) (Temporary 10 Miles Per Hour Speed Restriction) Order 1994 No. 2666. Enabling power: *Road Traffic Regulation Act 1984, s. 14 (1) (a)*. Made: 16.09.94. Coming into force: 17.09.94. Effect: None. – *Unpublished*

The A435 Trunk Road (Evesham Road) (Temporary 10 Miles Per Hour Speed Restriction) Order 1994 No. 739. Enabling power: *Road Traffic Regulation Act 1984, s. 14 (1) (a)*. Made: 25.02.94. Coming into force: 26.02.94. Effect: None. – *Unpublished*

The A435 Trunk Road (Layby, Alcester Road, Studley) (Restriction of Waiting) Order 1993 No.154. Enabling power: *Road Traffic Regulation Act 1984, ss. 1 (1), 2 (1) (2), 4 (1) (2)*. Made: 31.12.93. Coming into force: 05.01.94. Effect: None. – *Unpublished*

The A435 Trunk Road (M42 Portway to Gorcott Hill) (Clearway) Order 1994 No. 2067. Enabling power: *Road Traffic Regulation Act 1984, ss. 1 (1), 2 (1) (2), 4 (1)*. Made: 30.06.94. Coming into force: 04.07.94. Effect: None. *Unpublished*

The A435 Trunk Road (Puffin Crossing Alcester Road Studley) (Prohibition of Waiting and Overtaking) Experimental Order 1994 No. 2992. Enabling power: *Road Traffic Regulation Act 1984, s. 9 (1) (2)*. Made: 10.11.94. Coming into force: 14.11.94. Effect: None. – *Unpublished*

The A449 Trunk Road (Coven Heath) (Temporary Restriction of Traffic) Order 1994 No.2178. Enabling power: *Road Traffic Regulation Act 1984, s. 14 (1) (a)*. Made: 06.08.94. Coming into force: 07.08.94. Effect: None. – *Unpublished*

The A449 Trunk Road (Crateford to Four Ashes) (Temporary Restriction of Traffic) Order 1994 No. 270. Enabling power: *Road Traffic Regulation Act 1984, s. 14 (1) (a)*. Made: 29.01.94. Coming into force: 30.01.94. Effect: None. – *Unpublished*

The A449 Trunk Road (Hammers Culvert) (Temporary 30 Miles Per Hour Speed Restriction) Order 1994 No. 1093. Enabling power: *Road Traffic Regulation Act 1984, s. 14 (1) (a)*. Made: 08.04.94. Coming into force: 09.04.94. Effect: None. – *Unpublished*

The A449 Trunk Road (Stourbridge Road) (Temporary 40 Miles Per Hour Speed Restriction) Order 1994 No. 375. Enabling power: *Road Traffic Regulation Act 1984, s. 14 (1) (a)*. Made: 18.02.94. Coming into force: 19.02.94. Effect: None. – *Unpublished*

The A449 Trunk Road (Stourbridge Road, Wombourne) (Temporary 40 Miles Per Hour Speed Restriction) Order 1994 No. 2917. Enabling power: *Road Traffic Regulation Act 1984, s. 14 (1) (a)*. Made: 11.11.94. Coming into force: 12.11.94. Effect: None. – *Unpublished*

The A449 Trunk Road (Summerfield Crossroads, Summerfield, Kidderminster) (Prohibition of Waiting) Order 1994 No. 2175. Enabling power: *Road Traffic Regulation Act 1984, ss. 1 (1), 2 (1) (2)*. Made: 07.07.94. Coming into force: 08.07.94. Effect: None. – *Unpublished*

The A449 Trunk Road (Temporary 50 Miles per Hour Speed Restriction) Order 1994 No. 80. Enabling power: *Road Traffic Regulation Act 1984, ss. 14 (1) (a)*. Made: 23.02.94. Coming into force: 28.02.94. Effect: None. – *Unpublished*

The A449 Trunk Road (Wolverhampton Road) (Temporary Restriction of Traffic) Order 1994 No. 2648. Enabling power: *Road Traffic Regulation Act 1984, s. 14 (1) (a)*. Made: 07.10.94. Coming into force: 08.10.94. Effect: None. – *Unpublished*

The A453 Trunk Road (Ratcliffe-On-Soar Railway Bridge, Nottinghamshire) (Temporary 10 Miles Per Hour and 40 Miles Per Hour Speed) Order 1994 No. 456. Enabling power: *Road Traffic Regulation Act 1984, s. 14 (1) (a)*. Made: 24.02.94. Coming into force: 05.03.94. Effect: None. – *Unpublished*

The A458 Trunk Road (Berriew Street, Welshpool, Powys) (Temporary Prohibition of Vehicles) Order 1994 No. 1513. Enabling power: *Road Traffic Regulation Act 1984, s. 14 (1) (a)*. Made: 28.05.94. Coming into force: 31.05.94. Effect: None. – *Unpublished*

The A458 Trunk Road (South of Welshpool, Powys) (Temporary Prohibition of Vehicles and Pedestrians) Order 1994 No. 2320. Enabling power: *Road Traffic Regulation Act 1984, s. 14 (1) (4)*. Made: 30.08.94. Coming into force: 01.09.94. Effect: None. – *Unpublished*

The A458 Trunk Road (Temporary 40 Miles Per Hour Speed Restriction) Order 1994 No. 514. Enabling power: *Road Traffic Regulation Act 1984, s. 14 (1) (a)*. Made: 18.02.94. Coming into force: 21.02.94. Effect: None. – *Unpublished*

The A465 Trunk Road (Aberdulais-Llandarcy, West Glamorgan) (Prohibition of Pedestrians) Order 1994 No. 792. Enabling power: *Road Traffic Regulation Act 1984 ss. 1 (1), 2 (1) (3), 124 & sch.9, para. 27*. Made: 10.03.94. Coming into force: 21.03.94. Effect: S.I. 1975/643 revoked. – *Unpublished*

The A465 Trunk Road (Cefn-coed-y-cymmer, Merthyr Tydfil, Mid Glamorgan) (Temporary 30 MPH Speed Limit) Order 1994 No. 3324. Enabling power: *Road Traffic Regulation Act 1984, s. 14 (1) (4)*. Made: 22.12.94. Coming into force: 22.12.94. Effect: None. – *Unpublished*

The A465 Trunk Road (Hirwaun, Mid Glamorgan) (Temporary Prohibition of Vehicles and 50 MPH Speed Limit) Order 1994 No. 1616. Enabling power: *Road Traffic Regulation Act 1984, s. 14 (1)*. Made: 15.06.94. Coming into force: 20.06.94. Effect: None. – *Unpublished*

The A465 Trunk Road (Merthyr Tydfil, Mid Glamorgan) (Temporary Prohibition of Vehicles and 30 MPH Speed Limit) Order 1994 No. 2451. Enabling power: *Road Traffic Regulation Act 1984, s. 14 (1) (4)*. Made: 09.09.94. Coming into force: 12.09.94. Effect: None. – *Unpublished*

The A465 Trunk Road (Neath, West Glamorgan) (Temporary Prohibition of Vehicles) (No. 2) Order 1994 No. 2763. Enabling power: *Road Traffic Regulation Act 1984, s. 14 (1) (4)*. Made: 14.10.94. Coming into force: 15.10.94. Effect: None. – *Unpublished*

The A465 Trunk Road (Neath, West Glamorgan) (Temporary Prohibition of Vehicles) Order 1994 No. 3337. Enabling power: *Road Traffic Regulation Act 1984, s. 14 (1)*. Made: 01.03.94. Coming into force: 01.03.94. Effect: None. – *Unpublished*

The A465 Trunk Road (Neath, West Glamorgan) (Temporary Prohibition of Vehicles) Order 1994 No. 2523. Enabling power: *Road Traffic Regulation Act 1984, s. 14 (1) (4)*. Made: 19.09.94. Coming into force: 19.09.94. Effect: None. – *Unpublished*

The A465 Trunk Road (Neath, West Glamorgan) (Temporary Prohibition of Vehicles and 40 MPH Speed Limit) Order 1994 No. 2547. Enabling power: *Road Traffic Regulation Act 1984, s. 14 (1) (4)*. Made: 16.09.94. Coming into force: 17.09.94. Effect: None. – *Unpublished*

The A465 Trunk Road (Resolven - Glynneath, West Glamorgan) (Temporary Prohibition of Overtaking and 40 MPH Speed Limit) Order 1994 No. 2028. Enabling power: *Road Traffic Regulation Act 1984, s. 14 (1)*. Made: 25.07.94. Coming into force: 30.07.94. Effect: None. – *Unpublished*

The A465 Trunk Road (Resolven, West Glamorgan) (Temporary Prohibition of Vehicles) Order 1994 No. 2261. Enabling power: *Road Traffic Regulation Act 1984, s. 14 (1) (4)*. Made: 23.08.94. Coming into force: 03.09.94. Effect: None. – *Unpublished*

The A470 Trunk Road (Abercynon-Abercanaid, Mid Glamorgan) (Temporary 50 MPH Speed Limit) Order 1994 No. 1138. Enabling power: *Road Traffic Regulation Act 1984, s. 14 (1).* Made: 18.04.94. Coming into force: 23.04.94. Effect: None. – *Unpublished*

The A470 Trunk Road (Abercynon, Mid Glamorgan) (Temporary 40 MPH Speed Limit) Order 1994 No.1665. Enabling power: *Road Traffic Regulation Act 1984, s. 14 (1).* Made: 13.06.94. Coming into force: 22.06.94. Effect: None. – *Unpublished*

The A470 Trunk Road (Bontnewydd Bridge, Bontnewydd, Gwynedd) (Temporary Prohibition of Vehicles) Order 1994 No. 85. Enabling power: *Road Traffic Regulation Act 1984, ss. 14 (1).* Made: 13.01.94. Coming into force: 17.01.94. Effect: None. – *Unpublished*

The A470 Trunk Road (Bontnewydd Bridge, Bontnewydd, Gwynedd) (Temporary Prohibition of Vehicles) Order 1994 (Revocation) Order 1994 No. 713. Enabling power: *Road Traffic Regulation Act 1984, ss. 14 (1), 124 & sch. 9, para. 27.* Made: 28.02.94. Coming into force: 28.02.94. Effect: S.I. 1994/85 revoked. – *Unpublished*

The A470 Trunk Road (Cefn Coed, Mid Glamorgan) (Prohibition and Restriction of Waiting) Order 1994 No. 3300. Enabling power: *Road Traffic Regulation Act 1984, ss. 1 (1), 2 (1) (2), 4 (2), 124 & sch. 9, para. 27.* Made: 14.12.94. Coming into force: 22.12.94. Effect: S.I. 1973/1163 amended. – *Unpublished*

The A470 Trunk Road (Conway Road, Glan Conwy, Gwynedd) (Prohibition of Waiting) Order 1994 No. 3019. Enabling power: *Road Traffic Regulation Act 1984, ss. 1 (1), 2 (1) (2), 4 (2), 124, sch. 9, para. 27.* Made: 14.11.94. Coming into force: 25.11.94. Effect: S.I. 1983/518 revoked. – *Unpublished*

The A470 Trunk Road (Pontypridd, Mid Glamorgan) (Temporary 40 MPH Speed Limit) Order 1994 No.1700. Enabling power: *Road Traffic Regulation Act 1984, s. 14 (1).* Made: 24.06.94. Coming into force: 30.06.94. Effect: None. – *Unpublished*

The A470 Trunk Road (Station Road Bridge, Llanrwst, Gwynedd) (Temporary Prohibition of Vehicles) Order 1994 No. 1699. Enabling power: *Road Traffic Regulation Act 1984, s. 14 (1).* Made: 24.06.94. Coming into force: 29.06.94. Effect: None. – *Unpublished*

The A479 Trunk Road (Bronllys Castle Bridge, Bronllys, Powys) (Temporary Prohibition of Vehicles) Order 1994 No. 521. Enabling power: *Road Traffic Regulation Act 1984, s. 14 (1).* Made: 25.02.94. Coming into force: 07.03.94. Effect: None. – *Unpublished*

The A483 Trunk Road (Croesfoel, Wrexham, Clwyd) (Temporary Prohibition of Vehicles) Order 1994 No. 11. Enabling power: *Road Traffic Regulations Act 1984, s. 14 (1).* Made: 29.12.93. Coming into force: 04.01.94. Effect: None. – *Unpublished*

The A483 Trunk Road (Dolfor Road Junction, Newtown, Powys) (Temporary Prohibition of Traffic Order 1994 No. 2764. Enabling power: *Road Traffic Regulation Act 1984, s. 14 (1) (4).* Made: 17.10.94. Coming into force: 17.10.94. Effect: None. – *Unpublished*

The A483 Trunk Road (Lay-Bys, Welshpool Bypass, Welshpool, Powys) (Prohibition of Right-Hand Turns and No Entry) Order 1994 No. 1273. Enabling power: *Road Traffic Regulation Act 1984, ss. 1 (1), 2 (1) (2).* Made: 09.05.94. Coming into force: 16.05.94. Effect: None. – *Unpublished*

The A483 Trunk Road (Welshpool Bypass, Welshpool, Powys) (Prescribed Route and Prohibition of U-Turns) Order 1994 No. 1199. Enabling power: *Road Traffic Regulation Act 1984, ss. 1 (1), 2 (1) (2).* Made: 22.04.94. Coming into force: 09.05.94. Effect: None. – *Unpublished*

The A483 Trunk Road (Wrexham Bypass, Clwyd) (Temporary Traffic Restrictions) Order 1994 No.1530. Enabling power: *Road Traffic Regulation Act 1984, s. 14 (1).* Made: 03.06.94. Coming into force: 05.06.94. Effect: None. – *Unpublished*

The A487 and A489 Trunk Roads (Machynlleth, Powys) (Prohibiton and Restriction of Waiting) Order 1994 No. 3160. Enabling power: *Road Traffic Regulation Act 1984, ss. 1 (1), 2 (1) (2), 4 (2), 124, sch. 9, para. 27.* Made: 30.11.94. Coming into force: 12.12.94. Effect: S.I. 1984/1656; 1991/1960 revoked. – *Unpublished*

The A487 Trunk Road (Llanllyfni, Gwynedd) (Prohibition of Waiting) Order 1994 No.3020. Enabling power: *Road Traffic Regulation Act 1984, ss. 1 (1), 2 (1) (2), 4 (2).* Made: 17.11.94. Coming into force: 28.11.94. Effect: None. – *Unpublished*

The A487 Trunk Road (Newport, Dyfed) (Temporary Prohibition of Vehicles) Order 1994 No.150. Enabling power: *Road Traffic Regulation Act 1984, s. 14 (1).* Made: 14.01.94. Coming into force. 17.02.94. Effect: None. – *Unpublished*

The A487 Trunk Road (Port Dinorwic By-Pass, Gwynedd) (Clearway) Order 1994 No. 795. Enabling power: *Road Traffic Regulation Act 1984 ss. 1 (1), 2 91) (2).* Made: 09.03.94. Coming into force: 28.03.94. Effect: None. – *Unpublished*

The A487 Trunk Road (Port Dinorwic By-Pass, Gwynedd) (Restriction of Waiting in Lay-Bys) Order 1994 No. 794. Enabling power: *Road Traffic Regulation Act 1984 ss. 1 (1), 2 (1) (2), 4 (2).* Made: 09.03.94. Coming into force: 28.03.94. Effect: None. – *Unpublished*

The A487 Trunk Road (Talybont, Dyfed) (Prohibition of Waiting) Order 1994 No. 1366. Enabling power: *Road Traffic Regulation Act 1984, ss. 1 (1), 2 (1) (2), 4 (2), 124 & sch. 9, para 27.* Made: 11.05.94. Coming into force: 14.06.94. Effect: S.I. 1981/883 revoked. – *Unpublished*

The A494 Trunk Road (Alltami, Clwyd) (Temporary 30 MPH Speed Limit) Order 1994 No. 2933. Enabling power: *Road Traffic Regulation Act 1984, s.14 (1) (a) (4)*. Made: 04.11.94. Coming into force: 07.11.94. Effect: None. – *Unpublished*

The A494 Trunk Road (Lay-bys, Mold Bypass, Clwyd) (Restriction of Waiting) Order 1994 No. 2235. Enabling power: *Road Traffic Regulation Act 1984, ss. 1 (1), 2 (1) (2)*. Made: 15.08.94. Coming into force: 24.08.94. Effect: None. – *Unpublished*

The A494 Trunk Road (Mold Bypass, Clwyd) (Clearway) Order 1994 No. 2234. Enabling power: *Road Traffic Regulation Act 1984, ss. 1 (1), 2 (1) (2)*. Made: 15.08.94. Coming into force: 24.08.94. Effect: None. – *Unpublished*

The A500 Trunk Road (Nantwich Bypass) Nantwich (Temporary 10 Miles Per Hour Speed Restriction) (No. 2) Order 1994 No. 2378. Enabling power: *Road Traffic Regulation Act 1984, s. 14 (1) (a)*. Made: 23.08.94. Coming into force: 05.09.94. Effect: None. – *Unpublished*

The A500 Trunk Road (Nantwich Bypass) Nantwich (Temporary 10 Miles Per Hour Speed Restriction) Order 1994 No. 2315. Enabling power: *Road Traffic Regulation Act 1984, s. 14 (1) (a)*. Made: 23.08.94. Coming into force: 01.09.94. Effect: None. – *Unpublished*

The A500 Trunk Road (Newcastle Road, Crewe) (Temporary 30 MPH Speed Restriction) Order 1994 No. 2059. Enabling power: *Road Traffic Regulation Act 1984, s. 14 (1) (b)*. Made: 28.07.94. Coming into force: 29.07.94. Effect: None. – *Unpublished*

The A500 Trunk Road (Newcastle Road) Shavington (Temporary 30 Miles Per Hour Speed Restriction) Order 1994 No. 3336. Enabling power: *Road Traffic Regulation Act 1984, s. 14 (1) (a)*. Made: 16.12.94. Coming into force: 23.12.94. Effect: None. – *Unpublished*

The A500 Trunk Road (Queensway, Stoke On Trent) (Temporary 30 Miles Per Hour Speed Restriction) Order 1994 No. 1131. Enabling power: *Road Traffic Regulation Act 1984, s. 14 (1) (a)*. Made: 16.04.94. Coming into force: 17.04.94. Effect: None. – *Unpublished*

The A500 Trunk Road (Queensway) (Temporary Prohibition of Traffic) Order 1994 No. 2456. Enabling power: *Road Traffic Regulation Act 1984, s. 14 (1) (a)*. Made: 09.09.94. Coming into force: 10.09.94. Effect: None. – *Unpublished*

The A501 Trunk Road (Euston Road and Pentonville Road, Camden and Islington) (Temporary Prohibition of Traffic) Order 1994 No. 3242. Enabling power: *Road Traffic Regulation Act 1984, s. 14 (1) (4) (7)*. Made: 12.12.94. Coming into force: 18.12.94. Effect: None. – *Unpublished*

The A501 Trunk Road (Euston Road Underpass, Camden) (Temporary Prohibition of Traffic) Order 1994 No. 1236. Enabling power: *Road Traffic Regulation Act 1984, s. 14 (1) (4) (5) (7)*. Made: 03.05.94. Coming into force: 08.05.94. Effect: None. – *Unpublished*

The A523 Trunk Road (London Road) at Macclesfield, Cheshire (Temporary 30 Miles Per Hour Speed Restriction) Order 1994 No. 819. Enabling power: *Road Traffic Regulation Act 1984, s. 14 (1) (a)*. Made: 02.02.94. Coming into force: 06.02.94. Effect: None. – *Unpublished*

The A523 Trunk Road (London Road) at Macclesfield, Cheshire (Temporary 30 MPH Speed Restriction) (No.2) Order 1994 No. 820. Enabling power: *Road Traffic Regulation Act 1984, s. 14 (1) (a)*. Made: 04.02.94. Coming into force: 06.02.94. Effect: None. – *Unpublished*

The A523 Trunk Road (London Road South) Poynton (Temporary 10 Miles Per Hour Speed Restriction) Order 1994 No. 2313. Enabling power: *Road Traffic Regulation Act 1984, s. 14 (1) (a)*. Made: 19.08.94. Coming into force: 21.08.94. Effect: None. – *Unpublished*

The A523 Trunk Road (London Road) Sunny-Bank (Temporary 10 Miles Per Hour Speed Restriction) Order 1994 No. 2314. Enabling power: *Road Traffic Regulation Act 1984, s. 14 (1) (a)*. Made: 19.08.94. Coming into force: 21.08.94. Effect: None. – *Unpublished*

The A523 Trunk Road (The Silk Road) Bradley Mount (Temporary Prohibition and Restriction of Traffic) Order 1994 No. 2305. Enabling power: *Road Traffic Regulation Act 1984, s. 14 (1) (a)*. Made: 19.08.94. Coming into force: 22.08.94. Effect: None. – *Unpublished*

The A523 Trunk Road (The Silk Road) Macclesfield (Temporary 10 Miles Per Hour Speed Restriction) Order 1994 No. 2303. Enabling power: *Road Traffic Regulation Act 1984, s. 14 (1) (a)*. Made: 19.08.94. Coming into force: 23.08.94. Effect: None. – *Unpublished*

The A523 Trunk Road (The Silk Road) Tytherington (Temporary 10 Miles Per Hour Speed Restriction) Order 1994 No. 2304. Enabling power: *Road Traffic Regulation Act 1984, s. 14 (1) (a)*. Made: 19.08.94. Coming into force: 23.08.94. Effect: None. – *Unpublished*

The A527(M) Motorway (Junctions 1 - 2) Slip Roads (Temporary Prohibition of Traffic) Order 1994 No. 1165. Enabling power: *Road Traffic Regulation Act 1984, s. 14 (1) (a)*. Made: 19.04.94. Coming into force: 05.05.94. Effect: None. – *Unpublished*

The A550 Trunk Road (Welsh Road) Ellesmere Port (Temporary Prohibition of Traffic) Order 1994 No. 1799. Enabling power: *Road Traffic Regulation Act 1984, s. 14 (1) (a)*. Made: 27.06.94. Coming into force: 09.07.94. Effect: None. – *Unpublished*

The A556 Trunk Road (Chester Road) at Lostock Gralam, Cheshire (Temporary 30 Miles Per Hour Speed Restriction) Order 1994 No. 838. Enabling power: *Road Traffic Regulation Act 1984, s. 14 (1) (a)*. Made: 28.01.94. Coming into force: 31.01.94. Effect: None. – *Unpublished*

Price/availability are liable to change without notice

The A556 Trunk Road (Chester Road Junction with Flittogate Lane) (Prohibition of Right Turns) Order 1994 No. 3029. Enabling power: *Road Traffic Regulation Act 1984, ss. 1 (1), 2 (1) (2)*. Made: 15.08.94. Coming into force: 31.08.94. Effect: None. – *Unpublished*

The A556 Trunk Road (Chester Road) Lostock Gralam, Cheshire (Temporary 30 MPH Speed Restriction) Order 1994 No. 813. Enabling power: *Road Traffic Regulation Act 1984, s. 14 (1) (a)*. Made: 31.01.94. Coming into force: 31.01.94. Effect: None. – *Unpublished*

The A556 Trunk Road (Chester Road) Mere, Cheshire (Temporary Prohibition and Restriction of Traffic) Order 1994 No. 396. Enabling power: *Road Traffic Regulation Act 1984, s. 14 (1) (a)*. Made: 04.02.94. Coming into force: 06.02.94. Effect: None. – *Unpublished*

The A556 Trunk Road (Chester Road) Mere (Temporary 10 Miles Per Hour Speed Restriction) Order 1994 No. 2317. Enabling power: *Road Traffic Regulation Act 1984, s. 14 (1) (a)*. Made: 24.08.94. Coming into force: 15.09.94. Effect: None. – *Unpublished*

The A556 Trunk Road (Northwich Bypass) (Temporary Prohibition of U-Turns and Right Turns) Order 1994 No. 1354. Enabling power: *Road Traffic Regulation Act 1984, s. 14 (1) (b)*. Made: 11.04.94. Coming into force: 12.04.94. Effect: None. – *Unpublished*

The A565 Trunk Road (Formby Bypass) Formby, Merseyside (Temporary Prohibition of Traffic) Order 1994 No. 840. Enabling power: *Road Traffic Regulation Act 1984, s. 14 (1) (a)*. Made: 07.01.94. Coming into force: 09.01.94. Effect: None. – *Unpublished*

The A565 Trunk Road (Formby Bypass, Formby) (Prohibition of U-turn) Order 1993 No. 1400. Enabling power: *Road Traffic Regulation Act 1984, ss. 1 (1), 2 (1) (2)*. Made: 20.12.93. Coming into force: 05.01.94. Effect: None. – *Unpublished*

The A565 Trunk Road (Plough Inn Roundabout - Banks Roundabout) (Temporary Restriction of Traffic) Order 1994 No. 1344. Enabling power: *Road Traffic Regulation Act 1984, ss. 3 (2), 14 (1) (a), 5 (b), (6)*. Made: 04.05.94. Coming into force: 08.05.94. Effect: None. – *Unpublished*

The A570 Trunk Road (Rainford Bypass, St Helens (Prohibition of Use of Gaps in Central Reservation) Order 1993 No. 846. Enabling power: *Road Traffic Regulation Act 1984, ss. 1 (1), 2 (1) (2)*. Made: 16.12.93. Coming into force: 06.01.94. Effect: None. – *Unpublished*

The A570 Trunk Road (Rainford Bypass) St Helens (Temporary Prohibition of Traffic) Order 1994 No. 1798. Enabling power: *Road Traffic Regulation Act 1984, s. 14 (1) (a)*. Made: 24.06.94. Coming into force: 31.07.94. Effect: None. – *Unpublished*

The A570 Trunk Road (Rainford Bypass) West Lancashire and St Helens (Temporary 50 Miles Per Hour Speed Restriction) Order 1994 No. 366. Enabling power: *Road Traffic Regulation Act 1984, s. 14 (1) (a)*. Made: 11.02.94. Coming into force: 13.02.94. Effect: None. – *Unpublished*

The A570 Trunk Road (Southport Road, Ormskirk) Between A59 County Road and Derby Street (Temporary Prohibition of Traffic) Order 1993 No. 865. Enabling power: *Road Traffic Regulation Act 1984, s. 14 (1) (a)*. Made: 18.11.93. Coming into force: 20.11.93. Effect: None. – *Unpublished*

The A570 Trunk Road (Southport Road) Ormskirk (Temporary Prohibition of Traffic) Order 1994 No. 1660. Enabling power: *Road Traffic Regulation Act 1984, s. 14 (1) (a)*. Made: 13.06.94. Coming into force: 25.06.94. Effect: None. – *Unpublished*

The A570 Trunk Road (St Helens Road, Ormskirk) Between Moor Street and the Park Road Link Road (Temporary Prohibition of Traffic) Order 1994 No. 369. Enabling power: *Road Traffic Regulation Act 1984, s. 14 (1) (a)*. Made: 14.02.94. Coming into force: 15.02.94. Effect: None. – *Unpublished*

The A580 Trunk Road (East Lancashire Road) Lowton (Temporary Prohibition of Traffic) Order 1994 No. 605. Enabling power: *Road Traffic Regulation Act 1984, s. 14 (1) (a)*. Made: 25.02.94. Coming into force: 06.03.94. Effect: None. – *Unpublished*

The A580 Trunk Road (East Lancashire Road, Moss Lane Junction) (Prohibition of Use of Gap in Central Reservation) Order 1994 No. 2324. Enabling power: *Road Traffic Regulation Act 1984, ss. 1 (1), 2 (1) (2)*. Made: 14.06.94. Coming into force: 07.07.94. Effect: None. – *Unpublished*

The A580 Trunk Road (East Lancashire Road) St Helens (Temporary Prohibition of Traffic) Order 1994 No. 1274. Enabling power: *Road Traffic Regulation Act 1984, s. 14 (1) (a) (b)*. Made: 17.04.94. Coming into force: 15.05.94. Effect: None. – *Unpublished*

The A585 Trunk Road (Amounderness Way Roundabout Junction with the B5412) Thornton Cleveleys (Temporary Prohibition of Traffic) Order 1994 No. 395. Enabling power: *Road Traffic Regulation Act 1984, s. 14 (1) (a)*. Made: 04.02.94. Coming into force: 04.02.94. Effect: None. – *Unpublished*

The A585 Trunk Road (Copse Road Diversion, Fleetwood) (24 Hour Clearway) Order 1994 No. 1222. Enabling power: *Road Traffic Regulation Act 1984, ss. 1 (1), 2 (1) (2), 3 (2), 4 (1)*. Made: 07.02.94. Coming into force: 24.02.94. Effect: None. – *Unpublished*

The A585 Trunk Road (Copse Road Diversion, Fleetwood) (Prohibition of Right Turn) Order 1993 No. 1524. Enabling power: *Road Traffic Regulation Act 1984, ss. 1 (1), 2 (1) (2)*. Made: 07.10.93. Coming into force: 28.10.93. Effect: None. – *Unpublished*

The A585 Trunk Road (Fleetwood Diversion) Wyre (Temporary Prohibition of Traffic) Order 1994 No. 1032. Enabling power: *Road Traffic Regulation Act 1984, ss. 3 (2), 14 (1) (a), 5 (b) (6).* Made: 23.03.94. Coming into force: 25.03.94. Effect: None. – *Unpublished*

The A590 Trunk Road (Backbarrow to Newby Bridge) (Temporary 40 Miles Per Hour Speed Restriction) Order 1994 No. 2816. Enabling power: *Road Traffic Regulation Act 1984, s. 14 (1) (a).* Made: 27.10.94. Coming into force: 28.10.94. Effect: None. – *Unpublished*

The A590 Trunk Road (East of Gilkin House, Newby Bridge) (Temporary 10 Miles Per Hours Speed Restriction) Order 1994 No. 1857. Enabling power: *Road Traffic Regulation Act 1984, s. 14 (1) (a).* Made: 07.07.94. Coming into force: 10.07.94. Effect: None. – *Unpublished*

The A590 Trunk Road (Greenodd Bypass to Levens Interchange) (Temporary Prohibition and 10 Miles per Hour and 40 Miles Per Hour Speed Restriction) Order 1994 No. 2425. Enabling power: *Road Traffic Regulation Act 1984, s. 14 (1) (a).* Made: 01.09.94. Coming into force: 03.09.94. Effect: None. – *Unpublished*

The A590 Trunk Road (Old Backbarrow Retaining Wall) (Temporary 40 Miles Per Hour Speed Restriction) Order 1994 No. 593. Enabling power: *Road Traffic Regulation Act 1984, s. 14 (1) (a).* Made: 03.03.94. Coming into force: 06.03.94. Effect: None. – *Unpublished*

The A595 Trunk Road (Butts Wood to High Cross) (Temporary Prohibition of Traffic) Order 1994 No. 1287. Enabling power: *Road Traffic Regulation Act 1984, s. 14 (1) (a).* Made: 05.05.94. Coming into force: 07.05.94. Effect: None. – *Unpublished*

The A595 Trunk Road (Grizebeck to Duddon Bridge) (Temporary 10 Miles Per Hour Speed Restriction) Order 1994 No. 1855. Enabling power: *Road Traffic Regulation Act 1984, s. 14 (1) (a).* Made: 07.07.94. Coming into force: 10.07.94. Effect: None. – *Unpublished*

The A595 Trunk Road (Hallthwaites and Whicham) (Temporary Prohibition and 10 Miles Per Hour Speed Restriction) Order 1994 No. 740. Enabling power: *Road Traffic Regulation Act 1984, s. 14 (1) (a).* Made: 03.03.94. Coming into force: 06.03.94. Effect: None. – *Unpublished*

The A595 Trunk Road (Holegill to Moorgreen Farm) (Temporary Prohibition of Traffic) Order 1994 No. 2940. Enabling power: *Road Traffic Regulation Act 1984, s. 14 (1) (a).* Made: 10.11.94. Coming into force: 12.11.94. Effect: None. – *Unpublished*

The A595 Trunk Road (Loop Road Bridge No 1, Whitehaven) (Temporary Prohibition of Traffic) Order 1994 No. 1224. Enabling power: *Road Traffic Regulation Act 1984, s. 14 (1) (a).* Made: 28.04.94. Coming into force: 30.04.94. Effect: None. – *Unpublished*

The A595 Trunk Road (Muncaster Bridge) (Temporary Prohibition and Restriction of Traffic) Order 1994 No. 312. Enabling power: *Road Traffic Regulation Act 1984, s. 14 (1) (a).* Made: 10.02.94. Coming into force: 13.02.94. Effect: None. – *Unpublished*

The A595 Trunk Road (Whicham Valley) (Temporary Prohibition and Restriction of Traffic) Order 1994 No. 1848. Enabling power: *Road Traffic Regulation Act 1984, s. 14 (1) (a).* Made: 06.07.94. Coming into force: 10.07.94. Effect: None. – *Unpublished*

The A596 Trunk Road (Dunmail Park, Low Whinnow, Shawood Farm & Crosby) (Temporary 10 Miles Per Hour Speed Restriction) Order 1994 No. 1845. Enabling power: *Road Traffic Regulation Act 1984, s. 14 (1) (a).* Made: 06.07.94. Coming into force: 10.07.94. Effect: None. – *Unpublished*

The A596 Trunk Road (Heathfield) (Temporary 10 Miles Per Hour Speed Restriction) Order 1994 No. 2632. Enabling power: *Road Traffic Regulation Act 1984, s. 14 (1) (a).* Made: 29.09.94. Coming into force: 02.10.94. Effect: None. – *Unpublished*

The A596 Trunk Road (Thursby-Wigton) (Temporary 10 Miles Per Hour Speed Restriction) Order 1994 No. 437. Enabling power: *Road Traffic Regulation Act 1984, s. 14 (1) (a).* Made: 21.02.94. Coming into force: 26.02.94. Effect: None. – *Unpublished*

The A604 Trunk Road (Huntingdon Bypass, Cambridgeshire) (Temporary 50 Miles Per Hour Speed Restriction) Order 1994 No. 336. Enabling power: *Road Traffic Regulation Act 1984, s. 14 (1) (a).* Made: 11.02.94. Coming into force: 14.02.94. Effect: None. – *Unpublished*

The A614 Trunk Road (Howden Spur) and the M62 Motorway (Temporary Prohibition of Traffic) Order 1994 No. 2722. Enabling power: *Road Traffic Regulation Act 1984, s. 14 (1) (a).* Made: 19.10.94. Coming into force: 20.10.94. Effect: None. – *Unpublished*

The A614 Trunk Road (Leapool Roundabout, Gedling, Nottinghamshire) (Temporary Prohibition of Traffic) Order 1994 No. 2706. Enabling power: *Road Traffic Regulation Act 1984, s. 14 (1) (a).* Made: 09.10.94. Coming into force: 13.10.94. Effect: None. – *Unpublished*

The A614 Trunk Road (Ollerton, Nottinghamshire) (Temporary 30 Miles Per Hour Speed Restriction) Order 1994 No. 204. Enabling power: *Road Traffic Regulation Act 1984, s. 14 (1) (a).* Made: 28.01.94. Coming into force: 29.01.94. Effect: None. – *Unpublished*

The A616 Trunk Road (Flough Crossroads - Midhopestones) (Temporary Restriction and Prohibition of Traffic) Order 1994 No. 3112. Enabling power: *Road Traffic Regulation Act 1984, s. 14 (1) (a).* Made: 02.12.94. Coming into force: 04.12.94. Effect: None. – *Unpublished*

The A616 Trunk Road (Fox Wire Access Road) (Temporary 40 Miles Per Hour Speed Restriction) Order 1994 No. 445. Enabling power: *Road Traffic Regulation Act 1984, s. 14 (1) (a)*. Made: 23.02.94. Coming into force: 26.02.94. Effect: None. – *Unpublished*

The A616 Trunk Road (Stocksbridge Bypass) (Temporary 40 Miles Per Hour Speed Restriction) Order 1994 No. 1248. Enabling power: *Road Traffic Regulation Act 1984, s. 14 (1) (a)*. Made: 06.05.94. Coming into force: 08.05.94. Effect: None. – *Unpublished*

The A628 Trunk Road (Flouch Crossroads - Saltersbrook Bridge) (Temporary Restriction and Prohibition of Traffic) Order 1994 No. 2738. Enabling power: *Road Traffic Regulation Act 1984, s. 14 (1) (a)*. Made: 20.10.94. Coming into force: 22.10.94. Effect: None. – *Unpublished*

The A638 Trunk Road (Crofton Railway Bridge) (Temporary Prohibition of Traffic) Order 1994 No. 441. Enabling power: *Road Traffic Regulation Act 1984, s. 14 (1) (a)*. Made: 23.02.94. Coming into force: 25.02.94. Effect: None. – *Unpublished*

The A638 Trunk Road (Doncaster Road, Ackworth) (Temporary 40 Miles Per Hour Speed Restriction) Order 1994 No. 916. Enabling power: *Road Traffic Regulation Act 1984, s. 14 (1) (a)*. Made: 18.03.94. Coming into force: 21.03.94. Effect: None. – *Unpublished*

The A638 Trunk Road (Doncaster Road, Crofton) (Temporary 40 Miles Per Hour Speed Restriction) Order 1994 No. 1802. Enabling power: *Road Traffic Regulation Act 1984, s. 14 (1) (a)*. Made: 05.07.94. Coming into force: 08.07.94. Effect: None. – *Unpublished*

The A638 Trunk Road (Nostell Bridge) (Temporary Prohibition of Traffic) Order 1994 No.2006. Enabling power: *Road Traffic Regulation Act 1984, s. 14 (1) (a)*. Made: 20.07.94. Coming into force: 23.07.94. Effect: None. – *Unpublished*

The A638 Trunk Road (Oakenhshaw Railway Bridge, Doncaster Road) (Temporary 40 Miles Per Hour Speed Restriction) Order 1994 No. 2444. Enabling power: *Road Traffic Regulation Act 1984, s. 14 (1) (a)*. Made: 14.09.94. Coming into force: 17.09.94. Effect: None. – *Unpublished*

The A638 Trunk Road (York Road, Doncaster) (Ban on U Turns and Right Turns) Order 1994 No.2838. Enabling power: *Road Traffic Regulation Act 1984, ss. 1 (1), 2 (1) (2)*. Made: 24.10.94. Coming into force: 28.10.94. Effect: None. – *Unpublished*

The A638 Trunk Road (York Road, Doncaster) (Cycle Track) (Prohibition of Right and Left Turns) Order 1994 No. 2985. Enabling power: *Road Traffic Regulation Act 1984, ss. 1 (1), 2 (1) (2)*. Made: 23.11.94. Coming into force: 28.11.94. Effect: None. – *Unpublished*

The A646 Trunk Road (Burnley Road, Cornholme) (Temporary Restriction of Traffic) Order 1994 No. 2266. Enabling power: *Road Traffic Regulation Act 1984, s. 14 (1) (a)*. Made: 26.08.94. Coming into force: 01.09.94. Effect: None. – *Unpublished*

The A650 Trunk Road (Bradford Road, Bingley) (Bus Stop Clearway) Order 1994 No. 2752. Enabling power: *Road Traffic Regulation Act 1984, s. 1 (1), 2 (1) (2), 4 (1)*. Made: 18.10.94. Coming into force: 21.10.94. Effect: S.I. 1972/1183 amended. – *Unpublished*

The A696 Trunk Road (40 MPH Speed Limit at Belsay) Temporary Restriction of Traffic) Order 1994 No. 816. Enabling power: *Road Traffic Regulation Act 1984, s. 14 (1) (a)*. Made: 11.03.94. Coming into force: 13.03.94. Effect: None. – *Unpublished*

The A696 Trunk Road (Catleugh) (Temporary 40 Miles Per Hour and 10 Miles Per Hour Restriction of Traffic) Order 1994 No. 2503. Enabling power: *Road Traffic Regulation Act 1984, s. 14 (1) (a) (7)*. Made: 15.09.94. Coming into force: 17.09.94. Effect: None. – *Unpublished*

The A696 Trunk Road (Cottonshope, Redesdale Camp and Bennetsfield) (Temporary 40 Miles Per Hour and 10 Miles Per Hour Speed Restriction) Order 1994 No. 1617. Enabling power: *Road Traffic Regulation Act 1984, s. 14 (1) (a)*. Made: 10.06.94. Coming into force: 19.06.94. Effect: None. – *Unpublished*

The A696 Trunk Road (Kirkwhelpington and Newhouses) (Temporary 40 Miles Per Hour and 10 Miles Per Hour Restriction of Traffic) Order 1994 No. 1750. Enabling power: *Road Traffic Regulation Act 1984, s. 14 (1) (a)*. Made: 24.06.94. Coming into force: 03.07.94. Effect: None. – *Unpublished*

The A823 (M) Pitreavie Spur and the M90/A90 Trunk Road Inverkeithing-Aberdeen (Masterton and Admiralty Slip Roads (Temporary Prohibition of Traffic) Order 1994 No. 1193. Enabling power: *Road Traffic Regulation Act 1984, s. 14 (1) (a) (4) (a)*. Made: 28.04.94. Coming into force: 30.04.94. Effect: None. – *Unpublished*

The A823 (M) Pitreavie Spur (Westbound) (Temporary Prohibition of Traffic) Order 1994 No.2355. Enabling power: *Road Traffic Regulation Act 1984, s. 14 (4) (a)*. Made: 02.09.94. Coming into force: 10.09.94. Effect: None. – *Unpublished*

The A835/A893 Trunk Road Tore-Ullapool (Garve Railway Level Crossing) (Temporary Prohibition of Traffic) Order 1994 No. 1267. Enabling power: *Road Traffic Regulation Act 1984, s. 14 (1) (a) (4)*. Made: 09.05.94. Coming into force: 15.05.94. Effect: None. – *Unpublished*

The A977 Trunk Road (Drum to Crook of Devon) (Tayside Region) (Temporary 10 MPH Speed Limit) Order 1994 No. 2575. Enabling power: *Road Traffic Regulation Act 1984, s. 14 (1) (a) (4) (a), 121A*. Made: 03.10.94. Coming into force: 10.10.94. Effect: None. – *Unpublished*

Price/availability are liable to change without notice

154 ROAD TRAFFIC: TRAFFIC REGULATION

The A1016 Trunk Road (Webbs Farm Interchange - White Horse Roundabout, Essex) (Temporary 10 Miles Per Hour and 40 Miles Per Hour Speed Restriction) Order 1994 No. 2714. Enabling power: *Road Traffic Regulation Act 1984, s. 14 (1) (a)*. Made: 17.10.94. Coming into force: 24.10.94. Effect: None. – *Unpublished*

The A1053 Trunk Road (Greystone Road) (Temporary Restriction and Prohibition of Traffic) Order 1994 No. 1585. Enabling power: *Road Traffic Regulation Act 1984, s. 14 (1) (a)*. Made: 09.06.94. Coming into force: 12.06.94. Effect: None. – *Unpublished*

The A1079 Trunk Road (Grimston, Near York) (Box Junction) Order 1994 No. 1352. Enabling power: *Road Traffic Regulation Act 1984, s. 1 (1) 2 (1) (2)*. Made: 13.05.94. Coming into force: 23.05.94. Effect: None. – *Unpublished*

The A1079 Trunk Road (Market Weighton Bypass, Eastern Junction) (Prohibition of Various Traffic Movements) Order 1994 No. 2265. Enabling power: *Road Traffic Regulation Act 1984, ss. 1 (1), 2 (1) (2)*. Made: 19.08.94. Coming into force: 26.09.94. Effect: None. – *Unpublished*

The A1079 Trunk Road (York Road, Kexby) (Temporary 40 Miles Per Hour Speed Restriction) Order 1994 No. 2044. Enabling power: *Road Traffic Regulation Act 1984, s. 14 (1) (a)*. Made: 26.07.94. Coming into force: 29.07.94. Effect: None. – *Unpublished*

The A1089 Trunk Road (St. Andrews Road, Tilbury, Essex) (Temporary Restriction of Traffic) Order 1994 No. 2476. Enabling power: *Road Traffic Regulation Act 1984, s. 14 (1) (a)*. Made: 19.09.94. Coming into force: 26.09.94. Effect: None. – *Unpublished*

The A1089 Trunk Road (Tilbury, Essex) (Temporary Prohibition and Restriction of Traffic) Order 1994 No. 2580. Enabling power: *Road Traffic Regulation Act 1984, s. 14 (1) (a)*. Made: 03.10.94. Coming into force: 10.10.94. Effect: None. – *Unpublished*

The A1400 Trunk Road (Southend Road and Woodford Avenue, Redbridge) (Temporary Prohibition of Traffic) Order 1994 No. 319. Enabling power: *Road Traffic Regulation Act 1984, s. 14 (1) (4) (5) (7)*. Made: 14.02.94. Coming into force: 20.02.94. Effect: None. – *Unpublished*

The A3113 Trunk Road (Airport Way) (Temporary Restriction and Prohibition of Traffic) Order 1994 No. 1594. Enabling power: *Road Traffic Regulation Act 1984, s. 14 (1) (a), 5 (b)*. Made: 09.06.94. Coming into force: 10.06.94. Effect: None. – *Unpublished*

The A4042 Trunk Road (Llanfrechfa, Gwent) (Temporary 40 MPH Speed Limit) Order 1994 No. 41. Enabling power: *Road Traffic Regulation Act 1984, s. 14 (1)*. Made: 04.01.94. Coming into force: 10.01.94. Effect: None. – *Unpublished*

The A4042 Trunk Road (Llanyrafon-Llantarnam, Gwent) Temporary Prohibition of Vehicles) Order 1994 No. 901. Enabling power: *Road Traffic Regulation Act 1984, s. 14 (1)*. Made: 17.03.94. Coming into force: 18.03.94. Effect: None. – *Unpublished*

The A4042 Trunk Road (Mamhilad, Gwent) (Closure of Central Reservation Crossing) Order 1994 No. 248. Enabling power: *Road Traffic Regulation Act 1984, ss. 1 (1), 2 (1) (2)*. Made: 01.02.94. Coming into force: 11.02.94. Effect: None. – *Unpublished*

The A4123 Trunk Road (Titford Road) (Temporary Restriction of Traffic) Order 1994 No. 2839. Enabling power: *Road Traffic Regulation Act 1984, s. 14 (1) (a)*. Made: 07.10.94. Coming into force: 11.10.94. Effect: None. – *Unpublished*

The A4232 Trunk Road (Capel Llanilltern - Culverhouse Cross, South Glamorgan) (Temporary 50 MPH Speed Limit) Order 1994 No. 1810. Enabling power: *Road Traffic Regulation Act 1984, s. 14 (1)*. Made: 28.06.94. Coming into force: 01.07.94. Effect: None. – *Unpublished*

The A4232 Trunk Road (Culverhouse Cross Junction, Cardiff, South Glamorgan) (Temporary Prohibition of Vehicles) Order 1994 No. 2827. Enabling power: *Road Traffic Regulation Act 1984, s. 14 (1) (4)*. Made: 27.10.94. Coming into force: 27.10.94. Effect: None. – *Unpublished*

The A5036 Trunk Road (Between Copy Lane and Switch Island) (Closure of Gap in Central Reservation) Order 1994 No. 2008. Enabling power: *Road Traffic Regulation Act 1984, s. 1 (1), 2 (1) (2)*. Made: 22.04.94. Coming into force: 01.07.94. Effect: None. – *Unpublished*

The A5036 Trunk Road (Church Road) at Litherland, Merseyside (Temporary 20 Miles Per Hour Speed Restriction) Order 1993 No. 864. Enabling power: *Road Traffic Regulation Act 1984, s. 14 (1) (a)*. Made: 23.12.93. Coming into force: 02.01.94. Effect: None. – *Unpublished*

The A5036 Trunk Road (Dunnings Bridge Road) Netherton, Merseyside (Temporary Prohibition of Traffic) Order 1994 No. 370. Enabling power: *Road Traffic Regulation Act 1984, s. 14 (1) (a)*. Made: 14.01.94. Coming into force: 16.01.94. Effect: None. – *Unpublished*

The A5103 Trunk Road (Princess Parkway) Northbound Access Slip Road (Temporary Prohibition of Traffic) Order 1994 No. 1805. Enabling power: *Road Traffic Regulation Act 1984, s. 14 (1) (a)*. Made: 13.06.94. Coming into force: 15.06.94. Effect: None. – *Unpublished*

The A5103 Trunk Road (Princess Parkway Northenden Manchester) (Closure of Gaps in Central Reservation) Order 1993 No. 1619. Enabling power: *Road Traffic Regulation Act 1984, ss. 1 (1), 2 (1) (2)*. Made: 28.10.93. Coming into force: 19.11.93. Effect: None. – *Unpublished*

The A5103 Trunk Road (Princess Parkway) Northenden Southbound Exit Slip Road (Temporary Prohibition of Traffic) Order 1994 No. 2718. Enabling power: *Road Traffic Regulation Act 1984, s. 14 (1) (a)*. Made: 05.10.94. Coming into force: 09.10.94. Effect: None. – *Unpublished*

The A5103 Trunk Road (Princess Parkway) Northenden (Temporary Prohibition of Traffic) (No. 2) Order 1994 No. 2322. Enabling power: *Road Traffic Regulation Act 1984, s. 14 (1) (a)*. Made: 17.08.94. Coming into force: 01.09.94. Effect: None. – *Unpublished*

The A5103 Trunk Road (Princess Parkway) Northenden (Temporary Prohibition of Traffic) Order 1994 No. 1674. Enabling power: *Road Traffic Regulation Act 1984, s. 14 (1) (a)*. Made: 13.06.94. Coming into force: 01.07.94. Effect: None. – *Unpublished*

The A5111 and A52 Trunk Roads and Slip Roads (Raynesway, Borrowash Bypass, Derbyshire) (Temporary Prohibition of Traffic) Order 1994 No. 2220. Enabling power: *Road Traffic Regulation Act 1984, s. 14 (1) (4)*. Made: 22.08.94. Coming into force: 29.08.94. Effect: None. – *Unpublished*

The A5111 and A516 Trunk Roads (Uttoxeter New Road, Derbyshire) (Temporary Prohibition and Restriction of Traffic) Order 1994 No. 256. Enabling power: *Road Traffic Regulation Act 1984, s. 14 (1) (a)*. Made: 03.02.94. Coming into force: 12.02.94. Effect: None. – *Unpublished*

The A5111 Trunk Road (Osmaston Park Road, Derby, Derbyshire) (Temporary 30 Miles Per Hour Speed Restriction) Order 1994 No. 1126. Enabling power: *Road Traffic Regulation Act 1984, s. 14 (1) (a)*. Made: 05.04.94. Coming into force: 09.04.94. Effect: None. – *Unpublished*

The A5111 Trunk Road (Osmaston Park Road, Derby) (Prohibition of Right Turns) Order 1994 No. 2642. Enabling power: *Road Traffic Regulation Act 1984, s. 1 (1), 2 (1) (2)*. Made: 06.10.94. Coming into force: 17.10.94. Effect: None. – *Unpublished*

The A5148 Trunk Road (Lichfield Eastern Bypass) (Temporary Restriction and Prohibition of Traffic) Order 1994 No. 2726. Enabling power: *Road Traffic Regulation Act 1984, s. 14 (1) (a), 5 (a) (7)*. Made: 14.10.94. Coming into force: 15.10.94. Effect: None. – *Unpublished*

The A6119 Trunk Road (Brownhill Drive, Blackburn) (Temporary 40 Miles Per Hour Speed Restriction) Order 1993 No. 1110. Enabling power: *Road Traffic Regulation Act 1984, s. 14 (1) (b)*. Made: 24.09.93. Coming into force: 27.09.93. Effect: None. – *Unpublished*

The A6119 Trunk Road (Brownhill Drive) (Temporary Prohibition of 'U' Turns) Order 1993 No. 1363. Enabling power: *Road Traffic Regulation Act 1984, s. 14 (1) (a)*. Made: 30.09.93. Coming into force: 03.10.93. Effect: None. – *Unpublished*

The A6120 Trunk Road (Otley Road Roundabout - King Lane Roundabout, Eastbound Carriageway) (Temporary Prohibition of Traffic) Order 1994 No. 878. Enabling power: *Road Traffic Regulation Act 1984, s. 14 (1) (a)*. Made: 10.03.94. Coming into force: 12.03.94. Effect: None. – *Unpublished*

The A6514 Trunk Road (Nottingham Ring Road, Nottinghamshire) (Prohibition of "U" Turns) Order 1994 No. 2966. Enabling power: *Road Traffic Regulation Act 1984, ss. 1 (1), 2 (1) (2)*. Made: 17.11.94. Coming into force: 28.11.94. Effect: None. – *Unpublished*

The A6514 Trunk Road (Western Boulevard, Aspley, Nottinghamshire) (Temporary Prohibition of Traffic) Order 1994 No. 2172. Enabling power: *Road Traffic Regulation Act 1984, s. 14 (1) (a)*. Made: 03.08.94. Coming into force: 06.08.94. Effect: None. – *Unpublished*

The A6514 Trunk Road (Western Boulevard/Beechdale Road Junction, Nottinghamshire) (Temporary Prohibition of Traffic) Order 1994 No. 837. Enabling power: *Road Traffic Regulation Act 1984, s. 14 (1) (a)*. Made: 14.03.94. Coming into force: 18.03.94. Effect: None. – *Unpublished*

The Aberdeen-Fraserburgh Trunk Road (A956/A92/A952) (Parkway to Murcar) (Prohibition of Specified Turns) Order 1994 No. 2554. Enabling power: *Road Traffic Regulation Act 1984, s. 1 (1)*. Made: 29.09.94. Coming into force: 24.09.94. Effect: None. – *Unpublished*

The Aberdeen to Fraserburgh Trunk Road (A956) (Ellon Road, Aberdeen) (Restriction of Traffic) Order 1994 No. 1676. Enabling power: *Road Traffic Regulation Act 1984, s. 1 (1)*. Made: 20.06.94. Coming into force: 01.08.94. Effect: None. – *Unpublished*

The Glasgow-Carlisle Trunk Road (A74) (Beattock to Cleuchbrae (Clearway) Order 1994 No. 462. Enabling power: *Road Traffic Regulation Act 1984, ss. 1 (1), 2 (1), 2 (2), 121A (1) (b)*. Made: 18.02.94. Coming into force: 04.03.94. Effect: None. – *Unpublished*

The Glasgow-Carlisle Trunk Road (A74) (Cleuchbrae to Dinwoodie Green (Clearway) Order 1994 No. 463. Enabling power: *Road Traffic Regulation Act 1984, ss. 1 (1), 2 (1), 2 (2), 121A (1) (b)*. Made: 18.02.94. Coming into force: 04.03.94. Effect: None. – *Unpublished*

The Glasgow-Carlisle Trunk Road (A74) (Dinwoodie Green to Muirhouse (Clearway) Order 1994 No. 464. Enabling power: *Road Traffic Regulation Act 1984, ss. 1 (1), 2 (1), 2 (2), 121A (1) (b)*. Made: 18.02.94. Coming into force: 04.03.94. Effect: None. – *Unpublished*

The Glasgow-Carlisle Trunk Road (A74) (Eaglesfield to Kirkpatrick Fleming) (Clearway) Order 1994 No. 466. Enabling power: *Road Traffic Regulation Act 1984, ss. 1 (1), 2 (1), 2 (2), 121A (1) (b)*. Made: 18.02.94. Coming into force: 04.03.94. Effect: None. – *Unpublished*

The Glasgow-Carlisle Trunk Road (A74) (Ecclefechan Interchange to Eaglesfield) (Clearway) Order 1994 No. 467. Enabling power: *Road Traffic Regulation Act 1984, ss. 1 (1), 2 (1), 2 (2), 121A (1) (b)*. Made: 18.02.94. Coming into force: 04.03.94. Effect: None. – *Unpublished*

The Glasgow-Carlisle Trunk Road (A74) (Ecclefechan Railway Bridge to Ecclefechan Interchange) (Clearway) Order 1994 No. 477. Enabling power: *Road Traffic Regulation Act 1984, ss. 1 (1), 2 (1), 2 (2), 121A (1) (b)*. Made: 18.02.94. Coming into force: 04.03.94. Effect: None. – *Unpublished*

The Glasgow-Carlisle Trunk Road (A74) (Greenhillstairs to Beattock (Clearway) Order 1994 No.461. Enabling power: *Road Traffic Regulation Act.1984, ss. 1 (1), 2 (1), 2 (2), 121A (1) (b)*. Made: 18.02.94. Coming into force: 04.03.94. Effect: None. – *Unpublished*

The Glasgow-Carlisle Trunk Road (A74) (Muirhouse to Water of Milk) (Clearway) Order 1994 No.475. Enabling power: *Road Traffic Regulation Act 1984, ss. 1 (1), 2 (1), 2 (2), 121A (1) (b)*. Made: 18.02.94. Coming into force: 04.03.94. Effect: None. – *Unpublished*

The Glasgow-Carlisle Trunk Road (A74) (Nether Abington to Elvanfoot) (Clearway) Order 1994 No. 476. Enabling power: *Road Traffic Regulation Act 1984, ss. 1 (1), 2 (1), 2 (2), 121A (1) (b)*. Made: 18.02.94. Coming into force: 04.03.94. Effect: None. – *Unpublished*

The Glasgow-Carlisle Trunk Road (A74) (Paddy's Rickle Bridge to Greenhillstairs) (Clearway) Order 1994 No. 465. Enabling power: *Road Traffic Regulation Act 1984, ss. 1 (1), 2 (1), 2 (2), 121A (1) (b)*. Made: 18.02.94. Coming into force: 04.03.94. Effect: None. – *Unpublished*

The Glasgow-Carlisle Trunk Road (A74) (Water of Milk to Ecclefechan) (Clearway) Order 1994 No. 474. Enabling power: *Road Traffic Regulation Act 1984, ss. 1 (1), 2 (1), 2 (2), 121A (1) (b)*. Made: 18.02.94. Coming into force: 04.03.94. Effect: None. – *Unpublished*

The Glasgow-Inverness Trunk Road (A82) (Urquhart Castle) (Clearway) Order 1994 No.549. Enabling power: *Road Traffic Regulation Act 1984, ss. 1 (1), 2 (1) (2), 121A (1) (b)*. Made: 01.03.94. Coming into force: 10.03.94. Effect: None. – *Unpublished*

The Glasgow-Inverness Trunk Road (Route A82) (Clearways) (Variation) Order 1994 No.2389. Enabling power: *Road Traffic Regulation Act 1984, s. 1 (1)*. Made: 09.09.94. Coming into force: 07.10.94. Effect: S.I. 1976/1567 amended. – *Unpublished*

The London North Circular Trunk Road (A406) and the A1 Trunk Road (Great North Way, Barnet) (Temporary Restriction of Traffic) Order 1994 No. 1116. Enabling power: *Road Traffic Regulation Act 1984, s. 14 (1) (4)*. Made: 19.04.94. Coming into force: 25.04.94. Effect: None. – *Unpublished*

The London North Circular Trunk Road (A406) (Angel Road, Enfield) (Temporary Prohibition of Traffic) Order 1994 No. 1462. Enabling power: *Road Traffic Regulation Act 1984, s. 14 (1) (4) (7)*. Made: 26.05.94. Coming into force: 06.06.94. Effect: None. – *Unpublished*

The London North Circular Trunk Road (A406) (Barking Road Flyover, Newham) (Temporary Prohibition of Traffic) Order 1994 No. 2047. Enabling power: *Road Traffic Regulation Act 1984, s. 14 (1) (4)*. Made: 01.08.94. Coming into force: 07.08.94. Effect: None. – *Unpublished*

The London North Circular Trunk Road (A406) (Barnet) (Temporary Prohibition of Traffic) No. 2 Order 1994 No. 1166. Enabling power: *Road Traffic Regulation Act 1984, s. 14 (1) (4)*. Made: 25.04.94. Coming into force: 02.05.94. Effect: None. – *Unpublished*

The London North Circular Trunk Road (A406) (Barnet) (Temporary Prohibition of Traffic) (No.3) Order 1994 No. 2201. Enabling power: *Road Traffic Regulation Act 1984, s. 14 (1) (4) (5) (7)*. Made: 15.08.94. Coming into force: 20.08.94. Effect: None. – *Unpublished*

The London North Circular Trunk Road (A406) (Barnet) (Temporary Prohibition of Traffic) Order 1994 No. 751. Enabling power: *Road Traffic Regulation Act 1984 s. 14 (1) (4) (5) (7)*. Made: 14.03.94. Coming into force: 19.03.94. Effect: None. – *Unpublished*

The London North Circular Trunk Road (A406) (Barnet) (Temporary Prohibition of Use of Gap in Central Reserve) Order 1994 No. 2949. Enabling power: *Road Traffic Regulation Act 1984, s. 14 (1) (4)*. Made: 21.11.94. Coming into force: 25.11.94. Effect: None. – *Unpublished*

The London North Circular Trunk Road (A406) (Barnet) (Temporary Speed Restriction) Order 1994 No. 2291. Enabling power: *Road Traffic Regulation Act 1984, s. 14 (1) (4), 15 (2)*. Made: 26.08.94. Coming into force: 02.09.94. Effect: None. – *Unpublished*

The London North Circular Trunk Road (A406) (Crooked Billet Underpass, Waltham Forest) (Temporary Prohibition of Traffic) Order 1994 No. 1960. Enabling power: *Road Traffic Regulation Act 1984, s. 14 (1) (4)*. Made: 18.07.94. Coming into force: 24.07.94. Effect: None. – *Unpublished*

The London North Circular Trunk Road (A406) (Great Cambridge Road, Underpass, Enfield) (Temporary Prohibition of Traffic) Order 1994 No. 2290. Enabling power: *Road Traffic Regulation Act 1984, s. 14 (1) (4)*. Made: 26.08.94. Coming into force: 04.09.94. Effect: None. – *Unpublished*

The London North Circular Trunk Road (A406) (Gunnersbury Avenue and Hanger Lane, Ealing) (Temporary Prohibition of Traffic) Order 1994 No. 1078. Enabling power: *Road Traffic Regulation Act 1984, s. 14 (1) (4) (5) (7)*. Made: 11.04.94. Coming into force: 18.04.94. Effect: None. – *Unpublished*

The London North Circular Trunk Road (A406) (Ilford Viaduct and Redbridge Viaduct, Redbridge) (Temporary Prohibition of Traffic) Order 1994 No. 2292. Enabling power: *Road Traffic Regulation Act 1984, s. 14 (1) (4)*. Made: 26.08.94. Coming into force: 03.09.94. Effect: None. – *Unpublished*

The London North Circular Trunk Road (A406) (Lea Valley Viaduct, Waltham Forest) (Temporary Prohibition of Traffic) Order 1994 No. 1708. Enabling power: *Road Traffic Regulation Act 1984, s. 14 (1) (4) (7)*. Made: 27.06.94. Coming into force: 07.07.94. Effect: None. – *Unpublished*

The London North Circular Trunk Road (A406) (Sterling Way, Enfield) (Temporary Restriction of Traffic) Order 1994 No. 1406. Enabling power: *Road Traffic Regulation Act 1984, s. 14 (1) (4)*. Made: 23.05.94. Coming into force: 31.05.94. Effect: None. – *Unpublished*

The London North Circular Trunk Road (A406) (Waltham Forest) (Temporary Prohibition of Traffic) Order 1994 No. 2705. Enabling power: *Road Traffic Regulation Act 1984, s. 14 (1) (4)*. Made: 17.10.94. Coming into force: 23.10.94. Effect: None. – *Unpublished*

The London North Circular Trunk Road (A406) (Waltham Forest) (Temporary Restriction of Traffic) Order 1994 No. 1706. Enabling power: *Road Traffic Regulation Act 1984, s. 14 (1) (4) (7)*. Made: 27.06.94. Coming into force: 01.07.94. Effect: None. – *Unpublished*

The London North Circular Trunk Road (A406) (Woodford Viaduct, Redbridge) (Temporary Restriction of Speed) Order 1994 No. 1077. Enabling power: *Road Traffic Regulation Act 1984, s. 14 (1) (4)*. Made: 11.04.94. Coming into force: 17.04.94. Effect: None. – *Unpublished*

The London North Circular Trunk Road (A406) (Woodford Viaduct, Redbridge) (Temporary Prohibition of Traffic) Order 1994 No. 2604. Enabling power: *Road Traffic Regulation Act 1984, s. 14 (1) (4)*. Made: 03.10.94. Coming into force: 07.10.94. Effect: None. – *Unpublished*

The London South Circular Trunk Road (A205) (Atkins Road and Poynders Road, Lambeth) (Temporary Restriction of Traffic) Order 1994 No. 1997. Enabling power: *Road Traffic Regulation Act 1984, s. 14 (1) (4)*. Made: 25.07.94. Coming into force: 01.08.94. Effect: None. – *Unpublished*

The London South Circular Trunk Road (A205) (Cavendish Road, Lambeth) (Temporary Restriction of Traffic) Order 1994 No. 16. Enabling power: *Road Traffic Regulation Act 1984, s. 14 (1) (4) (5) (7)*. Made: 04.01.94. Coming into force: 10.01.94. Effect: None. – *Unpublished*

The London South Circular Trunk Road (A205) (Christchurch Road, Lambeth) (Temporary Prohibition of Traffic) Order 1994 No. 2132. Enabling power: *Road Traffic Regulation Act 1984, s. 14 (1) (4) (5) (7)*. Made: 08.08.94. Coming into force: 15.08.94. Effect: None. – *Unpublished*

The London South Circular Trunk Road (A205) (London Road, Lewisham) (Temporary Restriction of Traffic) Order 1994 No. 2209. Enabling power: *Road Traffic Regulation Act 1984, s. 14 (1) (4)*. Made: 15.08.94. Coming into force: 22.08.94. Effect: None. – *Unpublished*

The London South Circular Trunk Road (A205) (Thurlow Park Road, Lambeth) (Temporary Restriction of Traffic) Order 1994 No. 322. Enabling power: *Road Traffic Regulation Act 1984, s. 14 (1) (4)*. Made: 14.02.94. Coming into force: 20.02.94. Effect: None. – *Unpublished*

The M1 (Junction 6) and M25 (Junction 21) Motorways (Hertfordshire) (Temporary Prohibition of Traffic) Order 1994 No. 889. Enabling power: *Road Traffic Regulation Act 1984, s. 14 (1) (a)*. Made: 21.03.94. Coming into force: 28.03.94. Effect: None. – *Unpublished*

The M1 (Junction 6, Hertfordshire) (Slip Roads) (Temporary Prohibition of Traffic) Order 1994 No. 2834. Enabling power: *Road Traffic Regulation Act 1984, s. 14 (1) (a)*. Made: 31.10.94. Coming into force: 07.11.94. Effect: None. – *Unpublished*

The M1 (Junction 8) and M10 Motorways (Hertfordshire) (Temporary Prohibition of Traffic) Order 1994 No. 980. Enabling power: *Road Traffic Regulation Act 1984, s. 14 (1) (a)*. Made: 28.03.94. Coming into force: 05.04.94. Effect: None. – *Unpublished*

The M1 (Junction 8) and M10 Motorways (Hertfordshire) (Temporary Prohibition of Traffic) Order 1994 No. 2119. Enabling power: *Road Traffic Regulation Act 1984, s. 14 (1) (a)*. Made: 08.08.94. Coming into force: 15.08.94. Effect: None. – *Unpublished*

The M1 (Junction 8, Hertfordshire) and (Junction 10, Hertfordshire and Bedfordshire) (Temporary Prohibition of Traffic) Order 1994 No. 985. Enabling power: *Road Traffic Regulation Act 1984, s. 14 (1) (a)*. Made: 28.03.94. Coming into force: 05.04.94. Effect: None. – *Unpublished*

The M1 (Junctions 8-9) and M10 Motorways (Hertfordshire) (Temporary Prohibition and Restriction of Traffic) Order 1994 No. 2436. Enabling power: *Road Traffic Regulation Act 1984, s. 14 (1) (a)*. Made: 12.09.94. Coming into force: 19.09.94. Effect: None. – *Unpublished*

The M1 (Junctions 8 and 9, Slip Roads) and M10 Motorways (Hertfordshire) (Temporary Prohibition of Traffic) Order 1994 No. 2830. Enabling power: *Road Traffic Regulation Act 1984, s. 14 (1) (a)*. Made: 31.10.94. Coming into force: 07.11.94. Effect: None. – *Unpublished*

The M1 Motorway and the London North Circular Trunk Road (A406) (Barnet) (Temporary Prohibition of Traffic) Order 1994 No. 46. Enabling power: *Road Traffic Regulations Act 1984, s. 14 (1) (4)*. Made: 11.01.94. Coming into force: 18.01.94. Effect: None. – *Unpublished*

158 ROAD TRAFFIC: TRAFFIC REGULATION

The M1 Motorway (Barnet and Harrow) (Temporary Prohibition of Traffic and Speed Restriction) Order 1994 No. 1284. Enabling power: *Road Traffic Regulation Act 1984, s. 14 (1) (4) (5) (7)*. Made: 09.05.94. Coming into force: 16.05.94. Effect: None. –*Unpublished*

The M1 Motorway (Barnet) (Temporary Prohibition of Traffic) (No. 2) Order 1994 No.1868. Enabling power: *Road Traffic Regulation Act 1984, s. 14 (1) (4)*. Made: 11.07.94. Coming into force: 18.07.94. Effect: None. – *Unpublished*

The M1 Motorway (Barnet) (Temporary Prohibition of Traffic) (No. 3) Order 1994 No.3304. Enabling power: *Road Traffic Regulation Act 1984, s. 14 (1) (4)*. Made: 19.12.94. Coming into force: 09.01.95. Effect: None. – *Unpublished*

The M1 Motorway (Barnet) (Temporary Prohibition of Traffic) Order 1994 No. 1111. Enabling power: *Road Traffic Regulation Act 1984, s. 14 (1) (4) (5) (7)*. Made: 19.04.94. Coming into force: 25.04.94. Effect: None. – *Unpublished*

The M1 Motorway (Blaby, Leicestershire) (Temporary Restriction of Traffic) Order 1993 Amendment Order (No. 2) 1994 No. 348. Enabling power: *Road Traffic Regulation Act 1984, s. 14 (1) (a) (7)*. Made: 19.01.94. Coming into force: 21.01.94. Effect: S.I. 1993/2117 amended. –*Unpublished*

The M1 Motorway (Junction 6) and the A405 Trunk Road (North Orbital Road, St Albans, Hertfordshire) (Temporary Prohibition of Traffic) Order 1994 No. 1219. Enabling power: *Road Traffic Regulation Act 1984, s. 14 (1) (a)*. Made: 31.03.94. Coming into force: 07.04.94. Effect: None. –*Unpublished*

The M1 Motorway (Junction 6, Hertfordshire) (Temporary Prohibition of Traffic) Order 1994 No.1028. Enabling power: *Road Traffic Regulation Act 1984, s. 14 (1) (a)*. Made: 25.03.94. Coming into force: 26.03.94. Effect: None. –*Unpublished*

The M1 Motorway (Junction 8, Hertfordshire) (Temporary Prohibition and Restriction of Traffic) Order 1994 No. 3057. Enabling power: *Road Traffic Regulation Act 1984, s. 14 (1) (a)*. Made: 21.11.94. Coming into force: 28.11.94. Effect: None. –*Unpublished*

The M1 Motorway (Junction 9) Southbound Access Slip Road (Temporary Prohibition of Traffic) Order 1994 No. 1546. Enabling power: *Road Traffic Regulation Act 1984, s. 14 (1) (a)*. Made: 09.06.94. Coming into force: 16.06.94. Effect: None. –*Unpublished*

The M1 Motorway (Junction 9) Southbound Access Slip Road (Temporary Prohibition of Traffic) Order 1994 No. 2222. Enabling power: *Road Traffic Regulation Act 1984, s. 14 (1) (a)*. Made: 22.08.94. Coming into force: 29.08.94. Effect: None. –*Unpublished*

The M1 Motorway (Junction 10, Hertfordshire and Bedfordshire) (Temporary Prohibition of Traffic) Order 1994 No. 2715. Enabling power: *Road Traffic Regulation Act 1984, s. 14 (1) (a)*. Made: 17.10.94. Coming into force: 24.10.94. Effect: None. –*Unpublished*

The M1 Motorway (Junction 10, Luton, Bedfordshire) (Temporary Prohibition of Traffic) Order 1994 No. 1475. Enabling power: *Road Traffic Regulation Act 1984, s. 14 (1) (a)*. Made: 23.05.94. Coming into force: 31.05.94. Effect: None. –*Unpublished*

The M1 Motorway (Junction 12, Bedfordshire) (Temporary Prohibition and Restriction of Traffic) Order 1994 No. 409. Enabling power: *Road Traffic Regulation Act 1984, s. 14 (1) (a)*. Made: 21.02.94. Coming into force: 28.02.94. Effect: None. –*Unpublished*

The M1 Motorway (Junction 13, Bedfordshire) (Temporary Prohibition and Restriction of Traffic) Order 1994 No. 2649. Enabling power: *Road Traffic Regulation Act 1984, s. 14 (1) (a)*. Made: 10.10.94. Coming into force: 17.10.94. Effect: None. –*Unpublished*

The M1 Motorway (Junction 13, Bedfordshire) (Temporary Prohibition and Restriction of Traffic) Order 1994 No. 410. Enabling power: *Road Traffic Regulation Act 1984, s. 14 (1) (a)*. Made: 21.02.94. Coming into force: 28.02.94. Effect: None. –*Unpublished*

The M1 Motorway (Junction 14, Buckinghamshire) (Temporary 50 Miles Per Hour Speed Restriction) Order 1994 No. 2177. Enabling power: *Road Traffic Regulation Act 1984, s. 14 (1) (a)*. Made: 15.08.94. Coming into force: 22.08.94. Effect: None. –*Unpublished*

The M1 Motorway (Junction 23-23A, Leicestershire) (Temporary Restriction of Traffic) Order 1994 No. 20. Enabling power: *Road Traffic Regulations Act 1984, s. 14 (1) (a)*. Made: 05.01.94. Coming into force: 08.01.94. Effect: None. –*Unpublished*

The M1 Motorway (Junction 27, Slip Roads, Nottinghamshire) (Temporary Prohibition of Traffic) Order 1994 No. 2221. Enabling power: *Road Traffic Regulation Act 1984, s. 14 (1) (a)*. Made: 22.08.94. Coming into force: 01.09.94. Effect: None. –*Unpublished*

The M1 Motorway (Junction 28, Pinxton, Derbyshire) Southbound Exit Slip Road (Temporary Prohibition of Traffic) Order 1994 No. 845. Enabling power: *Road Traffic Regulation Act 1984, s. 14 (1) (a)*. Made: 15.03.94. Coming into force: 19.03.94. Effect: None. –*Unpublished*

The M1 Motorway (Junction 28, Tibshelf, Derbyshire) (Temporary 50 Miles Per Hour Speed Restriction) Order 1994 No. 438. Enabling power: *Road Traffic Regulation Act 1984, s. 14 (1) (a)*. Made: 22.02.94. Coming into force: 26.02.94. Effect: None. –*Unpublished*

The M1 Motorway (Junction 30 - Woodall) (Temporary Restriction and Prohibition of Traffic) Order 1994 No. 126. Enabling power: *Road Traffic Regulation Act 1984, s. 14 (1) (a) (7)*. Made: 13.01.94. Coming into force: 16.01.94. Effect: None. –*Unpublished*

The M1 Motorway (Junction 30-34, Slip Roads) (Temporary Restriction of Traffic) Order 1994 No. 1471. Enabling power: *Road Traffic Regulation Act 1984, s. 14 (1) (a)*. Made: 31.05.94. Coming into force: 01.06.94. Effect: None. –*Unpublished*

The M1 Motorway (Junction 35A, Southbound Entry Slip Road) (Temporary Prohibition of Traffic) Order 1994 No. 1588. Enabling power: *Road Traffic Regulation Act 1984, s. 14 (1) (a)*. Made: 03.06.94. Coming into force: 04.06.94. Effect: None. –*Unpublished*

The M1 Motorway (Junction 37, Northbound Exit Slip Road) (Temporary Restriction of Traffic) Order 1994 No. 2240. Enabling power: *Road Traffic Regulation Act 1984, s. 14 (1) (a) (7)*. Made: 18.08.94. Coming into force: 20.08.94. Effect: None. –*Unpublished*

The M1 Motorway (Junction 40, Southbound Carriageway and Southbound Exit Slip Road) (Temporary Prohibition of Traffic) Order 1994 No. 1281. Enabling power: *Road Traffic Regulation Act 1984, s. 14 (1) (a)*. Made: 09.05.94. Coming into force: 11.05.94. Effect: None. –*Unpublished*

The M1 Motorway (Junction 40, Southbound Entry Slip Road) (Temporary Prohibition of Traffic) Order 1994 No. 1473. Enabling power: *Road Traffic Regulation Act 1984, s. 14 (1) (a)*. Made: 27.05.94. Coming into force: 02.06.94. Effect: None. –*Unpublished*

The M1 Motorway (Junction 43, Southbound Exit Slip Road) (Temporary Prohibition of Traffic) Order 1994 No. 2605. Enabling power: *Road Traffic Regulation Act 1984, s. 14 (1) (a)*. Made: 05.10.94. Coming into force: 07.10.94. Effect: None. –*Unpublished*

The M1 Motorway (Junctions 12 - 13, Bedfordshire) (Temporary Restriction of Traffic) Order 1994 No. 1361. Enabling power: *Road Traffic Regulation Act 1984, s. 14 (1) (a) (7)*. Made: 16.05.94. Coming into force: 23.05.94. Effect: None. –*Unpublished*

The M1 Motorway (Junctions 15 - 16) and Slip Roads (Temporary Prohibition and Restriction of Traffic) Order 1994 No. 1938. Enabling power: *Road Traffic Regulation Act 1984, s. 14 (1) (a) (7)*. Made: 14.07.94. Coming into force: 27.07.94. Effect: None. –*Unpublished*

The M1 Motorway (Junctions 15, 15A and 16) (Temporary Prohibition of Traffic) Order 1994 No. 1185. Enabling power: *Road Traffic Regulation Act 1984, s. 14 (1) (a)*. Made: 21.04.94. Coming into force: 21.04.94. Effect: None. –*Unpublished*

The M1 Motorway (Junctions 21-22) Leicestershire (Temporary Prohibition of Traffic) Order 1994 No. 1843. Enabling power: *Road Traffic Regulation Act 1984, s. 14 (1) (a)*. Made: 05.07.94. Coming into force: 13.07.94. Effect: None. –*Unpublished*

The M1 Motorway (Junctions 31-37, Slip Roads) (Temporary 30 Miles Per Hour Speed Restriction) Order 1994 No. 2173. Enabling power: *Road Traffic Regulation Act 1984, s. 14 (1) (a)*. Made: 11.08.94. Coming into force: 15.08.94. Effect: None. –*Unpublished*

The M1 Motorway (Junctions 34-38, Slip Roads) (Temporary Restriction of Traffic) Order 1994 No. 1941. Enabling power: *Road Traffic Regulation Act 1984, s. 14 (1) (a)*. Made: 16.06.94. Coming into force: 18.06.94. Effect: None. –*Unpublished*

The M1 Motorway (Junctions 36-37, Southbound Carriageway) (Temporary Restriction of Traffic) Order 1994 No. 406. Enabling power: *Road Traffic Regulation Act 1984, ss. 14 (1) (a) 7*. Made: 24.02.94. Coming into force: 26.02.94. Effect: None. –*Unpublished*

The M1 Motorway (Junctions 37 - 39) (Temporary Restriction and Prohibition of Traffic) Order 1994 No. 2242. Enabling power: *Road Traffic Regulation Act 1984, s. 14 (1) (a) (7)*. Made: 19.08.94. Coming into force: 20.08.94. Effect: None. –*Unpublished*

The M2 Motorway (Junction 7) Londonbound Access Slip Road (Temporary Prohibition of Traffic) Order 1994 No. 2376. Enabling power: *Road Traffic Regulation Act 1984, s. 14 (1) (a)*. Made: 05.09.94. Coming into force: 10.09.94. Effect: None. –*Unpublished*

The M2 Motorway (Junctions 5-7) (Temporary Restriction and Prohibition of Traffic) Order 1994 No. 120. Enabling power: *Road Traffic Regulation Act 1984, s. 14 (1) (a) (7)*. Made: 24.01.94. Coming into force: 05.02.94. Effect: None. –*Unpublished*

The M2 Motorway (Marker Posts 59.8-63.0) (Temporary Restriction of Traffic) Order 1994 No. 1944. Enabling power: *Road Traffic Regulation Act 1984, s. 14 (1) (a) (7)*. Made: 18.07.94. Coming into force: 23.07.94. Effect: None. –*Unpublished*

The M2 Motorway (Marker Posts 74.0 - 78.0) (Temporary 50 Miles Per Hour Speed Restriction) Order 1994 No. 3034. Enabling power: *Road Traffic Regulation Act 1984, s. 14 (1) (a)*. Made: 28.11.94. Coming into force: 29.11.94. Effect: None. –*Unpublished*

The M2 Motorway (Medway Bridge) (Temporary Prohibition and Restriction of Use of Special Tracks) Order 1994 No. 1876. Enabling power: *Road Traffic Regulation Act 1984, s. 14 (1) (a) (7)*. Made: 11.07.94. Coming into force: 16.07.94. Effect: None. –*Unpublished*

Price/availability are liable to change without notice

The M3 and M25 Motorways (Thorpe Interchange) (Temporary Restriction of Traffic) Order 1994 No. 2481. Enabling power: *Road Traffic Regulation Act 1984, s. 14 (1) (a) (7).* Made: 19.09.94. Coming into force: 24.09.94. Effect: None. –*Unpublished*

The M3 and M25 Motorways (Thorpe Interchange) (Temporary Restriction of Traffic) (No. 2) Order 1994 No. 2864. Enabling power: *Road Traffic Regulation Act 1984, s. 14 (1) (a) (7).* Made: 07.11.94. Coming into force: 11.11.94. Effect: S.I. 1994/2481 revoked. –*Unpublished*

The M3 (Junction 14) and M27 (Junction 4) Motorways (Bassett Interchange) (Temporary Prohibition of Traffic) Order 1994 No. 1427. Enabling power: *Road Traffic Regulation Act 1984, s. 14 (1) (a).* Made: 23.05.94. Coming into force: 28.05.94. Effect: None. –*Unpublished*

The M3 Motorway and the A33 Trunk Road (Easton Lane to Oak Mount) (Temporary Restriction of Traffic) Order 1994 No. 1454. Enabling power: *Road Traffic Regulation Act 1984, s. 14 (1) (a).* Made: 31.05.94. Coming into force: 04.06.94. Effect: S.I. 1993/93, 137; 1994/387 revoked. –*Unpublished*

The M3 Motorway and the A316 Trunk Road (Marker Posts 23.0 30.0) (Temporary Restriction and Prohibition of Traffic) Order 1994 No. 2275. Enabling power: *Road Traffic Regulation Act 1984, s. 14 (1) (a) (7).* Made: 30.08.94. Coming into force: 03.09.94. Effect: None. –*Unpublished*

The M3 Motorway (Bar End to Alresford Road) (Temporary Restriction of Traffic) Order 1994 No. 1428. Enabling power: *Road Traffic Regulation Act 1984, s. 14 (1) (a) (7).* Made: 23.05.94. Coming into force: 28.05.94. Effect: None. –*Unpublished*

The M3 Motorway (Easton Lane Interchange to Bar End Interchange) (Temporary Prohibition of Traffic) Order 1994 No. 1593. Enabling power: *Road Traffic Regulation Act 1984, s. 14 (1) (a).* Made: 06.06.94. Coming into force: 11.06.94. Effect: None. –*Unpublished*

The M3 Motorway (Junction 3) (Temporary Prohibition of Traffic) Order 1994 No. 2902. Enabling power: *Road Traffic Regulation Act 1984, s. 14 (1) (a).* Made: 14.11.94. Coming into force: 19.11.94. Effect: None. –*Unpublished*

The M3 Motorway (Junction 7) Eastbound Exit Slip Road (Temporary Prohibition of Traffic) Order 1994 No. 1550. Enabling power: *Road Traffic Regulation Act 1984, s. 14 (1) (a).* Made: 06.06.94. Coming into force: 11.06.94. Effect: None. –*Unpublished*

The M3 Motorway (Junction 8-9) (Temporary Prohibition of Traffic) Order 1994 No. 2352. Enabling power: *Road Traffic Regulation Act 1984, s. 14 (1) (a).* Made: 05.09.94. Coming into force: 10.09.94. Effect: None. – *Unpublished*

The M3 Motorway (Junction 9) Southbound Entry Slip Road (Temporary Prohibition of Traffic) Order 1994 No. 2862. Enabling power: *Road Traffic Regulation Act 1984, s. 14 (1) (a).* Made: 07.11.94. Coming into force: 12.11.94. Effect: None. –*Unpublished*

The M3 Motorway (Junctions 5-6) (Temporary Prohibition of Traffic) Order 1994 No. 1429. Enabling power: *Road Traffic Regulation Act 1984, s. 14 (1) (a).* Made: 23.05.94. Coming into force: 28.05.94. Effect: None. – *Unpublished*

The M3 Motorway (Marker Posts 26.0-33.5) (Temporary Restriction of Traffic) (No. 2) Order 1994 No. 2701. Enabling power: *Road Traffic Regulation Act 1984, s. 14 (1) (a) (7).* Made: 17.10.94. Coming into force: 19.10.94. Effect: S.I. 1994/2572 revoked. –*Unpublished*

The M3 Motorway (Marker Posts 26.0-33.5) (Temporary Restriction of Traffic) Order 1994 No. 2572. Enabling power: *Road Traffic Regulation Act 1984, s. 14 (1) (a).* Made: 03.10.94. Coming into force: 08.10.94. Effect: None. –*Unpublished*

The M3 Motorway (Pitmore Interchange) (Temporary Prohibition of Traffic) Order 1994 No. 2636. Enabling power: *Road Traffic Regulation Act 1984, s. 14 (1) (a).* Made: 10.10.94. Coming into force: 15.10.94. Effect: None. –*Unpublished*

The M4 (Junctions 4 - 4A) and M25 (Junction 15) Motorways (Buckinghamshire) (Temporary Prohibition and Restriction of Traffic) Order 1994 No. 1651. Enabling power: *Road Traffic Regulation Act 1984, s. 14 (1) (a).* Made: 20.06.94. Coming into force: 27.06.94. Effect: None. –*Unpublished*

The M4 (Junctions 4 - 4B), M25 (Junctions 14 - 15, and 16) and M40 (Junctions 3 - 4) (Temporary Prohibition of Traffic) Order 1994 No. 412. Enabling power: *Road Traffic Regulation Act 1984, s. 14 (1) (a).* Made: 21.02.94. Coming into force: 22.02.94. Effect: None. –*Unpublished*

The M4 Motorway (Baglan-Briton Ferry, West Glamorgan) (Temporary 50 MPH Speed Limit) Order 1994 No. 3312. Enabling power: *Road Traffic Regulation Act 1984, s. 14 (1) (4) (7).* Made: 07.12.94. Coming into force: 12.12.94. Effect: None. –*Unpublished*

The M4 Motorway (Baglan-Briton Ferry, West Glamorgan) (Temporary Traffic Restrictions) Order 1994 No. 688. Enabling power: *Road Traffic Regulation Act 1984 ss. 14 (1) (a) (7).* Made: 03.03.94. Coming into force: 07.03.94. Effect: None. –*Unpublished*

The M4 Motorway (Baglan-Llandarcy, West Glamorgan) (Temporary Prohibition of Vehicles) Order 1994 No. 3092. Enabling power: *Road Traffic Regulation Act 1984, s. 14 (1) (4).* Made: 18.11.94. Coming into force: 19.11.94. Effect: None. –*Unpublished*

The M4 Motorway (Baglan, West Glamorgan) (Temporary 40 MPH Speed Limit) Order 1992 (Revocation) Order 1994 No. 3261. Enabling power: *Road Traffic Regulation Act 1984, ss. 14, 124 & sch. 9, para. 27.* Made: 12.12.94. Coming into force: 12.12.94. Effect: S.I. 1992/2756 revoked. –*Unpublished*

The M4 Motorway (Baglan, West Glamorgan) (Temporary Prohibition of Vehicles) Order 1994 No.1740. Enabling power: *Road Traffic Regulation Act 1984, s. 14 (1) (7)*. Made: 28.06.94. Coming into force: 05.07.94. Effect: None. – *Unpublished*

The M4 Motorway (Baglan, West Glamorgan) (Temporary Traffic Restrictons) Order 1994 No.2027. Enabling power: *Road Traffic Regulation Act 1984, s. 14 (1) (4) (7)*. Made: 22.07.94. Coming into force: 22.07.94. Effect: None. – *Unpublished*

The M4 Motorway (Brynglas Tunnels, Newport, Gwent) (Temporary Prohibition of Vehicles) Order 1994 No. 136. Enabling power: *Road Traffic Regulation Act 1984, s. 14 (1) (7)*. Made: 21.01.94. Coming into force: 21.01.94. Effect: None. – *Unpublished*

The M4 Motorway (Coldra - Malpas, Gwent) (Temporary Prohibition of Vehicles) Order 1994 No.1603. Enabling power: *Road Traffic Regulation Act 1984, s. 14 (1) (7)*. Made: 09.06.94. Coming into force: 11.06.94. Effect: None. – *Unpublished*

The M4 Motorway (Coryton-Capel Llanilltern, South Glamorgan) (Temporary Prohibition of Vehicles and 50 MPH Speed Limit) Order 1994 No. 1605. Enabling power: *Road Traffic Regulation Act 1984, s. 14 (1) (7)*. Made: 09.06.94. Coming into force: 11.06.94. Effect: None. – *Unpublished*

The M4 Motorway (Eastbound Carriageway, Llandarcy, West Glamorgan) (Temporary Prohibition of Vehicles) Order 1994 No. 3311. Enabling power: *Road Traffic Regulation Act 1984, s. 14 (1) (4) (7)*. Made: 08.12.94. Coming into force: 12.12.94. Effect: None. – *Unpublished*

The M4 Motorway (Hardy Lane Overbridge) (Temporary Restriction of Traffic) Order 1994 No.205. Enabling power: *Road Traffic Regulation 1984, s. 14 (1) (a)*. Made: 27.01.94. Coming into force: 29.01.94. Effect: None. – *Unpublished*

The M4 Motorway (Junction 4, Buckinghamshire) (Temporary Prohibition of Traffic) Order 1994 No. 344. Enabling power: *Road Traffic Regulation Act 1984, s. 14 (1) (a)*. Made: 14.02.94. Coming into force: 21.02.94. Effect: None. – *Unpublished*

The M4 Motorway (Junction 7) (Temporary Prohibition of Traffic) Order 1994 No. 971. Enabling power: *Road Traffic Regulation Act 1984, s. 14 (1) (a)*. Made: 28.03.94. Coming into force: 02.04.94. Effect: None. – *Unpublished*

The M4 Motorway (Junction 10 - Emergency Link Roads) (Prohibition of Entry) Order 1994 No.2749. Enabling power: *Road Traffic Regulation Act 1984, ss. 1 (1), 2 (1)*. Made: 24.10.94. Coming into force: 07.11.94. Effect: None. – *Unpublished*

The M4 Motorway (Junction 10) Slip Roads 2 and 4 (Temporary Prohibition of Traffic) Order 1994 No. 2959. Enabling power: *Road Traffic Regulation Act 1984, s. 14 (1) (a)*. Made: 21.11.94. Coming into force: 26.11.94. Effect: None. – *Unpublished*

The M4 Motorway (Junction 10) (Temporary Prohibition of Traffic) Order 1994 No.2638. Enabling power: *Road Traffic Regulation Act 1984, s. 14 (1) (a)*. Made: 10.10.94. Coming into force: 15.10.94. Effect: None. – *Unpublished*

The M4 Motorway (Junction 11) Westbound Exit Slip Road (Temporary Prohibition of Traffic) Order 1994 No. 2534. Enabling power: *Road Traffic Regulation Act 1984, s. 14 (1) (a)*. Made: 26.09.94. Coming into force: 01.10.94. Effect: None. – *Unpublished*

The M4 Motorway (Junction 17 - 18) (Temporary 50 Miles Per Hour Speed Restriction) Order 1994 No. 2259. Enabling power: *Road Traffic Regulation Act 1984, s. 14 (1) (a)*. Made: 17.08.94. Coming into force: 19.08.94. Effect: None. – *Unpublished*

The M4 Motorway (Junction 19, Bristol) (Temporary Restriction of Traffic) Order 1994 No.206. Enabling power: *Road Traffic Regulation 1984, s. 14 (1) (a) (7)*. Made: 27.01.94. Coming into force: 29.01.94. Effect: None. – *Unpublished*

The M4 Motorway (Junction 26, Malpas, Gwent) (Temporary Prohibition of Vehicles) Order 1994 No. 1369. Enabling power: *Road Traffic Regulation Act 1984, s. 14 (1)*. Made: 15.05.94. Coming into force: 16.05.94. Effect: None. – *Unpublished*

The M4 Motorway (Junctions 6 - 7) (Temporary Prohibition of Traffic) Order 1994 No.1596. Enabling power: *Road Traffic Regulation Act 1984, s. 14 (1) (a)*. Made: 13.06.94. Coming into force: 18.06.94. Effect: None. – *Unpublished*

The M4 Motorway (Junctions 11 - 12) (Temporary Restriction and Prohibition of Traffic) Order 1994 No. 3290. Enabling power: *Road Traffic Regulation Act 1984, s. 14 (1) (a) (7)*. Made: 19.12.94. Coming into force: 24.12.94. Effect: None. – *Unpublished*

The M4 Motorway (Junctions 11 - 13) (Temporary Restriction and Prohibition of Traffic) Order 1994 No. 1597. Enabling power: *Road Traffic Regulation Act 1984, s. 14 (1) (a) (7)*. Made: 13.06.94. Coming into force: 18.06.94. Effect: None. – *Unpublished*

The M4 Motorway (Junctions 16 - 18) (Temporary 50 Miles Per Hour Speed Restriction) Order 1994 No. 1073. Enabling power: *Road Traffic Regulation Act 1984, s. 14 (1) (a)*. Made: 28.03.94. Coming into force: 30.03.94. Effect: None. – *Unpublished*

The M4 Motorway (Junctions 20-21, Northavon) (Temporary Restriction of Traffic) Order 1994 No. 1436. Enabling power: *Road Traffic Regulation Act 1984, s. 14 (1) (a), 15 (2)*. Made: 18.05.94. Coming into force: 20.05.94. Effect: S.I. 1992/2999 revoked. – *Unpublished*

Price/availability are liable to change without notice

The M4 Motorway (Llandarcy, West Glamorgan) (Temporary 50 MPH Speed Limit) Order 1993 (Revocation) Order 1994 No. 3274. Enabling power: *Road Traffic Regulation Act 1984, ss. 14, 124 & sch. 9, para. 27.* Made: 08.12.94. Coming into force: 12.12.94. Effect: S.I. 1993/1058 revoked. – *Unpublished*

The M4 Motorway (Llangyfelach, West Glamorgan-Pont Abraham, Dyfed) (Temporary Prohibition of Vehicles and 50 MPH Speed Limit) Order 1994 No. 2300. Enabling power: *Road Traffic Regulation Act 1984, s. 14 (1) (4) (7).* Made: 30.08.94. Coming into force: 01.09.94. Effect: None. – *Unpublished*

The M4 Motorway (London Borough of Hounslow) (Temporary Prohibition of Traffic) Order 1994 No. 983. Enabling power: *Road Traffic Regulation Act 1984, s. 14 (1) (4).* Made: 28.03.94. Coming into force: 05.04.94. Effect: None. – *Unpublished*

The M4 Motorway (London Borough of Hounslow) (Temporary Restriction of Traffic and Speed Restriction) Order 1994 No. 89. Enabling power: *Road Traffic Regulation Act 1984, s. 14 (1) (4) (7).* Made: 17.01.94. Coming into force: 22.01.94. Effect: None. – *Unpublished*

The M4 Motorway (London Boroughs of Hounslow and Hillingdon) (Temporary Restriction of Traffic and Speed Restriction) Order 1994 No. 964. Enabling power: *Road Traffic Regulation Act 1984, s. 14 (1) (4) (7).* Made: 25.03.94. Coming into force: 11.04.94. Effect: None. – *Unpublished*

The M4 Motorway (London Boroughs of Hounslow and Hillingdon) (Temporary Restriction of Traffic and Speed Restriction) Order 1994 No. 1958. Enabling power: *Road Traffic Regulation Act 1984, s. 14 (1) (4) (7).* Made: 18.07.94. Coming into force: 25.07.94. Effect: None. – *Unpublished*

The M4 Motorway (Magor-Caldicot, Gwent) (Temporary 50 MPH Speed Limit) Order 1994 No.193. Enabling power: *Road Traffic Regulation 1984, s. 14 (1) (7).* Made: 24.01.94. Coming into force: 24.01.94. Effect: None. – *Unpublished*

The M4 Motorway (Magor, Gwent) (Temporary 50 MPH Speed Limit) Order 1994 No. 2134. Enabling power: *Road Traffic Regulation Act 1984, s. 14 (1) (4) (7).* Made: 14.09.94. Coming into force: 15.09.94. Effect: None. – *Unpublished*

The M4 Motorway (Margam-Baglan, West Glamorgan) (Temporary Prohibition of Vehicles) Order 1994 No. 2214. Enabling power: *Road Traffic Regulation Act 1984, s. 14 (1) (4) (7).* Made: 18.08.94. Coming into force: 20.08.94. Effect: None. – *Unpublished*

The M4 Motorway (Marker Posts 54.0-62.5) (Temporary Restriction and Prohibition of Traffic) Order 1994 No. 1051. Enabling power: *Road Traffic Regulation Act 1984, s. 14 (1) (a) (7).* Made: 11.04.94. Coming into force: 16.04.94. Effect: None. – *Unpublished*

The M4 Motorway (Marker Posts 67.7-72.7) (Temporary 50 Miles Per Hour Speed Restriction) Order 1994 No. 1551. Enabling power: *Road Traffic Regulation Act 1984, s. 14 (1) (a).* Made: 06.06.94. Coming into force: 11.06.94. Effect: None. – *Unpublished*

The M4 Motorway (Newbridge Roundabout) (Temporary Prohibition of Traffic) (No. 3) Order 1994 No. 3295. Enabling power: *Road Traffic Regulation Act 1984, ss. 14 (1) (a) (4) (a), 121A.* Made: 19.12.94. Coming into force: 09.01.95. Effect: None. – *Unpublished*

The M4 Motorway (Westbound Carriageway, Baglan, West Glamorgan) (Temporary Traffic Restrictions) Order 1994 No. 2237. Enabling power: *Road Traffic Regulation Act 1984, s. 14 (1) (4).* Made: 12.08.94. Coming into force: 14.08.94. Effect: None. – *Unpublished*

The M5 Motorway (Clapton Lane Underbridge) (Temporary Restriction of Traffic) Order 1994 No.2597. Enabling power: *Road Traffic Regulation Act 1984, s. 14 (1) (a) (7).* Made: 19.09.94. Coming into force: 26.09.94. Effect: None. – *Unpublished*

The M5 Motorway (Clingre Pipe Overbridge) (Temporary Restriction of Traffic) Order 1994 No.2908. Enabling power: *Road Traffic Regulation Act 1984, s. 14 (1) (a).* Made: 14.11.94. Coming into force: 21.11.94. Effect: None. – *Unpublished*

The M5 Motorway (Coaley to Dursley-Cambridge Overbridges) (Temporary Restriction of Traffic) Order 1994 No. 2909. Enabling power: *Road Traffic Regulation Act 1984, s. 14 (1) (a).* Made: 14.11.94. Coming into force: 21.11.94. Effect: None. – *Unpublished*

The M5 Motorway (Fiddington to Stoke Orchard to Piffs Elm Overbridges) (Temporary Restriction of Traffic) Order 1994 No. 2601. Enabling power: *Road Traffic Regulation Act 1984, s. 14 (1) (a) (7).* Made: 23.09.94. Coming into force: 30.09.94. Effect: None. – *Unpublished*

The M5 Motorway (Gambril Lane Overbridge) (Temporary 50 Miles Per Hour Speed Restriction) Order 1994 No. 752. Enabling power: *Road Traffic Regulation Act 1984 s. 14 (1) (a).* Made: 09.03.94. Coming into force: 11.03.94. Effect: None. – *Unpublished*

The M5 Motorway (Golden Valley Interchange) (Temporary 50 Miles Per Hour Speed Restriction) Order 1994 No. 2599. Enabling power: *Road Traffic Regulation Act 1984, s. 14 (1) (a) (7).* Made: 03.10.94. Coming into force: 10.10.94. Effect: None. – *Unpublished*

The M5 Motorway (Green Street Overbridge) (Temporary Restriction of Traffic) Order 1994 No.2600. Enabling power: *Road Traffic Regulation Act 1984, s. 14 (1) (a) (7).* Made: 23.09.94. Coming into force: 30.09.94. Effect: None. – *Unpublished*

The M5 Motorway (Junction 2) (Temporary Prohibition of Traffic) Order No. 68. Enabling power: *Road Traffic Regulation Act 1984, ss. 14 (1) (a).* Made: 05.01.94. Coming into force: 06.01.94. Effect: None. – *Unpublished*

ROAD TRAFFIC: TRAFFIC REGULATION 163

The M5 Motorway (Junction 3 and Frankley Service Area) (Temporary Restriction of Traffic) Order 1994 No. 1864. Enabling power: *Road Traffic Regulation Act 1984, s. 14 (1) (a) (7)*. Made: 28.06.94. Coming into force: 29.06.94. Effect: None. – *Unpublished*

The M5 Motorway (Junction 3) (Temporary Prohibition of Traffic) Order 1994 No. 1127. Enabling power: *Road Traffic Regulation Act 1984, s. 14 (1) (a)*. Made: 04.03.94. Coming into force: 05.03.94. Effect: None. – *Unpublished*

The M5 Motorway (Junction 13) (Temporary 50 Miles Per Hour Speed Restriction) Order 1994 No. 587. Enabling power: *Road Traffic Regulation Act 1984 s. 14 (1) (a)*. Made: 22.02.94. Coming into force: 24.02.94. Effect: None. – *Unpublished*

The M5 Motorway (Junction 14) Northbound Exit Slip Road (Temporary Prohibition of Traffic) Order 1994 No. 588. Enabling power: *Road Traffic Regulation Act 1984 s. 14 (1) (a)*. Made: 22.02.94. Coming into force: 24.02.94. Effect: None. – *Unpublished*

The M5 Motorway (Junction 18) Slip Roads) (Temporary Prohibition of Traffic) Order 1994 No. 1092. Enabling power: *Road Traffic Regulation Act 1984, s. 14 (1) (a)*. Made: 12.04.94. Coming into force: 14.04.94. Effect: None. – *Unpublished*

The M5 Motorway (Junction 18) Slip Roads (Temporary Prohibition of Traffic) Order 1994 No. 2881. Enabling power: *Road Traffic Regulation Act 1984, s. 14 (1) (a)*. Made: 09.11.94. Coming into force: 11.11.94. Effect: None. – *Unpublished*

The M5 Motorway (Junction 19) Northbound Exit Slip Road (Temporary Prohibition of Traffic) Order 1994 No. 235. Enabling power: *Road Traffic Regulation Act 1984, s. 14 (1) (a)*. Made: 01.02.94. Coming into force: 03.02.94. Effect: None. – *Unpublished*

The M5 Motorway (Junction 22, Edithmead) (Temporary Restriction of Traffic) Order 1994 No. 1844. Enabling power: *Road Traffic Regulation Act 1984, s. 14 (1) (a) (7)*. Made: 08.07.94. Coming into force: 18.07.94. Effect: None. – *Unpublished*

The M5 Motorway (Junctions 3-2) (Temporary Restriction and Prohibition of Traffic) Order 1994 No. 882. Enabling power: *Road Traffic Regulation Act 1984, s. 14 (1) (a) (7)*. Made: 18.03.94. Coming into force: 19.03.94. Effect: None. – *Unpublished*

The M5 Motorway (Junctions 9 - 11) (Temporary 50 Miles Per Hour Speed Restriction) Order 1994 No. 886. Enabling power: *Road Traffic Regulation Act 1984, s. 14 (1) (a)*. Made: 16.03.94. Coming into force: 18.03.94. Effect: None. – *Unpublished*

The M5 Motorway (Junctions 11-12) (Temporary Restriction of Traffic) Order 1994 No. 1124. Enabling power: *Road Traffic Regulation Act 1984, ss. 14 (1) (a) (7), 15 (2)*. Made: 05.04.94. Coming into force: 07.04.94. Effect: None. – *Unpublished*

The M5 Motorway (Junctions 11-12) (Temporary Restriction of Traffic) Order 1994 No. 1929. Enabling power: *Road Traffic Regulation Act 1984, ss. 14 (1) (4) (7), 15 (2)*. Made: 08.07.94. Coming into force: 09.07.94. Effect: S.I. 1994/1124 revoked. – *Unpublished*

The M5 Motorway (Junctions 13-14) (Temporary Restriction of Traffic) Order 1994 No. 2426. Enabling power: *Road Traffic Regulation Act 1984, s. 14 (1) (a) (7)*. Made: 05.09.94. Coming into force: 09.09.94. Effect: None. – *Unpublished*

The M5 Motorway (Junctions 15 and 21) (Slip Roads) (Temporary Prohibition of Traffic) Order 1994 No. 2681. Enabling power: *Road Traffic Regulation Act 1984, s. 14 (1) (a)*. Made: 29.09.94. Coming into force: 01.10.94. Effect: None. – *Unpublished*

The M5 Motorway (Junctions 17-18) (Temporary Prohibition of Traffic) Order 1994 No. 292. Enabling power: *Road Traffic Regulation Act 1984, s. 14 (1) (a)*. Made: 08.02.94. Coming into force: 10.02.94. Effect: None. – *Unpublished*

The M5 Motorway (Junctions 19-20, Gordano-Clevedon) (Temporary Restriction of Traffic) Order 1994 No. 1068. Enabling power: *Road Traffic Regulation Act 1984, s. 14 (1) (a) (7)*. Made: 28.03.94. Coming into force: 30.03.94. Effect: None. – *Unpublished*

The M5 Motorway (Junctions 22-23) (Temporary Restriction of Traffic) Order 1994 No. 1159. Enabling power: *Road Traffic Regulation Act 1984, s. 14 (1) (a) (7)*. Made: 05.04.94. Coming into force: 09.04.94. Effect: None. – *Unpublished*

The M5 Motorway (Junctions 26-27) (Temporary Restriction and Prohibition of Traffic) Order 1994 No. 2742. Enabling power: *Road Traffic Regulation Act 1984, s. 14 (1) (a) (7)*. Made: 19.10.94. Coming into force: 21.10.94. Effect: None. – *Unpublished*

The M5 Motorway (Lower Wick - Coaley) (Temporary Restriction of Traffic) Order 1994 No. 1174. Enabling power: *Road Traffic Regulation Act 1984, s. 14 (1) (a) (7)*. Made: 29.03.94. Coming into force: 31.03.94. Effect: None. – *Unpublished*

The M5 Motorway (NAAS Lane to Haresfield Overbridges) (Temporary Restriction of Traffic) Order 1994 No. 2602. Enabling power: *Road Traffic Regulation Act 1984, s. 14 (1) (a) (7)*. Made: 23.09.94. Coming into force: 30.09.94. Effect: None. – *Unpublished*

The M5 Motorway (Poltimore - Hele Straight) (Temporary Restriction of Traffic) Order 1994 No. 1158. Enabling power: *Road Traffic Regulation Act 1984, s. 14 (1) (a) (7)*. Made: 30.03.94. Coming into force: 01.04.94. Effect: None. – *Unpublished*

Price/availability are liable to change without notice

The M5 Motorway (Quinton to Lydiate Ash) (Temporary 50 Miles Per Hour Speed Restriction) Order 1994 No. 2531. Enabling power: *Road Traffic Regulation Act 1984, s. 14 (1) (a)*. Made: 23.09.94. Coming into force: 24.09.94. Effect: None. – *Unpublished*

The M5 Motorway, The A38 Trunk Road, A380 Non-Trunk Road (Splatford to Pearces Hill) (Temporary Prohibition and Restriction of Traffic) Order 1994 No. 2640. Enabling power: *Road Traffic Regulation Act 1984, s. 14 (1) (a) (7)*. Made: 30.09.94. Coming into force: 03.10.94. Effect: None. – *Unpublished*

The M5 Motorway (Woodford Lane Overbridge) (Temporary Restriction of Traffic) Order 1994 No.2907. Enabling power: *Road Traffic Regulation Act 1984, s. 14 (1) (a)*. Made: 14.11.94. Coming into force: 21.11.94. Effect: None. – *Unpublished*

The M6 Motorway and the M61 Motorway, Preston (Temporary Restriction and Prohibition of Traffic) Order 1994 No. 1117. Enabling power: *Road Traffic Regulation Act 1984, ss. 14 (1) (a) (7), 15 (2)*. Made: 12.04.94. Coming into force: 12.04.94. Effect: None. – *Unpublished*

The M6 Motorway (Junction 15 Slip Roads) (Temporary Prohibition of Traffic) Order 1994 No.2149. Enabling power: *Road Traffic Regulation Act 1984, s. 14 (1) (a)*. Made: 11.08.94. Coming into force: 12.08.94. Effect: None. – *Unpublished*

The M6 Motorway (Junction 23) Northbound Exit Slip Road (Temporary Prohibition of Traffic) Order 1994 No. 2116. Enabling power: *Road Traffic Regulation Act 1984, s. 14 (1) (a)*. Made: 01.08.94. Coming into force: 12.08.94. Effect: None. – *Unpublished*

The M6 Motorway (Junction 33) Slip Roads (Temporary Prohibition and Restriction of Traffic) Order 1994 No. 821. Enabling power: *Road Traffic Regulation Act 1984, s. 14 (1) (a)*. Made: 11.02.94. Coming into force: 13.02.94. Effect: None. – *Unpublished*

The M6 Motorway (Junction 34) Slip Roads (Temporary Prohibition of Traffic) Order 1994 No.2647. Enabling power: *Road Traffic Regulation Act 1984, s. 14 (1) (a)*. Made: 30.09.94. Coming into force: 02.10.94. Effect: None. – *Unpublished*

The M6 Motorway (Junction 37 and Killington Service Area) (Temporary Restriction and Prohibition of Traffic) Order 1994 No. 721. Enabling power: *Road Traffic Regulation Act 1984 s. 14 (1) (a)*. Made: 01.03.94. Coming into force: 03.03.94. Effect: None. – *Unpublished*

The M6 Motorway (Junctions 10-9) Walsall (Temporary Restriction of Traffic) Order 1994 No.2432. Enabling power: *Road Traffic Regulation Act 1984, s. 14 (1) (a) (7)*. Made: 09.09.94. Coming into force: 10.09.94. Effect: None. – *Unpublished*

The M6 Motorway (Junctions 15-16) (Temporary Restriction and Prohibition of Traffic) Order 1994 No. 1659. Enabling power: *Road Traffic Regulation Act 1984, s. 14 (1) (a) (7)*. Made: 15.06.94. Coming into force: 16.06.94. Effect: None. – *Unpublished*

The M6 Motorway (Junctions 25 - 27) Wigan (Temporary Restriction and Prohibition of Traffic) Order 1994 No. 1589. Enabling power: *Road Traffic Regulation Act 1984, s. 14 (1) (a) (7)*. Made: 31.05.94. Coming into force: 05.06.94. Effect: None. – *Unpublished*

The M6 Motorway (Junctions 25-28) Chorley and Wigan (Temporary Restriction of Traffic) Order 1994 No. 822. Enabling power: *Road Traffic Regulation Act 1984, s. 14 (1) (a) (7)*. Made: 18.02.94. Coming into force: 20.02.94. Effect: None. – *Unpublished*

The M6 Motorway (Junctions 32 - 34) (Temporary Restriction of Traffic) Order 1993 No.393. Enabling power: *Road Traffic Regulation Act 1984, s. 14 (1) (a)*. Made: 22.12.93. Coming into force: 31.12.93. Effect: None. – *Unpublished*

The M6 Motorway (Junctions 36-39) (Temporary Prohibition of Traffic) Order 1994 No.1847. Enabling power: *Road Traffic Regulation Act 1984, s. 14 (1) (a)*. Made: 06.07.94. Coming into force: 16.07.94. Effect: None. – *Unpublished*

The M6 Motorway (Junctions 39-41) (Temporary Restriction and Prohibition of Traffic) Order 1994 No. 1724. Enabling power: *Road Traffic Regulation Act 1984, s. 14 (1) (a) (7)*. Made: 22.06.94. Coming into force: 24.06.94. Effect: None. – *Unpublished*

The M6 Motorway (Junctions 43-44) (Temporary 50 Miles Per Hour Speed Restriction) Order 1994 No. 1854. Enabling power: *Road Traffic Regulation Act 1984, s. 14 (1) (a) (7)*. Made: 07.07.94. Coming into force: 10.07.94. Effect: None. – *Unpublished*

The M6 Motorway (Loups Fell and Tebay Bridges) (Temporary 50 Miles Per Hour Speed Restriction) Order 1994 No. 2474. Enabling power: *Road Traffic Regulation Act 1984, s. 14 (1) (a)*. Made: 15.09.94. Coming into force: 17.09.94. Effect: None. – *Unpublished*

The M6 Motorway (Marker Posts 429/7 to 425/8) (Temporary 50 Miles Per Hour Speed Restriction) Order 1994 No. 439. Enabling power: *Road Traffic Regulation Act 1984, s. 14 (1) (a)*. Made: 24.02.94. Coming into force: 25.02.94. Effect: None. – *Unpublished*

The M6 Motorway (Marker Posts 460/3 - 495/3) (Temporary 50 Miles Per Hour Speed Restriction) Order 1994 No. 1079. Enabling power: *Road Traffic Regulation Act 1984, s. 14 (1) (a)*. Made: 06.04.94. Coming into force: 08.04.94. Effect: None. – *Unpublished*

The M6 Motorway (Marker Posts 461/4 - 462/8) (Temporary 50 Miles Per Hour Speed Restriction of Traffic) Order 1994 No. 879. Enabling power: *Road Traffic Regulation Act 1984, s. 14 (1) (a)*. Made: 03.03.94. Coming into force: 06.03.94. Effect: None. – *Unpublished*

The M6 Motorway (MP 176/6 to MP 182/3) (Temporary Prohibition and Restriction of Traffic) Order 1994 No. 756. Enabling power: *Road Traffic Regulation Act 1984 ss. 14 (1) (a) (7)*. Made: 04.03.94. Coming into force: 05.03.94. Effect: None. – *Unpublished*

The M6, M61 and M55 Motorways and the A59 Trunk Road (Temporary Restriction and Prohibition of Traffic) Order 1993 Amendment Order 1994 No. 1881. Enabling power: *Road Traffic Regulation Act 1984, s. 14 (1) (a)*. Made: 10.06.94. Coming into force: 11.06.94. Effect: None. – *Unpublished*

The M8 Motorway (Junctions 3, 3A and 4) (Slip Roads) (Temporary Prohibition of Traffic) Order 1994 No. 2511. Enabling power: *Road Traffic Regulation Act 1984, s. 14 (1) (a) (4)*. Made: 23.09.94. Coming into force: 01.10.94. Effect: None. – *Unpublished*

The M8 Motorway (Junctions 26-29) (Temporary Prohibition of Traffic) (No. 2) Order 1994 No.3310. Enabling power: *Road Traffic Regulation Act 1984, s. 14 (1) (a) (4)*. Made: 23.12.94. Coming into force: 01.01.95. Effect: None. – *Unpublished*

The M8 Motorway (Newbridge Roundabout) (Temporary Prohibition of Traffic) (No. 2) Order 1994 No. 2925. Enabling power: *Road Traffic Regulation Act 1984, s.14 (1) (a) (4) (a), 121A*. Made: 16.11.94. Coming into force: 21.11.94. Effect: None. – *Unpublished*

The M8 Motorway (Newbridge Roundabout) (Temporary Prohibition of Traffic) Order 1994 No.2293. Enabling power: *Road Traffic Regulation Act 1984, s. 14 (1) (a) (4) (a)*. Made: 02.09.94. Coming into force: 12.09.94. Effect: None. – *Unpublished*

The (M8) Motorway (Junctions 26-29) (Temporary Prohibition of Traffic) Order 1994 No.365. Enabling power: *Road Traffic Regulation Act 1984, s. 14 (1) (a) (4)*. Made: 17.02.94. Coming into force: 28.02.94. Effect: None. – *Unpublished*

The M9/A9/A882 Trunk Road Edinburgh-Thurso (Auchterarder Junction) (Temporary Prohibition of Specified Turns) Order 1994 No. 2182. Enabling power: *Road Traffic Regulation Act 1984, s. 14 (1) (a) (4)*. Made: 17.08.94. Coming into force: 21.08.94. Effect: None. – *Unpublished*

The M10 (Junction 1) and M1 (Junctions 7-8) Motorways (Temporary Prohibition of Traffic) Order 1994 No. 2776. Enabling power: *Road Traffic Regulation Act 1984, s. 14 (1) (a)*. Made: 24.10.94. Coming into force: 31.10.94. Effect: None. – *Unpublished*

The M11 Motorway and A11 Trunk Road (M11 J9 to A11, Worsted Lodge) (Temporary 50 Miles Per Hour Speed Restriction) Order 1994 No. 735. Enabling power: *Road Traffic Regulation Act 1984, s. 14 (1) 15 (2)*. Made: 10.03.94. Coming into force: 10.03.94. Effect: S.I. 1993/3272 amended. – *Unpublished*

The M11 Motorway and A14 Trunk Road (Girton Interchange, Cambridgeshire) (Temporary 50 Miles Per Hour Speed Restriction) Order 1994 No. 2820. Enabling power: *Road Traffic Regulation Act 1984, s. 14 (1) (a)*. Made: 28.10.94. Coming into force: 04.11.94. Effect: None. – *Unpublished*

The M11 Motorway, Essex (Spur Road) (Temporary Restriction and Prohibition of Traffic) Order 1994 No. 3031. Enabling power: *Road Traffic Regulation Act 1984, s. 14 (1) (a) (7)*. Made: 28.11.94. Coming into force: 30.11.94. Effect: None. – *Unpublished*

The M11 Motorway (Junction 4, Essex) (Temporary Prohibition of Traffic) Order 1994 No.1217. Enabling power: *Road Traffic Regulation Act 1984, s. 14 (1) (a)*. Made: 31.03.94. Coming into force: 05.04.94. Effect: None. – *Unpublished*

The M11 Motorway (Junction 6, Essex) (Link Roads) (Temporary Restriction of Traffic) Order 1994 No. 2398. Enabling power: *Road Traffic Regulation Act 1984, s. 14 (1) (a) (7)*. Made: 05.09.94. Coming into force: 12.09.94. Effect: None. – *Unpublished*

The M11 Motorway (Junction 7, Essex) (Temporary Prohibition of Traffic) Order 1994 No.3048. Enabling power: *Road Traffic Regulation Act 1984, s. 14 (1) (a)*. Made: 28.11.94. Coming into force: 03.12.94. Effect: None. – *Unpublished*

The M11 Motorway (Junction 8, Bishops Stortford, Essex) (Temporary Prohibition of Traffic) Order 1994 No. 2002. Enabling power: *Road Traffic Regulation Act 1984, s. 14 (1) (a)*. Made: 25.07.94. Coming into force: 01.08.94. Effect: None. – *Unpublished*

The M11 Motorway (Junctions 7-8, Essex) Slip Roads (Temporary Prohibition and Restriction of Traffic) Order 1994 No. 893. Enabling power: *Road Traffic Regulation Act 1984, s. 14 (1) (a)*. Made: 21.03.94. Coming into force: 28.03.94. Effect: None. – *Unpublished*

The M11 Motorway (Junctions 7-8, Essex) (Temporary Prohibition and Restriction of Traffic) No. 2 Order 1994 No. 2179. Enabling power: *Road Traffic Regulation Act 1984, s. 14 (1) (a) (7)*. Made: 15.08.94. Coming into force: 22.08.94. Effect: None. – *Unpublished*

The M18 and the A1(M) Motorways (Wadworth Roundabout and Slip Roads) (Temporary Restriction of Traffic) Order 1994 No. 1250. Enabling power: *Road Traffic Regulation Act 1984, s. 14 (1) (a) (7)*. Made: 04.05.94. Coming into force: 05.05.94. Effect: None. – *Unpublished*

The M18 Motorway (Junction 2, Northbound and Southbound Entry Slip Roads) (Temporary 30 Miles Per Hour Speed Restriction) Order 1994 No. 2781. Enabling power: *Road Traffic Regulation Act 1984, s. 14 (1) (a)*. Made: 26.10.94. Coming into force: 28.10.94. Effect: None. – *Unpublished*

The M18 Motorway (Junction 5, Slip Roads) (Temporary Restriction of Traffic) Order 1994 No.345. Enabling power: *Road Traffic Regulation Act 1984, s. 14 (1) (a) (7)*. Made: 28.01.94. Coming into force: 30.01.94. Effect: None. – *Unpublished*

The M18 Motorway (Junctions 1-5, Slip Roads) (Temporary 30 Miles Per Hour Speed Restriction) Order 1994 No. 2198. Enabling power: *Road Traffic Regulation Act 1984, s. 14 (1) (a)*. Made: 15.08.94. Coming into force: 17.08.94. Effect: None. – *Unpublished*

The M18 Motorway (Junctions 3-4) (Temporary Restriction and Prohibition of Traffic) Order 1994 No. 125. Enabling power: *Road Traffic Regulation Act 1984, s. 14 (1) (a) (7)*. Made: 14.01.94. Coming into force: 16.01.94. Effect: None. – *Unpublished*

The M18 Motorway (Junctions 3-4) (Temporary Restriction of Traffic) Order 1994 No.95. Enabling power: *Road Traffic Regulation Act 1984, s. 14 (1) (a) (7)*. Made: 04.01.94. Coming into force: 05.01.94. Effect: None. – *Unpublished*

The M18 Motorway (Junctions 5 and 6) (Temporary Restriction and Prohibition of Traffic) Order 1994 No. 2724. Enabling power: *Road Traffic Regulation Act 1984, s. 14 (1) (a)*. Made: 19.10.94. Coming into force: 21.10.94. Effect: None. – *Unpublished*

The M18 Motorway (Junction with M1 Motorway to Junction 1) (Temporary Restriction of Traffic) Order 1994 No. 1466. Enabling power: *Road Traffic Regulation Act 1984, s. 14 (1) (a) (7)*. Made: 25.05.94. Coming into force: 31.05.94. Effect: None. – *Unpublished*

The M18 Motorway (M1-M1/M18 Link Road, Southbound Carriageway) (Temporary Prohibition of Traffic) Order 1994 No. 414. Enabling power: *Road Traffic Regulation Act 1984, s. 14 (1) (a)*. Made: 05.01.94. Coming into force: 07.01.94. Effect: None. – *Unpublished*

The M20 Motorway and the A20 Trunk Road (Ashford to Folkestone) (Temporary Prohibition of Traffic) Order 1994 No. 2533. Enabling power: *Road Traffic Regulation Act 1984, s. 14 (1) (a)*. Made: 26.09.94. Coming into force: 30.09.94. Effect: None. – *Unpublished*

The M20 Motorway and the A20 Trunk Road (Round Hill Tunnels) (Temporary Restriction and Prohibition of Traffic) Order 1994 No. 3240. Enabling power: *Road Traffic Regulation Act 1984, s. 14 (1) (a) (7)*. Made: 12.12.94. Coming into force: 01.01.95. Effect: None. – *Unpublished*

The M20 Motorway (Junctions 12-13) (Temporary Prohibition of Traffic) Order 1994 No.48. Enabling power: *Road Traffic Regulations Act 1984, s. 14 (1) (a)*. Made: 10.01.94. Coming into force: 15.01.94. Effect: None. – *Unpublished*

The M20 Motorway (Marker Post 99.2 to Junction 13) (Temporary Restriction of Traffic) Order 1994 No. 1052. Enabling power: *Road Traffic Regulation Act 1984, s. 14 (1) (a) (7)*. Made: 08.04.94. Coming into force: 10.04.94. Effect: None. – *Unpublished*

The M20 Motorway (Marker Posts 52.0-65.0) (Temporary Prohibition and Restriction of Traffic) Order 1994 No. 1785. Enabling power: *Road Traffic Regulation Act 1984, s. 14 (1) (a) (7)*. Made: 04.07.94. Coming into force: 09.07.94. Effect: None. – *Unpublished*

The M23 Motorway and the A23 Trunk Road (Pease Pottage to Handcross) (Temporary 40 Miles Per Hour Speed Restriction) Order 1994 No. 1348. Enabling power: *Road Traffic Regulation Act 1984, s. 14 (1) (a)*. Made: 16.05.94. Coming into force: 21.05.94. Effect: None. – *Unpublished*

The M23 Motorway (Junctions 10-11) (Temporary Prohibition of Traffic) Order 1994 No.1652. Enabling power: *Road Traffic Regulation Act 1984, s. 14 (1) (a)*. Made: 20.06.94. Coming into force: 25.06.94. Effect: None. – *Unpublished*

The M25 and M26 Motorways (Sevenoaks Interchange) (Temporary Restriction and Prohibition of Traffic) Order 1994 No. 1036. Enabling power: *Road Traffic Regulation Act 1984, s. 14 (1) (a) (7)*. Made: 05.04.94. Coming into force: 09.04.94. Effect: None. – *Unpublished*

The M25 (Junction 15) and M4 (Junction 4B) Motorways (Slough, Buckinghamshire and Hillingdon, Greater London) (Slip Roads) (Temporary Prohibition of Traffic) Order 1994 No. 3058. Enabling power: *Road Traffic Regulation Act 1984, s. 14 (1) (a)*. Made: 29.11.94. Coming into force: 01.12.94. Effect: None. – *Unpublished*

The M25 London Orbital Motorway (Junction 18 Hertfordshire) (Temporary Prohibition of Traffic) Order 1994 No. 1091. Enabling power: *Road Traffic Regulation Act 1984, s. 14 (1) (a)*. Made: 11.04.94. Coming into force: 18.04.94. Effect: None. – *Unpublished*

The M25 Motorway and M40 Motorway (Link Roads, Buckinghamshire) (Temporary Prohibition of Traffic) Order 1994 No. 337. Enabling power: *Road Traffic Regulation Act 1984, s. 14 (1) (a)*. Made: 14.02.94. Coming into force: 21.02.94. Effect: None. – *Unpublished*

The M25 Motorway (Bell Common Tunnel, Essex) (Temporary Prohibition and Restriction of Traffic) No. 2 Order 1994 No. 3333. Enabling power: *Road Traffic Regulation Act 1984, s. 14 (1) (a) (7)*. Made: 21.12.94. Coming into force: 30.12.94. Effect: None. – *Unpublished*

The M25 Motorway (Bell Common Tunnel, Essex) (Temporary Restriction of Traffic) Order 1994 No. 138. Enabling power: *Road Traffic Regulation Act 1984, ss. 14 (1) (a) (7).* Made: 24.01.94. Coming into force: 27.01.94. Effect: None. – *Unpublished*

4@TS D = The M25 Motorway (Holmesdale Tunnel, Hertfordshire) (Temporary Prohibition and Restriction of Traffic) No. 2 Order 1994 No. 3335. Enabling power: *Road Traffic Regulation Act 1984, s. 14 (1) (a) (7).* Made: 21.12.94. Coming into force: 30.12.94. Effect: None. – *Unpublished*

The M25 Motorway (Holmesdale Tunnel, Hertfordshire) (Temporary Restriction of Traffic) Order 1994 No. 139. Enabling power: *Road Traffic Regulation Act 1984, ss. 14 (1) (a) (7).* Made: 24.01.94. Coming into force: 27.01.94. Effect: None. – *Unpublished*

The M25 Motorway (Junction 4) (Temporary Restriction and Prohibition of Traffic) Order 1994 No. 1035. Enabling power: *Road Traffic Regulation Act 1984, s. 14 (1) (a) (7).* Made: 05.04.94. Coming into force: 09.04.94. Effect: None. – *Unpublished*

The M25 Motorway (Junction 16, Buckinghamshire) (Temporary Prohibition and Restriction of Traffic) Order 1994 No. 1712. Enabling power: *Road Traffic Regulation Act 1984, s. 14 (1) (a).* Made: 27.06.94. Coming into force: 04.07.94. Effect: None. – *Unpublished*

The M25 Motorway (Junction 18, Hertfordshire) (Temporary Prohibition of Traffic) Order 1994 No. 1710. Enabling power: *Road Traffic Regulation Act 1984, s. 14 (1) (a).* Made: 27.06.94. Coming into force: 02.07.94. Effect: None. – *Unpublished*

The M25 Motorway (Junction 19 to Hunton Bridge Roundabout, Hertfordshire) (Temporary 50 Miles Per Hour Speed Restriction) Order 1994 No. 1656. Enabling power: *Road Traffic Regulation Act 1984, s. 14 (1) (a).* Made: 10.06.94. Coming into force: 10.06.94. Effect: None. – *Unpublished*

The M25 Motorway (Junction 19 to Hunton Bridge Roundabout, Hertfordshire) (Temporary Restriction and Prohibition of Traffic) No. 2 Order 1994 No. 3317. Enabling power: *Road Traffic Regulation Act 1984, s. 14 (1) (a).* Made: 23.12.94. Coming into force: 03.01.95. Effect: None. – *Unpublished*

The M25 Motorway (Junction 19 to Hunton Bridge Roundabout, Hertfordshire) (Temporary Restriction and Prohibition of Traffic) Order 1994 No. 2818. Enabling power: *Road Traffic Regulation Act 1984, s. 14 (1) (a).* Made: 27.10.94. Coming into force: 31.10.94. Effect: S.I. 1994/1656 revoked. – *Unpublished*

The M25 Motorway (Junction 21A, Hertfordshire) (Slip Roads) (Temporary Prohibition of Traffic) Order 1994 No. 1999. Enabling power: *Road Traffic Regulation Act 1984, s. 14 (1) (a).* Made: 25.07.94. Coming into force: 01.08.94. Effect: None. – *Unpublished*

The M25 Motorway (Junction 22, Hertfordshire) (Temporary Prohibition of Traffic) Order 1994 No. 2634. Enabling power: *Road Traffic Regulation Act 1984, s. 14 (1) (a).* Made: 23.09.94. Coming into force: 30.09.94. Effect: None. – *Unpublished*

The M25 Motorway (Junction 24, Hertfordshire) (Temporary Prohibition of Traffic) Order 1994 No. 49. Enabling power: *Road Traffic Regulations Act 1984, s. 14 (1) (a).* Made: 10.01.94. Coming into force: 17.01.94. Effect: None. – *Unpublished*

The M25 Motorway (Junction 25, Hertfordshire) (Temporary Prohibition of Traffic) Order 1994 No. 214. Enabling power: *Road Traffic Regulation 1984, s. 14 (1) (a).* Made: 31.01.94. Coming into force: 07.02.94. Effect: None. – *Unpublished*

The M25 Motorway (Junction 25, Hertfordshire) (Temporary Prohibition of Traffic) Order 1994 No. 385. Enabling power: *Road Traffic Regulation Act 1984, s. 14 (1) (a).* Made: 21.02.94. Coming into force: 28.02.94. Effect: None. – *Unpublished*

The M25 Motorway (Junction 27, Essex) (Temporary Restriction of Traffic) Order 1994 No.1539. Enabling power: *Road Traffic Regulation Act 1984, s. 14 (1) (a) (7).* Made: 31.05.94. Coming into force: 06.06.94. Effect: None. – *Unpublished*

The M25 Motorway (Junction 27, Theydon Interchange, Essex) (Temporary Prohibition and Restriction of Traffic) Order 1994 No. 518. Enabling power: *Road Traffic Regulation Act 1984, s. 14 (1) (a).* Made: 28.02.94. Coming into force: 07.03.94. Effect: None. – *Unpublished*

The M25 Motorway (Junction 28, Essex) (Temporary Prohibition of Traffic) Order 1994 No.1540. Enabling power: *Road Traffic Regulation Act 1984, s. 14 (1) (a).* Made: 31.05.94. Coming into force: 06.06.94. Effect: None. – *Unpublished*

The M25 Motorway (Junction 28, Essex) (Temporary Prohibition of Traffic) Order 1994 No.2775. Enabling power: *Road Traffic Regulation Act 1984, s. 14 (1) (a).* Made: 21.10.94. Coming into force: 28.10.94. Effect: None. – *Unpublished*

The M25 Motorway (Junction 28, Southbound Access Slip Road, Essex) (Temporary Prohibition of Traffic) Order 1994 No.2245. Enabling power: *Road Traffic Regulation Act 1984, s. 14 (1) (a).* Made: 22.08.94. Coming into force: 30.08.94. Effect: None. – *Unpublished*

The M25 Motorway (Junction 29, Codham Hall Interchange, Essex) (Temporary Prohibition of Traffic) Order 1994 No. 2223. Enabling power: *Road Traffic Regulation Act 1984, s. 14 (1) (a).* Made: 19.08.94. Coming into force: 26.08.94. Effect: None. – *Unpublished*

The M25 Motorway (Junctions 6-8) (Temporary Restriction and Prohibition of Traffic) (No. 2) Order 1994 No. 1455. Enabling power: *Road Traffic Regulation Act 1984, s. 14 (1) (a) (7)*. Made: 31.05.94. Coming into force: 04.06.94. Effect: None. – *Unpublished*

The M25 Motorway (Junctions 6-8) (Temporary Restriction and Prohibition of Traffic) Order 1994 No. 122. Enabling power: *Road Traffic Regulation Act 1984, s. 14 (1) (a) (7)*. Made: 24.01.94. Coming into force: 29.01.94. Effect: None. – *Unpublished*

The M25 Motorway (Junctions 6-8) (Temporary Restriction and Prohibition of Traffic) (No. 3) Order 1994 No. 2212. Enabling power: *Road Traffic Regulation Act 1984, s. 14 (1) (a) (7)*. Made: 22.08.94. Coming into force: 27.08.94. Effect: S.I. 1994/1455 revoked. – *Unpublished*

The M25 Motorway (Junctions 10-11) (Temporary Restriction and Prohibition of Traffic) Order 1994 No. 2570. Enabling power: *Road Traffic Regulation Act 1984, s. 14 (1) (a) (7)*. Made: 03.10.94. Coming into force: 08.10.94. Effect: S.I. 1993/3180 revoked. – *Unpublished*

The M25 Motorway (Junctions 10-14) (Temporary Prohibition of Traffic) Order 1994 No.3033. Enabling power: *Road Traffic Regulation Act 1984, s. 14 (1) (a)*. Made: 28.11.94. Coming into force: 03.12.94. Effect: None. – *Unpublished*

The M25 Motorway (Junctions 13-15) (Temporary Prohibition of Traffic) Order 1994 No.1176. Enabling power: *Road Traffic Regulation Act 1984, s. 14 (1) (a)*. Made: 25.04.94. Coming into force: 30.04.94. Effect: None. – *Unpublished*

The M25 Motorway (Junctions 14-15, Buckinghamshire and Surrey) (Temporary Prohibition and Restriction of Traffic) Order 1994 No. 2535. Enabling power: *Road Traffic Regulation Act 1984, s. 14 (1) (a)*. Made: 26.09.94. Coming into force: 03.10.94. Effect: None. – *Unpublished*

The M25 Motorway (Junctions 18 and 22, Hertfordshire) (Slip Roads) (Temporary Prohibition of Traffic) Order 1994 No.2835. Enabling power: *Road Traffic Regulation Act 1984, s. 14 (1) (a)*. Made: 31.10.94. Coming into force: 07.11.94. Effect: None. – *Unpublished*

The M25 Motorway (Junctions 20-21A) and the M1 Motorway (Junction 6A) (Hertfordshire) (Temporary Prohibition of Traffic) Order 1994 No. 325. Enabling power: *Road Traffic Regulation Act 1984, s. 14 (1) (a)*. Made: 14.02.94. Coming into force: 21.02.94. Effect: None. – *Unpublished*

The M25 Motorway (Junctions 21-21A, Hertfordshire) (Temporary Prohibition of Traffic) Order 1994 No. 943. Enabling power: *Road Traffic Regulation Act 1984, s. 14 (1) (a)*. Made: 17.03.94. Coming into force: 21.03.94. Effect: None. – *Unpublished*

The M25 Motorway (Junctions 21-21A, Hertfordshire) (Temporary Prohibition of Traffic) Order 1994 No. 1943. Enabling power: *Road Traffic Regulation Act 1984, s. 14 (1) (a)*. Made: 18.07.94. Coming into force: 25.07.94. Effect: None. – *Unpublished*

The M25 Motorway (Junctions 21-23, Hertfordshire) (Temporary Prohibition and Restriction of Traffic) Order 1994 No. 1784. Enabling power: *Road Traffic Regulation Act 1984, s. 14 (1) (a)*. Made: 04.07.94. Coming into force: 11.07.94. Effect: None. – *Unpublished*

The M25 Motorway (Junctions 21A-22, Hertfordshire) (Temporary Prohibition and Restriction of Traffic) Order 1994 No. 984. Enabling power: *Road Traffic Regulation Act 1984, s. 14 (1) (a)*. Made: 28.03.94. Coming into force: 04.04.94. Effect: None. – *Unpublished*

The M25 Motorway (Junctions 21A-22, Hertfordshire) (Temporary Prohibition of Traffic) Order 1994 No. 742. Enabling power: *Road Traffic Regulation Act 1984 s. 14 (1) (a)*. Made: 07.03.94. Coming into force: 14.03.94. Effect: None. – *Unpublished*

The M25 Motorway (Junctions 23 and 25, Hertfordshire) (Temporary Prohibition of Traffic) Order 1994 No. 2306. Enabling power: *Road Traffic Regulation Act 1984, s. 14 (1) (a)*. Made: 26.08.94. Coming into force: 05.09.94. Effect: None. – *Unpublished*

The M25 Motorway (Junctions 25 - 26, Essex) (Temporary Restriction of Traffic) Order 1994 No.1538. Enabling power: *Road Traffic Regulation Act 1984, s. 14 (1) (a) (7)*. Made: 31.05.94. Coming into force: 06.06.94. Effect: None. – *Unpublished*

The M25 Motorway (Junctions 28 - 31, Essex) (Temporary Prohibition of Traffic) Order 1994 No.1223. Enabling power: *Road Traffic Regulation Act 1984, s. 14 (1) (a)*. Made: 29.04.94. Coming into force: 04.05.94. Effect: None. – *Unpublished*

The M25 Motorway (Junctions 30 - 31, Thurrock, Essex) (Temporary Prohibition of Traffic) Order 1994 No. 1957. Enabling power: *Road Traffic Regulation Act 1984, s. 14 (1) (a)*. Made: 04.07.94. Coming into force: 11.07.94. Effect: None. – *Unpublished*

The M26 Motorway (Marker Posts 7.0 - 9.4) (Temporary Restriction of Traffic) Order 1994 No.2532. Enabling power: *Road Traffic Regulation Act 1984, s. 14 (1) (a) (7)*. Made: 26.09.94. Coming into force: 30.09.94. Effect: None. – *Unpublished*

The M27 Motorway and the A27 Trunk Road (Junctions 11 - 12) (Temporary Restriction and Prohibition of Traffic) Order 1994 No. 3291. Enabling power: *Road Traffic Regulation Act 1984, s. 14 (1) (a) (7)*. Made: 19.12.94. Coming into force: 31.12.94. Effect: None. – *Unpublished*

The M27 Motorway and the A31 Trunk Road (Cadnam to Ower) (Temporary Restriction and Prohibition of Traffic) (No. 2) Order 1994 No. 2558. Enabling power: *Road Traffic Regulation Act 1984, s. 14 (1) (a) (7)*. Made: 28.09.94. Coming into force: 30.09.94. Effect: S.I. 1994/1945 revoked. – *Unpublished*

The M27 Motorway and the A31 Trunk Road (Cadnam to Ower) (Temporary Restriction and Prohibition of Traffic) Order 1994 No. 1945. Enabling power: *Road Traffic Regulation Act 1984, s. 14 (1) (a) (7)*. Made: 18.07.94. Coming into force: 23.07.94. Effect: None. – *Unpublished*

The M27 Motorway (Junctions 11-12) (Temporary Restriction and Prohibition of Traffic) Order 1994 No. 2536. Enabling power: *Road Traffic Regulation Act 1984, s. 14 (1) (a) (7)*. Made: 26.09.94. Coming into force: 01.10.94. Effect: None. – *Unpublished*

The M27 Motorway (Marker Posts 14.8-16.2) (Temporary Restriction of Traffic) Order 1994 No.3032. Enabling power: *Road Traffic Regulation Act 1984, s. 14 (1) (a) (7)*. Made: 28.11.94. Coming into force: 03.12.94. Effect: None. – *Unpublished*

The M27 Motorway (Marker Posts 35.6-44.6) (Temporary Restriction of Traffic) Order 1994 No.210. Enabling power: *Road Traffic Regulation 1984, s. 14 (1) (a) (7)*. Made: 31.01.94. Coming into force: 05.02.94. Effect: None. – *Unpublished*

The M27 Motorway (Portsmouth) (Temporary Prohibition of Traffic) Order 1994 No. 1426. Enabling power: *Road Traffic Regulation Act 1984, s. 14 (1) (b)*. Made: 23.05.94. Coming into force: 28.05.94. Effect: None. – *Unpublished*

The M32 Motorway (M4/M32 Junction, Hambrook) (Temporary 30 Miles Per Hour Speed Restriction) Order 1994 No. 1727. Enabling power: *Road Traffic Regulation Act 1984, s. 14 (1) (a)*. Made: 29.06.94. Coming into force: 01.07.94. Effect: None. – *Unpublished*

The M32 Motorway (Stoke Lane Overbridge) (Temporary 50 Miles Per Hour Speed Restrictons) Order 1994 No. 2055. Enabling power: *Road Traffic Regulation Act 1984, s. 14 (1) (a)*. Made: 01.08.94. Coming into force: 15.08.94. Effect: None. – *Unpublished*

The M40 Motorway (District of Stratford-Upon-Avon in the County of Warwickshire) (Temporary 50 Miles Per Hour Speed Restriction) Order 1994 No. 1625. Enabling power: *Road Traffic Regulation Act 1984, s. 14 (1) (a)*. Made: 09.06.94. Coming into force: 14.06.94. Effect: None. – *Unpublished*

The M40 Motorway (Junction 4 and Connecting Roads, Handycross, Buckinghamshire) (Temporary Restriction and Prohibition of Traffic) Order 1994 No. 885. Enabling power: *Road Traffic Regulation Act 1984, ss. 14 (1) (a) (5) (b)*. Made: 14.03.94. Coming into force: 15.03.94. Effect: None. – *Unpublished*

The M40 Motorway (Junctions 4-5) (Temporary 50 Miles per Hour Speed Restriction) Order 1994 No. 147. Enabling power: *Road Traffic Regulation Act 1984, s. 14 (1) (a)*. Made: 21.01.94. Coming into force: 24.01.94. Effect: None. – *Unpublished*

The M40 Motorway (Marker Posts 61.8-70.8) (Temporary Restriction and Prohibition of Traffic) Order 1994 No. 1786. Enabling power: *Road Traffic Regulation Act 1984, s. 14 (1) (a) (7)*. Made: 04.07.94. Coming into force: 09.07.94. Effect: None. – *Unpublished*

The M41, A40(M) and A501 Trunk Roads (West Cross Route, Westway and Marlybone Flyover) (Temporary Prohibition of Traffic) Order 1994 No. 88. Enabling power: *Road Traffic Regulation Act 1984, ss. 14 (1) (4) (5) (7)*. Made: 17.01.94. Coming into force: 24.01.94. Effect: None. – *Unpublished*

The M41 Trunk Road (West Cross Route, Hammersmith and Fulham) (Temporary Prohibition of Traffic) Order 1994 No. 981. Enabling power: *Road Traffic Regulation Act 1984, s. 14 (1) (4)*. Made: 28.03.94. Coming into force: 05.04.94. Effect: None. – *Unpublished*

The M42 Motorway (Junction 6) (Temporary Prohibition of Traffic) Order 1994 No. 3243. Enabling power: *Road Traffic Regulation Act 1984, s. 14 (1) (a)*. Made: 14.09.94. Coming into force: 16.09.94. Effect: None. – *Unpublished*

The M50 Motorway (Junctions 1-2) (Temporary Restriction and Prohibition of Traffic) Order 1994 No. 1618. Enabling power: *Road Traffic Regulation Act 1984, s. 14 (1) (a) (7)*. Made: 10.06.94. Coming into force: 11.06.94. Effect: None. – *Unpublished*

The M50 Motorway (Queenhill Bridge) (Temporary Restriction of Traffic) Order 1994 No.3113. Enabling power: *Road Traffic Regulation Act 1984, s. 14 (1) (a) (7)*. Made: 02.12.94. Coming into force: 03.12.94. Effect: None. – *Unpublished*

The M50 Motorway (Ross Spur) (Temporary Restriction of Traffic) Order 1994 No. 2091. Enabling power: *Road Traffic Regulation Act 1984, s. 14 (1) (a) (7)*. Made: 30.07.94. Coming into force: 31.07.94. Effect: None. – *Unpublished*

The M53 Motorway (Junction 1) Bidston Viaduct, Wallasey (Temporary Prohibition of Traffic) Order 1994 No. 377. Enabling power: *Road Traffic Regulation Act 1984, s. 14 (1) (a)*. Made: 02.02.94. Coming into force: 07.02.94. Effect: None. – *Unpublished*

The M53 Motorway (Junction 1) Northbound Exit Slip Road (Temporary Prohibition of Traffic) Order 1994 No. 2057. Enabling power: *Road Traffic Regulation Act 1984, s. 14 (1) (a)*. Made: 29.07.94. Coming into force: 07.08.94. Effect: None. – *Unpublished*

The M53 Motorway (Junction 2) (Moreton Spur Link Road) (Southbound Entry and Exit Slip Roads) (Temporary Prohibition of Traffic) Order 1994 No. 907. Enabling power: *Road Traffic Regulation Act 1984, s. 14 (1) (a)*. Made: 15.03.94. Coming into force: 20.03.94. Effect: None. – *Unpublished*

The M53 Motorway (Junction 2) Slip Road) (Temporary Prohibition of Traffic) Order 1994 No.2646. Enabling power: *Road Traffic Regulation Act 1984, s. 14 (1) (a)*. Made: 04.10.94. Coming into force: 03.11.94. Effect: None. *– Unpublished*

The M53 Motorway (Junction 2) Slip Road (Temporary Prohibition of Traffic) Order 1994 No.2929. Enabling power: *Road Traffic Regulation Act 1984, s. 14 (1) (a)*. Made: 10.11.94. Coming into force: 10.11.94. Effect: None. *– Unpublished*

The M53 Motorway (Junction 5) Northbound Exit Slip Road (Temporary Prohibition of Traffic) Order 1994 No. 2496. Enabling power: *Road Traffic Regulation Act 1984, s. 14 (1) (a)*. Made: 04.09.94. Coming into force: 08.09.94. Effect: None. *– Unpublished*

The M53 Motorway (Junction 5) Slip Roads (Temporary Prohibition of Traffic) Order 1994 No.3060. Enabling power: *Road Traffic Regulation Act 1984, s. 14 (1) (a)*. Made: 24.11.94. Coming into force: 02.12.94. Effect: None. *– Unpublished*

The M53 Motorway (Junction 8) Slip Road (Temporary Prohibition of Traffic) Order 1994 No.2717. Enabling power: *Road Traffic Regulation Act 1984, s. 14 (1) (a)*. Made: 05.10.94. Coming into force: 27.10.94. Effect: None. *– Unpublished*

The M53 Motorway (Junction 9) Northbound Exit Slip Road (Temporary Prohibition of Traffic) Order 1994 No. 2060. Enabling power: *Road Traffic Regulation Act 1984, s. 14 (1) (a)*. Made: 29.07.94. Coming into force: 09.08.94. Effect: None. *– Unpublished*

The M53 Motorway (Junction 10) Slip Roads (Temporary Prohibition of Traffic) Order 1994 No.2401. Enabling power: *Road Traffic Regulation Act 1984, s. 14 (1) (a)*. Made: 31.08.94. Coming into force: 01.09.94. Effect: None. *– Unpublished*

The M53 Motorway (Junctions 10 - 11) Little Stanney (Temporary Prohibition of Traffic) Order 1994 No. 2400. Enabling power: *Road Traffic Regulation Act 1984, s. 14 (1) (a)*. Made: 31.08.94. Coming into force: 08.09.94. Effect: None. *– Unpublished*

The M53 Motorway (Marker Posts 9/3 to 26/5) Wirral (Temporary Restriction of Traffic) Order 1994 No. 823. Enabling power: *Road Traffic Regulation Act 1984, s. 14 (1) (a) (7)*. Made: 10.02.94. Coming into force: 11.02.94. Effect: None. *– Unpublished*

The M53 Motorway (Marker Posts 13/5-19/5) (Temporary Restriction of Traffic) Order 1994 No.2501. Enabling power: *Road Traffic Regulation Act 1984, s. 14 (1) (a) (7)*. Made: 16.09.94. Coming into force: 17.09.94. Effect: None. *– Unpublished*

The M53 Motorway (Through Junction 1) Wallasey (Temporary Prohibition of Traffic) Order 1994 No. 2379. Enabling power: *Road Traffic Regulation Act 1984, s. 14 (1) (a)*. Made: 23.08.94. Coming into force: 02.09.94. Effect: None. *– Unpublished*

The M54 Motorway and the A5 Trunk Road (Cluddley Interchange) (Temporary Prohibition of Traffic) Order 1994 No. 906. Enabling power: *Road Traffic Regulation Act 1984, s. 14 (1) (a)*. Made: 17.03.94. Coming into force: 18.03.94. Effect: None. *– Unpublished*

The M54 Motorway (Junction 1) and M6 Motorway (Junction 10A) (Temporary Restriction of Traffic) Order 1994 No. 2396. Enabling power: *Road Traffic Regulation Act 1984, s. 14 (1) (a) (7)*. Made: 01.09.94. Coming into force: 02.09.94. Effect: None. *– Unpublished*

The M54 Motorway (Junctions 2 - 4) (Temporary Restriction and Prohibition of Traffic) Order 1994 No. 1549. Enabling power: *Road Traffic Regulation Act 1984, s. 14 (1) (a) (7)*. Made: 03.06.94. Coming into force: 04.06.94. Effect: None. *– Unpublished*

The M54 Motorway (Priorslee to Forge) (Temporary Restriction of Traffic) Order 1994 No.2397. Enabling power: *Road Traffic Regulation Act 1984, s. 14 (1) (a) (7)*. Made: 26.08.94. Coming into force: 30.08.94. Effect: None. *– Unpublished*

The M56 Motorway (Junction 1) Slip Road (Temporary Prohibition of Traffic) Order 1994 No.2644. Enabling power: *Road Traffic Regulation Act 1984, s. 14 (1) (a)*. Made: 27.09.94. Coming into force: 27.09.94. Effect: None. *– Unpublished*

The M56 Motorway (Junction 3) Slip Roads (Temporary Prohibition of Traffic) Order 1994 No.1722. Enabling power: *Road Traffic Regulation Act 1984, s. 14 (1) (a)*. Made: 13.06.94. Coming into force: 30.06.94. Effect: None. *– Unpublished*

The M56 Motorway (Junctions 2-7) Sharston - Rostherne (Temporary Restriction and Prohibition of Traffic) Order 1993 Amendment Order 1994 No. 1794. Enabling power: *Road Traffic Regulation Act 1984, s. 14 (1) (a)*. Made: 23.06.94. Coming into force: 24.06.94. Effect: None. *– Unpublished*

The M56 Motorway (Junctions 11-12) Preston Brook, Cheshire (Temporary Restriction and Prohibition of Traffic) Order 1993 No. 394. Enabling power: *Road Traffic Regulation Act 1984, ss. 14 (1) (a) 7*. Made: 25.11.93. Coming into force: 26.11.93. Effect: None. *– Unpublished*

The M56 Motorway (Junctions 14-16) (Temporary Prohibition of Traffic) Order 1994 No.869. Enabling power: *Road Traffic Regulation Act 1984, s. 14 (1) (a)*. Made: 09.03.94. Coming into force: 11.03.94. Effect: None. *– Unpublished*

The M56 Motorway (Marker Posts 55/9 - 61/0) Stoak - Dunkirk (Temporary Prohibition of Traffic) Order 1994 No. 1793. Enabling power: *Road Traffic Regulation Act 1984, s. 14 (1) (a)*. Made: 27.06.94. Coming into force: 15.07.94. Effect: None. – *Unpublished*

The M57 Motorway (Junction 2) Southbound Access Slip Road (Temporary Prohibition of Traffic) Order 1994 No. 2098. Enabling power: *Road Traffic Regulation Act 1984, s. 14 (1) (a)*. Made: 02.08.94. Coming into force: 15.08.94. Effect: None. – *Unpublished*

The M57 Motorway (Junction 2) Southbound Exit Slip Road (Temporary Prohibition of Traffic) Order 1994 No. 2434. Enabling power: *Road Traffic Regulation Act 1984, s. 14 (1) (a)*. Made: 02.08.94. Coming into force: 14.08.94. Effect: None. – *Unpublished*

The M57 Motorway (Junction 3) Southbound Exit Slip Road (Temporary Prohibition of Traffic) Order 1994 No. 2984. Enabling power: *Road Traffic Regulation Act 1984, s. 14 (1) (a)*. Made: 10.11.94. Coming into force: 24.11.94. Effect: None. – *Unpublished*

The M57 Motorway (Junction 4) Northbound Exit Slip Road (Temporary Prohibition of Traffic) Order 1994 No. 839. Enabling power: *Road Traffic Regulation Act 1984, s. 14 (1) (a)*. Made: 13.01.94. Coming into force: 21.01.94. Effect: None. – *Unpublished*

The M58 Motorway (Junction 3 to M6 Motorway, Junction 26) (Temporary Restriction of Traffic) Order 1994 No. 380. Enabling power: *Road Traffic Regulation Act 1984, s. 14 (1) (a) (7)*. Made: 28.01.94. Coming into force: 31.01.94. Effect: None. – *Unpublished*

The M58 Motorway (Junctions 1-3) (Temporary Restriction and Prohibition of Traffic) Order 1994 No. 2502. Enabling power: *Road Traffic Regulation Act 1984, s. 14 (1) (a) (7)*. Made: 13.09.94. Coming into force: 13.09.94. Effect: None. – *Unpublished*

The M61 Motorway (Junction 4) Slip Roads (Temporary Prohibition of Traffic) Order 1994 No.1109. Enabling power: *Road Traffic Regulation Act 1984, s. 14 (1) (a)*. Made: 30.03.94. Coming into force: 16.05.94. Effect: None. – *Unpublished*

The M61 Motorway (Junction 4) Slip Road (Temporary Prohibition of Traffic) Order 1994 No.2506. Enabling power: *Road Traffic Regulation Act 1984, s. 14 (1) (a)*. Made: 20.09.94. Coming into force: 06.10.94. Effect: None. – *Unpublished*

The M61 Motorway (Junctions 2-3) Kearsley (Temporary Restriction of Traffic) Order 1994 No.433. Enabling power: *Road Traffic Regulation Act 1984, s. 14 (1) (a) 7*. Made: 14.02.94. Coming into force: 17.02.94. Effect: None. – *Unpublished*

The M61 Motorway (Junctions 2-3) Slip Roads (Temporary Prohibition of Traffic) Order 1994 No. 1147. Enabling power: *Road Traffic Regulation Act 1984, s. 14 (1) (a)*. Made: 25.03.94. Coming into force: 15.05.94. Effect: None. – *Unpublished*

The M61 Motorway (Kearsley Spur-A666) (Temporary Prohibition of Traffic) Order 1994 No.1183. Enabling power: *Road Traffic Regulation Act 1984, s. 14 (1) (a)*. Made: 18.04.94. Coming into force: 13.05.94. Effect: None. – *Unpublished*

The M61 Motorway (Marker Posts 4/6 - 4/0) (Temporary Prohibition of Traffic) Order 1994 No.1119. Enabling power: *Road Traffic Regulation Act 1984, s. 14 (1) (a)*. Made: 25.03.94. Coming into force: 16.05.94. Effect: None. – *Unpublished*

The M61 Motorway (Marker Posts 5/4 - 4/0) (Temporary 50 Miles Per Hour Speed Restriction) Order 1994 No. 2424. Enabling power: *Road Traffic Regulation Act 1984, s. 14 (1) (a)*. Made: 05.08.94. Coming into force: 21.08.94. Effect: None. – *Unpublished*

The M61 Motorway (Marker Posts 8/0 - 11/2) (Temporary Prohibition of Traffic) Order 1994 No.2399. Enabling power: *Road Traffic Regulation Act 1984, s. 14 (1) (a)*. Made: 24.08.94. Coming into force: 08.09.94. Effect: None. – *Unpublished*

The M61 Motorway (Marker Posts 8/5 to 3/5) Bolton (Temporary Restriction of Traffic) Order 1994 No. 2494. Enabling power: *Road Traffic Regulation Act 1984, s. 14 (1) (a) (7)*. Made: 16.09.94. Coming into force: 18.09.94. Effect: None. – *Unpublished*

The M62 and M1 Motorways (Lofthouse Interchange) (Temporary Restriction of Traffic) Order 1994 No. 2263. Enabling power: *Road Traffic Regulation Act 1984, s. 14 (1) (a) (7)*. Made: 25.08.94. Coming into force: 30.08.94. Effect: None. – *Unpublished*

The M62 and the A627(M) Motorways (Thornham Roundabout) (Temporary Prohibition of Traffic) Order 1994 No. 1870. Enabling power: *Road Traffic Regulation Act 1984, s. 14 (1) (a)*. Made: 13.06.94. Coming into force: 16.06.94. Effect: None. – *Unpublished*

The M62 Motorway (Junction 6) Westbound Exit Slip Road (Temporary Prohibition of Traffic) Order 1994 No. 1464. Enabling power: *Road Traffic Regulation Act 1984, s. 14 (1) (a)*. Made: 25.05.94. Coming into force: 18.06.94. Effect: None. – *Unpublished*

The M62 Motorway (Junction 7) and the A568 Trunk Road (Temporary 30 Miles Per Hour Speed Restriction) Order 1994 No. 2043. Enabling power: *Road Traffic Regulation Act 1984, s. 14 (1) (a) (5) (b)*. Made: 15.07.94. Coming into force: 02.08.94. Effect: None. – *Unpublished*

Price/availability are liable to change without notice

172 ROAD TRAFFIC: TRAFFIC REGULATION

The M62 Motorway (Junction 7) Eastbound Exit Slip Road (Temporary Prohibition of Traffic) Order 1994 No. 2061. Enabling power: *Road Traffic Regulation Act 1984, s. 14 (1) (a)*. Made: 29.07.94. Coming into force: 11.08.94. Effect: None. – *Unpublished*

The M62 Motorway (Junction 9) Eastbound Access Slip Road (Temporary Prohibition of Traffic) Order 1994 No. 2058. Enabling power: *Road Traffic Regulation Act 1984, s. 14 (1) (a)*. Made: 29.07.94. Coming into force: 10.08.94. Effect: None. – *Unpublished*

The M62 Motorway Junction 12 and the M63 Motorway Junction 1 Interchange) (Temporary Prohibition of Traffic) Order 1994 No. 2885. Enabling power: *Road Traffic Regulation Act 1984, s. 14 (1) (a)*. Made: 04.11.94. Coming into force: 07.11.94. Effect: None. – *Unpublished*

The M62 Motorway Junction 12 Interchange (Between Marker Posts 43/7 and 44/5) (Temporary Prohibition of Traffic) Order 1994 No. 2719. Enabling power: *Road Traffic Regulation Act 1984, s. 14 (1) (a)*. Made: 11.10.94. Coming into force: 13.10.94. Effect: None. – *Unpublished*

The M62 Motorway (Junction 12) (Temporary Prohibition of Traffic) Order 1994 No. 1399. Enabling power: *Road Traffic Regulation Act 1984, s. 14 (1) (a)*. Made: 16.05.94. Coming into force: 24.05.94. Effect: None. – *Unpublished*

The M62 Motorway (Junction 13) Slip Roads (Temporary Prohibition of Traffic) Order 1994 No.1179. Enabling power: *Road Traffic Regulation Act 1984, s. 14 (1) (a)*. Made: 18.04.94. Coming into force: 17.05.94. Effect: None. – *Unpublished*

The M62 Motorway (Junction 13) (Temporary Restriction of Traffic) Order 1994 No. 1118. Enabling power: *Road Traffic Regulation Act 1984, s. 14 (1) (a) (7)*. Made: 30.03.94. Coming into force: 17.05.94. Effect: None. – *Unpublished*

The M62 Motorway (Junction 13) Westbound Access Slip Road (Temporary Prohibition of Traffic) Order 1994 No. 1672. Enabling power: *Road Traffic Regulation Act 1984, s. 14 (1) (a)*. Made: 13.06.94. Coming into force: 14.06.94. Effect: None. – *Unpublished*

The M62 Motorway (Junction 13) Westbound Access Slip Road (Temporary Prohibition of Traffic) Order 1994 No. 1796. Enabling power: *Road Traffic Regulation Act 1984, s. 14 (1) (a)*. Made: 23.06.94. Coming into force: 09.07.94. Effect: None. – *Unpublished*

The M62 Motorway (Junction 14) Slip Roads (Temporary Prohibition of Traffic) Order 1994 No.1164. Enabling power: *Road Traffic Regulation Act 1984, s. 14 (1) (a)*. Made: 19.04.94. Coming into force: 08.07.94. Effect: None. – *Unpublished*

The M62 Motorway (Junction 17) Slip Roads (Temporary Prohibition of Traffic) Order 1994 No.1178. Enabling power: *Road Traffic Regulation Act 1984, s. 14 (1) (a)*. Made: 18.04.94. Coming into force: 08.07.94. Effect: None. – *Unpublished*

The M62 Motorway (Junction 18) Simister Roundabout (Temporary 50 Miles per Hour Speed Restriction) Order 1994 No. 112. Enabling power: *Road Traffic Regulation Act 1984, s. 14 (1) (a)*. Made: 13.01.94. Coming into force: 16.01.94. Effect: None. – *Unpublished*

The M62 Motorway (Junction 18) Simister (Temporary Restriction of Traffic) Order 1994 No.2377. Enabling power: *Road Traffic Regulation Act 1984, s. 14 (1) (a) (7)*. Made: 30.08.94. Coming into force: 01.09.94. Effect: None. – *Unpublished*

The M62 Motorway (Junction 18) Slip Roads (Temporary Prohibition of Traffic) Order 1994 No.1181. Enabling power: *Road Traffic Regulation Act 1984, s. 14 (1) (a)*. Made: 18.04.94. Coming into force: 09.05.94. Effect: None. – *Unpublished*

The M62 Motorway (Junction 19) Slip Roads (Temporary Prohibition of Traffic) Order 1994 No.868. Enabling power: *Road Traffic Regulation Act 1984, s. 14 (1) (a)*. Made: 10.03.94. Coming into force: 03.05.94. Effect: None. – *Unpublished*

The M62 Motorway (Junction 20) Slip Roads (Temporary Prohibition of Traffic) Order 1994 No.871. Enabling power: *Road Traffic Regulation Act 1984, s. 14 (1) (a)*. Made: 08.03.94. Coming into force: 27.04.94. Effect: None. – *Unpublished*

The M62 Motorway (Junction 21) Milnrow (Temporary Restriction of Traffic) Order 1994 No.304. Enabling power: *Road Traffic Regulation Act 1984, s. 14 (1) (a) (7)*. Made: 02.02.94. Coming into force: 05.02.94. Effect: None. – *Unpublished*

The M62 Motorway (Junction 21) Slip Roads (Temporary Prohibition of Traffic) Order 1994 No.789. Enabling power: *Road Traffic Regulation Act 1984 s. 14 (1) (a)*. Made: 02.03.94. Coming into force: 24.04.94. Effect: None. – *Unpublished*

The M62 Motorway (Junction 22) Slip Roads (Temporary Prohibition of Traffic) Order 1994 No.382. Enabling power: *Road Traffic Regulation Act 1984, s. 14 (1) (a)*. Made: 15.02.94. Coming into force: 04.03.94. Effect: None. – *Unpublished*

The M62 Motorway (Junction 26, Slip Roads) (Temporary Restriction and Prohibition of Traffic) Order 1994 No. 357. Enabling power: *Road Traffic Regulation Act 1984, s. 14 (1) (a)*. Made: 04.02.94. Coming into force: 05.02.94. Effect: None. – *Unpublished*

ROAD TRAFFIC: TRAFFIC REGULATION

The M62 Motorway (Junction 29, Eastbound Entry Slip Road) (Temporary Prohibition of Traffic) Order 1994 No. 1749. Enabling power: *Road Traffic Regulation Act 1984, s. 14 (1) (a)*. Made: 29.06.94. Coming into force: 30.06.94. Effect: None. – *Unpublished*

The M62 Motorway (Junction 32, Westbound Entry Slip Road) (Temporary Prohibition of Traffic) Order 1994 No. 76. Enabling power: *Road Traffic Regulation Act 1984, ss. 14 (1) (a)*. Made: 14.01.94. Coming into force: 16.01.94. Effect: None. – *Unpublished*

The M62 Motorway (Junctions 12 and 13)) (Temporary Prohibition of Traffic) Order 1994 No.2886. Enabling power: *Road Traffic Regulation Act 1984, s. 14 (1) (a)*. Made: 04.11.94. Coming into force: 06.11.94. Effect: None. – *Unpublished*

The M62 Motorway (Junctions 14, 14A, 15 and 17) (Temporary Restriction and Prohibition of Traffic) Order 1993 Amendment Order 1994 No. 1863. Enabling power: *Road Traffic Regulation Act 1984, s. 14 (1) (a)*. Made: 14.06.94. Coming into force: 15.06.94. Effect: S.I. 1993/1427 amended. – *Unpublished*

The M62 Motorway (Junctions 14-17) Wardley - Prestwich (Temporary Restriction of Traffic) Order 1994 No. 137. Enabling power: *Road Traffic Regulation Act 1984, ss. 14 (1) (a), 15 (2)*. Made: 19.01.94. Coming into force: 20.01.94. Effect: None. – *Unpublished*

The M62 Motorway (Junctions 24-25) (Temporary Restriction and Prohibition of Traffic) Order 1994 No. 1346. Enabling power: *Road Traffic Regulation Act 1984, s. 14 (1) (a) (7)*. Made: 10.05.94. Coming into force: 11.05.94. Effect: None. – *Unpublished*

The M62 Motorway (Junctions 24-25) (Temporary Restriction and Prohibition of Traffic) Order 1994 Amendment Order 1994 No. 1998. Enabling power: *Road Traffic Regulation Act 1984, s. 14 (1) (a) (7)*. Made: 21.07.94. Coming into force: 22.07.94. Effect: None. – *Unpublished*

The M62 Motorway (Junctions 26-27) (Temporary Restriction of Traffic) Order 1994 No.2771. Enabling power: *Road Traffic Regulation Act 1984, s. 14 (1) (a) (7)*. Made: 25.10.94. Coming into force: 27.10.94. Effect: None. – *Unpublished*

The M62 Motorway (Junctions 31-32) (Temporary Restriction and Prohibition of Traffic) Order 1994 No. 2307. Enabling power: *Road Traffic Regulation Act 1984, s. 14 (1) (a) (7)*. Made: 30.08.94. Coming into force: 31.08.94. Effect: None. – *Unpublished*

The M62 Motorway (M62/M606 Link Roads, Chain Bar Junction) (Temporary Prohibition of Traffic) Order 1994 No. 1075. Enabling power: *Road Traffic Regulation Act 1984, s. 14 (1) (a)*. Made: 25.03.94. Coming into force: 26.03.94. Effect: None. – *Unpublished*

The M62 Motorway (Marker Posts 44/5 - 43/8) (Temporary Prohibition of Traffic) Order 1994 No.1276. Enabling power: *Road Traffic Regulation Act 1984, s. 14 (1) (a)*. Made: 18.04.94. Coming into force: 20.05.94. Effect: None. – *Unpublished*

The M62 Motorway (Marker Posts 64/0 - 66/0) (Temporary Restriction of Traffic) Order 1994 No.2453. Enabling power: *Road Traffic Regulation Act 1984, s. 14 (1) (a) (7)*. Made: 10.08.94. Coming into force: 11.08.94. Effect: None. – *Unpublished*

The M63 Motorway (Junction 1) Southbound Access Slip Road (Temporary Prohibition of Traffic) Order 1994 No. 1797. Enabling power: *Road Traffic Regulation Act 1984, s. 14 (1) (a)*. Made: 23.06.94. Coming into force: 15.07.94. Effect: None. – *Unpublished*

The M63 Motorway (Junction 1) Winton (Temporary Restriction of Traffic) Order 1994 No.2872. Enabling power: *Road Traffic Regulation Act 1984, s. 14 (1) (a) (7)*. Made: 03.11.94. Coming into force: 11.11.94. Effect: None. – *Unpublished*

The M63 Motorway (Junction 2) Slip Roads (Temporary Prohibition of Traffic) Order 1994 No.1368. Enabling power: *Road Traffic Regulation Act 1984, s. 14 (1) (a)*. Made: 16.05.94. Coming into force: 24.05.94. Effect: None. – *Unpublished*

The M63 Motorway (Junction 3) Slip Roads (Temporary Prohibition of Traffic) Order 1994 No.1995. Enabling power: *Road Traffic Regulation Act 1984, s. 14 (1) (a)*. Made: 14.07.94. Coming into force: 15.07.94. Effect: None. – *Unpublished*

The M63 Motorway (Junction 4) Slip Road (Temporary Prohibition of Traffic) Order 1994 No.1163. Enabling power: *Road Traffic Regulation Act 1984, s. 14 (1) (a)*. Made: 19.04.94. Coming into force: 19.05.94. Effect: None. – *Unpublished*

The M63 Motorway (Junction 4) Slip Road (Temporary Prohibition of Traffic) Order 1994 No.1244. Enabling power: *Road Traffic Regulation Act 1984, s. 14 (1) (a)*. Made: 26.04.94. Coming into force: 09.06.94. Effect: None. – *Unpublished*

The M63 Motorway (Junction 4) Slip Road (Temporary Prohibition of Traffic) Order 1994 No.2643. Enabling power: *Road Traffic Regulation Act 1984, s. 14 (1) (a)*. Made: 27.09.94. Coming into force: 27.09.94. Effect: None. – *Unpublished*

The M63 Motorway (Junction 6) Carrington Spur (Temporary Prohibition of Traffic) Order 1994 No. 1416. Enabling power: *Road Traffic Regulation Act 1984, s. 14 (1) (a)*. Made: 12.05.94. Coming into force: 30.06.94. Effect: None. – *Unpublished*

Price/availability are liable to change without notice

ROAD TRAFFIC: TRAFFIC REGULATION

The M63 Motorway (Junction 7) Stretford (Temporary Restriction of Traffic) Order 1994 No.74. Enabling power: *Road Traffic Regulation Act 1984, ss. 14 (1) (a) (7)*. Made: 12.01.94. Coming into force: 13.01.94. Effect: None. – *Unpublished*

The M63 Motorway (Junction 8) Slip Roads (Temporary Prohibition of Traffic) Order 1994 No.1180. Enabling power: *Road Traffic Regulation Act 1984, s. 14 (1) (a)*. Made: 18.04.94. Coming into force: 13.06.94. Effect: None. – *Unpublished*

The M63 Motorway (Junction 8) Slip Road (Temporary Prohibition of Traffic) Order 1994 No.2321. Enabling power: *Road Traffic Regulation Act 1984, s. 14 (1) (a)*. Made: 15.08.94. Coming into force: 18.08.94. Effect: None. – *Unpublished*

The M63 Motorway (Junction 9) Northbound Exit Slip Road (Temporary Prohibition of Traffic) Order 1994 No. 1345. Enabling power: *Road Traffic Regulation Act 1984, s. 14 (1) (a)*. Made: 04.05.94. Coming into force: 02.06.94. Effect: None. – *Unpublished*

The M63 Motorway (Junction 9) Slip Roads (Temporary Prohibition of Traffic) Order 1994 No.1241. Enabling power: *Road Traffic Regulation Act 1984, s. 14 (1) (a)*. Made: 25.04.94. Coming into force: 14.06.94. Effect: None. – *Unpublished*

The M63 Motorway (Junction 10) Slip Roads (Temporary Prohibition of Traffic) Order 1994 No.1242. Enabling power: *Road Traffic Regulation Act 1984, s. 14 (1) (a)*. Made: 25.04.94. Coming into force: 16.06.94. Effect: None. – *Unpublished*

The M63 Motorway (Junction 10) Slip Roads (Temporary Prohibition of Traffic) Order 1994 No.1871. Enabling power: *Road Traffic Regulation Act 1984, s. 14 (1) (a)*. Made: 13.06.94. Coming into force: 17.06.94. Effect: None. – *Unpublished*

The M63 Motorway (Junction 10) Westbound Access Slip Road (Temporary Prohibition of Traffic) Order 1994 No. 332. Enabling power: *Road Traffic Regulation Act 1984, s. 14 (1) (a)*. Made: 09.02.94. Coming into force: 17.02.94. Effect: None. – *Unpublished*

The M63 Motorway (Junction 11) Cheadle (Temporary Restriction of Traffic) Order 1994 No.215. Enabling power: *Road Traffic Regulation 1984, s. 14 (1) (a) (7)*. Made: 25.01.94. Coming into force: 27.01.94. Effect: None. – *Unpublished*

The M63 Motorway (Junction 11) Slip Road (Temporary Prohibition of Traffic) Order 1994 No.1245. Enabling power: *Road Traffic Regulation Act 1984, s. 14 (1) (a)*. Made: 27.04.94. Coming into force: 17.06.94. Effect: None. – *Unpublished*

The M63 Motorway (Junction 12) Eastbound Exit Slip Road (Temporary Prohibition of Traffic) Order 1994 No. 1874. Enabling power: *Road Traffic Regulation Act 1984, s. 14 (1) (a)*. Made: 17.06.94. Coming into force: 20.06.94. Effect: None. – *Unpublished*

The M63 Motorway (Junction 12) Slip Roads (Temporary Prohibition of Traffic) Order 1994 No.1161. Enabling power: *Road Traffic Regulation Act 1984, s. 14 (1) (a)*. Made: 18.04.94. Coming into force: 16.06.94. Effect: None. – *Unpublished*

The M63 Motorway (Junction 12) Westbound Access Slip Road (Temporary Prohibition of Traffic) Order 1994 No. 1631. Enabling power: *Road Traffic Regulation Act 1984, s. 14 (1) (a)*. Made: 13.06.94. Coming into force: 22.06.94. Effect: None. – *Unpublished*

The M63 Motorway (Junction 13) Portwood (Temporary Prohibition of Traffic) Order 1994 No.334. Enabling power: *Road Traffic Regulation Act 1984, s. 14 (1)*. Made: 01.02.94. Coming into force: 04.02.94. Effect: None. – *Unpublished*

The M63 Motorway (Junction 13) Stockport (Temporary Restriction of Traffic) Order 1994 No.1873. Enabling power: *Road Traffic Regulation Act 1984, s. 14 (1) (a) (7)*. Made: 13.06.94. Coming into force: 16.06.94. Effect: None. – *Unpublished*

The M63 Motorway (Junction 14) Westbound Exit Slip Road (Temporary Prohibition of Traffic) Order 1994 No. 841. Enabling power: *Road Traffic Regulation Act 1984, s. 14 (1) (a)*. Made: 07.01.94. Coming into force: 09.01.94. Effect: None. – *Unpublished*

The M63 Motorway (Junction 15) Eastbound Exit Slip Road (Temporary Prohibition of Traffic) Order 1994 No. 1872. Enabling power: *Road Traffic Regulation Act 1984, s. 14 (1) (a)*. Made: 13.06.94. Coming into force: 20.06.94. Effect: None. – *Unpublished*

The M63 Motorway (Junctions 1 - 2) Southbound Exit Slip Roads (Temporary Prohibition of Traffic) Order 1994 No. 2045. Enabling power: *Road Traffic Regulation Act 1984, s. 14 (1) (a)*. Made: 20.07.94. Coming into force: 21.07.94. Effect: None. – *Unpublished*

The M63 Motorway (Junctions 6-7) Carrington Spur and Stretford (Temporary Prohibition of Traffic) Order 1994 No. 1243. Enabling power: *Road Traffic Regulation Act 1984, s. 14 (1) (a)*. Made: 27.04.94. Coming into force: 08.06.94. Effect: None. – *Unpublished*

The M63 Motorway (Junctions 6-7) Stretford (Temporary Prohibition of Traffic) Order 1994 No.1483. Enabling power: *Road Traffic Regulation Act 1984, s. 14 (1) (a)*. Made: 17.05.94. Coming into force: 09.06.94. Effect: None. – *Unpublished*

Price/availability are liable to change without notice

The M63 Motorway (Junctions 8 - 9) Sale (Temporary Restriction of Traffic) Order 1994 No.866. Enabling power: *Road Traffic Regulation Act 1984, s. 14 (1) (a) (7)*. Made: 02.03.94. Coming into force: 27.03.94. Effect: None. – *Unpublished*

The M63 Motorway (Junctions 9 - 11) (Temporary Restriction and Prohibition of Traffic) Order 1994 No. 2871. Enabling power: *Road Traffic Regulation Act 1984, s. 14 (1) (a) (7)*. Made: 02.11.94. Coming into force: 02.11.94. Effect: None. – *Unpublished*

The M63 Motorway (Marker Posts 0/0 - 0/6) (Temporary Prohibition of Traffic) Order 1994 No.1966. Enabling power: *Road Traffic Regulation Act 1984, s. 14 (1) (a)*. Made: 14.07.94. Coming into force: 14.07.94. Effect: None. – *Unpublished*

The M63 Motorway (Marker Posts 10/0 - 12/0) Sale (Temporary Restriction of Traffic) Order 1994 No. 1626. Enabling power: *Road Traffic Regulation Act 1984, s. 14 (1) (a) (7)*. Made: 15.06.94. Coming into force: 28.07.94. Effect: None. – *Unpublished*

The M63 Motorway (Marker Posts 12/6 - 13/4) Northenden (Temporary Restriction of Traffic) Order 1994 No. 1162. Enabling power: *Road Traffic Regulation Act 1984, s. 14 (1) (a)*. Made: 18.04.94. Coming into force: 10.06.94. Effect: None. – *Unpublished*

The M63 Motorway (Marker Posts 19/8 - 2/3) (Temporary Restriction of Traffic) Order 1994 No.1407. Enabling power: *Road Traffic Regulation Act 1984, s. 14 (1) (a)*. Made: 16.05.94. Coming into force: 16.06.94. Effect: None. – *Unpublished*

The M63 Motorway (Marker Posts 24/3 - 23/1) (Temporary Prohibition of Traffic) Order 1994 No.1465. Enabling power: *Road Traffic Regulation Act 1984, s. 14 (1) (a)*. Made: 25.05.94. Coming into force: 19.06.94. Effect: None. – *Unpublished*

The M66 Motorway (Junction 1) Slip Roads (Temporary Prohibition of Traffic) Order 1994 No.870. Enabling power: *Road Traffic Regulation Act 1984, s. 14 (1) (a)*. Made: 09.03.94. Coming into force: 08.05.94. Effect: None. – *Unpublished*

The M66 Motorway (Junction 2) Slip Roads (Temporary Prohibition of Traffic) Order 1994 No.891. Enabling power: *Road Traffic Regulation Act 1984, s. 14 (1) (a)*. Made: 17.03.94. Coming into force: 05.05.94. Effect: None. – *Unpublished*

The M66 Motorway (Junction 2) Southbound Access Slip Road (Temporary Prohibition of Traffic) Order 1994 No. 58. Enabling power: *Road Traffic Regulations Act 1984, s. 14 (1) (a)*. Made: 06.01.94. Coming into force: 15.01.94. Effect: None. – *Unpublished*

The M66 Motorway (Junction 3 - 5) and M62 Motorway (Junction 18) Bury (Temporary Prohibition and Restriction of Traffic) Order 1994 No. 2983. Enabling power: *Road Traffic Regulation Act 1984, s. 14 (1) (a) (7)*. Made: 11.11.94. Coming into force: 13.11.94. Effect: S.I. 1993/1873 revoked. – *Unpublished*

The M66 Motorway (Junction 3) Slip Roads (Temporary Prohibition of Traffic) Order 1994 No.892. Enabling power: *Road Traffic Regulation Act 1984, s. 14 (1) (a)*. Made: 17.03.94. Coming into force: 05.05.94. Effect: None. – *Unpublished*

The M66 Motorway (Marker Posts 0/0 - 3/5) Bury (Temporary Prohibition of Traffic) Order 1994 No. 1792. Enabling power: *Road Traffic Regulation Act 1984, s. 14 (1) (a)*. Made: 23.06.94. Coming into force: 15.07.94. Effect: None. – *Unpublished*

The M66 Motorway (Marker Posts 9/2 - 7/1) (Temporary Restriction of Traffic) Order 1994 No.1277. Enabling power: *Road Traffic Regulation Act 1984, s. 14 (1) (a)*. Made: 29.04.94. Coming into force: 05.05.94. Effect: None. – *Unpublished*

The M66 Motorway (Marker Posts 13/1 -10/1) (Temporary 50 Miles Per Hour Speed Restriction) Order 1994 No. 788. Enabling power: *Road Traffic Regulation Act 1984 s. 14 (1) (a)*. Made: 02.03.94. Coming into force: 10.03.94. Effect: None. – *Unpublished*

The M66 Motorway (Marker Posts 34/7-31/0) and the M63 Motorway (Marker Posts 23/4-24/1) (Temporary Prohibition of Traffic) Order 1994 No. 2663. Enabling power: *Road Traffic Regulation Act 1984, s. 14 (1) (a)*. Made: 27.09.94. Coming into force: 27.09.94. Effect: None. – *Unpublished*

The M67 Motorway (Junction 2) Westbound Exit Slip Road (Temporary Prohibition of Traffic) Order 1994 No. 786. Enabling power: *Road Traffic Regulation Act 1984 s. 14 (1) (a)*. Made: 09.03.94. Coming into force: 19.03.94. Effect: None. – *Unpublished*

The M67 Motorway (Junction 2) Westbound Exit Slip Road (Temporary Restriction of Traffic) Order 1994 No. 1930. Enabling power: *Road Traffic Regulation Act 1984, s. 14 (1) (a) (7)*. Made: 04.07.94. Coming into force: 10.07.94. Effect: None. – *Unpublished*

The M67 Motorway (Junction 3) Westbound Exit Slip Road at Hyde (Temporary Prohibition of Traffic) Order 1994 No. 596. Enabling power: *Road Traffic Regulation Act 1984 s. 14 (1) (a)*. Made: 21.02.94. Coming into force: 26.02.94. Effect: None. – *Unpublished*

The M67 Motorway (Marker Posts 1/1 - 8/4) (Temporary Prohibition of Traffic) Order 1994 No.1628. Enabling power: *Road Traffic Regulation Act 1984, s. 14 (1) (a)*. Made: 13.06.94. Coming into force: 23.06.94. Effect: None. – *Unpublished*

Price/availability are liable to change without notice

The M67 Motorway (Marker Posts 3/8 to 2/8) (Temporary Restriction of Traffic) Order 1994 No.2495. Enabling power: *Road Traffic Regulation Act 1984, s. 14 (1) (a) (7)*. Made: 09.09.94. Coming into force: 09.09.94. Effect: None. – *Unpublished*

The M67 Motorway (Marker Posts 8/4 - 1/0) (Temporary Prohibition of Traffic) Order 1994 No.1627. Enabling power: *Road Traffic Regulation Act 1984, s. 14 (1) (a)*. Made: 13.06.94. Coming into force: 24.06.94. Effect: None. – *Unpublished*

The M74 Motorway (Junction 6 Slip Roads From A723) (Temporary Prohibition of Traffic) Order 1994 No. 2185. Enabling power: *Road Traffic Regulation Act 1984, s. 14 (1) (a) (4)*. Made: 18.08.94. Coming into force: 03.09.94. Effect: None. – *Unpublished*

The M74 Motorway (Junction 6) (Temporary Prohibition of Traffic) Order 1994 No.1840. Enabling power: *Road Traffic Regulation Act 1984, s. 14 (1) (a) (4)*. Made: 08.07.94. Coming into force: 17.07.94. Effect: None. – *Unpublished*

The M74 Motorway (Junction 9 Slip Road) (Temporary Prohibition of Traffic) Order 1994 No.1512. Enabling power: *Road Traffic Regulation Act 1984, s. 14 (1) (a) (4)*. Made: 03.06.94. Coming into force: 12.06.94. Effect: None. – *Unpublished*

The (M74) Motorway (Junction 6 Slip Road) (Temporary Prohibition of Traffic) (No 2) Order 1994 No. 1213. Enabling power: *Road Traffic Regulation Act 1984, s. 14 (1) (4)*. Made: 29.04.94. Coming into force: 13.05.94. Effect: None. – *Unpublished*

The (M74) Motorway (Junction 6 Slip Road) (Temporary Prohibition of Traffic) Order 1994 No.936. Enabling power: *Road Traffic Regulation Act 1984, s. 14 (1) (4)*. Made: 25.03.94. Coming into force: 08.04.94. Effect: None. – *Unpublished*

The (M74) Trunk Road (Glasgow-Carlisle) (Maryville to West of Fullarton Road) (Temporary Prohibition of Traffic) Order 1994 No.2168. Enabling power: *Road Traffic Regulation Act 1984, s. 14 (1)*. Made: 16.08.94. Coming into force: 04.09.94. Effect: None. – *Unpublished*

The (M74) Trunk Road (Glasgow-Carlisle) (Maryville to West of Fullarton Road) (Temporary Prohibition of Traffic) Order 1994 No.2252. Enabling power: *Road Traffic Regulation Act 1984, s. 14 (1)*. Made: 31.08.94. Coming into force: 04.09.94. Effect: None. – *Unpublished*

The (M74) Trunk Road (Glasgow-Carlisle) (Maryville to West of Fullarton Road) (Temporary Prohibition of Traffic) Order 1994 No.2596. Enabling power: *Road Traffic Regulation Act 1984, s. 14 (1)*. Made: 16.09.94. Coming into force: 18.09.94. Effect: None. – *Unpublished*

The M90/A90 Trunk Road Inverkeithing-Aberdeen (Admiralty Southbound Slip Road) (Temporary Prohibition of Traffic) Order 1994 No.1370. Enabling power: *Road Traffic Regulation Act 1984, s. 14 (1) (a) (4) (a)*. Made: 20.05.94. Coming into force: 22.05.94. Effect: None. – *Unpublished*

The M180 Motorway (Junction 2, Slip Roads) (Temporary Prohibition of Traffic) Order 1994 No.3059. Enabling power: *Road Traffic Regulation Act 1984, s. 14 (1) (a)*. Made: 29.11.94. Coming into force: 01.12.94. Effect: None. – *Unpublished*

The M180 Motorway (Junction 4, Slip Roads) (Temporary Prohibition of Traffic) Order 1994 No.734. Enabling power: *Road Traffic Regulation Act 1984 s. 14 (1) (a)*. Made: 09.03.94. Coming into force: 10.03.94. Effect: None. – *Unpublished*

The M180 Motorway (Junctions 4 - 5) and the A180 Trunk Road (Temporary Restriction and Prohibition of Traffic) Order 1994 No.1586. Enabling power: *Road Traffic Regulation Act 1984, s. 14 (1) (a) (7)*. Made: 10.06.94. Coming into force: 11.06.94. Effect: None. – *Unpublished*

The M271 Motorway (Nursling Interchange to Redbridge Roundabout) (Temporary Prohibition of Traffic) Order 1994 No.2052. Enabling power: *Road Traffic Regulation Act 1984, s. 14 (1) (a)*. Made: 01.08.94. Coming into force: 06.08.94. Effect: None. – *Unpublished*

The M602 Motorway (Junction 1) Link Road to the Northbound M63 Motorway (Temporary Prohibition of Traffic) Order 1994 No. 3334. Enabling power: *Road Traffic Regulation Act 1984, s. 14 (1) (a)*. Made: 16.12.94. Coming into force: 17.12.94. Effect: None. – *Unpublished*

The M602 Motorway (Junction 2) Slip Roads (Temporary Prohibition of Traffic) Order 1994 No.1398. Enabling power: *Road Traffic Regulation Act 1984, s. 14 (1) (a)*. Made: 16.05.94. Coming into force: 22.05.94. Effect: None. – *Unpublished*

The M602 Motorway (Junction 2) - The M62 Motorway (Junction 12) (Temporary Restriction and Prohibition of Traffic) Order 1994 No. 381. Enabling power: *Road Traffic Regulation Act 1984, s. 14 (1) (a) (7)*. Made: 17.02.94. Coming into force: 17.02.94. Effect: None. – *Unpublished*

The M602 Motorway (Junctions 3 - 2) Eccles (Temporary Prohibition of Traffic) Order 1994 No.1795. Enabling power: *Road Traffic Regulation Act 1984, s. 14 (1) (a)*. Made: 23.06.94. Coming into force: 21.07.94. Effect: None. – *Unpublished*

The M602 Motorway (Marker Posts 4/0 - 3/4) (Temporary Prohibition of Traffic) Order 1994 No.1146. Enabling power: *Road Traffic Regulation Act 1984, s. 14 (1) (a)*. Made: 18.04.94. Coming into force: 20.05.94. Effect: None. – *Unpublished*

The M602 Motorway (Marker Posts 4/0 - 44/0) (Temporary Prohibition of Traffic) Order 1994 No. 1425. Enabling power: *Road Traffic Regulation Act 1984, s. 14 (1) (a)*. Made: 20.05.94. Coming into force: 22.05.94. Effect: None. – *Unpublished*

The M602 Motorway (Marker Posts 6/7 - 4/0) (Temporary Restriction of Traffic) Order 1994 No. 1182. Enabling power: *Road Traffic Regulation Act 1984, s. 14 (1) (a) (7)*. Made: 18.04.94. Coming into force: 20.05.94. Effect: None. – *Unpublished*

The M606 Motorway (Chain Bar Junction, Slip Roads) (Temporary Prohibition of Traffic) Order 1994 No. 354. Enabling power: *Road Traffic Regulation Act 1984, s. 14 (1) (a)*. Made: 04.02.94. Coming into force: 05.02.94. Effect: None. – *Unpublished*

The M606 Motorway (M606/M62 Link Roads, Southbound Carriageway) (Temporary Restriction of Traffic) Order 1994 No. 1282. Enabling power: *Road Traffic Regulation Act 1984, s. 14 (1) (a) (7)*. Made: 22.04.94. Coming into force: 23.04.94. Effect: None. – *Unpublished*

The M606 Motorway (M606/M62 Southbound Link Road) (Temporary 50 Miles Per Hour Speed Restriction) Order 1994 No. 2199. Enabling power: *Road Traffic Regulation Act 1984, s. 14 (1) (a)*. Made: 12.08.94. Coming into force: 15.08.94. Effect: None. – *Unpublished*

The M621 Motorway (M1/M621 Link Road) (Temporary Prohibition of Traffic) Order 1994 No. 2939. Enabling power: *Road Traffic Regulation Act 1984, s. 14 (1) (a)*. Made: 10.11.94. Coming into force: 12.11.94. Effect: None. – *Unpublished*

The M876/A876/A977 Trunk Road (Checkbar Interchange Slip Road) (Temporary Prohibition of Traffic) Order 1994 No. 2814. Enabling power: *Road Traffic Regulation Act 1984, s. 14 (1) (a), 14 (4)*. Made: 01.11.94. Coming into force: 14.11.94. Effect: None. – *Unpublished*

The North London Circular Trunk Road (A406) (Barnet) (Temporary Restriction of Traffic) Order 1994 No. 585. Enabling power: *Road Traffic Regulation Act 1984, ss. 14 (1) (4) (7)*. Made: 07.03.94. Coming into force: 14.03.94. Effect: None. – *Unpublished*

The Stirling-Crianlarich Trunk Road (A84/A85) (Callander) (Yellow Box Junction) Order 1994 No. 2766. Enabling power: *Road Traffic Regulation Act 1984, ss. 2 (1) (2), 121A*. Made: 25.10.94. Coming into force: 07.11.94. Effect: None. – *Unpublished*

The Trunk Road (A3) (Robin Hood Way Service Road, Kingston Upon Thames) (Restriction of Entry) Order 1982 (Variation) Experimental Order 1994 No. 1115. Enabling power: *Road Traffic Regulation Act 1984, ss. 9 (1), 10 (1) (2)*. Made: 18.04.94. Coming into force: 03.05.94. Effect: None. – *Unpublished*

The Trunk Road (A40) (Lay-bys, East of Haverfordwest) (Prohibition of Traffic) Order 1983 (Revocation) Order 1994 No. 399. Enabling power: *Road Traffic Regulation Act 1984, ss. 1 (1), 124 & sch. 9, para. 27*. Made: 16.02.94. Coming into force: 26.02.94. Effect: None. – *Unpublished*

The Trunk Road (A470) (Carno, Powys) (Prohibition of Waiting) (Variation) Order 1994 No. 2039. Enabling power: *Road Traffic Regulation Act 1984, ss. 1 (1), 2 (1) (2), 4 (2), 124, sch. 9, para. 27*. Made: 20.07.94. Coming into force: 01.08.94. Effect: S.I. 1989/691 amended. – *Unpublished*

The Trunk Road (A4042) (Mamhilad, Gwent) (Prohibition of Right-Hand Turn) Order 1983 (Revocation) Order 1994 No. 261. Enabling power: *Road Traffic Regulation Act 1984, s. 1 (1), 124, sch. 9, para. 27*. Made: 31.01.94. Coming into force: 11.02.94. Effect: S.I. 1983/1084 revoked. – *Unpublished*

The Trunk Roads in Scotland (Temporary Restriction of Traffic, Temporary Prohibition of Overtaking and Temporary 30 MPH, 40 MPH and 50 MPH Speed Limit) (No. 2) Order 1994 No. 2743. Enabling power: *Road Traffic Regulation Act 1984, s. 14 (1) (a), 14 (4) (a), 121A*. Made: 21.10.94. Coming into force: 28.10.94. Effect: S.I. 1994/811 revoked. – *Unpublished*

The Trunk Roads in Scotland (Temporary Restriction of Traffic, Temporary Prohibition of Overtaking and Temporary 30 MPH, 40 MPH and 50 MPH Speed Limit) Order 1994 No. 811. Enabling power: *Road Traffic Regulation Act 1984 ss. 14 (1) (a) (4) (a), 121A*. Made: 11.03.94. Coming into force: 01.04.94. Effect: None. – *Unpublished*

The Trunk Roads (Routes A75 and A77) (Stranraer) (Prohibition of Waiting) (Varitation) Order 1994 No. 297. Enabling power: *Road Traffic Regulation Act 1984, s. 1 (1)*. Made: 09.02.94. Coming into force: 09.03.94. Effect: None. – *Unpublished*

The Trunk Road (Various Roads, Belper) (Prohibition of Waiting, Loading and Unloading) Order 1977 (Amendment) Order 1994 No. 1791. Enabling power: *Road Traffic Regulation Act 1984, ss. 1 (1), 2 (1) (2)*. Made: 24.06.94. Coming into force: 29.08.94. Effect: None. – *Unpublished*

The Trunk Road (Wakley Street, Islington) (Temporary Prohibition of Traffic) (No. 2) Order 1994 No. 2528. Enabling power: *Road Traffic Regulation Act 1984, s. 14 (1) (4) (7)*. Made: 26.09.94. Coming into force: 03.10.94. Effect: None. – *Unpublished*

The Trunk Road (Wakley Street, Islington) (Temporary Prohibition of Traffic) Order 1994 No. 814. Enabling power: *Road Traffic Regulation Act 1984, s. 14 (1) (4) (7)*. Made: 14.03.94. Coming into force: 18.03.94. Effect: None. – *Unpublished*

Price/availability are liable to change without notice

The Unclassified Road Adjacent to the (A74) Trunk Road Glasgow-Carlisle (Dumfries and Galloway Region) Dinwoodie Green Farm to Muirhouse Farm, Lockerbie (Temporary 50 MPH Speed Limit) Order 1994 No. 2106. Enabling power: *Road Traffic Regulation Act 1984, ss. 14 (1) (a) (4) (a), 124 (2)*. Made: 05.08.94. Coming into force: 06.08.94. Effect: None. – *Unpublished*

The Unclassified Road Adjacent to the (A74) Trunk Road Glasgow-Carlisle (Dumfries and Galloway Region) (Muirhouse Farm to Norwood, Lockerbie) (Temporary 30 MPH and 50 MPH Speed Limit) Order 1994 No. 2. Enabling power: *Road Traffic Regulation Act 1984, ss. 14 (1) (a) (4) (a), 124 (2)*. Made: 05.01.94. Coming into force: 07.01.94. Effect: None. – *Unpublished*

The Unclassified Road Adjacent to the (A74) Trunk Road Glasgow-Carlisle (Dumfries and Galloway Region) (Muirhouse Farm to Norwood, Lockerbie) (Temporary 50 MPH Speed Limit) Order 1994 No.2105. Enabling power: *Road Traffic Regulation Act 1984, ss. 14 (1) (a) (4) (a), 124 (2)*. Made: 05.08.94. Coming into force: 06.08.94. Effect: None. – *Unpublished*

The Unclassified Road Adjacent to the (A74) Trunk Road Glasgow-Carlisle (Dumfries and Galloway Region) (Water of Milk to Ecclefechan) (Temporary 50 MPH Speed Limit) Order 1994 No.186. Enabling power: *Road Traffic Regulation Act 1984, ss. 14 (1) (a) (4) (a), 124 (2)*. Made: 31.01.94. Coming into force: 01.02.94. Effect: None. – *Unpublished*

The Unclassified Road Adjacent to the (A74) Trunk Road Glasgow-Carlisle (Dumfries and Galloway Region) (Water of Milk to Ecclefechan) (Temporary 50 MPH Speed Limit) Order 1994 No.2108. Enabling power: *Road Traffic Regulation Act 1984, ss. 14 (1) (a) (4) (a), 124 (2)*. Made: 05.08.94. Coming into force: 06.08.94. Effect: None. – *Unpublished*

The Unclassified Road at Johnstonebridge, Near Lockerbie (Dumfries and Galloway Region) (Temporary 50 MPH Speed Limit) Order 1994 No. 2107. Enabling power: *Road Traffic Regulation Act 1984, ss. 14 (1) (a) (4) (a), 121A*. Made: 05.08.94. Coming into force: 06.08.94. Effect: None. – *Unpublished*

The Unclassified Road Near Eaglesfield (Dumfries and Galloway Region) (Temporary 50 MPH Speed Limit) Order 1994 No. 2188. Enabling power: *Road Traffic Regulation Act 1984, ss. 14 (1) (a) (4) (a), 124 (2)*. Made: 19.08.94. Coming into force: 20.08.94. Effect: None. – *Unpublished*

The Unclassified Road Near Ecclefechan (Dumfries and Galloway Region) (Temporary 50 MPH Speed Limit) Order 1994 No. 2187. Enabling power: *Road Traffic Regulation Act 1984, ss. 14 (1) (a) (4) (a), 124 (2)*. Made: 19.08.94. Coming into force: 20.08.94. Effect: None. – *Unpublished*

SALMON AND FRESHWATER FISHERIES

The Diseases of Fish (Control) Regulations 1994 No. 1447. Enabling power: *European Communities Act 1972, s. 2 (2)*. Issued: 10.06.94. Made: 26.05.94. Laid: 10.06.94. Coming into force: 01.07.94. Effect: None. Territorial extent & classification: E/W/S. General. – 10p. – 0 11 044477 7 *£2.40*

The Fish Health (Amendment) Regulations 1994 No. 1448. Enabling power: *European Communities Act 1972, s. 2 (2)*. Issued: 10.06.94. Made: 26.05.94. Laid: 10.06.94. Coming into force: 01.07.94. Effect: S.I. 1992/3300 amended. Territorial extent & classification: E/W/S. General. – 6p. – 0 11 044448 5 *£1.55*

SCIENTIFIC RESEARCH

The Biotechnology and Biological Sciences Research Council Order 1994 No. 423. Enabling power: *Science and Technology Act 1965, s. 1 (1)*. Issued: 04.03.94. Made: 24.02.94. Coming into force: 01.04.94. Effect: None. Territorial extent & classification: GB. General. – 2p. – 0 11 043423 4 *£0.65*

The Engineering and Physical Sciences Research Council Order 1994 No. 424. Enabling power: *Science and Technology Act 1965, s. 1 (1)*. Issued: 04.03.94. Made: 24.02.94. Coming into force: 01.04.94. Effect: None. Territorial extent & classification: GB. General. – 2p. – 0 11 043424 2 *£0.65*

The Particle Physics and Astronomy Research Council Order 1994 No. 425. Enabling power: *Science and Technology Act 1965, s. 1 (1)*. Issued: 04.03.94. Made: 24.02.94. Coming into force: 01.04.94. Effect: None. Territorial extent & classification: GB. General. – 2p. – 0 11 043425 0 *£0.65*

The Research Councils (Transfer of Property etc.) Order 1994 No. 611. Enabling power: *Science and Technology Act 1965, s. 3 (6) (7)*. Issued: 24.03.94. Made: 05.03.94. Laid: 10.03.94. Coming into force: 01.04.94. Effect: 1965 c. 4 amended. Territorial extent & classification: GB. General. – 16p. – 0 11 043611 3 *£3.20*

SCOTTISH LAND COURT

The Scottish Land Court (Fees) Order 1994 No. 498 (S. 20). Enabling power: *Courts of Law Fees (Scotland) Act 1895, s. 2*. Issued: 11.03.94. Made: 01.03.94. Laid: 11.03.94. Coming into force: 01.04.94. Effect: S.I. 1993/297 revoked. With correction slip. Territorial extent & classification: S. General. – 4p. – 0 11 043498 6 *£1.10*

SEA FISHERIES

The Brancaster Staithe Fishery (Variation) Order 1994 No. 2230. Enabling power: *Sea Fisheries (Shellfish) Act 1967, s. 1*. Issued: 05.09.94. Made: 12.08.94. Laid: 30.08.94. Coming into force: 20.09.94. Effect: S.I. 1979/1066 amended. Territorial extent & classification: E. Local. – 2p. – 0 11 045230 5 *£0.65*

The Diseases of Fish (Control) Regulations 1994 No. 1447. Enabling power: *European Communities Act 1972, s. 2 (2)*. Issued: 10.06.94. Made: 26.05.94. Laid: 10.06.94. Coming into force: 01.07.94. Effect: None. Territorial extent & classification: E/W/S. General. – 10p. – 0 11 044477 7 *£2.40*

The Fish Health (Amendment) Regulations 1994 No. 1448. Enabling power: *European Communities Act 1972, s. 2 (2)*. Issued: 10.06.94. Made: 26.05.94. Laid: 10.06.94. Coming into force: 01.07.94. Effect: S.I. 1992/3300 amended. Territorial extent & classification: E/W/S. General. – 6p. – 0 11 044448 5 *£1.55*

Price/availability are liable to change without notice

The Inshore Fishing (Prohibition of Fishing and Fishing Methods) (Scotland) Amendment Order 1994 No. 326 (S. 10). Enabling power: *Inshore Fishing (Scotland) Act 1984, s. 1*. Issued: 23.02.94. Made: 14.02.94. Laid: 21.02.94. Coming into force: 14.03.94. Effect: S.I. 1989/2307 amended. Territorial extent & classification: S. General. – 4p. – 0 11 043326 2 *£1.10*

The Inshore Fishing (Prohibition of Fishing for Cockles) (Scotland) (No. 2) Order 1994 No.2613 (S. 128). Enabling power: *Inshore Fishing (Scotland) Act 1984, s. 1*. Issued: 18.10.94. Made: 06.10.94. Laid: 10.10.94. Coming into force: 01.11.94. Effect: S.I. 1994/1828 revoked. Territorial extent & classification: S. General. – 2p. – 0 11 045613 0 *£0.65*

The Inshore Fishing (Prohibition of Fishing for Cockles) (Scotland) Order 1994 No.1828 (S. 83). Enabling power: *Inshore Fishing (Scotland) Act 1984, s. 1*. Issued: 15.07.94. Made: 05.07.94. Laid: 11.07.94. Coming into force: 01.08.94. Effect: S.I. 1993/1709 revoked. Territorial extent & classification: S. General. – 2p. – 0 11 044828 6 *£0.65*

The Inshore Fishing (Scotland) Act 1994 (Commencement) Order 1994 No. 2124 (C. 41)(S. 110). Enabling power: *Inshore Fishing (Scotland) Act 1994, s. 5 (1). Bringing into operation various provisions of the 1994 act on 08.08.94.* Issued: 17.08.94. Made: 03.08.94. Effect: None. Territorial extent & classification: S. General. – 2p. – 0 11 045124 4 *£0.65*

The Sea Fishing (Enforcement of Community Conservation Measures) Order 1994 No. 1680. Enabling power: *Fisheries Act 1981, s. 30 (2) (3)*. Issued: 19.07.94. Made: 24.06.94. Laid: 24.06.94. Coming into force: 15.07.94. Effect: S.I. 1986/2090 amended & S.I. 1992/2936 revoked. Territorial extent & classification: GB. General. – 2p. – 0 11 044680 1 *£0.65*

SEA FISHERIES: COMMUNITY RESTRICTIONS

The Sea Fishing (Enforcement of Community Control Measures) Order 1994 No. 451. Enabling power: *Fisheries Act 1981, s. 30 (2) (3)*. Issued: 08.03.94. Made: 28.02.94. Laid: 01.03.94. Coming into force: 22.03.94. Effect: S.I. 1993/2016 revoked. With correction slip dated March 1994 Territorial extent & classification: GB. General. – 10p. – 0 11 043451 X *£2.40*

The Sea Fishing (Enforcement of Community Quota Measures) Order 1994 No. 1679. Enabling power: *Fisheries Act 1981, s. 30 (2) (3)*. Issued: 19.07.94. Made: 24.06.94. Laid: 24.06.94. Coming into force: 15.07.94. Effect: S.I. 1993/387 revoked. Territorial extent & classification: GB. General. – 8p. – 0 11 044679 8 *£1.95*

The Third Country Fishing (Enforcement) Order No. 1681. Enabling power: *Fisheries Act 1981, s. 30 (2) (3)*. Issued: 19.07.94. Made: 24.06.94. Laid: 24.06.94. Coming into force: 15.07.94. Effect: S.I. 1993/1197 revoked. Territorial extent & classification: GB. General. – 6p. – 0 11 044681 X *£1.55*

SEA FISHERIES: CONSERVATION OF SEA FISH

The Plaice and Sole (Specified Sea Areas) (Prohibition of Fishing) Order 1994 No.2169. Enabling power: *Sea Fish (Conservation) Act 1967, ss. 5 (1), 15 (3), 22 (2) (A)*. Issued: 12.09.94. Made: 16.08.94. Laid: 18.08.94. Coming into force: 19.08.94. Effect: None. Territorial extent & classification: GB. General. – 6p. – 0 11 045169 4 *£1.55*

The Sea Fishing (Licences and Notices) Regulations 1994 No. 2813. Enabling power: *Sea Fish (Conservation) Act 1967, ss. 4B, 22 (2) (a)*. Issued: 01.11.94. Made: 01.11.94. Laid: 03.11.94. Coming into force: 19.12.94. Effect: None. Territorial extent & classification: GB. General. – 4p. – 0 11 045813 3 *£1.10*

The Sole and Nephrops (Prohibition of Fishing) Order 1994 No. 3273. Enabling power: *Sea Fish Conservation Act 1967, ss. 5 (1), 15 (3), 22 (2) (a)*. Issued: 09.02.95. Made: 18.12.94. Laid: 19.12.94. Coming into force: 20.12.94. Effect: None. Territorial extent & classification: GB. Local. – 6p. – 0 11 043941 4 *£1.55*

SEA FISHERIES: MARKETING

The Sea Fishing (Marketing Standards) (Amendment) Regulations 1994 No. 452. Enabling power: *European Communities Act 1972, s. 2 (2)*. Issued: 08.03.94. Made: 28.02.94. Laid: 01.03.94. Coming into force: 22.03.94. Effect: S.I. 1986/1272 amended. Territorial extent & classification: E/W/S. General. – 4p. – 0 11 043452 8 *£1.10*

SEA FISHERIES: SEA FISH INDUSTRY

The Fishing Vessels (Decommissioning) Scheme 1994 No. 1568. Enabling power: *Fisheries Act 1981, ss. 15 (1) (2), 18 (1)*. Issued: 12.08.94. Made: 15.06.94. Laid: 15.06.94. Coming into force: 06.07.94. Effect: None. Supersedes SI of same no. & ISBN published 30.06.94. Territorial extent & classification: GB. General. – 6p. – 0 11 044568 6 *£1.55*

SEA FISHERIES: SHELLFISH

The Loch Ewe, West Ross, Scallops Fishery Order 1994 No. 1946 (S. 86). Enabling power: *Sea Fisheries (Shellfish) Act 1967, s. 1, sch. 1*. Issued: 27.07.94. Made: 14.07.94. Laid: 27.07.94. Coming into force: 17.08.94. Effect: None. Territorial extent & classification: S. Local. – 4p., ill. – 0 11 044946 0 *£1.10*

The Thames Estuary Cockle Fishery Order 1994 No. 2329. Enabling power: *Sea Fisheries (Shellfish) Act 1967, s. 1*. Issued: 10.10.94. Made: 05.09.94. Laid: 07.09.94. Coming into force: 28.09.94. Effect: None. Territorial extent & classification: E. Local. – 6p. – 0 11 045329 8 *£1.55*

SEEDS

The Oil and Fibre Plant Seeds (Amendment) Regulations 1994 No. 1423. Enabling power: *Plant Varieties and Seeds Act 1964, ss. 16 (1) (8), 36.* Issued: 10.06.94. Made: 18.05.94. Laid: 10.06.94. Coming into force: 01.07.94. Effect: S.I. 1993/2007 amended. Territorial extent & classification: E/W/S. General. – 2p. – 0 11 044423 X £0.65

The Seed Potatoes (Amendment) Regulations 1994 No. 2592. Enabling power: *Plant Varieties and Seeds Act 1964, ss. 16 (1) (1A) (2) (3) (5) (8), 36.* Issued: 14.10.94. Made: 30.09.94. Laid: 14.10.94. Coming into force: 04.11.94. Effect: S.I. 1991/2206 amended. Territorial extent & classification: E/W/S. General. – 4p. – 0 11 045592 4 £1.10

The Seeds (National List of Varieties) (Fees) Regulations 1994 No. 676. Enabling power: *Plant Varieties and Seeds Act 1964, ss. 16 (1), 1 (a) (e) (8), 36.* Issued: 25.03.94. Made: 09.03.94. Laid: 11.03.94. Coming into force: 01.04.94. Effect: S.I. 1990/617; 1991/657; 1993/416 revoked. Territorial extent & classification: GB. General. – 6p. – 0 11 043676 8 £1.55

SEX DISCRIMINATION

The Sex Discrimination Act 1975 (Application to Armed Forces etc) Regulations 1994 No.3276. Enabling power: *European Communities Act 1972, s. 2 (2).* Issued: 29.12.94. Made: 20.12.94. Laid: 20.12.94. Coming into force: 01.02.95. Effect: 1975 c. 65 amended. Territorial extent & classification: GB. General. – Implements DIR 76/207 (OJ L 39/76) in relation to the armed forces of the Crown. – 2p. – 0 11 043755 1 £0.65

SHERIFF COURT, SCOTLAND

Act of Sederunt (Copyright, Designs and Patents) (Amendment) 1994 No. 3066 (S. 160). Enabling power: *Sheriff Courts (Scotland) Act 1971, s. 32 & Trade Marks Act 1994, s. 19 (3).* Issued: 09.12.94. Made: 30.11.94. Coming into force: 22.12.94. Effect: S.I. 1990/380 amended. Territorial extent & classification: S. General. – 2p. – 0 11 043302 5 £0.65

Act of Sederunt (Fees of Sheriff Officers) 1994 No. 392 (S. 13). Enabling power: *Sheriff Courts (Scotland) Act 1907, s. 40 & Execution of Diligence (Scotland) Act 1926, s. 6.* Issued: 02.03.94. Made: 18.02.94. Laid: 02.03.94. Coming into force: 23.03.94. Effect: S.I. 1990/381; 1991/290; 1992/82, 773; 1993/120 revoked. Territorial extent & classification: S. General. – 8p. – 0 11 043392 0 £1.95

Act of Sederunt (Fees of Sheriff Officers) (No. 2) 1994 No. 3267 (S. 187). Enabling power: *Sheriff Courts (Scotland) Act 1907, s. 40 & Execution of Diligence (Scotland) Act 1926, s. 6.* Issued: 12.01.95. Made: 16.12.94. Laid: 20.12.94. Coming into force: 09.01.95. Effect: S.I. 1994/392 amended. Territorial extent & classification: S. General. – 6p. – 0 11 043866 3 £1.55

Act of Sederunt (Fees of Shorthand Writers in the Sheriff Court) 1994 No. 1141 (S. 61). Enabling power: *Sheriff Courts (Scotland) Act 1907, s. 40.* Issued: 03.05.94. Made: 21.04.94. Laid: 03.05.94. Coming into force: 24.05.94. Effect: S.I. 1992/1878 amended. Territorial extent & classification: S. General. – 2p. – 0 11 044141 9 £0.65

Act of Sederunt (Fees of Solicitors in the Sheriff Court) (Amendment) 1994 No. 1142 (S. 62). Enabling power: *Sheriff Courts (Scotland) Act 1907, s. 40.* Issued: 03.05.94. Made: 21.04.94. Laid: 03.05.94. Coming into force: 24.05.94. Effect: S.I. 1993/3080 amended. Territorial extent & classification: S. General. – 6p. – 0 11 044142 7 £1.55

Act of Sederunt (Judicial Factors Rules) Amendment 1994 No. 2354 (S. 113). Enabling power: *Judicial Factors (Scotland) Act 1880, s. 5 & Sheriff Courts (Scotland) Act 1971, s. 32.* Issued: 19.09.94. Made: 06.09.94. Coming into force: 01.10.94. Effect: S.I. 1992/272 amended. Territorial extent & classification: S. General. – 2p. – 0 11 045354 9 £0.65

Act of Sederunt (Proceedings in the Sheriff Court under the Debtors (Scotland) Act 1987) (Amendment) 1994 No. 3086 (S. 166). Enabling power: *Sheriff Courts (Scotland) Act 1971, s. 32; Finance Act 1994, sch. 7, para. 7 (8).* Issued: 16.12.94. Made: 30.11.94. Coming into force: 22.12.94. Effect: S.I. 1988/2013 amended. Territorial extent & classification: S. General. – 4p. – 0 11 043379 3 £1.10

Act of Sederunt (Sheriff Court Parental Orders (Human Fertilisation and Embryology) Rules) 1994 No. 2805 (S. 142). Enabling power: *Sheriff Courts (Scotland) Act 1971, s. 32 & Adoption (Scotland) Act 1978, s. 59.* Issued: 09.11.94. Made: 21.10.94. Coming into force: On the date of coming into force of the Parental Orders (Human Fertilisation and Embryology) (Scotland) Regulations 1994 Effect: None. Territorial extent & classification: S. General. – 16p. – 0 11 045805 2 £3.20

SHOPS AND OFFICES

The Sunday Trading Act 1994 Appointed Day Order 1994 No. 1841 (C. 34). Enabling power: *Sunday Trading Act 1994, s. 1. Bringing various provisions of the 1994 act into operation on 26.08.94.* Issued: 19.07.94. Made: 11.07.94. Effect: None. Territorial extent & classification: E/W. General. – 2p. – 0 11 044841 3 £0.65

SOCIAL SECURITY

The Council Tax Benefit (Permitted Total) Order 1994 No. 2138. Enabling power: *Social Security Administration Act 1992, ss. 139 (10), 189 (1) (4) (5).* Issued: 19.08.94. Made: 12.08.94. Laid: 19.08.94. Coming into force: 03.10.94. Effect: S.I. 1993/689 revoked. Territorial extent & classification: E/W/S. General. – 2p. – 0 11 045138 4 £0.65

The Housing Benefit and Council Tax Benefit (Amendment) Regulations 1994 No. 470. Enabling power: *Social Security Contributions and Benefits Act 1992, ss. 131 (3) (b), 137 (1) (2) (i), 175 (1) to (4)*. Issued: 03.03.94. Made: 01.03.94. Laid: 03.03.94. Coming into force: 01.04.94. for regs. 1, 2 & 3 in part. 04.04.94. for remaining purposes of reg. 3. Effect: S.I. 1987/1971; 1992/1814 amended. Territorial extent & classification: E/W/S. General. – 6p. – 0 11 043470 6 £1.55

The Housing Benefit and Council Tax Benefit (Miscellaneous Amendments) (No. 2) Regulations 1994 No. 2137. Enabling power: *Social Security Contributions and Benefits Act 1992, ss. 123 (1) (d) (e), 131 (10), 135 (1) (6), 136 (3) (4) (5) (a) (b), 137 (1), 175 (1) (3) to (5) & Social Security Administration Act 1992, ss. 5 (1) (p), 63, 127 (1) (2), 128 (1) (2), 139 (6) (b), 189 (1) (4) to (6)*. Issued: 19.08.94. Made: 12.08.94. Laid: 19.08.94. Coming into force: 03.10.94. Effect: S.I. 1987/1971; 1988/662; 1992/1814 amended. Territorial extent & classification: E/W/S. General. – 12p. – 0 11 045137 6 £2.80

The Housing Benefit and Council Tax Benefit (Miscellaneous Amendments) Order 1994 No. 578. Enabling power: *Social Security Contributions and Benefits Act 1992, ss. 123 (1) (d) (e), 130 (4), 136 (3) to (5), 137 (1), 175 (1) to (5) & Social Security Administration Act 1992, ss. 63 (3), 127 (3), 128 (3), 189 (1) (3) to (5)*. Issued: 10.03.94. Made: 07.03.94. Laid: 10.03.94. Coming into force: 01.04.94, 04.04.94. Effect: S.I. 1987/1971; 1988/662; 1992/1814 amended. Territorial extent & classification: E/W/S. General. – 12p. – 0 11 043578 8 £2.40

The Housing Benefit and Council Tax Benefit (Subsidy) Order 1994 No. 523. Enabling power: *Social Security Administration Act 1992, ss. 135 (2) (4) (5), 136 (1), 140 (2) to (6), 189 (1) (3) to (7)*. Issued: 10.03.94. Made: 03.03.94. Laid: 10.03.94. Coming into force: 31.03.94. Effect: None. With correction slip. Territorial extent & classification: E/W/S. General. –76p. – 0 11 043523 0 £8.70

The Housing Benefit and Council Tax Benefit (Subsidy) Regulations 1994 No. 781. Enabling power: *Social Security Administration Act 1992, ss. 137 (2) (3), 140 (7), 189 (1) (3) to (6), 191*. Issued: 21.03.94. Made: 15.03.94. Laid: 21.03.94. Coming into force: 11.04.94. Effect: S.I. 1991/441; 1992/701; 1993/945 revoked. Territorial extent & classification: E/W/S. General. – 6p. – 0 11 043781 0 £1.55

The Housing Benefit (General) Amendment Regulations 1994 No. 1003. Enabling power: *Social Security Contributions and Benefits Act 1992, ss. 123 (1) (d), 130 (4), 135 (1), 137 (1), 175 (1) to (4)*. Issued: 08.04.94. Made: 31.03.94. Laid: 06.04.94. Coming into force: 01.05.94. Effect: S.I. 1987/1971 amended. Territorial extent & classification: E/W/S. General. – 2p. – 0 11 044003 X £0.65

The Housing Benefit (Permitted Totals) Order 1994 No. 579. Enabling power: *Social Security Administration Act 1992, ss. 134 (12), 189 (1) (3) to (6)*. Issued: 10.03.94. Made: 07.03.94. Laid: 10.03.94. Coming into force: 01.04.94. Effect: S.I. 1990/534 revoked. Territorial extent & classification: E/W/S. General. – 2p. – 0 11 043579 6 £0.65

The Housing Benefit (Supply of Information) and Council Tax Benefit (General) Amendment Regulations 1994 No. 1925. Enabling power: *Social Security Administration Act 1992, ss. 127 (1) (2), 128 (1) (2), 189 (1) (4) to (6)*. Issued: 21.07.94. Made: 18.07.94. Laid: 21.07.94. Coming into force: 01.09.94. Effect: S.I. 1988/662; 1992/1814 amended. Territorial extent & classification: E/W/S. General. – 4p. – 0 11 044925 8 £1.10

The Immigration Act 1988 (Commencement No. 3) Order 1994 No. 1923 (C. 35). Enabling power: *Immigration Act 1988, s. 12 (4)*. Bringing into operation various provisions of this Act on 20.07.94. Issued: 25.07.94. Made: 16.07.94. Effect: None. Territorial extent & classification: UK. General. – 2p. – 0 11 044923 1 £0.65

The Income-Related Benefits Schemes (Miscellaneous Amendments) (No. 2) Regulations 1994 No. 1608. Enabling power: *Social Security Contributions and Benefits Act 1992, ss. 123 (1), 130 (2) (4), 136 (3) (5), 137 (1), 175 (1) to (5)*. Issued: 23.06.94. Made: 16.06.94. Laid: 23.06.94. Coming into force: In accord. with reg. 1 (1). Effect: S.I. 1987/1967, 1971, 1973; 1991/2887; 1992/1814 amended. Territorial extent & classification: E/W/S. General. – 4p. – 0 11 044608 9 £1.10

The Income-Related Benefits Schemes (Miscellaneous Amendments) (No. 3) Regulations 1994 No. 1807. Enabling power: *Social Security Contributions and Benefits Act 1992, ss. 131 (3) (b), 135 (1), 137 (1) (2) (i), 175 (1) (3) (4)*. Issued: 11.07.94. Made: 07.07.94. Laid: 11.07.94. Coming into force: 01.08.94. Effect: S.I. 1987/1967, 1971; 1992/1814 amended. With correction slip dated July 1994. Territorial extent & classification: E/W/S. General. –4p. – 0 11 044807 3 £1.10

The Income-Related Benefits Schemes (Miscellaneous Amendments) (No. 4) Regulations 1994 No. 1924. Enabling power: *Social Security Contributions and Benefits Act 1992, ss. 123 (1) (b) to (e), 136 (3) (5) (b), 137 (1), 175 (1) (3) to (5)*. Issued: 25.07.94. Made: 18.07.94. Laid: 19.07.94. Coming into force: 03.10.94. Effect: S.I. 1987/1971, 1973; 1991/2887; 1992/1814 amended. Territorial extent & classification: E/W/S. General. – 10p. – 0 11 044924 X £2.40

The Income-Related Benefits Schemes (Miscellaneous Amendments) (No. 5) Regulations 1994 No. 2139. Enabling power: *Social Security Contributions and Benefits Act 1992, ss. 123 (1) (a) (b) (c), 128 (3) (4) (b), 129 (6) (7) (b), 135 (1) (6), 136 (3) (4) (5) (a) to (c), 137 (1) (2) (c) (d), 175 (1) (3) to (5) & Social Security Administration Act 1992, 5 (1) (k), 27 (1), 33 (3), 189 (1) (4) (5)*. Issued: 19.08.94. Made: 12.08.94. Laid: 19.08.94. Coming into force: 03.10.94. for this reg. & regs. 22, 23 & 04.10.94. for regs. 2 to 21 in accord. with reg 1 (1). Effect: S.I. 1987/1967; 1987/1973; 1991/2887 amended. Territorial extent & classification: E/W/S. General. – 16p. – 0 11 045139 2 £3.20

The Income-Related Benefits Schemes (Miscellaneous Amendments) (No. 6) Regulations 1994 No. 3061. Enabling power: *Social Security Contributions and Benefits Act 1992, ss. 135 (1) (6), 137 (1), 175 (1) (3) (4)*. Issued: 16.12.94. Made: 01.12.94. Laid: 01.12.94. Coming into force: 02.12.94. Effect: S.I. 1987/1967, 1971; 1992/1814 amended. Territorial extent & classification: E/W/S. General. – 2p. – 0 11 043410 2 £0.65

SOCIAL SECURITY

The Income-Related Benefits Schemes (Miscellaneous Amendments) Regulations 1994 No.527. Enabling power: *Social Security Contributions and Benefits Act 1992, ss. 123 (1), 124 (1) (d) (i), 135 (1), 136 (3) (4) (5) (a) (b), 137 (1), 175 (1) to (5).* Issued: 10.03.94. Made: 03.03.94. Laid: 10.03.94. Coming into force: 31.03.94, 11.04.94, 12.04.94. Effect: S.I. 1987/1967, 1973; 1991/2887 amended. Territorial extent & classification: E/W/S. General. – 12p. – 0 11 043527 3 £2.80

The Income Support (General) Amendment Regulations 1994 No. 1004. Enabling power: *Social Security Contributions and Benefits Act 1992, ss. 135 (1), 137 (1), 175 (1) to (4).* Issued: 08.04.94. Made: 31.03.94. Laid: 08.04.94. Coming into force: 02.05.94. Effect: S.I. 1987/1967 amended. Territorial extent & classification: E/W/S. General. – 4p. – 0 11 044004 8 £1.10

The Maternity Allowance and Statutory Maternity Pay Regulations 1994 No. 1230. Enabling power: *European Communities Act 1972, s. 2 (2).* Issued: 11.05.94. Made: 04.05.94. Laid: 24.03.94. Coming into force: 04.09.94. for reg. 5; 16.10.94. for all others Effect: 1992 c.4. amended. Supersedes Draft ISBN 0110458931 previously published on 24.03.94. Territorial extent & classification: E/W/S. Local. – 4p. – 0 11 044230 X £1.10

The Social Fund Cold Weather Payments (General) Amendment Regulations 1994 No. 2593. Enabling power: *Social Security Contibutions and Benefits Act 1992, ss. 138 (2) (4), 175 (2) (3) (4).* Issued: 11.10.94. Made: 06.10.94. Laid: 11.10.94. Coming into force: 01.11.94. Effect: S.I. 1988/1724 amended. Territorial extent & classification: E/W/S. General. – 4p. – 0 11 045593 2 £1.10

The Social Fund Maternity and Funeral Expenses (General) Amendment Regulations 1994 No.506. Enabling power: *Social Security Contributions and Benefits Act 1992, ss. 138 (1) (a) (4), 175 (1) to (4).* Issued: 09.03.94. Made: 02.03.94. Laid: 09.03.94. Coming into force: 01.04.94. Effect: S.I. 1987/481 amended. Territorial extent & classification: E/W/S. General. –4p. – 0 11 043506 0 £1.10

The Social Security Act 1989 (Commencement No. 5) Order 1994 No. 1661 (C.30). Enabling power: *Social Security Act 1989, s. 33 (2). Bringing various provisions of the 1989 act into operation on 23.06.94.* Issued: 28.06.94. Made: 22.06.94. Effect: None. Territorial extent & classification: E/W/S. General. – 4p. – 0 11 044661 5 £1.10

The Social Security (Adjudication) Amendment (No. 2) Regulations 1994 No. 2686. Enabling power: *Social Security Administration Act 1992, ss. 61 (1), 189 (1) (6).* Issued: 24.10.94. Made: 18.10.94. Laid: 24.10.94. Coming into force: 14.11.94. Effect: S.I. 1986/2218 amended. Territorial extent & classification: E/W/S. General. – 4p. – 0 11 045686 6 £1.10

The Social Security (Adjudication) Amendment Regulations 1994 No. 1082. Enabling power: *Social Security Administration Act 1992, ss. 46 (3) (a), 59 (1), 189 (6), 191, sch. 3, paras. 2, 3.* Issued: 20.04.94. Made: 13.04.94. Laid: 20.04.94. Coming into force: 11.05.94. Effect: S.I. 1986/2218 amended. Territorial extent & classification: E/W/S. General. –4p. – 0 11 044082 X £1.10

The Social Security (Attendance Allowance and Disability Living Allownace) (Amendment) Regulations 1994 No. 1779. Enabling power: *Social Security Contributions and Benefits Act 1992, ss. 67 (2), 72 (8), 73 (5), 122 (1), 175 (1) (3) & Social Security Administration Act 1992, ss. 73 (1), 189 (1) (4), 191.* Issued: 11.07.94. Made: 05.07.94. Laid: 11.07.94. Coming into force: 01.08.94. Effect: S.I. 1991/2740, 2890; 1992/3147; 1993/518 amended. Territorial extent & classification: E/W/S. General. – 8p. – 0 11 044779 4 £1.95

The Social Security Benefit (Persons Abroad) Amendment (No. 2) Regulations 1994 No.1832. Enabling power: *Social Contributions and Benefits Act 1992, ss. 113 (1), 175 (1) to (4).* Issued: 15.07.94. Made: 11.07.94. Laid: 15.07.94. Coming into force: 06.08.94. Effect: S.I. 1975/563 amended. Territorial extent & classification: E/W/S. General. – 4p. – 0 11 044832 4 £1.10

The Social Security Benefit (Persons Abroad) Amendment Regulations 1994 No. 268. Enabling power: *Social Security Contributions and Benefits Act 1992, ss. 113 (1) (a), 175 (1) (3).* Issued: 15.02.94. Made: 08.02.94. Laid: 15.02.94. Coming into force: 08.03.94. Effect: S.I. 1975/563 amended. Territorial extent & classification: E/W/S. General. – 4p. – 0 11 043268 1 £1.10

The Social Security Benefits Up-Rating Order 1994 No. 542. Enabling power: *Social Security Administration Act 1992, ss. 150, 189 (1) (3) (4).* Issued: 14.03.94. Made: 03.03.94. Laid: 10.02.94. Coming into force: 01.04.94, 03.04.94, 06.04.94, 11.12.94, 12.04.94. Effect: 1965 c. 51; 1992 c. 4,, 5; 1993 c. 48; S.I. 1976/1267; 1978/393; 1986/1960; 1987/1967, 1969, 1971, 1973; 1991/2887, 2890; 1992/1814 amended & S.I. 1993/349 revoked. Supersedes Draft ISBN 0110458710 Territorial extent & classification: E/W/S. General. – 38p. – 0 11 043542 7 £6.10

The Social Security Benefits Up-Rating Regulations 1994 No. 559. Enabling power: *Social Security Contributions and Benefits Act 1992, ss. 57 (1) (a) (ii), 113 (1) (a), 122 (1), 175 (1) to (4), sch. 7, para. 2 (3) & Social Security Administration Act 1992, ss. 155 (3), 189 (1) (3) (4), 191.* Issued: 14.03.94. Made: 07.03.94. Laid: 14.03.94. Coming into force: 11.04.94. Effect: S.I. 1982/1408; 1983/1598 amended & S.I. 1993/723 revoked. Territorial extent & classification: E/W/S. General. – 2p. – 0 11 043559 1 £0.65

The Social Security (Categorisation of Earners) Amendment Regulations 1994 No. 726. Enabling power: *Social Security Contributions and Benefits Act 1992, ss. 2 (2), 7 (2), 122 (1), 175 (1).* Issued: 16.03.94. Made: 14.03.94. Laid: 16.04.94. Coming into force: 06.04.94. Effect: S.I. 1978/1689 amended. Territorial extent & classification: E/W/S. General. –4p. – 0 11 043726 8 £1.10

The Social Security (Claims and Payments) Amendment (No. 2) Regulations 1994 No. 2943. Enabling power: *Social Security Administration Act 1992, ss. 5 (1) (a) (f) (i), 7 (1), 189 (1) (4) (6) & Social Security (Incapacity for Work) Act 1994, s. 12.* Issued: 24.11.94. Made: 21.11.94. Laid: 24.11.94. Coming into force: 13.04.95. Effect: S.I. 1987/1968 amended. Territoral extent & classification: E/W/S. General. – 6p. – 0 11 043123 5 £1.55

Price/availability are liable to change without notice

The Social Security (Claims and Payments) Amendment (No. 3) Regulations 1994 No. 2944. Enabling power: *Social Security Administration Act 1992, ss. 15A (2) (b), 189 (1)*.Issued: 28.11.94. Made: 21.11.94. Laid: 28.11.94. Coming into force: 01.04.95. Effect: S.I. 1987/1968 amended. Territorial extent & classification: E/W/S. General. –2p. – 0 11 043122 7 *£0.65*

The Social Security (Claims and Payments) Amendment (No. 4) Regulations 1994 No. 3196. Enabling power: *Social Security Administration Act 1992, ss. 5 (1) (i), 189 (1) (4) (5) (6)*. Issued: 20.12.94. Made: 13.12.94. Laid: 20.12.94. Coming into force: 10.01.95. Effect: S.I. 1987/1968 amended. Territorial extent & classification: E/W/S. General. –4p. – 0 11 043508 7 *£1.10*

The Social Security (Claims and Payments) Amendment Regulations 1994 No. 2319.Enabling power: *Social Security Administration Act 1992, ss. 5 (1) (a) (c) (g) (i) (m) (o) (p), 189 (1) (4) (6)*. Issued: 12.09.94. Made: 06.09.94. Laid: 12.09.94. Coming into force: 03.10.94. Effect: S.I. 1987/1968 amended. Territorial extent & classification: E/W/S. General. –4p. – 0 11 045319 0 *£1.10*

The Social Security (Contributions) Amendment (No. 2) Regulations 1994 No. 1553. Enabling power: *Social Security Contributions and Benefits Act 1992, ss. 1 (4) (a), 3 (2) (3), 116 (3), 122 (1), 175 (1) to (3), sch. 1, para. 8 (1) (d) & Social Security Contributions and Benefits Act (Northern Ireland) Act 1992, s. 116 (3)*. Issued: 15.06.94. Made: 13.06.94. Laid: 15.06.94. Coming into force: 06.07.94. Effect: S.I. 1979/591 amended. Territorial extent & classification: E/W/S. General. –4p. – 0 11 044553 8 *£1.10*

The Social Security (Contributions) Amendment (No. 3) Regulations 1994 No. 2194. Enabling power: *Social Security Contributions and Benefits Act 1992, ss. 3 (2) (3), 122 (1), 175 (1) to (3)*. Issued: 02.09.94. Made: 23.08.94. Laid: 23.08.94. 0oming into force: 24.08.94. Effect: S.I. 1979/591 amended. Territorial extent & classification: E/W/S. General. –4p. – 0 11 045194 5 *£1.10*

The Social Security (Contributions) Amendment (No. 4) Regulations 1994 No. 2299. Enabling power: *Social Security Contributions and Benefits Act 1992, ss. 1 (4), 122 (1), 175 (1) to (3), sch. 1, para. 6 (1)*. Issued: 09.09.94. Made: 05.09.94. Laid: 09.09.94. Coming into force: 30.09.94. Effect: S.I. 1979/591 amended. Territorial extent & classification: E/W/S. General. –2p. – 0 11 045299 2 *£0.65*

The Social Security (Contributions) Amendment Regulations 1994 No. 563. Enabling power: *Social Security Contributions and Benefits Act 1992, ss. 5, 119, 175 (1) to (3)*.Issued: 14.03.94. Made: 07.03.94. Laid: 14.03.94. Coming into force: 06.04.94. Effect: S.I. 1979/591 amended. Territorial extent & classification: E/W/S. General. –2p. – 0 11 043563 X *£0.65*

The Social Security (Contributions) (Miscellaneous Amendments) Regulations 1994 No.667. Enabling power: *Social Security Contributions and Benefits Act 1992, ss. 1 (4), 10 (7) (9), 122 (1), 175 (1) to (3), sch. 1, para. 6 (1)*. Issued: 16.03.94. Made: 09.03.94. Laid: 16.03.94. Coming into force: 06.04.94. Effect: 1992 c.4; S.I. 1979/591 amended. Territorial extent & classification: E/W/S. General. –4p. – 0 11 043667 9 *£1.10*

The Social Security (Contributions) (Re-rating and National Insurance Fund Payments) Order 1994 No. 544. Enabling power: *Social Security Administration Act 1992, ss. 141 (4) (5), 142 (2), 143 (1), 145 (2), 189 (1) (3), & Social Security Act 1993, s. 2 (2) (8)*. Issued: 11.03.94. Made: 03.03.94. Laid: 10.02.94. Coming into force: 06.04.94. Effect: 1992 c.4 amended. Supersedes Draft ISBN 0110458729 previously published 10.02.94. Territoral extent & classification: E/W/S. General. –4p. – 0 11 043544 3 *£1.10*

The Social Security (Credits) Amendment Regulations 1994 No. 1837. Enabling power: *Social Security Contributions and Benefits Act 1992, ss. 22 (5), 122 (1), 175 (1) to (3)*. Issued: 18.07.94. Made: 11.07.94. Laid: 18.07.94. Coming into force: 08.08.94. Effect: S.I. 1975/556 amended. Territorial extent & classification: E/W/S. General. –4p. – 0 11 044837 5 *£1.10*

The Social Security (Cyprus) Order 1994 No. 1646. Enabling power: *Social Security Administration Act 1992, s. 179 (1) (a) (2)*. Issued: 04.07.94. Made: 22.06.94. Coming into force: 04.07.94. Effect: 1992 c. 4, c. 5; S.I. 1983/1698; 1988/591 amended. Territorial extent & classification: E/W/S. General. –8p. – 0 11 044646 1 *£1.95*

The Social Security (Incapacity Benefit–Increases for Dependants) Regulations 1994 No.2945. Enabling power: *Social Security Contributions and Benefits Act 1992, ss. 3 (2), 80 (7), 86A, 87, 89, 90, 114 (1), 122 (1) (5)*. Issued: 24.11.94. Made: 21.11.94. Laid: 24.11.94. Coming into force: 13.04.95, except for reg. 15 (6) (b) (i) & (c) (i). 13.05.95, for reg. 15 (6) (b) (i) & (c) (i). Effect: S.I. 1977/343 amended. Territorial extent & classification: E/W/S. General. –10p. – 0 11 043121 9 *£2.40*

The Social Security (Incapacity Benefit) Regulations 1994 No. 2946. Enabling power: *Social Security Contributions and Benefits Act 1992, ss. 30B (7), 30C (3) (4) (a) (6), 30D (3), 30E (1) (2), 122, 175 (1) (3) & Social Security (Incapacity for Work) Act 1994, ss. 2 (1), 3 (1)*. Issued: 24.11.94. Made: 21.11.94. Laid: 24.11.94. Coming into force: 13.04.95. Effect: None. Territorial extent & classification: E/W/S. General. –6p. – 0 11 043120 0 *£1.55*

The Social Security (Incapacity for Work) Act 1994 (Commencement) Order 1994 No. 2926 (C. 65). Enabling power: *Social Security (Incapacity for Work) Act 1994, s. 16 (3)*. Bringing into operation various provisions of the 1994 act on 18.11.94, 06.01.95, 13.04.95. Issued: 24.11.94. Made: 17.11.94. Effect: None. Territorial extent & classification: E/W/S. General. –4p. – 0 11 043096 4 *£1.10*

The Social Security (Industrial Injuries) (Prescribed Diseases) Amendment Regulations 1994 No. 2343. Enabling power: *Social Security Contributions and Benefits Act 1992, ss. 108 (2), 109 (2), 122 (1), 175 (1) (3) & Social Security Administration Act 1992, s. 184*.Issued: 14.09.94. Made: 07.09.94. Laid: 13.09.94. Coming into force: 10.10.94. Effect: S.I. 1985/967 amended. Territorial extent & classification: E/W/S. General. –4p. – 0 11 045343 3 *£1.10*

The Social Security (Jersey and Guernsey) Order 1994 No. 2802. Enabling power: *Social Security Administration Act 1992, s. 179 (1) (a) (2)*. Issued: 14.11.94. Made: 02.11.94. Coming into force: 02.11.94. Effect: 1992 c. 4, c. 5; S.I. 1976/963; 1988/591 amended & S.I. 1973/1085; 1977/592; 1978/1527; 1982/1527; 1983/604; 1992/1735 revoked. Territorial extent & classification: E/W/S. General. – 20p. – 0 11 045802 8 *£3.70*

The Social Security Maternity Benefits and Statutory Sick Pay (Amendment) Regulations 1994 No. 1367. Enabling power: *Social Security and Contributions Benefits Act 1992, ss. 35 (3) (b) (i) (c), 119, 153 (6), 164 (4) (9) (e), 165 (1) (3), 166 (3), 171 (1), 175 (1) to (4), sch. 11, para. 1*. Issued: 26.05.94. Made: 19.05.94. Laid: 20.05.94. Coming into force: 11.06.94. Effect: S.I. 1982/894; 1986/1960; 1987/416, 417 amended. Territorial extent & classification: E/W/S. General. – 6p. – 0 11 044367 5 *£1.55*

The Social Security (Medical Evidence) Amendment Regulations 1994 No. 2975. Enabling power: *Social Security Administration Act 1992, s. 59, sch. 3*. Issued: 12.12.94. Made: 23.11.94. Laid: 24.11.94. Coming into force: 13.04.95. Effect: S.I. 1976/615 amended. Territorial extent & classification: E/W/S. General. – 6p. – 0 11 043344 0 *£1.55*

The Social Security Pensions (Home Responsibilities) Regulations 1994 No. 704. Enabling power: *Social Security Contributions and Benefits Act 1992, ss. 21 (3), 175 (1) to (5), sch. 3, para. 5 (7) (b)*. Issued: 15.03.94. Made: 11.03.94. Laid: 15.03.94. Coming into force: 06.04.94. Effect: S.I. 1978/508 amended & S.I. 1981/330; 1988/623 revoked. Territorial extent & classification: E/W/S. General. – 4p. – 0 11 043704 7 *£1.10*

The Social Security Revaluation of Earnings Factors Order 1994 No. 1105. Enabling power: *Social Security Administration Act 1992, s. 148 (3) (4)*. Issued: 25.04.94. Made: 19.04.94. Laid: 25.04.94. Coming into force: 16.05.94. Effect: None. Territorial extent & classification: E/W/S. General. – 2p. – 0 11 044105 2 *£0.65*

The Social Security (Severe Disablement Allowance) Amendment Regulations 1994 No. 2947. Enabling power: *Social Security Contributions and Benefits Act 1992, ss. 68 (11) (b) (c) (d) & Social Security (Incapacity for Work) Act 1994, s. 12 (1)*. Issued: 24.11.94. Made: 21.11.94. Laid: 24.11.94. Coming into force: 13.04.95. Effect: S.I. 1984/1303 amended. Territorial extent & classification: E/W/S. General. – 4p. – 0 11 043114 6 *£1.10*

The Social Security (Severe Disablement Allowance and Invalid Care Allowance) Amendment Regulations 1994 No. 2556. Enabling power: *European Communities Act 1972, s. 2 (2)*. Issued: 07.10.94. Made: 03.10.94. Laid: 07.10.94. Coming into force: 28.10.94. Effect: 1992 c.4; 1994 c. 18; S.I. 1976/409; 1984/1303 amended. Territorial extent & classification: E/W/S. General. – 6p. – 0 11 045556 8 *£1.55*

The Social Security (Sickness and Invalidity Benefit and Severe Disablement Allowance) Miscellaneous Amendments Regulations 1994 No. 1101. Enabling power: *Social Security Contributions and Benefits Act 1992, ss. 57 (1) (a) (ii), 68 (11) (e) (ii), 175 (1) (3)*. Issued: 22.04.94. Made: 18.04.94. Laid: 22.04.94. Coming into force: 16.05.94. Effect: S.I. 1983/1598; 1984/1303 amended. Territorial extent & classification: E/W/S. General. – 2p. – 0 11 044101 X *£0.65*

The Statutory Maternity Pay (Compensation of Employers) and Miscellaneous Amendment Regulations 1994 No. 1882. Enabling power: *Social Security Contributions and Benefits Act 1992, ss. 35 (3), 167 (1) (1A) (1B) (4), 171 (1), 175 (1) to (4)*. Issued: 21.07.94. Made: 14.07.94. Laid: 15.07.94. Coming into force: 31.07.94. for regs. 1 & 9; 04.09.94. for regs. 2 to 8. Effect: S.I. 1987/416 amended & S.I. 1987/91 revoked. Territorial extent & classification: E/W/S. General. – 4p. – 0 11 044882 0 *£1.10*

The Workmen's Compensation (Supplementation) (Amendment) Scheme 1994 No. 671. Enabling power: *Social Security Contributions and Benefits Act 1992, sch. 8, para. 2 & Social Security Administration Act 1992, sch. 9, para. 1*. Issued: 16.03.94. Made: 09.03.94. Laid: 16.03.94. Coming into force: 13.04.94. Effect: S.I. 1982/1489 amended. Territorial extent & classification: E/W/S. General. – 4p. – 0 11 043671 7 *£1.10*

SOLICITORS

The Solicitors' (Non-Contentious Business) Remuneration Order 1994 No. 2616 (L. 16). Enabling power: *Solicitors Act 1974, s. 56*. Issued: 17.10.94. Made: 05.10.94. Laid: 10.10.94. Coming into force: 01.11.94. Effect: S.I. 1972/1139 revoked. Territorial extent & classification: E/W. General. – 6p. – 0 11 045616 5 *£1.55*

SPORTS GROUNDS AND SPORTING EVENTS

The Football Spectators (Seating) Order 1994 No. 1666. Enabling power: *Football Spectators Act 1989, s. 11 (1) to (3)*. Issued: 04.07.94. Made: 22.06.94. Laid: 24.06.94. Coming into force: 15.07.94. Effect: None. Territorial extent & classification: E/W. General. – 6p. – 0 11 044666 6 *£1.55*

The Safety of Sports Grounds (Designation) Order 1994 No. 2239. Enabling power: *Safety of Sports Grounds Act 1975, ss. 1 (1), 18 (2)*. Issued: 05.09.94. Made: 23.08.94. Laid: 05.09.94. Coming into force: 26.09.94. Effect: S.I. 1983/962; 1986/1296 amended. Territorial extent & classification: E. General. – 2p. – 0 11 045239 9 *£0.65*

STATISTICS OF TRADE

The Statistics of Trade (Customs and Excise) (Amendment) Regulations 1994 No. 2914. Enabling power: *European Communities Act 1972, s. 2 (2)*. Issued: 06.12.94. Made: 29.11.94. Laid: 29.11.94. Coming into force: 01.01.95. Effect: S.I. 1992/707; 1993/2790 amended. Territorial extent & classification: GB. General. – Implements REG 2256/92 (OJ L 219/92). – 2p. – 0 11 043273 8 *£0.65*

Price/availability are liable to change without notice

SUGAR

The Sugar Beet (Research and Education) Order 1994 No. 407. Enabling power: *Food Act 1984, s. 68 (1)*. Issued: 14.03.94. Made: 22.02.94. Laid: 03.03.94. Coming into force: 01.04.94. Effect: None. With correction slip dated May 1994 Territorial extent & classification: E/W. General. – 6p. – 0 11 043407 2 *£1.55*

SUMMARY JURISDICTION, SCOTLAND

Act of Adjournal (Consolidation Amendment) (Miscellaneous) 1994 No. 1769 (S. 78). Enabling power: *Criminal Procedure (Scotland) Act 1975, ss. 282, 457*. Issued: 14.07.94. Made: 01.07.94. Coming into force: 01.08.94. Effect: S.I. 1988/110 amended. Territorial extent & classification: S. General. – 4p. – 0 11 044769 7 *£1.10*

The Backing of Warrants (Republic of Ireland) (Rule of Speciality) Order 1994 No. 1952. Enabling power: *Backing of Warrants (Republic of Ireland) Act 1965, ss. 2 (5), 6A, 6B, 6C*. Issued: 28.07.94. Made: 20.07.94. Laid: 28.07.94. Coming into force: 22.08.94. Effect: None. Territorial extent & classification: UK/CI/IOM. General. – 4p. – 0 11 044952 5 *£1.10*

SUMMER TIME

The Summer Time Order 1994 No. 2798. Enabling power: *Summer Time Act 1972, s. 2 (1) (a) (2)*. Issued: 11.11.94. Made: 02.11.94. Coming into force: 16.11.94. Effect: S.I. 1980/1089; 1982/1673; 1986/223; 1988/931; 1989/985 revoked. Supersedes Draft ISBN 0110459407 published on 08.07.94. Territorial extent & classification: GB/Guernsey. General. – Implements the 7th Summer Time Dir 94/21 (OJ no. L164 1994). – 2p. – 0 11 045798 6 *£0.65*

SUPREME COURT OF ENGLAND AND WALES

The Civil Courts (Amendment No. 2) Order 1994 No. 1536. Enabling power: *Supreme Court Act 1981, s. 99 (1) & County Courts Act 1984, ss. 2 (1), 26 & Insolvency Act 1986, ss. 117 (4), 374*. Issued: 24.06.94. Made: 09.06.94. Laid: 13.06.94. Coming into force: 04.07.94. Effect: S.I. 1983/713 amended. Territorial extent & classification: E/W. General. – 4p. – 0 11 044536 8 *£1.10*

The Civil Courts (Amendment No. 3) Order 1994 No. 2626. Enabling power: *Supreme Court Act 1981, s. 99 (1) & County courts Act 1984, ss. 2 (1), 26 & Insolvency Act 1986, ss. 117 (4), 374*. Issued: 26.10.94. Made: 11.10.94. Laid: 11.10.94. Coming into force: 02.11.94. Effect: S.I. 1983/713 amended. Territorial extent & classification: E/W. General. – 2p. – 0 11 045626 2 *£0.65*

The Civil Courts (Amendment No. 4) Order 1994 No. 2893. Enabling power: *Supreme Court Act 1981, s. 99 (1) & County Court Act 1984, ss. 2 (1), 26 & Insolvency Act 1986, ss. 117, 374*. Issued: 25.11.94. Made: 14.11.94. Laid: 14.11.94. Coming into force: 05.12.94, except for art. 5 (a). 09.01.95, for art. 5 (a). Effect: S.I. 1983/713 amended. Territorial extent & classification: E/W. General. – 2p. – 0 11 043095 6 *£0.65*

The Crown Court (Amendment) (No. 2) Rules 1994 No. 3153 (L. 19). Enabling power: *Supreme Court Act 1981, ss. 84 (1), 86*. Issued: 20.12.94. Made: 08.12.94. Laid: 12.12.94. Coming into force: 03.02.95. Effect: S.I. 1982/1109 amended. Territorial extent & classification: E/W. General. – 4p. – 0 11 043512 5 *£1.10*

The Crown Court (Amendment) Rules 1994 No. 1480 (L. 9). Enabling power: *Supreme Court Act 1981, ss. 84 (1), 86*. Issued: 13.06.94. Made: 26.05.94. Laid: 06.06.94. Coming into force: 27.06.94. Effect: S.I. 1982/1109 amended. Territorial extent & classification: E/W. General. – 6p. – 0 11 044480 9 *£1.55*

The Enrolment of Deeds (Change of Name) Regulations 1994 No. 604 (L. 3). Enabling power: *Supreme Court Act 1981, s. 133 (1)*. Issued: 11.03.94. Made: 03.03.94. Laid: 10.03.94. Coming into force: 01.04.94. Effect: S.I. 1983/680; 1990/2471 revoked. Territorial extent & classification: E/W. General. – 4p. – 0 11 043604 0 *£1.10*

The Enrolment of Deeds (Fees) Regulations 1994 No. 601 (L. 2). Enabling power: *Supreme Court Act 1981, s. 133 (4)*. Issued: 11.03.94. Made: 07.03.94. Laid: 10.03.94. Coming into force: 01.04.94. Effect: S.R. & O. 1922/210; S.I. 1951/1937 revoked. Territorial extent & classification: E/W. General. – 4p. – 0 11 043601 6 *£1.10*

The Family Proceedings (Amendment) (No. 2) Rules 1994 No. 2165 (L. 13). Enabling power: *Matrimonial and Family Proceedings Act 1984, s. 40 (1)*. Issued: 24.08.94. Made: 11.08.94. Laid: 24.08.94. Coming into force: 01.11.94. Effect: S.I. 1991/1247 amended. Territorial extent & classification: E/W. General. – 20p. – 0 11 045165 1 *£3.70*

The Family Proceedings (Amendment) (No. 3) Rules 1994 No. 2890 (L. 17). Enabling power: *Matrimonial and Family Proceedings Act 1984, s. 40 (1)*. Issued: 21.11.94. Made: 25.10.94. Laid: 14.11.94. Coming into force: 06.12.94. Effect: S.I. 1991/1247 amended. Territorial extent & classification: E/W. General. – 4p. – 0 11 043077 8 *£1.10*

The Family Proceedings (Amendment) (No. 4) Rules 1994 No. 3155 (L. 21). Enabling power: *Matrimonial and Family Proceedings Act 1984, s. 40*. Issued: 22.12.94. Made: 08.12.94. Laid: 12.12.94. Coming into force: 03.01.95. Effect: S.I. 1991/1247 amended. Territorial extent & classification: E/W. General. – 92p. – 0 11 043515 X *£9.40*

The Family Proceedings (Amendment) Rules 1994 No. 808 (L. 4). Enabling power: *Matrimonial and Family Proceedings Act 1984, s. 40 (1)*. Issued: 25.03.94. Made: 21.03.94. Laid: 21.03.94. Coming into force: 11.04.94. Effect: S.I. 1991/1247, 21113 amended. Territorial extent & classification: E/W. General. – 8p. – 0 11 043808 6 *£1.95*

The Maximum Number of Judges Order 1994 No. 3217. Enabling power: *Administration of Justice Act 1968, s. 1 (2) & Supreme Court Act 1981, s. 2 (4).* Issued: 22.12.94. Made: 14.12.94. Laid: 16.11.94. Coming into force: 15.12.94. Effect: 1968 c. 5 & 1981 c. 54 amended. Territorial extent & classification: E/W. General. – 2p. – 0 11 043584 2 £0.65

The Rules of the Supreme Court (Amendment) 1994 No. 1975 (L. 10). Enabling power: *Supreme Court Act 1981, s. 85.* Issued: 28.07.94. Made: 18.07.94. Laid: 28.07.94. Coming into force: 01.09.94. Effect: S.I.1965/1776 amended. With correction slip dated September 1994 Territorial extent & classification: E/W. General. – 8p. – 0 11 044975 4 £1.95

SUPREME COURT OF ENGLAND AND WALES: COMPOSITION OF THE COURT OF APPEAL

The Criminal Justice and Public Order Act 1994 (Commencement No. 3) Order 1994 No.3258 (C. 82). Enabling power: *Criminal Justice and Public Order Act 1994, s. 172 (2). Bringing into operation various provisions of the 1994 act on 11.01.95.* Issued: 22.12.94. Made: 15.12.94. Effect: None. Territorial extent & classification: E/W. General. – 2p. – 0 11 043734 9 £0.65

SUPREME COURT OF ENGLAND AND WALES: OFFICES AND REGISTRIES

The District Probate Registries (Amendment No. 2) Order 1994 No. 3079 (L. 18). Enabling power: *Supreme Court Act 1981, s. 104 (1).* Issued: 14.12.94. Made: 01.12.94. Laid: 14.12.94. Coming into force: 16.01.95. Effect: S.I. 1982/379 amended. With correction slip dated January 1995 (corrrecting the laid date). Territorial extent & classification: E/W. General. –2p. – 0 11 043380 7 £0.65

The District Probate Registries (Amendment) Order 1994 No. 1103 (L. 6). Enabling power: *Supreme Court Act 1981, s. 104.* Issued: 25.04.94. Made: 18.04.94. Laid: 25.04.94. Coming into force: 23.05.94. Effect: S.I. 1982/379 amended. Territorial extent & classification: E/W. General. – 2p. – 0 11 044103 6 £0.65

TAXES

The Capital Gains Tax (Annual Exempt Amount) Order 1994 No. 3008. Enabling power: *Taxation of Chargeable Gains Act 1992, s. 3 (4).* Issued: 07.12.94. Made: 29.11.94. Coming into force: 06.04.95. Effect: None. Territorial extent & classification: GB. General. – 2p. – 0 11 043292 4 £0.65

The Capital Gains Tax (Gilt-Edged Securities) Order 1994 No. 2656. Enabling power: *Taxation of Chargeable Gains Act 1992, sch. 9, para. 1.* Issued: 26.10.94. Made: 11.10.94. Effect: None. Territorial extent & classification: GB. General. – 2p. – 0 11 045656 4 £0.65

The General and Special Commissioners (Amendment of Enactments) Regulations 1994 No.1813. Enabling power: *Taxes Management Act 1970, ss. 46A, 56B.* Issued: 14.07.94. Made: 06.07.94. Laid: 14.07.94. Coming into force: 01.09.94. Effect: 1970 c. 9; 1972 c. 41; 1975 c. 22; 1984 c. 43, 51; 1988 c. 1; 1988 c. 39; 1989 c. 26; 1994 c. 9 & S.I. 1959/452; 1967/149; 1986/1711; 1989/421; 1990/627; 1991/851; 1992/511; 1993/415, 744; 1994/728 amended & S.I. 1987/1422 revoked. Territorial extent & classification: E/W. General. – 12p. – 0 11 044813 8 £2.80

The Petroleum Revenue Tax (Nomination Scheme for Disposals and Appropriations) (Amendment) Regulations 1994 No. 939. Enabling power: *Finance Act 1987, s. 61 (8).* Issued: 05.04.94. Made: 25.03.94. Laid: 28.03.94. Coming into force: 18.04.94. Effect: S.I. 1987/1338 amended. Territorial extent & classification: GB. General. – 2p. – 0 11 043939 2 £0.65

The Special Commissioners (Jurisdiction and Procedure) Regulations 1994 No. 1811. Enabling power: *Taxes Management Act 1970, ss. 46A, 56B to 56D.* Issued: 14.07.94. Made: 06.07.94. Laid: 14.07.94. Coming into force: 01.09.94. Effect: None. Territorial extent & classification: E/W. General. – 16p. – 0 11 044811 1 £3.20

The Taxes (Interest Rate) (Amendment No. 2) Regulations 1994 No. 1567. Enabling power: *Finance Act 1989, s. 178 & Income and Corporation Taxes Act 1988, s. 160 (5).* Issued: 30.06.94. Made: 14.06.94. Laid: 15.06.94. Coming into force: 06.07.94. Effect: S.I. 1989/1297 amended. Territorial extent & classification: GB. General. – 2p. – 0 11 044567 8 £0.65

The Taxes (Interest Rate) (Amendment No. 3) Regulations 1994 No. 2657. Enabling power: *Finance Act 1989, s. 178.* Issued: 24.10.94. Made: 11.10.94. Laid: 12.10.94. Coming into force: 06.11.94. Effect: None. Territorial extent & classification: GB. General. – 2p. – 0 11 045657 2 £0.65

The Taxes (Interest Rate) (Amendment) Regulations 1994 No. 1307. Enabling power: *Finance Act 1989, s. 178 & Income and Corporation Taxes Act 1988, s. 160 (5).* Issued: 26.05.94. Made: 13.05.94. Laid: 16.05.94. Coming into force: 06.06.94. Effect: S.I. 1989/1297 amended. Territorial extent & classification: GB. General. – 2p. – 0 11 044307 1 £0.65

TELECOMMUNICATIONS

The British Telecommunications (Dissolution) Order 1994 No. 2162. Enabling power: *Telecommunications Act 1984, s. 69 (2).* Issued: 06.09.94. Made: 16.08.94. Coming into force: 06.09.94. Effect: None. Territorial extent & classification: GB. General. – 2p. – 0 11 045162 7 £0.65

The Public Telecommunication System Designation (Bradford Cable Communications Limited) Order 1994 No. 1190. Enabling power: *Telecommunications Act 1984, s. 9.* Issued: 13.05.94. Made: 12.04.94. Laid: 05.05.94. Coming into force: 03.06.94. Effect: S.I. 1993/2172 revoked. Territorial extent & classification: E. General. – 2p. – 0 11 044190 7 £0.65

Price/availability are liable to change without notice

The Public Telecommunication System Designation (Comment Cablevision Wearside Partnership) Order 1994 No. 2654. Enabling power: *Telecommunications Act 1984, s. 9.* Issued: 24.10.94. Made: 10.10.94. Laid: 17.10.94. Coming into force: 15.11.94. Effect: None. Territorial extent & classification: E/W. General. – 2p. – 0 11 045654 8 £0.65

The Public Telecommunication System Designation (Comment Cablevision Worcester Limited) Order 1994 No. 952. Enabling power: *Telecommunications Act 1984, s. 9.* Issued: 11.04.94. Made: 24.03.94. Laid: 30.03.94. Coming into force: 28.04.94. Effect: None. Territorial extent & classification: E. General. – 2p. – 0 11 043952 X £0.65

The Public Telecommunication System Designation (Encom Cable TV & Telecommunications Limited) (Dartford) Order 1994 No. 874. Enabling power: *Telecommunications Act 1984, s. 9.* Issued: 05.04.94. Made: 22.03.94. Laid: 28.03.94. Coming into force: 25.04.94. Effect: None. Territorial extent & classification: E. General. – 2p. – 0 11 043874 4 £0.65

The Public Telecommunication System Designation (Encom Cable TV & Telecommunications Limited) (Epping Forest) Order 1994 No. 875. Enabling power: *Telecommunications Act 1984, s. 9.* Issued: 05.04.94. Made: 22.03.94. Laid: 28.03.94. Coming into force: 25.04.94. Effect: None. Territorial extent & classification: E. General. – 2p. – 0 11 043875 2 £0.65

The Public Telecommunication System Designation (Insight Communications Cardiff Limited) Order 1994 No. 1007. Enabling power: *Telecommunications Act 1994, s. 9.* Issued: 22.04.94. Made: 28.03.94. Laid: 14.04.94. Coming into force: 13.05.94. Effect: S.I. 1991/172 revoked. Territorial extent & classification: E. General. – 2p. – 0 11 044007 2 £0.65

The Public Telecommunication System Designation (Insight Communications Guildford Limited) Order 1994 No. 1006. Enabling power: *Telecommunications Act 1984, s. 9.* Issued: 19.03.94. Made: 28.03.94. Laid: 12.04.94. Coming into force: 11.05.94. Effect: S.I. 1987/827 revoked. Territorial extent & classification: E. General. – 2p. – 0 11 044006 4 £0.65

The Public Telecommunication System Designation (NORWEB plc) Order 1994 No. 1008. Enabling power: *Telecommunications Act 1994, s. 9.* Issued: 22.04.94. Made: 28.03.94. Laid: 14.04.94. Coming into force: 13.05.94. Effect: None. Territorial extent & classification: E. General. – 2p. – 0 11 044008 0 £0.65

The Public Telecommunication System Designation (NYNEX CableComms Bury and Rochdale) Order 1994 No. 234. Enabling power: *Telecommunications Act 1984, s. 9.* Issued: 14.02.94. Made: 02.02.94. Laid: 07.02.94. Coming into force: 07.03.94. Effect: None. Territorial extent & classification: E. General. – 2p. – 0 11 043234 7 £0.65

The Public Telecommunication System Designation (NYNEX CableComms Oldham and Tameside) Order 1994 No. 876. Enabling power: *Telecommunications Act 1984, s. 9.* Issued: 05.04.94. Made: 22.03.94. Laid: 28.03.94. Coming into force: 25.04.94. Effect: None. Territorial extent & classification: E. General. – 2p. – 0 11 043876 0 £0.65

The Public Telecommunication System Designation (NYNEX CableComms Wessex) Order 1994 No.1071. Enabling power: *Telecommunications Act 1984, s. 9.* Issued: 28.04.94. Made: 14.04.94. Laid: 20.04.94. Coming into force: 19.05.94. Effect: None. Territorial extent & classification: E. General. – 2p. – 0 11 044071 4 £0.65

The Public Telecommunication System Designation (Racal Network Services Limited) Order 1994 No. 2655. Enabling power: *Telecommunications Act 1984, s. 9.* Issued: 24.10.94. Made: 10.10.94. Laid: 17.10.94. Coming into force: 15.11.94. Effect: None. Territorial extent & classification: E/W. General. – 2p. – 0 11 045655 6 £0.65

The Public Telecommunication System Designation (Sprint Holding (UK) Limited) Order 1994 No.1202. Enabling power: *Telecommunications Act 1984, s. 9.* Issued: 13.05.94. Made: 28.04.94. Laid: 05.05.94. Coming into force: 03.06.94. Effect: None. Territorial extent & classification: GB. General. – 2p. – 0 11 044202 4 £0.65

The Public Telecommunication System Designation (Telecom Securicor Cellular Radio Limited) Order 1994 No. 954. Enabling power: *Telecommunications Act 1984, s. 9.* Issued: 18.04.94. Made: 24.03.94. Laid: 30.03.94. Coming into force: 28.04.94. Effect: None. Territorial extent & classification: E. General. – 2p. – 0 11 043954 6 £0.65

The Public Telecommunication System Designation (Telstra (UK) Limited) Order 1994 No.1204. Enabling power: *Telecommunications Act 1984, s. 9.* Issued: 17.05.94. Made: 28.04.94. Laid: 09.05.94. Coming into force: 07.06.94. Effect: None. Territorial extent & classification: GB. General. – 2p. – 0 11 044204 0 £0.65

The Public Telecommunication System Designation (United Artists Communications) (London South) PLC) Order 1994 No. 1072. Enabling power: *Telecommunications Act 1984, s. 9.* Issued: 27.04.94. Made: 14.04.94. Laid: 19.04.94. Coming into force: 18.05.94. Effect: None. Territorial extent & classification: E. General. – 2p. – 0 11 044072 2 £0.65

The Public Telecommunication System Designation (Videotron City and Westminster Limited) Order 1994 No. 953. Enabling power: *Telecommunications Act 1984, s. 9.* Issued: 11.04.94. Made: 24.03.94. Laid: 30.03.94. Coming into force: 28.04.94. Effect: None. Territorial extent & classification: E. General. – 2p. – 0 11 043953 8 £0.65

The Public Telecommunication System Designation (Vodafone Limited) Order 1994 No.1. Enabling power: *Telecommunications Act 1984, s. 9.* Issued: 20.01.94. Made: 01.01.94. Laid: 11.01.94. Coming into force: 09.02.94. Effect: None. Territorial extent & classification: GB. General. – 2p. – 0 11 043001 8 £0.65

Price/availability are liable to change without notice

The Public Telecommunication System Designation (WORLDCOM INTERNATIONAL, INC) Order 1994 No.1203. Enabling power: *Telecommunications Act 1984, s. 9*. Issued: 18.05.94. Made: 28.04.94. Laid: 10.05.94. Coming into force: 08.06.94. Effect: None. Territorial extent & classification: GB. General. – 2p. – 0 11 044203 2 £0.65

The Telecommunications Act 1984 (Government Shareholding) Order 1994 No. 744. Enabling power: *Telecommunications Act 1984, s. 65 (4)*. Issued: 23.03.94. Made: 14.03.94. Laid: 15.03.94. Coming into force: 05.04.94. Effect: S.I. 1992/631 revoked. Territorial extent & classification: GB. General. – 2p. – 0 11 043744 6 £0.65

The Telecommunications (Leased Lines) (Amendment) Regulations 1994 No. 2251. Enabling power: *European Communities Act 1972, s. 2 (2)*. Issued: 14.09.94. Made: 31.08.94. Laid: 07.09.94. Coming into force: 01.10.94. Effect: S.I. 1993/2330 amended. Territorial extent & classification: GB. General. – 4p. – 0 11 045251 8 £1.10

The Telecommunications Meters (Approval Fees) (BABT) (Amendment) Order 1994 No. 3163. Enabling power: *Telecommunications Act 1984, s. 24 (13)*. Issued: 20.12.94. Made: 12.12.94. Laid: 13.12.94. Coming into force: 03.01.95. Effect: S.I. 1992/712 amended. Territorial extent & classification: GB. General. – 4p. – 0 11 043475 7 £1.10

The Telecommunications Terminal Equipment (Amendment and Extension) Regulations 1994 No.3129. Enabling power: *European Communities Act 1972, s. 2 (2)*. Issued: 09.01.95. Made: 07.12.94. Laid: 08.12.94. Coming into force: 01.01.95. for pts. I, II, III; 01.05.95. for part IV. Effect: S.I. 1985/718; 1992/2423 amended. Territorial extent & classification: GB. General. – Amends provisions derived from DIR 91/263 & implements provisions of DIR 93/68, DIR 91/263, DIR 89/336. – 16p.; ill. – 0 11 043870 1 £3.20 Replaced by ISBN 0110523962

The Wireless Telegraphy (Guernsey) Order 1994 No. 1064. Enabling power: *Wireless Telegraphy Act 1949, s. 20 (3), & Marine, etc., Broadcasting (Offences) Act 1967, s. 10, & Telecommunications Act 1984, s. 108, & Broadcasting Act 1990, s. 204 (6)*. Issued: 25.04.94. Made: 13.04.94. Coming into force: 01.06.94. Effect: S.I. 1991/1709 amended. Territorial extent & classification: Guernsey. General. – 6p. – 0 11 044064 1 £1.55

The Wireless Telegraphy (Short Range Devices) (Exemption) (Amendment) Regulations 1994 No.2250. Enabling power: *Wireless Telegraphy Act 1949, s. 1 (1), 3 (1) (a) (b) & Telecommunications Act 1984, s. 84 (1) (b)*. Issued: 14.09.94. Made: 31.08.94. Laid: 07.09.94. Coming into force: 01.10.94. Effect: S.I. 1993/1591 amended. Territorial extent & classification: GB. General. – 4p. – 0 11 045250 X £1.10

TELEGRAPHS

The Wireless Telegraphy (Guernsey) Order 1994 No. 1064. Enabling power: *Wireless Telegraphy Act 1949, s. 20 (3), & Marine, etc., Broadcasting (Offences) Act 1967, s. 10, & Telecommunications Act 1984, s. 108, & Broadcasting Act 1990, s. 204 (6)*. Issued: 25.04.94. Made: 13.04.94. Coming into force: 01.06.94. Effect: S.I. 1991/1709 amended. Territorial extent & classification: Guernsey. General. – 6p. – 0 11 044064 1 £1.55

The Wireless Telegraphy (Licence Charges) (Amendment) Regulations 1994 No. 659. Enabling power: *Wireless Telegraphy Act 1949, s. 2 (1)*. Issued: 29.03.94. Made: 08.03.94. Laid: 10.03.94. Coming into force: 01.04.94. Effect: S.I. 1991/542 amended. Territorial extent & classification: GB/IOM/CI. General. – 16p. – 0 11 043659 8 £3.20

The Wireless Telegraphy (Television Licence Fees) (Amendment) Regulations 1994 No.595. Enabling power: *Wireless Telegraphy Act 1949, s. 2*. Issued: 15.03.94. Made: 04.03.94. Laid: 08.03.94. Coming into force: 01.04.94. Effect: S.I. 1991/436 amended. Territorial extent & classification: UK/CI/IOM. General. – 4p. – 0 11 043595 8 £1.10

TERMS AND CONDITIONS OF EMPLOYMENT

The Guarantee Payments (Exemption) (No. 29) Order 1994 No. 1409. Enabling power: *Employment Protection (Consolidation) Act 1978, s. 18 (1) (5)*. Issued: 06.06.94. Made: 23.05.94. Coming into force: 01.07.94. Effect: S.I. 1977/158 revoked. Territorial extent & classification: E/W/S. General. – 4p. – 0 11 044409 4 £1.10

The Maternity Allowance and Statutory Maternity Pay Regulations 1994 No. 1230. Enabling power: *European Communities Act 1972, s. 2 (2)*. Issued: 11.05.94. Made: 04.05.94. Laid: 24.03.94. Coming into force: 04.09.94. for reg. 5; 16.10.94. for all others Effect: 1992 c.4. amended. Supersedes Draft ISBN 0110458931 previously published on 24.03.94. Territorial extent & classification: E/W/S. Local. – 4p. – 0 11 044230 X £1.10

The Maternity (Compulsory Leave) Regulations 1994 No. 2479. Enabling power: *European Communities Act 1972, s. 2 (2)*. Issued: 28.09.94. Made: 21.09.94. Laid: 28.09.94. Coming into force: 19.10.94. Effect: None. Territorial extent & classification: E/W/S. General. – 2p. – 0 11 045479 0 £0.65

The Redundancy Payments (Local Government) (Modification) (Amendment) Order 1994 No.417. Enabling power: *Employment Protection (Consolidation) Act 1978, ss. 149 (1) (b), 154 (3) (4)*. Issued: 04.03.94. Made: 23.02.94. Laid: 04.03.94. Coming into force: 01.04.94. Effect: S.I. 1983/1160 amended. Territorial extent & classification: E/W/S. General. – 2p. – 0 11 043417 X £0.65

The Social Security Benefits Up-rating Order 1994 No. 542. Enabling power: *Social Security Administration Act 1992, ss. 150, 189 (1) (3) (4)*. Issued: 14.03.94. Made: 03.03.94. Laid: 10.02.94. Coming into force: 01.04.94, 03.04.94, 06.04.94, 11.12.94, 12.04.94. Effect: 1965 c. 51; 1992 c. 4,, 5; 1993 c. 48; S.I. 1976/1267; 1978/393; 1986/1960; 1987/1967, 1969, 1971, 1973; 1991/2887, 2890; 1992/1814 amended & S.I. 1993/349 revoked. Supersedes Draft ISBN 0110458710 Territorial extent & classification: E/W/S. General. – 38p. – 0 11 043542 7 £6.10

Price/availability are liable to change without notice

The Social Security Maternity Benefits and Statutory Sick Pay (Amendment) Regulations 1994 No. 1367. Enabling power: *Social Security and Contributions Benefits Act 1992, ss. 35 (3) (b) (i) (c), 119, 153 (6), 164 (4) (9) (e), 165 (1) (3), 166 (3), 171 (1), 175 (1) to (4), sch. 11, para. 1.* Issued: 26.05.94. Made: 19.05.94. Laid: 20.05.94. Coming into force: 11.06.94. Effect: S.I. 1982/894; 1986/1960; 1987/416, 417 amended. Territorial extent & classification: E/W/S. General. – 6p. – 0 11 044367 5 £1.55

The Statutory Maternity Pay (Compensation of Employers) Amendment Regulations 1994 No.592. Enabling power: *Social Security Contributions and Benefits Act 1992, ss. 167 (1) (c), 171 (1), 175 (1) to (3).* Issued: 14.03.94. Made: 08.03.94. Laid: 14.03.94. Coming into force: 06.04.94. Effect: S.I. 1987/91 amended. Territorial extent & classification: E/W/S. General. –2p. – 0 11 043592 3 £0.65

The Statutory Maternity Pay (Compensation of Employers) and Miscellaneous Amendment Regulations 1994 No. 1882. Enabling power: *Social Security Contributions and Benefits Act 1992, ss. 35 (3), 167 (1) (1A) (1B) (4), 171 (1), 175 (1) to (4).* Issued: 21.07.94. Made: 14.07.94. Laid: 15.07.94. Coming into force: 31.07.94. for regs. 1 & 9; 04.09.94.for regs. 2 to 8. Effect: S.I. 1987/416 amended & S.I. 1987/91 revoked. Territorial extent & classification: E/W/S. General. – 4p. – 0 11 044882 0 £1.10

The Statutory Sick Pay Act 1994 (Consequential) Regulations 1994 No. 730. Enabling power: *Social Security Contributions and Benefits Act 1992, ss. 158 (1), 163 (1) & Social Security Administration Act 1992, ss. 81 (1), 191 & Statutory Sick Pay Act 1994, s. 2.* Issued: 25.03.94. Made: 14.03.94. Laid: 15.03.94. Coming into force: 06.04.94. Effect: S.I. 1983/376; 1990/322 amended. Territorial extent & classification: E/W/S. General. – 4p. – 0 11 043730 6 £1.10

The Statutory Sick Pay (Rate of Payment) Order 1994 No. 562. Enabling power: *Social Security Contributions and Benefits Act 1992, ss. 157 (2), 175 (1) (3) (4).* Issued: 14.03.94. Made: 07.03.94. Laid: 10.02.94. Coming into force: 06.04.94. Effect: 1992 c. 4; S.I. 1993/350 amended & S.I. 1991/506 revoked. Supersedes Draft ISBN 011045880X published on 15.02.94. Territorial extent & classification: E/W/S. General. – 2p. – 0 11 043562 1 £0.65

The Statutory Sick Pay (Small Employers' Relief) Amendment Regulations 1994 No. 561. Enabling power: *Social Security Contributions and Benefits Act 1992, ss. 158 (2) (3), 163 (1), 175 (1).* Issued: 14.03.94. Made: 07.03.94. Laid: 10.02.94. Coming into force: 06.04.94. Effect: S.I. 1991/428 amended. Supersedes Draft ISBN 0110458796 published on 15.02.94. Territorial extent & classifcation: E/W/S. General. – 2p. – 0 11 043561 3 £0.65

The Suspension from Work (on Maternity Grounds) Order 1994 No. 2930. Enabling power: *Employment Protection (Consolidation) Act 1978, s. 45 (3).* Issued: 25.11.94. Made: 21.11.94. Laid: 21.11.94. Coming into force: 01.12.94. Effect: None. Territorial extent & classification: E/W/S. General. – Gives effect, in GB, DIR 92/85 arts. 5 (2), 7 (2).(OJ L 348/92). – 2p. – 0 11 043139 1 £0.65

The Trade Union Reform and Employment Rights Act 1993 (Commencement No. 3 and Transitional Provisions) Order 1994 No. 1365 (C.23). Enabling power: *Trade Union Reform and Employment Rights Act 1993, s. 52, sch. 9, para . 1.* Bringing into operation various provisions of the 1993 act on 10.06.94. Issued: 25.05.94. Made: 19.05.94. Effect: None. Territorial extent & classification: E/W/S. General. – 2p. – 0 11 044365 9 £0.65

TOWN AND COUNTRY PLANNING, ENGLAND AND WALES

The Ecclesiastical Exemption (Listed Buildings and Conservation Areas) Order 1994 No.1771. Enabling power: *Planning (Listed Buildings and Conservation Areas) Act 1990, ss. 60 (5) (6), 75 (7) (8), 93 (6).* Issued: 15.07.94. Made: 30.06.94. Laid: 15.07.94. Coming into force: 01.10.94. Effect: None. Territorial extent & classification: E/W. General. – 6p. – 0 11 044771 9 £1.55

The Town and Country Planning (Assessment of Environmental Effects) (Amendment) Regulations 1994 No. 677. Enabling power: *European Communities Act 1972, s. 2 (2) & Town & Country Planning Act 1990, s. 71A.* Issued: 18.03.94. Made: 09.03.94. Laid: 18.03.94. Coming into force: 08.04.94. Effect: S.I. 1988/1199 amended. Territorial extent & classification: E/W. General. – 4p. – 0 11 043677 6 £1.10

The Town and Country Planning (Control of Advertisements) (Amendment) Regulations 1994 No.2351. Enabling power: *Town and Country Planning Act 1990, ss. 220, 221, 333 (1).* Issued: 16.09.94. Made: 07.09.94. Laid: 09.09.94. Coming into force: 01.10.94. Effect: S.I. 1992/666 amended. Territorial extent & classification: E/W. General. – 4p. – 0 11 045351 4 £1.10

The Town and Country Planning General Development (Amendment) Order 1994 No. 678. Enabling power: *Town & Country Planning Act 1990, ss. 59, 60, 61 (1), 65, 74 (1), 333 (7).* Issued: 18.03.94. Made: 09.03.94. Laid: 18.03.94. Coming into force: 08.04.94. Effect: S.I. 1988/1813 amended. Territorial extent & classification: E/W. General. – 4p. – 0 11 043678 4 £1.10

The Town and Country Planning General Development (Amendment) (No. 2) Order 1994 No.2595. Enabling power: *Town and Country Planning Act 1990, ss. 59, 60, 61 (1), 65, 74, 333 (7) & Coal Industry Act 1994, s. 54.* Issued: 17.10.94. Made: 06.10.94. Laid: 10.10.94. Coming into force: 31.10.94. Effect: S.I. 1988/1813 amended. Territorial extent & classification: E/W. General. – 6p. – 0 11 045595 9 £1.55

The Town and Country Planning (Simplified Planning Zones) (Amendment) Regulations 1994 No.267. Enabling power: *Town and Country Planning Act 1990, ss. 333 (1), 336 (1), sch. 7, paras. 5 (2), 13.* Issued: 15.02.94. Made: 04.02.94. Laid: 15.02.94. Coming into force: 08.03.94. Effect: S.I. 1992/2414 amended. Territorial extent & classification: E/W. General. – 2p. – 0 11 043267 3 £0.65

The Town and Country Planning (Use Classes) (Amendment) Order 1994 No. 724. Enabling power: *Town and Country Planning Act 1990, ss. 55 (2) (f), 333 (7).* Issued: 18.03.94. Made: 14.03.94. Coming into force: 04.04.94. Effect: S.I. 1987/764 amended. Territorial extent & classification: E/W. General. – 2p. – 0 11 043724 1 £0.65

Price/availability are liable to change without notice

TOWN AND COUNTRY PLANNING, SCOTLAND

The Environmental Assessment (Scotland) Amendment Regulations 1994 No. 2012 (S. 91). Enabling power: *European Communities Act 1972, s. 2 (2) & Town and Country Planning (Scotland) Act 1972, s. 26B.* Issued: 09.08.94. Made: 19.07.94. Laid: 29.07.94. Coming into force: 19.08.94. Effect: S.I. 1988/1221; 1984 c. 54 amended. Territorial extent & classification: S. General. – 8p. – 0 11 045012 4 *£1.95*

The Planning and Compensation Act 1991 (Commencement No. 16) (Scotland) Order 1994 No.398 (C. 8) (S. 14). Enabling power: *Planning and Compensation Act 1991, s. 84 (2). Bringing into operation various provisions of this act on 07.03.94.* Issued: 04.03.94. Made: 21.02.94. Effect: None. Territorial extent & classification: S. General. – 6p. – 0 11 043398 X *£1.55*

The Planning and Compensation Act 1991 (Commencement No. 17 and Transitional Provision) (Scotland) Order 1994 No. 3292 (C. 84) (S. 191). Enabling power: *Planning and Compensation Act 1991, s. 84 (2) (3). Bringing into operation various provisions of the 1991 act on 03.02.95.* Issued: 11.01.95. Made: 15.12.94. Effect: None. With correction slip, dated February 1995 (issued 22nd February) substituting (C. 84) for (C. 83) in the SI number. Territorial extent & classification: S. General. – 6p. – 0 11 043842 6 *£1.55*

The Town and Country Planning (Fees for Applications and Deemed Applications) (Scotland) Amendment Regulations 1994 No. 3269 (S. 189). Enabling power: *Local Government, Planning and Land Act 1980, s. 87.* Issued: 10.01.95. Made: 16.12.94. Laid: 16.11.94. Coming into force: 03.01.95. Effect: S.I. 1990/563; 1993/3211 amended. Territorial extent & classification: S. General. – 8p. – 0 11 043815 9 *£1.95*

The Town and Country Planning (General Development Procedures) (Scotland) Amendment Order 1994 No. 2585 (S. 121). Enabling power: *Town and Country Planning (Scotland) Act 1972, ss. 28 (1) (c), 273 (3).* Issued: 14.10.94. Made: 05.10.94. Laid: 10.10.94. Coming into force: 31.10.94. Effect: S.I. 1992/224 amended. Territorial extent & classification: S. General. –2p. – 0 11 045585 1 *£0.65*

The Town and Country Planning (General Development Procedure) (Scotland) Amendment (No. 2) Order 1994 No. 3293 (S. 192). Enabling power: *Town and Country Planning (Scotland) Act 1972, ss. 21 (1) (2) (3), 22 (1) (b) (c) (2), 24 (1) (2) (3) (7), 26 (3) (3A), 28 (1) (c) (d) (dd), 32 (4), 33 (2) (5), 34, 273 (3).* Issued: 11.01.95. Made: 15.12.94. Laid: 29.12.94. Coming into force: 03.02.95. Effect: S.I. 1992/224 amended. Territorial extent & classification: S. General. – 16p. – 0 11 043841 8 *£3.20*

The Town and Country Planning (General Permitted Development) (Scotland) Amendment (No. 2) Order 1994 No. 2586 (S. 122). Enabling power: *Town and Country Planning (Scotland) Act 1972, ss. 21, 273 (3) & Coal Industry Act 1994, s. 54.* Issued: 14.10.94. Made: 05.10.94. Laid: 10.10.94. Coming into force: 31.10.94. Effect: S.I. 1992/223 amended. Territorial extent & classification: S. General. – 6p. – 0 11 045586 X *£1.55*

The Town and Country Planning (General Permitted Development) (Scotland) Amendment (No. 3) Order 1994 No. 3294 (S. 193). Enabling power: *Town and Country Planning (Scotland) Act 1972, ss. 21, 273.* Issued: 11.01.95. Made: 15.12.94. Laid: 29.12.94. Coming into force: 03.02.95. Effect: S.I. 1992/223 amended. Territorial extent & classification: S. General. – 8p. – 0 11 043839 6 *£1.95*

The Town and Country Planning (General Permitted Development) (Scotland) Amendment Order 1994 No. 1442 (S. 68). Enabling power: *Town and Country Planning (Scotland) Act 1972, ss. 21 and 273 (3).* Issued: 08.06.94. Made: 24.05.94. Laid: 08.06.94. Coming into force: 29.06.94. Effect: S.I. 1992/223 amended. Territorial extent & classification: S. General. – 4p. – 0 11 044442 6 *£1.10*

TRADE DESCRIPTIONS

The Textile Products (Indications of Fibre Content) (Amendment) Regulations 1994 No.450. Enabling power: *European Communities Act 1972, s. 2 (2).* Issued: 16.03.94. Made: 25.02.94. Laid: 28.02.94. Coming into force: 01.06.94. Effect: S.I. 1986/26 amended. Territorial extent & classification: GB. General. – 2p. – 0 11 043450 1 *£0.65*

TRADE MARKS

The Registered Trade Mark Agents (Mixed Partnerships and Bodies Corporate) Rules 1994 No.363. Enabling power: *Copyright, Designs and Patents Act 1988, s. 283 (4).* Issued: 10.03.94. Made: 17.02.94. Laid: 03.03.94. Coming into force: 24.03.94. Effect: None. Territorial extent & classification: GB. General. – 2p. – 0 11 043363 7 *£0.65*

The Trade Marks Act 1994 (Commencement) Order 1994 No. 2550 (C. 52). Enabling power: *Trade Marks Act 1994, s. 109. Bringing into operation various provisions of the 1994 act on 31.10.94.* Issued: 11.10.94. Made: 29.09.94. Effect: None. Territorial extent & classification: GB/IOM. General. – 4p. – 0 11 045550 9 *£1.10*

The Trade Marks and Service Marks (Amendment) Rules 1994 No. 2549. Enabling power: *Trade Marks Act 1938, ss. 40, 68 (1).* Issued: 11.10.94. Made: 29.09.94. Laid: 04.10.94. Coming into force: 28.10.94. Effect: S.I. 1986/1319 amended. Territorial extent & classification: GB/IOM. General. – 2p. – 0 11 045549 5 *£0.65*

The Trade Marks and Service Marks (Fees) (Amendment) Rules 1994 No. 2581. Enabling power: *Trade Marks Act 1938, ss. 40, 41, 68 (1).* Issued: 14.10.94. Made: 05.10.94. Laid: 07.10.94. Coming into force: 28.10.94. Effect: S.I. 1992/1069 amended. Territorial extent & classification: GB/IOM. General. – 2p. – 0 11 045581 9 *£0.65*

The Trade Marks and Service Marks (Forms) (Amendment) Rules 1994 No. 2551. Enabling power: *Trade Marks Act 1938, ss. 40, 68 (1).* Issued: 11.10.94. Made: 29.09.94. Laid: 04.10.94. Coming into force: 28.10.94. Effect: S.I. 1986/1367 amended. Territorial extent & classification: GB/IOM. General. – 2p. – 0 11 045551 7 *£0.65*

Price/availability are liable to change without notice

The Trade Marks and Service Marks (Forms) (Revocation) Rules 1994 No. 2582.Enabling power: *Trade Marks Act 1938, ss. 40, 68 (1)*. Issued: 17.10.94. Made: 05.10.94. Laid: 07.10.94. Coming into force: 31.10.94. Effect: S.I. 1986/1367; 1988/1112; 1990/1811; 1994/2551 revoked. With correction slip dated November 1994. Territorial extent & classification: GB/IOM. General. – 2p. – 0 11 045582 7 *£0.65*

The Trade Marks (Claims to Priority from Relevant Countries) Order 1994 No. 2803. Enabling power: *Trade Marks Act 1994, s. 36 (1) (2)*. Issued: 14.11.94. Made: 02.11.94. Laid: 14.11.94. Coming into force: 05.12.94. Effect: None. Territorial extent & classification: GB/IOM. General. – 4p. – 0 11 045803 6 *£1.10*

The Trade Marks (Customs) Regulations 1994 No. 2625. Enabling power: *Trade Marks Act 1994, s. 90 (1) (2) (3)*. Issued: 27.10.94. Made: 11.10.94. Laid: 11.10.94. Coming into force: 31.10.94. Effect: S.I. 1970/212 revoked. Territorial extent & classification: GB. General. – 4p. – 0 11 045625 4 *£1.10*

The Trade Marks (Fees) Rules 1994 No. 2584. Enabling power: *Trade Marks Act 1994, s. 79*. Issued: 17.10.94. Made: 05.10.94. Laid: 07.10.94. Coming into force: 31.10.94. Effect: S.I. 1992/1069; 1993/3029; 1994/2581 revoked. Territorial extent & classification: GB/IOM. General. – 4p. – 0 11 045584 3 *£1.10*

The Trade Marks Rules 1994 No. 2583. Enabling power: *Trade Marks Act 1994, ss. 4 (4), 13 (2), 25 (1), (5) (6), 34 (1), 35 (5), 38 (1) (2), 39 (3), 40 (4), 41 (1) (3), 43 (2) (3) (5) (6), 44 (3), 45 (2), 63 (2) (3), 64 (4), 65, 66 (2), 67 (1) (2), 68 (1) (3), 69, 76 (1), 78, 80 (3), 81, 82, 88, sch. 1, para. 6 (2), sch. 2, para. 7 (2), sch. 3, paras. 10 (2), 11 (2), 12, 14 (5)*. Issued: 18.10.94. Made: 05.10.94. Laid: 07.10.94. Coming into force: 31.10.94. Effect: S.I. 1986/1319; 1988/1112; 1989/1117; 1990/1459, 1799; 1991/1431; 1994/2549 revoked. Territorial extent & classification: GB. General. – 26p. – 0 11 045583 5 *£4.70*

TRADE UNIONS

The Certification Officer (Amendment of Fees) Regulations 1994 No. 546. Enabling power: *Trade Union and Labour Relations (Consolidation) Act 1992, ss. 108, 293*. Issued: 10.03.94. Made: 02.03.94. Laid: 10.03.94. Coming into force: 01.04.94. Effect: SS.I. 1975/536 amended & .I. 1993/936 revoked. Territorial extent & classification: E/W/S. General. – 4p. – 0 11 043546 X *£1.10*

The Trade Union Reform and Employment Rights Act 1993 (Commencement No. 3 and Transitional Provisions) Order 1994 No. 1365 (C.23). Enabling power: *Trade Union Reform and Employment Rights Act 1993, s. 52, sch. 9, para . 1. Bringing into operation various provisions of the 1993 act on 10.06.94*. Issued: 25.05.94. Made: 19.05.94. Effect: None. Territorial extent & classification: E/W/S. General. – 2p. – 0 11 044365 9 *£0.65*

TRANSPORT

The Bowes Extension Light Railway Order 1994 No. 691. Enabling power: *Light Railways Act 1896, ss. 3, 7, 9, 10, 11, 12*. Issued: 17.03.94. Made: 03.03.94. Coming into force: 04.03.94. Effect: None. With correction slip dated June 1994 Territorial extent & classification: E. Local. – 4p. – 0 11 043691 1 *£1.10*

The British Railways Act 1990 (Arpley Chord) (Extension of Time) Order 1994 No. 1039. Enabling power: *Transport and Works Act 1992, s. 1, 5*. Issued: 15.04.94. Made: 30.03.94. Coming into force: 20.04.94. Effect: 1990 c. 42 amended. Territorial extent & classification: E. General. – 2p. – 0 11 044039 0 *£0.65*

The British Transport Police Force Scheme 1963 (Amendment) Order 1994 No. 609.Enabling power: *Railways Act 1993, ss. 143 (3) (4), sch. 10, para. 3 (2)*. Issued: 22.04.94. Made: 08.03.94. Laid: 08.03.94. Coming into force: 01.04.94. Effect: S.I. 1964/1456 amended. Territorial extent & classification: E/W/S. General. – 8p. – 0 11 043609 1 *£1.95*

The Chappel and Wakes Colne Light Railway Order 1994 No. 84. Enabling power: *Light Railways Act 1896, ss. 7, 9 to 12, 18*. Issued: 26.01.94. Made: 05.01.94. Coming into force: 06.01.94. Effect: None. Territorial extent & classification: E. Local. – 4p. – 0 11 043084 0 *£1.10*

The Chinnor and Princes Risborough Railway Order 1994 No. 1803. Enabling power: *Transport and Works Act 1992, ss. 1, 5 & Transport Act 1968, s. 121 (2)*. Issued: 14.07.94. Made: 04.07.94. Coming into force: 26.07.94. Effect: None. Territorial extent & classification: E. General. – 6p. – 0 11 044803 0 *£1.55*

The Greater Manchester (Light Rapid Transit System) (Modification) Order 1994 No.701. Enabling power: *Transport and Works Act 1992, s. 1*. Issued: 18.03.94. Made: 07.03.94. Coming into force: 28.03.94. Effect: None. Territorial extent & classification: E. General. – 2p. – 0 11 043701 2 *£0.65*

The International Transport Conventions Act 1983 (Amendment) Order 1994 No. 1907. Enabling power: *International Transport Conventions Act 1983, s. 8 (1)*. Issued: 29.07.94. Made: 19.07.94. Laid: 26.01.94. Coming into force: In accord. with art. 1. Effect: 1983 c. 14 amended. Supersedes Draft ISBN 0 11 045860 5 published 26.01.94. Territorial extent & classification: GB. General. – 2p. – 0 11 044907 X *£0.65*

The Lydney and Parkend Light Railway (Extension and Amendment) Order 1994 No. 1331. Enabling power: *Light Railways Act 1896, ss. 7, 9, 10, 11, 12, 18, 24*. Issued: 25.05.94. Made: 13.05.94. Coming into force: 14.05.94. Effect: S.I. 1985/844 amended. Territorial extent & classification: E. Local. – 12p. – 0 11 044331 4 *£2.80*

The Railtrack (Marsh Lane, Leeds, Footbridge) Order 1994 No. 1532. Enabling power: *Transport and Works Act 1992, s. 1, 5*. Issued: 17.06.94. Made: 01.06.94. Coming into force: 22.06.94. Effect: 1857 c. xlvi amended. Territorial extent & classification: E. Local. – 2p. – 0 11 044532 5 *£0.65*

The Railway Heritage Scheme Order 1994 No. 2032. Enabling power: *Railways Act 1993, s. 125 (1) (4) (8)*. Issued: 10.08.94. Made: 01.08.94. Laid: 10.08.94. Coming into force: 01.09.94. Effect: None. Territorial extent & classification: E/W/S. General. – 4p. – 0 11 045032 9 *£1.10*

Price/availability are liable to change without notice

The Railway Pensions (Protection and Designation of Schemes) Order 1994 No. 1432. Enabling power: *Railways Act 1993, s. 143 (3) (4), sch. 11, paras. 1 (1), 5 (b) (iii), 6 (1) (2) (4) (b) (6) (8) (9), 7 (1) (3), 8 (1) (2) (b) (iii) (6) to (11)*. Issued: 06.06.94. Made: 27.05.94. Laid: 10.05.94. Coming into force: 31.05.94. Effect: None. Supersedes Draft ISBN 0110459075 previously published on 20.05.94. Territorial extent & classification: GB. General. – 16p. – 0 11 044432 9 *£3.20*

The Railway Pensions (Substitution) Order 1994 No. 2388. Enabling power: *Transport Act 1980, ss. 52B, 52D (4) (5)*. Issued: 10.10.94. Made: 12.09.94. Laid: 12.09.94. Coming into force: 13.09.94. Effect: None. Territorial extent & classification: GB. General. – 16p. – 0 11 045388 3 *£3.20*

The Railway Pensions (Transfer and Miscellaneous Provisions) Order 1994 No. 2005. Enabling power: *Railways Act 1993, s. 143 (3) (4), sch. 11, paras. 2 to 4, 6 to 8, 10, 12*. Issued: 02.08.94. Made: 28.07.94. Laid: 07.07.94. Coming into force: 01.08.94. for arts 1, 3 to 5; 01.10.94. for arts 2 (1) to (10), 6, 7,; 02.10.94. for art 2 (11). Effect: S.I. 1964/1329; 1969/1824; 1994/1432, 1433 & the Trust Deed of the B.R. (1974) Pensions Fund; 1986 c.xxvi amended. Supersedes Draft ISBN 0110459423 published 14.07.94. Territorial extent & classification: GB. General. – 24p. – 0 11 045005 1 *£4.15*

The Railways Act 1993 (Commencement No. 2) Order 1994 No. 202 (C. 6). Enabling power: *Railways Act 1993, s. 154 (2)*. Bringing into operation various provisions of the 1993 act on 02.02.94. Issued: 09.02.94. Made: 01.02.94. Effect: None. Territorial extent & classification: GB. General. – 2p. – 0 11 043202 9 *£0.65*

The Railways Act 1993 (Commencement No. 3) Order 1994 No. 447 (C. 9). Enabling power: *Railways Act 1993, s. 154 (2)*. Bringing into operation various provisions of this act on 22.02.94. Issued: 04.03.94. Made: 21.02.94. Effect: None. Territorial extent & classification: E/W/S. General. – 2p. – 0 11 043447 1 *£0.65*

The Railways Act 1993 (Commencement No. 4 and Transitional Provision) Order 1994 No. 571 (C. 11). Enabling power: *Railways Act 1993, ss. 143 (3), 154 (2)*. Bringing into operation various provisions of this act on 08.03.94. Issued: 22.04.94. Made: 07.03.94. Effect: None. Territorial extent & classification: GB. General. – 4p. – 0 11 043571 0 *£1.10*

The Railways Act 1993 (Commencement No. 5 and Transitional Provisions) Order 1994 No. 1648 (C. 29). Enabling power: *Railways Act 1993, ss. 143 (3), 154 (2)*. Bringing various provisions of the 1993 act into operation on 15.07.94. Issued: 29.06.94. Made: 22.06.94. Effect: None. Territorial extent & classification: E/W/S. General. – 4p. – 0 11 044648 8 *£1.10*

The Railways Act 1993 (Commencement No. 6) Order 1994 No. 2142 (C. 42). Enabling power: *Railways Act 1993, s. 154 (2)*. Bringing into operation various provisions of the 1993 act on 16.08.94. Issued: 22.08.94. Made: 15.08.94. Effect: None. Territorial extent & classification: GB. General. – 4p. – 0 11 045142 2 *£1.10*

The Railways Act 1993 (Consequential Modifications) (No. 2) Order 1994 No. 1649. Enabling power: *Railways Act 1993, s. 153*. Issued: 29.06.94. Made: 22.06.94. Laid: 22.06.94. Coming into force: 14.07.94. Effect: 1947 c. 48; 1985 c. 67 amended. Territorial extent & classification: E/W/S. General. – 4p. – 0 11 044649 6 *£1.10*

The Railways Act 1993 (Consequential Modifications) (No. 4) Order 1994 No. 2520. Enabling power: *Railways Act 1993, s. 153*. Issued: 07.10.94. Made: 27.09.94. Laid: 28.09.94. Coming into force: 01.10.94. Effect: 1981 c. xv amended. Territorial extent & classification: E/W/S. General. – 4p. – 0 11 045520 7 *£1.10*

The Railways Act 1993 (Consequential Modifications) Order 1994 No. 857. Enabling power: *Railways Act 1993, s. 153*. Issued: 15.04.94. Made: 22.03.94. Laid: 22.03.94. Coming into force: 01.04.94. Effect: 1845 c. 20, c. 33; 1868 c. 119: 1871 c. 78; 1889 c. 57; 1968 c. 73; S.I. 1986/1456 amended. Territorial extent & classification: E/W/S. General. – 4p. – 0 11 043857 4 *£1.10*

The Railways (Alternative Closure Procedure) Order 1994 No. 607. Enabling power: *Railways Act 1993, ss. 49 (3), 143 (4)*. Issued: 28.03.94. Made: 08.03.94. Laid: 08.03.94. Coming into force: 01.04.94. Effect: None. Territorial extent & classification: E/W/S. General. – 2p. – 0 11 043607 5 *£0.65*

The Railways (Amendment) Regulations 1994 No. 608. Enabling power: *European Communities Act 1972, s. 2 (2)*. Issued: 28.03.94. Made: 08.03.94. Laid: 08.03.94. Coming into force: 31.03.94. Effect: S.I. 1992/3060 amended. Territorial extent & classification: E/W/S. General. – 4p. – 0 11 043608 3 *£1.10*

The Railways and Other Transport Systems (Approval of Works, Plant and Equipment) Regulations 1994 No. 157. Enabling power: *Transport and Works Act 1992, s. 41*. Issued: 08.02.94. Made: 31.01.94. Laid: 08.02.94. Coming into force: 05.04.94. Effect: None. Territorial extent & classification: E/W/S. General. – 12p. – 0 11 043157 X *£2.80*

The Railways (Class and Miscellaneous Exemptions) Order 1994 No. 606. Enabling power: *Railways Act 1993, ss. 7 (1) (2) (9) (10), 20 (1) (8) (9) (11) (12), 24 (1) (2) (8) (11), 49 (2) (4) (5), 143 (4), 151 (5)*. Issued: 27.04.94. Made: 08.03.94. Laid: 08.03.94. Coming into force: 01.04.94. for arts. 1 to 4, 6, 7. 02.04.94. for art. 5. Effect: None. Territorial extent & classification: E/W/S. General. – 12p. – 0 11 043606 7 *£2.80*

The Railways (Heathrow Express) (Exemptions) Order 1994 No. 574. Enabling power: *Railways Act 1993, ss. 7 (1) (2) (9) (10), 20 (1) (2) (8) (9) (12), 24 (1) (2) (8) (11), 49 (4) (5), 143 (4), 151 (5)*. Issued: 28.03.94. Made: 07.03.94. Laid: 08.03.94. Coming into force: 01.04.94. for arts. 1, 2, 4, 5. 02.04.94. for art. 3. Effect: None. Territorial extent & classification: E/W/S. General. – 4p. – 0 11 043574 5 *£1.10*

The Railways (Licence Application) Regulations 1994 No. 572. Enabling power: *Railways Act 1993, ss. 8 (3), 143 (3)*. Issued: 28.03.94. Made: 07.03.94. Laid: 08.03.94. Coming into force: 01.04.94. Effect: None. Territorial extent & classification: E/W/S. General. – 4p. – 0 11 043572 9 *£1.10*

Price/availability are liable to change without notice

The Railways (London Regional Transport) (Exemptions) Order 1994 No. 573. Enabling power: *Railways Act 1993, ss. 7 (1) (2) (10), 20 (1) (2) (9) (12), 24 (1) (2) (11), 49 (2) (4) (5), 143 (4), 151 (5).* Issued: 28.03.94. Made: 07.03.94. Laid: 08.03.94. Coming into force: 01.04.94, for arts. 1 to 3, 4, 6. & 02.04.94, for art. 4. Effect: None. Territorial extent & classification: E/W/S. General. – 4p. – 0 11 043573 7 *£1.10*

The Railways (Penalty Fares) Regulations 1994 No. 576. Enabling power: *Railways Act 1993, ss. 130, 143 (3) (4).* Issued: 28.03.94. Made: 07.03.94. Laid: 08.03.94. Coming into force: 01.04.94. Effect: None. Territorial extent & classification: E/W/S. General. –6p. – 0 11 043576 1 *£1.55*

The Railways Pension Scheme Order 1994 No. 1433. Enabling power: *Railways Act 1993, s. 143 (3) (4), sch. 11, paras. 1 (1), 2.* Issued: 06.06.94. Made: 27.05.94. Laid: 10.05.94. Coming into force: 31.05.94. Effect: None. Supersedes Draft ISBN 0110459083 previously published on 20.05.94. Territorial extent & classification: GB. General. –140p. – 0 11 044433 7 *£12.30*

The Railways Pensions Guarantee (Prescribed Persons) Order 1994 No. 2150. Enabling power: *Railways Act 1993. sch. 11, para. 1 (5).* Issued: 05.09.94. Made: 16.08.94. Laid: 16.08.94. Coming into force: 18.08.94. Effect: None. Territorial extent & classification: GB. General. – 2p. – 0 11 045150 3 *£0.65*

The Railways (Registers) Order 1994 No. 575. Enabling power: *Railways Act 1993, ss. 72 (7), 73 (5) (6).* Issued: 28.03.94. Made: 07.03.94. Laid: 08.03.94. Coming into force: 01.04.94. Effect: None. Territorial extent & classification: E/W/S. General. – 2p. – 0 11 043575 3 *£0.65*

The Service Subsidy Agreements (Tendering) (Amendment) Regulations 1994 No. 1227. Enabling power: *Transport Act 1985, s. 91 (1).* Issued: 10.05.94. Made: 29.04.94. Laid: 10.05.94. Coming into force: 01.06.94. Effect: S.I. 1985/1921 amended. Territorial extent & classification: GB. General. – 2p. – 0 11 044227 X *£0.65*

The Swinford Bridge (Revision of Tolls and Traffic Classification) Order 1994 No.2927. Enabling power: *Transport Charges etc. (Miscellaneous Provisions) Act 1954, s. 6.* Made: 16.11.94. Coming into force: 27.11.94. Effect: None. – *Unpublished*

The Tamar Bridge and Torpoint Ferry (Revision of Tolls and Traffic Classification) Order 1994 No.1060. Enabling power: *Transport Charges etc. (Miscellaneous Provisions) Act 1954, s. 6.* Made: 13.04.94. Coming into force: 13.04.94. Effect: None. – *Unpublished*

The Transport and Works Act 1992 (Commencement No. 5 and Transitional Provisions) Order 1994 No. 718 (C. 14). Enabling power: *Transport and Works Act 1992, s. 70 (1) (2). Bringing into operation various provisions of the 1992 act on 05.04.94.* Issued: 18.03.94. Made: 10.03.94. Effect: None. Territorial extent & classification: E/W/S. General. – 4p. – 0 11 043718 7 *£1.10*

The Wells and Walsingham Light Railway (Amendment) Order 1994 No. 260. Enabling power: *Light Railways Act 1896, s. 24.* Issued: 15.02.94. Made: 03.02.94. Coming into force: 04.02.94. Effect: S.I. 1982/521 amended. Territorial extent & classification: E. Local. –2p. – 0 11 043260 6 *£0.65*

The Wirral Tramway Light Railway Order 1994 No. 1761. Enabling power: *Light Railways Act 1896, ss. 3, 7, 9 to 12.* Issued: 12.07.94. Made: 30.06.94. Coming into force: 01.07.94. Effect: None. Territorial extent & classification: E. Local. – 12p. – 0 11 044761 1 *£2.80*

TRANSPORT AND WORKS

The British Railways Act 1990 (Arpley Chord) (Extension of Time) Order 1994 No. 1039. Enabling power: *Transport and Works Act 1992, s. 1, 5.* Issued: 15.04.94. Made: 30.03.94. Coming into force: 20.04.94. Effect: 1990 c. 42 amended. Territorial extent & classification: E. General. – 2p. – 0 11 044039 0 *£0.65*

The Chinnor and Princes Risborough Railway Order 1994 No. 1803. Enabling power: *Transport and Works Act 1992, ss. 1, 5 & Transport Act 1968, s. 121 (2).* Issued: 14.07.94. Made: 04.07.94. Coming into force: 26.07.94. Effect: None. Territorial extent & classification: E. General. – 6p. – 0 11 044803 0 *£1.55*

The Docklands Light Railway (Penalty Fares and Provision of Police Services) Order 1994 No.371. Enabling power: *Transport and Works Act 1992, s. 1.* Issued: 28.02.94. Made: 14.02.94. Coming into force: 25.02.94.; for arts. 1, 2, 8 & 9. 03.04.94.; for the remainder. Effect: 1984 c.iv; 1985 c.vi; 1986 c.xxiii; 1989 c.ii, ix; 1991 c.xxii; 1993 c.vii amended. Territorial extent & classification: E. General. – 6p. – 0 11 043371 8 *£1.55*

The Greater Manchester (Light Rapid Transit System) (Modification) Order 1994 No.701. Enabling power: *Transport and Works Act 1992, s. 1.* Issued: 18.03.94. Made: 07.03.94. Coming into force: 28.03.94. Effect: None. Territorial extent & classification: E. General. – 2p. – 0 11 043701 2 *£0.65*

The Railtrack (Marsh Lane, Leeds, Footbridge) Order 1994 No. 1532. Enabling power: *Transport and Works Act 1992, s. 1, 5.* Issued: 17.06.94. Made: 01.06.94. Coming into force: 22.06.94. Effect: 1857 c. xlvi amended. Territorial extent & classification: E. Local. – 2p. – 0 11 044532 5 *£0.65*

TRANSPORT AND WORKS: INLAND WATERWAYS

The River Humber (Upper Burcom Cooling Works) Order 1994 No. 1753. Enabling power: *Transport and Works Act 1992, ss. 3, 5 & S.I. 1992/3230.* Issued: 12.07.94. Made: 01.07.94. Coming into force: 21.07.94. Effect: None. Territorial extent & classification: E/W/S. General. – 4p. – 0 11 044753 0 *£1.10*

Price/availability are liable to change without notice

TRANSPORT CHARGES

The Swinford Bridge (Revision of Tolls and Traffic Classification) Order 1994 No. 2927. Enabling power: *Transport Charges etc. (Miscellaneous Provisions) Act 1954, s. 6.* Made: 16.11.94. Coming into force: 27.11.94. Effect: None. – *Unpublished*

The Tamar Bridge and Torpoint Ferry (Revision of Tolls and Traffic Classification) Order 1994 No. 1060. Enabling power: *Transport Charges etc. (Miscellaneous Provisions) Act 1954, s. 6.* Made: 13.04.94. Coming into force: 13.04.94. Effect: None. – *Unpublished*

TRIBUNALS AND INQUIRIES

The Compulsory Purchase by Ministers (Inquiries Procedure) Rules 1994 No. 3264. Enabling power: *Tribunals and Inquiries Act 1992, s. 9.* Issued: 05.01.95. Made: 15.12.94. Laid: 20.12.94. Coming into force: 10.01.95. Effect: S.I. 1967/720 revoked. With correction slip dated January 1995 Territorial extent & classification: E/W. General. – 10p. – 0 11 043824 8 *£2.40*

The Fees for Inquiries (Standard Daily Amount) Regulations 1994 No. 642. Enabling power: *Housing and Planning Act 1986, s. 42 (1).* Issued: 15.03.94. Made: 28.02.94. Laid: 15.03.94. Coming into force: 05.04.94. Effect: None. Territorial extent & classification: GB. General. – Relates to recovery, by MAFF, of costs incurred for inquiries. – 2p. – 0 11 043642 3 *£0.65*

The Highways (Inquiries Procedure) Rules 1994 No. 3263. Enabling power: *Tribunals and Inquiries Act 1992, s. 9.* Issued: 05.01.95. Made: 15.12.94. Laid: 20.12.94. Coming into force: 10.01.95. Effect: S.I. 1976/721 revoked. Territorial extent & classification: E/W. General. – 16p. – 0 11 043823 X *£3.20*

TRUSTEES

The Public Trustee (Custodian Trustee) Rules 1994 No. 2519. Enabling power: *Public Trustee Act 1906, s. 14 (1).* Issued: 05.10.94. Made: 23.09.94. Laid: 05.10.94. Coming into force: 31.10.94. Effect: S.R. & O. 1912/348 amended. Territorial extent & classification: E/W. General. – 2p. – 0 11 045519 3 *£0.65*

The Public Trustee (Fees) (Amendment) Order 1994 No. 714. Enabling power: *Public Trustee Act 1906, s. 9 & Public Trustee (Fees) Act 1957, s. 1.* Issued: 17.03.94. Made: 09.03.94. Coming into force: 01.04.94. Effect: S.I. 1985/373 amended. Territorial extent & classification: E/W. General. – 2p. – 0 11 043714 4 *£0.65*

The Trustee Investments (Additional Powers) (No. 2) Order 1994 No. 1908. Enabling power: *Trustee Investments Act 1961, s. 12 & European Communities Act 1972, s. 2 (2).* Issued: 29.07.94. Made: 19.07.94. Laid: 29.07.94. Coming into force: 22.08.94. Effect: None. Territorial extent & classification: GB. General. – 4p. – 0 11 044908 8 *£1.10*

The Trustee Investments (Additional Powers) Order 1994 No. 265. Enabling power: *Trustee Investments Act 1961, s. 12.* Issued: 18.02.94. Made: 08.02.94. Laid: 18.02.94. Coming into force: 11.03.94. Effect: None. Territorial extent & classification: GB. General. – 2p. – 0 11 043265 7 *£0.65*

UNITED NATIONS

The Former Yugoslavia (United Nations Sanctions) (Channel Islands) (Amendment) Order 1994 No. 2797. Enabling power: *United Nations Act 1946, s. 1.* Issued: 11.11.94. Made: 02.11.94. Laid: 03.11.94. Coming into force: 04.11.94. Effect: S.I. 1994/2675 amended. This SI has been made in consequence of a defect in SI 1994/2675 and is being sent free of charge to all known recipients of that SI. Territorial extent & classification: GB. General. – 2p. – 0 11 045797 8 *£0.65*

The Former Yugoslavia (United Nations Sanctions) (Channel Islands) Order 1994 No. 2675. Enabling power: *United Nations Act 1946, s. 1.* Issued: 24.10.94. Made: 17.10.94. Laid: 18.10.94. Coming into force: 19.10.94. Effect: None. Territorial extent & classification: GB. General. – 10p. – 0 11 045675 0 *£2.80* Replaced by ISBN 0110459598

The Former Yugoslavia (United Nations Sanctions) (Dependent Territories) Order 1994 No. 2674. Enabling power: *United Nations Act 1946, s. 1.* Issued: 24.10.94. Made: 17.10.94. Laid: 18.10.94. Coming into force: 19.10.94. Effect: S.I. 1993/1195 amended. Territorial extent & classification: GB. General. – 10p. – 0 11 045674 2 *£2.40*

The Former Yugoslavia (United Nations Sanctions) (Isle of Man) Order 1994 No. 2676. Enabling power: *United Nations Act 1946, s. 1.* Issued: 24.10.94. Made: 17.10.94. Laid: 18.10.94. Coming into force: 19.10.94. Effect: None. Territorial extent & classification: GB. General. – 8p. – 0 11 045676 9 *£1.95*

The Former Yugoslavia (United Nations Sanctions) Order 1994 No. 2673. Enabling power: *United Nations Act 1946, s. 1.* Issued: 24.10.94. Made: 17.10.94. Laid: 18.10.94. Coming into force: 19.10.94. Effect: S.I. 1993/1188 amended. Territorial extent & classification: GB. General. – 10p. – 0 11 045673 4 *£2.40*

The Haiti (United Nations Sanctions) (Channel Islands) Order 1994 No. 1325. Enabling power: *United Nations Act 1946, s. 1.* Issued: 26.05.94. Made: 18.05.94. Laid: 19.05.94. Coming into force: 23.05.94. Effect: S.I. 1993/1793 revoked. Territorial extent & classification: GB. General. – 16p. – 0 11 044326 8 *£3.20*

The Haiti (United Nations Sanctions) (Dependent Territories) Order 1994 No. 1324. Enabling power: *United Nations Act 1946, s. 1.* Issued: 26.05.94. Made: 18.05.94. Laid: 19.05.94. Coming into force: 23.05.94. Effect: S.I. 1993/1785 revoked. Territorial extent & classification: GB. General. – 16p. – 0 11 044324 1 *£3.20*

The Haiti (United Nations Sanctions) (Isle of Man) Order 1994 No. 1326. Enabling power: *United Nations Act 1946, s. 1.* Issued: 26.05.94. Made: 18.05.94. Laid: 19.05.94. Coming into force: 23.05.94. Effect: S.I. 1993/1794 revoked. Territorial extent & classification: GB. General. – 16p. – 0 11 044325 X *£3.20*

Price/availability are liable to change without notice

The Haiti (United Nations Sanctions) Order 1994 No. 1323. Enabling power: *United Nations Act 1946, s. 1.* Issued: 26.05.94. Made: 18.05.94. Laid: 19.05.94. Coming into force: 23.05.94. Effect: S.I. 1993/1784 revoked. Territorial extent & classification: GB. General. – 16p. – 0 11 044323 3 *£3.20*

The South Africa (United Nations Arms Embargo) (Prohibited Transactions) Revocations Order 1994 No. 1636. Enabling power: *United Nations Act 1946, s. 1.* Issued: 29.06.94. Made: 22.06.94. Laid: 23.06.94. Coming into force: 22.06.94. Effect: S.I. 1978/277, 1034, 1052, 1053, 1054, 1624, 1895, 1896, 1898, 1897; 1981/1671; 1982/153, 154, 1531 revoked. With correction slip dated August 1994 Territorial extent & classification: GB. General. – 4p. – 0 11 044636 4 *£1.10*

The United Nations Arms Embargoes (Amendment) (Rwanda) Order 1994 No. 1637. Enabling power: *United Nations Act 1946, s. 1.* Issued: 29.06.94. Made: 22.06.94. Laid: 23.06.94. Coming into force: 24.06.94. Effect: S.I. 1993/1787 amended. Territorial extent & classification: GB. General. – 2p. – 0 11 044637 2 *£0.65*

UNIVERSITY AND COLLEGES

The Education (University Commissioners) Order 1994 No. 3106. Enabling power: *Education Reform Act 1988, sch. 11, para. 3 (2) (b).* Issued: 15.12.94. Made: 06.12.94. Laid: 07.12.94. Coming into force: 30.12.94. Effect: None. Territorial extent & classification: E/W/S. General. – 2p. – 0 11 043390 4 *£0.65*

URBAN DEVELOPMENT

The Leasehold Reform, Housing and Urban Development Act 1993 (Commencement No. 4) Order 1994 No. 935 (C. 16). Enabling power: *Leasehold Reform, Housing and Urban Development Act 1993, s. 188 (2) (3).* Issued: 30.03.94. Made: 25.03.94. Coming into force: 01.04.94. Effect: None. Territorial extent & classification: E/W. General. – 4p. – 0 11 043935 X *£1.10*

The London Docklands Development Corporation (Alteration of Boundaries) Order 1994 No. 2578. Enabling power: *Local Government, Planning and Land Act 1980, s. 134 (3A) (5).* Issued: 13.10.94. Made: 01.10.94. Laid: 07.10.94. Coming into force: 31.10.94. Effect: None. With correction slip dated November 1994 Territorial extent & classification: E. Local. – 4p., ill. – 0 11 045578 9 *£1.10*

VALUE ADDED TAX

The Finance Act 1994, section 45, (Appointed Day) Order 1994 No. 1257 (C. 22). Enabling power: *Finance Act 1994, s. 45 (4). Bringing into operation s. 45 of the 1994 act on 01.06.94.* Issued: 02.06.94. Made: 09.05.94. Coming into force: 01.06.94. Effect: None. Territorial extent & classification: GB. General. – 2p. – 0 11 044257 1 *£0.65*

The Finance Act 1994, section 47 (Appointed Day) (No. 2) Order 1994 No. 1253 (C. 21). Enabling power: *Finance Act 1994, s. 47. Bringing into operation s. 47 of the 1994 act on 09.05.94.* Issued: 09.06.94. Made: 09.05.94. Effect: S.I. 1994/1234 revoked. Territorial extent & classification: GB. General. – 2p. – 0 11 044253 9 *£0.65*

The Value Added Tax (Accounting and Records) (Amendment) Regulations 1994 No. 803. Enabling power: *Value Added Tax Act 1983, sch. 7, para. 2 (4) & Finance Act 1985, ss. 14 (5A) (b), 14A (4).* Issued: 29.03.94. Made: 17.03.94. Laid: 18.03.94. Coming into force: 01.05.94. Effect: S.I. 1989/2248 amended. Territorial extent & classification: GB. General. – 2p. – 0 11 043803 5 *£0.65*

The Value Added Tax Act 1994 (Interest on Tax) (Prescribed Rate) Order 1994 No. 2542. Enabling power: *Value Added Tax Act 1994, s. 74 (6).* Issued: 24.10.94. Made: 28.09.94. Laid: 30.09.94. Coming into force: 06.10.94. Effect: None. Territorial extent & classification: GB. General. – 2p. – 0 11 045542 8 *£0.65*

The Value Added Tax (Buildings and Land) Order 1994 No. 3013. Enabling power: *Value Added Tax Act 1994, s. 51.* Issued: 08.12.94. Made: 29.11.94. Laid: 29.11.94. Coming into force: 30.11.94. Effect: 1994 c. 23 amended. Territorial extent & classification: GB. General. – 2p. – 0 11 043314 9 *£0.65*

The Value Added Tax (Buildings and Land) Order 1994 No. 3013. Enabling power: *Value Added Tax Act 1994, s. 51.* Issued: 27.02.95. Made: 29.11.94. Laid: 29.11.94. Coming into force: 30.11.94. Effect: 1994 c. 23 amended. Supersedes SI of same no. published 8th December 1994 ISBN 0 11 043314 9. Territorial extent & classification: GB. General. – 2p. – 0 11 052482 9 *£0.65*

The Value Added Tax (Education) (No. 2) Order 1994 No. 2969. Enabling power: *Value Added Tax 1994, ss. 31 (2), 96 (9).* Issued: 01.12.94. Made: 22.11.94. Laid: 23.11.94. Coming into force: 01.01.95. Effect: 1994 c.23 amended. Territorial extent & classification: GB. General. – 2p. – 0 11 043203 7 *£0.65*

The Value Added Tax (Education) Order 1994 No. 1188. Enabling power: *Value Added Tax Act 1983, ss. 17 (2), 48 (6).* Issued: 31.05.94. Made: 27.04.94. Laid: 28.04.94. Coming into force: 01.08.94. Effect: 1983 c. 55 amended. Territorial extent & classification: GB. General. – 4p. – 0 11 044188 5 *£1.10*

The Value Added Tax (General) (Amendment) Regulations 1994 No. 3015. Enabling power: *Value Added Tax 1994, s. 26 (1) (3) (4).* Issued: 06.12.94. Made: 29.11.94. Laid: 29.11.94. Coming into force: In accord. with reg. 1. Effect: S.I. 1985/886 amended. Territorial extent & classification: GB. General. – 4p. – 0 11 043271 1 *£1.10*

The Value Added Tax (Increase of Registration Limits) Order 1994 No. 2905. Enabling power: *Value Added Tax Act 1994, sch. 1, para. 15, sch. 3, para. 9.* Issued: 07.12.94. Made: 29.11.94. Laid: 29.11.94. Coming into force: 30.11.94. for arts. 1 & 2; 01.01.95. for art. 3. Effect: 1994 c. 23 amended. Territorial extent & classification: GB. General. – 2p. – 0 11 043290 8 *£0.65*

Price/availability are liable to change without notice

The Value Added Tax (Means of Transport) Order 1994 No. 3128. Enabling power: *Value Added Tax Act 1994, s. 95 (4)*. Issued: 16.12.94. Made: 07.12.94. Laid: 08.12.94. Coming into force: 01.01.95. Effect: 1994 c.23 amended. Territorial extent & classification: GB. General. – Part of a package of measures which implement DIR 94/5 [OJ L60/94]. – 2p. – 0 11 043393 9 *£0.65*

The Value Added Tax (Sport, Physical Education and Fund-Raising Events) Order 1994 No.687. Enabling power: *Value Added Tax Act 1983, ss. 17 (2), 48 (6)*. Issued: 13.04.94. Made: 10.03.94. Laid: 10.03.94. Coming into force: 01.04.94. Effect: 1983 c. 55 amended. Territorial extent & classification: GB. General. – 2p. – 0 11 043687 3 *£0.65*

The Value Added Tax (Tax Free Shops) Order 1994 No. 686. Enabling power: *Value Added Tax Act 1983, ss. 16 (4), 48 (6)*. Issued: 18.03.94. Made: 09.03.94. Laid: 10.03.94. Coming into force: 01.04.94. Effect: 1983 c. 55 amended. Territorial extent & classification: GB.General. – 2p. – 0 11 043686 5 *£0.65*

The Value Added Tax (Transport) Order 1994 No. 3014. Enabling power: *Value Added Tax Act 1994, ss. 30 (4), 96 (9)*. Issued: 08.12.94. Made: 29.11.94. Coming into force: 01.04.95. Effect: 1994 c. 23 amended. Territorial extent & classification: GB. General. –2p. – 0 11 043301 7 *£0.65*

The Value Added Tax (Transport) Order 1994 No. 3014. Enabling power: *Value Added Tax Act 1994, ss. 30 (4), 96 (9)*. Issued: 27.02.95. Made: 29.11.94. Coming into force: 01.04.95. Effect: 1994 c. 23 amended. Supersedes SI of same no. published 8h February 1995 ISBN 0 11 043301 7. Territorial extent & classification: GB. General. – 2p. – 0 11 052480 2 *£0.65*

The Value Added Tax Tribunals (Amendments) Rules 1994 No. 2617. Enabling power: *Value Added Tax Act 1994, sch. 12, para. 9*. Issued: 17.10.94. Made: 05.10.94. Laid: 10.10.94. Coming into force: 01.11.94. Effect: S.I. 1986/590 amended. Territorial extent & classification: E/W/NI. General. – 4p. – 0 11 045617 3 *£1.10*

The Value Added Tax Tribunals Appeals (Northern Ireland) Order 1994 No. 1978. Enabling power: *Finance Act 1985, s. 26*. Issued: 16.08.94. Made: 22.07.94. Laid: 26.07.94. Coming into force: 01.10.94. Effect: None. Territorial extent & classification: NI. General. – 2p. – 0 11 044978 9 *£0.65*

VETERINARY SURGEONS

The Veterinary Surgeons and Veterinary Practitioners (Registration) (Amendment) Regulations Order of Council 1994 No. 305. Enabling power: *Veterinary Surgeons Act 1966, s. 11*. Issued: 17.02.94. Made: 08.02.94. Coming into force: 31.03.94. Effect: S.I. 1967/395; 1993/610 amended & S.I. 1975/2212 revoked. Territorial extent & classification: GB. General. – 2p. – 0 11 043305 X *£0.65*

WALES: CHANGES IN LOCAL GOVERNMENT AREAS

The Ogwr (Ogwr Valley and Garw Valley Communities) Order 1994 No. 3168. Enabling power: *Local Government Act 1972, s. 58 (2)*. Issued: 12.01.95. Made: 12.12.94. Coming into force: 01.03.95. for purposes described in art. 1 (2). 01.04.95. for all other purposes. Effect: None. Territorial extent & classification: E/W. Local. – 4p.; ill. – 0 11 043885 X *£1.10*

WATER, ENGLAND AND WALES

The Reservoirs (Panels of Civil Engineers) (Application Fees) (Amendment) Regulations 1994 No. 1533. Enabling power: *Reservoirs Act 1975, ss. 4 (2), 5*. Issued: 17.06.94. Made: 08.06.94. Coming into force: 01.07.94. Effect: S.I. 1992/1527 amended. Territorial extent & classification: E/W/S. General. – 2p. – 0 11 044533 3 *£0.65*

The Southern Water Authority (Dissolution) Order 1994 No. 1150. Enabling power: *Water Act 1989, s. 4 (3)*. Made: 21.04.94. Coming into force: 22.04.94. Effect: None. – *Unpublished*

The Thames Water Authority (Dissolution) Order 1994 No. 1149. Enabling power: *Water Act 1989, s. 4 (3)*. Made: 21.04.94. Coming into force: 22.04.94. Effect: None. – *Unpublished*

The Urban Waste Water Treatment (England and Wales) Regulations 1994 No. 2841. Enabling power: *European Communities Act 1972, s. 2 (2)*. Issued: 17.11.94. Made: 04.11.94. Laid: 09.11.94. Coming into force: 30.11.94. Effect: None. Territorial extent & classification: E/W. General. – Implements DIR 91/271 [L 135/91]. – 12p. – 0 11 045841 9 *£2.80*

The Welsh Water Authority (Dissolution) Order 1994 No. 1947. Enabling power: *Water Act 1989, sch. 2*. Made: 14.07.94. Coming into force: 20.07.94. Effect: None. – *Unpublished*

The Wrexham and East Denbighshire Water Company) (Constitution and Regulation) Order 1994 No.2205. Enabling power: *Statutory Water Companies Act 1991, ss. 12 (1), 14*. Issued: 07.09.94. Made: 20.08.94. Laid: 25.08.94. Coming into force: 22.09.94. Effect: 1864 c. lxxxv; 1874 c. lvii; 1880 c. lxx; 1902 c. ix; 1921 c. xxx; 1936 c. cvii; 1921 c. xxx; 1936 c. cvii; Wrexham Waterworks Order 1898; Wrexham & East Denbighshire Water Order 1933; S.I. 1952/1235; 1954/813; 1955/927; 1960/583; 1964/600; 1973/2236; 1975/978 amended & S.I. 1971/349; 1977/799; 1979/801; 1983/965 revoked. Territorial extent & classification: W. Local. – 4p. – 0 11 045205 4 *£1.10*

WATER INDUSTRY, ENGLAND AND WALES

The Bournemouth and West Hampshire Water (Amendment of Local Enactments etc.) Order 1994 No.1650. Enabling power: *Water Industry Act 1991, sch. 2, para. 7*. Issued: 28.06.94. Made: 20.06.94. Coming into force: 01.07.94. Effect: 1896 c. cxcvi; 1940 c. xxviii; 1951 c. xxxiv amended & West Hampshire Water Order 1919 revoked. Territorial extent & classification: E. Local. – 4p. – 0 11 044650 X *£1.10*

Price/availability are liable to change without notice

The Suffolk and Essex Water (Amendment of Local Enactments etc.) Order 1994 No. 978. Enabling power: *Water Act 1989, sch. 2, para. 7.* Issued: 06.04.94. Made: 29.03.94. Coming into force: 31.03.94. Effect: 1901 c. cclxix; 1907 c. lxxxiv; 1931 c. xxvii; S.I. 1961/2291 amended & S.I. 1972/2050; 1977/295; 1985/240 revoked. Territorial extent & classification: E/W. Local. – 4p. – 0 11 043978 3 £1.10

The Thames Water Utilities Limited (North London Discharge) Order 1994 No. 3077. Enabling power: *Water Industry Act 1991, s. 167.* Made: 02.12.94. Coming into force: 05.12.94. Effect: None. – *Unpublished*

The Three Valleys, Rickmansworth and Colne Valley Water (Amendment of Local Enactments etc.) Order 1994 No. 977. Enabling power: *Water Act 1989, sch. 2, para. 7.* Issued: 06.04.94. Made: 29.03.94. Coming into force: 31.03.94. Effect: 1939 c. lxxviii; 1945 c, viii amended & S.I. 1970/1790: 1984/785 revoked. Territorial extent & classification: E/W. Local. –4p. – 0 11 043977 5 £1.10

The Water Enterprises (Merger) (Modification) Regulations 1994 No. 73. Enabling power: *Water Industry Act 1991, s. 33 (4).* Issued: 21.01.94. Made: 11.01.94. Laid: 19.01.94. Coming into force: 09.02.94. Effect: 1991 c.56 amended. Territorial extent & classification: E/W. General. – 2p. – 0 11 043073 5 £0.65

The Wrexham and East Denbighshire and Chester (Pipelaying and Other Works) (Codes of Practice) Order 1994 No. 2915. Enabling power: *Water Industry Act 1991, s. 182 (2).* Issued: 24.11.94. Made: 25.10.94. Coming into force: 25.10.94. Effect: None. Territorial extent & classification: E/W. Local. – 2p. – 0 11 043097 2 £0.65

WATER RESOURCES, ENGLAND AND WALES

The Surface Waters (River Ecosystem) (Classification) Regulations 1994 No. 1057. Enabling power: *Water Resources Act 1991, ss. 82, 219 (2).* Issued: 19.04.94. Made: 12.04.94. Laid: 19.04.94. Coming into force: 10.05.94. Effect: None. Territorial extent & classification: E/W. General. – 4p. – 0 11 044057 9 £1.10

WATER SUPPLY, SCOTLAND

The Borders Regional Council (Galashiels Mill Lade) (Amendment) Water Order 1994 No.810 (S. 35). Enabling power: *Water (Scotland) Act 1980, ss. 17 (2), 107 (1) (b), 107 (3).* Issued: 24.03.94. Made: 16.03.94. Coming into force: 15.07.94. Effect: S.I. 1969/945 amended. Territorial extent & classification: S. Local. – 2p. – 0 11 043810 8 £0.65

The Council Tax (Discounts) (Scotland) Amendment Order 1994 No. 626 (S. 26). Enabling power: *Local Government Finance Act 1992, s. 113 (1), sch. 1, paras. 2, 4.* Issued: 17.03.94. Made: 04.03.94. Laid: 11.03.94. Coming into force: 01.04.94. Effect: S.I. 1992/1408 amended & S.I. 1993/343 revoked. Territorial extent & classification: S. General. – 2p. – 0 11 043626 1 £0.65

The Council Tax (Discounts) (Scotland) Amendment Regulations 1994 No. 629 (S. 28). Enabling power: *Local Government Finance Act 1992, ss. 113 (1), 116 (1), sch. 1, para. 9.* Issued: 17.03.94. Made: 04.03.94. Laid: 11.03.94. Coming into force: 01.04.94. Effect: S.I. 1992/1409 amended. Territorial extent & classification: S. General. – 2p. – 0 11 043629 6 £0.65

The Council Tax (Exempt Dwellings) (Scotland) Amendment Order 1994 No. 628 (S. 27). Enabling power: *Local Government Finance Act 1992, ss. 72 (6) (7), sch. 11, para. 7 (2) (3).* Issued: 17.03.94. Made: 04.03.94. Laid: 11.03.94. Coming into force: 01.04.94. Effect: S.I. 1992/1333 amended. Territorial extent & classification: S. General. – 2p. – 0 11 043628 8 £0.65

The Council Tax (Reduction of Liability) (Scotland) Regulations 1994 No. 3170 (S. 177). Enabling power: *Local Government Finance Act 1992, ss. 80, 84 (3), 113 (1), 116 (1), sch. 2, paras. 1 (1), 2 (4) (e).* Issued: 21.12.94. Made: 12.12.94. Laid: 21.12.94. Coming into force: 12.01.95. Effect: S.I. 1992/1330, 1332 amended. Territorial extent & classification: S. General. – 4p. – 0 11 043438 2 £1.10

The Reservoirs (Panels of Civil Engineers) (Application Fees) (Amendment) Regulations 1994 No. 1533. Enabling power: *Reservoirs Act 1975, ss. 4 (2), 5.* Issued: 17.06.94. Made: 08.06.94. Coming into force: 01.07.94. Effect: S.I. 1992/1527 amended. Territorial extent & classification: E/W/S. General. – 2p. – 0 11 044533 3 £0.65

The Shetland Islands Council (Laxa Burn, Mid Yell) (Amendment) Water Order 1994 No.2758 (S. 139). Enabling power: *Water (Scotland) Act 1980, s. 107 (1) (b) (3).* Issued: 03.11.94. Made: 25.10.94. Coming into force: 01.11.94. Effect: S.I. 1965/460 amended. Territorial extent & classification: S. Local. – 2p. – 0 11 045758 7 £0.65

The Strathclyde Regional Council (Ayr Burgh Act 1885) (Amendment) Water Order 1994 No.3309 (S. 196). Enabling power: *Water (Scotland) Act 1980, ss. 107 (1) (b) (3).* Issued: 10.01.95. Made: 22.12.94. Coming into force: 01.01.95. Effect: 1885 c. lxxxiii (18 & 19 Vict.) amended. Territorial extent & classification: S. Local. – 4p. – 0 11 043871 X £1.10

The Strathclyde Regional Council (Kilduskland) Water Order 1994 No. 1556 (S. 70). Enabling power: *Water (Scotland) Act 1980, ss. 17 (2), 29 (1).* Issued: 22.06.94. Made: 10.06.94. Coming into force: 17.06.94. Effect: None. Territorial extent & classification: S. Local. – 4p. – 0 11 044556 2 £1.10

The Strathclyde Regional Council (Loch Assapol) Water Order 1994 No. 3308 (S. 195). Enabling power: *Water (Scotland) Act 1980, ss. 17 (2), 29 (1), 107 (1) (b).* Issued: 10.01.95. Made: 22.12.94. Coming into force: 01.01.95. for all purposes except for art.4. In accord. with art. 1(2) for art. 4. Effect: S.I. 1959/2298; 1962/435; 1981/1787 revoked. Territorial extent & classification: S. Local. – 4p. – 0 11 043872 8 £1.10

The Water Byelaws (Loch an Sgoltaire) Extension Order 1994 No. 3053 (S. 159). Enabling power: *Water (Scotland) Act 1980, s. 72 (4).* Issued: 08.12.94. Made: 29.11.94. Coming into force: 10.12.94. Effect: None. Territorial extent & classification: S. Local. – 1p. – 0 11 043319 X £0.65

Price/availability are liable to change without notice

WEIGHTS AND MEASURES

The Measuring Equipment (Capacity Measures) (Amendment) Regulations 1994 No. 1259. Enabling power: *Weights and Measures Act 1985, s. 5 (9), 11 (1) (4), 86 (1).* Issued: 29.07.94. Made: 09.05.94. Laid: 10.05.94. Coming into force: In accord. with reg. 1. Effect: S.I. 1963/1710; 1990/2626 amended. Territorial extent & classification: E/W/S. General. –2p. – 0 11 044259 8 £0.65

The Units of Measurement Regulations 1994 No. 2867. Enabling power: *European Communities Act 1972, s. 2 (2).* Issued: 28.11.94. Made: 06.11.94. Laid: 19.07.94. Coming into force: Immediately after the Weights & Measures Act 1985 (Metrication) (Amendment) Order 1994 [SI 1994/2866] comes into force. Effect: 1985 c. 72; S.I. 1986/1082 amended. Supersedes Draft ISBN 0110459563 published on 28.07.94. Territorial extent & classification: GB. General. – Implements amendments made by DIR 89/617 (OJ L 357/89) to DIR 80/181 (OJ L 39/80). –10p. – 0 11 043126 X £2.40

The Weights and Measures Act 1985 (Metrication) (Amendment) Order 1994 No. 2866. Enabling power: *Weights and Measures Act 1985, ss. 8 (6), 22 (1) (2).* Issued: 28.11.94. Made: 06.11.94. Laid: 19.07.94. Coming into force: 07.11.94. Effect: 1985 c. 72 amended. Supersedes Draft ISBN 0110459555 published on 28.07.94. Territorial extent & classification: E/W/S. General. – Implements amendments made by DIR 89/617 (OJ L 357/89) to DIR 80/181 (OJ L 39/80). – 4p. – 0 11 043125 1 £1.10

The Weights and Measures (Cosmetic Products) Order 1994 No. 1884. Enabling power: *Weights and Measures Act 1985, s. 22 (1) (2), 24 (1), 86 (1).* Issued: 25.07.94. Made: 13.07.94. Laid: 10.05.94. Coming into force: 31.07.94. Effect: 1985 c. 72 amended & S.I. 1974/874 revoked. Supersedes Draft ISBN 0110459121 published 23.05.94. Territorial extent & classification: E/W/S. General. – 4p. – 0 11 044884 7 £1.10

The Weights and Measures (Intoxicating Liquor) (Amendment) Order 1994 No. 1883. Enabling power: *Weights and Measures Act 1985, ss. 8 (6), 22 (1) (2).* Issued: 22.07.94. Made: 13.07.94. Laid: 10.05.94. Coming into force: 14.07.94. Effect: 1985 c. 72; S.I. 1988/2039 amended. Supersedes Draft ISBN 0110459113 published 23.05.94. Territorial extent & classification: E/W/S. General. – 2p. – 0 11 044883 9 £0.65

The Weights and Measures (Metrication Amendments) Regulations 1994 No. 1851. Enabling power: *Weights and Measures Act 1985, s. 4 (5) (6), 5 (a), 11 (1) (4), 15 (1), 94 (1).* Issued: 28.07.94. Made: 13.07.94. Laid: 19.07.94. Coming into force: Immediately after the Units of Measurement Regulations 1994 come into force, in accord. with reg. 1. Effect: S.I. 1983/914, 1390, 1656; 1986/1320, 1682, 1684, 1685: 1988/120, 128, 876; 1990/2626 amended. With correction slip dated January 1995. Territorial extent & classification: E/W/S. General. – These Regs. implement the amendments made by Council DIR 89/617/EEC (OJ No. L357, 7.12.89, p. 28) to Council DIR 80/181/EEC (OJ No. L39, 15.2.80, p. 40). – 12p. – 0 11 044851 0 £2.80

The Weights and Measures (Metrication) (Miscellaneous Goods) (Amendment) Order 1994 No.2868. Enabling power: *Weights and Measures Act 1985, ss. 22 (1), 24 (1), 86 (1).* Issued: 28.11.94. Made: 06.11.94. Laid: 19.07.94. Coming into force: 07.11.94. Effect: S.I. 1988/2039, 2040 amended. Supersedes Draft ISBN 0110459547 published on 28.07.94. Territorial extent & classification: E/W/S. General. – Implements amendments made by DIR 89/617 (OJ L 357/89) to DIR 80/181 (OJ L 39/80). – 6p. – 0 11 043127 8 £1.55

The Weights and Measures (Packaged Goods) (Amendment) Regulations 1994 No. 1258. Enabling power: *Weights and Measures Act 1985, ss. 48, 49, 66, 86, 94 (1).* Issued: 18.05.94. Made: 09.05.94. Laid: 10.05.94. Coming into force: 31.07.94. Effect: S.I. 1986/2049 amended. Territorial extent & classification: E/W/S. General. – 2p. – 0 11 044258 X £0.65

The Weights and Measures (Packaged Goods and Quantity Marking and Abbreviations of Units) (Amendment) Regulations 1994 No. 1852. Enabling power: *Weights and Measures Act 1985, ss. 15 (1) (g), 23 (1) (a) (d), 48 (1) (a), (1A) (ii), 49, 65, 66, 68 (1A), 94 (1).* Issued: 28.07.94. Made: 13.07.94. Laid: 19.07.94. Coming into force: Immediately after the Units of Measurement Regulations 1994 come into force, in accord. with reg. 1. Effect: S.I. 1986/2049; 1987/1538 amended. With correction slip dated January 1995. Territorial extent & classification: E/W/S. General. – These regs. implement the amendments made by the Council DIR 89/617/EEC (OJ No. L 357, 7.12.89, p. 28) to Council DIR 80/181/EEC (OJ No. L 39. 15.2.80, p. 40). –6p. – 0 11 044852 9 £1.55

WELSH LANGUAGE

The Alternative Names in Welsh Order 1994 No. 2889. Enabling power: *Welsh Language Act 1993, ss. 25 (1), 27 (3).* Issued: 25.11.94. Made: 04.11.94. Laid: 16.11.94. Coming into force: 14.12.94. Effect: None. Territorial extent & classification: W.General. – In English & Welsh. – 2p. – 0 11 043100 6 £0.65

WILDLIFE

The Conservation (Natural Habitats, &c.) Regulations 1994 No. 2716. Enabling power: *European Communities Act 1972, s. 2 (2).* Issued: 31.10.94. Laid: 13.07.94. Coming into force: 30.10.94. Effect: None. Supersedes Draft ISBN 0110459458 published on 18/07/94. Territorial extent & classification: E/W/S. General. – Implements DIR 92/43 [L 206/92]. –60p. – 0 11 045716 1 £8.70

The Wildlife and Countryside Act 1981 (Variation of Schedule 4) Order 1994 No. 1151. Enabling power: *Wildlife and Countryside Act 1981, s. 22 (1).* Issued: 03.05.94. Made: 25.04.94. Laid: 03.05.94. Coming into force: 24.05.94. Effect: 1981 c. 69 amended. Territorial extent & classification: E/W/S. General. – 4p. – 0 11 044151 6 £1.10

Price/availability are liable to change without notice

The Wildlife and Countryside (Registration and Ringing of Certain Captive Birds) (Amendment) Regulations 1994 No. 1152. Enabling power: *Wildlife and Countryside Act 1981, s. 7 (1) (2)*. Issued: 03.05.94. Made: 25.04.94. Laid: 03.05.94. Coming into force: 24.05.94. Effect: S.I. 1982/1221 amended. Territorial extent & classification: E/W/S. General. –2p. – 0 11 044152 4 *£0.65*

YOUNG OFFENDER INSTITUTIONS, ENGLAND AND WALES

The Young Offender Institution (Amendment) Rules 1994 No. 3194. Enabling power: *Prison Act 1952, s. 47*. Issued: 20.12.94. Made: 10.12.94. Laid: 16.12.94. Coming into force: 09.01.95. Effect: S.I. 1988/1422 amended. Territorial extent & classification: E/W. General. –4p. – 0 11 043476 5 *£1.10*

YOUNG OFFENDERS INSTITUTIONS, SCOTLAND

The Prisons and Young Offenders Institutions (Scotland) Rules 1994 No. 1931 (S. 85). Enabling power: *Prisons (Scotland) Act 1989, s. 39*. Issued: 01.08.94. Made: 15.07.94. Laid: 19.07.94. Coming into force: 01.11.94. for all purposes except those specified in rule 1 (3) (5): 01.10.94. for purposes specified in rule 1 (3): 01.01.95. for purposes specified in rule 1 (5). Effect: S.I. 1952/565; 1954/240; 1956/671; 1965/195; 1966/1551, 1552; 1970/2013; 1979/1630; 1981/1222, 1223; 1984/2058; 1987/2231; 1988/537; 1993/2227, 2228 revoked. Territorial extent & classification: S. General. –64p. – 0 11 044931 2 *£8.05*

YOUTH COURTS AND OFFENDERS

The Essex Youth Court Panel Order 1994 No. 2761. Enabling power: *Children and Young Persons Act 1933, sch. 2, paras. 6, 20, 21*. Made: 21.10.94. Coming into force: 01.01.96. exc. for making appointments to the first youth court panel appointed after the date of this Order it shall come into force forwith Effect: None. – *Unpublished*

The Gloucestershire Youth Court Panels Order 1994 No. 716. Enabling power: *Children and Young Persons Act 1993, sch. 2, paras. 6 20 21*. Made: 03.03.94. Coming into force: 01.07.94. Effect: S.I. 1989/1811 revoked. – *Unpublished*

The Hertfordshire Youth Court Panels Order 1994 No. 1107. Enabling power: *Children and Young Persons Act 1933, sch. 2, paras. 6, 20, 21*. Made: 18.04.94. Coming into force: In accord with art. 1. Effect: None. – *Unpublished*

The Humberside Youth Court Panel Order 1994 No. 1775. Enabling power: *Children and Young Persons Act 1933, sch. 2, paras. 6, 20, 21*. Made: 01.07.94. Coming into force: 01.09.94. Effect: None. – *Unpublished*

The Lancashire Youth Courth Panels Order 1994 No. 949. Enabling power: *Children and Young Persons Act 1933, sch. 2, paras. 6, 20, 21*. Made: 25.03.94. Coming into force: 01.04.94. Effect: None. – *Unpublished*

The Lincolnshire Youth Court Panel Order 1994 No. 420. Enabling power: *Children and Young Persons Act 1933, sch. 2, paras. 6, 20, 21*. Made: 23.02.94. Coming into force: 01.03.94. Effect: None. – *Unpublished*

The Oxfordshire Youth Court Panel Order 1994 No. 1207. Enabling power: *Children and Young Persons Act 1933, sch. 2, paras. 6, 20, 21*. Made: 28.04.94. Coming into force: 28.04.94. for the purpose of making appointments to the first youth court panel appointed after 28/04/94 & 01.07.94 for all other purposes. Effect: None. – *Unpublished*

The Staffordshire Youth Court Panel Order 1994 No. 2757. Enabling power: *Children and Young Persons Act 1933, sch. 2, paras. 6, 20, 21*. Made: 21.10.94. Coming into force: 01.01.95. exc. for making appointments to the first youth court panel appointed after the date of this Order it shall come into force forwith Effect: None. – *Unpublished*

The Suffolk Youth Court Panel (No. 2) Order 1994 No. 1718. Enabling power: *Children and Young Persons Act 1933, sch. 2, para. 4*. Made: 27.06.94. Coming into force: 01.09.94. Effect: None. – *Unpublished*

The Suffolk Youth Court Panels Order 1994 No. 479. Enabling power: *Children and Young Persons Act 1933, sch. 2, paras. 6 20 21*. Made: 24.02.94. Coming into force: 01.01.95. Effect: S.I. 1988/607 revoked. – *Unpublished*

The Youth Courts (London) Order 1994 No. 1695. Enabling power: *Children and Young Persons Act 1933, sch. 2, paras. 14, 20*. Issued: 07.07.94. Made: 28.06.94. Coming into force: 01.09.94. Effect: S.I. 1975/1385; 1984/713; 1990/766 revoked. Territorial extent & classification: E/W. General. –2p. – 0 11 044695 X *£0.65*

NUMERICAL LIST OF STATUTORY INSTRUMENTS

1	Telecommunications
2	Road traffic
3	Roads and bridges, Scotland
4	Roads and bridges, Scotland
5	Roads and bridges, Scotland
6	Roads and bridges, Scotland
7	Road traffic
8	Road traffic
9	Road traffic
10	Road traffic
11	Road traffic
12	Highways, England and Wales
13	Road traffic
14	Road traffic
15	Local government, England and Wales
16	Road traffic
17	Road traffic
18	Road traffic
19	Road traffic
20	Road traffic
21	Road traffic
22	National Health Service, England and Wales
23	National Health Service, England and Wales
24	National Health Service, England and Wales
25	National Health Service, England and Wales
26	National Health Service, England and Wales
27	National Health Service, England and Wales
28	Highways, England and Wales
29	National Health Service, England and Wales
30	National Health Service, England and Wales
31	National Health Service, England and Wales
32	National Health Service, England and Wales
33	National Health Service, England and Wales
34	National Health Service, England and Wales
35	National Health Service, England and Wales
36	National Health Service, England and Wales
37	Local government, England and Wales
38	Road traffic
39	Road traffic
40	Road traffic
41	Road traffic
42	Housing, England and Wales
43	Highways, England and Wales
44	Road traffic
45	Road traffic
46	Road traffic
47	Road traffic
48	Road traffic
49	Road traffic
50	Public health, England and Wales
	Public health, Scotland
	Public Health, Northern Ireland
51	National Health Service, England and Wales
52	National Health Service, England and Wales
53	National Health Service, England and Wales
54	National Health Service, England and Wales
55	National Health Service, England and Wales
56	Road traffic
57	Road traffic
58	Road traffic
59	National Health Service, England and Wales
60	National Health Service, England and Wales
61	National Health Service, England and Wales
62	National Health Service, England and Wales
63	Public health, England and Wales
	Public health, Scotland
	Public health, Northern Ireland
64	
(S. 1)	Rating and valuation
65	Public health, England and Wales
	Public health, Scotland
	Public health, Northern Ireland
66	Local government, England and Wales
67	Local government, England and Wales
68	Road traffic
69	Road traffic
70	Opticians
71	
(C. 1)	Criminal law, England and Wales
	Criminal law, Scotland
	Criminal law, Northern Ireland
72	Monopolies and mergers
73	Water industry, England and Wales
74	Road traffic
75	Road traffic
76	Road traffic
77	Road traffic
78	Road traffic
79	Road traffic
80	Road traffic
81	
(C. 2)	Road traffic
82	Road traffic
83	Representation of the people
84	Transport
85	Road traffic
86	
(C. 3)	Pensions
87	
(C. 4)	Income tax
88	Road traffic
89	Road traffic
90	Road traffic

NUMERICAL LIST OF STATUTORY INSTRUMENTS 201

91	Road traffic	141	European Communities
92	Road traffic	142	Local government, England and Wales
93	Road traffic	143	Customs and excise
94	Agriculture	144	Customs and excise
95	Road traffic	145	
96	Road traffic	(S. 5)	National Health Service, Scotland
97	Road traffic	146	Road traffic
98	Road traffic	147	Road traffic
99	Road traffic	148	Road traffic
100	Road traffic	149	Road traffic
101	Medicines	150	Road traffic
102	Medicines	151	Road traffic
103	Medicines	152	Road traffic
104	Medicines	153	Road traffic
105	Medicines	154	Road traffic
106		155	Road traffic
(S. 2)	Housing, Scotland	156	Education, England and Wales
107		157	Transport
(S. 3)	National Health Service, Scotland	158	Employment and training
108	Highways, England and Wales	159	Employment and training
109	Race relations	160	Food
110	Highways, England and Wales	161	National Health Service, England and Wales
111		162	National Health Service, England and Wales
(S. 4)	River, Scotland	163	National Health Service, England and Wales
112	Road traffic	164	National Health Service, England and Wales
113	Road traffic	165	National Health Service, England and Wales
114	Road traffic	166	National Health Service, England and Wales
115		167	National Health Service, England and Wales
(C. 5)	Companies	168	National Health Service, England and Wales
116	Road traffic	169	National Health Service, England and Wales
117	Companies	170	National Health Service, England and Wales
118	Health and safety	171	National Health Service, England and Wales
119	Criminal law, England and Wales	172	National Health Service, England and Wales
120	Road traffic	173	National Health Service, England and Wales
121	Road traffic	174	National Health Service, England and Wales
122	Road traffic	175	National Health Service, England and Wales
123	Road traffic	176	National Health Service, England and Wales
124	Road traffic	177	National Health Service, England and Wales
125	Road traffic	178	National Health Service, England and Wales
126	Road traffic	179	National Health Service, England and Wales
127	Road traffic	180	National Health Service, England and Wales
128	Road traffic	181	National Health Service, England and Wales
129	Agriculture	182	National Health Service, England and Wales
130	Local government, England and Wales	183	National Health Service, England and Wales
131	National Health Service, England and Wales	184	National Health Service, England and Wales
132	Friendly societies	185	National Health Service, England and Wales
133	Housing, England and Wales	186	Road traffic
134	Road traffic	187	Insider dealing
135	Council tax, England and Wales	188	Insider dealing
136	Road traffic	189	National lottery
137	Road traffic	190	Road traffic
138	Road traffic	191	Road traffic
139	Road traffic	192	Road traffic
140	Road traffic		

NUMERICAL LIST OF STATUTORY INSTRUMENTS

193	Road traffic	242	
194	National Health Service, England and Wales	(C. 7)	Criminal law, England and Wales
195	National Health Service, England and Wales		Criminal law, Scotland
196	National Health Service, England and Wales		Criminal law, Northern Ireland
197	National Health Service, England and Wales	243	Road traffic
198	National Health Service, England and Wales	244	Road traffic
199	Environmental protection	245	Land drainage
200		246	Local government, England and Wales
(S. 6)	New towns	247	Copyright
201		248	Road traffic
(S. 7)	Armorial bearings, ensigns and flags	249	Agriculture
202		250	Revoked and replaced by SI 1994/933 before published
(C. 6)	Transport	251	Revoked and replaced by SI 1994/932 before published
203	Road traffic	252	Revoked and replaced by SI 1994/931 before published
204	Road traffic	253	Revoked and replaced by SI 1994/930 before published
205	Road traffic	254	Revoked and replaced by SI 1994/929 before published
206	Road traffic	255	Road traffic
207	Road traffic	256	Road traffic
208	Road traffic	257	Road traffic
209	Road traffic	258	Road traffic
210	Road traffic	259	
211	Road traffic	(S. 9)	Local government, Scotland
212	Road traffic	260	Transport
213	Road traffic	261	Road traffic
214	Road traffic	262	Children and young persons
215	Road traffic	263	Copyright
216	Road traffic	264	Rights in performances
217	Road traffic	265	Trustees
218	Local government, England and Wales	266	Housing, England and Wales
219	Local government, England and Wales	267	Town and country planning, England and Wales
220	Road traffic	268	Social security
221		269	Road traffic
(S. 8)	Court of Session, Scotland	270	Road traffic
222	Education, England and Wales	271	Road traffic
223	National Health Service, England and Wales	272	Road traffic
224	National Health Service, England and Wales	273	Road traffic
225	National Health Service, England and Wales	274	Road traffic
226	National Health Service, England and Wales	275	Food
227	Family law	276	Medicines
228	Legal aid and advice, England and Wales	277	Education, England and Wales
229	Legal aid and advice, England and Wales	278	National Health Service, England and Wales
230	Legal aid and advice, England and Wales	279	National Health Service, England and Wales
231	Road traffic	280	National Health Service, England and Wales
232	Health and safety	281	National Health Service, England and Wales
233	Companies	282	Agriculture
234	Telecommunications	283	Road traffic
235	Road traffic	284	National Health Service, England and Wales
236	Income tax	285	Road traffic
237	Health and safety	286	Land charges
238	Agriculture		
239	Agriculture		
240	Agriculture		
241	Agriculture		

No.	Subject
287	Land charges
288	Legal profession
289	Road traffic
290	Road traffic
291	Road traffic
292	Road traffic
293	Road traffic
294	Road traffic
295	Income tax
296	Income tax
297	Road traffic
298	Food
299	Health and safety
300	Road traffic
301	Road traffic
302	Road traffic
303	Road traffic
304	Road traffic
305	Veterinary surgeons
306 (L. 1)	County courts
307	National Health Service, England and Wales
308	National Health Service, England and Wales
309	National Health Service, England and Wales
310	Land drainage
311	Public health, England and Wales
312	Road traffic
313	Road traffic
314	Road traffic
315	Road traffic
316	National Health Service, England and Wales
317	National Health Service, England and Wales
318	National Health Service, England and Wales
319	Road traffic
320	Road traffic
321	Road traffic
322	Road traffic
323	Education, England and Wales
324	Road traffic
325	Road traffic
326 (S. 10)	Sea fisheries
327	Civil aviation
328	Road traffic
329	Road traffic
330	Local government, England and Wales
331	Local government, England and Wales
332	Road traffic
333	Road traffic
334	Road traffic
335	Road traffic
336	Road traffic
337	Road traffic
338	Local government, England and Wales
339	Local government, England and Wales
340	Financial services
341	Industrial and provident societies
342	Representation of the people
343	National debt
344	Road traffic
345	Road traffic
346	Road traffic
347	Road traffic
348	Road traffic
349	Education, England and Wales
350	Pensions
351 (S. 11)	Education, Scotland
352	Civil aviation
353	Road traffic
354	Road traffic
355	Road traffic
356	Road traffic
357	Road traffic
358	National Health Service, England and Wales
359	National Health Service, England and Wales
360	National Health Service, England and Wales
361	Revoked and replaced by SI 1994/694 before published
362	Patents
363	Trade marks
364	Road traffic
365	Road traffic
366	Road traffic
367	Road traffic
368	Road traffic
369	Road traffic
370	Road traffic
371	Transport and works
372	Offshore installations
373	Road traffic
374	Road traffic
375	Road traffic
376	Road traffic
377	Road traffic
378	Road traffic
379	Road traffic
380	Road traffic
381	Road traffic
382	Road traffic
383	Road traffic
384	Road traffic
385	Road traffic
386	Road traffic
387	Road traffic
388	Road traffic
389	Road traffic
390	Road traffic

391 (S. 12)	Court of Session, Scotland	436 (C. 13)	Education, England and Wales
392 (S. 13)	Sheriff Court, Scotland	437	Road traffic
393	Road traffic	438	Road traffic
394	Road traffic	439	Road traffic
395	Road traffic	440	Clean air
396	Road traffic	441	Road traffic
397	Health and safety	442	Road traffic
398 (C. 8) (S. 14)	Town and country planning, Scotland	443	Road traffic
399	Road traffic	444	Road traffic
400	National Health Service, England and Wales	445	Road traffic
401	National Health Service, England and Wales	446	Road traffic
402	National Health Service, England and Wales	447 (C. 9)	Transport
403	National Health Service, England and Wales	448	Road traffic
404	National Health Service, England and Wales	449	Insurance
405	National Health Service, England and Wales	450	Trade descriptions
406	Road traffic	451	Sea fisheries
407	Sugar	452	Sea fisheries
408	Road traffic	453	Broadcasting
409	Road traffic	454	Broadcasting
410	Road traffic	455	Road traffic
411	Road traffic	456	Road traffic
412	Road traffic	457	Road traffic
413	Road traffic	458	Road traffic
414	Road traffic	459	Road traffic
415	Rating and valuation	460	Road traffic
416	Road traffic	461	Road traffic
417	Terms and conditions of employment	462	Road traffic
418	Road traffic	463	Road traffic
419	Road traffic	464	Road traffic
420	Youth courts and offenders	465	Road traffic
421	Rating and valuation	466	Road traffic
422	Merchant shipping	467	Road traffic
423	Scientific research	468	Acquisition of land
424	Scientific research	469	Acquisition of land
425	Scientific research	470	Social security
426 (NI. 1)	Northern Ireland	471	Probation
427	Representation of the people	472	Animals
428	Representation of the people	473	Probation
429 (NI. 2)	Northern Ireland	474	Road traffic
430 (S. 15)	Housing, Scotland	475	Road traffic
431 (S. 16)	Education, Scotland	476	Road traffic
432	Open spaces	477	Road traffic
433	Road traffic	478 (S. 17)	Education, Scotland
434	Road traffic	479	Youth courts and offenders
435	Housing, England and Wales	480	Justices of the Peace, England and Wales
		481	National Health Service, England and Wales
		482	National Health Service, England and Wales
		483	National Health Service, England and Wales
		484	National Health Service, England and Wales
		485	National Health Service, England and Wales
		486	National Health Service, England and Wales

NUMERICAL LIST OF STATUTORY INSTRUMENTS

487	National Health Service, England and Wales	533	Electricity
488	National Health Service, England and Wales	534	Customs and excise
489	National Health Service, England and Wales	535	Dangerous drugs
490	National Health Service, England and Wales	536	Industrial tribunals
491	National Health Service, England and Wales	537	Education, England and Wales
492	National Health Service, England and Wales	538	Industrial tribunals
493	National Health Service, England and Wales	539	Council tax, England and Wales
494	National Health Service, England and Wales	540	Council tax, England and Wales
495	National Health Service, England and Wales	541	Merchant shipping
496		542	Social security
(S. 18)	National Health Service, Scotland		Terms and conditions of employment
497		543	Council tax, England and Wales
(S. 19)	Lands Tribunal	544	Social security
498		545	National Health Service, England and Wales
(S. 20)	Scottish Land Court	546	Trade unions
499	Agriculture	547	Rating and valuation
500	Pensions	548	Housing, England and Wales
501	Cultural objects		Housing, Scotland
502	Merchant shipping	549	Road traffic
503	Civil aviation	550	Road traffic
504	Community charges, England and Wales	551	Highways, England and Wales
505	Council tax, England and Wales	552	Road traffic
506	Social security	553	Local government, England and Wales
507		554	Road traffic
(C. 10)	Education, England and Wales	555	Employment and training
508	Road traffic	556	British nationality
509	Road traffic	557	Local government, England and Wales
510		558	Medicines
(S. 21)	National Health Service, Scotland	559	Social security
511	Road traffic	560	Local government, England and Wales
512	Road traffic	561	Terms and conditions of employment
513	Road traffic	562	Terms and conditions of employment
514	Road traffic	563	Social security
515	Road traffic	564	Highways, England and Wales
516	Road traffic	565	Housing, England and Wales
517	Road traffic	566	Housing, England and Wales
518	Road traffic	567	Local government, England and Wales
519	Road traffic	568	Housing, England and Wales
520	Insurance	569	Local government, England and Wales
521	Road traffic	570	Channel tunnel
522	Environmental protection	571	
523	Social security	(C. 11)	Transport
524	Banks and banking	572	Transport
525	Building societies	573	Transport
526	Financial services	574	Transport
527	Social security	575	Transport
528		576	Transport
(S. 22)	Local government, Scotland	577	Public passenger transport
529		578	Social security
(S. 23)	Local government, Scotland	579	Social security
530	National Health Service, England and Wales	580	Education, England and Wales
531		581	Education, England and Wales
(S. 24)	Pensions	582	
532	Education, England and Wales	(S. 25)	Housing, Scotland

583	Road traffic		Water supply, Scotland
584	Road traffic	630	
585	Road traffic	(S. 29)	Local government, Scotland
586	National Health Service, England and Wales	631	Parliament
587	Road traffic	632	
588	Road traffic	(S. 30)	Housing, Scotland
589	National Health Service, England and Wales	633	National Health Service, England and Wales
590	National Health Service, England and Wales	634	National Health Service, England and Wales
591	Road traffic	635	
592	Terms and conditions of employment	(S. 31)	National Health Service, Scotland
593	Road traffic	636	
594	Road traffic	(S. 32)	National Health Service, Scotland
595	Telegraphs	637	Energy conservation
596	Road traffic	638	Road traffic
597	Road traffic	639	Road traffic
598	Road traffic	640	National Health Service, England and Wales
599	Medicines	641	Police
600	Clerk of the Crown in Chancery	642	Tribunals and inquiries
601		643	Insurance
(L. 2)	Supreme Court of England and Wales	644	Partnership
602	National Health Service, England and Wales	645	Education, England and Wales
603	National Health Service, England and Wales	646	Education, England and Wales
604		647	Education, England and Wales
(L. 3)	Supreme Court of England and Wales	648	Housing, England and Wales
605	Road traffic	649	Road traffic
606	Transport	650	Education, England and Wales
607	Transport	651	Education, England and Wales
608	Transport	652	Education, England and Wales
609	Transport	653	Education, England and Wales
610	Education, England and Wales	654	Education, England and Wales
611	Scientific research	655	Building societies
612	Education, England and Wales	656	Building societies
613	Housing, England and Wales	657	Friendly societies
614	Road traffic	658	Industrial and provident societies
615	Local government, England and Wales	659	Telegraphs
616	Road traffic	660	Industrial and provident societies
617	Road traffic	661	National Health Service, England and Wales
618	Road traffic	662	National Health Service, England and Wales
619	National Health Service, England and Wales	663	National Health Service, England and Wales
620	National Health Service, England and Wales	664	National Health Service, England and Wales
621	National Health Service, England and Wales	665	National Health Service, England and Wales
622	National Health Service, England and Wales	666	National Health Service, England and Wales
623	National Health Service, England and Wales	667	Social security
624	National Health Service, England and Wales	668	Housing, England and Wales
625	National Health Service, England and Wales	669	Health and safety
626		670	Health and safety
(S. 26)	Council tax, Scotland	671	Social security
	Water supply, Scotland	672	Food
627	Housing, England and Wales	673	Animals
628		674	Agriculture
(S. 27)	Council tax, Scotland	675	Plant breeders' rights
	Water supply, Scotland	676	Seeds
629		677	Town and country planning, England and Wales
(S. 28)	Council tax, Scotland		

NUMERICAL LIST OF STATUTORY INSTRUMENTS

678	Town and country planning, England and Wales	723	Land drainage
679	National Health Service, England and Wales	724	Town and country planning, England and Wales
680	National Health Service, England and Wales	725	Landlord and tenant, England and Wales
681	National Health Service, England and Wales	726	Social security
682	National Health Service, England and Wales	727	Companies
683	National Health Service, England and Wales	728	Income tax
684	National Health Service, England and Wales	729	Opticians
685 (S. 33)	Agriculture	730	Terms and conditions of employment
686	Value added tax	731	Family law
687	Value added tax	732	Road traffic
688	Road traffic	733	Road traffic
689	Road traffic	734	Road traffic
690	National Health Service, England and Wales	735	Road traffic
691	Transport	736	Road traffic
692	Education, England and Wales	737	Road traffic
693	Housing, England and Wales	738	Road traffic
694	Customs and excise	739	Road traffic
695	Housing, England and Wales	740	Road traffic
696	Medicines	741	Road traffic
697 (S. 34)	National Health Service, Scotland	742	Road traffic
698	Revoked by SI 1994/699 before published	743	Food
699	Due to short life of this SI this was also never published	744	Telecommunications
		745	National Health Service, England and Wales
700 (C. 12)	Criminal law, England and Wales	746	Road traffic
	Criminal law, Scotland	747	Representation of the people
	Criminal law, Northern Ireland	748	Representation of the people
701	Transport and works	749	Building societies
	Transport	750	Building societies
702	Public passenger transport	751	Road traffic
703	Ecclesiastical law, England	752	Road traffic
704	Social security	753	Road traffic
705	Road traffic	754	Road traffic
706	County courts	755	Road traffic
707	Agriculture	756	Road traffic
708	Agriculture	757	European Communities
709	Agriculture	758	European Communities
710	Agriculture	759	European Communities
711	Agriculture	760	European Communities
712	Agriculture	761	European Communities
713	Road traffic	762 (NI. 3)	Northern Ireland
714	Trustees	763	Northern Ireland
715	Pensions	764	Northern Ireland
716	Youth courts and offenders	765 (NI. 4)	Northern Ireland
717	Education, England and Wales	766 (NI. 5)	Northern Ireland
718 (C. 14)	Transport	767	Income tax
719	Justices of the Peace, England and Wales	768	Income tax
720	Road traffic	769	Income tax
721	Road traffic	770	Income tax
722	Road traffic	771	Pensions
		772	Pensions

773	Pensions	821	Road traffic
774	Merchant shipping	822	Road traffic
775	Income tax	823	Road traffic
776	Pensions	824	Road traffic
777	Income tax	825	National assistance services
778	Income tax	826	National assistance services
779	Education, England and Wales	827	National Health Service, England and Wales
780		828	National Health Service, England and Wales
(C. 15)	Environmental protection	829	National Health Service, England and Wales
781	Social security	830	National Health Service, England and Wales
782	Representation of the people	831	National Health Service, England and Wales
783	Civil aviation	832	National Health Service, England and Wales
784	Civil aviation	833	National Health Service, England and Wales
785	Civil aviation	834	Rating and valuation
786	Road traffic	835	Prevention and suppression of terrorism
787	Medicines	836	Road traffic
788	Road traffic	837	Road traffic
789	Road traffic	838	Road traffic
790	Road traffic	839	Road traffic
791	Merchant shipping	840	Road traffic
792	Road traffic	841	Road traffic
793	Road traffic	842	Road traffic
794	Road traffic	843	Road traffic
795	Road traffic	844	Housing, England and Wales
796	Road traffic	845	Road traffic
797	National Health Service, England and Wales	846	Road traffic
798	National Health Service, England and Wales	847	Road traffic
799	Highways, England and Wales	848	National Health Service, England and Wales
800	Highways, England and Wales	849	National Health Service, England and Wales
801	Highways, England and Wales	850	National Health Service, England and Wales
802	Highways, England and Wales	851	National Health Service, England and Wales
803	Value added tax	852	National Health Service, England and Wales
804	Food	853	National Health Service, England and Wales
805	Legal aid and advice, England and Wales	854	National Health Service, England and Wales
806	Legal aid and advice, England and Wales	855	National Health Service, England and Wales
807	Legal aid and advice, England and Wales	856	National Health Service, England and Wales
808		857	Transport
(L. 4)	Family proceedings Supreme Court of England and Wales County courts	858	National Health Service, England and Wales
		859	National Health Service, England and Wales
		860	National Health Service, England and Wales
809		861	National Health Service, England and Wales
(L. 5)	Magistrates' courts	862	National Health Service, England and Wales
810		863	National Health Service, England and Wales
(S. 35)	Water supply, Scotland	864	Road traffic
811	Road traffic	865	Road traffic
812	Road traffic	866	Road traffic
813	Road traffic	867	Local government, England and Wales
814	Road traffic	868	Road traffic
815	Road traffic	869	Road traffic
816	Road traffic	870	Road traffic
817	Road traffic	871	Road traffic
818	Harbours, docks, piers and ferries	872	Road traffic
819	Road traffic	873	Road traffic
820	Road traffic		

Number	Subject
874	Telecommunications
875	Telecommunications
876	Telecommunications
877	Road traffic
878	Road traffic
879	Road traffic
880	Road traffic
881	Road traffic
882	Road traffic
883	Road traffic
884 (S. 36)	National Health Service, Scotland
885	Road traffic
886	Road traffic
887	Road traffic
888	Road traffic
889	Road traffic
890	Road traffic
891	Road traffic
892	Road traffic
893	Road traffic
894	Representation of the people
895	Pensions
896	National Health Service, England and Wales
897	Road traffic
898	Highways, England and Wales
899	Medicines
900	Road traffic
901	Road traffic
902	Local government, England and Wales
903	Rating and valuation
904	Civil aviation
905	Civil aviation
906	Road traffic
907	Road traffic
908	Road traffic
909	Atomic energy and radioactive substances
910	Education, England and Wales
911 (S. 37)	Rating and valuation
912 (S. 38)	Rating and valuation
913 (S. 39)	Rating and valuation
914	Road traffic
915	Road traffic
916	Road traffic
917	Road traffic
918	Agriculture
919	Agriculture
920	Agriculture
921	Agriculture
922	Agriculture
923	Agriculture
924	Agriculture
925	Agriculture
926	Agriculture
927	Agriculture
928	Agriculture
929	Agriculture
930	Agriculture
931	Agriculture
932	Agriculture
933	Agriculture
934	Education, England and Wales
935 (C. 16)	Housing, England and Wales Urban development
936	Road traffic
937	Education, England and Wales
938	Education, England and Wales
939	Taxes
940	Road traffic
941	Road traffic
942	Road traffic
943	Road traffic
944	Animals
945	National Health Service, England and Wales
946	Justices of the Peace, England and Wales
947	Agriculture
948	Pensions
949	Youth courts and offenders
950	Companies
951	Agriculture
952	Telecommunications
953	Telecommunications
954	Telecommunications
955	Customs and excise
956	Betting, gaming and lotteries
957	Betting, gaming and lotteries
958	Betting, gaming and lotteries
959	Education, England and Wales
960 (S. 40)	Food
961	Local government, England and Wales
962	Ecclesiastical law, England
963	Pensions
964	Road traffic
965	Road traffic
966	Road traffic
967	Road traffic
968	Official secrets
969	Probation
970	Channel tunnel
971	Road traffic
972	Road traffic
973	Road traffic
974	Road traffic

No.	Subject
975	Road traffic
976	Road traffic
977	Water industry, England and Wales
978	Water industry, England and Wales
979	Food
980	Road traffic
981	Road traffic
982	Road traffic
983	Road traffic
984	Road traffic
985	Road traffic
986	National Health Service, England and Wales
987	National Health Service, England and Wales
988	National Health Service, England and Wales
989	National Health Service, England and Wales
990	National Health Service, England and Wales
991	National Health Service, England and Wales
992	National Health Service, England and Wales
993	National Health Service, England and Wales
994	National Health Service, England and Wales
995	National Health Service, England and Wales
996	Road traffic
997	
(S. 41)	Legal aid and advice, Scotland
998	
(S. 42)	Legal aid and advice, Scotland
999	Rating and valuation
1000	
(S. 43)	Legal aid and advice, Scotland
1001	
(S. 44)	Legal aid and advice, Scotland
1002	Highways, England and Wales
1003	Social security
1004	Social security
1005	New towns, England and Wales
1006	Telecommunications
1007	Telecommunications
1008	Telecommunications
1009	Highways, England and Wales
1010	Highways, England and Wales
1011	Highways, England and Wales
1012	Injuries in war compensation
1013	
(S. 45)	Crofters, cottars and small landholders
1014	
(S. 46)	Crofters, cottars and small landholders
1015	
(S. 47)	Legal aid and advice, Scotland
1016	
(S. 48)	Legal aid and advice, Scotland
1017	
(S. 49)	Legal aid and advice, Scotland
1018	
(S. 50)	Legal aid and advice, Scotland
1019	
(S. 51)	Legal aid and advice, Scotland
1020	Highways, England and Wales
1021	Highways, England and Wales
1022	Highways, England and Wales
1023	Highways, England and Wales
1024	Highways, England and Wales
1025	Highways, England and Wales
1026	Road traffic
1027	Road traffic
1028	Road traffic
1029	Food
1030	Road traffic
1031	Road traffic
1032	Road traffic
1033	Road traffic
1034	Road traffic
1035	Road traffic
1036	Road traffic
1037	Highways, England and Wales
1038	Highways, England and Wales
1039	Transport and works
1040	Road traffic
1041	Education, England and Wales
1042	
(S. 52)	Betting, gaming and lotteries
1043	
(S. 53)	Betting, gaming and lotteries
1044	Representation of the people
1045	Road traffic
1046	
(S. 54)	Housing, Scotland
1047	Education, England and Wales
1048	Education, England and Wales
1049	
(S. 55)	Legal aid and advice, Scotland
1050	
(S. 56)	Legal aid and advice, Scotland
1051	Road traffic
1052	Road traffic
1053	National Health Service, England and Wales
1054	National Health Service, England and Wales
1055	
(C. 16)	National lottery
	Betting, gaming and lotteries
1056	Environmental protection
1057	Water resources, England and Wales
1058	Education, England and Wales
1059	Education, England and Wales
1060	Transport
	Transport and works
1061	
(S. 57)	Legal aid and advice, Scotland
1062	Pensions

NUMERICAL LIST OF STATUTORY INSTRUMENTS

1063	Children and young persons	1112	Road traffic
1064	Telegraphs	1113	Road traffic
	Telecommunications	1114	Road traffic
	Broadcasting	1115	Road traffic
1065	Cinemas and films	1116	Road traffic
1066	Road traffic	1117	Road traffic
1067	Road traffic	1118	Road traffic
1068	Road traffic	1119	Road traffic
1069	Road traffic	1120	Road traffic
1070	Electricity	1121	Road traffic
1071	Telecommunications	1122	Road traffic
1072	Telecommunications	1123	Road traffic
1073	Road traffic	1124	Road traffic
1074	Road traffic	1125	
1075	Road traffic	(S. 58)	Education, Scotland
1076	Road traffic	1126	Road traffic
1077	Road traffic	1127	Road traffic
1078	Road traffic	1128	Road traffic
1079	Road traffic	1129	Road traffic
1080	Road traffic	1130	Land registration, England and Wales
1081	Road traffic	1131	Road traffic
1082	Social security	1132	Road traffic
1083	Education, England and Wales	1133	Road traffic
1084	Education, England and Wales	1134	Agriculture
1085	Education, England and Wales	1135	Education, England and Wales
1086	National Health Service, England and Wales	1136	Education, England and Wales
1087	Metropolitan and City police districts	1137	Environmental protection
1088	Highways, England and Wales	1138	Road traffic
1089		1139	
(C. 17)	Representation of the people	(S. 59)	Court of Session, Scotland
1090	Road traffic	1140	
1091	Road traffic	(S. 60)	Court of Session, Scotland
1092	Road traffic	1141	
1093	Road traffic	(S. 61)	Sheriff Court, Scotland
1094	Road traffic	1142	
1095	Restrictive trade practices	(S. 62)	Sheriff Court, Scotland
1096		1143	Road traffic
(C. 18)	Environmental protection	1144	Road traffic
1097	Road traffic	1145	Road traffic
1098	Road traffic	1146	Road traffic
1099	Road traffic	1147	Road traffic
1100	Road traffic	1148	Road traffic
1101	Social security	1149	Water, England and Wales
1102	Police	1150	Water, England and Wales
1103		1151	Wildlife
(L. 6)	Supreme Court of England and Wales	1152	Wildlife
1104	Merchant shipping	1153	Civil aviation
1105	Social security	1154	Civil aviation
1106	Justices of the Peace, England and Wales	1155	Civil aviation
1107	Youth courts and offenders	1156	Civil aviation
1108	Road traffic	1157	Civil aviation
1109	Road traffic	1158	Road traffic
1110	Road traffic	1159	Road traffic
1111	Road traffic	1160	Road traffic

1161	Road traffic	1213	Road traffic
1162	Road traffic	1214	Road traffic
1163	Road traffic	1215	Road traffic
1164	Road traffic	1216	Road traffic
1165	Road traffic	1217	Road traffic
1166	Road traffic	1218	Road traffic
1167	Local government, England and Wales	1219	Road traffic
1168	Road traffic	1220	Road traffic
1169	Road traffic	1221	Road traffic
1170	National lottery	1222	Road traffic
1171	Civil aviation	1223	Road traffic
1172	Civil aviation	1224	Road traffic
1173	Road traffic	1225	Road traffic
1174	Road traffic	1226	Road traffic
1175	Road traffic	1227	Transport
1176	Road traffic	1228	Probation
1177	Road traffic	1229	Civil aviation
1178	Road traffic	1230	Social security
1179	Road traffic		Terms and conditions of employment
1180	Road traffic	1231	Education, England and Wales
1181	Road traffic	1232	Education, England and Wales
1182	Road traffic	1233	
1183	Road traffic	(S. 64)	Legal aid and advice, Scotland
1184	Road traffic	1234	
1185	Road traffic	(C. 20)	Revoked by 1994/1253 before published
1186	Education, England and Wales	1235	Charities
1187		1236	Road traffic
(S. 63)	Acquisition of land	1237	Road traffic
1188	Value added tax	1238	Road traffic
1189	Public health, England and Wales	1239	Road traffic
1190	Telecommunications	1240	Road traffic
1191	Customs and excise	1241	Road traffic
1192	Government trading funds	1242	Road traffic
1193	Road traffic	1243	Road traffic
1194	Civil aviation	1244	Road traffic
1195	Education, England and Wales	1245	Road traffic
1196	Education, England and Wales	1246	Road traffic
1197	Civil aviation	1247	Road traffic
1198	Road traffic	1248	Road traffic
1199	Road traffic	1249	Road traffic
1200	National lottery	1250	Road traffic
1201		1251	Education, England and Wales
(C. 19)	Merchant shipping	1252	Road traffic
1202	Telecommunications	1253	
1203	Telecommunications	(C. 21)	Value added tax
1204	Telecommunications	1254	Road traffic
1205	National Health Service, England and Wales	1255	Education, England and Wales
1206	National Health Service, England and Wales	1256	Education, England and Wales
1207	Youth courts and offenders	1257	
1208	Justices of the Peace, England and Wales	(C. 22)	Value added tax
1209	Road traffic	1258	Weights and measures
1210	Local government, England and Wales	1259	Weights and measures
1211	National Health Service, England and Wales	1260	National Health Service, England and Wales
1212	Income tax	1261	National Health Service, England and Wales

NUMERICAL LIST OF STATUTORY INSTRUMENTS 213

1262	National Health Service, England and Wales	1311	National Health Service, England and Wales
1263	Housing, England and Wales	1312	National Health Service, England and Wales
1264	Civil aviation	1313	National Health Service, England and Wales
1265	Road traffic	1314	National Health Service, England and Wales
1266		1315	National Health Service, England and Wales
(S. 65)	Building and buildings	1316	National Health Service, England and Wales
1267	Road traffic	1317	National Health Service, England and Wales
1268	National Health Service, England and Wales	1318	National Health Service, England and Wales
1269	National Health Service, England and Wales	1319	National Health Service, England and Wales
1270	Education, England and Wales	1320	National Health Service, England and Wales
1271	Environmental protection	1321	Education, England and Wales
1272	Road traffic	1322	Children and young persons
1273	Road traffic	1323	United Nations
1274	Road traffic	1324	United Nations
1275	Road traffic	1325	United Nations
1276	Road traffic	1326	United Nations
1277	Road traffic	1327	European Communities
1278	Road traffic	1328	Public passenger transport
1279	Road traffic	1329	Environmental protection
1280	Road traffic	1330	Highways, England and Wales
1281	Road traffic	1331	Transport
1282	Road traffic	1332	National Health Service, England and Wales
1283	Road traffic	1333	National Health Service, England and Wales
1284	Road traffic	1334	National Health Service, England and Wales
1285	Road traffic	1335	National Health Service, England and Wales
1286	Road traffic	1336	National Health Service, England and Wales
1287	Road traffic	1337	National Health Service, England and Wales
1288		1338	National Health Service, England and Wales
(L.7)	County courts	1339	National Health Service, England and Wales
1289		1340	National Health Service, England and Wales
(L.8)	County courts	1341	National Health Service, England and Wales
1290	Education, England and Wales	1342	National lottery
1291	Agriculture	1343	National Health Service, England and Wales
1292	Agriculture	1344	Road traffic
1293	Agriculture	1345	Road traffic
1294	National Health Service, England and Wales	1346	Road traffic
1295	National Health Service, England and Wales	1347	Road traffic
1296	National Health Service, England and Wales	1348	Road traffic
1297	National Health Service, England and Wales	1349	Road traffic
1298	National Health Service, England and Wales	1350	Road traffic
1299	National Health Service, England and Wales	1351	Road traffic
1300	National Health Service, England and Wales	1352	Road traffic
1301	National Health Service, England and Wales	1353	Road traffic
1302	Agriculture	1354	Road traffic
1303	Education, England and Wales	1355	Road traffic
1304	Education, England and Wales	1356	Road traffic
1305	Road traffic	1357	Road traffic
1306	Road traffic	1358	Road traffic
1307	Income tax	1359	Road traffic
	Inheritance tax	1360	Road traffic
	Taxes	1361	Road traffic
1308	Police	1362	Road traffic
1309	National Health Service, England and Wales	1363	Road traffic
1310	National Health Service, England and Wales		

1364	Road traffic	1413	Representation of the people
1365		1414	Education, England and Wales
(C.23)	Trade unions	1415	Road traffic
	Terms and conditions of employment	1416	Road traffic
1366	Road traffic	1417	Road traffic
1367	Social security	1418	Income tax
	Terms and conditions of employment	1419	Council tax, England and Wales
1368	Road traffic	1420	Education, England and Wales
1369	Road traffic	1421	Education, England and Wales
1370	Road traffic	1422	Coal industry
1371	Roads and bridges, Scotland	1423	Seeds
1372	Roads and bridges, Scotland	1424	Agriculture
1373	Roads and bridges, Scotland	1425	Road traffic
1374	Roads and bridges, Scotland	1426	Road traffic
1375	Roads and bridges, Scotland	1427	Road traffic
1376	Road traffic	1428	Road traffic
1377	Road traffic	1429	Road traffic
1378	Road traffic	1430	Road traffic
1379	Representation of the people	1431	Rating and valuation
1380	Oaths	1432	Transport
	Legal services	1433	Transport
1381	Ancient monuments	1434	Education, England and Wales
1382	Hovercraft	1435	Education, England and Wales
1383	Merchant shipping	1436	Road traffic
1384	Road traffic	1437	
1385	Education, England and Wales	(C. 24)	Criminal law, England and Wales
1386	Environmental protection	1438	Criminal law, England and Wales
1387	Road traffic	1439	Local government, England and Wales
1388	National Health Service, England and Wales	1440	Harbours, docks, piers and ferries
1389	Local government, England and Wales	1441	
1390	Channel tunnel	(S. 67)	Plant health
1391	Civil aviation	1442	
1392	Civil aviation	(S. 68)	Town and country planning, Scotland
1393	Civil aviation	1443	
1394	Civil aviation	(S. 69)	Highways, England and Wales
1395	Civil aviation	1444	Civil aviation
1396	Civil aviation	1445	
1397	Road traffic	(C. 25)	Local government, England and Wales
1398	Road traffic		Local government, Scotland
1399	Road traffic	1446	Food
1400	Road traffic	1447	River, England and Wales
1401	Road traffic		River, Scotland
1402	Medicines		Salmon and freshwater fisheries
1403	Agriculture		Sea fisheries
1404	Agriculture	1448	River, England and Wales
1405	Channel tunnel		River, Scotland
1406	Road traffic		Salmon and freshwater fisheries
1407	Road traffic		Sea fisheries
1408		1449	Education, England and Wales
(S. 66)	National Health Service, Scotland	1450	Education, England and Wales
1409	Terms and conditions of employment	1451	Road traffic
1410	Customs and excise	1452	Road traffic
1411	Land drainage	1453	Road traffic
1412	Representation of the people	1454	Road traffic

NUMERICAL LIST OF STATUTORY INSTRUMENTS

1455	Road traffic		1505	Road traffic
1456	Road traffic		1506	Road traffic
1457	Road traffic		1507	Road traffic
1458	Road traffic		1508	Road traffic
1459	Road traffic		1509	Road traffic
1460	Road traffic		1510	Road traffic
1461	Road traffic		1511	Children and young persons
1462	Road traffic		1512	Road traffic
1463	Road traffic		1513	Road traffic
1464	Road traffic		1514	Civil aviation
1465	Road traffic		1515	Insurance
1466	Road traffic		1516	Insurance
1467	Road traffic		1517	Financial services
1468	Civil aviation		1518	Income tax
1469	Road traffic		1519	Road traffic
1470	Road traffic		1520	Education, England and Wales
1471	Road traffic		1521	Civil aviation
1472	Road traffic		1522	Civil aviation
1473	Road traffic		1523	Road traffic
1474	Road traffic		1524	Road traffic
1475	Road traffic		1525	Road traffic
1476	Road traffic		1526	Road traffic
1477	Legal aid and advice, England and Wales		1527	Income tax
1478	Education, England and Wales		1528	Agriculture
1479	Income tax		1529	Consumer protection
1480 (L. 9)	Supreme Court of England and Wales		1530	Road traffic
			1531	Medicines
1481 (L. 10)	Magistrates' courts		1532	Transport and works Transport
1482 (C. 26)	Road traffic		1533	Water, England and Wales Water supply, Scotland
1483	Road traffic		1534	National Health Service, England and Wales
1484 (C. 27)	Road traffic		1535	National Health Service, England and Wales
1485	Road traffic		1536	Supreme Court of England and Wales County courts
1486	Food		1537	Road traffic
1487	Road traffic		1538	Road traffic
1488	Road traffic		1539	Road traffic
1489	Road traffic		1540	Road traffic
1490	Road traffic		1541	Road traffic
1491	Road traffic		1542	Probation
1492	Road traffic		1543	Probation
1493	Road traffic		1544	Education, England and Wales
1494	Road traffic		1545	Road traffic
1495	Road traffic		1546	Road traffic
1496	Road traffic		1547	Road traffic
1497	Road traffic		1548	Road traffic
1498	Road traffic		1549	Road traffic
1499	Road traffic		1550	Road traffic
1500	Road traffic		1551	Road traffic
1501	Road traffic		1552	Road traffic
1502	Road traffic		1553	Social security
1503	Road traffic		1554	Medicines
1504	Road traffic			

1555	National Health Service, England and Wales	1605	Road traffic
1556		1606	Education, England and Wales
(S. 70)	Water supply, Scotland	1607	
1557	Competition	(S. 71)	National Health Service, Scotland
1558		1608	Social security
(C. 28)	Education, England and Wales	1609	Patents
1559	National Health Service, England and Wales	1610	Agriculture
1560	National Health Service, England and Wales	1611	Road traffic
1561	National Health Service, England and Wales	1612	Civil aviation
1562	National Health Service, England and Wales	1613	Road traffic
1563	National Health Service, England and Wales	1614	Highways, England and Wales
1564	National Health Service, England and Wales	1615	Education, England and Wales
1565	Road traffic	1616	Road traffic
1566	Road traffic	1617	Road traffic
1567	Income tax	1618	Road traffic
	Inheritance tax	1619	Road traffic
	Taxes	1620	Road traffic
1568	Sea fisheries	1621	Roads and bridges, Scotland
1569	Northern Ireland	1622	Road traffic
1570	Road traffic	1623	Industrial tribunals
1571	National Health Service, England and Wales	1624	Industrial tribunals
1572	National Health Service, England and Wales	1625	Road traffic
1573	National Health Service, England and Wales	1626	Road traffic
1574	National Health Service, England and Wales	1627	Road traffic
1575	National Health Service, England and Wales	1628	Road traffic
1576	National Health Service, England and Wales	1629	Road traffic
1577	Road traffic	1630	Road traffic
1578	Road traffic	1631	Road traffic
1579	Road traffic	1632	Customs and excise
1580	Road traffic	1633	Education, England and Wales
1581	Road traffic	1634	British nationality
1582	Road traffic	1635	Dangerous drugs
1583	Road traffic	1636	United Nations
1584	Road traffic	1637	United Nations
1585	Road traffic	1638	Caribbean and North Atlantic territories
1586	Road traffic	1639	Criminal law, England and Wales
1587	Road traffic	1640	Criminal law, England and Wales
1588	Road traffic		Criminal law, Northern Ireland
1589	Road traffic	1641	Criminal law, England and Wales
1590	Road traffic	1642	Defence
1591	Road traffic	1643	Defence
1592	Road traffic	1644	
1593	Road traffic	(S. 72)	Criminal law, Scotland
1594	Road traffic	1645	
1595	Road traffic	(S. 73)	Criminal law, Scotland
1596	Road traffic	1646	Social security
1597	Road traffic	1647	Harbours, docks, piers and ferries
1598	Road traffic	1648	
1599	Road traffic	(C. 29)	Transport
1600	Road traffic	1649	Transport
1601	Civil aviation	1650	Water industry, England and Wales
1602	Road traffic	1651	Road traffic
1603	Road traffic	1652	Road traffic
1604	Road traffic	1653	Road traffic

NUMERICAL LIST OF STATUTORY INSTRUMENTS 217

1654	Road traffic	1702	
1655	Road traffic	(S. 76)	Education, Scotland
1656	Road traffic	1703	Road traffic
1657	Road traffic	1704	Road traffic
1658	Road traffic	1705	Road traffic
1659	Road traffic	1706	Road traffic
1660	Road traffic	1707	Road traffic
1661		1708	Road traffic
(C. 30)	Social security	1709	Road traffic
1662	European parliament	1710	Road traffic
1663	European parliament	1711	Road traffic
1664	Road traffic	1712	Road traffic
1665	Road traffic	1713	Road traffic
1666	Sports grounds and sporting events	1714	Road traffic
1667	Channel tunnel	1715	
1668	Road traffic	(S. 77)	Education, Scotland
1669	Road traffic	1716	Animals
1670	Road traffic	1717	Justices of the peace, England and Wales
1671	Local government, England and Wales	1718	Youth courts and offenders
	Local government, Scotland	1719	Highways, England and Wales
1672	Road traffic	1720	Local government, England and Wales
1673	Education, England and Wales	1721	Agriculture
1674	Road traffic	1722	Road traffic
1675		1723	Road traffic
(S. 74)	Mental health	1724	Road traffic
1676	Road traffic	1725	Road traffic
1677	Road traffic	1726	Road traffic
1678	Road traffic	1727	Road traffic
1679	Sea fisheries	1728	Road traffic
1680	Sea fisheries	1729	Agriculture
1681	Sea fisheries	1730	Police
1682	Highways, England and Wales	1731	Civil aviation
1683	Electricity	1732	Civil aviation
1684	Road traffic	1733	Civil aviation
1685	Road traffic	1734	Civil aviation
1686	Road traffic	1735	Civil aviation
1687	Road traffic	1736	Civil aviation
1688	Highways, England and Wales	1737	Customs and excise
1689	Road traffic	1738	Customs and excise
1690		1739	Customs and excise
(C. 31)	Customs and excise	1740	Road traffic
1691	Road traffic	1741	Education, England and Wales
1692	Revoked by 1994/1739 before it was published	1742	Rating and valuation
1693	Harbours, docks, piers and ferries	1743	Education, England and Wales
1694	Road traffic	1744	Education, England and Wales
1695	Youth courts and offenders	1745	Road traffic
1696	Insurance	1746	Council tax, England and Wales
1697	Education, England and Wales	1747	Council tax, England and Wales
1698	Insurance premium tax	1748	Race relations
1699	Road traffic	1749	Road traffic
1700	Road traffic	1750	Road traffic
1701		1751	Pensions
(S. 75)	Agriculture	1752	Road traffic
		1753	Transport and works

1754	Education, England and Wales	1795	Road traffic
1755	Education, England and Wales	1796	Road traffic
1756	Criminal law, England and Wales	1797	Road traffic
	Criminal law, Scotland	1798	Road traffic
	Criminal law, Northern Ireland	1799	Road traffic
1757	Criminal law, England and Wales	1800	Road traffic
1758	Criminal law, England and Wales	1801	Road traffic
	Criminal law, Scotland	1802	Road traffic
	Criminal law, Northern Ireland	1803	Transport and works
1759	Criminal law, England and Wales		Transport
	Criminal law, Scotland	1804	Road traffic
1760	Criminal law, England and Wales	1805	Road traffic
	Criminal law, Scotland	1806	Environmental protection
	Criminal law, Northern Ireland		Health and safety
1761	Transport	1807	Social security
1762	Housing, England and Wales	1808	
1763	Housing, England and Wales	(S. 80)	Criminal law, Scotland
1764	Civil aviation	1809	Rating and valuation
1765	Civil aviation	1810	Road traffic
1766	Civil aviation	1811	Income tax
1767	Civil aviation		Inheritance tax
1768	Consumer protection		Taxes
1769		1812	Income tax
(S. 78)	High court of justiciary, Scotland	1813	Income tax
	Summary jurisdiction, Scotland		Inheritance tax
1770			Taxes
(S. 79)	National Health Service, Scotland	1814	Education, England and Wales
1771	Town and country planning, England and Wales	1815	Education, England and Wales
		1816	Education, England and Wales
1772	Northern Ireland	1817	Education, England and Wales
1773		1818	Education, England and Wales
(C. 32)	Insurance premium tax	1819	Insurance premium tax
1774	Insurance premium tax	1820	Customs and excise
1775	Youth courts and offenders	1821	Customs and excise
1776		1822	Legal aid and advice, England and Wales
(C. 33)	Human fertilisation and embryology	1823	Legal aid and advice, England and Wales
1777	Highways, England and Wales	1824	Legal aid and advice, England and Wales
1778	Harbours, docks, piers and ferries	1825	Legal aid and advice, England and Wales
1779	Social security	1826	
1780	Road traffic	(S. 81)	Education, Scotland
1781	Road traffic	1827	
1782	Road traffic	(S. 82)	Education, Scotland
1783	Road traffic	1828	
1784	Road traffic	(S. 83)	Sea fisheries
1785	Road traffic	1829	Road traffic
1786	Road traffic	1830	Education, England and Wales
1787	Road traffic	1831	National Health Service, England and Wales
1788	Road traffic	1832	Social security
1789	Road traffic	1833	Road traffic
1790	Road traffic	1834	Road traffic
1791	Road traffic	1835	Road traffic
1792	Road traffic	1836	Offshore installations
1793	Road traffic	1837	Social security
1794	Road traffic	1838	Road traffic

NUMERICAL LIST OF STATUTORY INSTRUMENTS

1839	Road traffic	1890	International immunities and privileges
1840	Road traffic	1891	
1841		(NI. 6)	Northern Ireland
(C. 34)	Shops and offices	1892	
1842	Protection of wrecks	(NI. 7)	Northern Ireland
1843	Road traffic	1893	
1844	Road traffic	(NI. 8)	Northern Ireland
1845	Road traffic	1894	
1846	Road traffic	(NI. 9)	Northern Ireland
1847	Road traffic	1895	Immigration
1848	Road traffic	1896	
1849	Road traffic	(NI. 10)	Northern Ireland
1850	Building and buildings	1897	
1851	Weights and measures	(NI. 11)	Northern Ireland
1852	Weights and measures	1898	
1853	Prices	(NI. 12)	Northern Ireland
1854	Road traffic	1899	
1855	Road traffic	(NI. 13)	Northern Ireland
1856	Road traffic	1900	Contracts
1857	Road traffic	1901	Judgments
1858	Road traffic	1902	Maintenance of dependants
1859		1903	Defence
(S. 84)	Fees and charges	1904	Cinemas and films
1860	Roads and bridges, Scotland	1905	Charities
1861	Education, England and Wales	1906	Pensions
1862	Road traffic	1907	Transport
1863	Road traffic	1908	Trustees
1864	Road traffic	1909	Pensions
1865	Road traffic	1910	Education, England and Wales
1866	Road traffic	1911	Road traffic
1867	Road traffic	1912	Education, England and Wales
1868	Road traffic	1913	National Health Service, England and Wales
1869	Road traffic	1914	National Health Service, England and Wales
1870	Road traffic	1915	National Health Service, England and Wales
1871	Road traffic	1916	National Health Service, England and Wales
1872	Road traffic	1917	National Health Service, England and Wales
1873	Road traffic	1918	National Health Service, England and Wales
1874	Road traffic	1919	National Health Service, England and Wales
1875	Road traffic	1920	National Health Service, England and Wales
1876	Road traffic	1921	National Health Service, England and Wales
1877	Road traffic	1922	Monopolies and Mergers
1878	Road traffic	1923	
1879	Road traffic	(C. 35)	Social security
1880	Road traffic	1924	Social security
1881	Road traffic	1925	Social security
1882	Social security	1926	Road traffic
	Terms and conditions of employment	1927	Road traffic
		1928	Road traffic
1883	Weights and measures	1929	Road traffic
1884	Weights and measures	1930	Road traffic
1885	Local government, England and Wales	1931	
1886	Health and safety	(S. 85)	Prisons
1887	European Communities		Young offenders institutions, Scotland
1888	Local government, England and Wales	1932	Medicines
1889	Children and young persons		

1933	Medicines	1976	
1934	Monopolies and mergers	(S. 89)	Industrial development
1935	Companies	1977	Public health, England and Wales
1936			Public health, Scotland
(L. 9)	County courts		Public health, Northern Ireland
1937	Road traffic	1978	Value added tax
1938	Road traffic	1979	Road traffic
1939	Road traffic	1980	
1940	Road traffic	(S. 90)	Education, Scotland
1941	Road traffic	1981	Friendly societies
1942	Road traffic	1982	Friendly societies
1943	Road traffic	1983	Friendly societies
1944	Road traffic	1984	Friendly societies
1945	Road traffic	1985	Agriculture
1946		1986	Race relations
(S. 86)	Sea fisheries	1987	Housing, England and Wales
1947	Water, England and Wales	1988	
1948	Registration of births, deaths, marriages, etc.	(C. 37)	Merchant shipping
1949		1989	Agriculture
(S. 87)	River, Scotland	1990	Agriculture
1950	Public health, England and Wales	1991	Civil aviation
	Public health, Scotland	1992	Civil aviation
	Public health, Northern Ireland	1993	
1951		(NI. 14)	Northern Ireland
(C. 36)	Criminal law, England and Wales	1994	Pipe-lines
	Criminal law, Scotland	1995	Road traffic
	Criminal law, Northern Ireland	1996	Road traffic
1952	Magistrates' courts	1997	Road traffic
	Summary jurisdiction, Scotland	1998	Road traffic
1953		1999	Road traffic
(S. 88)	Police	2000	Road traffic
1954	Road traffic	2001	Road traffic
1955	Road traffic	2002	Road traffic
1956	Road traffic	2003	Education, England and Wales
1957	Road traffic	2004	Food
1958	Road traffic	2005	Transport
1959	Road traffic	2006	Road traffic
1960	Road traffic	2007	Road traffic
1961	Road traffic	2008	Road traffic
1962	Road traffic	2009	Ecclesiastical law, England
1963	Road traffic	2010	Ecclesiastical law, England
1964	Road traffic	2011	Ecclesiastical law, England
1965	Road traffic	2012	
1966	Road traffic	(S. 91)	Town and country planning, Scotland
1967	Road traffic		Roads and bridges, Scotland
1968	Civil aviation		Electricity
1969	Civil aviation		Land drainage
1970	Civil aviation	2013	Merchant shipping
1971	Road traffic	2014	Merchant shipping
1972	Highways, England and Wales	2015	Road traffic
1973	Road traffic	2016	Education, England and Wales
1974	Land registration, England and Wales	2017	Education, England and Wales
1975		2018	Education, England and Wales
(L. 10)	Supreme Court of England and Wales	2019	Education, England and Wales

NUMERICAL LIST OF STATUTORY INSTRUMENTS

2020	Building and buildings	2068		
2021	Pensions	(S. 93)	Rating and valuation	
2022	Medical profession	2069		
2023	Police	(S. 94)	Rating and valuation	
2024	Police	2070		
2025		(S.95)	Rating and valuation	
(C. 38)	Police	2071		
2026	Public health, England and Wales	(S. 96)	Rating and valuation	
2027	Road traffic	2072		
2028	Road traffic	(S. 97)	Rating and valuation	
2029	Public health, England and Wales	2073		
	Public health, Scotland	(S. 98)	Rating and valuation	
	Public health, Northern Ireland	2074		
2030		(S. 99)	Rating and valuation	
(S. 92)	Housing, Scotland	2075		
2031	Highways, England and Wales	(S. 100)	Rating and valuation	
2032	Transport	2076		
2033	Highways, England and Wales	(S. 101)	Rating and valuation	
2034	Education, England and Wales	2077		
2035	Education, England and Wales	(S. 102)	Rating and valuation	
2036	Education, England and Wales	2078		
2037	Education, England and Wales	(S. 103)	Rating and valuation	
2038		2079		
(C. 39)	Education, England and Wales	(S. 104)	Rating and valuation	
2039	Road traffic	2080		
2040	Highways, England and Wales	(S. 105)	Rating and valuation	
2041	Highways, England and Wales	2081		
2042	Highways, England and Wales	(S. 106)	Rating and valuation	
2043	Road traffic	2082	Merchant shipping	
2044	Road traffic		Marine pollution	
2045	Road traffic	2083	Marine pollution	
2046	Road traffic	2084	Marine pollution	
2047	Road traffic	2085	Marine pollution	
2048	Road traffic	2086	Highways, England and Wales	
2049	Road traffic	2087	Highways, England and Wales	
2050	Road traffic	2088	Road traffic	
2051	Road traffic	2089	Road traffic	
2052	Road traffic	2090	Road traffic	
2053	Road traffic	2091	Road traffic	
2054	Road traffic	2092	Education, England and Wales	
2055	Road traffic	2093	Education, England and Wales	
2056	Road traffic	2094	Education, England and Wales	
2057	Road traffic	2095		
2058	Road traffic	(S. 107)	Police	
2059	Road traffic	2096		
2060	Road traffic	(S. 108)	Police	
2061	Road traffic	2097		
2062	Road traffic	(S. 109)	Housing, Scotland	
2063	Health and safety	2098	Road traffic	
2064	Harbours, docks, piers and ferries	2099	Education, England and Wales	
2065	Civil aviation	2100	Education, England and Wales	
2066	Civil aviation	2101	Education, England and Wales	
2067	Road traffic	2102	Education, England and Wales	
		2103	Education, England and Wales	
		2104	Education, England and Wales	

2105	Road traffic	2151	
2106	Road traffic	(C. 44)	Northern Ireland
2107	Road traffic	2152	Highways, England and Wales
2108	Road traffic	2153	Highways, England and Wales
2109		2154	Local government, England and Wales
(C. 40)	Local government, England and Wales	2155	Agriculture
2110		2156	Education, England and Wales
(L. 11)	County courts	2157	Medicines
2111	Education, England and Wales	2158	Highways, England and Wales
2112	Education, England and Wales	2159	Civil aviation
2113	Road traffic	2160	Civil aviation
2114	Road traffic	2161	Civil aviation
2115	Road traffic	2162	Telecommunications
2116	Road traffic	2163	Education, England and Wales
2117	Road traffic	2164	
2118	Road traffic	(L. 12)	Family law
2119	Road traffic	2165	
2120	Road traffic	(L. 13)	Family law
2121	Road traffic		Supreme Court of England and Wales
2122	Road traffic		County courts
2123	Road traffic	2166	
2124		(L. 14)	Magistrates' courts
(C. 41)		2167	Education, England and Wales
(S. 110)	Sea fisheries	2168	Road traffic
2125	Road traffic	2169	Sea fisheries
2126	Animals	2170	Highways, England and Wales
2127	Agriculture	2171	Road traffic
2128	Education, England and Wales	2172	Road traffic
2129	Road traffic	2173	Road traffic
2130	Road traffic	2174	Road traffic
2131	Road traffic	2175	Road traffic
2132	Road traffic	2176	Road traffic
2133	Road traffic	2177	Road traffic
2134	Road traffic	2178	Road traffic
2135	Road traffic	2179	Road traffic
2136	Road traffic	2180	Road traffic
2137	Social security	2181	Charities
2138	Social security	2182	Road traffic
2139	Social security	2183	Landlord and tenant, England and Wales
2140	Road traffic	2184	Fire precautions
2141	Highways, England and Wales	2185	Road traffic
2142		2186	Road traffic
(C. 42)	Transport	2187	Road traffic
2143		2188	Road traffic
(C. 43)	Customs and excise	2189	
2144	Public health, England and Wales	(C. 45)	Coal industry
	Public health, Scotland	2190	Road traffic
	Public health, Northern Ireland	2191	Road traffic
2145	Acquisition of land	2192	Road traffic
2146	Road traffic	2193	Public health, England and Wales
2147	Road traffic		Public health, Scotland
2148	Road traffic		Public health, Northern Ireland
2149	Road traffic	2194	Social security
2150	Transport	2195	Police

2196	Local government, England and Wales	2248	
2197	Road traffic	(C. 47)	Education, England and Wales
2198	Road traffic	2249	Environmental protection
2199	Road traffic	2250	Telecommunications
2200	Road traffic	2251	Telecommunications
2201	Road traffic	2252	Road traffic
2202	Road traffic	2253	Harbours, docks, piers and ferries
2203	Road traffic	2254	Education, England and Wales
2204		2255	National Health Service, England and Wales
(C. 46)	Education, England and Wales	2256	National Health Service, England and Wales
2205	Water, England and Wales	2257	National Health Service, England and Wales
2206	Education, England and Wales	2258	National Health Service, England and Wales
2207	Road traffic	2259	Road traffic
2208	Road traffic	2260	Civil aviation
2209	Road traffic	2261	Road traffic
2210	Road traffic	2262	Road traffic
2211	Road traffic	2263	Road traffic
2212	Road traffic	2264	Road traffic
2213	Road traffic	2265	Road traffic
2214	Road traffic	2266	Road traffic
2215	Highways, England and Wales	2267	Road traffic
2216	Customs and excise	2268	Road traffic
2217	Companies	2269	Road traffic
2218	Legal aid and advice, England and Wales	2270	Road traffic
2219	Road traffic	2271	Road traffic
2220	Road traffic	2272	Road traffic
2221	Road traffic	2273	Road traffic
2222	Road traffic	2274	Road traffic
2223	Road traffic	2275	Road traffic
2224	Road traffic	2276	Road traffic
2225	Road traffic	2277	Road traffic
2226	Education, England and Wales	2278	Road traffic
2227	Education, England and Wales	2279	Road traffic
2228	Education, England and Wales	2280	Road traffic
2229	Railways	2281	Education, England and Wales
2230	Sea fisheries	2282	Road traffic
2231		2283	Road traffic
(S. 111)	Police	2284	Road traffic
2232	Roads and bridges, Scotland	2285	Road traffic
2233	Roads and bridges, Scotland	2286	Agriculture
2234	Road traffic	2287	Agriculture
2235	Road traffic	2288	National Health Service, England and Wales
2236	Road traffic	2289	National Health Service, England and Wales
2237	Road traffic	2290	Road traffic
2238	Road traffic	2291	Road traffic
2239	Sports grounds and sporting events	2292	Road traffic
2240	Road traffic	2293	Road traffic
2241	Road traffic	2294	Road traffic
2242	Road traffic	2295	Public health, England and Wales
2243	Road traffic		Public health, Scotland
2244	Road traffic		Public health, Northern Ireland
2245	Road traffic	2296	Local government, England and Wales
2246	Road traffic	2297	Local government, England and Wales
2247	Education, England and Wales		

2298	Harbours, docks, piers and ferries	2349	Agriculture
2299	Social security	2350	Road traffic
2300	Road traffic	2351	Town and country planning, England and Wales
2301	Road traffic		
2302	Road traffic	2352	Road traffic
2303	Road traffic	2353	Public records
2304	Road traffic	2354	
2305	Road traffic	(S. 113)	Sheriff court, Scotland
2306	Road traffic	2355	Road traffic
2307	Road traffic	2356	Road traffic
2308	Road traffic	2357	National Health Service, England and Wales
2309	Road traffic	2358	National Health Service, England and Wales
2310		2359	National Health Service, England and Wales
(S. 112)	Court of Session, Scotland	2360	National Health Service, England and Wales
2311	Road traffic	2361	National Health Service, England and Wales
2312	Road traffic	2362	National Health Service, England and Wales
2313	Road traffic	2363	National Health Service, England and Wales
2314	Road traffic	2364	National Health Service, England and Wales
2315	Road traffic	2365	National Health Service, England and Wales
2316	Road traffic	2366	National Health Service, England and Wales
2317	Road traffic	2367	National Health Service, England and Wales
2318	Income tax	2368	National Health Service, England and Wales
2319	Social security	2369	National Health Service, England and Wales
2320	Road traffic	2370	National Health Service, England and Wales
2321	Road traffic	2371	
2322	Road traffic	(S. 114)	Education, Scotland
2323	Road traffic	2372	Protection of wrecks
2324	Road traffic	2373	Road traffic
2325	Civil aviation	2374	Road traffic
2326	Consumer protection Health and safety	2375	Road traffic
		2376	Road traffic
2327	Fees and charges	2377	Road traffic
2328	Consumer protection	2378	Road traffic
2329	Sea fisheries	2379	Road traffic
2330	Education, England and Wales	2380	Road traffic
2331	Police	2381	Road traffic
2332	National Health Service, England and Wales	2382	Road traffic
2333	National Health Service, England and Wales	2383	Road traffic
2334	National Health Service, England and Wales	2384	Road traffic
2335	National Health Service, England and Wales	2385	Road traffic
2336	National Health Service, England and Wales	2386	National assistance services
2337	National Health Service, England and Wales	2387	Education, England and Wales
2338	National Health Service, England and Wales	2388	Transport
2339	National Health Service, England and Wales	2389	Road traffic
2340	National Health Service, England and Wales	2390	Highways, England and Wales
2341	National Health Service, England and Wales	2391	Road traffic
2342	National Health Service, England and Wales	2392	Road traffic
2343	Social security	2393	Road traffic
2344	Road traffic	2394	Road traffic
2345	Road traffic	2395	Road traffic
2346	Road traffic	2396	Road traffic
2347	Road traffic	2397	Road traffic
2348	Road traffic	2398	Road traffic
		2399	Road traffic

2400	Road traffic	2451	Road traffic
2401	Road traffic	2452	Road traffic
2402	National Health Service, England and Wales	2453	Road traffic
2403		2454	Road traffic
(L. 15)	County courts	2455	Road traffic
2404	Agriculture	2456	Road traffic
2405	Highways, England and Wales	2457	Building societies
2406	Highways, England and Wales	2458	Building societies
2407	Roads and bridges, Scotland	2459	Building societies
2408		2460	Agriculture
(C. 48)	Medicines	2461	Road traffic
	National Health Service, England and Wales	2462	Highways, England and Wales
2409	Medicines	2463	Education, England and Wales
2410	Medicines	2464	Merchant shipping
2411	Medicines	2465	Food
2412	National Health Service, England and Wales	2466	Road traffic
2413	Highways, England and Wales	2467	Road traffic
2414	Highways, England and Wales	2468	Road traffic
2415	Highways, England and Wales	2469	Road traffic
2416	Highways, England and Wales	2470	Road traffic
2417	Highways, England and Wales	2471	Road traffic
2418	Highways, England and Wales	2472	Road traffic
2419	Highways, England and Wales	2473	Road traffic
2420	Consumer credit	2474	Road traffic
2421	Insolvency	2475	Road traffic
2422	Local government, England and Wales	2476	Road traffic
2423	Road traffic	2477	Road traffic
2424	Road traffic	2478	Channel tunnel
2425	Road traffic	2479	Terms and conditions of employment
2426	Road traffic	2480	Road traffic
2427	Road traffic	2481	Road traffic
2428	Road traffic	2482	Road traffic
2429	Road traffic	2483	
2430	Road traffic	(S. 115)	Court of Session, Scotland
2431	Road traffic	2484	
2432	Road traffic	(S. 116)	National Health Service, Scotland
2433	Road traffic	2485	
2434	Road traffic	(S. 117)	National Health Service, Scotland
2435	Road traffic	2486	Road traffic
2436	Road traffic	2487	
2437	Road traffic	(C. 49)	Environmental protection
2438	Road traffic	2488	
2439	Road traffic	(S. 118)	Roads, Scotland
2440	Road traffic	2489	Civil aviation
2441	Road traffic	2490	Civil aviation
2442	Road traffic	2491	Civil aviation
2443	Road traffic	2492	Civil aviation
2444	Road traffic	2493	Civil aviation
2445	Road traffic	2494	Road traffic
2446	Education, England and Wales	2495	Road traffic
2447	Road traffic	2496	Road traffic
2448	Food	2497	Road traffic
2449	Education, England and Wales	2498	Road traffic
2450	Education, England and Wales	2499	Road traffic

2500	Road traffic	2548	Road traffic
2501	Road traffic	2549	Trade marks
2502	Road traffic	2550	
2503	Road traffic	(C. 52)	Trade marks
2504	Road traffic	2551	Trade marks
2505	Road traffic	2552	
2506	Road traffic	(C. 53)	Coal industry
2507	Insolvency	2553	Coal industry
	Insolvency	2554	Road traffic
2508		2555	Public health, England and Wales
(C. 50)	Income tax		Public health, Scotland
2509	Customs and excise		Public health, Northern Ireland
2510	Agriculture	2556	Social security
2511	Road traffic	2557	Road traffic
2512	Road traffic	2558	Road traffic
2513	Road traffic	2559	Road traffic
2514	Road traffic	2560	Road traffic
2515	Highways, England and Wales	2561	Road traffic
2516	Highways, England and Wales	2562	Coal industry
2517	Highways, England and Wales	2563	Coal industry
2518	Customs and excise	2564	Coal industry
2519	Trustees	2565	Coal industry
2520	Transport	2566	Coal industry
2521	National Health Service, England and Wales	2567	Coal industry
2522	National Health Service, England and Wales	2568	
2523	Road traffic	(C. 54)	Gas
2524		2569	Insurance
(S. 119)	River, Scotland	2570	Road traffic
2525	Road traffic	2571	Road traffic
2526	Road traffic	2572	Road traffic
2527	Road traffic	2573	Road traffic
2528	Road traffic	2574	Road traffic
2529	Road traffic	2575	Road traffic
2530	Road traffic	2576	Coal industry
2531	Road traffic	2577	Coal industry
2532	Road traffic	2578	Urban development
2533	Road traffic	2579	Opticians
2534	Road traffic	2580	Road traffic
2535	Road traffic	2581	Trade marks
2536	Road traffic	2582	Trade marks
2537	Road traffic	2583	Trade marks
2538	Road traffic	2584	Trade marks
2539	Road traffic	2585	
2540	Broadcasting	(S. 121)	Town and country planning, Scotland
2541	Insolvency	2586	
	Insolvency	(S. 122)	Town and country planning, Scotland
2542	Value added tax	2587	
2543		(S. 123)	National Health Service, Scotland
(C. 51)	Friendly societies	2588	
2544		(C. 56)	
(S. 120)	Food	(S. 124)	Land registration, Scotland
2545	Roads and bridges, Scotland	2589	
2546	Roads and bridges, Scotland	(S. 125)	Agriculture
2547	Road traffic		

2590		2633	Road traffic
(S. 126)	Agriculture	2634	Road traffic
2591		2635	Road traffic
(S. 127)	Agriculture	2636	Road traffic
2592	Seeds	2637	Road traffic
2593	Social security	2638	Road traffic
2594		2639	Road traffic
(C. 55)	Magistrates' courts	2640	Road traffic
2595	Town and country planning, England and Wales	2641	Road traffic
		2642	Road traffic
2596	Road traffic	2643	Road traffic
2597	Road traffic	2644	Road traffic
2598	Road traffic	2645	Road traffic
2599	Road traffic	2646	Road traffic
2600	Road traffic	2647	Road traffic
2601	Road traffic	2648	Road traffic
2602	Road traffic	2649	Road traffic
2603	Road traffic	2650	Road traffic
2604	Road traffic	2651	Highways, England and Wales
2605	Road traffic	2652	
2606	Road traffic	(S. 134)	Arms and ammunition
2607	Road traffic	2653	
2608	Road traffic	(S. 135)	Road traffic
2609	Roads and Bridges, Scotland	2654	Telecommunications
2610	Roads and Bridges, Scotland	2655	Telecommunications
2611	Roads and Bridges, Scotland	2656	Taxes
2612	Roads and Bridges, Scotland	2657	Income tax
2613			Inheritance tax
(S. 128)	Sea fisheries		Taxes
2614	Arms and ammunition	2658	
2615	Arms and ammunition	(C. 57)	
2616		(S. 136)	National Health Service, Scotland
(L. 16)	Solicitors	2659	
2617	Value added tax	(C. 58)	National lottery
2618			Betting, gaming and lotteries
(S. 129)	Education, Scotland	2660	Highways, England and Wales
2619	National Health Service, England and Wales	2661	Road traffic
2620	National Health Service, England and Wales	2662	Road traffic
2621		2663	Road traffic
(S. 130)	River, Scotland	2664	Road traffic
2622		2665	Road traffic
(S. 131)	River, Scotland	2666	Road traffic
2623		2667	Road traffic
(S. 132)	River, Scotland	2668	Road traffic
2624		2669	Road traffic
(S. 133)	National Health Service, Scotland	2670	Road traffic
2625	Trade marks	2671	Road traffic
2626	Supreme Court of England and Wales	2672	Road traffic
	County courts	2673	United Nations
2627	Animals	2674	United Nations
2628	Food	2675	United Nations
2629	Civil aviation	2676	United Nations
2630	Civil aviation	2677	Local government, England and Wales
2631	Road traffic	2678	Police
2632	Road traffic		

2679		2729	Road traffic
(C. 59)	Customs and excise	2730	Road traffic
2680	Rating and valuation	2731	Agriculture
2681	Road traffic	2732	Education, England and Wales
2682	Road traffic	2733	Harbours, docks, piers and ferries
2683	Road traffic	2734	
2684	Road traffic	(C. 60)	Intelligence services
2685	Road traffic	2735	Northern Ireland
2686	Social security	2736	Police
2687	National Health Service, England and Wales	2737	Road traffic
2688	National Health Service, England and Wales	2738	Road traffic
2689	National Health Service, England and Wales	2739	Road traffic
2690	National Health Service, England and Wales	2740	Agriculture
2691	National Health Service, England and Wales	2741	Agriculture
2692	National Health Service, England and Wales	2742	Road traffic
2693	National Health Service, England and Wales	2743	Road traffic
2694	National Health Service, England and Wales	2744	Local government, England and Wales
2695	National Health Service, England and Wales	2745	Road traffic
2696	National Health Service, England and Wales	2746	Road traffic
2697	National Health Service, England and Wales	2747	Road traffic
2698	National Health Service, England and Wales	2748	Road traffic
2699		2749	Road traffic
(S. 137)	Education, Scotland	2750	Road traffic
2700	Road traffic	2751	Road traffic
2701	Road traffic	2752	Road traffic
2702	Road traffic	2753	Road traffic
2703	Road traffic	2754	Road traffic
2704	Road traffic	2755	Road traffic
2705	Road traffic	2756	Road traffic
2706	Road traffic	2757	Youth courts and offenders
2707	Road traffic	2758	
2708	National Health Service, England and Wales	(S. 139)	Water supply, Scotland
2709	National Health Service, England and Wales	2759	Agriculture
2710		2760	Justices of the Peace, England and Wales
(S. 138)	Agriculture	2761	Youth courts and offenders
2711	Customs and excise	2762	Animals
2712	Civil aviation	2763	Road traffic
2713	Civil aviation	2764	Road traffic
2714	Road traffic	2765	Housing, England and Wales
2715	Road traffic	2766	Road traffic
2716	Wildlife	2767	Human fertilisation and embryology
	Countryside	2768	Legal aid and advice, England and Wales
2717	Road traffic	2769	Road traffic
2718	Road traffic	2770	
2719	Road traffic	(S. 140)	Animals
2720	Road traffic	2771	Road traffic
2721	Road traffic	2772	Road traffic
2722	Road traffic	2773	National Health Service, England and Wales
2723	Road traffic	2774	Education, England and Wales
2724	Road traffic	2775	Road traffic
2725	Road traffic	2776	Road traffic
2726	Road traffic	2777	Road traffic
2727	Road traffic	2778	Road traffic
2728	Road traffic	2779	Road traffic

NUMERICAL LIST OF STATUTORY INSTRUMENTS 229

2780	Road traffic		2827	Road traffic
2781	Road traffic		2828	Road traffic
2782	Food		2829	Road traffic
2783	Food		2830	Road traffic
2784	National Health Service, England and Wales		2831	Road traffic
2785	Road traffic		2832	Road traffic
2786	Road traffic		2833	Road traffic
2787	Road traffic		2834	Road traffic
2788	Marine pollution		2835	Road traffic
2789			2836	Road traffic
(C. 61)	Merchant shipping		2837	Road traffic
2790			2838	Road traffic
(C. 62)	Local government, England and Wales		2839	Road traffic
2791	European Communities		2840	Road traffic
2792	Children and young persons		2841	Water, England and Wales
2793	Diplomatic service		2842	
2794	Extradition		(S. 144)	Local government, Scotland
2795				Public health, Scotland
(NI. 15)	Northern Ireland		2843	Local government, England and Wales
2796	Extradition		2844	Consumer protection
2797	United Nations		2845	Education, England and Wales
2798	Summer time		2846	Harbours, docks, piers and ferries
2799	Children and young persons		2847	Environmental protection
2800	Children and young persons		2848	Education, England and Wales
2801	Highways, England and Wales		2849	Education, England and Wales
2802	Social security		2850	
2803	Trade marks		(C. 63)	
2804			(S. 145)	Local government, Scotland
(S. 141)	Human fertilisation and embryology		2851	Land drainage
2805			2852	Medicines
(S. 142)	Sheriff Court, Scotland		2853	Agriculture
2806			2854	
(S. 143)	Court of Session, Scotland		(C. 64)	Environmental protection
2807	Road traffic		2855	Education, England and Wales
2808	Road traffic		2856	Road traffic
2809			2857	Road traffic
(NI. 16)	Northern Ireland		2858	Road traffic
2810	Northern Ireland		2859	Road traffic
2811	Magistrates' courts		2860	Road traffic
2812	Local government, England and Wales		2861	Road traffic
2813	Sea fisheries		2862	Road traffic
2814	Road traffic		2863	Road traffic
2815	Road traffic		2864	Road traffic
2816	Road traffic		2865	Health and safety
2817	Road traffic		2866	Weights and measures
2818	Road traffic		2867	Weights and measures
2819	Road traffic		2868	Weights and measures
2820	Road traffic		2869	Road traffic
2821	Road traffic		2870	Road traffic
2822	Road traffic		2871	Road traffic
2823	Road traffic		2872	Road traffic
2824	Road traffic		2873	Road traffic
2825	Local government, England and Wales		2874	Road traffic
2826	Local government, England and Wales		2875	Road traffic

2876	Education, England and Wales	2921	Agriculture
2877	Monopolies and mergers	2922	Agriculture
2878	Port health authorities, England and Wales	2923	Road traffic
2879	Companies	2924	Education, England and Wales
2880	Overseas development and co-operation	2925	Road traffic
2881	Road traffic	2926	
2882	Road traffic	(C. 65)	Social security
2883	Road traffic	2927	Transport
2884	Local government, England and Wales		Transport charges
	Local government, Scotland	2928	Road traffic
2885	Road traffic	2929	Road traffic
2886	Road traffic	2930	Terms and conditions of employment
2887	Road traffic	2931	Housing, England and Wales
2888	Local government, England and Wales	2932	Housing, England and Wales
	Local government, Scotland	2933	Road traffic
2889	Welsh language	2934	Road traffic
2890		2935	
(L. 17)	Family proceedings	(C. 66)	Criminal law, England and Wales
	Supreme Court of England and Wales		Criminal law, Scotland
	County courts		Criminal law, Northern Ireland
2891	Pensions	2936	Medicines
2892	Education, England and Wales	2937	Road traffic
2893	Supreme Court of England and Wales	2938	Road traffic
	County courts	2939	Road traffic
	Insolvency	2940	Road traffic
2894	Agriculture	2941	Road traffic
2895	Housing, England and Wales	2942	Road traffic
2896	Education, England and Wales	2943	Social security
2897	Highways, England and Wales	2944	Social security
2898	Customs and excise	2945	Social security
2899	Betting, gaming and lotteries	2946	Social security
2900		2947	Social security
(S. 146)	Agriculture	2948	Road traffic
2901		2949	Road traffic
(S. 147)	Court of Session, Scotland	2950	National Health Service, England and Wales
2902	Road traffic	2951	National Health Service, England and Wales
2903	Cancelled and number never used	2952	National Health Service, England and Wales
2904	Customs and excise	2953	Monopolies and mergers
2905	Value added tax	2954	National Health Service, England and Wales
2906	Road traffic	2955	Intelligence services
2907	Road traffic	2956	Charities
2908	Road traffic	2957	Education, England and Wales
2909	Road traffic	2958	
2910	Road traffic	(S. 148)	Local government, Scotland
2911	Road traffic	2959	Road traffic
2912	Highways, England and Wales	2960	Road traffic
2913	Highways, England and Wales	2961	Road traffic
2914	Statistics of trade	2962	Road traffic
2915	Water industry, England and Wales	2963	Road traffic
2916	Housing, England and Wales	2964	Local government, England and Wales
2917	Road traffic	2965	Animals
2918	Road traffic	2966	Road traffic
2919	Food	2967	Customs and excise
2920	Animals		

NUMERICAL LIST OF STATUTORY INSTRUMENTS

2968		3012	Income tax
(C. 67)	Customs and excise	3013	Value added tax
2969	Value added tax	3014	Value added tax
2970	Road traffic	3015	Value added tax
2971		3016	Medicines
(C. 68)	Merchant shipping	3017	Consumer protection
2972	Customs and excise	3018	Local government, England and Wales
2973	Coal industry	3019	Road traffic
2974	Coal industry	3020	Road traffic
2975	Social security	3021	Electricity
2976	Road traffic	3022	Arms and ammunition
2977	Road traffic	3023	
2978	Prevention and suppression of terrorism	(C. 69)	Charities
2979	Education, England and Wales	3024	Charities
2980	Road traffic	3025	Local government, England and Wales
2981	Registration of births, deaths, marriages, etc.	3026	Local government, England and Wales
2982	Road traffic	3027	Road traffic
2983	Road traffic	3028	Road traffic
2984	Road traffic	3029	Road traffic
2985	Road traffic	3030	Road traffic
2986	Medicines	3031	Road traffic
2987	Medicines	3032	Road traffic
2988	National Health Service, England and Wales	3033	Road traffic
2989	National Health Service, England and Wales	3034	Road traffic
2990	National Health Service, England and Wales	3035	Road traffic
2991	National Health Service, England and Wales	3036	Income tax
2992	Road traffic	3037	
2993	Police	(C. 70)	Deregulation
2994		3038	
(S. 149)	National Health Service, Scotland	(S. 157)	National Health Service, Scotland
2995		3039	
(S. 150)	National Health Service, Scotland	(S. 158)	Police
2996		3040	Housing, England and Wales
(S. 151)	National Health Service, Scotland	3041	Isle of Man
2997		3042	Education, England and Wales
(S. 152)	National Health Service, Scotland	3043	Education, England and Wales
2998		3044	Education, England and Wales
(S. 153)	National Health Service, Scotland	3045	Education, England and Wales
2999			Education, Scotland
(S. 154)	National Health Service, Scotland	3046	Mental health
3000		3047	Powers of attorney
(S. 155)	National Health Service, Scotland		Mental health
3001		3048	Road traffic
(S. 156)	National Health Service, Scotland	3049	Merchant shipping
3002	Agriculture	3050	Medicines
3003	Agriculture	3051	Building and buildings
3004	Road traffic	3052	Road traffic
3005	Road traffic	3053	
3006	Road traffic	(S. 159)	Water supply, Scotland
3007	Road traffic	3054	Local government, England and Wales
3008	Taxes	3055	Civil aviation
3009	Income tax	3056	Highways, England and Wales
3010	Income tax	3057	Road traffic
3011	Inheritance tax	3058	Road traffic

3059	Road traffic	3102	Agriculture
3060	Road traffic	3103	Magistrates' courts
3061	Social security	3104	London government
3062	Coal industry	3105	Education, England and Wales
3063 (C. 71)	Coal industry	3106	University and colleges
3064	Coal industry	3107 (S. 168)	Local government, Scotland
3065	Coal industry	3108 (S. 169)	Housing, Scotland
3066 (S. 160)	Sheriff Court, Scotland	3109	Road traffic
3067 (S. 161)	Agriculture	3110	Road traffic
3068 (S. 162)	Local government, Scotland	3111	Road traffic
3069	Insurance	3112	Road traffic
3070	Coal industry	3113	Road traffic
3071	Civil aviation	3114	Road traffic
3072	Civil aviation	3115	Local government, England and Wales
3073	Civil aviation	3116 (C. 73)	Marriage
3074	Road traffic	3117	Consumer protection
3075 (C. 72) (S.163)	Police	3118	Ecclesiastical law, England
3076	Energy conservation	3119	Medicines
3077	Water industry, England and Wales	3120	Medicines
3078	Education, England and Wales	3121	Rating and valuation
3079 (L. 18)	Supreme court of England and Wales	3122	Rating and valuation
3080	Electromagnetic compatibility	3123	Rating and valuation
3081	Coal industry	3124	Local government, England and Wales
3082	Food	3125	Rating and valuation
3083	Energy conservation	3126	Road traffic
3084 (S. 164)	Local government, Scotland	3127	Road traffic
3085 (S. 165)	Agriculture	3128	Value added tax
3086 (S. 166)	Sheriff Court, Scotland	3129	Telecommunications
3087	Road traffic	3130	National Health Service, England and Wales National Health Service, Scotland Medical profession
3088	Road traffic	3131	Agriculture
3089	Road traffic	3132	Insurance
3090	Road traffic	3133	Insurance
3091	Road traffic	3134	Highways, England and Wales
3092	Road traffic	3135	Highways, England and Wales
3093	Plant health	3136	Legal aid and advice, England and Wales
3094	Plant health	3137	Revoked by SI 1995/362 before published
3095	Road traffic Northern Ireland	3138	Family law
3096 (S. 167)	European Communities	3139	Rating and valuation
3097	Coal industry	3140	Health and safety
3098	Health and safety	3141	Animals
3099	Agriculture	3142	Medicines
3100	Agriculture	3143	Medicines
3101	Agriculture	3144	Medicines
		3145	Road traffic
		3146 (S. 170)	Rating and valuation
		3147 (S. 171)	Registration of births, deaths, marriages, etc.

3148		3187	Civil aviation
(S. 172)	Education, Scotland	3188	
3149		(C. 76)	Deregulation
(S. 173)	Education, Scotland		Road traffic
3150			Public passenger transport
(C. 74)		3189	Local government, England and Wales
(S. 174)	Rating and valuation	3190	Local government, England and Wales
3151		3191	
(S. 175)	Registration of births, deaths, marriages, etc.	(C. 77)	Criminal law, England and Wales
3152		3192	
(C. 75)		(C. 78)	Criminal law, England and Wales
(S. 176)	Rating and valuation		Criminal law, Scotland
3153		3193	Prisons
(L. 19)	Supreme Court of England and Wales	3194	Young offender institutions, England and Wales
3154			
(L. 20)	Magistrates' courts	3195	Prisons
3155		3196	Social security
(L. 21)	Family proceedings	3197	National Health Service, England and Wales
	Supreme Court of England and Wales	3198	
	County courts	(S. 178)	Arms and ammunition
3156		3199	
(L. 22)	Magistrates' courts	(S. 179)	Rating and valuation
3157	Children and young persons	3200	
3158	Highways, England and Wales	(S. 180)	Rating and valuation
3159	Consumer protection	3201	Children and young persons
3160	Road traffic	3202	Diplomatic service
3161	Local government, England and Wales	3203	Extradition
3162	Harbours, docks, piers and ferries	3204	
3163	Telecommunications	(NI. 17)	Northern Ireland
3164	Local government, England and Wales	3205	Marine pollution
3165	Local government, England and Wales	3206	Parliament
3166	Local government, England and Wales	3207	Income tax
3167	Local government, England and Wales	3208	Income tax
3168	Local government, England and Wales	3209	Income tax
	Wales	3210	Income tax
3169	Medicines	3211	Income tax
3170		3212	Income tax
(S. 177)	Council tax, Scotland	3213	Income tax
	Water supply, Scotland	3214	Inheritance tax
3171	Medical profession	3215	Income tax
3172	Broadcasting	3216	Income tax
3173	National Health Service, England and Wales	3217	House of Lords
3174	National Health Service, England and Wales		Supreme Court of England and Wales
3175	National Health Service, England and Wales	3218	Cinemas and films
3176	National Health Service, England and Wales	3219	Designs
3177	National Health Service, England and Wales	3220	Patents
3178	National Health Service, England and Wales	3221	Pensions
3179	National Health Service, England and Wales	3222	Cinemas and films
3180	National Health Service, England and Wales	3223	Local government, England and Wales
3181	National Health Service, England and Wales	3224	
3182	National Health Service, England and Wales	(C. 79)	Income tax
3183	National Health Service, England and Wales	3225	
3184	National Health Service, England and Wales	(C. 80)	Income tax
3185	National Health Service, England and Wales	3226	Income tax
3186	National Health Service, England and Wales	3227	Income tax

234 NUMERICAL LIST OF STATUTORY INSTRUMENTS

3228	Income tax
3229	Income tax
3230	Income tax
3231	Income tax
3232	Income tax
3233	Income tax
3234 (C. 81)	Environmental protection
3235	Civil aviation
3236	Civil aviation
3237	Civil aviation
3238	Civil aviation
3239	Road traffic
3240	Road traffic
3241	Road traffic
3242	Road traffic
3243	Road traffic
3244	Road traffic
3245	Marine pollution
	Merchant shipping
3246	Health and safety
3247	Health and safety
3248	Consumer protection
3249	Animals
3250 (L. 23)	Magistrates' courts
3251	Education, England and Wales
3252	Road traffic
3253 (S. 181)	Housing, Scotland
3254 (S. 182)	National Health Service, Scotland
3255 (S. 183)	Local government, Scotland
	Representation of the people
3256 (S. 184)	Rating and valuation
3257	Registration of births, deaths, marriages, etc.
3258 (C. 82)	Supreme court of England and Wales
3259	Electricity
3260	Consumer protection
3261	Road traffic
3262 (C. 83)	Police
3263	Tribunals and inquiries
3264	Tribunals and inquiries
3265 (S. 185)	Court of Session, Scotland
3266 (S. 186)	High Court of Justiciary, Scotland
3267 (S. 187)	Sheriff Court, Scotland
3268 (S. 188)	Court of Session, Scotland
3269 (S. 189)	Town and country planning, Scotland
3270	Road traffic
3271	Public passenger vehicles
3272	Public passenger vehicles
3273	Sea fisheries
3274	Road traffic
3275 (S. 190)	Electricity
3276	Sex discrimination
3277	National debt
3278	Income tax
3279	Rating and valuation
3280	Rating and valuation
3281	Rating and valuation
3282	Rating and valuation
3283	Rating and valuation
3284	Rating and valuation
3285	Rating and valuation
3286	Channel tunnel
3287	Road traffic
3288	Road traffic
3289	Road traffic
3290	Road traffic
3291	Road traffic
3292 (C. 84) (S. 191)	Town and country planning, Scotland
3293 (S. 192)	Town and country planning, Scotland
3294 (S. 193)	Town and country planning, Scotland
3295	Road traffic
3296	Road traffic
3297	Road traffic
	Northern Ireland
3298	Medical profession
3299	Road traffic
3300	Road traffic
3301	Insurance
3302 (S. 194)	River, Scotland
3303	Legal aid and advice, England and Wales
3304	Road traffic
3305	Road traffic
3306	Road traffic
3307	Highways, England and Wales
3308 (S. 195)	Water supply, Scotland
3309 (S. 196)	Water supply, Scotland
3310	Road traffic
3311	Road traffic
3312	Road traffic

3313	Probation
3314	Probation
3315	Probation
3316	Road traffic
3317	Road traffic
3318	Road traffic
3319	Road traffic
3320	Road traffic
3321	Road traffic
3322	Civil aviation
3323	Civil aviation
3324	Road traffic
3325	Road traffic
3326	Road traffic
3327	Opticians
3328	Number never used
3329	Road traffic
3330	Road traffic
3331	Road traffic
3332	Civil aviation
3333	Road traffic
3334	Road traffic
3335	Road traffic
3336	Road traffic
3337	Road traffic

LIST OF SUBSIDIARY NUMBERS

C.   Commencement orders (bring an Act or part of an Act into operation).

L.   Instruments relating to fees or procedure in courts in England and Wales.

N.I.   Certain orders in Council relating to Northern Ireland.

S.   Instruments that extend only to Scotland.

(C.)	(S.I.)	(C.)	(S.I.)
1	71	36	1951
2	81	37	1988
3	86	38	2025
4	87	39	2038
5	115	40	2109
6	202	41	2124
7	242	42	2142
8	398	43	2143
9	447	44	2151
10	507	45	2189
11	571	46	2204
12	700	47	2248
13	436	48	2408
14	718	49	2487
15	780	50	2508
16	935	51	2543
16	1055	52	2550
17	1089	53	2552
18	1096	54	2568
19	1201	55	2594
20	1234	56	2588
21	1253	57	2658
22	1257	58	2659
23	1365	59	2679
24	1437	60	2734
25	1445	61	2789
26	1482	62	2790
27	1484	63	2850
28	1558	64	2854
29	1648	65	2926
30	1661	66	2935
31	1690	67	2968
32	1773	68	2971
33	1776	69	3023
34	1841	70	3037
35	1923	71	3063
		72	3075

LIST OF SUBSIDIARY NUMBERS 237

73	3116		6	1891
74	3150		7	1892
75	3152		8	1893
76	3188		9	1894
77	3191		10	1896
78	3192		11	1897
79	3224		12	1898
80	3225		13	1899
81	3234		14	1993
82	3258		15	2795
83	3262		16	2809
84	3292		17	3204

(L.)	(S.I.)		(S.)	(S.I.)
1	306		1	64
2	601		2	106
3	604		3	107
4	808		4	111
5	809		5	145
6	1103		6	200
7	1288		7	201
8	1289		8	221
9	1480		9	259
9	1936		10	326
10	1481		11	351
10	1975		12	391
11	2110		13	392
12	2164		14	398
13	2165		15	430
14	2166		16	431
15	2403		17	478
16	2616		18	496
17	2890		19	497
18	3079		20	498
19	3153		21	510
20	3154		22	528
21	3155		23	529
22	3156		24	531
23	3250		25	582
			26	626
(N.I.)	(S.I.)		27	628
1	426		28	629
2	429		29	630
3	762		30	632
4	765		31	635
5	766		32	636

LIST OF SUBSIDIARY NUMBERS

33	685		79	1770
34	697		80	1808
35	810		81	1826
36	884		82	1827
37	911		83	1828
38	912		84	1859
39	913		85	1931
40	960		86	1946
41	997		87	1949
42	998		88	1953
43	1000		89	1976
44	1001		90	1980
45	1013		91	2012
46	1014		92	2030
47	1015		93	2068
48	1016		94	2069
49	1017		95	2070
50	1018		96	2071
51	1019		97	2072
52	1042		98	2073
53	1043		99	2074
54	1046		100	2075
55	1049		101	2076
56	1050		102	2077
57	1061		103	2078
58	1125		104	2079
59	1139		105	2080
60	1140		106	2081
61	1141		107	2095
62	1142		108	2096
63	1187		109	2097
64	1233		110	2124
65	1266		111	2231
66	1408		112	2310
67	1441		113	2354
68	1442		114	2371
69	1443		115	2483
70	1556		116	2484
71	1607		117	2485
72	1644		118	2488
73	1645		119	2524
74	1675		120	2544
75	1701		121	2585
76	1702		122	2586
77	1715		123	2587
78	1769		124	2588

125	2589		171	3147
126	2590		172	3148
127	2591		173	3149
128	2613		174	3150
129	2618		175	3151
130	2621		176	3152
131	2622		177	3170
132	2623		178	3198
133	2624		179	3199
134	2652		180	3200
135	2653		181	3253
136	2658		182	3254
137	2699		183	3255
138	2710		184	3256
139	2758		185	3265
140	2770		186	3266
141	2804		187	3267
142	2805		188	3268
143	2806		189	3269
144	2842		190	3275
145	2850		191	3292
146	2900		192	3293
147	2901		193	3294
148	2958		194	3302
149	2994		195	3308
150	2995		196	3309
151	2996			
152	2997			
153	2998			
154	2999			
155	3000			
156	3001			
157	3038			
158	3039			
159	3053			
160	3066			
161	3067			
162	3068			
163	3075			
164	3084			
165	3085			
166	3086			
167	3096			
168	3107			
169	3108			
170	3146			

ALPHABETICAL INDEX

A

Abduction & custody: Children: Parties to conventions	10
Aberdeen & District Milk Marketing Board	1
Academic awards & distinctions: Royal Scottish Academy of Music & Drama	33
Accident hazards: Industrial: Major: Control	41
Accountants: Banks	7
Accounts & audits	58
Accumulators: Dangerous substances	41
Acquisition of land	1
Acquisition of land: Compensation	1
Rate of interest after entry	1
Rate of interest after entry: Scotland	1
Act of Adjournal	42, 185
Act of Sederunt: Copyright, designs & patents	180
Court of Session: Rules	19
Shorthand writers': Fees	19
Solicitors: Fees	19
Human fertilisation & embryology: Parental orders	19, 180
Judicial factors: Rules	180
Messengers-at-arms: Fees	19
Registration Appeal Court	19
Sheriff Court: Parental orders	180
Proceedings	180
Shorthand writers: Fees	180
Solicitors: Fees	180
Sheriff officers: Fees	180
Solicitors: Right of audience	19
Addenbrooke's: National Health Service Trust	69
Administration & control system: Integrated: Agriculture	4
Adoption: Parental orders: Forms of entry	104
Advertisements: Control: Town & country planning	189
Advertising: Medicines	65
Medicines: Monitoring	66
Advice & assistance: Financial contributions: Scotland	57
Representation: Scotland	57
Aeroplanes: Noise	11
Agricultural grants: Crofting counties: Scotland	22
Agricultural holdings: Units of production	56
Agricultural marketing: Milk	1
Agricultural Training Board	35
Agriculture	1, 2, 3, 4, 5
Agriculture: Administration & control system: Integrated	4
Beef: Special premium	1
Broadleaved woodland: Habitat: Wales	3
Cereals: Marketing	5
Coastal belt: Habitat: Wales	3
Farm & conservation grant: Variation	3, 46
Hill livestock: Compensatory allowances	4
Horticulture	5
Milk Marketing Board: Reorganisation	4
Milk marketing schemes: Scotland	4
Nitrate sensitive areas	4
Northern Ireland	90
Organic aid: Scotland	5
Organic farming: Aid	5
Pesticides	6
Potato Marketing Scheme	5

    Set-aside access: Scotland 5
    Sheep: Annual premium 5
        Annual premium: Quotas 5
    Species rich grassland: Habitat: Wales 4
    Suckler cows: Annual premium 5
        Annual premium: Quotas 5
      Water fringe: Habitat: Wales 4
Aintree Hospitals: National Health Service Trust 69
Air: Clean 14
  Rules 14
Air carriers: Licensing: European Communities 14
Aircraft operators: Accounts & records 22
Aire & Calder: Navigation: Coal industry 14
Airedale: National Health Service Trust 69
Air fares 11
Air Force: Disablement & death: Pensions 94
    Discipline acts 24
Air navigation: Dangerous goods 11
    Flying restrictions: Ballahulish 11
        Bournemouth 11
        Brentwood 11
        Chequers 11
        Coventry 11
        Cowden 11
        Cranfield 11
        Edinburgh 11
        Epsom racecourse 11
        Exhibition of flying 11, 12
        Fairford 12
        Farnborough 12
        Finningley 12
        Gawcott 12
        Glen Ogle 12
        Great Longstone 12
        Guidon ceremony 12
        Hackney 12
        Higher Chisworth 12
        Inverness 12
        Kensington 12
        Kintyre 12
        Leicester 12
        Middle Wallop 13
        Official opening of the Channel Tunnel 13
        Piper Bravo 13
        Portsmouth & D Day 50th anniversary commemoration 13
        Queen's birthday parade 13
        Remembrance day ceremony 13
        Ripon 13
        Runnymede 13
        Silverstone Aerodrome 13
        State opening of Parliament 13
        State visit of the King & Queen of Norway 13
        State visit of the President of Zimbabwe 13
        Stevenage 13
        St Mawgan 13
        Tour de France (United Kingdom stages) 13
        Visit of the President of the United States 13
        Wigan 13
Air passenger duty: Connected flights 22
  Customs & excise 22
  Prescribed rates of interest 22
Airports: Birmingham: Free zone 23
  Northern Ireland 91
  Slot allocation 13

242 ALPHABETICAL INDEX

Air routes: Access: European Communities ... 11
Alcan Aluminium UK Ltd.: Rateable values: Scotland ... 100
Alcoholic liquor: Duties ... 23
Alexandra Health Care: National Health Service Trust ... 69
Allington: National Health Service Trust ... 69
Allowances: Travellers ... 24
Ammunition & arms ... 7
Ancient monuments: Class consents ... 6
Andover District Community Health Care ... 69
Anglia: East Anglian Ambulance: National Health Service Trust ... 73
    Mid Anglia Community Health: National Health Service Trust ... 78
Anglian Harbours: National Health Service Trust ... 69
Anglian Regional Flood Defence Committee area: Boundaries ... 56
Anguilla: Drugs: Criminal justice: International co-operation ... 24
Animal health: Animal & poultry products: Importation ... 6
    Brucellosis ... 6
    Diseases: Approved disinfectants ... 6
    Racing pigeons: Vaccination ... 6
    Scotland ... 6
Animal products: Importation ... 6
Animals ... 6
Animals: Animal health: Scotland ... 6
    Brucellosis ... 6
    Cruelty: Prevention ... 7
    Diseases: Approved disinfectants ... 6
    Feedingstuffs: Medicated ... 66
    Health ... 6
    Meat & meat products: Residues: Examinations ... 38
    Medicinal products: Fees ... 65
    Welfare: Transport ... 6
Anti-competitive practices: Exclusions ... 16
Appeal Court: Registration: Act of Sederunt ... 19
Apple orchards: Grubbing up ... 1
Appropriation: Northern Ireland ... 91
Arable area: Payments ... 1
Argyll & Bute: National Health Service Trust ... 88
Armed forces: Sex discrimination ... 180
Armorial bearings: Local authorities ... 58
Armorial bearings, ensigns & flags ... 7
Arms & ammunition ... 7
Arms & ammunition: Scotland ... 7
Army: Disablement & death: Pensions ... 94
    Discipline acts ... 24
Arpley Chord: British railways ... 191, 193
Ashford Hospitals (Middx.): National Health Service Trust ... 69, 70
Associated Community Services: National Health Service Trust ... 83
Atomic energy & radioactive substances ... 7
Attendance allowance ... 182
Audit exemption: Companies ... 16
Auditors: Building societies ... 9
    Financial services ... 38
    Friendly societies ... 40
    Insurance ... 53
Australia: Foreign judgments: Reciprocal enforcement ... 55
Austria: Double taxation relief: Income tax ... 49
Avalon, Somerset: National Health Service Trust ... 70
Aviation: Civil: Navigation services: Route charges ... 14
Avon Ambulance Service: National Health Service Trust ... 70
Avon Valley: Environmentally sensitive areas ... 1
Aylesbury Vale Community Healthcare: National Health Service Trust ... 70
Ayr Burgh: Water ... 197

B
Bail ... 20

Bail: Magistrates' courts 64
    Prosecuting authorities: Prescription 20
Ballet schools: Grants 28
Bank accounts: Companies 16
Bankers' games: Gaming clubs 7
Banks & banking 7
Banks: Accountants 7
Barclays Bank plc: Thomas Cook Group Ltd.: Merger reference 68, 69
Bareboat charter ships 67
Barking & Dagenham (London Borough): Special parking areas 109
Barnet: Special parking areas 110
Barnet Community Healthcare: National Health Service Trust 70
Barnet (London Borough): Special parking areas 109
Barnsley District General Hospital: National Health Service Trust 70
Barry & Dinas Powys communities 62
Barts Hospital: National Health Service Trust 83
Basildon & Thurrock General Hospitals: National Health Service Trust 70
Batteries: Dangerous substances 41
Bedford & Shires Health & Care: National Health Service Trust 70
Bedford Hospital: National Health Service Trust 70
Bedfordshire & Hertfordshire Ambulance & Paramedic Service: National Health Service Trust 70
Beef: Carcases: Classification 1
    Special premium 1
Beer-based beverages: Duties 23
Benefices: Incumbents: Vacation 25
Benefits: Scheme: Income-related 181
Berkshire: Changes in local government areas 61
    East Berkshire Community Health: National Health Service Trust 73
    East Berkshire NHS Trust for People with Learning Disabilities: National Health Service Trust 73
    West Berkshire Priority Care Service: National Health Service Trust 87
Bethlem & Maudsley: National Health Service Trust 70
Betting, gaming & lotteries 7, 8, 23, 90
Betting, gaming & lotteries: Gaming clubs: Bankers' games 7
    Northern Ireland 91
Bexley Community Health: National Health Service Trust 70
Bexley (London Borough): Special parking areas 109
Bingo duty: Exemptions 23
Biotechnology & Biological Sciences Research Council 178
Birds: Registration & ringing 199
Birmingham & Fazeley Canal Bridge 42
Birmingham: East Birmingham Hospital: National Health Service Trust 73
    Northern: Mental Health: National Health Service Trust 80
    South: Mental Health: National Health Service Trust 84
    South Birmingham Community Health: National Health Service Trust 84
Birmingham airport: Free zone 23
Birmingham Children's Hospital: National Health Service Trust 70
Birmingham City Council: Birmingham & Fazeley Canal Bridge 42
Births & deaths: Registration 104
Births, deaths & marriages: Registration: Fees 104
Births, deaths, marriages, etc.: Registration: England & Wales 104
Bivalve molluscs: Live: Food safety 39
Blackburn, Hyndburn & Ribble Valley Health Care: National Health Service Trust 71
Black Country Mental Health: National Health Service Trust 71
Blackdown Hills: Environmentally sensitive areas 2
Blackpool Victoria Hospital: National Health Service Trust 71
Blackpool, Wyre & Fylde Community: National Health Service Trust 71
Blood: National Blood Authority 76
Blood Authority: National: Establishment 78
Boilers: Efficiency 35
Bonito: Preserved: Marketing standards 5
Borders Community Health Services: National Health Service Trust .88
Borders General Hospital: National Health Service Trust 88
Borders Regional Council: Galashiels Mill Lade: Water 197
Bosnian & Croatian territories: Goods: Export: Control 23

244 ALPHABETICAL INDEX

Bournemouth & West Hampshire Water 196
Bournewood Community & Mental Health: National Health Service Trust 71
Bovine offal: Prohibition 38
    Prohibition: Scotland 38
Bovine spongiform encephalopathy: Compensation 6
Bowes Extension Light Railway 191
Bradford Cable Communications Ltd.: Public telecommunication systems 186
Brancaster Staithe: Fishery 178
Breckland: Environmentally sensitive areas 2
Brent (London Borough): Special parking areas 109
Bridgend District: National Health Service Trust 71
Bridges: Birmingham & Fazeley Canal 42
    Kitty Brewster Bridge: Duplicate: Scheme 43
Brighton Borough Council: Local government: Defined activities: Exemption 59
Brighton Health Care: National Health Service Trust 71
British citizenship: Designated service 8
British Coal: Staff superannuation scheme 14
British Gas plc.: Rateable values 101
    Rateable values: Scotland 101
British nationality 8
British nationality: South Africa 8
British railways: Arpley Chord 191, 193
British Telecommunications plc.: Dissolution 186
    Rateable values: Scotland 101
British Transport Police Force 191
British Waterways Board & telecommunications industry: Rateable values 101
Broadcasting: Foreign satellite programmes: Specified countries 8
    Networking arrangements 8
    Prescribed countries 8
    Television services: Unlicensed 8
    Wireless telegraph: Guernsey 8, 188
Broadleaved woodland: Habitat: Wales 3
Broads (The Broads): Environmentally sensitive areas 3
Bromley: Special parking areas 110
Bromley Hospitals: National Health Service Trust 71
Bromley (London Borough): Special parking areas 110
Broxtowe Borough Council: Defined activities: Exemption 59
Brucellosis 6
Brucellosis: Scotland 6
Buckingham: Internal Drainage Board: Reconstitution 56
Buckinghamshire: Changes in local government areas 61
    Combined probation areas 97
Building 8
Building & buildings 8
Building & buildings: Standards: Scotland 8
Building: Prescribed fees 8
Buildings: Value added tax 195
Building societies 9
Building societies: Accounts, etc. 8
   Auditors 9
   Capital resources: Designated 9
   Debt: Undated subordinated 9
   Dividends & interest: Income tax 51
   EFTA states 9
   General charge & fees 9
   Qualifying bodies 9
Building standards: Scotland 8
Bulgaria: European Communities: Treaties 36
    Extradition: European convention 37
Burnley Health Care: National Health Service Trust 71

C
Cabs: London 68
Calderdale Healthcare: National Health Service Trust 71

Calderstones: National Health Service Trust 71
Caledonian MacBrayne: Rateable values: Scotland 101
Cambrian Mountains: Environmentally sensitive areas 2
Canada: Navigation services: Civil aviation 13, 14
Canadian navigation services 13, 14
Canals: Non-domestic rating 103
Canterbury & Kent Hospitals: National Health Service Trust 76
Canterbury & Thanet Community Health Care: National Health Service Trust 71
Capacity measures: Measuring equipment 198
Capital gains tax: Annual exempt amount 186
    Gilt-edged securities 186
Carcases: Pigs: Grading 5
Cardiff: Changes in local government areas 61
Care proceedings: Legal aid 57
Car fuel benefits: Income tax: Cash equivalents 51
Caribbean & north Atlantic territories: Virgin Islands: Constitution 9
Carlisle: Diocese: Educational endowments 25
Cars: Benefits: Replacement accessories: Income tax 51
    Driving instruction 108
    Replacement: Income tax 51
Castle Vale Housing Action Trust: Transfer of property 46
Categorisation of earners: Social security 182
Cats: Importation: Rabies 6
Central Manchester: National Health Service Trust 71
Central Middlesex Hospital: National Health Service Trust 71
Central rating lists 101
Central Scotland Healthcare: National Health Service Trust: Scotland 88
Cereals: Home-grown: Authority: Levy: Rate 5
    Marketing 5
Certification officer: Fees 191
Chancery: Clerk of the Crown in Chancery 14
Channel Islands: Intelligence services 55
Channel tunnel 9
Channel tunnel: Fisheries 9
    Road traffic: Enactments: Application 9
    Security 9
    Shop & liquor licensing hours 9
    Sunday trading 9
Chappel & Wakes Colne Light Railway 191
Charitable institutions: Fund raising 9
Charities 9, 10
Charities: Exempt 10
    National Trust 10
    Royal Philanthropic Society 10
Chase Farm Hospitals: National Health Service Trust 71
Chelsea & Westminster Healthcare: National Health Service Trust .71
Chemicals: Hazard information & packaging 41
Cheshire: East: National Health Service Trust 73
Chester: Pipelaying: Code of practice 197
Chesterfield & North Derbyshire Hospital: National Health Service Trust 72
Child abduction & custody: Parties to conventions 10
Children & young persons 10
Children & young persons: Abduction & custody: Parties to conventions 10
    Parental responsibility: Agreement 10
    Proceedings: Allocation 37
Children's homes 10
Children's pensions: Superannuation: Earnings limit 95
Child safety: Medicines 65
Child support 37
Chinnor & Princes Risborough railway 191, 193
Chorley & South Ribble: National Health Service Trust 72
Chorley: Changes in local government areas 61
Church: Representation 24
Churches: Redundant: Fund: Grants 25

Churchill John Radcliffe: National Health Service Trust 72
Church of England 25
Cinemas & films 11
Cinemas & films: Cinematographic co-production: European convention 10
   Films co-production agreements 11
Cinematographic co-production: European Convention 10, 11
Citizenship: British: Designated service 8
City of London: Special parking areas 109
City of Worcester: Changes in local government areas 61
Civil aviation 11, 13, 14
Civil aviation: Aeroplanes: Noise 11
   Air fares 11
   Canadian navigation services 13, 14
   Dangerous goods 11
   Flying restrictions 11, 12, 13
   Joint financing 14
   Navigation services: Charges 14
   Personnel licences: Northern Ireland 14
Civil courts 18, 53, 185
Civil engineers: Panels: Reservoirs: Application fees 196, 197
Civilians: Personal injuries 94
Civil legal aid 56
Civil legal aid: Assessment of resources 56
   Fees: Scotland 58
   Financial contributions: Scotland 57
   Scotland 57
Civil service: Management functions: Northern Ireland 91
Claims & payments: Social security 182
Clean air 14
Clerk of the Crown in Chancery 14
Cleveland Ambulance: National Health Service Trust 72
Cleveland College of Further Education: Dissolution 25
Cleveland Tertiary College: Government 25
   Incorporation 25
Clubs: Gaming: Hours & charges 7
Clun: Environmentally sensitive areas 2
Clwydian Range: Environmentally sensitive areas 2
Clyde River catchment area: Protection 105
Coal: Opencast: Forms 15
Coal industry 14, 15
Coal industry: Aire & Calder navigation 14
   Copyhold interests: Retained 15
   Doncaster area: Drainage 15
   Local Acts 15
   Pensions: Protected persons 15
   Restructuring date 15
   Restructuring grants 15
   Staff: Superannuation schemes 15
Coal mining: Subsidence: Arbitration schemes 15
   Subsidence: Blight & compensation 15
      Information 15
      Land drainage 15
      Subsidence adviser 15
Coastal belt: Habitat: Wales 3
Cockle fishery: Thames estuary 179
Cockles: Fishing: Prohibition: Scotland 179
   Inshore fishing: Prohibition: Scotland 179
Cold weather payments: Social fund 182
Coleg Menai: Government 25
Coleg Pencraig: Dissolution 28
Collective enfranchisement & tenants' audit: Surveyors: Qualified 46
Collectors: Taxes: Distraint: Fees, costs & charges 49
Comment Cablevision Wearside Partnership: Public telecommunication systems 187
Comment Cablevision Worcester Ltd: Public telecommunication systems 187

Commissioners for oaths: Prescribed bodies	58, 92
Common agricultural policy	5
Common agricultural policy: Wine	1
Commonwealth Development Corporation: Additional enterprises	93
CommuniCare: National Health Service Trust	72
Community care: Scotland	89
Community charges: Administration & enforcement	16
Community Health Care: North Durham: National Health Service Trust	72
Community Health Care Service: North Derbyshire: National Health Service Trust	72
Community Health Services, Southern Derbyshire: National Health Service Trust	72
Companies	16
Companies: Audit exemption	16
Bank accounts	16
Fees	16
Foreign: Execution of documents	16
Forms & documents: Welsh language	16
Insolvency	53
Insurance	54
Insurance: Accounts & statements	54
Welsh language forms & documents	16
Compatibility: Electromagnetic	34
Compensation: Acquisition of land	1
Injuries in war	53
Workmen: Supplementation	184
Competition	16
Competitions & trials: Motor vehicles: Scotland	108
Compulsory purchase: Ministers: Inquiries procedure	194
Conservation: Farm: Grant: Variation	3, 46
Natural habitats	18, 198
Constables: Special: Scotland	96
Construction & property services: Local government: Competition: Defined activities	59, 62
Construction: Design & management	41
Local government: Competition: England	59
Construction Board: Industrial training levy	35
Construction products	8
Consular fees	24
Consumer contracts: Unfair terms	17
Consumer credit: Exempt agreements	16
Consumer protection	16, 17, 41
Consumer protection: Consumer contracts: Unfair terms	17
Cosmetic products: Safety	16
Electrical equipment: Safety	16
Motor vehicles: Tyres: Safety	17
Tickets: Resale: Price indications	17
Contempt of court: Legal aid: Fees: Scotland	58
Contracting-out: Deregulation	24, 100, 108
Contracts: Applicable law	17
Consumer: Unfair terms: Consumer protection	17
Conwy mussel fishery: Food safety: Live bivalve molluscs & other shellfish	39
Copyhold interests: Coal industry	15
Copyright: Act of Sederunt	180
Application to other countries	17
Licensing schemes: Educational Recording Agency Ltd	17
Core subjects: National curriculum: Assessment arrangments: Key stage 1	29
National curriculum: Assessment arrangments: Key stage 2	29
Assessment arrangments: Key stage 3	29
Cornwall & Devon: Local government: Committees	60
Cornwall & Isles of Scilly Learning Disabilities: National Health Service Trust	72
Cornwall Healthcare: National Health Service Trust	72
Cosmetic products: Safety	16
Cosmetics: Weights & measures	198
Cotswold Hills: Environmentally sensitive areas	2
Council tax: Administration & enforcement	17
Calculation of council tax base: England	60

248 ALPHABETICAL INDEX

Discount disregards	17
Discounts: Scotland	18, 197
Dwellings: Situation & valuation	18
England & Wales	17, 18
Exempt dwellings	17
Exempt dwellings: Scotland	18, 197
Liability: Reduction: Scotland	18, 197
Limitation: Sheffield City Council	18
Lists & appeals	17
Transitional reduction scheme: England	18
Council tax benefit	181
Council tax benefit: Permitted totals	180, 181
Subsidy	181
Countess of Chester: National Health Service Trust	72
Countryside	18, 198
Countryside: Access	1
County courts	18, 19, 37, 38, 53, 185
County courts: Family proceedings: Rules	19, 37, 185
Fees	18
Forms	19
Patents	93
Procedure	19
Rules	18
Court of Protection: Rules	67, 96
Court of Session: Fees	20
Rules	19
Rules: Act of Sederunt	19
Scotland	19, 20
Courts: Civil courts	18, 53, 185
County courts	18, 19, 37, 53, 185
County courts: Fees	18
Forms	19
Magistrates' courts	63, 185
Magistrates' courts: Police	63, 95, 96
Police: Northern Ireland	91
Police: Scotland	95
Scottish Land Court: Fees	178
Coventry Healthcare: National Health Service Trust	72
Cows: Suckler: Annual premium	5
Suckler: Annual premium: Quotas	5
Crawley Horsham: National Health Service Trust	72
Credit unions: Industrial & provident societies: Fees	52
Criminal & care proceedings: Legal aid	57
Criminal justice	20, 21, 22
Criminal justice: Crown servants	20, 22
Crown servants & regulators: Emergency provisions: Northern Ireland	21, 22
Scotland	22
Designated countries & territories	20
International co-operation: Crown servants	20, 21, 22
Drugs: Anguilla	24
Overseas forfeiture orders: Scotland	20, 22
Northern Ireland	91
Prisoner custody officer certificate: Suspension	97
Public order	20, 22, 186
Sentencing: Reviews	20
Criminal law	20, 21, 22
Criminal law: Designated countries & territories	20
Drug trafficking	20
England & Wales	20, 21, 22
Northern Ireland	20, 21, 22
Overseas forfeiture orders	20, 22
Scotland	20, 21, 22
Criminal legal aid: Fees: Scotland	58
Precribed proceedings: Scotland	58

  Scotland 58
Criminal proceedings: Legal aid 57
Croatian & Bosnian territories: Goods: Export: Control 23
Crofters: Livestock purchase loans: Scotland 22
Crofters, cottars & small landholders 22
Crofting counties: Agricultural grants: Scotland 22
Crops, food & feedingstuffs: Pesticides: Residue levels: Maximum 6
Crown Court: Rules 185
Crown Office: Fees 14
Crown servants: Criminal justice 20, 21, 22
  Criminal justice: International co-operation 20, 21, 22
  Drug trafficking: Offences 20
  Emergency provisions: Northern Ireland 21, 22
  Terrorism: Prevention 21, 22
Croydon (London Borough): Special parking areas 109
Cruelty: Animals: Prevention 7
Cultural objects: Return 22
Cumbria: West Cumbria Health Care: National Health Service Trust .87
Currency contracts & options 49
Curriculum: Assessment arrangements: Core subjects: Key stage 1: Wales 29
  Assessment arrangements: Core subjects: Key stage 3: Wales 29
  Exceptions: Wales 30
  Geography: Attainment targets & programmes of study 29
    Attainment targets & programmes of study: Wales 29
  History: Attainment targets & programmes of study 29
    Attainment targets & programmes of study: Wales 30
  Foundation subjects: Key stage 4 30
  Modern foreign languages 30
  Modern foreign languages & technology: Attainment targets & programmes of study . . .30
  National: Exceptions 30
  Science: Attainment targets & programmes of study 30
Customs & excise 22, 23, 24
Customs & excise: Free zone designation: Port of Sheerness 23
  Trade: Statistics 184
Customs: Trade marks 191
Customs duties: ECSC: Quota & other reliefs 23
Cycle racing: Highways: Tour de France 108
Cyprus: Social security 183
Czech Republic: European Communities: Treaties 36

D

Dacorum & St Albans Community: National Health Service Trust 72
Dairies: Charges 39
Dairy produce: Quotas 38
Dangerous drugs 24
Dangerous goods: Air navigation 11
  Carriage: Rail 41
    Rail: Classification, packaging & labelling 41
  Reporting requirements: Merchant shipping 64, 68
Dangerous substances & preparations: Safety 16
Dartford-Thurrock crossing 43
Dartford-Thurrock crossing: Tolls 43
Dartmoor: Environmentally sensitive areas 2
Deaths: Births: Registration 104
Deeds: Enrolment: Change of name 185
  Enrolment: Fees 185
  Execution: Land registration 56
Defence 24
Defence organisations: Designation & privileges 24
Defence services: Disablement & death: Pensions 94
  Discipline acts 24
Denbighshire: East: Wrexham: Pipelaying: Code of practice 197
Dental charges: National Health Service 79
  National Health Service: Scotland 89

Dependants: Maintenance 64
Dependent territories: Family law 10
Derby City General Hospital: National Health Service Trust 73
Derbyshire: Combined probation areas 97
    North Derbyshire & Chesterfield Hospital: National Health Service Trust 72
    North Derbyshrie Community Health Care Serivce: National Health Service Trust 72
Deregulation & contracting-out 24, 100, 108
Derwentside: Changes in local government areas 61
Designs: Act of Sederunt 180
    Convention countries 24
Development: Permitted: Town & country planning: Scotland 190
Development Board for Rural Wales: Housing stock 90
Development procedure: Town & country planning: Scotland 190
Devon & Cornwall: Local government: Committees 60
Diocese of Bangor: Educational endowments 25
Diocese of Canterbury: Educational endowments 25
Diocese of Carlisle: Educational endowments 25
Diocese of Chelmsford: Educational endowments 25
Diocese of Ely: Educational endowments 25
Diocese of Guildford: Educational endowments 25
Diocese of Norwich: Educational endowments 25
Diocese of Oxford: Educational endowments 25, 26
Diocese of St Asaph: Educational endowments 26
Diocese of Truro: Educational endowments 26
Diocese of Wakefield: Educational endowments 26
Diplomatic service: Consular fees 24
Direct labour organisations: Competition 61
    Local government: Changes: England 60
        Competition: Exemption 61
Disability living allowance 182
Disablement: Severe disablement allowance 184
Diseases: Fish 105, 106, 178
    Prescribed: Industrial injuries 183
District health authorities: National Health Service 79
District probate registries 186
Districts: National Health Service: Determination 79
Docklands Development Corporation: London: Boundaries 195
Docklands Light Railway: Penalty fares: Police services 193
Docks & harbours: Rateable values 101
Dogs: Importation: Rabies 6
Doncaster area: Drainage: Coal industry 15
Doncaster Healthcare: National Health Service Trust 73
Dorset Ambulance: National Health Service Trust 73
Dorset Community: National Health Service Trust 73
Double taxation: Deceased estates & inheritances: Relief: Switzerland 52
Double taxation relief: Austria 49
    Estonia 49
    Guernsey 49
    Indonesia 49
    Isle of Man 49
    Jersey 49
    Kazakhstan 49
    Mexico 49
    Russian Federation 50
    Saudi Arabia 49
    Switzerland 50
    United States of America 50
    Uzbekistan 50
    Vietnam 50
Downfields Canal Bridge: Scheme 42
Drainage: Land 55, 56
Drinking water: Containers 38
Driving instruction: Motor cars 108
Driving licences: Motor vehicles 108

Relevant external law: Designation	108
Drugs & appliances: Charges: National Health Service	79
Charges: National Health Service: Scotland	89
Drugs: Dangerous	24
Misuse: Licence fees	24
Veterinary: Products other than	66
Drug trafficking: Designated countries & territories	20
Extradition	37
Offences: Crown servants & regulators	20
Proceeds: Confiscation: Scotland	22
Dudley Group of Hospitals: National Health Service Trust	73
Dudley Priority Health: National Health Service Trust	73
Dumfries & Galloway College of Technology	33
Dumfries & Galloway Community Health: National Health Service Trust	88
Duncan of Jordanstone College of Art: Closure	33
Dundee: University of Abertay Dundee	34
Durham County Ambulance Service: National Health Service Trust	73
Duty: Air passengers: Connected flights	22
Air passengers: Prescribed rates of interest	22

E

Ealing Hospital: National Health Service Trust	73
Ealing (London Borough): Special parking areas	109
Earners: Categorisation: Social security	182
Earnings cap: Indexation: Retirement benefits schemes	51
Earnings factors: Revaluation: Social security	184
East Anglian Ambulance: National Health Service Trust	73
East Berkshire Community Health: National Health Service Trust	73
East Berkshire NHS Trust for People with Learning Disabilities: National Health Service Trust	73
East Birmingham Hospital: National Health Service Trust	73
Eastbourne & County Healthcare: National Health Service Trust	73
East Cheshire: National Health Service Trust	73
East Denbighshire: Wrexham: Pipelaying: Code of practice	197
East Glamorgan: National Health Service Trust	73
East Hertfordshire: National Health Service Trust	73
East Kilbride: New towns: Winding up: Scotland	90
East Suffolk Health Services: National Health Service Trust	74
East Surrey Hospital & Community Healthcare: National Health Service Trust	74
East Surrey Learning Disablity & Mental Health Service: National Health Service Trust	74
East Sussex Health Authority: National Health Service	74
East Yorkshire Borough Council: Local government: Defined activities: Exemption	59
East Yorkshire Hospitals: National Health Service Trust	74
Ecclesiastical exemption: Listed buildings & conservation areas	189
Ecclesiastical judges: Fees	25
Ecclesiastical law: Church representation	24
England	25
Fees: England	25
ECSC: Customs duties: Quota & other reliefs	23
Edinburgh: Queen Margaret College	33
Education	26, 30, 33
Education: Appeal committees: Lay members	28
Assisted places	26
Assisted places: Incidental expenses	26
Scotland	33
Chief Inspector of Schools: England	26
Cleveland Tertiary College: Government	25
Incorporation	25
Coleg Menai: Government	25
Curriculum: Exceptions: Wales	30
Geography: Attainments targets & programmes of study	29
Geography: Attainment targets & programmes of study: Wales	29
History: Attainment targets & programmes of study	29
History: Attainment targets & programmes of study: Wales	30
Foundation subjects: Key stage 4	30

        Modern foreign languages 30
        Modern foreign languages & technology: Attainment targets & programmes of study 30
        Science: Attainment targets & programmes of study 30
Diocese of Bangor: Educational endowments 25
Diocese of Canterbury: Educational endowments 25
Diocese of Carlisle: Educational endowments 25
Diocese of Chelmsford: Educational endowments 25
Diocese of Ely: Educational endowments 25
Diocese of Guildford: Educational endowments 25
Diocese of Norwich: Educational endowments 25
Diocese of Oxford: Educational endowments 25, 26
Diocese of St Asaph: Educational endowments 26
Diocese of Truro: Educational endowments 26
Diocese of Wakefield: Educational endowments 26
Duncan of Jordanstone College of Art: Closure 33
England & Wales 25, 30, 32, 33
European Community enlargement: Scotland 33
Fees & awards 27
Further education corporations 27
Grant 27
Grant-maintained schools: Finance 27
    Governors 27
    Groups 28
    Groups: Finance 28
    Groups: Government 27
    Groups: Initial government 28
    Initial governing instruments 27
Grant-maintained special schools 27
Grant-maintained special schools: Finance 27
    Initial governing instruments 27
    Initial government 28
Grants: Music & ballet schools 28
  Support & training 28
Gwynedd Technical College & Coleg Pencraig: Dissolution 28
Henrietta Barnett School: Grant 27
Independent schools: Particulars 30
Information: Provision 28
Inner London Education Authority: Property transfer 28
Inter-authority recoupment 28
London Residuary Body: Transfer of property 28
Maintained special schools: Becoming grant-maintained 29
Mandatory awards 29
Middle schools 29
National curriculum: Core subjects: Assessment arrangements: Key stage 1 29
    Core subjects: Assessment arrangements: Key stage 1: Wales 29
    Core subjects: Assessment arrangements: Key stage 2 29
    Core subjects: Assessment arrangements: Key stage 2: Wales 29
    Core subjects: Assessment arrangements: Key stage 3 29
    Core subjects: Assessment arrangements: Key stage 3: Wales 29
    Exceptions 30
    Welsh language: Key stage 4 30
Northern School of Contemporary Dance, Leeds Further Education Corporation 30
Norwich School of Art & Design Further Education Corporation 30
Physical: Value added tax 196
Pupil referral units 31
Pupils: Achievements: Information: Wales 28
  Excluded: Amount to follow 26
  Registration 32
Religious: Local conferences & councils 33
School Curriculum & Assessment Authority: Transfer of functions: Wales 31
Schools: Chief Inspector: Wales 26
  Conducted by education associations 31
  Education associations: Government: Initial articles 31
  Exclusions: Prescribed periods 27

ALPHABETICAL INDEX

  Financial delegations: Mandatory exceptions 27
  Financial statements 31
  Further education information: Wales 26
  Grant-maintained: Finance: Wales 27
  Grant-maintained special: Groups 28
  Grant-maintained status: Ballots: Wales 26
  Information 31
  Information: Wales 31
  Performance information: England 31
  Performance information: Wales 31
  Registered inspectors: Appeal tribunal: Procedure 31
  Self-governing: Scotland 34
School teachers: Pay & conditions 31, 32
Scotland 33, 34
Special needs 32
Special needs: Code of practice 32
  Independent schools: Approval 32
  Supplies: Payment 30
  Tribunal 33
Special schools 32
Special schools: Conducted by education associations 32
  Education associations 32
  Grant-maintained 27
  Grant maintained: Finance 27
  Grant-maintained: Initial governing instruments 27
  Grant-maintained: Initial government 28
  Notices: Publication 30
Student loans 32, 33
Teachers 32
Teachers' superannuation: Additional voluntary contributions .33
  England & Wales 33
  Scotland 34
Teacher training: Bursaries 26
Teaching As A Career Unit: Transfer of property 33
University commissioners 195
Value added tax 195
Writtle Agricultural Colleges Further Education Corporation 32
Educational Recording Agency Ltd: Copyright: Licensing schemes 17
Education associations: Schools 31
  Schools: Government: Initial articles 31
  Special schools 32
EFTA states: Building societies 9
Elections: Day of election: European Parliament 104
  European Parliament 104
  European Parliament: Returning officers 104
    Returning officers: Charges 104
    Returning officers: Charges: Northern Ireland 104
  Local: Candidates: Expenses: Northern Ireland 91
Electrical equipment: Safety 16
Electricity: Licence requirements: Class exemptions 34
 Non-fossil fuel: Scotland 34
 Non-fossil fuel sources 34
 Scotland 34, 56, 106, 190
 Supply 34
Electricity generators: Rateable values: Scotland 101
Electricity supply industry: Rateable values 101
Electromagnetic compatibility 34
Embryology & human fertilisation 48
Embryology & human fertilisation: Parental orders 49
Employers: Small: Statutory sick pay: Relief 189
Employers' liability: Compulsory insurance 54
 Compulsory insurance: Exemption 53
Employment & training 35
Employment & training: Agricultural Training Board 35

Employment: Terms & conditions 182, 184, 188, 189
    Wages councils: Abolition 189, 191
Employment protection: Guarantee payments: Exemption 188
    Suspension: Maternity grounds 189
Employment rights: Trade unions: Reform 189, 191
Employments: Income tax 51
Encom Cable TV & Telcommunications Ltd.: Dartford: Public telecommunication systems 187
    Epping Forest: Public telecommunication systems 187
Energy conservation 35
Energy information: Refrigerators & freezers 35
Enfield Community Care: National Health Service Trust 74
Enfield (London Borough): Special parking areas 109
Engineering & Physical Sciences Research Council 178
Engineering Construction Board: Industrial training levy 35
Environmental assessment: Scotland 34, 56, 106, 190
Environmental effects: Highways: Assessment 43
Environmentally sensitive areas: Avon Valley 1
    Blackdown Hills 2
    Breckland 2
    The Broads 3
    Cambrian Mountains 2
    Clun 2
    Clwydian Range 2
    Cotswold Hills 2
    Dartmoor 2
    Essex coast 2
    Exmoor 2
    Lake District 2
    Lleyn Peninsula 2
    North Kent Marshes 2
    North Peak 2
    Pennine Dales 2
    Preseli 2
    Radnor 2
    Scotland 2
    Shropshire Hills 2
    Somerset levels & moors 3
    South Downs 3
    South Wessex Downs 3
    South West Peak 3
    Suffolk River Valleys 3
    Test Valley 3
    Upper Thames tributaries 3
    West Penwith 3
    Ynys Môn 2
Environmental protection 35, 36, 41
Environmental protection: Prescribed processes & substances 35, 36
    Processes: Authorisation 35
    Waste recycling payments 36
Epsom School of Art & Design: Dissolution 32
Essex & Herts Community: National Health Service Trust 74
Essex & Suffolk: Water 197
Essex: Petty sessional divisions 55
    Youth court panel 199
Essex coast: Environmentally sensitive areas 2
Essex Rivers Healthcare: National Health Service Trust 74
Estonia: Double taxation relief: Income tax 49
European Communities: Air carriers: Licencing 14
    Bulgaria: Treaties 36
    Czech Republic: Treaties 36
    Designation 36
    Highlands & Islands: Agricultural programme 37
    Intra-community air routes: Access 11
    Iron & steel: Employees re-adaptation benefits scheme: Termination 37

ALPHABETICAL INDEX

Romania: Treaties 36
Sea fisheries: Restrictions 179
Sea fishing: Conservation measures 179
Slovak Republic: Treaties 36
European convention: Cinematographic co-production 11
Extradition 37
European Economic Area: Immigration 49
European Economic Interest Grouping: Fees 38
European Free Trade Association: Building societies 9
European Molecular Biology Laboratory: Immunities & privileges 55
European Parliament: Constituencies 105
Constituencies: Wales 105
Elections 104
Elections: Day of election 104
Northern Ireland 104
Representatives: Franchise & qualification 104
Returning officers 104
Returning officers: Charges 104
Returning officers: Charges: Northern Ireland 104
Pay & pensions 37
United Kingdom representatives: Pensions 37
Exchange gains & losses 50
Exchange gains & losses: Calculation: Alternative method 50
Debts: Varying amounts 50
Deferral 50
Excess 50
Insurance companies 50
Excise duty: Isle of Man 55
Exempt charities 10
Exeter & North Devon Health Authority: National Health Service 74
Exmoor: Environmentally sensitive areas 2
Export of goods: Control 23
Control: Croatian & Bosnian territories 23
Extradition: Bulgaria: European convention 37
Drug trafficking 37
European Convention 37

F

Fair trading: Merger prenotification 68
Monopoly references 69
Family health services authorities: National Health Service: London: Functions 79
Family law 19, 37, 185
Family law: Children: Proceedings: Allocation 37
Child support 37
Dependent territories 10
Family proceedings 19, 37, 38, 185
Family proceedings: Courts 63
Courts: Rules 63
Legal aid: Remuneration 57
Rules 19, 37, 185
Farm & conservation grants 5
Farm & conservation grants: Variation 3, 5, 46
Farming: Organic: Aid 5
Feedingstuffs: Medicated 66
Sampling & analysis 3
Fees & charges 38
Fertilisation: Human: Embryology 48
Fertilisers: Sampling & analysis 3
Fibre & oil plant seeds 180
Films: Cinemas 11
Cinematographic co-production: European convention 10
Co-production agreements 11
Finance 23, 50, 54, 195
Finance: Local government: England & Wales 62

Finance Act: Appointed day 50
    Chapter II of Part IV: Appointed day 50
Financial services 38
Financial services: Auditors 38
    Information: Disclosure: Designated authorities 38
Financial statements: Schools 31
Firearms 7
Firearms: Fees 7
    Fees: Scotland 7
    Northern Ireland 91
    Period of certificate 7
    Scotland 7
Fire precautions: Sub-surface railway stations 38
Fish: Diseases 105, 178
    Health 105, 178
    Oil & chemical pollution: Food protection 98, 100
Fisheries: Channel tunnel 9
    Salmon & freshwater 105, 178
    Salmon & freshwater: Scotland 105
    Sea 105, 178, 179
    Sea: Community restrictions 179
        Conservation of sea fish 179
        Marketing 179
Fishery products: Food safety 39
Fishing: Cockles: Prohibition: Scotland 179
    Inshore: Scotland 179
    Plaice & Sole: Prohibition 179
    Sole & Nephrops: Prohibition 179
    Third country 179
Fishing vessels: Decommissioning 179
    Radio 68
Flavourings: Food 38
Food 38, 39
Food: Dairy produce: Quotas 38
    Flavourings 38
    Labelling 39
    Labelling: Scotland 39
    Materials & articles in contact with food 39
    Meat products: Hygiene 39
    Quick-frozen foodstuffs 39
Food protection: Emergency prohibitions 99, 100
    Emergency prohibitions: Fish: Oil & chemical pollution 98, 100
        Paralytic shellfish 98, 99, 100
        Radioactivity in sheep 99, 100
    Isle of Man 64
Food safety: Conwy mussel fishery 39
    Fishery products 39
    Live bivalve molluscs & other shellfish 39
Football grounds: Rateable values: Scotland 101
Football spectators: Seating 184
Footbridges: Leeds: Marsh Lane: Railtrack plc 191, 193
    Shifford Island: Oxfordshire County Council 43
Foreign companies: Execution of documents 16
Foreign judgments: Reciprocal enforcement: Australia 55
Forest Healthcare: National Health Service Trust 74
Forestry: Plant health 95
Forth Ports plc.: Rateable values: Scotland 101
Foss Bank bridge: Scheme confirmation 43
Fosse Health, Leicestershire Community: National Health Service Trust 74
Freeman Group of Hospitals: National Health Service Trust 74
Freezers: Energy information 35
Free zone: Humberside: Designation 23
    Prestwick airport: Designation 23
    Southampton: Designation 23

Tilbury Port: Designation 23
Frenchay Healthcare: National Health Service Trust 74
Freshwater & salmon fisheries: Scotland 105
Friendly societies 39
Friendly societies: Accounts 39
    Auditors 40
    Authorisation 40
    General charge & fees 40
    Insurance business 40
Frimley Park Hospital: National Health Service Trust 74
Fuel: Motor: Composition & content 97, 100
Fund-holding practices: National Health Service 79
Fund-raising: Charitable institutions 9
Fund-raising events: Value added tax 196
Funeral expenses: Social Fund 182
Furness Hospitals: National Health Service Trust 74
Further education corporations 27

G

Galashiels Mill Lade: Water 197
Galloway & Dumfries College of Technology 33
Game meat: Farmed: Hygiene & inspection 39
Gaming: Clubs: Hours & charges 7
    Monetary limits: Variation 7
        Variation: Scotland 7
Gaming clubs: Bankers' games 7
    Hours & charges: Scotland 8
Garw valley community 61, 196
Gas: Exempt supplies 40
    Safety 41
Gas carriers: Merchant shipping 68
Gas oil: Sulphur content: Marketing 36
Gateshead: Local government: Defined activities: Exemptions 59
Gateshead Community Health: National Health Service Trust 75
Gateshead Healthcare: National Health Service Trust 75
General & special commissioners: Taxes: Management 50, 52, 186
General commissioners: Taxes: Management 50
General Medical Council: Fitness to Practise Committees: Constitution 64
    Professional Conduct Committee: Preliminary proceedings 64
General Optical Council: Companies Committee: Rules 93
    Maximum penalty 93
    Registration & enrolment: Rules 93
    Testing of sight: Trainee ophthalmic opticians: Rules 93
General product safety 17
Geography: Curriculum: Attainment targets & programmes of study 29
    Curriculum: Attainment targets & programmes of study: Wales 29
Gillingham Borough Council: Defined activies: Exemption 59
Gilt-edged securities: Capital gains tax 186
Gipsy encampments: Rushmoor & Hart 97
    Wychavon District 97
Glamorgan: East: National Health Service Trust 73
    Vale: Changes in local government areas 61
Glasgow Community & Mental Health Services: National Health Service Trust 89
Glasgow Dental Hospital & School: National Health Service Trust 89
Glasgow Underground: Rateable values: Scotland 101
Glenfield Hospital: National Health Service Trust 75
Gloucester Harbour: Revision 40
Gloucestershire: Combined probation areas 97
    Petty sessional divisions 55
    Youth courts & offenders 199
Gloucestershire Ambulance Service: National Health Service Trust 75
Good Hope Hospital: National Health Service Trust 75
Goods: Dangerous: Air navigation 11
    Dangerous: Carriage: Rail 41

258 ALPHABETICAL INDEX

Carriage: Rail: Classification, packaging & labelling 41
Export: Control 23
    Control: Croatian & Bosnian territories 23
Packaged: Weights & measures 198
Goods vehicles: Operators' licences, qualifications & fees 108
    Plating & testing 108
    Type approval 108
Government trading funds 40
Grantham & District Hospital: National Health Service Trust 75
Grant-maintained schools 28
Grant-maintained schools: Finance 27, 28
    Finance: Wales 27
    Governors 27
    Groups 28
    Groups: Government 27
        Initial government 28
    Initial governing instruments 27
Grant-maintained special schools 27
Grant-maintained special schools: Finance 27
    Initial governing instruments 27
    Initial government 28
Grant-maintained status: Maintained special schools 29
    Schools: Ballots: Wales 26
Grants: Education: Support & training 28
Grassland: Species rich: Habitat: Wales 4
Greater London: Changes in local government areas 61
Greater Manchester: Combined probation areas 97
Greater Manchester Buses Ltd.: Superannuation 94
Greater Manchester Buses North Ltd.: Superannuation 94
Greater Manchester light rapid transit system 191, 193
Great Ormond Street Hospital for Children: National Health Service Trust 75
Greenwich (London Borough): Special parking areas 109
Grimsby Health: National Health Service Trust 75
Guaranteed minimum pensions increase 93
Guarantee payments: Exemption: Employment protection 188
Guernsey: Double taxation relief: Income tax 49
    Emergency provisions: Northern Ireland 91
    Social security 184
    Wireless telegraphy 8, 188
Gwynedd Technical College: Dissolution 28

H

Habitat: Former set-aside land 3
    Salt-marsh 4
    Water fringe 4
Habitats: Scotland 4
Hague Convention countries: Maintenance orders: Reciprocal enforcement 64
Haiti: United Nations: Sanctions 195
    United Nations: Sanctions: Channel Islands 194
        Sanctions: Dependent territories 194
        Sanctions: Isle of Man 194
Halton General Hospital: National Health Service Trust 75
Hammersmith & Fulham: Special parking areas 110
Hammersmith Hospitals: National Health Service Trust 75
Hampshire: Petty sessional divisions 55
Hampshire Ambulance Service: National Health Service Trust 75
Harbours: Lancaster Port Commission 40
    North Killingholme Haven 40
    Saundersfoot 40
    Shetland Islands Council 40
    Ventnor 40
Harbours, docks, piers & ferries 40
Haringey: Bus lanes: Red route traffic: A1 107
    Red route traffic: A1 107

Haringey (London Borough): Special parking areas 109
Harlow District Council: Defined activities: Exemptions 59
Harrogate Borough Council: Defined activities: Exemption 59
Harrow & Hillingdon Healthcare: National Health Service Trust 75
Harrow Community Health Services: National Health Service Trust 75
Harrow (London Borough): Special parking areas 109
Hartlepool Community Care: National Health Service Trust 76
Hartlepool Hospital: National Health Service Trust 75
Haven Road Bridge: Scheme confirmation 43
Havering (London Borough): Special parking areas 109
Health & personal social services: Northern Ireland 91
Health & safety 36, 41
Health & safety: Electrical equipment 16
   Fees 41
   Machinery supply 42
   Personal protective equipment: EC directive 17, 41
   Pressure vessels: Simple: Safety 42
   Railways 42
   Substances hazardous to health: Control 41
   Transport 41, 42
   Work: Management 41
Health: Animals 6
   Fish 105, 106, 178
Health Service: National 80
   National: Dental charges 79
      District health authorities 79
      Districts 79
      Districts: Determination 79
      Drugs & appliances: Charges 79
      East Sussex Health Authority 74
      England & Wales 65, 76, 77, 78, 87, 90
      Exeter & North Devon Health Authority 74
      Family health services authorities: London: Functions 79
      Functions 79
      Fund-holding practices 79
      General medical & pharmaceutical services: Scotland 89
      Isles of Scilly 76
      Medical & pharmaceutical services: Scotland 89
      Medical Practices Committee: Composition 79
      Optical charges & payments 80
      Overseas visitors: Charges 79
      Regional & district health authorities 80
      Regional health authorities 80
      Regions: Determination 79
      Scotland 65, 87, 89, 90
      Service committees & tribunal 80
      Trustees: Appointment: Scotland 89
   National Trusts 69, 70, 71, 72, 73, 74, 75, 76, 77, 78, 80, 81, 82, 83, 84, 85, 86, 87, 88, 89, 90
   National Trusts: Originating capital debt 80
      Originating capital debt: Scotland 90
   Regional & District Health Authorities 83
Health Service Commissioner: National Blood Authority 76
Health visiting, nursing, midwifery: National Board: England 79
Heatherwood & Wexham Park Hospitals: National Health Service Trust 76
Heathlands Mental Health: National Health Service Trust 76
Heathrow Express: Railways: Exemption 192
Hemel Hempstead & St Albans: National Health Service Trust 85
Henrietta Barnett School: Grant 27
Hereford & Worcester Ambulance Service: National Health Service Trust 76
Heritable securities indemnities: Local authorities: Recognised bodies: Scotland 48
Hertfordshire & Bedfordshire Ambulance & Paramedic Service: National Health Service Trust 70
Hertfordshire: Combined probation areas 97
   East: National Health Service Trust 73
   Petty sessional divisions 55

Youth court panel ... 199
High Court of Justiciary: Fees: Scotland ... 42
　Scotland ... 42, 185
Highlands & Islands: Agricultural programme ... 37
Highways: England & Wales ... 42, 43, 45
　England & Wales: Special roads ... 43, 44
　　Trunk roads ... 44, 45, 46
　Environmental effects: Assessment ... 43
　Inquiries procedure ... 194
　Trunk roads ... 44, 46
Hillingdon & Harrow Healthcare: National Health Service Trust ... 75
Hillingdon Community Health: National Health Service Trust ... 76
Hillingdon Hospital: National Health Service Trust ... 76
Hillingdon (London Borough): Special parking areas ... 110
Hill livestock: Compensatory allowances ... 4
Hinchingbrooke Health Care: National Health Service Trust ... 76
History: Curriculum: Attainment targets & programmes of study ... 29
　Curriculum: Attainment targets & programmes of study: Wales ... 30
HMSO Trading fund ... 40
Home energy efficiency: Grants ... 35
Home-grown Cereals Authority: Levy: Rate ... 5
Home guard ... 93
Homerton Hospital: National Health Service Trust ... 76
Homewood: National Health Service Trust ... 76
Homoeopathic medicinal products: Human use: Medicines ... 66
Homoeopathic products: Advisory Board on the Registration of Homoeopathic Products ... 65
Horticulture ... 3, 5
Hospitals: Post-graduate teaching: Authorities: National Health Service ... 70
Household appliances: Noise emission ... 36
House of Commons: Members' Fund ... 93
House of Lords ... 46, 186
Housing: England & Wales ... 46, 47, 48, 195
　Landlord: Change: Disposal cost: Payment instalments ... 46
　Local authorities: Improvements: Compensation ... 47
　Management: Local government: Competition ... 59
　Purchasing assistance ... 46, 48
　Renovation: Grants: Forms & particulars ... 47
　　Grants: Prescribed forms & particulars: Welsh ... 47
　　Grants: Reduction ... 47
　Rent officers: Additional functions ... 47
　　Additional functions: Scotland ... 48
　Revenue account: General fund contribution limits: Scotland ... 48
　Right to buy: Prescribed forms: Welsh forms ... 47
　　Priority of charges ... 47
　Right to manage ... 47
　Scotland ... 48
　Welfare services ... 47
Housing Action Trusts ... 46, 48
Housing associations: Permissible additional purposes ... 46
　Registered: Accounting: Wales ... 47
Housing benefit ... 181
Housing benefit: Information ... 181
　Permitted totals ... 181
　Subsidy ... 181
Housing management: Competition: Defined activities: Local government ... 59, 62
Housing renovation: Grants ... 47
Housing support grant: Scotland ... 48
Hovercrafts: Fees ... 48
Huddersfield Health Care Services: National Health Service Trust ... 76
Human fertilisation & embryology ... 48, 49
Human fertilisation & embryology: Parental orders ... 49
　Parental orders: Act of Sederunt ... 19, 180
Humber river: Upper Burcom cooling works ... 193
Humberside: Free zone: Designation ... 23

Youth court panel 199
Humberside Ambulance Service: National Health Service Trust 76
Hyde Park & Regent's Park: Vehicle parking 92
Hydrocarbon oil 24

I
Immigration 181
Immigration: European Economic Area 49
Incapacity benefit 183
Incapacity benefit: Dependants: Increases 183
Incapacity for work: Social security 183
Income-related benefits schemes 181, 182
Income support 182
Income tax 49, 50, 51, 52, 53, 186
Income tax: Building societies: Dividends & interest 51
    Car benefits: Replacement accessories 51
    Car fuel benefits 51
    Cars: Replacement cars 51
    Deposit-takers: Interest payments 51
    Double taxation relief: Austria 49
        Estonia 49
        Guernsey 49
        Indonesia 49
        Isle of Man 49
        Jersey 49
        Kazakhstan 49
        Mexico 49
        Russian Federation 50
        Switzerland 50
        United States of America 50
        Uzbekistan 50
        Vietnam 50
    Employments 51
    Employments: Notional payments 51
    Indexation 51
    Interest rate 52, 53, 186
    Unit trusts: Interest distributions 51
    Unit trust scheme: Definition 51
Incumbents: Benefices: Vacation 25
Independent schools: Particulars 30
    Special needs: Approval 32
Individuals: Insolvency 53
Indonesia: Double taxation relief: Income tax 49
Industrial & freight transport: Rateable values: Scotland 101
Industrial & provident societies 52
Industrial & provident societies: Credit unions: Fees 52
    Fees 52
Industrial development 52
Industrial injuries: Prescribed diseases 183
Industrial major accident hazards: Control 41
Industrial training levy: Construction Board 35
    Engineering Construction Board 35
Industrial tribunals: Constitution & rules of procedure 52
    Constitution & rules of procedure: Scotland 52
    Jurisdiction 52
    Jurisdiction: Scotland 52
Inheritance tax 50, 51, 52, 53, 186
Inheritance tax: Double taxation relief: Switzerland 52
    Indexation 52
    Interest rate 52, 53, 186
Injuries: Personal: Civilians 94
Injuries in war: Shore employments: Compensation 53
Inner London Education Authority: Property transfer 28
Inquiries: Costs: Recovery: Ministry of Agriculture, Fisheries & Food 194

Inshore fishing: Cockles: Prohibition: Scotland 179
    Scotland 179
Insider dealing: Securities & regulated markets 53
    Traded securities 53
Insight Communications Cardiff Ltd.: Public telecommunication systems 187
Insight Communications Guildford Ltd.: Public telecommunication systems 187
Insolvency 18, 53, 185
Insolvency: Fees 53
    Partnerships 53
Inspectors: Registered: Schools: Appeal tribunal: Procedure 31
Insurance 53, 54
Insurance: Auditors 53
    Companies 54
    Compulsory: Employers' liability 54
    Fees 54
    Medical: Private: Tax relief 51
    Taxable 54
Insurance Brokers Registration Council: Code of conduct 54
    Registration & enrolment 54
Insurance business: Friendly societies 40
Insurance companies 54
Insurance companies: Accounts & statements 54
    Exchange gains & losses 50
    Pension business 51
Insurance premium tax 54
Intelligence services 55
Intelligence services: Channel Islands 55
International headquarters: Designation & privileges 24
    Law: Application 24
International transport conventions 191
Invalid care allowance 184
Ipswich Hospital: National Health Service Trust 76
Irish Republic: Warrants: Backing 63, 185
Iron & steel: Employees re-adaptation benefits scheme: Termination: European Communities 37
Isle of Man: Children: Abduction & custody 10
    Double taxation relief: Income tax 49
    Excise duty 55
    Food protection 64
Isle of Wight: Harbours 40
    Structural change 58
Isles of Scilly: National Health Service 76
Islington (London Borough): Special parking areas 110

J

James Paget Hospital: National Health Service Trust 76
Jersey: Double taxation relief: Income tax 49
    Social security 184
Judges: Maximum number 46, 186
Judgments 55
Justice: Criminal 20, 21, 22
    Criminal: Crown servants 20, 22
        Crown servants & regulators: Emergency provisions: Northern Ireland 21, 22
        Crown servants & regulators: Scotland 22
        Designated countries & territories 20
        International co-operation: Crown servants 20, 21, 22
        International co-operation: Drugs: Anguilla 24
        International co-operation: Overseas forfeiture orders: Scotland 20, 22
        Northern Ireland 91
        Prisoner custody officer certificate: Suspension 97
        Public order 20, 22, 186
        Sentencing: Reviews 20
Justices of the Peace: Petty sessional divisions 55

K

Kazakhstan: Double taxation relief: Income tax 49

Kensington & Chelsea (Royal Borough): Special parking areas 110
Kent & Canterbury Hospitals: National Health Service Trust 76
Kent & Sussex Weald: National Health Service Trust 76
Kent: South: Hospitals: National Health Service Trust 85
    Weald of Kent Community: National Health Service Trust 87
Kilbride: East: New towns: Winding up: Scotland 90
Kilduskland: Water 197
Kingston & District Community: National Health Service Trust 77
Kingston upon Thames (London Borough): Special parking areas 110
Kitty Brewster Bridge: Duplicate: Scheme 43

L
Labelling & leaflets: Medicines 66
Lake District: Environmentally sensitive areas 2
Lambeth (London Borough): Special parking areas 110
Lanarkshire Healthcare: National Health Service Trust 89
Lancashire: Combined probation areas 97
    Petty sessional divisions 55
    Youth court panel 199
Lancaster Port Commission Harbour 40
Land: Acquisition 1
    Acquisition: Rate of interest after entry 1
        Rate of interest after entry: Scotland 1
    Compulsory purchase 1
    Value added tax 195
Land charges 55
Land charges: Fees 55
Land compensation: Additional development: Forms: Scotland 1
Land drainage 55, 56
Land drainage: Scotland 34, 56, 106, 190
Landlord & tenant: England & Wales 56
Landlord: Change: Disposal cost: Payment instalments 46
Land registration: Execution of deeds 56
    Fees 56
    Scotland 56
Land searches: Charges 59
Lands Tribunal: Fees: Scotland 56
Langport District Drainage Board: Reconstitution 56
Large goods & passenger-carrying vehicles: Driving licences 108
Law: Family law: Child support 37
Laxa Burn, Mid Yell: Water 197
Lay members: Appeal committees: Education 28
Lazy Acres: Natural gas pipe-line 95
Leasehold reform, housing & urban development 47, 195
Leeds: Footbridges: Marsh Lane: Railtrac plc 191, 193
    United Leeds Teaching Hospital: National Health Service Trust 86
Leeds Community & Mental Health Services Teaching: National Health Service Trust 77
Legal advice & assistance 57
Legal advice & assistance: Police stations 57
    Police stations: Remuneration 57
Legal aid & advice: England & Wales 56, 57
    Scotland 57, 58
Legal aid: Children: Scotland 58
    Civil 56
    Civil: Fees: Scotland 58
    Civil proceedings: Contempt: Scotland 58
        Remuneration 57
    Contempt of court: Fees: Scotland 58
    Criminal & care proceedings 57
    Criminal & care proceedings: Costs 57
    Family proceedings: Remuneration 57
    Scope 57
Legal officers: Fees 25
Legal profession 58

Legal services 58, 92
Legal services: Local government: Competition: England 59
Leicester General Hospital: National Health Service Trust 77
Leicester Royal Infirmary: National Health Service Trust 77
Leicestershire: Fosse Health, Leicestershire Community: National Health Service Trust 74
Lerwick Harbour: Revision 40
Lewisham: Special parking areas 110
Lewisham (London Borough): Special parking areas 110
Liability: Shipowners, etc.: Interest rate 67
Licences & certificates: Medicines: Standard provisions 66
Licences: Driving: Relevant external law: Designation 108
Licensing: Channel tunnel: Shop & liquor licensing hours 9
    Fees 63
Licensing schemes: Copyright: Educational Recording Agency Ltd 17
Light rail transit: Penalty fares: South Yorkshire 100
Light railways: Bowes extension 191
    Chappel & Wakes Colne Light Railway 191
    Lydney & Parkend 191
    Wells & Walsingham light railway 193
Lincoln District Healthcare: National Health Service Trust 77
Lincolnshire: South Lincolnshire Community & Mental Health Services: National Health Service Trust ... 85
    Youth court panel 199
Lincolnshire College of Agriculture & Horticulture: Dissolution 32
Lincolnshire College of Art & Design: Dissolution 32
Lindsey: West: National Health Service Trust 88
Liquor: Weights & measures 198
Litter: Northern Ireland 91
Liverpool: Royal Liverpool & Broadgreen University Hospitals: National Health Service Trust 83
Liverpool Obstetric & Gynaecology Services: National Health Service Trust 77
Livestock: Hill: Compensatory allowances 4
    Purchase loans: Crofters: Scotland 22
    Welfare 7
Livingston Development Corporation: Local government: Defined activities: Exempt 62
Lleyn Peninsula: Environmentally sensitive areas 2
Lloyd's underwriters: Tax 51
Local authorities: Armorial bearings 58
    Capital finance 58
    Funds: Wales 62
    Goods & services: Public bodies 59
    Heritable securities indemnities: Recognised bodies: Scotland 48
    Housing: Improvements: Compensation 47
    Land searches: Charges 59
    Members' allowances 59
    Requisite calculations & funds: Alteration 62
Local currency: Elections 51
Local elections: Candidates: Expenses: Northern Ireland 91
Local government: Allowances: Scotland 62
    Changes: Direct labour & services organisations: England 60
        England 60
    Changes in areas 61, 62, 196
    Collection fund: Surpluses & deficits: Changes: England 60
    Competition: Construction & property services: England 59
        Defined activities 59, 62
        Defined activities: Construction & property services 59, 62
        Defined activities: Housing management 59, 62
        Defined activities: Parking supervision, vehicle management & security work 59
        Defined activities: Scotland 59, 62
        Direct labour organisations 61
        Direct labour organisations: Exemption 61
        Housing management 59
        Legal services: England 59
    Council tax base: Calculation: England 60
    Defined activities 60
    Defined activities: Exemption 59, 60

ALPHABETICAL INDEX

    Exemption: Brighton Borough Council 59
    Exemption: Broxtowe Borough Council 59
    Exemption: East Yorkshire Borough Council 59
    Exemption: Gateshead 59
    Exemption: Harlow District Council 59
    Exemption: Harrogate Borough Council 59
    Exemption: Hastings, Worthing, Barnet 60
    Exemption: Livingston Development Corporation 62
    Exemption: South Norfolk District Council 60
    Exemption: Southwark London Borough Council 60
Devon & Cornwall: Committees 60
England & Wales 58, 59, 60, 61, 62
England: Changes 60
Finance: England & Wales 62
    Scotland 63, 101
Local authorities: Funds: Wales 62
Magistrates' Courts 61
Manpower information: Publication 61
    Wales 61
Non-domestic rating: Contributions: Changes: England 60
Parking: Supervision: Exemption: Scotland 62
Redundancy: Compensation 60
    Compensation: Scotland 62
Redundancy payments 188
Reorganisation: Superannuation 94
    Wales 62
Scotland 59, 60, 62, 63, 100, 101
Superannuation 61, 94
Superannuation: Greater Manchester Buses Ltd. 94
    Greater Manchester Buses North Ltd. 94
    Investments 94
Transitional election arrangements: Scotland 63, 104
Wales 60, 61, 62
Local Government Staff Commission: Scotland 63
Local housing authorities: Tenants: Secure: Right to repair 48
Lochaber Power Co.: Rateable values: Scotland 102
Loch an Sgoltaire: Water byelaws 197
Loch Assapol: Water 197
Loch Ewe, West Ross: Scallops fishery 179
Lomond Healthcare: National Health Service Trust 89
London: Family health services authorities: Functions 79
    Government 63
London cabs 68
London Chest Hospital: National Health Service Trust 83
London Docklands Development Corporation: Boundaries 195
London Regional Transport: Exemptions 193
    Penalty fares 100
London Residuary Body: Pits at Stone 63
    Transfer of property 28
Lothian Region: Electoral arrangements 63
Lotteries 8, 90
Lottery: National 8, 90
    National: Licences: Revocation 90
Louth & District Healthcare: National Health Service Trust 77
Luton & Dunstable Hospital Trust: National Health Service Trust 77
Lydney & Parkend light railway 191
Lyon Court & Office: Fees 7

M

Machinery: Supply: Safety 42
Magistrates' courts 63, 185
Magistrates' courts: Bail 64
    Committees: Constitution 63
    Family proceedings: Rules 63

Fees	.63
Licensing: Fees	.63
Local government	.61
Police	63, 95, 96
Police: Northern Ireland	.91
Scotland	.95
Procedure	.64
Rules	.64
Maidstone Priority Care: National Health Service Trust	.77
Maintained special schools: Becoming grant-maintained	.29
Maintenance of dependants	.64
Maintenance orders: Reciprocal enforcement: Hague Convention countries	.64
Mammals: Importation: Rabies	6
Manchester: Central Manchester: National Health Service Trust	.71
Mancunian Community Health: National Health Service Trust	.77
South: University Hospitals: National Health Service Trust	.85
Manchester Children's Hospitals: National Health Service Trust	.77
Mancunian Community Health: National Health Service Trust	.77
Manpower information: Local government: Wales	.61
Marek's disease: Vaccination: Restriction	6
Margaret Danyers College: Incorporation	.32
Marine pollution: Food protection	.64
Merchant shipping	.64
Merchant shipping: BCH code	.64
Dangerous or polluting goods: Reporting requirements	64, 68
IBC code	64, 68
Oil pollution: Prevention	.64
Sterling equivalents	.64
Marketing: Sea fisheries	179
Marketing development scheme	4
Marriage	.64
Marsh Drive, Great Linford: Scheme confirmation	.42
Masters & seamen: Merchant shipping	.68
Materials & articles in contact with food	.39
Maternity & funeral expenses: Social Fund	182
Maternity: Compulsory leave	188
Work: Suspension	189
Maternity allowance	182, 188
Maternity benefits: Social security	184, 189
Maternity pay: Statutory	182, 188
Maudsley: Bethlem & Maudsley: National Health Service Trust	.70
Measurement: Units	198
Measuring equipment: Capacity measures	198
Meat & meat products: Residues: Examinations	.38
Meat products: Hygiene	.39
Medical devices	17, 65
Medical evidence: Social security	184
Medical insurance: Private: Tax relief: Disentitlement	.51
Medical Practices Committee: Composition	.79
Medical profession: General Medical Council: Fitness to practise Committees: Constitution	.64
General Medical Council: Preliminary Proceedings & Professional Conduct Committees: Procedure	.64
Vocational training: General medical practice	65, 87, 90
Medical services: National Health Service	.80
Scotland	.89
Medicines	65, 77
Medicines: Advertising	.65
Advertising: Monitoring	.66
Advisory Board on the Registration of Homoeopathic Products	.65
Animals: Feedingstuffs: Medicated	.66
Fees	.65
Child safety	.65
Committee on Dental & Surgical Materials: Revocation	.65
Control	.65
Homoeopathic medicinal products: Human use	.66

    Human use: Fees 66
        Marketing authorisations 65
    Labelling & leaflets 66
    Licences & certificates: Standard provisions 66
    Manufacturers' licences: Veterinary medicinal products 66
    Other than veterinary drugs: General sale list 66
    Pharmacies: Registration & fees: Applications 66
    Pharmacy & general sale: Exemption 66
    Prescription by nurses 65, 77
    Products other than veterinary drugs: Prescription only 66
    Sale or supply 66
    Veterinary: Product licences: Applications 67
    Veterinary drugs: Licences & animal test certificates 67
        Pharmacy & merchants' list 67
    Veterinary medicinal products: Administration 66
            Marketing authorisations 65
                Veterinary surgeons: EEA states 67
Mental health 67, 96
Mental health: Nurses: Class: Scotland 67
Merchant shipping 67
Merchant shipping: Accident reporting & investigation 67
    Bareboat charter ships 67
    BCH code 64
    Dangerous or polluting goods: Reporting requirements 64, 68
    Fees 67
    Gas carriers 68
    IBC code 64, 68
    Liability: Interest rate 67
    Masters & seamen 68
    Noxious liquid substances: Pollution: Control 64
    Oil pollution: Prevention 64
    Radio: Fishing vessels 68
    Ro-Ro passenger ship survivability 68
    Safety 68
    Safety: Ro-Ro passenger ship survivability 68
    Safety officials: Accidents & dangerous occurrences: Reporting 68
    Salvage & pollution 68
    Seamen's wages & accounts 68
    Ships: Registration 67
    Sterling equivalents 64
Mercury Communications Ltd.: Rateable values: Scotland 102
Merger references: Assets: Increase in value 68
Mergers: Prenotification 68
Merton & Sutton Community: National Health Service Trust 77
Merton (London Borough): Special parking areas 110
Messengers-at-arms: Fees 19
    Fees: Act of Sederunt 19
Metrication: Weights & measures: Miscellaneous goods 198
Metropolitan & City police districts 68
Metropolitan Police Force: Loss of office: Compensation 95
Mexico: Double taxation relief: Income tax 49
Microbiological Research Authority 77, 78
Mid Anglia Community Health: National Health Service Trust 78
Middle schools 29
Middlesex: Central Middlesex Hospital: National Health Service Trust 71
Mid Essex: National Health Service Trust 78
Mid Essex Community Health: National Health Service Trust 78
Mid Kent Healthcare: National Health Service Trust 78
Mid-Staffordshire General Hospitals: National Health Service Trust 78
Mid-Sussex: National Health Service Trust 78
Midwifery, nursing & health visiting: National Board: England 79
Military services: Disablement & death: Pensions 94
Milk: Agricultural marketing 1
    Charges 39

Milk marketing: Aberdeen & District Board 1
    North of Scotland Board 5
    Scottish Milk Marketing Board 5
Milk Marketing Board: Reorganisation 4
    Reorganisation scheme: 3rd party rights 4
    Residuary functions 4
Milk marketing scheme: Revocation: Certification 4
    Revocation: Substitution of date 4
Milk marketing schemes: Revocation: Certification: Scotland 4
    Scotland 4
Milton Keynes Community Health: National Health Service Trust 78
Milton Keynes General: National Health Service Trust 78
Mines & quarries: Rateable values: Scotland 102
Mineworkers: Pension scheme 15
Ministerial & other salaries 93
Ministers: Compulsory purchase: Inquiries procedure 194
Ministry of Agriculture, Fisheries & Food: Inquiries: Costs: Recovery 194
Ministry of Defence: Police committee 95
Modern foreign languages: Curriculum 30
    Curriculum: Attainment targets & programmes of study 30
Molecular Biology Laboratory: European: Immunities & privileges 55
Monopolies & mergers 68, 69
Monopoly references: Fair trading 69
Moorfields Eye Hospital: National Health Service Trust 78
Morriston Hospital: National Health Service Trust 78
Mortgage indemnities: Recognised bodies 47
Motor cars: Driving instruction 108
Motor fuel: Composition & content 97, 100
Motor vehicles: Competitions & trials: Scotland 108
    Driving licences 108
    EC type approval 108
    Tests 108
    Type approval 108
    Type approval: Fees 108
    Tyres: Safety 17
Motorways: A1(M): Blyth roundabout 117
    A1(M): Bowburn interchange 117
        Bowburn interchange to Bradbury interchange 118
        Burtree interchange-Barton interchange 118
        Hatfield tunnel, Hertfordshire 118
        Junction 1 117
        Junction 1-4, Hertfordshire 118
        Junction 2, Hertfordshire 118
        Junction 3-4, Hertfordshire 118
        Junction 3, Colney Heath, Hertfordshire 146
        Junction 4-2, Hertfordshire 118
        Junction 4-6, Hertfordshire 116
        Junction 6-7, Hertfordshire 118
        Junction 7-8, Hertfordshire 118
        Junction 9-10, Hertfordshire & Bedfordshire 118
        Junction 10, Hertfordshire & Bedfordshire 118
        Junction 37, Marr, northbound exit slip road 118
        Marr-Redhouse 118
        Marr-Wadworth 118
        Redhouse-Wadworth, slip roads 118
        Sprotborough-Marr 118
        Wadworth roundabout & slip roads 165
    A3(M): Marker post 2.10-8.80 120
    A40(M): West Cross route, Westway & Marylebone flyover 169
        Westway & Marylebone flyover 133
    A74: Gretna bypass 142
    A74(M): Ecclefechan to Kirkpatrick-Fleming 106
        Ecclefechan to Kirkpatrick-Fleming, side roads 106
    A194(M): Birtley to Whitemare Pool roundabout 144

ALPHABETICAL INDEX

Follingsby, Havannah interchanges ... 144
Whitemare Pool roundabout ... 144
A627(M): Junction 1-2 slip roads ... 150
A823(M): Pitreavie spur, westbound ... 153
M1: A406, Barnet ... 157
  Barnet ... 158
  Barnet & Harrow ... 158
  Belle Isle ... 43
  Blaby, Leicestershire ... 158
  Junction 1, Barnet ... 111
  Junction 6 ... 158
  Junction 6, Hertfordshire ... 157, 158
  Junction 6, Hertfordshire, slip roads ... 157
  Junction 6A, Hertfordshire ... 168
  Junction 7-8 ... 165, 167
  Junction 8 & 9, slip roads ... 157
  Junction 8 & M10 motorways, Hertfordshire ... 157
  Junction 8, Hertfordshire ... 157, 158
  Junction 8, Hertfordshire, junction 10, Hertfordshire, Bedfordshire ... 157
  Junction 8-9, Hertfordshire ... 157
  Junction 9, southbound access slip road ... 158
  Junction 10, Hertfordshire & Bedfordshire ... 158
  Junction 10, Luton, Bedfordshire ... 158
  Junction 12-13, Bedfordshire ... 159
  Junction 12, Bedfordshire ... 158
  Junction 13, Bedfordshire ... 158
  Junction 14, Buckinghamshire ... 158
  Junction 15, 15A & 16 ... 159
  Junction 15-16 & slip roads ... 159
  Junction 21-22, Leicestershire ... 159
  Junction 23-23A, Leicestershire ... 158
  Junction 27, slip roads, Nottinghamshire ... 158
  Junction 28, Pinxton, Derbyshire, southbound exit slip road ... 158
  Junction 28, Tibshelf, Derbyshire ... 158
  Junction 30-34, slip roads ... 159
  Junction 30, Woodall ... 159
  Junction 31-37, slip roads ... 159
  Junction 34-38, slip roads ... 159
  Junction 35A, southbound entry slip road ... 159
  Junction 36-37, southbound carriageway ... 159
  Junction 37-39 ... 159
  Junction 37, northbound exit slip road ... 159
  Junction 40, southbound carriageway & southbound exit slip road ... 159
  Junction 40, southbound entry slip road ... 159
  Junction 43, southbound exit slip road ... 159
  Lockington ... 43
  Lofthouse interchange ... 171
M1: M1/A1 link: Belle Isle to Bramham crossroads ... 43
M2: Junction 5-7 ... 159
  Junction 7, Londonbound access slip road ... 159
  Marker post 59.8-63.0 ... 159
  Marker post 74.0-78.0 ... 159
  Medway Bridge ... 159
M3: Bar End to Alresford Rd. ... 160
  Easton Lane interchange to Bar End interchange ... 160
  Easton Lane to Oak Mount ... 160
  Junction 3 ... 160
  Junction 5-6 ... 160
  Junction 7, eastbound exit slip road ... 160
  Junction 8-9 ... 160
  Junction 9, southbound entry slip road ... 160
  Junction 14 ... 160
  Marker post 23.0-30.0 ... 160
  Marker post 26.0-33.5 ... 160

    Pitmore interchange 160
    Thorpe interchange 160
  M4: Baglan-Briton ferry, West Glamorgan 160
    Baglan-Llandarcy, West Glamorgan 160
    Baglan, West Glamorgan 160, 161
    Brynglas tunnels, Newport, Gwent 161
    Coldra-Malpas, Gwent 161
    Coryton-Capel Lanilltern, South Glamorgan 161
    Hardy Lane Overbridge 161
    Heathrow Airport spur 111
    Hounslow 162
    Junction 4-4B 160
    Junction 4-4A, Buckinghamshire 160
    Junction 4B, Slough, Buckinghamshire & Hillingdon, Greater London 166
    Junction 5, Buckinghamshire 161
    Junction 6-7 161
    Junction 7 161
    Junction 10 161
    Junction 10, slip roads 2 & 4 161
    Junction 11-12 161
    Junction 11-13 161
    Junction 11, westbound exit slip road 161
    Junction 16-18 161
    Junction 17-18 161
    Junction 19, Bristol 161
    Junction 21-21 161
    Junction 26, Malpas, Gwent 161
    Llandarcy, West Glamorgan 161, 162
    Llangyfelach, West of Glamorgan-Pont Abraham, Dyfed 162
    London borough of Hounslow 162
    London boroughs of Hounslow & Hillingdon 162
    M4/M32 junction, Hambrook 169
    Magor-Caldicot, Gwent 162
    Magor, Gwent 162
    Margam-Baglan, West Glamorgan 162
    Marker post 54.0-62.5 162
    Marker post 67.7-72.7 162
    Newbridge roundabout 162
    Westbound carriageway, Baglan, West Glamorgan 162
  M5: A30 trunk road: Honiton to Exeter 44
    Clapton Lane underbridge 162
    Clingre Pipe overbridge 162
    Coaley to Dursley-Cambridge overbridges 162
    Fiddington to Stoke Ochard to Piffs Elm overbridges 162
    Gambril lane overbridge 162
    Golden Valley interchange 162
    Green St. overbridge 162
    Junction 2 162
    Junction 3 163
    Junction 3 & Frankley Service Area 163
    Junction 3-2 163
    Junction 9-11 163
    Junction 11-12 163
    Junction 13 163
    Junction 13-14 163
    Junction 14, Northbound exit slip road 163
    Junction 15 & 21, slip roads 163
    Junction 17-18 163
    Junction 18, slip roads 163
    Junction 19, northbound exit slip road 163
    Junction 19-20, Gordano-Clevedon 163
    Junction 22, Edithmead 163
    Junction 22-23 163
    Junction 26-27 163

ALPHABETICAL INDEX

Lower Wick-Coaley	163
Naas Lane to Haresfield overbridges	163
Poltimore, Hele Straight	163
Quinton to Lydiate Ash	164
Splatford to Pearces Hill	164
Woodford Lane overbridge	164
M6	165
M6: Junction 10-9, Walsall	164
Junction 10A	170
Junction 15-16	164
Junction 15, slip roads	164
Junction 23, northbound exit slip road	164
Junction 25-27, Wigan	164
Junction 25-28, Chorley, Wigan	164
Junction 32-34	164
Junction 33, slip roads	164
Junction 34, slip roads	164
Junction 36-39	164
Junction 39-41	164
Junction 43-44	164
Junction 47, Killington service area	164
Loups Fell & Tebay Bridges	164
Marker post 429/7 to 425/8	164
Marker post 460/3-495/3	164
Marker post 461/4-462/8	165
MP 176/6 to MP 182/3	165
Preston	164
M8: Junction 3, 3A, 4	165
Junction 26-29	165
Langbank to West Ferry interchange	122
Newbridge roundabout	165
M9/A9/A882: Auchterarder junction	165
Scrabster	115
M10: Hertfordshire	157
Junction 1	165, 167
Junction 8-9, Hertfordshire	157
M1 junction 8, Hertfordshire	157
M11: Girton interchange, Cambridgeshire	165
Junction 4, Essex	165
Junction 6, Essex	165
Junction 7-8, Essex	165
Junction 7, Essex	165
Junction 8, Bishops Stortford, Essex	165
Junction 9 to A11, Worsted Lodge	165
Spur road, Essex	165
M18: Junction with M1 motorway to junction 1	166
Junction 1-5, slip roads	166
Junction 2, northbound & southbound entry slip roads	166
Junction 3-4	166
Junction 5 & 6	166
Junction 5, slip roads	166
M1-M1/M18 Link road, southbound carriageway	166
Wadworth roundabout & slip roads	165
M20: Ashford to Folkestone	166
Junction 12-13	166
Marker post 52.0-65.0	166
Marker post 99.2 to junction 13	166
Round Hill Tunnels	166
M23: Junction 10-11	166
Pease Pottage to Handcross	166
M25: Bell Common Tunnel, Essex	166, 167
Holmesdale Tunnel, Hertfordshire	167
Junction 4	167
Junction 6-8	168

272 ALPHABETICAL INDEX

    Junction 10-11 ... 168
    Junction 10-14 ... 168
    Junction 13-15 ... 168
    Junction 14-15, & 16 ... 160
    Junction 14-15, Buckinghamshire & Surrey ... 168
    Junction 15, Buckinghamshire ... 160
    Junction 15, Slough, Buckinghamshire & Hillingdon, Greater London ... 166
    Junction 16, Buckinghamshire ... 167
    Junction 18 & 22, Hertfordshire, slip roads ... 168
    Junction 18, Hertfordshire ... 167
    Junction 19 to Hunton Bridge roundabout, Hertfordshire ... 167
    Junction 20-21A, Hertfordshire ... 168
    Junction 21, Hertfordshire ... 157
    Junction 21-21A, Hertfordshire ... 168
    Junction 21-23, Hertfordshire ... 168
    Junction 21A, Hertfordshire ... 167
    Junction 21A-22, Hertfordshire ... 168
    Junction 22, Hertfordshire ... 167
    Junction 23, Hertfordshire ... 117
    Junction 23-25, Hertfordshire ... 168
    Junction 24, Hertfordshire ... 167
    Junction 25-26, Essex ... 168
    Junction 25, Hertfordshire ... 167
    Junction 27, Essex ... 167
    Junction 27, Theydon interchange, Essex ... 167
    Junction 28, Essex ... 167
    Junction 28, southbound access slip road ... 167
    Junction 28-31, Essex ... 168
    Junction 29, Codham Hall interchange, Essex ... 167
    Junction 30-31, Thurrock, Essex ... 168
    Link roads, Buckinghamshire ... 166
    London Orbital, junction 18, Hertfordshire ... 166
    Sevenoaks interchange ... 166
    Staines ... 129
    Thorpe interchange ... 160
M26: Marker post 7.0-9.4 ... 168
    Sevenoaks interchange ... 166
M27: Cadnam to Ower ... 169
    Junction 4 ... 160
    Junction 11-12 ... 168, 169
    Marker post 14.8-16.2 ... 169
    Marker post 35.6-44.6 ... 169
    Ower-Chilworth: Connecting roads scheme ... 44
    Portsmouth ... 169
M32: Stoke Lane overbridge ... 169
M40: Junction 3-4 ... 160
    Junction 4-5 ... 169
    Junction 4 & connecting roads, Handycross, Buckinghamshire ... 169
    Link roads, Buckinghamshire ... 166
    Marker post 61.8-70.8 ... 169
    Stratford-Upon-Avon, Warwickshire: District ... 169
M41: West Cross route, Westway & Marylebone flyover ... 169
M42: Junction 6 ... 169
M50: Junction 1-2 ... 169
    Queenhill Bridge ... 169
    Ross Spur ... 169
M53: Junction 1, northbound exit slip road ... 169
    Junction 1, Bidston viaduct, Wallasey ... 169
    Junction 1, Wallasey ... 170
    Junction 2, Moreton Spur link road, southbound entry & exit slip road ... 169
    Junction 2, slip road ... 170
    Junction 5, northbound exit slip road ... 170
    Junction 5, slip roads ... 170
    Junction 8, slip road ... 170

ALPHABETICAL INDEX

Junction 9 170
Junction 10-11, Little Stanney 170
Junction 10, slip roads 170
Marker post 9/3 to 26/5 170
Marker post 13/5-19/5 170
M54: Cluddley interchange 170
   Junction 1 170
   Junction 2-4 170
   Priorslee to Forge 170
M56: Junction 1, slip road 170
   Junction 2-7, Sharston-Rostherne 170
   Junction 3, slip roads 170
   Junction 11-12, Preston Brook, Cheshire 170
   Junction 14-16 170
   Marker post 55/9-61/0, Stoak-Dunkirk 171
M57: Junction 2, southbound access slip road 171
   Junction 2, southbound exit slip road 171
   Junction 3, southbound exit slip road 171
   Junction 4, northbound exit slip road 171
M58: Junction 1-3 171
   Junction 3 to M6 motorway, junction 26 171
M61: Junction 2-3, Kearsley 171
   Junction 2-3, slip roads 171
   Junction 4, slip roads 171
   Kearsley Spur-A666 171
   Marker post 4/6-4/0 171
   Marker post 5/4-4/0 171
   Marker post 8/0-11/2 171
   Marker post 8/5 to 3/5 171
   Preston 164
M61/M55 165
M62 152
M62: Junction 6, westbound exit slip road 171
   Junction 7 172
   Junction 7 & the A568 trunk road 171
   Junction 9 172
   Junction 12 172
   Junction 12 & 13 173
   Junction 12 & M63 junction 1 interchange 172
   Junction 12 interchange: Between marker post 43/7 & 44/5 172
   Junction 13 172
   Junction 13, slip roads 172
   Junction 13, westbound access slip road 172
   Junction 14, 14A, 15 & 17 173
   Junction 14-17: Wardley-Prestwich 173
   Junction 14, slip roads 172
   Junction 17, slip roads 172
   Junction 18, Bury 175
   Junction 18, Simister 172
   Junction 18, slip roads 172
   Junction 19 172
   Junction 20, slip roads 172
   Junction 21, Milnrow 172
   Junction 21, slip roads 172
   Junction 22, slip roads 172
   Junction 24-25 173
   Junction 26-27 173
   Junction 26, slip roads 172
   Junction 29, eastbound entry slip road 173
   Junction 31-32 173
   Junction 32, westbound entry slip road 173
   Lofthouse interchange 171
   M62/M606 link roads, Chain Bar junction 173
   Marker post 44/5-43/8 173

       Marker post 64/0-66/0 … 173
       Thornham roundabout … 171
   M62/M1: Lofthouse interchange … 44
M63: Junction 1-2 … 174
   Junction 1 … 173
   Junction 1 & M62 junction 12 interchange … 172
   Junction 1, southbound access slip road … 173
   Junction 2, slip roads … 173
   Junction 3, slip roads … 173
   Junction 4, slip road … 173
   Junction 6-7, Carrington Spur & Stretford … 174
   Junction 6, Carrington Spur … 173
   Junction 7, Stretford … 174
   Junction 8-9, Sale … 175
   Junction 8, slip roads … 174
   Junction 9-11 … 175
   Junction 9, northbound exit slip road … 174
   Junction 9, slip roads … 174
   Junction 10, slip roads … 174
   Junction 10, westbound access slip road … 174
   Junction 11, Cheadle … 174
   Junction 11, slip road … 174
   Junction 12 … 174
   Junction 12, eastbound exit slip road … 174
   Junction 12, westbound access slip road … 174
   Junction 13, Portwood … 174
   Junction 13, Stockport … 174
   Junction 14, westbound exit slip road … 174
   Junction 15, eastbound exit slip road … 174
   Marker post 0/0-0/6 … 175
   Marker post 10/0-12/0, Sale … 175
   Marker post 12/6-13/4, Northenden … 175
   Marker post 19/8-20/3 … 175
   Marker post 23/4-24/1 … 175
   Marker post 24/3-23/1 … 175
M66: Junction 1, slip roads … 175
   Junction 2, slip roads … 175
   Junction 2, southbound access slip road … 175
   Junction 3-5, Bury … 175
   Junction 3, slip roads … 175
   Marker post 0/0-3/5, Bury … 175
   Marker post 34/7-31/0 … 175
   Marker post 9/2-7/1 … 175
   Marker post 13/1-10/1 … 175
M67: Junction 2, westbound exit slip road … 175
   Junction 3, westbound exit slip road, Hyde … 175
   Marker post 1/1-8/4 … 175
   Marker post 3/8 to 2/8 … 176
   Marker post 8/4-1/0 … 176
M74: Junction 6 … 176
   Junction 6 slip road … 176
   Junction 6 slip roads from A723 … 176
   Junction 9, slip road … 176
   Maryville to west of Fullarton … 176
   Maryville to west of Fullarton Rd. … 176
M90/A90: Admiralty southbound slip road … 176
M180: Junction 2, slip roads … 176
   Junction 4-5 … 176
   Junction 4, slip roads … 176
M271: Nursling interchange to Redbridge roundabout … 176
M602: Junciton 1, link road to the northbound M63 … 176
   Junction 2, M62 Junction 12 … 176
   Junction 2 slip roads … 176
   Junction 3-2, Eccles … 176

Marker post 4/0-3/4	176
Marker post 6/7-4/0	177
Marker post 4/0-44/0	177
M606: Chain Bar junction slip roads	177
M606/M62 link roads, southbound carriageway	177
M606/M62 southbound link road	177
Staygate extension	44
M621: M1/M621 link road	177
M627(M): Thornham roundabout	171
M876/A876/A977: Checkbar interchange	177
Mount Vernon & Watford Hospitals: National Health Service Trust	78
Mount Vernon Hospital: National Health Service Trust	78
Music schools: Grants	28
MV Braer: Wrecks: Protection	97

N

Names: Welsh alternatives	198
National assistance: Assessment of resources	69
Personal requirements: Sums	69
National Blood Authority	76
National Blood Authority: Establishment	78
National curriculum: Core subjects: Assessment arrangements: Key stage 1	29
Core subjects: Assessment arrangements: Key stage 1: Wales	29
Assessment arrangements: Key stage 2	29
Assessment arrangements: Key stage 3	29
Assessment arrangements: Key stage 3: Wales	29
Exceptions	30
Exceptions: Wales	30
Foundation subjects: Key stage 4	30
Geography: Attainment targets & programmes of study	29
Attainment targets & programmes of study: Wales	29
History: Attainment targets & programmes of study	29
Attainment targets & programmes of study: Wales	30
Modern foreign languages	30
Modern foreign languages & technology: Attainment targets & programmes of study	30
Science: Attainment targets & programmes of study	30
Welsh language: Key stage 4	30
National debt	69
National debt: National savings: Stock register	69
National Health Service: Dental charges	79
Dental charges: Scotland	89
District health authorities	79
Districts: Determination	79
Drugs & appliances: Charges	79
Charges: Scotland	89
East Sussex Health Authority	74
England & Wales	65, 76, 77, 78, 87, 90
Exeter & North Devon Health Authority	74
Family health services authorities: London: Functions	79
Functions	79
Fund-holding practices	79
General medical & pharmaceutical services: Scotland	89
Isles of Scilly	76
Medical & pharmaceutical services: Scotland	89
Medical Practices Committee: Composition	79
Medical services	79, 80
Optical charges & payments	80
Optical charges & payments: Scotland	89
Overseas visitors: Charges	79
Charges: Scotland	89
Pharmaceutical services & charges: Drugs & appliances	80
Regional & district health authorities	80
Regional & district health authorities: Membership & procedure	83
Regional health authorities	80

276 ALPHABETICAL INDEX

  Scotland 65, 87, 89, 90
   Service committees & tribunal 80
   Service committees & tribunal: Scotland 89
   Teaching hospitals: Post-graduate: Authorities 70
   Trustees: Appointment: Scotland 89
National Health Service Trusts: Addenbrooke's 69
  Aintree Hospitals 69
  Airedale 69
  Alexandra Health Care 69
  Allington 69
  Andover District Community Health Care 69
  Anglian Harbours 69
  Argyll & Bute 88
  Ashford Hospitals (Middx.) 69, 70
  Avalon, Somerset 70
  Avon Ambulance Service 70
  Aylesbury Vale Community Healthcare 70
  Barnet Community Healthcare 70
  Barnsley District General Hospital 70
  Basildon & Thurrock General Hospitals 70
  Bedford & Shires Health & Care 70
  Bedford Hospital 70
  Bedfordshire & Hertfordshire Ambulance & Paramedic Service 70
  Bethlem & Maudsley 70
  Bexley Community Health 70
  Birmingham Children's Hospital 70
  Blackburn, Hyndburn & Ribble Valley Health Care 71
  Black Country Mental Health 71
  Blackpool Victoria Hospital 71
  Blackpool, Wyre & Fylde Community 71
  Borders Community Health Services 88
  Borders General Hospital 88
  Bournewood Community & Mental Health 71
  Bridgend & District 71
  Brighton Health Care 71
  Bromley Hospitals 71
  Burnley Health Care 71
  Calderdale Healthcare 71
  Calderstones 71
  Canterbury & Thanet Community Health Care 71
  Central Manchester 71
  Central Middlesex Hospital 71
  Central Scotland Healthcare: Scotland 88
  Chase Farm Hospitals 71
  Chelsea & Westminister Healthcare 71
  Chesterfield & North Derbyshire Hospital 72
  Chorley & South Ribble 72
  Churchill John Radcliffe 72
  Cleveland Ambulance 72
  CommuniCare 72
  Community Health Care: North Durham 72
  Community Health Care Service (North Derbyshire) 72
  Community Health Services, Southern Derbyshire 72
  Cornwall & Isles of Scilly Learning Disabilities 72
  Cornwall Healthcare 72
  Countess of Chester Hospital 72
  Coventry Healthcare 72
  Crawley Horsham 72
  Dacorum & St Albans Community 72
  Derby City General Hospital 73
  Doncaster Healthcare 73
  Dorset Ambulance 73
  Dorset Community 73
  Dudley Group of Hospitals 73

ALPHABETICAL INDEX

Dudley Priority Health 73
Dumfries & Galloway Community Health 88
Durham County Ambulance Service 73
Ealing Hospital 73
East Anglian Ambulance 73
East Berkshire Community Health 73
East Berkshire NHS Trust for People with Learning Disabilities 73
East Birmingham Hospital 73
Eastbourne & County Healthcare 73
East Cheshire 73
East Glamorgan 73
East Hertfordshire 73
East Suffolk Local Health Services 74
East Surrey Hospital & Community Healthcare 74
East Surrey Learning Disability & Mental Health Service 74
East Yorkshire Hospitals 74
Enfield Community Care 74
Essex & Herts Community 74
Essex Rivers Healthcare 74
Forest Healthcare 74
Fosse Health, Leicestershire Community 74
Freeman Group of Hospitals 74
Frenchay Healthcare 74
Frimley Park Hospital 74
Furness Hospitals 74
Gateshead Community Health 75
Gateshead Healthcare 75
Glasgow Community & Mental Health Services 89
Glasgow Dental Hospital & School 89
Glenfield Hospital 75
Gloucestershire Ambulance Service 75
Good Hope Hospital 75
Grantham & District Hospital 75
Great Ormond Street Hospital for Children 75
Grimsby Health 75
Halton General Hospital 75
Hammersmith Hospitals 75
Hampshire Ambulance Service 75
Harrow & Hillingdon Healthcare 75
Harrow Community Health Services 75
Hartlepool & Peterlee Hospitals 75
Hartlepool Community Care 76
Heatherwood & Wexham Park Hospitals 76
Heathlands Mental Health 76
Hereford & Worcester Ambulance Service 76
Hillingdon Community Health 76
Hillingdon Hospital 76
Hinchingbrooke Health Care 76
Homerton Hospital 76
Homewood 76
Huddersfield Health Care Services 76
Humberside Ambulance Service 76
Ipswich Hospital 76
James Paget Hospital 76
Kent & Canterbury Hospitals 76
Kent & Sussex Weald 76
Kingston & District Community 77
Lanarkshire Healthcare 89
Leeds Community & Mental Health Services Teaching 77
Leicester General Hospital 77
Leicester Royal Infirmary 77
Lincoln District Healthcare 77
Liverpool Obstetric & Gynaecology Services 77
Lomond Healthcare 89

ALPHABETICAL INDEX

London Chest Hospital 83
Louth & District Healthcare 77
Luton & Dunstable Hospital Trust 77
Maidstone Priority Care 77
Manchester Children's Hospitals 77
Mancunian Community Health 77
Membership & procedure: Scotland 90
Merton & Sutton Community 77
Mid Anglia Community Health 78
Mid Essex 78
Mid Essex Community Health 78
Mid Kent Healthcare 78
Mid-Staffordshire General Hospitals 78
Mid-Sussex 78
Milton Keynes Community Health 78
Milton Keynes General 78
Moorfields Eye Hospital 78
Morriston Hospital 78
Mount Vernon & Watford Hospitals 78
Mount Vernon Hospital 78
Newcastle City Health 80
Newcastle Mental Health 80
Newham Healthcare 80
New Possibilities 80
Norfolk & Norwich Health Care 80
North East Essex Mental Health 80
Northern Birmingham Mental Health 80
Northgate 81
Northgate & Prudhoe 81
North Hampshire Hospitals 81
North Hertfordshire 81
North Kent Healthcare 81
North Staffordshire Hospital Centre 81
North Warwickshire 81
North West Anglia Health Care 81
North West London Mental Health 81
Northwick Park & St. Mark's 81
Northwick Park Hospital 81
North Yorkshire Ambulance Service 81
Nottingham City Hospital 81
Nottingham Community Health 81
Nottingham Healthcare 81
Nottinghamshire Ambulance Service 81
Nuffield Orthopaedic Centre 82
Originating capital debt 80, 90
Papworth Hospital 82
Parkside 82
Pathfinder 82
Peterborough Hospitals 82
Phoenix 82
Pinderfields Hospitals 82
Plymouth Community Services 82
Pontefract Hospitals 82
Premier Health 82
Princess Alexendra Hospital 82
Queen Mary's Sidcup 82
Redbridge Health Care 82
Regions: Determination 79
Richmond, Twickenham & Roehampton Healthcare 83
Robert Jones & Agnes Hunt Orthopaedic & District Hospital 83
Rotherham General Hospital 83
Rotherham Priority Health Services 83
Royal Berkshire & Battle Hospitals 83
Royal Berkshire Ambulance 83

ALPHABETICAL INDEX

Royal Brompton Hospital .83
Royal Cornwall Hospitals .83
Royal Devon & Exeter Healthcare .83
Royal Hospital of St Bartholomew .83
Royal Hull Hospitals .83
Royal Liverpool & Broadgreen University Hospital .83
Royal London Hospital .83
Royal London Hospital & Associated Community Service .83
Royal Marsden .83
Royal Scottish National Hospital & Community: Scotland .90
Royal Shrewsbury Hospitals .83
Royal Victoria Infirmary & Associated Hospitals .84
Royal West Sussex .84
Rugby .84
Salford Hospitals .84
Sandwell Healthcare .84
Scottish Ambulance Service .90
Scunthorpe & Goole Hospitals .84
Scunthorpe Community Health Care .84
Shropshire's Community Health Service .84
Shropshire's Mental Health .84
Southampton University Hospitals .84
South Bedfordshire Community Health Care .84
South Birmingham Community Health .84
South Birmingham Mental Health .84
South Downs Health .84
South East London Mental Health .85
Southend Community Care Services .85
Southend Health Care Services .85
Southern Derbyshire Mental Health .85
South Kent Hospitals .85
South Lincolnshire Community & Mental Health Services .85
South Manchester University Hospitals .85
South Tees Acute Hospitals .85
South Tees Community & Mental Health .85
South Warwickshire General Hospitals .85
South Warwickshire Health Care .85
South West Durham Mental Health .85
South Western Regional Health Authority .85
South Yorkshire Metropolitan Ambulance & Paramedic Service .85
St Albans & Hemel Hempstead .85
St. George's Healthcare .86
St Helens & Knowsley Community Health .86
St. James's & Seacroft University Hospitals .86
Surrey Ambulance .86
Sussex Ambulance Service .86
Swansea .86
Tavistock & Portman .86
Thameside Community Health Care .86
Thameslink Healthcare Services .86
Thanet Health Care .86
Trafford Healthcare .86
Two Shires Ambulance .86
United Leeds Teaching Hospitals .86
University College London Hospitals .87
Wakefield & Pontefract Community Health .87
Walsall Community Health .87
Warrington Community Health Care .87
Warrington Hospital .87
Weald of Kent Community .87
Wellhouse .87
West Berkshire Priority Care Service .87
Westcountry Ambulance Service .87
West Cumbria Health Care .87

280 ALPHABETICAL INDEX

  West Dorset Community Health 87
  West Dorset Mental Health 87
  West Herts Community Health 87
  West Lindsey 87, 88
  West London Healthcare 88
  West Middlesex University Hospital 88
  West Suffolk Hospitals 88
  Wiltshire Ambulance Service 88
  Wolverhampton Health Care 88
  Worcester Royal Infirmary 88
  Worthing Priority Care 88
  York Health Services 88
National insurance fund: Payment 183
Nationality: British 8
National lottery 8, 90
National lottery: Licence fees 90
 Licences: Revocation 90
National Rivers Authority: Boundaries 56
 South Holland internal drainage district 56
National savings: Stock register 69
National Trust: Charities 10
Natural habitats: Conservation 18, 198
Naval, Military & Air Forces: Disablement & death: Service pensions .94
Navigation services: Canada: Civil aviation 14
 Civil aviation: Route charges 14
Navy: Disablement & death: Pensions 94
 Discipline acts 24
Nephrops: Fishing: Prohibition: Specified sea areas 179
Net fishing & construction of nets: Salmon: Scotland 105
Networking arrangements: Broadcasting 8
Newark Area & Upper Witham Internal Drainage Districts: Boundaries: Alteration 55
Newcastle City Health: National Health Service Trust 80
Newcastle Mental Health: National Health Service Trust 80
Newham Healthcare: National Health Service Trust 80
Newham (London Borough): Special parking areas 110
New Possibilities: National Health Service Trust 80
New Shoreham Port Health Authority 96
New towns: East Kilbride: Winding up: Scotland 90
 England & Wales 90
Nitrate sensitive areas 4
Noise emission: Household appliances 36
Non-domestic rates: Scotland 102
Non-domestic rating 102
Non-domestic rating: Chargeable amounts 102
 Contributions 102
 Contributions: England 60, 102
  Scotland 102
  Wales 102
 Demand notices: Wales 102
 Lists & appeals 102
 Railways: Central rating lists 102
 Railways, telecommunications & canals 103
 Unoccupied property: Scotland 103
  Wales 102
Non-fossil fuel sources: Electricity 34
Norfolk & Norwich Health Care: National Health Service Trust 80
North Derbyshire & Chesterfield Hospital: National Health Service Trust 72
North Derbyshire: Community Health Care Service: National Health Service Trust 72
North Durham: Community Health Care: National Health Service Trust 72
North East Essex Mental Health: National Health Service Trust 80
Northern Birmingham Mental Health: National Health Service Trust .80
Northern Ireland 92
Northern Ireland: Agriculture 90
 Airports 91

    Appropriation 91
    Betting & lotteries 91
    Civil aviation: Personnel licences 14
    Civil service: Management functions 91
    Criminal justice 91
    Criminal justice: Crown servants & regulators: Emergency provisions 21, 22
    Criminal law 20, 22
    Emergency provisions: Guernsey 91
    European Parliament: Elections 104
        Elections: Returning officer's charges 104
    Firearms 91
    Health & personal social services 91
    Interim period extension 91
    Litter 91
    Local elections: Candidates: Expenses 91
    Parliament: Elections: Returning officer's charges 104
    Police & magistrates' courts 91
    Ports 91, 92
    Public health 97, 100
    Rates 92
    Remand 92
    Road vehicles: Registration & licensing 92, 111
    Social security: Contributions 92
        Work: Incapacity 92
    Statutory sick pay 92
    Terrorism provisions: Emergency & prevention 91
    Value added tax tribuanls: Appeals 196
    Vehicle licences: First licences: Duty 92, 111
    Wills & administration proceedings 92
Northern School of Contemporary Dance, Leeds Further Education Corporation 30
Northgate & Prudhoe: National Health Service Trust 81
Northgate: National Health Service Trust 81
North Hampshire Hospitals: National Health Service Trust 81
North Hertfordshire: National Health Service Trust 81
North Kent Healthcare: National Health Service Trust 81
North Kent Marshes: Environmentally sensitive areas 2
North Killingholme Haven Harbour 40
North of Scotland Milk Marketing Board 5
North Peak: Environmentally sensitive areas 2
North Staffordshire Hospital Centre: National Health Service Trust 81
Northumberland County Council: Kitty Brewster Bridge 43
North Warwickshire: National Health Service Trust 81
North West Anglia Health Care: National Health Service Trust 81
North West London Mental Health: National Health Service Trust 81
North West Sutherland: Protection: Salmon & freshwater fisheries 105
Northwick Park & St. Mark's: National Health Service Trust 81
Northwick Park Hospital: National Health Service Trust 81
North Yorkshire Ambulance Service: National Health Service Trust 81
NORWEB plc: Public telecommunication systems 187
Norwich & Norfolk Health Care: National Health Service Trust 80
Norwich School of Art & Design Further Education Corporation 30
Nottingham City Hospital: National Health Service Trust 81
Nottingham Community Health: National Health Service Trust 81
Nottingham Healthcare: National Health Service Trust 81
Nottinghamshire Ambulance Service: National Health Service Trust 81
Nuclear installations: Operators: Liability: Limits 7
Nuffield Orthopaedic Centre: National Health Service Trust 82
Nurses: Prescriptions: Medicinal products 65, 77
Nursing, midwifery & health visiting: National Board: England 79
NYNEX CableComms Bury & Rochdale: Public telecommunication systems 187
NYNEX CableComms Oldham & Tameside: Public telecommunication systems 187
NYNEX CableComms Wessex: Public telecommunication systems 187

O

Oaths: Commissioners: Prescribed bodies	58, 92
Occupational & personal pension schemes	94
Occupational pensions: Revaluation	94
Occupational pension schemes: Winding up: Deficiency	94
Offal: Bovine: Prohibition	38
Bovine: Prohibition: Scotland	38
Offices: Shops	180
Official secrets: Prohibited places	92
Offshore installations: Safety zones	92
Ogwr Valley community	61, 196
Oil & chemical pollution: Fish: Food protection	98, 100
Oil & fibre plant seeds	180
Oil: Hydrocarbon	24
Opencast coal: Forms	15
Open spaces: Hyde Park & the Regent's Park: Vehicle parking	92
Ophthalmic opticians: Trainees: Testing of sight: Rules: General Optical Council	93
Optical charges & payments: National Health Service	80, 89
National Health Service: Scotland	89
Optical Council: General: Maximum penalty	93
General: Registration & enrolment: Rules	93
Testing of sight: Trainee ophthalmic opticians: Rules	93
Opticians	93
Opticians: General Optical Council: Maximum penalty	93
General Optical Council: Registration & enrolment: Rules	93
Testing of sight: Trainee ophthalmic opticians: Rules	93
Orchards: Apples: Grubbing up	1
Organic aid: Scotland	5
Organic farming: Aid	5
Organic products: Agriculture	5
Overseas development & co-operation: Commonwealth Development Corporation	93
Overseas forfeiture orders: Criminal justice: International co-operation: Scotland	20, 22
Overseas Life Assurance Fund	51
Overseas visitors: National Health Service: Charges	79
Oxfordshire: Combined probation areas	97
Petty sessional divisions	55
Youth court panel	199
Oxfordshire County Council: Shifford Island footbridge	43
Ozone monitoring & information	14

P

Packaged goods: Weights & measures	198
Papworth Hospital: National Health Service Trust	82
Paralytic shellfish: Food protection	98, 99, 100
Parental order register: Scotland	103
Parental orders: Forms of entry	104
Human fertilisation & embryology	19, 48, 49, 180
Parental responsibility: Agreement	10
Parking: Local government: Supervision: Exemption: Scotland	62
Supervision: Local government: Defined activites: Competition	59
Parkside: National Health Service Trust	82
Parliament	93
Parliament: Ministerial & other salaries	93
Parliamentary elections: Returning officers: Charges	104
Returning officers: Charges: Northern Ireland	104
Parliamentary pensions	93
Parochial: Fees	25
Particle Physics & Astronomy Research Council	178
Partnerships	93
Partnerships: Insolvency	53
Passenger & goods vehicles: Recording equipment	109
Passenger ships: Ro-Ro: Survivability	68
Patents: Act of Sederunt	180

ALPHABETICAL INDEX

Agents	.93
Convention countries	.93
County court	.93
Pathfinder: National Health Service Trust	.82
Peasholme Green bridge: Scheme confirmation	.43
Penalty fares: British Railways	100
London Regional Transport	100
Pennine Dales: Environmentally sensitive areas	2
Pensions	93, 94, 95
Pensions: Children: Earnings limit	.95
Coal industry: Protected persons	.15
Defence services: Disablement & death	.94
European Parliament: United Kingdom representatives	.37
Guaranteed minimum pensions increase	.93
Home responsibilities: Social security	184
Increase: Review	.94
Parliamentary	.93
Police	.96
Protected rights: Transfer payment	.94
Railways	192
Railways: Guarantee: Prescribed persons	193
Superannuation: Local government	.94
Pension schemes	.94
Pension schemes: Mineworkers	.15
Occupational & personal	.94
Occupational: Winding up: Deficiency	.94
Railways	192, 193
Performances: Reciprocal protection: Convention countries	105
Personal injuries: Civilians	.94
Personal pension schemes	.94
Personal protective equipment: EC directive	17, 41
Persons abroad: Social security benefit	182
Pesticides: Residue levels: Maximum: Crops, food & feedingstuffs	6
Peterborough Hospitals: National Health Service Trust	.82
Peterlee Hospital: National Health Service Trust	.75
Petroleum: Sulphur content: Marketing	.36
Petroleum revenue tax: Nomination scheme for disposals & appropriations	186
Petty sessional divisions	.55
Pharmaceutical services & charges: Drugs & appliances: National Health Service	.80
Pharmaceutical services: Scotland	.89
Pharmacies: Registration, applications & fees	.66
Phoenix: National Health Service Trust	.82
Physical education: Value added tax	196
Pig carcases: Grading	5
Pigeons (Racing): Vaccination	6
Pinderfields Hospitals: National Health Service Trust	.82
Pipe-lines: Natural gas: Lazy Acres	.95
Plaice: Fishing: Prohibition: Specified sea areas	179
Planning & compensation: Scotland	190
Town & country planning: Scotland	190
Planning: Town & country: Advertisements: Control	189
Town & country: Development	189
Development: Permitted: Scotland	190
Development: Procedure: Scotland	190
Scotland	190
Simplified planning zones	189
Plant & machinery: Rating valuation	103
Plant breeders' rights: Fees	.95
Plant health: Fees: Scotland	.95
Forestry	.95
Spruce bark: Treatment	.95
Plant seeds: Oil & fibre	180
Plugs & sockets: Safety	.17
Plymouth Community Services: National Health Service Trust	.82

Police	95, 96
Police & magistrates' courts	63, 95, 96
Police & magistrates' courts: Northern Ireland	91
Scotland	95
Police: British Transport Police Force	191
Legal advice & assistance: Remuneration	57
Metropolitan & City districts	68
Metropolitan: Loss of office: Compensation	95
Pensions	96
Police committee: Ministry of Defence	95
Promotion: Scotland	96
Scotland	96
Secretary of State's objectives	96
Special constables: Scotland	96
Police authorities: Members: Numbers	96
Names: Welsh language	96
Selection panel	96
Police cadets: Scotland	96
Police stations: Legal advice & assistance	57
Polluting goods: Reporting requirements: Merchant shipping	64, 68
Pollution & salvage: Merchant shipping	68
Pontefract Hospitals: National Health Service Trust	82
Portman & Tavistock: National Health Service Trust	86
Port of Sheerness: Free zone designation	23
Ports: Northern Ireland	91, 92
Tees & Hartlepool Port Authority: Dissolution	40
Portsmouth College of Art, Design & Further Education: Dissolution	32
Portsmouth Mile End Quay: Continental ferry port phase 7: Harbour revision	40
Post-graduate teaching hospitals: Authorities: National Health Service	70
Potatoes: Seed potatoes	180
Seed potatoes: Fees	38
Potato marketing scheme	5
Poultry: Diseases	6
Poultry meat: Farmed game meat: Rabbit meat: Hygiene & inspection	39
Poultry products: Importation	6
Powers of attorney	67, 96
Premier Health: National Health Service Trust	82
Prescribed diseases: Industrial injuries	183
Preseli: Environmentally sensitive areas	2
Pressure vessels: Simple: Safety	42
Prestwick airport: Free zone: Designation	23
Prevention & suppression of terrorism	96
Price indications: Tickets: Resale: Consumer protection	17
Price marking	96
Prices	96
Princess Alexandra Hospital: National Health Service Trust	82
Prisoner custody officer certificate: Suspension	97
Prisons	97
Prisons: Prisoner custody officer certificate: Suspension	97
Scotland	97, 199
Private medical insurance: Tax relief	51
Probate: District registries	186
Probation	97
Probation: Combined areas	97
Combined areas: Buckinghamshire	97
Greater Manchester	97
Lancashire: Combined areas	97
Products: Safety: General	17
Prohibited places: Official secrets	92
Property: Unoccupied: Non-domestic rating: Scotland	103
Property services: Local government: Competition: England	59
Protected rights: Transfer payment	94
Protection of wrecks	97
Public health	97, 98, 99, 100

Public health: Contamination of food 98, 99, 100
    International trains 98
    Scotland 63, 100
Public health authorities: New Shoreham 96
Public order: Criminal justice 20, 22, 186
Public passenger transport 100
Public passenger transport: Deregulation & contracting out 24, 100, 108
Public passenger vehicles 100
Public Record Office: Fees 100
Public records 100
Public service vehicles: Services: Registration 100
    Traffic regulation: Conditions 100
Public telecommunication systems: Bradford Cable Communications Ltd 186
    Comment Cablevision Wearside Partnership 187
    Comment Cablevision Worcester Ltd 187
    Encom Cable TV & Telecommunications Ltd.: Dartford 187
        Epping Epping Forest 187
    Insight Communications Cardiff Ltd. 187
    Insight Communications Guildford Ltd. 187
    NORWEB plc 187
    NYNEX CableComms Bury & Rochdale 187
    NYNEX CableComms Oldham & Tameside 187
    NYNEX CableComms Wessex 187
    Racal Network Services Ltd. 187
    Sprint Holding (UK) Ltd 187
    Telecom Securicor Cellular Radio Ltd. 187
    Telstra (UK) Ltd. 187
    United Artists Communications (London South) PLC. 187
    Videotron City & Westminster Ltd 187
    Vodafone Ltd 187
    Worldcom International Inc. 188
Public trustees: Custodian trustee 194
    Fees 194
Pupils: Achievements: Information: Wales 28
    Excluded: Amount to follow 26
    Registration 32

Q
Queen Margaret College, Edinburgh 33
Queen Mary's Sidcup: National Health Service Trust 82
Quick-frozen foodstuffs 39

R
Rabbit meat: Hygiene & inspection 39
Rabies: Dogs, cats & other mammals: Importation 6
Racal Network Services Ltd.: Public telecommunication systems 187
Race relations 100
Race relations: Awards: Interest 100
    Prescribed public bodies 100
Racing pigeons: Vaccination 6
Radioactive substances: Atomic energy 7
Radioactivity in sheep: Food protection 99, 100
Radnor: Environmentally sensitive areas 2
Railtrack plc: Leeds: Footbridges: Marsh Lane 191, 193
Railways 100, 192
Railways & other transport systems: Works, plant & equipment: Approval 192
Railways: Alternative closure procedure 192
    British: Arpley Chord 191, 193
        Penalty fares 100
    Class & miscellaneous exemptions 192
    Docklands Light Railways: Penalty fares: Police services 193
    Heathrow Express: Exemptions 192
    Heritage scheme 191
    Licence application 192

286 ALPHABETICAL INDEX

- Light: Bowes extension ... 191
  - Chappel & Wakes Colne Light Railway ... 191
  - Lydney & Parkend ... 191
  - Wells & Walsingham light railway ... 193
- London Regional Transport: Exemptions ... 193
- Non-domestic rating ... 102, 103
- Penalty fares ... 193
- Pensions ... 192
- Pensions: Schemes ... 193
  - Schemes: Protection & designation ... 192
- Pensions guarantee: Prescribed persons ... 193
- Rateable values ... 103
- Rateable values: Scotland ... 103
- Registers ... 193
- Safety case ... 41
- Safety critical work ... 42

Railway stations: Sub-surface: Fire precautions ... 38
Rateable values: British Gas plc ... 101
- British Waterways Board & telecommunications industry ... 101
- Docks & harbours ... 101
- Electricity supply industry ... 101
- Railways ... 103

Rates: Non-domestic: Scotland ... 102
- Northern Ireland ... 92

Rating & valuation ... 100, 101, 102, 103
Rating & valuation: Central rating lists ... 101
- Contributions: Wales ... 102
- Decapitalisation rate: Scotland ... 103
- Local government: Scotland ... 101
- Plant & machinery ... 103

Rating: Central lists ... 101
- Non-domestic: Chargeable amounts ... 102
  - Contributions ... 102
  - Contributions: England ... 60, 102
  - Contributions: Wales ... 102
  - Demand notices: Wales ... 102
  - Lists & appeals ... 102
  - Railways, telecommunications & canals ... 103
  - Unoccupied property: Scotland ... 103
  - Wales ... 102

Recording equipment: Passenger & goods vehicles ... 109
Redbridge Health Care: National Health Service Trust ... 82
Redbridge (London Borough): Special parking areas ... 110
Red route traffic: Bus lanes: Haringey: A1 ... 107
- Haringey: A1 ... 107

Redundancy: Local government ... 60, 188
- Premature retirement: Compensation: Teachers ... 33

Redundant churches: Fund: Grants ... 25
Refrigerant containers: Non-refillable ... 35
Refrigerators: Energy information ... 35
Regent's Park & Hyde Park: Vehicle parking ... 92
Regional & district health authorities: National Health Service ... 80, 83
Regions: Determination: National Health Service ... 79
Registered housing associations: Accounting: Wales ... 47
Registration Appeal Court: Act of Sederunt ... 19
Registration marks: Retention ... 109
- Sale ... 111

Registration of births, deaths, marriages, etc.: England & Wales ... 104
- Scotland ... 103

Religious education: Local conferences & councils ... 33
Renovation: Grants: Housing; Prescribed forms & particulars: Welsh ... 47
- Housing: Grants: Reduction ... 47

Rent: Forms: Welsh language ... 56
Rent officers: Additional functions ... 47, 48

Additional functions: Scotland ... 48
Replacement cars: Income tax ... 51
Representation of the people ... 63, 104
Representation of the people: Candidates: Election expenses: Limits ... 104
    European parliamentary elections ... 105
Research Councils: Property: Transfer ... 178
Reservoirs: Civil engineers: Panels: Application fees ... 196, 197
Restrictive trade practices ... 105
Restrictive trading agreements: Registration: EEC documents ... 105
Retirement: Premature: Redundancy: Compensation: Teachers ... 33
Retirement benefits schemes: Indexation of earnings cap ... 51
Revenue support grant: Scotland ... 63
Richmond, Twickenham & Roehampton Healthcare: National Health Service Trust ... 83
Rights: Protected: Transfer payment ... 94
Rights in performances ... 105
Right to purchase: Housing: Prescribed persons: Scotland ... 48
River: England & Wales ... 105, 178
    Scotland ... 105, 106, 178
River Clyde catchment area: Protection ... 105
River ecosystem: Surface waters: Classification ... 197
River Eye: Protection ... 105
River Humber: Upper Burcom cooling works ... 193
River Lunan: Protection ... 105
River Nene: Dog-in-a-Doublet Bridge: Scheme confirmation ... 42
River Tummel: Protection ... 105
River Tweed: Protection ... 105
Roads & bridges: Scotland ... 34, 56, 106, 190
Roads: B1040: River Nene Dog-in-a-Doublet Bridge: Scheme confirmation ... 42
    Traffic calming: Scotland ... 106
Road traffic ... 107, 108, 109, 110, 111
Road traffic: Channel tunnel: Enactments: Application ... 9
    Cycle racing ... 108
    Deregulation & contracting out ... 24, 100, 108
    Driving licences ... 108
    M4: Heathrow Airport spur ... 111
    Special parking areas ... 109, 110
    Special roads ... 111
    Speed limits ... 107, 111, 112, 113, 114, 115
    Traffic regulation ... 107, 115, 116, 117, 118, 119, 120, 121, 122, 123, 124, 125, 126, 127, 128, 129,
    ... 130, 131, 132, 133, 134, 135, 136, 137, 138, 139, 140, 141, 142, 143, 144, 145,
    ... 146, 147, 148, 149, 150, 151, 152, 153, 154, 155, 156, 157, 158, 159, 160, 161, 162, 163,
    ... 164, 165, 166, 167, 168, 169, 170, 171, 172, 173, 174, 175, 176, 177, 178
    Traffic signs ... 111
Road vehicles: Construction & use ... 111
    Lighting ... 111
    Plating & testing ... 111
    Registration & licensing ... 111
    Registration & licensing: Northern Ireland ... 92, 111
Robert Jones & Agnes Hunt Orthopaedic & District Hospital: National Health Service Trust ... 83
Rochford: Changes in local government areas ... 61
Romania: European Communities: Treaties ... 36
Rotherham: Changes in local government areas ... 62
Rotherham General Hospital: National Health Service Trust ... 83
Rotherham Priority Health Services: National Health Service Trust ... 83
Royal Berkshire & Battle Hospitals: National Health Service Trust ... 83
Royal Berkshire Ambulance: National Health Service Trust ... 83
Royal Brompton Hospital: National Health Service Trust ... 83
Royal Cornwall Hospitals: National Health Service Trust ... 83
Royal Devon & Exeter Healthcare: National Health Service Trust ... 83
Royal Hospital of St Bartholomew: National Health Service Trust ... 83
Royal Hull Hospitals: National Health Service Trust ... 83
Royal Liverpool & Broadgreen University Hospitals: National Health Service Trust ... 83
Royal London Hospital: National Health Service Trust ... 83
Royal Marsden: National Health Service Trust ... 83

Royal Philanthropic Society: Charities ... 10
Royal Scottish Academy of Music & Drama: Academic awards & distinctions ... 33
Royal Scottish National Hospital & Community: National Health Service Trust: Scotland ... 90
Royal Shrewsbury Hospitals: National Health Service Trust ... 83
Royal Victoria Infirmary & Associated Hospitals: National Health Service Trust ... 84
Royal West Sussex: National Health Service Trust ... 84
Rugby: National Health Service Trust ... 84
Russian Federation: Double taxation relief: Income tax ... 50
Rwanda: United Nations: Arms embargo ... 195

S

Safety: Dangerous substances & preparations ... 16
    Electrical equipment ... 16
    Gas ... 41
    Machinery supply ... 42
    Medicines: Child safety ... 65
    Merchant shipping ... 68
    Plugs & sockets ... 17
    Products: General ... 17
    Railways ... 41
    Railways: Critical work ... 42
    Sports grounds ... 184
Safety zones: Offshore installations ... 92
Salford Hospitals: National Health Service Trust ... 84
Salmon & freshwater fisheries ... 105, 178
Salmon & freshwater fisheries: Scotland ... 105
Salmon: Fish passes & screens ... 105
    Net fishing & construction of nets: Scotland ... 105
Salt-marsh: Habitat ... 4
Salvage & pollution: Merchant shipping ... 68
Sandwell Healthcare: National Health Service Trust ... 84
Saudi Arabia: Double taxation relief: Air transport ... 49
Saundersfoot: Harbour ... 40
Savings certificates ... 69
Scallops fishery: Loch Ewe, West Ross ... 179
School Curriculum & Assessment Authority: Transfer of functions: Wales ... 31
School performance: Information: Wales ... 31
Schools: Ballet: Grants ... 28
    Chief Inspector: England ... 26
        Wales ... 26
    Conducted by education associations ... 31
    Education associations: Government: Initial articles ... 31
    Exclusions: Prescribed periods ... 27
    Financial delegations: Mandatory exceptions ... 27
    Financial statements ... 31
    Further education information: Wales ... 26
    Grant-maintained ... 28
    Grant-maintained: Finance ... 27
        Finance: Wales ... 27
        Governors ... 27
        Groups: Finance ... 28
        Groups: Government ... 27
        Groups: Initial government ... 28
        Initial governing instruments ... 27
    Grant-maintained special schools: Grant-maintained ... 27
        Finance ... 27
        Groups ... 28
        Initial governing instruments ... 27
        Initial government ... 28
    Grant-maintained status: Ballots: Wales ... 26
    Henrietta Barnett School: Grant ... 27
    Independent: Particulars ... 30
        Special needs: Approval ... 32
    Information ... 31

Information: Wales 31
Maintained special schools: Becoming grant-maintained 29
Middle schools 29
Music: Grants 28
Performance information: England 31
        Wales 31
Pupils: Registration 32
Registered inspectors: Appeal tribunal: Procedure 31
Self-governing: Grant & recovery: Scotland 34
    Scotland 33, 34
Special educational needs 32
Special needs: Supplies: Payment 30
Special schools 32
Special schools: Education associations 32
      Grant-maintained 27
      Grant-maintained: Finance 27
      Grant-maintained: Groups 28
      Grant-maintained: Initial governing instruments 27
      Grant-maintained: Initial government 28
      Notices: Publication 30
Teachers: Pay & conditions 31, 32
Science: Curriculum: Attainment targets & programmes of study 30
Scientific research 178
Scientific research: Biotechnology & Biological Sciences Research Council 178
    Engineering & Physical Sciences Research Council 178
    Particle Physics & Astronomy Research Council 178
Scotland: Aberdeen & District Milk Marketing Board 1
    Act of Sederunt: Court of Session: Shorthand writers': Fees 19
        Court of Session: Solicitors: Fees 19
        Sheriff Court: Shorthand writers: Fees 180
        Sheriff Court: Solicitors: Fees 180
        Solicitors: Right of audience 19
    Advice & assistance 57
    Advice & assistance: Financial contributions 57
        Representation 57
    Alcan Aluminium UK Ltd.: Rateable values 100
    Animal health 6
    Argyll & Bute National Health Service Trust 88
    Borders Comunity Health Services National Health Service Trust 88
    Borders General Hospital National Health Service Trust 88
    Bovine offal: Prohibition 38
    British Gas plc.: Rateable values 101
    British Telecommunications plc.: Rateable values 101
    Brucellosis 6
    Building standards 8
    Caledonian MacBrayne: Rateable values 101
    Central Scotland Healthcare: National Health Service Trust 88
    Civil legal aid 57
    Civil legal aid: Fees 58
        Financial contributions 57
    Council tax: Discounts 18, 197
        Exempt dwellings 18, 197
        Liability: Reduction 18, 197
    Court of Session 19, 20
    Court of Session: Rules 19
    Criminal justice: Crown servants & regulators 22
        International co-operation 22
    Criminal law 20, 22
    Criminal legal aid 58
    Criminal legal aid: Fees 58
        Prescribed proceedings 58
    Crofters: Livestock purchase loans 22
    Crofting counties: Agricultural grants 22
    Drug trafficking: Proceeds: Confiscation 22

Dumfries & Galloway Community Health National Health Service Trust 88
Duncan of Jordanstone College of Art: Closure 33
Education 33, 34
Education: Assisted places 33
    European Community enlargement 33
Electricity: Non-fossil fuel 34
Electricity generators: Rateable values 101
Environmental assessment 34, 56, 106, 190
Environmentally sensitive areas 2
Firearms 7
Firearms: Fees 7
Fishing: Cockles: Prohibition 179
Food: Labelling 39
Football grounds: Rateable values 101
Forth Ports plc.: Rateable values 101
Freshwater & salmon fisheries 105
Gaming: Monetary limits: Variation 7
Gaming clubs: Hours & charges 8
Glasgow Dental Hospital & School National Health Service Trust .89
Glasgow Underground: Rateable values 101
Habitats 4
High Court of Justiciary: Fees 42
Housing 46, 48
Housing: Right to purchase: Prescribed persons 48
Industrial & freight transport: Rateable values 101
Industrial tribunals: Constitution & rules of procedure 52
        Jurisdiction 52
Inshore fishing 179
Inshore fishing: Cockles: Prohibition 179
Lanarkshire Healthcare National Health Service Trust 89
Land: Acquisition: Rate of interest after entry: Scotland 1
Land compensation: Additional development: Forms 1
Land Court: Fees 178
Land registration 56
Lands Tribunal: Fees 56
Legal aid & advice 57, 58
Legal aid: Contempt of court: Fees 58
    Contempt of court: Proceedings 58
    Scotland 58
Local authorities: Heritable securities indemnities: Recognised bodies 48
Local government 59, 60, 62, 63, 100, 101
Local government: Allowances 62
      Competition: Defined activities 59, 62
      Defined activities: Exemption: Livingston Development Corporation 62
      Finance 63, 101
      Parking: Supervision: Exemption 62
      Redundancy 62
      Transitional election arrangments 63, 104
Local Government Staff Commission 63
Lochaber Power Co.: Rateable values 102
Lomond Healthcare National Health Service Trust 89
Lyon Court & Office: Fees 7
Mental health: Nurses: Class 67
Mercury Communications Ltd.: Rateable values 102
Milk: Marketing schemes 4
    Marketing schemes: Revocation: Certification 4
Mines & quarries: Rateable values 102
Motor vehicles: Competitions & trials 108
National Health Service 88, 89, 90
National Health Service & community care 89
National Health Service: Dental charges 89
      Drugs & appliances: Charges 89
      Medical & pharmaceutical services 89
      Optical charges & payments 89

ALPHABETICAL INDEX

Overseas visitors: Charges	89
Service committees & tribunal	89
Trustees: Appointment	89
National Health Service Trusts: Membership & procedure	90
New towns: East Kilbride: Winding up	90
Non-domestic rates	102
Non-domestic rating: Contributions	102
North of Scotland Milk Marketing Board	5
Organic aid	5
Parental order register	103
Planning & compensation	190
Plant health: Fees	95
Police	96
Police & magistrates' courts	95
Police: Promotion	96
Special constables	96
Police cadets	96
Prisons & young offender institutions	97, 199
Public health	63, 97, 100
Queen Margaret College, Edinburgh	33
Railways: Rateable values	103
Rating valuation: Decapitalisation rate	103
Registration of births, still-births, deaths & marriages	103
Rent officers: Additional functions	48
Revenue support grant	63
River	105, 106, 178
Roads & bridges	106
Royal Scottish Academy of Music & Drama: Academic awards & distinction	33
Royal Scottish National Hospital & Community National Health Service Trust	90
Salmon: Fish passes & screens	105
Net fishing & construction of nets	105
Schools: Self-governing	34
Self-governing: Grant & recovery: Scotland	34
Scottish Ambulance Service National Health Service Trust	90
Scottish Hydro-Electric plc.: Rateable values	103
Scottish Milk Marketing Board	5
Scottish Nuclear Ltd.: Rateable values	103
Scottish Power plc.: Rateable values	103
Self-governing schools	34
Set-aside access	5
Sheriff Court	180
Sheriff Court: Fees	180
St Mary's Music School: Aided places	34
Strathclyde Regional Council: Kilduskland: Water	197
Summary jurisdiction	63, 185
Teachers: Superannuation	34
Teaching Council: Election	34
Tenants: Secure: Repair: Right	48
Town & country planning	34, 56, 106, 190
Town & country planning: Development: Permitted	190
Development: Procedure	190
Traffic calming	106
Waste water: Urban: Treatment	63, 100
Water supply	18, 196, 197
Water undertakings: Rateable values	103
Scottish Ambulance Service: National Health Service Trust	90
Scottish Development Agency: Dissolution	52
Scottish Hydro-Electric plc.: Rateable values: Scotland	103
Scottish Land Court: Fees	178
Scottish Milk Marketing Board	5
Scottish Nuclear Ltd.: Rateable values: Scotland	103
Scottish Power plc.: Rateable values: Scotland	103
Scunthorpe & Goole Hospitals: National Health Service Trust	84
Scunthorpe Community Health Care: National Health Service Trust	84

Sea fisheries 105, 178, 179
Sea fisheries: Community restrictions 179
    Conservation 179
    Marketing 179
    Sea fish industry 179
    Shellfish 179
Sea fishing: Community conservation measures: Enforcement 179
    Community control: Enforcement 179
    Community quota measures: Enforcement 179
    Licences & notices 179
    Marketing standards 179
Seamen: Wages & accounts 68
Secure tenants: Local housing authorities: Right to repair 48
    Repair: Right: Scotland 48
Securities & regulated markets: Insider dealing 53
Securities: Traded: Disclosure 53
Security work: Local government: Defined activities: Competition 59
Seed potatoes 180
Seed potatoes: Fees 38
Seeds 180
Seeds: Varieties: National list: Fees 180
Self-governing schools: Grant & recovery: Scotland 34
    Scotland 33, 34
Sentencing: Criminal law: Reviews 20
Service marks 190
Service marks: Fees 190
    Forms 190, 191
Service organisations: Local government: Changes: England 60
Service subsidy: Agreements: Tendering: Transport 193
Set-aside access: Scotland 5
Set-aside land: Former: Habitat 3
Severe disablement allowance 184
Severn Bridges 43
Severn-Trent Flood Defence Committee area: Boundaries 56
Sex discrimination: Armed forces 180
Sheep: Annual premium 5
    Annual premium: Quota 5
    Radioactivity: Food protection 99, 100
Sheerness: Port: Free zone designation 23
Sheffield: Broughton Lane Bridge scheme 42
Sheffield City Council: Council tax: Limitation 18
Shellfish: Food safety 39
    Paralytic: Food protection 98, 99, 100
    Sea fisheries 179
Sheriff Court: Act of Sederunt: Judicial factors: Rules 180
    Proceedings 180
    Scotland 180
    Shorthand writers: Fees 180
    Solicitors: Fees 180
Sheriff officers: Act of Sederunt: Fees 180
Shetland Islands: Water 197
Shetland Islands Council: Harbours 40
Shipowners, etc.: Liability: Interest rate 67
Ships: Bareboat charter 67
    Passenger: Ro-Ro: Survivability 68
    Registration: Merchant shipping 67
Shops & offices 180
Shorthand writers: Fees: Court of Session 19
    Fees: Sheriff Court 180
Shropshire: Community Health Service: National Health Service Trust 84
    Mental Health: National Health Service Trust 84
Shropshire Hills: Environmentally sensitive areas 2
Sickness, invalidity benefit & severe disablement allowance 184
Sick pay: Statutory 189

ALPHABETICAL INDEX

Statutory: Northern Ireland	92
Payment: Rate	189
Sir William Turners' Sixth Form College, Redcar: Dissolution	25
Slovak Republic: European Communities: Treaties	36
Small employers' relief: Statutory sick pay	189
Social fund: Cold weather payments	182
Social Fund: Maternity & funeral expenses	182
Social security	181, 182, 184, 188
Social security: Adjudication	182
Attendance allowance & disability living allowance	182
Benefits: Persons abroad	182
Up-rating	182, 188
Claims & payments	182, 183
Contributions	183
Contributions: Northern Ireland	92
Re-rating & national insurance fund payments	183
Council tax benefit	180, 181
Credits	183
Cyprus	183
Earners: Categorisation	182
Earnings factors: Revaluation	184
Housing & council tax benefits	181
Housing benefit	181
Incapacity benefit	183
Incapacity benefit: Dependents: Increases	183
Incapacity for work	183
Income-related benefits schemes	181
Industrial injuries: Prescribed diseases	183
Jersey & Guernsey	184
Maternity benefits & statutory sick pay	184, 189
Medical evidence	184
Pensions: Home responsibilities	184
Severe disablement allowance	184
Sickness, invalidity benefit & severe disablement allowance	184
Statutory maternity pay: Compensation	184, 189
Work: Incapacity: Northern Ireland	92
Sockets: Plugs: Safety	17
Sole: Fishing: Prohibition: Specified sea areas	179
Solicitors: Disciplinary proceedings	58
Fees: Court of Session	19
Sheriff Court	180
Non-contentious business	184
Right of audience: Act of Sederunt	19
Somerset: Avalon: National Health Service Trust	70
Somerset levels & moors: Environmentally sensitive areas	3
South Africa: British Nationality	8
United Nations: Arms embargo	195
Southampton: Free zone designation	23
Southampton University Hospitals: National Health Service Trust	84
South Bedfordshire Community Health Care: National Health Service Trust	84
South Birmingham Community Health: National Health Service Trust	84
South Birmingham Mental Health: National Health Service Trust	84
South Downs: Environmentally sensitive areas	3
South Downs Health: National Health Service Trust	84
South East London Mental Health: National Health Service Trust	85
Southend Community Care Service: National Health Service Trust	85
Southend Health Care Services: National Health Service Trust	85
Southern Derbyshire Community Health Services: National Health Service Trust	72
Southern Derbyshire Mental Health: National Health Service Trust	85
Southern Water Authority	196
South Holland internal drainage district: Boundaries	56
South Kent Hospitals: National Health Service Trust	85
South Lincolnshire Community & Mental Health Services: National Health Service Trust	85
South Manchester University Hospitals: National Health Service Trust	85

South Norfolk District Council: Defined activities: Exemptions 60
South Tees Acute Hospitals: National Health Service Trust 85
South Tees Community & Mental Health: National Health Service Trust 85
Southwark London Borough Council: Defined activities: Exemptions 60
South Warwickshire General Hospitals: National Health Service Trust 85
South Warwickshire Health Care: National Health Service Trust 85
South Wessex Downs: Environmentally sensitive areas 3
South West Durham Mental Health: National Health Service Trust 85
South Western Regional Health Authority: National Health Service Trust 85
South West Peak: Environmentally sensitive areas 3
South Yorkshire: Light rail transit: Penalty fares 100
South Yorkshire Metropolitan Ambulance & Paramedic Service: National Health Service Trust 85
Special commissioners: Taxes: Management 51, 52, 186
Special constables: Scotland 96
Special education 32
Special educational needs 32
Special educational needs: Code of practice 32
    Independent schools: Approval 32
    Supplies: Payment 30
Special Educational Needs Tribunal 33
Special roads: A1: Edinburgh-Berwick upon Tweed, old Craighall roundabout to east of Tranent 106
    A1: Kirk Deighton new junction to Walshford 43
    A74(M): Ecclefechan to Kirkpatrick-Fleming 106
        Ecclefechan to Kirkpatrick-Fleming, side roads 106
        Harthope-Middlegill 106
        Harthope-Middlegill side roads 107
        Harthope-Middlegill special road 107
        Lockerbie 106
        Middlegill-Beattock 107
        Middlegill-Beattock, side roads 107
    M4: Heathrow Airport spur 111
    Road traffic 111
Special schools 32
Special schools: Grant-maintained 27
    Grant-maintained: Finance 27
        Initial governing instruments 27
        Initial government 28
    Groups 28
    Notices: Publication 30
Species rich grassland: Habitat: Wales 4
Spongiform encephalopathy 6
Sport: Value added tax 196
Sports grounds & sporting events 184
Sports grounds & sporting events: Football spectators: Seating 184
Sports grounds: Safety 184
Sprint Holding (UK) Ltd.: Public telecommunication systems 187
Spruce bark: Treatment 95
Staffordshire: Mid-Staffordshire General Hospitals: National Health Service Trust 78
    North Staffordshire Hospital Centre: National Health Service Trust 81
    Youth court panel 199
St Albans & Dacorum Community: National Health Service Trust 72
St Albans & Hemel Hempstead: National Health Service Trust 85
Statutory maternity pay 189
Statutory maternity pay: Compensation 184, 189
Statutory sick pay 189
Statutory sick pay: Northern Ireland 92
    Payment: Rate 189
    Small employers' relief 189
    Social security 184, 189
St George's Healthcare: National Health Service Trust 86
St Helens & Knowsley Community Health: National Health Service Trust 86
St James's & Seacroft University Hospitals: National Health Service Trust 86
St Mark's & Northwick Park: National Health Service Trust 81
St Mary's Music School: Aided places: Scotland 34

Stonebridge Housing Action Trust 48
Stone (Kent): Pits 63
Strathclyde Regional Council: Ayr Burgh: Water 197
    Kilduskland: Water 197
    Loch Assapol: Water 197
Student loans 32, 33
Subsidence: Coal mining: Arbitration schemes 15
    Coal mining: Blight & compensation 15
        Information 15
        Subsidence adviser 15
Substances: Existing: Notification: Safety 36, 41
Substances hazardous to health: Control 41
Sub-surface railway stations: Fire precautions 38
Suckler cows: Annual premium 5
Suckler cow: Annual premium: Quotas 5
Suffolk & Essex: Water 197
Suffolk: Combined probation areas 97
    East Suffolk Health Services: National Health Service Trust 74
    Petty sessional divisions 55
    West Suffolk Hospitals: National Health Service Trust 88
    Youth court panel 199
Suffolk River Valleys: Environmentally sensitive areas 3
Sugar 185
Sugar beet: Research & education 185
Summary jurisdiction: Scotland 42, 63, 185
Summer time 185
Sunday trading 180
Sunday trading: Channel tunnel 9
Superannuation: Children's pensions: Earnings limit 95
    Greater Manchester Buses Ltd. 94
    Greater Manchester Buses North Ltd. 94
    Local government 61, 94
    Local government: Investments 94
    Teachers 33
Superannuation schemes: Coal industry: Staff 15
Supreme Court: Court of Appeal: Composition 186
    District probate registries 186
    England & Wales 18, 19, 37, 38, 46, 53, 185, 186
    Family proceedings: Rules 19, 37, 185
    Offices & registries 186
    Rules 186
Surface waters: River ecosystem: Classification 197
Surrey: Changes in local government areas 61
    East Surrey Hospital & Community Healthcare: National Health Service Trust 74
    East Surrey Learning Disablity & Mental Health Service: National Health Service Trust 74
Surrey Ambulance: National Health Service Trust 86
Surveyors: Qualified: Collective enfranchisement & tenants' audit 46
Sussex: East Sussex Health Authority: National Health Service 74
    Mid-Sussex: National Health Service Trust 78
    Royal West Sussex: National Health Service Trust 84
Sussex Ambulance Service: National Health Service Trust 86
Sutton (London Borough): Special parking areas 110
Swansea: National Health Service Trust 86
Swinford Bridge: Tolls & traffic classification: Revision 193, 194
Switzerland: Double taxation relief: Deceased estates & inheritances 52
    Double taxation relief: Income tax 50

T
Tamar Bridge & Torpoint Ferry: Tolls & traffic classification: Revision 193, 194
TASC: Transfer of property 33
Tavistock & Portman: National Health Service Trust 86
Tax: Lloyd's underwriters 51
Taxes 186
Taxes: Air passenger duty: Connected flights 22

Air passenger duty: Prescribed rates of interest 22
Capital gains: Gilt-edged securities 186
Capital gains tax: Annual exempt amount 186
Collectors: Distraint: Fees, costs & charges 49
Double taxation relief 49, 50, 52
Income tax 49, 50, 51
Income tax: Car fuel benefits 51
    Indexation 51
    Unit trusts: Interest distributions 51
    Unit trust scheme: Definition 51
Inheritance tax 52
Inheritance tax: Indexation 52
Insurance 54
Insurance premiums 54
Insurance premiums: Prescribed rates of interest 54
Interest rates 52, 53, 186
Management: General & special commissioners 50, 52, 186
    General commissioners 50
    Special commissioners 51, 52, 186
Petroleum revenue tax: Nomination scheme for disposals & appropriations 186
Value added tax 195
Value added tax: Buildings & land 195
    Education 195
    Interest 195
    Registration limits 195
    Tax free shops 196
    Transport 196
    Tribunals 196
Tax free shops 196
Tax relief: Private medical insurance 51
Teachers: Pay & conditions 32
    Redundancy: Premature retirement: Compensation 33
    Schools: Pay & conditions 31
    Superannuation 33
    Superannuation: Additional voluntary contributions 33
        Scotland 34
Teacher training: Bursaries 26
Teaching As A Career Unit: Transfer of property 33
Teaching Council: Election: Scotland 34
Teaching hospitals: Post-graduate: Authorities: National Health Service 70
Technology: Curriculum: Attainment targets & programmes of study 30
Tees & Hartlepool Harbour: Revision 40
Tees & Hartlepool Port Authority: Dissolution 40
Telecommunications 186, 187
Telecommunications: Government shareholding 188
    Leased lines 188
    Meters: Approval fees: BABT 188
    Non-domestic rating 103
    Public systems: Bradford Cable Communications Ltd. 186
        Comment Cablevision Wearside Partnership 187
        Comment Cablevision Worcester Ltd. 187
        Encom Cable TV & Telecommunications Ltd.: Dartford 187
        Encom Cable TV & Telecommunications Ltd.: Epping Forest 187
        Insight Communications Cardiff Ltd. 187
        Insight Communications Guildford Ltd. 187
        NORWEB plc. 187
        NYNEX CableComms Bury & Rochdale 187
        NYNEX CableComms Oldham & Tameside 187
        NYNEX CableComms Wessex 187
        Racal Network Services Ltd. 187
        Sprint Holding (UK) Ltd 187
        Telecom Securicor Cellular Radio Ltd. 187
        Telstra (UK) Ltd. 187
        United Artists Communications (London South) PLC 187

ALPHABETICAL INDEX

Videotron City & Westminster Ltd 187
Vodaphone Ltd 187
Worldcom International Inc. 188
Terminal equipment 188
Wireless telegraph: Guernsey 8, 188
Telecommunications industry: Rateable values 101, 103
Telecom Securicor Cellular Radio Ltd.: Public telecommunication systems 187
Telegraphs 188
Telegraphs: Wireless: Guernsey 8, 188
Telegraphy: Television licence fees 188
Wireless: Shore range devices 188
Television licence fees 188
Television services: Unlicensed: Broadcasting 8
Telstra (UK) Ltd.: Public telecommunication systems 187
Tenant & landlord: England & Wales 56
Tenants: Secure: Compensation for improvements: Scotland 48
Secure: Local authorities: Improvements: Compensation 47
Right to repair: Local housing authorities 48
Right to repair: Scotland 48
Terms & conditions of employment 182, 184, 188, 189
Terrorism: Prevention: Crown servants & regulators 21, 22
Prevention: Temporary provisions: Continuance 96
Suppression: Designation of countries 96
Terrorism provisions: Emergency & prevention: Northern Ireland 91
Test Valley: Environmentally sensitive areas 3
Textile products: Fibre content: Indications 190
Thames estuary: Cockle fishery 179
Thameside Community Health Care: National Health Service Trust 86
Thameslink Healthcare Services: National Health Service Trust 86
Thames Water Authority 196
Thames Water Utilities Ltd.: North London discharge 197
Thanet & Canterbury Community Health Care: National Health Service Trust 71
Thanet Health Care: National Health Service Trust 86
Third country fishing 179
Thomas Cook Group Ltd.: Barclays Bank plc: Merger reference 68, 69
Three Holes Bridge, Norfolk: Reconstruction 42, 43
Three Valleys, Ricksmansworth & Colne Valley: Water 197
Tickets: Resale: Price indications: Consumer protection 17
Tilbury Port: Free zone: Designation 23
Tour de France: Cycle racing: Highways 108
Tower Hamlets Council: Local government: Defined activities 60
Tower Hamlets Housing Action Trust 48
Tower Hamlets (London Borough): Special parking area 110
Town & country planning: Advertisements: Control 189
Applications & deemed applications: Fees 190
Development 189
Development: Permitted: Scotland 190
Procedure: Scotland 190
England & Wales 189
Environmental effects: Assessment 189
Planning & compensation: Scotland 190
Scotland 34, 56, 106, 190
Simplified planning zones 189
Use classes 189
Towns: New: England & Wales 90
Trade: Statistics: Customs & excise 184
Trade descriptions 190
Traded securities: Disclosure 53
Trade marks 190, 191
Trade marks: Agents 190
Customs 191
Fees 190, 191
Forms 190, 191
Priority claims: Relevant countries 191

Trade unions	191
Trade unions: Reform: Employment rights	189, 191
Trading: Sunday	180
Trading agreements: Restrictive: Registration: EEC documents	105
Trading funds: Government	40
Traffic calming: Scotland	106
Traffic signs	111
Trafford Healthcare: National Health Service Trust	86
Training: Employment	35
Vocational: General medical services	65, 87, 90
Trains: International: Public health	98
Transfrontier shipment: Waste	36
Transport	191, 192, 193, 194
Transport & works	191, 193
Transport & works: Inland waterways	193
Transport: Animals: Welfare	6
Charges	193, 194
Conventions: International	191
Health & safety	41, 42
Public passenger	100
Railways	192
Service subsidy: Agreements: Tendering	193
Value added tax	196
Travellers: Allowances	24
Trent & Mersey Canal Bridge, Wheelock: Scheme confirmation	42
Tribunals & inquiries: Costs: Recovery: Ministry of Agriculture, Fisheries & Food	194
Highways: Inquiries procedure	194
Ministers: Compulsory purchase: Inquiries procedure	194
Tribunals: Industrial: Constitution & rules of procedure	52
Industrial: Constitution & rules of procedure: Scotland	52
Trunk roads: A1 & slip roads: Newark-on-Trent, Nottinghamshire	116
A1: A1/A645 junction	116
Alconbury, Cambridgeshire	115
Aycliffe interchange	116
B1288 northside overbridge to Blaydon Bridge	116
Bedfordshire	111
Brotherton-Ferrybridge, southbound carriageway	116
Burneston Hargill	116
Carlton-on-Trent & Tuxford, Nottinghamshire	116
Causey Park, Long Horsley	116
Dish Hill flyover-Fairburn	116
Ducketts hill layby, North of Scurragh House lane junction	116
East Appleton junction-Angleham House junction	116
Falloden Way, Lyttleton Rd. & Aylmer Rd., Barnet & Haringey	116
Five Lanes End to Top Farm, Nottinghamshire	116
Girtford, Bedfordshire	116
Great North Rd., Colsterworth & North Witham, Lincolnshire	116
Great North Way, Barnet	156
Haringey: Red route traffic	107
Haringey: Red route traffic: Bus lanes	107
Islington: Red route traffic	107
Islington: Red route traffic: Bus lanes	107
Kirk Deighton new junction to Walshford	43
Leases Hall-East Appleton junction	116
Little Paxton, Cambridgeshire	116
Little Ponton, Lincolnshire	117
Lobley Hill-Northside overbridge	112
Long Bennington bypass, Lincolnshire	117
Markham Moor, Basseltaw	115
Micklefied & Bramham	44
Micklefield-Selby Fork interchange	117
Northway culvert, Stotfold, Bedfordshire	117
Ossington Lane Bridge, near Sutton on Trent, Nottinghamshire	117
Overbridge & southbound entry slip road, Cromwell, Nottinghamshire	117

Rochester way relief road, Greenwich & Bexley 119
Selby Fork interchange 117
Slip road, Eighton Lodge interchange 117
Southbound slip road, Barrowby, Lincolnshire 115
South Mimms, Hertfordshire 117
Southoe to Little Paxton, Cambridgeshire 117
Stamford & Norman Cross, various lengths 117
Stannington south junction-Seaton Burn junction 117
Swalwell roundabout southbound entry slip road 117
Tempsford Bridge, Bedfordshire 117
Wetherby to Kirk Deighton 44
Wetherby to Walshford 44
Wideopen/Seaton Burn bypass 117
Woolfox, South Witham, Leicestershire 116
Wyboston footbridge, Wyboston, Bedfordshire 117
A2: Bean 118
Canterbury bypass 118
Dunkirk 119
Eastern docks roundabout to Guston roundabout 119
Jubilee Way 119
Patrixbourne 119
Rochester Way relief road, Greenwich & Bexley 119
A3: B366, Redhill Rd. 119
Berelands interchange 119
Beverley Way, Merton 119
Bramshott 119
Bramshott to Hindhead 112
Copsem to Painshill 119
Guildford bypass 119
Guildford bypass-Hog's Back junction 119
Hindhead to Bramshott 119
Hog's Back junction, Guildford 119, 120
Hook to Bramshott 120
Kingston bypass, Kingston Upon Thames & Merton 120
Kingston Upon Thames & Surrey 120
Liphook-Petersfield bypass 112
Milford bypass 120
Robin Hood Way & Beverley Way, Kingston upon Thames 120
Robin Hood Way service road, Kingston Upon Thames 177
Tibbet's Corner underpass, Wandsworth 120
A4: Bath Rd. & Colnbrook bypass, Hillingdon 107
Bath Rd., Hillingdon, Hounslow 120
Bath Rd., Keynsham 112
Great West Rd., Hounslow 107, 120
Hammersmith flyover, Hammersmith & Fulham 120
Hogarth roundabout, Hounslow 120
A5: A460 Longford Is. to M6 junction 12 120
Anglesey, Gwynedd 120
Caergeiliog, Anglesey, Gwynedd 120
Cluddley interchange 170
Glyn Bends Dinmael, Clwyd 121
Glyn Bends, Tynant-Dinmael, Clwyd 121
Holyhead, Gwynedd 112
Llangristiolus, Anglesey, Gwynedd 121
Milton Keynes, Buckinghamshire 121
Muckley Corner to Newtown 121
Oswestry bypass 120
Valley, Gwynedd 112, 121
Watling St., Hinckley, Leicestershire 121
Wibtoft, Leicestershire 121
A6: Bakewell Rd., Devonshire Arms to Topley Pike, Derbyshire 121
Barton-le-Clay & Streatley, Bedfordshire 112
Bedfordshire 112
Buxton Rd.-Hazel Grove-High lane, Stockport 121

Desborough Rd., Rothwell, Northamptonshire	112
Dove Holes, Nr. Buxton, Derbyshire	121
Fillingate junction, Wanlip, Leicestershire	121
Houghton conquest/Haynes, Bedfordshire	112
Kegworth to Hathern, Leicestershire	121
Kibworth Harcourt, Leicestershire	121
Leicester Rd./Harborough Rd., Oadby, Leicestershire	121
Leicester Rd. railway bridge, Loughborough, Leicestershire	121
Lockington, Leicestershire	121
London Rd., Hazel Grove	121
London Rd., near Hemington, Leicestershire	121
Ranch Corner, Matlock Rd., Derbyshire	122
Wanlip, Leicestershire	122
A7: Binks-Castleweary diversion	106
Binks-Castleweary diversion side roads	106
Dumfries & Galloway region	122
Gilmerton Rd. roundabout to Melville Rd. roundabout	122
Highmill Bridge, Langholm, Dumfries & Galloway region	122
A8: Chapelhall junction slip roads	122
Langbank to West Ferry interchange	122
A9: Edinburgh-Thurso, Dalrachney Rd., Carrbridge	122
A10: Foxton level crossing, Cambridgeshire	122
Great Cambridge Rd., Enfield	122
Hoddesden bypass, Hertfordshire	122
Melbourn	112
Puckeridge, Royston, Hertfordshire	122
Reed, Hertfordshire	122
Rush Green interchange, Hertfordshire	122
Thundridge, Hertfordshire	122
Ware bypass, Hertfordshire	122
A11: Besthorpe-Wymondham improvement	123
Fiveways roundabout to Elveden, Suffolk	123
Heath Rd. Bridge, Newmarket, Cambridgeshire & Suffolk	122
Hethersett	112
London to Norwich, Barton Mills, Suffolk	123
M11 J9 to A11, Worsted Lodge	165
Stump Cross to Four Went Ways improvement	123
Thetford, Norfolk	123
Wymondham bypass, Wymondham, Norfolk	123
A12: A12/A45 Copdock Mill interchange, Ipswich, Suffolk	123
A12/A127: Gallows Corner flyover, Havering	124
A12/M25 interchange, Essex	123
Bascule Bridge, Lowestoft	124
Bentley & Capel St Mary interchanges, Suffolk	123
Blythburgh, Suffolk	123
Boreham interchange, northbound access slip road, Essex	123
Boxted Rd. Bridge to Spring Lane, Colchester, Essex	123
Brook St. interchange, Essex	123
Brook St. interchange to Maryland interchange, Brentwood, Essex	123
Capel St Mary to Four Sisters interchange, Suffolk	123
Copdock to Washbrook bypass	123
Crown interchange, Essex	123
Crown interchange, Essex-Stratford St Mary, Suffolk	123
Darsham level crossing, Suffolk	123
Darsham, Suffolk	123
Feering to Marks Tey, Essex	124
London, Great Yarmouth, Bascule Bridge, Lowestoft	124
Lowestoft eastern relief road	44
Marlesford to Benhall	112
Mountnessing	112
Mountnessing bypass, Brook St. interchange, Essex	124
Mountnessing to Margaretting, Essex	124
Pakefield & Lowestoft, Suffolk	124
Rivenhall	112

ALPHABETICAL INDEX

Spring Lane to Crown interchange, Colchester, Essex	124
Wangford bypass, Suffolk	124
Western bypass, Great Yarmouth	124
Witham pass	124
A13: Bus lanes	**107**
A406 interchange underpass, Newham	124
Beckton & Canning Town flyovers, Newham	124
Commercial Rd., Tower Hamlets	124
Mardyke roundabout, Essex	124
Movers Lane & Lodge Ave., flyovers	124
New Rd., Havering	124
North Stifford & Baker St. interchange, Essex	124
Purfleet, Essex	125
Ripple Rd. & New Rd., Barking & Dagenham	125
Ripple Rd., Barking & Dagenham	125
Sandy Lane, Wennington, Essex	125
Tower Hamlets: Bus lanes	107
A14: A1 & B1514 interchanges, Brampton, Cambridgeshire	**125**
A141 interchange slip road, Cambridgeshire	125
Brampton, Cambridgeshire	125
Brington to Barham, Cambridgeshire	125
Catthorpe interchange, Leicestershire	112, 125
Cow Lane & Rusts Lane interchanges, Cambridgeshire	125
Cranford St John & Thrapston, Northamptonshire	125
Girton interchange, Cambridgeshire	165
Heth Rd., Bridge, Newmarket, Cambridgeshire	122
Kettering southern bypass, Northamptonshire	125
Milton interchange, Cambridgeshire, eastbound entry slip road	125
Risby-Beyton, Suffolk	125
Rothwell interchange, Northamptonshire	125
Stowmarket bypass	125
St Saviours interchange, Bury St Edmunds, Suffolk, slip roads	125
Various lengths between Alconbury & Fen Ditton, Cambridgeshire	125
A15: Barton interchange-Bonby Lodge interchange & slip roads	**125, 126**
Ermine St., Hackthorn & Spridlington, Lincolnshire	126
Ermine St., Scampton, Lincolnshire	126
A16: Brazenose Lane, Stamford, Lincolnshire	**126**
High ferry level crossing, Lincolnshire	126
Littleworth Drove, Spalding, Lincolnshire	126
Littleworth Station Level Crossing, Lincolnshire	126
London Rd., Spalding, Lincolnshire	126
Louth bypass & Grimsby Rd., Louth, Lincolnshire	126
Main Rd., Sibsey, Lincolnshire	126
Main Rd., Tallington, Lincolnshire	126
Pinchbeck Rd./Spalding Rd., Spalding, Lincolnshire	126
Spalding Rd., Sutterton, Lincolnshire	126
Spilsby bypass, Lincolnshire	126
Town Bridge, Stamford, Lincolnshire	126
A17: Heckington bypass & Boston Rd., Lincolnshire	**126**
Leadenham, Lincolnshire	126
Main Rd., Swineshead, Lincolnshire	126
Sleaford Rd., Leadenham, Fubeck, Windmill hill, North Rauceby, Lincolnshire	126
Swineshead level crossing, Lincolnshire	126, 127
A18: Junction 5/M180 motorway	**44**
A19: A139 overbridge to Thames Rd. overbridge	**127**
A19/A64 junction, Fulford interchange	127
A66 junction-Tees viaduct	127
A66 Stockton Rd. interchange, slip road	127
B1280 to A690 interchange	127
Easington	127
Easington interchange slip roads	128
Eden Vale	127
Escrick Village	127
Fisher Lane roundabout to Moor Farm roundabout	127

Haverton Hill interchange, northbound & southbound entry slip road ... 127
Herrington interchange slip road ... 127
Knayton & Borrowby bypass ... 127
Mandale interchange, Crathorne interchange ... 127
New St., Selby ... 127
Peterlee interchange slip road ... 127
Portrack roundabout ... 44
Sheraton to Peterlee interchange ... 127
Stainsby Grange-Redhill overbridge ... 128
Tees viaduct ... 128
Wellfield interchange ... 128

A20: Ashford to Folkestone ... 166
Court Wood to South Military Rd. ... 128
Round Hill Tunnels ... 166
Sidcup bypass, Bexley ... 128
Sidcup Rd., Greenwich ... 107, 128

A21: Flimwell ... 128
Flimwell bypass ... 128
North of Lamberhurst ... 128
Somerhill Park link ... 128
Tonbridge bypass north ... 128

A23: Brighton Rd., Croydon ... 107, 128
Coulsdon inner relief road ... 44
Lombard roundabout, Croydon ... 128
London Rd., Croydon ... 128
Muddleswood to Patcham ... 128
Orchard Way service road ... 128
Patcham & Coldean ... 112
Pease Pottage to Handcross ... 166
Purley Way, Croydon ... 128
Purley Way, Croydon, box junction ... 107
Streatham High Rd., Lambeth ... 107, 128, 129
Streatham Hill, Lambeth ... 129
Thornton Rd., Croydon ... 129

A27: Arundel, Fishbourne roundabout ... 129
Beddingham level crossing ... 129
Chichester bypass ... 129
Falmer, Ashcombe roundabout ... 129
Falmer to Hove ... 112
Junction 11-12 ... 168
Langstone roundabout, westbound exit slip road ... 129
Patcham & Coldean ... 112
Patching ... 129
Tangmere roundabout to Fontwell roundabout ... 129
Tangmere to Fontwell ... 129
Wade Court Bridge ... 129

A30: Blackhorse Lane ... 129
Great South West Rd., Hounslow ... 129
Honiton to Exeter ... 44
Indian Queens/Fraddon ... 129
Little Silver to Shillingford ... 129
Shallowater Hill ... 130
Staines ... 129

A31: Ashley Heath roundabout-Woolsbridge roundabout ... 130
Bere Regis-World's End ... 130
Cadnam to Ower ... 169
Roundhouse roundabout-Winterborne Zelston ... 130
Verwood Rd. junction, eastbound exit slip road ... 130

A33: Compton ... 130
Easton Lane to Oak Mount ... 160
Hockley traffic lights ... 130
Poles Lane Bridge to Shepherds Lane Bridge ... 130
Shawford slip roads ... 130

A34: Abingdon bypass ... 130

    Aston-By-Stone ... 130
    Beedon to east Ilsley ... 130
    Burghclere ... 130
    Chieveley ... 130
    Chieveley to Donnington ... 130
    Marker post 3.05-6.45 ... 130
    Marker post 13.30-18.80 ... 130
    Walsall Rd. ... 130
A36: Alderbury bypass ... 130
    Landford ... 130
    Ower link ... 131, 161
    Plaitford to West Wellow ... 131
    Stapleford, Wiltshire ... 112
    Wylye bypass, Wiltshire ... 131
A38: Abbey Hill, Derbyshire ... 131
    Alfreton & South Normanton bypass, Derbyshire ... 131
    Alfreton, Ripley, Derbyshire ... 131
    Barton Turn to Branston interchange ... 131
    Birchwood Lane Bridge, near Alfreton, Derbyshire ... 131
    Claymills junction Bridge ... 131
    Exeter-Plymouth slip roads, Devonshire ... 131
    Exeter to Plymouth ... 131
    Fernhill Heath railway bridge ... 131
    Forder valley, Marsh Mills link road ... 131
    Haldon Hill ... 131
    Kingsway, Derby, Derbyshire ... 131
    Little Eaton bypass, Derbyshire ... 131
    Monks Bridge, Derbyshire ... 131
    Nix's Hill Bridge, Nr. Alfreton, Derbyshire ... 131
    Splatford to Pearces Hill ... 164
    Trerulefoot roundabout S. Hellier to Heskyn junction S. Hellier ... 131
    Trethawle, Tinkers lake ... 131
    Voss Farm Bridge ... 132
    Wrangaton to Lower Dean ... 132
A39: Camelford ... 132
    Fore St., Camelford ... 132
    Old River Camel Bridge, Wadebridge ... 132
    Wadebridge ... 132
A40: Churchdown footbridge ... 132
    Denham interchange, Buckinghamshire ... 132
    Dowdeswell reservoir ... 132
    Forest Hill ... 132
    Glangrwyney Bridge, Powys ... 132
    Glangrwyney village, Powys ... 132
    Hanger Lane underpass, Ealing ... 132
    Haverfordwest bypass, Dyfed ... 112
    Hillingdon ... 112
    Lay-bys, East of Haverfordwest ... 177
    Llandeilo, Dyfed ... 132
    London-Fishguard: Whitland bypass ... 46
    New Manor Farm, Oxford northern bypass ... 132
    Old Bath Rd., Cheltenham ... 132
    Raglan-Abergavenny, Gwent ... 132
    Raglan junction, Gwent ... 132
    Shipton hill ... 132
    Suffolk Rd. ... 133
    Westal Green, Cheltenham ... 133
    Western Ave., Ealing ... 133
    Western Ave., Hillingdon ... 133
    Whitchurch to Ross-on-Wye ... 133
    Witney bypass ... 133
A40/A449: Coldra-Monmouth, Gwent ... 133
A40(M): Westway & Marylebone flyover ... 133
A41: A41 ring road ... 133

Aylesbury	134
Aylesbury, Buckinghamshire	133
Berkhamsted bypass	133
Brent Cross flyover, Barnet	133
Finchley Rd., Westminster	133
Kings Langley & Berkhamsted bypasses	133
Kings Langley, Berkhamsted, Tring bypass, Hertfordshire	133
Kings Langley-Tring, Hertfordshire, slip roads	133
New Ferry/Rock Ferry bypass, Wirral	133
South of Prees Island	134
Whitchurch bypass	134
Whitchurch Rd., Christleton	134
Whitchurch Rd., Chowley, Cheshire	134
Whitchurch Rd., Hampton Heath, Cheshire	134
A43: Blisworth & Milton Malsor bypass	112, 134
Holcot-Sywell junction, Northamptonshire	112
Stamford Rd., Northamptonshire	113, 134
A45: Birmingham Rd.	134
Cambridge northern bypass, Cambridgeshire	134
Caxton-Eltisley, Cambridgeshire	134
Coventry	134
Coventry Rd., Stonebridge	134
Daventry Rd., Dunchurch	113
Fishponds Way, Suffolk	134
Ipswich western bypass, Suffolk	134
London Rd., Stretton-on-Dunsmore	134
Orwell Bridge, Ipswich southern bypass, Ipswich, Suffolk	134
Packington junction	134
Risby, Suffolk	135
Stonebridge highway	135
Stonebridge improvement	135
Stowmarket bypass	135
Whitehouse interchange slip roads, Suffolk	135
A46: Farndon, Nottinghamshire	135
Gloucester Rd., Tadwick	135
Near Syston, Leicestershire	135
Saxondale roundabout, Widmerpool, Nottinghamshire	135
Swainswick, Avon	135
Thurmaston roundabout, Widmerpool interchange, Leicestershire	135
Warwick bypass	135
Widmerpool interchange, Nottinghamshire	135
A47: A47/A1122 junction 1-5, Swaffham	135
Allexton-Belton in Rutland improvement	44
C258 Church Rd., Great Plumstead	135
East Norton bypass, Harborough, Leicestershire	135
Great Plumstead	135
Hockering, Norfolk	135
Nab Lane subway, Peterborough	136
Necton, Norfolk	136
Norwich Rd., West Bilney, Norfolk	136
Soke Parkway, Peterborough, Cambridgeshire	135, 136
Southorpe & Thornaugh, Cambridgeshire	136
Swaffham bypass, Swaffham, Norfolk	136
The Causeway, Eye, Cambridgeshire	136
Thorney, Cambridgeshire	136
Walpole highway, Tilney high end	136
West Bilney, East Winch, Norfolk	136
Western bypass, Great Yarmouth	136
Wisbech Rd., Thorney, Cambridgeshire	113
A48: Blakeney, Newnham	136
Briton Ferry roundabout-Earlswood roundabout, West Glamorgan	136
A49: Tarporley Rd., Cuddington	136
Warrington Rd., Acton Bridge, Dones Green, Cheshire	136
Weaverham diversion, Weaverham	113

ALPHABETICAL INDEX

Whitchurch bypass ... 134
Whitchurch Rd., Spurstow, Cheshire ... 136
A50: Blythe Bridge to Queensway & connecting roads ... 44
   Doveridge, Derbyshire ... 136
   Sudbury bypass, Derbyshire ... 136
A51: Chester Rd., Hurleston ... 137
   Chester Rd., Nantwich ... 137
   Nantwich Rd. ... 137
   Roundabout junction ... 137
A52: Birdsgrove Lane to Stanton Lane ... 137
   Clifton Boulevard, Nottingham, Nottinghamshire ... 137
   Elton, Nottinghamshire ... 137
   Leek/Ashbourne Rd. ... 115
   Nottingham Knight roundabout, Dunkirk roundabout, Nottinghamshire ... 137
   Radcliffe on Trent, Nottinghamshire ... 137
   Raynesway, Borrowash bypass, Derbyshire ... 155
   Southbound slip road, Barrowby, Lincolnshire ... 115
   Spondon, Derbyshire ... 137
A54: Chester Rd., Tarvin & Kelsall, Chester ... 113
   Chester Rd., Vale Royal, Cheshire ... 113
A55: Abergwyngregyn, Gwynedd ... 113, 137
   Burntwood, Clwyd ... 137
   Bus stop & turning lay-bys, Abergwyngregyn, Gwynedd ... 137
   Chester-Bangor, Holywell-Glan Conwy, Clwyd & Gwynedd ... 137
   Chester Southerly bypass, Cheshire/Clwyd boundary ... 137
   Conwy crossing tunnel, Gwynedd ... 137
   Eastbound carriageway, Penmaenbach headland, Gwynedd ... 138
   Eastbound carriageway, Pen-y-Clip section, Gwynedd ... 138
   Ewloe, Clwyd ... 137
   Llanfairfechan, Gwynedd ... 138
   Nant-y-Faenol Lane, St. Asaph, Clwyd ... 138
   Northop, Clwyd ... 138
   Old Telford Rd., Pen-y-Clip section, Gwynedd ... 138
   Penmaenbach-Dwygyfylchi, Gwynedd ... 113
   Penmaenbach, Gwynedd ... 138
   Penmaenbach tunnel, Gwynedd ... 138
   Penmaenmawr West junction, Pen-y-Clip Tunnel, Gwynedd ... 138
   Pen-y-Clip, Gwynedd ... 113, 138
   Pen-y-Clip tunnel, Gwynedd ... 138
   Rhuallt, Clwyd ... 138
   Roundabout junction ... 137
A56: Haslingden bypass ... 138
A57: Manchester Rd., Denton ... 138
   Markham Moor, Basseltaw ... 115
   Newton On Trent bypass, Lincolnshire ... 138
   Retford Rd. Bridge ... 138
A59 ... 165
A59: Liverpool Rd., Aughton ... 139
   Liverpool Rd., Howick ... 113
   Liverpool Rd., Penwortham ... 139
   Longsight Rd., Whalley Clithcroc bypass ... 139
   Longton bypass ... 139
   Longton bypass, South Ribble ... 139
   Mellor Brook bypass ... 113
   Northway at Sefton ... 139
   Northway, Aughton ... 139
   Northway, Aughton, West Lancashire ... 139
   Preston New Rd., Service Rd. ... 139
   Skipton bypass, Low Lodge ... 139
   Whalley-Clitheroe bypass, Chatburn ... 113
A60: Nottingham Knight roundabout, Dunkirk roundabout ... 137
A61: Alfreton hill, Alfreton, Derbyshire ... 139
   Chesterfield, Derbyshire ... 139
   Dronfield bypass, Derbyshire ... 139

306 ALPHABETICAL INDEX

A63: Austhorpe, Leeds 113
    Barrowby Rd. 139
    Long's Corner roundabout, Barnhill junction, Howden 139
    Monk Fryston 113
    Mount Pleasant roundabout-Great Union St. roundabout 139
    Mytongate roundabout, Hull 139
    Mytongate roundabout-Market Place, Hull 139
    Osgodby Railway Bridge 140
    School Lane & Austhorpe Grove junction 140
    School Lane & Bullerthorpe Lane junctions 140
    Selby Rd., Colton 140
    Selby Rd. junction 44
    Thorpe Willoughby railway crossing 140
A64: Bramham crossroads 44
    Copmanthorpe-Fulford interchange 140
    Grimston Bar interchange-Fulford 140
    Grimston Bar interchange, Westbound entry slip road 140
    Marrs Farm to Scagglethorpe junction 140
    Potter Brompton layby, Western End 140
    York Rd., Kiddal to Bramham 140
A65: A59 Harrogate Rd. roundabout, Skibeden-Ellenber Farm 140
    Boxtree & Stanley Bridge 140
    Cowan Bridge 113
    Greta Bridge-Bradford House junction, Ingleton 140
    Harden Bridge, Rawlingshaw 140
    Hellifield railway bridge 140
    Ilkley Rd., Burley in Wharfedale 140
    New Rd., Ingleton 113
    Skipton Rd., Addingham 140
    Skipton Rd., Ilkley 140
    Skir Beck Farm-Long Preston 141
    Spital Bridge 140
A66: Bowes-Cumbrian county boundary 141
    Braithwaite to Woodend Brow 141
    Brougham junction to Winderwath junction 141
    Cockermouth bypass 141
    County of Cumbria 141
    Culgaith Rd. junction 141
    Elton interchange 141
    Fitz Cottage to Brigham 141
    Glendermackin, Troutbeck Climbing Lane 141
    Great Clifton, Naddle Beck & Smithy Green 141
    Kempley Bank, Countless Pillar 141
    Kempley Bank to Countess Pillar improvement 141
    Keswick bypass 141
    Penruddock 141
    Teesside Park interchange 141
    Thornaby Rd. interchange 141
    Warcop junction-Musgrove Bridge 141
A68: Dalkeith 141
A69: Byegill Farm 142
    Constantius Bridge, Kingshaw Green railway bridge 142
    Cross Bank, Halwhistle 142
    East of Bush Cottage 142
    Haltwhistle bypass 44
    Haltwhistle town 45
    Haydon Bridge: West of 142
    Hayton 142
    Rosehill interchange 142
    Scotby junction to Wetheral Plains 142
    Wetheral Plains to Algionby & Broomriggs 142
    Wetheral Plains, Warwick Bridge, Burnrigg junction 142
A73: Roberton Bridge 142
A74: Carlisle-Gretna 142

ALPHABETICAL INDEX

Dumfries & Galloway region, Water of Milk to Ecclefechan	178
Beattock, Cleuchbrae	155
Cleuchbrae, Dinwoodie Green	155
Dinwoodie Green, Muirhouse	155
Eaglesfield, Kirkpatrick Fleming	155
Ecclefechan interchange, Eaglesfield	156
Ecclefechan railway bridge, Ecclefechan interchange	156
Greenhillstairs, Beattock	156
Muirhouse Farm to Lockerbie	178
Muirhouse, Water of Milk	142, 156
Nether Abington, Elvanfoot	156
Paddy's Rickle Bridge, Greenhillstairs	156
River Sark to Guards Mill section	142
Water of Milk, Ecclefechan	156
A74(M): Middlegill-Beattock	106
A75: Dumfries & Galloway region	122
Stranraer	177
A76: Dumfries & Galloway region	122
A77: Stranraer	177
Turnberry	142
A80: Crow Wood roundabout to Muirhead	106
A82	156
A82: Glasgow-Inverness	142
Glasgow-Inverness, Urquhart Castle	156
Kilbowie roundabout improvement side roads	106
A84/A85: Callander, Yellow Box junciton	177
A87: Inverinate	113
A90/M90: Inverkeithing-Perth-Dundee-Aberdeen, Barnhill interchange	142
A91: Cupar	142
A92: Aberdeen-Fraserburgh	155
Aberdeen-Fraserburgh, Stirling village, Boddam	115
Preston roundabout to Markinch Rd. junction	143
A92/A914: Preston roundabout to Markinch Rd. junction	143
A96: Aberdeen, Inverness, Nairn	114
Fochabers	115
Fochabers & Mosstodloch	115
Kintore	114
A98: Fochabers	115
Fraserburgh-Fochabers, Castle St., Banff	143
A102: Blackwall Tunnel	143
Blackwall Tunnel, approach roads	143
Blackwall Tunnel, northern approach	143
A127: A127/A129 interchange, Rayleigh Weir, Essex	143
Basildon, Essex	143
Basildon flyover, A176 interchange, Essex	143
Essex	143
Fairglen to Nevendon, Essex	143
Halfway House interchange, Essex	143
A134: Stradsett	114
Thetford Rd., Northwold, Norfolk	143
Wereham	144
A140: Creeting St Mary Culvert, Suffolk	144
A160: Habrough roundabout, Manby Rd. roundabout	144
A167: Chester-Le-Street, County of Durham	114
Cock O' the North to Browney Bridge	144
Croxdale Station layby	144
Croxdale to Thinford	144
Hermitage to Ropery Lane	144
Park Rd. South, Chester-Le-Street	144
Picktree lane roundabout	144
A168: Topcliffe bypass	144
A174: A171 & A172 junctions, Parkway	144
Parkway, Stokesley Rd.	144
Stainton interchange	144

A180 176
A180: Stallingborough interchange, westbound exit slip road 144
A205: Atkins Rd. & Poynders Rd., Lambeth 157
   Cavendish Rd., Lambeth 157
   Christchurch Rd., Lambeth 157
   London Rd., Lewisham 157
   Thurlow Park Rd., Lambeth 157
   Westhorne Ave., Greenwich 119
A220: Brookside junction, Northop Hall, Clwyd 137
A249: Brielle Way 144
   Kingsferry Bridge 144
   Queenborough bypass 144, 145
   Stockbury roundabout to Kingsferry Bridge 145
A259: A20 Castle Hill interchange to A260 Canterbury Rd. roundabout 45
   Dymchurch Rd. 145
   East Guldeford to Kent Ditch 145
   Ferry Hill & Tanyard Lane, Winchelsea 114
   Guestling Thorn 145
   Guldeford lane 145
   Hythe Rd. 145
   King Offa Way-De La Warr Rd. 145
A282: Dartford-Thurrock crossing 145
   Dartford-Thurrock crossing & approach roads 114
   Dartford Tunnels 145
   Dartford Tunnels & approaches 145
A303: Andover to Bransbury 145
   Barton Stacey 145
   Blackford junction-Yarlington junction 145
   Harewood Forest to Bransbury 145
   Hunton Down 145
   Ilchester bypass 146
   Marsh bypass 146
   Tidbury Farm 146
   Winterbourne Stoke, Wiltshire 114
A316: Country Way, Hounslow 146
   Great Chertsey Rd., Hounslow & Richmond 146
   Hogarth Car Bridge, Hounslow 146
   Hounslow 146
   Marker post 23.0-30.0 160
   Richmond Upon Thames 146
A339: Basingstoke northern bypass 146
   Kingsclere 146
   North of Headley 114
   Sandford Springs service road 146
A380: Non-trunk road: Splatford to Pearces Hill 164
A404: Bisham 146
   Maidenhead Thicket, Handy Cross 146
A405: Bricket Wood, Hertfordshire 146
   Horseshoe Lane/St Albans Rd. junction to Leavesden interchange 146
   Kingsway North Orbital Rd., Watford, Hertfordshire 146
   North orbital road, St Albans, Hertfordshire 158
   St Albans Rd., Watford 146
A406: Angel Rd., Enfield 156
   Barking Rd. flyover, Newham 156
   Barnet 156
   Barnet, Brent & Ealing 108
   Crooked Billet underpass, Waltham Forest 156
   Golders Green Rd./Brent St. junction 45
   Great Cambridge Rd. underpass, Enfield 156
   Ilford viaduct & Redbridge viaduct, Redbridge 157
   Lea Valley viaduct, Waltham Forest 157
   London North Circular 156
   London North Circular, Barnet 156
   London North Circular, Gunnersbury Ave., Hangar lane, Ealing 156

ALPHABETICAL INDEX

   London North Circular, Woodford viaduct, Redbridge 157
   M1, Barnet 157
   North London Circular trunk road, Barnet 177
   Staples Corner flyover, Barnet & Brent 146
   Sterling Way, Enfield 157
   Waltham Forest 157
   Woodford viaduct, Redbridge 157
A414: A1(M) junction 3, Colney Heath, Hertfordshire 146
   Eastbound slip road to Napsbury lane, St Albans 146
   London Rd. junction 147
   Two Waters Link 114
A417: A417/419: Cirencester & Stratton bypass & slip roads 45
   Barnwood bypass 147
   Brockworth bypass 147
   Crickley Hill 147
   Daglingworth Quarry junction 45
   New Mills footbridge 147
   North of Stratton to Nettleton improvement 45
A419: A417/419: Cirencester & Stratton bypass & slip roads 45
   Cirencester bypass 147
   Junction 15-Commonhead roundabout 147
   Latton bypass & slip roads 45
   Stratton St Margaret bypass 147
A420: Bessels Leigh, Tubney 147
   Faringdon bypass 147
   Kingston Bagpuize with Southmoor bypass 114
A423: Banbury to Southam 147
A428: Bedfordshire 111
   St.Neots bypass & Tithe Farm roundabout 147
A435: Evesham bypass 147
   Evesham Rd., Harvington 147
   Layby, Alcester Rd., Studley 147
   M42 Portway to Gorcott Hill 147
   Puffin crossing, Alcester Rd., Studley 147
A449 148
A449: Coven Heath 147
   Crateford to Four Ashes 147
   Stourbridge Rd., Wombourne 148
   Summerfield crossroads, Summerfield, Kidderminster 148
   Wolverhampton Rd. 148
A453: Nottingham Knight roundabout, Dunkirk roundabout 137
   Ratcliffe-On-Soar railway bridge, Nottinghamshire 148
A458 148
A458: Berriew St., Welshpool, Powys 148
   South of Welshpool, Powys 148
A465: Aberdulais-Llandarcy, West Glamorgan 148
   Cefn-coed-y-cymmer, Merther Tydfil, Mid Glamorgan 148
   Hirwaun, Mid Glamorgan 148
   Merthyr Tydfil, Mid Glamorgan 148
   Neath, West Glamorgan 148
   Resolven-Glynneath, West Glamorgan 148
   Resolven, West Glamorgan 148
   Tredegar-Dowlais Top, Gwent & Mid Glamorgan 114
A466: Wye Valley Link Rd., Chepstow, Gwent 114
A470: Abercynon-Abercanaid, Mid Glamorgan 149
   Abercynon, Mid Glamorgan 149
   Bontnewydd Bridge, Bontnewydd, Gwynedd 149
   Cardiff-Glan Conwy 46
   Carno, Powys 177
   Cefn Coed, Mid Glamorgan 149
   Conway Rd., Glan Conwy, Gwynedd 149
   Cwmbach, Powys 114
   Pontypridd, Mid Glamorgan 149
   Station Rd Bridge, Llanrwst, Gwynedd 149

ALPHABETICAL INDEX

A479: Bronllys Castle Bridge, Bronllys, Powys 149
A483: Croesfoel, Wrexham, Clwyd 149
    Crossgates, near Llandrindod Wells, Powys 114
    Dolfor Rd. junction, Newton, Powys 149
    Howey, near Llandrindod Wells, Powys 114
    Lay-by, Welshpool bypass, Welshpool, Powys 149
    Llaneilo, Dyfed 132
    Oswestry bypass 120
    Welshpool bypass, Welshpool, Powys 149
    Wrexham bypass, Clwyd 149
A487: Caernarfon, Gwynedd 114
    Fishguard-Bangor 46
    Llanllyfni, Gwynedd 149
    Machynlleth, Powys 149
    Newport, Dyfed 149
    Port Dinorwic bypass, Gwynedd 114, 149
    Talybont, Dyfed 149
A489: Machynlleth, Powys 149
A494: Alltami, Clwyd 150
    Ewloe, Clwyd 137
    Lay-bys, Mold bypass, Clwyd 150
    Mold bypass, Clwyd 150
A499: Hammers culvert 148
A500: M6 junction 16 to A34 at Talke 114
    Nantwich bypass, Nantwich 114, 150
    Newcastle Rd., Crewe 150
    Newcastle Rd., Shavington 150
    Queensway, Stoke on Trent 150
A501: Euston Rd. & Pentonville Rd., Camden & Islington 150
    Euston Rd. underpass, Camden 150
    West Cross route, Westway & Marylebone flyover 169
    Westway & Marylebone flyover 133
A516: Uttoxeter New Rd., Derbyshire 155
A523: Bradley Mount 150
    Leek/Ashbourne Rd. 115
    London Rd., Macclesfield, Cheshire 150
    London Rd., Sutton, Macclesfield 114
    Macclesfield 150
    Poynton 150
    Sunny-Bank 150
    Tytherington 150
A550: Improvement between Deeside Park & Ledsham 45
    Welsh Rd., Ellesmere Port 150
A556: Chester Rd., junction with Flittogate Lane 151
    Chester Rd., Lostock Gralam, Cheshire 150, 151
    Chester Rd., Mere, Cheshire 151
    Chester Rd., Vale Royal, Cheshire 113
    Northwich bypass 151
A564: Derby southern bypass 45
    Derby southern bypass & slip roads 45
    Derby southern bypass, Derby spur, junctions & slip roads 45
A565: Formby bypass, Formby 151
    Formby bypass, Formby, Merseyside 151
    Plough Inn roundabout-Banks roundabout 151
A570: Moor St. & St. Helens Rd., Ormskirk 45
    Rainford bypass, St Helens 151
    Rainford bypass, West Lancashire & St Helens 151
    Southport Rd., Ormskirk 114, 151
    Southport Rd., Ormskirk, Between A59 County road & Derby St. 151
    St Helens Rd., Ormskirk 151
A580: East Lancashire Rd., Lowton 151
    East Lancashire Rd., Moss Lane junction 151
    East Lancashire Rd., St Helens 151
    East Lancashire Rd., Wigan 114

A585: Amounderness way roundabout junction with B5412, Thornton, Cleveleys 151
   Copse Rd. diversion, Fleetwood 115, 151
    Fleetwood diversion, Wyre 152
A590: Backbarrow to Newby Bridge 152
   Gilkin House: East of Newby Bridge 152
   Greenodd bypass to Levens interchange 152
   Old Backbarrow retaining wall 152
A595: Butts Wood to High Cross 152
   Grizebeck to Duddon Bridge 152
   Hallthwaites, Whicham 152
   Holegill to Moorgreen farm 152
   Loop Rd. Bridge no 1, Whitehaven 152
   Muncaster Bridge 152
   Whicham Valley 152
A596: Dunmail Park, Low Whinnow, Shawood Farm & Crosby 152
   Heathfield 152
   Thursby-Wigton 152
A604: Alconbury, Cambridgeshire 115
   Huntingdon bypass, Cambridgeshire 152
A614: Howden Spur 152
   Leapool roundabout, Gedling, Nottinghamshire 152
   Ollerton, Nottinghamshire 152
A616: Flough crossroads-Midhopestones 152
   Fox Wire access road 153
   Stocksbridge bypass 153
A628: Flouch crossroads-Saltersbrook Bridge 153
A628/A616: Flouch junction 45
A630: Doncaster 45
A638: Crofton railway bridge 153
   Doncaster Rd., Ackworth 153
   Doncaster Rd., Crofton 153
   Nostell Bridge 153
   Oakenshaw Railway Bridge, Doncaster Rd. 153
   York Rd., Doncaster 153
A646: Burnley Rd., Cliviger 115
   Burnley Rd., Cornholme 153
   Burnley Rd., Friendly, Luddendenfoot 115
   Burnley Rd., Mytholmroyd & Luddendenfoot 115
   Burnley Rd., Todmorden 115
A650: Bradford Rd., Bingley 153
A689: Wolviston interchange 127
A696: Belsay 153
   Catleugh 153
   Cottonshope, Redesdale Camp & Bennetsfield 153
   Kirkwhelpington & Newhouses 153
A823(M): Pitreavie Spur 153
   Pitreavie spur, westbound 153
A835: Tore-Ullapool, Garve railway level crossing 153
A876: Checkbar interchange 177
A893: Tore-Ullapool, Garve railway level crossing 153
A898: Erskine Bridge, Dalnottar interchange 142
A914: Preston roundabout to Markinch Rd. junction 143
A952: Aberdeen-Fraserburgh 155
   Aberdeen-Fraserburgh, Stirling village, Boddam 115
A956: Aberdeen-Fraserburgh 155
   Aberdeen-Fraserburgh, Stirling village, Boddam 115
   Ellon Rd., Aberdeen 107, 155
A977: Checkbar interchange 177
   Drum to Crook of Devon 153
A985: Kincardine-Rosyth 115
A1016: Webbs Farm interchange, White Horse roundabout, Essex 154
A1033: Hedon Rd. 46
A1053: Greystone Rd. 154
A1079: Grimston, near York 154

   Market Weighton bypass, eastern junction 154
   York Rd., Kexby 154
  A1089: St. Andrew's Rd., Tilbury 154
   Tilbury, Essex 154
  A1400: Southend Rd. & Woodford Ave. Redbridge 154
  A3113: Airport way 154
  A4042: Llanfrechfa, Gwent 154
   Llanyrafon-Llantarnam, Gwent 154
   Mamhilad, Gwent 154, 177
  A4123: Titford Rd. 154
  A4232: Capel Llanilltern-Culverhouse Cross, South Glamorgan 154
   Culverhouse Cross junction, Cardiff, South Glamorgan 154
  A5036: Between Copy Lane & Switch Island 154
   Church Rd., Litherland, Merseyside 154
   Dunnings Bridge Rd., Netherton, Merseyside 154
  A5092: Greenodd to Penny Bridge 115
  A5103: Northenden southbound exit slip road 155
   Princess Parkway, Northenden, Manchester 154
  A5111: Osmaston Park Rd., Derby, Derbyshire 155
   Raynesway, Borrowash bypass, Derbyshire 155
   Uttoxeter New Rd., Derbyshire 155
  A5117: Improvement between Deeside Park & Ledsham 45
  A5148: Lichfield eastern bypass 155
  A6119: Brownhill drive 155
   Brownhill Drive, Blackburn 115, 155
  A6120: Austhorpe, Leeds 113
   Otley Rd. roundabout-King lane roundabout, Eastbound carriage 155
  A629/650: Kildwick to Crossflatts 45
  A6514: Nottingham ring road, Nottinghamshire 155
   Western Boulevard, Aspley, Nottinghamshire 155
   Western Boulevard/Beechdale road junction, Nottinghamshire 155
  B4260: Ross-on-Wye 46
  Dunbartonshire 115
  Gwalchmai bypass 46
  M9/A9/A882: Auchterarder junction 165
  M41: West cross route, Hammersmith, Fulham 169
  M74: Maryville to west of Fullarton Rd. 176
  M90/A90: Inverkeithing-Aberdeen, Masterton & Admiralty slip roads 153
  Restricted roads: Scotland 115
  Scotland 177
  Speed limits 115
  Various roads: Belper 177
  Wakely St., Islington 177
Trustee investments: Additional powers 194
Trustees 194
Tuna: Preserved: Marketing standards 5
Two Shires Ambulance: National Health Service Trust 86
Tyres: Motor vehicles: Safety 17

U
Ulster Defence Regiment 95
Unclassified roads: Dumfries & Galloway region: Dinwoodie Green Farm to Muirhouse Farm 178
  Dumfries & Galloway region: Johnstonebridge, near Lockerbie 178
    Muirhouse Farm to Norwood, Lockerbie 178
    Near Eaglesfield 178
    Near Ecclefechan 178
    Water of Milk to Ecclefechan 178
United Artists Communications (London South) PLC: Public telecommunication systems 187
United Leeds Teaching Hospital: National Health Service Trust 86
United Leeds Teaching Hospitals: National Health Service Trust 86
United Nations: Former Yugoslavia: Sanctions 194
  Former Yugoslavia: Sanctions: Channel Islands 194
   Sanctions: Dependent Territories 194
    Sanctions: Isle of Man 194

Haiti: Sanctions	195
Sanctions: Channel Islands	194
Sanctions: Dependent territories	194
Sanctions: Isle of Man	194
Rwanda: Arms embargo	195
South Africa: Arms embargo	195
United States of America: Double taxation relief: Income tax	50
Unit trusts: Income tax: Interest distributions	51
University & colleges: University commissioners	195
University College London Hospitals: National Health Service Trust	87
University commissioners	195
University of Abertay Dundee	34
Unoccupied property: Non-domestic rating: Scotland	103
Upper Thames tributaries: Environmentally sensitive areas	3
Urban development	47, 195
Uzbekistan: Double taxation relief: Income tax	50

V

Vaccination: Pigeons (Racing)	6
Vale of Glamorgan: Barry & Dinas Powys communities	62
Valuation: Rating: Plant & machinery	103
Value added tax	195, 196
Value added tax: Accounting & records	195
Buildings & land	195
Education	195
Interest on tax	195
Registration limits	195
Sport, physical education & fund-raising events	196
Tax free shops	196
Transport	196
Tribunals	196
Tribunals: Appeals: Northern Ireland	196
Vehicle licences: First licences: Duty	92, 111
Vehicles: Goods: Plating & testing	108
Goods vehicles: Type approval	108
Management: Local government: Defined activities: Competition	59
Motor: Competitions & trials: Scotland	108
Driving instruction	108
Driving licences	108
EC type approval	108
Tests	108
Type approval: Fees	108
Tyres: Safety	17
Motor vehicles: Type approval	108
Passenger & goods vehicles: Recording equipment	109
Public passenger	100
Removal & disposal	109
Road: Lighting	111
Plating & testing	111
Registration & licensing	111
Registration & licensing: Northern Ireland	92
Road vehicles: Construction & use	111
Ventnor: Harbour	40
Veterinary drugs: Animal test certificates: Renewal applications	67
Licences: Renewal applications	67
Pharmacy & merchants' list	67
Products other than	66
Veterinary medicinal products: Administration: Restrictions	66
Manufacturers' licences	66
Marketing authorisations	65
Product licences: Applications	67
Veterinary surgeons: EEA states	67
Veterinary surgeons	196
Veterinary surgeons & practitioners: Registration	196

Veterinary surgeons: EEA states 67
Videotron City & Westminster Ltd: Public telecommunication systems 187
Vietnam: Double taxation relief: Income tax 50
Virgin Islands: Constitution 9
Visiting forces: Law: Application 24
Vocational training: General medical practice 65, 87, 90
Vodafone Ltd: Public telecommunication systems 187

W

Wages Councils: Abolition 189, 191
Wakefield & Pontefract Community Health: National Health Service Trust 87
Wales: Bridgend District: National Health Service Trust 71
    Broadleaved woodland: Habitat 3
    Coastal belt: Habitat 3
    Curriculum: Geography: Attainment targets & programmes of study 29
        History: Attainment targets & programmes of study 30
    Development Board for Rural Wales: Housing stock 90
    Education: National Curriculum: Assessment arrangements 29
        Pupils: Achievements: Information 28
        Schools: Grant-maintained: Finance 27
        Schools: Performance information 31
    Housing: Renovation: Grants: Forms & particulars: Prescribed 47
        Right to buy: Prescribed forms: Welsh forms 47
    Housing associations: Registered: Accounting 47
    Local authorities: Funds 62
    Local government 60, 61, 62
    Local government: Changes in areas 61, 196
        Manpower information 61
        Reorganisation 62
    National curriculum: Assessment arrangements: Core subjects: Key stage 1 29
        Assessment arrangements: Core subjects: Key stage 3 29
    Non-domestic rating 102
    Non-domestic rating: Contributions 102
        Demand notices 102
    Police authorities: Names: Welsh language 96
    Principal councils: Election day 61
    Radnor: Environmentally sensitive areas 2
    Rent: Forms: Welsh language 56
    School Curriculum & Assessment Authority: Transfer of functions 31
    School performance: Information 31
    Schools: Chief Inspector 26
        Further education information 26
        Grant-maintained status: Ballots 26
        Information 31
    Species rich grassland: Habitat 4
    Trunk roads: Gwalchmai bypass 46
    Vale of Glamorgan: Barry & Dinas Powys communities 62
    Water fringe: Habitat 4
    Welsh alternative names 198
    Wrexham & East Denbighshire Water Company: Constitution & regulation 196
Walsall Community Health: National Health Service Trust 87
Waltham Forest (London Borough): Special parking areas 110
Wandsworth: Special parking areas 110
War: Injuries: Shore employments: Compensation 53
Warrants: Backing: Irish Republic 63, 185
Warrington: Changes in local government areas 62
Warrington Community Health Care: National Health Service Trust 87
Warrington Hospital: National Health Service Trust 87
Warwickshire: South Warwickshire General Hospitals: National Health Service 85
Waste: Transfrontier shipment 36
Waste management: Licensing 36
Waste recycling payments 36
Waste water: Urban: Treatment 196
    Urban: Treatment: Scotland 63, 100

Water 196, 197
  Water: Ayr Burgh, Strathclyde 197
    Bournemouth & West Hampshire 196
    Drinking: Containers 38
    England & Wales 196
    Kilduskland, Strathclyde 197
    Loch Assapol, Strathclyde 197
    Shetland Islands 197
    Southern Water Authority 196
    Thames Water Authority 196
    Waste: Urban: Treatment 196
      Urban: Treatment: Scotland 63, 100
Water byelaws: Loch an Sgoltaire 197
Water enterprises: Merger: Modification 197
Water fringe: Habitat 4
  Habitat: Wales 4
Water industry: England & Wales 196, 197
Water resources: England & Wales 197
Water supply: Council tax: Liability: Reduction: Scotland 18, 197
  Scotland 18, 196, 197
Water undertakers: Rateable values 103
Water undertakings: Rateable values: Scotland 103
Watford & Mount Vernon Hospitals: National Health Service Trust 78
Weald of Kent Community: National Health Service Trust 87
Weights & measures 198
Weights & measures: Cosmetic products 198
  Intoxicating liquor 198
  Metrication 198
  Miscellaneous goods: Metrication 198
  Packaged goods 198
  Packaged goods & quantity marking 198
Welfare food 39
Welfare services: Housing 47
Wellhouse: National Health Service Trust 87
Wells & Walsingham light railway 193
Wells Harbour: Revision 40
Welsh alternative names 198
Welsh language 16
Welsh language: Companies: Forms & documents 16
  Forms & documents: Companies 16
  National curriculum: Exceptions: Key stage 4 30
Welsh Water Authority: Dissolution 196
West Berkshire Priority Care Service: National Health Service Trust 87
Westcountry Ambulance Service: National Health Service Trust 87
West Cumbria Health Care: National Health Service Trust 87
West Dorset Community Health: National Health Service Trust 87
West Dorset Mental Health: National Health Service Trust 87
West Herts Community Health: National Health Service Trust 87
West Lindsey: National Health Service Trust 87, 88
West London Healthcare: National Health Service Trust 88
West Middlesex University Hospital: National Health Service Trust 88
Westminster (City of) (London): Special parking areas 109
West Penwith: Environmentally sensitive areas 3
West Suffolk Hospitals: National Health Service Trust 88
West Sussex: Royal: National Health Service Trust 84
Wildlife 18, 198
Wildlife & countryside 198
Wildlife & countryside: Birds: Registration & ringing 199
Wills & administration proceedings: Northern Ireland 92
Wiltshire Ambulance Service: National Health Service Trust 88
Wine: Common agricultural policy 1
Wireless telegraphy: Guernsey 8, 188
  Licence charges 188
  Short range devices 188

    Television licence fees 188
Wirral tramway light railway 193
Wolverhampton Health Care: National Health Service Trust 88
Worcester Royal Infirmary: National Health Service Trust 88
Work: Incapacity: Northern Ireland 92
    Suspension: Maternity grounds 189
Workmen's compensation: Supplementation 184
Worldcom International Inc.: Public telecommunication systems 188
Worthing Priority Care: National Health Service Trust 88
Wrecks: Protection 97
    Protection: MV Braer 97
Wrexham & East Denbighshire: Pipelaying: Code of practice 197
Wrexham & East Denbighshire Water Company: Constitution & regulation 196
Writtle Agricultural Colleges Further Education Corporation 32
Wychavon District: Gipsy encampments 97

Y
Ynys Môn: Environmentally sensitive areas 2
York Health Services: National Health Service Trust 88
Yorkshire: East Yorkshire Borough Council: Local government: Defined activities: Exemption 59
    East Yorkshire Hospitals: National Health Service Trust 74
Young offender institutions: England & Wales 199
    Scotland 97, 199
Young persons & children: Abduction & custody: Parties to conventions 10
Youth courts & offenders 199
Youth courts: London 199
Yugoslavia: Former: United Nations: Sanctions 194
    Former: United Nations: Sanctions: Channel Islands 194
        United Nations: Sanctions: Dependent Territories 194
        United Nations: Sanctions: Isle of Man 194

List of
Statutory Rules
of
Northern Ireland

Preface

The *List* contains:

(a) a list of the 1994 Northern Ireland statutory rules which appeared in the *Daily list*, arranged under their subject headings. The information given includes the enabling power, as set out in italics, and the date when the rule was issued, made and laid and comes into force, so far as applicable to each rule; pagination; ISBN and price;

(b) a numerical list of the same statutory rules, with their subject headings;

(c) a list of commencement orders;

(d) an alphabetical subject index.

Details of statutory rules from 1983 may be found in the monthly and annual *List of statutory instruments together with the list of statutory rules of Northern Ireland ...*

The full text of statutory rules may be found in the annual volumes of statutory rules which are issued in two parts.

Please note that statutory rules of Northern Ireland are only available from HMSO's Belfast Bookshop (address on back cover).

LIST OF STATUTORY RULES OF NORTHERN IRELAND BY SUBJECT HEADING

ACCESS TO HEALTH RECORDS

The Access to Health Records (1993 Order) (Commencement) Order (Northern Ireland) 1994 No.151 (C. 6). Enabling power: *S.I. 1993/1250 (NI 4), art. 1 (2) & Norther Ireland Act 1974, sch. 1, para. 2 (1). Bringing into operation various provisions of S.I. 1993/1250 (NI 4) on 18.04.94., 30.05.94.* Issued: 25.04.94. Made: 15.04.94. Effect: None. – 2p. – 0 337 91151 7 £0.65

The Access to Health Records (Control of Access) Regulations (Northern Ireland) 1994 No.159. Enabling power: *S.I. 1993/1250 (NI. 4), art. 7 (5).* Issued: 09.05.94. Made: 25.04.94. Coming into force: 30.05.94. Effect: None. – 2p. – 0 337 91159 2 £0.65

The Access to Health Records (Steps to Secure Compliance and Complaints Procedures) Regulations (Northern Ireland) 1994 No. 158. Enabling power: *S.I. 1993/1250 (NI. 4), art. 10 (2) (3).* Issued: 09.05.94. Made: 25.04.94. Coming into force: 30.05.94. Effect: None. –4p. – 0 337 91158 4 £1.10

AGRICULTURE

Agriculture (Environmental Areas) (Amendment) Regulations (Northern Ireland) 1994 No.419. Enabling power: *European Communities Act 1972, s. 2 (2).* Issued: 01.11.94. Made: 27.10.94. Coming into force: 05.12.94. Effect: S.I. 1987/458 (N.I. 3) amended. –2p. – 0 337 91419 2 £0.65

Arable Area Payments (Amendment) Regulations (Northern Ireland) 1994 No. 405. Enabling power: *European Communities Act 1972, s. 2 (2).* Issued: 01.11.94. Made: 24.10.94. Coming into force: 21.11.94. Effect: S.R. 1994/181 amended. – 4p. – 0 337 91405 2 *£1.10*

Arable Area Payments Regulations (Northern Ireland) 1994 No. 181. Enabling power: *European Communities Act 1972, s. 2 (2).* Issued: 25.05.94. Made: 10.05.94. Coming into force: 13.05.94. Effect: None. – 24p. – 0 337 91181 9 £4.15

Artificial Breeding of Sheep and Goats (EEC) Regulations (Northern Ireland) 1994 No.391. Enabling power: *S.I. 1975/1834 (N.I. 17), art. 5 (1) (2).* Issued: 24.10.94. Made: 14.10.94. Coming into force: 16.11.94. Effect: None. – 4p. – 0 337 91391 9 £1.10

The Beef Carcase (Classification) (Amendment) Regulations (Northern Ireland) 1994 No.486. Enabling power: *European Communities Act 1972, s. 2 (2).* Issued: 21.12.94. Made: 14.12.94. Coming into force: 12.01.95. Effect: S.R. 1992/1 amended. – 2p. – 0 337 91486 9 £0.65

Beef Special Premium (Protection of Payments) (Amendment) Regulations (Northern Ireland) 1994 No. 476. Enabling power: *European Communities Act 1972, s. 2 (2).* Issued: 09.01.95. Made: 06.12.94. Coming into force: 01.01.95. Effect: S.R. 1992/569 amended. – 4p. – 0 337 91476 1 £0.65

Deseasonalisation Premium (Protection of Payments) (Amendment) Regulations (Northern Ireland) 1994 No. 360. Enabling power: *European Communities Act 1972, s. 2 (2).* Issued: 28.09.94. Made: 21.09.94. Coming into force: 29.09.94. Effect: S.R. 1993/475 amended. –2p. – 0 337 91360 9 £0.65

Environmentally Sensitive Areas (Antrim Coast, Glens and Rathlin) Designation (Amendment) Order (Northern Ireland) 1994 No.376. Enabling power: *S.I. 1987/458 (N.I. 3), art. 3 (1) (3) (a).* Issued: 12.10.94. Made: 04.10.94. Coming into force: 07.11.94. Effect: S.I. 1993/179 amended. – 4p. – 0 337 91376 5 £1.10

Environmentally Sensitive Areas (Mourne Mountains and Slieve Croob) Designation (Amendment) Order (Northern Ireland) 1994 No.375. Enabling power: *S.I. 1987/458 (N.I. 3), art. 3 (1) (3) (a).* Issued: 12.10.94. Made: 04.10.94. Coming into force: 07.11.94. Effect: S.I. 1993/178 amended. – 4p. – 0 337 91375 7 £1.10

Environmentally Sensitive Areas (Slieve Gullion) Designation Order (Northern Ireland) 1994 No. 212. Enabling power: *S.I. 1987/458 (N.I. 3), art. 3 (1) (3).* Issued: 22.06.94. Made: 09.06.94. Coming into force: 11.07.94. Effect: None. – 12p. – 0 337 91212 2 £2.80

Environmentally Sensitive Areas (Sperrins) Designation Order (Northern Ireland) 1994 No.213. Enabling power: *S.I. 1987/458 (N.I. 3), art. 3 (1) (3).* Issued: 22.06.94. Made: 09.06.94. Coming into force: 11.07.94. Effect: None. – 12p. – 0 337 91213 0 £2.80

Environmentally Sensitive Areas (West Fermanagh and Erne Lakeland) Designation (Amendment) Order (Northern Ireland) 1994 No.377. Enabling power: *S.I. 1987/458 (N.I. 3), art. 3 (1) (3) (a).* Issued: 12.10.94. Made: 04.10.94. Coming into force: 07.11.94. Effect: S.I. 1993/180 amended. – 4p. – 0 337 91377 3 £1.10

Farm and Conservation Grant (Amendment) Scheme (Northern Ireland) 1994 No. 463. Enabling power: *S.I. 1987/166 (N.I. 1), art. 16 (1) (2).* Issued: 05.01.95. Made: 29.11.94. Coming into force: 30.11.94. Effect: S.R. 1989/38 amended. – 2p. – 0 337 91463 X £0.65

Farm Conservation Grant (Amendment) Regulations (Northern Ireland) 1994 No. 464. Enabling power: *European Communities Act 1972, s. 2 (2).* Issued: 05.01.94. Made: 29.11.94. Coming into force: 30.11.94. Effect: S.R. 1991/264 amended. – 2p. – 0 337 91464 8 £0.65

Price/availability are liable to change without notice

Feeding Stuffs (Amendment) (No. 2) Regulations (Northern Ireland) 1994 No. 502. Enabling power: *European Communities Act 1972, s. 2 (2) & Agriculture Act 1970, ss. 66 (1), 68 (1) (1A) (3), 69 (1) (3) (6) (7), 70 (1), 73 (3), 74 (1), 74A, 84, 86.* Issued: 09.01.95. Made: 29.12.94. Coming into force: 06.02.95. Effect: S.R. 1992/270 amended. – 20p. – 0 337 91102 9 *£3.70*

Feeding Stuffs (Amendment) Regulations (Northern Ireland) 1994 No. 123. Enabling power: *European Communities Act 1972. s. 2 (2) & Agriculture Act 1970, ss. 66 (1), 68 (1) (1A) (3), 69 (1) (3) (6) (7), 70 (1), 73 (3), 74 (1), 74A, 84, 86.* Issued: 01.04.94. Made: 29.03.94. Coming into force: 28.04.94. Effect: S.R. 1992/270 amended. – 8p. – 0 337 91123 1 *£1.95*

The Feeding Stuffs (Sampling and Analysis) (Amendment) Regulations (Northern Ireland) 1994 No. 309. Enabling power: *Agriculture Act 1970, ss. 66 (1), 77 (4), 78 (6), 79 (2), 84, 86.* Issued: 17.08.94. Made: 04.08.94. Coming into force: 16.09.94. Effect: S.R. 1982/338 amended. – 20p. – 0 337 91309 9 *£3.70*

Fertilisers (Sampling and Analysis) (Amendment) Regulations (Northern Ireland) 1994 No.166. Enabling power: *Agriculture Act 1970, ss. 66 (1), 74A, 75 (1), 76 (1), 77, 78 (2) (4) (6), 79 (1) (2) (9), 84, 86 (1) (2) (3) (9).* Issued: 09.05.94. Made: 27.04.94. Coming into force: 27.05.94. Effect: S.R. 1991/540 amended. – 28p. – 0 337 91166 5 *£4.70*

The Hill Livestock (Compensatory Allowances) Regulations (Northern Ireland) 1994 No.417. Enabling power: *European Communities Act 1972, s. 2 (2).* Issued: 28.11.94. Made: 25.10.94. Coming into force: 15.11.94. Effect: S.R. 1993/449, 474 amended. – 16p. – 0 337 91417 6 *£3.20*

Marketing of Potatoes (Amendment) Regulations (Northern Ireland) 1994 No. 385. Enabling power: *Marketing of Potatoes Act (Northern Ireland) 1964, ss. 3 (3), 7 (2), 11 (1).* Issued: 17.10.94. Made: 10.10.94. Coming into force: 14.11.94. Effect: S.R. 1989/221 amended & S.R. 1992/353 revoked. – 2p. – 0 337 91385 4 *£0.65*

Milk Marketing (Period for Making Applications) (Extension No. 2) Order (Northern Ireland) 1994 No. 341. Enabling power: *S.I. 1993/2665 (NI. 10) art. 5 (7).* Issued: 06.09.94. Made: 05.09.94. Coming into force: 29.09.94. Effect: S.I. 1993/2665 (NI. 10) amended. – 2p. – 0 337 91341 2 *£0.65*

Milk Marketing (Period for Making Applications) (Extension) Order (Northern Ireland) 1994 No.60. Enabling power: *S.I. 1993/2665 (NI. 10), art. 5 (7).* Issued: 08.03.94. Made: 28.02.94. Coming into force: 30.03.94. Effect: None. – 2p. – 0 337 91060 X *£0.65*

Milk Marketing Scheme (Postponement of Date of Revocation No. 2) Order (Northern Ireland) 1994 No. 340. Enabling power: *S.I. 1993/2665 (NI. 10) art. 4 (3).* Issued: 06.09.94. Made: 05.09.94. Coming into force: 01.12.94. Effect: S.I. 1993/2665 (NI. 10) amended. – 2p. – 0 337 91340 4 *£0.65*

Milk Marketing Scheme (Postponement of Date of Revocation) Order (Northern Ireland) 1994 No.59. Enabling power: *S.I. 1993/2665 (NI. 10), art. 4 (3).* Issued: 08.03.94. Made: 28.02.94. Coming into force: 30.03.94. Effect: S.I. 1993/2665 (NI. 10) amended. – 2p. – 0 337 91059 6 *£0.65*

Pig Carcase (Grading) Regulations (Northern Ireland) 1994 No. 384. Enabling power: *European Communities Act 1972, s. 2 (2).* Issued: 17.10.94. Made: 10.10.94. Coming into force: 14.11.94. Effect: S.R. 1988/358 revoked. – 12p. – 0 337 91384 6 *£2.40*

Poultry Meat, Farmed Game Bird Meat and Rabbit Meat (Hygiene and Inspection) Regulations (Northern Ireland) 1994 No. 346. Enabling power: *European Communities Act 1972, s. 2 (2) & Finance Act 1973, s. 56.* Issued: 16.09.94. Made: 07.09.94. Coming into force: 08.10.94. Effect: S.R. 1991/6; 1992/167 amended & S.R. 1977/165; 1979/261; 1981/260 revoked. – 68p. – 0 337 91346 3 *£7.65*

Seed Potatoes (Crop Fees) Regulations (Northern Ireland) 1991 No. 128. Enabling power: *Seeds Act (Northern Ireland) 1965; s. 1.* Issued: 06.04.94. Made: 29.03.94. Coming into force: 02.05.94. Effect: None. – 4p. – 0 337 91128 2 *£1.10*

Seed Potatoes (Tuber and Label Fees) (Amendment) Regulations (Northern Ireland) 1994 No.386. Enabling power: *Seeds Act (Northern Ireland) 1965, s. 1 (1) (2) (2A).* Issued: 17.10.94. Made: 10.10.94. Coming into force: 14.11.94. Effect: S.R. 1982/236 amended & S.R. 1992/352 revoked. – 2p. – 0 337 91386 2 *£0.65*

The Sheep Annual Premium (Amendment) Regulations (Northern Ireland) 1994 No. 404. Enabling power: *European Communities Act 1972, s. 2 (2).* Issued: 22.11.94. Made: 24.10.94. Coming into force: 15.11.94. Effect: S.R. 1992/476 amended. – 4p. – 0 337 91404 4 *£1.10*

Sub-Programme for Agriculture and Rural Development Regulations (Northern Ireland) 1994 No.413. Enabling power: *European Communities Act 1972, s. 2 (2).* Issued: 11.11.94. Made: 25.10.94. Coming into force: 28.11.94. Effect: None. – 8p. – 0 337 91413 3 *£1.55*

The Suckler Cow Premium (Amendment) Regulations (Northern Ireland) 1994 No.211. Enabling power: *European Communities Act 1972, s. 2 (2).* Issued: 03.08.94. Made: 09.06.94. Coming into force: 01.07.94. Effect: S.R. 1993/280 amended. – 4p. – 0 337 91211 4 *£1.10*

AIRPORTS

Airports (Nominated Successor Company) Order (Northern Ireland) 1994 No. 194. Enabling power: *S.I. 1994/426 (NI. 1), arts. 51 (1), 67 (a).* Issued: 01.06.94. Made: 24.05.94. Coming into force: 30.06.94. Effect: None. – 2p. – 0 337 91194 0 *£0.65*

Northern Ireland Airports Limited (Transfer Date) Order (Northern Ireland) 1994 No.275. Enabling power: *S.I. 1994/426 (N.I. 1), art 54 (2).* Issued: 03.08.94. Made: 20.07.94. Coming into force: 20.07.94. Effect: None. – 2p. – 0 337 91275 0 *£0.65*

Price/availability are liable to change without notice

ANIMALS

Aujeszky's Disease Order (Northern Ireland) 1994 No. 198. Enabling power: *S.I. 1981/1115 (N.I. 22), arts. 4, 5 (1), 10 (6), 12 (1), 14, 19, 44, 60 (1)*. Issued: 14.06.94. Made: 25.05.94. Coming into force: 01.09.94. Effect: None. – 8p. – 0 337 91198 3 *£1.95*

Aujeszky's Disease Scheme Order (Northern Ireland) 1994 No. 199. Enabling power: *S.I. 1981/1115 (N.I. 22), art. 8 (1) (2)*. Issued: 14.06.94. Made: 25.05.94. Coming into force: 01.09.94. Effect: None. – 8p. – 0 337 91199 1 *£1.95*

Bovine Embryo Collection and Transplantation Regulations (Northern Ireland) 1994 No.35. Enabling power: *S.I. 1975/1834 (NI.17), art. 5 (1) (2), Welfare of Animals Act (Northern Ireland) 1972, s. 2 (1)*. Issued: 09.02.94. Made: 31.01.94. Coming into force: 07.03.94. Effect: None. – 12p. – 0 337 91035 9 *£2.80*

Breeding Flocks, Hatcheries and Animal Protein (Fees) Order (Northern Ireland) 1994 No.119. Enabling power: *S.I. 1981/1115 (NI. 22), art. 50 (1)*. Issued: 06.04.94. Made: 28.03.94. Coming into force: 18.04.94. Effect: S.R. 1990/175; 1992/251 revoked. – 8p. – 0 337 91119 3 *£1.55*

The Diseases of Animals (Amendment) Regulations (Northern Ireland) 1994 No. 161. Enabling power: *European Communities Act 1972, s. 2 (2)*. Issued: 04.05.94. Made: 25.04.94. Coming into force: 06.06.94. Effect: S.I. 1981/1115 (NI. 22) amended. – 4p. – 0 337 91161 4 *£1.10*

Diseases of Animals (Modification) Order (Northern Ireland) 1994 No. 11. Enabling power: *S.I. 1981/1115 (NI. 22), arts. 2 (3), 16 (2)*. Issued: 26.01.94. Made: 14.01.94. Coming into force: 21.02.94. Effect: S.I. 1981/1115 (NI. 22) amended. – 4p. – 0 337 91011 1 *£1.10*

Poultry Breeding Flocks and Hatcheries (Registration and Testing etc) (Revocation) Order (Northern Ireland) 1994 No. 120. Enabling power: *S.I. 1981/1115 (NI. 22), arts. 5 (1), 19 (h), 44, 60 (1)*. Issued: 06.04.94. Made: 28.03.94. Coming into force: 18.04.94. Effect: S.R. 1990/50 revoked. – 2p. – 0 337 91120 7 *£0.65*

Poultry Breeding Flocks and Hatcheries Scheme Order (Northern Ireland) 1994 No. 118. Enabling power: *S.I. 1981/1115 (NI. 22), arts. 8 (1) (2)*. Issued: 06.04.94. Made: 28.03.94. Coming into force: 18.04.94. Effect: None. – 20p. – 0 337 91118 5 *£3.70*

The Rabies (Importation of Dogs, Cats and Other Mammals) (Amendment) Order (Northern Ireland) 1994 No. 402. Enabling power: *S.I. 1981/1115 (N.I. 22), arts. 29 (1) (2), 60 (1) (2), 62 (2), sch. 6, para. 2*. Issued: 01.11.94. Made: 21.10.94. Coming into force: 18.11.94. Effect: S.R. 1977/113 amended. – 8p. – 0 337 91402 8 *£1.55*

Specified Diseases (Notification and Movement Restrictions) (Amendment) Order (Northern Ireland) 1994 No. 130. Enabling power: *S.I. 1981/1115 (N.I. 22), arts. 5 (1), 10 (6), 19 (e) (f) (k), 60 (1)*. Issued: 25.04.94. Made: 29.03.94. Coming into force: 30.03.94. Effect: S.R. 1991/455 amended. – 2p. – 0 337 91130 4 *£0.65*

Tuberculosis Control (Amendment) Order (Northern Ireland) 1994 No. 216. Enabling power: *S.I. 1981/1115 (N.I. 22), arts. 5 (1) (b), 60 (1)*. Issued: 21.06.94. Made: 09.06.94. Coming into force: 10.06.94. Effect: S.R. & O. (N.I.) 1964/31 amended. – 4p. – 0 337 91216 5 *£1.10*

Welfare of Animals during Transport Order (Northern Ireland) 1994 No. 244. Enabling power: *S.I. 1981/1115 (N.I. 22), arts. 5 (1) (k), 19 (b) (c) (e) (i), 21, 23, 60 (1)*. Issued: 08.07.94. Made: 28.06.94. Coming into force: 01.08.94. Effect: S.R. & O. (N.I.) 1927/38; 1953/87; 1958/5; 1973/300; S.R. 1989/165, 166, 167 amended. – 12p. – 0 337 91244 0 *£2.80*

BETTING, GAMING AND LOTTERIES

The Betting and Lotteries (1994 Order) (Commencement) Order (Northern Ireland) 1994 No.466 (C. 16). Enabling power: *S.I. 19904/1893 (N.I. 8), art. 1 (2) & Northern Ireland Act 1974, sch. 1, para. 2 (1). Bringing into operation various provisions of the 1994 order on 09.01.95.* Issued: 05.12.94. Made: 29.11.94. Effect: None. – 2p. – 0 337 91466 4 *£0.65*

Lotteries Regulations (Northern Ireland) 1994 No. 467. Enabling power: *S.I. 1985/1204 (N.I. 11), arts. 137 (17), 138 (1)*. Issued: 07.12.94. Made: 29.11.94. Coming into force: 09.01.95. Effect: S.R. 1987/193; 1990/237 revoked. – 8p. – 0 337 91467 2 *£1.95*

BUILDING REGULATIONS

Building Regulations (Northern Ireland) 1994 No. 243. Enabling power: *S.I. 1979/1709 (N.I. 16), arts. 3, 5 (1) (2) (3), 15 (2) (7), 16 (1) (2), 17 (1) (2), sch. 1, paras. 1 to 7, 9 to 13, 17 to 22*. Issued: 08.07.94. Made: 28.06.94. Coming into force: 28.11.94. Effect: S.R. 1990/59 (NI); 1991/169; 1993/84 revoked with savings. – 92p. – 0 337 91243 2 *£9.50*

CHILD SUPPORT

The Child Support (Miscellaneous Amendments and Transitional Provisions) Regulations (Northern Ireland) 1994 No.37. Enabling power: *S.I. 1991/2628 (NI. 23), arts. 18, 19 (6), 32 (1) (2), 39 (3) (4), 44, 47, 48 (4), sch. 1, paras. 1 (3), 4 (1), 6 (6), 8 (a)*. Issued: 09.02.94. Made: 03.02.94. Coming into force: 07.02.94. Effect: S.R. 1992/340; 1992/341; 1992/390; 1993/73 amended. – 12p. – 0 337 91037 5 *£2.80*

The Child Support (Northern Ireland) Order 1991 (Consequential Amendments) Order (Northern Ireland) 1994 No. 259. Enabling power: *S.I. 1991/2628 (N.I. 23), art. 51 (1)*. Issued: 08.07.94. Made: 01.07.94. Coming into force: 15.08.94. Effect: S.I. 1981/1675 (N.I. 26) amended. – 2p. – 0 337 91259 9 *£0.65*

CLEAN AIR

The Air Quality Standards (Amendment) Regulations (Northern Ireland) 1994 No. 339. Enabling power: *European Communities Act 1972, s. 2 (2)*. Issued: 06.09.94. Made: 02.09.94. Coming into force: 04.10.94. Effect: S.R. 1990/145 amended. – 2p. – 0 33791339 0 £0.65

The Alkali, etc. Works (Amendment No. 2) Order (Northern Ireland) 1994 No. 444. Enabling power: *Clean Air (Northern Ireland) Order 1981, art. 25 (9)*. Issued: 22.11.94. Made: 15.11.94. Coming into force: 03.01.95. Effect: None. – 2p. – 0 337914443 £0.65

The Alkali, etc. Works (Amendment) Order (Northern Ireland) 1994 No.104. Enabling power: *S.I. 1981/158 (NI. 4), art. 25 (9)*. Issued: 31.03.94. Made: 23.03.94. Coming into force: 06.05.94. Effect: 1906 c.14 amended. – 4p. – 0 337911045 £1.10

COMPANIES

Companies (1986 Order) (Insurance Companies Accounts) Regulations (Northern Ireland) 1994 No.428. Enabling power: *S.I. 1986/1032 (N.I. 6), arts. 2 (3), 265 (1) (3)*. Issued: 09.11.94. Made: 02.11.94. Coming into force: 16.12.94. Effect: S.I. 1986/1032 (N.I. 6) amended. – 48p. – 0 337914281 £6.35

Companies (1990 Order) (Commencement No. 5) Order (Northern Ireland) 1994 No. 47 (C. 2). Enabling power: *S.I. 1990/593 (NI. 5), art. 1, & Northern Ireland Act 1974, sch. 1, para. 2 (1). Bringing into operation various provisions of the 1990 order on 07.04.94*. Issued: 22.02.94. Made: 10.02.94. Effect: None. – 4p. – 0 337910472 £1.10

Disclosure of Interests in Shares (Amendment) Regulations (Northern Ireland) 1994 No.2. Enabling power: *S.I. 1986/1032 (NI. 6), art. 218A*. Issued: 21.01.94. Made: 10.01.94. Coming into force: 11.03.94. Effect: S.I. 1986/1032 (NI. 6) amended & S.R. 1979/229 revoked. – 12p. – 0 337910022 £2.80

Partnerships and Unlimited Companies (Accounts) Regulations (Northern Ireland) 1994 No.133. Enabling power: *European Communities Act 1972, s. 2 (2)*. Issued: 14.04.94. Made: 30.03.94. Coming into force: 12.05.94. Effect: S.I. 1986/1032 (NI 6) amended. – 12p. – 0 337911339 £2.80

CONTRACTS OF EMPLOYMENT AND REDUNDANCY PAYMENTS

Redundancy Payments (Health and Personal Social Services) (Modification) Order (Northern Ireland) 1994 No. 8. Enabling power: *Contracts of Employment and Redundancy Payments Act (Northern Ireland) 1965, ss. 58A (a), 59 (3)*. Issued: 21.01.94. Made: 14.01.94. Coming into force: 11.02.94. Effect: 1965 c.19 amended. – 8p. – 0 337910081 £1.55

Redundancy Payments (Local Government etc.) (Modification) (Amendment) (No. 2) Order (Northern Ireland) 1994 No. 148. Enabling power: *Contracts of Employment and Redundancy Payments Act (Northern Ireland) 1965, ss. 58A (a), 59 (3)*. Issued: 20.04.94. Made: 14.04.94. Coming into force: 16.05.94. Effect: S.R. 1986/206 amended. – 2p. – 0 337911487 £0.65

Redundancy Payments (Local Government etc.) (Modification) (Amendment) Order (Northern Ireland) 1994 No. 9. Enabling power: *Contracts of Employment and Redundancy Payments Act (Northern Ireland) 1965, ss. 58A (a), 59 (3)*. Issued: 21.01.94. Made: 14.01.94. Coming into force: 11.02.94. Effect: S.I. 1986/206 amended. – 4p. – 0 33791009 X £1.10

COUNTY COURTS

County Court (Amendment) Rules (Northern Ireland) 1994 No. 472. Enabling power: *S.I. 1980/397 (N.I. 3), art. 46*. Issued: 15.12.94. Made: 30.11.94. Coming into force: 01.01.95. Effect: S.I. 1981/1675 (N.I. 26) amended. – 4p. – 0 337914729 £1.10

County Court Divisions Order (Northern Ireland) 1994 No. 471. Enabling power: *S.I. 1980/397 (N.I. 3), art. 3 (1)*. Issued: 15.12.94. Made: 24.11.94. Coming into force: 02.01.95. Effect: S.R. 1990/197 revoked. – 4p. – 0 337914710 £1.10

The County Court Fees Order (Northern Ireland) 1994 No. 280. Enabling power: *Judicature (Northern Ireland) Act 1978, s. 116 (1) (4)*. Issued: 11.08.94. Made: 21.07.94. Coming into force: 01.09.94. Effect: S.R. 1989/279; 1990/108; 1991/121; 1992/221, 425 revoked. – 16p. – 0 337912807 £3.20

The Matrimonial Causes Fees (Amendment) Order (Northern Ireland) 1994 No. 281. Enabling power: *Judicature (Northern Ireland) Act 1978, s. 116 (1)*. Issued: 11.08.94. Made: 21.07.94. Coming into force: 01.09.94. Effect: S.R. 1991/292 amended. – 8p. – 0 337912815 £1.55

CREDIT UNIONS

Credit Unions (Fees) Regulations (Northern Ireland) 1994 No. 436. Enabling power: *S.I. 1985/1205 (N.I. 12), arts. 31 (2) (3), 78 (1)*. Issued: 16.11.94. Made: 08.11.94. Coming into force: 21.12.94. Effect: S.R. 1993/421 revoked. – 4p. – 0 337914362 £1.10

CRIMINAL PROCEDURE

The Criminal Justice (1994 Order) (Commencement) Order (Northern Ireland) 1994 No.446 (C. 14). Enabling power: *S.I. 1994/2795 (N.I. 15), art. 1 (2). Bringing into operation various provisions fo the 1994 order on 09.01.95.* Issued: 22.11.94. Made: 15.11.94. Effect: None. – 2p. – 0 33791446 X £0.65

Price/availability are liable to change without notice

The Criminal Justice (Confiscation) (1993 Order) (Commencement) Order (Northern Ireland) 1994 No. 129 (C.4). Enabling power: *S.I. 1993/3146 (NI. 13), art. 1 (2). Bringing various provisions of the 1993 order into operation on 01.04.94.* Issued: 11.04.94. Made: 28.03.94. Effect: None. – 2p. – 0 337 91129 0 £0.65

The Criminal Justice (Confiscation) (Designated Countries and Territories) (1991 Order) (Amendment No. 2) (Northern Ireland) Order 1994 No. 350. Enabling power: *S.I. 1990/2588 (NI. 17), art. 27.* Issued: 22.09.94. Made: 06.09.94. Coming into force: 01.11.94. Effect: S.I. 1990/2588 (NI. 17); S.R. 1991/221 amended. – 4p. – 0 337 91350 1 £1.10

The Criminal Justice (Confiscation) (Designated Countries and Territories) (1991 Order) (Amendment) (Northern Ireland) Order 1994 No. 164. Enabling power: *S.I. 1990/2588 (NI. 17), art. 27.* Issued: 09.05.94. Made: 22.04.94. Coming into force: 17.06.94. Effect: S.R. 1991/221 amended. – 4p. – 0 337 91164 9 £1.10

The Criminal Justice (Confiscation) (Designated Countries and Territories) (1992 Order) (Amendment No. 2) (Northern Ireland) Order 1994 No. 351. Enabling power: *S.I. 1990/2588 (NI. 17), art. 27.* Issued: 22.09.94. Made: 06.09.94. Coming into force: 01.11.94. Effect: S.I. 1990/2588 (NI. 17); S.R. 1992/198 amended. – 4p. – 0 337 91351 X £1.10

The Criminal Justice (Confiscation) (Designated Countries and Territories) (1992 Order) (Amendment) (Northern Ireland) Order 1994 No. 165. Enabling power: *S.I. 1990/2588 (NI. 17), art. 27.* Issued: 11.05.94. Made: 22.04.94. Coming into force: 17.06.94. Effect: S.R. 1992/198 amended. – 4p. – 0 337 91165 7 £1.10

The Criminal Justice (Serious Fraud) (Northern Ireland) Order 1988 (Notice of Transfer) (Amendment) Regulations 1994 No. 344. Enabling power: *S.I. 1988/1846 (NI. 16), art. 4 (7).* Issued: 22.09.94. Made: 01.09.94. Coming into force: 01.11.94. Effect: S.R. 1989/338 amended. – 8p. – 0 337 91344 7 £1.55

The Remand (Temporary Provisions) (Northern Ireland) Order 1994 (Cessation) Order 1994 No. 369. Enabling power: *S.I. 1994/1993 (N.I. 14), art. 4 (2) (b).* Issued: 28.11.94. Made: 23.09.94. Coming into force: 23.09.94. Effect: S.I. 1994/1993 (N.I. 14) amended. – 2p. – 0 337 91369 2 £0.65

The Remand (Temporary Provisions) (Northern Ireland) Order 1994 (Continuance) Order 1994 No. 329. Enabling power: *S.I. 1994/1993 (N.I. 14), art. 4 (2) (a).* Issued: 28.11.94. Made: 19.08.94. Coming into force: 27.08.94. Effect: None. – 2p. – 0 337 91329 3 £0.65

EDUCATION

Colleges of Education (Grant Conditions) Regulations (Northern Ireland) 1994 No. 12. Enabling power: *S.I. 1986/594 (N.I. 3), arts. 66 (3) (4) (5), 134 (1).* Issued: 27.01.94. Made: 17.01.94. Coming into force: 07.02.94. Effect: S.R. & O. (N.I.) 1956/9; 1968/284; 1969/160; 1970/13 revoked. – 8p. – 0 337 91012 X £1.95

Curriculum (Programme of Study and Attainment Targets in Geography) Order (Northern Ireland) 1994 No. 257. Enabling power: *S.I. 1989/2406 (N.I. 20), art. 7 (1) (a) (2) (b) (5).* Issued: 08.07.94. Made: 01.07.94. Coming into force: 01.08.94. Effect: S.R. 1991/253 revoked. – 4p. – 0 337 91257 2 £1.10

Curriculum (Programme of Study and Attainment Targets in History) Order (Northern Ireland) 1994 No. 256. Enabling power: *S.I. 1989/2406 (N.I. 20), art. 7 (1) (a) (2) (b) (5).* Issued: 08.07.94. Made: 01.07.94. Coming into force: 01.08.94. Effect: S.R. 1991/254 revoked. – 4p. – 0 337 91256 4 £1.10

Curriculum (Programmes of Study and Attainment Targets) (Amendment) Order (Northern Ireland) 1994 No. 258. Enabling power: *S.I. 1989/2406 (N.I. 20), art. 7 (1) (a) (2) (b) (5).* Issued: 08.07.94. Made: 01.07.94. Coming into force: 01.08.94. Effect: S.R. 1990/289, 292; 1992/180, 233; 1993/273 amended & S.R. 1993/252, 253 revoked. – 4p. – 0 337 91258 0 £1.10

Curriculum (Programmes of Study and Attainment Targets in Physical Education) Order (Northern Ireland) 1994 No. 264. Enabling power: *S.I. 1989/2406 (N.I. 20), art. 7 (1) (a) (2) (b) (5).* Issued: 26.07.94. Made: 08.07.94. Coming into force: 01.08.94. In accord. with art. 1 (2). Effect: S.R. 1991/252 revoked. – 4p. – 0 337 91264 5 £1.10

Educational and Library Services Etc. Grants Regulations (Northern Ireland) 1994 No. 55. Enabling power: *S.I. 1986/594 (NI. 3), arts. 115 (1), 134 (1).* Issued: 01.03.94. Made: 18.02.94. Coming into force: 01.04.94. Effect: S.R. & O. (NI) 1973/439 revoked. – 4p. – 0 337 91055 3 £1.10

The Education and Libraries (1993 Order) (Commencement No. 1) Order (Northern Ireland) 1994 No. 127 (C. 3). Enabling power: *S.I. 1993/2810 (NI. 12), art. 1 (4). Bringing into operation various provisions of the 1993 order 01.04.94. for art. 3 & 01.09.94. for art. 4.* Issued: 11.04.94. Made: 28.03.94. Effect: None. – 2p. – 0 337 91127 4 £0.65

Education and Libraries (Competition in Functional Work) Regulations (Northern Ireland) 1994 No. 323. Enabling power: *S.I. 1993/2810 (N.I. 12), arts. 2 (3), 6 (3) (4).* Issued: 24.08.94. Made: 17.08.94. Coming into force: 26.09.94. Effect: None. – 4p. – 0 337 91323 4 £1.10

Education and Libraries (Defined Activities) (Exemptions) Order (Northern Ireland) 1994 No. 325. Enabling power: *S.I. 1993/2810 (N.I. 12), arts. 2 (3), 4 (8), 17 (3).* Issued: 24.08.94. Made: 17.08.94. Coming into force: 26.09.94. Effect: None. – 8p. – 0 337 91325 0 £1.55

Education and Libraries (Specified Periods for Functional Work) Regulations (Northern Ireland) 1994 No. 324. Enabling power: *S.I. 1993/2810 (N.I. 12), arts. 2 (3), 8 (1).* Issued: 24.08.94. Made: 17.08.94. Coming into force: 26.09.94. Effect: None. – 4p. – 0 337 91324 2 £1.10

Education (Individual Pupils' Achievements) (Information) (Amendment) Regulations (Northern Ireland) 1994 No. 122. Enabling power: *S.I. 1986/594 (NI. 3), art. 17A; S.I. 1989/2406 (NI. 20), art. 31 (2) (3).* Issued: 06.04.94. Made: 28.03.94. Coming into force: 28.04.94. Effect: S.R. 1991/351 amended. – 2p. – 0 337 91122 3 £0.65

The Education Reform (1989 Order) (Commencement No. 7) Order (Northern Ireland) 1994 No.296 (C. 10). Enabling power: *S.I. 1989/2406 (N.I. 20), art. 1 (3) (4). Bringing into operation various provisions of the 1989 order on 01.08.94.* Issued: 05.08.94. Made: 26.07.94. Effect: None. –8p. – 0 33791296 3 £1.55

The Education Reform (1989 Order) (Commencement Orders No. 4 and 5) (Amendment) Order (Northern Ireland) 1994 No.295 (C.9). Enabling power: *S.I. 1989/2406 (N.I. 20), art. 1 (3) (4). Bringing into operation various provisions of the 1989 order on 01.08.94.* Issued: 05.08.94. Made: 26.07.94. Effect: S.R. 1991/391 (C. 17); 1993/169 (C. 6) amended. –8p. – 0 33791295 5 £1.95

Education (School Information and Prospectuses) (Amendment No. 2) Regulations (Northern Ireland) 1994 No. 361. Enabling power: *S.I. 1989/2406 (N.I. 20), art. 42 (3) (6).*Issued: 28.09.94. Made: 22.09.94. Coming into force: 18.10.94. Effect: S.R. 1993/370 amended. –2p. – 0 33791361 7 £0.65

Education (School Information and Prospectuses) (Amendment) Regulations (Northern Ireland) 1994 No. 315. Enabling power: *S.I. 1989/2406 (N.I. 20), art. 42 (3) (6).*Issued: 16.08.94. Made: 10.08.94. Coming into force: 03.09.94. Effect: S.R. 1993/370 amended. –4p. – 0 33791315 3 £1.10

The Education (Student Loans) Regulations (Northern Ireland) 1994 No. 230. Enabling power: *S.I. 1990/1506 (N.I. 11), art. 3 (2), paras. 1 (1) (3) (4), 2 (1), 3 (4), sch. 2 & European Economic Area Act 1993, s. 2 (2).* Issued: 29.06.94. Made: 21.06.94. Coming into force: 01.08.94. Effect: S.R. 1993/288 revoked. –20p. – 0 33791230 0 £3.70

Maintenance Allowances (Pupils over Compulsory School Age) Regulations (Northern Ireland) 1994 No. 298. Enabling power: *S.I. 1986/594 (N.I. 3), arts. 50 (1) (2), 134 (1).*Issued: 05.08.94. Made: 28.07.94. Coming into force: 01.09.94. Effect: S.R. 1993/335 revoked. –8p. – 0 33791298 X £1.55

School Admissions (Appeal Tribunals) (Amendment) Regulations (Northern Ireland) 1994 No.238. Enabling power: *S.I. 1989/2406 (N.I. 20), arts. 37 (7), 164 (6) & S.I. 1986/594 (N.I. 3), art. 134 (1).* Issued: 29.07.94. Made: 24.06.94. Coming into force: 01.07.94. Effect: S.R. 1990/126 amended. –2p. – 0 33791238 6 £0.65

Schools (Expulsion of Pupils) (Appeal Tribunals) Regulations (Northern Ireland) 1994 No.13. Enabling power: *S.I. 1986/2810 (NI. 12), arts. 49 (10), 134 (1).* Issued: 26.01.94. Made: 17.01.94. Coming into force: 17.02.94. Effect: None. –6p. – 0 33791013 8 £1.55

Secondary Schools (Admissions Criteria) Regulations (Northern Ireland) 1994 No. 342. Enabling power: *S.I. 1989/2406 (NI. 20), art. 38 (6).* Issued: 16.09.94. Made: 05.09.94. Coming into force: 05.09.94. Effect: S.R. 1990/328; 1993/376 revoked. –4p. – 0 33791342 0 £1.10

ELECTRICITY

Electricity Generating Stations (Permitted Capacity) Order (Northern Ireland) 1994 No.180. Enabling power: *S.I. 1992/231 (NI. 1), art. 39 (3).* Issued: 25.05.94. Made: 05.05.94. Coming into force: 01.07.94. Effect: S.I. 1992/231 (NI. 1) amended. –2p. – 0 33791180 0 £0.65

Electricity (Non-Fossil Fuel Sources) Order (Northern Ireland) 1994 No. 132.Enabling power: *S.I. 1992/231 (NI. 1), art. 35 (1).* Issued: 14.04.94. Made: 31.03.94. Coming into force: 31.03.94. Effect: None. – 8p. – 0 33791132 0 £1.95

ENERGY CONSERVATION

Domestic Energy Efficiency Grants Regulations (Northern Ireland) 1994 No. 306.Enabling power: *S.I. 1990/1511 (N.I. 15), art. 17 (1) (2) (3) (4) (5) (6) (7) (10).* Issued: 11.08.94. Made: 04.08.94. Coming into force: 01.09.94. for regs. 1, 2, 3, 16, 18; 01.01.95. for other regs. Effect: None. – 16p. – 0 33791306 4 £3.20

ENVIRONMENTAL PROTECTION

The Genetically Modified Organisms (1991 Order) (Commencement No. 1) Order (Northern Ireland) 1994 No. 141 (C. 5). Enabling power: *S.I. 1991/1714 (NI. 19), art. 1 (2); Northern Ireland Act 1974, sch. 1, para. 2 (1). Bringing into operation various provisions of the 1991 order on 01.06.94.* Issued: 04.05.94. Made: 12.04.94. Effect: None.–2p. – 0 33791141 X £0.65

The Genetically Modified Organisms (Contained Use) (No. 2) Regulations (Northern Ireland) 1994 No. 145. Enabling power: *S.I. 1991/1714 (NI. 19), arts. 5 (5) (7), 24.* Issued: 04.05.94. Made: 12.04.94. Coming into force: 01.06.94. Effect: None. –4p. – 0 33791145 2 £1.10

The Genetically Modified Organisms (Deliberate Release) Regulations (Northern Ireland) 1994 No. 144. Enabling power: *European Communities Act 1972, s. 2 (2); S.I. 1991/1714 (NI. 19), arts. 3 (4) (5), 4 (8), 8 (1) (4) (5) (7) (11), 19 (1), 20 (7).* Issued: 04.05.94. Made: 12.04.94. Coming into force: 01.06.94. Effect: None. – 24p. – 0 33791144 4 £4.15

The Genetically Modified Organisms (Modification of Article 9 of the 1991 Order) Regulations (Northern Ireland) 1994 No. 142. Enabling power: *European Communities Act 1972, s. 2 (2).* Issued: 04.05.94. Made: 12.04.94. Coming into force: 01.06.94. Effect: S.I. 1991/1714 (NI. 19) amended. –2p. – 0 33791142 8 £0.65

EUROPEAN COMMUNITIES

The Air Quality Standards (Amendment) Regulations (Northern Ireland) 1994 No. 339. Enabling power: *European Communities Act 1972, s. 2 (2).* Issued: 06.09.94. Made: 02.09.94. Coming into force: 04.10.94. Effect: S.R. 1990/145 amended. –2p. – 0 33791339 0 £0.65

Price/availability are liable to change without notice

The Diseases of Animals (Amendment) Regulations (Northern Ireland) 1994 No. 161. Enabling power: *European Communities Act 1972, s. 2 (2)*. Issued: 04.05.94. Made: 25.04.94. Coming into force: 06.06.94. Effect: S.I. 1981/1115 (NI. 22) amended. – 4p. – 0 337 91161 4 *£1.10*

The Genetically Modified Organisms (Deliberate Release) Regulations (Northern Ireland) 1994 No. 144. Enabling power: *European Communities Act 1972, s. 2 (2); S.I. 1991/1714 (NI. 19), arts. 3 (4) (5), 4 (8), 8 (1) (4) (5) (7) (11), 19 (1), 20 (7)*. Issued: 04.05.94. Made: 12.04.94. Coming into force: 01.06.94. Effect: None. – 24p. – 0 337 91144 4 *£4.15*

The Genetically Modified Organisms (Modification of Article 9 of the 1991 Order) Regulations (Northern Ireland) 1994 No. 142. Enabling power: *European Communities Act 1972, s. 2 (2)*. Issued: 04.05.94. Made: 12.04.94. Coming into force: 01.06.94. Effect: S.I. 1991/1714 (NI. 19) amended. – 2p. – 0 337 91142 8 *£0.65*

The Marketing and Use of Dangerous Substances (No. 2) Regulations (Northern Ireland) 1994 No.223. Enabling power: *European Communities Act 1972, s. 2 (2)*. Issued: 26.06.94. Made: 17.06.94. Coming into force: 01.08.94. Effect: None. – 8p. – 0 337 91223 8 *£1.95*

The Marketing and Use of Dangerous Substances (No. 3) Regulations (Northern Ireland) 1994 No.224. Enabling power: *European Communities Act 1972, s. 2 (2)*. Issued: 29.06.94. Made: 17.06.94. Coming into force: 01.08.94. Effect: None. – 4p. – 0 337 91224 6 *£1.10*

The Marketing and Use of Dangerous Substances Regulations (Northern Ireland) 1994 No.222. Enabling power: *European Communities Act 1972, s. 2 (2)*. Issued: 26.06.94. Made: 17.06.94. Coming into force: 01.08.94. Effect: None. – 8p. – 0 337 91222 X *£1.95*

The Maternity Allowance and Statutory Maternity Pay Regulations (Northern Ireland) 1994 No.176. Enabling power: *European Communities Act 1972, s. 2 (2)*. Issued: 16.05.94. Made: 04.05.94. Coming into force: 04.09.94. for Regulation 5. 16.10.94. for all other purposes. Effect: 1992 c.7 amended. – 8p. – 0 337 91176 2 *£1.55*

Motor Vehicles (Construction and Use) (Amendment No. 3) Regulations (Northern Ireland) 1994 No. 452. Enabling power: *S.I. 1981/154 (N.I. 1), arts. 28 (1), 214 (1), 218 (1)*. Issued: 28.11.94. Made: 18.11.94. Coming into force: 01.01.95. Effect: S.R. 1989/299 amended. – 12p. – 0 337 91452 4 *£2.40*

Motor Vehicles (Type Approval) (EEC) (Revocation) Regulations (Northern Ireland) 1994 No.240. Enabling power: *European Communities Act 1972, s. 2 (2)*. Issued: 08.07.94. Made: 27.06.94. Coming into force: 15.08.94. Effect: S.R. 1987/306; 1988/310, 403 amended. – 2p. – 0 337 91240 8 *£0.65*

The Pollution of Groundwater by Dangerous Substances Regulations (Northern Ireland) 1994 No.147. Enabling power: *European Communities Act 1972, s. 2 (2)*. Issued: 20.04.94. Made: 13.04.94. Coming into force: 04.05.94. Effect: None. – 4p. – 0 337 91147 9 *£1.10*

The Public Health (Metrication) Regulations (Northern Ireland) 1994 No. 193. Enabling power: *S.I. 1978/1049 (NI. 19), art. 82 (1)*. Issued: 26.05.94. Made: 23.05.94. Coming into force: 04.07.94. Effect: 1878 c. 52, 1907 c. 53 amended. – 2p. – 0 337 91193 2 *£0.65*

Roads (Assessment of Environmental Effects) Regulations (Northern Ireland) 1994 No.316. Enabling power: *European Communities Act 1972, s. 2 (2)*. Issued: 19.08.94. Made: 12.08.94. Coming into force: 30.09.94. Effect: S.I. 1993/3160 (N.I. 15) amended. – 2p. – 0 337 91316 1 *£0.65*

FAIR EMPLOYMENT

Fair Employment (Increase of Compensation Limit) Order (Northern Ireland) 1994 No.50. Enabling power: *Fair Employment (Northern Ireland) Act 1989, s. 26 (9)*. Issued: 22.02.94. Made: 15.02.94. Coming into force: 15.03.94. Effect: None. – 2p. – 0 337 91050 2 *£0.65*

FAMILY LAW

The Child Support (Miscellaneous Amendments and Transitional Provisions) Regulations (Northern Ireland) 1994 No.37. Enabling power: *S.I. 1991/2628 (NI. 23), arts. 18, 19 (6), 32 (1) (2), 39 (3) (4), 44, 47, 48 (4), sch. 1, paras. 1 (3), 4 (1), 6 (6), 8 (a)*. Issued: 09.02.94. Made: 03.02.94. Coming into force: 07.02.94. Effect: S.R. 1992/340; 1992/341; 1992/390; 1993/73 amended. – 12p. – 0 337 91037 5 *£2.80*

The Child Support (Northern Ireland) Order 1991 (Consequential Amendments) Order (Northern Ireland) 1994 No. 259. Enabling power: *S.I. 1991/2628 (N.I. 23), art. 51 (1)*. Issued: 08.07.94. Made: 01.07.94. Coming into force: 15.08.94. Effect: S.I. 1981/1675 (N.I. 26) amended. – 2p. – 0 337 91259 9 *£0.65*

FIRE SERVICES

Fire Services (Appointments and Promotion) (Amendment) Regulations (Northern Ireland) 1994 No. 228. Enabling power: *S.I. 1984/1821 (N.I. 11), art. 9 (5)*. Issued: 30.06.94. Made: 16.06.94. Coming into force: 01.08.94. Effect: S.R. 1979/167 amended. – 4p. – 0 337 91228 9 *£1.10*

FISHERIES

Angling (Department of Agriculture Waters) Amendment Byelaws (Northern Ireland) 1994 No.40. Enabling power: *Fisheries Act (Northern Ireland) 1966, s. 26 (1)*. Issued: 15.02.94. Made: 04.02.94. Coming into force: 09.03.94. Effect: S.R. 1989/482 amended. – 2p. – 0 337 91040 5 *£0.65*

Angling (Department of Agriculture Waters) (Amendment No. 2) Byelaws (Northern Ireland) 1994 No. 314.
Enabling power: *Fisheries Act (Northern Ireland) 1966, s. 26 (1).* Issued: 19.08.94. Made: 08.08.94. Coming into force: 13.09.94. Effect: S.R. 1989/482 amended. –4p. – 0 337 91314 5 £1.10

Eel Fishing (Amendment) Regulations (Northern Ireland) 1994 No. 441. Enabling power: *Fisheries Act (Northern Ireland) 1966, s. 15.* Issued: 28.11.94. Made: 10.11.94. Coming into force: 30.12.94. Effect: S.R. 1979/19 amended. – 2p. – 0 337 91441 9 £0.65

Eel Fishing (Licence Duties) Regulations (Northern Ireland) 1994 No. 438. Enabling power: *Fisheries Act (Northern Ireland) 1966, ss. 15 (1), 19 (1).* Issued: 22.11.94. Made: 09.11.94. Coming into force: 01.01.95. Effect: S.R. 1993/440 revoked. – 4p. – 0 337 91438 9 £1.10

Fisheries Amendment Byelaws (Northern Ireland) 1994 No. 10. Enabling power: *Fisheries Act (Northern Ireland) 1966, ss. 26 (1), 37.* Issued: 21.01.94. Made: 10.01.94. Coming into force: 14.02.94. Effect: S.R. 1989/483 amended. – 2p. – 0 337 91010 3 £0.65

Fisheries (Licence Duties) Byelaws (Northern Ireland) 1994 No. 460. Enabling power: *Fisheries Act (Northern Ireland) 1966, ss. 261 (1), 114 (1) (b), 115 (1) (b).* Issued: 05.12.94. Made: 23.11.94. Coming into force: 01.01.95. Effect: S.R. (N.I.) 1989/483 amended. –8p. – 0 337 91460 5 £1.95

FOOD

The Drinking Water in Containers Regulations (Northern Ireland) 1994 No. 185. Enabling power: *S.I. 1991/762 (NI. 7), arts. 16 (1) (3), 26 (3), 47 (2).* Issued: 25.05.94. Made: 12.05.94. Coming into force: 20.06.94. Effect: None. –8p. – 0 337 91185 1 £1.95

The Flavourings in Food (Amendment) Regulations (Northern Ireland) 1994 No. 270. Enabling power: *S.I. 1991/762 (N.I. 7), arts. 15 (1) (a) (e), 25 (1) (3), 47 (2).* Issued: 02.08.94. Made: 14.07.94. Coming into force: 22.08.94. Effect: S.R. 1992/416; 1984/407 amended. – 4p. – 0 33791270 X £1.10

The Food Labelling (Amendment) Regulations (Northern Ireland) 1994 No. 214. Enabling power: *S.I. 1991/762 (N.I. 7), arts. 15 (1) (e), 16 (1), 25 (1) (a) (3), 26 (3), 47 (2).* Issued: 29.06.94. Made: 09.06.94. Coming into force: 01.03.95. Effect: S.R. 1984/407 amended. – 12p. – 0 337 91214 9 £2.80

The Materials and Articles in Contact with Food (Amendment) Regulations (Northern Ireland) 1994 No. 174. Enabling power: *European Communities Act 1972, s. 2 (2).* Issued: 11.05.94. Made: 04.05.94. Coming into force: 08.06.94. for all exc. reg. 2 (6); 01.07.94. for reg 2 (6). Effect: S.R. 1987/432 amended. – 8p. – 0 337 91174 6 £1.55

The Preserved Tuna and Bonito (Marketing Standards) Regulations (Northern Ireland) 1994 No. 425. Enabling power: *S.I. 1991/762 (N.I. 7), art. 16 (2).* Issued: 03.11.94. Made: 28.10.94. Coming into force: 01.12.94. Effect: S.R. 1984/407 amended. – 4p. – 0 337 91425 7 £1.10

The Quick-frozen Foodstuffs (Amendment) Regulations (Northern Ireland) 1994 No. 52. Enabling power: *S.I. 1991/762 (NI. 7), arts. 15 (1), 16 (1), 25 (1) (a) (2) (a) (3), 26 (3), 47 (2).* Issued: 23.02.94. Made: 17.02.94. Coming into force: 01.09.94. Effect: S.R. 1990/455 amended. – 4p. – 0 337 91052 9 £1.10

GAME

Game Birds Preservation Order (Northern Ireland) 1994 No. 220. Enabling power: *Game Preservation Act (Northern Ireland) 1928, ss. 7C (1), 7F & Northern Ireland Act 1974, sch. 1, para. 2 (1).* Issued: 22.06.94. Made: 14.06.94. Coming into force: 11.08.94. Effect: None. – 2p. – 0 337 91220 3 £0.65

GAS

Gas Supply Code (Premier Energy Suppliers Limited) Order (Northern Ireland) 1994 No. 367. Enabling power: *S.I. 1977/596 (N.I. 7), art 3 (2).* Issued: 12.10.94. Made: 27.09.94. Coming into force: 07.11.94. Effect: None. – 2p. – 0 337 91367 6 £0.65

Gas Undertaker (Premier Energy Suppliers Limited) Order (Northern Ireland) 1994 No. 293. Enabling power: *S.I. 1977/596 (N.I. 7), art. 14 (1).* Issued: 03.08.94. Made: 25.07.94. Coming into force: 12.09.94. Effect: None. – 2p. – 0 337 91293 9 £0.65

Gas Undertaker (Premier Transco Limited) Order (Northern Ireland) 1994 No. 41. Enabling power: *S.I. 1977/596 (NI. 7), art. 14 (1).* Issued: 15.02.94. Made: 07.02.94. Coming into force: 01.04.94. Effect: None. – 2p. – 0 337 91041 3 £0.65

GENERAL MEDICAL SERVICES

Medical Practitioners (Vocational Training) (Amendment) Regulations (Northern Ireland) 1994 No. 499. Enabling power: *S.I. 1978/1907 (NI. 26), art. 8.* Issued: 31.01.95. Made: 22.12.94. Coming into force: 01.01.95. Effect: S.R. 1979/460 amended. – 8p. – 0 337 91206 8 £1.55

HARBOURS, DOCKS, ETC.

The Warrenpoint Harbour Authority (Amendment) Order (Northern Ireland) 1994 No. 399. Enabling power: *Harbours Act (Northern Ireland) 1970, sch. 1, s. 1.* Issued: 01.11.94. Made: 20.10.94. Coming into force: 01.12.94. Effect: S.R.& O. (N.I.) 1971/136 amended. –4p. – 0 337 91399 4 £1.10

Price/availability are liable to change without notice

HEALTH AND PERSONAL SOCIAL SERVICES

The Belfast City Hospital Health and Social Services Trust (Establishment) (Amendment) Order (Northern Ireland) 1994 No. 108. Enabling power: *S.I. 1991/194 (NI 1), art. 10 (1), sch. 3, paras. 1, 3, 3A.* Issued: 25.04.94. Made: 25.03.94. Coming into force: 01.04.94. Effect: S.R. 1992/490 amended. – 4p. – 0 337911088 *£1.10*

Charges for Drugs and Appliances (Amendment) Regulations (Northern Ireland) 1994 No.124. Enabling power: *S.I. 1972/1265 (NI. 14), arts. 98, 106, sch. 15.* Issued: 11.03.94. Made: 29.03.94. Coming into force: 01.04.94. Effect: SR & O (NI) 1973/419 amended. – 4p. – 0 337 91124 X *£1.10*

The Craigavon and Banbridge Community Health and Social Services Trust (Establishment) (Amendment) Order (Northern Ireland) 1994 No. 114. Enabling power: *S.I. 1991/194 (NI 1), art. 10 (1), sch. 3, paras. 1, 3, 3A.* Issued: 25.04.94. Made: 25.03.94. Coming into force: 01.04.94. Effect: S.R. 1993/456 amended. – 8p. – 0 337 91114 2 *£1.55*

Dental Charges (Amendment) Regulations (Northern Ireland) 1994 No. 95. Enabling power: *S.I. 1972/1265 (NI. 14), arts. 98, 106, sch. 15.* Issued: 31.03.94. Made: 16.03.94. Coming into force: 01.04.94. Effect: S.R. 1989/111; 1993/139 amended. – 4p. – 0 337910952 *£1.10*

The Down Lisburn Health and Social Services Trust (Establishment) (Amendment) Order (Northern Ireland) 1994 No. 110. Enabling power: *S.I. 1991/194 (NI 1), art. 10 (1), sch. 3, paras. 1, 3, 3A.* Issued: 25.04.94. Made: 25.03.94. Coming into force: 01.04.94. Effect: S.R. 1993/355 amended. – 8p. – 0 337 91110 X *£1.55*

General Medical and Pharmaceutical Services (Amendment No. 2) Regulations (Northern Ireland) 1994 No. 403. Enabling power: *S.I. 1972/1265 (N.I. 14), arts. 56 (2), 63 (2), 106 (b), 107 (6).* Issued: 01.11.94. Made: 21.10.94. Coming into force: 01.11.94. Effect: S.R. & O. (N.I.) 1973/421 amended. – 8p. – 0 3379 14036 *£1.55*

General Medical and Pharmaceutical Services (Amendment No. 3) Regulations (Northern Ireland) 1994 No. 500. Enabling power: *S.I. 1972/1265 (N.I. 14), arts. 56, 106, 107 (6).* Issued: 17.01.95. Made: 22.12.94. Coming into force: 01.01.95. Effect: S.R. & O. (N.I.) 1973/421 amended. – 4p. – 0 337911053 *£1.10*

General Medical and Pharmaceutical Services (Amendment) Regulations (Northern Ireland) 1994 No. 117. Enabling power: *S.I. 1972/1265, arts. 56, 63, 106, 107 (6).* Issued: 06.04.94. Made: 28.03.94. Coming into force: 01.04.94. Effect: S.R. & O 1988/395 amended. – 8p. – 0 337911177 *£1.55*

The Health and Personal Social Services (Assessment of Resources) (Amendment) Regulations (Northern Ireland) 1994 No. 160. Enabling power: *S.I. 1972/1265 (NI. 14), arts. 36 (6), 99 (5).* Issued: 04.05.94. Made: 22.04.94. Coming into force: 02.05.94. Effect: S.R. 1993/127 amended. – 4p. – 0 337911606 *£1.10*

The Health and Personal Social Services (Superannuation) (Amendment No. 3) Regulations (Northern Ireland) 1994 No. 203. Enabling power: *S.I. 1972/1073 (N.I. 10), sch. 3, arts. 12, 14.* Issued: 14.06.94. Made: 26.05.94. Coming into force: 01.07.94. Effect: S.R. 1984/336 amended. – 4p. – 0 337912033 *£1.10*

The Health and Social Services Trusts (Consequential Amendments No. 2) Regulations (Northern Ireland) 1994 No. 66. Enabling power: *S.I. 1994/429 (NI. 2), art. 3 (11).* Issued: 08.03.94. Made: 01.03.94. Coming into force: 01.04.94. Effect: S.I. 1986/595 amended. – 2p. – 0 337910669 *£0.65*

The Health and Social Services Trusts (Consequential Amendments) Regulations (Northern Ireland) 1994 No. 65. Enabling power: *S.I. 1994/429 (NI. 2), art. 3 (11).* Issued: 08.03.94. Made: 01.03.94. Coming into force: 01.04.94. Effect: S.R. 1974/318; 1975/113, 293; 1976/19; 1984/245; 1985/365; 1986/174, 193; 1987/459, 461, 463, 465; 1989/253; 1992/20, 32, 78, 339, 340, 341; 1993/91, 92, 127, 163 amended. – 32p. – 0 337910650 *£5.20*

The Health and Social Services Trusts (Consultation on Dissolution) (Amendment) Regulations (Northern Ireland) 1994 No. 57. Enabling power: *S.I. 1991/194 (NI. 1), sch. 3, paras. 23 (3), 24 (3).* Issued: 08.03.94. Made: 21.02.94. Coming into force: 01.04.94. Effect: S.R. 1992/255 amended. – 4p. – 0 33791057 X *£1.10*

The Health and Social Services Trusts (Exercise of Functions) Regulations (Northern Ireland) 1994 No. 64. Enabling power: *S.I. 1994/429 (NI. 2), art. 3 (2).* Issued: 08.03.94. Made: 01.03.94. Coming into force: 01.04.94. Effect: None. – 4p. – 0 337910642 *£1.10*

The Health and Social Services Trusts (Membership and Procedure) Regulations (Northern Ireland) 1994 No. 63. Enabling power: *S.I. 1991/194 (NI. 1), art. 10 (6).* Issued: 08.03.94. Made: 01.03.94. Coming into force: 01.04.94. Effect: S.R. 1991/450 revoked. – 16p. – 0 337910634 *£3.20*

The Health and Social Services Trusts (Public Meetings) Regulations (Northern Ireland) 1994 No. 62. Enabling power: *S.I. 1991/194 (NI. 1), sch. 3, para. 7 (2) (3).* Issued: 08.03.94. Made: 01.03.94. Coming into force: 01.04.94. Effect: None. – 2p. – 0 337910626 *£0.65*

The Health and Social Services Trusts (Originating Capital Debt) Order (Northern Ireland) 1994 No. 303. Enabling power: *S.I. 1991/194 (N.I. 1), art. 14 (1) (4).* Issued: 08.08.94. Made: 02.08.94. Coming into force: 02.08.94. Effect: S.R. 1994/140 revoked. – 4p. – 0 33791303 X *£1.10*

The HSS Trusts (Originating Capital Debt) Order (Northern Ireland) 1994 No. 140. Enabling power: *S.I. 199/194 (NI. 1), art. 14 (1) (4).* Issued: 25.05.94. Made: 31.03.94. Coming into force: 31.03.94. Effect: None. – 4p. – 0337911401 *£1.10*

The Mater Infirmorum Hospital Health and Social Services Trust (Establishment) (Amendment) Order (Northern Ireland) 1994 No. 116. Enabling power: *S.I. 1991/194 (NI 1), art. 10 (1), sch. 3, paras. 1, 3, 3A.* Issued: 25.04.94. Made: 25.03.94. Coming into force: 01.04.94. Effect: S.R. 1994/67 amended. – 4p. – 0337911169 *£1.10*

Price/availability are liable to change without notice

The Mater Infirmorum Hospital Health and Social Services Trust (Establishment) Order (Northern Ireland) 1994 No. 67. Enabling power: S.I. 1991/194 (NI. 1), art. 10 (1), sch. 3, paras. 1, 3, 4, 5, 6 (2) (d). Issued: 08.03.94. Made: 01.03.94. Coming into force: 01.03.94. Effect: None. – 4p. – 0 337 91067 7 £1.10

The Newry and Mourne Health and Social Services Trust (Establishment) (Amendment) Order (Northern Ireland) 1994 No. 115. Enabling power: S.I. 1991/194 (NI. 1), art. 10 (1) & sch. 3, paras. 1, 3, 3A. Issued: 27.04.94. Made: 25.03.94. Coming into force: 01.04.94. Effect: S.R. 1993/455 amended. – 8p. – 0 337 91115 0 £1.55

The North and West Belfast Health and Social Services Trust (Establishment) (Amendment) Order (Northern Ireland) 1994 No. 112. Enabling power: S.I. 1991/194 (NI 1), art. 10 (1), sch. 3, paras. 1, 3, 3A. Issued: 25.04.94. Made: 25.03.94. Coming into force: 01.04.94. Effect: S.R. 1993/352 amended. – 8p. – 0 337 91112 6 £1.55

The North Down and Ards Community Health and Social Services Trust (Establishment) (Amendment) Order (Northern Ireland) 1994 No. 111. Enabling power: S.I. 1991/194 (NI 1), art. 10 (1), sch. 3, paras. 1, 3, 3A. Issued: 25.04.94. Made: 25.03.94. Coming into force: 01.04.94. Effect: S.R. 1993/354 amended. – 8p. – 0 337 91111 8 £1.55

The Northern Ireland Blood Transfusion Service (Special Agency) (Establishment and Constitution) Order (Northern Ireland) 1994 No. 175. Enabling power: S.I. 1990/247 (NI. 3), art. 3 (1) (2) (4) (6). Issued: 16.05.94. Made: 04.05.94. Coming into force: 01.06.94. Effect: None. – 4p. – 0 337 91175 4 £1.10

The Northern Ireland Regional Medical Physics Agency (Establishment and Constitution) Order 1994 No. 42. Enabling power: S.I. 1990/247 (NI. 3), art. 3 (1) (2) (4) (6). Issued: 14.02.94. Made: 08.02.94. Coming into force: 01.04.94. Effect: None. – 4p. – 0 337 91042 1 £1.10

Optical Charges and Payments (Amendment No. 2) Regulations (Northern Ireland) 1994 No.100. Enabling power: S.I. 1972/1265 (NI. 14), arts. 98, 106, sch. 15. Issued: 31.03.94. Made: 18.03.94. Coming into force: 01.04.94. Effect: S.R. 1989/114 amended. – 8p. – 0 337 91100 2 £1.55

Optical Charges and Payments (Amendment No. 3) Regulations (Northern Ireland) 1994 No.388. Enabling power: S.I. 1972/1265 (N.I. 14), arts. 98, 106, sch. 15. Issued: 26.10.94. Made: 13.10.94. Coming into force: 01.11.94. Effect: S.R. 1989/114 amended. – 2p. – 0 337 91388 9 £0.65

Optical Charges and Payments (Amendment) Regulations (Northern Ireland) 1994 No. 31. Enabling power: S.I. 1972/1265 (NI. 14), arts. 98, 106, sch. 15. Issued: 07.02.94. Made: 31.01.94. Coming into force: 21.02.94. Effect: S.R. 1989/114 amended. – 2p. – 0 337 91031 6 £0.65

The South and East Belfast Health and Social Services Trust (Establishment) (Amendment) Order (Northern Ireland) 1994 No. 113. Enabling power: S.I. 1991/194 (NI 1), art. 10 (1), sch. 3, paras. 1, 3, 3A. Issued: 25.04.94. Made: 25.03.94. Coming into force: 01.04.94. Effect: S.R. 1993/353 amended. – 8p. – 0 337 91113 4 £1.55

The Ulster, North Down and Ards Hospitals Health and Social Services Trust (Establishment) (Amendment) Order (Northern Ireland) 1994 No. 109. Enabling power: S.I. 1991/194 (NI 1), art. 10 (1), sch. 3, paras. 1, 3, 3A. Issued: 25.04.94. Made: 25.03.94. Coming into force: 01.04.94. Effect: S.R. 1992/494 amended. – 4p. – 0 337 91109 6 £1.10

HEALTH AND SAFETY

Asbestos (Licensing) (Fees Amendment) Regulations (Northern Ireland) 1994 No. 276. Enabling power: S.I. 1978/1039 (N.I. 9), art. 40 (2) (4). Issued: 02.08.94. Made: 21.07.94. Coming into force: 05.09.94. Effect: S.R. 1984/205 amended & S.R. 1992/34 revoked. – 2p. – 0 337 91276 9 £0.65

Control of Industrial Major Accident Hazards (Amendment) Regulations (Northern Ireland) 1994 No. 44. Enabling power: S.I. 1978/1039 (NI. 9), arts. 17 (1) (2) (3) (5) (6), 40 (2) (4), 55 (2), sch. 3, paras. 1 (1) (2), 14 (1), 19. Issued: 22.02.94. Made: 10.02.94. Coming into force: 21.03.94. Effect: S.R. 1985/175 amended. – 4p. – 0 337 91044 8 £1.10

Diving Operations at Work Regulations (Northern Ireland) 1994 No. 146. Enabling power: S.I. 1978/1039 (NI. 9), arts. 17 (1) (2) (3) (4) (5), 54 (1), 55 (2) & sch. 3, paras. 1 (1) (2), 4, 5, 6, 7, 8, 9, 10, 13, 14, 15, 19, 20 (a) (b) (c). Issued: 04.05.94. Made: 12.04.94. Coming into force: 01.08.94.;for some purposes.01.08.95;for other purposes. Effect: S.I. 1975/116; 1976/923; S.R. 1982/429 amended & S.R. 1983/209 revoked. – 36p. – 0 337 91146 0 £5.70

Genetically Modified Organisms (Contained Use) Regulations (Northern Ireland) 1994 No.143. Enabling power: *European Communities Act 1972, s. 2 (2)*. Issued: 20.04.94. Made: 12.04.94. Coming into force: 01.06.94. Effect: S.I. 1978/1039 (NI. 9) amended & S.R. 1991/238 revoked. – 36p. – 0 337 91143 6 £5.70

Health and Safety (Medical Fees) Regulations (Norhern Ireland) 1994 No. 277. Enabling power: S.I. 1978/1039 (N.I. 9), arts. 49, 55 (2). Issued: 02.08.94. Made: 21.07.94. Coming into force: 05.09.94. Effect: S.R. 1992/440 amended. – 8p. – 0 337 91277 7 £1.95

Health and Safety (Petroleum-Spirit License Fees) Regulations (Northern Ireland) 1994 No.260. Enabling power: S.I. 1978/1039 (N.I. 9), art. 40 (2) (3). Issued: 08.07.94. Made: 01.07.94. Coming into force: 01.08.94. Effect: S.R. 1992/396 amended. – 8p. – 0 337 91260 2 £1.55

Health and Safety (Training for Employment) Regulations (Northern Ireland) 1994 No.1. Enabling power: S.I. 1978/1039 (NI. 9). art. 2 (5). Issued: 21.01.94. Made: 10.01.94. Coming into force: 07.03.94. Effect: S.R. 1985/121 revoked. – 4p. – 0 337 91001 4 £1.10

Management of Health and Safety at Work (Amendment) Regulations (Northern Ireland) 1994 No.478. Enabling power: S.I. 1978/1039 (N.I. 9), arts. 17 (1) (2) (5), 43 (2), sch. 3, paras. 6, 7 (1). Issued: 15.12.94. Made: 07.12.94. Coming into force: 09.01.95. Effect: S.R. 1992/459 amended. – 8p. – 0 337 91478 8 £1.55

Price/availability are liable to change without notice

Notification of Cooling Towers and Evaporative Condensers Regulations (Northern Ireland) 1994 No. 38. Enabling power: *S.I. 1978/1039 (NI. 9), arts. 17 (1) (2) (4), 55 (2), sch. 3, para. 14 (1)*. Issued: 22.02.94. Made: 04.02.94. Coming into force: 29.03.94. Effect: None. – 4p. – 0 33791038 3 £1.10

Notification of New Substances Regulations (Northern Ireland) 1994 No. 6. Enabling power: *European Communities Act 1972, s. 2 (2), S.I. 1978/1039 (NI. 9), arts. 17 (1) (2) (3) (4) (5), 40 (2) (4), 55 (2), sch. 3, paras. 1 (1) (4) (5), 14 (1), 15*. Issued: 21.01.94. Made: 12.01.94. Coming into force: 28.02.94. Effect: S.R. 1993/412 amended & S.R. 1985/63, 1986/188, 1991/472 revoked. – 48p. – 0 33791006 5 £6.35

Offshore Installations (Life-saving Appliances and Fire-fighting Equipment) (Fees) Regulations (Northern Ireland) 1994 No. 239. Enabling power: *S.I. 1978/1039 (N.I. 9), arts. 17 (1) (3) (a), 40 (2) (3) (4)*. Issued: 08.07.94. Made: 27.06.94. Coming into force: 01.08.94. Effect: S.I. 1977/486; 1978/611 amended & S.I. 1990/707 revoked. – 8p. – 0 33791239 4 £1.55

HORSE RACING

Horse Racing (Charges on Bookmakers) Order (Northern Ireland) 1994 No. 189. Enabling power: *S.I. 1990/1508 (NI. 12), art. 9 (1)*. Issued: 01.06.94. Made: 18.05.94. Coming into force: 01.07.94. Effect: S.R. 1993/237 revoked. – 2p. – 0 33791189 4 £0.65

HORTICULTURAL PRODUCE

Apple Orchard Grubbing Up (Amendment) Regulations (Northern Ireland) 1994 No. 430. Enabling power: *European Communities Act 1972, s. 2 (2)*. Issued: 08.11.94. Made: 03.11.94. Coming into force: 03.11.94. Effect: S.R. 1991/157 amended. – 8p. – 0 33791430 3 £1.95

HORTICULTURE

Farm and Conservation Grant (Amendment) Scheme (Northern Ireland) 1994 No. 463. Enabling power: *S.I. 1987/166 (N.I. 1), art. 16 (1) (2)*. Issued: 05.01.95. Made: 29.11.94. Coming into force: 30.11.94. Effect: S.R. 1989/38 amended. – 2p. – 0 33791463 X £0.65

Farm Conservation Grant (Amendment) Regulations (Northern Ireland) 1994 No. 464. Enabling power: *European Communities Act 1972, s. 2 (2)*. Issued: 05.01.94. Made: 29.11.94. Coming into force: 30.11.94. Effect: S.R. 1991/264 amended. 2p. 0 33791464 8 £0.65

HOUSING

Homes Insulation Scheme and Grants (Amendment No. 2) Order (Northern Ireland) 1994 No.85. Enabling power: *S.I. 1981/156 (NI. 3), arts. 86 (1) (2) (3) (4) (a) (5) (7)*. Issued: 11.03.94. Made: 09.03.94. Coming into force: 01.04.94. Effect: S.R. 1991/29 amended & S.R. 1992/183 revoked. – 4p. – 0 33791085 5 £1.10

Homes Insulation Scheme and Grants (Amendment) Order (Northern Ireland) 1994 No. 53. Enabling power: *S.I. 1981/156 (NI. 3), art. 86 (1) (2) (3) (4) (a) (5) (7)*. Issued: 23.02.94. Made: 18.02.94. Coming into force: 24.02.94. Effect: S.R. 1991/29 amended. – 2p. – 0 33791053 7 £0.65

Homes Insulation Scheme and Grants (Revocation) Order (Northern Ireland) 1994 No.447. Enabling power: *S.I 1981/156 (N.I. 3), arts. 86 (1) (2) (3) (4) (a) (5) (7)*. Issued: 22.11.94. Made: 17.11.94. Coming into force: 01.01.95. Effect: S.R. 1991/29; 1994/53, 85 revoked. – 2p. – 0 33791447 8 £0.65

The Housing Benefit (General) (Amendment No. 2) Regulations (Northern Ireland) 1994 No.81. Enabling power: *Social Security Contributions and Benefits (Northern Ireland) Act 1992, ss. 122 (1) (d), 129 (4), 131 (1)*. Issued: 15.03.94. Made: 07.03.94. Coming into force: 01.04.94.; 04.04.94. Effect: S.R. 1987/461 amended & S.R. 1993/154 revoked. – 8p. – 0 33791081 2 £1.95

The Housing Benefit (General) (Amendment No. 3) Regulations (Northern Ireland) 1994 No.88. Enabling power: *Social Security Contributions and Benefits (Northern Ireland) Act 1992, ss. 122 (1) (d), 132 (3) (4) (a) (b), & Social Security Administration (Northern Ireland) Act 1992, s. 61 (3)*. Issued: 31.03.94. Made: 11.03.94. Coming into force: 01.04.94. for reg. 1, 04.04.94. for all others Effect: S.R. 1987/461 amended. – 8p. – 0 33791088 X £1.95

The Housing Benefit (General) (Amendment No. 4) Regulations (Northern Ireland) 1994 No.137. Enabling power: *Social Security Contributions and Benefits (Northern Ireland) Act 1992, ss. 122 (1) (d), 129 (4), 131 (1)*. Issued: 18.04.94. Made: 08.04.94. Coming into force: 01.05.94. Effect: S.R. 1987/461 amended. – 2p. – 0 33791137 1 £0.65

The Housing Benefit (General) (Amendment) Regulations (Northern Ireland) 1994 No.80. Enabling power: *Social Security Contributions and Benefits (Northern Ireland) Act 1992, ss. 122 (1) (d), 133 (2) (i)*. Issued: 15.03.94. Made: 07.03.94. Coming into force: 01.04.94.; 04.04.94. Effect: S.R. 1987/461 amended. – 8p. – 0 33791080 4 £1.95

The Housing Benefit (Miscellaneous Amendments) Regulations (Northern Ireland) 1994 No.335. Enabling power: *Social Security Contributions and Benefits (Northern Ireland) Act 1992, ss. 122 (1) (d), 131 (1) (6), 132 (3) (4) (a) (b) & Social Security Administration (Northern Ireland) Act 1992, ss. 5 (1) (q), 61, 120 (1) (2)*. Issued: 06.09.94. Made: 31.08.94. Coming into force: 03.10.94. Effect: S.R. 1987/461; 1988/118; 1993/145 amended. –12p. – 0 33791335 8 £2.80

Housing (Prescribed Forms) (Amendment) Regulations 1994 No. 481. Enabling power: *S.I. 1981/156 (NI. 3), arts. 162, sch. 4, paras. 1, 2, 6*. Issued: 20.12.94. Made: 30.11.94. Coming into force: 20.01.95. Effect: S.R. 1994/156 amended. – 12p. – 0 33791481 8 £2.80

Price/availability are liable to change without notice

Housing (Prescribed Forms) Regulations (Northern Ireland) 1994 No. 156. Enabling power: *S.I. 1981/156 (NI. 3), art. 162.* Issued: 01.06.94. Made: 15.04.94. Coming into force: 20.06.94. Effect: S.R. & O.(NI) 1963/9; 1968/241; 1971/275 revoked. – 36p. – 0 337911568 £5.70

Housing Renovation etc. Grants (Reduction of Grant) (Amendment) Regulations (Northern Ireland) 1994 No. 348. Enabling power: *S.I. 1992/1725, art. 47.* Issued: 16.09.94. Made: 08.09.94. Coming into force: 17.10.94. Effect: S.R. 1992/412 amended. – 16p. – 0 33791348 X £3.20

The Social Security Benefits Up-Rating Order (Northern Ireland) 1994 No. 74. Enabling power: *Social Security Administration (Northern Ireland) Act 1992, s. 132.* Issued: 17.03.94. Made: 07.03.94. Coming into force: 01.04.94.; 03.04.94.; 06.04.94.; 11.04.94.; 12.04.94.; 13.04.94. per art. 1 (1). Effect: 1966 c. 6 (NI); 1992 c. 7; S.R. 1976/223; 1978/105; 1987/30, 459, 460, 463; S.R. 1992/32, 78 amended & S.R. 1993/150 revoked. – 40p. – 0 33791074 X £5.70

INDUSTRIAL AND PROVIDENT SOCIETIES

Industrial and Provident Societies (Fees) (Amendment) Regulations (Northern Ireland) 1994 No.437. Enabling power: *Industrial and Provident Societies Act (Northern Ireland) 1969, ss. 29 (2) (3) (4), 97 (1).* Issued: 16.11.94. Made: 08.11.94. Coming into force: 21.12.94. Effect: S.R. & O. (N.I.) 1969/353 amended & S.R. 1993/422 revoked. – 8p. – 0 337914370 £1.95

INDUSTRIAL RELATIONS

Industrial Relations (1993 Order) (Commencement No. 2) Order (Northern Ireland) 1994 No.215 (C. 7). Enabling power: *S.I. 1993/2668 (N.I. 11), sch. 7, art. 1, para. 1. Bringing into operation various provisions of the 1993 order subject to para. 2 on 01.07.94.* Issued: 21.06.94. Made: 10.06.94. Effect: None. – 2p. – 0 337912157 £0.65

Industrial Relations (Continuity of Employment) Regulations (Northern Ireland) 1994 No.3. Enabling power: *S.I. 1976/1043 (NI. 16), art. 68 (4).* Issued: 21.01.94. Made: 11.01.94. Coming into force: 07.02.94. Effect: S.R. 1976/261 revoked. – 4p. – 0 337910030 £1.10

Industrial Relations (Deregulation and Contracting Out Act 1994) (Commencement) Order (Northern Ireland) 1994 No. 488 (C. 17). Enabling power: *Deregulation and Contracting Out Act 1994, s. 82 (6). Bringing into operation various provisions of the 1994 act on 03.01.95.* Issued: 21.12.94. Made: 15.12.94. Effect: None. – 4p. – 0 337914885 £1.10

Industrial Tribunals Extension of Jurisdiction Order (Northern Ireland) 1994 No. 308. Enabling power: *S.I. 1976/2147 (N.I. 28), arts. 57 (1) (4A) (5), 63 (4).* Issued: 08.08.94. Made: 04.08.94. Coming into force: 18.09.94. Effect: None. – 8p. – 0 337913080 £1.55

Maternity (Compulsory Leave) Regulations (Northern Ireland) 1994 No. 379. Enabling power: *European Communities Act 1972, s. 2 (2).* Issued: 12.10.94. Made: 07.10.94. Coming into force: 01.11.94. Effect: None. – 4p. – 0 33791379 X £1.10

Suspension from Work (on Maternity Grounds) Order (Northern Ireland) 1994 No. 479. Enabling power: *S.I. 1976/2147 (N.I. 28), art. 26 (3).* Issued: 15.12.94. Made: 07.12.94. Coming into force: 09.01.95. Effect: None. – 2p. – 0 337914796 £0.65

INDUSTRIAL TRAINING

The Industrial Training (Construction Board) (Amendment) Order (Northern Ireland) 1994 No.312. Enabling power: *S.I. 1984/1159 (NI. 9), art. 14 (1) (6).* Issued: 30.08.94. Made: 09.08.94. Coming into force: 31.08.94. Effect: S.R. & O. (NI) 1964/145 amended. – 2p. – 0 337913129 £0.65

Industrial Training Levy (Construction Industry) Order (Northern Ireland) 1994 No.273. Enabling power: *S.I. 1984/1159 (N.I. 9), arts. 23 (2) (3), 24 (3) (4).* Issued: 02.08.94. Made: 20.07.94. Coming into force: 31.08.94. Effect: None. – 8p. – 0 337912734 £1.95

INSOLVENCY

The Insolvency (Amendment) Rules (Northern Ireland) 1994 No.26. Enabling power: *S.I. 1989/2405 (NI. 19), art. 359 & Registration of Deeds Act (Northern Ireland) 1970, s. 19 (3).* Issued: 22.02.94. Made: 26.01.94. Coming into force: 01.03.94. Effect: S.R. 1991/364 amended. – 12p. – 0 33791026 X £2.80

INSURANCE

Companies (1986 Order) (Insurance Companies Accounts) Regulations (Northern Ireland) 1994 No.428. Enabling power: *S.I. 1986/1032 (N.I. 6), arts. 2 (3), 265 (1) (3).* Issued: 09.11.94. Made: 02.11.94. Coming into force: 16.12.94. Effect: S.I. 1986/1032 (N.I.6) amended. – 48p. – 0 337914281 £6.35

The Insurance Accounts Directive (Miscellaneous Insurance Undertakings) Regulations (Northern Ireland) 1994 No. 429. Enabling power: *European Communities Act 1972, s. 2 (2).* Issued: 09.11.94. Made: 02.11.94. Coming into force: 16.12.94. Effect: 1969 c. 24 (N.I.) amended. – 8p. – 0 33791429 X £1.95

JUDGMENTS (ENFORCEMENT)

The Judgment Enforcement Fees (Amendment) Order (Northern Ireland) 1994 No. 278. Enabling power: *Judicature (Northern Ireland) Act 1978, s. 116 (1).* Issued: 11.08.94. Made: 21.07.94. Coming into force: 01.09.94. Effect: S.R. 1992/19 amended. – 2p. – 0 337912785 £0.65

Price/availability are liable to change without notice

LAND

Compulsory Acquisition (Interest) Order (Northern Ireland) 1994 No. 91. Enabling power: *Public Health and Local Government (Miscellaneous Provisions) Act (Northern Ireland) 1955, s. 12.* Issued: 23.03.94. Made: 11.03.94. Coming into force: 14.04.94. Effect: S.R. 1992/567 revoked. – 2p. – 0 337 91091 X £0.65

LANDLORD AND TENANT

The Registered Rents (Increase) Order (Northern Ireland) 1994 No. 24. Enabling power: *S.I. 1978/1050 (NI. 20), art. 33 (2).* Issued: 03.02.94. Made: 25.01.94. Coming into force: 07.03.94. Effect: None. – 2p. – 0 337 910243 £0.65

LAND REGISTRATION

Land Registration Rules (Northern Ireland) 1994 No. 424. Enabling power: *Land Registration Act (Northern Ireland) 1970 & S.I. 1984/1984 (N.I. 4), & S.I. 1992/811 (N.I. 7).* Issued: 09.11.94. Made: 27.10.94. Coming into force: 09.12.94. Effect: S.R. 1977/154; 1989/270; 1991/7, 340, 381 revoked. – 228p. – 0 337 91424 9 £16.65

The Registration (Land and Deeds) (1992 Order) (Commencement No. 2) Order (Northern Ireland) 1994 No. 423 (C. 13). Enabling power: *S.I. 1992/811 (N.I. 7), art 1. (2) & Northern Ireland Act 1974, sch. 1, para. 2 (1).* Bringing into operation various provisions of the 1992 Order on 09.12.94. Issued: 03.11.94. Made: 27.10.94. Effect: None. – 4p. – 0 337 914230 £1.10

LANDS TRIBUNAL

Lands Tribunal (Salaries) Order (Northern Ireland) 1994 No. 157. Enabling power: *Lands Tribunal and Compensation Act (Northern Ireland) 1964, s. 2 (5) & Administrative and Financial Provisions Act (Northern Ireland) 1962, s. 18.* Issued: 04.05.94. Made: 19.04.94. Coming into force: 06.06.94. Effect: S.R. 1992/442 revoked. – 2p. – 0 337911576 £0.65

LEGAL AID, ADVICE AND ASSISTANCE

The Legal Aid in Criminal Proceedings (Costs) (Amendment) Rules (Northern Ireland) 1994 No.209. Enabling power: *S.I. 1981/228 (N.I. 8), art. 36 (3).* Issued: 21.06.94. Made: 03.06.94. Coming into force: 29.06.94. Effect: S.R. 1992/314 amended & S.R. 1993/266 revoked. – 2p. – 0 337912092 £0.65

LEGAL AID AND ADVICE

Legal Advice and Assistance (Amendment) Regulations (Northern Ireland) 1994 No. 98. Enabling power: *S.I. 1981/228 (NI. 8), arts. 7 (2), 22, 27.* Issued: 31.03.94. Made: 16.03.94. Coming into force: 11.04.94. Effect: S.R. 1981/366; 1993/124 amended. – 2p. – 0 337910987 £0.65

Legal Advice and Assistance (Financial Conditions) Regulations (Northern Ireland) 1994 No.96. Enabling power: *S.I. 1981/228 (NI. 8), arts. 3 (2), 7 (3), 22, 27.* Issued: 31.03.94. Made: 16.03.94. Coming into force: 11.04.94. Effect: S.R. 1981/228 (NI. 8) amended & S.R. 1993/123 revoked. – 2p. – 0 337910960 £0.65

Legal Aid (Financial Conditions) Regulations (Northern Ireland) 1994 No. 97. Enabling power: *S.I. 1981/228 (NI. 8), arts. 9 (2), 12 (2), 22, 27.* Issued: 31.03.94. Made: 16.03.94. Coming into force: 11.04.94. Effect: S.R. 1981/228 (NI. 8); 1992/107; 1993/121 amended. – 2p. – 0 337910979 £0.65

LOCAL GOVERNMENT

The General Grant (Specified Bodies) Regulations (Northern Ireland) 1994 No. 418. Enabling power: *S.I. 1972/1999 (N.I. 22), art. 4 (3).* Issued: 08.11.94. Made: 27.10.94. Coming into force: 08.12.94. Effect: S.R. 1986/154; 1989/362 revoked. – 2p. – 0 337914184 £0.65

Local Government (Employment of Group Building Control Staff) Order (Northern Ireland) 1994 No. 497. Enabling power: *Local Government Act (Northern Ireland) 1972, s. 41 (8) (8A) (8B).* Issued: 09.01.95. Made: 22.12.94. Coming into force: 01.04.95. Effect: S.R. & O. (N.I.) 1973/167; S.R. 1981/253 revoked. – 8p. – 0 337914974 £1.95

Local Government (Employment of Group Environmental Health Staff) Order (Northern Ireland) 1994 No. 498. Enabling power: *Local Government Act (Northern Ireland) 1972, s. 41 (8) (8A) (8B).* Issued: 09.01.95. Made: 22.12.94. Coming into force: 01.04.95. Effect: S.R. & O. (N.I.) 1973/168; S.R. 1981/254 revoked. – 8p. – 0 337914982 £1.95

The Local Government (General Grant) Order (Northern Ireland) 1994 No. 162. Enabling power: *S.I. 1972/1999 (NI. 22), sch. 1 Pt. 1, para. 3 (1).* Issued: 20.05.94. Made: 26.04.94. Coming into force: 21.06.94. Effect: S.R. 1991/197 revoked. – 2p. – 0 337911622 £0.65

MAGISTRATES' COURTS

Magistrates' Courts (Amendment) Rules (Northern Ireland) 1994 No. 387. Enabling power: *S.I. 1981/1675 (N.I. 26), art. 13, 126 (1) (3).* Issued: 24.10.94. Made: 08.10.94. Coming into force: 01.11.94. Effect: S.R. 1984/225 amended. – 8p. – 0 337913870 £1.95

Magistrates' Courts (Costs in Criminal Cases) (Amendment) Rules (Northern Ireland) 1994 No.285. Enabling power: *S.I. 1981/1675 (N.I. 26), art. 13 & Costs in Criminal Cases Act (Northern Ireland) 1968, s. 7.* Issued: 08.08.94. Made: 22.07.94. Coming into force: 01.09.94. Effect: None. – 8p. – 0 337912858 £1.95

Price/availability are liable to change without notice

The Magistrates' Courts Fees Order (Northern Ireland) 1994 No. 279. Enabling power: *Judicature (Northern Ireland) Act 1978, s. 116 (1) (4)*. Issued: 11.08.94. Made: 21.07.94. Coming into force: 01.09.94. Effect: S.R. 1989/280; 1991/122; 1992/265; 1993/133 revoked. – 10p. – 0 337912279 3 *£2.40*

Petty Sessions Districts Order (Northern Ireland) 1994 No. 470. Enabling power: *S.I. 1981/1675 (N.I. 26), art. 11 (2)*. Issued: 15.12.94. Made: 24.11.94. Coming into force: 02.01.95. Effect: S.R. 1990/196 revoked. – 4p. – 0 337 914702 *£1.10*

MATRIMONIAL CAUSES

The Matrimonial Causes Fees (Amendment) Order (Northern Ireland) 1994 No. 281. Enabling power: *Judicature (Northern Ireland) Act 1978, s. 116 (1)*. Issued: 11.08.94. Made: 21.07.94. Coming into force: 01.09.94. Effect: S.R. 1991/292 amended. – 8p. – 0 337912815 *£1.55*

MENTAL HEALTH

The Mental Health (Nurses, Guardianship, Consent to Treatment and Prescribed Forms) (Amendment) Regulations (Northern Ireland) 1994 No. 349. Enabling power: *S.I. 1986/595 (NI. 4), arts. 7(3), 135(1)*. Issued: 22.09.94. Made: 08.09.94. Coming into force: 01.11.94. Effect: S.R. 1986/174 amended. – 4p. – 0 337913498 *£1.10*

PARTNERSHIPS

Partnerships and Unlimited Companies (Accounts) Regulations (Northern Ireland) 1994 No.133. Enabling power: *European Communities Act 1972, s. 2 (2)*. Issued: 14.04.94. Made: 30.03.94. Coming into force: 12.05.94. Effect: S.I. 1986/1032 (NI 6) amended. –12p. – 0 337911339 *£2.80*

PENSIONS

The Guaranteed Minimum Pensions Increase Order (Northern Ireland) 1994 No. 69. Enabling power: *Pension Schemes (Northern Ireland) Act 1993, s. 105*. Issued: 10.03.94. Made: 03.03.94. Coming into force: 06.04.94. Effect: None. – 2p. – 0 337910693 *£0.65*

The Occupational and Personal Pension Schemes (Consequential Amendments) Regulations (Northern Ireland) 1994 No. 300. Enabling power: *Pension Schemes (Northern Ireland) Act 1993, ss. 3(1)(b)(6)(7), 4(3), 5(2)(3)(a)(5)(a), 6(2)(3), 7(5)(c), 8(3), 12(4), 13(6), 15(4)(5), 16, 17, 19(1)(6)(7), 20(3), 22, 23(3), 24(2)(a)(b)(3)(ii)(4)(5), 25(1)(b)(3)(b)(4), 26(1), 27(1), 28, 30(1)(8), 31(6), 33(6), 35, 39(1)(3)(4), 40, 41(3), 44(2)(4), 46(4)(5), 47(2)(4), 51(2) to (5), 52(1)(2), 53(1)(2)(4), 55(3), 56(7), 57(7)(11), 58(2), 59(2), 62, 67(6), 69, 70(8), 71(1)(7), 73(5)(6), 78, 84(1), 91, 93, 94(1)(2)(3), 107(1), 108(1), 109(1)(3), 84(1), 91, 93, 94(1)(2)(3), 107(1), 108(1), 109(1)(3)(4), 110, 112, 113, 115(3), 131(1), 132(1), 134(7), 142(4), 149, 150, 152, 156(1), 159(2)(4)(5)(6), 161(5), 170, 173, 176(1)(3)(4), 178, sch. 1, sch. 2, para. 5, sch.5, para. 17*. Issued: 05.08.94. Made: 29.07.94. Coming into force: 01.09.94. Effect: S.R. 1976/238; 1985/259, 356, 358; 1986/225, 320; 1987/279, 280, 281, 284, 288, 289, 290, 291, 295, 296; 1988/34, 449; 1990/204, 379, 384, 423; 1991/37, 38, 39, 93; 1992/47 amended. – 36p. – 0 337913005 *£5.70*

The Occupational Pension Schemes (Deficiency on Winding Up, etc.) Regulations (Northern Ireland) 1994 No. 107. Enabling power: *Pension Schemes (Northern Ireland) Act 1993, ss. 140 (5), 149 (5) (a) (b), 178 (3)*. Issued: 01.04.94. Made: 25.03.94. Coming into force: 19.04.94. Effect: S.R. 1992/300 revoked. – 8p. – 0 337 91107 X *£1.95*

The Occupational Pensions (Revaluation) Order (Northern Ireland) 1994 No. 445. Enabling power: *Pension Schemes Act 1993, sch. 3, para. 2 (1)*. Issued: 22.11.94. Made: 15.11.94. Coming into force: 01.01.95. Effect: None. – 2p. – 0 337914451 *£0.65*

The Pension Schemes (1993 Act) (Commencement No. 1) Order (Northern Ireland) 1994 No.17 (C. 1). Enabling power: *Pension Schemes (Northern Ireland) Act 1993, s. 186 (2) (3). Bringing into operation various provisions of the 1993 act on the 07.02.94*. Issued: 26.01.94. Made: 19.01.94. Effect: None. – 2p. – 0 337910170 *£0.65*

Pensions Increase (Review) Order (Northern Ireland) 1994 No. 99. Enabling power: *S.I. 1975/1503 (NI. 15), art. 69 (1) (2) (5) (5ZA)*. Issued: 25.03.94. Made: 16.03.94. Coming into force: 11.04.94. Effect: None. – 8p. – 0 337910995 *£1.95*

The Protected Rights (Transfer Payment) (Amendment) Regulations (Northern Ireland) 1994 No.261. Enabling power: *Pension Schemes (Northern Ireland) Act 1993, s. 24 (2) (b)*. Issued: 08.07.94. Made: 05.07.94. Coming into force: 29.07.94. Effect: S.R. 1987/296 amended. – 2p. – 0 337912610 *£0.65*

Superannuation (Museums Council) Order (Northern Ireland) 1994 No. 51. Enabling power: *S.I. 1972/1073 (NI. 10), art. 3 (4) (7)*. Issued: 08.03.94. Made: 07.02.94. Coming into force: 18.03.94. Effect: None. – 2p. – 0 337910510 *£0.65*

PHARMACY

Pharmaceutical Society of Northern Ireland (General) Regulations (Northern Ireland) 1994 No.202. Enabling power: *S.I. 1976/1213 (N.I. 22), art. 5*. Issued: 08.06.94. Made: 31.05.94. Coming into force: 28.06.94. Effect: S.R. 1992/192 revoked. – 8p. – 0 337912025 *£1.95*

PLANNING

Planning (Assessment of Environmental Effects) (Amendment) Regulations (Northern Ireland) 1994 No. 395. Enabling power: *European Communities Act 1972, s. 2 (2)*. Issued: 24.10.94. Made: 14.10.94. Coming into force: 28.11.94. Effect: S.R. 1989/20 amended. – 4p. – 0 33791395 1 £1.10

Planning (Development Plans) (Amendment) Regulations (Northern Ireland) 1994 No. 394. Enabling power: *S.I. 1991/1220 (N.I. 11), arts. 2 (2), 5 (3), 10, 129 (1)*. Issued: 24.10.94. Made: 14.10.94. Coming into force: 28.11.94. Effect: S.R. 1991/119 amended. – 2p. – 0 337 91394 3 £0.65

Planning (Fees) (Amendment) Regulations (Northern Ireland) 1994 No. 58. Enabling power: *S.I. 1991/1220 (NI. 11), arts. 127, 129 (1)*. Issued: 08.03.94. Made: 25.02.94. Coming into force: 01.04.94. Effect: S.R. 1992/97 amended. – 8p. – 0 337 91058 8 £1.95

Planning (Simplified Planning Zones) (Excluded Development) Order (Northern Ireland) 1994 No. 426. Enabling power: *S.I. 1991/1220 (N.I. 11), art. 18 (3) (b)*. Issued: 08.11.94. Made: 01.11.94. Coming into force: 12.12.94. Effect: None. – 2p. – 0 337 91426 5 £0.65

PLANT HEALTH

Plant Health (Amendment) (Potatoes) Order (Northern Ireland) 1994 No. 28. Enabling power: *Plant Health Act (Northern Ireland) 1967, ss. 2 (a), 3 (1) (b), 3A (c), 3B (1) (d), 4 (1) (e)*. Issued: 03.02.94. Made: 28.01.94. Coming into force: 01.03.94. Effect: S.R. 1993/256 amended. – 4p. – 0 337 91028 6 £1.10

POISONS

Poisons (Amendment) Regulations (Northern Ireland) 1994 No. 217. Enabling power: *S.I. 1976/1214 (N.I. 23), art. 9*. Issued: 21.06.94. Made: 09.06.94. Coming into force: 11.07.94. Effect: S.R. 1983/201 amended. – 2p. – 0 337 91217 3 £0.65

Poisons List (Amendment) Order (Northern Ireland) 1994 No. 218. Enabling power: *S.I. 1976/1214 (N.I. 23), art. 4 (6)*. Issued: 21.06.94. Made: 09.06.94. Coming into force: 11.07.94. Effect: S.R. 1983/200 amended. – 2p. – 0 337 91218 1 £0.65

POLICE

Royal Ulster Constabulary (Amendment No. 2) Regulations 1994 No. 186. Enabling power: *Police Act (Northern Ireland) 1970, s. 25*. Issued: 26.05.94. Made: 09.05.94. Coming into force: 01.07.94. Effect: S.R. 1984/62 amended. – 8p. – 0 337 91186 X £1.55

Royal Ulster Constabulary (Amendment No. 3) Regulations 1994 No. 331. Enabling power: *Police Act (Northern Ireland) 1970, s. 25*. Issued: 16.09.94. Made: 26.08.94. Coming into force: 01.09.94. Effect: S.R. 1984/62 amended. – 12p. – 0 337 91331 5 £2.80

Royal Ulster Constabulary (Amendment No. 4) Regulations 1994 No. 378. Enabling power: *Police Act (Northern Ireland) 1970, s. 25*. Issued: 12.10.94. Made: 05.10.94. Coming into force: 01.11.94. Effect: S.R. 1984/62 amended. – 4p. – 0 337 91378 1 £1.10

Royal Ulster Constabulary (Amendment No. 5) Regulations 1994 No. 431. Enabling power: *Police Act (Northern Ireland) 1970, s. 25 & Administrative and Financial Provisions Act (Northern Ireland) 1962, s. 18*. Issued: 11.11.94. Made: 07.11.94. Coming into force: 09.12.94. Effect: S.R. 1984/62; 1994/331 amended. – 12p. – 0 337 91431 1 £2.80

Royal Ulster Constabulary (Amendment) Regulations 1994 No. 71. Enabling power: *Police Act (Northern Ireland) 1970, s. 25*. Issued: 10.03.94. Made: 07.02.94. Coming into force: 31.03.94. Effect: S.R. 1984/62 amended. – 4p. – 0 337 91071 5 £1.10

Royal Ulster Constabulary (Discipline and Disciplinary Appeals) (Amendment No. 2) Regulations 1994 No. 291. Enabling power: *Police Act (Northern Ireland) 1970, ss. 25, 26*. Issued: 02.08.94. Made: 26.07.94. Coming into force: 01.09.94. Effect: S.R. 1988/10 amended. – 4p. – 0 337 91291 2 £1.10

Royal Ulster Constabulary (Discipline and Disciplinary Appeals) (Amendment) Regulations 1994 No. 48. Enabling power: *Police Act (Northern Ireland) 1970, ss. 25, 26*. Issued: 22.02.94. Made: 11.02.94. Coming into force: 31.03.94. Effect: S.R. 1988/10 amended. – 2p. – 0 337 91048 0 £0.65

Royal Ulster Constabulary Reserve (Full-Time) (Appointment and Conditions of Service) (Amendment No. 2) Regulations 1994 No. 187. Enabling power: *Police Act (Northern Ireland) 1970, s. 26*. Issued: 26.05.94. Made: 09.05.94. Coming into force: 01.07.94. Effect: S.R. 1988/36 amended. – 8p. – 0 337 91187 8 £1.55

Royal Ulster Constabulary Reserve (Full-Time) (Appointment and Conditions of Service) (Amendment No. 3) Regulations 1994 No. 332. Enabling power: *Police Act (Northern Ireland) 1970, s. 26*. Issued: 16.09.94. Made: 26.08.94. Coming into force: 01.09.94. Effect: S.R. 1988/36 amended. – 8p. – 0 337 91332 3 £1.95

Royal Ulster Constabulary Reserve (Full-Time) (Appointment and Conditions of Service) (Amendment No. 4) Regulations 1994 No. 432. Enabling power: *Police Act (Northern Ireland) 1970, s. 26*. Issued: 16.11.94. Made: 07.11.94. Coming into force: 09.12.94. Effect: S.R. 1988/36 amended. – 4p. – 0 337 91432 X £1.10

Royal Ulster Constabulary Reserve (Full-Time) (Appointment and Conditions of Service) (Amendment) Regulations 1994 No. 72. Enabling power: *Police Act (Northern Ireland) 1970, s. 26*. Issued: 10.03.94. Made: 07.02.94. Coming into force: 31.03.94. Effect: S.R. 1988/36 amended. – 4p. – 0 337 91072 3 £1.10

Royal Ulster Constabulary Reserve (Full-time) Pensions Regulations 1994 No. 197. Enabling power: *Police Act (Northern Ireland) 1970, s. 26.* Issued: 01.06.94. Made: 25.05.94. Coming into force: 01.07.94. Effect: S.R. 1988/374 amended. – 8p. – 0 33791 1975 £1.95

Royal Ulster Constabulary Reserve (Part-Time) (Appointment and Conditions of Service) (Amendment No. 2) Regulations 1994 No. 188. Enabling power: *Police Act (Northern Ireland) 1970, s. 26.* Issued: 25.05.94. Made: 22.04.94. Coming into force: 01.07.94. Effect: S.R. 1988/35 amended. – 2p. – 0 33791 1886 £0.65

Royal Ulster Constabulary Reserve (Part-Time) (Appointment and Conditions of Service) (Amendment) Regulations 1994 No. 73. Enabling power: *Police Act (Northern Ireland) 1970, s. 26.* Issued: 10.03.94. Made: 07.02.94. Coming into force: 31.03.94. Effect: S.R. 1988/35 amended. – 2p. – 0 33791 0731 £0.65

Royal Ulster Constabulary Reserve (Part-time) (Discipline and Disciplinary Appeals) (Amendment No. 2) Regulations 1994 No. 292. Enabling power: *Police Act (Northern Ireland) 1970, s. 26.* Issued: 02.08.94. Made: 26.07.94. Coming into force: 01.09.94. Effect: S.R. 1988/8 amended. – 4p. – 0 33791 2920 £1.10

Royal Ulster Constabulary Reserve (Part-time) (Discipline and Disciplinary Appeals) (Amendment) Regulations 1994 No. 49. Enabling power: *Police Act (Northern Ireland) 1970, s. 26.* Issued: 22.02.94. Made: 11.02.94. Coming into force: 31.03.94. Effect: S.R. 1988/8 amended. – 2p. – 0 33791 0499 £0.65

PRIVATE STREETS

The Private Streets (Construction) Regulations (Northern Ireland) 1994 No. 131. Enabling power: *S.I. 1980/1086 (NI. 12), art. 5 (1) (2).* Issued: 12.04.94. Made: 30.03.94. Coming into force: 11.05.94. Effect: S.R. & O. (N.I.) 1966/262 revoked. – 64p. – 0 33791 1312 £7.65

PUBLIC HEALTH

The Alkali, &c. Works and Clean Air (Metrication) Regulations (Northern Ireland) 1994 No.192. Enabling power: *S.I. 1978/1049 (NI. 19), art. 82 (1).* Issued: 26.05.94. Made: 23.05.94. Coming into force: 04.07.94. Effect: 1906 c. 14, S.I. 1981/158 (NI. 4) amended. –8p. – 0 33791 1924 £1.55

Food Protection (Emergency Prohibitions) (Amendment) Order (Northern Ireland) 1994 No.489. Enabling power: *Food and Environment Protection Act 1985, ss. 1 (1), 24 (3).* Issued: 21.12.94. Made: 16.12.94. Coming into force: 18.01.95. Effect: S.R. 1991/8 amended. –4p. – 0 33791 4893 £1.10

Food Protection (Emergency Prohibitions) Order (Northern Ireland) 1994 No. 204. Enabling power: *Food and Environment Protection Act 1985, ss. 1 (1), 24 (3).* Issued: 14.06.94. Made: 01.06.94. Coming into force: 01.06.94. Effect: None. – 4p. – 0 33791 2041 £1.10

Food Protection (Emergency Prohibitions) (Revocation) Order (Northern Ireland) 1994 No.229. Enabling power: *1985 c.48, ss. 1 (10), 24 (3).* Issued: 06.07.94. Made: 20.06.94. Coming into force: 20.06.94. Effect: S.R. 1994/204 revoked. – 2p. – 0 33791 2297 £0.65

Interest on Recoverable Sanitation Expenses Order (Northern Ireland) 1994 No. 90. Enabling power: *Public Health and Local Government (Miscellaneous Provisions) Act (Northern Ireland) 1962, s. 5.* Issued: 21.03.94. Made: 11.03.94. Coming into force: 14.04.94. Effect: S.R. 1992/568 revoked. – 2p. – 0 33791 0901 £0.65

The Litter (1994 Order) (Commencement) Order (Northern Ireland) 1994 No. 337 (C. 11). Enabling power: *Northern Ireland Act 1974, sch. 1, para. 2 (1) & S.I. 1994/1896 (NI. 10) art. 1 (2). Bringing into operation various provisions of the 1994 order on 01.10.94.* Issued: 06.09.94. Made: 02.09.94. Effect: None. –2p. – 0 33791 3374 £0.65

The Litter (Designated Educational Institutions) Order (Northern Ireland) 1994 No.338. Enabling power: *S.I. 1994/1896 (NI. 10) art. 2 (2).* Issued: 06.09.94. Made: 02.09.94. Coming into force: 04.10.94. Effect: None. – 2p. – 0 33791 3382 £0.65

The Litter (Designation of Roads) Order (Northern Ireland) 1994 No. 414. Enabling power: *S.I. 1994/1896 (N.I. 10), art. 2 (5).* Issued: 01.11.94. Made: 25.10.94. Coming into force: 25.11.94. Effect: None. – 4p. – 0 33791 4141 £1.10

The Litter (Fixed Penalty Notices) Regulations (Northern Ireland) 1994 No. 352. Enabling power: *S.I. 1994/1896 (NI. 10), art. 6 (5).* Issued: 22.09.94. Made: 14.09.94. Coming into force: 20.10.94. Effect: None. –4p. – 0 33791 3528 £1.10

The Litter (Statutory Undertaker) (Prescribed Body) Regulations (Northern Ireland) 1994 No.449. Enabling power: *S.I. 1994/1896 (N.I. 10), art. 2 (2).* Issued: 28.11.94. Made: 18.11.94. Coming into force: 20.12.94. Effect: None. – 2p. – 0 33791 4494 £0.65

The Marketing and Use of Dangerous Substances (No. 2) Regulations (Northern Ireland) 1994 No.223. Enabling power: *European Communities Act 1972, s. 2 (2).* Issued: 26.06.94. Made: 17.06.94. Coming into force: 01.08.94. Effect: None. – 8p. – 0 33791 2238 £1.95

The Marketing and Use of Dangerous Substances (No. 3) Regulations (Northern Ireland) 1994 No.224. Enabling power: *European Communities Act 1972, s. 2 (2).* Issued: 29.06.94. Made: 17.06.94. Coming into force: 01.08.94. Effect: None. – 4p. – 0 33791 2246 £1.10

The Marketing and Use of Dangerous Substances Regulations (Northern Ireland) 1994 No.222. Enabling power: *European Communities Act 1972, s. 2 (2).* Issued: 26.06.94. Made: 17.06.94. Coming into force: 01.08.94. Effect: None. – 8p. – 0 33791 222 X £1.95

Price/availability are liable to change without notice

The Pollution of Groundwater by Dangerous Substances Regulations (Northern Ireland) 1994 No.147. Enabling power: *European Communities Act 1972, s. 2 (2)*. Issued: 20.04.94. Made: 13.04.94. Coming into force: 04.05.94. Effect: None. – 4p. – 0 33791 1479 *£1.10*

The Public Health (Metrication) Regulations (Northern Ireland) 1994 No. 193. Enabling power: *S.I. 1978/1049 (NI. 19), art. 82 (1)*. Issued: 26.05.94. Made: 23.05.94. Coming into force: 04.07.94. Effect: 1878 c. 52, 1907 c. 53 amended. – 2p. – 0 33791 1932 *£0.65*

RATES

The Housing Benefit (General) (Amendment No. 2) Regulations (Northern Ireland) 1994 No.81. Enabling power: *Social Security Contributions and Benefits (Northern Ireland) Act 1992, ss. 122 (1) (d), 129 (4), 131 (1)*. Issued: 15.03.94. Made: 07.03.94. Coming into force: 01.04.94.; 04.04.94. Effect: S.R. 1987/461 amended & S.R. 1993/154 revoked. – 8p. – 0 33791 0812 *£1.95*

The Housing Benefit (General) (Amendment No. 3) Regulations (Northern Ireland) 1994 No.88. Enabling power: *Social Security Contributions and Benefits (Northern Ireland) Act 1992, ss. 122 (1) (d), 132 (3) (4) (a) (b), & Social Security Administration (Northern Ireland) Act 1992, s. 61 (3)*. Issued: 31.03.94. Made: 11.03.94. Coming into force: 01.04.94. for reg. 1, 04.04.94. for all others Effect: S.R. 1987/461 amended. – 8p. – 0 33791 088 X *£1.95*

The Housing Benefit (General) (Amendment No. 4) Regulations (Northern Ireland) 1994 No.137. Enabling power: *Social Security Contributions and Benefits (Northern Ireland) Act 1992, ss. 122 (1) (d), 129 (4), 131 (1)*. Issued: 18.04.94. Made: 08.04.94. Coming into force: 01.05.94. Effect: S.R. 1987/461 amended. – 2p. – 0 33791 1371 *£0.65*

The Housing Benefit (General) (Amendment) Regulations (Northern Ireland) 1994 No.80. Enabling power: *Social Security Contributions and Benefits (Northern Ireland) Act 1992, ss. 122 (1) (d), 133 (2) (i)*. Issued: 15.03.94. Made: 07.03.94. Coming into force: 01.04.94.; 04.04.94. Effect: S.R. 1987/461 amended. – 8p. – 0 33791 0804 *£1.95*

The Housing Benefit (Miscellaneous Amendments) Regulations (Northern Ireland) 1994 No.335. Enabling power: *Social Security Contributions and Benefits (Northern Ireland) Act 1992, ss. 122 (1) (d), 131 (1) (6), 132 (3) (4) (a) (b) & Social Security Administration (Northern Ireland) Act 1992, ss. 5 (1) (q), 61, 120 (1) (2)*. Issued: 06.09.94. Made: 31.08.94. Coming into force: 03.10.94. Effect: S.R. 1987/461; 1988/118; 1993/145 amended. –12p. – 0 33791 3358 *£2.80*

Rates (Regional Rate) Order (Northern Ireland) 1994 No. 56. Enabling power: *S.I. 1977/2157 (NI. 28), arts. 2 (2), 7 (1), 27 (4)*. Issued: 01.03.94. Made: 21.02.94. Coming into force: 01.04.94. Effect: None. – 2p. – 0 33791 0561 *£0.65*

REGISTRATION OF CLUBS

The Registration of Clubs (Required Information) (Amendment) Regulations (Northern Ireland) 1994 No. 354. Enabling power: *S.I. 1987/1278 (N.I. 14), sch. 2, para. 2 (2), sch. 3, para. 3 (2)*. Issued: 28.09.94. Made: 15.09.94. Coming into force: 24.10.94. Effect: S.R. 1988/27 amended. – 2p. – 0 33791 3544 *£0.65*

ROAD AND RAILWAY TRANSPORT

Buses (Section 10B Permits) Regulations (Northern Ireland) 1994 No. 23. Enabling power: *Transport Act (Northern Ireland) 1967, ss. 10D, 45, 81*. Issued: 15.02.94. Made: 24.01.94. Coming into force: 01.03.94. Effect: None. – 4p. – 0 33791 0235 *£1.10*

Bus Permits (Designated Bodies) (Northern Ireland) Order 1994 No. 22. Enabling power: *Transport Act (Northern Ireland) 1967, s. 10B (6)*. Issued: 15.02.94. Made: 24.01.94. Coming into force: 01.03.94. Effect: None. – 8p. – 0 33791 0227 *£1.95*

Level Crossing (Eglinton) Order (Northern Ireland) 1994 No. 29. Enabling power: *Transport Act (Northern Ireland) 1967, ss. 66 (1) (2)*. Issued: 15.02.94. Made: 28.01.94. Coming into force: 28.03.94. Effect: S.R. 1983/195 revoked. – 8p. – 0 33791 0294 *£1.95*

Level Crossing (Lock) Order (Northern Ireland) 1994 No. 30. Enabling power: *Transport Act (Northern Ireland) 1967, ss. 66 (1) (2)*. Issued: 15.02.94. Made: 28.01.94. Coming into force: 21.03.94. Effect: None. – 8p. – 0 33791 0308 *£1.95*

ROADS

Motorways Traffic (Amendment) Regulations (Northern Ireland) 1994 No. 190. Enabling power: *S.I. 119193/3160, art. 20 (3)*. Issued: 26.05.94. Made: 16.05.94. Coming into force: 01.07.94. Effect: S.R. 1984/160 amended. – 4p. – 0 33791 1908 *£1.10*

Roads (Assessment of Environmental Effects) Regulations (Northern Ireland) 1994 No.316. Enabling power: *European Communities Act 1972, s. 2 (2)*. Issued: 19.08.94. Made: 12.08.94. Coming into force: 30.09.94. Effect: S.I. 1993/3160 (N.I. 15) amended. – 2p. – 0 33791 3161 *£0.65*

ROAD TRAFFIC AND VEHICLES

Bus Lane (Nelson Street, Belfast) (Revocation) Order (Northern Ireland) 1994 No. 356. Enabling power: *S.I. 1981/154 (N.I. 1), art. 23 (1) (2)*. Issued: 28.09.94. Made: 19.09.94. Coming into force: 24.10.94. Effect: S.R. 1983/82 revoked. – 2p. – 0 33791 3560 *£0.65*

Control of Traffic (Ballynahinch) Order (Northern Ireland) 1994 No. 172. Enabling power: *S.I. 1981/154 (NI. 1), art. 21 (1)*. Issued: 16.05.94. Made: 03.05.94. Coming into force: 14.06.94. Effect: None. – 2p. – 0 33791172 X £0.65

Control of Traffic (Belfast) (No. 2) Order (Amendment) Order (Northern Ireland) 1994 No.7. Enabling power: *S.I. 1981/154 (NI. 1), art. 21 (1)*. Issued: 21.01.94. Made: 11.01.94. Coming into force: 22.02.94. Effect: S.R. 1987/159 amended. – 2p. – 0 337910073 £0.65

Control of Traffic (Belfast) (No. 2) Order (Northern Ireland) 1994 No. 433. Enabling power: *S.I. 1981/154 (N.I. 1), art. 21 (1)*. Issued: 16.11.94. Made: 07.11.94. Coming into force: 19.12.94. Effect: None. – 2p. – 0 337 914338 £0.65

Control of Traffic (Belfast) (No. 3) Order (Northern Ireland) 1994 No. 455. Enabling power: *S.I. 1981/154 (N.I. 1), art. 21 (1)*. Issued: 28.11.94. Made: 21.11.94. Coming into force: 22.01.94. Effect: None. – 2p. – 0 337914559 £0.65

Control of Traffic (Belfast) Order (Northern Ireland) 1994 No. 173. Enabling power: *S.I. 1981/154 (NI. 1), art. 21 (1)*. Issued: 15.05.94. Made: 03.05.94. Coming into force: 14.06.94. Effect: None. – 4p. – 0 337911738 £1.10

Control of Traffic (Carrickfergus) (No.2) Order (Northern Ireland) 1994 No.205. Enabling power: *S.I. 1981/154 (N.I. 1), art. 21 (1)*. Issued: 14.06.94. Made: 01.06.94. Coming into force: 20.07.94. Effect: None. – 2p. – 0 33791205 X £0.65

Control of Traffic (Carrickfergus) Order (Northern Ireland) 1994 No. 27. Enabling power: *S.I. 1981/154 (NI. 1), art. 21 (1)*. Issued: 07.02.94. Made: 28.01.94. Coming into force: 10.03.94. Effect: None. – 2p. – 0 337910278 £0.65

Control of Traffic (Holywood) Order (Northern Ireland) 1994 No. 305. Enabling power: *S.I. 1981/154 (N.I. 1), art. 21 (1)*. Issued: 08.08.94. Made: 03.08.94. Coming into force: 14.09.94. Effect: None. – 2p. – 0 337913056 £0.65

Control of Traffic (Larne) Order (Northern Ireland) 1994 No. 390. Enabling power: *S.I. 1981/154 (N.I. 1), art. 21 (1)*. Issued: 26.10.94. Made: 13.10.94. Coming into force: 24.11.94. Effect: None. – 2p. – 0 337913900 £0.65

Control of Traffic (Lisburn) Order (Northern Ireland) 1994 No. 139. Enabling power: *S.I. 1981/154 (N.I. 1), art. 2 (1)*. Issued: 25.04.94. Made: 11.04.94. Coming into force: 23.05.94. Effect: None. – 2p. – 0 337911398 £0.65

Control of Traffic (Portrush) Order (Northern Ireland) 1994 No. 304. Enabling power: *S.I. 1981/154 (N.I. 1), arts. 21 (1), 22 (1)*. Issued: 09.08.94. Made: 02.08.94. Coming into force: 01.10.94. Effect: S.R. 1979/268 amended. – 8p. – 0 337913048 £1.55

Control of Traffic (Woodhouse Street, Portadown) Order (Northern Ireland) 1994 No.473. Enabling power: *S.I. 1981/154 (N.I. 1), arts. 21 (1), 22 (1)*. Issued: 12.12.94. Made: 02.12.94. Coming into force: 16.01.95. Effect: S.R. 1980/85 amended & S.R. 1972/51 revoked. – 2p. – 0 337914737 £0.65

Cycle Racing on Roads (Amendment) Regulations (Northern Ireland) 1994 No. 442. Enabling power: *S.I. 1981/154 (N.I. 1), arts. 211 (2), 218 (1)*. Issued: 22.11.94. Made: 09.11.94. Coming into force: 19.12.94. Effect: S.R. 1986/321 amended. – 2p. – 0 337914427 £0.65

Goods Vehicles (Certification) (Amendment) Regulations (Northern Ireland) 1994 No.54. Enabling power: *S.I. 1981/154 (NI. 1), arts. 53 (3), 218 (1)*. Issued: 08.03.94. Made: 17.02.94. Coming into force: 01.04.94. Effect: S.R. 1990/224 amended. – 2p. – 0 337910545 £0.65

Goods Vehicles (Certification) (Fees) (Amendment) Regulations (Northern Ireland) 1994 No.410. Enabling power: *S.I. 1981/154 (N.I. 1), arts. 54 (1), 58 (1), 218 (1)*. Issued: 01.11.94. Made: 24.10.94. Coming into force: 01.12.94. Effect: S.R. 1990/224 amended & S.R. 1992/380 revoked. – 4p. – 0 337914109 £1.10

Large Private Passenger Vehicles (Certification) (Fees) (Amendment) Regulations (Northern Ireland) 1994 No. 411. Enabling power: *S.I. 1981/154 (N.I. 1), arts. 67 (3), 69, 218 (1)*. Issued: 01.11.94. Made: 24.10.94. Coming into force: 01.12.94. Effect: S.R. 1982/383 amended & S.R. 1991/354; 1992/383 revoked. – 2p. – 0 337914117 £0.65

Motor Cars (Driving Instruction) (Fees) (Amendment) Regulations (Northern Ireland) 1994 No.408. Enabling power: *S.I. 1981/154 (N.I. 1), arts. 132 (2) (d), 218 (1)*. Issued: 01.11.94. Made: 24.10.94. Coming into force: 01.12.94. Effect: S.R. 1991/373 amended. – 2p. – 0 337914087 £0.65

Motor Vehicles (Construction and Use) (Amendment no. 2) Regulations (Northern Ireland) 1994 No. 353. Enabling power: *S.I. 1981/154 (N.I. 1), arts. 28 (1), 218 (1)*. Issued: 28.09.94. Made: 14.09.94. Coming into force: 01.11.94. Effect: S.R. 1989/299 amended. – 12p. – 0 337913536 £2.80

Motor Vehicles (Construction and Use) (Amendment No. 3) Regulations (Northern Ireland) 1994 No. 452. Enabling power: *S.I. 1981/154 (N.I. 1), arts. 28 (1), 214 (1), 218 (1)*. Issued: 28.11.94. Made: 18.11.94. Coming into force: 01.01.95. Effect: S.R. 1989/299 amended. – 12p. – 0 337914524 £2.40

Motor Vechicles (Construction and Use) (Amendment) Regulations (Northern Ireland) 1994 No.231. Enabling power: *S.I. 1981/154 (N.I. 1), arts. 28 (1), 218 (1)*. Issued: 04.07.94. Made: 21.06.94. Coming into force: 01.08.94. Effect: S.R. 1989/299 amended. – 12p. – 0 337912319 £2.80

Motor Vehicles (Driving Licences) (Designation of Relevant External Law) Order (Northern Ireland) 1994 No. 43. Enabling power: *S.I. 1981/154 (NI. 1), art. 5 (2) (b) (c)*. Issued: 18.02.94. Made: 08.02.94. Coming into force: 14.03.94. Effect: None. – 2p. – 0 33791043 X £0.65

Motor Vehicles (Driving Licences) (Large Goods and Passenger-Carrying Vehicles) (Amendment) Regulations (Northern Ireland) 1994 No. 366. Enabling power: *S.I. 1981/154 (N.I. 1), arts. 5 (4), 9 (2), 19C (2), 218 (1)*. Issued: 12.10.94. Made: 29.09.94. Coming into force: 21.11.94. Effect: S.R. 1991/100 amended. – 4p. – 0 337913668 £1.10

Price/availability are liable to change without notice

Motor Vehicles (Driving Licences) Regulations (Northern Ireland) 1994 No. 365.Enabling power: *S.I. 1981/154 (N.I. 1)*, arts. 4 (7) (8), 5 (1) (3) (4), 8, 9 (2) (4), 11 (4) (5), 13 (1) (3), 14 (4), 17 (2), 19C (1), 194 (8), 214 (1), 218 (1). Issued: 12.10.94. Made: 29.09.94. Coming into force: 21.11.94. Effect: S.R. 1989/238; 1990/271, 311, 412; 1991/98, 279, 380; 1992/315, 384; 1993/107, 289, 390 revoked. – 32p. – 0 337 91365 X £5.20

Motor Vehicles (Exchangeable Licences) Order (Northern Ireland) 1994 No. 364.Enabling power: *S.I. 1981/154 (N.I. 1)*, art 19D (2). Issued: 17.10.94. Made: 29.09.94. Coming into force: 21.11.94. Effect: None. – 2p. – 0 337 91364 1 £0.65

Motor Vehicles (Payments in Respect of Applicants for Exemption from Wearing Seat Belts) Order (Northern Ireland) 1994 No. 170. Enabling power: *S.I. 1981/154 (NI. 1)*, art. 129C (3). Issued: 20.05.94. Made: 29.04.94. Coming into force: 08.06.94. Effect: S.I. 1981/154 (NI. 1) amended. – 2p. – 0 337 91170 3 £0.65

Motor Vehicles (Taxi Drivers' Licences) (Amendment) Regulations (Northern Ireland) 1994 No.363. Enabling power: *S.I. 1981/154 (N.I. 1)*, art. 79A (3). Issued: 12.10.94. Made: 29.09.94. Coming into force: 21.11.94. Effect: S.R. 1991/454 amended. – 2p. – 0 337 91363 3 £0.65

Motor Vehicles (Taxi Drivers' Licences) (Fees) (Amendment) Regulations (Northern Ireland) 1994 No. 412. Enabling power: *S.I. 1981/154 (N.I. 1)*, arts. 79A (2), 218 (1). Issued: 01.11.94. Made: 24.10.94. Coming into force: 01.12.94. Effect: S.R. 1991/454 amended & S.R. 1993/394 revoked. – 2p. – 0 337 91412 5 £0.65

Motor Vehicles (Third-Party Risks) Regulations (Northern Ireland) 1994 No. 46.Enabling power: *S.I. 1981/154 (NI. 1)*, arts. 103 (1), 218 (1). Issued: 22.02.94. Made: 10.02.94. Coming into force: 01.04.94. Effect: S.R. & O. 1972/235; 1973/447 & S.R. 1974/207; 1981/357 revoked. – 12p. – 0 337 91046 4 £2.80

Motor Vehicles (Type Approval) (EEC) (Revocation) Regulations (Northern Ireland) 1994 No.240. Enabling power: *European Communities Act 1972, s. 2 (2)*. Issued: 08.07.94. Made: 27.06.94. Coming into force: 15.08.94. Effect: S.R. 1987/306; 1988/310, 403 amended. – 2p. – 0 337 91240 8 £0.65

Motor Vehicle Testing (Fees) (Amendment) Regulations (Northern Ireland) 1994 No. 409. Enabling power: *S.I. 1981/154 (N.I. 1)*, arts. 33 (2) (6), 35 (3), 36 (4), 218 (1). Issued: 01.11.94. Made: 24.10.94. Coming into force: 01.12.94. Effect: S.R. 1989/234 amended & S.R. 1991/357; 1992/379; 1993/393 revoked. – 8p. – 0 337 91409 5 £1.55

Motorways Traffic (Amendment) Regulations (Northern Ireland) 1994 No. 190. Enabling power: *S.I. 119193/3160*, art. 20 (3). Issued: 26.05.94. Made: 16.05.94. Coming into force: 01.07.94. Effect: S.R. 1984/160 amended. – 4p. – 0 337 91190 8 £1.10

Off-Street Parking (Amendment) Bye-Laws (Northern Ireland) 1994 No. 415. Enabling power: *S.I. 1981/154 (N.I. 1)*, art. 105 (1). Issued: 01.11.94. Made: 25.10.94. Coming into force: 06.12.94. Effect: S.R. 1994/134 amended. – 4p. – 0 337 91415 X £1.10

Off-Street Parking Bye-laws (Northern Ireland) 1994 No. 134. Enabling power: *S.I. 1981/154 (NI. 1)*, art. 105 (1). Issued: 20.04.94. Made: 31.03.94. Coming into force: 04.04.94. Effect: S.R. 1983/240; 1984/35, 39, 183, 203, 330, 390; 1985/132, 140, 303; 1986/197, 271, 298; 1987/45, 49, 62, 109, 133, 181, 241, 324, 426; 1988/38, 106, 228, 277. 324, 399; 1989/161, 200, 220, 456; 1990/139, 140, 281; 1991/3, 59, 177, 209, 270, 273, 403, 545; 1992/317, 345, 389; 1993/56, 214, 264 revoked. – 117p. – 0 337 91134 7 £10.90

One-Way Traffic (Ballymena) (Amendment) Order (Northern Ireland) 1994 No. 246.Enabling power: *S.I. 1981/154 (N.I. 1)*, art. 2 (1). Issued: 08.07.94. Made: 29.06.94. Coming into force: 01.09.94. Effect: S.R. 1982/33 amended. – 2p. – 0 337 91246 7 £0.65

One-Way Traffic (Bangor) (Amendment) Order (Northern Ireland) 1994 No. 4. Enabling power: *S.I. 1981/154 (NI. 1)*, art. 21 (1). Issued: 21.01.94. Made: 10.01.94. Coming into force: 26.02.94. Effect: S.R. 1992/188 amended. – 2p. – 0 337 91004 9 £0.65

One-Way Traffic (Belfast) (Amendment No. 2) Order (Northern Ireland) 1994 No. 247. Enabling power: *S.I. 1981/154 (N.I. 1)*, art. 23 (1) (2). Issued: 08.07.94. Made: 29.06.94. Coming into force: 10.08.94. Effect: S.R. 1986/6 amended. – 2p. – 0 337 91247 5 £0.65

One-Way Traffic (Belfast) (Amendment No. 3) Order (Northern Ireland) 1994 No. 330. Enabling power: *S.I. 1981/154 (N.I. 1)*, art. 23 (1) (2). Issued: 02.09.94. Made: 23.08.94. Coming into force: 04.10.94. Effect: S.R. 1986/6 amended. – 2p. – 0 337 91330 7 £0.65

One-Way Traffic (Belfast) (Amendment No. 4) Order (Northern Ireland) 1994 No. 368. Enabling power: *S.I. 1981/154 (N.I. 1)*, art. 21 (1). Issued: 12.10.94. Made: 29.09.94. Coming into force: 10.11.94. Effect: S.R. 1986/6 amended. – 2p. – 0 337 91368 4 £0.65

One-Way Traffic (Belfast) (Amendment No. 5) Order (Northern Ireland) 1994 No. 434. Enabling power: *S.I. 1981/154 (N.I. 1)*, art. 21 (1). Issued: 17.11.94. Made: 08.11.94. Coming into force: 20.12.94. Effect: S.R. 1986/6 amended. – 2p. – 0 337 91434 6 £0.65

One-Way Traffic (Belfast) (Amendment) Order (Northern Ireland) 1994 No. 87.Enabling power: *S.I. 1981/154 (NI. 1)*, art. 23 (1) (2). Issued: 21.03.94. Made: 10.03.94. Coming into force: 21.04.94. Effect: S.R. 1986/6 amended. – 2p. – 0 337 91087 1 £0.65

One-Way Traffic (Londonderry) (Amendment) Order (Northern Ireland) 1994 No. 440. Enabling power: *S.I. 1981/154 (N.I.)*, 21 (1). Issued: 17.11.94. Made: 09.11.94. Coming into force: 21.12.94. Effect: S.R. 1981/161 amended. – 2p. – 0 337 91440 0 £0.65

One-Way Traffic (Newtownabbey) (Amendment) Order (Northern Ireland) 1994 No. 382. Enabling power: *S.I. 1981/154 (N.I. 1)*, art. 21 (1). Issued: 17.10.94. Made: 10.10.94. Coming into force: 21.11.94. Effect: S.R. 1986/5 amended. – 2p. – 0 337 91382 X £0.65

Price/availability are liable to change without notice

One-Way Traffic (Portrush) (Amendment) Order (Northern Ireland) 1994 No. 453. Enabling power: *S.I. 1981/154 (N.I. 1), art. 21 (1)*. Issued: 28.11.94. Made: 21.11.94. Coming into force: 10.01.95. Effect: S.R. 1979/268 amended. – 2p. – 0 33791453 2 *£0.65*

On-Street Parking (Amendment) Bye-Laws (Northern Ireland) 1994 No. 241. Enabling power: *S.I. 1981/154 (N.I.), arts. 107 (1), 109 (2), 110, 111 (1) (2)*. Issued: 08.07.94. Made: 27.06.94. Coming into force: 01.08.94. Effect: S.R. 1987/410 amended. – 8p. – 0 33791241 6 *£1.55*

Parking Places on Roads (Amendment No. 2) Order (Northern Ireland) 1994 No. 336. Enabling power: *S.I. 1981/154 (NI. 1), art. 104 (1) (c)*. Issued: 16.09.94. Made: 31.08.94. Coming into force: 12.10.94. Effect: S.R. 1993/201 amended. – 8p. – 0 33791336 6 *£1.95*

Parking Places on Roads (Amendment No. 3) Order (Northern Ireland) 1994 No. 416. Enabling power: *S.I. 1981/154 (N.I. 1), art. 104 (1) (c)*. Issued: 01.11.94. Made: 25.10.94. Coming into force: 05.12.94. Effect: S.R. 1993/201 amended. – 4p. – 0 33791416 8 *£1.10*

Parking Places on Roads (Amendment) Order (Northern Ireland) 1994 No. 207. Enabling power: *S.I 1981/154 (N.I. 1), art. 104 (1) (c)*. Issued: 14.06.94. Made: 02.06.94. Coming into force: 25.07.94. Effect: S.R. 1993/201 amended. – 4p. – 0 33791207 6 *£1.10*

Prohibition of Overtaking (Culcavey Road, Hillsborough) Order (Northern Ireland) 1994 No.392. Enabling power: *S.I. 1981/154 (N.I. 1), art. 22 (1)*. Issued: 26.10.94. Made: 14.10.94. Coming into force: 25.11.94. Effect: None. – 2p. – 0 33791392 7 *£0.65*

Prohibition of Traffic (Windsor Park, Bangor) Order (Northern Ireland) 1994 No. 475. Enabling power: *S.I. 1981/154 (N.I.), art. 22 (1)*. Issued: 12.12.94. Made: 05.12.94. Coming into force: 16.01.94. Effect: None. – 4p. – 0 33791475 3 *£1.10*

Public Service Vehicles (Amendment) Regulations (Northern Ireland) 1994 No. 225. Enabling power: *S.I. 1981/154 (N.I. 1), arts. 61 (1) (4) (5), 218 (1)*. Issued: 29.06.94. Made: 15.06.94. Coming into force: 01.08.94. Effect: S.R. 1985/123 amended. – 2p. – 0 33791225 4 *£0.65*

Public Service Vehicles (Construction) (Amendment) Regulations (Northern Ireland) 1994 No.435. Enabling power: *S.I. 1981/154 (N.I. 1), arts. 28 (1), 218 (1)*. Issued: 16.11.94. Made: 08.11.94. Coming into force: 20.12.94. Effect: S.R. & O. 1960/91 amended. – 36p. – 0 33791435 4 *£5.70*

Public Service Vehicles (Licence Fees) (Amendment) Regulations (Northern Ireland) 1994 No.407. Enabling power: *S.I. 1981/154 (N.I. 1), arts. 61 (1), 66 (1), 218 (1)*. Issued: 01.11.94. Made: 24.10.94. Coming into force: 01.12.94. Effect: S.R. 1985/123 amended & S.R. 1991/356; 1992/381; 1993/396 revoked. – 4p. – 0 33791407 9 *£1.10*

Roads (Speed Limit) (No. 2) Order (Northern Ireland) 1994 No. 154. Enabling power: *S.I. 1981/154 (NI. 1), art. 50 (4)*. Issued: 04.05.94. Made: 18.04.94. Coming into force: 31.05.94. Effect: S.R. 1991/316; 1992/499 amended. – 4p. – 0 33791154 1 *£1.10*

Roads (Speed Limit) (No. 3) Order (Northern Ireland) 1994 No. 195. Enabling power: *S.I. 1981/154 (N.I. 1), art. 50 (4) (c)*. Issued: 03.06.94. Made: 24.05.94. Coming into force: 18.07.94. Effect: S.R. 1978/290; 1979/61; 1988/322 amended. – 4p. – 0 33791195 9 *£1.10*

Roads (Speed Limit) (No. 4) Order (Northern Ireland) 1994 No. 196. Enabling power: *S.I. 1981/154 (N.I. 1), art. 50 (4)*. Issued: 03.06.94. Made: 24.05.94. Coming into force: 18.07.94. Effect: S.R. 1983/109; 1989/109; 1990/166 amended. – 4p. – 0 33791196 7 *£1.10*

Roads (Speed Limit) (No. 5) Order (Northern Ireland) 1994 No. 373. Enabling power: *S.I. 1981/154 (N.I. 1), art. 50 (4) (c)*. Issued: 12.10.94. Made: 04.10.94. Coming into force: 21.11.94. Effect: S.R. 1977/40; 1982/131; 1986/292; 1987/164; 1991/317; 1992/319 amended. – 8p. – 0 33791373 0 *£1.55*

Roads (Speed Limit) (No. 6) Order (Northern Ireland) 1994 No. 374. Enabling power: *S.I. 1981/154 (N.I. 1), art. 50 (4)*. Issued: 12.10.94. Made: 04.10.94. Coming into force: 21.11.94. Effect: S.R. 1977/40; 1982/134; 1986/293; 1987/165 amended. – 4p. – 0 33791374 9 *£1.10*

Roads (Speed Limit) (No. 7) Order (Northern Ireland) 194 No. 397. Enabling power: *S.I. 1981/154 (N.I. 1), art. 50 (4) (c)*. Issued: 01.11.94. Made: 20.10.94. Coming into force: 01.12.94. Effect: S.R. 1978/290; 1983/108; 1985/275; 1986/292 amended. – 4p. – 0 33791397 8 *£1.10*

Roads (Speed Limit) (No. 8) Order (Northern Ireland) 1994 No. 398. Enabling power: *S.I. 1981/154 (N.I. 1), art. 50 (4) (a)*. Issued: 01.11.94. Made: 20.10.94. Coming into force: 01.12.94. Effect: S.R. 1980/207; 1985/276 amended. – 4p. – 0 33791398 6 *£1.10*

Roads (Speed Limit) Order (Northern Ireland) 1994 No. 153. Enabling power: *S.I. 1981/154 (NI. 1), art. 50 (4) (c)*. Issued: 04.05.94. Made: 18.04.94. Coming into force: 31.05.94. Effect: S.R. & O. (N.I.) 1957/231; 1960/83; 1970/25, 57 & S.R. 1977/40; 1978/290; 1980/205; 1981/207; 1983/86; 1986/292; 1987/164; 1989/108; 1989/256; 1991/315, 317, 318; 1992/498 amended. – 16p. – 0 33791153 3 *£3.20*

Road Traffic (Third-Party Risks) Order (Northern Ireland) 1994 No. 18. Enabling power: *S.I. 1981/154 (NI. 1), art. 90 (2) (b)*. Issued: 03.02.94. Made: 19.01.94. Coming into force: 01.03.94. Effect: S.I. 1981/154 (NI. 1) amended. – 2p. – 0 33791018 9 *£0.65*

Taxis (Antrim) Bye-Laws (Northern Ireland) 1994 No. 451. Enabling power: *S.I. 1981/154 (N.I. 1), art. 65 (1) (2)*. Issued: 28.11.94. Made: 18.11.94. Coming into force: 21.12.94. Effect: None. – 4p. – 0 33791451 6 *£1.10*

Price/availability are liable to change without notice

Taxis (Downpatrick) (Revocation) Bye-laws (Northern Ireland) 1994 No. 135. Enabling power: *S.I. 1981/154 (N.I. 1), art. 65 (1)*. Issued: 25.04.94. Made: 31.03.94. Coming into force: 16.05.94. Effect: S.R. 1990/225 revoked. – 2p. – 0 33791135 5 *£0.65*

Temporary Speed Limit (Sydenham By-Pass, Route A2, Belfast) (No. 2) Order (Northern Ireland) 1994 No. 448. Enabling power: *S.I. 1981/154 (N.I. 1), art. 51 (4)*. Issued: 28.11.94. Made: 17.11.94. Coming into force: 01.01.95. Effect: None. – 2p. – 0 33791448 6 *£0.65*

Temporary Speed Limit (Sydenham By-Pass, Route A2, Belfast) Order (Northern Ireland) 1994 No.297. Enabling power: *S.I. 1981/154 (N.I. 1), art. 51 (1)*. Issued: 03.08.94. Made: 27.07.94. Coming into force: 01.09.94. Effect: None. – 2p. – 0 33791297 1 *£0.65*

Traffic Signs (Amendment No. 2) Regulations (Northern Ireland) 1994 No. 454. Enabling power: *S.I. 1981/154 (N.I. 1), art. 27*. Issued: 28.11.94. Made: 21.11.94. Coming into force: 02.11.94. Effect: S.R. 1979/386 amended. – 12p. – 0 33791454 0 *£2.80*

Traffic Signs (Amendment) Regulations (Northern Ireland) 1994 No. 201. Enabling power: *S.I. 1981/154 (N.I. 1), art. 27*. Issued: 08.06.94. Made: 31.05.94. Coming into force: 31.07.94. Effect: S.R. 1979/386 amended. – 12p. – 0 33791201 7 *£2.80*

Traffic Weight Restriction (Fergy's Bridge, Route U8047, Markethill) Order (Northern Ireland) 1994 No. 393. Enabling power: *S.I. 1981/154 (N.I. 1), 22 (1)*. Issued: 26.10.94. Made: 14.10.94. Coming into force: 25.11.94. Effect: None. – 2p. – 0 33791393 5 *£0.65*

Traffic Weight Restriction (Lisnabilla Road, Moira) Order (Northern Ireland) 1994 No.272. Enabling power: *S.I. 1981/154 (N.I. 1), art. 22 (1)*. Issued: 02.08.94. Made: 18.07.94. Coming into force: 01.09.94. Effect: None. – 2p. – 0 33791272 6 *£0.65*

Traffic Weight Restriction (Manooney Road, Killylea) Order (Northern Ireland) 1994 No.86. Enabling power: *S.I. 1981/154 (NI. 1), arts. 23 (1) (2)*. Issued: 21.03.94. Made: 10.03.94. Coming into force: 25.04.94. Effect: None. – 2p. – 0 33791086 3 *£0.65*

Traffic Weight Restriction Order (Northern Ireland) 1994 No. 465. Enabling power: *S.I. 1981/154 (N.I. 1), art. 22 (1)*. Issued: 07.12.94. Made: 29.11.94. Coming into force: 31.12.94. Effect: S.R. & O. (N.I.) 1961/36; 1963/121; 1967/182; 1969/269, 302; 1971/62, 390; 1972/292, 293, 294, 295, 296, 297, 298, 299, 300, 301, 302, 303, 304, 305, 306, 307, 308, 309, 310, 314; 1973/73, 74, 277, 284, 354, 407; 1974/41, 42, 238; 1975/126, 170; 1976/111; 1978/55, 295; 1980/272, 303, 308; 1981/316, 330; 1982/204 revoked. – 20p. – 0 33791465 6 *£3.70*

Urban Clearways (Belfast) (No. 2) Order (Amendment) Order (Northern Ireland) 1994 No.458. Enabling power: *S.I. 1981/154 (NI. 1), art. 21 (1)*. Issued: 01.12.94. Made: 23.11.94. Coming into force: 04.01.95. Effect: S.I. 1981/304 amended. – 4p. – 0 33791458 3 *£1.10*

SALARIES

Salaries (Parliamentary Commissioner and Commissioner for Complaints) Order (Northern Ireland) 1994 No. 400. Enabling power: *S.I. 1973/1086 (N.I. 14), art. 4 (2)*. Issued: 01.11.94. Made: 14.10.94. Coming into force: 02.12.94. Effect: S.R. 1993/333 revoked. – 2p. – 0 33791400 1 *£0.65*

SEEDS

Beet Seeds Regulations (Northern Ireland) 1994 No. 251. Enabling power: *Seeds Act (Northern Ireland) 1965, ss. 1 (1) (2A), 2, 4 (1) to (4)*. Issued: 26.07.94. Made: 30.06.94. Coming into force: 22.08.94. Effect: S.R. 1976/296 revoked. – 36p., ill. – 0 33791251 3 *£5.70*

Cereal Seeds Regulations (Northern Ireland) 1994 No. 254. Enabling power: *Seeds Act (Northern Ireland) 1965, ss. 1 (1) (2A), 2, 4 (1) to (4)*. Issued: 27.07.94. Made: 30.06.94. Coming into force: 22.08.94. Effect: S.R. 1976/300; 1979/419; 1988/317 revoked. –48p., ill. – 0 33791254 8 *£6.35*

Fodder Plant Seeds Regulations (Northern Ireland) 1994 No. 252. Enabling power: *Seeds Act (Northern Ireland) 1965, ss. 1 (1) (2A), 2, 4 (1) (2) (3) (4)*. Issued: 27.07.94. Made: 30.06.94. Coming into force: 22.08.94. Effect: S.R. 1976/299; 1977/232 revoked. –52p. – 0 33791252 1 *£6.95*

Oil and Fibre Plant Seeds Regulations (Northern Ireland) 1994 No. 255. Enabling power: *Seeds Act (Northern Ireland) 1965, ss. 1 (1) (2A), 2, 4 (1) to (4)*. Issued: 26.07.94. Made: 30.06.94. Coming into force: 22.08.94. Effect: S.R. 1976/298 amended. – 40p. – 0 33791255 6 *£5.70*

Seed Potatoes (Amendment) Regulations (Northern Ireland) 1994 No. 459. Enabling power: *Seeds Act (Northern Ireland) 1965, ss. 1, 2, 12 (1)*. Issued: 29.11.94. Made: 23.11.94. Coming into force: 30.12.94. Effect: S.R. 1981/243 amended. – 8p. – 0 33791459 1 *£1.95*

Seeds (Registration, Licensing and Enforcement) Regulations (Northern Ireland) 1994 No.253. Enabling power: *Seeds Act (Northern Ireland) 1965, ss. 1 (1) (2A), 2 (2) (3), 7 (3), 9 (1) (2) (3)*. Issued: 26.07.94. Made: 30.06.94. Coming into force: 22.08.94. Effect: S.R. 1974/146; 1975/152 revoked. –28p. – 0 33791253 X *£4.70*

Vegetable Seeds Regulations (Northern Ireland) 1994 No. 250. Enabling power: *Seeds Act (Northern Ireland) 1965, ss. 1 (1) (2A), 2, 4 (1) to (4)*. Issued: 26.07.94. Made: 30.06.94. Coming into force: 22.08.94. Effect: S.R. 1976/297 revoked. – 40p., ill. – 0 33791250 5 *£5.70*

SOCIAL SECURITY

The Income-Related Benefits (Miscellaneous Amendments No. 2) Regulations (Northern Ireland) 1994 No. 233. Enabling power: *Social Security and Benefits (Northern Ireland) Act 1992, ss. 122 (1), 129 (2) (4), 132 (3) (4) (b).* Issued: 29.06.94. Made: 21.06.94. Coming into force: 01.08.94., 01.09.94, 05.09.94, 06.09.94. Effect: S.R. 1987/459, 461, 463; 1992/78 amended & S.R. 1992/327; 1993/312 revoked. – 4p. – 0 337 91233 5 *£1.10*

The Income-Related Benefits (Miscellaneous Amendments No. 3) Regulations (Northern Ireland) 1994 No. 266. Enabling power: *Social Security Contributions and Benefits (Northern Ireland) Act 1992, ss. 122 (1) (a) (d), 131 (1), 133 (2) (i).* Issued: 26.07.94. Made: 11.07.94. Coming into force: 01.08.94. Effect: S.R. 1987/459, 461 amended. – 4p. – 0 337 91266 1 *£1.10*

The Income-Related Benefits (Miscellaneous Amendments No. 4) Regulations (Northern Ireland) 1994 No. 274. Enabling power: *Social Security Constributions and Benefits (Northern Ireland) Act 1992, ss. 122 (1) (b) (c) (d), 132 (3) (4) (b), 171 (5).* Issued: 02.08.94. Made: 19.07.94. Coming into force: 03.10.94. Effect: S.R. 1987/461, 463; 1992/78 amended. –12p. – 0 337 91274 2 *£2.40*

The Income-related Benefits (Miscellaneous Amendments No. 5) Regulations (Northern Ireland) 1994 No. 327. Enabling power: *Social Security Contributions and Benefits (Northern Ireland) Act 1992, ss. 122 (1) (a) (b) (c), 127 (3) (4) (b), 128 (6) (7) (b), 131 (1) (6), 132 (3) (4) (a) (b) (c), 133 (2) (c) (d) (i), 171 (5) & Social Security Administration (Northern Ireland) Act 1992, ss. 5 (1) (l), 25 (1), 28 (3).* Issued: 01.09.94. Made: 22.08.94. Coming into force: 03.10.94. for regs. 1 (1), 2 & 04.10.94. for regs. 3, 4. Effect: S.R. 1987/459, 463; 1992/78 amended. – 16p. – 0 337 91327 7 *£3.20*

The Income-Related Benefits (Miscellaneous Amendments No. 6) Regulations (Northern Ireland) 1994 No. 474. Enabling power: *Social Security Contributions and Benefits (Northern Ireland) Act 1992, s. 131 (1) (6).* Issued: 15.12.94. Made: 02.12.94. Coming into force: 02.12.94. Effect: S.R. 1987/459, 461 amended. – 4p. – 0 337 91474 5 *£1.10*

The Income-Related Benefits (Miscellaneous Amendments) Regulations (Northern Ireland) 1994 No. 77. Enabling power: *Social Security Contributions and Benefits (Northern Ireland) Act 1992, ss. 122 (1) (a) (b) (c), 123 (1) (d) (i), 131 (1), 132 (3) (4) (a) (b), 133 (2) (d) (ii), 171 (5).* Issued: 21.03.94. Made: 07.03.94. Coming into force: 31.03.94.; 11.04.94.; 12.04.94. in accord. with reg. 1 (1). Effect: S.R. 1987/459, 463; 1992/78 amended. – 16p. – 0 337 91077 4 *£3.20*

The Income Support (General) (Amendment) Regulations (Northern Ireland) 1994 No. 138. Enabling power: *Social Security Contributions and Benefits (Northern Ireland) Act 1992, ss. 122 (1) (a), 131 (1).* Issued: 18.04.94. Made: 08.04.94. Coming into force: 02.05.94. Effect: S.R. 1987/459 amended. – 4p. – 0 337 91138 X *£1.10*

The Maternity Allowance and Statutory Maternity Pay Regulations (Northern Ireland) 1994 No. 176. Enabling power: *European Communities Act 1972, s. 2 (2).* Issued: 16.05.94. Made: 04.05.94. Coming into force: 04.09.94. for Regulation 5. 16.10.94. for all other purposes. Effect: 1992 c.7 amended. – 8p. – 0 337 91176 2 *£1.55*

The Social Fund (Cold Weather Payments) (General) (Amendment) Regulations (Northern Ireland) 1994 No. 383. Enabling power: *Social Security Contributions and Benefits (Northern Ireland) Act 1992, s. 134 (2).* Issued: 24.10.94. Made: 10.10.94. Coming into force: 01.11.94. Effect: S.R. 1988/368 amended & S.R. 1991/48 revoked. – 2p. – 0 337 91383 8 *£0.65*

The Social Fund (Maternity and Funeral Expenses) (General) (Amendment) Regulations (Northern Ireland) 1994 No. 68. Enabling power: *Social Security Contributions and Benefits (Northern Ireland) Act 1992, s. 134 (1) (a).* Issued: 10.03.94. Made: 02.03.94. Coming into force: 01.04.94. Effect: S.R. 1987/150 amended. – 4p. – 0 337 91068 5 *£1.10*

The Social Security (1989 Order) (Commencement No. 3) Order (Northern Ireland) 1994 No. 234 (C. 8). Enabling power: *S.I. 1989/1342 (N.I. 13). art. 1 (2) & Northern Ireland Act 1974, sch. 1, para. 2 (1) Bringing into operation various provisions of the 1989 order on 23.06.94.* . Issued: 29.06.94. Made: 22.06.94. Effect: None. – 4p. – 0 337 91234 3 *£1.10*

The Social Security (Adjudication) (Amendment No. 2) Regulations (Northern Ireland) 1994 No. 150. Enabling power: *Social Security Administration (Northern Ireland) Act 1992, ss. 4 (3) (a), 57 (1), sch. 3 paras. 2, 3.* Issued: 25.04.94. Made: 15.04.94. Coming into force: 11.05.94. Effect: S.R. 1987/82; 1990/119 amended. – 4p. – 0 337 91150 9 *£1.10*

The Social Security (Adjudication) (Amendment No. 3) Regulations (Northern Ireland) 1994 No. 396. Enabling power: *Social Security Administration (Northern Ireland) Act 1992, s. 59 (1).* Issued: 26.10.94. Made: 19.10.94. Coming into force: 14.11.94. Effect: S.R. 1987/82 amended. – 4p. – 0 337 91396 X *£1.10*

The Social Security (Adjudication) (Amendment) Regulations (Northern Ireland) 1994 No. 21. Enabling power: *Social Security Administration (Northern Ireland) Act 1992, ss. 25 (1) (b), 30 (8), 33 (10), 59 (1) (2).* Issued: 26.01.94. Made: 21.01.94. Coming into force: 28.02.94. Effect: S.R. 1987/82 amended. – 2p. – 0 337 91021 9 *£0.65*

The Social Security (Attendance Allowance and Disability Living Allowance) (Amendment) Regulations (Northern Ireland) 1994 No. 263. Enabling power: *Social Security Contributions and Benefits (Northern Ireland) Act 1992, ss. 67 (2), 72 (8), 73 (5) & Social Security Administration (Northern Ireland) Act 1992, s. 71 (1).* Issued: 26.07.94. Made: 06.07.94. Coming into force: 01.08.94. Effect: S.R. 1992/20, 32; 1993/149 amended. – 12p. – 0 337 91263 7 *£2.40*

Price/availability are liable to change without notice

The Social Security Benefit (Persons Abroad) (Amendment No. 2) Regulations (Northern Ireland) 1994 No. 269. Enabling power: *Social Security Contributions and Benefits (Northern Ireland) Act 1992, s. 113 (1)*. Issued: 26.07.94. Made: 14.07.94. Coming into force: 06.08.94. Effect: S.R. 1978/114 amended. – 8p. – 0 33791269 6 £1.55

The Social Security Benefit (Persons Abroad) (Amendment) Regulations (Northern Ireland) 1994 No. 45. Enabling power: *Social Security Contributions and Benefits (Northern Ireland) Act 1992, s. 113 (1) (a)*. Issued: 18.02.94. Made: 11.02.94. Coming into force: 08.03.94. Effect: S.R. 1978/114; 1990/22 amended. – 8p. – 0 337910456 £1.55

The Social Security Benefits Up-Rating Order (Northern Ireland) 1994 No. 74. Enabling power: *Social Security Administration (Northern Ireland) Act 1992, s. 132*. Issued: 17.03.94. Made: 07.03.94. Coming into force: 01.04.94.; 03.04.94.; 06.04.94.; 11.04.94.; 12.04.94.; 13.04.94. per art. 1 (1). Effect: 1966 c. 6 (NI); 1992 c. 7; S.R. 1976/223; 1978/105; 1987/30, 459, 460, 463; S.R. 1992/32, 78 amended & S.R. 1993/150 revoked. – 40p. – 0 337 91074 X £5.70

The Social Security Benefits Up-rating Regulations (Northern Ireland) 1994 No. 75. Enabling power: *Social Security Contributions and Benefits (Northern Ireland) Act 1992, ss. 57 (1) (a) (ii), 113 (1) (a), sch. 7, para. 2 (3). & Social Security Administration (Northern Ireland) Act 1992, s. 135 (3)*. Issued: 11.03.94. Made: 07.03.94. Coming into force: 11.04.94. Effect: S.R. 1984/92, 245 amended & S.R. 1993/159 revoked. – 4p. – 0 337910758 £1.10

The Social Security (Categorisation of Earners) (Amendment) Regulations (Northern Ireland) 1994 No. 92. Enabling power: *Social Security Contributions and Benefits (Northern Ireland) Act 1992, ss. 2 (2), 7 (2)*. Issued: 23.03.94. Made: 14.03.94. Coming into force: 06.04.94. Effect: S.R. 1978/401 amended. – 4p. – 0 337910928 £1.10

The Social Security (Claims and Payments) (Amendment No. 2) Regulations (Northern Ireland) 1994 No. 456. Enabling power: *Social Security Administration (Northern Ireland) Act 1992, s. 5 (1) (a) (c) (f) (i) (j) & S.I. 1994/1898 (N.I. 12), art. 14*. Issued: 28.11.94. Made: 22.11.94. Coming into force: 13.04.95. Effect: S.R. 1987/465; 1988/141; 1990/398; 1992/7, 453 amended. – 8p. – 0 337914567 £1.95

The Social Security (Claims and Payments) (Amendment No. 3) Regulations (Northern Ireland) 1994 No. 457. Enabling power: *Social Security Administration (Northern Ireland) Act 1992, s. 13A (2) (b)*. Issued: 28.11.94. Made: 22.11.94. Coming into force: 01.04.95. Effect: S.R. 1987/465 amended & S.R. 1992/534 revoked. – 2p. – 0 337914575 £0.65

The Social Security (Claims and Payments) (Amendment No. 4) Regulations (Northern Ireland) 1994 No. 484. Enabling power: *Social Security Administration (Northern Ireland) Act 1992, ss. 5 (l) (j), 165 (6)*. Issued: 21.12.94. Made: 14.12.94. Coming into force: 10.01.95. Effect: S.R. 1987/465 amended. – 4p. – 0 337914842 £1.10

The Social Security (Claims and Payments) (Amendment) Regulations (Northern Ireland) 1994 No. 345. Enabling power: *Social Security Administration (Northern Ireland) Act 1992, s. 5 (1) (a) (c) (g) (j) (n) (p) (q)*. Issued: 16.09.94. Made: 06.09.94. Coming into force: 03.10.94. Effect: S.R. 1987/465; 1990/398; 1991/488 amended. – 8p. – 0 337913455 £1.55

The Social Security (Contributions) (Amendment No. 2) Regulations (Northern Ireland) 1994 No. 219. Enabling power: *Social Security Contributions and Benefits (Northern Ireland) Act 1992, sch. 1, para. 8 (1) (d), s. 3 (2) (3)*. Issued: 21.06.94. Made: 13.06.94. Coming into force: 06.07.94. Effect: S.R. 1979/186; 1992/138 amended. – 4p. – 0 33791219 X £1.10

The Social Security (Contributions) (Amendment No. 3) Regulations (Northern Ireland) 1994 No. 328. Enabling power: *Social Security Contributions and Benefits (Northern Ireland) Act 1992, s. 3 (2) (3)*. Issued: 30.08.94. Made: 23.08.94. Coming into force: 24.08.94. Effect: S.R. 1979/186; 1993/463 amended. – 4p. – 0 337913285 £1.10

The Social Security (Contributions) (Amendment No. 4) Regulations (Northern Ireland) 1994 No. 343. Enabling power: *Social Security Contributions and Benefits (Northern Ireland) Act 1992, sch. 1, para. 6 (1)*. Issued: 16.09.94. Made: 05.09.94. Coming into force: 30.09.94. Effect: S.R. 1979/186 amended. – 2p. – 0 337913439 £0.65

The Social Security (Contributions) (Amendment) Regulations (Northern Ireland) 1994 No. 78. Enabling power: *Social Security Contributions and Benefits (Northern Ireland) Act 1992, ss. 5, 119*. Issued: 11.03.94. Made: 07.03.94. Coming into force: 06.04.94. Effect: S.R. 1979/186 amended & S.R. 1991/80; 1993/61 revoked. – 4p. – 0 337910782 £1.10

The Social Security (Contributions) (Miscellaneous Amendments) Regulations (Northern Ireland) 1994 No. 94. Enabling power: *Social Security Contributions and Benefits (Northern Ireland) Act 1992, s. 10 (7) (9), sch. 1, para. 6 (1)*. Issued: 31.03.94. Made: 11.03.94. Coming into force: 06.04.94. Effect: 1992 c.7; S.R. 1979/186 amended. – 4p. – 0 337910944 £1.10

The Social Security (Contributions) (Re-Rating and Northern Ireland Natinal Insurance Fund Payments) Order (Northern Ireland) 1994 No. 79. Enabling power: *Social Security Administration Act 1992, ss. 141 (4) (5), 142 (2), 142 (1), 145 (2), 189 (1) (3) & Social Security Act 1993, s. 2 (2) (8)*. Issued: 11.03.94. Made: 07.03.94. Coming into force: 06.04.94. Effect: 1992 c. 7 amended. – 4p. – 0 337910790 £1.10

The Social Security (Credits) (Amendment) Regulations (Northern Ireland) 1994 No. 265. Enabling power: *Social Security Contributions and Benefits (Northern Ireland) Act 1992, s. 22 (5)*. Issued: 26.07.94. Made: 11.07.94. Coming into force: 08.08.94. Effect: S.R. 1975/113; 1983/76, 348; 1987/153; 1988/326 amended. – 4p. – 0 337912653 £1.10

The Social Security (Cyprus) Order (Northern Ireland) 1994 No. 262. Enabling power: *Social Security Administration (Northern Ireland) Act 1992, s. 155 (1) (2)*. Issued: 08.07.94. Made: 29.06.94. Coming into force: 04.07.94. Effect: 1992 c. 7, c. 8; S.R. 1983/387; 1988/120 amended. – 12p. – 0 337912629 £1.95

Price/availability are liable to change without notice

342 STATUTORY MATERNITY PAY

The Social Security (Incapacity Benefit Increases for Dependents) Regulations (Northern Ireland) 1994 No. 485. Enabling power: *Social Security Contributions and Benefits (Northern Ireland) Act 1992, ss. 3 (2), 80 (7), 86A, 87, 89, 90, 114 (1), 121 (5)*. Issued: 22.12.94. Made: 14.12.94. Coming into force: 13.04.95. for regs. 1 to 15 (6) (a), (6) (b) (ii) (c) (ii), (7) (8) & 13.05.95. for reg. 15 (6) (b) (i) (c) (i). Effect: S.R. 1977/74 amended. – 16p. – 0 337 91485 0 £3.20

The Social Security (Incapacity Benefit) Regulations (Northern Ireland) 1994 No. 461. Enabling power: *Social Security Contributions and Benefits (Northern Ireland) Act 1992, ss. 30B (7), 30C (3) (4) (a) (6), 30D (3), 30E (1) (2)*. Issued: 05.12.94. Made: 25.11.94. Coming into force: 13.04.95. Effect: None. – 8p. – 0 337 91461 3 £1.95

The Social Security (Incapacity for Work) (1994 Order) (Commencement) Order (Northern Ireland) 1994 No. 450 (C. 15). Enabling power: *S.I. 1994/1898 (N.I. 12), art. 1 (2). & Northern Ireland Act 1974, sch. 1, para. 2 (1)*. Bringing into operation various provisions of the 1994 order on 21.11.94, 06.04.95., 13.04.95. Issued: 28.11.94. Made: 18.11.94. Effect: None. – 4p. – 0 337 91450 8 £1.10

The Social Security (Industrial Injuries) (Prescribed Diseases) (Amendment) Regulations (Northern Ireland) 1994 No. 347. Enabling power: *Social Security Contributions and Benefits (Northern Ireland) Act 1992, ss. 108 (2), 109 (2), 171 (3)*. Issued: 22.09.94. Made: 08.09.94. Coming into force: 10.10.94. Effect: S.R. 1986/179 amended. – 4p. – 0 337 91347 1 £1.10

The Social Security (Jersey and Guernsey) Order (Northern Ireland) 1994 No. 427. Enabling power: *Social Security Administration (Northern Ireland) Act 1992, s. 155 (1) (2)*. Issued: 09.11.94. Made: 02.11.94. Coming into force: 02.11.94. Effect: S.R. & O. (N.I.) 1951/183; S.R. 1977/92; 1978/327; 1982/370; 1983/98; 1988/120; 1992/328 amended. – 28p. – 0 337 91427 3 £4.70

The Social Security Maternity Benefits, Statutory Maternity Pay and Statutory Sick Pay (Amendment) Regulations (Northern Ireland) 1994 No. 191. Enabling power: *Social Security Contributions and Benefits (Northern Ireland) Act 1992, ss. 35 (3) (b) (i) (c), 119, 149 (6), 160 (4) (9) (e), 161 (1) (3), 162 (3), sch. 11, para. 1*. Issued: 01.06.94. Made: 20.05.94. Coming into force: 11.06.94. Effect: S.R. 1987/30, 151, 170; 1982/263 amended. – 8p. – 0 337 91191 6 £1.95

The Social Security (Medical Evidence) (Amendment) Regulations (Northern Ireland) 1994 No. 468. Enabling power: *Social Security Administration (Northern Ireland) Act 1992, sch. 3, para. 4 & S.I. 1994/1898 (N.I. 12), art. 14 (1)*. Issued: 07.12.94. Made: 30.11.94. Coming into force: 13.04.95. Effect: S.R. 1976/175; 1984/317 amended. – 8p. – 0 337 91468 0 £1.95

The Social Security Pensions (Home Responsibilities) Regulations (Northern Ireland) 1994 No. 89. Enabling power: *Social Security Contributions and Benefits (Northern Ireland) Act 1992, ss. 21 (3), 171 (5), sch. 3, para 5 (7) (b)*. Issued: 21.03.94. Made: 11.03.94. Coming into force: 06.04.94. Effect: S.R. 1978/102; 1992/6 amended & S.R. 1981/71; 1988/125 revoked. – 8p. – 0 337 91089 8 £1.55

The Social Security Revaluation of Earnings Factors Order (Northern Ireland) 1994 No. 155. Enabling power: *Social Security Administration (Northern Ireland) Act 1992, s. 130*. Issued: 04.05.94. Made: 20.04.94. Coming into force: 24.05.94. Effect: None. – 4p. – 0 337 91155 X £1.10

The Social Security (Severe Disablement Allowance) (Amendment) Regulations (Northern Ireland) 1994 No. 462. Enabling power: *Social Security Contributions and Benefits (Northern Ireland) Act 1992, s. 68 (11) (b) (c) (d) & S.I. 1994/1898 (N.I. 12), art. 14 (1)*. Issued: 05.12.94. Made: 25.11.94. Coming into force: 13.04.94. Effect: S.R. 1984/317; 1986/337; 1989/443; 1992/146; 1994/152 amended. – 4p. – 0 337 91462 1 £1.10

The Social Security (Severe Disablement Allowance and Invalid Care Allowance) (Amendment) Regulations (Northern Ireland) 1994 No. 370. Enabling power: *European Communities Act 1972, s. 2 (2)*. Issued: 12.10.94. Made: 03.10.94. Coming into force: 28.10.94. Effect: 1992 c. 7; S.I. 1994/1898 (N.I. 12); S.R. 1976/99; 1984/317 amended. – 8p. – 0 337 91370 6 £1.95

The Social Security (Sickness and Invalidity Benefit and Severe Disablement Allowance) (Miscellaneous Amendments) Regulations (Northern Ireland)m 1994 No. 152. Enabling power: *Social Security Contributions and Benefits (Northern Ireland) Act 1992, ss. 57 (1) (a) (ii), 68 (11) (e) (ii)*. Issued: 25.04.94. Made: 18.04.94. Coming into force: 16.05.94. Effect: S.R. 1984/245, 317; 1992/146; 1994/75 amended & S.R. 1987/221 revoked. – 4p. – 0 337 91152 5 £1.10

The Statutory Maternity Pay (Compensation of Employers) and Miscellaneous Amendment Regulations (Northern Ireland) 1994 No. 271. Enabling power: *Social Security Contributions and Benefits (Northern Ireland) Act 1992, ss. 35 (3), 163 (1) (1B) (4)*. Issued: 02.08.94. Made: 18.07.94. Coming into force: 31.07.94. for regs 1, 8, 9 (b); 04.09.94. for all other regs. Effect: S.R. 1987/170; 1994/191 amended & S.R. 1987/80; 1988/95; 1994/84 revoked. – 8p. – 0 337 91271 8 £1.55

The Workmen's Compensation (Supplementation) (Amendment) Regulations (Northern Ireland) 1994 No. 83. Enabling power: *Social Security Contributions and Benefits (Northern Ireland) Act 1992, s. 171 (4), sch. 8, para. 2*. Issued: 15.03.94. Made: 08.03.94. Coming into force: 13.04.94. Effect: S.R. 1983/101 amended & S.R. 1993/153 revoked. – 4p. – 0 337 91083 9 £1.95

STATUTORY MATERNITY PAY

The Social Security Benefits Up-Rating Order (Northern Ireland) 1994 No. 74. Enabling power: *Social Security Administration (Northern Ireland) Act 1992, s. 132*. Issued: 17.03.94. Made: 07.03.94. Coming into force: 01.04.94.; 03.04.94.; 06.04.94.; 11.04.94.; 12.04.94.; 13.04.94. per art. 1 (1). Effect: 1966 c. 6 (NI); 1992 c. 7; S.R. 1976/223; 1978/105; 1987/30, 459, 460, 463; S.R. 1992/32, 78 amended & S.R. 1993/150 revoked. – 40p. – 0 337 91074 X £5.70

Price/availability are liable to change without notice

The Social Security Maternity Benefits, Statutory Maternity Pay and Statutory Sick Pay (Amendment) Regulations (Northern Ireland) 1994 No. 191. Enabling power: *Social Security Contributions and Benefits (Northern Ireland) Act 1992, ss. 35 (3) (b) (i) (c), 119, 149 (6), 160 (4) (9) (e), 161 (1) (3), 162 (3), sch. 11, para. 1.* Issued: 01.06.94. Made: 20.05.94. Coming into force: 11.06.94. Effect: S.R. 1987/30, 151, 170; 1982/263 amended. – 8p. – 0 337 91191 6 *£1.95*

The Statutory Maternity Pay (Compensation of Employers) (Amendment) Regulations (Northern Ireland) 1994 No. 84. Enabling power: *Social Security Contributions and Benefits (Northern Ireland) Act 1992, s. 163 (1) (c).* Issued: 11.03.94. Made: 08.03.94. Coming into force: 06.04.94. Effect: S.R. 1987/80 amended & 1991/94 revoked. – 2p. – 0 337 91084 7 *£0.65*

The Statutory Maternity Pay (Compensation of Employers) and Miscellaneous Amendment Regulations (Northern Ireland) 1994 No. 271. Enabling power: *Social Security Contributions and Benefits (Northern Ireland) Act 1992, ss. 35 (3), 163 (1) (1B) (4).* Issued: 02.08.94. Made: 18.07.94. Coming into force: 31.07.94. for regs 1, 8, 9 (b); 04.09.94. for all other regs. Effect: S.R. 1987/170; 1994/191 amended & S.R. 1987/80; 1988/95; 1994/84 revoked. – 8p. – 0 337 91271 8 *£1.55*

STATUTORY SICK PAY

The Social Security Benefits Up-Rating Order (Northern Ireland) 1994 No. 74. Enabling power: *Social Security Administration (Northern Ireland) Act 1992, s. 132.* Issued: 17.03.94. Made: 07.03.94. Coming into force: 01.04.94.; 03.04.94; 06.04.94; 11.04.94; 12.04.94; 13.04.94 per art. 1 (1). Effect: 1966 c. 6 (NI); 1992 c. 7; S.R. 1976/223; 1978/105; 1987/30, 459, 460, 463; S.R. 1992/32, 78 amended & S.R. 1993/150 revoked. – 40p. – 0 337 91074 X *£5.70*

The Social Security Maternity Benefits, Statutory Maternity Pay and Statutory Sick Pay (Amendment) Regulations (Northern Ireland) 1994 No. 191. Enabling power: *Social Security Contributions and Benefits (Northern Ireland) Act 1992, ss. 35 (3) (b) (i) (c), 119, 149 (6), 160 (4) (9) (e), 161 (1) (3), 162 (3), sch. 11, para. 1.* Issued: 01.06.94. Made: 20.05.94. Coming into force: 11.06.94. Effect: S.R. 1987/30, 151, 170; 1982/263 amended. – 8p. – 0 337 91191 6 *£1.95*

The Statutory Sick Pay (Northern Ireland) Order 1994 (Consequential) Regulations (Northern Ireland) 1994 No. 103. Enabling power: *Social Security Contributions and Benefits (Northern Ireland) Act 1992, s. 154 (1) (a) & Social Security Administration (Northern Ireland) Act 1992, s. 77 (1) & S.I. 1994/766 (NI. 5), art. 4.* Issued: 31.03.94. Made: 23.03.94. Coming into force: 06.04.94. Effect: S.R. 1983/54; 1990/85; 1991/138 amended. – 4p. – 0 337 91103 7 *£1.10*

The Statutory Sick Pay (Rate of Payment) Order (Northern Ireland) 1994 No. 82. Enabling power: *Social Security Contributions and Benefits (Northern Ireland) Act 1992, s. 153 (2) (a).* Issued: 11.03.94. Made: 08.03.94. Coming into force: 06.04.94. Effect: 1992 c. 7; S.R. 1993/152 amended & S.R. 1991/87 revoked. – 2p. – 0 337 91082 0 *£0.65*

The Statutory Sick Pay (Small Employers' Relief) (Amendment) Regulations (Northern Ireland) 1994 No. 76. Enabling power: *Social Security Contributions and Benefits (Northern Ireland) Act 1992, s. 154 (2) (3) & Social Security Administration (Northern Ireland) Act 1992, s. 131.* Issued: 11.03.94. Made: 07.03.94. Coming into force: 06.04.94. Effect: S.R. 1991/137; 1992/139 amended. – 2p. – 0 337 91076 6 *£0.65*

SUPREME COURT

The Matrimonial Causes Fees (Amendment) Order (Northern Ireland) 1994 No. 281. Enabling power: *Judicature (Northern Ireland) Act 1978, s. 116 (1).* Issued: 11.08.94. Made: 21.07.94. Coming into force: 01.09.94. Effect: S.R. 1991/292 amended. – 8p. – 0 337 91281 5 *£1.55*

Supreme Court Fees Order (Northern Ireland) 1994 No. 283. Enabling power: *Judicature (Northern Ireland) Act 1978, s. 116 (1) (4).* Issued: 16.08.94. Made: 21.07.94. Coming into force: 01.09.94. Effect: S.R. 1991/291, 440; 1992/220 revoked. – 16p. – 0 337 91283 1 *£3.20*

Supreme Court (Non-Contentious Probate) Fees (Amendment) Order (Northern Ireland) 1994 No.282. Enabling power: *Judicature (Northern Ireland) Act 1978, s. 116 (1).* Issued: 11.08.94. Made: 21.07.94. Coming into force: 01.09.94. Effect: S.R. 1991/293 amended. – 8p. – 0 337 91282 3 *£1.55*

SUPREME COURT, NORTHERN IRELAND: PROCEDURE

The Rules of the Supreme Court (Northern Ireland) (Amendment) 1994 No. 286. Enabling power: *Judicature (Northern Ireland) Act 1978, s. 55.* Issued: 08.08.94. Made: 22.07.94. Coming into force: 01.09.94. rule 5 (a) (c); 01.10.94. rules 1, 2, 3, 4, 5 (b), 6. Effect: None. – 8p. – 0 337 91286 6 *£1.95*

WATER AND SEWERAGE

The Prevention of Pollution (Erne System) Regulations (Northern Ireland) 1994 No.20. Enabling power: *Water Act (Northern Ireland) 1972, s. 12.* Issued: 26.01.94. Made: 20.01.94. Coming into force: 01.04.94. Effect: None. – 4p. – 0 337 91020 0 *£1.10*

The Private Water Supplies Regulations (Northern Ireland) 1994 No. 237. Enabling power: *S.I. 1973/70 (N.I. 2), arts. 2, 3C, 3D (3) (4).* Issued: 08.07.94. Made: 23.06.94. Coming into force: 01.11.94. Effect: S.R. 1994/221 amended. – 24p. – 0 337 91237 8 *£4.15*

The Water Quality Regulations (Northern Ireland) 1994 No. 221. Enabling power: *S.I. 1973/70 (N.I. 2), arts. 2, 3A, 3B, 3C.* Issued: 29.06.94. Made: 17.06.94. Coming into force: 01.10.94. Effect: None. – 32p. – 0 337 91221 1 *£5.20*

Price/availability are liable to change without notice

WEIGHTS AND MEASURES

Measuring Equipment (Capacity Measures) (Amendment) Regulations (Northern Ireland) 1994 No.322. Enabling power: *S.I. 1981/231 (NI. 10), art. 9 (1) (3)*. Issued: 30.08.94. Made: 17.08.94. Coming into force: 20.09.94. Effect: S.R. & O. (NI.) 1967/237 amended. –2p. – 0 33791322 6 £0.65

Weights and Measures (Cosmetic Products) Order (Northern Ireland) 1994 No. 319. Enabling power: *S.I. 1981/231 (NI. 10), arts. 19 (2) (3) (7)*. Issued: 30.08.94. Made: 17.08.94. Coming into force: 19.09.94. Effect: S.I. 1981/231 (NI. 10) amended & S.R. 1974/282 revoked. –4p. – 0 337 91319 6 £1.10

Weights and Measures (Intoxicating Liquor) (Amendment) Order (Northern Ireland) 1994 No.320. Enabling power: *S.I. 1981/231 (NI. 10), arts. 6 (4) (a) (c), 19 (2) (3)*. Issued: 30.08.94. Made: 17.08.94. Coming into force: 19.09.94. Effect: S.R. 1989/164 & S.I. 1981/231 (NI. 10) amended. –2p. – 0 33791320 X £0.65

Weights and Measures (Packaged Goods) (Amendment) Regulations (Northern Ireland) 1994 No.321. Enabling power: *S.I. 1981/231 (NI. 10), arts. 30, 31, 32, 33, 34, 37, 38 & sch. 8, para. 1*. Issued: 30.08.94. Made: 17.08.94. Coming into force: 19.09.94. Effect: S.R. 1990/410 amended. –8p. – 0 337 91321 8 £1.55

WELFARE FOODS

The Welfare Foods (Amendment) Regulations (Northern Ireland) 1994 No. 326. Enabling power: *S.I. 1988/594 (NI. 2), art. 13 (3) (4)*. Issued: 30.08.94. Made: 19.08.94. Coming into force: 23.09.94. Effect: S.R. 1988/137; 1993/219 amended. –2p. – 0 337 91326 9 £0.65

WILLS AND ADMINISTRATION OF ESTATES

Wills and Administration Proceedings (1994 Order) (Commencement No. 1) Order (Northern Ireland) 1994 No. 372 (C. 12). Enabling power: *S.I. 1994/1899 (N.I. 13), art. 1 (2) & Northern Ireland Act 1974, sch. 1, para. 2 (1). Bringing into operation various provisions of the 1994 order on 01.01.95.* Issued: 17.10.94. Made: 03.10.94. Effect: None. –2p. – 0 337 91372 2 £0.65

Price/availability are liable to change without notice

NUMERICAL LIST OF STATUTORY RULES OF NORTHERN IRELAND WITH SUBJECT HEADINGS

1	Health and safety	47	
2	Companies	(C. 2)	Companies
3	Industrial relations	48	Police
4	Road traffic and vehicles	49	Police
5	*	50	Fair employment
6	Health and safety	51	Pensions
7	Road traffic and vehicles	52	Food
8	Contracts of employment and redundancy payments	53	Housing
		54	Road traffic and vehicles
9	Contracts of employment and redundancy payments	55	Education
		56	Rates
10	Fisheries	57	Health and personal social services
11	Animals	58	Planning
12	Education	59	Agriculture
13	Education	60	Agriculture
14	*	61	*
15	*	62	Health and personal social services
16	*	63	Health and personal social services
17		64	Health and personal social services
(C. 1)	Pensions	65	Health and personal social services
18	Road traffic and vehicles	66	Health and personal social services
19	*	67	Health and personal social services
20	Water and sewerage	68	Social security
21	Social security	69	Pensions
22	Road and railway transport	70	*
23	Road and railway transport	71	Police
24	Landlord and tenant	72	Police
25	*	73	Police
26	Insolvency	74	Social security
27	Road traffic and vehicles		Statutory maternity pay
28	Plant health		Statutory sick pay
29	Road and railway transport		Housing
30	Road and railway transport	75	Social security
31	Health and personal social services	76	Statutory sick pay
32	*	77	Social security
33	*	78	Social security
34	*	79	Social security
35	Animals	80	Housing
36	*		Rates
37	Family law	81	Housing
	Child support		Rates
38	Health and safety	82	Statutory sick pay
39	*	83	Social security
40	Fisheries	84	Statutory maternity pay
41	Gas	85	Housing
42	Health and personal social services	86	Road traffic and vehicles
43	Road traffic and vehicles	87	Road traffic and vehicles
44	Health and safety	88	Housing
45	Social security		Rates
46	Road traffic and vehicles	89	Social security

*These rules were of a local nature and publication was not required

90	Public health	141	
91	Land	(C. 5)	Environmental protection
92	Social security	142	European Communities
93	*		Environmental protection
94	Social security	143	Health and safety
95	Health and personal social services	144	European Communities
96	Legal aid and advice		Environmental protection
97	Legal aid and advice	145	Environmental protection
98	Legal aid and advice	146	Health and safety
99	Pensions	147	European Communities
100	Health and personal social services		Public health
101	*	148	Contracts of employment and redundancy payments
102	*	149	*
103	Statutory sick pay	150	Social security
104	Clean air	151	
105	*	(C. 6)	Access to health records
106	*	152	Social security
107	Pensions	153	Road traffic and vehicles
108	Health and personal social services	154	Road traffic and vehicles
109	Health and personal social services	155	Social security
110	Health and personal social services	156	Housing
111	Health and personal social services	157	Lands tribunal
112	Health and personal social services	158	Access to health records
113	Health and personal social services	159	Access to health records
114	Health and personal social services	160	Health and personal social services
115	Health and personal social services	161	European Communities
116	Health and personal social services		Animals
117	Health and personal social services	162	Local government
118	Animals	163	*
119	Animals	164	Criminal procedure
120	Animals	165	Criminal procedure
121	*	166	Agriculture
122	Education	167	*
123	Agriculture	168	*
124	Health and personal social services	169	*
125	*	170	Road traffic and vehicles
126	*	171	*
127		172	Road traffic and vehicles
(C. 3)	Education	173	Road traffic and vehicles
128	Agriculture	174	Food
129		175	Health and personal social services
(C. 4)	Criminal procedure	176	European Communities
130	Animals		Social Security
131	Private streets	177	*
132	Electricity	178	*
133	Companies	179	*
	Partnerships	180	Electricity
134	Road traffic and vehicles	181	Agriculture
135	Road traffic and vehicles	182	*
136	*	183	*
137	Housing	184	*
138	Social security	185	Food
139	Road traffic and vehicles	186	Police
140	Health and personal social services		

These rules were of a local nature and publication was not required

NUMERICAL LIST OF STATUTORY RULES

187	Police	232	*
188	Police	233	Social security
189	Horse racing	234	
190	Roads	(C. 8)	Social security
	Road traffic and vehicles	235	*
191	Social security	236	*
	Statutory maternity pay	237	Water and sewerage
	Statutory sick pay	238	Education
192	Public health	239	Health and safety
193	Public health	240	European Communities
	Eurpoean Communities		Road traffic and vehicles
194	Airports	241	Road traffic and vehicles
195	Road traffic and vehicles	242	*
196	Road traffic and vehicles	243	Building regulations
197	Police	244	Animals
198	Animals	245	*
199	Animals	246	Road traffic and vehicles
200	*	247	Road traffic and vehicles
201	Road traffic and vehicles	248	*
202	Pharmacy	249	*
203	Health and personal social services	250	Seeds
204	Public health	251	Seeds
205	Road traffic and vehicles	252	Seeds
206	*	253	Seeds
207	Road traffic and vehicles	254	Seeds
208	*	255	Seeds
209	Legal aid, advice and assistance	256	Education
210	*	257	Education
211	Agriculture	258	Education
212	Agriculture	259	Family law
213	Agriculture		Child support
214	Food	260	Health and safety
215		261	Pensions
(C. 7)	Industrial relations	262	Social security
216	Animals	263	Social security
217	Poisons	264	Education
218	Poisons	265	Social security
219	Social security	266	Social security
220	Game	267	*
221	Water and sewerage	268	*
222	European Communities	269	Social security
	Public health	270	Food
223	European Communities	271	Social security
	Public health		Statutory maternity pay
224	European Communities	272	Road traffic and vehicles
	Public health	273	Industrial training
225	Road traffic and vehicles	274	Social security
226	*	275	Airports
227	*	276	Health and safety
228	Fire services	277	Health and safety
229	Public health	278	Judgments (Enforcement)
230	Education	279	Magistrates' courts
231	Road traffic and vehicles	280	County courts

These rules were of a local nature and publication was not required

281	Matrimonial Causes Supreme Court County Courts	329	Criminal procedure
		330	Road traffic and vehicles
		331	Police
282	Supreme Court	332	Police
283	Supreme Court	333	*
284	*	334	*
285	Magistrates' courts	335	Housing
286	Supreme Court, Northern Ireland Procedure	336	Road traffic and vehicles
		337	
287	*	(C. 11)	Public health
288	*	338	Public health
289	*	339	European Communities Clean air
290	*		
291	Police	340	Agriculture
292	Police	341	Agriculture
293	Gas	342	Education
294	*	343	Social security
295		344	Criminal procedure
(C. 9)	Education	345	Social security
296		346	Agriculture
(C. 10)	Education	347	Social security
297	Road traffic and vehicles	348	Housing
298	Education	349	Mental health
299	*	350	Criminal procedure
300	Pensions	351	Criminal procedure
301	*	352	Public health
302	*	353	Road traffic and vehicles
303	Health and personal social services	354	Registration of clubs
304	Road traffic and vehicles	355	*
305	Road traffic and vehicles	356	Road traffic and vehicles
306	Energy conservation	357	*
307	*	358	*
308	Industrial relations	359	*
309	Agriculture	360	Agriculture
310	*	361	Education
311	*	362	*
312	Industrial training	363	Road traffic and vehicles
313	*	364	Road traffic and vehicles
314	Fisheries	365	Road traffic and vehicles
315	Education	366	Road traffic and vehicles
316	European Communities Roads	367	Gas
		368	Road traffic and vehicles
317	*	369	Criminal procedure
318	*	370	Social security
319	Weights and measures	371	*
320	Weights and measures	372	
321	Weights and measures	(C. 12)	Wills and administration of estates
322	Weights and measures	373	Road traffic and vehicles
323	Education	374	Road traffic and vehicles
324	Education	375	Agriculture
325	Education	376	Agriculture
326	Welfare foods	377	Agriculture
327	Social security	378	Police
328	Social security	379	Industrial relations

*These rules were of a local nature and publication was not required

NUMERICAL LIST OF STATUTORY RULES 349

380	*	431	Police
381	*	432	Police
382	Road traffic and vehicles	433	Road traffic and vehicles
383	Social security	434	Road traffic and vehicles
384	Agriculture	435	Road traffic and vehicles
385	Agriculture	436	Credit unions
386	Agriculture	437	Industrial and provident societies
387	Magistrates' courts	438	Fisheries
388	Health and personal social services	439	*
389	*	440	Road traffic and vehicles
390	Road traffic and vehicles	441	Fisheries
391	Agriculture	442	Road traffic and vehicles
392	Road traffic and vehicles	443	*
393	Road traffic and vehicles	444	Clean air
394	Planning	445	Pensions
395	Planning	446	
396	Social security	(C. 14)	Criminal procedure
397	Road traffic and vehicles	447	Housing
398	Road traffic and vehicles	448	Road traffic and vehicles
399	Harbours, docks, etc.	449	Public health
400	Salaries	450	
401	*	(C. 15)	Social security
402	Animals	451	Road traffic and vehicles
403	Health and personal social services	452	European Communities
404	Agriculture		Road traffic and vehicles
405	Agriculture	453	Road traffic and vehicles
406	*	454	Road traffic and vehicles
407	Road traffic and vehicles	455	Road traffic and vehicles
408	Road traffic and vehicles	456	Social security
409	Road traffic and vehicles	457	Social security
410	Road traffic and vehicles	458	Road traffic and vehicles
411	Road traffic and vehicles	459	Seeds
412	Road traffic and vehicles	460	Fisheries
413	Agriculture	461	Social security
414	Public health	462	Social security
415	Road traffic and vehicles	463	Agriculture
416	Road traffic and vehicles		Horticulture
417	Agriculture	464	Agriculture
418	Local government		Horticulture
419	Agriculture	465	Road traffic and vehicles
420	*	466	
421	*	(C. 16)	Betting, gaming and lotteries
422	*	467	Betting, gaming and lotteries
423		468	Social security
(C. 13)	Land registration	469	*
424	Land registration	470	Magistrates' courts
425	Food	471	County courts
426	Planning	472	County courts
427	Social security	473	Road traffic and vehicles
428	Companies	474	Social security
	Insurance	475	Road traffic and vehicles
429	Insurance	476	Agriculture
430	Horticultural produce	477	*
		478	Health and safety

These rules were of a local nature and publication was not required

479	Industrial relations
480	*
481	Housing
482	*
483	*
484	Social security
485	Social security
486	Agriculture
487	*
488 (C. 17)	Industrial relations
489	Public health
490	*
491	*
492	*
493	*
494	*
495	*
496	*
497	Local government
498	Local government
499	General medical services
500	Health and personal social services
501	*
502	Agriculture

These rules were of a local nature and publication was not required

LIST OF COMMENCEMENT ORDERS

(C.)	(S.I.)
1	17
2	47
3	127
4	129
5	141
6	151
7	215
8	234
9	295
10	296
11	337
12	372
13	423
14	446
15	450
16	466
17	488

ALPHABETICAL INDEX TO STATUTORY RULES

A

Access to health records	319
Accident hazards: Major: Industrial: Control	328
Acquisition: Compulsory: Interest	331
Agriculture	319, 320, 329
Agriculture & rural development	320
Agriculture: Beef carcase: Classification	319
Environmental areas	319
Feedingstuffs	320
Fertilisers: Sampling & analysis	320
Milk marketing: Applications period	320
Applications period: Extension	320
Milk marketing scheme	320
Milk marketing scheme: Revocation: Postponement	320
Poultry meat, farmed game bird meat & rabbit meat: Hygiene & inspection	320
Airports	320
Airports: Nominated successor company	320
Airports Limited: Transfer date	320
Air quality: Standards	322, 324
Akali: Works	322
Alkali etc. works: Clean air	322
Clean air: Metrication	334
Angling: Department of Agriculture waters	325, 326
Animal protein: Breeding flocks & hatcheries: Fees	321
Animals	321
Animals: Bovine embryo collection & transplantation	321
Diseases	321
Diseases: European Communities	321, 325
Notification & movement restrictions	321
Welfare: Transport	321
Antrim: Taxis: Bye-laws	338
Antrim coast: Environmentally Sensitive areas	319
Apple orchard grubbing up	329
Arable area payments	319
Ards: North Down & Ards Community: Health & Social Services Trust	328
Ulster, North Down & Ards Hospitals: Health & Social Services Trust	328
Asbestos: Licensing: Fees	328
Aujeszky's disease	321

B

Ballymena: One-way traffic	337
Banbridge: Craigavon & Banbridge Community: Health & Social Services Trust	327
Bangor: One-way traffic	337
Windsor Park: Traffic	338
Beef carcase: Classification	319
Beef special premium: Protection of payments	319
Beet seeds	339
Belfast: Control of traffic	336
One-way traffic	337
North & West: Health & Social Services Trust	328
South & East: Health & Social Services Trust	328
Sydenham By-Pass: Speed limit	339
Urban clearways	339
Belfast City Hospital: Health & Social Services Trust	327
Belfast, New Street: Bus lane	335
Belfast, Sydenham by-pass: Speed limit	339

Betting, gaming & lotteries	321
Birds: Game: Preservation	326
Blood transfusion service: Health & personal social services	328
Bonito: Marketing standards	326
Bookmakers: Charges: Horse racing	329
Bovine embryo collection & transplantation	321
Breeding: Artificial: Sheep & goats	319
Breeding flocks & hatcheries: Animal protein: Fees	321
Building regulations	321
Buses: Section 10B permits	335
Bus lane: New Street, Belfast	335
Bus permits: Designated bodies	335

C

Carrickfergus: Control of traffic	336
Cars: Motor: Driving instruction: Fees	336
Cats: Rabies: Importation	321
Cereal seeds	339
Child support	321, 325
Clean air	322
Clean air: Air quality: Standards	322, 324
Alkali, etc. works	322
Alkali, etc. works: Metrication	334
Clubs: Registration	335
Cold weather payments: Social Fund	340
Colleges of education: Grant conditions	323
Commissioner for Complaints: Salaries	339
Companies	322, 330, 332
Companies: Shares: Disclosure of interests	322
Compulsory acquisition: Interest	331
Confiscation: Criminal justice	323
Construction Board: Industrial training	330
Construction industry: Industrial training levy	330
Contracts of employment & redundancy payments: Health & personal social services	322
Local government: Modification	322
Cooling towers & evaporative condensers: Notification	329
Cosmetic products: Weights & measures	344
County court: Divisions	322
Fees	322
Rules	322
County courts	322, 332, 343
Craigavon & Banbridge Community: Health & Social Services Trusts	327
Credit unions	322
Credit unions: Fees	322
Criminal justice	322
Criminal justice: Confiscation	323
Confiscation: Designated countries & territories	323
Serious fraud	323
Criminal procedure	322, 323
Criminal procedure: Criminal justice: Confiscation	323
Criminal justice: Confiscation: Designated countries & territories	323
Serious fraud	323
Criminal proceedings: Legal aid: Costs	331
Crop fees: Seed potatoes	320
Curriculum: History: Programme of study & attainment targets	323
Geography: Programme of study & attainment targets	323
Physical education: Programme of study & attainment targets	323
Programmes of study & attainment targets	323
Cycle racing: Roads	336
Cyprus: Social security	341

D

Dangerous substances: Marketing & use	325, 334
Dental charges	327

Department of Agriculture waters: Angling 325
Deregulation & contracting out: Industrial relations 330
Deseasonalisation premium: Protection of payments 319
Development plans: Planning 333
Diseases: Animals 321
    Animals: European Communities 321, 325
        Notification & movement restrictions 321
Diving operations: Health & safety 328
Dogs: Rabies: Importation 321
Domestic energy efficiency: Grants 324
Down Lisburn: Health & Social Services Trust 327
Downpatrick: Taxis 339
Drinking water in containers 326
Driving instruction: Motor cars: Fees 336
Driving licences: Large goods & passenger-carrying vehicles 336
    Motor vehicles 337
    Motor vehicles: Relevant external law: Designation 336

E

Earners: Categorisation: Social security 341
Education 323, 324
Education & libraries 323
Education & libraries: Functional work 323
    Functional work: Competition 323
Education: Colleges of education: Grant conditions 323
    Curriculum: History: Programme of study & attainment targets 323
        Geography: Programme of study & attainment targets 323
        Physical education: Programme of study & attainment targets 323
        Programmes of study & attainment targets 323
    Educational & library services: Grants 323
    Individual pupils' achievements: Information 323
    Libraries 327
    Reform 324
    School information & prospectuses 324
    Schools: Pupils expulsion: Appeals tribunals 324
    Secondary schools: Admissions criteria 324
    Student loans 324
Educational & library services: Grants 323
Educational institutions: Designated: Litter 334
Eel fishing 326
Eel fishing: Licence duties 326
Eglinton: Level crossing 335
Electricity: Generating stations: Permitted capacity 324
    Non-fossil fuel sources 324
Employers: Statutory maternity pay: Compensation 342, 343
Employment: Continuity: Industrial relations 330
Employment contracts & redundancy payments: Health & personal social services 322
    Local government: Modification 322
Employment: Fair: Compensation limit: Increase 325
    Training 328
Energy conservation 324
Energy efficiency: Domestic: Grants 324
Environmental areas: Agriculture 319
Environmental effects: Planning 333
Environmentally sensitive areas: Antrim coast, Glens & Rathlin 319
    Mourne Mountain & Slieve Croob 319
    Slieve Guillion 319
    West Fermanagh & Erne Lakeland 319
Environmental protection: Genetically modified organisms 324, 325
Erne system: Pollution prevention 343
European Communities 324, 325, 334, 335, 336, 337
European Communities: Air quality: Standards 322, 324
    Animals: Diseases 321, 325
    Environmental protection: Genetically modified organisms 324, 325

Public health: Groundwater: Pollution ... 325, 335
    Metrication ... 325, 335
Evaporative condensers & cooling towers: Notification ... 329

F
Fair employment: Compensation limit: Increase ... 325
Family law ... 321, 325
Family law: Child support ... 321, 325
Farm & conservation grant ... 319, 329
Farmed game bird meat, rabbit meat & poultry meat: Hygiene & inspection ... 320
Feeding stuffs ... 320
Feeding stuffs: Sampling & analysis ... 320
Fertilisers: Sampling & analysis ... 320
Fibre plant seeds ... 339
Fire services: Appointments & promotion ... 325
Fisheries ... 326
Fisheries: Angling: Department of Agriculture waters ... 325
    Byelaws ... 326
    Licence duties: Byelaws ... 326
Flavourings: Food ... 326
Fodder plant seeds ... 339
Food ... 326
Food: Drinking water in containers ... 326
    Flavourings ... 326
    Materials & articles in contact ... 326
    Quick-frozen foodstuffs ... 326
Food labelling ... 326
Food protection: Emergency prohibitions ... 334

G
Game birds: Preservation ... 326
Gas ... 326
Gas supply code: Premier Energy Suppliers Ltd. ... 326
Gas undertaker: Premier energy suppliers Ltd ... 326
    Premier Transco Ltd. ... 326
General grant: Local government ... 331
General medical & pharmaceutical services ... 327
General medical services: Medical practitioners: Vocational training ... 326
Genetically modified organisms: Environmental protection ... 324, 325, 328
Geography: Curriculum: Programme of study & attainment targets ... 323
Glens & Rathlin: Environmentally sensitive areas ... 319
Goats: Artificial breeding ... 319
Goods vehicles: Certification ... 336
    Certification: Fees ... 336
Grant: Specified bodies ... 331
Groundwater: Pollution: Dangerous substances ... 325, 335
Group building control: Employment: Local government ... 331
Group Environmental Health Staff: Employment: Local government ... 331
Guernsey: Social security ... 342

H
Harbours: Docks ... 326
Health & personal social services ... 327, 328
Health & personal social services: Blood transfusion services ... 328
    Dental charges ... 327
    Optical charges & payments ... 328
    Redundancy payments: Modification ... 322
    Resources: Assessment ... 327
Health & personal social services trusts: Originating capital & debt ... 327
Health & safety ... 328, 329
Health & safety: Accident hazards: Major: Industrial: Control ... 328
    Cooling towers & evaporative condensers: Notification ... 329
    Diving operations ... 328
    Employment: Training ... 328

Genetically modified organisms: Contained use 328
Medical fees 328
New substances: Notification 329
Work: Management 328
Health & social services trusts: Consequential amendments 327
Dissolution: Consultation 327
Functions: Exercise 327
Mater Infirmorum Hospital 328
Membership & procedure 327
Public meetings 327
Health: Records: Access 319
Health records: Access: Compliance & complaints: Procedures 319
Access: Control 319
Health Service: Trusts: Belfast City Hospitals 327
Trusts: Craigavon & Banbridge Community 327
Down Lisburn 327
Mater Infirmorum Hospital 327
North & West Belfast 328
North Down & Ards Community 328
South & East Belfast 328
Ulster, North Down & Ards Hospitals 328
Hill livestock: Compensatory allowances 320
Hillsborough, Culcavey Road: Overtaking: Prohibition 338
History: Curriculum: Programme of study & attainment targets 323
Holywood: Control of traffic 336
Homes: Insulation scheme & grants 329
Horse racing: Bookmakers: Charges 329
Horticultural produce 329
Horticulture 319, 329
Housing 329, 330, 341, 342, 343
Housing: Insulation scheme & grants 329
Prescribed forms 329, 330
Rates 329, 335
Rates: Benefit 329, 335
Renovation: Grants: Reduction 330
Housing benefit 329, 335

I

Incapacity benefit 342
Incapacity benefit: Dependents: Increases 342
Income-related benefits 340
Income support 340
Industrial & provident societies 330
Industrial & provident societies: Fees 330
Industrial injuries: Prescribed diseases 342
Industrial major accident hazards: Control 328
Industrial relations 330
Industrial relations: Deregulation & contracting out 330
Employment: Continuity 330
Jurisdiction: Extension 330
Industrial training: Construction Board 330
Industrial training levy: Construction industry 330
Insolvency 330
Insurance 322, 330
Insurance accounts directive 330
Intoxicating liquor: Weights & measures 344
Invalid care allowance: Social security 342
Invalidity benefit 342

J

Jersey: Social security 342
Judgment: Enforcement: Fees 330
Judgments: Enforcement 330
Justice: Criminal: Confiscation 323

L

Land	331
Land & deeds: Registration	331
Landlord & tenant: Registered rents: Increase	331
Land registration	331
Land registration: Rules	331
Lands tribunal: Salaries	331
Large goods vehicle: Driving licences	336
Large passenger vehicles: Certification: Fees	336
Larne: Control of traffic	336
Legal advice & assistance	331
Legal advice & assistance: Financial conditions	331
Legal aid & advice	331
Legal aid: Criminal proceedings: Costs	331
Financial conditions	331
Legal aid, advice & assistance	331
Libraries	323
Libraries: Education	323, 327
Education: Functional work	323
Functional work: Competition	323
Licences: Exchangeable: Motor vehicles	337
Lisburn: Control of traffic	336
Lisnabilla Road, Moira: Traffic weight restriction	339
Litter	334
Litter: Designated educational institutions	334
Fixed penalty notices	334
Roads	334
Statutory undertaker: Prescribed body	334
Local government	331
Local government: General grant	331
Group building control: Employment	331
Group Environmental Health Staff: Employment	331
Redundancy payments: Modification	322
Lock: Level crossing	335
Londonderry: One-way traffic	337
Lotteries	321

M

Magistrates' court	332
Magistrates' courts: Criminal cases: Costs	331
Fees	332
Rules	331
Maintenance allowances: Pupils: Compulsory school age	324
Mammals: Rabies: Importation	321
Management: Health & safety: Work	328
Manooney Rd., Killylea: Traffic weight restriction	339
Markethill: Fergy's Bridge: Traffic weight restriction	339
Marketing: Potatoes	320
Mater Infirmorum Hospital: Health & Social Services Trust	327, 328
Maternity & funeral expenses: Social Fund	340
Maternity: Compulsory leave	330
Maternity allowance	325, 340
Maternity benefits	342, 343
Maternity grounds: Suspension from work	330
Matrimonial causes: Fees	322, 332, 343
Measuring equipment: Capacity measures: Weights & measures	344
Medical & pharmaceutical services	327
Medical evidence: Social security	342
Medical fees: Health & safety	328
Medical practitioners: Vocational training	326
Medical services	327
Mental health: Nurses, guardianship, consent to treatment & prescribed forms	332
Metrication: Alkali, etc. works: Clean air: Public health	334

358 SRNI INDEX

      Public health: European Communities 325, 335
Milk marketing: Applications: Period 320
    Applications period: Extension 320
Milk marketing scheme 320
Milk marketing scheme: Revocation: Postponement 320
Motor cars: Driving instruction: Fees 336
Motor vehicles: Construction & use 325, 336
    Driving licences 337
    Driving licences: Large goods & passenger carrying vehicles 336
        Relevant external law: Designation 336
    Exchangeable licences 337
    Taxi drivers' licences 337
    Testing: Fees 337
    Third-party risks 337
    Type approval EEC 325, 337
Motor vehicles; Construction & use 336
Motorways traffic 335, 337
Mourne Mountain: Environmentaly sensitive areas 319
Museums Council: Superannuation 332

N

National curriculum: History: Programme of study & attainment targets 323
    Geography: Programme of study & attainment targets 323
    Physical education: Programme of study & attainment targets 323
    Programmes of study & attainment targets 323
National Health Service Trusts: Belfast City Hospital 327
    Craigavon & Banbridge Community 327
    Down Lisburn 327
    Mater Infirmorum Hospital 327
    North & West Belfast 328
    North Down & Ards Community 328
    South & East Belfast 328
    Ulster, North Down & Ards Hospitals 328
National insurance: Fund: Payments 341
Newry & Mourne Health & Social Services Trust 328
Newtownabbey: One-way traffic 337
Non-fossil fuel sources: Electricity 324
North & West Belfast: Health & Social Services Trust 328
North Down & Ards Community: Health & Social Services Trust 328
North Down: Ulster, North Down & Ards Hospitals: Health & Social Services Trust 328
Northern Ireland National Insurance Fund: Payments 341
Nurses, guardianship, consent to treatment & prescribed forms: Mental health 332

O

Occupational pensions: Revaluation 332
Occupational pension schemes 332
Occupational pension schemes: Winding up: Deficiency 332
Offshore installations: Fire fighting equipment: Fees 329
    Life saving appliances: Fees 329
Off-street parking: Bye-laws 337
Oil plant seeds 339
On-street parking: Bye-laws 338
Optical charges & payments 328
Organisms: Genetically modified: Contained use 328
Overtaking: Culcavey Road, Hillsborough: Prohibition 338

P

Packaged goods: Weights & measures 344
Parking: Off-street: Bye-laws 337
Parking places: Roads 338
Parliamentary Commissioner: Salaries 339
Partnerships: Unlimited companies: Accounts 322, 332
Pensions 332
Pensions: Guaranteed minimum increase 332

Increase: Review	332
Museums Council: Superannuation	332
Occupational pension schemes: Winding up: Deficiency	332
Social security: Home responsibilities	342
Personal pension schemes	332
Persons abroad: Social security benefit	341
Petroleum-spirit licence: Health & safety: Fees	328
Petty sessions districts	332
Pharmaceutical services	327
Pharmaceutical Society of Northern Ireland	332
Pharmacy	332
Physical education: Curriculum: Programme of study & attainment targets	323
Pig carcase: Grading	320
Planning	333
Planning: Development plans	333
Environmental effects	333
Fees	333
Zones	333
Plant health: Potatoes	333
Poisons	333
Poisons list	333
Police	333, 334
Police: Royal Ulster Constabulary	333
Royal Ulster Constabulary: Discipline & disciplinary appeals	333
Royal Ulster Constabulary Reserve: Full-time: Appointment & conditions of service	333
Full-time: Pensions	334
Part-time: Appointment & conditions of service	334
Part-time: Discipline & disciplinary appeals	334
Portadown: Woodhouse Street: Control of traffic	336
Portrush: Control of traffic	336
One way traffic	338
Potatoes: Marketing	320
Plant health	333
Seed: Tuber & label fees	320
Poultry breeding flocks & hatcheries: Animal protein: Fees	321
Registration & testing, etc.	321
Poultry breeding flocks & hatcheries scheme	321
Poultry meat, farmed game bird meat & rabbit meat: Hygiene & inspection	320
Premier Energy Suppliers Ltd.: Gas supply code	326
Premier Transco Ltd.: Gas undertaker	326
Private streets: Construction	334
Private water supplies	343
Protected rights: Transfer payment	332
Public health	325, 334
Public health: Metrication	325, 335
Food protection: Emergency prohibitions	334
Groundwater: Pollution: Dangerous substances	325, 335
Litter	334
Litter: Designated educational institutions	334
Fixed penalty notices	334
Public service vehicles	338
Public service vehicles: Construction	338
Licence fees	338
Pupils: Individual achievements: Information	323
Pupils expulsion: Appeals tribunals	324

Q

Quick-frozen foodstuffs	326

R

Rabbit meat, poultry meat & farmed game bird meat: Hygiene & inspection	320
Rabies: Importation	321
Rates: Housing benefits	329, 335
Regional rate	335

Redundancy payments: Health & personal social services: Modification 322
    Local government: Modification 322
Regional Medical Physics Agency: Establishment & constitution 328
Regional rate 335
Registration: Land & deeds 331
Registration of clubs 335
Remand 323
Rents: Registered: Increase 331
Road & railway transport: Buses: Section 10B permits 335
    Bus permits: Designated bodies 335
    Eglinton: Level crossing 335
    Lock: Level crossing 335
Roads 335, 337
Roads: Environmental effects: Assessment 325, 335
    Parking places 338
    Speed limit 338
Road traffic & vehicles 325, 335, 336, 337, 338, 339
Road traffic & vehicles: Driving licences: Relevant external law: Designation 336
    Motor vehicles: Third-party risks 337
    Off-street parking: Bye-laws 337
    Roads: Parking places 338
        Speed limit 338
    Seat belts: Exemption: Applicants: Payments 337
    Third party risks 338
    Urban clearways: Belfast 339
Royal Ulster Constabulary 333
Royal Ulster Constabulary: Discipline & disciplinary appeals 333
Royal Ulster Constabulary Reserve: Full-time: Appointment & conditions of service 333
    Full-time: Pensions 334
    Part-time: Appointment & conditions of service 334
        Discipline & disciplinary appeals 334
        Service 334

S

Salaries 339
Salaries: Lands tribunal 331
Sanitation expenses: Recoverable: Interest 334
School admissions: Appeal tribunals 324
School information & prospectuses: Education 324
Schools: Pupils expulsion: Appeals tribunals 324
Seat belts: Exemption: Applicants: Payments: Motor vehicles 337
Secondary schools: Admissions criteria 324
Seed potatoes 339
Seed potatoes: Crop fees 320
    Tuber & label fees 320
Seeds 339
Seeds: Registration, licensing & enforcement 339
Severe disablement allowance 342
Shares: Disclosure of interests 322
Sheep: Annual premium 320
    Artificial breeding 319
Sickness benefit 342
Sick pay: Statutory 343
Slieve Croob: Environmentally sensitive areas 319
Slieve Guillion: Environmentally sensitive areas 319
Social Fund: Cold weather payments 340
    Maternity & funeral expenses 340
Social security 340, 341, 342, 343
Social security: Adjudication 340
    Attendance allowance 340
    Benefit: Persons abroad 341
    Benefits: Up-rating 330, 341, 342, 343
    Claims & payments 341
    Contributions 341

    Credits 341
    Cyprus 341
    Disability living allowance 340
    Earners: Categorisation 341
    Earnings factors: Revaluations 342
    Incapacity benefit 342
    Incapacity benefit: Dependents: Increases 342
    Incapacity for work 342
    Income-related benefits 340
    Income support 340
    Industrial injuries: Prescribed diseases 342
    Medical evidence 342
    Re-rating 341
    Severe disablement allowance 342
    Severe disablement allowance & invalid care allowance 342
    Sickness & invalidity benefit & severe disablement allowance 342
    Social Fund: Maternity & funeral expenses 340
    Statutory maternity pay 343
    Statutory sick pay 343
    Workmen's compensation 342
Social security benefits: Persons abroad 341
Social security maternity benefits 342, 343
South & East Belfast: Health & Social Services Trust 328
Speed limit: Belfast, Sydenham by-pass 339
Statutory maternity pay 325, 330, 340, 341, 342, 343
Statutory maternity pay: Employers: Compensation 342, 343
Statutory sick pay 330, 341, 342, 343
Student loans: Education 324
Substances: New: Notification: Health & safety 329
Suckler cow: Premium 320
Supreme Court 322, 332, 343
Supreme Court: Fees 343
    Non-contentious probate: Fees 343
    Northern Ireland procedure 343
    Rules 343
Suspension from work: Maternity grounds 330

T

Taxi drivers' licences 337
Taxi drivers' licences: Fees 337
Taxis: Antrim: Bye-laws 338
    Downpatrick 339
Traffic signs 339
Traffic weight 339
Traffic weight restriction: Lisnabilla Road, Moira 339
Transport: Animals: Welfare 321
Tuberculosis: Control 321
Tuna: Marketing standards 326

U

Ulster, North Down & Ards Hospitals: Health & Social Services Trust 328
Unlimited companies: Partnerships: Accounts 322, 332
Urban clearways: Belfast 339

V

Vegetable seeds 339
Vehicles: Construction & use 325, 336
    Goods: Certification: Fees 336
    Motor: Construction & use 336
        Driving licences 337
        Driving licences: Large goods & passenger carrying vehicles 336
        Exchangeable licences 337
        Taxi drivers' licences 337
        Taxi drivers' licences: Fees 337

  Testing: Fees 337
  Type approval: EEC 325, 337
 Passenger: Certification: Fees 336
 Public service: Licence fees 338
 Road traffic 336, 339

W

Warrenpoint Harbour Authority 326
Water & sewerage 343
Water & sewerage: Pollution prevention: Erne system 343
Water: Drinking water in containers 326
Water quality 343
Water supplies: Private 343
Weights & measures: Cosmetic products 344
 Intoxicating liquor 344
 Measuring equipment: Capacity measures 344
 Packaged goods 344
Welfare foods 344
West Fermanagh & Erne Lakeland: Environmentally sensitive areas 319
Wills & administration proceedings 344
Work: Incapacity: Social security 342
 Management: Health & safety 328
 Suspension: Maternity grounds 330
Workmen's compensation 342

HMSO information and services

HMSO catalogues
HMSO provides a complete bibliographic service for titles published by HMSO or sold on an agency basis. The services ranges from a daily listing of new publications to annual catalogues and a database on CD-ROM. Full details are available from Bibliographic services, HMSO Publications Centre, 51 Nine Elms Lane, London SW8 5DR (tel. 0171 873 8275)

Publicity catalogues
HMSO produces a number of leaflets and catalogues on selected titles and themes. These concentrate on the more recent publications, and give a brief description of their contents. Subject areas covered, and updated regularly, include international organisation publications, education, agriculture, law, social issues, medicine and health, architecture and building, science and technology. Copies of these and other catalogues are available from Publicity Department, HMSO Books, St Crispins, Duke Street, Norwich NR3 1PD. Details of HMSO's mailing list, covering over thirty subject classifications, are available from the same address.

Publications Centre
This is the main warehouse and distribution centre for HMSO publications, and is the address for mail orders: HMSO Books, PO Box 276, London SW8 5DT.

HMSO bookshops
There are seven HMSO bookshops, in London, Edinburgh, Belfast, Bristol, Manchester, Birmingham and Cardiff (addresses on back cover.)

HMSO agents
HMSO's accredited agents are listed in the *Yellow pages*.

Prestel
Most HMSO publications (including all statutory instruments) are listed on the Prestel database on the day of publication, and agency titles on the date they are placed on sale. Details are displayed for one week. There is also much information about HMSO and its services. Enquiries and orders can be placed through Prestel (lead frame 50040.)

Selected subscription service
For a single advance subscription (representing a considerable saving on the total price of publications), customers can be supplied automatically with one copy of most publications published by HMSO (there are exceptions: details from address below). It is possible to break this down further into one or two of the following categories: Parliamentary, Non-Parliamentary, Statutory instruments. Further information and costs can be obtained from Selected Subscription Service, HMSO Publications Centre, 51 Nine Elms Lane, London SW8 5DR (0171 873 8491)

Standing order service
This service is open to all HMSO account holders, and allows customers to receive automatically all publications they require in a specified subject area. There are some 4000 categories to choose from. Further information is available from Standing Orders, HMSO Publications Centre, 51 Nine Elms Lane, London SW8 5DR (0171 873 8466)

Subscriptions
Annual subscriptions may be placed for all periodicals. Further information may be obtained from Subscriptions, HMSO Publications Centre, 51 Nine Elms Lane, London SW8 5DR (0171 873 8499) for HMSO publications, and from Agency Subscriptions for items sold but not published by HMSO (0171 873 8409)

Trade terms
Booksellers who would like further information on HMSO's trade terms and representatives should contact Sales Office, HMSO Publications Centre, London SW8 5DR (0171 873 8440)

Enquiries

The details given below are of services available in London and Norwich; customers may also contact HMSO's bookshops and agents.

By post

To enquire about an order already placed, to enquire about accounts or to make a general enquiry	HMSO Books PO Box 276 London SW8 5DT
To ask for free catalogues/information material	HMSO Books Publicity Department St Crispins Duke Street Norwich NR3 1PD

By telephone

To make a general publications enquiry (HMSO titles)	0171 873 0011*
To enquire whether an item is held at Holborn Bookshop, call the general enquiries number	0171 873 0011*
To enquire about an order previously placed and complaints	0171 873 0022*
Enquiries on agency publications (sold but not published by HMSO)	0171 873 8372
Enquiries from government departments	0171 873 8373/8367
To enquire about opening an account	0171 873 8346
Subscriptions (Parliamentary and non-Parliamentary)	0171 873 8499
Subscriptions (Agency publications)	0171 873 8409
Standing orders	0171 873 8466
HMSO catalogues	0171 873 8275
HMSO free catalogues and leaflets (publicity)	01603 694498
Copyright enquiries	01603 695506
London gazette office	0171 873 8300

By other means

Fax enquiries 0171 873 8463

Fax subscriptions/standing orders 0171 873 8222

Prestel (lead frame 50040)

* Queuing systems in operation, calls answered in turn.

Orders

HMSO books can be ordered from

- **HMSO Publications Centre**
  PO Box 276
  London SW8 5DT (mail and telephone orders only)

  Telephone orders 0171 873 9090

  General enquiries 0171 873 0011

  Enquiries about previously placed orders 0171 873 0022
  (Queuing systems in operation for above numbers)

  Fax orders 0171 873 8200

- **HMSO bookshops** at

  49 High Holborn, **London** WC1V 6HB
  (counter service only; telephone general enquiry no. above) Fax 0171 831 1326

  68/69 Bull Street, **Birmingham** B4 6AD 0121 236 9696 Fax 0121 236 9699

  33 Wine Street, **Bristol** BS1 2BQ 0117 9264306 Fax 0117 9294515

  9-21 Princess Street, Albert Square, **Manchester** M60 8AS 0161 834 7201 Fax 0161 833 0634

  16 Arthur Street, **Belfast** BT1 4GD 01232 238451 Fax 01232 235401

  71 Lothian Road, **Edinburgh** EH3 9AZ 0131 228 4181 Fax 0131 229 2734

  The HMSO Oriel Bookshop, The Friary, **Cardiff** CF1 4AA 01222 395 548 Fax 01222 384347

- HMSO bookshop agents (see *Yellow pages*)

- Through any good bookshop

- HMSO's Prestel frames (lead frame 50040); ISBN must be quoted

- Fax subscriptions/standing orders 0171 873 8222

The publications referred to in this catalogue shall be supplied to the customer only on the HMSO terms and conditions of sale (see p. xi-xii) and not on any additional terms which may be included with the customer's order.

Prices and availability are subject to alteration without notice.

SI-CD - Statutory instruments on CD-ROM

It contains the full text and graphics of Statutory Instruments from 1987 onwards and a short form of Statutory Instruments from 1980 onwards.

Annual subscription costs **£850.00** (excluding VAT in EC)

For further information please contact David Blake/Andrew Evans, HMSO Electronic Publishing Sales.

   Telephone No. +44 (0) 171-873 8236/8259

   Fax No.   +44 (0) 171-873 8203

If you would like to place an order contact HMSO Books Subscriptions on:

   Telephone No. +44 (0) 171-873 8499

   Fax No.   +44 (0) 171-873 8222

British Standards

Now available from all HMSO Bookshops

The seven HMSO Bookshops are now official distributors for the British Standards Institution (BSI). The bookshops stock a range of British, European and international (ISO) standards, and can order and obtain any standard within 24 hours. The HMSO Bookshops are at:

49 High Holborn, **London** WC1V 6HB
BSI Hotline 0171 404 1213 Fax 0171 831 1326

16 Arthur Street, **Belfast** BT1 4GD
Tel 01232 238451 Fax 01232 235401

68/69 Bull Street, **Birmingham** B1 2HE
Tel 0121 236 9696 Fax 0121 236 9699

HMSO Oriel, The Friary, **Cardiff** CF1 4AA
Tel 01222 395548 Fax 01222 384347

33 Wine Street, **Bristol** BS1 2BQ
Tel 0117 9264306 Fax 0117 9294515

71 Lothian Road, **Edinburgh** EH3 9AZ
Tel 0131 228 4181 Fax 0131 229 2734

9-21 Princess Street, **Manchester** M60 8AS
Tel 0161 834 7201 Fax 0161 833 0634
BSI Hotline 0161 834 4188

Our staff have been trained by BSI and can provide an informed service to help you determine which standards best suit your needs. British Standards promote quality in every sector of industry so make sure standards are playing their full part in your success.

Contact your nearest HMSO Bookshop for more details and to place your order.

HMSO BOOKS' TERMS AND CONDITIONS OF SALE

DEFINITIONS

1.1 In the following and any other conditions included in the Contract, the expressions listed below shall have the meaning shown:

Expression	Meaning
The Seller (We, Us)	the Controller of HMSO, his staff and authorised representatives and assignees.
The Customer (You)	whoever sends us the Order for the Goods.
Goods	the item fitting the description in your Order and as available from HMSO Books' lists of items.
Price	that quoted in HMSO Books' current price list plus any applicable Value Added Tax.
Force Majeure	any circumstances beyond our reasonable control, such as accidents, flood, fire or other natural disasters, and unlawful industrial disputes.
Contract	the agreement between us and you made by our acceptance of your Order.
Order	your request for the Goods.

APPLICABLE CONDITIONS

2.1 These are the only conditions which shall apply to the Contract. Any variations to them must be agreed in writing by our Head of Sales or Credit Controller.

ACCURACY OF DESCRIPTION

3.1 We shall only be liable to supply the Goods which you describe accurately in your Order.

3.2 When your Order does not accurately describe the Goods we will use our best endeavours to supply the correct Goods but you shall not rely on our skill and judgement in selecting these.

DELIVERY

4.1 You shall accept the Goods securely packaged, free of delivery charge by mail or carier at your address in the United Kingdom or Republic of Ireland, during normal business hours. Delivery in the United Kingdom shall be the later date of either 14 days from recieving your Order, or the publication date of the Goods

4.2 We may charge you for the cost of delivery byb any other method, or to other countries

4.3 Where we cannot deliver by the promised date we will promptly advise you of the reason. We may make a partial delivery of your Order where not all items are available. You have the right to return that partial delivery at our expense by the most economical method, within 5 working days of receiving it

INABILITY TO SUPPLY

5.1 If we notify you in writing that we are unable to deliver the Goods as specified for Force Majeure or "out of stock" reasons, you shall allow us to deliver within a further reasonable time. What is a further reasonable time shall depend on the nature and duration of the force majeure or out of stock position.

5.2 You may return any Goods that are not delivered within that further reasonable time, but not within 14 days of being notified of inability to supply. On safe return of the goods in saleable condition we will cancel the invoice.

OWNERSHIP OF THE GOODS

6.1 The Goods remain our property until you pay for them, but you shall be responsible for their condition once they are delivered to your premises. You shall insure them to cover any risk this involves.

6.2 If you become insolvent we may take the Goods back at your expense and if necessary, may enter your premises to do so, or to inspect the Goods.

DAMAGE OR LOSS IN TRANSIT

7.1 We will replace at no extra cost any Goods damaged before or on delivery, if you notify us by telephone or in writing within 5 days of their receipt.

7.2 We will replace at no extra cost any Goods which have been lost in transit if you notify us by telephone or in writing within 21 days of us receiving your Order or the publication date of the Goods, whichever shall be the later.

REJECTION

8.1 We aim to take care to provide goods of a merchantable quality which are fit for their purpose and value for money. These Terms and Conditions show how we aim to do this, and do not affect your legal rights.

8.2 If you notify us by telephone within 5 working days of receipt of any Goods which are defective, and confirm this in writing at our request, and then return them at our expense stating the reason you are rejecting them, we will promptly replace them with Goods in an acceptable condition.

8.3 We will refund the price of any Goods which we are unable to replace with Goods in acceptable condition.

8.4 If you accurately described the Goods in your Order form you may within 5 days of receipt return any Goods that do not conform with your description. We will replace at no extra charge the Goods with Goods that correspond to your description.

PAYMENT

9.1 You shall pay our invoice for the Price of the Goods and any special delivery charges, as defined in 4.2. above, within 28 days of the date of our invoice, unless our Head of Sales or Credit Controller has agreed otherwise in writing.

9.2 Your payment shall be in sterling, free from any bank or transmission charge.

INTELLECTUAL PROPERTY RIGHTS

10.1 You shall protect our copyright and all other intellectual property rights in the Goods, while they remain your property.

10.2 You shall notify any subsequent owner of such rights in the Goods.

CANCELLATION

11.1 We shall stop despatching Goods against a Standing Order within 3 working days of receiving your written request to do so. You shall pay us for any Goods despatched in that period.

11.2 You shall not cancel Orders that we have already entered into our Order processing system.

ENFORCEMENT

12.1 Our failure to enforce any of these Conditions shall not prevent us from enforcing them at a later date.

12.2 If any Condition is found to be invalid, it shall not prevent all other Conditions being enforced.

HEADINGS

13.1 The headings to each of these Conditions is for guidance only and shall not affect their interpretation.

COMMUNICATIONS

14.1 Any notification, request or other communication required under these Conditions shall be in writing, including facsimile transmission, unless specified otherwise and addressed to the Enquiries Manager.

GOVERNING LAW

15.1 These Conditions shall be governed by English Law and subject to the exclusive jurisdiction of the English Courts.